CONSTITUTIONAL AND ADMINISTRATIVE LAW

PEARSON EDUCATION

We work with leading authors to develop the strongest
educational materials in law, bringing cutting-edge thinking
and best learning practice to a global market.

Under a range of well-known imprints, including Longman,
we craft high quality print and electronic publications which
help readers to understand and apply their content,
whether studying or at work.

To find out more about the complete range of our
publishing, please visit us on the World Wide Web at:
www.pearsoneduc.com

CONSTITUTIONAL AND ADMINISTRATIVE LAW

THIRTEENTH EDITION

A W Bradley MA LLM, LLD (Hon)

Emeritus Professor of Constitutional Law,
University of Edinburgh;
Barrister of the Inner Temple

K D Ewing LLB PhD

Professor of Public Law,
King's College London

An imprint of **Pearson Education**

Harlow, England • London • New York • Boston • San Francisco • Toronto
Sydney • Tokyo • Singapore • Hong Kong • Seoul • Taipei • New Delhi
Cape Town • Madrid • Mexico City • Amsterdam • Munich • Paris • Milan

Pearson Education Limited
Edinburgh Gate
Harlow
Essex CM20 2JE

and Associated Companies throughout the world

Visit us on the World Wide Web at:
www.pearsoneduc.com

ISBN: 0 582 43807 1

First Edition 1931 (E C S Wade and G G Phillips)
Second Edition 1935 (E C S Wade and G G Phillips)
Third Edition 1946 (E C S Wade and G G Phillips)
Fourth Edition 1950 (E C S Wade and G G Phillips)
Fifth Edition 1955 (E C S Wade)
Sixth Edition 1960 (E C S Wade)
Seventh Edition 1965 (E C S Wade and A W Bradley)
Eighth Edition 1970 (E C S Wade and A W Bradley)
Ninth Edition 1977 (A W Bradley)
Tenth Edition 1985 (A W Bradley)
Eleventh Edition 1993 (A W Bradley and K D Ewing)
Twelfth Edition (A W Bradley and K D Ewing)
Thirteenth Edition 2003 (A W Bradley and K D Ewing)

British Library Cataloguing-in-Publication Data
A catalogue record for this book is available from the British Library

Typeset by 35 in 10/11.5pt Sabon
Print and bound by Ashford Colour Press, Gosport

Brief Contents

Full Contents

PART II – THE INSTITUTIONS OF GOVERNMENT

PART III – THE CITIZEN AND THE STATE

PART IV – ADMINISTRATIVE LAW

Preface

The great legal historian, F W Maitland, was in 2002 honoured with a memorial stone in Westminster Abbey. Of the lectures on constitutional history that he gave at Cambridge in 1887, he is remembered not only for what he had to say about the Crown (which 'as a matter of fact does nothing but lie in the Tower of London to be gazed at by sight-seers' and 'is a convenient cover for ignorance') but also for his remark that 'we are becoming a much governed nation' (page 635 below).

The United Kingdom has been a much governed nation for many years. The historical process of government growth has been held back neither by Thatcherism in the 1980s nor since 1997 by New Labour. Indeed, recent changes have led to the introduction of new institutions of government through devolution, and the reform of existing institutions, notably the House of Lords. Moreover, the Human Rights Act 1998 is now fully in force, imposing obligations on all public authorities, and in the process reshaping the role of the courts in the constitution. Other important changes have affected the voting system, and the operation of the civil service.

Not only do we continue to be a much governed nation, but we are now governed by procedures which are much more open and visible than in the past. Although there remains a need for more effective accountability, transparency in government has been encouraged by the codification and publication of many of the rules, standards and principles of government that apply to ministers, MPs, and civil servants, and in relation to public appointments. The Data Protection Act 1998 is already operating and the Freedom of Information Act 2000 is expected to come fully into force in 2005. Political parties must now also reveal the source of their income.

The growing powers of government directly affect the citizen. The events of September 11, 2001 led immediately to new legislation on terrorism which is considered in chapter 26. The balance between liberty and security is a delicate one which has troubled public lawyers for hundreds of years. In an era of international instability, fears for security must be taken seriously, but they must not lead governments to acquire powers which are unnecessary: powers taken in the interests of national security are rarely surrendered when the moment of crisis has passed. It is in these times of crisis that the need for due process of law becomes greater, not less.

This book seeks to provide readers with an informed understanding of the structure of law and government under which they live, and of the values of democracy and constitutionalism that underly that structure. Our aim is to provide significant signposts rather than a street-map of the whole terrain. In several of the areas covered, readers seeking a fuller treatment may wish to consult the more specialist texts we have mentioned. But in providing a full account of recent changes, we make no apology for retaining discussion of historic legal and constitutional topics, since the sometimes frenzied re-organisations to which government agencies are subject seldom alter matters of substance.

Events since 1997 have made necessary much re-writing to take account of devolution, progress of the European Union (where much of the power over the United Kingdom is exercised), and the incorporation of European human rights in national law. Where possible we have pruned older material for reasons of space, sometimes referring back to earlier editions where fuller accounts of the topics appeared. Although the book has fewer pages than the 12th edition, the text is in fact longer, with a new chapter on privacy and new material on many topics, including government finance and the growing power of the Treasury in the machinery of government

One feature of this edition is the appearance in the foot-notes of references to sites on the internet. For reading reports of decided cases, as well as parliamentary and official publications of all kinds, the internet is a most valuable research tool. More details of web-sites could have been given, but we believe that many readers will be adept at accessing information in electronic form and will be able to find their own way to relevant electronic sources.

In the task of revision, we have been assisted with information and advice by numerous people, some of whom we cannot name because of the official posts that they hold, but we thank publicly Robin Allan, Sionaidh Douglas Scott, Conor Gearty, Chris Himsworth, Richard Kay, Paul Mitchell, Alastair Mowbray, Peter Oliver, Adam Solomon, David O'Sullivan and Barry Winetrobe. We record warm thanks to the staff of the libraries in which most of the work for this edition has been undertaken, namely the Bodleian Law Library, Oxford; the Squire Law Library, Cambridge; the Inner Temple Library; and the Library of King's College, London. Our respective families must be thanked for having survived the transferred stress that preparation of the new edition has been liable to cause.

It is the custom today that legal texts should be enlivened with a pictorial cover. After completing our work on the text, we were faced by our publishers with a difficult choice between Westminster Bridge at the dawn of a new day and the Palace of Westminster seen in a setting sun. The fact that we have chosen the latter is not to be taken as expressing a belief on our part that the light of democracy is fading fast. But it is a matter of concern that the general election in 2001 saw a lower turn-out of voters than at any general election since the 'khaki' election in December 1918. This is despite the constitutional reforms since 1997 designed to strengthen democracy.

Anthony Bradley
Keith Ewing
15 June 2002

Note: The text in principle covers events occurring up to 31 December 2001, but where possible developments in the first few months of 2002 are noted. While we jointly accept responsibility for the whole book, the revision of chapters 1–7, 11, 15, 20, and 27–32 was undertaken by AWB; the new chapter on privacy and revision of the other chapters are the work of KDE. As in previous editions, case references are where possible given to the main Law Reports, or if necessary to All ER or WLR, but some specialist reports are cited. In the interests of space, abbreviated references are given to periodical articles and to official publications.

Table of Legislation

United Kingdom Orders and Statutory Instruments

Legislation from other jurisdictions

Australia

Table of Cases

Abbreviations

In addition to the standard abbreviations used for the citation of reported cases, the following abbreviations are used for the principal journals and other sources cited.

ACD   *Administrative Court Digest*
AJCL   *Americal Journal of Comparative Law*
AJIL   *American Journal of International Law*
ALJ   *Australian Law Journal*
APS   *Acts of Parliament of Scotland*
BHRC   *Butterworths Human Rights Cases*
BNIL   *Bulletin of Northern Ireland Law*
BYIL   *British Yearbook of International Law*
CJQ   *Civil Justice Quarterly*
CL   *Current Law*
CLJ   *Cambridge Law Journal*
CLP   *Current Legal Problems*
CMLR   *Common Market Law Reports*
CML Rev   *Common Market Law Review*
COD   *Crown Office Digest*
Crim LR   *Criminal Law Review*
Edin LR   *Edinburgh Law Review*
EHRR   *European Human Rights Reports*
ELR   *Education Law Reports*
EL Rev   *European Law Review*
HC   House of Commons Paper
HC Deb   House of Commons Debates (Hansard)
HEL   Sir William Holdsworth, *A History of English Law*
HL   House of Lords Paper
HL Deb   House of Lords Debates (Hansard)
HLE   *Halsbury's Laws of England* (4th edn, 1973 onwards)
ICLQ   *International and Comparative Law Quarterly*
ILJ   *Industiral Law Journal*
JR   *Juridical Review*
JSSL   *Journal of Social Security Law*
Kilbrandon Report   Report of Royal Commission on the Constitution, vol. 1, Cmnd 5460, 1973
LQR   *Law Quarterly Review*
LS   *Legal Studies*
MLR   *Modern Law Review*
MPR   Report of Committee of Ministers' Powers, Cmd 4060, 1932
NIJB   *Northern Ireland Judgment Bulletin*
NILQ   *Northern Ireland Legal Quarterly*
NLJ   *New Law Journal*
OJLS   *Oxford Journal of Legal Studies*
PL   *Public Law*
SI   Statutory Instrument
SO   Standing Order
SLT   *Scots Law Times*
TEU   *Treaty on European Union (Maastricht, 1992)*
WA   Written Answer
YBEL   *Yearbook of European Law*

Part I

GENERAL PRINCIPLES OF CONSTITUTIONAL LAW

Chapter 1

DEFINITION AND SCOPE OF CONSTITUTIONAL LAW

The starting-point for studying constitutional law should ideally be the same starting-point as for studying political philosophy or the role of law and government in society. How is individual freedom to be reconciled with the claims of social justice? Is society founded upon a reciprocal network of rights and duties or is the individual merely a pawn in the hands of state power?

These fundamental questions are often not pursued explicitly in the study of constitutional law. In fact, constitutional law concerns the relationship between the individual and the state, seen from a particular viewpoint, namely the notion of law. As a historian stated: 'It is inherent in the especial character of law, as a body of rules and procedures, that it shall apply logical criteria with reference to standards of universality and equity.'[1] Law is not merely a matter of the rules which govern relations between private individuals (for example between employer and employee or between landlord and tenant). Law also concerns the structure and powers of the state. The constitutional lawyer is always likely to insist that the relations between the individual and the state should be founded upon and governed by law.

But law does not exist in a social and political vacuum. Within a given society, the legal rules that concern relations between employer and employee will reflect that society's attitude to paid employment. So too the rules of constitutional law, that govern political relations, will, within a given society, reflect a particular distribution of political power. In a stable society, constitutional law expresses what may be a very high degree of consensus about the organs and procedures by which political decisions are taken. But when, within a community, political decisions are taken by recourse to armed force, gang warfare or the might of industrial muscle, the rules of constitutional law are either non-existent or, at best, no more than a transparent cover for a power struggle that is not conducted in accordance with anything deserving the name of law. Within a stable democracy, constitutional law reflects the value that people attach to orderly human relations, to individual freedom under the law and to institutions such as Parliament, political parties, free elections and a free press. Now the reality is often different from the rhetoric. Laws are the product of human decisions, not the gift of an all-perfect deity. As Lord Acton said: 'Power tends to corrupt and absolute power tends to corrupt absolutely.' But the weaknesses and imperfections of human nature are a reason for law, not a reason for discarding law as a means of regulating political conduct. The rules of football are often broken. But if we shoot the referee and tear up the rules, football as an organised activity ceases to exist.

Total disbelief in the value of the individual or in the possibility of public good is therefore a bad starting-point for studying constitutional law. But there is no need to go to the other extreme and hold the belief, fiercely savaged by Jeremy Bentham, that in Great Britain we have a 'matchless constitution'.[2] We ought not to be dominated

---

[1] Thompson, *Whigs and Hunters*, p 262.
[2] Bentham, *Handbook of Political Fallacies* (ed. Larrabee), pp 154–63.

by the lessons which our ancestors learned about constitutional government; neither should we reject those lessons out of hand or from sheer ignorance. A modest claim founded upon the past may be made – that constitutional law is one branch of human learning and experience that helps to make life in today's world more tolerable and less brutish than it might otherwise be.

What is a constitution?

Applied to the system of law and government by which the affairs of a modern state are administered, the word constitution has two meanings. In its narrower meaning, a constitution means a document having a special legal sanctity which sets out the framework and the principal functions of the organs of government within the state and declares the principles by which those organs must operate. In those countries in which the constitution has overriding legal force, there is often a constitutional court which applies and interprets the text of the constitution in disputed cases. Such a court is the Supreme Court in the USA or the Federal Constitutional Court in Germany. In these countries, legislative or administrative acts may be held by the constitutional court to be without legal force where they conflict with the constitution.

In this sense of the word, the United Kingdom of Great Britain and Northern Ireland has no constitution. There is no single document from which is derived the authority of the main organs of government, such as the Crown, the Cabinet, Parliament and the courts of law. No single document lays down the relationship of the primary organs of government one with another or with the people.[3] But the word constitution has a wider meaning. As Bolingbroke stated in 1733:

> By constitution we mean, whenever we speak with propriety and exactness, that assemblage of laws, institutions and customs, derived from certain fixed principles of reason, directed to certain fixed objects of public good, that compose the general system, according to which the community hath agreed to be governed.[4]

Or, in more modern words, constitution in its wider sense refers to 'the whole system of government of a country, the collection of rules which establish and regulate or govern the government'.[5] In this sense, the United Kingdom has a constitution since it has a complex and comprehensive system of government, which has been called 'one of the most successful political structures ever devised'.[6] This system is founded partly on Acts of Parliament and judicial decisions, partly upon political practice and partly upon detailed procedures established by the various organs of government for carrying out their own tasks, for example the law and custom of Parliament or the rules issued by the Prime Minister to regulate the conduct of ministers.[7]

The wider sense of the word constitution necessarily includes a constitution in the narrower sense. In Canada, the USA, India and many other states, the written constitution occupies the primary place among the 'assemblage of laws, institutions and customs' which make up the constitution in the wider sense. But no written document

---

[3] For what such a document might contain, see *The Constitution of the United Kingdom* (Institute for Public Policy Research, 1991). Also see King, *Does the United Kingdom still have a Constitution?* and G Marshall, 'The Constitution: its Theory and Interpretation' in Bogdanor (ed.), *The British Constitution in the Twentieth Century*.

[4] From *A Dissertation Upon Parties* (1733), reprinted in Bolingbroke, *Political Writings* (ed. Armitage), p 88.

[5] Wheare, *Modern Constitutions*, p 1.

[6] Hailsham, *On the Constitution*, p 1.

[7] See *Ministerial Code: A code of conduct and guidance on procedures for Ministers*; in an earlier form, the Code was first published in 1992; chs 7 and 13 B.

alone can ensure the smooth working of a system of government. A written document has no greater force than that which persons in authority are willing to attribute to it. Around a written constitution will evolve a wide variety of customary rules and practices which adjust the operation of the constitution to changing conditions.[8] These customary rules and practices may often be more easily changed than the constitution itself and their constant evolution will reduce the need for formal amendment of the written constitution. As has been said of the US constitution: 'The governing Constitution is a synthesis of legal doctrines, institutional practices, and political norms.'[9]

Neither can a written constitution contain all the detailed rules upon which government depends. Thus the rules for electing the legislature are usually found not in the written constitution but in ordinary statutes enacted by the legislature within limits laid down by the constitution. Such statutes can when necessary be amended by ordinary legislation, whereas amendments to the constitution may require a more elaborate process, such as a special majority in the legislature or approval by a referendum.

In 2001 the House of Lords appointed a select committee on the constitution (a) to examine the constitutional implications of all public Bills coming to the House and (b) 'to keep under review the operation of the constitution'. As a working guide for its own activities, the committee defined the constitution as:

the set of laws, rules and practices that create the basic institutions of the state, and its component and related parts, and stipulate the powers of those institutions and the relationship between the different institutions and between those institutions and the individual.[10]

While scarcely inspirational, this at least reflects the potential breadth of the committee's duty of review.

The making of written constitutions

It was in the late 18th century that the word constitution first came to be identified with a single document, mainly as a result of the American and French Revolutions. The political significance of the new concept of constitutions was stressed by the radical Tom Paine:

A constitution is a thing *antecedent* to a government, and a government is only the creature of a constitution. . . . A constitution is not the act of a government, but of a people constituting a government, and government without a constitution, is power without a right.[11]

In the modern world, the making of a constitution normally follows some fundamental political event – the conferment of independence on a colony; a successful revolution; the creation of a new state by the union of states which were formerly independent of one another; reconstruction of a country's institutions following a world war. A documentary constitution normally reflects the beliefs and political aspirations of those who have framed it. Within the United Kingdom, except between 1653 and 1660 when the country was governed under Cromwell's 'Instrument of Government', political circumstances have never required the enactment of a code of rules covering the whole of government. There have indeed been periods of acute political upheaval culminating in the reform of certain institutions, for example the revolution of 1688,

---

[8] For the argument that all constitutions leave important things unsaid, see Foley, *The Silence of Constitutions*; and King, ch 1.

[9] Whittington, *Constitutional Construction*, p 3.

[10] HL 11 (2001–02), ch 2; on reasons for the committee's appointment, see Cm 4534 2000, ch 5; and HL Deb, 17 July 2000, cols 584–9.

[11] *Rights of Man* (ed. Collins), pp 93 and 207.

which was the final act of the constitutional conflicts of the 17th century. Later there was the first major reform of the House of Commons in 1832 and the crisis over the Lords which led to the Parliament Act 1911. There have also been the union of England and Scotland in 1707, the union of Great Britain and Ireland in 1800, and the subsequent questions relating to the government of Ireland. There was the abdication crisis affecting the monarchy in 1936. And in 1973 the United Kingdom became a member of what was then the European Communities. But on none of these occasions was it necessary to reconstruct the whole system of government. Instead, legislation was passed to give effect in law to the particular consequences of each political event. A pragmatic approach has predominated that avoids the difficult task of stating the shared political beliefs and assumptions on which the system of government depends. In 1973, the Royal Commission on the Constitution reported that its task was to examine the need for devolution of power rather than to make a radical re-examination of the whole constitution.[12] And from 1997 to 2001 the government was criticised for making extensive constitutional changes without placing them in an integrated programme of reform.

Nevertheless, the Westminster system of government is not inherently incompatible with a written constitution. In the past, numerous written constitutions were framed for British territories overseas, whether as colonies or when they attained independence. The earliest constitutions contained no definition of responsible government and did not guarantee the rights of the citizen. Some of these older constitutions have stood the test of time virtually unchanged, for example the constitution of the Commonwealth of Australia, enacted in 1900. The need for constitutional reform has been much discussed by Australians and in 1986 surviving legal links with the United Kingdom Parliament were severed by the Australia Act; but many proposed constitutional amendments have failed to win majority support.[13] The Australian position presents a contrast with Canada: in 1982 the Canada Act, the last Act amending the Canadian constitution to be passed at Westminster, gave full powers of constitutional amendment to Canada and also enacted the Canadian Charter of Rights and Freedoms as part of the Canadian constitution.[14] After 1945, as British colonies acquired their independence, numerous variants of what was often referred to as the Westminster model constitution were created. It became common practice for guarantees of rights and declarations of broad political purpose to be included in the constitutions of the newly independent countries, as in 1979 when Rhodesia achieved independence as the republic of Zimbabwe.[15] Within the United Kingdom, interest in the idea of a written constitution is low on the political agenda. In reality, because of devolution to Scotland, Wales and Northern Ireland, the Human Rights Act 1998 and changes in electoral law, as well as the emergence of documents such as the *Ministerial Code* and the *Code of Conduct for MPs*, many areas of political conduct are subject to written rules, some of which have the force of law. The constitution is not as unwritten as it was in the past.

Legal consequences of the unwritten constitution

Where there is a written constitution, the legal structure of government may assume a wide variety of forms. Within a federal constitution, the tasks of government are divided

---

[12] Kilbrandon Report, para 14. And see ch 3 B.
[13] See H P Lee [1988] PL 535.
[14] See Hogg, *Constitutional Law of Canada*; and app 1 of the 10th edn of this book.
[15] Zimbabwe Constitution Order 1979, SI 1979 No 1600, part III; and see de Smith, *The New Commonwealth and its Constitutions*, ch 5.

into two classes, those entrusted to the federal (or central) organs of government, and those entrusted to the various states, regions or provinces which make up the federation. Thus in countries such as Canada, Australia or the USA, constitutional limits bind both levels of government, and these limits are enforceable in law. In many countries it may be desired to place certain rights of the citizen beyond reach of the organs of government created by the constitution; these fundamental rights may be entrenched by requiring a special legislative procedure if they are to be amended or even by rendering them in essence unalterable, as in Germany.[16] Again, many constitutions seek to avoid a concentration of power in the hands of any one organ of government by adopting the principle of separation of powers, vesting legislative power exclusively in the legislature, executive power in the executive and judicial power in the courts.[17]

Within the United Kingdom, there is no written constitution to secure these objects or serve as the foundation of the legal system. The resulting vacuum is occupied by the doctrines of the legislative supremacy of Parliament and the rule of law, their interrelation being one of the central questions of public law in Britain.[18] These doctrines will be examined later, but one result is that formal restraints upon the exercise of power which exist elsewhere do not exist in the United Kingdom. For example, no truly federal system can exist so long as Parliament's legislative supremacy is maintained. Just as Parliament passed the Government of Ireland Act 1920, devolving powers of self-government upon Northern Ireland, so in 1972 Parliament could suspend operation of the Act of 1920 by re-imposing direct rule upon Northern Ireland.[19] For a federal system to be established a written constitution would be necessary, limiting the powers of the Westminster Parliament and thus preventing it from taking back the devolved powers into its own hands. Thus, the powers of the Scottish Parliament and the Welsh Assembly could be cut down or revoked by further legislation at Westminster; the safeguards against this happening are political rather than legal.

Many written constitutions contain a chapter of fundamental rights, the enforcement of which is entrusted to the courts. The absence of a written constitution is widely considered to make it difficult and even impossible for the courts to be entrusted with the protection of such rights against legislation by Parliament. In later chapters this subject is examined in depth, but the Human Rights Act 1998 has significantly extended the role of the courts in protecting human rights, and there are some who would agree that the Act could have gone further.

What is certain is that the absence of a written constitution means that there is no special procedure prescribed for legislation of constitutional importance. Before the Republic of Ireland could join the EC, a constitutional amendment had to be approved by referendum of the people. In the United Kingdom, while the European Communities Act 1972 was debated at length in Parliament, the Act was passed by a procedure having the same basic form as applies to ordinary legislation. British membership of the EC was in 1975 confirmed by a consultative referendum; but this was a product of divisions in the Labour party. Other referendums have since been held, related to the government of Scotland, Wales and Northern Ireland, and more may be held in future, on the European currency and the electoral system. These referendums are held because they seem desirable or necessary on political grounds, not because of a constitutional obligation. By contrast with written constitutions, which may be described as *rigid* because of the special procedure required if they are to be altered, the United Kingdom has what at least in form is an extremely *flexible* constitution. It would seem that there is

---

[16] Basic Law of the Federal Republic of Germany, arts 19(2) and 79(3).
[17] Ch 5.
[18] See Allan, *Law, Liberty and Justice*; and Forsyth (ed.), *Judicial Review and the Constitution*.
[19] Ch 3 A.

no aspect of our constitutional arrangements which could not be altered by an Act of Parliament.

The absence of a written constitution affects the sources of constitutional law. Instead of the constitution being the formal source of all constitutional law, we look to Acts of Parliament and to judicial decisions, which settle the law on matters such as the principles of judicial review that have never been the subject of comprehensive legislation. Some major institutions, like the Cabinet, do not derive their authority from the law; many important constitutional rules are not rules of law at all.[20] To summarise, the absence of a written constitution means that British government depends less on legal rules and safeguards than upon political and democratic principles.

Constitutionalism[21]

According to the principle of constitutionalism as it has developed in the democratic tradition, one primary function assigned to a written constitution is that of controlling the organs of government. As Professor Vile remarked:

> Western institutional theorists have concerned themselves with the problems of ensuring that the exercise of governmental power, which is essential to the realisation of the values of their societies, should be controlled in order that it should not itself be destructive of the values it was intended to promote.[22]

An American commentator has written: 'The special virtue of constitutionalism . . . lies not merely in reducing the power of the state, but in effecting that reduction by the advance imposition of rules.'[23]

The absence of a written constitution does not, of course, mean that no restraints or limits upon government are required. In the United Kingdom, the problem is no less acute than in countries with written constitutions. The absence of a written constitution makes the more necessary the existence of a free political system in which official decisions are subject to discussion and scrutiny by Parliament. Thus, if the parliamentary process is seen to be failing to provide adequate protection, there is likely to be a call for other constitutional reforms. Between 1973 and 1997 strong advocacy was heard for various reforms including what was called a new 'constitutional settlement'.[24] Many demands were made for a new Bill of Rights to protect individual liberties.[25] In 1988 a cross-party movement, Charter 88, called for reform in the electoral system and urged that the courts be given new powers to protect the individual. In 1991, the text of a complete constitution for the United Kingdom was published by a research institute.[26] During the 1990s, the Labour party became increasingly committed to constitutional reform. Before the 1997 general election, the Labour and Liberal Democratic parties adopted a common platform of reforms, including devolution and incorporation of the European Convention on Human Rights. Much of this platform was implemented

---

[20] Ch 2 B.
[21] See Vile, *Constitutionalism and the Separation of Powers*; McIlwain, *Constitutionalism, Ancient and Modern*; and Alexander (ed.), *Constitutionalism: Philosophical Foundations*.
[22] Vile, p 1.
[23] R Kay, in Alexander (ed.), op cit, pp 16, 23.
[24] Notably from Scarman, *English Law – the New Dimension* and Hailsham, *The Dilemma of Democracy*. Contrast the provocative defence of the unwritten constitution as an expression of political culture in Thompson, *Writing by Candlelight*, pp 191–256. And see Brazier, *Constitutional Reform*; Foley, *The Politics of the British Constitution*; Mount, *The British Constitution Now*; Norton, *The Constitution in Flux*; Blackburn and Plant, *Constitutional Reform*.
[25] Ch 19 C.
[26] See note 3 above.

between 1997 and 2001. Although these reforms were criticised for lacking a coherent framework, their overall effect ought to strengthen values of constitutionalism.

What is constitutional law?

There is no hard and fast definition of constitutional law. According to one wide definition, constitutional law is that part of national law which governs the system of public administration and the relationships between the individual and the state.[27] Constitutional law presupposes the existence of the state[28] and includes those laws which regulate the structure and functions of the principal organs of government and their relationship to one another and to the citizen. Where there is a written constitution, emphasis is placed on the rules which it contains and on the way in which they have been interpreted by the highest court with constitutional jurisdiction. One problem of definition in the United Kingdom is that many of the rules and practices under which our system of government operates do not have the force of law.[29] Without knowledge of these rules and practices, knowledge of the legal rules alone is incomplete and sometimes misleading. These rules, principles and practices are essential to an understanding of the relationship between what may be called the 'political constitution' and the 'legal constitution', and give a constitutional meaning to apparently disparate events.[30]

A further problem of definition is that, unlike legal systems in which law is divided up into a series of codes, there is no hard and fast demarcation in Britain between constitutional law and other branches of law. A legal historian advised students of constitutional law that they should take a wide view of the subject: 'There is hardly any department of law which does not, at one time or another, become of constitutional importance.'[31] For example, in the field of family law, important protection for family life is given by the European Convention on Human Rights[32] and family status is an important basis for many rules of immigration control.[33] In employment law, the freedom of association and the law of picketing[34] are of constitutional importance. Numerous civil liberty issues arise out of criminal law and procedure. In property law, public control of private rights is a fertile field for the emergence of disputes. These examples are not meant to suggest that constitutional law comprehends the whole of the legal system, but that the manner in which the legal system allocates rights and duties and arbitrates on disputes is of direct concern to constitutional law.

Constitutional law and administrative law

In the past, constitutional law gave more emphasis to the role of the state in maintaining public order and national security than it did to the individual's right to employment and housing, education and health services and the conservation of the environment. We still look to the courts for protection in the sphere of public order and the criminal law. But in the administration of the social services, and in the exercise of economic regulation, individuals come into contact more often with officials

---

[27] HLE, vol 8 (2), para 1; and see Marshall, *Constitutional Theory*, ch 1.
[28] For the impact of the changing concept of the state, see N MacCormick (1993) 56 MLR 1, C M G Himsworth [1996] PL 639 and MacCormick, *Questioning Sovereignty*.
[29] Ch 2 B.
[30] Whittington, *Constitutional Construction*, ch 1. See also K D Ewing [2000] PL 405.
[31] Maitland, *Constitutional History*, p 538.
[32] Arts 8 and 12. Ch 19 B.
[33] Ch 20 B.
[34] Ch 24.

than with judges. When a dispute arises out of these activities, a citizen may wish to go to the courts to assert his or her rights and often the procedure of judicial review enables this to be done.[35] However, many prefer to seek redress of the grievance from a member of Parliament. Moreover, administrative tribunals and the Parliamentary Ombudsman provide important means of remedy for the citizen against official action or inaction.[36]

There is no precise demarcation between constitutional and administrative law in Britain. Administrative law may be defined as the law which determines the organisation, powers and duties of administrative authorities.[37] Like constitutional law, administrative law deals with the exercise and control of governmental power. A rough distinction is that constitutional law is mainly concerned with the structure of the primary organs of government, whereas administrative law is concerned with the work of official agencies in providing services and in regulating the activities of citizens. Within the vast field of government, questions often arise as to the sources of administrative power, the adjudication of disputes arising out of the public services and, above all, the means of securing a system of legal control over the activities of government which takes account of both public needs and the private interests of the individual.

Constitutional law and public international law

Public international law is that system of law whose primary function it is to regulate the relations of states with one another. The system:

> presupposes the state, a territorial unit of great power, possessing within its own sphere the quality of independence of any superior, a quality which we are accustomed to call sovereignty and possessing within that sphere the power and right to make law not only for its own citizens, but also for those of others.[38]

International law thus deals with the *external* relations of a state with other states; constitutional law deals with the legal structure of the state and its *internal* relations with its citizens and others on its territory. Both are concerned with regulating by legal process and values the great power that states wield. In the dualist tradition, national and international law operate at two distinct levels, but both are concerned with state power. Thus one important branch of constitutional law is the national law relating to a government's power to enter into treaties with other states and thus to create new international obligations.[39] So too, the procedure of extradition, by which a criminal who escapes from one state to another may be sent back to the state in which his crime was committed, operates in both international and national law.[40] International organisations have today established new forms of cooperation between states and have set standards of conduct for the international community, for example, in the creation of the International War Crimes Tribunal. Increasingly international law has become concerned with the protection of the human rights of individuals and national minorities. These developments make it necessary to reconsider the nature of internal sovereignty which the national system of constitutional law ascribes to the state.[41]

---

[35] Chs 30 and 31.
[36] Ch 29.
[37] Ch 27. Also Maitland, *Constitutional History*, pp 528–35, and Craig, *Public Law and Democracy in the UK and the USA*, pp 1–3.
[38] C Parry, in *Manual of Public International Law* (ed. Sorensen), p 3. And cf note 28 above.
[39] Ch 15 B.
[40] Ch 20 C.
[41] And see note 28 above.

Constitutional law and the law of the European Union

The European Union was created by the Maastricht Treaty in 1992, entered into by the member states of the European Community Itself created by means of treaties between the member states, the European Community is very different from other international organisations to which the United Kingdom belongs, being equipped with legislative, administrative and judicial organs, which exercise their powers with direct effect throughout the member states. The substantive rules of Community law in the economic and social fields lie outside the scope of this book. But there can be no doubt that the Community exercises powers of government over the member states, including the United Kingdom, in which the British electorate participates through elections to the Westminster and the European Parliaments: the public law of the United Kingdom has had to adapt to this reality. Accordingly, the main structure of the EU will be outlined and the implications of membership for constitutional law examined, including the relationship between Community law and national law.[42] In 2002 a keenly disputed issue was the extent to which the United Kingdom should take part in further European integration, requiring member states to relinquish aspects of national sovereignty in favour of European measures such as a common currency. It continues to be necessary for public law to be studied in a European perspective.

---

[42] Ch 8.

Chapter 2

SOURCES AND NATURE OF THE CONSTITUTION

A. The sources of constitutional law

If the United Kingdom possessed a written constitution, the main rules of constitutional law would be contained within it. Alterations to these rules would be made by the procedure laid down for amendment of the constitution. In all probability, Parliament would be authorised to make detailed provision for such matters as the machinery of elections and the structure of the courts. If a court exercised the function of interpreting and applying the constitution in disputed cases, its decisions would be an authoritative statement of the meaning of the constitution. The sources of constitutional law would comprise: (a) the constitution itself and amendments made to it; (b) Acts of Parliament dealing with matters of constitutional importance; (c) judicial decisions interpreting the constitution. By the word 'source' is meant the formal origin of a rule which confers legal force upon that rule. The word source may also be used in other senses: thus the historical sources of a written constitution include both the immediate circumstances in which it was framed and adopted, and also the long-term factors which influenced its making. So too, there are broad political principles which influence the content of particular legal rules. Thus a long-standing commitment to democracy explains why the people have the right to vote in elections. Such principles are given practical effect in legislation by Parliament and may influence decisions that the courts take on disputed questions of law. But in this section we are concerned solely with the formal sources of the legal rules of the United Kingdom constitution. Those constitutional rules which do not have the force of law are discussed in section B.

Sources of legal rules

In the absence of a written constitution, the two main sources of constitutional law are the same as those of law in general, namely:

(a) *Legislation* (or enacted law) including Acts of Parliament; legislation enacted by ministers and other authorities upon whom Parliament has conferred power to legislate;[1] exceptionally, legislative instruments issued by the Crown under its prerogative powers;[2] and, since 1973, legislation enacted by organs of the European Community.[3]
(b) *Judicial precedent* (or case law), i.e. the decisions of the courts expounding the common law or interpreting legislation. Since 1973, this includes decisions of the European Court of Justice in relation to Community law. The Human Rights Act 1998 requires all courts and tribunals to take account of relevant decisions of the European Court of Human Rights.[4]

---

[1] Ch 28.
[2] Ch 12 D.
[3] Ch 8.
[4] Ch 19 C.

Another source of legal rules is custom, i.e. rules of conduct based upon social or commercial custom which are recognised by judicial decision as having binding force. Custom of this kind is not an important source of constitutional law. However, if a customary practice of government is challenged in judicial proceedings, evidence of the practice may lead the court to decide that it is lawful.[5] Moreover, many rules of the constitution which do not have the force of law are based on the customary usages of various organs of government, and these rules will be considered in section B. In the case of Parliament, each House of Parliament has authority to regulate its internal affairs: the 'law and custom of Parliament' (*lex et consuetudo Parliamenti*) is therefore an important source of constitutional rules and practice. Another secondary source of constitutional law is to be found in the opinions and conclusions of writers of books of authority.[6]

(a) *Legislation*   In the absence of a written constitution, many Acts of Parliament have been enacted which relate to the system of government. There are few topics of constitutional law which have not been affected by legislation. Unlike some branches of private law, for example the general law of contract, a study of constitutional law involves frequent recourse to the statute book. Those statutes which deal with matters of constitutional law do not form sections of a complete constitutional code. If a collection were made of all the legislation (from medieval charters to the present day) which deals with the form and functions of government, the result would present a most imperfect description of the constitution.[7] Moreover, these enactments can each be repealed by another Act of Parliament. A few statutes, although in law in no different position from other Acts, have special constitutional significance.

1 *Magna Carta*[8]   Magna Carta was granted in 1215 by King John to the nobles at Runnymede, but in various forms the charter was confirmed by later kings with the approval of the English Parliament; it appears on the statute book in the form confirmed by Edward I in 1297. Its importance lies in the fact that it contained a statement of grievances, formulated on behalf of important sections of the community, which the king undertook to redress. The Charter set out the rights of various classes of the medieval community according to their different needs. The Church was to be free; London and other cities were to enjoy their liberties and customs; merchants were not to be subject to unjust taxation. Although both trial by jury and the writ of habeas corpus owe their origins to other sources, chapter 29 declared that no man should be punished except by the judgment of his peers or the law of the land and that to none should justice be denied. These clauses embodied a protest against arbitrary punishment and asserted the right to a fair trial and a just legal system. Today few provisions of Magna Carta remain on the statute book but it has been called 'the nearest approach to an irrepealable "fundamental statute" that England has ever had'.[9]

2 *Petition of Right*   Another document enacted by the English Parliament at a later period of constitutional conflict is the Petition of Right 1628, enrolled on the statute book as 3 Car 1 c 1.[10] This contained protests against taxation without consent of

---

[5] See, e.g., *Carltona Ltd* v *Commissioners of Works* [1943] 2 All ER 560; p 116 below.

[6] Section C below.

[7] See the statutes collected under the title 'Constitutional Law' in *Halsbury's Statutes*, 4th edn, vol 10 (2001 reissue).

[8] For a full historical account, see Holt, *Magna Carta*.

[9] Pollock and Maitland, *History of English Law*, vol I, p 173. See also *R* v *Home Secretary, ex p Phansopkar* [1976] QB 606; *R* v *Foreign Secretary, ex p Bancoult* [2001] QB 1067; and A Tomkins, [2001] PL 571.

[10] *Halsbury's Statutes*, vol 10, p 26.

Parliament, arbitrary imprisonment, the use of commissions of martial law in time of peace and the billeting of soldiers upon private persons. To these protests the king yielded, though the effect of the concessions was weakened by the view Charles I held that his prerogative powers were not thereby diminished.

3 *Bill of Rights and Claim of Right*   The 'glorious revolution' of 1688 brought about the downfall of James II of England and James VII of Scotland from his two thrones and the restoration of monarchy in the two kingdoms on terms laid down by the English and Scottish Parliaments respectively. These terms were accepted by the incoming joint monarchs, William and Mary. In England it was the House of Lords and the remnants of Charles II's last Parliament that in 1689 approved the Bill of Rights which was later confirmed by the post-revolution Parliament.[11] This laid the foundations of the modern constitution by disposing of the more extravagant claims of the Stuarts to rule by prerogative right.

Its principal provisions (known as 'articles'), many of which are still in force as part of English law, declared:

(1) That the pretended power of suspending of laws or the execution of laws by regal authority without consent of Parliament is illegal.

(2) That the pretended power of dispensing with laws or the execution of laws by regal authority as it hath been assumed and exercised of late is illegal.

(3) That the commission for erecting the late court of commissioners for ecclesiastical causes and all other commissions and courts of like nature are illegal and pernicious.

(4) That the levying money for or to the use of the crown by pretence of prerogative without grant of Parliament for longer time or in other manner than the same is or shall be granted is illegal.

(5) That it is the right of the subjects to petition the king and all commitments and prosecutions for such petitioning are illegal.

(6) That the raising or keeping of a standing army within the kingdom in time of peace unless it be with consent of Parliament is against the law.

(7) That the subjects which are protestants may have arms for their defence suitable to their conditions and as allowed by law.

(8) That election of members of Parliament ought to be free.

(9) That the freedom of speech and debates or proceedings in Parliament ought not to be impeached or questioned in any court or place out of Parliament.

(10) That excessive bail ought not be required nor excessive fines imposed nor cruel and unusual punishments inflicted.

(11) That jurors ought to be duly impannelled and returned. . . .

(12) That all grants and promises of fines and forfeitures of particular persons before conviction are illegal and void.

(13) And that for redress of all grievances and for the amending, strengthening and preserving of the laws, Parliaments ought to be held frequently.[12]

The Scottish Parliament enacted the Claim of Right in 1689. Its contents followed those of the Bill of Rights with certain modifications; for example, the distinction between the suspending and dispensing powers was not made, but all proclamations asserting

---

[11] Ibid, p 38.

[12] *Halsbury's Statutes*, vol 10, p 34. See *Congreve v Home Office* [1976] QB 629 (art 4); *Williams v Home Office (No 2)* [1981] 1 All ER 1211 (art 10); and *R v Home Secretary, ex p Herbage (No 2)* [1987] QB 1077 (art 10). Art 7, sometimes cited by the gun lobby, had no effect on the Firearms (Amendment) Act 1997. Art 9 was amended by the Defamation Act 1996, see chs 11 A and 23 F.

an absolute power to 'cass [quash], annul or disable laws' were declared illegal.[13] Many provisions of the Claim of Right are still in force within Scotland.

4 *The Act of Settlement* The Act of Settlement 1700, enacted by the English Parliament, not only provided for the succession to the throne, but added important provisions complementary to the Bill of Rights, especially:

> That whosoever shall hereafter come to the possession of this crown shall join in communion with the Church of England as by law established.
> That in case the crown and imperial dignity of this realm shall hereafter come to any person, not being a native of this kingdom of England, this nation be not obliged to engage in any war for the defence of any dominions or territories which do not belong to the crown of England, without consent of Parliament.
> That no person who has an office or place of profit under the King or receives a pension from the crown shall be capable of serving as a member of the House of Commons.
> That . . . judges' commissions be made *quamdiu se bene gesserint* [so long as they are of good behaviour], and their salaries ascertained and established, but upon the address of both Houses of Parliament it may be lawful to remove them.
> That no pardon under the great seal of England be pleadable to an impeachment by the Commons in Parliament.[14]

The Bill of Rights and the Act of Settlement marked the victory of Parliament over the claim of kings to govern by the prerogative. There was, however, nothing in these statutes to secure the responsibility of the king's ministers to Parliament. That important principle of parliamentary government developed in the 18th century and later, a product of constitutional practice rather than legislation.[15]

5 *Other statutes of constitutional importance* It is not intended to catalogue other principal statutes that form part of constitutional law. They include the Act of Union with Scotland 1707, the Parliament Acts 1911 and 1949, the Crown Proceedings Act 1947, the European Communities Act 1972, the British Nationality Act 1981 and the Public Order Act 1986. Those enacted since 1997 include the Scotland Act 1998, the Human Rights Act 1998, the House of Lords Act 1999 and the Terrorism Act 2000.

If the United Kingdom had a written constitution, this would be likely to require a special legislative procedure to be followed for the making of textual amendments to the constitution. As it is, in two respects a distinction is sometimes drawn between constitutional and other legislation. First, the House of Commons may refer Bills of constitutional significance for detailed consideration to a committee of the whole House rather than to a standing committee of the House,[16] but not all Bills of constitutional significance are treated in this way. Second, by the doctrine of implied repeal,[17] a later Act prevails over the provisions of an earlier Act which are inconsistent with the later Act; however, in the case of some statutes of special significance, the courts are sometimes reluctant to hold that they have been overridden by a later Act. Under this category might come such Acts as the Bill of Rights 1689, the Acts of Union with Scotland and Ireland, the European Communities Act 1972 and the Human Rights Act 1998.[18] As a senior judge said extra-judicially:

> In strict law there may be no difference in status . . . as between one Act of Parliament and another, but I confess to some reluctance in holding that an Act of such constitutional

---

[13] APS IX, 38.
[14] *Halsbury's Statutes*, vol 10, p 40.
[15] Ch 7.
[16] Ch 10 A.
[17] Ch 4 C.
[18] Chs 8 C, 19 C.

significance as the Union with Ireland Act is subject to the doctrine of implied repeal or of obsolescence.[19]

Moreover, although there is no settled custom requiring this, the practice of holding a referendum of electors when certain constitutional changes are proposed has developed since 1973.[20]

(b) *Case law*   The other main source of rules of law is found in the decisions of the superior courts, stated in authoritative form in the law reports. Under the doctrine of precedent, or 'stare decisis' (i.e. the duty of courts to observe decided cases), these decisions are binding on inferior courts and may, according to the relative status of the courts in question, bind other superior courts.[21] Judge-made law takes two principal forms.

1 *The common law*   This consists of the laws and customs which have from early times been declared to be law by the judges in deciding particular cases coming before them. In the reports of these cases are found authoritative expositions of the law relating to the prerogatives of the Crown,[22] the remedies of the subject against illegal acts by public authorities and officials,[23] and the writ of habeas corpus,[24] which in English law protects against unlawful invasion of personal liberty.

Examples of judicial decisions are *Entick* v *Carrington*, which held that a Secretary of State had no power to issue general warrants for the arrest and search of those publishing seditious papers;[25] and, in modern times, *Burmah Oil Co* v *Lord Advocate*, which held that the Crown must compensate the subject for property taken in the exercise of prerogative powers,[26] *Conway* v *Rimmer*, which held that the courts had power to order the production of documents in evidence for which Crown privilege had been claimed by the Home Secretary,[27] and *M* v *Home Office*, holding that the Home Secretary had committed contempt of court in not obeying a judge's order to bring a deported Zairean teacher back to the United Kingdom.[28] These decisions, made by the most senior judges in the United Kingdom, declare important rules of public law which often would not have been enacted by Parliament. In the absence of a written constitution, such decisions provide what have been called the legal foundations of British constitutionalism.[29] Even so, they are not binding for all time since they may be set aside or amended by Parliament, even retrospectively.[30] And as the final court of appeal, the House of Lords may in exceptional circumstances review and, if necessary, alter the law laid down by its own earlier decisions.[31] Moreover, if the case concerns rights under Community law, a House of Lords decision is subject to the European Court of Justice at

---

[19] Report by the Committee of Privileges on the Petition of the Irish Peers (1966) HL 53 (Lord Wilberforce), p 73.
[20] See p 164 below.
[21] See Cross and Harris, *Precedent in English Law*.
[22] Ch 12 D.
[23] Ch 31.
[24] Ch 21 E and ch 31.
[25] (1765) 19 St Tr 1030.
[26] [1965] AC 75.
[27] [1968] AC 910; ch 32 C.
[28] *Re M* [1994] 1 AC 377; chs 18 B, 32 C.
[29] See Allan, *Law, Liberty and Justice*, chs 1, 4. Also S Sedley, in Richardson and Genn (eds), *Administrative Law and Government Action*, ch 2 and (1994) 110 LQR 270.
[30] The War Damage Act 1965 reversed the *Burmah Oil* decision above; ch 12 D.
[31] See *Practice Statement (Judicial Precedent)* [1966] 3 All ER 77. For review of a previous decision for due process reasons, see *R* v *Bow Street Magistrate, ex p Pinochet Ugarte (No 2)* [2000] 1 AC 119.

Luxembourg;[32] in cases affecting human rights, the European Court of Human Rights may hold that the national decision conflicts with the European Convention on Human Rights.[33] Judicial decisions provide the foundations for such principles as the legislative supremacy of Parliament and judicial review of executive action.[34]

2 *Interpretation of statute law* The courts have no authority to rule on the validity of an Act of Parliament (although they have such authority in the case of subordinate legislation)[35] but they have the task of interpreting enacted law in cases where the correct meaning of an Act is disputed. Important issues of public law may arise out of the interpretation of statutes, as may be seen from two recent decisions of the House of Lords. In one, the House held, under the Human Rights Act 1998, that someone convicted at a trial held before the Act came into force, and who appealed against the conviction after the Act was in force, could not on appeal claim that his or her rights under the Act had been breached at the trial.[36] In the other, the Environment Secretary had, under an Act of 1985, a broad power to make regulations restricting increases in certain residential rents. He used this power to protect tenants against increases result-ing from judicial decisions on the assessment of rents; landlords claimed that the power could be used only as a measure against inflation. In upholding the regulations, the law lords discussed the court's approach to deciding the meaning of the 1985 Act. As Lord Bingham said, 'the overriding aim . . . must always be to give effect to the inten-tion of Parliament as expressed in the words used.'[37] Lord Nicholls said:

> The task of the court is often said to be to ascertain the intention of Parliament expressed in the language under consideration. This is correct and may be helpful, so long as it is remem-bered that the 'intention of Parliament' is an objective concept, not subjective. The phrase is a shorthand reference to the intention which the court reasonably imputes to Parliament in respect of the language used. It is not the subjective intention of the minister or other persons who promoted the legislation. Nor is it the subjective intention of the draftsman, or of indi-vidual members or even of a majority of individual members of either House.[38]

Lord Nicholls explained that in seeking the meaning of the words used by Parlia-ment, the courts employ established principles of interpretation as useful guides and, if necessary, use internal aids (found in the rest of the Act) or external aids (for example, material outside the Act) to identify the mischief that the statute is intended to cure and the purpose of the legislation.

Since most powers of government are derived from statute, the judge-made law which results from the interpretation of statutes is of great importance in administrative law. The principles (or presumptions) of statutory interpretation that the courts apply are seldom conclusive and sometimes point in opposite directions.[39] The task of the court in discovering the meaning or effect of words used by Parliament always requires analysis of the text of the legislation. But if the policy or purpose of a statute can be determined, it may be possible to give an interpretation consistent with that. There was formerly a rule that the courts may not look at Hansard (the record of debates in Parliament) to discover the meaning of legislation, although limited use might be made

---

[32] For the *Factortame* litigation, ch 8 D.
[33] Ch 19 B.
[34] Ch 4 and chs 30, 31.
[35] Ch 28.
[36] *R v Lambert* [2001] 3 All ER 577. Cf *R v Kansal* (No 2) [2002] 1 All ER 257.
[37] *R v Environment Secretary, ex p Spath Holme Ltd* [2001] 2 AC 349, 388.
[38] Ibid, 396.
[39] Marshall, *Constitutional Theory*, ch 4; Cross, *Statutory Interpretation*; Bennion, *Statutory Interpretation*.

of documents such as the reports of royal commissions and parliamentary committees as an aid to identifying the mischief which legislation was intended to remedy.[40] However, Hansard was used to discover the intention of Parliament in approving regulations which gave effect to a decision of the European Court of Justice.[41] In 1992 the House of Lords modified the former rule: a court may use Hansard as an aid to statutory construction where the legislation is ambiguous or obscure and the material relied on consists of clear statements made by a minister or other promoter of the Bill.[42]

Certain presumptions of interpretation are of constitutional importance. Thus many Acts do not in law bind central government departments, since the Crown is presumed not to be bound by legislation, unless this is expressly stated or necessarily implied.[43] It has often been presumed that Parliament does not intend to take away common law rights by mere implication, as distinct from express words. Thus the courts have presumed that Parliament does not intend to take away the property of a subject without compensation[44] or to deprive a subject of access to the courts,[45] and have interpreted penal statutes strictly in favour of the citizen: thus a statute creating a criminal offence will not in the absence of express words be held to be retrospective.[46] In recent decisions, the courts have used these presumptions to develop the idea of common law constitutional rights, such as the right of access to a court, which may be abrogated but only by express words or necessary implication.[47] It has been said that Parliament does not legislate in a vacuum, but against a background of constitutional democracy that includes the 'principle of legality'. According to Lord Hoffmann: 'The principle of legality means that Parliament must squarely confront what it is doing and accept the political cost. Fundamental rights cannot be overridden by general or ambiguous words.'[48]

Most principles of interpretation evolved from judicial decisions, but new rules of interpretation may be imposed on the courts by Parliament. Under the Human Rights Act 1998, all legislation, whenever made, must, 'so far as it is possible to do so', be read and given effect in a way that is compatible with the rights protected by the European Convention.[49]

British membership of the European Union directly affects our traditional approaches to interpretation, since in most European legal systems the methods of legislative drafting and the rules of statutory interpretation are very different from those in Britain. Where it is necessary for a provision of a European treaty or regulation to be interpreted in a British court, art 234 (ex 177) of the EC Treaty enables the question of interpretation to be settled by the European Court of Justice.[50] British courts must follow that court's practice by giving a purposive construction to regulations intended to comply with EC directives.[51]

It is an essential principle of the concept of law that enacted laws should be interpreted by judicial bodies independent of the legislature which made the law: statutory

---

[40] *Black-Clawson International Ltd* v *Papierwerke AG* [1975] AC 591; *Davis* v *Johnson* [1979] AC 264.
[41] *Pickstone* v *Freemans plc* [1989] AC 66.
[42] *Pepper* v *Hart* [1993] AC 593. And on use of Hansard, see *R* v *Environment Secretary, ex p Spath Holme Ltd* (above); and Lord Steyn (2001) 21 OJLS 59.
[43] *Lord Advocate* v *Dumbarton DC* [1990] 2 AC 580; ch 32 C.
[44] *Central Control Board* v *Cannon Brewery Co* [1919] AC 744, 752.
[45] *Chester* v *Bateson* [1920] 1 KB 829.
[46] *Waddington* v *Miah* [1974] 2 All ER 377.
[47] *R* v *Lord Chancellor, ex p Witham* [1998] QB 575. Also *R* v *Home Secretary, ex p Pierson* [1998] AC 539; and *R* v *Home Secretary, ex p Simms* [2000] 2 AC 115.
[48] *R* v *Home Secretary, ex p Simms*, at 131.
[49] See G Marshall [1998] PL 167, [1999] PL 377; and F Bennion [2000] PL 77. And ch 19 C.
[50] Ch 8 A.
[51] *Litster* v *Forth Dry Dock and Engineering Co Ltd* [1990] 1 AC 546.

provisions authorising the government to define the meaning of terms used in an Act of Parliament endanger this principle. While the courts must be able to act independently of the executive in interpreting legislation, their duty is to decide what Parliament must be taken to have intended and they are not free merely to decide what they believe may be in the public interest.[52]

B. Non-legal rules of the constitution

Many important rules of constitutional behaviour, which are observed by the Sovereign, the Prime Minister and other ministers, members of Parliament, judges and civil servants, are contained neither in Acts nor in judicial decisions. It will be shown below that disputes which arise out of these rules rarely lead to action in the courts and that judicial sanctions are not applicable if the rules are broken. Constitutional writers have applied a wide variety of names to these rules: the positive morality of the constitution,[53] the unwritten maxims of the constitution,[54] and 'a whole system of political morality, a whole code of precepts for the guidance of public men'.[55] Dicey referred to them as:

> conventions, understandings, habits or practices which, though they may regulate the conduct of the several members of the sovereign power . . . are not in reality laws at all since they are not enforced by the courts.[56]

Under Dicey's influence, the most common name given to this phenomenon is constitutional convention.

This meaning of the word convention is quite different from its meaning in international law, where a convention is a synonym for a treaty, or binding agreement between states. But the notion of conventional conduct does include a strong element of what is customarily expected, in the sense of ordinary or regular behaviour. In common speech a person may be described as conventional or unconventional, depending on whether he or she conforms to or departs from accepted patterns of social behaviour and opinion. Most discussion of constitutional conventions has gone beyond description of conduct which is merely a customary practice and has suggested that conventions give rise to binding rules of conduct.[57] John Mackintosh described a convention as 'a generally accepted political practice, usually with a record of successful applications or precedents'[58] but other authors describe conventions as:

> rules of constitutional behaviour which are considered to be binding by and upon those who operate the Constitution but which are not enforced by the law courts . . . nor by the presiding officers in the Houses of Parliament.[59]

---

[52] *Duport Steels Ltd* v *Sirs* [1980] 1 All ER 529.

[53] Austin, *The Province of Jurisprudence Determined*, p 259.

[54] Mill, *Representative Government*, ch 5.

[55] Freeman, *Growth of the English Constitution*, p 109, quoted in Dicey, p 418. And see O Hood Phillips (1966) 29 MLR 137.

[56] Dicey, *The Law of the Constitution*, p 24.

[57] See, e.g., Mitchell, *Constitutional Law*, p 39; Wheare, *The Statute of Westminster and Dominion Status*, p 10; Marshall, *Constitutional Conventions*, chs 1 and 13; Heard, *Canadian Constitutional Conventions*, ch 7.

[58] Mackintosh, *The British Cabinet*, p 13. Brazier, in *Constitutional Practice*, p 3, leaves it open whether the practices that he describes have the status of 'rules'; at (1992) 43 NILQ 262 he distinguishes conventions (which impose duties) from matters of practice.

[59] Marshall and Moodie, *Some Problems of the Constitution,* pp 22–3. Marshall, *Constitutional Conventions*, p 3, refers to conventions as 'non-legal rules of constitutional behaviour'.

Mackintosh here regarded conventions as merely *descriptive* statements of constitutional practice, based on observation of what actually happens; the latter approach regards conventions as *prescriptive* statements of what should happen, based in part upon observation but also upon constitutional principle. We return later to the choice between these two approaches;[60] but at present we will assume that conventions are concerned with matters of obligation and will explore the nature of that obligation.

In this section it is not possible to summarise all existing conventional rules; the aim is rather to discuss their general characteristics. Other chapters will examine the non-legal rules which apply to particular institutions. Some of the most important conventional rules will be discussed in the chapters dealing with responsible government, the Crown and the Cabinet. First, some examples will be given of non-legal rules and in each case relevant legal rules will be mentioned.

Non-legal rules of the constitution: some examples

1 It is a rule of common law that the royal assent must be given before a Bill which has been approved by both Houses of Parliament can become an Act of Parliament.[61] The manner in which the royal assent may be given is now regulated by statute and in certain circumstances the royal assent may be signified by others on behalf of the Sovereign.[62] These legal rules deal with a vital matter of legal form. But a more important conventional rule is that the royal assent is granted by the Sovereign on the advice of her ministers. Where a Bill has been passed by both Houses of Parliament, the royal assent will be given as a matter of course. The Sovereign's legal power to refuse assent was last exercised by Queen Anne in 1708, when (apparently with the approval of her ministers and without objection by Parliament) the royal assent was refused to the Scottish Militia Bill.[63] In the Irish crisis of 1912–14 the Unionists suggested to George V that he should withhold assent from the Bill to give home rule to Ireland. The Liberal Prime Minister, Asquith, advised the King against this and the royal assent was granted.[64] While the Queen may not of her own initiative refuse the royal assent the position may be different if ministers themselves advise this course, although this advice would have to be defended in Parliament and would be highly controversial.

2 At common law the Sovereign has unlimited power to appoint whom she pleases to be her ministers. Statutes provide for the payment of salaries to ministers and limit the number of appointments which may be made from the House of Commons.[65] There is no rule of law which prevents the Sovereign appointing to ministerial office a person who is outside Parliament. But all appointments are made by the Sovereign on the advice of the Prime Minister and the principle of ministerial responsibility[66] requires that a minister should belong to one or other House of Parliament. If a non-member is appointed to ministerial office, he or she will receive a life peerage: the earlier practice of expecting such a person appointed to win a seat at an early by-election (last seen in 1964) has lapsed since no government today willingly causes a by-election to be held in one of its own seats.

---

[60] Pages 26–8 below.
[61] Ch 4 C.
[62] Royal Assent Act 1967, Regency Acts 1937–53.
[63] Hearn, *The Government of England*, p 61.
[64] Jennings, *Cabinet Government*, pp 395–400. See also ch 12 B. Cf Brazier, *Constitutional Practice*, pp 193–6.
[65] Ch 9 G.
[66] Ch 7.

While therefore there is a rule that ministers of the Crown should be members of one or other House, limited exceptions to the rule may be accepted, as was formerly seen in respect of the Scottish Law Officers (the Lord Advocate and the Solicitor-General for Scotland).[67]

3 Although the conduct of a general election is governed by detailed statutory rules,[68] no legal rule regulates the conduct of the Prime Minister when the result of the election is known. But there is a conventional rule that the government must have the confidence of a majority in the Commons. Therefore when it is clear from the election results that the Prime Minister on whose advice the election was called has lost the election and another party has been successful, he must resign immediately without, as formerly, waiting for the new Parliament to meet.[69] Where the result of the election gives no party an overall majority in the Commons, the Prime Minister may continue in office for such period as is necessary to discover whether he is able to form a coalition or to govern with the support of other parties. In February 1974, when this situation arose, three days elapsed before Mr Heath decided to resign, having learned that the Liberal MPs would not support him. In 1979, an Opposition motion of no confidence in the Labour government was carried by one vote (on 28 March 1979) and forced Mr Callaghan to call an election in May 1979. He resigned as Prime Minister as soon as it was clear that the Conservative party had won the election.

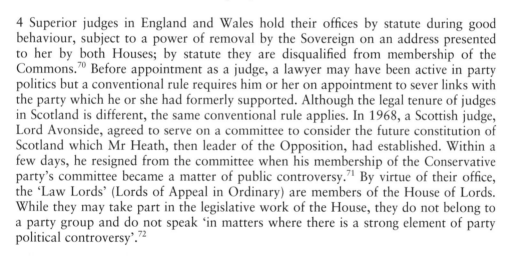

4 Superior judges in England and Wales hold their offices by statute during good behaviour, subject to a power of removal by the Sovereign on an address presented to her by both Houses; by statute they are disqualified from membership of the Commons.[70] Before appointment as a judge, a lawyer may have been active in party politics but a conventional rule requires him or her on appointment to sever links with the party which he or she had formerly supported. Although the legal tenure of judges in Scotland is different, the same conventional rule applies. In 1968, a Scottish judge, Lord Avonside, agreed to serve on a committee to consider the future constitution of Scotland which Mr Heath, then leader of the Opposition, had established. Within a few days, he resigned from the committee when his membership of the Conservative party's committee became a matter of public controversy.[71] By virtue of their office, the 'Law Lords' (Lords of Appeal in Ordinary) are members of the House of Lords. While they may take part in the legislative work of the House, they do not belong to a party group and do not speak 'in matters where there is a strong element of party political controversy'.[72]

5 Under the Scotland Act 1998, the Scottish Parliament has, since July 1999, had power to legislate on the subjects devolved to Scotland, but the Westminster Parliament retains full power to legislate for Scotland. By what is known as the 'Sewel convention', now based on an agreement between the government in London and the Scottish Executive, the Westminster Parliament is not asked to legislate for Scotland on devolved matters except with the agreement of the Scottish Parliament.[73]

---

[67] By the Scotland Act 1998, ss 44(1)(b) and 48, the Scottish Law Officers are now members of the Scottish Executive. The holder of the new office of Advocate General of Scotland is a minister in the UK government (s 87).

[68] Ch 9 D.

[69] Ch 12 B.

[70] Chs 9 G, 18 C.

[71] See *The Times* and *The Scotsman*, 26 July–6 August 1968.

[72] See statement by the senior Law Lord, Lord Bingham, HL Deb, 22 June 2000, col 419.

[73] See HL Deb, 21 July 1998, col 791; Cm 4444 (1999), para 13. Also ch 3 B.

6 The legal opinions which the Law Officers of the Crown give to the government are in law confidential and are protected by legal privilege from being produced as evidence in court proceedings. They may, however, be published by the government or quoted from in Parliament if (as rarely happens) a minister considers it expedient that the Commons should be told of their contents.[74] During the Westland affair in 1986, the Secretary of State for Trade and Industry (Mr Brittan) authorised civil servants to leak to the press extracts from a confidential letter to him from the Solicitor-General, without first seeking the latter's consent. 'Cover' but not approval for the leak was sought from the Prime Minister's office. Under a storm of criticism for these events, Mr Brittan had to resign, thus reinforcing the authority of the rule which the Law Officers sought to defend.[75] The code of conduct for ministers now states that the content of advice given by the Law Officers 'must not be disclosed outside Government without their authority'.[76]

Many more examples of conventional rules could be given. They serve a wide variety of purposes and vary widely in importance. Such rules develop under every system of government, whether a written constitution exists or not. Their special importance in Britain is that it is through such rules and practices that the system of Cabinet government develops and continues to evolve. In earlier times, conventional rules were important in the process by which self-governing colonies in the British Empire attained dominion status,[77] and they determine the Queen's role today in Commonwealth countries where she is head of state.[78] When amendments to the Canadian constitution could be made only by Act of the Westminster Parliament, an elaborate system of conventions and practices evolved as to how the process of amendment should be set in motion.[79] With such a diversity of subject matter, what general characteristics, if any, do these rules possess?

General characteristics[80]

Although some long-established conventional rules (like the rule that the Queen's speech, read at the opening of each session of Parliament, is prepared by her ministers) have great authority and are universally known, many have developed out of a desire to avoid the formality, explicitness and publicity associated with changes in the law. The development of a regular practice may enable legislation on a point of principle to be avoided. The role of the Sovereign in the conduct of government has almost disappeared since the 18th century without a series of statutes removing one royal power after another. In the same way, many powers have been acquired by the Prime Minister by the operation of convention rather than as the result of legislation. Conventional rules may be used for discreetly managing the internal relationships of government while the outward legal form is left intact.

The informality of such rules is often accompanied by the fact that the rules themselves are not formulated in writing, for example, the rule that judges should not

---

[74] Edwards, *The Law Officers of the Crown*, pp 256–61.
[75] See, e.g., Linklater and Leigh, *Not Without Honour*, ch 11; and G Marshall [1986] PL 184.
[76] *Ministerial Code*, para 24; and see chs 7 and 13 C.
[77] Ch 15 C.
[78] V Bogdanor and G Marshall [1996] PL 205.
[79] Marshall, *Constitutional Conventions*, ch 11.
[80] A full discussion by the Supreme Court of Canada is in *Reference re Amendment of the Constitution of Canada* (1982) 125 DLR (3d) 1. See also C R Munro (1975) 91 LQR 218, W Maley (1985) 48 MLR 121, R Brazier (1992) 43 NILQ 262 and G Wilson's postscript to Nolan and Sedley, *The Making and Remaking of the British Constitution*, pp 95–133.

undertake party political activities. But this is not always the case. The government may give to the Commons an undertaking about the future use of its powers – for example, about the laying of treaties before the House to enable them to be debated[81] – or may convey to the House undertakings regarding future practice in the making of certain appointments by the Sovereign or Prime Minister. Such undertakings are publicly recorded.[82] One result of the recent debate on ministerial responsibility is the publication of documents containing guidance for ministers and civil servants on their duties to Parliament.[83]

The development of unwritten rules is often an evolutionary process. In retrospect, it is possible to identify the time when the royal assent to a Bill was last refused (1708), when the Lord Chief Justice of England last held a seat in the Cabinet (1806), and when a member of the House of Lords last held office as Prime Minister (1902). The fact that each of these events is virtually inconceivable today and would be regarded as contrary to good constitutional practice, does not mean that this has been so ever since the last occurrence.[84] At a given moment of time, it may be impossible to tell whether practice on a certain matter has hardened into a rule, particularly where the practice is negative in character.

It is for these reasons, as well as the fact that they operate in a political context, that disputes may arise about the existence and content of conventional rules. Moreover, different rules are enforceable in different ways. While the Prime Minister interprets and enforces the rules regarding the duties and collective responsibility of ministers,[85] the enforcement of other conventional rules may depend essentially on the force of public and political opinion. Disputes about the existence and content of legal rules are typically settled by judicial decision. If many legal rules have an 'open texture',[86] how much more 'open' will be the texture of non-legal rules where there is no definite procedure for resolving disputes about existence and content.

In the past, accounts of constitutional conventions often concentrated on the rules by which powers legally vested in the Sovereign came to be exercised by ministers of the Crown. Dicey considered that conventions were 'rules intended to regulate the exercise of the whole of the remaining discretionary powers of the Crown'.[87] In fact, many non-legal rules fall outside this category. It is more accurate to say that conventional rules regulate the conduct of those holding public office. Our constitutional system allots different roles to the Sovereign, ministers, judges, civil servants and so on. Anyone who would play one of these roles must observe the restraints which the system imposes on those who accept that office. Edward VIII was not willing to accept these constraints and was required to abdicate.[88] So, too, a minister who does not observe or does not accept the constraints of his office must resign. Mr Nicholas Fairbairn, Solicitor-General for Scotland, resigned after making comments to the press on the Glasgow rape case, one day before an important statement on the subject was to be made to Parliament by the Lord Advocate.[89] In January 1986, Mr Michael Heseltine, Secretary of State for Defence, walked out of a Cabinet meeting and resigned his

---

[81] The so-called Ponsonby Rule: HC Deb, 1 April 1924, col 2001; ch 15 B.
[82] See HC Deb, 11 December 1962, cols 209–10 (appointment of Serjeant at Arms); and Cmnd 8323, 1981, para 23 (Comptroller and Auditor General).
[83] Ch 7.
[84] On the work of Reading LCJ and Darling J for the government during the 1914–18 war, see Ewing and Gearty, *The Struggle for Civil Liberties*, pp 80–93.
[85] See now the *Ministerial Code*; and chs 7 and 13 C.
[86] See Hart, *The Concept of Law*, pp 121–32.
[87] Dicey, p 426.
[88] Ch 12 A.
[89] HC Deb, 21 January 1982, col 423.

post because he was not prepared to accept Cabinet Office clearance for all further ministerial statements on the Westland affair.[90] Similar constraints operate at the institutional level. If the House of Lords does not accept its subordinate role when confronted with the determined will of the Commons, the House knows that its remaining legislative powers might be cut back still further.

Why are conventional rules observed?

Dicey, writing as a lawyer in a period dominated by Austinian jurisprudence according to which laws were observed because they could be enforced against the citizen by the coercive power of the state, said:

> the sanction which constrains the boldest political adventurer to obey the fundamental principles of the constitution and the conventions in which these principles are expressed, is the fact that the breach of these principles and of these conventions will almost immediately bring the offender into conflict with the courts and the law of the land.[91]

To support this view, Dicey argued that Parliament meets at least once a year because the government would be compelled to act unlawfully if this did not happen. This argument has been shown to be much weaker than Dicey had supposed.[92] In any event, the rule which the supposed legal sanction supports is antiquated. Today Parliament is expected not merely to meet once a year but to be in session at Westminster for about 34 weeks in the year, interspersed with holidays and the long summer recess. During these weeks there is a customary pattern of parliamentary work to be done. The Provisional Collection of Taxes Act 1968[93] imposes certain constraints upon the timetable of Parliament, but this in itself does not explain why Parliament meets regularly throughout the year. That Parliament should do so is expected by politicians and citizens alike.

It is nearer the mark to say, as did Sir Ivor Jennings, that conventions are observed because of the political difficulties which arise if they are not.[94] As these rules regulate the conduct of those holding public office, possibly the most acute political difficulty which can arise for such a person is to be forced out of office. But an explanation merely in terms of political difficulties is inadequate since not every event which gives rise to political difficulties (for example, an unpopular Bill) is a breach of a conventional rule. The Supreme Court of Canada stated that the main purpose of conventions is to ensure that the legal framework of the constitution is operated in accordance with the prevailing constitutional values of the period.[95] On this basis, conventions are observed for the positive reason that they express prevailing constitutional values and for the negative reason of avoiding the difficulties that may follow from 'unconstitutional' conduct.

The meaning of 'unconstitutional'

Where a written constitution ranks as fundamental law, acts which conflict with the constitution may be held unconstitutional and thus illegal. In the United Kingdom, the term 'unconstitutional' has no defined content. The 19th-century jurist, Austin, suggested that the Sovereign was acting unconstitutionally when he infringed the maxims of government which with popular approval he generally observed – but by definition

---

[90] See D Oliver and R Austin (1987) 40 Parliamentary Affairs 20; and note 75 above.
[91] Dicey, pp 445–6.
[92] For example, by Jennings, *The Law and the Constitution*, pp 128–9.
[93] Ch 10 C.
[94] *The Law and the Constitution*, p 134.
[95] *Reference re Amendment of the Constitution of Canada* (1982) 125 DLR (3d) 1, 84.

the Austinian Sovereign could not act illegally.[96] For Freeman, unconstitutional conduct was conduct contrary to 'the undoubted principles of the unwritten but universally accepted constitution'.[97] Where conduct breaches a written constitution, 'unconstitutional' is likely to mean 'illegal'; where it breaches unwritten values or principles of government, the term may mean 'wrong'. The two senses of 'unconstitutional' were illustrated in the Canadian constitutional controversy of 1981–82, when the Supreme Court dealt separately with the issues of whether it would be (a) illegal and (b) in breach of convention for the Federal Parliament to adopt resolutions requesting amendments to the constitution which were opposed by eight of the ten provinces.[98] On the first question, the court held (by seven to two) that such action would not be illegal, but on the second question (by six to three) that it would be in breach of convention.

While conduct may be unconstitutional without being illegal, illegal acts may also be unconstitutional. British politicians who instigated or covered up criminal offences for political ends would be in breach of the code of behaviour recognised by public opinion, as well as being in breach of the criminal law. Ministers are restrained from exceeding their powers not only by the likelihood of legal sanctions, but also by the obligation on government to conduct its affairs according to law. When used concerning executive decisions, 'unconstitutional' implies that a decision is not merely incorrect in law but also contrary to fundamental principle, for example where a policy of the Inland Revenue involved 'taxation by self asserted administrative discretion and not by law'.[99] It is in this sense that exemplary damages may in exceptional cases be awarded in the law of tort when public authorities or officials commit wrongful acts that are 'oppressive, arbitrary or unconstitutional'.[100]

However, it is often not easy to determine whether the boundary between constitutional and unconstitutional conduct has been crossed, especially where there is no universally accepted rule of conduct. Different politicians may take opposing views of the constitutional propriety of the acts of a government. Unpopular proposals for new legislation are not for that reason unconstitutional, but a Bill which sought to destroy essential features of the electoral system or to give the Cabinet power to overrule decisions of the courts could rightly be described as unconstitutional.

Another difficulty in determining what is constitutional in a given situation is that there may be no relevant precedent. When in 1932 the Cabinet of the National government agreed to differ on a major issue of economic policy, an attack on the government for unconstitutional conduct was met by the rejoinder:

> Who can say what is constitutional in the conduct of a National Government? It is a precedent, an experiment, a new practice, to meet a new emergency, a new condition of things.[101]

In 1975 the open disagreement of the Labour Cabinet over Britain's continued membership of the EEC was defended in similar terms.

Consequences of a breach of conventional rule

Various consequences may follow the breach of conventional rules. Loss of office or departure from public life is the severest consequence, as when a minister is forced to resign because of an open disagreement with stated government policy. The force of

---

[96] Austin, *The Province of Jurisprudence Determined*, pp 257–60.
[97] Freeman, *The Growth of the English Constitution*, p 112.
[98] Note 80 above.
[99] *Vestey v Inland Revenue Commissioners* [1980] AC 1148, 1173.
[100] *Rookes v Barnard* [1964] AC 1129; *Kuddus v Chief Constable of Leicestershire* [2001] 3 All ER 193.
[101] HC Deb, 8 February 1932, col 535 (Mr Baldwin).

public opinion may simply force the offender to think again: thus the Scottish judge who in 1968 joined a committee established by the Conservative party resigned rather than prejudice the work of the committee.[102] In these instances, the outcome reinforces the established rule. A less serious consequence would be a reprimand or a reminder not to act similarly in the future, given by someone in a position to enforce the rule. If no adverse consequences follow, the matter becomes more open. It may be expedient that, for instance, the Prime Minister should turn a blind eye to acts of colleagues that breach a rule for ministers: but if such acts are repeatedly condoned, it must be asked whether the rule has been abandoned or modified. Some departures from normal practice may not harm the core elements of government. Between 1997 and 2001 there existed a sub-committee of the Cabinet that included both Labour ministers and Liberal Democrat members. Its function was to provide liaison between the government and Liberal Democrats on reforms which the parties had both supported at the 1997 election. The utility of this device was limited and it was not revived after the election in 2001.

As constitutional rules often give rise to reciprocal obligations, one consequence of a breach may be to release another office-holder from the normal constraints that would otherwise be binding. When Ian Smith's Cabinet in 1965 unilaterally declared Rhodesia's independence, the immediate response of the UK government, conveyed through the Governor-General of Rhodesia, was to dismiss the entire Cabinet. This dismissal proved purely nominal. More significantly, the Southern Rhodesia Act 1965 was passed at Westminster to give the British government power to legislate for the domestic affairs of Rhodesia, overriding the previous convention that Westminster would not exercise its sovereignty in such matters except with the agreement of the Rhodesian government.[103]

Another consequence may be the passing of legislation to avoid a similar breach in the future. When in 1909 the Lords rejected the Liberal government's Finance Bill, the crisis was resolved only by the Parliament Act 1911, which removed the power of the Lords to veto or delay money Bills. The 1911 Act contained other provisions intended to place the Lords–Commons relationship on a new footing.[104] These provisions led in turn to new conventions regarding the use by the House of Lords of its residual powers. While the partial reform of the House of Lords in 1999 (when most hereditary peers were excluded) was not intended to alter the use by the House of these powers, it may nonetheless have opened up changes in the conduct of the House.

Should all constitutional rules be enacted as law?

In theory, all the non-legal rules of the constitution could be enacted in legal form by one or more Acts of Parliament. Written constitutions in the Commonwealth have adopted various means of incorporating conventions: express enactment of the main rules, wholesale adoption by reference to practice in the United Kingdom and so on.[105]

If a written constitution were to be drafted for the United Kingdom, many hard decisions on these matters would have to be made. It would, for example, be very difficult to anticipate every possible eventuality in which the Sovereign might be required to invite a new Prime Minister to form a government. There would be no real difficulty in framing the main principles of responsible government, but this would make little

---

[102] Note 71 above.
[103] Cf *Madzimbamuto* v *Lardner-Burke* [1969] AC 645, 723.
[104] Ch 10 B.
[105] de Smith, *The New Commonwealth and its Constitutions*, pp 78–87. For an Australian exercise in restating the conventions, see C Sampford and D Wood [1987] PL 231.

difference if the principles continued to govern an essentially political relationship between government and Parliament: to make the doctrine of responsible government enforceable by the courts would be to change its character entirely.[106]

While legislation may be useful in the case of particular rules that need to be clarified, there is little to be said for 'codifying' the non-legal rules of the constitution. They cover so diverse an area that they could not be included within a single code. Even if the attempt were made, it would be impossible to stop the process by which formal rules are gradually modified by informal rules, principles and practices from starting over again.

There is indeed an indistinct borderline between conduct that is a matter of habitual practice and conduct that occurs as a result of what is felt to be constitutional obligation. Textbooks on constitutional law often exaggerate the extent to which rules govern political life.

In 1963, by a procedure without precedent, the 14th Earl of Home was chosen to follow Harold Macmillan as Prime Minister and renounced his title so that he could enter the House of Commons as Sir Alec Douglas-Home. Commenting upon these events, Professor Griffith coined two aphorisms as an antidote against a convention-dominated view of the constitution: 'the constitution is what happens' and 'if it works, it's constitutional'. His comment concluded: 'So let us delete those pages in constitutional textbooks headed Conventions, and talk about what happens and why what happened yesterday may not happen tomorrow.'[107] In other words, it is better to discuss why it would be politically impossible today for a Prime Minister to govern from the House of Lords, than to try and read back into past events a rule to this effect.

One reply to this approach involves considering the relation between the reasons which give rise to a rule and the rule itself. Legal rules, whether made by the judges or by Parliament, may continue long after the original reasons for them have been forgotten. In the constitutional field, the informality of many non-legal rules enables them to disappear or to change as the underlying reasons for the rule change. This does not mean that so long as the original circumstances continue, there is no rule. Within a stable political system, what is learned by experience can be expressed in the form of rules for future conduct. The abdication of Edward VIII and the reasons for it must have influenced Elizabeth II and her advisers. The failure of the 'agreement to differ' in 1932 has not encouraged later Cabinets to repeat the experiment. One lesson from previous events is that short-term political expediency may be a temptation that an experienced government ought to resist, and that constitutional principle may provide more reliable norms of conduct. As Freeman wrote in 1872:

> Political men may debate whether such and such a course is or is not constitutional, just as lawyers may debate whether such a course is not legal. But the very form of the debate implies that there is a Constitution to be observed, just as in the other case it implies that there is a law to be observed.[108]

The motives for human conduct are usually mixed. If we seek to understand the behaviour of the Sovereign, a politician or a judge, we may discover a degree of enlightened self-interest and also a strong perception of constitutional obligation. If that

[106] In 1996 Sir Richard Scott said that if ministers did not accept the obligations of accountability, a statutory duty requiring them to keep Parliament informed should be enacted and enforced by the courts: [1996] PL 410, 426. And see pp 103, 114 below.

[107] [1963] PL 401–2. For criticism of the distinction between law and convention, see Jennings, *The Law and the Constitution*, p 132 and Mitchell, *Constitutional Law*, pp 34–8; and in reply, Marshall, *Constitutional Theory*, pp 7–12. See also note 80 above.

[108] *The Growth of the English Constitution*, p 112; cf Loughlin, *Public Law and Political Theory*, p 53.

perception is shared by others in a similar position, as well as by informed comment-
ators, it is difficult to explain such behaviour without reference to the perceived
obligation. The fact that conventional rules may change without formal amendment
does not mean that they are irrelevant to political behaviour.

The attitude of the courts

In this section it has been assumed that the rules under discussion are not capable
of being enforced through the courts. If, when a rule has been broken, a remedy is
available in the courts for securing relief or imposing a sanction upon the wrongdoer,
this would indicate that the rule has the quality of law. Where a non-legal rule has
been broken, no remedy will be available in the courts. Often the citizen's only
recourse will be political action – a complaint to an MP, a letter to the press, a public
demonstration or protest. In view of the political nature of most conventional rules,
the stress on political or parliamentary remedies is appropriate. Moreover, many
conventional rules, for example those relating to the Cabinet system, do not affect a
citizen's rights closely enough for a judicial remedy to be justified.

It may however be necessary for a court to take into account the existence of a conventional rule in making its decision on a point of law. This is likely to happen in
administrative law cases where the courts have taken judicial notice of the fact that
civil servants take decisions in the name of ministers and that ministers may be called
to account by Parliament for the decisions, but the courts are also aware that
such accountability may not provide an effective remedy for the individual.[109] The
Australian High Court took account of the conventional rules which in practice
restricted legislation by the UK Parliament for Australia before the rules were enacted
in the Statute of Westminster 1931.[110] But on an appeal from Rhodesia following
the unilateral declaration of independence, the Judicial Committee, referring to the
former convention by which Westminster would not legislate for Rhodesia except at
the request of the Rhodesian government, stated that the convention had no legal effect
and that the Judicial Committee were concerned only with the legal powers of
Parliament.[111]

The Crossman diaries case is an outstanding illustration of the interrelation of legal
and non-legal rules. As a last resort, an attempt was made by the Attorney-General to
prevent the breach of a conventional rule and to establish the existence of a legal obligation. The court held that former Cabinet ministers could be restrained by injunction
from publishing confidential information which came to them as ministers, since there
was a legal obligation to respect that confidentiality.[112] But the court was not simply
enforcing the convention of collective responsibility; that convention was no more
than one factor taken into account by the judge in establishing the limits of the legal
doctrine of confidence. In the different context of the Canadian constitution, by a
reference procedure which permits Canadian courts to give wide-ranging advisory
opinions, the Supreme Court of Canada in 1981 gave an opinion on the existence of
the conventions governing the process of constitutional amendment.[113] It is difficult to
imagine circumstances in which the British courts would have jurisdiction to give a
similar opinion.

---

[109] *Carltona Ltd* v *Commissioners of Works* [1943] 2 All ER 560; pp 116, 274 below. And see *R* v *Environment Secretary, ex p Notts CC* [1986] AC 240.
[110] *Copyright Owners Reproduction Society Ltd* v *EMI (Australia) Pty Ltd* (1958) 100 CLR 597.
[111] *Madzimbamuto* v *Lardner-Burke* [1969] AC 645.
[112] *A-G* v *Jonathan Cape Ltd* [1976] QB 752; ch 13 B.
[113] Note 80 above. Cf *Adegbenro* v *Akintola* [1963] AC 614.

It is however possible that developments in public law may broaden the scope for judicial decisions concerning the observance of conventional practices by public authorities. In the GCHQ case, concerning a decision by the Prime Minister that was imposed on the civil servants without prior consultation, evidence showed there to be an invariable practice by government of consulting with civil service unions before changing conditions of employment.[114] If this practice were viewed merely as a constitutional convention, the unions would have no enforceable rights in the matter. But the House of Lords held that, as a matter of public law, the unions had a legitimate expectation of being consulted that would have been protected,[115] had this not been overridden by national security considerations. Many aspects of ministerial conduct, that formerly rested on unwritten rules, are now contained in the *Ministerial Code*, issued by the Cabinet Office. Should an individual be adversely affected by the breach of a minister's duties under the Code, an argument based on legitimate expectations might possibly succeed that would have been certain to fail if phrased in terms of breach of an unwritten convention.

C. Other sources of the constitution

The law and custom of Parliament

While a distinction may be drawn between rules of the constitution which have the force of law and those which do not, it is difficult to classify the law and custom of Parliament under either heading. In earlier days, reference was often made to the 'High Court of Parliament'.[116] Each House has power over its own procedure and has certain privileges and immunities. The inherent authority of each House to control its own internal affairs is respected by the ordinary courts of law, who seek to avoid interfering in these matters.[117] Many rules of constitutional importance are contained in the standing orders of the House of Commons, as well as in resolutions of the House and in other sources of the practice of the House, such as rulings by the Speaker.[118]

Moreover, many informal practices and understandings are observed between the two main parties in the Commons, between the two front benches and the backbench members, and between the main parties and the smaller parties. These practices are not in standing orders, nor are they often mentioned in that authoritative guide to the procedure of Parliament, Erskine May, but they directly affect the conduct of parliamentary business. These practices resemble the conventional rules of the constitution which apply outside Parliament. Departure from these practices could lead to changed conduct within Parliament, for example the withdrawal of cooperation between government and opposition (such as agreed pairing between absent MPs) and possibly to changes in the formal rules of parliamentary business.

Within Parliament, therefore, there are formal rules, informal rules, principles and practices; and the distinction between these various categories is often no more certain in Parliament than outside. In general, courts have no jurisdiction to apply and enforce the law of Parliament.

---

[114] *CCSU v Minister for the Civil Service* [1985] AC 374.
[115] See ch 30 C.
[116] McIlwain, *The High Court of Parliament*, especially ch 2.
[117] Ch 11 A.
[118] Erskine May, *Parliamentary Practice*, pp 1–8, 190–1.

Legal and constitutional literature

In English law, as a general rule no legal textbook has intrinsic authority as a source of law: the authority of the most eminent textbook is confined to the extent to which a court considers that it accurately reproduces the law enacted by the legislature or decided by earlier courts. Where a statute has not yet been judicially interpreted or where no court has pronounced authoritatively on a matter of common law, the opinions of textbook writers and academic authors may be of great value when a case arises for decision.[119] Dicey's *Law of the Constitution* has profoundly influenced judicial reasoning; and the development of administrative law owes much to the writing of the late Professor de Smith and of Sir William Wade.

In Scots law, the position is different as regards the past. A series of eminent legal authors between the mid-17th and early 19th centuries, including Stair, Erskine and Hume, are known as the institutional writers. Their work expounded the private law and criminal law of Scotland in a systematic manner which derived much from the institutional writers of Roman law: in the absence of other authority, a statement in their works may be taken as settling the law.[120] The approach of the Scottish legal system to legal authority was seen in *Burmah Oil Co v Lord Advocate*,[121] relating to the Crown's prerogative: the case having reached the House of Lords on appeal from Scotland, counsel and judges referred extensively to the civilian writers of earlier centuries, in a manner untypical of the English common law.

Legal writers on the constitution are handicapped by the unreality of many of the legal terms which they must sometimes employ.[122] Statements about the prerogative powers of the Crown often seem archaic or to be conferring despotic powers upon the Sovereign, until it is realised that they concern powers of government exercised by ministers, civil servants and other Crown servants.

In some areas of the constitution, books such as Jennings's *Cabinet Government*, Mackintosh's *The British Cabinet*, Griffith and Ryle's *Parliament*, and Brazier's *Constitutional Practice* are a valuable record of practice. Since they are founded both on historical sources and on contemporary political accounts, it is not surprising that works on British government are seldom unanimous in their description of controversial events (for example, the differing interpretations of the political crisis in 1931 which led to the formation of the National government).[123] Rules of official secrecy may make it difficult to write about current practice. While most Cabinet papers are available in the Public Record Office after 30 years, the structure of Cabinet committees and the rules of conduct for ministers were, until 1992, regarded as secret.[124] Another problem is that historical precedents are often of doubtful relevance to present issues. Jennings, whose book was first published in 1936, used constitutional precedents dating from 1841.[125] But today the speed of change in government has accelerated to a point at which it may seldom be useful to look at precedents from before 1979, let alone as far back as 1945.

In the field of parliamentary procedure, a work which has especial authority is Erskine May's *Parliamentary Practice*. First published in 1844, this is revised regularly under the editorship of the Clerk to the House of Commons and it summarises the collective

---

[119] For clear recognition of this by the House of Lords, see *Woolwich BS v IRC (No 2)* [1993] AC 70, 163 (Lord Goff).
[120] See *Stair Memorial Encyclopedia, the Laws of Scotland*, vol 22, pp 212–19.
[121] [1965] AC 75; ch 12 D.
[122] Cf Bagehot, *The English Constitution*, pp 99–100.
[123] See Bassett, *1931: Political Crisis*.
[124] Ch 13 B.
[125] Jennings, *Cabinet Government*, p 9.

experience of the Clerks of the House.[126] It is essentially a means of reference to the original sources, which are found in standing orders, in resolutions of the House, and in rulings given by the Speaker and recorded in Hansard.

Finally, there is a more diverse source of information, namely the unending flow from government and Parliament of reports of such bodies as royal commissions, departmental committees, committees of Parliament and tribunals of inquiry. Many of these reports have concerned important constitutional topics, the most notable in recent years being the first report of the (Nolan) committee on standards in public life, and Sir Richard Scott's massive report on the 'arms for Iraq' inquiry.[127] There is also the prolific class of reports by select committees of the House of Commons into the activities of government departments.[128] The reports of the Parliamentary Ombudsman give a more detailed insight into the methods of central departments than can be obtained from the law reports or Hansard alone. British membership of the European Union has given rise to a flow of official publications from the headquarters of the European Community.

D. Constitutional government in Britain

Evolutionary development

The British system of government is flexible, not in the sense that it is unstable but in that most of its principles and rules can be changed by an Act of Parliament or the establishment of a new conventional rule. Perhaps because of this flexibility, the United Kingdom has, at least since 1688, escaped those revolutionary convulsions which may occur in countries with more rigid constitutions but less stable political or social systems. Since the settlement of 1688, there have been innumerable changes in the system of government, some freely conceded but many fought for by political action. The result has been a complete change from personal rule by the monarch to the ascendancy of the Prime Minister who, as leader of the majority party in Parliament and head of the executive branch of the state, is able with other ministers in the Cabinet to direct and coordinate the activities of central government.

Many of the older forms and organs have survived from earlier times and these are tolerated or respected because they represent historic continuity. Writing in 1867, Walter Bagehot in *The English Constitution* distinguished between the *dignified* parts of the constitution 'which excite and preserve the reverence of the population' and the *efficient* parts, 'by which it, in fact, works and rules'.[129] Bagehot called it the characteristic merit of the constitution, 'that its dignified parts are very complicated and somewhat imposing, very old and rather venerable; while its efficient part, at least when in great and critical action, is decidedly simple and rather modern.'[130] The apparent continuity can be misleading, causing the Royal Commission on the Constitution, which reported in favour of devolution in 1973, to say: 'The United Kingdom already possesses a constitution which in its essentials has served well for some hundreds of years.'[131] Such a complacent reflection draws attention away from many significant changes in government and politics that have occurred in the past, are now occurring, and are yet to come.

---

[126] See the 22nd edn by D Limon and W R McKay, 1997.
[127] Respectively Cm 2850–1, 1995, and HC 115 (1995–96).
[128] Ch 10 D.
[129] *The English Constitution*, p 61.
[130] Ibid, p 65.
[131] Kilbrandon Report, para 395.

The evolutionary nature of British government can be illustrated in many ways. While the Sovereign has lost the role of governing the country since 1688, further changes in the residual functions of the monarch may yet occur. Potential tension between Cabinet and Prime Ministerial government remains and the relationship between House of Commons and Whitehall is not entrenched. Labour's programme of reform from 1997 to 2001 stemmed from a belief in the need for change in the accountability of government, the electoral system, the composition of Parliament, the structure of the United Kingdom and the protection of human rights. In 2001, no one supposed that the changes already made had caused democratic government to reach a plateau of perfection.

The party system

Parliamentary government cannot be explained solely in terms of legal and conventional rules. It depends essentially upon the political base which underlies it, in particular on the party system around which political life is organised. Given the present political parties and the electoral system, it is accepted that, following a general election, the party with a majority of seats in the House of Commons will form the government. As the British system of politics is strongly centralised, power to direct national affairs passes to the leadership of the party which, in popular terms, has won the general election. Except for February 1974, every general election held between 1935 and 2001 produced an absolute majority in the Commons for one or other of the major parties. Even if that majority is counted in single figures (as it was in 1950–51, 1964–66 and after October 1974) it serves as a basis for the government's authority. In terms of the ability to govern for the time being, it is irrelevant that the majority of seats in the Commons represents only a minority of votes cast by the electorate – as it did in every election between 1906 and 1992 except in 1931 and 1935. The general election in 2001 led to a House of Commons in which there were 412 Labour MPs, 166 Conservative MPs, 52 Liberal Democrats and 29 other MPs. Where elections were held for the Scottish Parliament and the Welsh National Assembly in 1999, a different electoral system led in each country to a result in which Labour won the largest number of seats and votes, but (when members were added on a proportional basis) lacked an absolute majority of seats. In both countries, it was necessary for the Labour and Liberal Democrat parties to form a coalition government, in Scotland immediately and in Wales only after a year of minority government by Labour.

The tendency of the Westminster electoral system to reward the party with the largest number of votes by conferring on it a majority of seats is often said to provide strong government, on the assumption that the governing party will continue to be supported by its majority in the Commons. However, given the concentration of power in the hands of the executive, the British system is tolerable only because of the range of restraints upon government which exist. One restraint is the certainty of a general election, guaranteed by law to occur at least every five years and often likely to occur more frequently. Another restraint is that government policies run the gauntlet of criticism from Opposition parties and others in Parliament. Another is that no government can ignore the force of public reaction to its measures (as was seen when Mrs Thatcher was ousted from power in 1990): legislation which has passed through Parliament may not be enforceable unless it is accepted by the majority of those to whom it is intended to apply.

While there were periods during the 20th century when it was possible to think of the United Kingdom as forming a single political system, dominated by two national parties, this view became much less tenable after 1974. In part, this was because of the electoral advance made, albeit with difficulty in terms of winning seats at Westminster, by the third party (now the Liberal Democrats) and partly because other parties from Scotland, Wales and Northern Ireland made their presence felt in the House of Commons, sometimes influencing the outcome of important votes in a closely balanced House. This was reinforced by the devolution elections in 1999, when, both in Scotland and Wales, the nationalist party did strongly enough to become the leading Opposition party.

While the Conservative and Labour parties have a common interest in seeking to maintain a rigorous two-party system, the constitutional structure of Britain does not rest upon that system, even if for many politicians the ideal state of affairs is one in which they hold office with their party commanding an absolute majority in the Commons, as the Conservatives did after the elections in 1979, 1983, 1987 and 1992 and Labour did after overwhelming victories in 1945, 1997 and 2001. Periods of minority government, as occurred between February and October 1974, and again between 1976 and 1979, may lead to developments in government like the agreement between the Labour government and the Liberal party in 1977–78.[132] But there are no reasons based on constitutional principle for regretting such developments. Indeed, there would be real advantage from a democratic viewpoint if a government's proposals and performance could come under more effective scrutiny in the Commons than is possible when that House is dominated by the government. Coalitions, electoral pacts and unwritten understandings between the parties cannot be regarded as unconstitutional.[133] Nor should the occasional decision of an MP to switch allegiance to another party be seen as a threat to the democratic process.[134]

It is not possible in this book to give an account of the political system, or systems, of the United Kingdom, although many features of the political process determine the manner in which the formal constitutional structure operates. Indeed, the internal procedures of the parties are often of constitutional importance – for example, the election of a leader, the relationship between the parliamentary party and other bodies and the relationship between the party and interests such as the trade unions. We will be examining electoral law, including the new rules contained in the Political Parties, Elections and Referendums Act 2000 that aim to set limits within which the parties operate and to maintain a measure of democratic equality between the contesting parties.[135]

It is easy to criticise politicians and the role of the parties in public life. But it is not possible to imagine a democratic system of government for a population of millions in which there is no need for political organisation. In 2001, while many aspects of the political life and structure of the United Kingdom were changing, it was a salutary warning for the parties that at the general election the turn-out of voters (at 59.4%) was the lowest in recent times for Westminster elections. Was this a deep-seated trend caused by underlying social or cultural factors that are beyond the reach of politicians and government, or will a vigorous and campaigning party be able to reverse the trend and secure the benefit of so doing?

---

[132] See Steel, *A House Divided: the Lib-Lab Pact and the Future of British Politics*.

[133] See Butler (ed.), *Coalitions in British Politics*; Butler, *Governing without a Majority: Dilemmas for Hung Parliaments in Britain*; Bogdanor, *Multi-party Politics and the Constitution*.

[134] On MPs who cross the floor of the Commons between elections, see P Cowley [1996] PL 214.

[135] See ch 9 C–E.

Chapter 3

THE STRUCTURE OF THE UNITED KINGDOM

A. The historic structure

While the external identity of a state is a matter for international law, it is constitutional law which regulates the internal relationships of the various territories which make up the state. In the past, writers often used the word 'English' in referring to the constitution, a usage liable to give the false impression that English law prevailed throughout the United Kingdom. Dicey and Bagehot, for example, wrote about the English constitution when they were dealing with the British constitution or, to be completely accurate, with what was then the constitution of the United Kingdom of Great Britain and Ireland. The active political consciousness of Ireland since the 19th century, and that of Scotland and Wales more recently, means that constitutional lawyers must choose their geographical adjectives with care. When in 1969 a Royal Commission on the constitution was appointed, among its duties was 'to examine the present functions of the central legislature and government in relation to *the several countries, nations and regions* of the United Kingdom' and also to consider the constitutional and economic relationships between the United Kingdom and the Channel Islands and the Isle of Man.[1] Some of the deliberate vagueness of the words in italics was dispelled when the commission's report referred to England, Scotland, Wales and Northern Ireland as the four countries which make up the United Kingdom.

Legal definitions

In law, the expression 'United Kingdom' refers to the United Kingdom of Great Britain and Northern Ireland; it does not include the Channel Islands or the Isle of Man.[2] For purposes of international relations, however, the Channel Islands and the Isle of Man are represented by the UK government. So are the colonies and other dependent territories of the United Kingdom overseas.[3]

The expression 'British Islands' is defined in the Interpretation Act 1978 as meaning the United Kingdom, the Channel Islands and the Isle of Man. The British Islands do not in law include the Republic of Ireland, which is outside the United Kingdom.[4]

The expression 'Great Britain' refers to England, Scotland and Wales: these first became a single kingdom by virtue of art 1 of the Treaty of Union between England and Scotland in 1707.

---

[1] See section B in this chapter.

[2] Interpretation Act 1978, Sch 1. By the British Nationality Act 1981, s 50 (1), the United Kingdom includes the Channel Islands and the Isle of Man for purposes of nationality law.

[3] Ch 15 C.

[4] As to which, see Roberts-Wray, *Commonwealth and Colonial Law*, pp 32–5. For an account of the status of the Isle of Man and the Channel Islands, see 12th edition of this work, pp 46–8. The Islands have a special status in relation to the European Community: see Treaty of Rome, art 310 (ex 238). See also the Kilbrandon Report, part XI; HLE, vol 6, pp 381–90; and Kermode, *Devolution at Work: A Case Study of the Isle of Man.*

The Wales and Berwick Act 1746 provided that where the expression 'England' was used in an Act of Parliament, this should be taken to include the dominion of Wales and the town of Berwick on Tweed. But the Welsh Language Act 1967, s 4, provided that references to England in future Acts should not include the dominion of Wales. Concerning the boundary between Wales and England, a long-standing controversy was brought to an end by the Local Government Act 1972, which declared that Monmouthshire was to be within Wales.[5]

The adjective 'British' is used in common speech to refer to matters associated with Great Britain or the United Kingdom. It has no definite legal connotation and one authority has described the expression 'British law' as hopelessly ambiguous.[6] In legislation 'British' is sometimes used as an adjective referring to the United Kingdom, particularly in the context of nationality.[7]

Historical development of the United Kingdom

1 *Wales*[8]   While it is not possible to summarise the lengthy history by which the kingdom of England became a single entity, it is worthwhile briefly to examine the historical formation of the United Kingdom. The military conquest of Wales by the English reached its culmination in 1282, when Prince Llywelyn was killed and his principality passed by conquest to King Edward I of England. Thereafter the principality (which formed only part of what is now Wales) was administered in the name of the Prince, but the rest of Wales was subjected to rule by a variety of local princes and lords; at this period English law was not extended to Wales, where the local customs, laws and language prevailed. From 1471, a Council of Wales and the Marches brought Wales under closer rule from England and the accession of the Tudors did much to complete the process of assimilation. In 1536, an Act of the English Parliament united Wales with England, establishing an administrative system on English lines, requiring the English language to be used, and granting Wales representation in the English Parliament.[9] In 1543, a system of Welsh courts (the Courts of the Great Sessions) was established to apply the common law of England. The Council of Wales and the Marches was granted a statutory jurisdiction which it exercised until its abolition in 1689. In 1830, the Courts of the Great Sessions were abolished and in their place were set up two new circuits to operate as part of the English court system. After the union with England, Acts of Parliament applying exclusively to Wales were rare.[10]

The mid-19th century saw the beginning of a political and educational revival and occasional Acts of Parliament applying only to Wales began again to be passed.[11] In 1906 the Welsh Department of the Board of Education was established, the first central department created specifically to administer Welsh affairs.[12] In 1914 was passed the Welsh Church Act, which disestablished and disendowed the Church of England in Wales. Thereafter, from time to time, the identity of Wales was recognised as new administrative arrangements were made. Various advisory bodies were formed, including the

---

[5] Ss 1(12), 20(7) and 269; Interpretation Act 1978, Sch 1.
[6] Roberts-Wray, p 69.
[7] British Nationality Act 1981. See ch 20 A.
[8] Kilbrandon Report, ch 5, and Andrews (ed.), *Welsh Studies in Public Law*, specially chs 2 (D Jenkins), 3 (H Carter) and 4 (I L Gowan).
[9] 27 Hen VIII, c 26. The Statute Law Revision Act 1948 called this Act the Laws in Wales Act 1535, but recent Welsh writers have called it the Act of Union of 1536: *Welsh Studies*, p 28.
[10] See e.g. Welsh Bible and Prayer Book Act 1563: *Welsh Studies*, pp 38–9.
[11] See e.g. Sunday Closing (Wales) Act 1881: *Welsh Studies*, p 48.
[12] *Welsh Studies*, p 49.

Welsh Economic Planning Council in 1966 and the Welsh Council in 1968.[13] In 1964, the post of Secretary of State for Wales was established and the Welsh Office emerged as a department of the UK government. Thereafter the administration of Wales through the Welsh Office was largely based on the model of the Scottish Office,[14] except that the Welsh Office was never divided into departments and did not maintain a continuing legislative programme at Westminster. Wales and England share a common legal system, but some statutes make special provision for Wales. By the Welsh Language Act 1967, the Welsh language may be spoken in any legal proceedings within Wales, by any person who desires to use it; and ministers may prescribe the use of Welsh versions of any official document or form. The Welsh Language Act 1993 created the Welsh Language Board, to further the principle in Wales that public authorities and the courts should treat the English and Welsh languages on a basis of equality.

2 *Scotland*[15] Unlike Wales, Scotland maintained its national independence against English military and political pressures during the Middle Ages. Scotland retained its own monarchy and only in the 16th century did the two royal lines come closer together with the marriage of Henry VII's daughter, Margaret, to James IV of Scotland. On the death of Elizabeth in 1603, James VI of Scotland, great-great-grandson of Henry VII, became James I of England. This personal union of the two monarchies had the legal consequence that persons born in England and Scotland after the union both owed allegiance to the same King.[16] During the conflicts of the 17th century, events took a broadly similar course in both countries and for a brief period under Cromwell, the Commonwealth of England, Scotland and Ireland was subject to a single legislature and executive. But apart from this, and despite the personal union of the monarchies, the constitutions of the two countries were not united and both the English and the Scottish Parliaments maintained separate existences.[17] Following the ousting of James II/VII in 1688, the Scottish Parliament for the first time asserted independence of the royal will. There followed for some 20 years a contest of wills between the English and Scottish Parliaments, marked by religious disputation and by keen rivalry to profit from expanding ventures in world trade, against a deeply insecure European background. In 1704, the Scottish Parliament by the Act of Security went so far as to provide that if Anne died without heirs the Parliament would choose her successor, 'provided always that the same be not successor to the Crown of England', unless in the meantime acceptable conditions of government had been established between the two countries.[18] Following a strong initiative from the English government, the English and Scottish Parliaments authorised negotiations between two groups of commissioners representing each Parliament but appointed by the Queen. The Treaty of Union was drawn up by them and was approved by Act of each Parliament together with an Act to maintain Presbyterian church government within Scotland.[19]

The Treaty of Union came into effect on 1 May 1707: it united the two kingdoms of England and Scotland into one by the name of Great Britain; the Crown was to descend to the Hanoverian line after Anne's death; there was to be a Parliament of Great Britain including 16 Scottish peers and 45 elected members in the Commons.

---

[13] Ibid, pp 62–3.
[14] See Andrews (ed.), *Welsh Studies in Public Law*, ch 4 (I L Gowan); and HLE, vol 8(2), pp 50–4.
[15] Kilbrandon Report, ch 4; also Donaldson, *Scotland: James V–James VII*; Ferguson, *Scotland, 1689 to the Present*; HLE, vol 8(2), pp 54–72 and Devine, *The Scottish Nation 1700–2000*, pt. 1.
[16] *Calvin's* case (1608) 7 Co Rep 1a.
[17] See Donaldson, op cit, ch 15, and Terry, *The Scottish Parliament 1603–1707*.
[18] APS XI, 136.
[19] Scottish Act: APS XI, 406, English Act: 6 Anne c 11; *Halsbury's Statutes*, vol 10, p 44. For the making of the union, see Riley, *The Union of England and Scotland* and Devine, ch 1.

Extensive financial and economic terms were included in the Treaty. Guarantees were given for the continuance of Scottish private law (art 18) and the Scottish courts (art 19), as well as for the maintenance of the feudal jurisdictions in Scotland and the privileges of the royal burghs in Scotland. The Act to maintain the Presbyterian Church in Scotland was incorporated in the Treaty and also provided for the maintenance of the Scottish universities. While the Treaty was described as an incorporating union (it did not establish a federal system and did not maintain the previous Scottish and English legislatures for any purpose), it gave extensive guarantees to Scottish institutions. Guarantees of a similar kind for English institutions were not required as it was obvious that the English would be predominant in the new Parliament of Great Britain.[20]

In the years after 1707, the new unity of Great Britain was challenged by the Jacobite uprisings in 1715 and 1745 but without success. Various expedients were resorted to for governing Scotland from London and, from time to time, new laws were made for Scotland by the Parliament of Great Britain. Some of these, for example the abolition of the Scottish feudal jurisdictions in 1747, were considered in Scotland to be a breach of the Treaty of Union. The Scottish Privy Council having been abolished in 1708, for much of the 18th and 19th centuries the Lord Advocate, the Crown's chief law officer in Scotland, occupied the primary role in politics and government, managing affairs in Scotland on behalf of the Crown. In 1885, a new post of Secretary for Scotland was created and in 1928 the post was raised to Cabinet status with the title of Secretary of State for Scotland. Demands for home rule for Scotland were expressed from the late 19th century onwards: the response of the government was to develop the Scottish Office as the department responsible for Scottish affairs.[21] Political demands for a Scottish legislative assembly were firmly resisted, although greater use was made of committees of Scottish MPs in the Commons. Since 1707, Parliament has often legislated separately for the English and Scottish legal systems. In particular, the structure of private law, courts, education and local government in Scotland has always differed from the English pattern.

From 1945 to 1999 the Scottish Office comprised four or five departments of the UK government, located in Edinburgh but headed by a Cabinet minister (the Secretary of State for Scotland).[22] The officials in these departments were members of the British civil service. The functions of government entrusted to the Scottish Office included agriculture and fisheries, education, the environment, health, housing, local government, police, prisons, roads, social services, transport (except road freight and rail), tourism and town planning. Other functions (such as inland revenue, social security, employment and the control of immigration) were exercised in Scotland by British or UK departments. As well as having direct responsibility for the Scottish Office, the Secretary of State had an indirect interest in all matters affecting Scotland, entitling a Scottish voice to be heard in a wide variety of decisions made in Whitehall.

Although the political direction of government remained centralised in the Cabinet, the Scottish Office system enabled much Scottish business to be handled by civil servants resident in Scotland and, latterly, some financial autonomy was conferred on Scottish ministers. On certain matters, uniform social and economic standards were maintained throughout Great Britain (for example, financing of higher education) but in some services higher levels of expenditure were accepted and Scottish initiatives in administration could be taken. One drawback was that subjects on which separate

---

[20] On the legal effect of these guarantees, see ch 4 D.
[21] See H J Hanham in Wolfe (ed.) *Government and Nationalism in Scotland*, ch 4.
[22] See Drucker (ed.) *Scottish Government Yearbook*, ch 8 (M Macdonald and A Redpath); Keating and Midwinter, *The Government of Scotland*; Kellas, *The Scottish Political System*; Milne, *The Scottish Office*. And see HLE, vol 8(2), pp 69–71.

legislation for Scotland was customary had to compete for time and political support in Westminster's legislative programme. The political legitimacy of the system was in question whenever, as from 1970 to 1974 and from 1979 to 1997, the majority of MPs from Scotland were in the Opposition at Westminster; the system was then open to the charge that Scotland was being governed from England. For instance, despite the fact that only ten Conservative MPs (out of 72) were elected from Scotland at the 1987 election, the Conservative government in 1989 abolished domestic rates for financing local government in favour of the notorious poll tax (community charge), one year earlier in Scotland than in England and Wales.[23] Although the Scottish Office system was for a time referred to as 'administrative devolution', it did not provide 'home rule' but was a form of direct rule of Scotland by the UK government.

3 *Northern Ireland*[24]   The constitutional history of Northern Ireland is inextricably linked with the history of Ireland itself. As an entity Northern Ireland dates only from the partition of Ireland in the early 1920s. Ireland itself first came under English influence in the 12th century when Henry II of England became Lord of Ireland. As settlers came from England, courts modelled on those in England were established. While an Irish Parliament began to develop, some English legislation was extended to Ireland by ordinance of the King of England. In 1494, the Irish Parliament passed the statute known as Poyning's Law, which required that all Irish Bills should be submitted to the King and his Council in England; only such Bills as the English Council approved were to be returned for the Irish Parliament to pass. In 1541, the title of Lord of Ireland was changed to King of Ireland. During the 17th century, Ireland had its share of religious bitterness and conflict. William of Orange defeated the former King James II at the Battle of the Boyne in 1690. There followed a dispute over the power of the Irish House of Lords to hear appeals from Irish courts and in 1720 the British Parliament by statute declared that it retained full power to legislate for Ireland and deprived the Irish House of Lords of all its judicial powers. Pressure from Ireland for greater autonomy led in 1782 to the repeal of the Declaratory Act of 1720 and to the recognition by the British Parliament of the Irish Parliament's legislative independence of Britain, although there was no change in the position of the monarchy.[25] But legislative independence was shortlived and after the rising of the United Irishmen in 1798, the British government proceeded to a legislative union with Ireland.

The Union agreement between the two Parliaments was broadly similar to the Union with Scotland, although fewer constitutional guarantees were given to Ireland than had been given to Scotland. Article 1 created the United Kingdom of Great Britain and Ireland and arts 3 and 4 provided for Irish representation in the new Parliament of the United Kingdom. Article 5 provided for the (Protestant) United Church of England and Ireland, whose continuance was stated to be an essential and fundamental part of the Union. Within the enlarged United Kingdom, all trade was to be free; the laws in force in Ireland were to continue, subject to alteration by the UK Parliament from time to time. As with the Scottish union, the terms of the Union were separately adopted by Act of each of the two Parliaments concerned.[26]

---

[23] See C M G Himsworth and N C Walker [1987] PL 586 and authorities cited below in ch 4, note 158.

[24] For the earlier history, see Donaldson, *Some Comparative Aspects of Irish Law*; for the 1920 Constitution, see Calvert, *Constitutional Law in Northern Ireland*, and Kilbrandon Report, ch 6. Also Hadfield, *The Constitution of Northern Ireland*; Hadfield (ed.), *Northern Ireland: Politics and the Constitution*; C McCrudden, in Jowell and Oliver (eds), *The Changing Constitution*, 3rd edn, ch 12; McEldowney, *Public Law*, ch 19; Morison and Livingstone, *Reshaping Public Power*; HLE, vol 8(2), pp 72–93.

[25] Cf *Re Keenan* [1972] 1 QB 533.

[26] For the Union with Ireland Act 1800, see *Halsbury's Statutes*, vol 31 (1994 reissue), p 290.

The Irish Union with Britain was less stable than the Anglo-Scottish Union of 1707. For much of the 19th and 20th centuries, the Irish question proved to be one of the most difficult political and constitutional issues within the United Kingdom. Catholic emancipation occurred in 1829, opening the way for political demands for further reform, often associated with militant action and acts of violence. The Irish Church was disestablished in 1869 despite the guarantee for its existence contained in the Act of Union.[27] Gladstone's two Home Rule Bills in 1886 and 1893 were both defeated in Parliament, the first in the Commons, the second in the Lords. After the Parliament Act 1911 had taken away the power of the House of Lords to veto legislation[28] the Government of Ireland Act 1914 became law, but it never came into effect because of the outbreak of world war; its parliamentary history had been marked by the extreme determination of Ulster Protestants not to be separated from Britain.

The Easter rising in Dublin in 1916 was further evidence of the nationalist feeling in Catholic Ireland. In 1919 the Sinn Fein movement established a representative assembly for what was proclaimed to be the Irish Republic. In 1920 the Government of Ireland Act was passed by the UK Parliament, providing for two Parliaments in Ireland, one for six northern counties and one for the remainder of Ireland, with cooperation between the two to be maintained by means of a Council of Ireland. The 1920 Act was ignored by Sinn Fein and, after a period of bitter civil war, an Anglo-Irish Treaty was formally concluded in 1922. This recognised the emergence of the Irish Free State, on which Westminster conferred what was then described as the status of a self-governing dominion within the British Empire.[29] The six northern counties were excluded from the Irish Free State, acquiring their own government and Parliament under the 1920 Act.

The dominion status of the Irish Free State proved no more than a transitional stage and steps were taken by the state in the 1930s to assert a more complete independence of the United Kingdom. The Irish Constitution of 1937 declared that Eire was a sovereign independent state. During the Second World War, Eire was neutral. In 1949, the state became the Republic of Ireland and the UK Parliament at last recognised that Eire had ceased to be part of Her Majesty's dominions although it was, perhaps anomalously, also declared that Ireland was not to be regarded as a foreign country.[30]

The system of government established under the Act of 1920 in Northern Ireland survived in all essentials for 50 years. During this time, Northern Ireland possessed its own executive (Governor, Prime Minister and Cabinet) and a legislature of two houses (Senate and House of Commons) sitting at Stormont.[31] Northern Ireland elected a reduced number of MPs to sit at Westminster and was subject to the legislative supremacy of Westminster. By the 1920 Act, certain matters were reserved for the United Kingdom, including the Crown, treaties and foreign relations, the armed forces and defence, postal services and customs and excise. Subject to the reserved matters, the Stormont Parliament had power 'to make laws for the peace, order and good government of Northern Ireland'.[32] Constitutional issues could be referred for decision to the Privy Council, but if an Act of the Stormont Parliament exceeded its competence (for example, by legislating with respect to the armed forces),[33] it could be held invalid by the

---

[27] *Ex p Canon Selwyn* (1872) 36 JP 54, and see Calvert, pp 20–1.

[28] Ch 10 B.

[29] Ch 15 C.

[30] Ireland Act 1949, ss 1(1) and 2.

[31] See note 24. Also Birrell and Murie, *Policy and Government in Northern Ireland*; Buckland, *The Factory of Grievances*; Lawrence, *The Government of Northern Ireland*, ch 10.

[32] Government of Ireland Act 1920, s 4(1).

[33] See *R (Hume)* v *Londonderry Justices* [1976] NILR 91; Northern Ireland Act 1972.

courts. Stormont was heavily dependent on the United Kingdom for financial support, for example in maintaining a social security system that offered the same benefits as in Great Britain. The courts rarely had to interpret the Act of 1920 and no body of constitutional case-law developed.[34] Since the Unionist party representing the Protestant majority was in power throughout the life of Stormont, the Catholic community was in a permanent minority and their accumulated grievances led to civil unrest from 1968 onwards.[35] The UK government was required to intervene increasingly in Northern Ireland until, in 1972, direct rule of Northern Ireland was resumed and the constitution of Northern Ireland was suspended.[36] In 1973, after a poll of the electorate had shown a clear majority in favour of Northern Ireland remaining part of the United Kingdom, the system of government under the 1920 Act was finally ended. In its place, an attempt was made to establish a new Assembly and a new form of executive based on the concept of power sharing.[37] Elections for the Assembly were held by proportional representation, the Sunningdale agreement (to which the Dublin government was a party) was reached in December and the executive came into office in January 1974. But the experiment failed after a few months. The Northern Ireland Act 1974 restored direct rule, making temporary provision for governing the province through the Secretary of State for Northern Ireland and authorised the holding of an elected constitutional convention under the chairmanship of the Chief Justice of Northern Ireland. The convention met during 1975 but it failed to produce an agreed scheme,[38] and direct rule from Westminster continued.

Later developments included the Anglo-Irish Inter-governmental Council, established in 1981 by the governments of the United Kingdom and the Irish Republic for discussion of matters of common concern; the increase in Northern Ireland's representation at Westminster from 12 to 17 seats;[39] and the re-activation in 1982 of the Assembly first created in 1973.[40] Under the Northern Ireland Act 1982, elections for the Assembly were held in October 1982. However, the Assembly failed to find a way of making proposals to the Secretary of State for a resumption of the devolution of powers authorised by the Act of 1973 and it was dissolved in June 1986.

A notable development in November 1985 was the signing of the Anglo-Irish Agreement by the British and Irish Prime Ministers at Hillsborough.[41] The Agreement gave the assurance that no change in the status of Northern Ireland would come about without the consent of the majority of its people. It sought to increase cooperation between the two governments in relation to security, economic and social matters and to provide a framework (based on a standing Inter-governmental Conference) for discussion of issues affecting Northern Ireland (such as human rights, security and criminal justice). The Agreement endorsed the UK government's policy of seeking to devolve powers of government from the Secretary of State to democratic bodies within the province.

This Agreement attracted much support, apart from Unionist parties which protested vehemently at the increased recognition that it gave to the interest of the Dublin government in Northern Ireland affairs.[42]

---

[34] See *Londonderry CC v McGlade* [1925] NI 47; *Gallagher v Lynn* [1937] AC 863; *Belfast Corporation v OD Cars Ltd* [1960] AC 490.

[35] See Cmnd 532, 1969 (the Cameron report).

[36] Northern Ireland (Temporary Provisions) Act 1972.

[37] Cmnd 5259, 1973; Northern Ireland Assembly Act 1973; Northern Ireland Constitution Act 1973.

[38] HC 1 (1975–76); Cmnd 6387, 1976.

[39] House of Commons (Redistribution of Seats) Act 1979.

[40] See Cmnd 8541, 1982; the Northern Ireland Act 1982; and C Gearty [1982] PL 518.

[41] Cmnd 9690. And see Hadden and Boyle, *The Anglo-Irish Agreement*.

[42] For an unsuccessful legal challenge, see *Ex p Molyneaux* [1986] 1 WLR 331. And cf *McGimpsey v Ireland* [1990] ILRM 441.

Both direct rule and terrorist activity continued in the 1990s, as efforts were made to find a political solution. In December 1993, the 'Downing Street Declaration' of the two Prime Ministers sought to bring about by peaceful negotiation a settlement for Northern Ireland. It confirmed that the status of the province could not be changed without majority consent and that the British government would not oppose a united Ireland for which there was popular consent.[43] In August 1994, the IRA announced a cessation of military activities and this was followed by a loyalist ceasefire. Despite this, little progress towards all-party talks was made, mainly because of disagreement over the conditions on which Sinn Fein might take part in talks. In 1995, the Prime Ministers outlined framework proposals for a Northern Ireland Assembly, a cross-border body with executive and consultative functions and a Belfast/Dublin parliamentary forum.[44] The IRA resumed activities in February 1996, with the South Quay bombing in London. The British government caused elections to be held in May 1996[45] before the opening of multi-party talks in June, but only in October was some agreement reached on the agenda for discussion.

No new political initiative occurred until the change of government at the general election in 1997 opened the way for the 'Good Friday Agreement' in Belfast in 1998, the aftermath of which will be outlined in section B.

Three legal systems

The United Kingdom has often been described as a unitary state, since there is no structure of federalism. But this historical outline has shown that constitutional differences exist within the United Kingdom and that there is both diversity and political and economic unity. While the legislative competence of Parliament extends to all the United Kingdom, three distinct legal systems exist, each with its own courts and legal profession, namely, (a) England and Wales, (b) Scotland and (c) Northern Ireland. A unifying influence is that the House of Lords is the final court of appeal from all three jurisdictions, except for criminal cases in Scotland. When Parliament legislates, it may legislate for the whole United Kingdom (for example, income tax or immigration law), for Great Britain (for example, social security or trade union law) or separately for one or more of the countries within the United Kingdom.

In the next section, we examine aspects of the devolution legislation passed in 1998, applying to Scotland, Wales and Northern Ireland. Emphasis will be given to key structural aspects and it will not be possible in this work to describe how these schemes of devolution are operating.[46] A brief reference will be made to a related matter, the development of regional government in England.

B. Devolution of government

The Labour government elected in May 1997 was committed to securing devolution of government to both Scotland and Wales and to renewing efforts to establish peace and order in Northern Ireland. This commitment caused Westminster in 1998 to legislate separately for Scotland, Wales and Northern Ireland.[47] It is an indication of

---

[43] Cm 2442, 1994.
[44] Cm 2964, 1995.
[45] Cm 3232, 1996; and Northern Ireland (Entry to Negotiations, etc.) Act 1996.
[46] For the operation of the first two years of devolution, see Hazell (ed.) *The State and the Nations* and Trench (ed.) *The State of the Nations 2001*.
[47] Scotland Act 1998; Government of Wales Act 1998; and Northern Ireland Act 1998. See Bogdanor, *Devolution in the United Kingdom*; Burrows, *Devolution*; and A J Ward, in Jowell and Oliver (eds), *The Changing Constitution*, 4th edn, ch 5.

the asymmetric structure of the United Kingdom that the differences between the three Acts are almost greater than the similarities.

Devolution is not a term of art in constitutional law. Unlike federalism, its nature within the United Kingdom depends not on a written constitution, but on the legislation authorising devolution and on the practice that develops through use of the new structure for decision making.

Devolution has been defined as 'the delegation of central government powers without the relinquishment of sovereignty',[48] but this definition includes many different forms of delegation. In the United Kingdom, devolution has come to mean the vesting of legislative and executive powers in elected bodies in Scotland, Wales and Northern Ireland, who thus acquire political responsibility for the devolved functions. Legislation to create devolved government includes provision for: (1) an elected assembly for the area in question; (2) a political executive responsible to the assembly; (3) 'machinery of government' matters, including funding; (4) the functions to be devolved; and (5) legal and political control of those powers.

Precursors to devolution

The schemes of devolution created in 1998 were influenced by the abortive attempt in the 1970s to establish devolved government for Scotland and Wales. In 1973, the Royal Commission on the constitution (the Kilbrandon Report)[49] made proposals for devolution that were far from unanimous. For Scotland, eight of the 13 members recommended legislative devolution, with an elected assembly with power to make laws and an executive comprising ministers drawn from the assembly. For Wales, only six members (a minority) recommended a similar scheme. Two members of the Commission, taking a broader approach, recommended elected assemblies for Scotland, Wales and five English regions, to carry out social and economic policies within the framework of national laws.[50]

Although the Labour government of 1974–79 undertook to create elected assemblies for Scotland and Wales, it lacked an absolute majority in the House of Commons for much of this period and it experienced great difficulties with the devolution project. After lengthy proceedings in two sessions of Parliament, the Scotland Act and the Wales Act were enacted in 1978, to come into effect only if approved by referendum in each country. In the referendum held on 1 March 1979, the scheme for Wales was heavily defeated; in Scotland, a small majority of those voting supported devolution, but they were less than 40 per cent of the whole electorate and did not satisfy the '40 per cent rule' that had been applied to the referendum to guard against a low turn-out of voters. Orders repealing the Scotland and Wales Acts were approved in Parliament after the Conservatives were elected into office in May 1979.

Between 1979 and 1997, the Conservative government opposed all proposals for devolution within Great Britain, although in 1995 it supported minor changes in Scottish business at Westminster, extending the functions of the Scottish Grand Committee in the Commons.[51] The Labour and Liberal Democrat parties supported the Scottish Constitutional Convention, a non-governmental body endorsed by many groups and voluntary organisations in Scotland. In 1995, the Convention proposed a scheme of

---

[48] Kilbrandon Report, para 543.
[49] Cmnd 5460, 1973; and see T C Daintith (1974) 37 MLR 544.
[50] Cmnd 5460–I, 1973 (memorandum of dissent).
[51] See HC S0 94A–94H (1995); HC Deb, 29 November 1995, col 1228, and 19 December 1995, col 1410.

devolution which sought to improve upon the Scotland Act 1978.[52] In 1997 the Labour and Liberal Democrats agreed that there would be an early referendum in Scotland on the Convention's scheme. For Wales, the parties favoured an elected assembly to oversee Welsh affairs.

The Referendums (Scotland and Wales) Act 1997 authorised the holding of a referendum in Scotland and Wales respectively, to secure the approval of electors to the government's schemes for devolution.[53] The timing of the referendums thus differed from 1979, when the referendums were not held until legislation for devolution had received the royal assent. In 1997, of the 60 per cent who voted in the Scottish referendum, 74 per cent supported the proposed Scottish Parliament and 63.5 per cent agreed that the Parliament should be able to vary the basic rate of income tax for Scottish taxpayers. In Wales, only 50 per cent of the electorate voted, of whom 50.3 per cent supported the proposed Assembly. Thereafter, detailed legislation to implement the schemes was enacted at Westminster and the first elections to the Parliament and the Assembly were held in May 1999.

The Scotland Act 1998[54]

Part I of the Act created a unicameral Scottish Parliament. Of its 129 members, 73 are elected from single-member constituencies by simple majority vote and 56 are elected by regions (based on European Parliament constituencies) under an 'additional member' system of proportional representation. Elections are held every four years (s 2), but exceptionally elections may be held at other times, for example if two-thirds of the members vote for a resolution dissolving the Parliament (s 3). The electoral system is likely to ensure that no single party has an absolute majority, as was the outcome in 1999. Subject to this, most of the electoral rules are similar to those which apply to elections for Westminster.[55] Members of the Scottish Parliament (MSPs) are not prevented by law from being MPs at Westminster or members of the European Parliament.

The Scottish Parliament has a broad power to make laws for Scotland, to be known as Acts of the Scottish Parliament (s 28(1)), but this power is subject to limitations. Thus, it does not extend to matters reserved to Westminster. 'Reserved matters' include the Crown, the Union, foreign affairs, the civil service, defence of the realm and the armed forces and a long list of domestic matters under 11 headings, including finance and the economy (such as fiscal, economic and monetary policy and financial services), aspects of home affairs (such as the misuse of drugs, data protection, immigration and nationality), trade and industry (such as import and export policy), energy, social security, regulation of the professions, employment, broadcasting and equal opportunities.[56]

If the Scottish Parliament were to go outside its competence by legislating on a 'reserved matter', the provision in question would not be law (s 29(1)). Other limits on the Parliament's competence are that a Scottish Act may not affect the law of any country outside Scotland and may not conflict either with Community law or with rights under the European Convention on Human Rights.[57]

---

[52] *Scotland's Parliament, Scotland's Right* (1995); J McFadden [1995] PL 215 and D Millar (1997) 1 Edin LR 260. See also Constitution Unit, *Scotland's Parliament: Fundamentals for a new Scotland* (1996).
[53] *Scotland's Parliament*, Cm 3658, 1997; and *A Voice for Wales*, Cm 3718, 1997.
[54] Himsworth and Munro, *The Scotland Act 1998*; Page, Reid and Ross, *A Guide to the Scotland Act 1998*; McFadden and Lazarowicz, *The Scottish Parliament: An Introduction*; N Burrows (1999) 62 MLR 241.
[55] See ch 9 D.
[56] Schedule 5 to the Act contains general and specific reservations; detailed provisions modify the effect of the general headings.
[57] S 29(2)(a), (d). And see chs 8 and 19 B, C.

By Part II of the Act, the Scottish Executive comprises the First Minister, other ministers and the law officers (the Lord Advocate and the Solicitor General for Scotland) (s 44). The First Minister is appointed by the Queen after having been nominated by the Parliament (ss 45, 46). The First Minister and other ministers must be MSPs and the nomination of the other ministers must be approved by the Parliament before their formal appointment (s 47). The First Minister, other ministers, and the law officers must resign if the Parliament resolves that the Executive no longer enjoys the confidence of the Parliament (ss 45(2), 47(3)(c), 48(2)). The Executive is thereby accountable to the Parliament, which may scrutinise acts of the Executive and the civil servants who staff the Scottish Administration (s 51). For this purpose, the Parliament has developed a system of 16 committees, dealing with all aspects of the work of the Executive.

The Executive's powers are based on a transfer of functions to Scottish ministers from the UK government, those functions being linked to the legislative powers devolved. Thus, in general, the Scottish Executive exercises functions that relate to matters within the Parliament's legislative competence, except that there are certain matters on which executive power is devolved to the Executive without power to legislate being conferred on the Parliament. Like the Parliament, the Executive may not take decisions that are contrary to European Community law or conflict with Convention rights (s 57).

Parts III and IV of the Act deal with finance. The bulk of the income of the Scottish Administration is derived from a block grant made from Westminster. This (together with similar grants for devolved services in Wales and Northern Ireland) is calculated by what is called the 'Barnett formula', not found in the Scotland Act itself, which produces a sum that is treated as Scotland's share of public expenditure.[58] Within that total, the Scottish Administration may set its own priorities for expenditure on devolved matters, but it may not pass on the cost of doing so to the United Kingdom government. An early use of this freedom was the Scottish decision not to follow the policy on payment of tuition fees by university students that applies elsewhere in the United Kingdom.[59] The Scottish authorities have power (not yet exercised) to increase or reduce the basic rate of income tax paid by Scottish taxpayers[60] on their earned income by 3 pence in the pound, a power equivalent to an annual power to raise or forgo some £450 million.

It is important both that the Scottish Executive and Parliament can make autonomous decisions within their powers and that there should be safeguards against decisions that would exceed those powers. When a Bill is introduced in the Parliament, the responsible minister must be satisfied that it is within the competence of the Parliament, and the presiding officer must also consider the matter (s 31). The Judicial Committee of the Privy Council may be asked to decide whether a Bill is within competence (s 33). In addition to these procedures, the Scotland Act provides for the decision of 'devolution issues'. Such an issue arises when, in proceedings in a court or tribunal, a legislative or executive decision is challenged on the ground that it is not within devolved powers, including questions as to its compatibility with the European Convention on Human Rights.[61] A devolution issue may be referred by the court or tribunal in which

---

[58] The formula, dating from 1979, is used to calculate a population-based proportion for each of Scotland, Wales and Northern Ireland, of changes in planned spending on comparable UK services in England: see HC 341 (1997–98), HC 619 (1997–98) and HM Treasury, *Funding the Scottish Parliament, National Assembly for Wales and the Northern Ireland Assembly* (2nd edn, 2000). Also Bogdanor, pp 241–51, Hazell, op cit, pp 175–9; Trench, ch 6 (D Bell and A Christie).

[59] See Hazell, op cit, pp 25–6.

[60] For the meaning of Scottish taxpayers, see Scotland Act 1998, s 75.

[61] Scotland Act 1998, Sch 6. Significant decisions on devolution issues raising human rights questions are *Anderson, Docherty and Reid v Scottish Ministers* (detention of potentially dangerous psychiatric patients);

it is raised to a superior court (in Scotland, to the Court of Session or the High Court of Justiciary) and from such a decision appeal may lie to the Privy Council. If the Act is considered to be a written constitution for Scotland on devolved matters, its interpretation will have constitutional significance.[62]

The Westminster Parliament retains power to legislate for Scotland (s 28(7)) and in law it may override decisions taken in Edinburgh on devolved matters, but to do so would frustrate the purpose of devolution. A convention already exists that Westminster should not legislate on a devolved matter without the prior consent of the Scottish Parliament.[63] Scotland's representation in the Commons was not reduced by devolution, but the number of Westminster constituencies in Scotland may be reduced at the next boundary review.[64] Unless the Scotland Act is amended, a reduction in Westminster constituencies will mean a reduction in size of the Scottish Parliament.[65]

Although the Parliament's powers are limited in law, its political significance within Scotland is great, enabling the Scottish people to be represented in a forum that has resonances of Scotland's Parliament before 1707. It provides a means within Scotland for reforming Scottish law. Its existence requires the UK government to take seriously the commitment to 'subsidiarity' that has emerged as a principle of the European Union.[66]

The Government of Wales Act 1998[67]

By contrast with the Scottish Parliament, the National Assembly for Wales (created by s 1 of the 1998 Act) lacks a general power to make laws for Wales. The legislature for Wales is still the Westminster Parliament. But the Assembly exercises a secondary role in legislation, since the Assembly has had transferred to it (s 22) many powers of making delegated legislation previously exercised by the Secretary of State for Wales. In its composition, the Assembly is a smaller version of the Scottish Parliament: 40 members are elected in single-member constituencies by majority vote and 20 members by regions under proportional representation. Elections are held every four years. The Assembly has 18 areas of responsibility, including agriculture, economic development, education, the environment, health and health services, industry, social services and transport (Sch 2). There have been transferred to the Assembly many powers formerly exercised by the Secretary of State for Wales, and the Assembly may supervise, scrutinise and where necessary reform Welsh public bodies (ss 27, 28). The Assembly works through all-party subject committees, intended 'to have a strong and effective role in policy development and in scrutinising the work of public bodies'.[68]

By Part II of the 1998 Act, the Executive Committee (s 56) comprises the Assembly First Secretary (in effect, the leader of the Assembly) and the chairs of the subject committees (known as Assembly Secretaries) to provide overall direction to the Assembly. The Committee acts as a Cabinet; although it meets privately, its minutes are published. The First Secretary is accountable to the Assembly 'for the exercise of functions by the Executive Committee' (s 56(7)) and is regularly questioned by the Assembly. Draft

---

Brown v Stott [2001] 2 WLR 817 (car owner's duty to inform police of identity of driver); *Starrs v Ruxton* 2000 JC 208 (appointment of part-time sheriffs; see A O'Neill (2000) 63 MLR 429).

[62] See P Craig and M Walters [1999] PL 274 and S Tierney (2001) 5 Edin LR 49.

[63] Such consent has been given readily since 1999. For the 'Sewel convention', see Himsworth and Munro, p 37; *Memorandum of Understanding*, Cm 4444, 1999 para 13; Hazell, op cit, pp 158–9.

[64] Scotland Act 1998, s 86. And see ch 9 B.

[65] By reason of the Scotland Act 1998, s 1 and Sch 1.

[66] For assessments of the Scottish Parliament, see B K Winetrobe, *Realising the Vision: a Parliament with a Purpose* (Constitution Unit); Hazell, ch 2 (G Leicester), Trench, op cit, ch 3 (J Mitchell et al).

[67] See Hazell, ch 3 (J Osmond), Trench, op cit, ch 2 (J Osmond).

[68] Preamble to the Standing Orders of the National Assembly for Wales (1999).

subordinate legislation is considered by committees of the Assembly before the Assembly's power of approving the legislation is exercised. As with Scotland, the Assembly is primarily funded by an annual block grant from Westminster calculated by the Barnett formula and it can set its own expenditure priorities; unlike the Scottish Parliament, the Assembly may not vary the basic rate of income tax. Subordinate legislation made by the Assembly is void if it goes outside the Assembly's competence, for example if it is inconsistent with Westminster legislation, with European Community law or with the European Convention on Human Rights (ss 106(7), 107(1)). Devolution issues may arise in relation to Wales as they can in relation to Scotland; similar procedures exist for enabling them to be decided ultimately by the Judicial Committee of the Privy Council (s 109 and Sch 8).

Welsh representation at Westminster was not affected by the creation of the Assembly and there is a continuing, although diminished, role for the Secretary of State for Wales. Although the Secretary of State may not vote in the Assembly or take part in Assembly committees, he or she may attend and participate (without voting) in Assembly proceedings (s 76).

Although the formal role of the Assembly is to carry out executive functions formerly entrusted to the Secretary of State for Wales, the Assembly, like the Scottish Parliament, is likely to play a more important role of political representation than its functions suggest.

The Northern Ireland Act 1998

A new political initiative in Northern Ireland was taken after the general election in 1997. After lengthy talks, the Belfast (or Good Friday) Agreement was reached on 10 April 1998.[69] Strand One of the agreement provided for an elected Assembly in Northern Ireland of 108 members. Strand Two provided for a North/South Ministerial Council, comprising representatives of the Northern Ireland and Irish governments and machinery for implementing policies agreed by the council. Strand Three provided for a British–Irish Council, representing the British and Irish governments, as well as the devolved governments of Northern Ireland, Scotland and Wales, and also a British Irish Intergovernmental Conference to discuss Northern Ireland matters that were not devolved, such as policing.

The Belfast Agreement was endorsed on 22 May 1998 by separate referendums in both parts of Ireland and elections for the new Assembly were held on 25 June 1998. By the Northern Ireland Act 1998, Northern Ireland is to remain part of the United Kingdom until a majority of the electorate in the province voting in a poll held for the purpose, decide to the contrary (s 1); in that event, the Secretary of State shall lay proposals to give effect to the majority wish before the Westminster Parliament. The Assembly is, in principle, elected every four years. The electoral system is that of the single transferable vote, with each of the 18 Westminster constituencies returning six members. A complex scheme of power sharing between the main parties provides for key decisions to be taken on a cross-community basis, either by parallel consent of a majority of unionist and nationalist designations or by a weighted majority (60 per cent) of members present and voting, including at least 40 per cent of unionist and nationalist designations. Such key decisions include election of the Assembly chair, the First Minister and the Deputy First Minister.

---

[69] *The Belfast Agreement: An Agreement Reached at the Multi-Party talks on Northern Ireland*, Cm 3383, 1998. Annexed to the multi-party agreement is an agreement between the British and Irish governments. See B Hadfield [1999] PL 599 and D O'Sullivan [2000] Dublin Univ LJ 112.

Certain matters (such as the Crown, defence, immigration, elections and political parties) are *excepted* from devolution (s 4 and Sch 2). Other matters (including civil aviation, criminal law, emergency powers, telecommunications, consumer protection and data protection) are *reserved* from devolution (s 4 and Sch 3). *Transferred* matters, which fall within the scheme of devolution, are neither excepted nor reserved. The Assembly may make laws on transferred matters, but this does not affect the power of Westminster to make laws for Northern Ireland (s 5). The Assembly's legislative competence does not include matters that would extend outside Northern Ireland, would be incompatible with the Human Rights Act 1998 or European Community law or would discriminate on grounds of religious belief or political opinion (s 6). As in Scotland, there are safeguards against the Assembly exceeding its competence (ss 11, 14) and provision for the decision of 'devolution issues' (s 79, Sch 10). Unlike the Scottish Parliament, the Assembly has no power to vary the rate of United Kingdom income tax.

The Executive Committee of the Assembly comprises the First Minister, the Deputy First Minister and other ministers appointed by a formula for power sharing that divides the ministries between the main parties on the basis of voting at the previous election. All ministers must take the prescribed pledge of office.

The 1998 Act authorises other aspects of the Belfast Agreement, such as the North/South Ministerial Council and the British–Irish Council and the appointment in Northern Ireland of a new Human Rights Commission (ss 68–70) and an Equality Commission (s 73). All public authorities must promote equality of opportunity (s 75) and it is unlawful for a public authority to discriminate on grounds of religious belief or political opinion (s 76).

The progress of devolution has been impeded by continuing difficulties in the peace process, in particular as regards decommissioning of arms and other aspects of the security situation, including policing. Thus between February and May 2000, the operation of the Assembly was suspended while Northern Ireland returned to direct rule by the Secretary of State.[70]

Both the recent history and the background in Northern Ireland have contributed to the complexity of this scheme. But so long as the Executive and Assembly continue to operate, Northern Ireland may be grouped with Scotland and Wales as providing an instance of devolved government.

Conclusion

It may be said that Scotland, Wales and Northern Ireland have now each acquired a written constitution in the form of the Acts of 1998. Each constitution is subject to judicial interpretation and binds the devolved governments and each can be amended at Westminster. But each of these constitutions is no more than a partial account of the government of these countries. For one thing, their operation cannot be understood without reference to the elaborate array of 'Concordats', namely, the agreements reached between Whitehall departments and the devolved executives as to how the two levels of government will relate to each other.[71] Further, many important functions applying to Scotland, Wales and Northern Ireland are exercised by the Westminster Parliament and by Whitehall. The three offices of Secretary of State have been kept in being, albeit with reduced staffs and with altered functions.

---

[70] See Northern Ireland Act 2000.
[71] See *Memorandum of Understanding and Supplementary Agreements*, Cm 4444, 1999. Also Hazell, ch 6; R Rawlings (2000) 106 LQR 257 and J Poirier [2001] PL 134.

Generalisation is difficult because each scheme of devolution is different.[72] Although these various forms of devolution do not apply to England, many consequences for the United Kingdom will be felt. While the composition of the Commons has not been changed following devolution to Scotland and Wales, its procedures have had to adapt to the fact that questions regarding the exercise of devolved powers must be asked in Cardiff or Edinburgh, not at Westminster.[73] Difficult questions remain as to whether the House of Commons should continue to use its legislative authority without differentiation for the United Kingdom, Great Britain and England and Wales, whether its composition should vary according to the territory for which it is legislating and whether an English forum is needed for exclusively English issues.[74] Experience of devolution may also affect decisions about the electoral system used for the House of Commons and possibly about the future composition and functions of the House of Lords.

The impact of devolution is being felt at a time when the United Kingdom is experiencing the effects of European integration, both in the European Union and under the European Convention on Human Rights. We saw earlier that devolution involves 'the delegation of central government powers without the relinquishment of sovereignty'.[75] Even if 'sovereignty' is still retained by the central organs of the United Kingdom, exercise of that sovereignty will be affected both by Europe and by new centres of political power within the United Kingdom. Changing conceptions of sovereignty may enable the devolved bodies to enjoy a share of that sovereignty,[76] despite assertions to the contrary by those responsible for introducing devolution.

The asymmetric structure of the United Kingdom has been stressed in this chapter. A possible response to the challenge that this presents would be to create devolved forms of government at a regional level in England. In 1994, Whitehall divided England outside London for governmental purposes into eight regions and this structure has served as the basis for further administrative changes.[77] In May 2002, the government issued a white paper that proposed legislation to give electors in each of the eight regions an opportunity by referendum to choose whether to support the creation of a regional assembly for their region, comprising 23–35 members elected by means of proportional representation on the additional member system, with power to raise funds by means of a precept on council tax.[78]

---

[72] The schemes have been criticised for 'constitutional incoherence': see A J Ward, in Jowell and Oliver (eds), op cit, p 135.

[73] Procedure Committee, *Procedural Consequences of Devolution* HC 185 (1998–99) and HC 814 (1998–99); Scottish Affairs Committee, *Operation of Multi-Layer Democracy* HC 460-I (1997–98).

[74] See Hazell, ch 7 (M Russell and R Hazell); and R Hazell [2001] PL 268; Trench, op cit, ch 9 (R Masterman and R Hazell).

[75] See note 48 above.

[76] MacCormick, *Questioning Sovereignty*, p 74, says in respect of Scotland: 'The unitary sovereignty of the incorporating union agreed in 1707 seems to be at best in its twilight.'

[77] See especially the Regional Development Agencies Act 1998, creating development agencies for eight regions, which *inter alia* are to cooperate with the non-statutory regional chambers that represent industrial, commercial and public sector interests in each region. See pp 362–3 below; also Hazell, op cit, ch 5 (J Tomaney); Trench, op cit, ch 5 (J Tomaney).

[78] Cm 5511, 2002.

Chapter 4

PARLIAMENTARY SUPREMACY

Within a democracy, an elected assembly that represents the people deserves particular respect. The laws enacted by the legislature (including those imposing taxation) affect everyone, but this does not mean that it will exercise absolute law-making authority.

Where there is a written constitution, limits on the authority to make laws may be set out in that text. Without such a constitution, are there limits on legislative authority and, if so, where may they be found? And should measures from Parliament prevail over all other rules of law?

This chapter examines the extent of the formal authority exercised today by the Westminster Parliament. We first consider briefly the stages by which that authority was established, since without a written constitution, the historical background to the authority of legislation assumes great significance.

A. The growth of the legislative authority of Parliament

It is often claimed that the first Parliament was that assembled by Simon de Montfort in 1265 to give counsel to Henry III, which for the first time included representatives of the shires, cities and boroughs of England as well as the feudal barons. But to become a legislature in a modern sense, the enlarged council had to acquire a regular existence as a body with power to legislate and with settled procedure; and the measures which emerged from that procedure had to be accepted as law. By 1485, it was accepted that measures that had been considered by Parliament and enacted by the monarch could change the common law. With the English Reformation, there disappeared the belief that Parliament could not affect the authority of the Roman church. Henry VIII and Elizabeth I made the Crown of England supreme over all persons and causes and used the English Parliament to attain this end.

Although wide authority was attributed to acts of the 'King in Parliament', two views were held as to the justification for this.[1] The royalist view grounded legislative authority in the King, acting as sovereign in exercise of divine right, but with the approval of Lords and Commons. By contrast, the parliamentarian view stressed the role of the two Houses, acting on behalf of the nobility and the common people, in exercising supreme authority with the sovereign. There continued to be a view that certain natural laws could not be changed, even by the King in Parliament.[2] To set against this view there was much authority in the law reports and in political writing which indicated that the courts had no power to review the validity of Acts of Parliament.[3]

---

[1] For historical attitudes to the authority of Parliament, see Goldsworthy, *The Sovereignty of Parliament*, ch 4. Also P Craig [2000] PL 211.

[2] See *Bonham's* case (1610) 8 Co Rep 114a, quoted below in text at note 64.

[3] Goldsworthy (passim); and Gough, *Fundamental Law in English Constitutional History*.

The struggle for supremacy

Legislative supremacy involves not only the right to change the law but also that no one else should have that right. At the heart of the conflicts of the 17th century that led to the civil war, Charles I's execution, Cromwell's Protectorate and the restoration of the monarchy in 1660, was uncertainty as to whether the King could use his prerogative powers to govern without Parliament. In 1603, the King's prerogatives were undefined. Despite the existence of Parliament and the common law courts, the King, through his Council, exercised a residue of legislative and judicial power. Acts of Parliament which sought to take away any of the 'inseparable' prerogatives of the Crown were considered invalid.[4] Four instances of the struggle for authority can be considered.

1 *Ordinances and proclamations* A clear distinction between the statutes of the English Parliament and the ordinances of the King in Council was lacking long after the end of the 13th century. The Statute of Proclamations 1539 gave Henry VIII wide powers of legislating without reference to Parliament by proclamation, which had replaced the ordinance as a form of legislation. This statute did not give to the King and Council power to do anything that they pleased by royal ordinance, but sought to deal with the obscure position of the authority possessed by proclamations. It safeguarded the common law, existing Acts of Parliament and rights of property, and prohibited the infliction of the death penalty for breach of a proclamation.[5] 'Its chief practical purpose was undoubtedly to create machinery to enforce proclamations.'[6] Despite the repeal of this statute in 1547, Mary and Elizabeth continued to resort to proclamations. The judicial powers of the Council, and in particular of the Court of Star Chamber, were available to enforce proclamations. The scope of the royal prerogative to legislate remained undefined. James I made full use of this power, and in 1611 Chief Justice Coke was consulted by the Council, along with three of his brother judges, about the legality of proclamations. The resulting opinion is to be found in the *Case of Proclamations*:

> 1 The King by his proclamation cannot create any offence which was not one before; for then he might alter the law of the land in a high point; for if he may create an offence where none is, upon that ensues fine and imprisonment.
> 2 The King hath no prerogative but what the law of the land allows him.
> 3 But the King for the prevention of offences may by proclamation admonish his subjects that they keep the laws and do not offend them upon punishment to be inflicted by law; the neglect of such proclamation aggravates the offence.
> 4 If an offence be not punishable in the Star Chamber, the prohibition of it by proclamation cannot make it so.[7]

A definite limit was thus put upon the prerogative, the full force of which was effective only when the Star Chamber and other conciliar tribunals were abolished in 1640. The gist of the *Case of Proclamations* is that the King's prerogative is under the law and that Parliament alone can alter the law which the King is to administer.

2 *Taxation* The imposition of taxes is a matter for legislation. Inevitably taxation was a major issue between the Stuart Kings and Parliament. If the Crown could not levy

---

[4] 'No Act of Parliament can bar a King of his regality': *The Case of Ship Money* (1637) 3 St Tr 825, Finch CJ, at 1235. For the leading 17th-century cases on prerogative, see Keir and Lawson, *Cases in Constitutional Law*, ch II.
[5] HEL, vol IV, pp 102–3.
[6] G R Elton, in Fryde and Miller, *Historical Studies of the English Parliament*, II, p 206.
[7] (1611) 12 Co Rep 74. This case was applied by the Court of Session in *Grieve v Edinburgh and District Water Trustees* 1918 SC 700.

taxes without the consent of Parliament, the will of Parliament must prevail in the long run. It had been conceded by the time of Edward I that the consent of Parliament was necessary for direct taxation. The history of indirect taxation is more complicated, since the regulation of foreign trade was a part of the royal prerogative relating to foreign affairs. There was no clear distinction between the imposition of taxes by way of customs duties and the prerogative powers over foreign trade and defence of the realm:

> In the *Case of Impositions (Bate's Case)*,[8] John Bate refused to pay a duty on imported currants imposed by the Crown on the ground that its imposition was contrary to the statute 45 Edw 3 c 4 which prohibited indirect taxation without the consent of Parliament. The Court of Exchequer unanimously decided in favour of the Crown. The King could impose what duties he pleased for the purpose of regulating trade, and the court could not go behind the King's statement that the duty was in fact imposed for the regulation of trade.
>
> In the *Case of Ship Money (R v Hampden)*,[9] John Hampden refused to pay ship money, a tax levied by Charles I for the purpose of furnishing ships in time of national danger. Counsel for Hampden conceded that sometimes the existence of danger would justify taking the subject's goods without his consent, but only in actual as opposed to threatened emergency. The Crown conceded that the subject could not be taxed in normal circumstances without the consent of Parliament, but contended that the King was the sole judge of whether an emergency justified the exercise of his prerogative power to raise funds to meet a national danger. A majority of the Court of Exchequer Chamber gave judgment for the King.[10]

The decision was reversed by the Long Parliament,[11] and this aspect of the struggle for supremacy was concluded by the Bill of Rights, art 4, which declared that it was illegal for the Crown to seek to raise money without Parliamentary approval.[12]

3 *Dispensing and suspending powers* The power of the Crown to dispense with the operation of statutes within certain limits may at one time have been necessary having regard to the form of ancient statutes and the irregular meetings of Parliament. So long, however, as the limits on the dispensing power were not clearly defined, there was here a threat to the legislative supremacy of Parliament. In the leading case of *Thomas v Sorrell*,[13] the court took care to define the limits within which the royal power to dispense with laws was acceptable. But in *Godden v Hales* the court upheld a dispensation from James II to Sir Edward Hales excusing him from taking religious oaths and fulfilling other obligations imposed by the Test Act; it was held that it was an inseparable prerogative of the Kings of England to dispense with penal laws in particular cases and upon necessary reasons of which the King is sole judge.[14]

Thus encouraged, James II proceeded to set aside statutes as he pleased, granting a suspension of the penal laws relating to religion in the Declarations of Indulgence in 1687 and 1688. These acts of James were an immediate cause of the revolution of 1688. The Bill of Rights abolished the Crown's alleged power of suspending laws and also prohibited the Crown's power to dispense with the operation of statutes, except where this was authorised by Parliament.[15] Similar provision was made in the Scottish Claim of Right.[16]

---

[8] (1606) 2 St Tr 371; G D G Hall (1953) 69 LQR 200.

[9] (1637) 3 St Tr 825.

[10] For a full analysis, see D L Keir (1936) 52 LQR 546.

[11] Shipmoney Act 1640.

[12] Page 14 above.

[13] (1674) Vaughan 330.

[14] (1686) 11 St Tr 1165.

[15] Articles 1 and 2 of the Bill of Rights, p 14 above. The Bill of Rights did not curtail the prerogative of pardon or the power to enter a nolle prosequi. Cf the present practice of granting extrastatutory concessions in taxation, ch 17 C.

[16] Page 14 above.

4 *The independence of the judiciary*   So long as the tenure of judicial office depended on the royal pleasure, there was a risk of the subservience of judges to the Crown. To ensure that English judges should not hold office at pleasure of the Crown, the Act of Settlement 1700 provided that they should hold office *quamdiu se bene gesserint* (during good behaviour) but subject to a power of removal upon an address from both Houses of Parliament.[17]

Growth of ministerial responsibility

The Bill of Rights and the Act of Settlement established the legislative authority of the English Parliament vis-à-vis the Crown, while preserving the prerogatives of the Crown in matters which had not been called in question. The settlement reflected the fact that the common lawyers had joined with Parliament to defeat the Crown's claim to rule by prerogative; it is often said that the common lawyers thereby accepted that legislation by Parliament was of overriding authority as a source of law. Executive government itself was still conducted by and in the name of the monarch and democratic government had yet to be established. The changed role of the Sovereign thereafter was summarised in this way:

> The position of affairs has been reversed since 1714. Then the King or Queen governed through Ministers, now Ministers govern through the instrumentality of the Crown.[18]

The development after 1714 of Cabinet government and of ministerial responsibility[19] was accompanied by changes in the electoral system, beginning in 1832 with the first parliamentary reform and continuing until the universal franchise for adults was achieved in 1928. The political authority of the House of Commons increased as it became able to insist that the executive must be responsive to the will of the electorate.

The result of the conflict between Commons and Lords in 1909–11 was to leave the House of Commons in a dominant position within Parliament. Thus the legislative authority of Parliament came to be based on the political support of the electorate for the party with a majority of seats in the elected House.

B. Meaning of legislative supremacy

In this brief summary, we have examined the rise of Parliament to be at the centre of the constitutional system. We now consider the legal doctrine of the legislative supremacy of Parliament. This doctrine is referred to by many writers, notably by Dicey, as the sovereignty of Parliament. New constitutional developments are often debated in terms of their supposed effect on the sovereignty of Parliament. This was seen in the debate about British membership of the EC; those opposed to British membership proposed, without success, an amendment to the Bill which became the European Communities Act 1972 declaring that British membership would not affect the sovereignty of Parliament.[20] Critics of British membership of the European Union complain both at the loss of national sovereignty and at erosion of the sovereignty of Parliament. There is no doubt that Britain's place in Europe affects the role of Parliament, since many laws are now made at a European level. But the same applies to every state that is a member of the EU. Moreover, many states (including the USA)

---

[17] See now Supreme Court Act 1981, s 11(3). See also ch 18 A.
[18] Anson, *Law and Custom of the Constitution*, vol II, p 41.
[19] See ch 7.
[20] HC Deb, 5 July 1972, cols 556–644; HL Deb, 7 August 1972, cols 893–914. And see ch 8.

enjoy sovereignty in international law without having a 'sovereign' legislature. In this chapter, the expression legislative supremacy will be used, partly because it is less likely to be confused with the notion of national sovereignty; and to avoid supporting the jurisprudential doctrine of John Austin and his successors that in every legal system there must be a sovereign.[21]

By the legislative supremacy of Parliament is meant that there are no legal limitations on the legislative competence of Parliament. Parliament here does not refer to the two Houses of Parliament individually, for neither House has authority to legislate on its own, but to the constitutional phenomenon known as the Queen in Parliament: namely the legislative process by which a Bill approved by Lords and Commons receives the royal assent and thus becomes an Act of Parliament. Thus defined, Parliament, said Dicey, has 'under the English constitution, the right to make or unmake any law whatever; and further that no person or body is recognised by the law of England as having a right to override or set aside the legislation of Parliament'.[22] Now Dicey was writing at a time when England was often used as a loose synonym for Great Britain or the United Kingdom[23] and today it is necessary to discuss whether the law on this matter is the same throughout the United Kingdom.[24] But the positive and negative aspects of the doctrine emerge clearly from Dicey's formulation, namely that Parliament has power to legislate on any matter whatsoever and that there exists no competing authority with power to legislate for the United Kingdom or to impose limits upon the competence of Parliament.

British membership of the European Union gives rise to the difficult issue of competing supremacies, the supremacy of Parliament on the one hand and the supremacy, or primacy, of Community law, on the other. This question will be considered later,[25] but we first examine the issue in terms of the law of the United Kingdom alone.

Legal nature of legislative supremacy

This doctrine consists essentially of a legal rule which governs the relationship between the courts and the legislature, namely that the courts are under a duty to apply the legislation made by Parliament and may not hold an Act of Parliament to be invalid or unconstitutional. 'All that a court of law can do with an Act of Parliament is to apply it.'[26] In *Madzimbamuto* v *Lardner-Burke*, which concerned the effect of the unilateral declaration of independence in 1965 by the Rhodesian government on the Westminster Parliament's power to legislate for Rhodesia, Lord Reid said:

> It is often said that it would be unconstitutional for the United Kingdom Parliament to do certain things, meaning that the moral, political and other reasons against doing them are so strong that most people would regard it as highly improper if Parliament did these things. But that does not mean that it is beyond the power of Parliament to do such things. If Parliament chose to do any of them, the courts could not hold the Act of Parliament invalid.[27]

While the doctrine of legislative supremacy has great political significance, the legal rule is not to be confused with statements about the dominance of the House of Commons, the Cabinet or the Prime Minister within the legislative process. Certainly, how

---

[21] Austin, *The Province of Jurisprudence Determined*, Lecture 6. See MacCormick, *Questioning Sovereignty*; and (1993) 56 MLR 1.
[22] Dicey, *The Law of the Constitution*, pp 39–40.
[23] Ch 3 A.
[24] Section D in this chapter.
[25] Page 68; and ch 8.
[26] Keir and Lawson, *Cases in Constitutional Law*, p 1. For the power of the courts to disapply an Act of Parliament which conflicts with European Community law, see p 68 below.
[27] [1969] 1 AC 645, 723. And see *Manuel* v *A-G* [1983] Ch 77.

Parliament exercises its legislative authority is of great importance in the debate about whether its supremacy should be retained or modified. Craig has argued that Dicey's exposition of sovereignty was advanced on the basis of assumptions about representative democracy which (in Craig's view) were flawed even in 1885 and cannot be made today.[28] However, we must distinguish as far as possible between analysing the present law and considering how it should develop in future. Changes in the legislative process do not in themselves alter the legal effect of that process, although they might affect the case for parliamentary reform.

Only an Act of Parliament is supreme

The courts ascribe to an Act of Parliament legal force which they are not willing to ascribe to other instruments which for one reason or another fall short of being an Act of Parliament. Thus the following instruments do not enjoy legislative supremacy and the courts will if necessary decide whether or not they have legal effect:

(a) a resolution of the House of Commons;[29]

(b) a proclamation issued by the Crown under prerogative powers for which the force of law is claimed;[30]

(c) a treaty entered into by the government under prerogative powers which seeks to change the law within territory subject to British jurisdiction;[31]

(d) an instrument of subordinate legislation which appears to be issued under the authority of an Act of Parliament by a minister or a government department,[32] even though this has been approved by resolution of each House of Parliament;[33]

(e) an act of a subordinate legislature,[34] such as the Scottish Parliament or the Northern Ireland Assembly;

(f) byelaws made by a public corporation or local authority;[35]

(g) laws made by the governor of a dependent territory under powers conferred by Order in Council.[36]

In all such cases, the courts must consider whether the document for which legislative force is claimed is indeed legally binding. So too, when a party to litigation relies on an Act of Parliament, the court must if necessary decide whether the provision in question has been brought into force.

The difference between an Act of Parliament and lesser instruments is reflected in a distinction drawn by the Human Rights Act 1998 between 'primary legislation' and 'secondary legislation'. Unfortunately, the line drawn in the 1998 Act does not coincide with the distinctions just drawn. Thus various measures (including prerogative Orders in Council) are treated by the Act as primary legislation.[37]

---

[28] In *Public Law and Democracy*, ch 2, Craig argues that Dicey's notion of sovereignty was 'firmly embedded within a conception of self-correcting majoritarian democracy' (p 15) since, in Dicey's words, 'The electors can in the long run always enforce their will'; further, that the British system 'became one dominated by the top, by the executive and the party hierarchy' (p 42) and that the danger has always been one of majoritarian tyranny.

[29] *Stockdale v Hansard* (1839) 9 A & E 1; *Bowles v Bank of England* [1913] 1 Ch 57.

[30] *Case of Proclamations* (p 50 above).

[31] *The Parlement Belge* (1879) 4 PD 129, 154; *A-G for Canada v A-G for Ontario* [1937] AC 326. Cf *Malone v Metropolitan Police Commissioner* [1979] Ch 344. And ch 15 B.

[32] E.g. *Chester v Bateson* [1902] 1 KB 829; ch 28.

[33] *Hoffmann-La Roche v Secretary for Trade & Industry* [1975] AC 295.

[34] *Belfast Corpn v OD Cars Ltd* [1960] AC 490.

[35] E.g. *Kruse v Johnson* [1898] 2 QB 91.

[36] *R v Foreign and Commonwealth Secretary, ex p Bancoult* [2001] QB 1067.

[37] Human Rights Act 1998, s 21(1). See chs 19 C and 28; and P Billings and B Pontin [2001] PL 21.

Position different under written constitution

The doctrine of legislative supremacy distinguishes the United Kingdom from those countries in which a written constitution imposes limits on the legislature and entrusts the ordinary courts or a constitutional court to decide whether the acts of the legislature are in accordance with the constitution. In *Marbury* v *Madison*, the US Supreme Court held that the judicial function vested in the court necessarily carried with it the task of deciding whether an Act of Congress was or was not in conformity with the constitution.[38] In a legal system which accepts judicial review of legislation, legislation may be held invalid on a variety of grounds: for example, because it conflicts with the separation of powers where this is a feature of the constitution,[39] infringes human rights guaranteed by the constitution,[40] or has not been passed in accordance with the procedure laid down in the constitution.[41] By contrast, in the United Kingdom the legislative supremacy of Parliament appears to be the fundamental rule of constitutional law and this supremacy includes power to legislate on constitutional matters. In so far as constitutional rules are contained in earlier Acts, there seems to be no Act which Parliament could not repeal or amend by passing a new Act. The Bill of Rights could in law be repealed or amended by an ordinary Act of Parliament. This was done in the Defamation Act 1996, section 13 of which amended Article 9 of the Bill of Rights regarding the freedom of speech in Parliament.[42]

Legislative supremacy illustrated

The apparently unlimited powers of Parliament may be illustrated in many ways. The Tudor Kings used Parliament to legalise the separation of the English church from the church of Rome: Sir Thomas More was executed in 1535 for having denied the authority of Parliament to make Henry VIII supreme head of the Church. In 1715, Parliament passed the Septennial Act to extend the life of Parliament (including its own) from three to seven years, because it was desired to avoid an election so soon after the Hanoverian accession and the 1715 uprising in Scotland. In vain did opponents of the Act argue that the supreme legislature must be restrained 'from subverting the foundation on which it stands'.[43] Less controversially, during the two world wars, Parliament prolonged its own life by amending the rule in the Parliament Act 1911 that a general election must be held at least every five years.

Parliament has altered the succession to the throne (in the Act of Settlement 1700 and His Majesty's Declaration of Abdication Act 1936); removed prerogative powers from the Crown; reformed the composition of both Houses of Parliament; dispensed with the approval of the House of Lords for certain Bills (the Parliament Acts 1911 and 1949); given effect to British membership of the EC (the European Communities Act 1972); given effect to the Scottish and Irish Treaties of Union and later departed from those treaties;[44] and altered the territorial limits of the United Kingdom.[45] Between 1997 and 2001, constitutional legislation included the Scotland Act 1998, the Human Rights Act 1998 and the House of Lords Act 1999.

---

[38] 1 Cranch 137 (1803).
[39] *Liyanage* v *R* [1967] 1 AC 259; *Hinds* v *R* [1977] AC 195 and see p 83 below.
[40] E.g. *Aptheker* v *Secretary of State* 378 US 500 (1964) (Act of US Congress refusing passports to communists held an unconstitutional restriction on right to travel).
[41] *Harris* v *Minister of Interior* 1952 (2) SA 428. Generally see Brewer-Carias, *Judicial Review in Comparative Law*.
[42] See chs 11 A and 23 F.
[43] Quoted in Marshall, *Parliamentary Sovereignty and Commonwealth*, p 84.
[44] Ch 3 A, and section D in this chapter.
[45] Island of Rockall Act 1972.

Indemnity Acts and retrospective legislation

Parliament has exercised the power to legalise past illegalities and to alter the law retrospectively. This power has been used by an executive with a secure majority in Parliament to reverse inconvenient decisions made by the courts.[46] Retrospective legislation was passed after both world wars, protecting various illegal acts committed in the national interest.[47] Retrospective laws are, however,

> contrary to the general principle that legislation by which the conduct of mankind is to be regulated ought . . . to deal with future acts and ought not to change the character of past transactions carried on upon the faith of the then existing law . . . Accordingly the court will not ascribe retrospective force to new laws affecting rights unless by express words or necessary implication it appears that such was the intention of the legislature.[48]

Thus there is a rule of interpretation that a statute should not be interpreted retrospectively so as to impair an existing right or obligation unless that result is unavoidable.[49] The Immigration Act 1971 was held to have empowered the Home Office to deport Commonwealth citizens who had entered in breach of earlier immigration laws but against whom no such action could have been taken at the time the 1971 Act came into effect:[50] but the Act did not make punishable by criminal sanctions conduct which had occurred before the Act was passed.[51] Although art 7 of the European Convention on Human Rights provides that no one shall be held guilty of a criminal offence for conduct which did not constitute an offence at the time when it was committed,[52] Parliament has power to legislate retrospectively in breach of this: but, as Lord Reid said, 'It is hardly credible that any government department would promote or that Parliament would pass retrospective criminal legislation.'[53] Legislation which authorises payments to be made to individuals in respect of past events is also retrospective, but plainly less objectionable.[54]

Legislative supremacy and international law

The legislative supremacy of Parliament is not limited by international law. The courts may not hold an Act void on the ground that it contravenes general principles of international law.

> The Herring Fishery (Scotland) Act 1889 authorised a fishery board to make byelaws prohibiting certain forms of trawling within the Moray Firth, an area which included much sea that lay beyond British territorial waters. The Danish master of a Norwegian trawler was convicted in a Scottish court for breaking these byelaws. The High Court of Justiciary held

---

[46] War Damage Act 1965 (*Burmah Oil Co v Lord Advocate* [1965] AC 75); Northern Ireland Act 1972 (*R (Hume et al) v Londonderry Justices* [1972] NILR 91); Education (Scotland) Act 1973 (*Malloch v Aberdeen Corpn* 1974 SLT 253); National Health Service (Invalid Direction) Act 1980 (*Lambeth BC v Secretary of State* (1980) 79 LGR 61).

[47] Indemnity Act 1920 and War Charges Validity Act 1925; Enemy Property Act 1953, ss 1–3.

[48] Per Willes J in *Phillips v Eyre* (1870) LR 6 QB 1, 23.

[49] *Yew Bon Tew v Kenderaan Bas Mara* [1983] 1 AC 553, 558. And see *Plewa v Chief Adjudication Officer* [1995] 1 AC 249 (common law presumption applied to recovery of overpaid benefits).

[50] *Azam v Home Secretary* [1974] AC 18.

[51] *Waddington v Miah* [1974] 2 All ER 377.

[52] Ch 19 B. On the War Crimes Act 1991, see A T Richardson (1992) 55 MLR 73, 76–80; and S N McMurtrie (1992) 13 Statute Law Review 128. On retrospective penalties, see *R v Pora* [2001] 2 NZLR 37; and A Butler [2001] PL 586.

[53] [1974] 2 All ER 377, 379; and see *R v Home Secretary, ex p Bhajan Singh* [1976] QB 198.

[54] E.g. Employment Act 1982, s 2 and Sch 1.

that its function was confined to interpreting the Act and the byelaws, and that Parliament had intended to legislate for the conduct of all persons within the Moray Firth, whatever might be the position in international law. 'For us an Act of Parliament duly passed by Lords and Commons and assented to by the King is supreme, and we are bound to give effect to its terms.'[55]

Nor may the courts hold an Act invalid because it conflicts with a treaty to which the United Kingdom is a party.

An assessment to income tax was challenged on the ground that part of the tax raised was used for the manufacture of nuclear weapons, contrary to the Geneva Convention Act 1957. It was held that the unambiguous provisions of a statute must be followed even if they are contrary to international law. Regarding an argument that tax had been imposed for an improper purpose, the judge said: 'What the statute itself enacts cannot be unlawful, because what the statute says and provides is itself the law, and the highest form of law that is known to this country'.[56]

As far as British courts are concerned, there are no territorial restrictions on the legislative competence of Parliament. Generally Parliament legislates only in respect of its own territory or in respect of the conduct of its own citizens when they are abroad, but occasionally legislation is intended to operate outside the United Kingdom: thus the Continental Shelf Act 1964 vested in the Queen the rights of exploration and exploitation of the continental shelf; the Act provided for the application of criminal and civil law in respect of installations placed in the surface waters above the continental shelf.[57] A few serious crimes committed in a foreign state by British citizens are justiciable in British courts, such as treason, murder, manslaughter, bigamy and certain revenue offences.[58] The courts apply a rule of interpretation that statutes will not be given extra-territorial effect, unless this is expressly provided or necessarily implied.[59] By general principles of international law, the United Kingdom may not exercise jurisdiction in territory belonging to a foreign state. In practice Parliament does not pass laws which would be contrary to the comity of nations. Yet the law in Britain does not always keep pace with Britain's changing international obligations. While the government under the royal prerogative may enter into treaties, treaties must be approved or adopted by Act of Parliament if national law is to be altered.[60] The fact that a treaty has been ratified by the United Kingdom might in some instances create a legitimate expectation that this would be followed by legislation giving domestic effect to the treaty, but this possibility may be excluded by statutory provision to the contrary.[61]

British membership of the European Union raises questions as to the relationship between UK law and Community law which cannot be answered by reference to the general principles of international law.[62]

---

[55] Lord Dunedin in *Mortensen v Peters* (1906) 8 F(J) 93, 100. The Trawling in Prohibited Areas Prevention Act 1909 later made it an offence to land in the United Kingdom fish caught in prohibited areas of the sea, thus limiting the extra-territorial effect of the earlier ban.

[56] Ungoed-Thomas J in *Cheney v Conn* [1968] 1 All ER 779, 782; and see *Inland Revenue Commissioners v Collco Dealings Ltd* [1962] AC 1.

[57] See also the Antarctic Act 1994. Contrast the Sexual Offences (Conspiracy and Incitement) Act 1996 (P Alldridge [1997] Crim LR 30).

[58] Law Commission, Report No 91, 'Territorial and Extra-territorial Extent of Criminal Law', 1978, pp 36–41.

[59] *Treacy v DPP* [1971] AC 537, 552. And see *R v Kelly* [1982] AC 665; and Bennion, *Statutory Interpretation*, pp 274–294.

[60] Note 31 above.

[61] *Minister for Immigration and Ethnic Affairs v Teoh* (1995) 128 ALR 353; *R v DPP, ex p Kebeline* [2000] 2 AC 326; and ch 15 B.

[62] Page 68 below and ch 8.

No legal limitations on Parliament

Many illustrations may be given of the use which Parliament has made of its legislative supremacy in legislating on constitutional matters, retrospectively, in breach of international law, and so on. It does not follow from a recital of this kind that the powers of Parliament are unlimited. As Calvert has said:

> No one doubts that the powers of the UK Parliament are extremely wide . . . But that is not what is in issue. What is in issue is whether those powers are unlimited and one no more demonstrates this by pointing to a wide range of legislative objects than one demonstrates the contrary by pointing to matters on which Parliament has not, in fact, ever legislated.[63]

There is much evidence from the law reports that, at least since 1688, judges have been strongly inclined to accept the legislative omnicompetence of Parliament. Yet this has not always been the judicial attitude. In his note on *Dr Bonham's* case, Coke CJ said:

> In many cases, the common law will control Acts of Parliament, and sometimes adjudge them to be utterly void: for when an Act of Parliament is against common right and reason, or repugnant, or impossible to be performed, the common law will control it, and adjudge such Act to be void.[64]

While English judges made similar statements only rarely after 1688,[65] it is not possible from reported cases alone to demonstrate that they have utterly lost the power to 'control' an Act of Parliament – or to show that a judge who is confronted with a statute fundamentally repugnant to moral principle (for example, a law condemning all of a certain race to be executed) must either apply the statute or resign from office.[66] Support for this has come from New Zealand, where the former President of the Court of Appeal (Lord Cooke of Thorndon) urged that within the common law the judges exercise an authority which extends to upholding fundamental values that might be at risk from certain forms of legislation.[67] In 1995, Lord Woolf argued that 'if Parliament did the unthinkable' and legislated without regard for the role of the judiciary in upholding the rule of law, the courts might wish to make it clear that 'ultimately there are even limits on the supremacy of Parliament which it is the courts' inalienable responsibility to identify and uphold'.[68]

Short of such an extreme situation, it is very unlikely that the courts would of their volition exercise power derived solely from common law to review the validity of Acts of Parliament. Where in modern constitutional systems judicial review of legislation takes place, this is generally derived from a written constitution.[69] But in the United Kingdom, Parliament enjoys an unlimited power to legislate on constitutional matters. Is it therefore possible that, *on the initiative of Parliament itself*, the courts could begin to exercise a power of judicial review derived from constitutional legislation passed by

---

[63] *Constitutional Law in Northern Ireland*, p 14.
[64] (1610) 8 Co Rep 113b, 118a. And see S E Thorne (1938) 54 LQR 543; Goldsworthy, *The Sovereignty of Parliament*, pp 111–117; and Gough, *Fundamental Law*, pp 35–40.
[65] E.g. Holt CJ, *City of London* v *Wood* (1702) 12 Mod 669, 687.
[66] Cf Jennings, *The Law and the Constitution*, pp 159–60. For the attitude that British courts take to foreign legislation which infringes fundamental rights, see *Oppenheimer* v *Cattermole* [1976] AC 249 and F A Mann (1978) 94 LQR 512.
[67] See *Taylor* v *New Zealand Poultry Board* [1984] 1 NZLR 394, 398; also J L Caldwell [1984] NZLJ 357 and R Cooke [1988] NZLJ 158.
[68] Lord Woolf [1995] PL 57, 69. See also J Laws [1995] PL 72, 81–93 and cf Lord Irvine [1996] PL 59, 75–78.
[69] Israel is an apparent exception: I Zamir [1991] PL 523, 529–30, and C Klein (1996) 2 European Public Law 225.

Parliament? This possibility has often been dismissed out of hand by invocation of the principle that no Parliament may bind its successors. It has been said that the rule that the courts enforce without question all Acts of Parliament is the one rule of the common law which Parliament may not change.[70] But, it has been asked, 'Why cannot Parliament change that rule; since all other rules of the common law are subject to its sovereignty?'[71] It is to this difficult and fundamental question that we now turn.

[handwritten margin note: Why?]

[handwritten margin note: Supersede/repeal (future enactments)]

C. The continuing nature of parliamentary supremacy

Within a modern legal system, enacted laws remain in force until they are repealed or amended, unless they are declared when enacted to have a limited life.[72] It is inherent in the nature of a legislature that it should continue to be free to make new laws. The fact that legislation about, say, divorce or consumer protection was enacted five or 50 years ago is no reason why fresh legislation on the same subject should not be enacted today: even if social conditions have not changed, a new legislature may favour a fresh approach. If the legislature wishes to alter a law previously enacted, it is convenient if the new Act expressly repeals the old law or states the extent to which the old law is amended. Suppose that this is not done and a new Act is passed which conflicts with an older Act but does not expressly repeal it. There now appear to be two inconsistent statutes on the statute book. How is the apparent conflict to be resolved? And by whom?

The doctrine of implied repeal

It is for the courts to resolve this conflict because it is their duty to decide the law which applies to a given situation. Where two Acts conflict with each other, the courts apply the Act which is later in time and any earlier Act inconsistent with the later Act is taken to have been repealed by implication.

> If two inconsistent Acts be passed at different times, the last must be obeyed, and if obedience cannot be observed without derogating from the first, it is the first which must give way . . . Every Act is made either for the purpose of making a change in the law, or for the purpose of better declaring the law, and its operation is not to be impeded by the mere fact that it is inconsistent with some previous enactment.[73]

This doctrine is found in all legal systems, but in Britain its operation is sometimes considered to have special constitutional significance.

> Before 1919, many public and private Acts of Parliament empowered public authorities to acquire land compulsorily and laid down many differing rules of compensation. In 1919, the Acquisition of Land (Assessment of Compensation) Act was passed to provide a uniform code of rules for assessing the compensation to be paid in future. Section 7(1) provided: 'The provisions of the Act or order by which the land is authorised to be acquired, or of any Act incorporated therewith, shall, in relation to the matters dealt with in this Act, have effect subject to this Act, and so far as inconsistent with this Act those provisions shall cease to have or

---

[70] H W R Wade [1955] CLJ 172, 187–9; and (1996) 112 LQR 568.
[71] E C S Wade, Introduction to Dicey, p lv.
[72] This has always been the position in English law (Edgar, *Craies on Statute Law*, pp 406–12). But in respect of Scottish Acts passed before 1707, by the doctrine of desuetude a statute may cease to be law through non-use and change of circumstances: see *M'Ara* v *Magistrates of Edinburgh* 1913 SC 1059 and Mitchell, *Constitutional Law*, pp 21–2.
[73] Lord Langdale, in *Dean of Ely* v *Bliss* (1842) 5 Beav 574, 582. And see Bennion, *Statutory Interpretation*, pp 225–7.

shall not have effect.' The Housing Act 1925 sought to alter the 1919 rules of compensation by reducing the compensation payable in respect of slum-housing. In *Vauxhall Estates Ltd* v *Liverpool Corpn*,[74] it was held that the provisions of the 1925 Act must prevail over the 1919 Act so far as they were inconsistent with it. The court rejected the ingenious argument of counsel for the slum-owners that s 7(1) (and especially the words 'or shall not have effect') had tied the hands of future Parliaments so that the later Parliament could not (short of express repeal) legislate inconsistently with the 1919 Act. In a similar case, *Ellen Street Estates Ltd* v *Minister of Health*, Maugham LJ said: 'The Legislature cannot, according to our constitution, bind itself as to the form of subsequent legislation, and it is impossible for Parliament to enact that in a subsequent statute dealing with the same subject matter there can be no implied repeal. If in a subsequent Act Parliament chooses to make it plain that the earlier statute is being to some extent repealed, effect must be given to that intention just because it is the will of Parliament.'[75]

The correctness of these two decisions is not in doubt, for there were very weak grounds for suggesting that in 1919 Parliament had been attempting to bind its successors. But Maugham LJ went far beyond the actual situation in saying that Parliament could not bind itself as to the *form* of subsequent legislation. He would have been closer to the facts of the case had he said that Parliament could not bind itself as to the *contents* of subsequent legislation.[76] However, these cases, which illustrate the doctrine of repeal by implication, have been used to support a broad constitutional argument that Parliament may never bind its successors.[77]

Can Parliament bind its successors?

The rule that Parliament may not bind its successors (and that no Parliament is bound by Acts of its predecessors) is often cited both as a limitation on legislative supremacy and as an example of it. To adopt for a moment the language of sovereignty: if it is an essential attribute of a legal sovereign that there should be no legal restraints upon him or her, then, by definition, the rules laid down by a predecessor cannot bind the present sovereign, for otherwise the present holder of the post would not be sovereign. Dicey, outstanding exponent of the sovereignty of Parliament, accepted this point:

> The logical reason why Parliament has failed in its endeavours to enact unchangeable enactments is that a sovereign power cannot, *while retaining its sovereign character*, restrict its own powers by any parliamentary enactment.[78] (italics supplied)

Thus to state that no Parliament may bind its successors is to assume that all future Parliaments must have the same attribute of sovereignty as the present Parliament. But why must this be so? The problem is less intractable than the comparable conundrum of whether an omnipotent deity can bind itself,[79] for even sovereign Parliaments are human institutions; and there is nothing inherently impossible in the idea of a supreme Parliament having power to make fresh constitutional arrangements for the future. Merely to state that Parliament may not bind its successors leaves unclear both the nature of the obligation which a present Parliament is unable to impose on its successors and also the meaning of 'successors'.[80] Indeed, it may be shown that the doctrine that Parliament may not 'bind' its successors is an over-simplification.

---

[74] [1932] 1 KB 733.
[75] [1934] KB 590, 597.
[76] H R Gray (1953) 10 Univ of Toronto LJ 54, 67.
[77] Cf H W R Wade [1955] CLJ 172, 187.
[78] Dicey, p 68.
[79] Cf Hart, *The Concept of Law*, p 146; Marshall, *Parliamentary Sovereignty and the Commonwealth*, p 13; and H R Gray, note 76 above.
[80] R Stone (1966) 26 Louisiana LR 753, 755.

(*a*) Some matters authorised by legislation are of such a kind that once done, they cannot be undone by a later Act. Thus, over 60 years after Parliament approved the cession of Heligoland to Germany in 1890, Parliament repealed the statute by which cession was approved.[81] But in so doing, Parliament did not expect that this would recover the territory for the United Kingdom. When Parliament confers independence upon a colony, as it has done on many occasions, it has been the practice since 1960 to provide that no future Act of the United Kingdom Parliament 'shall extend or be deemed to extend' to the independent country as part of its law; and that the United Kingdom government should thereafter have no responsibility for the government of the country in question.[82] Earlier Independence Acts were less categorical, since it was thought that in some circumstances it might be convenient for the Westminster Parliament to continue to legislate for the territory at the request of the territory concerned.[83] At one time it was suggested that provisions conferring independence could be revoked by the Westminster Parliament.[84] The true position is that conferment of independence is an irreversible process; 'freedom once conferred cannot be revoked'.[85] Thus, by ceding territory or conferring independence, Parliament may restrict the geographical area over which future Parliaments may legislate effectively. In the Canada Act 1982, which conferred full power of constitutional amendment on Canada, it was provided that no subsequent Act of the UK Parliament 'shall extend to Canada as part of its law'. If Westminster in future should seek to reverse the historical clock by attempting to legislate for Canada, the Canadian courts would ignore any such attempt, unless the Canadian Parliament had authorised them to give effect to the legislation from Westminster. But British courts would be bound to give effect to the Westminster legislation so far as it lay within their jurisdiction to do so.[86]

(*b*) In a different way, Parliament may bind future Parliaments by altering the rules for the composition of the two Houses of Parliament or the succession to the throne. Thus in 1832, when Parliament reformed the House of Commons to secure more democratic representation, later Parliaments were bound by that legislation inasmuch as the only lawful House of Commons was one elected in accordance with the 1832 Act. Any further changes to the composition of the Commons had to be approved by the reformed House, since the pre-1832 House had ceased to exist. The present House of Commons was elected in accordance with election laws that are different from what they were in 1900 or in 1945. As for the House of Lords, in 1958 authority was given for creating life peerages and in 1999 all but 92 hereditary peers were removed from the House. Every change in the composition of the House of Lords must either be approved by that House (as constituted for the time being), or in the absence of such approval be enacted under the Parliament Acts 1911 and 1949.[87] In 1936, His Majesty's Declaration of Abdication Act altered the line of succession to the throne laid down by the Act of Settlement 1700, by removing Edward VIII and his issue from the succession: if a later Parliament had wished the throne to revert to Edward VIII, the assent of the Sovereign for the time being (i.e. George VI or his descendant) would have been required, just as Edward VIII's assent was needed for the Abdication Act itself. Thus, the supreme Parliament may alter the rules which determine who the

---

[81] Anglo-German Agreement Act 1890, repealed by Statute Law Revision Act 1953, s 1.
[82] E.g. Kenya Independence Act 1963, s 1; and see Roberts-Wray, *Commonwealth and Colonial Law*, p 261.
[83] Statute of Westminster 1931, s 4 and e.g. Ceylon Independence Act 1947, s 1; ch 15 C.
[84] *British Coal Corpn* v *R* [1935] AC 500, 520.
[85] *Ndlwana* v *Hofmeyr* 1937 AD 229, 237; *Ibralebbe* v *R* [1964] AC 900, 923; *Blackburn* v *A-G* [1971] 2 All ER 1380.
[86] *Manuel* v *A-G* [1983] Ch 77, 88.
[87] Ch 10 B.

successors of the component parts of Parliament are to be (and, it might be added, may abolish one of these component parts, e.g. the House of Lords, though this issue receives separate discussion below).

By contrast, in one situation successive Parliaments have taken care to ensure that their acts do not bind their successors. This situation arises when Westminster creates an assembly or parliament with devolved power to make law for part of the United Kingdom, but at the same time does not limit its own power to legislate for the whole United Kingdom. The Scotland Act 1998, s 28, empowered the Scottish Parliament to make laws on devolved matters; but the Act stated that conferment of that power to make laws 'does not affect the power' of the United Kingdom Parliament to make laws for Scotland (s 28(7)). A similar provision is found in the Northern Ireland Act 1998 (s 5(6)). The same declaration in grander language was in the Government of Ireland Act 1920, which established a parliament for Northern Ireland and by s 75 provided that the 'supreme authority' of the United Kingdom Parliament 'shall remain unaffected and undiminished over all persons, matters and things' in Northern Ireland. The power retained by Westminster includes in law the power to repeal the entire scheme of devolution. Thus in 1972 Westminster abolished the Stormont Parliament. On the Diceyan view of supremacy, it is not necessary in law to include express provision in a devolution Act to preserve Westminster's legislative powers. But such provision may serve a deeper political purpose, as the existence of the Scottish Parliament presents a definite challenge to Westminster's continuing legislative authority over Scotland.[88]

The rule that Parliament may not bind its successors presents difficulties for certain constitutional reforms (for example, the creation of an entrenched Bill of Rights, discussed below). But it presents no obstacle to the adoption of a wholly new constitutional structure for the United Kingdom. As was said about Gladstone's first Home Rule Bill for Ireland, 'if the Irish Government Bill had become law the Parliament of 1885 would have had no successors.'[89] The object of securing that no subsequent Parliament enjoyed the attribute of legislative supremacy could be achieved in a variety of ways, for example by creating a federal system in the United Kingdom under which England, Scotland, Wales and Northern Ireland would each have its own legislature and executive; these bodies, together with a federal legislature and executive, would all be subject to the constitution as interpreted by a federal court. The creation of such a system would be inconsistent with the continuance of the legislative supremacy of the present Parliament. The legislative ground for the new constitution would be laid by the supreme Parliament before it ceased to exist.

With the possible exception of the Union between Scotland and England in 1707 and the Union between Ireland and Great Britain in 1800,[90] no actual reforms have been intended to go as far as this. However, as with British accession to the European Community,[91] problems have arisen only where the clear intention of Parliament to divest itself of legislative supremacy has not been manifested and where it may be argued that the overriding rule of supremacy has not been affected. The question is not, 'May a supreme Parliament bind its successors?' but 'What must a supreme Parliament do (a) to express the definite intention that future Parliaments should not be supreme? and (b) to ensure (whether by positive direction or structural changes) that the courts will in future give effect to that intention?' The second part of the question is important: for if the matter were to rest merely on the stated intention of the

---

[88] And see ch 3 B.
[89] W R Anson (1886) 2 LQR 427, 436.
[90] Ch 3 A and section D in this chapter.
[91] Ch 8.

present Parliament, it is likely that the courts would hold that a later Parliament would be free to depart from that intention. Moreover, it is only by subsequent judicial decisions, taken in the light of relevant political developments, that it would be known whether or not the present (supreme) Parliament had successfully achieved its stated objective.

Before these matters are considered further, one question which has already been mentioned[92] needs to be more fully examined, namely the need for legal rules identifying the measures which are judicially accepted as Acts of Parliament.

What is an Act of Parliament?[93]

In an extremely simple community, where all powers within the human group are exercised by one person recognised as sovereign, no legal problems of identifying acts of the sovereign arise. But, as R T E Latham said:

> Where the purported sovereign is anyone but a single actual person, the designation of him must include the statement of rules for the ascertainment of his will, and these rules, since their observance is a condition of the validity of his legislation, are rules of law logically prior to him.[94]

Latham pointed out that Parliament, regarded only as an assembly of human beings, was not sovereign. 'It can only be sovereign when acting in a certain way prescribed by law. At least some rudimentary "manner and form" is demanded of it: the simultaneous incoherent cry of a rabble, small or large, cannot be law, for it is unintelligible.'[95]

In the absence of a written constitution to guide the courts in identifying an Act of Parliament, the definition of an Act of Parliament is primarily a matter of common law.[96] The rule of English common law is that for a Bill to become law, it must have been approved by Lords and Commons and have received the royal assent. In the ordinary case, this simple test will be satisfied by a rapid inspection of the Queen's Printer's copy of an Act of Parliament which will bear at its head formal words of enactment.[97] When Acts of Parliament have been challenged on the ground of procedural defects during their passage through Parliament, the judges have laid down the 'enrolled Act' rule.

> In *Edinburgh & Dalkeith Railway* v *Wauchope*, a private Act which adversely affected Wauchope's rights against a railway company was challenged by him on the ground that notice of its introduction as a Bill into Parliament had not been given to him, as required by standing orders of the House of Commons. The court rejected this challenge. Lord Campbell said: 'All that a court of justice can do is to look to the Parliament roll: if from that it should appear that a Bill has passed both Houses and received the Royal Assent, no court of justice can inquire into the mode in which it was introduced into Parliament, or into what was done previous to its introduction, or what passed in Parliament during its progress in its various stages through both Houses.'[98] And in *Lee* v *Bude & Torrington Railway Co* it was said: 'If an Act of Parliament has been obtained improperly, it is for the legislature to correct it by repealing it; but, so long as it exists as law, the courts are bound to obey it.'[99]

---

[92] Page 54 above.
[93] R T E Latham (1939) King's Counsel 152 and G Marshall (1954) 2 Political Studies 193.
[94] *The Law and the Commonwealth*, p 523; compare Hart's 'rule of recognition', *The Concept of Law* (pp 75, 245 and ch 6). And see on Latham, P Oliver (2000) II King's College Law Journal 153.
[95] (1939) King's Counsel, 153, quoted in Heuston, *Essays in Constitutional Law*, pp 7–8.
[96] Sir Owen Dixon (1957) 31 ALJ 240. And see *Prince's Case* (1606) 8 Co Rep 1, 20b.
[97] Interpretation Act 1978, s 3. And see *Manuel* v *A-G* [1983] Ch 77, 87.
[98] (1842) 8 Cl and F 710, 725.
[99] (1871) LR 6 CP 577, 582 (Willes J).

This principle was reaffirmed in 1974, when the House of Lords in *Pickin v British Railways Board* held that a local or private Act of Parliament was binding whether or not the standing orders of each House of Parliament had been complied with.

Private Acts of 1836 and 1845 authorised the taking of land for a railway and provided that, if the line were ever abandoned, the land should vest in the owners of the adjoining land. In 1968, another private Act was passed, promoted by the British Railways Board, which abolished this rule. In 1969, Pickin bought a small piece of adjoining land and, when the railway was discontinued, claimed a declaration that under the 1836 and 1845 Acts he was entitled to a strip of the old line. He alleged that the board had fraudulently misled Parliament when promoting the 1968 Act, and had not complied with the standing orders of each House requiring individual notice to be given to owners affected by private legislation. Although the Court of Appeal held that these allegations raised a triable issue,[100] the House of Lords held that the courts had no power to disregard an Act of Parliament, whether public or private, nor had they any power to examine proceedings in Parliament to determine whether an Act had been obtained by irregularity or fraud.[101]

There are several reasons for this reluctance of the courts to inquire into the internal procedures of Parliament. One important reason is the privilege of each House to regulate its own proceedings.[102] For officers of Parliament to be summoned before a court to give evidence about the internal proceedings of Parliament would create a danger of the courts infringing art 9 of the Bill of Rights.[103] On many matters of parliamentary procedure, the courts have declined to intervene whether or not alleged breaches of statute were involved.[104] The rule that a Bill must be read three times in each House is not a requirement of the common law but is part of the 'law and custom of Parliament' and on this the standing orders of each House are based. If one House wished to alter the requirement, say by abolishing the third reading, this change would not affect the duty of the courts to apply the 'enrolled Act' rule.

But some comments must be made on the 'enrolled Act' rule. First, there is today no Parliament roll: in case of necessity, all that a court could inspect is the two vellum prints of an Act which since 1849 have been signed by the Clerk of Parliaments and preserved in the Public Record Office and the House of Lords Record Office.[105] Second, the rule is reinforced by the rule in the Interpretation Act 1978 that every Act passed after 1850 shall be a public Act and judicially noticed as such, unless the contrary is expressly provided by the Act.[106] Third, if it should appear that a measure has not been approved by one House, then (unless the Parliament Acts 1911–49 apply) the measure is not an Act.[107] Fourth, where there is a written constitution, this may lay down the procedures which must be followed before a Bill can become an Act. Thus in South Africa, the former constitution provided that certain entrenched rights could be revoked only by legislation adopted at a joint sitting of both Houses of the South African Parliament, voting by a two-thirds majority: where this procedure was not followed, the result was not a valid Act of Parliament.[108]

---

[100] [1973] QB 219.

[101] [1974] AC 765.

[102] Ch 11 A. The Scottish Parliament does not enjoy this privilege (*Whaley v Lord Watson of Invergowrie* 2000 SC 125) but by the Scotland Act 1998, s 28(5), the validity of an Act of that Parliament is not affected by any invalidity in proceedings leading to its enactment.

[103] Page 14 above.

[104] *Bradlaugh v Gossett* (1884) 12 QBD 271; *Bilston v Wolverhampton Corpn* [1942] Ch 391; *Harper v Home Secretary* [1955] Ch 238; *Rediffusion (Hong Kong) Ltd v A-G of Hong Kong* [1970] AC 1136 (see O Hood Phillips (1971) 87 LQR 321). And see B Beinart [1954] SALR 135.

[105] Heuston, *Essays in Constitutional Law*, p 18; and Erskine May, *Parliamentary Practice*, p 571.

[106] For an explanation of this rule, see *Craies on Statute Law*, pp 55–8.

[107] *The Prince's Case* (1606) 8 Co Rep 1a; cf Erskine May, p 572.

[108] *Harris v Minister of Interior* 1952 (2) SA 428. For a full account, see Marshall, *Parliamentary Sovereignty and the Commonwealth*, part 3. Also Loveland, *By Due Process of Law*, chs 7 and 8.

Could the 'enrolled Act' rule be changed by Act of Parliament? To an extent this has already occurred. Thus the Regency Acts 1937–53 make permanent provision for the infancy, incapacity or temporary absence abroad of the Sovereign.[109] A regent appointed under these Acts may exercise all royal functions, including assenting to Bills, except that he may not assent to a Bill for changing the order of succession to the Crown or for repealing or altering the Act of 1707 securing Presbyterian Church Government in Scotland. If, which is unlikely, a regent did assent to a Bill for one of these purposes, there seems no reason why the courts should regard the resulting measure as an Act of Parliament.

Similarly, the Parliament Acts 1911–49[110] provide that in certain circumstances a Bill may become an Act without having been approved by the Lords. The 1911 Act provides special words of enactment which refer to the Parliament Acts (s 4(1)) and also provides that the Speaker's certificate that the requirements of the Acts have been complied with shall be conclusive for all purposes (s 3). But this procedure does not apply either to a Bill to extend the life of Parliament or to private or local Bills. If it were attempted to extend the life of Parliament by a measure which had not been approved by the Lords, a court should decline to regard the result as an Act of Parliament: the 'conclusiveness' of the Speaker's certificate would not bar such a decision by the court.[111]

In respect both of the Regency Acts and the Parliament Acts, it has been argued that measures which become law thereunder are not Acts of the supreme Parliament but are Acts of a subordinate legislature to which the supreme Parliament has made a limited delegation of its powers; such measures are thus no more than delegated legislation.[112] But in other contexts, courts have been reluctant to apply to a legislature the principle that delegated power may not be sub-delegated (*delegatus non potest delegare*)[113] and a preferable view is that, for all but the purposes excluded, Parliament has provided a procedure for legislation which is alternative to the procedure of legislation by the supreme Parliament recognised at common law.[114] On this view, the legal definition of an Act of Parliament may already differ according to the circumstances, as it may where a written constitution requires special procedures or special majorities for certain purposes.[115]

There continues to be doubt whether Parliament may by statute alter the legal rules for identifying an Act of Parliament. In *Pickin's* case, Lord Morris said:

> It must surely be for Parliament to lay down the procedures which are to be followed before a Bill can become an Act. It must be for Parliament to decide whether its decreed procedures have in fact been followed.[116]

This statement needs to be read with great care. First, it was made in the context of an alleged departure from the standing orders of the House of Commons. Second, where there is a written constitution prescribing special procedure for certain legislation, we have seen that the enforcement of these procedures may be a matter for the courts. Thirdly, Lord Morris's use of 'Parliament' is ambiguous. Are the procedures for

---

[109] For fuller details, see 12th edn of this work, pp 257–8.

[110] Ch 10 B.

[111] Section 3 of the 1911 Act requires that the Speaker's certificate shall be given 'under this Act'; in interpreting this section, a court could hold that the test of ultra vires had not been ousted: cf *Minister of Health v R* [1931] AC 494 and *Anisminic Ltd v Foreign Compensation Commission* [1969] 2 AC 147; ch 31.

[112] H W R Wade [1955] CLJ 172, 193–4 and *Constitutional Fundamentals*, pp 27–8.

[113] *R v Burah* (1878) 3 App Cas 889 and *Hodge v R* (1883) 9 App Cas 117 (power of colonial legislature to delegate).

[114] P Mirfield (1979) 95 LQR 36, 47–50.

[115] Note 108 above. And see J Jaconelli [1989] PL 587.

[116] [1974] AC 765, 790.

legislation to be laid down by the Queen in Parliament (i.e. by statute) or by each House of Parliament separately (i.e. by standing orders and resolutions)? If the procedures for legislation were to be laid down by statute, so that a new statutory definition of an Act of Parliament (for all or some purposes) replaced the former common law rule, why should the courts continue to observe the former rule rather than the new statutory definition? Finally, if the question whether a certain document was an Act of Parliament were to arise in the course of litigation between two parties, it would be for the court to decide whether the document satisfied the 'enrolled Act' rule or some other rule laid down in legislation. As Marshall CJ said in *Marbury* v *Madison*, 'It is emphatically the province and duty of the judicial department to say what the law is'.[117]

In the context of a colonial legislature, the case of *Attorney-General for New South Wales* v *Trethowan*[118] concerned the effects on the validity of legislation of a constitutional requirement of 'manner and form'.

> Under the Colonial Laws Validity Act 1865, the legislature of New South Wales had power to make laws respecting its own constitution, powers and procedure, provided that these laws were passed 'in such manner and form' as might be required by an Act of Parliament or other law for the time being in force in the state. In 1929 an Act provided that the upper House of the legislature should not be abolished until a Bill approved by both Houses had been approved by a referendum of the electorate; the requirement of a referendum applied also to amendments of the 1929 Act. Following a change of government, a Bill passed through both Houses which sought to abolish both the upper House and the requirement of a referendum. The government did not intend to submit the Bill to a referendum. An injunction was granted by the New South Wales court to restrain the government of New South Wales from presenting the Bill for the royal assent unless and until a majority of the electors had approved it. On appeal, the Judicial Committee held that the requirement of a referendum was binding on the legislature until it had been abolished by a law passed in the 'manner and form' required by law for the time being, i.e. with the approval of a referendum.

One view of *Trethowan's* case is that it depended solely on the fact that the legislature was a subordinate legislature, subject to the rule in the Colonial Laws Validity Act that a constitutional amendment had to be enacted 'in such manner and form' as the law required from time to time. On this view, *Trethowan* is not relevant to a supreme legislature, such as the Westminster Parliament.[119] Another view is that there is a common law rule that legislation may be enacted only in such manner and form as is laid down in law, that this rule applies to the UK Parliament and that the 1865 Act put into statutory form a rule that is fundamental to the court's task of deciding whether a measure has the force of law.[120] While the Judicial Committee's decision in *Trethowan* was expressly based on the 1865 Act, a British court might be reluctant to accept that the 'enrolled Act' rule had been changed by a similar requirement of a referendum and might take the view that the dispute raised an issue as to justiciability.[121]

The Human Rights Act 1998 provides an example of a change in legislative procedure that might possibly give rise to a 'manner and form' argument. By section 19 of the Act, a minister who is in charge of a Bill in Parliament must, before it is debated on second reading, state either that the Bill is compatible with the rights protected by

---

[117] 1 Cranch 137 (1803).

[118] [1932] AC 526, discussed in Marshall, *Parliamentary Sovereignty and the Commonwealth*, ch 8; W Friedmann (1950) 24 ALJ 103; and Loveland, *Constitutional Law*, pp 35–40.

[119] H W R Wade [1955] CLJ 172, 183; E C S Wade, Introduction to Dicey, *The Law of the Constitution*, pp lxxiii–v.

[120] E.g. Jennings, *The Law and the Constitution*, p 153; R T E Latham (1939) King's Counsel 152, 161; W G Friedmann (1950) 24 ALJ 103, 104; O Dixon (1935) 51 LQR 590, 603.

[121] Cf G Sawer (1944) 60 LQR 83; see also *Rediffusion (Hong Kong) Ltd* v *Attorney-General of Hong Kong* [1970] AC 1136.

the 1998 Act or, if it is not so compatible, that the government wishes the House to proceed with the Bill. Would failure by a minister in charge of a Bill to make such a statement affect the validity of the resulting Act? For several reasons, the courts would not hold the legislation to be invalid. The requirement of a ministerial statement would be seen as a parliamentary procedure, enforceable by Parliament and not by the court. Nor would the courts be likely to hold that in enacting s 19, Parliament was intending to alter the 'enrolled Act' rule.[122] This would be the case even if the ministerial statement was inaccurate.

Summary

The argument so far may be summarised as follows. In principle a legislature must remain free to enact new laws on matters within its competence: if a conflict occurs between the laws enacted by Parliament, the courts apply the later of the two laws. The authority of Parliament includes power to legislate on constitutional matters, including both the composition of Parliament and the 'manner and form' by which new legislation may be made. While the courts may not of their own accord review the internal proceedings of Parliament, the scope for judicial decision could be extended if, by statute, Parliament altered the common law rules according to which the courts recognise or identify an Act of Parliament. The doctrine of parliamentary supremacy is no bar to the adoption of a written constitution for the United Kingdom which imposes judicially enforceable limits upon a future legislature, at least if such structural changes are made that the new legislative process is radically different from the present process by Lords, Commons and royal assent. Difficulty would arise if changes were *not* made in the structure of the legislature but the attempt was made to impose limits or restrictions on the present legislature; in this situation, the courts might not regard the purported limits or restrictions as ousting the continuing legislative supremacy of Parliament. The matter remains open. While Parliament could alter the 'manner and form' of the legislative process, such an attempt would not be effective if the courts still gave allegiance to the supreme Parliament defined in common law.

These general principles will now be discussed briefly in relation to some specific constitutional issues.

1 *Constitutional guarantees for Northern Ireland*[123]   An account is given elsewhere of the events by which Southern Ireland broke from the United Kingdom.[124] In the Ireland Act 1949, the UK Parliament recognised the republican status of Southern Ireland and that it had ceased to be part of the Crown's dominions. The Act also declared that 'in no event' would Northern Ireland 'or any part thereof' cease to be part of the United Kingdom 'without consent of the Parliament of Northern Ireland'.[125]

The 1949 Act gave no express guarantee of the continued existence of the Parliament of Northern Ireland. When that Parliament was abolished in 1973 by Westminster, a new guarantee was given that Northern Ireland would not cease to be part of the United Kingdom without the consent of the majority of the people.[126] Today the Northern Ireland Act 1998, s 1, declares that Northern Ireland 'in its entirety remains

---

[122] See N Bamforth [1998] PL 572, 575–82, citing *Mangawaro Enterprises* v *Attorney-General* [1994] 2 NZLR 451.

[123] Calvert, *Constitutional Law in Northern Ireland*, pp 23–33; Heuston, *Essays in Constitutional Law*, ch 1; Hadfield, *Constitutional Law of Northern Ireland*, pp 104–5.

[124] Ch 3 A.

[125] For an analogous provision in Gladstone's first Home Rule Bill, see Marshall, *Parliamentary Sovereignty and the Commonwealth*, pp 63–6.

[126] Northern Ireland Act 1973, s 1.

part of the United Kingdom and shall not cease to be so without the consent of a majority of the people of Northern Ireland' voting in a poll held for the purpose. The guarantee is of great political significance. But has Parliament fettered itself from, say, ceding Londonderry to the Republic of Ireland without first obtaining the consent of the majority of the people of Northern Ireland? Or could Parliament at a future date repeal the 1998 Act and provide nothing in its place? The strongest legal argument for the proposition that Parliament could not breach the guarantee takes the form that for the purposes of legislating for the future status of Northern Ireland, Parliament has redefined itself so that an additional stage, namely approval by a border poll, is required. But would the courts hold that this intention had been so clearly expressed that a subsequent Parliament had lost the legal capacity to repeal the 1998 Act, expressly or by implication? At one time, a court might have been reluctant to recognise an individual's standing to challenge action by Parliament,[127] and reluctant to grant injunctive relief. However, standing to sue has presented few difficulties in recent public law cases and a declaratory judgment would be an appropriate remedy.[128] It has been suggested that the Northern Ireland guarantee is an example of a limitation which Parliament may impose on itself but which does not incapacitate Parliament from acting.[129] In reality, the political constraints against breach of the guarantee provide a greater safeguard for the Ulster Unionists than reliance on litigation that sought to establish that in 1998 Parliament had limited the powers of future Parliaments.

2 *British membership of the European Union*   A later chapter will outline the structure of the European Union and will discuss the relationship between national law and Community law. Community law has been held by the European Court of Justice to prevail over any inconsistent provisions of the national law of the member states:

> the law stemming from the Treaty, an independent source of law, cannot because of its very nature be overridden by rules of national law, however framed . . . without the legal basis of the Community itself being called into question.[130]

The European Communities Act 1972 gave legal effect within the United Kingdom to those provisions of Community law which were, according to the European treaties, intended to have direct effect within member states. This applied both to existing and future treaties and regulations. The Community organs therefore may legislate for the United Kingdom, as they do for other member states. While Britain remains a member of the Community, the Westminster Parliament is not the sole body with power to make new law for the United Kingdom. Nor can Community law appropriately be described as delegated legislation.[131]

The extent to which Community law overrides inconsistent national law was seen in *R v Transport Secretary, ex p Factortame Ltd*:[132]

> Spanish fishing interests that had formed companies registered in the United Kingdom challenged as contrary to Community law the Merchant Shipping Act 1988. This Act, by defining the term, British fishing vessels, in a restrictive way, sought to prevent non-British interests from having access to the British fishing quota. In interim proceedings to protect Spanish interests pending decision of the substantive case, the European Court of Justice held that a national court must set aside a rule of national law if this was the sole obstacle preventing it from

---

[127] Ch 31.
[128] See e.g. *R v Employment Secretary, ex p EOC* [1995] 1 AC 1.
[129] Mitchell, *Constitutional Law*, p 81.
[130] *Case 11/70, Internationale Handelsgesellschaft* case [1970] ECR 1125, 1134. And see ch 8 B.
[131] Cf Cmnd 3301, 1967, para 22.
[132] [1990] 2 AC 85 and ibid (*No 2*) [1991] 1 AC 603. See also N Gravells [1989] PL 568 and [1991] PL 180; and ch 8 D.

granting temporary relief to protect Community rights. Thus the British courts must disregard s 21 of the Crown Proceedings Act 1947 (no injunctions to be granted against the Crown)[133] and must also not apply the Merchant Shipping Act 1988. In the House of Lords, Lord Bridge challenged the view that 'this was a novel and dangerous invasion by a Community institution of the sovereignty of the United Kingdom Parliament'. He stated that long before the United Kingdom joined the Community, the supremacy of Community law over the laws of member states was well established. 'Thus whatever limitation of its sovereignty Parliament accepted when it enacted the European Communities Act 1972 was entirely voluntary'.[134]

In *R v Employment Secretary, ex p EOC*,[135] the House of Lords declared that provisions in the Employment Protection (Consolidation) Act 1978, making protection for part-time workers (who were mainly female) subject to conditions that did not apply to full-time workers (who were mainly male), were incompatible with the right of female workers under Community law to equal treatment with male workers.

These decisions establish that the British courts must not apply national legislation, whether enacted before or after the European Communities Act 1972, if to do so would conflict with Community law. In Sir William Wade's view, decisions such as *Factortame* have effected a 'constitutional revolution', by holding that Parliament in 1972 did bind its successors.[136] A narrower explanation is that the 1972 Act created a rule of construction requiring the courts to apply UK legislation consistently with Community law, except where an Act expressly overrides Community law.[137] Whichever explanation is preferred, the primacy of Community law is an inescapable, albeit indeterminate, consequence of membership of the European Union.

3 *The Human Rights Act 1998*   The doctrine that Parliament may not bind its successors is a major obstacle to enactment of a Bill of Rights intended to protect human rights against legislation by later Parliaments. In outlining its scheme for the Human Rights Act 1998, the government denied that it was trying to transfer power from future Parliaments to the courts:

> To make provision in the Bill for the courts to set aside Acts of Parliament would confer on the judiciary a general power over the decisions of Parliament which under our present constitutional arrangements they do not possess, and would be likely on occasions to draw the judiciary into serious conflict with Parliament. There is no evidence to suggest that they desire this power, nor that the public wish them to have it. Certainly this Government has no mandate for any such change.[138]

This stance applied to both existing and future Acts of Parliament, although Parliament in 1998 undoubtedly could have provided that the rights protected by the Human Rights Act should prevail over all *existing* statutes. On whether those rights should be entrenched against *subsequent* legislation, the government mentioned the procedure for amending the US constitution and stated:

> an arrangement of this kind could not be reconciled with our own constitutional traditions, which allow any Act of Parliament to be amended or repealed by a subsequent Act of Parliament. We do not believe that it is necessary or would be desirable *to attempt to devise such a special arrangement* for this Bill.[139]

---

[133] See ch 32 C.
[134] [1991] 1 AC at 659. And see *Thoburn v Sunderland Council* [2002] EWHC Admin 934.
[135] [1995] 1 AC 1. Cf *R v Social Security Secretary, ex p EOC* (Case C 9/91) [1992] 3 All ER 577 (upholding differential age in state pensions scheme).
[136] (1996) 112 LQR 568.
[137] P Craig (1991) 11 YBEL 221, 251. And see ch 8 D.
[138] *Rights Brought Home* Cm 3872 (1997), para 2.13. And see ch 19 C.
[139] Ibid, para 2.16 (emphasis supplied). Note the use of the word 'attempt' in the italicised phrase.

Certainly, if a wholly new constitution for the United Kingdom were to be created, it could include entrenched fundamental rights. Short of that, are there ways in which fundamental rights could be protected against infringement by a future Parliament? In 1979, a select committee of the House of Lords, considering the desirability of a Bill of Rights for the United Kingdom, said:

> there is no way in which a Bill of Rights could protect itself from encroachment, whether express or implied, by later Acts. The most that such a Bill could do would be to include an interpretation provision which ensured that the Bill of Rights was always taken into account in the construction of later Acts and that, so far as a later Act could be construed in a way that was compatible with a Bill of Rights, such a construction would be preferred to one that was not.[140]

That view had not been taken by the Northern Ireland Standing Advisory Commission on Human Rights in 1977, when the Commission recommended that no future Act that was inconsistent with the European Convention on Human Rights should have effect unless the later Act expressly declared that it should apply notwithstanding the Convention.[141] As will be seen later, the Human Rights Act 1998 does not attempt to bind future Parliaments in this way. Instead, the Act (s 3) imposes a new duty on the courts to interpret all legislation, whatever its date, consistently with the Convention, *if such an interpretation is possible.* If such an interpretation is not possible, then the conflicting provision remains in effect, but it may be declared by a superior court to be incompatible with Convention rights, in which case the government may exercise a novel power to make a 'remedial order' removing the incompatibility from the statute.[142] This scheme preserves the formal authority of an Act of Parliament, while extending the powers of the judiciary to subject Parliament's work to detailed scrutiny. As Judge LJ said in 2001, 'The Act is carefully drafted to ensure that the court cannot and must not strike down or dispense with any single item of primary legislation.'[143]

4 *Abolition of the House of Lords*   In chapter 10 B we examine the present role of the House of Lords under the Parliament Acts 1911 and 1949. Here we deal only with the issue of whether, as one of the component parts of the supreme legislature, the House of Lords can be abolished.[144] There would indeed be a significant change in fundamental doctrine if 'whatever the Queen, Lords and Commons enact is law' were to become 'whatever the Queen and Commons enact is law'. If, as argued earlier, the former proposition is ultimately grounded on decisions of the courts, the latter proposition would be authoritatively established only when the courts accepted the legislative supremacy of the Queen and Commons in place of the former supreme legislature. Arguably this change could be regarded as a legal revolution or a breach in legal continuity,[145] but this would seem to be inaccurate if the courts had given effect to a constitutional change initiated and authorised by the former legislature.

Two issues of practical significance might arise. First, if the Act abolishing the House of Lords included a Bill of Rights which was declared to be incapable of amendment by the new legislature (Queen and Commons), the courts would then have a choice

---

[140] HL 176 (1977–78), para 23.
[141] Cmnd 7009, 1977. Cf New Zealand Bill of Rights Act 1990, s 6: 'Wherever an enactment can be given a meaning that is consistent with [this Bill of Rights], that meaning shall be preferred to any other meaning.'
[142] Human Rights Act 1998, ss 4, 5 and 10.
[143] *Re K (a child)* [2001] Fam 377, para 121. And see *R v Lyons* [2001] EWCA Crim 2860.
[144] For the main arguments, see P Mirfield (1979) 95 LQR 36 and G Winterton (1979) 95 LQR 386. And Dicey, *The Law of the Constitution*, pp 64–70.
[145] Mirfield, op cit, pp 42–5.

between whether (a) to give effect to the stated intention of the former legislature, by holding that the Bill of Rights must prevail over any Acts passed by the new legislature or (b) to hold that the new legislature was as legislatively supreme as its predecessor. Since the courts might not wish to create a legislative vacuum (i.e. a situation in which certain legislation is totally impossible), the outcome might depend on whether any procedure was provided for use if it became necessary in an emergency to encroach upon the Bill of Rights.

Second, could the House of Lords be lawfully abolished against the wishes of the House, by use of the Parliament Acts 1911 and 1949? The answer depends essentially upon whether the legislative powers conferred by the Parliament Act 1911 on the House of Commons and the Queen are to be construed subject to implied limitations, over and above those that are expressed in the 1911 Act itself.[146] Since the analogy of delegated legislation does not seem a close one, it is submitted that an Act passed under the Parliament Act procedure could lawfully abolish the House of Lords; such a measure might be resisted on political grounds but not by challenge in the courts.[147]

D. The Treaty of Union between England and Scotland

In Section C, we discussed the question whether the Westminster Parliament may impose legal limitations upon its successors. The Anglo-Scottish Union of 1707 raises the different question, 'was the United Kingdom Parliament born unfree?'[148] The main features of the Treaty of Union have already been outlined.[149] Now it is necessary to examine more closely provisions of the Treaty concerning the power to legislate after the Union.

The Treaty contemplated that the new Parliament of Great Britain would legislate both for England and Scotland; but no grant of general legislative competence to Parliament was made in the Treaty. Article 18 provided that the laws concerning regulation of trade, as well as customs and excise duties, should be uniform throughout Britain; subject to this, all other laws within Scotland were to remain in force,

> but alterable by the Parliament of Great Britain, with this difference betwixt the laws concerning public right, policy, and civil government, and those which concern private right; that the laws which concern public right, policy and civil government may be made the same throughout the whole United Kingdom, but that no alteration be made in laws which concern private right except for evident utility of the subjects within Scotland.

By art 19, the Court of Session and the Court of Justiciary were to remain 'in all time coming' within Scotland as then constituted and with the same authority and privileges as before the Union, 'subject nevertheless to such regulations for the better administration of justice as shall be made by the Parliament of Great Britain'. Other courts were to be subject to regulation and alteration by Parliament. No causes in Scotland were to be cognisable (i.e. capable of being heard) by the Courts of Chancery, Queen's Bench, Common Pleas (or any other court in Westminster Hall). An Act for securing the Protestant religion and Presbyterian Church government in Scotland was passed at

---

[146] Ibid, pp 45–6 and Winterton, op cit, pp 390–2. See also ch 10 B.
[147] As suggested by Lord Denning in *What Next in the Law?*, p 320. In 2000, the Royal Commission on reform of the House of Lords recommended that the Parliament Acts be amended to exclude the possibility of their being further amended by use of Parliament Act procedures: Cm 4534, para 5.15.
[148] Mitchell, *Constitutional Law*, pp 69–74; T B Smith [1957] PL 99; D N MacCormick (1978) 29 NILQ 1. See also Munro, *Studies in Constitutional Law*, pp 137–42; M Upton (1989) 105 LQR 79; *Stair Encyclopedia: The Laws of Scotland*, vol 5, pp 137–62; HLE, vol 8(2), pp 54–8; MacCormick, *Questioning Sovereignty*, ch 4; Clyde and Edwards, *Judicial Review*, pp 86–91.
[149] Ch 3 A.

the same time by the English and Scottish Parliaments and was declared to be a fundamental and essential condition of the Treaty of Union 'in all time coming'.

There is substantial evidence in the Treaty that, while the framers of the Union intended
the new Parliament to be the sole legislature, they sought to distinguish between matters on which Parliament would be free to legislate, matters on which it would have a
limited authority to legislate, and matters which were declared fundamental and unalterable. The Treaty made no provision for future amendment of itself or for future
renegotiation of the terms of the Union. The former English and Scottish Parliaments
ceased to exist. No machinery was provided for applying the distinction drawn in art
18 between the laws concerning 'public right, policy and civil government' and the laws
concerning 'private right' or, in the latter case, for discovering what changes in those
laws might be for 'evident utility' of the Scottish people.

The argument that the Union imposed limitations upon the new Parliament can be
summarised as follows: the new Parliament entered into its life by virtue of the Union;
its powers were therefore limited by the guarantees in the Treaty, which guarantees
had been enacted by the separate Parliaments before the united Parliament was born.
The assertion that a sovereign Parliament may not bind its successors may be coun-
tered by the view that even if both the English and Scottish Parliaments were supreme
before 1707,[150] each committed suicide in favour of a common heir with limited powers.
The Treaty of Union, concludes the argument, is a fundamental constitutional text
which prevents the British Parliament from itself enjoying the attribute of legislative
supremacy. When, as in *Cheney v Conn*, an English judge remarks, 'what the statute
says and provides is the highest form of law that is known to this country',[151] a Scots
lawyer might reply: 'Not so: the Treaty of Union is a higher form of law and may
prevail over inconsistent Acts of Parliament.'

This viewpoint is subject to both theoretical and historical difficulties. First, no
legislature other than the British Parliament was created. If circumstances changed, and
amendments to the Union became desirable, how could they be made except by Act
of Parliament? Thus in 1748, the heritable jurisdictions were abolished and, when Scottish
local government was reformed in 1975, the royal burghs were abolished.[152] In 1853,
the Universities (Scotland) Act abolished the requirement that the professors of the ancient
Scottish universities should be confessing members of the Church of Scotland, thus repealing an 'unalterable' provision of the Act for securing the Presbyterian Church. Second,
the distinction between laws concerning 'public right, policy and civil government' and
laws concerning 'private right' is a very difficult one. For example, power to tax
private property or to acquire land compulsorily for public purposes concerns both
public and private right; and is the law of education or industrial relations a matter of
public or private right? Third, the test of 'evident utility' for changes in the law affecting private right is obscure: who is to decide – Scottish MPs, Scottish courts, public
opinion or institutions such as the General Assembly of the Church of Scotland?[153] Fourth,
after the Union the Westminster Parliament continued to conduct its affairs exactly
as before, subject only to its enlargement by members from Scotland.[154] As dominant
partners in the Union, the English assumed that continuity from pre-Union days

---

[150] On whether the Scottish Parliament was supreme before 1707, see Donaldson, *Scotland: James V–James VII*, ch 15; and Dicey and Rait, *Thoughts on the Union between England and Scotland*, pp 19–22, 242–4.

[151] Page 57 above.

[152] Cf arts 20 and 21 of the Treaty of Union.

[153] The court was prepared to find a statute to be of 'evident utility' in *Laughland v Wansborough Paper Co* 1921 1 SLT 341, but cf *Gibson v Lord Advocate* (p 73 below).

[154] See e.g. the comment by Bryce, *Studies in History and Jurisprudence*, vol 1, p 194, that, by fusing her-self with Scotland in 1707, England altered the constitution of the enlarged state no further than by the admission of additional members to Parliament and the suppression of certain offices in Scotland.

was unbroken. On a matter left silent by the Treaty of Union, the House of Lords in its judicial capacity has heard appeals from Scotland in civil cases since the case of *Greenshields* in 1709 (the House of Lords was not a court within Westminster Hall within the meaning of art 19 of the Union) but it has no jurisdiction in Scottish criminal cases. Fifth, even if the framers of the Union intended there to be limitations on the British Parliament, this might not in itself be sufficient to vest jurisdiction in the courts to hold Acts of that Parliament invalid on the ground that they conflicted with the Treaty. In Dicey's view, the subsequent history of the Union 'affords the strongest proof of the futility inherent in every attempt of one sovereign legislature to restrain the action of another equally sovereign body'.[155]

These matters have been debated in several important Scottish cases.

In *MacCormick* v *Lord Advocate*,[156] the Rector of Glasgow University challenged the Queen's title as 'Elizabeth the Second', on the grounds that this was contrary to historical fact and contravened art 1 of the Treaty of Union. At first instance, Lord Guthrie dismissed the challenge for the reason, inter alia, that an Act of Parliament could not be challenged in any court as being in breach of the Treaty of Union or on any other ground. In the Inner House of the Court of Session, the First Division dismissed the appeal against Lord Guthrie's decision, but on narrower grounds. After holding that MacCormick had no legal title or interest to sue, that the royal numeral was not contrary to the Treaty, and that the Royal Titles Act 1953 was irrelevant, Lord President Cooper said: 'The principle of the unlimited sovereignty of Parliament is a distinctively English principle which has no counterpart in Scottish constitutional law'. He had difficulty in seeing why it should have been supposed that the Parliament of Great Britain must have inherited all the peculiar characteristics of the English Parliament but none of the Scottish Parliament. He could find in the Union legislation no provision that the Parliament of Great Britain should be 'absolutely sovereign' in the sense that it should be free to alter the Treaty at will. He reserved opinion on whether breach of such fundamental law as is contained in the Treaty of Union would raise an issue justiciable in the courts; in his view there was no precedent that the courts of Scotland or England had authority to determine 'whether a governmental act of the type here in controversy is or is not conform to the provisions of a Treaty, least of all when that Treaty is one under which both Scotland and England ceased to be independent States and merged their identity in an incorporating union'. Lord Russell, who concurred, stressed the limited functions of the courts in dealing with political matters, suggesting that a political remedy would be more suitable for MacCormick than a judicial remedy.

Although Lord Cooper's judgment went beyond what was necessary for decision of the case, the fundamental issues remain confused. In particular, the denial that the courts have jurisdiction to decide whether 'a governmental act of the type here in controversy' conformed to the Treaty must be read in relation to the disputed royal title. If the Westminster Parliament were to pass an Act which sought to deprive persons in Scotland of access to the Scottish courts in matters of private right, the courts would seem bound to decide whether to give effect to that Act.

In 1975, a Scottish fisherman unsuccessfully claimed in the Court of Session that British membership of the European Community was incompatible with the Treaty of Union.

In *Gibson* v *Lord Advocate*, Gibson claimed that an EC regulation granting EC nationals the right to fish in Scottish waters and the European Communities Act 1972, which gave this legal effect in Britain, were contrary to art 18 of the Union, since this was a change in the law concerning a private right which was not for the 'evident utility' of the Scottish people. Lord Keith held that the control of fishing in territorial waters was a branch of public law, which might

---

[155] Dicey, *The Law of the Constitution*, p 65; and cf Dicey and Rait, p 252.
[156] 1953 SC 396.

be made the same throughout the United Kingdom and was not protected by art 18. Obiter, Lord Keith said that the question whether an Act of Parliament altering Scots private law was for the 'evident utility' of the Scottish people was not a justiciable issue. 'The making of decisions upon what must essentially be a political matter is no part of the function of the court.'[157] He considered the question of title to sue (locus standi) to be of secondary importance.

Both in *MacCormick* and in *Gibson* the question was held open of the validity of legislation seeking to abolish the Court of Session or the Church of Scotland, both being institutions safeguarded by the Union. Short of such an extreme situation, the Scottish courts appear reluctant to claim a power to review the validity of Acts of Parliament. This attitude was maintained when the Court of Session declined to hold that the community charge (or poll tax) legislation, which applied to Scotland a year earlier than in England and Wales, was contrary to art 4 of the Treaty of Union.[158]

The Scotland Act 1998 conferred on the courts a new jurisdiction to decide 'devolution issues', namely questions as to the extent of the powers of the Scottish Parliament and Executive.[159] But this new jurisdiction would not cause the Scottish courts to review the validity of Acts of the Westminster Parliament. A related question is whether the Scotland Act affected the historical jurisdiction of the Scottish courts on matters relating to government and the people. Section 37 of the 1998 Act declares that the Union with Scotland Act 1706 and the Union with England Act 1707 shall 'have effect subject to this Act'. This provision aims 'to ensure that neither the Scotland Act 1998 nor legislation or actions authorised under its terms should be vulnerable to challenge on the ground of their inconsistency with the Acts of Union'.[160]

In 1999, the Committee of Privileges in the House of Lords considered whether the proposal in the House of Lords Bill to remove Scottish hereditary peers from the House at the same time as other hereditary peers would breach the Treaty of Union, article 22 of which entitled 16 peers of Scotland to sit in the House. In fact, the Peerage Act 1963 had removed the limit of 16 and entitled all surviving Scottish peers to sit; and article 22 had later been repealed. The Committee of Privileges unanimously held that the removal of the Scottish peers would not breach the Treaty of Union.[161] Lord Hope left open, without deciding, whether the courts have jurisdiction to decide whether some provisions of the Treaty of Union might have binding force. Even if the exclusion of the Scottish peers had been considered to breach the Union, it is not at all likely that the validity of the House of Lords Act 1999 would have been affected.

E. Conclusions

This chapter has examined whether there are any legal limits on the legislative supremacy of Parliament, in particular whether there are, or could be, any limits capable of being enforced judicially. While British tradition has been strongly against the courts having power to review the validity of primary legislation, the courts cannot escape the task of deciding whether a document for which legislative authority is claimed is in law an Act of Parliament. While the basic rule of legislative supremacy is a matter of common law, as well as being an important political fact, it cannot be

---

[157] 1975 SLT 134.
[158] *Pringle, Petitioner* 1991 SLT 330 and *Murray v Rogers* 1992 SLT 221. See also N C Walker and C M G Himsworth [1991] JR 45 and D J Edwards (1992) 12 Legal Studies 34. Cf *R v Lord Chancellor, ex p Law Society, The Times*, 25 June 1993.
[159] See ch 3 B.
[160] Himsworth and Munro, *The Scotland Act 1998*, p 52.
[161] *Lord Gray's Motion* [2000] 1 AC 124.

demonstrated from existing precedents that under no circumstances could this rule be qualified by judicial decision – still less that the basic rule could not be changed by Act of Parliament. It is therefore not possible to assert dogmatically that the legislative supremacy of Parliament will continue to be the primary rule of constitutional law in the United Kingdom.[162] Indeed, the advancing pace of European integration (through Community law) has already made extensive inroads into the Diceyan doctrine of legislative supremacy; the Human Rights Act 1998 stops short of enabling the courts to set aside an Act of Parliament but authorises the courts to scrutinise legislation for compliance with the European Convention on Human Rights; and the advent of devolution means that the Westminster Parliament is not the only legislature in the United Kingdom.

Political significance of legislative supremacy

There are difficulties in attempting to assess the political significance of the legislative supremacy of Parliament. For one thing, constitutional and legal rules tend to reflect political facts, but sometimes only with a considerable time lag. Moreover, the doctrine has always been affected by a tinge of political unreality since it would empower Parliament to do many unlikely, immoral or undesirable things which no one wishes it to do. Does Parliament really need power to condemn all red-haired males to death or to make attendance at public worship illegal? Or to create criminal offences retrospectively?

Yet it would be wrong to ignore the strong political argument for retaining supremacy, particularly when the wishes of a newly elected House of Commons can be identified with the will of the majority. Legislative supremacy is well suited to a centralised, unitary system of government in which the needs of the executive are closely linked with the dominant political voice in Parliament: and in which the judiciary exercise an important but subordinate role. Even in such a system, there are many factors which limit the use to which the executive can put Parliament's legislative powers. Dicey suggested that political sovereignty, as opposed to legislative sovereignty, lay in the electorate and that ultimately the will of the electorate would prevail on all subjects to be determined by the British government.[163] Certainly, the electoral system serves as a limitation on the use of legislative powers, but the control which it provides is very generalised and sporadic in effect: and this effect depends in turn on the political parties, on the media, on economic and social interest groups and on other means by which public opinion is formed and expressed. Moreover, the voting system itself produces a House of Commons which does not accurately reproduce the distribution of views among the electorate[164] and provides only weak protection for unpopular minorities.

Parliament and the electorate

Under the British system, the electorate takes no direct part in legislative decision-making, save by electing the House of Commons. In some constitutions, for example the Republic of Ireland and the Commonwealth of Australia,[165] constitutional amendments may take effect only if they are approved by referendum. In other constitutions (for example, Denmark and Switzerland) legislative proposals may be subject to

---

[162] See A W Bradley, in Jowell and Oliver (eds), *The Changing Constitution*, 4th edn, ch 2.
[163] Dicey, *The Law of the Constitution*, p 73. And see p 54 above.
[164] Ch 9 F.
[165] See Cmnd 5925, 1975, annex B.

referendum. Until 1975, the United Kingdom found no place for the machinery of direct democracy, save in the case of the border poll in Northern Ireland.[166] Where major political issues are concerned, the outcome of a general election may indicate the degree of popular support for any changes. In 1910, two elections were held because of the legislative veto of the Lords and the necessity to establish popular support for the constitutional changes involved. In general, it is difficult to decide from the result of a general election the state of public opinion on particular issues. Since the party which wins a general election may be considered to have a mandate to implement its manifesto, a government can scarcely be criticised for seeking to carry out its election promises. Conversely, a government may be criticised for proposing major reforms of a constitutional nature which have never been before the electorate. The Conservative government elected in 1970 was criticised by those opposed to British membership of the European Communities for having completed the negotiations for membership, signed the Treaty of Accession and secured the passing of the European Communities Act 1972 without allowing the electorate the opportunity to vote on this issue. For these reasons, but mainly because of the internal division of opinion within the Labour party, a referendum on Britain's membership of the Communities was held in 1975. In 1979, devolution referendums were held in both Scotland and Wales.[167] In 1997, as we have seen, referendums were held in Scotland and Wales on whether the government should proceed with its proposals for a Scottish Parliament and a Welsh Assembly. It may be argued that the referendum should be used for deciding other constitutional issues and a referendum on whether the United Kingdom should join the European Monetary Union has been promised by the government. While advisory referendums do not directly affect the legislative authority of Parliament, if referendums were to be mandatory for certain reforms, this would affect the position of Parliament. It has been argued that referendums should be used 'as an extra check against government, an additional protection to that given by Parliament'.[168] This would give a form of entrenchment to certain matters against action by the elected majority in the Commons. Without all-party agreement on the matter, the selection of those aspects of the constitution to be protected would be contentious. There is a case to be made for requiring a referendum whenever it is proposed to transfer the powers of Parliament; as John Locke said, 'it being but a delegated power from the People, they who have it cannot pass it to others'.[169] Since 1975, the use of referendums has been on an ad hoc basis, but it is likely that the referendum will play a continuing role in respect of exceptional political issues. This in turn creates a need for regulating the use and conduct of referendums. The Political Parties, Elections and Referendums Act 2000 introduced rules on public funding for campaign groups, and broke new ground with rules on spending limits during a referendum campaign, and a supervisory role for the new Electoral Commission.[170]

Summary

The view taken in this chapter has been that Parliament's legislative authority includes power to make new arrangements under which future Parliaments would not enjoy legislative supremacy. The argument that the doctrine of legislative supremacy must be retained is strengthened if it can be shown that the political system provides

---

[166] Page 67 above.
[167] Ch 3 B.
[168] Bogdanor, *The People and the Party System*, p 69.
[169] *Second Treatise on Civil Government*, quoted in Bogdanor, p 77.
[170] See K D Ewing [2001] PL 542, 562–5; and ch 9 E.

adequate safeguards against legislation which would be contrary to fundamental constitutional principle or the individual's basic rights. It is, however, doubtful whether the present system, which relies so heavily on political controls, adequately protects individuals or minority groups who may be vulnerable to legislative oppression. Moreover, Parliament's importance within British government depends less on absolute legislative power than on its effectiveness as a political forum in expressing public opinion and in exercising control over government. In the case of the European Union, political necessity has brought about a situation, recognised by the judiciary, in which Community law prevails over inconsistent national legislation. A return of the United Kingdom to Diceyan orthodoxy would scarcely compensate for the disadvantages of an isolationist policy within Europe.

Chapter 5

THE RELATIONSHIP BETWEEN LEGISLATURE, EXECUTIVE AND JUDICIARY

Emphasis on the legislative supremacy of Parliament as the basic doctrine of constitutional law may cause principles of constitutionalism to be undervalued. The separation of powers is found, in stronger or weaker form, in many modern constitutions; it is opposed to the concentration of state power in a single person or group, since that is a clear threat to democratic government. The need for a separation of powers arises not only in political decision-making but also in the legal system, where an independent judiciary is essential if the rule of law is to have any substance.[1]

Distinguished observers of the system of British government have often minimised the significance of the separation of powers as a feature of that system. Thus Dicey referred in passing to the doctrine as being 'the offspring of a double misconception'[2] and Sir Ivor Jennings sought at considerable length to show that it was of little significance.[3] Today, with the growing recognition of the judicial role in public law, the legal significance of the separation of powers is more readily recognised. Lord Mustill has said:

> It is a feature of the peculiarly British conception of the separation of powers that Parliament, the executive and the courts have each their distinct and largely exclusive domain. Parliament has a legally unchallengeable right to make whatever laws it thinks right. The executive carries on the administration of the country in accordance with the powers conferred on it by law. The courts interpret the laws, and see that they are obeyed.[4]

This model for the exercise of legislative, executive and judicial powers is exemplified by the law of taxation: to authorise the levying of a new tax is a legislative function; to assess and collect the tax payable by individuals is an executive (or administrative) function; to settle disputes between the tax official and a taxpayer as to the tax due in a particular case is a judicial function, involving interpretation of the law and applying it to the facts. So too in criminal law: the creation of a new offence is a matter for legislation, enforcement of the law is an executive function, and the trial of alleged offenders is a judicial function. The same model is seen in the judicial review of executive decisions. In such cases, the court decides between the applicant's claim that the decision was not properly taken under powers granted by Parliament and the official's contention that it was.[5]

In this chapter, it is intended to examine two questions:

(*a*) to what extent are the three functions (legislative, executive and judicial) distinguishable today?

---

[1] Vile, *Constitutionalism and the Separation of Powers*; Allan, *Law, Liberty and Justice*, chs 1, 3, 8 and Allan, *Constitutional Justice*, ch 2. Also Mount, *The British Constitution Now*, pp 81–92; E Barendt [1995] PL 599; N W Barber [2001] CLJ 59.

[2] *Law of the Constitution*, p 338.

[3] *Law and the Constitution*, pp 18–28 and App 1.

[4] *R v Home Secretary, ex p Fire Brigades' Union* [1995] 2 AC 513, 567.

[5] Chs 30 and 31.

(*b*)   to what extent are these three functions exercisable separately by the institutions of Parliament, the executive and the courts?

The legislative function

The legislative function involves the enactment of general rules determining the structure and powers of public authorities and regulating the conduct of citizens and private organisations. In the United Kingdom, new law is enacted when, usually on the proposal of the government, a Bill has been approved by Commons and Lords and has received the royal assent. Under the Parliament Acts of 1911 and 1949, however, legislation may be enacted even though it has been rejected by the House of Lords.[6]

While legislative authority is vested in the Queen in Parliament, several qualifications need to be borne in mind:

(*a*)   By Act of Parliament, legislative powers may be conferred on executive bodies – for example on ministers, government departments and local authorities. While subordinate legislation of this kind is made under the authority of an Act, it is not directly made by Parliament.[7] Legislative powers, of varying width, are exercised by the Scottish Parliament and the Assemblies in Wales and Northern Ireland.[8]

(*b*)   In the European Communities Act 1972, Parliament recognised that the organs of the European Communities could legislate in respect of the United Kingdom. In Community matters, legislative powers for the United Kingdom are exercisable by the European Parliament, the Council and the Commission.[9]

(*c*)   While one result of the 17th-century constitutional conflict was to impose very severe limits on the authority of the Crown to make new law without the approval of Parliament, certain legislative powers of the Crown have survived.[10] It was the survival and exercise of such a power that lay behind a decision of the House of Lords in 1995 on separation of powers.[11]

(*d*)   While primary legislative authority is vested in Parliament, the two Houses have much work to do which does not involve legislating. The time devoted to the legislative programme seldom exceeds half the number of days in a session. The rest of Parliament's time is used in debating government policies and other national issues, and in scrutinising the work of government.[12]

(*e*)   Government Bills predominate in Parliament, with ministers being responsible for supervising their passage through each House and for implementing new Acts once they have received the royal assent. The executive therefore participates actively, and often decisively, in the process of legislation, especially when the government has a large majority of MPs in the Commons.

(*f*)   Once a new law has been enacted by Parliament, the authoritative interpretation of that law is a matter for the courts. The interpretation of statutes is in one sense a vital part of the law-making process, as it is only after such interpretation that it is known whether the intentions of those who framed the law have been carried into effect. In this task, the judges must not challenge the political authority of the legislature to

---

[6] Ch 10 B.
[7] Ch 28.
[8] See ch 3 B.
[9] Ch 8.
[10] Ch 12 D.
[11] *R v Home Secretary, ex p Fire Brigades' Union* [1995] 2 AC 513 (and see E Barendt [1995] PL 357). Cf *R v HM Treasury, ex p Smedley* [1985] QB 657, 666 (Donaldson MR).
[12] Ch 10 C and D.

decide what new laws should be made.[13] They must decide disputed questions by applying common law principles of interpretation as those principles have been modified by statute.[14]

The executive function

It is more difficult to give a simple account of the executive function than of the legislative function. The executive function broadly comprises the whole corpus of authority to govern, other than that which is involved in the legislative functions of Parliament and the judicial functions of the courts. The general direction of policy includes the initiation of legislation, the maintenance of order, the promotion of social and economic welfare, administration of public services and conduct of the external relations of the state. The executive function has therefore a residual character, its techniques ranging from the formation of broad policy to the detailed management of routine services. Historically, the executive was identified with the Sovereign, in whose name many acts are still performed by the Prime Minister and other ministers. Today, in a broad sense, the executive comprises all officials and public authorities by which functions of government are exercised, including the civil service and armed forces. Executive functions are also performed by the police, local authorities and many statutory bodies, as well as by the executives with devolved powers in Scotland, Wales and Northern Ireland. British membership of the European Union has meant that the Council and the Commission exercise executive functions in relation to the United Kingdom.[15]

The judicial function

The primary judicial function is to determine disputed questions of fact and law in accordance with the law laid down by Parliament and expounded by the courts. This function is exercised mainly in the civil and criminal courts by professional judges. Civil jurisdiction covers both private law issues (on such matters as contract and property) and also questions of public law. Lay magistrates exercise many powers of criminal justice in the lower courts and ordinary citizens contribute to justice by serving on juries at criminal trials. The civil and criminal courts do not have a monopoly of the judicial function. Many disputes which arise out of the conduct of government are entrusted to tribunals. Today these tribunals are a recognised part of the machinery of justice; they operate subject to the supervision of the superior civil courts.[16]

As well as their primary function of settling legal disputes, the courts exercise certain minor legislative functions (for example, making rules governing court procedure) and administrative functions (for example, administering the estates of deceased persons). In matters of Community law, judicial functions are exercised for the United Kingdom by the European Court of Justice and the Court of First Instance. Under the Human Rights Act 1998, British courts and tribunals must take account of decisions made by the European Court of Human Rights.

The doctrine of the separation of powers

Within a system of government based on law, there are legislative, executive and judicial functions to be performed; and the primary organs for discharging these functions

---

[13] *Stock* v *Frank Jones (Tipton) Ltd* [1978] 1 All ER 948; *Duport Steels Ltd* v *Sirs* [1980] 1 All ER 529.
[14] See ch 2 A and (for the Human Rights Act 1998, s 3) ch 19 C.
[15] Ch 8.
[16] Ch 29 A.

are respectively the legislature, the executive and the courts. A legal historian has remarked:

> This threefold division of labour, between a legislator, an administrative official, and an independent judge, is a necessary condition for the rule of law in modern society and therefore for democratic government itself.[17]

Admittedly, there is no clear-cut demarcation between some aspects of these functions, nor is there always a neat correspondence between the functions and the institutions of government. As a matter of history, Parliament, the courts and central government in Britain owe their origin to the monarchy; before these institutions developed as distinct entities, the King governed through his Council, with a mixture of legislative, executive and judicial work. Today these tasks are all performed in the name of the Crown, but in a mature democracy it is important that judges are independent both of Parliament and government, and that Parliament is not merely a rubber stamp for the Cabinet. Indeed, it may be argued that essential values of law, liberty and democracy are best protected if the three primary functions of a law-based government are discharged by distinct institutions. Robson described the separation of powers as 'that antique and rickety chariot . . . , so long the favourite vehicle of writers on political science and constitutional law for the conveyance of fallacious ideas'.[18] But this does not do justice to the contribution which the doctrine has made to the maintenance of liberty and the continuing need by constitutional means to restrain abuse of governmental power.[19] The rest of this chapter will examine the doctrine and how far it applies in Britain today.

Locke and Montesquieu

In 1690, the Englishman John Locke wrote in his *Second Treatise of Civil Government*:

> It may be too great a temptation to humane frailty, apt to grasp at power, for the same persons who have the power of making laws, to have also in their hands the power to execute them, whereby they may exempt themselves from obedience to the laws they make, and suit the law, both in its making and execution, to their own private advantage.[20]

The doctrine of the separation of powers was developed further by the French jurist, Montesquieu, who based his exposition on the British constitution of the early 18th century as he understood it. His division of power did not closely correspond except in name with the classification which has become traditional; for, although he followed the usual meaning of legislative and judicial powers, by executive power he meant only 'the power of executing matters falling within the law of nations', i.e. making war and peace, sending and receiving ambassadors, establishing order, and preventing invasion.[21] He stated the essence of the doctrine thus:

> When the legislative and executive powers are united in the same person, or in the same body of magistrates, there can be no liberty . . . Again, there is no liberty, if the judicial power be not separated from the legislative and executive. Were it joined with the legislative, the life and liberty of the subject would be exposed to arbitrary control; for the judge would then be

---

[17] Henderson, *Foundations of English Administrative Law*, p 5.
[18] Robson, *Justice and Administrative Law*, p 14.
[19] See Vile, *Constitutionalism and the Separation of Powers*, for reassessment of the link between legal values and separation of powers; also Marshall, *Constitutional Theory*, ch 5, and Munro, *Studies in Constitutional Law*, ch 9.
[20] Ch XII, para 143, quoted in Vile, p 62.
[21] But cf Vile, p 87.

the legislator. Were it joined to the executive however, the judge might behave with violence and oppression. There would be an end to everything, were the same man, or the same body, whether of the nobles or of the people, to exercise those three powers, that of enacting laws, that of executing the public resolutions, and of trying the causes of individuals.[22]

This statement emphasises that the judicial function should be exercised by a body separate from legislature and executive. Montesquieu did not mean that legislature and executive ought to have no influence or control over the acts of each other, but only that neither should exercise the whole power of the other.[23]

In observing the British constitution in the 18th century, Montesquieu saw that Parliament had achieved legislative dominance over the King by means of the Bill of Rights and that the independence of the judiciary had been declared, but that the King still exercised executive power. By 1800, however, there had been established in Britain the Cabinet system, under which the King governed only through ministers who were members of Parliament and responsible to it. This system, with its emphatic link between Parliament and the executive, in a major respect ran contrary to Montesquieu's doctrine. It is in the United States' constitution that his influence can best be seen.

Separation of powers in the US constitution

In the US constitution of 1787 the separation of powers formed one pillar of the new edifice.[24] The framers of the constitution intended that a balance of powers should be attained by vesting each primary function in a distinct organ. Possibly they were imitating the British constitution, but by that time in Britain executive power was passing from the Crown to the Cabinet. The US constitution vests legislative powers in Congress, consisting of a Senate and a House of Representatives (art 1), executive power in the President (art 2) and judicial power in the Supreme Court and such other federal courts as might be established by Congress (art 3). The President holds office for a fixed term of four years and is separately elected: he may therefore be of a different party from that which has a majority in either or both Houses of Congress. His powers, like those of Congress, are declared by the constitution. While the heads of the chief departments of state are known as the Cabinet, they are individually responsible to the President and not to Congress.

Neither the President nor members of his Cabinet sit or vote in Congress; they have no direct power of initiating Bills or securing their passage through Congress. The President may recommend legislation in his messages to Congress, but he cannot compel it to carry out his recommendations. While he has a power to veto legislation passed by Congress, this veto may be overridden by a two-thirds vote in each House of Congress. Treaties may be negotiated by the President, but must be approved by a two-thirds majority of the Senate. The President may nominate to key offices, including the justices of the Supreme Court, but the Senate must confirm these appointments and may refuse to do so. The President himself is not directly responsible to Congress for his conduct of affairs: in normal circumstances he is irremovable, but the constitution authorises the President to be removed from office by the process of impeachment at the hands of the Senate, 'for treason, bribery, or other high crimes and misdemeanours' (art 2(4)). The prospect of impeachment was the immediate cause of President Nixon's resignation in 1974 following his complicity in the Watergate affair; 25 years later, President Clinton successfully defended the impeachment proceedings that were brought

---

[22] *De l'Esprit des Lois*, Book XI, ch 6, quoted in Vile, p 90.
[23] Jennings, *The Law and the Constitution*, app 1.
[24] For a classic defence of the US approach to separation, see *The Federalist*, XLVII (Madison).

against him.[25] Once appointed, the judges of the Supreme Court are independent both of Congress and the President, although they too may be removed by impeachment. Early in its history, the Supreme Court assumed the power, expressed in the historic judgment of Chief Justice Marshall in *Marbury* v *Madison*,[26] to declare acts of the legislature and the President to be unconstitutional should they conflict with the constitution.

Even in the US constitution, there is not a complete separation of powers between the executive, legislative and judicial functions, if by this is meant that each power can be exercised in isolation from the others. Having established the threefold allocation of functions as a basis, the constitution constructed an elaborate system of checks and balances to enable control and influence to be exercised by each branch upon the others. The Watergate affair showed not only the strong position of a President elected into office by popular vote: it also showed how a combination of powers exercised by Congress and the Supreme Court, as well as such forces as public opinion and the press, could combine to remove even the President from office.[27]

Separation of powers in other constitutions

Many other constitutions have been influenced by the separation of powers. Written constitutions often contain distinct chapters dealing with legislative, judicial and executive powers, but display no uniformity in the extent to which these functions are separate. In France, the doctrine is of great importance but it has manifested itself very differently from the American version. Thus it is considered to flow from the separation of powers that the ordinary courts should have no jurisdiction to review the legality of acts of the legislature or executive. In place of the courts the Conseil d'Etat, structurally part of the executive, has developed a jurisdiction over administrative agencies and officials which is exercised independently of the political arm of the executive; a more recent creation, the Conseil Constitutionnel, may review the constitutionality of new laws.[28]

The constitutions of states in the Commonwealth have been influenced by the separation of powers in a variety of ways. Under the Australian constitution, for example, delegation of legislative powers to executive agencies has been accepted more readily than the delegation to them of judicial powers.[29] In Canada, the Constitution Act 1867 did not provide for a general separation of powers; legislative powers may be delegated by both the federal Parliament and the provincial legislatures, but the latter are subject to restrictions in seeking to confer judicial powers on tribunals that ought to be vested in the courts.[30] The former constitution of Sri Lanka was held to be based on an implied separation of powers; legislation to provide special machinery for convicting and punishing the leaders of an unsuccessful coup infringed the fundamental principle that judicial power was vested only in the courts.[31] Where the constitution is based on an express or implied separation of powers, the courts may have to decide whether a particular statutory power should be classified as legislative, executive or judicial.[32] British courts do not have this task but have sometimes classified

---

[25] See Gerhardt, *The Federal Impeachment Process*.
[26] 1 Cranch 137 (1803).
[27] See *US* v *Nixon* 418 US 683 (1974). For separation of powers issues under the US constitution, see Tribe, *Constitutional Choices*, part II. For re-assessment of US-style separation of powers as a constitutional model, see B Ackerman (2000) 113 Harv LR 634.
[28] See Brown and Bell, *French Administrative Law*, and Bell, *French Constitutional Law*.
[29] Howard, *Australian Federal Constitutional Law*, ch 4 B.
[30] See Hogg, *Constitutional Law of Canada*, section 7.3(a).
[31] *Liyanage* v *R* [1967] 1 AC 259.
[32] *Hinds* v *R* [1977] AC 195 (appeal from Jamaica).

powers for such purposes as applying the law of contempt of court and the rules of natural justice.[33]

Meaning of separation of powers

As the contrast between the United States and France shows, the doctrine of separation of powers has a variety of meanings. The concept of 'separation' may mean at least three different things:

(*a*)   that the same persons should not form part of more than one of the three organs of government, for example, that ministers should not sit in Parliament;

(*b*)   that one organ of government should not control or interfere with the work of another, for example, that the executive should not interfere in judicial decisions;

(*c*)   that one organ of government should not exercise the functions of another, for example, that ministers should not have legislative powers.

In considering these aspects of separation, it needs to be remembered that complete separation of powers is possible neither in theory nor in practice.

Legislature and executive   Writing in 1867, Bagehot described the 'efficient secret' of the constitution as 'the close union, the nearly complete fusion, of the legislative and executive powers'.[34] Bagehot's critics have rejected the concept of fusion, arguing that the close relationship between executive and legislature does not negate the constitutional distinction between the two. As Amery wrote:

> Government and Parliament, however closely intertwined and harmonized, are still separate and independent entities, fulfilling the two distinct functions of leadership, direction and command on the one hand, and of critical discussion and examination on the other. They start from separate historical origins, and each is perpetuated in accordance with its own methods and has its own continuity.[35]

The three meanings of separation mentioned earlier will be applied to the relationship between executive and legislature:

(*a*)   Do the same persons or bodies form part of both the legislature and executive? Leaving aside the formal position of the Sovereign, there is a strong convention that ministers are members of one or other House of Parliament. Their presence in Parliament goes along with their responsibility to Parliament for their acts as ministers. However, there is a statutory limit on the number of ministers who may be members of the Commons.[36] Moreover, except for these ministers, most persons who hold positions within the executive are disqualified from the Commons, namely the civil service, the armed forces, the police and the holders of many public offices; police officers and some civil servants are also restricted from taking part in political activities. Only ministers exercise a dual role as key figures in both Parliament and the executive.

(*b*)   Does the legislature control the executive or the executive the legislature? This question goes to the heart of parliamentary government in Britain and no brief answer can be adequate. In one sense, the Commons ultimately controls the executive since the Commons can oust a government which has lost the ability to command a majority

---

[33] Chs 18 D and 27.
[34] Bagehot, *The English Constitution*, p 65.
[35] Amery, *Thoughts on the Constitution*, p 28: also Vile, *Constitutionalism and the Separation of Powers*, pp 224–30, and Mount, *The British Constitution Now*, pp 39–47.
[36] Ch 9 G.

on an issue of confidence. The Commons did this to Mr Callaghan's minority government in March 1979. But so long as the Cabinet retains the confidence of the Commons, it exercises a decisive voice in the work of the House. In 1978 the Select Committee on Procedure concluded that

> the balance of advantage between Parliament and Government in the day to day working of the Constitution is now weighted in favour of the Government to a degree which arouses widespread anxiety and is inimical to the proper working of our parliamentary democracy.[37]

The period beginning with the Conservative government of 1970–74 has seen a developing willingness by MPs to use their voting power in the Commons to indicate when necessary their disapproval of particular government measures. This trend was at its height during the periods of minority government in 1974 and in 1976–79.[38] After 1979, during Conservative rule until 1997, and thereafter under Labour, the government could always rely on a clear majority in the Commons. The effects of a continuing majority are not confined to legislation but extend to the role of Parliament in calling government to account for its policies and decisions. The existence of an assured majority in the Commons is not incompatible with there being a body of MPs who are vigilant in scrutinising the work of the executive, but it does not ensure that fully accountable government is achieved.[39]

(c)   Do the legislature and the executive exercise each other's functions? The most substantial area in which the executive exercises legislative functions is in respect of delegated legislation. In Britain there is no formal limit on the power of Parliament to delegate legislative powers to the government. While democratic reasoning means that the most important legal rules should be contained in Acts of Parliament, it is convenient to the executive that ministers and departments can implement primary legislation by making regulations. But it is essential that parliamentary procedures should exist for scrutinising the use made of delegated power.[40]

Executive and judiciary   We now examine the relationship between the judiciary and the other two organs of government. Again the three questions may be asked:

(a)   Do the same persons form part of the judiciary and the executive? The courts are the Queen's courts, but judicial functions are exercised by the judges. The Judicial Committee of the Privy Council is in form an executive organ, but in fact it is an independent court of law.[41] The Lord Chancellor, who is a member of the Cabinet, is also head of the judiciary and is entitled to preside over the Lords, which is the final court of appeal from the courts of the United Kingdom. In fact, he sits infrequently to hear appeals today and could not properly decide appeals in which a government department is a party or has an interest in the outcome.[42]

The law officers of the Crown (in particular the Attorney-General in England and the Lord Advocate in Scotland) have duties of enforcing the criminal law which are sometimes described as 'quasi-judicial'; it must be emphasised that the law officers are members of the executive and are not judges.[43]

---

[37] HC 588–1 (1977–78), p viii.
[38] See works by Norton: *Dissension in the House of Commons, 1945–74*; (same title) *1974–79*; *The Commons in Perspective*; and [1978] PL 360.
[39] Ch 7.
[40] Ch 28.
[41] Ch 18 E.
[42] Under the Human Rights Act 1998 and art 6(1) ECHR, it is doubtful whether a court including the Lord Chancellor would be an 'independent' tribunal. See ch 19 C and cf *Starrs v Ruxton* (2000) JC 208.
[43] Ch 18 E.

(*b*)   Does the executive control the judiciary or the judiciary control the executive? Although judges are appointed by the executive, judicial independence of the executive is secured by law, by constitutional custom, and by professional and public opinion.[44] Since the Act of Settlement 1700, judges of the superior English courts have held office during good behaviour and not at pleasure of the executive. The lay magistracy in England and Wales apart, inferior judges have statutory protection against arbitrary dismissal by the executive. Under the Tribunals and Inquiries Act 1992, members of most tribunals are protected against being removed by the appointing government department.[45]

One essential function of the judiciary is to protect the citizen against unlawful acts of government agencies and officials.[46] In applying judicial review in administrative law, the judges must have regard to 'the peculiarly British conception of the separation of powers'.[47] Within the EC, the Court of Justice and the Court of First Instance must ensure that the acts of Community organs comply with the treaties on which the Community system is based.

(*c*)   Do the executive and judiciary exercise each other's functions? The value of an independent judiciary would be reduced if essential judicial functions, for example the conduct of civil and criminal trials, were removed from the courts and entrusted to administrative authorities. But many disputes which arise out of public services today are decided not by litigation in the ordinary courts, but are entrusted to tribunals for decision. Tribunals such as employment and social security tribunals form part of the machinery of justice and carry out their work independently of the departments concerned.[48] Many matters are entrusted not to tribunals but to government departments and ministers for decision. Procedures such as the public inquiry have been established to maintain standards of fairness and openness before a decision is made by the department concerned. It is because a decision is required in which full account may be taken of departmental policy, rather than a decision based on a judicial application of legal rules, that these matters remain subject to departmental or ministerial decision.[49]

It is not possible to draw a sharp distinction between decisions which should be entrusted to courts and tribunals on the one hand, and decisions which should be entrusted to administrative authorities on the other. When a new statutory scheme is introduced, there is often a wide choice to be made between the different procedures available for deciding disputes likely to arise under the scheme. The separation of powers affords little direct guidance as to how particular categories of dispute should be settled, except to indicate that decisions which are to be made independently of political influence should be entrusted to courts or tribunals, and decisions for which ministers are to be responsible to Parliament should be entrusted to government departments.

In *Gouriet* v *Union of Post Office Workers*, the House of Lords reasserted the distinction between executive responsibility for enforcing the criminal law and the judicial function, and denied that the civil courts had any executive authority in criminal law.[50] In *M* v *Home Office*, the House held that ministers and civil servants were subject to the contempt jurisdiction of the courts, and that the Home Secretary was in contempt when he disobeyed a judge's order to return to London a Zairean

---

[44] Ch 18 C.
[45] Ch 29 A.
[46] Chs 30–2.
[47] *R* v *Home Secretary, ex p Fire Brigades Union* [1995] 2 AC 513, 567 (Lord Mustill).
[48] Ch 29 A.
[49] Ch 29 B. And see *R (Alconbury Developments Ltd)* v *Environment and Transport Secretary* [2001] 2 All ER 929 (HL).
[50] [1978] AC 435; ch 31.

teacher who had sought asylum in England.[51] A perceptive summary of the position was given by Nolan LJ:

> The proper constitutional relationship of the executive with the courts is that the courts will respect all acts of the executive within its lawful province, and that the executive will respect all decisions of the courts as to what its lawful province is.[52]

This is a subtle statement of a sensitive relationship. But it does not prevent there being continuing tension, in relation to serious offenders serving life imprisonment, between the Home Secretary's duty to ensure public confidence in the penal system and the role of the judges in sentencing.[53]

Judiciary and legislature   Finally, the relationship between the judiciary and the legislature:

(*a*)   Do the same persons exercise legislative and judicial functions? All full-time judicial appointments disqualify for membership of the Commons, but potential problems arise in the House of Lords, where the Lord Chancellor presides over the House as a legislature and, when circumstances permit, may preside over the Appellate Committee in its judicial work. The Lords of Appeal in Ordinary who sit as judges in the Appellate Committee take some part in the legislative business of the House, but they do so as cross-benchers. Their place in the upper house of the legislature is an open breach of the separation of powers and would have to be terminated if a Supreme Court were created for the United Kingdom. Lay peers by long-established convention do not take part in the hearing of appeals.[54]

(*b*)   Is there any control by the legislature over the judiciary or by the judiciary over the legislature? By statute judges of the superior courts may be removed by the Crown on an address from both Houses, but only once since the Act of Settlement has Parliament exercised the power of removal.[55] The rules of debate in the Commons protect judges from certain forms of criticism.

While the courts may examine acts of the executive to ensure that they conform with the law, the doctrine of legislative supremacy denies the courts the power to review the validity of legislation. The judges are under a duty to apply and interpret the laws enacted by Parliament. The effect of their decisions may be altered by Parliament both prospectively and also, if necessary, retrospectively. In one sense, therefore, the courts are constitutionally subordinate to Parliament, but the courts are bound only by Acts of Parliament and not by resolutions of each House, which may have no legal force.[56] The European Communities Act 1972 provides an outstanding example of the control which the legislature may exercise over the judiciary: by s 3, the courts are required to follow the case law of the European Court of Justice in dealing with matters of Community law and to take full account of the reception of Community law into the United Kingdom. This duty may require the courts to disapply an Act of Parliament which clashes with rights in Community law.[57] Under the Human Rights Act 1998,

---

[51] [1994] 1 AC 377; see G Marshall [1992] PL 7, M Gould [1993] PL 568.
[52] *M v Home Office* [1992] QB 270, 314.
[53] See e.g. *R v Home Secretary, ex p Pierson* [1998] AC 539 and *R v Home Secretary, ex p Hindley* [2001] 1 AC 410.
[54] Ch 18 A.
[55] Ch 18 C.
[56] E.g. *Bowles v Bank of England* [1913] 1 Ch 57; ch 4 B.
[57] See the *Factortame* litigation, p 68 above and *R v Employment Secretary, ex p EOC* [1995] 1 AC 1.

the superior courts may declare an Act of Parliament to be inconsistent with European Convention rights but may not disapply it.[58]

(*c*)   Do the legislature and judiciary exercise each other's functions? The judicial functions of the House of Lords have already been discussed. Each House of Parliament has power to enforce its own privileges and to punish those who offend against them. This power might in some circumstances lead to a direct conflict with the courts.[59]

Because of the doctrine of precedent, the judicial function of declaring and applying the law has a quasi-legislative effect. The ability of the judges to create law by their decisions is narrower than the ability of Parliament to legislate, since Parliament may at will change established rules of law, whether contained in statutes or in decisions of the courts. However, there is much scope for judicial law making in relation to individual liberties and the principles of public law. Decisions in these areas may be welcomed as bringing old law up to date (for example, by reversing the rule that a married man cannot, in law, rape his wife or by broadening the meaning of 'family' to include a long-standing homosexual relationship)[60] or may be criticised for failing to do so.[61] The rules of precedent themselves are judge made, except where, as in the European Communities Act 1972 and the Human Rights Act 1998, statute has intervened. In 1966 the House of Lords announced that it would in future be prepared to depart from a former decision by the House when it appeared right to do so.[62] An important instance of this occurred when in *Conway* v *Rimmer*[63] the House held that the courts might overrule a minister's claim on grounds of public interest immunity to withhold evidence in civil litigation.

As *Conway* v *Rimmer* illustrates, judicial decision is important as a source of law on matters where the government is unwilling to ask Parliament to legislate. The executive is slow to propose new measures exposing itself to more effective judicial control. Some judicial decisions directly affect the formal relationship between the courts and Parliament.[64]

Summary

In the absence of a written constitution, there is no formal separation of powers in the United Kingdom. No Act of Parliament may be held unconstitutional on the ground that it seeks to confer powers in breach of the doctrine. The functions of legislature and executive are closely interrelated and ministers are members of both. Yet '[it] is a feature of the peculiarly British conception of the separation of powers that Parliament, the executive and the courts each have their distinct and largely exclusive domain'.[65] The formal process of legislation is different from the day-to-day conduct of government, just as the legal effect of an Act of Parliament differs from that of an executive

---

[58] Ch 19 C.
[59] Ch 11 A.
[60] Respectively, *R* v *R (Rape: marital exemption)* [1992] 1 AC 599; *Fitzpatrick* v *Sterling Housing Association Ltd* [2001] 1 AC 27.
[61] *R* v *Lemon* [1979] AC 617 (offence of blasphemy), ch 23 D; *R* v *Brown* [1994] AC 212 (criminal nature of consensual sado-masochistic acts).
[62] [1966] 3 All ER 77. Between 1898 and 1966, a contrary rule prevailed: *London Street Tramways Co* v *LCC* [1898] AC 375.
[63] *Conway* v *Rimmer* [1968] AC 910; ch 32 C.
[64] E.g. *R* v *Home Secretary, ex p Fire Brigades' Union* [1995] 2 AC 513; and *Pepper* v *Hart* [1993] AC 593.
[65] *R* v *Home Secretary, ex p Fire Brigades' Union* [1995] 2 AC at 567 (Lord Mustill). The case concerned the 'separation' of legislative functions between Parliament and the Home Secretary. See E Barendt [1995] PL 357.

decision.[66] Practical necessity demands a large measure of delegation by Parliament to the executive of power to legislate. The independence of the judiciary is especially necessary given the role of the courts in judicial review of executive decisions.

The effect of British membership of the European Union is that the organs of the Community now exercise legislative, executive and judicial powers in respect of the United Kingdom. While judicial powers are exercised by the European Court of Justice, whose independence is guaranteed, legislative authority is vested in the Council, representing the governments of the member states. In general this authority is exercised only after extensive preparatory work by the Commission and after consultation or by co-decision with the European Parliament.[67] Experience at a national level suggests that the excessive concentration of power in any single organ of government is a greater danger to liberty than departures from a formal separation of powers. The Human Rights Act 1998 brought to UK courts a need to consider aspects of the separation of powers (such as the independence of courts and tribunals) that are central to rights protected by the European Convention on Human Rights, such as the right to a fair trial.[68]

While the classification of the powers of government into legislative, executive and judicial powers involves certain conceptual difficulties, within a system of government based on law it remains important to distinguish in constitutional structure between the primary functions of law-making, law-executing and law-adjudicating. If these distinctions are abandoned, the concept of law itself can scarcely survive.

---

[66] It was the government's failure to observe this distinction which gave rise to the *Fire Brigades' Union* case.

[67] Ch 8 A.

[68] And see Allan, *Constitutional Justice*, ch 2.

Chapter 6

THE RULE OF LAW

During 1971, at what we now know was an early stage of open strife between the communities in Northern Ireland, the IRA increased the ferocity of its campaign of violence in Northern Ireland, shooting soldiers and police and blowing up buildings. Early in August, the government of Northern Ireland, after consulting with the UK government, decided to exercise the power of internment available to it under the Civil Authorities (Special Powers) Act (Northern Ireland) 1922.[1] This power could be used against persons suspected of having acted or being about to act in a manner prejudicial to the preservation of peace or the maintenance of order. On 9 August, 342 men were arrested. By November 1971, when the total arrested had risen to 980, 299 of those arrested were being interned indefinitely; the remainder were held under temporary detention orders or had already been released.

The security forces saw in internment an opportunity of obtaining fresh intelligence about the IRA. In August 1971, 12 detainees and in October two more were interrogated in depth. The procedures of interrogation included keeping the detainees' heads covered with black hoods; subjecting them to continuous and monotonous noise; depriving them of sleep; depriving them of food and water, except for one slice of bread and one pint of water at six-hourly intervals; making them stand facing a wall with legs apart and hands raised. It was later held by a committee of inquiry that these procedures constituted physical ill-treatment.[2]

In November 1971, after these facts had been established, three Privy Councillors were asked to consider whether the procedures 'currently authorised' for interrogating persons suspected of terrorism needed to be changed. They produced two reports.[3] Two members, a former Lord Chief Justice and a former Conservative Cabinet minister, recommended that the procedures could continue to be used subject to certain safeguards, including the express authority of a UK minister for their use, the presence of a doctor with psychiatric training at the interrogation centre, and a complaints procedure. This report did not express any view on the legality of the interrogation procedures, but stated that valuable information about the IRA had been discovered through the interrogation.

The minority report, by Lord Gardiner, a former Labour Lord Chancellor, held that the interrogation procedures had never been authorised:

> If any document or minister had purported to authorise them, it would have been invalid because the procedures were and are illegal by the domestic law and may also have been illegal by international law.

Should legislation be introduced enabling a minister in time of emergency to fix in secret the limits of permissible ill-treatment to be used in interrogating suspects? Lord

---

[1] Such power did not survive into the Terrorism Act 2000; see ch 26 E. On the internments in 1971–76, see R J Spjut (1986) 49 MLR 712.
[2] Cmnd 4823, 1971 (Compton Report).
[3] Cmnd 4901, 1972 (Parker Report).

Gardiner viewed with abhorrence any proposal that a minister should be empowered to make secret law. Neither could he agree that a minister should fix secret limits without the authority of Parliament, 'that is to say illegally', and then if found out ask Parliament for an Act of Indemnity: that, he said, would be a flagrant breach of the whole basis of the rule of law and of the principles of democratic government.

The government accepted Lord Gardiner's report and abandoned the interrogation procedures. When those who had been interrogated sued the government for damages for their unlawful treatment, liability was not contested and substantial awards of damages were made. The European Commission on Human Rights held that the interrogation procedures amounted to inhuman and degrading treatment and also torture, contrary to art 3 of the European Convention on Human Rights. When the Irish government referred the case to the European Court of Human Rights, the court held that the procedures were inhuman and degrading treatment but did not amount to torture.[4]

No clearer illustration could be given of the need to adhere to the rule of law if citizens are to be protected against arbitrary and harsh acts of government. However lawless may have been the acts of the IRA, and however seriously those acts infringed life and liberty, government must not retaliate with measures which are not only unlawful but are of such a nature that it would be impossible on moral and political grounds to make them lawful. Controversial as the power of internment was, it was authorised by the legislature and its use was a matter of public knowledge and admitted political responsibility. But in law the power to intern does not include power to interrogate or to administer physical ill-treatment or torture.[5]

By similar reasoning, while use of reasonable force is permitted in self-defence or in the prevention of crime or the arrest of offenders, and in some circumstances the use of firearms may be justified,[6] the adoption of a 'shoot to kill' policy by the police or armed forces would be seriously objectionable. This was alleged to have occurred in 1988 when three IRA members were shot dead by British forces in Gibraltar while organising a terrorist attack. The European Court of Human Rights held that force resulting in the taking of life could be used only in 'absolute necessity' for purposes stated in the European Convention on Human Rights (art 2). Claims that the three deaths were premeditated were not upheld; but the Court held (by 10–9) that, on what was known of the arrest operation, the killings were not justified by 'absolute necessity'.[7] The British government was angered by this decision, but reluctantly complied with the Court's order to reimburse the dead terrorists' families for their legal costs.

These instances illustrate the complexity of the values associated with the 'rule of law' and the scope for disagreement about what they may require in concrete situations.

A. Historical development

For many centuries it has been recognised that the possession by the state of coercive powers that may be used to oppress individuals presents a fundamental problem both for legal and political theory.[8] Since the days of the Greek philosophers there has been

---

[4] *Ireland v UK* (1978) 2 EHRR 25; and see ch 19 B.
[5] For the report of the Bennett committee of inquiry into police interrogation procedures in Northern Ireland in 1975–78, see Cmnd 7497, 1979.
[6] See ch 26 A, B.
[7] *McCann v UK* (1995) 21 EHRR 97. And see Windlesham and Rampton, *Report on 'Death on the Rock'*.
[8] See d'Entrèves, *The Notion of the State*. Also Heuston, *Essays in Constitutional Law*, ch 2.

recourse to the notion of law as a primary means of subjecting governmental power to control. Aristotle argued that government by laws was superior to government by men.[9]

The legal basis of the state was developed further by Roman lawyers. In the middle ages, the theory was held that there was a universal law which ruled the world. Gierke wrote: 'Medieval doctrine, while it was truly medieval, never surrendered the thought that law is by its origin of equal rank with the state and does not depend on the state for its existence.'[10] Bracton, writing in the 13th century, maintained that rulers were subject to law: 'The King shall not be subject to men, but to God and the law: since law makes the King.'[11] Justice according to law was due both to ruler and subject. Magna Carta and its later confirmations expressed this principle in seeking to remedy the grievances of certain classes in the community. When renaissance and reformation in the 16th century weakened the idea of a universal natural law, emphasis shifted to the national legal system as an aspect of the sovereignty of the state.[12] In Britain, the 17th-century contest between Crown and Parliament led to a rejection of the Divine Right of Kings and to an alliance between common lawyers and Parliament. The abolition in 1640 of the Court of Star Chamber ensured that the common law should apply to public as well as private acts, except as the common law was modified by Parliament.

The Bill of Rights in 1689 finally affirmed that the monarchy was subject to the law. Not only was the Crown thereby forced to govern through Parliament, but also the right of individuals to be free of unlawful interference in their private affairs was established.

> In *Entick* v *Carrington*, two King's Messengers were sued for having unlawfully broken and entered the plaintiff's house and seized his papers: the defendants relied on a warrant issued by the Secretary of State ordering them to search for Entick and bring him with his books and papers before the Secretary of State for examination. The Secretary of State claimed that the power to issue such warrants was essential to government, 'the only means of quieting clamours and sedition'. The court held that, in the absence of a statute or a judicial precedent upholding the legality of such a warrant, the practice was illegal. Lord Camden said: 'what would the Parliament say if the judges should take upon themselves to mould an unlawful power into a convenient authority, by new restrictions? That would be, not judgement, but legislation . . . And with respect to the argument of State necessity, or a distinction that has been aimed at between State offences and others, the common law does not understand that kind of reasoning, nor do our books take notice of any such distinction.'[13]

Such decisions stressed the value of personal liberty and the necessity of protecting private property against official interference. At the same time, the remedy of habeas corpus was being developed. Formal adherence to the law was one of the public values of 18th-century Britain, although not all the people gained equally from it.[14] Economic and social developments since 1765 have qualified the forthright declaration of Lord Camden that in the absence of precedent no common law powers of search and seizure will be recognised,[15] but *Entick* v *Carrington* still exercises influence on judicial attitudes to the claims of government.

---

[9] d'Entrèves, p 71.
[10] Quoted in d'Entrèves, p 83.
[11] d'Entrèves, p 86; Maitland, *Constitutional History*, pp 100–4; McIlwain, *Constitutionalism Ancient and Modern*, ch 4.
[12] For the rule of law in 16th-century England, see Elton, *Studies in Tudor and Stuart Politics and Government*, vol 1, p 260.
[13] (1765) 19 St Tr 1030, 1067, 1073.
[14] Thompson, *Whigs and Hunters: the Origin of the Black Act*, pp 258–69.
[15] Ch 21 D. And see *Malone* v *Metropolitan Police Commissioner* [1979] Ch 344.

Dicey's exposition of the rule of law

One reason for this is to be found in the work of A V Dicey, whose lectures at Oxford were first published in 1885 under the title, *Introduction to the Study of the Law of the Constitution*.[16] Dicey's aim was to introduce students to 'two or three guiding principles' of the constitution, foremost among these being the rule of law. The spirit of *Entick* v *Carrington* seems to run through Dicey's arguments, but he expressed the general doctrine of the rule of law in the form of several detailed statements describing the English constitution, some of them derived from authors who immediately preceded him.[17] Dicey gave to the rule of law three meanings:

> It means, in the first place, the absolute supremacy or predominance of regular law as opposed to the influence of arbitrary power, and excludes the existence of arbitrariness, of prerogative, or even of wide discretionary authority on the part of the government . . . ; a man may with us be punished for a breach of law, but he can be punished for nothing else.

Thus none could be made to suffer penalties except for a distinct breach of law established before the ordinary courts. In this sense Dicey contrasted the rule of law with systems of government based on the exercise by those in authority of wide or arbitrary powers of constraint, such as a power of detention without trial.

Secondly, the rule of law meant:

> equality before the law, or the equal subjection of all classes to the ordinary law of the land administered by the ordinary law courts.

In Dicey's view, this implied that no one was above the law; that officials like private citizens were under a duty to obey the same law; and that there were no administrative courts to decide claims by the citizens against the state or its officials.

Thirdly, the rule of law meant:

> that with us the law of the constitution, the rules which in foreign countries naturally form part of a constitutional code, are not the source but the consequence of the rights of individuals, as defined and enforced by the courts; that, in short, the principles of private law have with us been by the action of the courts and Parliament so extended as to determine the position of the Crown and of its servants; thus the constitution is the result of the ordinary law of the land.[18]

Therefore the rights of the individual were secured not by guarantees set down in a formal document but by the ordinary remedies of private law available against those who unlawfully interfered with his or her liberty, whether they were private citizens or officials.

Assessment of Dicey's views[19]

These three meanings of the rule of law raise considerable problems. In the first, for example, what is meant by 'regular law'? Does this include, for example, social security law, anti-discrimination law or the Terrorism Act 2000? Does 'arbitrary power' refer to powers of government that are so wide they could be used for a wide

---

[16] Dicey's text is reprinted in the 10th edn, with an introduction by E C S Wade. See also Cosgrove, *The Rule of Law: Albert Venn Dicey, Victorian Jurist*, and the symposium of articles at [1985] PL 587.

[17] H W Arndt (1957) 31 ALJ 117.

[18] Dicey, pp 202–3.

[19] See Jennings, *The Law and the Constitution*, ch 2 and app 2; F H Lawson (1959) 7 Political Studies 109, 207; H W Arthurs (1979) Osgoode Hall LJ 1; Craig, *Public Law and Democracy*, ch 2; Loughlin, *Public Law and Political Theory*, ch 7. For endorsement of Dicey's approach, see Allan, *Law Liberty and Justice*, ch 2, and (the same) *Constitutional Justice*, ch 1.

variety of different purposes; powers that are capable of abuse if not subjected to proper control; or powers that directly infringe individual liberty (for example, power to detain a citizen without trial)?[20] If 'arbitrary power' and 'wide discretionary authority' alike are unacceptable, how are the limits of acceptable discretionary authority to be settled? If it is contrary to the rule of law that discretionary authority should be given to government departments or public officers, then the rule of law applies to no modern constitution. Today the state regulates national life in multifarious ways. Discretionary authority in most spheres of government is inevitable. While there are still certain powers which we are unwilling to trust to the executive (for example, the power to detain individuals without trial) except when national emergencies dictate otherwise,[21] attention has to be concentrated not so much on attacking the existence of discretionary powers as on establishing a system of legal and political safeguards by which the exercise of such powers may be controlled.[22] Doubtless Dicey would have regarded as arbitrary many of the powers of government on which social welfare and economic organisation now depend.

Dicey's second meaning stresses the equal subjection of all persons to the ordinary law. The 14th Amendment to the United States Constitution provides, inter alia, that no state shall 'deny to any person within its jurisdiction the equal protection of the law', a provision which has been a fertile source of constitutional challenges to discriminatory state legislation.[23] Similar provisions are found in the constitutions of India, Germany and Canada.[24] In fact the legislature must frequently distinguish between categories of person by reference to economic or social considerations or legal status. Landlords and tenants, employers and employees, company directors and shareholders, British citizens and aliens – these and innumerable other categories are subject to differing legal rules. What a constitutional guarantee of equality before the law may achieve is to enable legislation to be invalidated which distinguishes between citizens on grounds which are considered irrelevant, unacceptable or offensive (for example, improper discrimination on grounds of sex, race, origin or colour).[25] Dicey had in mind no such jurisdiction. The specific meaning he attached to equality before the law was that all citizens (including officials) were subject to the jurisdiction of the ordinary courts should they transgress the law which applied to them and that there should be no separate administrative courts, as in France, to hear complaints of unlawful conduct by officials.[26] He believed that *droit administratif* in France favoured the officials and that English law through decisions such as *Entick* v *Carrington* gave better protection to the citizens. These views of Dicey long impeded the proper understanding of administrative law, but today the need for such law in a democracy cannot be denied. Administrative courts as they exist in many European countries, not least in France, protect the individual against unlawful acts by public bodies. Britain has no system of administrative courts on the French model, but in October 2000 a section of the High Court in London was named the Administrative Court. The name reflects the expansion in public law litigation that has occurred since the procedure of judicial review was created in that name in 1977.[27]

---

[20] Cf Report of the Franks Committee, Cmnd 218, 1957, para 29.
[21] Chs 21 C and 25.
[22] Davis, *Discretionary Justice*.
[23] Marshall, *Constitutional Theory*, ch 7; and Polyviou, *The Equal Protection of the Laws*.
[24] India, 1949 Constitution, art 14; Federal Republic of Germany, Basic Law, art 3; Canadian Charter of Rights and Freedoms, s 15.
[25] Ch 19 A; and Feldman, *Civil Liberties and Human Rights*, ch 3.
[26] See Brown and Bell, *French Administrative Law*; and ch 27.
[27] See chs 30 and 31.

Dicey's third meaning of the rule of law expressed a strong preference for the principles of common law declared by the judges as the basis of the citizen's rights and liberties. Dicey had in mind the fundamental political freedoms – freedom of the person, freedom of speech, freedom of association. The citizen whose freedoms were infringed could seek a remedy in the courts and did not need to rely on constitutional guarantees. Dicey believed that the common law gave better protection to the citizen than a written constitution. The Habeas Corpus Acts, which made effective a remedy by which persons unlawfully detained might obtain their freedom were, said Dicey, 'for practical purposes worth a hundred constitutional articles guaranteeing individual liberty'.[28] Today it is difficult to share Dicey's faith in the common law as the primary legal means of protecting the citizen's liberties against the state. First, fundamental liberties at common law may be eroded by Parliament and thus acquire a residual character (namely, what remains after all statutory restrictions have taken effect). Second, the common law does not assure the citizen's economic or social well-being. Third, while it remains essential that legal remedies are effective, there is value in a declaration of the individual's basic rights, as in the European Convention on Human Rights, and in creating judicial procedures for protecting those rights.[29]

Dicey's view of the rule of law, like his view of parliamentary sovereignty, is based on assumptions about the British system of government which in many respects no longer apply. Although he did not satisfactorily resolve the potential conflict between the two notions of the rule of law and the supremacy of Parliament,[30] a recent formulation of the relationship implies equilibrium rather than conflict:

> The maintenance of the rule of law is in every way as important in a free society as the democratic franchise. In our society the rule of law rests upon twin foundations: the sovereignty of the Queen in Parliament in making the law and the sovereignty of the Queen's courts in interpreting and applying the law.[31]

While Dicey's views have greatly influenced attitudes to constitutional law in Britain, what follows in this chapter seeks to explore the main features of the rule of law in the British system of government today, a discussion which is not cast in the Diceyan mould.

B. Rule of law and its implications today

Emphasis will be placed on three related but separate ideas. First, statements of the rule of law embody a preference for orderly life within an organised community ('law and order'), rather than a situation of anarchy or strife in which there is no security for persons, their well-being or their possessions. Some stability in society is a precondition for the existence of a legal system. Second, the rule of law expresses a principle of fundamental importance, namely that government must be conducted according to law and that in disputed cases what the law requires is declared by judicial decision. Third, the rule of law refers to a body of opinion, both about what powers the government should have (for example, that the executive should have no power to detain without trial) and about the procedures to be followed when action is taken by the state (for example, the right to a fair hearing in criminal trials). The second of these

---

[28] Dicey, p 199. And see ch 31.
[29] Ch 19 B.
[30] Dicey, ch 13. For an approach that sees no such conflict, see Allan, *Law, Liberty and Justice*, chs 3 and 11; and (same author) *Constitutional Justice*, ch 7.
[31] *X v Morgan-Grampian Ltd* [1991] AC 1, 48 (Lord Bridge).

ideas is founded on innumerable decisions of the courts and thus it expresses existing legal doctrine. The third idea is relevant to debate in Parliament and in the media on proposals for changing the law, that are liable to be made when the community is challenged by events such as unrest on British streets or international terrorism in New York.

The relation between the second and third ideas may be put in this way. The requirement that government be conducted according to law (the principle of legality) is a necessary condition for the rule of law; but insistence on legality alone does not ensure that the state's powers are consistent with values such as liberty and due process. This emphasis is found in case-law of the European Court of Human Rights.[32] Few doubt that governments should observe the law, but there is no unanimity as to the powers that should be available to them.

These three aspects of the rule of law are now examined in more depth.

Three aspects of the rule of law

1 *Law and order better than anarchy.*   In the limited sense of law and order, the rule of law may appear to be preserved by a dictatorship or a military occupation as well as by a democratic form of government. Under a government which is not freely elected, the courts of law may continue to function, settling disputes between private citizens and such disputes between a citizen and government officials as the regime permits to be so decided. However, constitutionalism and the rule of law will not thrive unless legal restraints apply to the government. The maintenance of law and order and the existence of political liberty are not mutually exclusive, but interdependent. As the Supreme Court of Canada has said, 'democracy in any real sense of the word cannot exist without the rule of law.'[33] And the Universal Declaration of Human Rights states: 'It is essential if man is not to be compelled to have recourse, as a last resort, to rebellion against tyranny and oppression, that human rights should be protected by the rule of law.'[34] In a democracy, it must be possible by political means to change a government without threatening the existence of the state. Unless this possibility exists, the state becomes identified with coercive might and the role of law within the state is emptied of moral content, 'the State cannot be conceived in terms of force alone.'[35]

2 *Government according to law.*   The principle of legality requires that the organs of government operate through law. If the police need to detain a citizen or if taxes are to be levied, the officials concerned must be able to show legal authority for their actions. In Britain, they may be challenged to do so before a court of law, as they were in *Entick* v *Carrington*. Acts of public authorities which are beyond their legal powers may be declared ultra vires and invalid by the courts.[36] In a striking instance, the High Court held (some 30 years after the event) that the enforced removal of 1,500 British citizens from islands in the Indian Ocean to make way for the US base on Diego Garcia had lacked any legal authority.[37] It is because of the principle of legality that legislation

---

[32] See p 100 below and ch 19 B.
[33] *Reference Concerning Certain Questions Relating to the Secession of Quebec* (1998) 161 DLR (4th) 385, 416–17.
[34] Preamble, 3rd para.
[35] d'Entrèves, *The Notion of the State*, p 69.
[36] Ch 30.
[37] *R* v *Foreign and Commonwealth Secretary, ex p Bancoult* [2001] QB 1067; see A Tompkins [2001] PL 571. According to Ewing and Gearty, *The Struggle for Civil Liberties*, ch 1, the principle of legality is the essence of the rule of law.

must be passed through Parliament if (for instance) the police are to have additional powers to combat terrorism. The rule of law serves as a buttress for democracy, since new powers of government may be conferred only by Parliament.[38]

In the British tradition of government according to law, it is from the ordinary courts that a remedy for unlawful acts of government is to be obtained. Within this tradition, the Human Rights Act 1998 extended to all courts a duty where possible to interpret legislation consistently with the European Convention on Human Rights.[39] In some legal systems, jurisdiction in public law is assigned not to the ordinary civil courts, but to specialised courts, such as the administrative courts in France headed by the Conseil d'Etat. Provided that those courts are independent and impartial, judicial control of government can be secured.

Public authorities and officials must be subject to effective sanctions if they depart from the law. Often the sanction is that their acts are declared invalid by the courts. But another sanction is the duty to compensate citizens whose rights have been infringed. Today it is unlikely that the British Prime Minister would be sued for damages, not because he is immune from such action but because his political decisions do not normally have direct legal effect; but in 1959 the Premier of Quebec was held liable in damages for having maliciously and without legal authority directed a liquor licensing authority to cancel the licence of a restaurant proprietor who had repeatedly provided bail for Jehovah's Witnesses accused of police offences.[40] In Britain, government departments became liable to be sued for their wrongful acts under the Crown Proceedings Act 1947.[41] That Act preserved the personal immunity of the Sovereign, an immunity which in other legal systems is enjoyed by the head of state. Thus in the USA, the President while in office is immune from liability for his unlawful acts and he is irremovable except by a successful impeachment. If the President is so removed, he may then be sued or prosecuted for unlawful acts which he may have committed while in office. Even a President while in office may not disregard the law.

> In the course of criminal investigations into the Watergate affair, the special prosecutor appointed by the Attorney-General requested President Nixon to produce tape-recordings of discussions which the President had had with his advisers. When presidential privilege was claimed for the tapes, the US Supreme Court held that this claim had to be considered 'in the light of our historic commitment to the rule of law'. The court rejected the claim and ordered the tapes to be produced, since 'the generalised assertion of privilege must yield to the demonstrated, specific need for evidence in a pending criminal trial'.[42]

Nixon thereafter resigned rather than face impeachment proceedings before a hostile Congress. In 1998–99, when President Clinton was impeached, he was acquitted by the Senate on charges that included one of giving false testimony to a federal grand jury in the Lewinsky affair.[43] In 1999, presidential immunity of a different kind came before the House of Lords in the case of General Pinochet, former President of Chile: he was held liable to be extradited to Spain to stand trial on charges of conspiring to commit torture contrary to international law, relating to events while he was in office.[44] In 1993, the House of Lords held that the Home Secretary was liable for contempt of court, in that he decided not to order the return to the United Kingdom of a

---

[38] For the contribution that law can make to government, see J Jowell, in Jowell and Oliver (eds), *The Changing Constitution*, 4th edn, ch 1.
[39] Ch 19 C.
[40] *Roncarelli* v *Duplessis* (1959) 16 DLR (2d) 689.
[41] Ch 32.
[42] *US* v *Nixon* 418 US 683 (1974); for public interest immunity in Britain, see ch 32 C.
[43] Gerhardt, *The Federal Impeachment Process*, ch 14. And see Berger, *Impeachment*.
[44] *R* v *Bow Street Magistrate, ex p Pinochet Ugarte (No 3)* [2000] 1 AC 147.

Zairean teacher who was claiming refugee status, despite an order by a High Court judge that this should be done.[45] This was the first time that the English courts had to decide whether a minister of the Crown could be guilty of contempt of court. Lord Templeman said: 'For the purpose of enforcing the law against all persons and institutions, . . . the courts are armed with coercive powers exercisable in proceedings for contempt of court.' The Home Secretary's argument that the courts had no such powers against ministers 'would, if upheld, establish the proposition that the executive obey the law as a matter of grace and not as a matter of necessity, a proposition which would reverse the result of the Civil War'.[46]

The doctrine of government according to law stresses the importance of legal authority and form for the acts of government. In a system in which Parliament is supreme and in which the Cabinet is supported by a majority in the Commons, executive decisions may readily be clothed with legality. In the absence of constitutional guarantees for individual rights, the need for legal authority does not protect these rights from legislative invasion. A detainee's right to come to a court for a ruling on the legality of his or her detention is of little value if the government has taken care to obtain the requisite power to detain from a compliant legislature.

In the United Kingdom, Parliament may authorise the executive to exercise powers which drastically affect the liberty of the individual: for example, by authorising the detention of persons suspected of involvement in terrorist offences.[47] If all that the rule of law means is that official acts must be clothed with legality, this gives no guarantee that other fundamental values are not infringed. The Human Rights Act 1998 may reduce the likelihood of legislation that is inconsistent with the European Convention on Human Rights, but it provides no guarantee against such legislation.

3 *The rule of law as a broad political doctrine.*   If the law is not to be merely a means of achieving whatever ends a particular government may favour, the rule of law must go beyond the principle of legality. The experience and values of the legal system are relevant both to the question, 'What legal authority *does* the government have for its acts?' and also to the question, 'What powers *ought* the government to have?' If, for example, the government wishes to introduce criminal sanctions for conduct contrary to its economic or social policies, the new legislation ought to respect principles of fair criminal procedure. If a Bill seeks to depart from these principles, arguments invoking the rule of law will be used in the debates on the Bill. Such arguments are reinforced by the fact that the right to due process is protected by the European Convention on Human Rights, art 6.

As a broad principle influencing the content of new legislation, the content of the 'rule of law' has been much debated. What *are* the essential values which have emerged from centuries of legal experience? Are they absolute values or may there be circumstances in which political necessity justifies the legislature in departing from them? To revert to the example of interrogation in depth with which this chapter began, would it ever be justified to use such methods to compel detainees suspected of terrorist activities to reveal information? Could legislation to authorise this be framed that would not also permit measures amounting to torture or degrading treatment in breach of article 3, ECHR? One approach might be to authorise the interrogation of detainees, but to grant the interrogators immunity from liability for all action taken in the process of interrogation. The dangers of such legislation are evident. To deprive a

---

[45] *M v Home Office* [1994] 1 AC 377.
[46] [1994] 1 AC 377 at 395.
[47] For the Terrorism Act 2000 and the Anti-terrorism, Crime and Security Act 2001, see ch 26 E.

detainee of a remedy in such circumstances could aptly be described as eroding the rule of law.

The 'rule of law' implications are not always clear-cut. Thus, company directors may be obliged to give evidence about their business activities to an inspector, but it does not follow that the evidence so given should be admissible in criminal proceedings against the directors.[48] In such situations, the political parties may well disagree as to what legislation should contain to protect the rights and interests of those persons who are primarily affected.

Is the rule of law then in this broad sense too subjective and uncertain to be of any value? Would discussion of new legislation be clearer if the rule of law were excluded from the vocabulary of debate? One attempt to ascertain the values inherent in the system of law was made by Lon Fuller, who argued that the enactment of secret laws would be contrary to the essential nature of a legal system, as would heavy reliance on retrospective legislation or on legislation imposing criminal sanctions for conduct which is not defined but may be deemed undesirable by an official.[49]

Joseph Raz argues that the term 'rule of law' should be limited to formal values associated with the legal system. Thus, laws should be prospective, open, certain and capable of guiding human conduct; judges should be independent and the courts accessible; litigants should receive a fair hearing and so on. While these standards should ensure conformity to the rule of law, Raz emphasises both that they do not ensure that the substance of the law meets the needs of the people; and that conformity to legal values is a matter of degree, to be balanced against competing claims.[50]

While Raz regards the rule of law as a concept confined to matters of form, others favour a more substantive concept.[51] But the distinction between form and substance is not clear-cut (is the case against 'arbitrary power' based on matters of form or substance or both?). Raz accepted that the rule of law is 'compatible with gross violations of human rights', but also argued that 'deliberate disregard for the rule of law violates human dignity'.[52] Raz rightly warns against identifying the rule of law with utopia. But is the rule of law observed under a dictatorship in which the judges diligently apply the dictator's decrees, including one that permits indefinite detention without trial for those suspected of subversive activity? Many would conclude that the rule of law in a strong sense thrives only alongside values of human dignity, liberty and democracy.

Among British judges there is an important vein of belief in the values to be upheld in a legal system. The nature of these values can be discovered from judicial decisions[53] and from a growing body of articles and lectures by judges.[54] Today courts in Britain are required under the Human Rights Act 1998 to have regard to the values inherent in the European Convention on Human Rights.

International movement to promote the rule of law

Since 1945 the rule of law, in parallel with the human rights movement, has been a matter of much international discussion. The Universal Declaration of Human Rights,

---

[48] *Saunders* v *UK* (1996) 23 EHRR 313.
[49] Fuller, *The Morality of Law*. For endorsement of Fuller's approach, see Allan, *Constitutional Justice*.
[50] J Raz (1977) 93 LQR 195. See also Raz, *Ethics in the Public Domain*, ch 16.
[51] The different approaches are examined in P Craig [1997] PL 467.
[52] J Raz (1977) 93 LQR 195, 204 and 205.
[53] See e.g. D Feldman (1990) 106 LQR 246.
[54] These include Lord Bingham (1993) 109 LQR 390; J Laws (1994) 57 MLR 213, [1995] PL 72, [1996] PL 622, [1997] PL 455 and [1998] PL 221; R Scott [1996] PL 410 and 427; S Sedley (1994) 110 LQR 260; Lord Steyn [1997] PL 84; and Lord Woolf [1995] PL 57.

adopted in 1948, was followed by the European Convention on Human Rights, signed at Rome in 1950.[55] The Convention recognised that European countries have 'a common heritage of political traditions, ideals, freedom and the rule of law' and sought to create machinery for protecting certain human rights. In *Golder's* case, which concerned the right of a convicted prisoner in the United Kingdom to have access to legal advice regarding a possible civil action against the prison authorities, the European Court of Human Rights referred to the rule of law and said, 'in civil matters one can scarcely conceive of the rule of law without there being a possibility of having access to the courts.'[56]

Both the Convention and the case law of the Strasbourg Court support the analysis of the rule of law made in this chapter. The Convention seeks to protect individuals against the arbitrary or unlawful exercise of state power, and it requires national legal systems to bear the primary burden of protecting Convention rights. Some Convention rights (for instance, the right not to be tortured, art 3) are absolute. Others (for instance, the right to freedom of expression, art 10) are not absolute and may be restricted in the public interest; such restrictions must satisfy various criteria, including that of being 'prescribed by law'. This criterion means (in outline) (1) that the restriction must be authorised in national law and (2) that the 'quality' of the national law must be compatible with the Convention.[57] In English law, it was formerly held that public authorities might do anything which did not interfere with the rights of individuals, even if they had no express authority for such action.[58] This approach is not acceptable where Convention rights are concerned.

The European Convention is one of the most successful multilateral treaties that encourage national legal systems to provide increased protection for human rights.[59] This movement in international law has taken inspiration from many sources, including conferences held by the International Commission of Jurists, which have urged lawyers from many countries to improve their national systems.[60]

Within the Commonwealth, the heads of government at their meetings have often expressed support for the rule of law. In 1991 at Harare they linked the rule of law, the independence of the judiciary and the protection of human rights, with 'democratic processes and institutions which reflect national circumstances' and 'just and honest government' as being among the fundamental values of the Commonwealth association.[61]

Social and economic aspects of the rule of law

The rule of law movement has been broadened to include social and economic goals which lie far beyond the typical values associated with the legal profession and the practice of law. Such a broadening is opposed by those critics of the mixed economy and the welfare state who wish to see a return to the restricted functions of government in the 19th century. Believing in the market economy and wishing to minimise state

---

[55] Ch 19 B. For the background, see Simpson, *Human Rights and the End of Empire*.
[56] *Golder* v *UK* (1975) 1 EHRR 524.
[57] See *Sunday Times* v *UK* (1979) 2 EHRR 245; *Malone* v *UK* (1984) 7 EHRR 14. Also Clayton and Tomlinson, *The Law of Human Rights*, paras 6.126–138.
[58] *Malone* v *Metropolitan Police Commissioner* [1979] Ch 344; cf *R* v *Somerset CC, ex p Fewings* [1995] 3 All ER 20.
[59] Others include the International Covenant on Civil and Political Rights 1966; and International Convention on Elimination of Racial Discrimination 1966.
[60] See e.g. the Declaration of Delhi (1959) 2 Jl of ICJ 7; and ICJ, *The Rule of Law and Human Rights – Principles and Definitions*, 1966.
[61] The Harare Communiqué, 1991; ch 15 C.

intervention, they argue that individuals must be able to plan their own affairs and to predict with reasonable certainty how the powers of the state will be used.[62] Now certainty and predictability are values often associated with law; in a different context, Lord Diplock said in 1975: 'The acceptance of the rule of law as a constitutional principle requires that a citizen, before committing himself to any course of action, should be able to know what are the legal consequences that will flow from it.'[63] But however desirable it may be that discretionary powers of government should be controlled by rules,[64] this is not attainable so long as the state has responsibilities for economic and social affairs.

A related question is whether constitutional protection for the classic civil and political rights (such as personal liberty and freedom of expression) can or should be extended to economic and social rights (such as rights to employment or housing).[65] In the absence of constitutional protection for such rights, individuals ought nevertheless to have (and in many areas of government already have) enforceable rights to the delivery of public goods (such as education or medical care). Much detailed legislation has long existed in these areas, and individuals may typically enforce their rights under that legislation by appealing to the appropriate tribunal (where one exists) or, where there is no relevant right of appeal, by recourse to judicial review.[66] Thus, in respect of immigration control, the creation of immigration adjudicators and an immigration appeal tribunal to hear appeals from the decisions of immigration officials was based on the principle that 'it is fundamentally wrong and inconsistent with the rule of law that power to take decisions affecting a man's whole future should be vested in officers of the Executive, from whose findings there is no appeal.'[67] Legal protection in the form of appeal to a tribunal and procedure for judicial review is of great practical significance, but it does not necessarily meet the need for constitutional protection of the rights involved.

Conclusion

It is not possible to formulate a simple and clear-cut statement of the rule of law as a broad political doctrine. As the needs of national and international communities change, so we may need to restate the received values of law in response to those changes. A government's changing programme must not lead it to suppose that new areas of public action (such as the function of regulating the public utilities)[68] can be isolated from the scope of law and subjected only to administrative or political controls. Through membership of the European Union, the United Kingdom is part of a supranational system which is intended (inter alia) to exercise control in legal form over important areas of economic activity. Indeed, the powers granted to European organs are capable of enlarging the effective scope of the rule of law, for example by granting to the individual rights of legal protection against the governments of member states.[69]

Challenges to the orderly working of law and society are presented by phenomena such as hijacking, urban terrorism, direct action by militant groups, campaigns of civil

---

[62] Hayek, *The Constitution of Liberty*, makes a profound analysis of rule of law concepts; for a critique, see Loughlin, *Public Law and Political Theory*, pp 84–101.
[63] *Black-Clawson International Ltd* v *Papierwerke AG* [1975] AC 591, 638.
[64] Davis, *Discretionary Justice*, ch 3.
[65] See K D Ewing (2001) 5 Edin LR 297.
[66] Ch 29 A.
[67] Report of Committee on Immigration Appeals, Cmnd 3387, 1967, p 23; ch 20 B.
[68] See ch 14.
[69] See Case 11/70, *Internationale Handelsgesellschaft* [1970] ECR 1125; Case 5/88, *Wachauf* v *Germany* [1989] ECR 2609. See further, ch 8 B. See also the EU Charter of Fundamental Rights 2000, said in the preamble to be based on 'the principles of democracy and the rule of law'. But the Charter is not directly enforceable in legal proceedings, though it may be referred to by the European Court of Justice.

disobedience, and violent protests and demonstrations. All these are sometimes described indiscriminately as a growing threat to the rule of law (by which may simply be meant the authority and stability of established institutions). There are many important distinctions to be drawn between these different forms of political or criminal action. But, if we leave aside acts of criminal violence at one end of the scale and law-abiding political expression at the other end, do acts of non-violent civil disobedience endanger the legal system? In particular, does the rule of law require complete obedience to the law from all citizens and organisations?[70] It would be casting an impossible burden on the courts to require them to base decisions as to whether certain conduct constitutes a criminal offence on the political motives of the accused.[71] It may be argued both that, in a democratic society, there are important reasons for obeying the law which do not exist in other forms of government, but also that there are forms of principled disobedience that do not run counter to the democratic reasons for obedience, particularly those which are designed to improve the working of democratic procedures for political decisions.[72] While individuals may be driven by conscience to resist a particular law that they regard as unjust or immoral, there is a danger that decisions to disobey particular laws taken by organised groups (whether public authorities, private bodies, or individuals, or business corporations) might cumulatively suggest that there is no general obligation to obey the law, but only the law of which one approves. In fact, the maintenance of life in modern society requires a willingness from most citizens for most of the time to observe the laws, even when individually they may not agree with them. It deserves to be remembered that law, like the democratic process, may be used to protect the weaker, underprivileged sections of society against those who can exercise physical or economic force.

---

[70] Marshall, *Constitutional Theory*, ch 9; Dworkin, *Taking Rights Seriously*, ch 8; Allan, *Law, Liberty, and Justice*, ch 5.

[71] Cf *Chandler* v *DPP* [1964] AC 763.

[72] Singer, *Democracy and Disobedience*. For the Strasbourg Court's recognition that direct action may involve Convention rights to freedom of expression and association, see *Steel* v *UK* (1998) 28 EHRR 603. Also H Fenwick and G Phillipson [2000] PL 627 and (2001) 21 LS 535.

Chapter 7

RESPONSIBLE AND ACCOUNTABLE GOVERNMENT

Within a democracy, those who govern must be accountable, or responsible, to those whom they govern. The power to govern derives directly from the votes of the electors, as well as from their continuing willingness to be governed by the elected government. Between general elections, one function of the elected representatives is to call the government to account for its acts and policies on a continuing basis. This both requires government to justify its decisions by giving the reasons for them and enables decisions that appear unjustified or mistaken to be criticised. The process enables electors to make an informed appraisal of the government's record on their next opportunity to vote; until then it influences the formation of public opinion regarding the government.

In ordinary speech, the words 'responsible' and 'accountable' have several meanings; and the concept of responsible government takes several forms.[1] During the 1990s, possibly because of some serious failures of accountability, attempts were made to clarify the essential meaning of accountable government and to strengthen the procedures which apply it. In 1996, the Scott report on the 'arms for Iraq' affair contained penetrating criticism of numerous incomplete and misleading answers given in Parliament by ministers to questions about the government's policy.[2] Also in 1996, an influential report by the Public Service Committee of the House of Commons, while affirming that ministerial responsibility 'is a central principle of the British Constitution', examined the difficulties inherent in the principle.[3] In 2001, a report by an independent committee urged that Parliament must be at the apex of the system of scrutiny of the executive and must develop both a culture of scrutiny and more effective methods of securing accountability.[4]

This chapter examines the political responsibility of government to Parliament, including both collective and individual responsibility. Another form of responsibility is the legal responsibility of ministers and officials for their acts. Whereas legal responsibility may be enforced in the courts, political responsibility is enforced through Parliament. A government's relationship with Parliament is too complex to be summarised in a code of precise rules, but the essential features of responsibility to Parliament give rise to obligations which are (or ought to be) observed in the regular practice of government. The debate on accountability has led to the publication of documents summarising these essential obligations and recording official practice.[5]

---

[1] Related principles include popular control of decision-making and political equality: see Weir and Beetham, *Political Power and Democratic Control in Britain*, ch 1. Also see Birch, *Representative and Responsible Government*, pp 17–21.

[2] HC 115 (1995–96), vol IV, section K.8, pp 1799–1806; and see R Scott [1996] PL 410.

[3] HC 313–I (1995–96). For the government's response, see HC 67 (1996–97).

[4] Hansard Society, *The Challenge for Parliament: Making Government Accountable* (the Newton report). See also HC 300 and 748 (1999–2000), Cm 4737, 2000, HC 321 (2000–01) and D Oliver [2001] PL 666.

[5] And see ch 2 B.

Early origins of responsible government

So long as government was carried on by the King, the nature of monarchy made it difficult to establish any responsibility for acts of government. In medieval times, the practice developed by which the royal will was signified in documents bearing a royal seal, which would be applied by one of the King's ministers. Maitland detected in this practice 'the foundation for our modern doctrine of ministerial responsibility – that for every exercise of the royal power some minister is answerable'.[6] With the responsibility of ministers came the rule that 'the King can do no wrong'. This meant not that everything done on behalf of the King was lawful, but that the King's advisers and ministers were punishable for illegal measures that occurred in the course of government.[7] Today the use of various seals or forms for recording decisions taken in the name of the Sovereign by ministers is regulated partly by statute and partly by custom.[8] These rules formerly ensured that, since the Sovereign could not be called personally to account, responsibility could be laid on those ministers who carried out his decisions.

This responsibility was at one time enforced by the English Parliament through impeachment. Officers of state were liable to be impeached by the Commons at the bar of the House of Lords for the treason, high crimes and misdemeanours they were alleged to have committed. In the 17th century, impeachment became a political weapon wielded by Parliament for striking at unpopular royal policies.[9] Following the granting of a royal pardon to Danby in 1679 to forestall his impeachment, the Act of Settlement provided that a royal pardon could not be pleaded in bar of an impeachment. The last instance of a purely political impeachment came when the Tory ministers who in 1713 negotiated the Peace of Utrecht were later impeached by a Whig House of Commons. Thereafter, only two impeachments occurred, of Warren Hastings between 1788 and 1795 for misgovernment in India and of Lord Melville in 1806 for alleged corruption. The power of impeachment is still available to Parliament: but more modern means of achieving ministerial responsibility have rendered it an obsolete weapon in the United Kingdom.[10]

The legal responsibility of government

The principle that government must be conducted according to law has already been discussed.[11] The Sovereign may not personally be sued or prosecuted in the courts. But servants or officers of the Crown who commit crimes or civil wrongs are, and always have been, subject to the jurisdiction of the courts. This jurisdiction extends to contempt of court.[12] Superior orders or the interest of the state are no defence to such proceedings.[13] Public authorities other than the Crown are at common law liable for the wrongful acts of their officials or servants.[14] The departments of central government

---

[6] Maitland, *Constitutional History*, p 203. Cf art 64 of the Belgian Constitution of 1831.

[7] Chitty, *Prerogatives of the Crown*, p 5.

[8] Anson, *Law and Custom of the Constitution*, vol II, part I, pp 62–72; HLE, vol 8(2), pp 233, 518–19.

[9] Maitland, *Constitutional History*, pp 317–18; Taswell-Langmead, *English Constitutional History*, pp 164–5, 353–4, 529–38; Clayton Roberts, *The Growth of Responsible Government in Stuart England*; Berger, *Impeachment*, ch 1.

[10] See A W Bradley, in Carnall and Nicholson (eds), *The Impeachment of Warren Hastings*, ch 7. Cf Dicey, *The Law of the Constitution*, p 499.

[11] Ch 6.

[12] *M v Home Office* [1994] 1 AC 377.

[13] Smith and Hogan, *Criminal Law*, pp 263–4; Dicey, pp 302–6; *Entick v Carrington*, p 92 above.

[14] *Mersey Docks and Harbour Board Trustees v Gibbs* (1866) LR 1 HL 93.

became liable to be sued under the Crown Proceedings Act 1947 and their decisions are subject to control by means of judicial review.[15] It is with political responsibility that this chapter is concerned.

Development of responsibility to Parliament

After 1688 the doctrine of collective responsibility developed in fits and starts as the Cabinet system came into being.[16] For much of the 18th century the Cabinet was a body of holders of high office whose relationship with one another was ill-defined; the body as a whole was not responsible to Parliament. Although the King rarely attended Cabinet meetings after 1717, it was the King's government in fact as well as in name, and the King could act on the advice of individual ministers. Under Walpole, ministries were relatively homogeneous. Other Cabinets in the century were less united. Parliament could force the dismissal of individual ministers who were disapproved, but could not dictate appointments to the King. The King sometimes consulted those who were out of office without the prior approval of his ministers. There was no clear dividing line between matters dealt with by individual ministers and matters dealt with in the Cabinet. As late as 1806, it was debated in the Commons whether ministers must accept collective responsibility for the general affairs of government or whether only those ministers who carried policies into execution were individually responsible.[17]

By the early 19th century, as the scope for personal government by the Sovereign sharply declined, so the tendencies towards the collective responsibility of the Cabinet became more marked. After 1832, it became evident that the Cabinet must retain the support of the majority in the House of Commons if it wished to continue in office. Just as it had earlier been recognised that a single minister could not retain office against the will of Parliament, so it became clear that all ministers must stand or fall together in Parliament, if the Cabinet were to function effectively.

By the mid-19th century, ministerial responsibility was the accepted basis of parliamentary government in Britain.[18] As the Victorian foundations of the system were laid, critics of the rule of Cabinet unity were reminded that 'the various departments of the Administration are but parts of a single machine . . . and that the various branches of the Government have a close connection and mutual dependence upon each other'.[19]

The development of collective responsibility during the 19th century was accompanied by an expansion in government, not least in the period of reform after 1832 when new central agencies were created to oversee areas of social administration, such as the reformed poor law and public health. After some experimenting with appointed public boards that were not directly responsible to Parliament and might have no one in Parliament to defend them against their critics,[20] a strong political preference was expressed for vesting the new powers in a minister who sat in Parliament and could account to Parliament for what was done. The development of parliamentary procedures for financial scrutiny and for obtaining information through questions addressed to ministers enabled members to influence matters within the minister's responsibility.[21]

---

[15] Chs 30–2.
[16] Mackintosh, *British Cabinet*, ch 2.
[17] Williams, *The 18th Century Constitution*, pp 123–5.
[18] For a notable summary, see Grey, *Parliamentary Government*, p 4.
[19] Grey, p 57.
[20] F M G Willson (1955) 33 Public Administration 43, 44.
[21] Chester and Bowring, *Questions in Parliament*, ch 2.

The corollary of this, as the civil service itself was reformed following the Northcote-Trevelyan report of 1854, was the anonymity and permanence of the civil servants who administered the new departments under the control or oversight of ministers.[22]

The meaning of collective responsibility

The doctrine of collective responsibility was stated in absolute terms by Lord Salisbury in 1878:

> For all that passes in Cabinet every member of it who does not resign is absolutely and irretrievably responsible and has no right afterwards to say that he agreed in one case to a compromise, while in another he was persuaded by his colleagues . . . It is only on the principle that absolute responsibility is undertaken by every member of the Cabinet, who, after a decision is arrived at, remains a member of it, that the joint responsibility of Ministers to Parliament can be upheld and one of the most essential principles of parliamentary responsibility established.[23]

In 2001, the Prime Minister's statement of the doctrine took this form:

> Collective responsibility requires that Ministers should be able to express their views frankly in the expectation that they can argue freely in private while maintaining a united front when decisions have been reached. This in turn requires that the privacy of opinions expressed in Cabinet and Ministerial Committees should be maintained.[24]

Yet it is difficult to control political behaviour in absolute terms. In the 19th century, the degree of political cohesion was variable. Cabinet unity could not always be achieved when ministers held deeply divided opinions. Some subjects were regarded as 'open questions', for example women's suffrage between 1906 and 1914 and more recently capital punishment.[25] But it was a sign of political weakness if many issues were accepted as open questions. Except for open questions, ministers who did not wish to be publicly identified with Cabinet policies were expected to resign.

Today collective responsibility embodies a number of related aspects. Like other principles of government, it is neither static nor unchangeable and may give way before more pressing political forces.

1 The Prime Minister and other ministers are collectively responsible to Parliament, and to the Commons in particular, for the conduct of national affairs. In practice, so long as the governing party retains its majority in the House, the Prime Minister is unlikely to be forced to resign (although this was Mrs Thatcher's fate in 1990, after over 11 years in office) or to seek a dissolution of Parliament.

2 When a Prime Minister dies or resigns office, then even if the same party continues in power, all ministerial offices are at the disposal of the new Prime Minister.

3 Although ministers are individually responsible to Parliament for the conduct of their departments, if members of the Commons seek to censure an individual minister, the government generally will rally to his or her defence: collective responsibility is a means of defending an incompetent or unpopular minister, but this may not succeed when there is a sustained media campaign to pillory and remove a particular minister.

4 Ministers while in office share in the collective responsibility of all ministers. As the Ministerial Code states bluntly: 'Decisions reached by the Cabinet or Ministerial

---

[22] Parris, *Constitutional Bureaucracy*, ch 3.
[23] *Life of Robert, Marquis of Salisbury*, vol II, pp 219–20.
[24] *Ministerial Code*, para 17.
[25] Jennings, *Cabinet Government*, pp 277–9; Hanham, *The 19th Century Constitution*, pp 79, 84–94; Grey, p 116.

Committees are binding on all members of the Government.'[26] A Cabinet minister may, however, ask for dissent from a Cabinet decision to be recorded in the private minutes of Cabinet.[27] He or she is expected nonetheless to support the government by voting in Parliament. Cabinet ministers who were also members of the National Executive of the Labour party were in 1974 told by the Prime Minister that they must observe the conventions of collective responsibility at Executive meetings.[28]

5 As a former Cabinet minister said, an element of concealment is inherent in the concept of collective responsibility. 'Ministers must in the nature of things have differences, but they must outwardly appear to have none.'[29] In principle, secrecy attaches to Cabinet discussions, Cabinet documents and the proceedings of Cabinet committees, except where the Cabinet or the Prime Minister decides that disclosures shall be made.[30] Exceptionally, where a minister resigns because of a disagreement with the Cabinet, he or she may explain in detail the reasons for the resignation, both to Parliament and in the press.[31] Today leakages about controversial matters frequently occur and the principle of secrecy is under pressure to give way to a more open system of government. In response to the media, a minister may state the obvious, namely that a controversial decision does not directly relate to his or her departmental responsibilities.

6 Similarly, in principle secrecy attaches to communications between departments. 'Decisions that may have been taken in the Cabinet or a ministerial committee are normally announced and explained as the decision of the Minister concerned.'[32] Thus collective responsibility reinforces the principle of the indivisibility of the executive.[33] Again, an element of concealment is inherent in the principle: departments are expected to agree with each other because their ministerial heads are members of the same Cabinet. In real life, serious disagreements between departments occur, and often cannot be kept secret. A government's reputation is not enhanced by attempts to create a wall of complete secrecy for communications within Whitehall.

7 Where necessary, decisions of the Cabinet are communicated to the Sovereign by or on behalf of the Prime Minister. Certain exceptions exist to the principle of collective responsibility for advice to the Sovereign. Thus, in advising the Sovereign on the prerogative of mercy, the Home Secretary acts on his or her own responsibility.[34]

Collective responsibility thus serves a variety of political uses. As most governments are drawn from one party, it reinforces party unity and prevents back-bench MPs from inquiring too far into the processes of government. It helps to maintain the government's control over legislation and public expenditure and to contain public disagreement between departments. It reinforces the traditional secrecy of the decision-making process within government. It helps to maintain the authority of the Prime Minister.[35]

Some purposes for which the doctrine is maintained are controversial, in particular over the degree of protection which should be afforded to the secrecy of decision making, to the authority of the Prime Minister and to the need for external unanimity. In some open processes of government, especially public inquiries, the separate views

---

[26] *Ministerial Code*, para 16. And see ch 13 C.
[27] Mackintosh, *British Cabinet*, p 534, but cf *Ministerial Code*, para 13. And see ch 13 C.
[28] Wilson, *The Governance of Britain*, pp 74–5, 191–3; and see D L Ellis [1980] PL 367, 379–83.
[29] Gordon Walker, *The Cabinet*, pp 27–8.
[30] Ch 13 B.
[31] See R Brazier [1990] PL 300.
[32] *Ministerial Code*, para 16.
[33] Heclo and Wildavsky, *The Private Government of Public Money*, p 116.
[34] Ch 12 D.
[35] See ch 13 A. Cf Crossman's comment that collective responsibility had come to mean collective obedience to the Prime Minister (Introduction to Bagehot, p 53). And see T Benn (1980) 33 Parliamentary Affairs 7.

of government departments are regularly made public.[36] But there is an obvious political advantage in being able to maintain an outward appearance of unity, which is why some aspects of collective responsibility apply also to the 'shadow Cabinet' of the main opposition party in the Commons. The political authority of the Labour 'shadow Cabinet' was weakened when, in a Commons debate about denationalisation, two inconsistent policies were advocated by the leading speakers for the Opposition.[37]

An assessment of collective responsibility must take account of the fact that not all important decisions of national policy are taken in full Cabinet. The decision to manufacture the British atomic bomb,[38] to mount the Suez operation in 1956, to raise the bank rate in 1957[39] and to devalue the pound in 1967[40] were effectively taken by a few ministers meeting with the Prime Minister. So were the decisions to ban trade union membership for staff at Government Communications Headquarters,[41] and to give the Bank of England responsibility for setting interest rates in 1997. In such cases other members of the Cabinet are in no better position than ministers outside the Cabinet to influence the decision before it is taken. During Mr Blair's period as Prime Minister, he appears to have made little use of meetings of the Cabinet for collective decision making.

Whether decisions are taken by the Cabinet or are merely reported to it, a minister may at any time resign in protest against decisions with which he or she strongly disagrees. Such resignations may indicate a deep disagreement over the way in which the Prime Minister is conducting government. Sir Geoffrey Howe's resignation in November 1990 after a series of other Cabinet resignations set in train the events leading to Mrs Thatcher's own resignation on 23 November 1990. But by its nature a resignation does not affect decisions that have already been taken.[42]

Agreements to differ

In exceptional circumstances, it may be politically impossible for the Cabinet to maintain a united front. In 1932, the coalition or 'National' government, formed in 1931 to deal with the economic crisis adopted an 'agreement to differ'. The majority of the Cabinet favoured the adoption of a general tariff of 10%, against the strong opposition of three Liberal ministers and one National Labour minister. It was announced that the dissenting ministers would be free to oppose the proposals of the majority by speech and vote, both in Parliament and outside. When the Labour opposition criticised the government for violating 'the long-established constitutional principle of Cabinet responsibility', the motion of censure was defeated by an overwhelming majority.[43] Eight months later the dissenting ministers resigned on the related issue of imperial preference. This short-lived departure from the principle of unanimity in fact demonstrated the virtues of that principle and the departure was justifiable, if at all, only in the special circumstances of a coalition government formed to deal with a national crisis.

In 1975, the Labour Cabinet agreed to differ over Britain's continued membership of the European Communities. Many in the Labour party were opposed to British membership. Party unity was maintained in the two general elections in 1974 by an undertaking from Mr Wilson to renegotiate the terms of British membership and to

---

[36]   Ch 29 B.
[37]   HC Deb, 10 November 1981, cols 438, 499.
[38]   Crossman, Introduction to Bagehot, pp 54–5. This was not an isolated event: Hennessy, *Cabinet*, ch 4.
[39]   Cmnd 350, 1957; and R A Chapman (1965) 43 Public Administration 199.
[40]   Wilson, *The Labour Government 1964–70*, ch 23.
[41]   See *CCSU v Minister for the Civil Service* [1985] AC 374.
[42]   Cf Alderman and Cross, *The Tactics of Resignation*.
[43]   Jennings, *Cabinet Government*, pp 279–81.

submit the outcome to the people for decision, either at a general election or by referendum. When in April 1975 the renegotiation of terms was completed, the Cabinet by a majority of 16–7 decided to recommend continued membership to the electorate. It was agreed that ministers who opposed this policy should be free to speak and campaign against it, but only outside Parliament.[44] When a junior minister, Eric Heffer, insisted on opposing Britain's membership in the Commons,[45] he had to resign from office. Other difficulties arose over the answering of parliamentary questions on European subjects by ministers opposed to British membership.[46]

In 1932, the agreement to differ occurred within a coalition between parties; in 1975, within the Labour party. Indeed, in 1975 majorities against Cabinet policy were recorded in the Parliamentary Labour Party, in the National Executive Committee and at a special party conference. Such agreements to differ on the part of the Cabinet give rise to many political difficulties, but neither in 1932 nor in 1975 did they lead to the downfall of the government. It is difficult to describe these rather desperate expedients as 'unconstitutional'. If conventions are observed because of the political difficulties which follow if they are not,[47] both in 1932 and 1975 it was less difficult to depart from Cabinet unanimity than to seek to enforce it. During a period of minority government, a free vote was allowed to the Labour party (including ministers) on the second reading of the European Assembly Elections Bill.[48] But there are other issues, notably capital punishment, on which ministers like other MPs are free to vote according to their conscience.[49]

Ministers not in the Cabinet

In any government there are more ministers outside the Cabinet than within it. Some have full departmental duties; others (for example, the parliamentary secretaries) merely assist in the work of their departments. These ministers are bound by Cabinet decisions and must refrain from criticising or opposing them in public. 'Ministers cannot speak on public affairs for themselves alone. In all cases, other than those [relating to certain constituency matters], they speak as Ministers; and the principle of collective responsibility applies.'[50] If ministers are to mention matters that 'affect the conduct of the Government as a whole or are of a constitutional character', the Prime Minister must first be consulted.[51]

Similar restraints apply to junior ministers. Thus, while in office they are barred from writing and publishing books relating to their ministerial experience. In 1969, a parliamentary secretary resigned to publish a book on the economy and the machinery of government. Refusing him permission to publish the book and remain a minister, the Prime Minister stated that he had no alternative 'but to uphold the principles which every Prime Minister must maintain in relation to the collective responsibility of the Administration'.[52] Collective responsibility is thus invoked to control the behaviour of ministers and this control is exercised by the Prime Minister. The consequences of collective responsibility are thus in part what the Prime Minister of the day chooses to

[44] See Cmnd 6003, 1975; HC Deb, 23 January 1975, col 1745; HC Deb, 7 April 1975, col 351 (WA). And see Wilson, *The Governance of Britain*, pp 194–7.
[45] HC Deb, 9 April 1975, cols 1325–32.
[46] Eg HC Deb, 5 May 1975, cols 989–1015.
[47] Page 24 above.
[48] HC Deb, 23 March 1977, col 1307; and see D L Ellis [1980] PL 367, 388.
[49] Eg HC Deb, 13 July 1983, col 972.
[50] *Ministerial Code* (2001), para 97.
[51] *Ministerial Code* (2001), para 98.
[52] *The Times*, 26 and 29 September 1969. See *Ministerial Code*, para 107.

make them. The obligation to support government policy on important issues extends to the backbench MPs who act as unpaid parliamentary secretaries to ministers and may be dismissed for stepping too far out of line. They are not members of the government, but they must not vote against the government or embarrass it in other ways.[53]

Operation of individual responsibility today[54]

Ministerial responsibility remains important, but structural changes in government have affected the application of the concept. During the 20th century, as the tasks of the state expanded and vast Whitehall departments were created, officials continued to act in their minister's name, but the ability of ministers to oversee their work declined. The state's economic and social functions led to the creation of non-departmental bodies, public corporations and other agencies. Many of these (especially the boards of the nationalised industries after 1945) were planned to operate beyond the reach of ministerial responsibility, at least for day-to-day decisions. By contrast, the executive agencies created since 1988 under the 'Next Steps' initiative were intended to achieve effective delegation of managerial power, without necessarily reducing overall ministerial control.[55]

By constitutional tradition, a minister answers to Parliament for his or her department. In the practice of Parliament, praise and blame are addressed to the minister, not civil servants. Ministers may not excuse the failure of policies by turning on their expert advisers and administrators.[56] Attempts to do so may seriously damage the minister's reputation, as the Home Secretary (Michael Howard) discovered in 1995; after intervening repeatedly in the operation of the Prison Service, Howard denied responsibility for defects in prison security and dismissed the Service's director, saying that the defects had been an operational matter entrusted to the director.[57] The corollary of the minister's responsibility is that civil servants are not directly responsible to Parliament for government policies or decisions, although they are responsible *to ministers* for their own actions and conduct. In 1996 the government defended 'the fundamental principle that civil servants are servants of the Crown, accountable to the duly constituted government of the day, and not servants of the House'.[58]

Much of the work of Parliament rests on this basis. Government Bills (drafted on the instructions of ministers) are introduced by ministers, who are responsible for the proposals they contain. Question time emphasises the responsibility of ministers.[59] Although civil servants have no voice in most parliamentary proceedings, they appear before select committees to give evidence on departmental policies and decisions. In giving such evidence, they 'do so on behalf of their Ministers and under their directions' and their stated purpose 'is to contribute to the central process of Ministerial accountability, not to offer personal views or judgments on matters of political controversy, or to become involved in what would amount to disciplinary investigations'.[60]

---

[53] *Ministerial Code*, para 46–48. And see P Norton [1989] PL 232.
[54] Marshall, *Constitutional Conventions*, ch 4; Brazier, *Ministers of the Crown*, ch 15; Woodhouse, *Ministers and Parliament*.
[55] See chs 13 D and 14.
[56] In 1963, it was plainly exceptional when the Prime Minister named a former Secretary to the Cabinet as responsible for failing to inform him of a security warning given by the Secretary to a minister of Cabinet rank (HC Deb, 17 June 1963, col 59).
[57] See HC Deb, 16 October 1995, col 30 and 19 October 1995, col 502, and ch 13 D. Also A Barker (1998) 76 Public Administration 21 and, for later events, C Polidano (2000) 71 Political Quarterly 177.
[58] HC 67 (1996–7), app, para 10. And see ch 13 D.
[59] Ch 10 D. Chester and Bowring, pp 251–68, and app II; Franklin and Norton (eds), *Parliamentary Questions*.
[60] *Departmental Evidence and Response to Select Committees*, para 38.

The sanctions for individual responsibility

What are the sanctions which underlie this general practice of Parliament? The system assumes that ministers will fulfil the parliamentary duties of their office, such as introducing legislation and answering questions. By a rota system, departments are assigned days for answering questions and a minister could not refuse to appear on the assigned day. But ministers may refuse to answer a question if they consider that it does not fall within their responsibility, that it would be contrary to the public interest to answer the question or that the expense of obtaining the information requested would be excessive.[61] If a minister persistently refused to answer questions that were properly asked, political pressure would be likely to build up against such refusals. If the Opposition were then to table a motion of censure on the minister, the motion would stand little chance of succeeding in view of the government majority in the House. But situations may occur in which a Prime Minister is unable or unwilling to protect a minister from pressure to resign exerted in other ways. In 1986, the Westland affair caused the Trade and Industry Secretary (Mr Brittan) to resign for having improperly released to the press a confidential letter from the Solicitor-General. Mr Brittan refused to answer questions from the Commons Defence Committee about his role in the matter.[62]

Ministerial responsibility for departmental maladministration

Ministers are, or ought to be, responsible to Parliament for their own decisions and policies and the efficient administration of their departments. The position in respect of the errors of civil servants is less clear. Two questions arise: (a) to what extent is a minister responsible for acts of maladministration in the department? (b) if serious maladministration occurs, does such responsibility involve a duty to resign? The Crichel Down affair has long been the starting-point for discussion of these questions.

> Farm land in Dorset known as Crichel Down had been acquired under compulsory powers from several owners by the Air Ministry in 1937. After the war, the land was transferred to the Ministry of Agriculture, for whom it was administered by a commission set up under the Agriculture Act 1947. While the future of the land was being considered, Lieutenant-Commander Marten, whose wife's family had previously owned much of the land, asked that it be sold back to the family. Misleading replies and false assurances were given when this and similar requests were refused, and a seriously inaccurate report was prepared by a junior civil servant which led the ministry to adhere to a scheme which it had prepared for letting all the land to a single tenant. Inadequate financial information was supplied to the headquarters of the ministry. When Conservative MPs took up Marten's case with the Minister of Agriculture, Sir Andrew Clark QC was appointed to hold an inquiry. His report established that there had been muddle, inefficiency, bias and bad faith on the part of some officials named in the report.[63] A subsequent inquiry to consider disciplinary action against the civil servants reported that some of the deficiencies were due as much to weak organisation within the ministry as to the faults of individuals.[64]

---

[61] And see Erskine May, *Parliamentary Practice*, pp 296–303. Since 1993, the practice of the House of Commons Table Office has been to reject questions only when a minister has refused to answer them in the same session: HC 313–I (1995–96), para 39; and R Scott [1996] PL 410, 416–17. On ministerial accountability and parliamentary questions, see HC 820 (1997–98), HC 821 (1998–99) and HC 61 (2000–01).

[62] HC (1985–86) 519; and see HC Deb, 29 October 1986, col 339; also A Tomkins (1996) 16 LS 63, 76–7.

[63] Cmd 9176, 1954.

[64] Cmd 9220, 1954.

During a Commons debate on these reports, the Minister of Agriculture, Sir Thomas Dugdale, resigned. Speaking in the debate, the Home Secretary, Sir David Maxwell Fyfe, reaffirmed that a civil servant is wholly and directly responsible to his minister and can be dismissed at any time by the minister – a 'power none the less real because it is seldom used'. He went on to give a number of categories where differing considerations apply.

1 A minister must protect a civil servant who has carried out his explicit order.

2 Equally a minister must defend a civil servant who acts properly in accordance with the policy laid down by the minister.

3 'Where an official makes a mistake or causes some delay, but not on an important issue of policy and not where a claim to individual rights is seriously involved, the Minister acknowledges the mistake and he accepts the responsibility although he is not personally involved. He states that he will take corrective action in the Department.'

4 Where action has been taken by a civil servant of which the minister disapproves and has no previous knowledge, and the conduct of the official is reprehensible, there is no obligation on a minister to endorse what he believes to be wrong or to defend what are clearly shown to be errors of his officers. He remains however, 'constitutionally responsible to Parliament for the fact that something has gone wrong', but this does not affect his power to control and discipline his staff.[65]

This statement and the implications of the Crichel Down affair have been much discussed.[66] Was the resignation due to the part which the minister had played, to the unpopularity of his department's policy among Conservative MPs or was he accepting vicarious responsibility for the civil servants? There have been no directly comparable resignations since 1954. In his analysis of the minister's duties, Maxwell Fyfe's four categories sought to identify situations in which a minister must 'accept responsibility' for the acts of civil servants. The analysis did not state that a minister's duty to accept responsibility carried with it a duty to resign.[67]

Subsequent events have confirmed that there is no duty on a minister to resign when maladministration has occurred within his or her department. Whether a minister may resign depends on a variety of political factors, including the attitude of the Prime Minister, the mood of the party, the temperament of the minister and other political factors.[68] Different considerations apply where the personal conduct of a minister is in issue: inadvertent disclosure of a Budget secret caused Hugh Dalton to resign as Chancellor of the Exchequer in 1947;[69] and in 1963 the Secretary of State for War resigned for having lied to the Commons in a personal statement.[70] Ministers resigned in 1973[71] and on many occasions thereafter because of personal improprieties. Of the resignations since 1973, apart from those caused by disagreement on policy, many were brought about by personal misconduct which made it too difficult for the individuals to perform their duties in the face of continuing criticism in the media.[72] By contrast, there have been no resignations directly because of departmental failures.

---

[65] HC Deb, 20 July 1954, cols 1286–7.

[66] See e.g. J A G Griffith (1955) 8 MLR 557; (1954) 32 Public Administration 385 (C J Hamson) and 389 (D N Chester). For a reinterpretation, see Nicolson, *The Mystery of Crichel Down*.

[67] And see Sir R Scott [1996] PL 410 at 412–13.

[68] S E Finer (1956) 34 Public Administration 377.

[69] HC 20 (1947–48).

[70] HC Deb, 22 March 1963, col 809; 17 June 1963, cols 34–170. And Cmnd 2152, 1963.

[71] Cmnd 5367, 1973.

[72] See D Woodhouse, *Ministers and Parliament*, and (1993) 46 Parliamentary Affairs 277; and R Brazier [1994] PL 431.

In 1968, when the first major investigation by the Parliamentary Commissioner for Administration (the Parliamentary Ombudsman) established that there had been maladministration within the Foreign Office in the Sachsenhausen affair[73] the Foreign Secretary, George Brown, assumed direct personal responsibility for the decisions of the Foreign Office, which he maintained were correct, while agreeing to provide compensation for the claimants. In the debate he said: 'We will breach a very serious constitutional position if we start holding officials responsible for things that are done wrong . . . If things are wrongly done, then they are wrongly done by ministers.'[74] This statement did not take full account of the duties of the Parliamentary Ombudsman, whose investigation into departmental conduct must inevitably probe behind statements made for the department by the minister. But the creation of the Ombudsman did not mean a complete change in the relationship between minister and civil servant. As the Attorney-General, Sir Elwyn Jones, said in 1968:

> It is only in exceptional cases that blame should be attached to the individual civil servant and it follows from the principle that the minister alone has responsibility for the actions of his department that the individual civil servant who has contributed to the collective decision of the department should remain anonymous.[75]

In terms of this statement, an 'exceptional case' was provided by the investigation into the affairs of the Vehicle and General Insurance company.

In March 1971, the company collapsed, leaving a million policy holders uninsured. The Department of Trade and Industry had statutory powers of supervision and control of insurance companies but it had failed to exercise these powers. Following allegations of misconduct, the government appointed a tribunal of inquiry[76] to inquire, inter alia, whether there had been negligence or misconduct by persons in the service of the Crown 'directly or indirectly responsible' for the government's statutory functions. The tribunal reported that Mr C W Jardine, under-secretary, and two named assistant secretaries were responsible for the failure to deal with the risk of the company's insolvency before 1971, and that the under-secretary's conduct fell below the standard which could reasonably be expected of an official in that position, and constituted negligence. Under a scheme of delegation within the department, almost all the work allocated to a division was dealt with at the level of under-secretary or below. 'The responsibility for deciding whether or not to exercise the Department's powers lay with Mr Jardine as the Under-Secretary in charge of the Insurance and Companies Division.'[77]

The significance of the report lies in the fact that, after a full public examination into the affair, the tribunal held that a single official should bear the entire responsibility for the department's inactivity. While the tribunal may have correctly described the facts that they had found, did this resolve the question of political responsibility to Parliament? If so, what is left of the principle that a minister takes the praise for the successes of his or her department and the blame for its failures?[78] If a tribunal of inquiry had not been appointed in the Vehicle and General case, the Commons would not have accepted a statement from the Secretary for Trade and Industry pillorying the luckless Mr Jardine.

---

[73] Ch 29 D, and see G K Fry [1970] PL 336.
[74] HC Deb, 5 February 1968, col 112.
[75] HC 350 (1967–68), para 24.
[76] Under the Tribunals of Inquiry (Evidence) Act 1921: ch 29 C.
[77] HL 80, HC 133 (1971–72), para 344.
[78] See HC Deb, 1 May 1972, col 34; and R J S Baker (1972) 43 Political Quarterly 340. The collapse of the Barlow Clowes investment business in 1988 led to a detailed investigation of the role of the civil service in the affair by the Parliamentary Ombudsman: no ministers were implicated and no civil servants were named, although serious faults were found. See R Gregory and G Drewry [1991] PL 192, 408 and ch 29 D.

In April 1982 the Argentine invasion of the Falkland Islands led to the resignation of the Foreign Secretary, Lord Carrington, and two Foreign Office ministers. The ministers stated that they accepted responsibility for the conduct of policy on the Falkland Islands and insisted against the express wishes of the Prime Minister that they should resign. A committee of privy councillors later reviewed the way in which government responsibilities had been discharged before the invasion, found that there had been a misjudgment of the situation within the Foreign Office and recommended changes in the intelligence organisation; but no blame was attached to any individual, nor did the committee consider that criticism for the circumstances leading to the invasion could be attached to the government.[79] The report thus cleared the ministers who had resigned of any culpability. Since Lord Carrington's resignation in 1982, ministers have been resolutely reluctant to resign for errors by civil servants; the resignation of Mr Brittan in 1986 was due to his own role in the Westland affair, not to the conduct of civil servants.

In 1996 Sir Richard Scott's report on the 'arms for Iraq' affair detailed numerous occasions on which ministers failed to inform Parliament adequately about their policy on exporting arms and machine tools to Iraq and did not reveal changes they had made in the policy. Their answers to repeated questions had been misleading,[80] but ministers persuaded the inquiry that they had not intentionally misled Parliament. However, without the provision of full information it is not possible for Parliament

> to assess what consequences, in the form of attribution or blame, ought to follow . . . A failure by Ministers to meet the obligations of Ministerial accountability by providing information about the activities of their departments undermines . . . the democratic process.[81]

When the report was debated in the Commons, the government survived by one vote. No ministers resigned.[82]

Failings in a different context were revealed by the massive inquiry conducted by Lord Phillips and two scientists into the adequacy of the response of five government departments to the problems for health and agriculture posed by BSE and variant CJD.[83] The Phillips report examined in detail the actions of ministers, civil servants and scientific advisers from 1986 to 1996. For many reasons, it was much less critical in tone than the Scott report. Indeed, no question of resignations arose, since the Conservative government was no longer in power. What is clear is that a fact-finding judicial inquiry, with access to relevant material in Whitehall, enables informed conclusions to be drawn that will not emerge from the political process in Parliament. Even when an inquiry into a departmental affair is made by a Commons committee, this is likely to be less effective than an independent inquiry.[84]

Responsibility and accountability restated

A central theme in the Scott report was the tension between government power and democratic accountability. In 1986, during the Defence Committee's inquiry into the Westland affair, the head of the civil service restated the duties of ministers towards Parliament;[85] in revised form, the statement was presented to other Commons

---

[79]   Cmnd 8787, 1983.
[80]   See e.g. the summary at HC 115 (1995–96), vol IV, pp 1799–1800.
[81]   HC 115 (1995–96), vol IV, p 1801.
[82]   HC Deb, 26 February 1996, col 589. On the Scott report, see articles at [1996] PL 357–507; Thompson and Ridley (eds), *Under the Scott-light* and Tomkins, *The Constitution after Scott*.
[83]   HC 887–I (1999–2000).
[84]   See C Polidano (2001) 79 Public Administration 249, discussing inquiries into the Sandline affair: HC 1016 (1997–98), HC 116–I (1998–99).
[85]   HC 92–II (1985–86). And Cmnd 9916, 1986, para 40.

committees and the Scott inquiry.[86] The statement contrasts 'accountability' (in its non-financial sense) with 'responsibility'. A minister is *accountable* to Parliament for everything which occurs in a department: the duty, which may not be delegated, is to inform Parliament about policies and decisions of the department, except in rare cases where secrecy is an overriding necessity (as with currency devaluation or sensitive defence secrets). If something goes wrong, the minister owes it to Parliament to find out what has happened, ensure necessary disciplinary action and take steps to avoid a recurrence.

By contrast, a minister is said to be *responsible* only for broad policies, the framework of administration and issues in which he or she has been involved, not for all departmental affairs. The emphasis is on matters for which the minister may be personally praised or blamed. This form of 'responsibility' may be delegated, and the minister is not responsible for what is done by civil servants (for example, by the chief executive of an executive agency) within the authority assigned to them.

This distinction between accountability and responsibility requires close scrutiny, since it provides a means by which a minister may avoid personal liability for unpopular or mistaken decisions; and it opens up potential areas of government for which no one is 'responsible' to Parliament, even though a minister remains 'accountable'. In 1996 the Public Service Committee of the Commons insisted that no clear dividing line can be drawn between accountability and responsibility, and that the two main aspects of ministerial responsibility are (i) the duty to give an account and (ii) the liability to be held to account.[87]

These matters were much discussed throughout the 1992–97 Parliament. Shortly before that Parliament was dissolved, both Houses adopted a resolution stating that the following principles should govern the conduct of ministers in relation to Parliament:

1 Ministers have a duty to Parliament to account, and be held to account, for the policies, decisions and actions of their Departments and Next Steps Agencies.
2 It is of paramount importance that Ministers give accurate and truthful information to Parliament, correcting any inadvertent error at the earliest opportunity. Ministers who knowingly mislead Parliament will be expected to offer their resignation to the Prime Minister.
3 Ministers should be as open as possible with Parliament, refusing to provide information only when disclosure would not be in the public interest, which should be decided in accordance with relevant statute and the Government's Code of Practice on Access to Government Information.
4 Similarly, Ministers should require civil servants who give evidence before Parliamentary Committees on their behalf and under their directions to be as helpful as possible in providing accurate, truthful and full information in accordance with the duties and responsibilities of civil servants as set out in the Civil Service Code.[88]

These principles are now included in the *Ministerial Code* issued by the Prime Minister. Although they lack the force of law, they are endorsed by both Houses and the Prime Minister. Even if some aspects of the *Ministerial Code* have an uncertain status, this statement of principle is of great authority on the relationship between government and Parliament.

The pre-eminent duty of ministers is indeed to keep Parliament informed and to do so without misleading Parliament by providing inaccurate or incomplete information.

---

[86] E.g. HC 390 (1992–93), para 25; HC 27 (1993–94), paras 118–20; Cm 2748, 1995, para 16; HC 313–I (1995–96), paras 15–18. See also the wealth of evidence in HC 313–II and 313–III (1995–96); and the Scott report, HC 115 (1995–96), vol IV, pp 1805–6.
[87] HC 313 (1995–96), paras 21 and 32. For the BSE inquiry's views on ministerial accountability, see HC 887 (1999–2000), vol 15, paras 8.7, 8.8.
[88] HC Deb, 19 March 1997, col 1046. Also HL Deb, 20 March 1997, col 1055. And see ch 13 D.

For a minister knowingly to mislead Parliament is a contempt of Parliament,[89] for which he or she must resign.[90] For other forms of maladministration, the Opposition may call for a resignation, but will know that this is unlikely.

Progress towards a more open system of government is to be welcomed, but difficulties remain. One is the government's restrictive approach to the giving of evidence by civil servants (and retired civil servants) to select committees:[91] should ministers be able to censor evidence as to matters of fact which civil servants give to a committee? Another is the abusive manner in which the government controlled publication of the Scott report in 1996 and sought to dominate the initial response to it in the Commons and the media.

The British system has emphasised the need to place departments under the control of ministers, who are the link between executive and Parliament. But the ability of ministers to exercise control is limited and may be misused. An independent means of scrutinising administration is provided by the Parliamentary Ombudsman.[92] Remarkably, the doctrine of ministerial responsibility was used as an argument *against* creating both the Ombudsman in 1967, and the present select committees of the Commons in 1979 – fortunately on each occasion without success. In fact, at any given moment the boundaries of ministerial responsibility are not necessarily drawn in the right place.[93] The principle of accountable government is ultimately more important than ministerial responsibility. If there appears to be any conflict between the two, the former principle ought to prevail.

Ministerial responsibility and the courts

The courts play no part in determining the duty of ministers to Parliament to account for themselves and their departments, but judicial decisions may take account of the practice of Parliament in interpreting legislation. Thus, by legislative practice, administrative powers are usually vested in a specified minister. Does this mean in law that only the minister may exercise these powers?

> In *Carltona Ltd* v *Commissioners of Works*, an order to requisition a factory was issued under defence regulations by an assistant secretary in the Ministry of Works, and it was challenged on the ground that the relevant minister had not personally considered the matter. The order was upheld by the court. Lord Greene MR said that government could not be carried on unless civil servants could take decisions on behalf of the minister. 'Constitutionally, the decision of such an official [i.e. the assistant secretary] is, of course, the decision of the minister. The minister is responsible. It is he who must answer before Parliament for anything that his officials have done under his authority.'[94]

While therefore a minister's powers may in law be exercised by civil servants and it is not necessary to establish a formal delegation of authority to them (in the absence of a statutory provision requiring such delegation),[95] the courts have maintained that the minister remains responsible to Parliament. However, there may be cases where

---

[89] See ch 11 A. Whether or not ministers had knowingly misled Parliament was a central issue in the Scott inquiry.

[90] HC 313 (1995–96), para 34; HC 67 (1996–97), para 3; *Ministerial Code*, para 1. iii; and see HC Deb, 18 July 1995, col 457.

[91] See *Departmental Evidence and Response to Select Committees*, paras 37–75. See ch 13 D.

[92] Ch 29 D.

[93] Fulton Report on the Civil Service, Cmnd 3638, 1968, para 190.

[94] [1943] 2 All ER 560, 563. Also *Lewisham MB* v *Roberts* [1949] 2 KB 608; *R* v *Skinner* [1968] 2 QB 700; and *Re Golden Chemical Products Ltd* [1976] Ch 300. See ch 13 D.

[95] *Commissioners of Customs and Excise* v *Cure & Deeley Ltd* [1962] 1 QB 340.

from the nature of the power or because of an express statutory provision the general principle does not apply and powers must be exercised personally by the minister.[96] Where a statutory duty is vested in one minister, he or she may not adopt a policy whereby decisions are effectively made by another minister.[97]

Judicial discussion of ministerial responsibility has generally occurred when an individual has sought judicial review of a decision by a minister or department. In such proceedings, the legality of the decision may be questioned, but judges may not substitute their view of the merits of the decision for that taken by the minister. When an applicant for review fails to establish any matters that go to legality, the judge may comment that the court may not intervene in matters for which the minister is accountable to Parliament. Such statements were made in 1915, when the House of Lords held, regarding a public inquiry into the compulsory purchase of private property, that the owner was entitled to be heard at the inquiry but had no right to a hearing in person before the minister.[98] Similar statements have often been made, most recently in 2001 when the House of Lords held that statutory decision making in certain town planning and compulsory purchase matters did not breach article 6 of the European Convention on Human Rights.[99] However, while a minister's decision is a matter for which he or she is responsible to Parliament, it is wholly incorrect to argue that, because the minister is responsible for the decision, therefore the decision is not subject to judicial review.

For many decades of the 20th century, before the emergence of judicial review in its present form, the development of administrative law was impeded by the fact that some courts relied on ministerial responsibility as a reason for not reviewing the legality of ministers' decisions.[100] In contrast, the rapid evolution of administrative law since 1980 may have been influenced by the failure of Parliament to take adequate steps to enforce the accountability of ministers.[101] Today, it is accepted that judicial review and ministerial responsibility serve different purposes and are not mutually exclusive.[102]

Devolution and ministerial responsibility

This chapter has been concerned with the customs and practices relating to the responsibility of UK ministers at Westminster. It must not be supposed that what is described here applies to the new Parliament for Scotland or the Assemblies in Northern Ireland and Wales. As we have seen, the three forms of devolution differ a great deal, both from each other and from the Westminster model.[103] In Scotland, where the structure is closest to that at Westminster, the Scottish ministers may not continue in office if Parliament resolves that it has lost confidence in the Executive[104] and Parliament is developing its own procedures for calling Scottish ministers to account for their departmental functions. The position in Wales differs in that the Assembly is in law, subject

---

[96] E.g. Immigration and Asylum Act 1999, s 70(1)(a), s 570(3)(b), s 570(6)(b). And see *R v Home Secretary, ex p Oladehinde* [1991] 1 AC 254.

[97] *Lavender and Son Ltd v Minister of Housing* [1970] 3 All ER 871.

[98] *Local Government Board v Arlidge* [1915] AC 120; ch 30 B. In similar vein, see also *Johnson and Co (Builders) Ltd v Minister of Health* [1947] 2 All ER 395, 400 and *Liversidge v Anderson* [1942] AC 206.

[99] *R (Alconbury Developments Ltd) v Environment and Transport Secretary* [2001] 2 All ER 929.

[100] See J D B Mitchell [1965] PL 95; and Dicey, *Law of the Constitution*, app 2.

[101] See, e.g., *R v Home Secretary, ex p Fire Brigades' Union* [1995] 2 AC 513, 572–3 and 575 (Lord Mustill).

[102] See *R v IRC, ex p National Federation of Self-Employed* [1982] AC 617, 644 and *R v Home Secretary, ex p Fire Brigades' Union* [1995] 2 AC 513, 572–3 and 575.

[103] Ch 3 B; and Burrows, *Devolution*, pp 82–90.

[104] Scotland Act 1998, s 45(2). And see the *Scottish Ministerial Code*.

to delegation of powers to the First Secretary and other secretaries, itself the executive decision-maker.[105] In Northern Ireland, the structure of government is based on an elaborate scheme of power sharing and this necessarily affects the operation of ministerial responsibility.

---

[105] In the Government of Wales Act 1998, s 56, the term 'accountability' is used in relation to functions exercised by the Assembly First Secretary and other secretaries. No definition is offered, but by s 56(7) Assembly members must be able to question the secretaries about use of the Assembly's functions in fields in which they are accountable.

Chapter 8

THE UNITED KINGDOM AND
THE EUROPEAN UNION

The European Economic Community was created in 1957, the original six member states being West Germany, France, Italy, Belgium, Netherlands and Luxembourg. It was not until 1973 that Britain became a member, along with the Republic of Ireland and Denmark. There are now 15 member states of what has become the European Union with an expectation that this may eventually become 27.[1] From the earliest days membership has caused great constitutional anxiety to some in Britain, despite the fact that the United Kingdom allegedly has the most flexible and the only unwritten constitution among the member states. Nevertheless, attempts to challenge entry were made on the ground that it constituted an abuse of the prerogative treaty-making power to the extent that it would allegedly undermine the sovereignty of Parliament[2], and on the ground also that the Treaty would breach art 18 of the Treaty of Union of 1707.[3] More recently the renegotiation of the Treaty at Maastricht in 1992 led to further challenges in the British courts, an unsuccessful attempt being made to prevent the government from ratifying it.[4] But if British membership has caused constitutional difficulties of a legal nature, this is as nothing when compared with the controversies of a political nature which it has generated. Thus political parties have been divided, constitutional conventions have been formally and informally suspended, and the only national referendum in the 20th century was held in 1975 on continued membership of what was then the EEC.[5] There is no sign of the controversy abating, with the first election of the 21st century being dominated by the question of British membership of the European single currency, on which the Labour government has promised to hold a referendum before taking any decision about entry.

Apart from enlargement, the EEC has undergone many significant changes since its formation in 1957. One of these was the Single European Act of 1986,[6] although this is now overshadowed by the changes wrought at Maastricht in 1992 which led in the Treaty on European Union to substantial revisions of the EC Treaty and the creation of new structures and procedures.[7] The Maastricht Treaty provides a number of objectives for the EU, which include the strengthening of social and economic cohesion, the implementation of a common foreign and security policy, the introduction of a

---

[1] The full list of member states, apart from those already mentioned, includes Greece, Spain, Portugal, Sweden, Austria and Finland.
[2] *Blackburn v A-G* [1971] 1 WLR 1037. See ch 12 D.
[3] *Gibson v Lord Advocate* 1975 SLT 134. See ch 4 D.
[4] *R v Foreign Secretary, ex p Rees-Mogg* [1994] QB 552. See G Marshall [1993] PL 402, and also R Rawlings [1994] PL 254, 367.
[5] Referendum Act 1975. See also Cmnd 5925, 1975 and 6251, 1975.
[6] Cm 372, 1986. See European Communities (Amendment) Act 1986. The Single European Act increased the scope for decision-making by majority vote, dispensing with the unanimity rule in many areas.
[7] See J C Piris (1994) 19 EL Rev 447 and J A Usher (1993) 14 Statute Law Rev 28. See also European Communities (Amendment) Act 1993.

common citizenship[8] and the development of close cooperation on matters relating to justice and home affairs.[9] The Treaty also provides that the EU shall respect the national identities of its member states, as well as fundamental rights as guaranteed by the European Convention on Human Rights and 'as they result from the constitutional traditions common to the member States'.[10] But the Treaty also contains a number of important amendments to the EC Treaty, which, on the one hand, increase the opportunity for law making by majority or qualified majority voting by the Council and, on the other, increase the power of the Parliament in the legislative process. It also adds a number of Protocols to the EC Treaty, dealing with matters such as the establishment of the European Central Banks as well as European Monetary Union. Other important changes were made or proposed by the Treaties of Amsterdam in 1997 and Nice in 2000.[11] One effect of recent changes is that the articles of the EC Treaty have been re-numbered; the new numbers are used in this chapter unless the contrary is indicated.

EC law has now become a vast subject with an ever-expanding literature. It is calculated to grow even larger as the powers of the Community grow and as its institutions become more powerful. In this chapter we are concerned principally with the consequences of EC membership for the constitutional law of the United Kingdom, for as we shall see there is a distinctive EC constitutional law, the fundamentals of which were in place before Britain's accession in 1973, but which makes claims that are not easy for the British public lawyer, schooled in the traditions of Dicey and others, to embrace. Although the focus is thus on the European impact on the UK constitution, it is necessary to deal first with the institutions and law-making process of the Community and with the relationship between the various sources of EC law and domestic law.[12] The most important constitutional questions clearly relate to the sovereignty of Parliament (politically as well as legally). Although the matter has been considered by the House of Lords on several occasions, it remains to be settled as a matter of English and Scottish constitutional law precisely where legal sovereignty ultimately resides, so long as the United Kingdom remains in membership of the European Community.

A. European Community institutions

There are five principal institutions of the EC, which is now said to constitute one of the three pillars of the EU (the others being (a) the common foreign and security policy and (b) police and judicial cooperation in criminal matters).[13] Art 7 of the EC Treaty provides that the tasks entrusted to the Community are to be carried out by the European Parliament, the Council, the Commission, the Court of Justice and the

---

[8] See esp EC Treaty, art 19 (every EU citizen residing in a member state of which he is not a national to have the right to vote and stand as a candidate at elections of the state in which he resides under the same conditions as nationals of that state). And ch 20 A.

[9] TEU, art 2.

[10] TEU, art 6. See J Weiler and N Lockhart (1995) 32 CML Rev 51.

[11] On Amsterdam, see Duff (ed), *The Treaty of Amsterdam*; and on Nice, see A Dashwood (2001) 26 EL Rev 215. See also European Communities (Amendment) Acts 1998 and 2001, dealing with Amsterdam and Nice respectively. But by the end of 2001 the Nice Treaty had not been formally ratified.

[12] For fuller treatment of these matters, see Douglas-Scott, *The Constitutional Law of the European Union*; Hartley, *The Foundations of EC Law*; Mathijsen, *A Guide to EC Law*; and Weatherill and Beaumont, *EC Law*. Also valuable are Craig and de Burca, *EC Law: Text, Cases and Materials* and Tridimas, *The General Principles of EC Law*.

[13] HC 642–I (1992–93), para 25.

Court of Auditors. The Council is not to be confused with the European Council, which consists of heads of state or government and meets at least twice a year to 'provide the Union with the necessary impetus for its development'.[14] Other institutions include the Economic and Social Committee and the Committee of the Regions,[15] while in the field of social policy law-making activity is, to an extent, delegated to the so-called social partners.[16] The Parliament is listed as the first Community institution, but it is not the most powerful, although its role has become more prominent since 1957, particularly after the amendments to the EC Treaty in 1992 and again in 1997.

The Commission

1 *Composition.* The Commission consists of 20 members,[17] appointed for renewable periods of five years.[18] There must be at least one Commissioner from each member state, with a maximum of two Commissioners with a common nationality. In practice two Commissioners are nominated by the larger states (France, Germany, Italy, Spain and the United Kingdom), with the remaining ten states nominating one Commissioner each.[19] The practice in the UK (where nominations are made by the Prime Minister) is for Commissioners to be senior political figures, the convention being that one should have a record of service in the Conservative party and the other in the Labour party. Each Commissioner is responsible for one or more of the 24 departments, known as Directorates-General, such as Industry, Employment, Industrial Relations and Social Affairs, Agriculture and Environment. The President of the Commission is nominated by the member states, though 'by common accord' and only after consulting the Parliament. Once nominated both the President and the other members of the Commission are 'subject as a body to a vote of approval by the European Parliament', following which they are appointed again 'by common accord of the governments of the member states'.[20] The Parliament thus has no power to veto an individual nomination to the Commission, which must be accepted or rejected as a whole. But Commissioners may be removed from office by the Court of Justice on a reference by the Council or the Commission if they no longer fulfil the conditions required for the performance of their duties or if guilty of serious misconduct.[21] In dramatic circumstances, the Commission resigned en bloc in March 1999 following allegations of corruption and nepotism levelled against some of them.[22]

2 *Functions.* The Commission – which works under the political guidance of the President – has two principal functions under the Treaty.[23] The first is to initiate proposals for legislation, to be considered by the Council and the Parliament. In this way the Commission plays a central role in the development of Community policy in the different areas of its competence and in initiating legislative proposals to give effect to that policy. In doing so it consults widely with pressure groups, both at Community

[14] TEU, art 4.
[15] EC Treaty, art 7.
[16] EC Treaty, art 137. See *Case T-135/96, UEAPME v Council* [1998] IRLR 602; B Bercusson (1999) 28 ILJ 153; L Betten (1998) 23 EL Rev 20.
[17] EC Treaty, art 213.
[18] EC Treaty, art 214, to be amended by the Treaty of Nice, art 2.
[19] After further enlargement, this will change: see Mathijsen, p 91.
[20] EC Treaty, art 214(2), to be amended by the Treaty of Nice, art 2.
[21] EC Treaty, art 216.
[22] See Weatherill and Beaumont, pp 1059–64.
[23] For the main functions of the Commission, see EC Treaty, art 211; other powers are found elsewhere in the Treaty, e.g. art 39.

and national level.[24] However, Commission initiatives are not always endorsed by the Council, particularly where the unanimity of the Council is required.[25] The Commission's second main function is to ensure that the provisions of the Treaty, as well as Community law generally, are implemented and applied. This may mean initiating enforcement proceedings in the Court of Justice against any member state which is in breach of the EC Treaty or which has failed to implement directives or regulations.[26] So in case *C-382/92, Re Business Transfers: EC Commission v UK*[27] enforcement proceedings were initiated in respect of failure to implement directives protecting workers in the event of business restructuring; and in *Case C-222/94, EC Commission v UK*[28] proceedings were initiated in respect of a failure to implement correctly a directive on television broadcasting.[29] In exercising their functions, members of the Commission are required to act 'in the general interest of the Community' as a whole and to be 'completely independent in the performance of their duties'.[30] Specifically, they must 'neither seek nor take instructions from any government or from any other body'.[31]

The Council

1 *Composition and functions.*   The Council consists of political representatives of the member states, each being represented by a minister who is 'authorised to commit the government of that member state'.[32] The representative at any particular session will depend on the subject of the meeting, so that for example on transport matters the United Kingdom representative will be a minister with responsibility for transport. The Presidency of the Council rotates between member states every six months,[33] and the Council meets when convened by the President or at the request of one of its members or the Commission.[34] The Council's functions include the coordination of general economic policies of member states. It also has a pivotal role in the legislative process, in the sense that it must approve Commission initiatives and indeed is in a real sense the principal legislative authority within the Community,[35] although unusually for a 'legislative' body its deliberations are not in public. The Council is assisted by the Committee of Permanent Representatives (COREPER) which is responsible for preparing the work of the Council and carrying out tasks assigned to it.[36] In practice Commission proposals are referred to COREPER for consideration before they are formally considered by the Council itself. Indeed, although all decisions must be taken by ministers, on less important matters they may be taken without debate if they have been agreed to by COREPER. The Commission is represented at all meetings of both the Council and COREPER.[37]

---

[24] See A B Philip, 'Pressure Groups and Policy Making in the European Community', in Lodge (ed), *Institutions and Policies of the European Community*. On the role of advisory committees, see G J Buitendijk and M P C M Van Schendelen (1995) 20 EL Rev 37.
[25] On voting procedures in the Council, see p 123 in this chapter.
[26] EC Treaty, art 226. See pp 125–6 below
[27] [1995] 1 CMLR 345. For the sequel, see SI 1995 No 2587. See also *R v Trade and Industry Secretary, ex p UNISON* [1997] 1 CMLR 459. See further M Radford and A Kerr (1997) 60 MLR 23.
[28] [1996] 3 CMLR 793.
[29] See also *Case C-246/89, Commission v UK* [1991] ECR I-4585.
[30] EC Treaty, art 213(2).
[31] Ibid.
[32] EC Treaty, art 203.
[33] EC Treaty, art 203.
[34] EC Treaty, art 204.
[35] D Curtin (1993) 30 CML Rev 17.
[36] EC Treaty, art 207.
[37] See generally Noel, *Working Together – The Institutions of the European Community*, p 38.

2 *Procedure and transparency.*   In performing its functions the Council may act by a majority of its members, although usually it will be required to act by a qualified majority vote or in some cases unanimously.[38] On a qualified majority vote (QMV), the votes of each country are weighted broadly by population, with France, Germany, Italy and the United Kingdom each having ten out of a total of 87 votes.[39] Where QMV is required, acts of the Council require at least 62 votes before they may be adopted, which means that no one country can veto any Commission initiative. In some cases where QMV operates, the proposal must also be supported by ten states. Although there has been an extension of the areas in which the Council can act by QMV, there remain important areas where unanimity is required and where one country does have a power of veto; this problem has arisen in the approximation of laws affecting social policy, where the unanimity of the Council continues to be required for measures on matters such as the social protection of workers and the protection of workers where their contracts of employment are terminated.[40] By EC Treaty article 255, any citizen of the Union, and any natural or legal person residing or based in the Union, has 'a right of access' to documents of the Parliament, Council and Commission. The principles governing access are to be determined by the Council.[41] Moreover, Commission staff are entitled to the protection of article 10 of the ECHR (freedom of expression), this does not permit them to disclose information in breach of staff regulations.[42]

European Parliament

1 *Composition.*   The status and powers of the European Parliament have greatly increased since its inception. In 1973 the Parliament was indirectly elected, Britain's delegation including members of both Houses of Parliament. Now it is elected for periods of five years by direct universal suffrage,[43] with the number of representatives elected in each state varying according to the population of the state in question. There are 626 seats in the unicameral Parliament, made up as follows: Austria, 21; Belgium, 25; Denmark, 16; Finland, 16; France, 87; Germany, 99; Greece, 25; Ireland, 15; Italy, 87; Luxembourg, 6; Netherlands, 31; Portugal, 25; Spain, 64; Sweden, 22; and United Kingdom, 87.[44] The EC Treaty emphasises the importance of political parties as a factor for integration within the EU, on the ground that they 'contribute to forming a European awareness and to expressing the political will of the citizens of the Union'.[45] But there are no European political parties as such, although parties in the European Parliament are placed in nine political groupings. The Labour party belongs to the Party of European Socialists along with other socialist and social democratic parties; the Conservative party forms part of the European People's Party; and the Liberal Democrats take part in the European Liberal Democratic and Reformist Group.[46] Elections

---

[38] EC Treaty, art 205.

[39] These weightings will change on 1 January 2005 as a result of the proposed enlargement of the Community.

[40] EC Treaty, art 137(3).

[41] See Regulation 1049/2001/EC. For fuller treatment, see Douglas Scott, ch 3.

[42] *Case C-274/99P, Connolly v Commission* [2001] 3 CMLR 1491.

[43] See European Parliamentary Elections Act 1978, amended by the European Parliamentary Elections Act 1999.

[44] It is proposed that the number of representatives of existing member states will be reduced in 2004 to make way for the new member states. It is anticipated that membership will increase to 732.

[45] EC Treaty, art 191.

[46] See Day, *Directory of European Union Political Parties.*

in Great Britain are conducted on the basis of a regional list system, by which the country is divided into 11 electoral regions (the number of members returned varying according to the size of the region), with votes being cast for registered parties rather than candidates. Seats are then allocated to individuals on the party lists (in the order in which they appear on the list) to reflect the votes cast in favour of each party in the region in question. So the more votes cast for a party, the larger the number of seats it will be allocated. Three members are elected from Northern Ireland by single transferable vote.

2 Functions. The European Parliament has been said to represent 'the principal form of democratic, political accountability in the Community system'.[47] Its most important functions relate to its role in the legislative process on the one hand, and its powers in relation to the Community budget on the other. So far as the former is concerned, we have seen that the Council is the principal legislative body of the Community; the focus in recent years has been not to substitute the Parliament for the Council but to develop a system which would enable the Parliament to play a fuller part in the law-making process.[48] Initially the Parliament enjoyed only a consultative status and this remains the case in a number of areas. But a failure to consult could nevertheless lead to the annulment of an instrument[49] and the Court of Justice has 'consistently held that the duty to consult the Parliament in the cases provided for by the Treaty includes a require-ment that the Parliament be re-consulted on each occasion on which the text finally adopted, viewed as a whole, departs substantially from the text on which the Parlia-ment has already been consulted'.[50] Treaty amendments introduced at Maastricht and Amsterdam significantly extend the power of the Parliament in a number of areas. The most important of these is the co-decision procedure (now in article 251) under which Council Decisions are submitted to both the Council and the Parliament, with the assent of the Parliament being required if the proposal is to be accepted. Although the pro-cedure by no means applies to all Commission proposals, it does nevertheless apply in a number of controversial areas relating to the internal market and to social policy[51] and it is to be further extended by the Treaty of Nice of 2000.[52] So far as the budget is concerned, this must be adopted by the Parliament which, acting by a majority of its members and two-thirds of the votes cast, is empowered to reject it 'if there are important reasons'.[53] It can adopt amendments or propose modifications which it may ultimately insist on being carried. The Parliament has powers to question and censure the Commission,[54] although it has no power to censure individual Commissioners. It is required to appoint an ombudsman to investigate maladministration by Community institutions.[55]

[47] *Matthews* v *UK* 1999 28 EHRR 361. It was held in this important case that the European Parliament was a legislature for the purposes of Article 1 (3) of the First Protocol to the European Convention on Human Rights and that the United Kingdom was in breach of the article for failing to make provision permitting the applicant – a British citizen resident in Gibraltar – to vote in the 1994 elections to the European Parliament.

[48] D Curtin (1993) 30 CML Rev 17.

[49] *Case C-21/94, Re Road Taxes: European Parliament* v *EU Council* [1996] 1 CMLR 94.

[50] *Case C-417/93, Re: Continuation of the Tacis Programme: European Parliament* v *EU Council* [1995] ECRI-1185 at p 1213. See earlier *Case 138/79, SA Roquette Frères* v *EC Council* [1980] ECR 3333.

[51] For a good account, see Weatherill and Beaumont, pp 117–43.

[52] See A Dashwood (2001) 26 EL Rev 215. Also on Nice, J Wouters (2001) 26 EL Rev 342.

[53] EC Treaty, art 272.

[54] EC Treaty, arts 197 and 201 respectively.

[55] EC Treaty, art 195.

The European Court of Justice[56]

1 *Composition and jurisdiction.*   The function of the Court (ECJ) is to 'ensure that in the interpretation and application of [the] Treaty the law is observed'.[57] It consists of one judge for each member state and may sit in chambers (of 3 or 5 judges) or in a Grand Chamber (of 11 judges) as provided by its own statute, which is annexed as a protocol to the EU Treaty.[58] The Court is assisted by eight Advocates-General, an office without parallel in the United Kingdom.[59] Under art 222, the duty of the Advocates-General is to make reasoned submissions on cases brought before the Court in order to assist the Court in the performance of its tasks. These submissions will include an assessment of the legal position in the matter referred for determination, an assessment which will often be endorsed by the Court. The submissions of the Advocates-General are reported along with the judgment of the Court. Both judges and Advocates-General are appointed from among people who are eligible for the highest judicial offices in their respective countries and appointments are made 'by common accord of the Governments of the member states for a term of six years'.[60] Every three years there is a partial replacement of both the judges and the Advocates-General, although retiring judges and Advocates-General are eligible for reappointment. The judges elect the President of the Court from among their number for a period of three years, a retiring President being eligible for re-election.[61] There is now a Court of First Instance attached to the ECJ to hear and determine a defined class of cases, the aim being to reduce the pressure of work on the ECJ itself, but to which there is a right of appeal on a point of law. The Court of First Instance deals with a 'wide and important' range of matters[62] and its jurisdiction is to be extended by the Treaty of Nice.[63]

Cases may be brought before the Court in a number of ways. First, as already suggested, proceedings may be brought by the Commission against a member state where it considers that the state has failed to comply with a Treaty obligation.[64] However, if the Commission considers that a member state has failed to fulfil a Treaty obligation, it must first deliver a reasoned opinion on the matter after giving the state concerned an opportunity to submit its observations. It is only if the state does not comply with the opinion that the Commission may bring the matter before the Court.[65] Secondly, one state may initiate proceedings against another where the former considers that the latter has failed to comply with a Treaty obligation.[66] Before doing so the matter must first be referred to the Commission, which will deliver a reasoned opinion in this

---

[56] For the work of the ECJ, see D Edward (1995) 20 EL Rev 539. For its jurisprudential approach, see T Tridimas (1996) 21 EL Rev 199. And see generally, Brown and Kennedy, *The Court of Justice of the European Communities*.

[57] EC Treaty, art 220.

[58] EC Treaty, art 221.

[59] See A Dashwood (1982) 2 LS 202.

[60] EC Treaty, art 223.

[61] Ibid.

[62] L Neville Brown (1995) 32 CML Rev 743.

[63] See EC Treaty, art 225.

[64] EC Treaty, art 226. Liability under art 226 arises whatever the agency of the state whose action or inaction is the cause of the failure to fulfil its obligations, even in the case of a constitutionally independent institution: *Case 77/69, EC Commission* v *Belgium* [1970] ECR 237 (difficulty in securing parliamentary approval because Parliament had been dissolved). See A C Evans (1979) 4 EL Rev 442, and A Dashwood and R White (1989) 14 EL Rev 388.

[65] See *Case 293/85, EC Commission* v *Belgium* [1988] ECR 305, and *Case 74/82, EC Commission* v *Ireland* [1984] ECR 317.

[66] See *Case 141/78, France* v *UK* [1979] ECR 2923.

situation too. Where the ECJ finds that a state has failed to comply with a Treaty obligation, 'the state shall be required to take the necessary measures to comply with the judgment of the Court',[67] and failure to do so could lead to subsequent proceedings before the Court initiated by the Commission with a view to imposing a financial penalty on the state.[68] Apart from actions brought against member states, it is possible for the ECJ 'to review the legality' of measures adopted by the different Community institutions,[69] in proceedings which may be commenced by 'a member state, the European Parliament, the Council or the Commission on grounds of lack of competence, infringement of an essential procedural requirement, infringement of [the] Treaty or of any rule of law relating to its application or misuse of powers'.[70] In some circumstances, a natural or legal person may challenge decisions which are either addressed to them personally or are of 'direct and individual concern' to him or her where addressed to another.[71] In the highly publicised *Case C-84/94, UK v EU Council*[72] the British government unsuccessfully argued that the Working Time Directive (93/104/EC) exceeded the power under what was then art 118a to make by way of qualified majority measures designed to encourage improvements, especially in the working environment, as regards the health and safety of workers.[73] If the action under art 230 is well founded the Court shall declare the act concerned to be void.[74] It may be possible in some cases to challenge the validity of a Community instrument in national courts.[75]

2 *Article 234.* Apart from proceedings brought against member states or Community institutions, the Court also has jurisdiction under art 234 (previously article 177) to give preliminary rulings concerning the interpretation of the Treaty, the validity and interpretation of acts of the institutions (and of the European Central Bank), as well as other matters.[76] A preliminary ruling may be sought by a national court or tribunal where the court or tribunal 'considers that a decision on the question is necessary to enable it to give judgment'.[77] In the case of a court or tribunal 'against whose decisions there is no judicial remedy under national law', the court or tribunal must bring before the ECJ for a ruling any question on a matter which is necessary for it to give judgment.[78] Where a ruling is sought, it is done on the basis of specific questions, the

---

[67] EC Treaty, art 228(1). In the *Factortame* affair (pp 129–31, 141 below), secondary legislation was introduced to remove the discriminatory effect of the vessel registration scheme set out in the Merchant Shipping Act 1988. See note 102 below.

[68] EC Treaty, art 228(2).

[69] On the scope of reviewable acts, see *Case 22/70, EC Commission v EC Council* [1971] ECR 263, and *Case 34/86, EC Council v Parliament* [1986] ECR 2155. Cf *Cases C-181 and 248/91, Parliament v EC Council and Commission* [1993] ECR I-3685.

[70] EC Treaty, art 230. This includes a power to review acts of the Parliament. See *Case 294/83, Les Verts v Parliament* [1986] ECR 1339.

[71] EC Treaty, art 230. See *Case C-321/95P, Greenpeace International v Commission* [1998] ECR I-1651.

[72] [1996] 3 CMLR 671. Other important cases include *Case C-376/98, Germany v European Parliament* [2000] All ER (EC) 769 annulling Directive 98/43 on advertising and sponsoring tobacco products.

[73] It was subsequently held that key provisions of the Directive were insufficiently precise for the Directive to have direct effect, thereby preventing workers from recovering holiday pay for the period in which the United Kingdom failed to implement the Directive: *Gibson v East Riding Council* [2000] ICR 890.

[74] EC Treaty, art 231.

[75] *Case C-408/95, Eurotunnel SA v SeaFrance* [1998] 2 CMLR 293.

[76] EC Treaty, art 234(1).

[77] EC Treaty, art 234(2).

[78] EC Treaty, art 234(3). This would apply to the House of Lords (but see *R v Employment Secretary, ex p EOC* [1995] 1 AC 1), and possibly also to bodies whose decisions are protected by a privative clause. On the meaning of a court or tribunal for this purpose, see *Case C-416/96, El-Yassini v Home Secretary* [1999] All ER (EC) 193 (immigration adjudicator a court or tribunal).

role of the ECJ being to answer these questions: the Court does not resolve the dispute between the parties, it being for the national court to apply the ruling to the facts of the case before it. Indeed, the Court 'has consistently held that under art 234 it has no jurisdiction to rule on the compatibility of national measures with Community law'.[79] Similarly, a national court or tribunal is not empowered to refer a matter unless it is pending before the court.[80] This means that the national case must be adjourned pending the ruling of the Court.

In *Bulmer Ltd* v *Bollinger SA*,[81] Lord Denning gave detailed guidance first on when 'a decision on the question is necessary to enable [a court] to give judgment' and, secondly, when in such a case the court should exercise its discretion to make a reference. As to the former, (i) the point must be conclusive of the case; (ii) substantially the same point must not have already been decided by the ECJ, unless there are reasons to believe that an earlier decision of the ECJ is wrong; and (iii) the court may decline to make a reference where the point is reasonably clear or free from doubt (*acte claire*). Lord Denning said that a reference should not be made until all the facts were determined, because it is only at that stage that it is possible to say whether it is necessary to resolve the matter. But even if a point of EC law is necessary to dispose of the case, there is no obligation to make a reference: 'The English court has a discretion either to decide the point itself or to refer it to the European court.'[82] In exercising that discretion it is to have regard to a number of factors, including (i) the length of time it may take to get a ruling; (ii) the importance of not overwhelming or overloading the ECJ; (iii) the difficulty and importance of the point; (iv) the expense to the parties of getting a ruling from the ECJ; and (v) the wishes of the parties. Although they have been very influential,[83] these guidelines have been replaced in practice by a new formulation by Lord Bingham, who before referring to *Bulmer* said:

> if the facts have been found and the Community law issue is critical to the court's final decision, the appropriate course is ordinarily to refer the issue to the Court of Justice unless the national court can with complete confidence resolve the issue itself. In considering whether it can with complete confidence resolve the issue itself the national court must be fully mindful of the differences between national and Community legislation, of the pitfalls which face a national court venturing into what may be an unfamiliar field, of the need for uniform interpretation throughout the Community and of the great advantages enjoyed by the Court of Justice in construing Community instruments. If the national court has any real doubt, it should ordinarily refer.[84]

---

[79] *Case C-458/93, Saddik* [1995] 3 CMLR 318.

[80] *Cases C-422–424/93, Zabala Erasun* v *Instituto Nacional de Empleo* [1995] All ER (EC) 758 (matter resolved by Spanish government amending the law to comply with a contested Council regulation).

[81] [1974] 1 Ch 401. See J D B Mitchell (1974) 11 CMLR 351.

[82] *Bulmer Ltd* v *Bollinger SA* [1974] 1 Ch 401, at p 423.

[83] See for example *Customs and Excise Commissioners* v *ApS Samex* [1983] 1 All ER 1042; *R* v *Pharmaceutical Society of Great Britain, ex p Association of Pharmaceutical Importers* [1987] 3 CMLR 951; *BLP Group* v *Customs and Excise Commissioners* [1994] STC 41; *Feehan* v *Commissioners of Customs and Excise* [1995] 1 CMLR 193. For Scotland, see *Prince* v *Secretary of State for Scotland*, 1985 SLT 74; *Wither* v *Cowie*, 1990 SCCR 741.

[84] *R* v *International Stock Exchange, ex p Else* [1993] QB 534, at p 545. Also *R* v *Secretary of State for Defence, ex p Perkins* [1997] 3 CMLR 310, *Booker Aquaculture Ltd* v *Secretary of State for Scotland* 2000 SC 9, and *Trinity Mirror plc* v *Commissioners of Customs and Excise* [2001] 2 CMLR 759. See Weatherill and Beaumont, pp 334–40.

B. European Community law

The unique qualities of Community law were addressed by the ECJ in several ground-breaking early decisions, including *Case 26/62, Van Gend en Loos v Nederlandse Administratie der Belastingen*,[85] in which it was noted that the EEC Treaty 'is more than an agreement which merely creates mutual obligations between the contracting states'. The point was reinforced forcefully in *Case 6/64, Costa v ENEL*,[86] a case concerning the nationalisation of the Italian electricity industry, in which the Court asserted:

> By contrast with ordinary international treaties, the EEC Treaty has created its own legal system which, on the entry into force of the Treaty, became an integral part of the legal systems of the member states and which their courts are bound to apply. By creating a Community of unlimited duration, having its own institutions, its own personality, its own legal capacity and capacity of representation on the international plane and, more particularly, real powers stemming from a limitation of sovereignty or a transfer of powers from the states to the Community, the member states have limited their sovereign rights, albeit within limited fields, and have thus created a body of law which binds both their nationals and themselves.[87]

Various principles underpin the Community legal system. The first is the principle of legality, namely that the Community 'shall act within the limits of the powers conferred upon it' by the Treaty;[88] the second is the principle of subsidiarity, whereby, in areas falling within its exclusive competence, the Community shall take action 'only if and in so far' as its objectives 'cannot be sufficiently achieved by the member states';[89] the third is what has been referred to as the principle of solidarity,[90] whereby member states shall take all appropriate measures 'to ensure fulfilment of the obligations arising out of [the] Treaty';[91] and the fourth is the principle of non-discrimination, prohibiting discrimination on the ground of nationality.[92] In addition to these principles to be found in the Treaty, the ECJ has developed principles (such as legal certainty, proportionality, equal treatment and the protection of human rights)[93] which it employs in determining points of Community law.

The supremacy of Community law

1 *The general principle.*   Within the Community legal order, EC law takes priority over national law. In *Case 6/64, Costa v ENEL*,[94] Mr Costa claimed that he was not obliged to pay for electricity supplied to him by ENEL on the ground that the supplier was an entity which had been nationalised in 1962 in breach of provisions of the EEC Treaty. The Italian court (the Giudice Conciliatore of Milan) referred to the ECJ for consideration whether Italian law violated the Treaty in the manner suggested, only to be faced with the argument by the Italian government that the reference was 'absolutely inadmissible' inasmuch as 'a national court which is obliged to apply a national law cannot avail itself of art 177 [now 234]'. In rejecting this argument, the ECJ held:

---

[85] [1963] ECR 1.
[86] [1964] ECR 585.
[87] Ibid, p 593.
[88] EC Treaty, art 5.
[89] Ibid. See A Toth (1992) 29 CML Rev 1079.
[90] See Weatherill, *Law and Integration in the European Union*, pp 45–9.
[91] EC Treaty, art 10.
[92] EC Treaty, art 12.
[93] See e.g. *Case C-331/88, Fedesa* [1990] ECR I-4023. See pp 133–4 below.
[94] [1964] ECR 585.

The integration into the laws of each member state of provisions which derive from the Community, and more generally the terms and the spirit of the Treaty, make it impossible for the states, as a corollary, to accord precedence to a unilateral and subsequent measure over a legal system accepted by them on a basis of reciprocity. Such a measure cannot therefore be inconsistent with that legal system. The executive force of Community law cannot vary from one state to another in deference to subsequent domestic laws, without jeopardising the attainment of the objectives of the Treaty.[95]

The ECJ further asserted that 'the laws stemming from the Treaty, an independent source of law, could not, because of its special and original nature, be overidden by domestic legal provisions, however framed, without being deprived of its character as Community law, and without the legal basis of the Community itself being called into question'.[96]

This case thus unequivocally declares the supremacy of Community law over inconsistent domestic law, including in particular domestic law introduced after accession.[97] Community law also takes priority over inconsistent provisions of national constitutional law. The leading case, *Case 11/70, Internationale Handelsgesellschaft v Einfuhr- und Vorratsstelle für Getreide und Futtermittel*,[98] was concerned with regulations which required applicants for export and import licences to pay a deposit which was forfeited if terms of the licence were violated. The German authorities were of the view that the system of licences violated certain principles of German constitutional law 'which must be protected within the framework of the German Basic Law'. But the ECJ disagreed and held:

Recourse to the legal rules or concepts of national law in order to judge the validity of measures adopted by the institutions of the Community would have an adverse effect on the uniformity and efficacy of Community law. The validity of such measures can only be judged in the light of Community law. In fact, the law stemming from the Treaty, an independent source of law, cannot because of its very nature be overridden by rules of national law, however framed, without being deprived of its character as Community law and without the legal basis of the Community itself being called into question.[99]

Further, 'the validity of a Community measure or its effect within a member state cannot be affected by allegations that it runs counter to either fundamental rights as formulated by the constitution of that state or the principles of a national constitutional structure'.[100] Although Community law thus prevails over even fundamental rights guaranteed by national constitutions, the ECJ did, nevertheless, hold that 'respect for fundamental rights forms an integral part of the general principles of law protected by the Court of Justice' and that 'protection of such rights, whilst inspired by the constitutional traditions common to the member states, must be ensured within the framework of the structure and objectives of the Community'.[101] On the facts it was held that the system of licences in question did not violate any such rights.

2 *EC law and the United Kingdom.* The implications of this for the United Kingdom were revealed by the *Factortame* series of cases in which the company challenged the Merchant Shipping Act 1988 and regulations made thereunder on the ground that they violated provisions of the EEC Treaty, including arts 7 and 52 (now 14 and 43

---

[95] Ibid, pp 593–4.
[96] Ibid, p 594.
[97] See also *Case 106/77, Amministrazione delle Finanze dello Stato v Simmenthal SpA* [1978] ECR 629.
[98] [1970] ECR 1125.
[99] Ibid, p 1134.
[100] See also *Case 44/79, Hauer v Land Rheinland-Pfalz* [1980] 3 CMLR 42.
[101] [1970] ECR 1125, 1134.

respectively).[102] The Act had been introduced to prevent what was called 'quota hopping' and amended the rules relating to the licensing of fishing vessels by providing that only British-owned vessels could be registered, a requirement which excluded the Spanish-owned vessels of the applicants. In judicial review proceedings in *Factortame (No 1)* the Divisional Court made a reference under art 177 (now 234) for a preliminary ruling on the issues of Community law raised by the proceedings and ordered by way of interim relief that the application of the 1988 Act should be suspended as regards the applicants. This latter order was set aside by the Court of Appeal on the ground that the court had no power to suspend the application of an Act, since 'it is fundamental to our (unwritten) constitution that it is for Parliament to legislate and for the judiciary to interpret and apply the fruits of Parliament's labours'.[103] By the time the case reached the House of Lords, however, the question of parliamentary sovereignty had been diluted, although not completely displaced. Lord Bridge said:

> If the applicants fail to establish the rights they claim before the ECJ, the effect of the interim relief granted would be to have conferred upon them rights directly contrary to Parliament's sovereign will and correspondingly to have deprived British fishing vessels, as defined by Parliament, of the enjoyment of a substantial proportion of the United Kingdom quota of stocks of fish protected by the common fisheries policy. I am clearly of the opinion that, as a matter of English law, the court has no power to make an order which has these consequences.[104]

It was also held that under English law it was not possible (at that time) to grant an interlocutory injunction against the Crown.

In the view of the ECJ, 'the full effectiveness' of Community law would be impaired 'if a rule of national law could prevent a court seised of a dispute governed by Community law from granting interim relief in order to ensure the full effectiveness of the judgment to be given on the existence of the rights claimed under community law'. It therefore followed that 'a court which in those circumstances would grant interim relief, if it were not for a rule of national law, is obliged to set aside that rule'. As a result EC law must take priority over domestic legislation, even if this means that the British courts are required to set aside a fundamental constitutional principle. However, there is nothing novel about such a conclusion, the ECJ holding on a number of occasions that the supremacy of Community law applies even in respect of provisions of national constitutional law. The position was reinforced by *Factortame (No 4)* which was concerned with whether the government was liable to the plaintiffs in damages for loss suffered as a result of the legislation.[105] It had already been held that failure to implement a directive could in some circumstances give rise to liability in damages on the part of a state to a citizen who suffered loss as a result.[106] In *Factortame (No 4)*, the ECJ held:

---

[102] For the *Factortame* litigation, see *R v Transport Secretary, ex p Factortame Ltd (No 1)* [1989] 2 CMLR 353 (CA), [1990] 2 AC 85 (HL); *Case C-213/89, R v Transport Secretary, ex p Factortame Ltd (No 2)* [1991] AC 603 (ECJ and HL); *Case C-221/89, R v Transport Secretary, ex p Factortame Ltd (No 3)* [1992] QB 680 (ECJ); *Case C-48/93, R v Transport Secretary, ex p Factortame Ltd (No 4)* [1996] QB 404 (ECJ); *R v Secretary of State for Transport, ex parte Factortame (No 5)* [2000] 1 AC 524. For proceedings by the Commission under art 169 (now 226) see *Case C-246/89, Commission v UK* [1991] ECR I-4585. For the sequel, see Merchant Shipping Act 1988 (Amendment) Order 1989, SI 1989 No 2006. For an account of the costs of the *Factortame* case, see HL Deb, 4 July 2000, WA 132.

[103] [1989] 2 CMLR 353, 397 (Lord Donaldson MR).

[104] [1990] 2 AC 85, 143.

[105] [1996] QB 404. Although the government moved quickly to repair the legislation, losses were sustained from the time the 1988 Act came into force (31 March 1989) until the offending discrimination was removed (2 November 1989).

[106] *Cases C-6&9/90, Francovich and Bonifaci v Italy* [1991] ECR I-5357. Also *Case C-91/92, Faccini Dori v Recreb Srl* [1994] ECR I-3325; Case C-261/95, *Palmisani v INPS* [1997] 3 CMLR 1356.

The fact that, according to national rules, the breach complained of is attributable to the legislature cannot affect the requirements inherent in the protection of the rights of individuals who rely on Community law and, in this instance, the right to obtain redress in the national courts for damage caused by the breach.[107]

So not only may an Act of Parliament be 'disapplied'; the courts may also be called on to make an award of damages for losses suffered as a result of its terms where the conditions for state liability are met. In *Factortame (No 5)*, the House of Lords held that the 'deliberate adoption of legislation which was clearly discriminatory on the ground of nationality and which inevitably violated [what was then] article 52 of the Treaty' was a sufficiently serious breach to give rise under Community law to a right to compensatory damages.[108]

The sources of EC law

1 *EC Treaty.* EC law takes a number of different forms. The highest form of law is the Treaty itself which not only sets out the constitution of the EC, but also deals with substantive matters, some of which give rise to rights which are directly effective in national courts. *Case 26/62, Van Gend en Loos* v *Nederlandse Administratie der Belastingen*[109] was concerned with the interpretation of what was then art 12 of the EEC Treaty, this requiring member states to refrain from introducing between themselves new customs duties, or increasing those already in force, in trade with each other. The question referred by the Dutch tribunal to the ECJ was whether the then art 12 had direct effect in the domestic courts 'in the sense that nationals of member states may on the basis of [the] article lay claim to rights which the national court must protect'. The ECJ held:

Independently of the legislation of member states, Community law . . . not only imposes obligations on individuals but is also intended to confer upon them rights which become part of their legal heritage. These rights arise not only where they are expressly granted by the Treaty, but also by reason of obligations which the Treaty imposes in a clearly defined way upon individuals as well as upon the member states and upon the institutions of the Community.[110]

But not all terms of the Treaty have direct effect in the sense that they will be enforceable by individuals in their own national courts.[111] Much will depend on the nature of the Treaty provision in question, it being stated in *Van Gend en Loos* that the then art 12 contained 'a clear and unconditional prohibition' which was unqualified 'by any reservation on the part of states which would make its implementation conditional upon a positive legislative measure enacted under national law'.[112] This made it 'ideally adapted to produce direct effects in the legal relationship between member states and their subjects'.

---

[107] [1996] QB 404, 497.
[108] *R v Secretary of State for Transport, ex parte Factortame Ltd (No 5)* [2000] 1 AC 524, at p 545 (Lord Slynn). See A Cygan (2000) 25 EL Rev 452. Article 52 is now article 43.
[109] [1963] ECR 1.
[110] Ibid, p 12.
[111] See e.g. *R v Home Secretary, ex p Flynn* [1995] 3 CMLR 397 (EC Treaty, art 7a (now 14) held not to have direct effect).
[112] [1963] ECR 1, p 13.

Among the cases in which the ECJ has held that Treaty provisions have direct effect, *Case 43/75, Defrenne v Sabena*,[113] was concerned with the then art 119 (now art 141), which provides that 'each member state shall during the first stage ensure and subsequently maintain the application of the principle that men and women should receive equal pay for equal work'. The article was said to promote a double aim, one economic and the other social, the former seeking to eliminate unfair competition and the latter furthering social objectives of the Community 'which is not merely an economic union, but is at the same time intended, by common action, to ensure social progress and seek the constant improvement of living and working conditions'.[114] The principle of equal pay formed part of 'the foundations of the Community', and art 119 was held to have direct effect even though its complete implementation 'may in certain cases involve the elaboration of criteria whose implementation necessitates the taking of appropriate measures at Community and national level'. There were, however, forms of pay discrimination which could be addressed by a court, and it was appropriate at least in those circumstances for art 119 (now art 141) to have direct effect. Even though the full implementation of art 119 (now art 141) would require legislation, the ECJ held that direct effect would apply in particular to 'those types of discrimination arising directly from legislative provisions or collective labour agreements, as well as in cases where men and women receive unequal pay for equal work which is carried out in the same establishment or service, whether private or public'. In an important qualification of its decision, however, the ECJ ruled that the effect of the decision would not in the circumstances of the case be retrospective in the sense that it could not be relied upon to permit claims concerning pay periods prior to the date of the judgment.[115]

2 *Community legislation.* The Treaty also confers law-making powers on the Community institutions, these taking a number of different forms. By art 249 'the European Parliament, acting jointly with the Council, the Council and the Commission', are empowered to 'make regulations and issue directives, take decisions, make recommendations or deliver opinions'. These different measures have different legal consequences. Thus regulations have 'general application' in the sense that they are binding in their entirety and directly applicable in all member states. Like terms of the Treaty, regulations may have direct effect, a point established in *Case 93/71, Leonesio v Italian Ministry of Agriculture*[116] which was concerned with an EEC regulation of 1969 providing a subsidy for those who slaughtered milk cows. The question for the ECJ was whether the regulation conferred on farmers a right to payment of the subsidy enforceable in national courts. In holding that it did, the Court held that, as a general principle, 'because of its nature and its purpose within the system of sources of Community law', a regulation 'has direct effect and is, as such, capable of creating individual rights which national courts must protect'. It was no excuse in this case that the national Parliament had not allocated the necessary funds to meet the costs of the subsidy, for to hold otherwise would have the effect of placing Italian farmers in a less favourable position than their counterparts elsewhere 'in disregard of the fundamental rule requiring the uniform application of regulations throughout the Community'.[117] Directives generally require implementing legislation in each member state before they give rise to enforceable obligations, the EC Treaty providing that they

---

[113] [1976] ECR 455.

[114] Ibid, p 472.

[115] See also on the temporal effect of art 141, *Case C-262/88, Barber v Guardian Royal Exchange Assurance Group* [1990] ECR I-1889. See too TEU (Protocol concerning art 141 of the Treaty establishing the European Community).

[116] [1972] ECR 287.

[117] See also *Case 128/78, Re Tachographs: Commission v UK* [1979] 2 CMLR 45.

are binding 'as to the result to be achieved', the national authorities being left 'the choice of form and methods'.[118] So 'where different options are available for and effective to achieve the objects of the Directive it is for Member States to choose between them'.[119] Decisions are binding in their entirety on those to whom they are addressed, while recommendations and opinions have no binding force.[120]

Directives also may have direct effect, the point having been established in *Case 41/74, Van Duyn v Home Office* where the ECJ said that it would be 'incompatible with the binding effect attributed to a directive by 189 (now art 249) to exclude, in principle, the possibility that the obligation which it imposes may be invoked by those concerned'.[121] The jurisprudence has developed considerably since then so that 'a member state which has not adopted the implementing measures required by [a] directive in the prescribed periods may not rely, as against individuals, on its own failure to perform the obligations which the directive entails'.[122] Another line of authority concludes that 'wherever the provisions of a directive appear, as far as their subject-matter is concerned, to be unconditional and sufficiently precise, those provisions may be relied upon by an individual against the state where that state fails to implement the directive in national law by the end of the prescribed period or where it fails to implement the directive correctly'.[123] In *Case 152/84, Marshall v Southampton and South West Hampshire AHA*,[124] it was held that art 5(1) of the Equal Treatment Directive (76/207/EEC) was directly effective, thereby allowing a woman (who had been dismissed at the age of 62 in circumstances where men would not have been dismissed until the age of 65) to bring proceedings in domestic law for sex discrimination on an issue to which domestic legislation did not then apply. It was held, however, that unlike art 141 of the Treaty (then article 119), directives have only 'vertical' rather than 'horizontal' direct effect, which means that they can be enforced in national courts only against public authorities and not against individuals.[125] On the other hand, a directive may be relied on against the state 'regardless of the capacity in which the latter is acting, whether employer or public authority'.[126]

The EC, the ECHR and fundamental rights

An issue of growing interest is the extent to which fundamental rights play a part in the developing law of the EC.[127] It is of course the case that many national constitutions

---

[118] Implementing legislation may impose greater obligations than those required by the Directive: *Case C-2/97, Societa Italiana Petroli SpA v Borsana Srl* [2001] 1 CMLR 27.

[119] *Wilson v St Helens Borough Council* [1999] 2 AC 52, per Lord Slynn.

[120] On decisions, see R Greaves (1996) 21 EL Rev 3.

[121] [1974] ECR 1337.

[122] *Case 148/78, Pubblico Ministero v Ratti* [1979] ECR 1629.

[123] *Case 8/81, Becker v Finanzamt Münster-Innenstadt* [1982] ECR 53.

[124] [1986] ECR 723. See A Arnull [1987] PL 383. See also *Case C-91/92, Faccini Dori v Recreb Srl* [1995] ECR I-3325 665; and see J Coppel (1994) 57 MLR 859.

[125] The Area Health Authority was a public authority for this purpose. See further *Case C-222/84, Johnston v Chief Constable of the RUC* [1987] QB 129 (police authority); *Case 188/89, Foster v British Gas* [1991] 2 AC 306 (nationalised industry); and *Griffin v South West Water* [1995] IRLR 15 (privatised water company). See ch 14. It has also been said that a directive may be 'relied on against organisations or bodies which are subject to the authority or control of the State or have special powers beyond those which result from the normal rules applicable to relations between individuals, such as local or regional authorities or other bodies which, irrespective of their legal form, have been given responsibility, by the public authorities and under their supervision, for providing a public service': *Joined Cases C-253/96 to C-258/96, Kampelmann v Landschaftsverband Westfalen-Lippe* [1998] IRLR 333.

[126] *Marshall*, at p 749.

[127] See Betten and Grief, *EU Law and Human Rights*.

include protection for fundamental rights, the nature of the protection varying from state to state. All member states have also ratified the European Convention on Human Rights as well as the Council of Europe's Social Charter of 18 October 1961. The EU is not a party to the ECHR and it has been held by the ECJ that the EC had no power under the treaties to accede to the ECHR,[128] as some have proposed.[129] The EU Treaty includes a clear commitment in the Preamble to the fundamental social rights as defined in the Social Charter of 18 October 1961[130] and an undertaking to 'respect fundamental rights, as guaranteed by the [European Convention on Human Rights] as they result from the constitutional provisions common to Member States'.[131] For its part, the ECJ has for some time held that 'respect for fundamental rights forms an integral part of the general principles of Community law protected by the Court of Justice'.[132] In this way the Court has been willing in a developing line of jurisprudence (i) to construe Community legal instruments in a manner which is consistent with fundamental rights;[133] and (ii) to set aside or annul decisions by Community institutions which are in breach of fundamental rights.[134] In this context, the ECHR is said to have 'special significance'[135] and must be observed by Community institutions in their dealings with their own staff.[136] National courts may also have to deal with fundamental rights when deciding matters of Community law.[137]

An important initiative in reinforcing the role of fundamental rights in EU law is the EU Charter of Fundamental Rights, adopted at Nice in December 2000. This is a wide-ranging document which is particularly important for its commitment to 'the indivisible, universal values of human dignity, freedom, equality and solidarity'. A document of 54 articles, it is divided in seven chapters, entitled respectively dignity (articles 1–5); freedoms (articles 6–19); equality (articles 20–26); solidarity (articles 27–38); citizens' rights (articles 39–46); justice (articles 47–50); and general provisions (articles 51–54). The Charter draws freely on other texts for its contents, including the ECHR and the Council of Europe's Social Charter, as well as the Community's Charter of the Fundamental Social Rights of Workers of 1989. The Nice Charter is addressed to the institutions and bodies of the Union and to the member states only when they are implementing Union law. Where the Charter includes rights which are also to be found in the ECHR, 'the meaning and scope of those rights shall be the same as those laid down' by the Convention. The Charter is not, however, legally binding (although it is said to be 'legally enforceable')[138] and is likely to have a significant influence in litigation, being relied on by the Advocate-General (although not referred to in the decision of the Court) only a few months after its adoption.[139] While there are many criticisms to be made of the Charter – which is very loosely drafted in some respects and highly qualified in others – it has nevertheless been described as 'a prelude to a European constitution'.[140]

---

[128] *Opinion 2/94, Re the Accession of the Community to the European Human Rights Convention* [1996] 2 CMLR 265.

[129] House of Lords, Select Committee on European Union, 8th Report (1999–2000), for discussion of this issue.

[130] See also EC Treaty, art 136.

[131] TEU, art 6. See also art 7 (to be amended by the Treaty of Nice, art 1).

[132] *Internationale Handelsgesellschaft* [1974] 2 CMLR 277. For a full treatment, see Craig and De Burca, ch 7; and Tridimas, ch 6.

[133] See *Case-13/94, P v S and Cornwall County Council* [1996] 2 CMLR 247.

[134] *Case C-185/95, Baustahlgewerbe GmbH v Commission* [1998] ECR I-8417.

[135] *Case C-260/89, ERT v Dimotiki Etairia Pliroforissis* [1991] ECR I-2925, para 41.

[136] *Case C-274/99P, Connolly v Commission* [2001] 3 CMLR 1491.

[137] See *Booker Aquaculture Ltd v Secretary of State for Scotland*, 2000 SC 9.

[138] K Lenaerts and E E De Smijter (2001) 38 CMLR 273, 300.

[139] See F Jacobs [2001] 26 EL Rev 331.

[140] Ibid.

C. European Community law and British constitutional law[141]

We have seen so far that the EC Treaty has created a new legal order, that the ECJ has asserted the supremacy of EC law over national law and that EC law, may have direct effect in national legal systems. In each of these respects EC law presents a challenge to traditional English (but perhaps not Scottish) constitutional law, in so far as this is deeply rooted in parliamentary supremacy and in the obligation of the courts to give effect to legislation passed by Parliament. Britain is not alone in experiencing difficulties in reconciling Community law with the principles of national constitutional law.[142] But the question of legislative supremacy is not the only potential flashpoint, with the courts being presented with difficulties of a more practical nature which some see as a challenge to their authority. Apart from the differences of style in the drafting of English and Community law,[143] there is the more serious point that British judges must determine questions of Community law in accordance with the principles laid down by and in accordance with any relevant decisions of the European Court of Justice.[144] Before considering the response of the courts, it is necessary to consider in some detail the constitutional issues presented by Community membership.

The constitutional implications of UK membership of the EC

The constitutional implications of EC membership were canvassed in a white paper published by the Labour government in 1967 which formed an important basis for the European Communities Act 1972.[145] It was pointed out that complex legislation would need to be introduced to implement measures which did not have direct effect and that further legislation would be needed to give effect to subsequent Community instruments. Legislation would also be required in the case of those provisions of Community law which are 'intended to take direct internal effect within the member states':

> This legislation would be needed, because, under our constitutional law, adherence to a treaty does not of itself have the effect of changing our internal law even where provisions of the treaty are intended to have direct internal effect as law within the participating states.[146]

The white paper further pointed out that 'the legislation would have to cover both provisions in force when we joined and those coming into force subsequently as a result of instruments issued by the Community institutions'. Although 'no new problem would be created by the provisions which were in force at the time we became a member of the Communities', a constitutional innovation would lie 'in the acceptance in advance as part of the law of the United Kingdom of provisions to be made in the future by instruments issued by the Community institutions – a situation for which there is no precedent in this country'. These instruments were said like ordinary delegated legislation to 'derive their force under the law of the United Kingdom from the original enactment passed by Parliament'.[147]

---

[141] See Jowell and Oliver (eds), *The Changing Constitution*, ch 2 (A W Bradley), and ch 3 (P Craig).
[142] See Weatherill and Beaumont, pp 443–53.
[143] See *Bulmer v Bollinger SA* [1974] Ch 401, 425.
[144] European Communities Act 1972, s 3.
[145] Cmnd 3301, 1967.
[146] Para 22.
[147] Ibid. Today this analogy is seen to be badly misconceived. Ordinarily, delegated legislation (see ch 28) does not give rise to an autonomous body of law claiming supremacy over the source of its legal authority in domestic law.

Quite whether this constitutional innovation could be successfully implemented is a question which was not resolved before the introduction of the 1972 Act. The 1967 white paper noted:

> The Community law having direct internal effect is designed to take precedence over the domestic law of the member states. From this it follows that the legislation of the Parliament of the United Kingdom giving effect to that law would have to do so in such a way as to override existing national law so far as inconsistent with it.[148]

But this merely rehearses rather than resolves the question: what happens if Parliament should legislate in a manner inconsistent with the directly effective terms of the Treaty? The answer it seemed was that 'within the fields occupied by Community law Parliament would have to refrain from passing fresh legislation inconsistent with that law as for the time being in force', although this 'would not however involve any constitutional innovation', for 'many of our treaty obligations already impose such restraints – for example, the Charter of the United Nations, the European Convention on Human Rights and GATT'.[149] But this did not provide an answer either: what would be the position of a post-accession statute which is incompatible with a subsequently introduced regulation having direct effect or a statute introduced to comply with the Treaty the terms of which are expanded in a novel and unpredictable way by the ECJ? In this context, the examples of the UN Charter or the ECHR are beside the point, for unlike the EC Treaty these provisions do not seek to create directly effective obligations but rely on implementing legislation for any obligations they generate.

The European Communities Act 1972

Britain's application for membership was made in 1967. The Treaty of Accession was signed on 22 January 1972 and was implemented by the European Communities Act 1972.[150] This deals with two central questions which were said to be 'fundamental to the structure and contents' of the Act,[151] the first being those provisions intended to embody in domestic law the provisions of Community law designed to have direct effect and the second being the provisions which did not have direct effect but where action was necessary for their implementation. So far as the former is concerned, s 2(1) of the 1972 Act, said to be 'at the heart of the Bill',[152] provides:

> All such rights, powers, liabilities, obligations and restrictions from time to time created or arising by or under the Treaties, and all such remedies and procedures from time to time provided for by or under the Treaties, as in accordance with the Treaties are without further enactment to be given legal effect or used in the United Kingdom shall be recognised and available in law, and be enforced, allowed and followed accordingly.

What this does is to provide that insofar as Community law has direct effect, it shall be enforceable in the UK courts. It is also designed to ensure that directly effective Community obligations take precedence over national law. But it does not address the question of what should happen where there is a statute which is inconsistent with directly effective Community obligations. This, however, is addressed by s 2(4) which provides (inter alia):

---

[148] Para 23.
[149] Ibid.
[150] As amended by the European Communities (Amendment) Act 1986 and the European Communities (Amendment) Acts 1993, 1998 and 2001. Also important is the European Parliamentary Elections Act 1978, esp s 6. On the interaction of these measures, see *R v Foreign Secretary, ex p Rees-Mogg* [1994] QB 552.
[151] HC Deb, 15 February 1972, col 271.
[152] Ibid, col 650.

any enactment passed or to be passed [i.e. by the Westminster Parliament], other than one contained in this part of this Act, shall be construed and have effect subject to the foregoing provisions of this section.

Together with s 2(1), this is expressly designed to mean that 'the directly applicable provisions ought to prevail over future Acts of Parliament in so far as they might be inconsistent with them'.[153] As such, s 2 is an attempt by one Parliament to fetter the continuing supremacy of another by providing that, while future Parliaments may legislate in breach of Community law, the courts must (to the extent of any inconsistency) deny it any effect.[154]

The provisions of Community law which do not have direct effect were addressed in two ways by the 1972 Act. The first was by making a number of amendments to existing legislation to bring it into line with Community law; and the second was by introducing a general power to make subordinate legislation to cover future as well as some present Community instruments. Although there was concern about the new power to make subordinate legislation, the government did not expect the power to be frequently used,[155] an expectation which was clearly unfulfilled. By s 2(2) of the 1972 Act, regulations may be introduced by a designated minister for the purpose of implementing any Community obligation. This is subject to Sched 2 which provides that regulations may not be used for a number of purposes, these being (i) an imposition of or increase in taxation; (ii) a provision having retrospective effect; (iii) a power delegating legislative authority; and (iv) a measure creating a new criminal offence punishable with imprisonment for more than two years, or punishable on summary conviction with imprisonment for more than three months or with a fine of more than level 5 on the standard scale. The power to make regulations under these provisions is exercisable by statutory instrument which, if not made following a draft being approved by resolution of each House of Parliament, is subject to annulment by either House.[156] Fresh obligations under Community law continue to be implemented by both primary and secondary legislation.[157] Although the power to make subordinate legislation has been widely construed,[158] the government must indicate in clear terms what primary legislation is being repealed or amended when this procedure is invoked.[159]

Parliamentary scrutiny of EC legislation

In addition to the need to give effect to Community law, there was also a need to put in place procedures for ensuring the accountability of ministers who were engaged in the making of new Community law, in particular where the Community instruments would have direct effect without the need for implementing legislation or other intervention by Parliament. The government expressed the view that 'Parliament should be informed about and have an opportunity to consider at the formative stage those Community instruments which, when made by the Council, will be binding in this country'.[160] Traditional parliamentary procedures, such as questions, adjournment debates and (the now discontinued) supply days, would continue to apply and an undertaking

---

[153] Ibid, col 278.
[154] See S A de Smith (1971) 34 MLR 597, H W R Wade (1972) 88 LQR 1, J D B Mitchell et al. (1972) 9 CML Rev 134, F A Trindade (1972) 35 MLR 375, G Winterton (1976) 92 LQR 591.
[155] HC Deb, 15 February 1972, col 282.
[156] For parliamentary scrutiny of delegated legislation, see ch 28.
[157] See e.g. Trade Union Reform and Employment Rights Act 1993 and SI 1995 No 2587.
[158] See *R v Trade and Industry Secretary, ex p UNISON* [1997] 1 CMLR 459.
[159] *R (on the Application of Orange Personal Communications Ltd) v Secretary of State for Trade and Industry* [2001] 3 CMLR 36.
[160] HC Deb, 15 February 1972, col 274.

was given that 'No Government would proceed on a matter of major policy in the Council unless they knew that they had the approval of the House'.[161]

Nevertheless, the government expressed the view that the traditional means of parliamentary accountability needed to be strengthened and that 'special arrangements' should be made under which the House would be 'apprised of draft regulations and directives before they go to the Council of Ministers for decision'.[162] In 1974 special committees were set up by both Houses of Parliament, now the Select Committee on European Scrutiny in the case of the Commons, and the European Union Committee in the case of the Lords. The Commons committee (which may appoint sub-committees) is empowered to examine European Community documents (a term defined to include proposed legislation) and to report its opinion on the legal and political importance of each and to consider any issue arising on any such document.[163] The revised terms of reference of the highly respected Lords' committee enable it to 'consider European Union documents and other matters relating to the European Union'. The Lords Committee also has the power to appoint sub-committees, of which there are in fact six, and it is mainly through the medium of these six sub-committees that business is conducted.[164] Debates on matters identified by the Commons Scrutiny Committee now take place in one of three European Standing Committees where ministers may make a statement and be questioned.[165]

The impact which these procedures have in the process of Community law-making is difficult to assess, although they no doubt ensure that at least some parliamentarians are well informed about European issues.[166] But in no sense do they provide effective scrutiny of EC legislation, as the Commons Procedure Committee pointed out as long ago as 1978:

> the ability of the House to influence the legislative decisions of the Communities is inhibited by practical as well as legal and procedural obstacles. The practical obstacles stem from the sheer volume of EEC legislation, the complexity of the Communities' own decision-making structure, and the very limited time available for the consideration of many of the proposals, including some of the most important. The legal and procedural obstacles include the fact that national parliaments have no right to be consulted, and the absence of direct control by national parliaments over legislation made by the Commission on its own authority. Moreover, the collective nature of decisions by the Council of Ministers necessarily weakens the responsibilities of the Government to Parliament for Council decisions to which they assent.[167]

These difficulties notwithstanding, Parliament does purport to exercise some measure of accountability on the part of ministers who participate in the Community legislative process. By a Commons resolution of 17 November 1998, no Minister of the Crown should give 'agreement' to any 'proposal for European Community legislation', '(a) which is still subject to scrutiny (that is, on which the European Scrutiny Committee has not completed its scrutiny) or (b) which is awaiting consideration by the House (that is,

---

[161] Ibid.

[162] Ibid, col 275.

[163] HC SO 143. The committee has 16 members.

[164] The sub-committees deal with Economic and Financial Affairs, Trade and External Relations (A), Energy, Industry and Transport (B), Common Foreign and Security Policy (C), Environment, Agriculture, Public Health and Consumer Protection (D), Law and Institutions (E), and Social Affairs, Education and Home Affairs (F).

[165] HC SO 119. See generally, Cygan, *The United Kingdom Parliament and European Union Legislation*. There is also now a European Committee of the Scottish Parliament with wide-ranging scrutiny functions.

[166] It has been said that 'the nature of the Community is such that it is inherently difficult to make Community decision-makers accountable to any Parliament, national or European' (D Marquand (1981) 19 Journal of Common Market Studies 223).

[167] HC 588–I (1977–78), para 4.1.

which has been recommended by the European Scrutiny Committee for consideration)'.[168] However, these obligations may be waived in the case of a proposal which is confidential, routine, or trivial, or is substantially the same as a proposal on which scrutiny has been completed. The minister may also give agreement before scrutiny is complete with the agreement of the Committee or if there are 'special reasons', although the minister should explain the reasons to the Scrutiny Committee and in some cases the House itself. It is uncertain to what extent a minister is bound by a resolution of one of the European Standing Committees and views predictably differ between government and Parliament. But ministers are unlikely to accept any formal constraint and in many cases departure from a Committee resolution is a decision which is unlikely to be taken lightly without the involvement of other ministers, thereby raising the possibility that the matter would become one of collective rather than individual responsibility.[169]

D. Response of the courts

As we have seen, the questions of parliamentary supremacy presented by Britain's membership were identified but not resolved in the pre-accession era. It would clearly be possible in principle for the United Kingdom to leave the Community and to that extent the supremacy of Parliament is preserved. But this is a theoretical point which bears no relationship to contemporary reality, any more than do claims in another context that Parliament could legislate to regain sovereignty over former colonies.[170] The real problem is whether Parliament can legislate in a manner which is expressly in defiance of Community law. Should that happen, how should the United Kingdom courts respond? It is on this question that the politicians abdicated all responsibility in the pre-accession debates. The point was made by the Lord Chancellor in 1967:

> There is in theory no constitutional means available to us to make it certain that no future Parliament would enact legislation in conflict with Community law. It would, however, be unprofitable to speculate on the academic possibility of a future Parliament enacting legislation expressly designed to have that effect. Some risk of inadvertent contradiction between United Kingdom legislation and Community law could not be ruled out.[171]

EC law and parliamentary supremacy

For the first decade after the passing of the 1972 Act, the courts vacillated between mutually conflicting positions. In *Felixstowe Dock and Railway Co v British Transport Docks Board*[172] Lord Denning commented that once a Bill 'is passed by Parliament and becomes a statute, that will dispose of all discussion about the Treaty. These courts will then have to abide by the statute without regard to the Treaty at all'.[173] Only three years later, Lord Denning appeared to change his mind. In *Macarthys Ltd v Smith*[174] the question was whether the Equal Pay Act 1970 permitted a woman to claim equal pay only with men currently in the employment of the employer or whether she could use as a comparator her male predecessor. The Court of Appeal were divided on the question: the majority (Lawton and Cumming Bruce LJJ) were of the view that

---

[168] HC Deb, 17 November 1998, col 778. Also HL Deb, 6 December 1999, col 1019. The European Committee of the Scottish Parliament considers and reports on proposed European Communities legislation and EU issues.
[169] For further discussion, see Cygan, (note 165 above).
[170] See ch 4 above.
[171] HL Deb, 8 May 1967, col 1203.
[172] [1976] 2 LlL Rep 656.
[173] Ibid, p 663.
[174] [1979] ICR 785. See T R S Allan (1983) 3 OJLS 22.

domestic law did not permit such claims, but that EC law was unclear. They were there-fore minded to make a reference under art 177 (now art 234) to determine whether equal pay for equal work under art 119 (now art 141) was 'confined to situations in which men and women are contemporaneously doing equal work for their employer'. Lord Denning was of the view that EC law permitted the woman's claim and that domestic law should be construed accordingly, saying:

> In construing our statute, we are entitled to look at the Treaty as an aid to its construction: and even more, not only as an aid but as an overriding force. If on close investigation it should appear that our legislation is deficient – or is inconsistent with Community law – by some oversight of our draftsmen – then it is our bounden duty to give priority to Community law. Such is the result of section 2(1) and (4) of the European Communities Act 1972.[175]

The ECJ confirmed the interpretation of art 119 (now art 141) which had been sug-gested by Lord Denning[176] following which the Court of Appeal sought to make it plain that the provisions of the Treaty 'take priority over anything in our English statute on equal pay which is inconsistent with art 119 (now art 141)', this priority having been 'given by our own law'. According to Lord Denning:

> Community law is now part of our law: and, whenever there is any inconsistency, Com-munity law has priority. It is not supplanting English law. It is part of our law which over-rides any other part which is inconsistent with it.[177]

Although Lord Denning appeared thus to have changed his mind, he also observed:

> Thus far I have assumed that our Parliament, whenever it passes legislation, intends to fulfil its obligations under the Treaty. If the time should come when our Parliament deliberately passes an Act – with the intention of repudiating the Treaty or any provision in it – or inten-tionally of acting inconsistently with it – and says so in express terms – then I should have thought that it would be the duty of our courts to follow the statute of our Parliament.[178]

On this basis the European Communities Act 1972, s 2, effected only a limited form of entrenchment: it would have the effect that Community law will apply in prefer-ence to any post-1972 statute and to that extent Parliament would have bound its successors. In these cases the courts would assume that Parliament had not intended to depart from Community obligations. But Lord Denning left open the possibility that Parliament might wish to assert its supremacy by stating clearly that a domestic statute is to apply notwithstanding Community law. In this case the domestic statute would displace to that extent s 2 of the 1972 Act. Further support in the early cases for the view that s 2 of the 1972 Act had only qualified the supremacy of Parliament was provided by *Case 12/81, Garland v British Rail Engineering Ltd.*[179] In an important passage which potentially goes further than Lord Denning in preserving the priority to be given to domestic legislation, Lord Diplock raised the question whether 'having regard to the express direction as to the construction of enactments "to be passed" . . . contained in section 2(4), anything short of an express positive statement in an Act of Parliament passed after January 1, 1973, that a particular provision is intended to be made in breach of an obligation assumed by the United Kingdom under a Community treaty, would justify an English court in construing that provision in a manner incon-sistent with a Community treaty obligation of the United Kingdom'.[180]

---

[175] Ibid, p 789.
[176] *Case 129/79, Macarthys Ltd v Smith* [1981] 1 QB 180.
[177] [1981] 1 QB 180, 200. See also Cumming Bruce LJ at p 201.
[178] [1979] ICR 785, 789.
[179] [1983] 2 AC 751.
[180] [1983] 2 AC 751, 771. For a more recent examination of the issues raised here, see *Thoburn v Sunderland City Council* [2001] EWCH (Admin) 934 (the market traders' case).

Factortame

The most recent and authoritative view is that expressed in the *Factortame* series of cases.[181] In *Factortame (No 1)* it was said by Lord Bridge (in upholding the Court of Appeal's refusal to grant interim relief to restrain the operation of the Merchant Shipping Act 1988 pending the outcome of the art 177 (now art 234) reference) that s 2(4) was to be regarded as having

> precisely the same effect as if a section were incorporated in Part II of the Act of 1988 which in terms enacted that the provisions with respect to registration of British fishing vessels were to be without prejudice to the directly enforceable Community rights of nationals of any member state of the EEC.[182]

As we have seen, however, the House of Lords held that they had no jurisdiction to grant the interim relief sought; on a reference under art 177, the ECJ ruled that a national court must set aside a rule of national law which precludes it from granting interim relief in a case concerning Community law. When the matter returned to the House of Lords, relief was granted, thereby restraining the operation of the Merchant Shipping Act 1988 in relation to the plaintiffs pending the final resolution of the case.[183] In a much quoted passage in *Factortame (No 2)*, Lord Bridge said:

> Some public comments on the decision of the European Court of Justice, affirming the jurisdiction of the courts of member states to override national legislation if necessary to enable interim relief to be granted in protection of rights under Community law, have suggested that this was a novel and dangerous invasion by a Community institution of the sovereignty of the UK Parliament. But such comments are based on a misconception. If the supremacy . . . of Community law over the national law of member states was not always inherent in the EEC Treaty it was certainly well established in the jurisprudence of the European Court of Justice long before the UK joined the Community. . . . Thus, whatever limitation of its sovereignty Parliament accepted when it enacted the European Communities Act 1972 was entirely voluntary. Under the terms of the Act of 1972 it has always been clear that it was the duty of a UK court, when delivering final judgment, to override any rule of national law found to be in conflict with any directly enforceable rule of Community law. Similarly, when decisions of the European Court of Justice have exposed areas of UK statute law which failed to implement Council directives, Parliament has always loyally accepted the obligation to make appropriate and prompt amendments. Thus there is nothing in any way novel in according supremacy to rules of Community law in those areas to which they apply and to insist that, in the protection of rights under Community law, national courts must not be inhibited by rules of national law from granting interim relief in appropriate cases is no more than a logical recognition of that supremacy.[184]

In this way, the House of Lords appears to have effected a form of entrenchment of s 2(4) of the 1972 Act which thereby does what no statute has done before, namely fetter the continuing supremacy of Parliament.[185] Sir William Wade refers to this as a constitutional revolution: 'The Parliament of 1972 had succeeded in binding the Parliament of 1988 and restricting its sovereignty, something that was supposed to be

---

[181] See note 102. On the question of parliamentary sovereignty, see P P Craig (1991) 11 YBEL 221; N Gravells [1989] PL 568, [1991] PL 180; and H W R Wade (1991) 107 LQR 1, (1996) 112 LQR 568.

[182] [1990] 2 AC 85, 140.

[183] [1991] 1 AC 603.

[184] Ibid, pp 658–9.

[185] See also *R v Employment Secretary, ex p EOC* [1995] 1 AC 1 where declarations were made that provisions of the Employment Protection (Consolidation) Act 1978 were incompatible with art 119 (now art 141) of the EEC Treaty and Council Directive 75/117/EEC and that other provisions of the Act were incompatible with the latter. For subsequent developments see D Nicol [1996] PL 579.

constitutionally impossible.'[186] But although this may be necessary as a matter of European integration, it is unclear whether the House of Lords in *Factortame (Nos 1 and 2)* satisfactorily dealt with the issue as a matter of domestic constitutional law; neither is it clear that the decision answers all the questions which arise. Indeed, it is open to question whether the decisions advance the matter much beyond the Court of Appeal decision in *Macarthys Ltd v Smith*.[187] It is unfortunate that in a case of such constitutional significance, the full range of constitutional authorities were not addressed in the course of argument, even if it would have been difficult for the defendants to have mounted a full frontal attack on the constitutional implications of s 2(4). But in terms of unanswered questions, what would be the position in the (admittedly unlikely) event that Parliament should say expressly (or by clear implication) that a statutory provision should apply notwithstanding any Community obligation to the contrary? Wade has argued that: 'If there had been any such provision in the Act of 1988 we can be sure that the European Court of Justice would hold that it was contrary to Community law to which by the Act of 1972 the Act of 1988 is held to be subject.'[188] But does it follow that in such a case national courts would be required to give effect to the 1972 Act rather than the 1988 Act? As a matter of British constitutional law (and regardless of what the ECJ might say), it would appear in such an eventuality that Parliament had repudiated the 'voluntary' 'limitation of its sovereignty' which it accepted when it enacted the 1972 Act (at least insofar as the 1988 Act is concerned).[189]

Parliamentary supremacy and the principle of indirect effect

Questions about parliamentary supremacy also arise, although rather less acutely, in the context of the interpretation of domestic legislation where questions are raised about its compatibility with directives. This presents problems of what is sometimes referred to as the indirect effect of directives, a matter which has given rise to a degree of inconsistency on the part of the ECJ and a degree of resistance initially on the part of the House of Lords. So far as the former is concerned, in one case (*Von Colson*),[190] a question arose about the relationship between German national law and the Equal Treatment Directive (76/207/EEC). In the view of the ECJ, 'in applying the national law and in particular the provisions of a national law specifically introduced in order to implement [a directive], national courts are required to interpret their national law in the light of the wording and the purpose of the directive'. But it is for the national court 'to interpret and apply the legislation adopted for the implementation of the directive in conformity with the requirements of Community law, insofar as it is given discretion to do so under national law'. In a more recent case (*Marleasing*),[191] the ECJ took a wider view of the application of directives, concluding now that 'in applying

---

[186] (1996) 112 LQR 568.
[187] [1979] ICR 785.
[188] (1996) 112 LQR 568, p 570.
[189] This is not to deny that such a decision would give rise to serious political and constitutional problems at Community level. But it would be for the Commission to take appropriate action by way of enforcement proceedings or otherwise, and it is perhaps in that way that any problems should be resolved rather than in the British courts.
[190] *Case 14/83, Von Colson and Kamann v Land Nordrhein-Westfalen* [1984] ECR 1891.
[191] *Case 106/89, Marleasing SA v La Comercial Internacional de Alimentación SA* [1992] 1 CMLR 305. See also *Case C-334/92, Wagner Miret v Fondo de Garantía Salarial* [1993] ECR I-6911; and *Case C-2/97, Societa Italiana Petroli SpA v Borsana Srl* [2001] 1 CMLR 27. But cf *Case C-185/97, Coote v Granada Hospitality Ltd* [1999] ICR 100, where the *Von Colson* formulation appears to have been preferred, with *Marleasing* cited as authority.

national law, whether the provisions in question were adopted before or after the directive, the national court called upon to interpret it is required to do so, as far as possible, in the light of the wording and the purpose of the directive in order to achieve the result pursued by the latter.' *Marleasing* thus involves an important reconsideration, with the domestic courts now being required to construe domestic law in line with the requirements of a directive, regardless of whether the legislation pre-dates or post-dates the directive. But it would appear that there is no overriding obligation to construe legislation in this way: the obligation arises only where it is possible to do so.[192] In some instances this plainly may not be the case.

The issue first arose for consideration by the House of Lords in *Duke v Reliance Systems Ltd*[193] which was concerned with the differential retirement ages for men and women which were permitted by UK law but which were in breach of the Equal Treatment Directive. As we have seen, however, the directive does not have horizontal direct effect and so could not be enforced in the domestic courts by someone who was not employed by a public authority. It was argued, nevertheless, that the Sex Discrimination Act 1975 should be construed so as to conform to the directive, a contention which drew the following response from Lord Templeman:

> a British court will always be willing and anxious to conclude that United Kingdom law is consistent with Community law. Where an Act is passed for the purpose of giving effect to an obligation imposed by a directive or other instrument a British court will seldom encounter difficulty in concluding that the language of the Act is effective for the intended purpose.[194]

In the *Duke* case, however, the Act in question was not passed to give effect to the directive. Indeed it was expressly intended to preserve discriminatory retirement ages and was not reasonably capable of bearing any construction to the contrary. In these circumstances, it was held that s 2(4) of the 1972 Act does not 'enable or constrain a British court to distort the meaning of a British statute in order to enforce against an individual a Community directive which has no direct effect between individuals'. In more recent decisions, however, the House of Lords has adopted a radically different approach in cases where statutory instruments had been introduced quite clearly to give effect to a directive. Indeed, in two cases the House was prepared to take the extraordinary step of implying words into the legislation quite consciously to change its literal meaning,[195] for fear that the measures would otherwise have 'failed their object and the United Kingdom would have been in breach of its treaty obligations to give effect to directives'.[196] The courts now freely refer to directives to discover 'the correct application' of domestic law[197] and in doing so provoke claims that they distort the meaning of statutes.[198] But what about legislation (primary and secondary) which covers the field occupied by a directive but which was not passed necessarily in order to implement it? The approach in *Duke* no longer appears to be followed, it now being accepted in *Webb v EMO Air Cargo (UK) Ltd*[199] (following *Marleasing*) that an English court should construe a statute to comply with a directive regardless of whether the statute was passed before or after the directive was made.

---

[192] See *Webb v EMO Air Cargo (UK) Ltd (No 2)* [1996] 2 CMLR 990.
[193] [1988] AC 618.
[194] Ibid, p 638.
[195] *Pickstone v Freemans plc* [1989] AC 66 (see A W Bradley [1988] PL 485) and *Litster v Forth Dry Dock & Engineering Co Ltd* [1990] 1 AC 546.
[196] *Litster*, ibid, at p 558.
[197] *Whitehouse v Chas A Blatchford & Sons Ltd* [2000] ICR 542. See also *A v National Blood Authority* [2001] 3 All ER 289; A Arnull (2001) 26 EL Rev 213.
[198] *Coote v Granada Hospitality Ltd* [1999] ICR 942.
[199] [1992] 4 All ER 929. See N Gravells [1993] PL 44.

The *Marleasing* principle applies only to legislation (primary or secondary), but not also to other instruments implementing a Directive. In *White v Motor Insurers' Bureau*[200] the Motor Insurance Directive was implemented by an agreement between the government and the MIB. The House of Lords held that the *Marleasing* principle cannot be stretched to the length of requiring contracts to be interpreted in a manner which would impose obligations which the contract did not impose. This was so even though the government was one of the parties to the contract. Although on the facts the agreement was found to be consistent with the requirements of the directive, this is nevertheless a highly unsatisfactory decision. It means that the rights under domestic law of the insured third party in this case are left to depend on the means by which the government elects to implement a Directive. This could be an issue in the social policy field where the EC Treaty provides expressly that directives may be implemented by collective agreements between trade unions and employers.

E. Conclusion

Whether or not Sir William Wade is correct in his assertion that a revolution has taken place,[201] British membership of the European Union continues to generate political controversy and legal uncertainty. At least three issues of constitutional law are likely to continue to be of interest. The first is the pressure towards ever closer political union in Europe and with it an enhancement of the role of the Community institutions.[202] Constitutional law will have a role to play in this process, although whether the current arrangements are adequate to the task is open to argument. So far as they apply to extending the powers of the Community, these are to be found in the European Parliamentary Elections Act 1978. This simply requires by s 6 that no treaty which provides for an increase in the powers of the European Parliament shall be ratified by the United Kingdom unless it has been approved by an Act of Parliament.[203] Second, there is the concern about what some refer to as the democratic deficit in the European Community, which takes a number of forms. But at the heart of the matter is a legislative process in which the still dominant part (the Council) is at best only indirectly elected and whose activities are in need of greater transparency. Yet it has been said persuasively by one commentator that 'neither the Council nor Parliament is capable, on its own, of assuring a satisfactory level of democratic accountability, in the complex political nexus of a constitutional order of States'.[204] The challenge for constitutional lawyers and others will be to extend the principles of liberal democracy into this important arena, while at the same time ensuring a greater degree of parliamentary accountability on the part of those who represent the United Kingdom in the process. Third, there is the matter of the constitutional base on which the whole enterprise is constructed. Although constitutional dogma has been shaken, the problem of sovereignty has not been adequately resolved; it is, however, unlikely that everyone would agree now with the view expressed in 1972 that 'the ultimate supremacy of Parliament will not be affected, and it will not be affected because it cannot be affected'.[205] Only time will tell whether this is a problem of any practical significance and, if so, whether closer political union at Community level can be built on such foundations.

---

[200] [2001] 2 CMLR 1.
[201] Cf J Eekelaar (1997) 113 LQR 185 and T R S Allan (1997) LQR 443.
[202] On some of the wider implications of this, see S Douglas-Scott (2001) 12 KCLJ 75, MacCormick, *Questioning Sovereignty*, and Weiler, *The Constitution of Europe*. Also J C Piris (1999) 24 EL Rev 557.
[203] See *R v Foreign Secretary, ex p Rees-Mogg*, note 4 above.
[204] A Dashwood (2001) 26 EL Rev 215, 220.
[205] HC Deb, 5 July 1972, col 627. See also HL Deb, 7 August 1972, col 911.

Part II

THE INSTITUTIONS OF GOVERNMENT

Chapter 9

COMPOSITION AND MEETING
OF PARLIAMENT

In this and the next two chapters, we examine the structure of Parliament, the functions of the two Houses and their privileges. Although both the House of Commons
and the House of Lords meet in the palace of Westminster, they sit separately and
are constituted on entirely different principles. The process of legislation is a matter in
which both Houses take part and the two-chamber structure is an integral part of the
parliamentary system. Within Parliament the House of Commons is the dominant House,
as it is on the ability to command a majority in the Commons that a government depends
for holding office. Under the Parliament Acts of 1911 and 1949, the formal power of
the Lords in legislation is limited to imposing a temporary veto on public Bills, a power
which may sometimes be an effective check on controversial legislation. The role of
the Lords as a revising chamber is important, especially for securing amendments to
Bills which have been subjected to closure in the Commons[1] and the House serves other
constitutional purposes. The Queen is formally also part of Parliament. Thus she opens
each session of Parliament and the royal assent is necessary for primary legislation.
These functions are performed on the advice of the government, but in very rare
circumstances the Queen may have a personal discretion to exercise in relation to
Parliament.

A. The electoral system

Before 1918 the right to vote was largely dependent on the ownership or occupation
of property. It was also affected by the ancient distinction between counties and
boroughs. For more than five centuries after Simon de Montfort's Parliament of 1265,
the English people were represented in the Commons by two knights from every county
and by two burgesses from every borough. Before the Reform Act of 1832 the franchise
was exercisable in the counties by those men who owned freehold land worth 40 shillings
per year. In the boroughs, the franchise varied according to the charter of the borough
and to local custom. In fact, many seats in the House before 1832 were controlled by
members of the landowning aristocracy who had sufficient influence by purchasing votes
or other means to nominate the successful candidates. In Scotland 'the principle of
representation', according to 'ancient rules', was said to depend on 'the payment of
direct taxes; and those who were excluded from voting for representatives, or from the
privilege of being elected, were such persons only as, while they shared in the benefits
and protection afforded by the government, contributed nothing directly towards the
expense of upholding it'.[2] Such people could nevertheless be expected to share in
other obligations of the state, such as military service in war. Acts for widening the
franchise were passed in 1832, 1867, 1884, 1918, 1928, 1948 and 1969 until today
the total electorate is over 43 million. The details of the earlier Acts have passed into

---

[1] Ch 10 A.
[2] More, *Lectures on the Law of Scotland*, vol II, pp 214–15.

history. In 1918 a uniform franchise based on residence was established for county and borough constituencies.[3] Votes for women over 30 were introduced in 1918 and in 1928 for women over 21. After 1918 various categories of person had the right to vote more than once either by reason of occupying land for business purposes or because of the right of graduates to vote in separate constituencies representing the universities. These elements of plural voting were abolished in 1948.

The franchise

The law is now contained in Part I of the Representation of the People Act 1983, which consolidated earlier legislation and which has itself been amended, notably in 1985 when the right to vote was extended to certain British citizens resident outside the United Kingdom.[4] As amended in 2000, s 1 of the 1983 Act provides that the right to vote at parliamentary elections is exercisable by all Commonwealth citizens (which in law includes all British citizens and British subjects),[5] and citizens of the Republic of Ireland who are (a) registered in the register of electors for the constituency in which they wish to vote; (b) not subject to any legal incapacity to vote (on which see below); and (c) of voting age (now 18 years or over). Under the 1983 Act a person is entitled to be registered in a constituency if he or she is resident there and is otherwise entitled to vote.[6] There is not now a qualifying period of residence before an elector may register in a particular constituency (except in Northern Ireland where the elector must be resident in the Province – not necessarily a particular constituency – for at least three months);[7] and it is no longer necessary to be resident in the constituency on a particular date (which until the 2000 amendments used to be 10 October, which was referred to as the qualifying date).

The meaning of residence for electoral purposes is governed by the 1983 Act, s 5 (as amended). This provides rather enigmatically that in determining whether someone is resident in a particular constituency, 'regard shall be had, in particular, to the purpose and other circumstances, as well as to the fact, of his presence at, or absence from, the address on that date'. A person who is staying at one place otherwise than on a permanent basis may be taken to be resident there if he or she has no home elsewhere, or not resident there if he or she does have a home elsewhere.[8] Residence is not to be taken as interrupted by reason of an absence 'in the performance of any duty arising from or incidental to any office, service or employment'; and for this purpose a temporary absence for educational purposes may be treated in the same way as a temporary absence for the performance of an aforementioned duty.[9] This means that students living away from home may register in their home constituencies or in the constituency where they are studying.[10] Specific provision is made for the registration of patients in

[3] See Butler, *The Electoral System in Britain since 1918* and, for the law and practice today, Clayton (ed.), *Parker's Law and Conduct of Elections*; also Blackburn, *The Electoral System in Britain* and Rawlings, *Law and the Electoral Process*.

[4] Representation of the People Act 1985, s 1; amended by the Political Parties, Elections and Referendums Act 2000, s 141, reducing from 20 to 15 years the period which British citizens formerly resident in this country may continue to be registered to vote.

[5] See British Nationality Act 1981, s 37; see ch 20 A below.

[6] 1983 Act, s 1 (as amended by the Representation of the People Act 2000).

[7] 1983 Act, s 4 (as amended by the Representation of the People Act 2000).

[8] 1983 Act, s 5(2) (as amended by the Representation of the People Act 2000). See *Scott v Phillips* 1974 SLT 32 (ownership of a country cottage as a second home is not enough to make the owner resident there if, on the facts, the owner's use of it is incidental to the owner's main home); and *Hipperson v Newbury Registration Officer* [1985] QB 1060 (Greenham Common women resident in peace camp for electoral purposes).

[9] 1983 Act, s 5(3), (5).

[10] See (on the law pre-2000 amendments), *Fox v Stirk* [1970] 2 QB 463.

mental hospitals, remand prisoners and homeless people.[11] In the case of the last, a homeless person may make a 'declaration of local connection' which enables him or her to be registered in the constituency where he or she 'commonly spends a substantial part' of his or her time. A person may be resident at more than one address and may be entered on the register for more than one constituency. But no one may vote more than once as an elector at a parliamentary election.[12]

The parliamentary franchise may not be exercised by:

(a)   persons who are subject to legal incapacity (such as those who because of mental illness, drunkenness or infirmity lack the capacity at the moment of voting to understand what they are about to do);[13]

(b)   persons who are neither Commonwealth citizens nor citizens of the Republic of Ireland;[14]

(c)   persons who have not attained the age of 18 by the date of the poll;[15]

(d)   persons convicted of a criminal offence and detained in a penal institution in pursuance of a sentence.[16] Remand prisoners may vote if they are on the register;[17]

(e)   persons detained in mental hospitals under statutory authority, including the Mental Health Act 1983 and the Criminal Procedure (Insanity) Act 1964;[18]

(f)   persons who are members of the House of Lords. Hereditary peers were previously disqualified; but they may now vote in a parliamentary election unless they have retained a place in Lords by virtue of the House of Lords Act 1999;[19]

(g)   persons convicted of corrupt or illegal practices at elections, the extent of disqualification depending on the nature of the offence.[20]

Perhaps the most controversial of these disqualification is (d): it is not clear why convicted prisoners should be denied the right to vote. But it has been held that this disqualification does not breach the Human Rights Act 1998.[21]

The register of electors

As already pointed out, it is a condition precedent to exercising the vote that the elector should be placed on the register of electors. The register is prepared by the registration officer of each constituency, who in England and Wales is appointed by each district council or London borough.[22] Each registration officer is required to conduct an annual canvass of the area to determine who is entitled to be on the register and for this purpose may conduct door-to-door inquiries.[23] The canvass for any year is to be conducted by reference to residence on 15 October and a revised version of the register must then be published after the annual canvass by 1 December each year.[24] But it is also possible for an elector to be added to the register between annual canvasses.

---

[11] 1983 Act, ss 7, 7A and 7B (as amended by the Representation of the People Act 2000).

[12] 1983 Act, s 1(2) (as amended by the Representation of the People Act 2000).

[13] 1983 Act, s 1(1)(b) (as amended by the Representation of the People Act 2000).

[14] 1983 Act, s 1(1)(c) (as amended by the Representation of the People Act 2000). Citizens of the European Union resident in the UK may vote and stand in local government elections and in elections to the European Parliament: see SI 1995 No 1948 and SI 1994 No 342.

[15] 1983 Act, s 1(1)(d) (as amended by the Representation of the People Act 2000).

[16] 1983 Act, s 3.

[17] On which see 1983 Act, s 7A (as amended by the Representation of the People Act 2000).

[18] 1983 Act, s 3A (as amended by the Representation of the People Act 2000).

[19] House of Lords Act 1999, s 3.

[20] 1983 Act, ss 51, 160.

[21] R (Pearson) v Home Secretary, The Times, 17 April 2001.

[22] 1983 Act, s 8.

[23] 1983 Act, ss 9, 10 (as amended by the Representation of the People Act 2000).

[24] 1983 Act, s 13 (as amended by the Representation of the People Act 2000).

The amendments to the Representation of the People Act 1983 in 2000 introduced the principle of the 'rolling register', designed to remove obstacles to registration and voting. We have thus moved from what was referred to as a 'fixed register' (amended annually) to a 'rolling register' (amended constantly): the former may be said to be more sensitive to the needs of the administration responsible for maintaining the register; and the latter more responsive to the interests of electors.

Under the new arrangements, an elector may apply to be registered at any time and the registration officer must issue alterations to the register at regular intervals.[25] So if someone moves house, for example, it is now possible to register immediately in a new constituency without the need to wait for the annual canvass. But in order to be effective for an election, a new registration must take effect before the close of nominations for candidates, a measure which can be justified as a device to prevent electoral fraud and for administrative convenience.[26] If the registration officer's decision including or excluding someone from the register is disputed,[27] an appeal lies to the county court (in Scotland to the sheriff court) and thence on a point of law to the Court of Appeal (in Scotland to the Electoral Registration Court of three judges).[28] The decision of the county court may also be reviewed on jurisdictional grounds.[29] It is the practice for electoral registers to be made available by registration officers to third parties, such as political parties for canvassing and other electoral purposes and companies which engage in direct mailing and telesales.[30] The 2000 amendments permit regulations to be made requiring registration officers to compile a full and an edited register. Electors will be permitted to have their names and addresses withheld from the latter.[31]

Manner of voting and conduct of elections

Normally voting takes place in person at the polling station assigned to the area in which the elector is resident.[32] But there are circumstances in which absent voting may take place, the term absent voting meaning voting by proxy or by post. The Representation of the People Act 2000 relaxed the rules with the aim of enabling more people to vote by post if they so wish. Under the existing rules, the registration officer must grant an application to vote by post if satisfied that the elector is registered[33] and otherwise meets prescribed statutory requirements.[34] The registration officer must also grant an application to vote by proxy where the applicant is a registered service voter, blind or suffers another physical disability; is unable to attend the polling station because of work or educational commitments; or unable to go to the polling station in person without making a journey by sea or air (as in the case of overseas voters).[35] It is likely that more flexibility and less formality in voting procedures (as well as ambitions for

---

[25] 1983 Act, s 13A (as amended by the Representation of the People Act 2000).

[26] 1983 Act, s 13B (as amended by the Representation of the People Act 2000).

[27] See SI 2001 No 341, regs 23–49.

[28] 1983 Act, ss 56–8. Additions or alterations to the register may be ordered by the High Court: *R v Hammond, ex parte Nottingham Council, The Times*, 10 October 1974. For Scotland, see *John Ferguson* 1965 SC 16.

[29] *R v Hurst, ex parte Smith* [1960] 2 QB 133.

[30] It was held in *R (Robertson) v Wakefield DC* [2002] 2 WLR 889, that the disclosure of this information containing personal details of electors is contrary to EC Directive 95/46/EC, as well as the Human Rights Act 1998 (ECHR, art 8 and First Protocol, art 3).

[31] 1983 Act, Sch 2(10) and (11) (as amended by the Representation of the People Act 2000).

[32] 1983 Act, s 19.

[32] Representation of the People Act 2000, Sch 4(3).

[34] SI 2001 No 341, Part IV. Some 1.4 million votes were cast by post at the general election in 2001, almost double the number in 1997.

[35] Representation of the People Act 2000, Sch 4(3).

internet voting) will develop in the future to encourage more people to vote, particularly in view of alarmingly low turnouts.[36] The proceedings at parliamentary elections are to be conducted in accordance with the Parliamentary Elections Rules in Schedule 1 of the 1983 Act. These detailed rules deal with the nomination of candidates, as well as the procedure to be followed at the polling station and in particular help to ensure the secrecy of the ballot.[37]

Responsibility for the official conduct of an election in each constituency rests with the returning officer, who in England and Wales in the case of a county constituency wholly contained within the area of a county council is the sheriff and in the case of a borough constituency wholly contained within a local government district is the chairman of the district council.[38] Most functions of the returning officer are, however, discharged by the registration officer or by an appointed deputy. Certain matters, for example the declaration of the poll, may be reserved to the returning officer. The official costs of an election, as distinct from the expenses of the candidates, are paid out of public funds in accordance with a scale prescribed by the Treasury. In the past, office holders who conducted elections did not always exercise their functions impartially. In the great case of *Ashby* v *White*, the Mayor of Aylesbury as returning officer wrongfully refused to allow Ashby to vote and Ashby sued him for damages. The House of Lords upheld the view of Chief Justice Holt (dissenting in the Queen's Bench) that the remedy of damages should be given. In Holt's words: 'To allow this action will make public officers more careful to observe the constitution of cities and boroughs, and not to be so partial as they commonly are in all elections.'[39] Today, officials concerned with the conduct of elections are required to carry out their duties impartially and are subject to criminal penalties if they do not, but they cannot be sued for damages if breach of official duty is alleged.[40]

B. Distribution of constituencies

Before 1832, the unreformed House of Commons was composed on the general principle that every county and borough in England and Wales was entitled to be represented by two members. A similar principle applied to Scottish representation at Westminster, subject to the limit of numbers imposed in the Treaty of Union, which led to the grouping of certain shires and royal burghs for this purpose. Representation thus depended on the status of the unit of local government and bore no regard to population. Counties such as Cornwall, which contained many tiny boroughs, were grossly over-represented by comparison with areas of rapidly growing industrial population. From the Reform Act 1832 onwards, successive measures of redistributing constituencies to remove glaring differences were undertaken, usually at the same time as reforms in the franchise were made.[41] Only since 1917 has there come to be general acceptance of the principle of broad mathematical equality in the size of constituencies[42] and only since 1945 has there been permanent machinery to enable boundaries to be

---

[36] See Representation of the People Act 2000, s 10 (pilot schemes for local elections). On the potential of the internet see Electoral Commission, *Election 2001*, pp 74–5.

[37] Also 1983 Act, s 66.

[38] 1983 Act, s 24(1).

[39] (1703) 2 Ld Raym 938, 956.

[40] 1983 Act, s 63.

[41] Butler, app II.

[42] Report of Speaker's Conference, Cd 8463, 1917; Report of Committee on Electoral Machinery, Cmd 6408, 1943.

adjusted from time to time to take account of shifting population and to avoid excessive disparities developing between constituencies. The legislation has sought to establish impartial machinery, but in practice the system has not operated without controversy. The system does not try to achieve strict arithmetical equality between constituencies, but lays emphasis also on the territorial aspect of representation, on the link between elected member and his or her constituency, and on the desirability of parliamentary boundaries not clashing with local government boundaries. The degree of discretion built into the system of electoral apportionment makes it particularly necessary to ensure that the machinery is impartial and charges of gerrymandering are avoided.

Machinery for determining constituency boundaries

By the Parliamentary Constituencies Act 1986, which consolidated the former House of Commons (Redistribution of Seats) Acts 1949 and 1958, there are four permanent boundary commissions, for England, Wales, Scotland and Northern Ireland.[43] The Speaker is the chairman of each commission, but in practice does not sit, and a judge from the appropriate High Court (in Scotland, from the Court of Session) is appointed deputy chairman of each commission. Each commission includes two other members, those for England being appointed by ministers. Each commission has two official assessors, those for England being the Registrar General and the Director General of Ordnance Survey. Each commission must undertake a general review of constituencies in that part of the United Kingdom assigned to it, at intervals of not less than ten or more than 15 years (reduced in 1992 to an interval of from eight to 12 years);[44] changes in particular constituencies may be proposed from time to time when necessary. Notice must be given to the constituencies affected by any provisional recommendations. If objections are received from an interested local authority or from a body of at least 100 electors, a local inquiry must be held into the recommendations. Having received a report on the inquiries, a commission must submit its report to the Secretary of State. The 1986 Act, by s 3(5), imposes a duty on the Secretary of State, 'as soon as may be after a Boundary Commission has submitted a report', to lay the report before Parliament together with a draft Order in Council for giving effect, with or without modifications, to the recommendations in the report (reasons must be given to Parliament for any modifications). The draft Order must be approved by resolution of each House before the final Order can be made by the Queen in Council. The validity of any Order in Council which purports to be made under the 1986 Act and recites that approval was given by each House is not to be called into question in any legal proceedings.[45]

The 1986 Act contains the rules which the commissions must observe in redistributing seats. Wales must be represented by not fewer than 35 seats, Northern Ireland by from 16 to 18 seats and Great Britain by 'not substantially greater or less than 613'.[46] It is no longer the case that Scotland must be represented by at least 71 seats.[47] These rules are not easy to apply, particularly in the case of England, but their effect is that Scotland and Wales are currently represented on a population basis more generously than England. Thus in 1997 the average electorate in English constituencies was 69,578, compared with 55,563 in Wales and 55,339 in Scotland. Northern Ireland

---

[43] A revision of the procedures in the Political Parties, Elections and Referendums Act 2000 whereby responsibility for redistribution is transferred to the Electoral Commission is not scheduled to take effect until after the next boundary review in 2005: HL Deb, 3 April 2000, col 1094.
[44] Boundary Commissions Act 1992.
[45] 1986 Act, s 4(7).
[46] 1986 Act, Sch 2.
[47] Scotland Act 1998, s 86.

was formerly represented at Westminster by only 12 members, since until 1973 it had its own Parliament for devolved matters; but with direct rule continuing, increased representation was granted in 1979. The legislation provides for the calculation of a separate electoral quota for each of the four countries (namely, the total electorate in each country divided by the number of constituencies existing when each commission starts on its general review). Each commission must secure that the electorate of a constituency shall be as near the relevant electoral quota as is practicable, having regard to certain other rules, for example, that parliamentary constituencies shall as far as practicable not cross certain local government boundaries. Strict application of these principles may be departed from if special geographical considerations make it desirable; and account must be taken of inconveniences that may follow the alteration of constituencies and of local ties that might be broken by alteration. The commissions thus have a broad discretion to decide how much priority should be given to achieving arithmetical equality between constituencies.[48]

Boundary review in practice

General reviews were completed by the four boundary commissions in 1954, 1969, 1982 and 1994. In 1954 the review resulted in the abolition of six constituencies and the creation of 11 new ones, all in England, to bring membership of the House up to 630. As well as other difficulties experienced by the English commission,[49] the method of calculating the electoral quota for England under the 1949 Act resulted in the draft Orders in Council being challenged in the courts

> In *Harper* v *Home Secretary*, two electors in Manchester sought an injunction to restrain the Home Secretary from submitting the draft Order in Council, already approved by both Houses of Parliament, to the Queen in Council. The injunction was granted by Roxburgh J but was discharged by the Court of Appeal, which held that the English commission had not departed from the statutory rules which vested a wide discretion in them. 'In so far as the matter was not within the discretion of the commission, it was certainly to be a matter for Parliament to determine', said Evershed MR, who reserved his position on the power of the court where the commission had made recommendations which were manifestly in complete disregard of the Act.[50]

In 1954 the government gave effect without modification to the recommendations of the four commissions. But events took a different turn in 1969 when the next general review was completed. The commission for England proposed major changes to 271 constituencies and five new constituencies for England.

At the time the commissions submitted their reports, a radical reorganisation of local government in England (outside Greater London) and in Wales was in train and the Labour government decided that revision of parliamentary boundaries should wait until local government had been reorganised. The government therefore delayed laying the commissions' reports in Parliament and instead introduced a Bill which gave effect only to the changes affecting Greater London and a few abnormally large constituencies elsewhere. The government thus sought by legislation to depart from its obligations under the Acts of 1949 and 1958. The Bill passed the Commons against severe criticism but was drastically amended by the Lords and was abandoned by the government when in October 1969 that House refused to give way to the Commons.

---

[48] *R v Boundary Commission for England, ex p Foot* [1983] QB 600.
[49] D E Butler (1955) 33 Public Administration 125.
[50] [1955] Ch 238, 251. See also Marshall and Moodie, *Some Problems of the Constitution*, ch 5; and S A de Smith (1955) 18 MLR 281.

An elector for the borough of Enfield then sought an order of mandamus from the High Court requiring the Home Secretary to perform his statutory duty of laying before Parliament the commission reports together with draft Orders in Council.[51] Thereupon the Home Secretary laid before Parliament the reports and the draft Orders in Council, but invited the Commons to reject them, using the government majority for this purpose.

The politics of boundary review

By this tangled course of events, the Labour government succeeded in postponing the much needed adjustments of constituency boundaries until after the 1970 general election, following which the new Conservative government promptly secured parliamentary approval to the changes recommended in 1969. Some MPs complained that Parliament had fettered its hands by setting up the boundary commissions and argued that Parliament must retain the right to make the final decisions. But the Conservative Home Secretary considered it 'enormously important' that Parliament comply with the impartial recommendations of the four commissions.[52] In 1983 the general review again led to extensive changes in constituencies, with seats in Great Britain being increased by ten and the total in the House rising to 650. The Labour party leader challenged the English changes in the High Court, but with no success.[53] The review which was completed in 1994 increased the number of seats in England from 524 to 529 and the total in the Commons to 659.[54] The review underway in December 2001 is expected to lead to a significant reduction in the number of Scottish constituencies. In view of the large number of prominent government members representing existing Scottish seats, this could prove to be contentious on a number of grounds.

The boundary commission procedure, which derives from Act of Parliament, is liable to be set aside or modified by a later Act and this may tempt a government to do this should the government think that this will benefit its own electoral interests. But, as the late Aneurin Bevan said, 'I can think of nothing that could undermine the authority of Parliament more than that people outside should feel that the constitutional mechanism by which the House of Commons is elected has been framed so as to favour one party in the State.'[55] In the United States, the Supreme Court has acted to protect the value of the individual elector's vote in state elections, holding that the voter has a plain, direct and adequate interest in maintaining the effectiveness of his or her vote which falls within the 'equal protection of the laws' guaranteed in the US constitution.[56] In Britain the process of boundary reviews is more likely to be blocked in Parliament than to be set aside by the courts. The matter was not identified by the Electoral Commission as an issue in its report on the 2001 general election, although there is a sense in some quarters that the House of Commons is too large, with the effect of recent reviews being to raise its membership to 659.

---

[51] *R v Home Secretary, ex p McWhirter, The Times,* 21 October 1969. The application was dismissed in view of the Home Secretary's action in October 1969 in laying the reports and draft Orders in Parliament. Previously on 19 June 1969 the reports alone had been laid in Parliament 'by Command' of the Crown rather than 'by Act', a distinction which it was difficult for the Home Secretary to sustain in view of the principle in *A-G v De Keyser's Royal Hotel Ltd* [1920] AC 508 (ch 12 E) and which was shown to be non-existent in *R v Immigration Appeals Tribunal, ex p Joyles* [1972] 3 All ER 213.

[52] HC Deb, 28 October 1970, col 241 ff.

[53] *R v Boundary Commission for England, ex p Foot,* note 48 above.

[54] The boundary commission reports for England (HC 433-i (1994–95)), Scotland and Wales were implemented by SIs 1995 Nos 1626, 1037 and 1036, and took effect at the 1997 election.

[55] HC Deb, 15 December 1954, col 1872.

[56] *Baker v Carr* 369 US 186 (1962); *Reynolds v Sims* 377 US 533 (1964). See I Loveland [1994] PL 332.

C. Political parties

Central to the role of modern democracy are political parties: they provide the policies and personnel of government (and opposition) and have other important functions as well.[57] Although electors vote for individuals to represent them in Parliament, the candidates will typically be chosen by a political party. It is very rare (but not unknown) for a candidate who is not representing one of the established parties to be elected to Parliament, or for an independent to be elected.[58] The parties also dominate appointments to the House of Lords. Yet political parties remain voluntary associations in the eyes of the law: bodies exercising a public function but governed by private law.[59] The relationship between a political party and its members is one based on contract and the contract may be enforced in the courts by an aggrieved member. Cases arise from time to time from individuals who claim to have been expelled from a party in breach of the rules, and from individuals challenging the procedures for the selection of a party's candidate for election to public office.[60] In some cases legislation may override the contract of membership, as in one case where it was held that all-women shortlists for the selection of parliamentary candidates were contrary to the Sex Discrimination Act 1975.[61] The Labour Party had introduced all-women shortlists for the selection of some candidates in order to increase the number of women MPs. There are currently proposals to amend the Sex Discrimination Act to allow the practice to be restored. The law governing political parties was overhauled by the Political Parties, Elections and Referendums Act 2000 which imposes a number of statutory duties on what remain voluntary associations.

The registration of political parties

Provision for the registration of political parties was first made in 1998[62] and is now to be found in the Political Parties, Elections and Referendums Act 2000.[63] Registration was first introduced in anticipation of the elections to the European Parliament for which a new electoral system was introduced by the European Elections Act 1999. This was known as a party list system whereby members are elected from large regional constituencies in proportion to the votes cast in favour of the different parties in the region in question. For this system to work effectively it was thought that only registered political parties should take part. Registration is now important for other reasons. Only candidates representing a registered party may be nominated for election; other candidates must be nominated as independents or without description.[64] This overcomes an irritant of British elections whereby individuals would present themselves in a manner which was calculated to confuse electors, as in one case where a candidate stood as a Literal Democrat.[65] The other principal reason why registration

---

[57] See Fisher, *British Political Parties*, pp 194–9, and Webb, *The Modern British Party System*.

[58] In 2001 a seat was won by a party registered as the Independent Kidderminster Hospital and Health Concern. And in 1997 the broadcaster Martin Bell was famously elected as an independent for Tatton.

[59] But see on the special and complex position of the Conservative Party, *Conservative and Unionist Central Office v Burrell* [1982] 2 All ER 1.

[60] *Lewis v Heffer* [1978] 1 WLR 1061; *Weir v Hermon* [2001] NIJB 260; *Mortimer v Labour Party, The Independent*, 28 February 2000.

[61] *Jepson v Labour Party* [1996] IRLR 116.

[62] Registration of Political Parties Act 1998; for comment, see O Gay [2001] PL 245.

[63] For a fuller account of the Act, see K D Ewing [2001] PL 542.

[64] Political Parties, Elections and Referendums Act 2000, ss 22 and 28.

[65] *Sanders v Chichester* (1994) SJ 225.

is important relates to party political broadcasts which broadcasters may carry only if made by registered parties.[66]

It is important to stress that registration of political parties is not compulsory, but that it is necessary in order to enjoy a number of prescribed benefits. There is no definition of a political party for this purpose, with registration being open to any party that declares that it intends to contest one or more 'relevant elections' in Great Britain or Northern Ireland.[67] There are separate registers for Great Britain and Northern Ireland. A party seeking registration must register its principal office holders (including its leader and treasurer) and its financial structure.[68] The latter obligation is in pursuance of a requirement that the parties adopt a scheme approved by the Electoral Commission which 'sets out the arrangements for regulating the financial affairs of the party'.[69] An application must be made to the Electoral Commission and must be granted unless the proposed name (i) is the same (or sufficiently similar to cause confusion) as that of a party already registered; (ii) comprises more than six words; (iii) is obscene or offensive; (iv) includes words which if published would be likely to amount to the commission of an offence; (v) includes any script other than Roman; or (vi) includes any words or expression prohibited by order made by the Secretary of State.[70] A registered party may also register three emblems to be used on ballot papers.[71] No fewer than 179 parties were registered in 2001, of which 75 fielded candidates.[72]

The funding of political parties

The funding of political parties has been a constant source of controversy.[73] The obligations of parties are such that it is not possible for them to rely on the subscriptions of members alone. Concern is frequently expressed about large private donations to political parties, which are sometimes associated with allegations of corruption.[74] The Political Parties, Elections and Referendums Act 2000 imposes obligations of transparency on political party funding and restricts the sources of party funding. The Act was passed to implement the recommendations of the Committee on Standards in Public Life,[75] the terms of reference of which were extended in 1997 to enable it to investigate party funding following a number of incidents involving both the Conservative party and the Labour party. All donations to a political party in excess of £5,000 nationally, and £1,000 locally must be reported to the Electoral Commission on a quarterly basis,[76] with the names of donors and the amount of donation published by the Electoral Commission.[77] Donations may only be received from a permissible donor, defined to mean individuals who are on the electoral register in this country or organisations

---

[66] Political Parties, Elections and Referendums Act 2000, s 37.
[67] Ibid, ss 22 and 28.
[68] Ibid, ss 24–7.
[69] Ibid, s 26(2). Where the party is composed of a number of separate 'accounting units' (such as the headquarters and each constituency party or association, as is the practice with the main parties), the treasurer of each accounting unit must also be registered (s 27).
[70] Ibid, s 28(4).
[71] Ibid, s 29.
[72] But of these 35 fielded candidates in only one constituency.
[73] See Ewing, *The Funding of Political Parties in Britain*, and Pinto-Duschinsky, *British Political Finance 1830–1980*.
[74] Under the Honours (Prevention of Abuses) Act 1925 it is an offence to make or receive a donation in return for an honour. But the problems of proof are overwhelming.
[75] Cm 4057, 1998. See L Klein (1999) 31 Case Western Reserve Journal of International Law 1.
[76] Political Parties, Elections and Referendums Act 2000, ss 62, 63.
[77] Ibid, ss 69, 149. The information is made available by the Electoral Commission on its website: www.electoralcommission.org.uk. It is possible to track the main donors to the parties. The information is also reported in the press on a quarterly basis.

(such as companies and trade unions) that are based here and conduct business and activity here.[78] The aim is to stop the foreign funding of British political parties, although as we have seen it is possible to be resident overseas and yet be on the electoral register.

There are no limits on the size of donations which may be made to political parties. Individual donations of £5m and £2m to the Conservative party and Labour party respectively before the 2001 general election renewed calls for a contribution cap. But contribution limits were rejected by the Committee on Standards in Public Life in 1998[79] and any such limit would have implications for those parties that operate on the basis of individual and collective membership. This would be a particular problem for the Labour party which is an organisation of individual and affiliated members (trade unions and socialist societies), the latter paying a membership or affiliation fee based to some extent on the number of members in the trade union or society in question. A ceiling on contributions would disturb this arrangement unless a convincing distinction could be drawn between a membership fee and a donation. Trade union funding of the Labour Party has been regulated by legislation since 1913:[80] trade unions may only pursue political objects with the approval of their members in a ballot which must be held every ten years; and trade union political contributions must be made from a separate fund to which members are entitled not to contribute.[81] Amendments made to the Companies Act 1985 in 2000 require companies to secure shareholder approval at least every four years for political donations and expenditures.[82]

State support for political parties

In many countries, political parties receive annual subventions of public funds to enable them more effectively to perform their functions without the need for excessive reliance on wealthy private donors.[83] In other countries the parties are assisted by the provision of income tax relief for donations to political parties, designed to encourage more people to make small donations. A scheme for public funding of political parties was proposed by the Houghton committee in 1976 but never implemented;[84] and proposals by the Committee on Standards in Public Life (Neill committee) in 1998 for income tax relief for small contributions to political parties were rejected by the government.[85] Media disquiet about large donations to the parties has revived interest in public funding, to relieve the parties of the need to rely on such donations. Indeed the Electoral Commission has already signalled that it proposes to consider the argument for a cap on political donations and state funding of political parties.[86] Given the choice between public funding based on votes cast at the previous general election (as proposed by Houghton) and income tax relief (as proposed by Neill), the disadvantage of the latter is that it benefits only those who are taxpayers and mainly those parties supported by individuals with higher discretionary income.

This is not to say that there is no state support for political parties in Britain, although it is limited when compared to some other countries. Parliamentary candidates are

---

[78] Political Parties, Elections and Referendums Act 2000, s 54.
[79] Cm 4057, 1998, ch 6.
[80] Ewing, *Trade Unions, The Labour Party and the Law: A Study of the Trade Union Act 1913*.
[81] Trade Union and Labour Relations (Consolidation) Act 1992, ch VI. See Collins, Ewing and McColgan, *Labour Law*, ch 7; Deakin and Morris, *Labour Law*, ch 10.
[82] Political Parties, Elections and Referendums Act 2000, s 139; Sch 19.
[83] Ewing (ed.), *The Funding of Political Parties: Europe and Beyond* (chapters on France, Spain, Italy and Japan). See also D Z Cass and S Burrows (2000) 22 Sydney Law Review 477 (Australia).
[84] Cmnd 6601, 1976.
[85] HC Deb, 10 January 2000, col 114 (Mike O'Brien).
[86] Electoral Commission, *Election 2001*, p 76.

provided with free postage for one election communication and are permitted to use school halls for election meetings free of charge.[87] Free time is made available to the political parties for party political broadcasts and party election broadcasts by both the BBC and the independent broadcasters, a facility which in the latter case exists as a matter of legal obligation.[88] The amount of time made available for the parties is determined by the broadcasters in consultation with the parties.[89] Finally, public money is made available to the Opposition parties in Parliament to assist them in the performance of their parliamentary activities;[90] and a small sum of money (£2m) is now available for distribution to eligible parties (those with parliamentary representation) to assist with policy development.[91] In the case of the former the amounts involved are not inconsiderable, the principal Opposition party now receiving in excess of £3m, with correspondingly smaller sums being made available to the other Opposition parties in Parliament.[92] Concern has been expressed by the Public Administration Committee of the House of Commons about the lack of effective scrutiny to ensure that the money is spent only for parliamentary purposes.[93] There is also provision for the public funding of campaign groups (up to £600,000 to each side) in the event of a national referendum.[94]

D. The conduct of elections

There is now a substantial body of law which has developed to regulate both local and national election campaigns. There are a number of objectives which legislation must promote, with the overriding objective being the need to maintain public confidence in the fairness and integrity of the electoral process. So it is necessary to ensure that neither electors nor candidates are subject to improper influences or pressures, and necessary also to ensure that there is a measure of equality of arms between candidates representing major strands of opinion. It has been acknowledged judicially that there is a need

> to achieve a level financial playing field between competing candidates, so as to prevent perversion of the voters' democratic choice between competing candidates within constituencies by significant disparities of local expenditure. At the constituency level it is the voters' perception of the personality and policies of the candidates, and the parties which they represent, which is intended to be reflected in the voting, not the weight of the parties' expenditure on local electioneering.[95]

It is important also that no party is able to secure an electoral advantage because of its greater financial resources or because it has better access to radio and television. British law has now developed detailed, sophisticated and in some respects uncompromising rules to help promote electoral fairness between the main parties and to reduce the influence of money in electoral politics. But because campaigning is expensive (yet of contestable effect), money cannot be removed completely from the scene; there will

---

[87] Representation of the People Act 1983, ss 91, 95.
[88] Broadcasting Act 1990, s 6. See pp 161–2 in this chapter.
[89] For an account of the arrangements, see L Klein at note 75 above.
[90] These are the so-called Short and Cranborne monies for the House of Commons and House of Lords respectively. See Cm 4057, 1998, ch 9.
[91] Political Parties, Elections and Referendums Act 2000, s 12.
[92] HC Deb, 10 January 2000, col 35. A similar scheme operates in the Scottish Parliament: SI 1999 No 1745.
[93] HC 238 (1999–2000); HC 293 (2000–1). There is also uncertainty about what is covered by the term parliamentary purposes.
[94] Political Parties, Elections and Referendums Act 2000, s 110. Provision is also made for referendum campaign broadcasts (ibid). Cf on the latter, *Wilson v IBA* 1979 SC 351.
[95] *R v Jones* [1999] 2 Cr App R 253, at p 255.

thus inevitably be disagreements about the content of some of the regulatory means which have been chosen to control its influence.

The campaign in the constituency

Under Part II of the Representation of the People Act 1983 every candidate must appoint an election agent, but a candidate may appoint himself or herself to act in that capacity. There are now restrictions on who may donate to candidates,[96] but the most important control is the limit on candidates' election expenses in s 76 of the 1983 Act, knowingly to breach which is an illegal practice. First introduced in 1883, the amount which a candidate may spend 'on account of or in respect of the conduct or management of the election' depends on the number of electors in the constituency and on whether it is a borough or county constituency. But at the time of writing a maximum sum of £10,000 would not be atypical.[97] There is a great deal of uncertainty about what falls within the scope of election expenses, a term which has been poorly defined in the Act,[98] there being 'no simple and decisive test to determine whether an expense is or is not an election expense within the meaning of the Act'.[99] In addition to this limit on the amount of permitted expenditure, certain forms of expenditure are forbidden. These include the payment to an elector for the display of election posters unless payment is made in the ordinary course of the elector's business as an advertising agent; and payments to canvassers.[100] Corrupt practices include bribery, treating and undue influence, such as the making of threats and attempts to intimidate an elector.[101] Election agents must submit a return of their candidate's election expenses to the returning officer within 35 days of the result being declared.[102]

Also important is s 75 which contains a measure first introduced in 1918 imposing a limit on the election expenses which may be incurred by third parties promoting or opposing a candidate. These third parties may be local businessmen, trade unions or local interest groups who believe that their cause would be well served by the election of one particular candidate or poorly served by the election of another. They may wish as a result to campaign in the election and in the absence of controls could, in theory, exceed the permitted expenditure of the candidates themselves. It is thus a corrupt practice under the widely construed s 75 to (i) incur an election expenditure with a view to promoting or procuring the election of a candidate, (ii) on account of holding public meetings, issuing advertisements or circulars or otherwise presenting the candidate or his views to the electorate, (iii) except with the authority of the candidate (in which case the authorised expenditure falls to be treated as part of the candidate's expenses).[103] This is subject to an exception for the media to ensure that press and

---

[96] 1983 Act, s 71A, as inserted by s 30 and Sch 16.

[97] A much higher level of expenditure is permitted at by-elections. In 2001, this was £100,000.

[98] 1983 Act, s 118.

[99] *R v Jones*, note 95 above, at p 258. There is now a much expanded definition in ss 90A–D which was inserted by the Political Parties, Elections and Referendums Act 2000, s 134.

[100] 1983 Act, ss 109 and 111.

[101] 1983 Act, s 115. See *R v Rowe, ex p Mainwaring* [1992] 4 All ER 821.

[102] 1983 Act, s 81 (amended by the Political Parties, Elections and Referendums Act 2000, Sch 18 (7)). The return which must now also include a statement of donations to the candidate (Sch 2A, inserted by the Political Parties, Elections and Referendums Act 2000, s 130) must be accompanied by a declaration made by the agent and the candidate that the return is a true record of expenses incurred. For a recent high-profile but unsuccessful prosecution of a candidate for allegedly making a false declaration, see *R v Jones* [1999] 2 Cr App R 253. See p 158 above.

[103] In *DPP v Luft* [1977] AC 962 it was held that expenditure on negative publicity aimed at preventing the election of a candidate was covered by this provision, as well as expenditure on positive promotional material aimed at procuring the election of a candidate.

broadcasting activity is not inadvertently caught, and another to a limit of what was £5. That limit was found to be too low by the European Court of Human Rights as violating article 10 of the ECHR.[104] Following an amendment introduced by the Political Parties, Elections and Referendums Act 2000,[105] the limit is now £500, which means that individuals and campaign groups may spend up to £500 promoting or attacking candidates without any candidate having to account for the expense.

National spending limits

The spending limits on candidates are now accompanied by spending limits on the national election spending incurred by political parties and others during a general election. It was for a long time the case that, although the expenditure of candidates was subject to limits, there was no corresponding limit on the national election campaigns of the parties.[106] These campaigns were becoming more sophisticated and more expensive: at the general election in 1997 the Conservative and Labour parties were thought to have spent £28 and £26.5m respectively, which in each case was more than double the amount spent at the general election in 1992. The Committee on Standards in Public Life recommended that national spending should be limited[107] and this recommendation forms the basis of Part 5 of the Political Parties, Elections and Referendums Act 2000 (with corresponding limits on national referendum expenditure in Part VII). This imposes a limit on the campaign expenditure of political parties,[108] the limit depending on the number of constituencies which are contested by party candidates.[109] But a national party which puts up a candidate in every constituency would be able to spend up to about £20m to promote the electoral success of the party. This is in addition to the £10,000 or so which may be spent by each candidate under the Representation of the People Act 1983 on the conduct or management of his or her campaign. There are also spending limits on political parties during referendum campaigns (£5m for each of the largest in a national referendum).[110]

It is not only the national campaigns of political parties which are subject to restrictions. Spending limits are also imposed on the campaigns of so-called third parties, such as trade unions, companies and pressure groups (such as the Countryside Alliance). These bodies may take part in an election by incurring expensive national advertising to promote particular issues which may tend to benefit one party at the expense of the others. Under Part VI of the 2000 Act, third parties may incur 'controlled expenditure' of up to £10,000 in England and £5,000 in each of Scotland, Wales and Northern Ireland without restraint. 'Controlled expenditure' is defined to mean expenses incurred in connection with the production or publication of election material which is made available to the public at large or any section of the public (s 85). A third party which wishes to spend more must register with the Electoral Commission to become a 'recognised third party'. A recognised third party may incur controlled expenditure of up to just under £1m, though part of it must be spent in each of England (£793,500), Scotland (£108,000), Wales (£60,000) and Northern Ireland (£27,000). A recognised third party must also submit an election return after the election, giving details of income

---

[104] *Bowman v UK* (1998) 26 EHRR 1.

[105] Political Parties, Elections and Referendums Act 2000, s 131.

[106] *R v Tronoh Mines Ltd* [1952] 1 All ER 697.

[107] Cm 4057, 1998, ch 10.

[108] For the definition of campaign expenditure, see Political Parties, Elections and Referendums Act 2000, s 72 and Sch 8.

[109] Ibid, s 79 and Sch 9.

[110] Political Parties, Elections and Referendums Act 2000, Part VII. There are also limits on campaign groups and others. See K D Ewing [2001] PL 542 for fuller treatment of this issue.

received and controlled expenditure incurred. At the general election in 2001, there were only seven third party registrations, fewer than anticipated:[111] they included a few trade unions and interest groups associated with countryside issues and the euro.

Broadcasting and elections

Political broadcasting at election times has also given rise to difficulties. It is an illegal practice for any person to procure the use of transmitting stations outside the United Kingdom with intent to influence voters at an election.[112] The Independent Television Commission is under a statutory duty to secure that news programmes are accurate and impartial and that due impartiality is preserved in political programmes.[113] Political advertising is banned on ITV and on local radio stations,[114] a measure justified judicially in part as legitimate response to 'the danger of the wealthy distorting the democratic process'.[115] But as already pointed out, free time is provided to the parties by the broadcasters for party election broadcasts. The allocation of time presents particular problems for the small parties and has given rise to a number of unsuccessful challenges in the courts on different grounds by parties which have been denied a broadcast or allocated an amount of time which they consider to be unfair.[116] At the general election in 2001, the Labour party and the Conservative party were allocated five broadcasts each and the Liberal Democrats four broadcasts in England; whereas in Scotland each of these parties was allocated four broadcasts, as was the Scottish National party. An equal four-way distribution was adopted in Wales where Plaid Cymru was the fourth party. Time was also provided for one broadcast for six of the other 75 parties which had candidates standing in the election.[117] These other parties had to contest at least one-sixth of the parliamentary seats to qualify: for a party contesting seats in England it would have to stand in 88 constituencies to qualify for an election broadcast.[118]

The other major issue relating to broadcasting concerns the ability of the broadcasters to report about activities in particular constituencies. The curious effect of the Representation of the People Act 1983, s 93 was that if a candidate took part in an item about a constituency election, the item could not be broadcast without his or her consent; and it was an offence for a candidate to take part in such an item for the purpose of promoting his or her election unless the broadcast had the consent of every other candidate for the constituency.[119] To 'take part' in a constituency item meant to participate actively, for example in an interview or discussion; a candidate could not prevent the BBC from filming while he or she was campaigning in streets.[120] These measures – which effectively gave individual candidates a veto over what might be

---

[111] Electoral Commission, *Election 2001*, p 53.

[112] 1983 Act, s 92.

[113] Broadcasting Act 1990, s 6(1)(b) and (c) and cf for radio, s 90(1)(b). The BBC, which exists under royal charter, seeks to maintain due impartiality although it is not subject to statutory restrictions. And see p 58 above

[114] Broadcasting Act 1990, s 8(2)(a).

[115] *R v Radio Authority, ex parte Bull* [1995] 4 All ER 481, at p 495 (Kennedy LJ); also [1997] 2 All ER 561.

[116] See *Grieve v Douglas-Home* 1965 SLT 186, *R v Broadcasting Complaints Commission* [1985] QB 1153 and *R v BBC and ITC, ex p Referendum Party* [1997] COD 459. Also *R (Prolife Alliance) v BBC* [2002] 2 All ER 756. Cf *Wilson v IBA* 1979 SC 351 (restraints on referendum broadcasts; see now Political Parties, Elections and Referendums Act 2000, s 110).

[117] This does not include the arrangements in Northern Ireland where six parties had broadcasts.

[118] See Electoral Commission, *Election 2001*, p 60.

[119] 1983 Act, s 93(1).

[120] *Marshall v BBC* [1979] 3 All ER 80. And see *McAliskey v BBC* [1980] NI 44.

broadcast – were widely criticised and they were replaced by the Political Parties, Elections and Referendums Act 2000. Section 93 now provides that each broadcasting authority must adopt a code of practice to deal with 'the participation of candidates at a parliamentary or local government election in items about the constituency'. Before drawing up the code, the broadcasters must 'have regard' to any views expressed by the Electoral Commission. The broadcasters thus now have a free hand, perhaps inevitably after the Human Rights Act 1998.

E. Supervision of elections

If elections are to be conducted according to law there must be effective machinery for investigating alleged breaches of the law and for imposing appropriate sanctions. Since the House of Commons has a direct interest in its own composition, it formerly claimed as a matter of privilege to determine questions of disputed elections. The Commons exercised the right to determine such questions from 1604 to 1868; and objected, not always with success, to breaches of election law being raised in the ordinary courts.[121] From 1672 election disputes were decided by the whole House, but the growth of party government resulted in disputes being settled by purely party voting. In 1868, Parliament entrusted the duty of deciding disputed elections to the courts. The procedure is now regulated by the Representation of the People Act 1983, which provides a procedure for contesting elections and for these contests to be dealt with in the courts. Also important, however, is the Electoral Commission established under the Political Parties, Elections and Referendums Act 2000.[122] Apart from supervising the new regulatory regime introduced by the Act, the Commission has wide-ranging responsibilities for the conduct of elections.

Election petitions

The principal way of challenging an election is by way of an election petition. This can be done only to challenge the election of a candidate: there is no way by which a general election result can be challenged. Within 21 days of the official return of the result of an election, an election petition complaining of an undue election may be presented by a registered elector for the constituency in question, by a person who claims the right to have been elected at the election, or by any person claiming to have been validly nominated as a candidate. The petition may raise a wide variety of issues, including the improper conduct of the election by officials,[123] the legal qualification of the successful candidate to be a member of the Commons[124] and the commission of election offences such as unauthorised election expenditure.[125] The petition is heard by an Election Court consisting of two judges of the Queen's Bench Division in England or of the Court of Session in Scotland. The Election Court, which 'has the authority of the High Court and is a court of record'[126] has a wide range of powers, including the power to order a recount or a scrutiny of the votes. The court determines whether the person whose election is complained of was duly elected and whether any alleged corrupt or illegal practices at the election were proved.

---

[121] *Ashby* v *White* (1703) 2 Ld Raym 938; *R* v *Paty* (1704) 2 Ld Raym 1105. And ch 11 A.
[122] For the Commission, see www.electoralcommission.org.uk.
[123] E.g. *Re Kensington North Parliamentary Election* [1960] 2 All ER 150.
[124] E.g. *Re Parliamentary Election for Bristol South East* [1964] 2 QB 257.
[125] E.g. *Grieve* v *Douglas-Home* 1965 SC 186.
[126] *Attorney-General* v *Jones* [2000] QB 66, at p 69.

If the court finds the candidate to have been disqualified from membership of the House, the court may, if satisfied that the cause of the disqualification was known to the electorate, deem the votes cast for him or her to be void and declare the runner-up to have been elected.[127] If the election has not been conducted substantially in accordance with the law or if there have been irregularities which have affected the result, the court must declare the election void and require a fresh election to be held.[128] The decision of the court – from which there is no appeal, although there may be a possibility of judicial review[129] – is notified to the Speaker and is entered on the journals of the House of Commons. The House must then give the necessary directions for confirming or altering the return or for issuing a writ for a new election, as the case may be.[130] In recent years there have been very few petitions in respect of parliamentary elections. The last instance of a successful candidate being unseated for election practices arose after the general election in December 1923.[131] Election petitions are more frequent in respect of local elections, where the procedure for challenging an irregular election is broadly the same.[132]

Prosecution of election offences

The other way by which election law can be enforced is by a criminal prosecution.[133] A person convicted on indictment of a corrupt practice is liable to imprisonment of up to one year and a fine; summary conviction carries a lesser penalty which may still lead to three months' imprisonment.[134] Conviction for an illegal practice carries a penalty of a fine not exceeding level 3 on the standard scale.[135] Equally important, conviction brings certain political disabilities, in the sense that a person found guilty of a corrupt or illegal practice is disqualified from being registered as an elector 'or voting at any parliamentary election in the United Kingdom or at any local government election in Great Britain'. A person found guilty of a corrupt or illegal practice is also incapable of being elected to the House of Commons and of holding 'any elective office' for five years. Anyone elected to the House of Commons who is subsequently found to have committed a corrupt practice, is required to vacate his or her seat.[136] In the case of a conviction for a corrupt practice the disqualification is for five years and three years in the case of an illegal practice. Similar disqualifications may face anyone found to have committed a corrupt or illegal practice by an election court following an election petition. Prosecutions must be brought within a year of the alleged offence being committed.[137]

In *Attorney-General* v *Jones*,[138] the defendant – the Labour member for Newark – had been convicted of the corrupt practice of knowingly making a false declaration of her election expenses. As a result her seat became vacant by the operation of s 160(4) of the 1983 Act. The conviction was reversed on appeal, at which point it was held that the seat ceased to be vacant, and that the existing member was entitled to resume her seat. Following this case the law was changed so that where a sitting member is convicted of a corrupt or illegal practice, the seat

---

[127] As in the *Bristol South East* case.
[128] *Morgan* v *Simpson* [1975] QB 151; *Ruffle* v *Rogers* [1982] QB 1220 (local election cases).
[129] *R* v *Cripps, ex p Muldoon* [1984] QB 686.
[130] 1983 Act, s 144(7).
[131] Butler, p 57.
[132] See *Sanders* v *Chichester*, p 155 above.
[133] See *Attorney-General* v *Jones* [2000] QB 66, at p 69.
[134] 1983 Act, s 168.
[135] Ibid, s 169.
[136] Political Parties, Elections and Referendums Act 2000, s 137, inserting a new s 173 into the 1983 Act.
[137] 1983 Act, s 176.
[138] [2000] QB 66.

does not become vacant until the end of the period within which an appeal may be lodged against the conviction. If notice of appeal is given, the seat becomes vacant three months after the conviction, unless the appeal is withdrawn or is unsuccessful (in which case it is vacated immediately), or unless the appeal is heard and succeeds (in which case the seat is not vacated). Where a seat is vacated and the appeal ultimately succeeds, this will not entitle the member to resume his or her seat.[139]

Failure to comply with the provisions of the Political Parties, Elections and Referendums Act 2000 has altogether much less dramatic consequences, although these are not to be underestimated. The main provisions here are the national spending limits. Although it recommended that there should be such a limit, the Committee on Standards in Public Life thought it 'wholly unrealistic' to suppose that a general election could be set aside and 'the runner-up party to be declared the winner' where the winning party exceeded the national limit.[140] The 'only realistic sanction' was thought to be the imposition of a 'heavy financial penalty' on the defaulting party.[141] It is the criminal law which must thus bear the greater part of the burden of enforcing the limits in the 2000 Act, although financial penalties are combined with the possibility of imprisonment of party officials in the event of a breach. So in the event of expenditure in excess of the statutory maximum, an offence is committed by both the party and the treasurer who authorised the expenditure, in this case the penalty on the party being an unlimited fine.[142] But it is the treasurer who must accept responsibility for any failure to deliver a return of campaign expenditure to the Commission or for making a false declaration about its contents.[143]

The role of the Electoral Commission

One of the other major innovations of the Political Parties, Elections and Referendums Act 2000 is the creation of the Electoral Commission. Every effort has been made to ensure that the Commission is independent of government and the political parties. The members are appointed by the Crown, but only with the agreement of the Speaker and after consultation with the leaders of the registered parties that have at least two MPs.[144] The appointments must be approved by the House of Commons; the Electoral Commissioners may be removed from office only on prescribed grounds and only after an address by the House of Commons. An individual is not eligible for appointment as an Electoral Commissioner if he or she is a member of a political party, an officer or employee of a political party or has at any time in the preceding ten years been an officer or employee of a party, a holder of elective office or a donor who appears in the register of donors. A donation of as little as £1,001 would thus serve to disqualify.[145] Also helping to ensure the independence of the Commission are the arrangements for its financing, which is not determined by the government but by a Speaker's Committee established by the Political Parties, Referendums and Elections Act 2000. The committee consists of two ministers, the chairman of the Home Affairs Committee and five backbench MPs selected by the Speaker.[146]

The Electoral Commission has a wide range of functions. It must publish a report on the conduct of elections and referendums, keep under review a number of electoral

---

[139] Political Parties, Elections and Referendums Act 2000, s 137 (as amended).
[140] Cm 4057, 1998, para 10.25.
[141] Ibid, para 10.26.
[142] 2000 Act, s 79(2).
[143] Ibid, ss 80–3.
[144] Ibid, s 3.
[145] Ibid and Sch 1.
[146] Ibid, s 2 and Sch 1.

matters (including political party income and expenditure and political advertising in the broadcast media).[147] The Commission must also be consulted about any changes to electoral law[148] and is empowered to give advice and assistance (but not financial assistance) to registration officers, returning officers, political parties and others.[149] This advice may be sought during election campaigns about election law.[150] Independent broadcasters must take into account the views of the Commission before making rules relating to party political broadcasts and the £2m made available to the parties for policy development is to be distributed in accordance with a scheme drawn up by the Commission and approved by the Home Secretary.[151] As we have also seen the Commission plays a crucial part in the administration of the law relating to donations to political parties and electoral expenditure. Under s 145 of the 2000 Act the Commission has a general duty to monitor compliance not only with the provisions of the Political Parties, Elections and Referendums Act, but also 'the restrictions and other requirements imposed by other enactments' relating to 'election expenses incurred by or on behalf of candidates at elections', which extends obviously to the Representation of the People Act 1983.[152] But although the Commission has wide powers of investigation, it bears no responsibility for the prosecution of offenders.

F. Electoral systems and electoral reform

Under the present electoral system in the United Kingdom, each constituency returns a single member. Each elector can vote for only one candidate and the successful candidate is the one who receives the highest number of valid votes. This system of 'first past the post' is known as the relative majority system since whenever there are more than two candidates in a constituency, the successful candidate may not have an absolute majority of votes but merely a majority relative to the vote of the runner-up. This system is simple, but as a means of providing representation in Parliament it is very crude. It makes no provision for the representation of minority interests, neither does it ensure that the distribution of seats in the Commons is at all proportionate to the national distribution of votes. In Britain, the general tendency of the system has been to exaggerate the representation of the two largest parties and to reduce that of the smaller parties; but even for the larger parties there is no consistent relation between the votes and the seats they obtain. The distortion felt by some is illustrated by the General Election of 2001 which saw the Labour party win 412 of the 659 seats (with a majority of 165) with only 41% of the vote.[153] The advantages claimed for the system include the simplicity of the voting method, the close links which develop between the member and his or her constituency, and its tendency to produce an absolute majority of seats in the House out of a large minority of votes. In defence of the system it is claimed that the function of a general election is to elect a government as well as a

---

[147] Ibid, ss 5 and 6. See Electoral Commission, *Election 2001*.
[148] Ibid, s 7.
[149] Ibid, s 9.
[150] See Electoral Commission, *Election 2001*, for details of the range of advice sought.
[151] Political Parties, Elections and Referendums Act 2000, ss 11 and 12. The Commission also has an important educational function regarding the electoral systems (s 13).
[152] With the exception of Scottish local government elections, unless the Scottish Ministers so provide (s 145(2)).
[153] It works the other way too. In 1983 the Conservatives won 42% of the votes and 61% of the seats and in 1992 they won 42% of the votes and 52% of the seats. The main losers have been the Liberal Democrats whose parliamentary representation regularly falls far short of votes cast nationally. In 2001 the Liberal Democrats polled 18% of the vote for 8% of seats. (The Conservatives polled 32% of the vote for 25% of the seats.)

Parliament and that the system produces strong government. This last claim needs to be examined with care, since a relatively small change of political support in a few constituencies may be exaggerated into an apparent change of mind from one party to the other by a majority of the electorate.

Other voting systems

Other electoral systems have long been devised with a view to securing better representation of minorities and a distribution of seats which bears a less haphazard relation to the votes cast. Many different systems are used in other countries.[154] One method, the alternative vote system, retains single-member constituencies but allows the elector to express a choice of candidates in order of preference. If no candidate has an absolute majority of first preferences, the lowest on the list is eliminated and his or her votes are distributed according to the second preference shown on the voting papers. The procedure continues until one candidate obtains an absolute majority. This system eliminates the return of a candidate on a minority vote when account is taken of second and later preferences, but it does not necessarily secure representation in the Commons proportional to the first preferences of the electorate on a national basis. Other systems have been designed to secure representation in Parliament directly proportional to the national voting strengths of the parties. Thus by the list system, as used in Israel, voting for party lists of candidates takes place in a national constituency, with each party receiving that number of seats which comes closest to its national votes; this system does not provide for any local links between voters and their representatives. In Germany, a mixed system is used by which each elector has two votes, one to elect a candidate in a single-member constituency, the other to vote for a party list; the list seats are assigned to parties to compensate for disproportionate representation arising from the constituency elections, but a party must record 5% of the national vote or win three constituencies to gain any list seats.

The system which is likely to produce a reasonably close relationship between votes and seats while maintaining a local basis for representation is that of the single transferable vote. This method has been used within the United Kingdom for several purposes.[155] It would require the country to be divided into multi-member constituencies, each returning between three and, say, seven members. Each elector would have a single vote but would vote for candidates in order of preference. Any candidate obtaining the quota of first preferences necessary to guarantee election would be immediately elected, the quota being calculated by a simple formula: in a five-member constituency, this quota would be one vote more than one-sixth of the total votes cast. The surplus votes of a successful candidate would be distributed to other candidates proportionately according to the second preference expressed; any candidate then obtaining the quota would be elected and a similar distribution of the surplus would follow. If at any count no candidate obtained the quota figure, the candidate with the lowest number of votes would be eliminated and all those votes distributed among the others. Under this scheme, parties would both nationally and locally be likely to secure representation according to their true strength; minority parties and independent

---

[154] Bogdanor, *The People and the Party System*, parts III–V; and Blackburn, ch 8.

[155] E.g. for university constituencies between 1918 and 1948; in Northern Ireland for elections to Stormont in 1922–28, to the Assembly in 1973 and 1982, to the Constitutional Convention in 1975 and to the European Parliament. Its use for electing assemblies in Scotland and Wales was proposed by the Royal Commission on the Constitution in 1973 (Cmnd 5460, 1973, paras 779–88), but this has been overtaken by events.

candidates would stand a better chance of election; and the number of ineffective votes would be reduced. Within the constituency, electors could in their order of preference choose between candidates from the same party and could base their choice of candidates on non-party considerations. Unless voting habits were to change, one party would be less likely to secure an absolute majority of seats in the Commons than at present; and Britain would become used to periods of minority or coalition government.[156]

Electoral reform

The case for electoral reform has been examined many times and a number of different electoral systems have been introduced in Britain since 1997. Under the Scotland Act 1998, a form of the additional member system has been adopted for elections to the Scottish Parliament, which contains 73 constituency members and 56 regional members.[157] Registered parties may submit lists of candidates to be regional members for a particular region, with up to 12 names on each party list, although only seven may be elected.[158] Electors have two votes: one for a constituency member; and the other for regional members to be exercised by voting for a political party which has submitted a regional list.[159] Constituency members are to be elected by first past the post as is currently the case for Westminster elections, and a measure of proportionality is secured by the regional member seats which are allocated to the parties on the basis of a complex formula which allocates seats according to votes cast for the party in the region.[160] The regional member constituencies are the same constituencies which existed for the purposes of the European Parliament, before the European Parliamentary Elections Act 1999. The new electoral system for European Parliament elections is very different (based on closed party lists in much larger regional constituencies) and is considered in chapter 8. A system similar to the Scottish system is in place for the National Assembly for Wales.[161]

Different systems have been adopted for the Northern Ireland Assembly and the Greater London Authority. In the case of the former, the single transferable vote is used to elect six candidates from each of the parliamentary constituencies for Northern Ireland.[162] The single transferable vote is defined in the Act as a vote (a) 'capable of being given so as to indicate the voter's order of preference for the candidates for election as members for the constituency' and (b) 'capable of being transferred to the next choice when the vote is not needed to give a prior choice the necessary quota of votes or when a prior choice is eliminated from the list of candidates because of a deficiency in the number of votes given for him'.[163] In the case of London, the system is different again. An elector has three votes: one for a mayoral candidate; one (a constituency vote) for an Assembly candidate; and one (a London vote) for a registered party or an individual candidate standing for election as London member.[164] Mayoral candidates are elected by simple majority unless there are more than two in which case

[156] Ch 2 D.
[157] Scotland Act 1998, s 1. This contrasts with the first past the post system which had been proposed in the Scotland Act 1978. See Cmnd 6348, 1975, p 9.
[158] Scotland Act 1998, s 5(6).
[159] Ibid, s 6.
[160] Ibid, s 1; Sch 1.
[161] Government of Wales Act 1998, Part 1. This contrasts with the first past the post system which had been proposed in the Wales Act 1978.
[162] Northern Ireland Act 1998, s 34.
[163] Northern Ireland Act 1998, s 34(3).
[164] Greater London Authority Act 1999, s 4(1).

the supplementary vote system is used: this means that where none of the candidates has a majority of the votes cast, all but the first two are eliminated with the second preference votes of the eliminated candidates then distributed to the candidates still in the contest.[165] The Assembly is elected on the basis of a variation of the additional member system used in Scotland and Wales.[166]

The Jenkins Commission

There are thus new electoral systems for the European Parliament and for the devolved bodies. But what about Westminster? There have been many proposals for reforming the Westminster system, one of the earliest being a recommendation by a royal commisssion in 1910 for the introduction of the alternative vote.[167] This was followed in 1917 by the recommendations of a Speaker's Conference on electoral reform for the adoption of the single transferable vote.[168] But after some vacillation Parliament refused to accept either this or the alternative vote. The matter was revived by the second Labour government in 1929[169] and a Bill which sought to introduce the alternative vote was passed by the Commons but abandoned when the government fell in 1931. The Speaker's Conference on electoral reform in 1944 rejected by a large majority proposals for change, as did a similar conference in 1967.[170] Electoral reform nevertheless continued to have its strong advocates, with few countries electing their legislatures on the basis of first past the post and with all the new electoral regimes adopted in Britain in recent years rejecting it in favour of a system which is perceived to be fairer in terms of producing a more representative outcome. Before the general election in 1997, the Labour and Liberal Democratic parties agreed that an early referendum should be held on electoral reform and a commitment to this effect was included in the Labour Party's general election manifesto of that year.

In acknowledgement of the manifesto commitment, in December 1997 the Prime Minister appointed the Independent Commission on the Voting System under the chairmanship of Lord Jenkins to consider and recommend alternatives to the voting system for Westminster elections. By its terms of reference the commission was required to 'observe the requirement for broad proportionality, the need for stable Government, an extension of voter choice and the maintenance of a link between MPs and geographical constituencies'. The commission recommended the introduction of 'a two-vote mixed system which can be described as either limited AMS or AV top-up'. The majority of MPs (80–85%) would continue to be elected from single-member constituencies, but by alternative vote; and the remainder 'elected on a corrective top-up basis which would significantly reduce the disproportionality and the geographical divisiveness' which were said to be inherent in first past the post.[171] Although the report and its proposals were widely praised for their elegance and subtlety, at the time of writing no referendum on these or other proposals has been held and there is no likelihood in the foreseeable future of the Labour government proposing any change to the voting system for the House of Commons. It is, however, proposed by the government that 120 members

---

[165] The candidate with the largest number of first preference votes and distributed second preferences from the other candidates is the winner. See Greater London Authority Act 1999, s 4(3).
[166] Ibid, s 4(4) (Assembly members elected under simple majority system) and s 4(5) (London members elected from party lists in a single London-wide constituency). It is in this latter respect (one rather than several additional member constituencies) that London differs from Scotland and Wales.
[167] Cd 5163, 1910.
[168] Cd 8463, 1917 and Representation of the People Act 1918, s 20. See Butler, part 1.
[169] Cmd 3636, 1930.
[170] Cmd 6534, 1944; Cmnd 3202, 1967.
[171] *The Report of the Independent Commission on the Voting System* (1998), p 50.

of the House of Lords out of a proposed total membership of 600 should be elected in the future on the basis of the regional list system which is already used for European Parliament elections.[172]

G. Membership of the House of Commons

The following are the main categories of persons who are disqualified from sitting and voting in the House of Commons.[173]

(a)   Both by common law and by statute, aliens are disqualified; citizens of Commonwealth countries and the Republic of Ireland are not disqualified.[174]

(b)   Persons under 21.[175]

(c)   Mental patients. Under the Mental Health Act 1983, s 141, when a member is ordered to be detained on grounds of mental illness, the detention must be reported to the Speaker. The Speaker obtains a medical report from two medical specialists, followed by a second report after six months. If the member is still detained and suffering from mental illness, his or her seat is vacated.

(d)   Peers and peeresses. But following the House of Lords Act 1999, hereditary peers are no longer disqualified unless they are one of the 92 hereditary peers (on which see below) who have retained their membership of the House under s 2 of the Act.

(e)   Bankrupts. Under the Insolvency Act 1986, s 427, a debtor who is adjudged bankrupt is disqualified from election to the Commons (and from sitting in the House or on a committee). Where a sitting member is adjudged bankrupt, his or her seat becomes vacant when six months have elapsed without the judgment being annulled.

(f)   Persons guilty of corrupt or illegal practices, under the Representation of the People Act 1983. A person found to have committed a corrupt practice is disqualified from being elected to the Commons for five years; and anyone found to have committed an illegal practice is disqualified for three years.[176]

(g)   Under the Forfeiture Act 1870, a person convicted of treason is disqualified from membership until expiry of the sentence or receipt of a pardon. The effect of the Criminal Law Act 1967 was that other criminal convictions, even where a substantial prison sentence was imposed, did not disqualify from the House. Thus prisoners convicted of terrorist offences in Northern Ireland could be nominated and elected to the Commons, although they were unable to attend at Westminster.[177] Since 1981, a person convicted of an offence and sentenced to prison for more than a year by a court in the United Kingdom or elsewhere is, while detained in the British Isles or in the Republic of Ireland or unlawfully at large, disqualified from being nominated and from being a member. If he or she is already a member, the seat is vacated.[178]

It is within the disciplinary powers of the House to expel a member, but expulsion does not prevent him or her from being re-elected.[179] Formerly a person who held contracts with the Crown for the public service was disqualified from membership. But this disqualification was abolished in 1975 along with the disqualification of those

---

[172] Cd 5291, 2001, paras 48–53. And see pp 178–9 below.

[173] For greater detail, see Erskine May, *Parliamentary Practice*, ch 3.

[174] British Nationality Act 1981, Sch 7, first item.

[175] Parliamentary Elections Act 1695, s 7 was expressly preserved by the Family Law Reform Act 1969, Sch 2, para 2, when the age of majority was reduced to 18. And see P Norton [1980] PL 55.

[176] 1983 Act, ss 160, 173.

[177] See G J Zellick [1977] PL 29.

[178] Representation of the People Act 1981; and see C P Walker [1982] PL 389.

[179] Ch 11A below.

who held pensions from the Crown. It was also the case that ordained clergy and ministers of the Church of Scotland were disqualified for membership of the House of Commons.[180] But these disqualifications were removed in 2001,[181] although it is still provided that a person is disqualified from being or being elected as a member of the House of Commons if he is a Lord Spiritual (that is to say, one of the Bishops of the Church of England who is a member of the House of Lords).

Disqualification of office holders

In addition to the above, there are a number of office-holders who are also disqualified. Until 1957 the law governing the disqualification which arose from the holding of public offices was 'archaic, confused and unsatisfactory'.[182] That law had grown out of ancient conflicts between Crown and Commons. During the early 17th century, the House secured recognition of the right to control its own composition. In particular, the House asserted the principle that a member could not continue to serve when appointed by the Crown to a position the duties of which entailed prolonged absence from Westminster. After 1660, the House feared that the Crown would exercise excessive influence over it by the use of patronage and sought to avert a situation in which members held positions of profit at pleasure of the Crown. This fear led in 1700 to a provision in the Act of Settlement to the effect that no one who held an office or place of profit under the Crown should be capable of serving as a member of the House. This provision, which would have excluded ministers from the Commons, was repealed before it took effect. In its place, the Succession to the Crown Act 1707 enabled certain ministers to retain their seats in the House, subject to re-election after appointment, but excluded those who held office of a non-political character, for example in what today would be regarded as the civil service. But much legislation was necessary to establish the distinction between ministerial, or political, office-holders, who were eligible for membership and non-political office-holders, who were excluded. Moreover, it was necessary to restrict the number appointed to ministerial office from the Commons, to avoid a situation in which the executive (now in the form of the Prime Minister) exercised excessive control by patronage over the House.

The House of Commons Disqualification Act 1957 (re-enacted in 1975) replaced disqualification for holding 'an office or place of profit under the Crown' by disqualification attached to the holding of specified offices. There are three broad reasons for disqualification: (1) the physical impossibility for certain office holders of attendance at Westminster, (2) the risk of patronage and (3) the conflict of constitutional duties. Under s 1 of the 1975 Act, the disqualifying offices fall into six categories:

(a)   A great variety of judicial offices, listed in Sch 1 of the Act, including judges in the High Court and the Court of Session, circuit judges in England and Wales, sheriffs in Scotland, resident magistrates in Northern Ireland and stipendiary magistrates. The principle is that no person may hold full-time judicial office and be a practising politician. Lay magistrates are not affected.

(b)   Employment in the civil service of the Crown, whether in an established or temporary capacity, whole-time or part-time. The disqualification extends to members of the civil service of Northern Ireland and the diplomatic service. Civil servants who

---

[180] House of Commons (Clergy Disqualification) Act 1801, Roman Catholic Relief Act 1829, s 9. There was no similar disqualification from membership of the European Parliament, the Scottish Parliament, the National Assembly for Wales or the Northern Ireland Assembly.
[181] House of Commons (Removal of Clergy Disqualification) Act 2001. The Act implements a recommendation of the Home Affairs Committee (HC 768-I, 1997–98, para 127). See Blackburn, ch 5.
[182] HC 120 (1940–41) and HC 349 (1955–56).

wish to stand for election to Parliament are required by civil service rules to resign before becoming candidates.[183]

(c)   Membership of the regular armed forces of the Crown. Members of the reserve and auxiliary forces are not disqualified if recalled for active service. Members of the armed forces, like civil servants, must resign before becoming candidates for election to Parliament and they may apply for release to contest an election. A spate of such applications in 1962 led to the appointment of an advisory committee of seven members to examine the credentials of applicants and to test the sincerity of their desire to enter Parliament.[184]

(d)   Membership of any police force maintained by a police authority, or the National Criminal Intelligence Service, or the National Crime Squad.

(e)   Membership of the legislature of any country or territory outside the Commonwealth, except – following the Disqualification Act 2001 – in the case of the Republic of Ireland. It is likely that members of a legislature other than that of the Irish Republic would be debarred by their status as aliens from membership of the Commons.

(f)   A great variety of disqualifying offices arising from chairmanship or membership of commissions, boards, administrative tribunals, public authorities and undertakings; in a few cases the disqualification attaches only to particular constituencies (Sch 1, Parts 2–4). As these offices cover such a wide range, each office is specified by name. The Schedule may be amended by Order in Council made following a resolution approved by the House of Commons. This power obviates the need for amendment by statute as and when new offices (s 5) are created. The Queen's Printer is authorised to print copies of the 1975 Act as it is amended by subsequent Orders in Council.

For one purpose alone acceptance of an office of profit continues to disqualify. From early times a member of the House was in law unable to resign his seat and acceptance of an office of profit under the Crown was the only legal method of release from membership. The offices commonly used for the purpose were the office of Steward or Bailiff of the Chiltern Hundreds or of the Manor of Northstead. Under the Act of 1975 these offices are disqualifying offices (s 4). Appointment to them is made by the Chancellor of the Exchequer on the request of the member concerned.

Other matters

1. *Ministers in the House of Commons*   British practice requires that the holders of ministerial office should be members of either the Commons or the Lords and that the great majority should be drawn from the Commons. But it has long been necessary for limits to be imposed on the number of ministers who may sit in the Commons, lest excessive powers of patronage be exercised by the Prime Minister over the House. The present law is found partly in the House of Commons Disqualification Act 1975 and partly in the Ministerial and Other Salaries Act 1975. Section 2 of the former Act allows no more than 95 holders of ministerial office (whether paid or unpaid, it would seem) to sit and vote in the Commons; this limit had been raised from 70 to 91 in 1964[185] and to 95 in 1974.[186] If more members of the Commons are appointed to ministerial office than are allowed by law, those appointed in excess must not sit or vote in the House until the number has been reduced to the permitted figure (s 2(2)). The

---

[183] Servants of the Crown (Parliamentary European Assembly and Northern Ireland Assembly) Order 1987, paras 4.4.20–4.4.21. See also ch 13 D.

[184] HC 111 and 262 (1962–63); HC Deb, 18 February 1963, col 163.

[185] Ministers of the Crown Act 1964, noted by A E W Park (1965) 28 MLR 338.

[186] Ministers of the Crown Act 1974.

Ministerial and Other Salaries Act sets out the salaries payable to various categories of ministerial office, these salaries being subject to revision.[187] Schedule 1 to the Act imposes limits on the total number of such salaries payable at any one time to the various categories. Thus, in category 1 (holders of posts in the Cabinet apart from the Lord Chancellor) not more than 21 salaries are payable. Not more than 50 salaries are payable to posts in category 1 taken together with category 2 (ministers of state and departmental ministers outside the Cabinet). Not more than 83 salaries are payable to posts in categories 1, 2 and 3 (parliamentary secretaries) taken together. In addition, salaries are paid to the four law officers of the Crown, to five Junior Lords to the Treasury (government whips in the Commons) and to seven assistant whips in the Commons, as well as to various political posts in the royal household, some of which may be held only by members of the Lords.

2. *Effects of disqualification*   If any person is elected to the House while disqualified by the 1975 Act, the election is void (s 6(1)) and this could be so determined on an election petition. If a member becomes disqualified after election, his or her seat is vacated and the House may so resolve. Before 1957, Parliament might pass an Act of Indemnity in favour of members who had unwittingly become subject to disqualification. Today, the House may direct by order that a disqualification under the 1975 Act which existed at the material time be disregarded if it has already been removed (for example, by the member's resignation from the office in question) (s 6(2)). Thus a new election is unnecessary where the House itself has dispensed with the consequences of the disqualification, but no such order can affect the proceedings on an election petition (s 6(3)). Disputed cases of disqualification are in general determined by the House after consideration by a select committee. Thus in 1961 the Committee of Privileges reported that Mr Tony Benn was disqualified because he had succeeded to his father's peerage while a member of the Commons.[188] While disputes under the 1975 Act as to disqualifying offices arise rarely, the Judicial Committee of the Privy Council has jurisdiction to declare whether a person has incurred a disqualification under that Act (s 7). Any person may apply to the Judicial Committee for a declaration of disqualification but must give security for costs. Issues of fact may on the direction of the Judicial Committee be tried by the High Court in England, the Court of Session in Scotland or the High Court in Northern Ireland (s 7(4)). A declaration may not be made if an election petition is pending, if one has been tried in which disqualification on the same grounds was in issue, nor where the House has given relief by order (s 7(5)). This jurisdiction replaces the former procedure by which a common informer could sue a disqualified member for financial penalties. Another procedure open where there is a dispute over disqualification is for the Commons to petition the Crown to refer the matter to the Judicial Committee of the Privy Council for an advisory opinion on the law.[189]

H. The House of Lords

Historically membership of the House of Lords was confined to hereditary peers and the bishops of the Church of England.[190] The former inherited their status and a considerable body of law has developed to regulate title to the peerage.[191] The latter

---

[187] See Ministerial and Other Salaries Act 1997.
[188] HC 142 (1960–61).
[189] Under the Judicial Committee Act 1833, s 4; and see *Re MacManaway* [1951] AC 161.
[190] A good history is provided by Lowell, *The Government of England*, ch 21. See also Maitland, *The Constitutional History of England*, pp 166–72.
[191] HLE, vol 35. See also 12th edition of this work, pp 164–6.

held their position ex officio and ceased to occupy a seat in the Lords on resignation or retirement. In 1876, provision was made for the appointment of Lords of Appeal in Ordinary to conduct the judicial business of the House;[192] and in 1958 the Life Peerages Act allowed for the appointment of others to the peerage for life, without the conferring of a title which would pass to succeeding generations. Membership of the House of Lords was thus confined to those who inherited their position or who were appointed by the Crown (in the case of the bishops, the law lords and the life peers). The House of Lords Act 1999 broke the link between the hereditary peerage and membership of the House of Lords:[193] until then all hereditary peers were entitled to a seat in the Lords. There continue to be four categories of members of the House of Lords, although the effect of the House of Lords Act 1999 has been greatly to alter the balance between the different categories, with hereditary peers displaced by the life peers as the largest group. The four categories of membership are as follows:

(a)   Life peers created under the Life Peerages Act 1958.
(b)   Law lords appointed under the Appellate Jurisdiction Act 1876.
(c)   Lords Spiritual, being 26 senior clergy of the Church of England.
(d)   Hereditary peers, of whom there are 92.

Life peers

It was decided in 1856 that the Crown, although able to create a life peerage, could not create such a peerage carrying with it the right to a seat in the House of Lords.[194] If life peers were to be created to sit in the Lords, legislation was thus necessary. The Life Peerages Act 1958 both strengthened the Lords and weakened the hereditary principle. The Act enabled the Queen by letters patent to confer a peerage for life with a seat in Parliament on a man or woman. It did not restrict the power of the Crown to confer hereditary peerages, although it made it unnecessary for new hereditary peerages to be created. In fact very few hereditary peerages have since been created, although Mrs Thatcher revived the practice of making such appointments when she nominated Viscount Whitelaw and Speaker Thomas in 1983.[195] An appointment under the 1958 is irrevocable: there is no room for second thoughts; unlike a hereditary peerage, a life peerage cannot be disclaimed.[196] In October 2000 there were 549 life peers, of whom 107 were women. Life peers may not vote in House of Commons elections and they may not stand as parliamentary candidates.[197] But they may vote and stand for election to the devolved parliament and assemblies.[198]

There is a great deal of criticism that the system of appointment on the recommendation of the Prime Minister is an inappropriate way to recruit a legislative chamber and that it allows too much patronage on the part of the Prime Minister. In order to address such criticism, Mr Blair took steps to reduce his powers of patronage by establishing the House of Lords Appointments Commission which is a non-statutory, non-departmental public body, attached to the Cabinet Office.[199] It is chaired by a peer and its members include nominees of the three main national political parties and three

---

[192] Appellate Jurisdiction Act 1876.
[193] House of Lords Act 1999, s 1: 'No one shall be a member of the House of Lords by virtue of a hereditary peerage.' This is subject to s 2, on which see below.
[194] *Wensleydale Peerage case* (1856) 5 HLC 958.
[195] See Brazier, *Constitutional Practice*, p 241.
[196] See pp 175–6 below.
[197] See pp 149, 169 above.
[198] See Scotland Act 1998, s 16; Government of Wales Act 1998, s 13; and Northern Ireland Act 1998, s 36(6).
[199] For full details of its work, see www.house of lords appointmentscommission.gov.uk.

independent members. The role of the Commission is to make recommendations for non-political peers and to vet all nominations for peerages by the political parties on grounds of propriety. Prior to the creation of the Commission in 2000,[200] this latter role was performed by the Political Honours Scrutiny Committee which still operates to scrutinise political honours other than peerages (such as knighthoods).[201] But it remains the case that although Canada also has a nominated second chamber (the Senate), nomination is nevertheless an uncommon method of composition when compared to other countries, where second chambers are typically elected, either directly (as in Australia or the USA) or indirectly (as in France and Germany).[202]

Law Lords and Lords Spiritual

The 12 peers appointed under the Appellate Jurisdication Act 1876 to perform the judicial functions of the House of Lords are styled Lords of Appeal in Ordinary. They may sit and vote for life, notwithstanding resignation or retirement from their judicial appointment. To be qualified for appointment, they must have held high judicial office for two years in the United Kingdom, or in England and Wales have had a right of audience in relation to all proceedings of the Supreme Court, in Scotland have been an advocate (or a solicitor entitled to appear in the Court of Session), or in Northern Ireland have been a practising barrister, in each case for at least 15 years.[203] In practice at least two of the law lords are appointed from Scotland and one from Northern Ireland, reflecting the fact that the House of Lords continues to be the final court of appeal from these jurisdictions (although only in civil matters in relation to Scotland). In addition to the 12 serving law lords, there are always a number of retired law lords who are members of the House of Lords. Both serving and retired members may and do take part in the political business of the House, particularly on matters where their legal experience can be brought to bear. The judicial members of the House have in the past taken an active and notable part in debates about the reform of the legal profession on the one hand[204] and human rights on the other.[205] It is nevertheless unusual for the senior judges to be members of a legislature, although the practice is not without its merits.[206]

The Lords Spiritual are 26 bishops of the Church of England; they hold their seats in the Lords until they resign from their episcopal office. The Archbishops of Canterbury and York and the Bishops of London, Durham and Winchester have the right to a seat. The remaining Lords Spiritual are the 21 other diocesan bishops having seniority of date of appointment, with the exception of the Bishop of Sodor and Man who may not take a seat. When a bishop with a seat in the Lords resigns or retires, his place in the Lords is taken by the next senior diocesan bishop.[207] Since 1847, whenever a new diocesan bishopric has been created, it had been enacted that the number of bishops sitting in Parliament should not be increased.[208] This right of

---

[200] See Cm 4183, 1999.
[201] For an account of the work of the Committee, see Cm 4057, 1998, ch 14.
[202] For a full account, see Russell, *Reforming the House of Lords*.
[203] Appellate Jurisdiction Act 1876, s 6, as amended by the Courts and Legal Services Act 1990, s 71, and Sch 10. See ch 18B below.
[204] See HL Deb, 7 April 1999, cols 1307–1480.
[205] Particularly on the proceedings relating to the Human Rights Bill: see K D Ewing (1999) 62 MLR 79.
[206] Cm 4534, 2000, paras 9.6–9.7. Cf pp 21 and 87 above.
[207] Under the Ecclesiastical Offices (Age Limit) Measure 1975, bishops retire from their sees, and therefore from membership of the House, at age 70. Retired bishops are entitled to use the facilities of the House available to members of the House outside the Chamber.
[208] Ecclesiastical Commissioners Act 1847, s 2; Bishoprics Act 1878, s 5.

representation is nevertheless not extended to other faiths or churches and its continued existence reflects the special constitutional position of the Church of England. Although justified historically, such representation is bound to be closely questioned in an age which is simultaneously both more multi-cultural and more secular. It is possible for members and clergy of other churches and faiths to be appointed under the Life Peerages Act 1958, in the case of those churches and faiths which do not prohibit their senior clergy from accepting positions of political authority. But this is not the same as an entitlement to a guaranteed number of places.

Hereditary peers

It was previously the case that a hereditary peerage carried with it the right to a seat in the House of Lords. The House of Lords Act 1999 now provides that hereditary peers are no longer entitled to membership of the Lords. But hereditary peers have not been excluded altogether. In order to expedite the passing of the House of Lords Act 1999, the government accepted an arrangement whereby 90 hereditary peers (plus the Earl Marshal and the Lord Great Chamberlain)[209] would remain in the Lords until the process of reform was completed.[210] These 90 are elected by secret ballot from the hereditary peers in accordance with the Standing Orders of the House. In 2000, the House of Lords was thus still graced by two dukes, one marquess, 28 earls and countesses and 17 viscounts. The removal of the hereditary peers was nevertheless challenged as breaching the Treaty of Union, which provides a guarantee that 16 Scottish peers would be accepted into membership of the House of Lords. But this was rejected by the House of Lords Committee of Privileges, which concluded that the Treaty of Union did not provide an unalterable restraint on the power of Parliament.[211] Hereditary peers are now eligible to vote and to stand for election to Parliament, unless they are members of the House of Lords.[212]

Under the Standing Orders of the House governing the election of hereditary peers,[213] 15 of the 90 places were set aside for those hereditary peers who were office holders in the House: deputy speakers and deputy chairmen of committees. They are elected by the whole House. The remaining 75 places are elected by the hereditary peers to reflect the strength of the different parties from among their number. So 42 places were allocated to the Conservatives; three to the Liberal Democrats; two to Labour; and 28 to the cross-benchers. These members were elected from constituencies of their own party or group (so that, for example, only Conservative hereditary peers elected the 42 Conservatives).[214] A peerage cannot be alienated or surrendered, although under

---

[209] The Earl Marshal has responsibility for ceremonial matters and the Lord Chamberlain is 'the hereditary officer of state to whom the sovereign entrusts the custody and control of those parts of the Palace of Westminster not assigned to the two Houses' (such as the Queen's Robing Room): House of Lords, *Companion to the Standing Orders and Guide to the Proceedings of the House of Lords*, para 1.49.

[210] House of Lords Act 1999, s 2. For an account of how these figures were arrived at, see R Brazier, House of Lords Act 1999, *Current Law Statutes 1999*. In addition to the places reserved to hereditary peers by the House of Lords Act 1999, another ten were made life peers to enable them to remain. These were mainly hereditary peers of first creation. Another two hereditary peers reverted to sitting under the authority of life peerages which they already had.

[211] *Lord Gray's Motion* 2000 SC (HL) 46.

[212] House of Lords Act 1999, s 3.

[213] HL Standing Order 9.

[214] Should a vacancy arise, provision is made in Standing Order 10 for a by-election, at which only those hereditary peers who remain in membership of the House may vote. So only the 41 remaining Conservative hereditary peers could vote in a by-election for a new Conservative hereditary peer to become a member of the House.

the Peerages Act 1963 a hereditary peer may disclaim his or her title for life.[215] The primary purpose of granting this right was to enable hereditary peers to sit in the Commons, following an unsuccessful action by Tony Benn, then Viscount Stansgate by succession, who challenged the existing law which disqualified members of the Lords from standing for election to Parliament.[216] But the 1963 Act has been largely over-taken by the House of Lords Act 1999, as a result of which a hereditary peer may be a member of the House of Commons, provided that he or she is not also a member of the House of Lords.

I. Reforming the Membership of the House of Lords

Although there are thus a number of different routes to membership of the House of Lords, a member may not take his or her seat until he or she has obtained a writ of summons, which is issued at the direction of the Lord Chancellor by the Clerk of the Crown in Chancery (a senior officer of the House; also the Lord Chancellor's Permanent Secretary). New writs are issued before the meeting of each Parliament to all Lords – temporal and Spiritual –who are entitled to receive them.[217] Writs are also issued to peers newly created during the life of a Parliament. But no writs are issued to any peer who is known to be disqualified from sitting and there are currently four categories of disqualification:[218] aliens;[219] those under the age of 21;[220] bankrupts;[221] and those convicted of treason (until they have served their sentence or been pardoned).[222] Convicted persons may resume their seats after serving a prison sentence.[223] It is also necessary for a new peer to be formally introduced into the House. A day for this purpose is fixed by the Lord Chancellor and by custom not more than two introduc-tions may take place on any one day. Lords are normally introduced by two peers 'of the same degree in the House'.[224] It is not to be overlooked that despite the manner of its composition and the formality of its proceedings, the House of Lords exists principally to transact political business. This gives rise to questions about the polit-ical balance of the chamber and the obligations of its members.

---

[215] Under the Act existing peers were given 12 months from royal assent to disclaim and new peers were given 12 months from the date of their succession (s 1). This still applies unless the peer is excepted from s 1 of the 1999 Act by s 2 of the same Act. A sitting member of the Commons was given one month from the death of his predecessor in which to disclaim (1963 Act, s 2); but this has been repealed by the 1999 Act. Where a peer disclaims his title, it could not be restored to him, although the title would pass to the next generation following the death of the person who disclaimed. A person who disclaimed could be restored to the House of Lords by a life peerage under the 1958 Act. It would presumably be possible – if unlikely – for a new hereditary peerage to be conferred on the person who disclaimed.

[216] *Re Parliamentary Election for Bristol South East* [1964] 2 QB 257. It was under the 1963 Act that the Earl of Home disclaimed his title on being appointed Prime Minister in 1964 in succession to Mr Harold Macmillan.

[217] House of Lords, *Companion to the Standing Orders and Guide to the Proceedings of the House of Lords*, para 1.09.

[218] The Peerage Act 1963, s 6 removed the disqualification on peeresses in their own right to receive a writ of summons. See *Viscountess Rhondda'a Claim* [1922] 2 AC 339.

[219] Act of Settlement 1701, s 3 (as amended by the British Nationality Act 1981, Sch 7).

[220] HL Standing Order 2.

[221] Insolvency Act 1986, s 427.

[222] Forfeiture Act 1870.

[223] This is a matter which gave rise to some concern following the imprisonment of Lord Archer of Weston-super-Mare in 2001.

[224] House of Lords, *Companion to the Standing Orders and Guide to the Proceedings of the House of Lords*, para 1.13.

The political composition of the House of Lords

The effect of the House of Lords Act 1999 was significantly to reduce the size of the House of Lords: in 1999, there were 1,295 members who were culled to 695 by October in the following year. This still makes the House of Lords the largest second chamber in Europe. Of these 695, 549 were life peers; 28 law lords; 26 bishops and archbishops; and 92 hereditaries. A common refrain about the unreformed House was that it had an inbuilt Conservative bias. This is because most of the hereditary peers (who were the largest category of peers) were supporters of the Conservative party. Conservative governments thus always had a majority in the Lords, while governments of other parties were always in a minority.[225] But although the House has been reformed by the 1999 Act and although a large number of Labour peers have been created since 1997, the Conservative party remains the largest party, although it does not now have an overall majority: 232 of the 695 members in 2000 are declared as Conservatives; 200 Labour; 63 Liberal Democrat; and 164 as cross-benchers (non-party political or independent members). The others include the bishops and those who are undeclared or who were on leave of absence (on which see below). The government consequently does not have a majority in the House of Lords, which is distinguished from the House of Commons also by its strong independent element, with neither the cross-benchers nor the judges or bishops taking a party whip.

The legislative role of the House of Lords makes it inevitable that the government should have some presence in the chamber, to ensure that business is conducted efficiently and that an account is given of government proposals. There are two Cabinet ministers who must be members of the House of Lords: the Lord Chancellor and the Leader of the House of Lords. By convention the Prime Minister must be a member of the House of Commons and the same is true of other senior Cabinet posts: it is inconceivable in particular that the Chancellor of the Exchequer could be a member of the House of Lords.[226] But there is no reason in principle why other ministers should not be based in the Lords and the life peerage provides an opportunity for the Prime Minister to bring into his or her government an individual who may not be a member of Parliament (as in the case of Lord Young by Mrs Thatcher). It also provides an opportunity for the Prime Minister to retain the services of a minister who may have lost his or her Commons seat in a general election (as in the case of Mrs Lynda Chalker who lost her seat in 1992 but who was elevated to the peerage, retaining her position as minister for overseas development in Mr Major's government). In 2000 there were in fact 20 ministers who held seats in the Lords. Apart from the Lord Chancellor and the Leader of the House already referred to, these were the Attorney-General, seven whips, five ministers of state and five parliamentary secretaries.

Obligations of membership

Unlike the House of Commons, many members of the House of Lords are not engaged full time in the business of the House or activities incidental thereto. Indeed it is one of the strengths of the House that its many part-time members are occupied in other pursuits, on the experience of which they may draw in their work in the upper chamber. But there must be some obligation of attendance and participation, particularly on the part of the life peers who have voluntarily assumed the benefits of office. House of Lords Standing Order 22 – introduced on 16 June 1958 – provides that 'Lords are to

---

[225] On this, see Miliband, *Capitalist Democracy in Britain*, p 125.
[226] Lord Carrington was Foreign Secretary in the House of Lords in Mrs Thatcher's government until he resigned in 1982 following the invasion of the Falkland Islands.

attend the sittings of the House or, if they cannot do so, obtain leave of absence, which the House may grant at pleasure'. It is also provided, however, that this particular standing order 'shall not be understood as requiring a Lord who is unable to attend regularly to apply for leave of absence if he proposes to attend as often as he reasonably can'.[227] At any time during a Parliament, a Lord may obtain leave of absence for the rest of the Parliament by applying in writing to the Clerk of the Parliaments.[228] Before the beginning of every new Parliament, the Clerk of the Parliaments (a senior officer of the House) writes to each Lord who was on leave in the previous Parliament asking whether he wishes to apply for leave in the forthcoming Parliament.[229]

A peer who has been granted leave of absence is expected not to attend sittings of the House during the period of leave, although provision is made for a peer who wishes to terminate his or her leave of absence to give a month's notice.[230] The House has no power to prevent the attendance of a peer who, having received a writ of summons, does not observe the leave of absence rules.[231] Apart from the law lords, who receive a salary so long as they hold their judicial appointment, members of the House do not receive a salary. Since 1957 a daily attendance allowance has been paid and travel costs are met; attending peers also receive allowances for overnight stays away from home, as well as for secretarial and research assistance. There is a sense, however, that membership of a part-time legislative chamber on an unpaid basis is difficult for people from outside London and the south east. The average daily attendance in the House is said to have more than trebled since the introduction of life peers: from 136 in 1959/60 to 446 in 1998/99. It has also been said that the introduction of life peers has broadened the areas of expertise of the Lords, 'beyond the traditional fields of agriculture, the armed forces and the law'.[232]

Further reform

The House of Lords Act 1999 is designed to be only the first step in the process of reform. In the reformed House it is proposed to remove the hereditary peers altogether and to move to a position in which the House is seen to have more legitimacy. But it is difficult to produce a solution for a reformed House which commands agreement across the political spectrum.[233] Democratic instinct suggests that the only credible solution is a wholly or largely elected (directly or indirectly) Upper House (perhaps one renamed as a Senate).[234] But the difficulty with this is that it could end up with a House wholly dominated by the political parties and, depending on election results, with the same party in control of both the Commons and the Lords. In that case, there would be little prospect of effective scrutiny or revision of government business. Conversely, election could lead to a House with a majority different from that of the Commons, leading to the alternative result of stalemate or gridlock in the legislative process, with both Houses claiming a mandate for their actions and each claiming a

---

[227] HL Standing Order 22(1).
[228] HL Standing Order 22(2).
[229] HL Standing Order 22(3).
[230] HL Standing Order 22(4). It was hoped in this way to diminish the influence of backwoodsmen – mainly hereditary peers who played little part in the work of the House but who might be summoned by their party leaders to vote on crucial and contentious divisions. After the culling of the hereditary peers, this ought to be much less of a problem today.
[231] See HL 7, 66-1, 67 (1955–56), paras 37–8.
[232] Cm 4534, 2000, paras 2.8–2.10.
[233] For good accounts of the difficulties, see Bogdanor, *Politics and the Constitution*, ch 14; Brazier, *Constitutional Reform*, ch 11; and Shell, *The House of Lords*.
[234] See Richard and Welfare, *Unfinished Business*. See also R Blackburn, in Blackburn and Plant, *Constitutional Reform*, ch 1 and Billy Bragg, *A Genuine Expression of the Will of the People*.

superior mandate to the other. It is thus a curious paradox that a nominated House without an electoral mandate is able to produce a revising chamber which simultane-ously provides a greater measure of independent scrutiny of government than the House of Commons, without at the same time unduly impeding or frustrating the implementation of the government's programme.[235]

Any proposal for the reform of the composition of the House of Lords ought logically to begin by asking what it is we expect the House of Lords to do and to tailor composition to function. If the purpose is to act as a restraint on government, the case for an elected chamber would be irresistible (provided election were guar-anteed to produce a House with a different political majority from the Commons). If, however, the purpose is (as currently) that of revision and scrutiny, there may be a case for other methods of composition. A white paper published in 2001, *The House of Lords – Completing the Reform*, proposed the removal of the existing hereditary peers and the inclusion of a small number of members (20% of the total number) who would be directly elected from regional constituencies (in closed party lists), to ensure an appropriate level of regional representation.[236] But it was also proposed that the overwhelming majority should be nominated for renewable fixed periods of 15 years or less, with most of the nominations to be made by the political parties.[237] This seems to be the worst of all options, in the sense that it may no longer be possible to say that doubts about the legitimacy of the composition of the House are balanced by the independence which only life tenure can provide for its members. It is now unlikely that this white paper will be implemented in view of the considerable opposition to it, causing it thus to suggest the same fate as earlier proposals for reform in 1918, 1945 and 1968.[238]

J. Meeting of Parliament

In law, a new Parliament is summoned by means of a royal proclamation. It is by the Sovereign that Parliament is prorogued, which occurs when a session of Parliament is terminated, and dissolved, when the life of one Parliament is brought to an end. These powers of the Sovereign are prerogative powers, that is they are derived from the common law powers of the Crown, not from statutes.[239] They were used as political weapons by the Stuart kings during their struggles with Parliament in the 17th century; since then they have been subjected to both legal and political controls, originally to ensure that the King could not govern without Parliament. In 1689, art 13 of the Bill of Rights provided that 'for redress of all grievances, and for the amending, strength-ening and preserving of the laws, Parliament ought to be held frequently'.[240] In 1694, the Meeting of Parliament Act (formerly the Triennial Act) supplemented this rather vague demand by requiring that Parliament should meet at least once every three years, a requirement which still forms part of the law.

---

[235] The elected option was rejected by the Wakeham royal commission which had been appointed in 1999, although it did recommend that there should be an elected element: Cm 4534 (2000).

[236] Cm 5291, 2001. For background and an account of Labour's plans for reform of the Lords, see D Shell (2000) 53 Parliamentary Affairs 290.

[237] 120 members would be nominated by the independent House of Lords Appointments Commission (which would be retained), in order to ensure the continuing presence of cross-benchers.

[238] Cd 9038, 1918, Cmd 7380, 1948 and Cmnd 3799, 1968.

[239] Ch 12 D. And see Blackburn, *The Meeting of Parliament*.

[240] Ch 2 A.

Frequency and duration of Parliament

Although there is no rule of law expressly requiring this, in practice Parliament has met annually ever since 1689. One reason for this is that since that time it has been the practice for some essential legislation, including authority for certain forms of taxation and expenditure, to be passed only for a year at a time; this legislation must therefore be renewed annually if lawful government is to be maintained.[241] Today the many pressures on government to maintain a flow of legislation through Parliament and the expectation of all politicians that Parliament should meet regularly ensure that, subject to customary periods of holiday, Parliament is in constant session. The Meeting of Parliament Act 1694 also regulated the life of a Parliament: no Parliament was to last for more than three years and, unless sooner dissolved, was then to expire by lapse of time. The Septennial Act 1715 extended the life of Parliament to seven years but the Parliament Act 1911 reduced the period to five years; the five-year period runs from the day appointed by writ of summons for Parliament to meet after a general election.[242] In practice, apart from the two world wars, when the life of Parliament was extended annually to avoid the holding of a general election during wartime, all modern Parliaments have been dissolved by the Sovereign, rather than expiring by lapse of time. The length of recent Parliaments has varied: that elected in February 1974 lasted only until October 1974; by contrast, the Parliaments elected in 1987 and 1992 lasted for almost the full five years, whereas that elected in 1997 lasted for four years.

Parliament continues for five years unless it is dissolved sooner by the Sovereign on the advice of the Prime Minister. Save in exceptional circumstances, the Sovereign must give effect to the Prime Minister's request. The opportunity to choose the timing of a general election is an important power at the disposal of the Prime Minister who may choose a time when there is a revival in the economy or when the government's popularity is rising. It is sometimes said that the right to request a dissolution is a powerful weapon in the hands of a Prime Minister to compel recalcitrant supporters in the Commons to conform. Where government policies are challenged by major national interests, the Prime Minister may take the dispute to the electorate in the hope of getting renewed support, as happened in February 1974 when Mr Heath called an election because the miners' strike challenged his economic policy. But dissolution is too ultimate a deterrent to be a convenient means of bringing pressure to bear on government members of the Commons, since an election at an unfavourable time may mean that the party goes out of office sooner than it otherwise would have done. Nevertheless, the possibility of a dissolution before the statutory life of a Parliament has run its course leaves the executive with a means of controlling Parliament which would not be available if the law required an election of a new Parliament at prescribed intervals (for example, once every four years).[243] Since the Representation of the People Act 1867, the duration of Parliament had been independent of the life of the Sovereign.[244]

---

[241] So too authority for the maintenance of the army has been continued in force annually, although this is now done by resolution of Parliament and not by Act. Ch 16.

[242] Septennial Act 1715 and Parliament Act 1911, s 5.

[243] Ch 12 B.

[244] If Parliament should be prorogued or adjourned when the Sovereign dies, Parliament must reassemble at once without a summons (Succession to the Crown Act 1707, s 5). Should the Sovereign die after a dissolution, but before the date fixed for the election, the former Parliament must meet immediately and polling day is postponed for 2 weeks (Representation of the People Act 1985, s 20, repealing the Meeting of Parliament Act 1797, ss 3–5).

Dissolution and prorogation of Parliament

Modern practice is that the same proclamation both dissolves Parliament and summons a new one. Formerly Parliament would be dissolved only after it had first been prorogued, but dissolution may now occur while the two Houses are adjourned.[245] After the summoning of Parliament by proclamation, individual writs are issued to the members of the Lords and writs are issued to returning officers commanding an election of members of the Commons to be held.[246] Between general elections, a session of Parliament usually runs from late October or early November for about one year. After the long summer adjournment of both Houses, there is usually a short resumption of the two Houses to complete necessary legislative business. Parliament is then prorogued and a new session opens a few days later. When a vacancy occurs in the House during a Parliament, for example by the death of a member, the Speaker may by warrant authorise the issue of a writ for the holding of a by-election. When the House is sitting, the Speaker issues the warrant upon the order of the House.[247] By long-established custom of the House, the motion for the issue of a writ is moved by the Chief Whip of the party which held the seat before the vacancy occurred. There is no time limit for filling the vacancy. In 1973 the Speaker's Conference on electoral law recommended that the writ for a by-election should normally be moved within three months of the vacancy occurring.[248]

Prorogation brings to an end a session of Parliament. Parliament is prorogued not by the Sovereign in person but by a royal commission, through whom the prorogation speech reviewing the work of the session is delivered to Parliament. Parliament may be recalled by proclamation at one day's notice during a prorogation, if this should be necessary.[249] Prorogation terminates all business pending in Parliament, with the exception of the judicial work of the House of Lords. Any public Bills which have not passed through all stages in both Houses lapse. In the case of private Bills a resolution may be passed before prorogation directing that a Bill be held over till the next session. Each House may adjourn for such time as it pleases, but this does not end any uncompleted business. The Sovereign may call on Parliament to meet before the conclusion of an adjournment intended to last for more than 14 days.[250] The standing orders of each House authorise an adjournment of either House to be terminated at short notice, should the Lord Chancellor or the Speaker be satisfied on the request of the government that public interest requires it. Parliament must be recalled within five days if a state of emergency is declared or the reserve forces are called out during an adjournment or prorogation.[251]

Opening of Parliament

After a dissolution or a prorogation, Parliament is opened by the Sovereign in person or by royal commissioners. When a new Parliament meets, the House of Commons first elects a Speaker, for which purpose the MP who has the longest continuous period of membership and is not a minister of the Crown presides over the proceedings.[252]

---

[245] See R Blackburn [1987] PL 533.
[246] See section D of this chapter.
[247] By the Recess Elections Act 1975, which re-enacted an Act of 1784, the Speaker may order the issue of a writ during a recess caused by prorogation or adjournment.
[248] Cmnd 5500, 1973.
[249] Parliament (Elections and Meetings) Act 1943, s 34.
[250] Meeting of Parliament Act 1870, amending the Meeting of Parliament Act 1799.
[251] Emergency Powers Act 1920 (ch 26 D); Reserve Forces Act 1996, s 68(10).
[252] HC SO 1(1) and see HC 111 (1971–72).

After this the House adjourns until the election of the Speaker has been announced to the Lord Chancellor in the House of Lords.[253] The Lords take the oath of allegiance as soon as Parliament has been opened and the Commons as soon as the Speaker has taken the oath.[254] At the beginning of every session, the first business is the debate on the speech from the throne. This speech announces in outline the government's plans for the principal business of the session. It is delivered in the House of Lords, to which the Commons are summoned to hear the speech read by the Sovereign or by the Lord Chancellor. In each House an address is moved in answer to the speech and a general debate of national affairs takes place, lasting some four or five days.

The chief officer of the House of Commons is the Speaker. Except when the House is in committee, he is its chairman and is responsible for the orderly conduct of debate. It is through the Speaker that the House communicates with the Sovereign. Today, the Speaker is expected to act with complete impartiality between the parties and to preserve the rights of minorities in the House.[255] A member of the House is elected to be Speaker at the beginning of each new Parliament and whenever a vacancy otherwise occurs. It is customary for the party with a majority in the House to select a candidate from among its own number, but that person will not necessarily be elected. When Michael Martin from the Labour backbenches was elected to succeed Betty Boothroyd in 2000, it was the first time in recent years that a retiring Speaker had been succeeded by someone from the same side of the House. The election of Speaker Martin proved controversial for a number of reasons and led to the introduction of formal rules for dealing with contested elections for Speaker in new standing orders of the House.[256] If the Speaker in the previous Parliament is re-elected as an MP at the general election, it is customary for him or her to be re-elected as Speaker when the new Parliament meets. In such a case, he or she will have fought the election as Speaker, not as a member of his or her former party. While the Speaker is unable to represent his or her constituency's interests in debate, he or she is able to take up the grievances of constituents privately with the departments concerned. The Speaker's salary is payable out of the Consolidated Fund. A retired Speaker receives a peerage by convention, and a statutory pension. If a Speaker dies in office, all business of the House comes to a halt until a successor is appointed.

The officers and administration of Parliament

The chief permanent officer of the House of Lords is the Clerk of the Parliaments, appointed by the Crown and removable only by the Crown on address from the Lords. His duties include the endorsement of every Act of Parliament with the date on which it received the royal assent and the custody of one copy of every Act printed on vellum. The Lord Chairman of Committees is assisted in his work on private legislation by Counsel to the Chairman of Committees. The Clerk of the House of Commons is appointed by the Crown; two clerk assistants are appointed by the Crown on the nomination of the Speaker. These officers may be removed only on an address from the House. The Clerk of the House is responsible for the records and journals of all proceedings in the Commons, endorsing all Bills sent to the Lords and laying documents on the table of the House. He is the Accounting Officer for House of Commons expenditure. The Speaker's Counsel advises the Speaker and officers of the House on matters of law and his duties include the oversight of private legislation and the scrutiny

---

[253] On the Lord Chancellor, see ch 18 E below.
[254] Under the Oaths Act 1978, s 5, members may make a solemn affirmation in lieu of the oath.
[255] See Laundy, *The Office of Speaker*.
[256] HC SO 1A and 1B.

of statutory instruments. The Serjeant at Arms, appointed by the Crown, is responsible for enforcing the orders of the House. Before the Queen appoints a new Serjeant at Arms, she consults with the Speaker, who may take soundings in the House before the appointment is made.[257] By the Parliamentary Corporate Bodies Act 1992, the Clerk of the Parliaments and the Clerk of the House of Commons were respectively designated as the Corporate Officers of the two Houses, each with capacity as a corporation sole to hold property, make contracts and so on for the House in question.

The Palace of Westminster was formerly controlled on the Sovereign's behalf by the Lord Great Chamberlain but in 1965 control of the Palace (except for Westminster Hall) passed to the two Houses. Control of that part occupied by the House of Lords is vested in the Lord Chancellor and is exercised by the House of Lords Offices Committee; and of that part occupied by the Commons in the Speaker. Administration of the Commons was reformed with the establishment of a House of Commons Commission under the House of Commons (Administration) Act 1978.[258] The commission consists of the Speaker, the Leader of the House, a member nominated by the Leader of the Opposition and three other members appointed by the House. The commission is responsible for the staff of the House, for preparing annual estimates of House expenditure and for supervising the departments into which the work of the House is organised. Underlying these arrangements are such problems as how much should be paid to service the activities of the House, what these activities should be and whether the government should control the House's expenditure. Acting on his own authority, the Speaker in 1987 directed that a BBC film on the Zircon defence project, alleged to have been made in breach of the Official Secrets Act 1911, should not be shown in a committee room at Westminster by backbench MPs. This action was upheld by the Committee of Privileges.[259] A number of select committees known generally as domestic committees advise the House of Commons Commission and the Speaker on provision of services to the House. These deal with accommodation and works; administration; catering; and information. The Finance and Services Committee considers the financial and administrative implications of their recommendations and has a more general remit to improve financial management in the House, after a report by Sir Robin Ibbs in 1990.[260]

---

[257] HC Deb, 11 December 1962, cols 209–10.
[258] Largely based on the Bottomley report (HC 624, 1974–75). And see G F Lock [2001] PL 465.
[259] See HC 365 (1986–87); A W Bradley [1987] PL 1, 487.
[260] For full details, see www.parliament.uk/commons/selcom/ctteesys.htm.

Chapter 10

FUNCTIONS OF PARLIAMENT

We have already examined the relationship between Parliament, the executive and the judiciary and the principle of responsible government. In looking more closely at the functions of Parliament, we will focus attention on the House of Commons, since it is the composition of this House that determines which party will form the government, it is from the Commons that most ministers are drawn and it is the House of Commons that by withdrawing its support can cause the Prime Minister to resign or to seek a dissolution. But the work of the House of Commons must not be exaggerated beyond its context. First, the role of the House of Lords in Parliament, especially in legislation, is significant, although the political role of the House is secondary to that of the Commons. Second, the political authority of the House of Commons does not extend to its undertaking the work of government itself. Most members of the Commons are not members of the government. Neither could an elected assembly of 659 members itself take on the executive role in national affairs.

A classic statement of both the importance of parliamentary control of government and its limitations was made by the political philosopher, John Stuart Mill:

> There is a radical distinction between controlling the business of government, and actually doing it. The same person or body may be able to control everything, but cannot possibly do everything; and in many cases its control over everything will be more perfect, the less it personally attempts to do . . . It is one question, therefore, what a popular assembly should control, another what it should itself do . . . Instead of the function of governing, for which it is radically unfit, the proper office of a representative assembly is to watch and control the government; to throw the light of publicity on its acts; to compel a full exposition and justification of all of them which anyone considers questionable; to censure them if found condemnable, and, if the men who compose the government abuse their trust, or fulfil it in a manner which conflicts with the deliberate sense of the nation, to expel them from office, and either expressly or virtually appoint their successors.[1]

Mill stressed that an important function of the Commons was also to be a sounding board for the nation's grievances and opinions, 'an arena in which not only the general opinion of the nation, but that of every section of it . . . can produce itself in full light and challenge discussion'.[2]

This high-principled analysis is still of value, even though the strength of the executive power today, the present electoral and party system and the fact that economic and industrial power is located outside the House of Commons, together present a formidable challenge to the political authority of the House. If it is a duty of the House to find out about, scrutinise and influence the many acts of government agencies, two consequences follow: first, the House needs procedures and resources that match the scale of the task; second, the members of the House who do not hold ministerial office need the political will to do more than simply sustain the government in office while voting through the measures laid before it. The creation by the Commons in 1979 of

---

[1] Mill, *Representative Government*, ch 5.
[2] Ibid.

a system of specialist committees to scrutinise the main departments of government was a notable reform,[3] but the committees operate within a House which for many tasks still adopts an adversarial approach to politics in its proceedings.[4] And although parliamentary procedure has undergone a process of modernisation since 1997, the reformer's scalpel has been less keenly felt in this area than in others. Indeed it has been suggested – perhaps with only some exaggeration – that the government's approach to legislative modernisation 'always owed more to its desire to secure the passage of its business than a desire to improve the effectiveness of parliamentary scrutiny'.[5]

Many writers have sought to list the principal functions of Parliament. Bagehot in *The English Constitution* included within the functions of the House of Commons the expressive function (expressing the opinion of the people), the teaching function and the informing function ('it makes us hear what otherwise we should not'),[6] as well as the functions of legislation and finance. In 1978, the House's Select Committee on Procedure, whose report led to the reform of the committee system in 1979, considered that the major tasks of the Commons fell into four main categories: legislation, the scrutiny of the activities of the executive, the control of finance and the redress of grievances.[7] Inevitably these categories overlap and the list does not include the broader political functions of the House that underlie its more detailed tasks. Here the work of Parliament will be examined under five headings: (*a*) legislation; (*b*) conflict between the two Houses; (*c*) financial procedure; (*d*) scrutiny of administration; and (*e*) its role as constitutional watchdog.[8] The redress of collective grievances is related to all these headings; the redress of individual grievances is an aspect of the scrutiny of administration and also relevant is the Parliamentary Ombudsman, whose work will be considered in chapter 29 D.

A. Legislation

In chapter 4, we saw that the legislative supremacy of Parliament does not mean that the whole work of legislating is carried on within Parliament or that the parliamentary stage is the most formative stage in the process of legislation. Many government policies can be achieved within the framework of existing legislation: for example, by the provision of more money for certain purposes or by the use of existing powers to direct local authorities. But other policies require legislation and most legislation is initiated by the government. The scope for legislative initiatives by individual MPs is severely limited, both because of restricted parliamentary time and of the tight hold the government maintains over departmental action. The process by which government policies are turned into law falls into three broad stages:

(*a*)   before publication of the Bill;
(*b*)   the passage of the Bill through Parliament;
(*c*)   after the Bill has received the royal assent.

In this section, emphasis is placed on the second of these stages. But stages (*a*) and (*c*) are both important to an understanding of the legislative process.[9] The process of

---

[3] Section D in this chapter.
[4] Cf Finer (ed), *Adversary Politics and Electoral Reform*.
[5] P Cowley and M Stuart (2001) Parliamentary Affairs 238.
[6] Bagehot, p 153. And see Norton, *The Commons in Perspective*, ch 4.
[7] HC 588–1 (1977–78), p viii.
[8] See also Ryle and Richards (eds), *The Commons Under Scrutiny*; Walkland (ed), *The House of Commons in the Twentieth Century*; Norton, *The Commons in Perspective*; Griffith and Ryle, *Parliament*.
[9] Cf the analysis made in Hansard Society, *Making the Law*.

legislation, like most aspects of parliamentary procedure, is complicated.[10] A distinction must be drawn between public and private Bills. A public Bill seeks to alter the general law and is introduced into Parliament under the standing orders of the two Houses relating to public business. A private Bill is a Bill relating to a matter of individual, corporate or local interest and is subject to separate standing orders relating to private business.[11] A private Bill must not be confused with a public Bill introduced by a private member, which is known as a private member's Bill.[12]

The pre-Bill stage

The life history of a Bill has usually begun long before it is laid before Parliament. The source of a Bill may be in a party's political programme or in the efforts of a pressure group to get the law reformed. Public authorities may have experienced difficulties in administering the existing law and may seek wider powers. A royal commission, the Law Commissions or bodies such as the Commission on Standards in Public Life may have published reports recommending reform. Economic problems or the action of terrorists may have made it necessary for government to take preventive measures. A decision of the courts, including the European Court of Human Rights and the European Court of Justice, may have shown the need for legislation. The government may have entered into a treaty which imposes an obligation to change the law of the United Kingdom. Whatever the circumstances which cause legislation to be seen as necessary, before a Bill can be introduced into Parliament by the minister of the sponsoring department, it must be adopted into the government's legislative programme. In 2001, it was the task of the Cabinet Committee on the Legislative Programme to prepare and submit to Cabinet drafts of the Queen's speeches and proposals for the legislative programme. The Committee also monitors the progress of Bills, both in preparation and during their passage through Parliament.[13]

Within the limits of Cabinet approval, it is for the department primarily concerned to decide what a Bill should contain and these instructions are conveyed to Parliamentary Counsel, who are responsible for drafting all government Bills. While a Bill is being drafted, extensive consultation may take place with other departments affected and successive revisions of the draft Bill are circulated confidentially within government. There may also be consultation with organisations outside government representing the interests primarily affected but until recently it was uncommon for a draft Bill to be disclosed. If more open consultation is desired, the government may publish a consultative document, for example a 'green paper', which states the government's provisional views, or a 'white paper', which while stating the government's decided position may leave certain matters open for further discussion. Where green or white papers are published, they are sometimes debated in Parliament, but the pre-Bill stage is essentially an administrative and political process which is carried on within government and behind the closed doors of Whitehall. The House of Commons Modernisation Committee has, however, welcomed the recent government practice of publishing a number of bills in draft form as providing a 'real chance for the House to exercise its powers of pre-legislative scrutiny in an effective way'. Although it was unrealistic to expect all or most major bills to be published in draft, it is said that there is almost universal agreement

---

[10] See HC 538 (1970–71); Griffith, *Parliamentary Scrutiny of Government Bills*; Miers and Page, *Legislation*; Erskine May *Parliamentary Practice* (esp ch 22); Griffith and Ryle, *Parliament*, chs 6–8; and *Making the Law* (note 9).

[11] Page 193 below.

[12] Page 190 below.

[13] www.cabinet-office.gov.uk/cabsec/2001/cabcom/lp.htm.

that pre-legislative scrutiny is right in principle: it provides an opportunity for the House as a whole, individual backbenchers and the Opposition to have a real input into the form of the legislation which ultimately emerges.[14] The government has undertaken to make more legislation available in draft for scrutiny by Select Committees. It was also suggested that legislation applying only in Wales could be scrutinised by the National Assembly for Wales.[15]

Public Bill procedure

1. *From first reading to committee* In the case of government Bills, the sponsoring minister presents the Bill to the Commons; it receives a formal first reading and is then printed and published. There follows the second reading of the Bill, when the House may debate the general proposals contained in the Bill. If the second reading is opposed, a division may take place on an opposition amendment to postpone the second reading for three or six months or (more usually) on a reasoned amendment opposing the Bill. For a government Bill to be lost on second reading would be a serious political defeat. This setback has been avoided by most modern governments, but not by the government in 1986 when the Shops Bill, to reform the law on Sunday opening of shops, was defeated on second reading in the Commons by 296 votes to 282.[16] In the Commons, a whole day (i.e. from 3.30 pm to 10 pm) may be set aside for the second reading of a major Bill, but many Bills are debated for less than two hours and two or more days may be allotted to the debate of Bills of exceptional political importance.[17] Where a Bill involves new public expenditure or new taxation, the Commons must approve a financial resolution on the proposal of a minister before the clauses concerned may be considered in committee; the financial resolution is approved immediately after a Bill's second reading.[18] In some cases the second reading may take place either in the Scottish Grand Committee[19] or in a second reading committee.[20] An expedited procedure exists for Consolidation Bills.[21]

After second reading, a Bill is normally referred for detailed consideration to a standing committee, consisting of between 16 and 50 members nominated by the Committee of Selection.[22] The Committee of Selection must have regard to the qualifications of the members and to the composition of the House, which means in practice that the parties are represented as nearly as possible in proportion to their representation in the House. If the government came into office with an overall majority over other parties and later loses that majority, it ceases to have a majority on standing committees.[23] Despite its name, a standing committee is constituted afresh for each Bill. The chairman of a standing committee is a member of the chairmen's panel appointed by the Speaker. Not more than two standing committees may be appointed for the committee stage of Bills which relate exclusively to Scotland.[24] Instead of referring a Bill to a standing committee, the House may commit the Bill to a committee

---

[14] HC 190 (1997–8), paras 19, 20.
[15] HC 440 (2001–2) (Memorandum by the Leader of the House), paras 17–19.
[16] HC Deb, 14 April 1986, cols 584–702. See Brazier, *Constitutional Practice*, pp 219–20.
[17] Griffith, ch 2; Griffith and Ryle, pp 322–9.
[18] Page 201 below; Erskine May, ch 31; Griffith and Ryle, pp 231, 251–2, 330–1.
[19] HC Standing Order (HC SO) 93. See C M G Himsworth (1996) 1 Edin LR 79.
[20] HC SO 90; Griffith, ch 2; Griffith and Ryle, pp 230, 312.
[21] HC SO 140. See Lord Simon of Glaisdale and J V D Webb [1975] PL 285.
[22] HC SOs 84, 86; Griffith, ch 3.
[23] HC Deb, 11 January 1995, col 158.
[24] HC SO 101. For a public Bill relating exclusively to Wales, the standing committee includes all members for Welsh constituencies (SO 86(2)).

of the whole House,[25] for which purpose the Speaker's place is taken by the Chairman of Ways and Means or one of the deputy chairmen. In practice this happens only on the proposal of the government, whether for minor Bills on which the committee stage is purely formal, for Bills of outstanding political or constitutional importance, or for Bills which the government wishes to see become law as soon as possible.[26]

2. *From committee to third reading* Whether a Bill is considered in standing committee or in committee of the whole House, the object of the committee stage is to consider the individual clauses of the Bill and to enable amendments to be made. While general approval has been given to the Bill on second reading, members opposed to the Bill may use the committee stage to propose amendments narrowing the scope of the Bill or in other ways rendering it more acceptable to them. Members may be able to persuade the minister in charge of the Bill to reconsider a specific point, but the government expects to maintain its majority in committee and an amendment is not often made against the wishes of the government. As has been commented, 'the direct impact of the committee stage on the contents of Bills is very small: only rarely is an amendment successfully moved against the wishes of the government and only rarely does the government accept an amendment moved by the Opposition.'[27] The indirect impact is much greater than this, as the debate in committee often causes the government to propose amendments at a later stage. In committee, members may speak any number of times supporting or opposing amendments. After the amendments to a clause have been considered, there may take place a further debate on the motion that the clause, or the clause as amended, should stand part of the Bill. Occasionally Bills will be referred to a select committee. But although this was a common procedure in the past, it has been used in recent years only for the quinquennial armed forces bills.[28]

When a Bill has completed its committee stage, it is reported as amended to the whole House. On the report stage, further amendments may be made to the Bill on the proposal of ministers, sometimes to give effect to undertakings which they have given in committee, sometimes to remove amendments made in committee but not accepted by the government. The Opposition may use the report stage to urge further amendments upon the government, although it is rare for these amendments to succeed and the Speaker has the discretion to select the amendments which will be debated.[29] A Bill committed to the whole House and not amended in committee is not considered by the House on report. Bills which were considered by a second reading committee or the Scottish Grand Committee (but not the Welsh or Northern Ireland Grand Committees) may be referred to a standing committee or to the Scottish Grand Committee for the report stage, but there has been reluctance to deprive the whole House of its opportunity to consider Bills on report.[30] After a Bill has been considered on report, it receives its third

---

[25] HC SO 63, 66.

[26] It is a 'long-standing convention of the House' that 'bills of first class constitutional importance' should 'have all their stages on the floor of the House'. This is said to derive from a memorandum submitted by the Labour Government to the Procedure Committee in 1945. See HC 190 (1997–98), paras 74–5. Major Bills taken in committee of the whole House have included the Bills for the European Communities Act 1972, the Scotland Act 1998, the Government of Wales Act 1998, the Northern Ireland Act 1998, the Human Rights Act 1998, the House of Lords Act 1999, the Representation of the People Act 2000 and parts of the Political Parties, Elections and Referendums Act 2000.

[27] Griffith and Ryle, p 317. For confirmation of this, see the fate of all amendments to government Bills in 1967–68, 1968–69 and 1970–71, recorded in Griffith, ch 3.

[28] HC, *The Committee System of the House of Commons* (1998), para 11. See ch 10 D (on select committees) and ch 16 A (on the quinquennial armed forces bills).

[29] HC SO 32(1).

[30] HC SO 92; HC 588–1 (1977–78), p xx; HC 350 (1986–87), p iv; Griffith and Ryle, pp 235–7.

reading; only verbal amendments may be made to a Bill at this stage.[31] Such debates as there are tend to be brief and formal, although with a controversial Bill the Opposition may wish once more to vote against it.

Government business and the role of backbenchers

1. *Allocation of time*   In the legislative work of the Commons, the time factor is always of importance both to the government, which wishes to see its Bills pass through Parliament without delay, and to the Opposition and backbench MPs, who may seek to prolong proceedings as a means of persuading the government to make concessions. Exceptionally, as in the case of the Prevention of Terrorism (Additional Powers) Act 1996, the Criminal Justice (Terrorism and Conspiracy) Act 1998 and the Anti-terrorism, Crime and Security Act 2001, the government may see the passage of legislation as being of extreme urgency. But even in matters which are not themselves urgent, the more time which one Bill takes, the less time is available in the House for other legislation. As well as the power of the Speaker or chairman to require a member to discontinue speaking who persists in irrelevance or tedious repetition,[32] various methods of curtailing debates have been adopted by the House. The simplest method is that known as the closure, by which any member (in practice usually a government whip) may, either in the House or in Committee, move 'that the question be now put'. The chairman may refuse to put the motion on the ground that it is an abuse of the rules of the House or an infringement of the rights of the minority; but if the chairman does not so refuse, the closure motion must be put forthwith and it is voted on without debate. It can be carried in the House only if not fewer than 100 members vote for the motion; if so carried, the debate cannot be resumed and the motion under discussion must then be voted on.[33]

A second method is the power of the chairman at the committee stage and of the Speaker at the report stage to select those amendments which are to be discussed; this power is exercised more strictly at the report stage than in committee. A third and more drastic method is the 'guillotine', by which a minister may move an allocation of time order in the House to allot a specified number of days or portions of days to the consideration of a Bill in committee of the whole House or on report. The guillotine motion may be debated for no more than three hours. If it is carried, it is the duty of the Business Committee, which consists of the Chairman of Ways and Means and up to eight other members nominated by the Speaker, to divide the Bill into parts and to allot to each part a specified period of time.[34] A similar procedure exists by which the House may allocate time for the proceedings of a standing committee on any Bill; the detailed allocation of time is then made by a business sub-committee.[35] The effect of an allocation of time order is that at the end of each allotted period, the portion of the Bill in question is voted on without further discussion. Compulsory timetabling of this kind can have the result that substantial parts of a Bill have not been considered at all by the Commons before it is sent to the Lords. Business is traditionally conducted on the basis of informal agreements between party managers in the House; but more recently an initiative has been taken for the formal timetabling of Bills by means of programme

---

[31] HC SO 76.
[32] HC SO 42.
[33] HC SOs 36, 37. In the 1993–4 session, 22 closures were claimed in the House; only two were refused by the chairman (HC 257 (1994–95)).
[34] HC SOs 82, 83. For the history, see Jennings, *Parliament*, pp 241–6; for recent practice, Griffith and Ryle, pp 302–7, and G Ganz [1990] PL 496.
[35] HC SO 120.

orders. This had been proposed by the House of Commons Procedure Committee as long ago as 1985 and was supported by the Modernisation Committee 'to secure a better discussion of legislation', to the benefit of all sides of the House: 'The Government gets its legislation, the Opposition chooses what areas get the focus of debate, and individual Members get greater certainty about the progress of business and the timing of votes.'[36]

2. *Private members' Bills*   Although the bulk of the legislative programme is taken up by government Bills, a small but significant part consists of Bills introduced by backbench MPs. Standing orders generally give precedence to government business but they set aside 13 Fridays in each session on which private members' Bills have priority. On the first eight of these Fridays, precedence is given to the second reading of Bills presented by members who have secured the best places in the ballot for private members' Bills held at the beginning of each session. On the remaining Fridays, precedence is given to the later stages of those Bills which received their second readings earlier in the session.[37] One of the standing committees is used primarily for the committee stage of private members' Bills, but these Bills may instead be referred to other standing committees which are not occupied with government Bills; the composition of a standing committee on a private member's Bill usually reflects the voting of the House on second reading, so that the supporters of the Bill form a majority. Private members' Bills are used for a variety of purposes including matters of social reform (for example, abortion and divorce law reform) on which public opinion may be too sharply divided for the government to wish to take the initiative, matters of special interest to minority groups (for example, rights of disabled persons) and topics of law reform which may be useful but have too low a priority to find a place in the government's programmes.[38]

A private member may not propose a Bill the main object of which is the creation of a charge on the public revenue;[39] where a Bill proposes charges on the revenue which are incidental to its main object, a financial resolution moved by a minister is needed before the financial clauses can be considered in committee. It is not the practice for the government to use its majority to defeat a private member's Bill by applying the whips.[40] Where a government supports a Bill, it may offer the services of a draftsman to the member concerned and other assistance; the government may also provide extra time for the later stages of a Bill for which there is much parliamentary support. Such assistance may be vital but it may, as with the Disabled Persons (Services, Consultation and Representation) Act 1986, be offered only at a very late stage in the procedure.[41] Not all private members' Bills become law: many are talked out by their opponents. The guillotine is not applied and the closure of debate needs the support of 100 members, which may not be easy to achieve on a Friday. A Bill which has not become law by the end of the session lapses. In addition to the ballot for Bills at the beginning of each session, there are two other procedures by which a private member's Bill may be introduced. A member may simply present a Bill for its first

---

[36] HC 589 (1999–2000), para 44. See also HC 382 (2000–01). These changes take the form of temporary standing orders and sessional orders.

[37] HC SO 14(4), (5).

[38] See Richards, *Parliament and Conscience*, and (same author) in Walkland (ed.), *The House of Commons in the Twentieth Century*, ch 6; Bromhead, *Private Members' Bills in the British Parliament*; Griffith and Ryle, pp 385–400; and Cowley (ed.), *Conscience and Parliament*.

[39] HC SO 48.

[40] Richards, *Parliament and Conscience*, p 27, describes this as a 'strong convention'.

[41] See Griffith and Ryle, p 387; cf HC 588 (1970–71), evidence of A Morris MP, pp 57–62.

reading, after giving notice but without previously obtaining the leave of the House.[42] Under the 'ten-minute rule' procedure, on Tuesdays and Wednesdays a private member may seek leave to bring in a Bill; he or she may speak briefly in support of the Bill, an opponent may reply and the House may then divide on the issue.[43] Under each of these procedures the chances of a Bill proceeding further depend on whether it is completely unopposed or on whether some time can be found for a second reading debate and later stages, either by the government or on a Friday devoted to private members' business. While it is a hazardous business for a backbencher to pilot the passage of a Bill through the House, private members' initiatives form a small but valuable part of the whole legislative work of Parliament.[44]

The House of Lords and the royal assent

1. *Procedure in the House of Lords*[45]   Except under the Parliament Acts 1911 and 1949, which are considered later, a Bill may be presented for the royal assent only when it has been approved by both Houses. After a public Bill has had its third reading in the Commons, it will be introduced into the Lords. The various stages in the Lords are broadly similar to those in the Commons, although they are governed by separate standing orders. The main differences have been that standing committees are not used in the Lords and the committee stage of Bills is usually taken in committee of the whole House. In 1995 for the first time the 'committee of the whole House' sat in a separate room at Westminster to consider the Children (Scotland) Bill, enabling the House itself to deal with other business.[46] Experiments have also been conducted in recent years for scrutinising draft Bills.[47] As recommended by the Jellicoe report on the committee work of the House,[48] the House in 1994 appointed a 'special standing committee' to receive evidence on proposals in a law reform Bill drafted by the Law Commission before considering the text.[49] In committee, there is no provision for the selection of amendments so that any amendments tabled may be moved. Even if no amendments are made in committee, there may be a report stage; unlike the position in the Commons, there is no limitation on the amendments which may be moved at the third reading. But by convention, all government business is considered within a reasonable time.

The distinctive procedures of the House, in contrast with those of the Commons, facilitate the submission and consideration of amendments.[50] While some Bills coming from the Commons are approved by the Lords unchanged and with little debate, it is more usual for Bills to be considered in detail by the Lords and amendments made. This is particularly valuable when the effect of the guillotine has been that only part of a Bill has been considered in detail by the Commons. The government itself tables many amendments in the Lords, some in response to undertakings given in the Commons. The passage of a Bill through the Lords thus enables the drafting of Bills to be improved as well as substantial amendments to be made and new material introduced. While the foregoing account has assumed that Bills are always introduced in

---

[42] HC SO 57(1).
[43] HC SO 23.
[44] HC 190 (1997–98), para 82.
[45] Griffith and Ryle, pp 480–8, 503–11; Shell, *The House of Lords*, chs 5 and 6.
[46] HL Deb, 6 June 1995, col CWH 1.
[47] Cm 4534, 2000, para 4.32.
[48] HL 35 (1991–92); HL Deb, 3 June 1992, col 899; 9 July 1992, col 1271.
[49] H Brooke [1995] PL 351. See also HL Deb, 21 January 1997, col 555. On the use of select committees on private members' Bills, see Griffith and Ryle, pp 486–7 and Shell, pp 236–9.
[50] See D N Clarke and D Shell [1994] PL 409, 412.

the Commons, in principle Bills may originate in either House. The major exception is that by ancient privilege of the Commons, Bills of 'aids and supplies', i.e. those which relate to national taxation and expenditure or to local rates and charges upon them, must begin in the Commons.[51] Moreover, the democratic character of the Commons and the fact that most ministers are MPs mean that Bills of major political importance start there. These factors often mean that early in a session the Lords have too little legislative work and have too much later in the session when a load of Bills approved by the Commons reaches them. In 1972 a standing order was adopted by the Commons which relaxed the extent of the Commons' financial privilege in the case of government Bills and made it easier for Bills with financial provisions to begin in the Lords.[52]

2. *The royal assent*   Parliament cannot legislate without the concurrence of all its parts and therefore the assent of the Sovereign is required after a Bill has passed through both Houses. The Sovereign does not attend Parliament to assent in person, since an Act of 1541 authorised the giving of the assent by commissioners in the presence of Lords and Commons and this became the invariable practice. Formerly the business of the Commons was interrupted to enable the Commons to attend the Lords for the purpose. But by the Royal Assent Act 1967, the assent, having been signified by letters patent under the Great Seal signed by the Sovereign, is notified separately to each House by its Speaker.[53] The traditional procedure has not, however, been abolished. In giving the royal assent ancient forms are used.[54] A public Bill, unless dealing with finance, as also a private Bill other than one of a personal nature, is accepted by the words '*La Reyne le veult*'. A financial Bill is assented to with the words '*La Reyne remercie ses bons sujets, accepte leur benevolence et ainsi le veult*'. The formula for the veto was '*La Reyne s'avisera*'. The right of veto has not been exercised since the reign of Queen Anne. The veto could now only be exercised on ministerial advice and no government would wish to veto Bills for which it was responsible or for the passage of which it had afforded facilities through Parliament.[55] The consent of the Sovereign is requested before legislation which affects any matter relating to the royal prerogative is debated. Although the seeking of such consent may today be no more than an act of courtesy so far as government Bills are concerned, the need for this consent presents an obstacle for a private member's Bill which seeks to abolish one of the Sovereign's prerogatives, since it enables the government to prevent the House considering any such proposals.[56]

While the royal assent concludes the formal process by which Bills become law, it would be wrong to assume that the assent also marks the end of the legislative process. The royal assent may bring the Act into force immediately,[57] but the operation of all or part of an Act is often suspended by provisions in the Act itself. Thus the Act may specify a later date on which it is to come into force or may give power to the government by Order in Council or to a minister by statutory instrument to specify when the Act, or different parts of it, will operate.[58] Moreover, many Acts confer

---

[51] Erskine May, ch 33; HC 538 (1970–71), paras 19–21. And see M Ryle, in Walkland (ed), *The House of Commons in the Twentieth Century*, pp 355–9.

[52] HC Deb, 8 August 1972, col 1656; Erskine May, p 799.

[53] See HL Deb, 2 March 1967, col 1181.

[54] Erskine May, p 565.

[55] See ch 2 B.

[56] Erskine May, pp 603–4.

[57] Acts of Parliament (Commencement) Act 1793 and Interpretation Act 1978, s 4: Acts deemed in force at beginning of day on which royal assent given, if no other provision made.

[58] Even if power to bring an Act into force has not been exercised, existence of the power may prevent the minister from acting under the prerogative to make provision inconsistent with the Act: *R v Home Secretary, ex p Fire Brigades Union* [1995] 2 AC 513; and E Barendt [1995] PL 357.

powers on the government to regulate in detail topics which are indicated only in outline in the Acts. While some Acts are complete in themselves, others, particularly those affecting complex social services, cannot take effect until the powers of delegated legislation which they confer are exercised. Exercise of these powers is primarily a matter for the executive, subject to scrutiny by Parliament.[59] Parliamentary interest in what happens after a Bill becomes law is not confined to delegated legislation, but traditional procedures are not designed for enabling MPs to monitor the operation of legislation. In 1971 the Select Committee on Procedure recommended that use should be made of 'post-legislation' committees. These committees would examine the working of a statute within a short period of its enactment and would consider whether there was a need for early amending legislation to deal with difficulties arising in the administration of the Act.[60] Select committees may be appointed to review the working of a particular Act (the Abortion Act of 1967 has been the subject of several reviews) and the select committees created in 1979 may also review the effects of legislation, but no scheme of post-legislation committees has been adopted.

Private Bills

A private Bill is a Bill to alter the law relating to a particular locality or to confer rights on or relieve from liability a particular person or body of persons (including local authorities and statutory undertakers, providing public utilities). The procedure is regulated by the standing orders of each House relating to private business.[61] When the objects of the Bill have been advertised and plans and other documents have been displayed in the locality concerned, a petition for the Bill together with the Bill itself must be deposited in Parliament by 27 November each year. Landowners and others whose interests are directly affected are separately notified by the promoters and they may petition against the Bill. The second reading of the Bill does not determine its desirability, as in the case of a public Bill, but merely that, assuming the facts stated in the preamble to the Bill to be true, it is unobjectionable from the point of view of national policy. If read a second time, the Bill is committed to a committee of four members in the Commons or of five members in the Lords. The committee stage is usually the most important stage in the passage of a private Bill, particularly if there are many petitions of objection to the Bill. The promoters and opponents of the Bill are usually represented by counsel and call evidence in support of their arguments. The views of relevant government departments are made known to the committee.

The committee first consider whether or not the facts stated in the preamble, which sets out the special reasons for the Bill, have been proved. If the preamble is accepted, the clauses are taken in order and may be amended. If the preamble is rejected, the Bill is dead. After the committee stage the Bill is reported to the House and its subsequent stages are similar to those of a public Bill. When a private Bill is opposed, the procedure is expensive, each side having to bear the fees of counsel, expert witnesses and parliamentary agents and the expense of preparing the necessary documents. Unopposed Bills are scrutinised closely by officers of each House. This method of obtaining special statutory powers is useful to local authorities who seek wider powers than are generally conferred or who have special needs for which the general law does not provide. One reason for the elaborate procedure is to ensure that Parliament does not inadvertently take away an individual's private rights.[62] But there are other means of

---

[59] Ch 28.
[60] HC 538 (1970–71), pp vii–ix; and HC 588–1 (1977–78), p xxvii.
[61] See Williams, *History of Private Bill Procedure*, vol I; and Erskine May, chs 36–41.
[62] Cf *Pickin v British Railways Board* [1974] AC 765; ch 4 C.

obtaining statutory authority for the exercise of special powers and ministerial orders are of more general importance today, for example by the provisional order procedure, a version of which is used in Scotland as a form of private legislation.[63] Another variant is 'special parliamentary procedure' under the Statutory Orders (Special Procedure) Act 1945: this must be observed if, for example, a government department wishes to acquire compulsorily certain types of land (such as land held inalienably by the National Trust). The subject of private legislation was subject to a broad review by a joint committee of both Houses in 1988, and changes made by the Transport and Works Act 1992 will reduce the need for private Bills.[64]

A hybrid Bill has been defined as 'a public Bill which affects a particular private interest in a manner different from the private interests of other persons or bodies of the same category or class'.[65] Thus a Bill to confer a general power on the Secretary of State to acquire land for the construction of railway tunnels is not a hybrid Bill since all landowners are potentially affected: but the Bill which became the Channel Tunnel Act 1987, after a protracted parliamentary battle, was a hybrid Bill since it sought to confer power to acquire specific land and construct specific works. After its second reading, a hybrid Bill is referred to a select committee and those whose rights are adversely affected by the Bill may petition against it and bring evidence in support of their objections. The Bill may then pass through committee and later stages as if it were an ordinary Bill. Whether a public Bill is hybrid and therefore subject to the standing orders for private business is a matter decided initially by the Examiners of Petitions for Private Bills, usually before the second reading. In 1976, after a government Bill to nationalise the aircraft and shipbuilding industries had completed a lengthy committee stage in the Commons, the Speaker ruled that the Bill was prima facie a hybrid Bill: rather than submit the Bill to a select committee to enable petitions against the Bill to be considered and evidence received, the government proposed and the Commons resolved that the standing orders relative to private business should not be applied to the Bill, a reminder that the House is master of its own procedure.[66] When the Bill reached the Lords in the same form in the next session, the government withdrew the hybrid clauses affecting ship repairers rather than cause further delay to the Bill.

B. Conflict between the two Houses

In recent years the House of Lords has been more prepared to amend Bills against the government's wishes, often on issues of principle and policy.[67] In 1999–2000 the government was defeated 36 times on 14 separate Bills. In the previous two sessions, the Lords had defeated the government on 39 and 31 occasions respectively.[68] Where a Bill approved by the Commons has been amended in the Lords, the Bill in its amended form goes back to the Commons so that the Lords' amendments may be approved or rejected. If all the amendments are approved, the House of Commons sends a message notifying the Lords of this. If not, the message will contain reasons for disagreement

[63] Private Legislation Procedure (Scotland) Act 1936; Erskine May, ch 41. But this does not apply where the public authority or persons are seeking parliamentary powers wholly within the competence of the Scottish Parliament: Scotland Act 1998, Sch 8.

[64] HL 625 (1987–88); and ch 29 B.

[65] Erskine May, p 554 and also pp 554–560.

[66] The complex saga may be followed at HC Deb, 25 May 1976 (col 299), 26 May (col 445), 27 May (col 632), 29 June (col 218) and 20 July (col 1527).

[67] Between 1970 and 1995, there were 603 government defeats in the Lords: HL Deb, 16 October 1995, col 90 (WA) and 27 November 1995, col 23 (WA), an average of 24 per session.

[68] Cowley and Stuart, note 5 above.

and possibly counter-amendments. It then is for the Lords to decide whether to persist in its earlier decisions or to give way to the views of the Commons. Disagreements between the two Houses tend to be resolved 'through a variety of informal procedures' and the Wakeham Commission considered whether the matter should be formalised in a Joint Committee in order to replace the current arrangements which can see a Bill 'ping-pong back and forward before agreement is reached'.[69] Usually the Lords give way; but if the House insists on maintaining its position, the disagreement between the two Houses must be resolved if the Bill is to receive the royal assent. The ultimate resolution of these conflicts is governed by the Parliament Acts 1911–49.

The Parliament Acts 1911–49

What happens when there are disputes between the two Houses which cannot be settled by consultation and compromise while the Bill is passing to and fro between the Houses? Today it is generally accepted that the will of the elected House should ultimately prevail. In the 19th century, the only means of coercing the Lords available to a government was to advise the Sovereign to create enough new peers to obtain a majority for the government in the Lords. Thus in 1832 the Lords abandoned their opposition to the Reform Bill when William IV eventually agreed to accept Grey's advice to create peers. Thereafter a rather uncertain convention developed that the Lords should give way in the event of a deadlock between the two Houses, whenever the will of the people was clearly behind the Commons, as it had been in 1832. This proved unsatisfactory for the Liberal party, since it gave the Lords a virtual claim to decide when a general election should be held to find out the will of the people.[70] More definite rules applied to Bills relating to public finance. Since the 17th century, the Commons had asserted privilege in proposals for taxation and public expenditure: it was clear that the Lords might not *amend* such Bills, for this would trespass on the exclusive right of the Commons to grant or refuse supplies to the Crown.[71] But, however contradictory to that exclusive right it seems to us today, it was still asserted by the Lords that they had the right to *reject* financial Bills.[72] With the widening of the electoral system, the growth of the Liberal party and the appearance of a perpetual Conservative majority in the Lords, the surviving powers of that House were bound to cause conflict. This conflict became an acute problem for the Liberal government after 1906. The Lords rejected measures of social reform which had been approved by the Commons; and in 1909 the Lords rejected the Finance Bill based on the budget which Lloyd George had presented to the Commons.

The Commons had in 1907 resolved that the powers of the Lords should be restricted by law to secure that within the limits of a single Parliament the final decision of the Commons should prevail. This principle of a suspensory veto became law in the Parliament Act 1911, passed after a prolonged constitutional crisis. This crisis was resolved only when, after two general elections in 1910, the Liberal government made known George V's willingness on the Prime Minister's advice to create over 400 new Liberal peers to coerce the Lords into giving way.[73] The 1911 Act, which did not

---

[69] Cm 4534, 2000, pp 40–1.
[70] See Lovell, *The Government of England*, p 410.
[71] Ibid, pp 400–02.
[72] In 1860 the Lords rejected the Bill to repeal the paper duty. The Commons challenged the propriety of this rejection and from 1861 all proposals for taxation were included in a single Finance Bill: Taswell-Langmead, *English Constitutional History*, pp 548–9.
[73] See Jenkins, *Mr Balfour's Poodle*; Nicolson, *King George V*, chs 9 and 10; Jennings, *Cabinet Government*, pp 428–48. For an account of why the 1911 Act took the form it did, see J Jaconelli (1991) 10 Parliamentary History 277.

alter the composition of the upper House, made three main changes: (a) it reduced the life of Parliament from seven to five years; (b) it removed the power of the Lords to veto or delay money Bills; and (c) in the case of other public Bills, apart from a Bill to prolong the life of Parliament, the veto of the Lords was abolished and there was substituted a power to delay legislation for two years. The Act enabled the Welsh Church Act 1914 and the Government of Ireland Act 1914 to become law. But the period of delay which the Lords could impose meant that in the fourth and fifth years of a Parliament the Lords could hold up a Bill knowing that it could not become law until after a general election. After 1945, faced with a massive programme of nationalisation which it wished to get through Parliament, the Labour government proposed to reduce the period of delay from two years to one year. After extensive discussions on the reform of the House of Lords, which broke down on the period of delay, the Parliament Act 1949 became law under the 1911 Act procedure.

Under the Parliament Acts 1911–49, Bills may in certain circumstances receive the royal assent after having been approved only by the Commons. This may happen (a) if the Lords fail within one month to pass a Bill which, having passed the Commons, is sent up at least one month before the end of the session and is endorsed by the Speaker as a money Bill;[74] or (b) if the Lords refuse in two successive sessions, whether of the same Parliament or not, to pass a public Bill (other than a Bill certified as a money Bill or a Bill to extend the maximum duration of Parliament beyond five years) which has been passed by the Commons in those two sessions, provided that one year has elapsed between the date of the Bill's second reading in the Commons in the first of those sessions and the date of its third reading in that House in the second of those sessions.[75] A money Bill is a public Bill which, in the opinion of the Speaker, contains only provisions dealing with: the imposition, repeal, remission, alteration or regulation of taxation; the imposition of charges on the Consolidated Fund or the National Loans Fund or on money provided by Parliament for the payment of debt or other financial purposes or the variation or repeal of such charges; supply; the appropriation, receipt, custody, issue or audit of public accounts; or the raising or guarantee or repayment of loans. Bills dealing with taxation, money or loans raised by local authorities or bodies for local purposes are not certifiable as money Bills.[76] The statutory definition has been so strictly interpreted that most annual Finance Bills have not been endorsed with the Speaker's certificate.[77]

Where a Bill is presented for the royal assent under s 2 of the 1911 Act, it must be endorsed with the Speaker's certificate that s 2 has been complied with. As the Speaker must certify that it is the same Bill which has been rejected in two successive sessions, there are strict limits on the alterations which may be made to a Bill between the first and second sessions. But the Bill in the second session may include amendments which have already been approved by the Lords and, in sending up the Bill in the second session, the Commons may accompany it with further suggested amendments without inserting them into the Bill.[78] Any certificate of the Speaker given under the 1911 Act 'shall be conclusive for all purposes, and shall not be questioned in any court of law',[79] a formula which seeks to exclude any challenge to the validity of an Act passed under

---

[74] 1911 Act, s 1.

[75] 1911 Act, s 2 (as amended by the 1949 Act).

[76] 1911 Act, s 1 (as amended by the National Loans Act 1968). See D Morris (2001) 22 Statute LR 211.

[77] Erskine May, pp 806–8; and Jennings, *Parliament*, pp 416–19. Before giving the certificate, the Speaker must, if practicable, consult two members appointed from the chairmen's panel each session by the Committee of Selection of the House of Commons.

[78] 1911 Act, s 2(4). The procedure was used in relation to the Bill which became the Trade Union and Labour Relations (Amendment) Act 1976.

[79] 1911 Act, s 3.

the Parliament Acts based on alleged defects in procedure. Apart from not applying to Bills which seek to extend the maximum duration of Parliament beyond five years, the Parliament Acts do not apply to local and private legislation or to public Bills which confirm provisional orders. Nor do they apply to delegated legislation: here the formal powers of the Lords will depend on whether the parent Act expressly empowers the Lords to approve or disapprove of the delegated legislation in question.[80]

The Parliament Acts in operation

Apart from the Welsh Church Act 1914 and the Government of Ireland Act 1914, only the Parliament Act 1949 became law under the Parliament Act procedure before 1991. Under Labour governments after 1945, it was the practice of the Lords to give way when Lords' amendments to government Bills were rejected by the Commons. Lord Salisbury, leader of the Conservative majority in the Lords during the Labour government of 1945–51, stated that the broad rule followed was that what had been in the Labour programme at the previous general election would be accepted as having been approved by the people; but that the Conservative peers 'reserved full liberty of action' as to measures that had not been in the election manifesto.[81] This became known as the Salisbury convention.[82] Direct confrontation between the Lords and the Commons was thus avoided, the general practice of the Lords being to allow a second reading to Bills coming from the Commons. In the late 1960s the Lords, strengthened by the appointment of life peers, adopted a more resolute policy, causing the Labour government in 1969 to abandon the House of Commons (Redistribution of Seats) (No 2) Bill.[83] In the 1974–75 session, failure to reach agreement between the Commons and Lords meant that the Trade Union and Labour Relations (Amendment) Bill did not become law. In the 1975–76 session, the Labour government invoked the Parliament Acts procedure but a much amended Bill was in March 1976 accepted by the Lords. The Aircraft and Shipbuilding Industries Act 1977 was similarly delayed by opposition from the Lords until the government abandoned the proposal to nationalise certain ship-repairing firms.[84]

In 1990–91, opposition from the Lords to the War Crimes Bill caused the Parliament Acts to be invoked for the first time by a Conservative government. The Bill retrospectively authorised prosecutions in Britain in respect of war crimes in Germany between 1939 and 1945 by persons who had become British citizens. It had not been part of the Conservative programme at the 1987 election and was carried on free votes in the Commons. It was, however, twice defeated on second reading in the Lords: following the second such defeat, the royal assent was given to it. The debates in the Lords were confused on the constitutional issues,[85] but those peers who voted against the Bill on the second occasion knew that their action would not prevent the Bill from becoming law. Although the Parliament Acts applied in a clear way to the War Crimes Bill, the procedure under the Acts has potential difficulties (for example, at what stage has a Bill 'not been passed' by the Lords subsequently, once it has been given a second reading?). The statutory method of calculating the one year's delay means that the effective delay may be considerably less than 12 months.

The willingness on the part of the House of Lords more readily to challenge the Commons led to the Parliament Acts being used on several occasions in the 1997–2001 Parliament: on one occasion following the defeat of the European Parliamentary

[80] Ch 28.
[81] HL Deb, 4 November 1964, col 66; Griffith and Ryle, p 504; and see HL Deb, 19 May 1993, col 1780.
[82] See Cm 4534, 2000, pp 39–40 for a discussion of the origins and purpose of the Convention.
[83] Ch 9 B.
[84] Page 194 above.
[85] G Ganz (1992) 55 MLR 87.

Election Bill, and on another following the defeat of the Sexual Offences (Amendment) Bill. But paradoxically, it was not necessary to invoke the Acts to secure the passage of the House of Lords Act 1999. Events in the 1997–2001 Parliament were a reminder of some of the limitations of the Parliament Acts: they do not apply to Bills which begin in the Lords (and so could not be invoked when the Lords voted down the Criminal Justice (Mode of Trial) Bill);[86] or to secondary legislation (and so could not be invoked when the Lords rejected the Greater London Authority (Election Expenses) Order 2000 – the first time an affirmative order had been rejected by the Lords since 1968).[87] These features of the Parliament Acts were acknowledged by the Royal Commission on House of Lords Reform, as were others: it had been argued that it should be possible for the Commons to amend a Bill before presenting it to the Lords on the second occasion without the Bill losing the protection of the Parliament Acts; at present the Commons may only 'suggest' amendments. But such technical questions were not thought to have given rise to any 'real difficulty in practice'[88] and no amendment to the Act was proposed, although it was proposed that the House of Lords should lose its power to veto secondary legislation, a recommendation accepted by the government.[89]

The Wakeham Commission had also broadly endorsed the present statutory procedures and conventional practices (including specifically the Salisbury Convention) relating to the distribution of powers between the two Houses. But the Committee apparently felt it unnecessary to address the argument that the Parliament Act 1949 is invalid since the Parliament Act procedure was never intended to be used for amending the 1911 Act itself, and since a delegate may not use delegated authority to increase the scope of his or her authority.[90] While there are indeed limits on the Bills which may become law under the Parliament Act procedure, the argument that the 1949 Act is invalid depends on the view that measures passed by the Commons and the Crown alone should be regarded as delegated legislation: yet the interpretation of Commonwealth constitutions suggests that a legislature is not subject to the limitations implied by the maxim *delegatus non potest delegare*.[91] While the 1911 Act was not intended to provide a final solution to the House of Lords question, it is doubtful whether the scope of the Act should be subject to such implied limitations; if so, it would follow that, for example, a Bill to reform the Lords or to vary the succession to the throne could not become law under the Parliament Act procedure.[92] Although the point has resurfaced during the debates about Lords reform in the late 1990s,[93] with the passage of time and more frequent use of the Parliament Act procedure, it is one which may be more appropriate for the classroom than the courtroom.

House of Lords reform

The preamble to the 1911 Act looked forward to the creation of a new second chamber constituted on a popular instead of a hereditary basis and with its own powers,

---

[86] One practical effect of this is that the House of Lords has an absolute veto over Commons amendments to Lords Bills.

[87] HL Deb, 22 February 2000, cols 134–82. On the same day the Lords also, for the first time, rejected an instrument subject to a annulment (Greater London Authority Election Rules 2000.) See HL Deb, 22 February, cols 182–5.

[88] Cm 4534 (2000), p 36.

[89] Ibid, pp 77–8. See p 199 below.

[90] Hood Phillips and Jackson, *Constitutional and Administrative Law*, pp 79–81; Hood Phillips, *Reform of the Constitution*, pp 18–19, 91–3. If it could be shown that the 1949 Act were invalid, would this also invalidate the War Crimes Act 1991, the European Parliamentary Elections Act 1999 (and the results?) and the Sexual Offences Amendment Act 2000?

[91] *R v Burah* (1878) 3 App Cas 889; *Hodge v R* (1883) 9 App Cas 117.

[92] And see ch 4 C.

[93] Hood Phillips and Jackson, p 81.

but this has never occurred. In 1918, an all-party conference chaired by Viscount Bryce agreed that the primary functions of the second chamber included (*a*) the examination and revision of Bills brought from the Commons; (*b*) the initiation and discussion of non-controversial Bills; (*c*) 'the interposition of so much delay (and no more) in the passing of a Bill into law as may be needed to enable the opinion of the nation to be adequately expressed upon it'; and (*d*) full and free discussion of current issues of policy which the Commons might not have time to consider. Yet the Bryce conference did not agree as to the composition of the House, although many members favoured indirect election of the second chamber by the House of Commons. Disputes between the Houses could, it was suggested, be settled by a joint conference of 60 members, chosen equally from each House, meeting in secret.[94] At an inter-party conference in 1948, agreement was reached on broad questions such as the need for a second chamber which should complement and not rival the Commons; the need to secure that a permanent majority was not assured to any one party; the admission of women; and the ending of admission based solely on succession to an hereditary peerage. The conference broke down through disagreement over the Lords' delaying powers: the Labour government would have accepted a delay of 12 months from second reading in the Commons or nine months from third reading, whichever was the longer, but the Conservatives insisted on 18 months from second reading or 12 months from third reading.[95] In the event the Parliament Act 1949 became law and no general reform of the House of Lords took place.

Another attempt at House of Lords reform was frustrated in 1969[96] and it was not until 1997 that the matter was revisited, with House of Lords reform forming a part of the Blair government's programme of constitutional change.[97] The main concern now, however, was with composition;[98] and in removing most of the hereditary peers from membership, the House of Lords Act 1999 did not in any way alter the legal powers of the House. In the subsequent White Paper, *The House of Lords – Completing the Reform*,[99] the government has argued that there 'is no case for giving specific new functions to the House of Lords', in addition to (i) revising legislation and (ii) scrutinising government.[100] Paradoxically, the greater legitimacy claimed for the House by the government as a result of this reform has led some of its members to be less cautious about exercising the not inconsiderable powers that they do have. The House of Lords has inflicted important defeats on recent governments, from not all of which it has been possible to recover by using the Parliament Acts. The government nevertheless is content to accept 'a delaying power, exercised only in exceptional circumstances, but not an absolute veto'.[101] With one exception no changes were proposed 'to the legislative or conventional framework governing the relationship between the two Houses'.[102] The exception related to secondary legislation, with the white paper endorsing the recommendation of the Wakeham Commission that the House should have a power to delay secondary legislation for up to three months, but not to veto it as is currently the case.[103]

---

[94] Cd 9038, 1918. See also Jennings, *Parliament*, ch 12 and Bromhead, *The House of Lords and Contemporary Politics 1911–1957*.

[95] Cmd 7390, 1948.

[96] Cmnd 3799, 1968; Morgan, *The House of Lords and the Labour Government 1964–70*, chs 7 and 8. And see 12th edn of this book pp 216–17.

[97] On which see D Shell (2000) 53 Parliamentary Affairs *290*.

[98] See ch 9 H, I above.

[99] Cm 5291, 2000.

[100] Ibid, para 24. Although it was accepted that the House of Lords should have a role in reviewing the impact of constitutional reform, this was said to be 'something which should develop within the existing constitutional framework' (para 24).

[101] Ibid, para 29.

[102] Ibid, paras 31–3.

[103] Ibid, para 7.38; Cm 5291, 2000, paras 30–3.

C. Financial procedure[104]

No government can exist without raising and spending money. In the Bill of Rights 1689, art 4, the levying of money for the use of the Crown without grant of Parliament was declared illegal. Relying on the principle that the redress of grievances preceded supply, the Commons could after 1689 insist that the Crown pursued acceptable policies before granting the taxes or other revenue which the Crown needed. It has been said of the financial procedure of Parliament that the Crown demands money, the Commons grants it, and the Lords assents to the grant.[105] Today, the assent of the Lords is only nominal and it is generally regarded as vital to a government's existence that its financial proposals be accepted by the Commons. It is unlikely that a government would accept that the Commons should modify its expenditure proposals. A government which failed to ensure supply would have to resign or to seek a general election.[106] The requirement of statutory authority before a government can impose charges on the citizen is a fundamental principle which gives the citizen protection in the courts against unauthorised charges.[107] Another principle is that no payment out of the national Exchequer may be made without the authority of an Act, and then only for the purposes for which the statute has authorised the expenditure.[108] By contrast with the rule on taxation, this is less likely to give rise to litigation in the courts since the rights of individuals are not in issue if it is broken. Yet taxpayers and certain interest groups may have a sufficient interest in an expenditure decision to seek judicial review of its legality.[109] The elaborate system of controlling expenditure which exists today still owes much to reforms linked with Gladstone's tenure of office as Chancellor of the Exchequer in the 1860s, though they have been overhauled by the Government Resources and Accounts Act 2000.[110]

Basic principles and rules of financial procedure

The basic principles of financial control by, and accountability to, Parliament form part of a broader public expenditure process, which has helpfully been described as having four stages: (i) expenditure planning by the executive; (ii) parliamentary debate and approval of the executive's request for supply; (iii) spending by the executive of the money voted by Parliament; and (iv) accounting for the money spent.[111] Our concern in this chapter is principally with the second of these steps in the process, with the other three being considered more fully in chapter 17. But although the 'power of the purse' is 'central to the the ability of Parliament to call government to account',[112] it ought not to be assumed that Parliament has developed adequate methods for this

---

[104] See also ch 17, with which this section must be read and J F McEldowney, in Jowell and Oliver (eds), *The Changing Constitution*, ch 8.

[105] Erskine May, p 732.

[106] Hence the necessity for a general election after the Lords had rejected the Liberal government's Finance Bill in 1909. In 1975, the failure of the Prime Minister of Australia to ensure supply (because of opposition from the Australian Senate to two Appropriation Bills) was the reason given by the Governor-General for dismissing him; ch 12 B.

[107] Ch 17. And see *Woolwich Building Society v IRC (No 2)* [1993] AC 70.

[108] *Auckland Harbour Board v R* [1924] AC 318.

[109] *R v Foreign and Commonwealth Secretary, ex p World Development Movement* [1995] 1 All ER 611: decision to finance Pergau Dam in Malaysia declared to be ultra vires the Overseas Development and Cooperation Act 1980. The government made up the money from other public funds: HC Deb, 13 December 1994, col 773.

[110] See ch 17 and HC 841 (1999–2000), Annex A.

[111] White and Hollingsworth, *Audit, Accountability and Government*, p 1.

[112] Ibid.

purpose. For as has been pointed out, 'in reality little substantial scrutiny is involved' in these procedures, for 'the policy objectives on which the money is spent are not determined by the Commons but by the government of the day'.[113] This is perhaps inevitable in a parliamentary democracy which operates on the basis of a mandate claimed by government for a range of actions: the government can normally expect that its promises will not be frustrated by the Commons. Yet although government can properly claim the opportunity to implement its mandate, this ought not to be at the expense of rigorous and effective financial scrutiny of how money is to be spent, as well as of how money has been spent.

The financial procedures of the Commons are intricate and can only be outlined here. According to Erskine May, three key rules govern present procedure.[114] For the purpose of these rules, the word 'charge' includes both charges upon the public revenue, i.e. expenditure, and charges upon the people, i.e. taxation:

1 A charge does not become fully valid until authorised by legislation; it must generally originate in the Commons, and money to meet authorised expenditure must be appropriated in the same session of Parliament as that in which the relevant estimate is laid before Parliament.

2 A charge may not be considered by the Commons unless it is proposed or recommended by the Crown. The financial initiative of the Crown is expressed in a standing order of the Commons which in part dates from 1713: 'This House will receive no petition for any sum relating to public service or proceed upon any motion for a grant or charge upon the public revenue . . . unless recommended from the Crown.'[115] This rule gives the government formal control over almost all financial business in the Commons, and severely restricts the ability of Opposition and backbenchers to propose additional expenditure or taxation.

3 A charge must first be considered in the form of a resolution which, when agreed to by the House, forms an essential preliminary to the Bill or clause by which the charge is authorised. Before 1967, these resolutions had to be passed by the whole House sitting as the Committee of Supply, in the case of expenditure, or as the Committee of Ways and Means, in the case of taxation.[116] These committees no longer exist and the resolutions are now passed by the House itself. Certain financial Bills must be preceded by a Commons resolution before they can be read a second time. But for most Bills, whether the main object or an incidental object is the creation of a public charge, the financial resolution normally follows the second reading and must be proposed by a minister.[117]

The work of the Commons is conducted on a sessional basis, each session usually running for a year from early November. However, the government's financial year begins on 1 April (the income tax year begins on 6 April). The result is a complex annual financial cycle, which will now be described – first in relation to the authorisation of expenditure (supply), and secondly in relation to taxation.

The system of supply: government estimates

Funds are requested by the government by means of estimates. These are prepared in government departments and examined by the Treasury to ensure that they are

---

[113] J F McEldowney, in Jowell and Oliver, p 198.

[114] Erskine May, ch 29. For discussion of earlier forms of the rules, see Reid, *The Politics of Financial Control* and M Ryle, in Walkland (ed), ch 7.

[115] For the history of SO 46, see Reid, pp 35–45.

[116] See HC 122 (1965–66).

[117] HC SO 48.

consistent with the government's overall spending plans.[118] After scrutiny by and debate in Parliament, the estimates are approved by a Resolution of the House of Commons. According to *Government Accounting*, scrutiny of individual departmental estimates is now mainly undertaken by select committees (although there is no suggestion that the estimates should be 'cleared' by the select committees before being put to the House for approval),[119] which may take evidence from ministers and officials. There is also an opportunity for the House as a whole to debate and vote on individual estimates on three estimates days set aside for this purpose under the Commons standing orders.[120] But a department may need to exceed its estimated expenditure during the current financial year – because of unforeseen circumstances or new policy initiatives; in that case supplementary estimates will have to be submitted for approval later in the year. There is also the possibility that a department may spend more than provided for in the estimate, but has not been able to cure the excess before the end of the financial year. This will have to be authorised after the event by what is referred to as an excess vote. These are examined annually by the Public Accounts Committee on a report from the Comptroller and Auditor-General before they are granted.

It has been emphasised that, 'presentation of the main estimates to Parliament does not provide sufficient authority for expenditure. Statutory authority from the Appropriation Act is required.'[121] Once the House of Commons has agreed the grants set out in the estimates, the Consolidated Fund (Appropriation) Bill is introduced and passed through all stages before the summer recess. The Act will do the following:

(*a*)   authorise the issue from the Consolidated Fund of the balance of the grant of the estimates for the current financial year.[122] To add to the complexity of the foregoing procedures, some money will already have been voted to meet departmental expenditure. This is because the Appropriation Act will not normally be passed until after the financial year has started, which means that unless some other method were available to supply money to the departments, they would be unable to carry out their business. So in the Consolidated Fund Act passed in the previous session, money will be provided by a vote on account to fund activities pending the enactment of the Appropriation Act. The vote on account is typically 45% of the amount voted to the service or activity in the year in which the vote is made (that is the year previous to the year for which it is to be applied);

(*b*)   specify in a table in the Act the total receipts that may be applied as appropriations in aid to each department or service to be funded. These appropriations in aid appear beside the amount of grant authorised to be made from the Consolidated Fund to the department or service in question. So there will be three columns next to each department or service. One will specify the total resources that may be used; a second will specify the amount to be issued from the Consolidated Fund for spending by the department or service; and a third will specify the amount of the appropriations in aid, which will be much smaller in amount than the second column. Appropriations in aid represent income received by departments (usually in return for services provided) and retained to meet departmental expenditure. Any additional income received by a department beyond the appropriation in aid must be paid into the Consolidated Fund.

---

[118]   This section draws heavily on HM Treasury, *Government Accounting*, esp ch 11.
[119]   HC 321 (2000–01), para 5.
[120]   HC SOs 54, 55.
[121]   J F McEldowney, in Jowell and Oliver, p 198.
[122]   On the Consolidated Fund, see ch 17.

The Act also provides an excess vote where required and authorises any supplementary estimates which may be required. It may also give statutory authority to any services or functions specified in the estimates where the authority for the activity rests on the Appropriation Act alone. There will not normally be a debate on the Consolidated Fund (Appropriation) Bill (known when passed as the Appropriation Act).[123]

The system of supply: statutory authorisation

The two principal statutes annually for the grant of supply are thus the Consolidated Fund Act and the Appropriation Act. The former meets standing consolidated fund expenditure (about 30% of total annual expenditure);[124] and by means of votes on account provides interim funding for departmental expenditure. There will then be legislation later in the year in the form of a subsequent Appropriation Act authorising further supply to departments or programmes. By way of illustration, between March and December 2001, there were four pieces of financial legislation, crossing the boundaries of two financial years (1 April), as follows:

(1)   The Consolidated Fund Act 2001, which received the royal assent on 22 March 2001, and authorised the use of resources of *circa* £120 billion for unspecified purposes for 'the service of the year ending on 31 March 2002' (that is to say, providing money for expenditure in the forthcoming year). The Act also authorised the Treasury to issue out of the Consolidated Fund sums of £447,616.60; £2,327,637,000; and £120,857,218,000.

(2)   The Appropriation Act 2001, which received the royal assent on 11 May 2001 (after the financial year had started). This authorised the use of additional resources of circa £149 billion and the issuing out of the Consolidated Fund to 'apply to the service of the year ending on 31st March 2002' the sum of circa £144 billion. The Act also specified the total amount of resources which it and other Acts (such as the Consolidated Fund Act 2001) authorised for use in the year ending 31 March 2002. This was circa £270 billion. A greater sum than this was authorised to be issued from the Consolidated Fund for the year. This was to meet excess votes for 1999–2000 and supplementary estimates for 2000–2001.

Schedule 2 of the Act set out the maximum amount of resources that may be applied to different services or departments. If this is not enough, fresh parliamentary authority will be required to authorise the use of additional resources by the services or departments in question. The schedule set out 61 different appropriations (including the excess vote and the supplementary estimates for 2000–2001). These include all the government departments as well as other public bodies such as the utility regulators, the security services and the Electoral Commission. It also set out both the grants to be made from the Consolidated Fund as well as Appropriations in Aid.

(3)   The Appropriation (No 2) Act 2001, which received the royal assent on 19 July 2001, long after the financial year had started. This gave effect to supplementary estimates by authorising the use of additional resources; and the making of additional grants from the Consolidated Fund, as well as additional appropriations in aid. Eleven departments or agencies came back for additional funding to finance their programmes, from circa £1 billion authorised for use by the Department of Trade and Industry to the £1,000 to the Forestry Commission.[125]

---

[123] Ibid.
[124] Ibid. See ch 17.
[125] £1,000 was authorised for the United Kingdom Atomic Energy Superannuation Funds.

(4)   The Consolidated Fund (No 2) Act 2001, which received the royal assent on 18 December 2001, and authorised the use of additional resources of circa £6 billion for unspecified purposes 'for the year ending on 31st March 2002' (that is to say providing money for expenditure in the current year). The Act also authorised the Treasury to issue out of the Consolidated Fund the sum of £7,238,134,000. Just as importantly, the same measure authorised the use of resources for the service of the following financial year (ending on 31 March 2003) and the issuing of money from the Consolidated Fund. The amount in each case was £125 billion.

Although the foregoing accounts for the main items of expenditure, there may be other forms of authorisation required for government programmes. In cases of urgent or temporary expenditure, the general provision made for the department in the Appropriation Act may be sufficient authority: but this is not acceptable if the Appropriation Act is thereby used to override limits imposed by existing legislation. Money may be spent in anticipation of express statutory authority when by a supplementary estimate expenditure is proposed for purposes to be authorised by a future Act. In 1967 the government was strongly criticised for paying the salaries of the Parliamentary Commissioner for Administration designate and his staff before the Bill to create this office had become law: the money had in fact come out of the Civil Contingencies Fund, a statutory reserve fund to meet items of expenditure which could not have been foreseen.[126] The maximum capital in the Fund, now renamed the Contingencies Fund, is fixed at an amount equal to 2% of the authorised supply expenditure for the previous year:[127] it may not now be drawn upon for any purpose for which legislation is necessary until a second reading has been given to the Bill in question. The existence of the Fund is a striking exception to the principle that parliamentary authority should be obtained before expenditure is incurred; effective scrutiny of the Fund depends on the Treasury, backed up by the Comptroller and Auditor-General's powers of audit. The legality of payments from the Fund appears uncertain, but is not likely to arise for decision in the courts.[128]

The raising of money: taxation and the budget

Government expenditure must be paid for from taxation, which must in turn be authorised by Parliament.[129] While many forms of revenue, such as customs and excise duties, are raised under Acts which continue in force from year to year, some taxes, notably income tax and corporation tax, are authorised from year to year. The machinery for the collection of these taxes is permanent but Parliament must approve each year the rates of tax. Until 1993 the traditional practice was that the Chancellor of the Exchequer presented his budget early in April. Since then the budget speech has in the same years been combined with the annual statement on public expenditure and delivered in December, so that expenditure decisions are announced at the same time as the Chancellor appraises the economy and proposes tax changes. The contents of the budget are kept secret until the speech is delivered. While the government is collectively responsible for the budget speech and the Chancellor prepares it in close consultation with the Prime Minister, the contents are made known to the Cabinet only on the previous day or even on the morning of the speech. 'The budget is seen, not as a simple balancing of tax receipts against expenditure, but as a sophisticated process

---

[126] HC 257, 326 (1966–67); HC Deb, 7 February 1967, col 1357.
[127] Miscellaneous Financial Provisions Act 1946; Contingencies Fund Act 1974.
[128] HC 118–1 (1980–81) p xiv; HC 137 (1981–82), app 20; HC 24–1 (1982–83), p xliii. And see J F McEldowney, in Jowell and Oliver, pp 200–1.
[129] See *Congreve* v *Home Office* [1976] QB 629.

in which the instruments of taxation and expenditure are used to influence the course of the economy.'[130] The Chancellor may find it necessary to announce changes in indirect taxation and expenditure decisions at other times in the year.

As soon as the Chancellor's speech is completed, the House passes formal resolutions which enable immediate changes to be made in the rates of existing taxes and duties and give renewed authority for the collection of the annual taxes. These resolutions are confirmed by the House at the end of the budget debate. The taxing resolutions are later embodied in the annual Finance Act. The effect of any changes made by the Finance Act may be made retrospective to the date of the budget or any selected date. It was for long the practice to begin at once to collect taxes under the authority of the budget resolutions alone. But in *Bowles* v *Bank of England*,[131] Bowles successfully sued the Bank for a declaration that it was not entitled to deduct any sum by way of income tax from dividends, until such tax had been imposed by Act of Parliament. This decision illustrates the principle in *Stockdale* v *Hansard*[132] that no resolution of the House of Commons can alter the law of the land. The decision made it necessary to pass a law which has now been re-enacted in the Provisional Collection of Taxes Act 1968.

This Act gives statutory force for a limited period to resolutions of the House varying an existing tax or renewing a tax imposed during the preceding year. Under the Act (as amended by the Finance Act 1993),[133] the Finance Bill which embodies the resolution must be read a second time within 30 sitting days of the resolution having been approved by the House; and an Act confirming the resolutions must become law within four months from the date of the resolution, or by 5 May in the next calendar year if voted in November or December. As now amended the Act applies to income tax and corporation tax, as well as a range of other taxes and duties.[134] Because the Finance Bill must become law by a set date, the government must ensure that it is passed by the Commons and sent to the Lords as quickly as possible. Although the House of Lords generally debates the Finance Bill on its second reading, its passage through the Lords is unopposed. Even if the Finance Bill is not certified as a 'money Bill' for the purposes of the Parliament Act 1911, it would be a serious breach of the financial privileges of the Commons for the Lords to seek to amend it as it comes within the hallowed class of 'Bills of Aids and Supplies'.[135] However, no such breach occurs if the Lords amend a Bill concerning the revenue-raising powers of local government.[136]

Parliamentary scrutiny of government expenditure

We have seen that the formal machinery for control of the government's estimates by the Commons has traditionally been used for broader political purposes. Before the creation of the present system of select committees in 1979,[137] the House appointed a succession of committees to examine government expenditure. After 1945 the House each year appointed a committee to examine such of the estimates presented to the House as it saw fit 'and to report what, if any, economies consistent with the policy implied in those estimates (might) be effected therein'. In fact, rather than making a detailed examination of estimates in order to propose economies, the committee

---

[130] Plowden Report, Cmnd 1432, 1961, para 10.
[131] [1913] 1 Ch 57.
[132] (1839) 9 A & E 1; p 219 below.
[133] Finance Act 1993, s 205.
[134] For details, see Erskine May, pp 788–91.
[135] Erskine May, ch 33.
[136] Ibid 76 above; and R Brazier (1988) 17 Anglo-American LR 131.
[137] Section D in this chapter.

inquired more broadly into the effectiveness of the work of departments; thus the Estimates Committee 'became an instrument of general administrative review and scrutiny and a major source of information about how the departments operate'.[138] In 1965, the committee's sub-committees began to specialise in particular areas of activity as the demand was raised for the appointment of specialised investigatory committees. In 1971, the Estimates Committee gave way to a new Expenditure Committee of 49 members; its remit was 'to consider any papers on public expenditure presented to this House and such of the estimates as may seem fit to the Committee and in particular to consider how, if at all, the policies implied in the figures of expenditure and in the estimates may be carried out more economically'.[139]

The committee, composed of backbench members, carried out its work through six sub-committees, concerned with such broad fields as defence and external affairs; the environment; trade and industry; social services and employment. Within these areas, each sub-committee inquired into a selected departmental activity. The aim of the committee was to inform the House about particular areas of the government's work so that they might be better debated in Parliament and outside. As with many committees of the Commons, the Expenditure Committee sought to avoid working in an atmosphere of party politics and to produce unanimous reports. The committee's work extended into matters that might have no financial implications, but this scrutiny of government derived directly from the constitutional function of the Commons in authorising expenditure. The Expenditure Committee was abolished in 1979, having prepared the way for the scheme of select committees described in the next section. Parliamentary scrutiny of expenditure as such is maintained through the audit procedures applied to departmental accounts by the Comptroller and Auditor-General and the Public Accounts Committee and described in chapter 17.

D. Scrutiny of administration

In chapter 7, the principle of responsible government was discussed. We are now concerned with the procedures within the Commons by which the conduct of administration may be scrutinised by the House. The legislative and financial procedures of Parliament have strongly influenced the means by which Parliament finds out about the work of government. But certain procedures have an importance which is related neither to legislation nor to finance.

Parliamentary questions[140]

At the start of each day that the House is sitting, except on Fridays, 45 to 55 minutes are set aside to enable members to question ministers. As well as receiving oral answers to written questions of which prior notice has been given, members may ask oral supplementary questions on matters arising out of the minister's reply to the written question. Members may ask questions for written answer at any time. According to Erskine May, 'the purpose of a question is to obtain information or press for action'; questions to ministers 'should relate to the public affairs with which they are officially connected, to proceedings pending in Parliament or to matters of

---

[138] Johnson, *Parliament and Administration: The Estimates Committee 1945–65*, p 128.

[139] See Robinson, *Parliament and Public Spending: The Expenditure Committee 1970–76*.

[140] Chester and Bowring, *Questions in Parliament*; H Irwin, in Ryle and Richards (eds), ch 5; Franklin and Norton (eds), *Parliamentary Questions*; Griffith and Ryle, pp 254–62, 352–9, 366–76; HC 393 (1971–72); HC 379 (1989–90); HC 178 (1990–91); Erskine May, pp 291–306.

administration for which they are responsible'.[141] Because of the existence of question time, matters concerning their constituencies may be raised by members in correspondence with ministers, who know that an unsatisfactory reply may lead to the tabling of a question. For this reason questions are used more for concentrating public attention on topics of current concern than for securing the redress of individual grievances. Civil servants are aware that action which they take may result in a parliamentary question. While ministers customarily answer those questions which have been accepted as being in order by the clerks of the House, acting under the Speaker's direction, it is for the minister to decide whether and how to reply to questions.

There are a number of grounds on which the information sought may be withheld, for example, if the cost of obtaining the information would be excessive or if it would be contrary to the public interest for the information to be given (for example, matters relating to Cabinet proceedings or to the security services). 'An answer to a question cannot be insisted upon, if the answer be refused by a Minister.'[142] Question time, it has been said, is 'pre-eminently a device for emphasizing the individual responsibility of ministers'.[143] Thus questions may be ruled out of order or refused an answer if they relate to matters for which ministers are not responsible: for example, decisions by local authorities, the BBC, courts and tribunals, the universities, trade unions and so on. When a question to a minister concerns a matter which has been assigned to an executive agency set up under the 'next steps' initiative,[144] it is generally answered by a letter to the MP from the agency's chief executive (the minister may be consulted on what is said). MPs may require a ministerial response if they are dissatisfied with the chief executive's reply. The answers from chief executives to MPs have since 1992 (in an unusual departure from principle) been printed in Hansard.[145]

Departmental ministers attend for questioning by rota. In May 1997, the allocation for questions to the Prime Minister was changed from 15 minutes every Tuesday and Thursday to 30 minutes every Wednesday. Members may not ask more than two starred questions (i.e. questions for oral answer) on any day and not more than one to a particular minister. Notice of starred questions cannot be given more than ten sitting days in advance.[146] Starred questions which are not reached during question time receive a written answer. While question time dramatises the personal responsibility of ministers for government policy and departmental action, its effectiveness as a means of securing information which the government does not wish to make available has often been limited. Since 1994 the government has operated a code of practice on access to government information[147] and expects ministers to comply with the code in answering MPs' questions. In 1996, the Scott report on 'arms for Iraq' extensively criticised attitudes within government to the answering of questions.[148] Civil servants are now instructed that in preparing answers they must be as open as possible with Parliament, although ministers are entitled to present government actions in a positive light; information should not be omitted merely because disclosure could lead to political embarrassment; and answers should be avoided 'which are literally true but likely to give rise to misleading inferences'.[149] The regular questioning of the Prime Minister

---

[141] Erskine May, pp 295–6.
[142] Ibid, p 302.
[143] Chester and Bowring, p 287.
[144] Ch 13 D.
[145] See P Evans, in Giddings (ed.), *Parliamentary Accountability*, ch 7. Also HC 178 (1990–91) and HC 14 (1996–97).
[146] HC SO 22.
[147] See Cm 2290, 1993; a revised version was issued in January 1997. And see ch 13 E, F.
[148] HC 115 (1995–96), esp vol IV, section K.8.
[149] See HC 671 (1996–97), annex C. See also Civil Service Code, para 5. See further ch 13 E.

receives much attention in the media and the use of 'open' questions to the Prime Minister (for example, asking him to list his engagements for the day) is permitted as a device for enabling a wide range of supplementary questions to be asked.[150] A member who is dissatisfied with a reply may take the matter further, for example by raising the matter in an adjournment debate. The marked increase in the number of questions asked for written answer, which is linked with the use by some MPs of research assistants, is not considered to make necessary any limit on the number of questions which MPs may ask.[151]

Debates

At the end of every day's public business, when the adjournment of the House is formally moved, half an hour is available for a private member to raise a particular issue and for a ministerial reply.[152] Members periodically ballot for the right to initiate an adjournment debate and advance notice of the subject is given so that the relevant minister may reply. While this gives more time for discussion of an issue than is possible in question time, the minister's reply, which often consists of a reasoned defence of the department's decision, may not advance the matter very far. During the debate, incidental reference to the need for legislation may be permitted by the Speaker. These brief debates are not followed by a vote of the House.[153] More substantial debates may be held at short notice on motions for the adjournment of the House for the purpose of discussing a specific and important matter that should have urgent consideration. The Speaker must be satisfied that the matter is proper to be discussed under the urgency procedure and either the request must be supported by at least 40 members or leave for the debate must be given by the House, if necessary upon a division. In deciding whether the matter should be debated, the Speaker considers the extent to which it concerns the administrative responsibilities of ministers or could come within the scope of ministerial action, but he does not give reasons for his decision.[154] Only one or two requests for such debates are granted each year, requests from the Opposition front bench succeeding more often than those from backbench MPs.[155]

In recent times a number of other opportunities have been provided for backbenchers wishing to raise matters in debate. Some of these follow the reform of financial procedures, described earlier. Before 1982, 29 'supply days' were assigned for debate on topics chosen by the Opposition, taken during the session at times when the estimates were formally approved. In 1982, the House severed the connection between debates initiated by the Opposition and formal consideration of the estimates.[156] In each session 20 days in the whole House are allotted for Opposition business,[157] 17 at the disposal of the Leader of the Opposition and three at the disposal of the leader of the second largest opposition party. The other opportunity follows the abolition in 1995 of the procedure whereby the formal passage of the Consolidated Fund or Appropriation Bill 'was followed by a series of private Members' debates on a motion for the adjournment of the House, often lasting all night'.[158] This has been replaced

---

[150] HC Deb, 3 February 1983, col 427; and HC 178 (1990–91).
[151] HC 178 (1990–91), p xx.
[152] HC SO 9(7).
[153] See Erskine May, pp 324–7.
[154] HC SO 24.
[155] Griffith and Ryle, pp 264–5, 350–2, 377–9. For an outstanding example of such a debate, see that on the Westland affair on 27 January 1986.
[156] See HC 118 (1980–81) and HC Debs, 19 July 1982, col 117.
[157] HC SO 14(2).
[158] Erskine May, p 761, note 1.

by arrangements whereby every Wednesday morning is given over to a motion for the adjournment of the House.[159] These Wednesday morning debates provide an opportunity for backbenchers to raise matters and initiate debates in a manner which is similar to the daily adjournment debates described earlier. In three of the Wednesday mornings time is set aside to debate select committee reports.

Despite these initiatives, 'there is a huge unsatisfied demand for private members' adjournment debates', which were said by the Modernisation Committee to be 'highly effective ways of bringing a constituency problem or some other topic to the personal attention of Ministers and putting to them a case to which they have both an opportunity and an obligation to make a full reply'.[160] The establishment of a parallel chamber in Westminster Hall was one attempt to meet this demand and it is the perception of the government that the introduction of debates there has 'greatly widened the opportunities for members to raise matters of concern to them'.[161] Although there are other opportunities for members to debate the administration of government departments (including debates on the Queen's Speech), it remains the case that these initiatives notwithstanding, all such debates are limited by the adversary framework in which they are held, and individual members may have no means of probing behind the statements made by ministers. These limitations have given rise to demands for other procedures by which the House may inform itself more directly of the work of government. Where it is alleged that maladministration by a department has caused injustice to individual citizens, a member may refer the citizen's complaint for investigation to the Parliamentary Ombudsman.[162] Another method of investigating an issue is for the matter to be examined by a select committee.

Select committees

Select committees were much used to investigate social and administrative problems in the 19th century. A group of MPs would examine a topic of current concern, with power on behalf of the House to take evidence from witnesses with first-hand knowledge of the issues. Their report, published with the supporting evidence, might convince the House of the need for legislative reforms. The use of select committees declined as departments grew in strength and resources, as the primary initiative for legislation moved to the government, and as the party system established stricter control over backbench MPs. The experience of the select committee on the Marconi scandal, when Liberal ministers were accused of reaping financial rewards through their prior knowledge of a government contract, showed that a select committee was not appropriate for investigations directly involving the reputation of Cabinet ministers.[163] However, the Public Accounts Committee has since 1861 had the task of reporting to the House on the financial and accounting practices of departments.[164] In the period after 1945, little use was made of committees for scrutinising administration, apart from the work of the Estimates Committee described in section C, the technical scrutiny of delegated legislation by the committee on statutory instruments[165] and (from 1956 to 1979) the work of the select committee on nationalised industries.

---

[159] Ibid, pp 276–7. See HC SO 10.
[160] HC 194 (1998–99), para 24.
[161] HC 440 (2001–02) (Memorandum by the Leader of the House), para 8.
[162] Ch 29 D.
[163] Donaldson, *The Marconi Scandal*; and ch 29 C.
[164] Ch 17.
[165] Ch 28.

One obstacle to the development of such committees was the fear that their investigations would interfere with the running of departments and conflict with ministerial responsibility. In 1959 the Select Committee on Procedure rejected a proposal for a committee on colonial affairs, on the ground that this was 'a radical constitutional innovation': 'there is little doubt that the activities of such a committee would be aimed at controlling rather than criticising the policy and actions of the department concerned. It would be usurping a function which the House itself has never attempted to exercise.'[166] By the mid-1960s the mood of the Commons had changed. In 1965, the Committee on Procedure declared that lack of knowledge of how the executive worked was the main weakness of the House.[167] Some limited reforms were made in 1966–68 while Richard Crossman MP was Leader of the House. Two specialised committees were created in 1966, one to consider the activities of a department (the Ministry of Agriculture, Fisheries and Food), the other to consider the subject of science and technology. The latter committee was regularly reappointed, but the Committee on the Ministry of Agriculture survived only for two sessions. Other committees established piecemeal at this time included committees to examine the activities of two departments, (Education and Science, and Overseas Development), race relations and immigration and Scottish affairs. During the 1970s, such committees existed alongside the Expenditure Committee and its sub-committees.[168]

In 1978, an influential report by the Select Committee on Procedure recommended a complete reorganisation of the select committees to produce a more rational structure and to provide means by which MPs could regularly scrutinise the activities of the main departments.[169] The incoming Conservative government moved with notable speed to adopt these recommendations.[170] Now embodied in the House's standing orders,[171] the system of select committees is directly related to the principal government departments.

Sixteen committees are appointed for the life of a Parliament to examine the 'expenditure, administration and policy' of the main departments, the list in 2001 being: Culture, Media and Sport; Defence; Education and Skills; Environment, Food and Rural Affairs; Foreign Affairs; Health; Home Affairs; International Development; Northern Ireland Affairs; Science and Technology; Scottish Affairs; Trade and Industry; Transport, Local Government and the Regions; Treasury; Welsh Affairs; and Work and Pensions. Each committee has 11 members, except Northern Ireland Affairs, which has 13, and Environment, Food and Rural Affairs, and Transport, Local Government and the Regions, each of which has 17. Each committee may appoint a sub-committee and the last two mentioned committees may appoint two sub-committees. As well as examining the work of the principal department specified for the committee, each committee has power to look at 'associated public bodies', that is, executive agencies, public corporations, boards and advisory bodies in the relevant field. The controversial work of the Child Support Agency has been examined more than once by committees, while the energy regulators have been examined by several committees on a number of occasions.[172]

---

[166] HC 92–1 (1958–59), para 47; Crick, *The Reform of Parliament*, ch 7.

[167] HC 303 (1964–65).

[168] See Morris (ed), *The Growth of Parliamentary Scrutiny by Committee*; and Mackintosh, *Specialist Committees in the House of Commons – Have they failed?*

[169] HC 588–1 (1977–78), chs 5–7; and see HC Deb, 19 and 20 February 1979, cols 44, 276.

[170] HC Deb, 25 June 1979, col 33. The literature on the select committees includes Drewry (ed), *The New Select Committees*; Englefield (ed), *Commons Select Committees*; Griffith and Ryle, ch 11; and N Johnson, in Ryle and Richards (eds), *The Commons under Scrutiny*, ch 9.

[171] HC SOs 121–138, 152.

[172] See ch 14 D in this volume.

The work of the select committees

The committees are chaired by senior backbenchers, with positions allocated by the Committee of Selection, which is dominated by the party whips. This can give rise to difficulty if it appears that the government is seeking to control appointments to these key positions, as appears to have occurred in 2001. After the general election the chairs of the Transport Committee (Gwyneth Dunwoody) and the Foreign Affairs Committee (Donald Anderson) in the previous Parliament were not renominated. In the ensuing row which followed, the government allowed a free vote when nominations of committee chairs came forward for approval and both Dunwoody and Anderson were reinstated. But it has been pointed out that 'this surrender on the part of the government did not involve making new arrangements for appointments to select committees in the future'.[173] Only backbench MPs serve on the committees. Each committee has a majority of members from the government side of the House, but some committee chairmen are Opposition members. The committees are serviced by House of Commons clerks and they may appoint specialist advisers. Within its subject area, each committee may choose the topics for investigation, subject only (through the Liaison Committee) to the avoidance of duplication with other committees. While evidence is usually heard in public, departments may ask for private sittings and for sections of the evidence to be deleted from the published report, on grounds of public interest.

> The topics investigated by select committees vary widely, ranging from major subjects that may take a year or longer to complete, to the latest departmental estimates and issues of topical concern which a committee may seek to influence by holding one or two hearings and publishing the evidence with a brief report. This freedom for a committee to decide for itself what to investigate is very important and no government approval is needed. Thus the Foreign Affairs Committee explored the role of the Westminster Parliament in the Canadian constitutional controversy at a time when the government had indicated that its policy was to accept without question any proposals coming from the Canadian government in Ottawa; the committee came to a different conclusion, after studying the matter in much greater depth than the Foreign and Commonwealth Office had done.[174] Similarly, the Employment Committee chose to examine the government's decision banning trade union membership at GCHQ;[175] the Foreign Affairs Committee examined the sinking of the *General Belgrano* during the Falklands conflict;[176] the Treasury and Civil Service Committee examined the relations between ministers and civil servants following Clive Ponting's acquittal under the Official Secrets Act;[177] no fewer than three committees examined aspects of the Westland affair;[178] and the Foreign Affairs Committee examined the government's support for the Pergau dam project in Malaysia.[179]

Such reports would be valueless if they merely reproduced the government's justification of its policies. The committees are aware that, even though they seldom change government decisions, as all-party committees they exercise an important critical function. Voting on party lines can occur when a committee is deciding the contents of its report, but this is exceptional and not the rule. For criticism of the government to be made, it must have been supported in the committee by one or more MPs from the government side of the House. The committee's report contains only

---

[173] D Oliver [2001] PL 666, at p 668, on which this account draws.
[174] HC 42 and 295 (1980–81); Cmnd 8450, 1981; HC 128 (1981–82).
[175] HC 238 (1983–84).
[176] HC 11 (1984–85).
[177] HC 92 (1985–86).
[178] Defence Committee, HC 518, 519 (1985–86); Trade and Industry Committee, HC 176 (1986–87); Treasury and Civil Service Committee, HC 92 (1985–86).
[179] HC 271 (1993–94). So did the Public Accounts Committee: HC 155 (1993–94); see F White et al. [1994] PL 526.

the majority view; but the extent of unity or division is revealed in the minutes of proceedings that are published with the report. In 1979, some MPs believed that such committees might detract from the adversary quality of parliamentary procedure, might develop consensus politics, might develop too close a relationship with the departments concerned and so on. These fears have not been borne out. But the 1979 reform of committees did not transform the power relationship between government and Parliament. The government has undertaken to cooperate fully with the committees[180] but it lays down the rules by which civil servants may give evidence; these rules seek to protect from investigation the process of decision-making within government.[181] In the 1997–2001 Parliament, some Committees encountered difficulties in securing evidence, whether from individuals who refused to attend or were prohibited by government from attending; or from departments that refused to release documents.[182] Nevertheless, it has been said by the House of Commons Liaison Committee in a comprehensive review of the select committee system that 20 years after it had been established, the system was now:

> widely acknowledged to be a success. Select Committees had become a vital source of scrutiny, analysis and ideas; they had made the political process more accessible; and they had provided a much-needed climate of Parliamentary accountability. In so doing, they became more visible and widely known, and an entrenched part of our constitutional arrangements.[183]

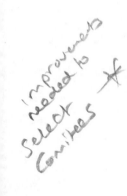

This is not to say that the system does not need to be improved and in an important report – *Shifting the Balance: Select Committees and the Executive*[184] – the Liaison Committee made a number of recommendations for the committees to be more effective and independent. Concern was expressed about the system for the nomination of members which was 'too much under the control of the Whips', with members kept off or removed 'on account of their views'. The committee also recommended that more time should be spent on the floor of the House considering select committee reports. Although an opportunity for greater consideration has arisen by the use of Westminster Hall (where debates on committee reports do take place), this was thought not to be a substitute for 'debating time on the floor of the House, on substantive motions'. The committee also proposed a 'select committee half hour once a week on a Tuesday', in which a minister would respond to a recently published report followed by contributions from committee members, and other members of the House. Other recommendations related to better scrutiny of government expenditure; more pre-legislative scrutiny of legislation by select committees; and more joint work by committees: 'Joined-up government must be scrutinised by joined-up committees.' There was also a need to address the 'insufficient knowledge of select committees and of Parliament generally, among departmental officials'.

E. Constitutional watchdog

This account has focused on the departmentally related select committees in the Commons. Of the other select committees appointed by the House,[185] the Public Accounts Committee, the Public Administration Committee, and the Deregulation

---

[180] HC Deb, 25 June 1979, col 45; and 16 January 1981, col 1697.
[181] See ch 13 D where this matter is fully explored.
[182] HC 321 (2000–01), paras 118–26.
[183] HC 321 (2000–01), para 2.
[184] HC 300 (1999–2000); also HC 748 (2000–01); and HC 321 (2000–01).
[185] See HC SOs 140–51.

Committee are each concerned with the scrutiny of executive action.[186] As well as the procedures of the House considered earlier, each MP's office provides a means by which individual grievances, particularly those emanating from his or her constituency, may be raised with the public body concerned.[187] Yet despite the means that exist for enabling the Commons to scrutinise the actions of public bodies, there remains some concern that the balance of power is weighted too heavily in favour of the executive and that the House lacks the political will to secure due accountability. Thus the House appears to accept that ministers control the flow of information from departments to the select committees of the House.[188] The Scott report in 1996[189] delivered a challenge to traditional assumptions within Westminster and Whitehall which deserved a more positive response than it received.

It is clear also that although the Labour administration has been responsive to calls to reform the legislative process and to enhance parliamentary scrutiny of the government's legislative proposals, it needs to be equally responsive to proposals – from within Parliament and beyond – to enhance parliamentary scrutiny of other executive action.[190] The House of Commons Liaison Committee expressed disappointment that the government's 'warm approval of the principles of more effective Parliamentary accountability were not matched by a willingness to make the modest changes that [the Committee] had put forward'.[191] An important step forward is the undertaking in 2002 by the Prime Minister to be a witness in select committee proceedings, Mr Blair having previously refused requests by both the Public Administration Committee and the Liaison Committee that he appear before them.[192] But the steps that have been taken in recent years ought not to be underestimated. In addition to the measures already discussed in this chapter, a Joint Committee on Human Rights was established in 2001,[193] along with a Constitutional Committee of the House of Lords.[194] Both these developments emphasise the additional role of Parliament as constitutional watchdog, and in this capacity some notable work was done by the Joint Committee on Human Rights in its scrutiny of the Anti-terrorism, Crime and Security Bill 2001, even if its conclusions about the disproportionate nature of the British government's response to the terrorist events in the United States on 11 September 2001 appeared to fall on deaf ears.[195]

---

[186] See respectively chs 17, 28 and 29 D.

[187] On the MP's 'complaints service', see R Rawlings (1990) 53 MLR 22, 149.

[188] Ch 7.

[189] Page 207 above.

[190] See esp Hansard Society, *The Challenge for Parliament: Making Government Accountable*; D Oliver [2001] PL 666.

[191] HC 321 (2000–01), para 6.

[192] See the exchange of correspondence in HC 321 (2000–01), paras 143–51.

[193] See ch 19 C in this volume.

[194] The responsibility of the latter is to examine the constitutional implications of all Bills brought before the House; and to keep under review the operation of the Constitution. For background, see Cm 4534, 2000, Ch 5.

[195] This matter is considered more fully in ch 19.

Chapter 11

PRIVILEGES OF PARLIAMENT

> Parliamentary privilege consists of the rights and immunities which the two Houses of Parliament and their members and officers possess to enable them to carry out their parliamentary functions effectively. Without this protection members would be handicapped in performing their parliamentary duties, and the authority of Parliament itself in confronting the executive and as a forum for expressing the anxieties of citizens would be correspondingly diminished.[1]

With these words the report of a committee of both Houses chaired by Lord Nicholls in 1999 emphasised that parliamentary privilege provides the necessary framework by which each House and its members can fulfil their duties. The privileges of each House have both external and internal aspects: they protect it against outside interference that would erode freedom to conduct its own proceedings; and they impose duties on its members, restraining them from conduct that would abuse their privileged position.

Privilege is an important part of the law and custom of Parliament, but aspects of the law are still obscure. It has been developed over centuries by the response of Parliament, especially the Commons, to changing circumstances and also, since privilege affects those outside Parliament, by decisions of the courts. Since neither House separately exercises legislative supremacy, neither House can by its own resolution create new privileges. When a matter of privilege is disputed, 'it is for the courts to decide whether a privilege exists and for the House to decide whether such privilege has been infringed.'[2] The Nicholls report recommended the enactment of a Parliamentary Privileges Act that would remove uncertainties, make essential changes and abolish obsolete aspects of privilege.

This chapter does not discuss the application of privilege to the Scottish Parliament and the Assemblies for Wales and Northern Ireland. These bodies enjoy certain rights and immunities enacted by legislation,[3] but beyond this they do not share in Westminster's inherited privileges.[4] Emphasis in this chapter is placed on the House of Commons, but questions of privilege may also arise in relation to the Lords.

A. House of Commons

For centuries certain privileges and immunities have been attached both to the House and its members. At the opening of each Parliament, the Speaker formally claims from the Crown for the Commons 'their ancient and undoubted rights and privileges' and, in particular, 'freedom of speech in debate, freedom from arrest, freedom of access to

---

[1] Report of joint committee on parliamentary privilege (HL 43–I, HC 214–I, 1998–99), para 3 (cited here as the 'Nicholls report'). And see P M Leopold [1999] PL 604. Also Erskine May, chs 5–11; Griffith and Ryle, *Parliament*, ch 3; Oliver and Drewry (eds), *The Law and Parliament*, chs 1, 2, 4, 5, 7.

[2] *Pepper* v *Hart* [1993] AC 595, 645 (Lord Browne-Wilkinson).

[3] See e.g. Scotland Act 1998, ss 22 and Sch 3 (standing orders), ss 23–26 (witnesses and documents), 39 (members' interests), 41 (defamatory statements), 42 (contempt of court), and 43 (corrupt practices).

[4] See *Whaley* v *Lord Watson of Invergowrie* 2000 SLT 475. And C R Munro [2000] PL 347.

Her Majesty whenever occasion shall require; and that the most favourable construction should be placed upon all their proceedings.' The privileges of individual members are primarily freedom from arrest and freedom of speech.

Freedom from arrest[5]

This ancient privilege developed to enable individual members to attend meetings of the House. It protects a member from arrest in connection with civil proceedings for the customary period from 40 days before to 40 days after a session of Parliament. But MPs have no privilege from arrest in connection with criminal proceedings.

Since it applies only to civil arrest, the privilege has been of little importance since the virtual abolition of imprisonment for debt. A member is protected against committal for contempt of court where the imprisonment is sought to compel performance of a civil obligation.[6] Members have no general immunity from having civil actions brought against them,[7] but they retain minor privileges in regard to civil litigation. It is a contempt of the House to seek to serve a writ or other legal process on a member within the precincts of the House.[8] A subpoena addressed to a member to give evidence in a civil court probably cannot be enforced by the High Court while the House is in session, but the House may grant a member leave of absence to attend as a witness. Members are not protected against bankruptcy proceedings, but are exempt from jury service.[9] In 1967, and again in 1999, it was recommended that any surviving freedom from arrest should be abolished.[10]

As regards criminal law, members have no privilege from arrest. Nor are they protected in cases of refusal to give surety to keep the peace or security for good behaviour nor against committal for contempt of court where contempt has a criminal character.[11] An MP was held in preventive detention under defence regulations during the Second World War,[12] but detention because of words spoken in Parliament would violate the privilege of freedom of speech. The House has always insisted on receiving immediate information of the imprisonment of a member, with reasons for the detention. In 1970, the Committee of Privileges inquired into the rights of members who were detained in prison whether awaiting trial or after conviction. The committee reported that a member awaiting trial could carry out many duties as a constituency representative, but that a member who had been convicted could do so only if granted exceptional concessions under prison rules. The committee considered that no special advantages in the conditions of detention should be granted to members.[13]

Freedom of speech[14]

Freedom of speech is today the most substantial privilege of the House. Its essence is that no penal or coercive action should be taken against members for what is said or

---

[5] Erskine May, ch 7; and Nicholls report, paras 325–28.
[6] As in *Stourton* v *Stourton* [1963] P 302. As ministers are subject to the contempt jurisdiction (*M* v *Home Office* [1994] 1 AC 377, ch 32 C), would an MP who is a minister be protected by parliamentary privilege from committal for contempt of court? Cf Erskine May, pp 102–4.
[7] *Re Parliamentary Privilege Act 1770* [1958] AC 331.
[8] HC 221 (1969–70) and HC 144 (1972–73).
[9] Insolvency Act 1986, s 427. For detention under the Mental Health Act 1983, see p 169 above. And see Juries Act 1974, s 9 and Sch 1.
[10] Nicholls report, para 327.
[11] Ch 18 D. And see note 6 above.
[12] HC 164 (1939–40) (Captain Ramsay's case).
[13] HC 185 (1970–71). And see G J Zellick [1977] PL 29.
[14] Erskine May, ch 6; Nicholls report, paras 36–134, 189–228. And P M Leopold [1981] PL 30.

done in Parliament. Claims for the privilege were regularly made by the Speaker from the end of the 16th century. The right of the Commons to criticise the King's government was called in question in 1629 when Eliot, Holles and Valentine were convicted by the Court of King's Bench for seditious words spoken in the Commons and for tumult in the House.[15] This judgment was reversed in 1668 by the House of Lords on the ground that words spoken in Parliament could be judged only in Parliament. In art 9 of the Bill of Rights 1689 it was declared 'that the freedom of speech and debates or proceedings in Parliament ought not to be impeached or questioned in any court or place out of Parliament.'[16]

The main effect of this is that no member may be made liable in the courts for words spoken in the course of parliamentary proceedings. Thus members may speak in the House knowing that they are immune from the law of defamation.[17] Neither can what is said in Parliament be examined by a court for the purpose of deciding whether it supports a cause of action in defamation which has arisen outside Parliament: 'a member must have a complete right of free speech in the House without any fear that his motives or intentions or reasoning will be questioned or held against him thereafter.'[18] And the courts may not receive in any proceedings 'evidence, questioning or submissions designed to show that a witness in parliamentary proceedings deliberately misled Parliament'.[19] Since 1818, leave of the House has been required before clerks or officers of the House may give evidence in court of proceedings in the House. In 1980, the House relaxed its practice to the extent of permitting reference to be made in court to Hansard and to the published evidence and reports of committees, without special leave from the House.[20] This change did not diminish the continuing force of art 9 of the Bill of Rights, nor did it alter the rule that Hansard may not be used in court as an aid to statutory interpretation. In 1993, the House of Lords in its appellate capacity changed the rule, holding that courts may use ministerial statements in Hansard to resolve ambiguities in legislation; such use would not 'impeach or question' freedom of speech in the Commons.[21] Moreover, ministerial statements in Parliament announcing new policies or executive decisions are frequently used as evidence in court in judicial review proceedings.[22]

The protection of members for words spoken extends to criminal as well as civil liability. Thus, disclosures to Parliament may not be made the subject of prosecution under the Official Secrets Acts,[23] although the MP concerned may be liable to the disciplinary jurisdiction of the House. Speeches or questions in Parliament may be in breach of the House's *sub judice* rule if they concern pending judicial proceedings, but may not be held to be in contempt of court.[24]

In protecting MPs from liability for speaking in Parliament, one indirect effect of the Bill of Rights was to restrict the ability of MPs to sue in defamation. The reason for this was that if an MP sued a newspaper for a defamatory report about his or her

---

[15] *Eliot's* case (1629) 3 St Tr 294.
[16] And see *Re Parliamentary Privilege Act 1770*, note 7 above.
[17] E.g. *Dillon v Balfour* (1887) 20 LR Ir 600. And *Lake v King* (1667) 1 Saunders 131.
[18] *Church of Scientology of California v Johnson-Smith* [1972] 1 QB 522, 530 (Browne J).
[19] *Hamilton v Al Fayed* [2001] 1 AC 395, 403 (Lord Browne-Wilkinson).
[20] HC Deb, 3 December 1979, col 167, and 31 October 1980, col 879; HC 102 (1978–79); and P M Leopold [1981] PL 316.
[21] *Pepper v Hart* [1993] AC 593; and ch 2 A.
[22] Ibid, 639 (Lord Browne-Wilkinson); Nicholls report, paras 46–59. The Nicholls committee considered that such statements could be used even to question the minister's good faith: cf *Prebble* v *Television New Zealand Ltd* [1995] 1 AC 321, 333.
[23] *Duncan Sandys* case, HC 101 (1938–39). On liability for criminal conspiracy, see *Ex p Wason* (1869) LR 4 QB 573.
[24] E.g. the disclosure of Colonel B's identity on 20 April 1978; HC 667 (1977–78) and 222 (1978–79); and p 385 below.

conduct, art 9 of the Bill of Rights prevented the newspaper from justifying the report by bringing evidence of what had been said or done in Parliament: thus, in the interests of justice, the court would require the case to be stayed.[25] In 1996, concern at 'cash for questions' allegations caused Parliament hastily to amend the Bill of Rights to enable Neil Hamilton MP to sue *The Guardian*; by s 13 of the Defamation Act 1996, any individual (whether an MP or not) may waive parliamentary privilege so that an action can proceed.[26] For several reasons, this was an unsatisfactory change in the law. In 1999, the Nicholls committee recommended that s 13 of the 1996 Act be repealed; in its place, each House should have power to waive privilege in court proceedings, subject to safeguards to maintain the protection of the Bill of Rights for individuals.[27]

The meaning of 'proceedings in Parliament'

Protection for members is not confined to debates in the House. It covers asking questions, giving written notice of questions and 'everything said or done by a member in the exercise of his functions as a member in a committee in either House, as well as everything said or done in either House in the transaction of parliamentary business'.[28] Protection extends to officials of the House acting in course of their duties, as well as to witnesses giving evidence to committees of the House. It may be that privilege is not confined to words spoken or acts done within the precincts of the House, and includes words spoken outside Parliament, for example, a conversation between a minister of the Crown and a member on parliamentary business in a minister's office. Conversely, it may not extend to a casual conversation within the House on private affairs. The posting of alleged libels to members in the House on matters unconnected with proceedings in the House is not protected.[29]

The question of whether a member's letter to a minister concerning a publicly owned industry was a 'proceeding in Parliament' arose in 1957.

> G R Strauss MP had written to the minister responsible for the electricity industry (the Paymaster-General) complaining of the methods of disposal of scrap cable followed by the London Electricity Board. The minister referred the letter to the board, who protested to Mr Strauss about its contents. Finally, the solicitors to the board told him that they had instructions to sue for libel unless he withdrew and apologised. Mr Strauss drew the attention of the House to this threat and the matter was referred to the Committee of Privileges. The crucial question was whether the original letter from the member to the Paymaster-General was a 'proceeding in Parliament' within the meaning of the Bill of Rights. The committee concluded that Mr Strauss was engaged in a proceeding in Parliament; accordingly the threat by the board to sue for libel was a threat to impeach or question his freedom of speech in a court or place outside Parliament. Thus the board and their solicitors had acted in breach of privilege. On 8 July 1958, the House decided on a free vote (218 to 213) to disagree with the committee, and resolved (*a*) that the original letter was not a proceeding in Parliament and (*b*) that nothing in the subsequent correspondence constituted a breach of privilege.[30]

In support of the majority view, it was argued that members should not widen the scope of absolute parliamentary privilege and should rely on the defence of qualified privilege in the law of defamation. There is no doubt that a complaint addressed by a

---

[25] *Prebble* v *Television New Zealand Ltd*; see ch 23 F below and P M Leopold (1995) 15 LS 204.
[26] By using s 13, Mr Hamilton later sued Mr Al Fayed over allegations already examined by a Commons committee: *Hamilton* v *Al Fayed* [2001] 1 AC 395 (and see A W Bradley [2000] PL 556). See ch 23 F for full consideration.
[27] Nicholls report, paras 60–82.
[28] HC 101 (1938–39).
[29] *Rivlin* v *Bilainkin* [1953] 1 QB 485.
[30] HC 305 (1956–57); *Re Parliamentary Privilege Act 1770* [1958] AC 331; HC 227 (1957–58). Also S A de Smith (1958) 21 MLR 465; D Thompson [1959] PL 10.

member of Parliament to a minister on an issue of public concern in which the minister has an interest has the protection of qualified privilege.[31] But qualified privilege may be rebutted by proof of express malice and it might possibly be held to constitute malice if a member passed on to a minister without any inquiry a letter from a constituent containing defamatory allegations.

In support of the view that a member's letter to a minister should be regarded as a proceeding in Parliament, it is certain that if a member tabled a parliamentary question instead of writing to the minister, he or she would be absolutely protected: many matters are raised in correspondence with ministers that may or may not become the subject of questions.

One issue not addressed in the Strauss case was whether for a claimant to sue for defamation in respect of a proceeding in Parliament is itself a breach of privilege. It has been argued that members should leave it to the courts to reject such an action and that the House should not treat the action itself as a breach of privilege.[32]

The 1957 Commons resolution in the Strauss case binds neither the House itself nor the courts. For this and other reasons, it has often been argued that the meaning of 'proceedings in Parliament' should be defined by legislation.[33] In 1999, the Nicholls committee agreed with this and proposed a definition that should have statutory force. But the committee did not agree that the absolute protection given by art 9 of the Bill of Rights should be extended to letters between MPs and ministers.[34]

Publication of parliamentary proceedings outside Parliament

The House has always maintained the right to secure privacy for its own debates. In wartime the House occasionally excluded the press and the public to enable matters to be discussed in secret for security reasons. The House formerly maintained the right to control publication of its debates outside Parliament. By resolution of 3 March 1762, any publication in the press of speeches made by members was declared a breach of privilege. In modern times this resolution bore no relation to reality. On 16 July 1971, the House resolved that in future it would entertain no complaint of contempt or breach of privilege regarding the publication of debates in the House or its committees, except when the House or a committee sat in private session. The House thus retained the power to permit committees and sub-committees to meet in private.[35] While select committees generally take evidence in public, their deliberations, especially when a draft report is being considered, take place in private. Premature reporting of these proceedings is a serious breach of privilege,[36] but the reporting of evidence taken at public sittings of committees is no longer restricted.[37]

The public interest in reports of parliamentary proceedings is recognised in the law of defamation; unless a defamed person can prove malice, a fair and accurate unofficial report of proceedings in Parliament is privileged, as is an article founded upon

---

[31] *Beach v Freeson* [1972] 1 QB 14 (MP forwarding constituent's complaint about solicitors to the Law Society and Lord Chancellor); and ch 23 F.

[32] S A de Smith (1958) 21 MLR 465, 468–75. Lord Denning's unpublished dissent in *Re Parliamentary Privilege Act 1770* (above) is at [1985] PL 80.

[33] HC 261 (1969–70), pp 8–12; Cmnd 5909, 1975, p 51; HC 417 (1976–77), p v. Cf *Rost v Edwards* [1990] 2 QB 460 (register of members' interests not a proceeding in Parliament), doubted in *Prebble*'s case, [1995] 1 AC 321 at p 337; P M Leopold [1990] PL 475.

[34] Nicholls report, paras 97–129.

[35] HC 34 (1966–77), paras 116–29.

[36] E.g. HC 357 (1967–68), debated on 24 July 1968; HC 185 (1969–70); HC 180 (1971–72); and HC 22 (1975–76), debated on 16 December 1975.

[37] HC Deb, 31 October 1980, col 917; and HC SO 136.

such proceedings, provided it is an honest and fair comment upon the facts.[38] The defence of qualified privilege thus protects the public interest in discovering what was said in Parliament. It applies to a 'parliamentary sketch', that is, an impressionistic and selective account of a debate,[39] but not to reports of detached parts of speeches published with intent to injure individuals or the publication of a single speech which contains libellous matter. Thus a member who repeats outside Parliament what is said in Parliament is liable if the speech contains defamatory material.[40] It is doubtful if qualified privilege attaches to the publication of a member's speech for the information of constituents.[41]

After long discussion within Parliament, regular sound broadcasting of proceedings in both Houses began in 1978.[42] Debates in the Lords were first televised in 1985 and the Commons followed suit in 1989. The broadcasting authorities have full editorial control to select what is broadcast, but the use of extracts for light entertainment or political satire is excluded. It is likely that those who broadcast Parliament are protected against liability for defamation by the common law defence of qualified privilege and by the Parliamentary Papers Act 1840 (considered later), section 3 of which was extended to radio broadcasting in 1952 and to television in 1990.[43] If parliamentary privilege is to be the subject of new legislation, this should re-enact the main provisions of the 1840 Act, drafted afresh in clear language.

Parliamentary papers

A difficult question at common law concerned the authority of the House to publish accounts of debates and reports of committees outside Parliament. In 1839, after a protracted dispute between the House and the courts, it was established that at common law the authority of the House was no defence when defamatory material was published outside the House and, more fundamentally, that the House could not create a new privilege by its own resolution.

In *Stockdale* v *Hansard*,[44] Hansard had by order of the Commons printed and sold to the public a report by the inspectors of prisons which stated that an indecent book published by Stockdale was circulating in Newgate Prison. The first action in defamation raised by Stockdale against Hansard was decided for Hansard on the ground that the statement in the report was true. When Stockdale brought a second action, after the report had been re-published, Hansard was ordered by the House to plead that he had acted under an order of the Commons, a court superior to any court of law; and further that the House had declared that the case was a case of privilege; that each House was the sole judge of its own privileges; and that a resolution of the House declaratory of its privileges could not be questioned in any court. The court rejected the defence, holding that only the Queen and both Houses of Parliament could make or unmake laws; that no resolution of either House could place anyone beyond the control of the law; and that, when it was necessary in order to decide the rights of private individuals outside Parliament, the courts should determine the nature and existence of privileges of the Commons. It was held further that the House had no privilege to permit the publication outside the House of defamatory matter.

---

[38] *Wason* v *Walter* (1868) LR 4 QB 73. And see ch 23 F.
[39] *Cook* v *Alexander* [1974] QB 279.
[40] *R* v *Creevey* (1813) 1 M & S 278.
[41] Cf *Davison* v *Duncan* (1857) 7 E & B 229.
[42] See HC 376 (1981–82) for the history and the Nicholls report (paras 358–361) for the present position.
[43] Nicholls report, paras 355–375. See P M Leopold [1987] PL 524, (1989) 9 LS 53 and [1999] PL 604, 614.
[44] (1839) 9 A & E 1. For the background, see P and G Ford (eds), *Luke Graves Hansard's Diary 1814–1841*. And E Stockdale [1990] PL 30.

One sequel to *Stockdale v Hansard* was the *Case of the Sheriff of Middlesex*, which will be considered later. The other sequel was the Parliamentary Papers Act 1840. By s 1, any civil or criminal proceedings arising out of the publication of papers, reports etc. made by the authority of either House must be stayed on the production of a certificate of such authority from an officer of the House. Thus Parliament as a whole gave the protection of absolute privilege to parliamentary papers. The official report of debates in the House (Hansard) is covered by absolute privilege under the 1840 Act and so are documents in the series of House of Commons papers. But Command papers as such are not considered to be covered; if the report of an inquiry may contain defamatory material, a minister will move an order calling for the report to be produced to Parliament, so bringing it within the 1840 Act.[45] Section 3 of the 1840 Act protects in the absence of malice the publication of fair and accurate extracts from, or abstracts of, papers published under the authority of Parliament: thus press reports of parliamentary papers are protected by qualified privilege, and the same privilege now applies to broadcast reports.[46] But the 1840 Act does not apply to reports of debates appearing in the press which are based not on Hansard but on the reporter's own notes.

Right to control internal proceedings

The House has the right to control its own proceedings and to regulate its internal affairs without interference by the courts. This principle in part explains why the courts refuse to investigate alleged defects of procedure when the validity of an Act of Parliament is challenged on this ground.[47] The courts will not consider whether the report of a committee of the House is invalid because of procedural defects[48] and will not issue an injunction to restrain a local authority from breaking a contractual obligation not to oppose in Parliament a Bill promoted by another local authority.[49]

The House is considered to have the right to provide for its own proper constitution as established by law.[50] At one time this included the right to determine disputed elections; today election disputes are decided by the courts.[51] But the House retains (*a*) the right to regulate the filling of vacancies by ordering the issue of a warrant by the Speaker for a writ for a by-election;[52] (*b*) the right to determine whether a member is qualified to sit in the House and to declare a seat vacant if a member is not so qualified;[53] and (*c*) the right to expel a member whom it considers unfit to continue as a member. When the House expels a member, he or she is not disqualified from re-election to the House. Subject to this, expulsion is the ultimate disciplinary sanction which the House can exercise over its members.

In 1947, Mr Allighan MP published an article which accused MPs of disclosing for reward or under the influence of drink the proceedings of confidential party meetings held in the precincts of the House but not forming any part of the formal business of Parliament. It was held by the House, after investigation by the Committee of Privileges, that the article was a gross contempt of the House; other grave contempts had been committed by Mr Allighan since he

---

[45] Cmnd 5909, 1975, p 55; P M Leopold [1990] PL 183; Nicholls report, paras 343–354.
[46] Defamation Act 1952, s 9(1); Broadcasting Act 1990, s 203(1) and Sch 20, para 1.
[47] *Pickin v British Railways Board* [1974] AC 765; cf *Harper v Home Secretary* [1955] Ch 238, p 153 above.
[48] *Dingle v Associated Newspapers Ltd* [1961] 2 QB 162.
[49] *Bilston Corpn v Wolverhampton Corpn* [1942] ch 391.
[50] Erskine May, pp 79–80.
[51] Ch 9 E.
[52] Page 180 above.
[53] Cf *A-G v Jones* [2000] QB 66 (Speaker asking court to decide whether MP's seat, vacated on her conviction for an election offence, reverted to her when she won her appeal against conviction).

had corruptly accepted payment for disclosing information and, except for a single case, he had been unable to substantiate any of the charges against his fellow-members. The House voted to expel Mr Allighan.[54]

By contrast with the position in the United States,[55] no court in Britain may review the legality of a resolution of the House to exclude or expel a member. One safeguard against abuse of this power is that a constituency may re-elect an expelled member, as in the case of John Wilkes in the 18th century. Today, the House would generally prefer a member to resign rather than be expelled.[56] While the House has power to enforce the attendance of members at Westminster, this power is not now used.[57]

This right of the House to regulate its own proceedings includes the right to maintain order and discipline during debates. A member guilty of disorderly conduct who refuses to withdraw may, on being named by the Speaker, be suspended from the service of the House either for a specified time or for the remainder of the session.[58] While in *Eliot*'s case[59] the question of whether the courts could deal with an assault on the Speaker committed in the House was left open when the judgment was declared illegal by resolutions of both Houses, in principle criminal acts in the Palace of Westminster may be dealt with in the ordinary courts. In the case of a statutory offence, it is necessary to show that the statute in question applies to the Palace of Westminster: an attempt to convict members of the Kitchen Committee of the House for breaches of licensing law failed, primarily on the ground of the right of the House to regulate its internal affairs.[60]

Breaches of privilege and contempt of the House

The House has inherent power to protect its privileges and to punish those who violate its privileges or commit contempt of the House. The penal powers of the House include power to order the offender to be reprimanded or admonished by the Speaker. Members may be suspended or expelled; officials of the House may be dismissed; and non-members such as lobby correspondents, who are granted certain facilities in the Palace of Westminster, may have those facilities withdrawn.[61] Although the House has no power to impose a fine, it has power to commit any person to the custody of its own officers or to prison for contempt of the House or breach of its privileges. Such commitment cannot last beyond the end of the session.

In parliamentary speech, the term 'breach of privilege' has often been used as synonymous with contempt of the House. However, while most breaches of privilege are likely to be contempts, a person may be adjudged to be guilty of a contempt who has not infringed any existing privilege of the House. Thus in *Allighan*'s case[62] the unfounded allegation about the proceedings of party meetings held in private at Westminster involved an affront to the House: but information about such meetings was not in itself a breach of privilege. Contempt of the House, like contempt of court, is a very wide concept. In Erskine May's words:

---

[54] HC 138 (1946–47).
[55] *Powell* v *McCormack* 395 US 486 (1970).
[56] For the case of the disappearing MP, John Stonehouse, who was eventually convicted of fraud and resigned, see HC 273, 357, 373, 414 (1974–75), and HC Deb, 11 June 1975, col 408.
[57] Erskine May, p 179.
[58] HC SOs 42–45A.
[59] Page 216 above.
[60] *R* v *Graham-Campbell, ex p Herbert* [1935] 1 KB 594. Cf Nicholls report, paras 240–51.
[61] Cf HC 22 (1975–76).
[62] Page 220 above.

any act or omission which obstructs or impedes either House of Parliament in the performance of its functions, or which obstructs or impedes any member or officer of such House in the discharge of his duty, or which has a tendency, directly or indirectly, to produce such results may be treated as a contempt even though there is no precedent of the offence.[63]

Contempt has been held by the House to include: disorderly conduct by members or strangers within the precincts of the House;[64] refusal of a person without reasonable excuse to give evidence to a committee of the House;[65] interference with the giving of evidence by others to a committee;[66] obstruction of a member in coming to and from the House;[67] inclusion by a member in a personal statement to the House of words which he knew to be untrue; bribery and corruption, or attempts thereat, in relation to the conduct of members as such;[68] molestation of a member on account of conduct in the House (for example, publication of a newspaper article inviting readers to telephone a member at his home to express their views about a question which he had tabled);[69] publication of material which is derogatory of the House (for example, an allegation of drunkenness among members);[70] an allegation that members 'have surrendered for money their freedom of action as parliamentarians';[71] premature disclosure of the proceedings of a committee of the House;[72] obstructing or assaulting an officer of the House while in the execution of his duty; and the secret recording by a journalist of his conversations with MPs at Westminster while trying to persuade them to accept cash for asking questions.[73] But it was held not to constitute a contempt for pressure to be brought to bear on a citizen to withdraw a complaint which he had asked his MP to raise in Parliament.[74] The fact that certain action may be a contempt of the House does not mean that the House will take action against the offender. In 1978, it was agreed that the House should use its penal jurisdiction as sparingly as possible and only when the House

> is satisfied that to do so is essential to provide reasonable protection for the House, its members or its officers, from such improper obstruction or attempt at or threat of obstruction as is causing or is liable to cause, substantial interference with the performance of their respective functions.[75]

The courts and contempt of the House

While the courts assert jurisdiction to decide the existence and extent of privileges of the House, what constitutes a contempt of the House is a matter which only the House can decide. If a contempt issue arises relating to the internal proceedings of the House, the courts will decline to interfere. The House has an undoubted power (but not exercised since 1880) to detain persons for contempt. There was in the past much debate as to whether the courts might review the House's decision to detain an individual.

---

[63] Erskine May, p 108; see HC 34 (1967–68), pp xi–xviii and 95–101; Nicholls report, paras 262–70.
[64] For the precedents and full references, see Erskine May, chs 8 and 9.
[65] On the power to compel evidence to be given to a select committee, see P M Leopold [1992] PL 516.
[66] The House resolved in 1688 that all witnesses summoned to the House should have the privilege of the House 'in coming, staying and returning'; and see the Witnesses (Public Inquiries) Protection Act 1892.
[67] Cf *Papworth v Coventry* [1967] 2 All ER 41.
[68] And see section B of this chapter.
[69] The *Daily Graphic* case, HC 27 (1956–57).
[70] *Duffy*'s case, HC 129 (1964–65) and see HC 302 (1974–75).
[71] *Ashton*'s case, HC 228 (1974).
[72] See notes 36 above and 90 below.
[73] HC 351–I (1994–95).
[74] *Stevenson*'s case, HC 112 (1954–55).
[75] HC 34 (1967–68), para 15; HC Deb, 6 February 1978, cols 1155–98.

In *Paty*'s case, which arose after five electors of Aylesbury had sued returning officers for the malicious refusal of their votes and thereby had annoyed the Commons, Chief Justice Holt in a dissenting judgment held that a writ of habeas corpus would go to release anyone committed for contempt by the House, where the cause of committal stated in the return to the writ was insufficient in law.[76] This view of the law is accepted today. But if only the bald statement of contempt of the House is shown in the return, the court will not make further inquiry into the reasons for the committal.[77] This principle was applied in the *Case of the Sheriff of Middlesex*.

> As a sequel to *Stockdale* v *Hansard*, the sheriffs attempted to recover for Stockdale by execution on Hansard's property £600 damages awarded in the third action of the series. The money recovered from Hansard was in the hands of the sheriffs when a new parliamentary session opened. The House first committed Stockdale and then, on the sheriffs refusing to refund the money to Hansard, also committed the two sheriffs for contempt, without expressing the reason for the committal. In habeas corpus proceedings it was held that the court had to accept the statement by the House that the sheriffs had been committed for contempt.[78]

Thus the House of Commons has power to commit persons for contempt and need not tell the courts of the reasons for doing so. However, except for the power to detain briefly anyone who tries to disrupt a sitting of the House, does the House need powers of detention? In 1999, the Nicholls committee concluded that the High Court should be granted power to punish non-members of the House for contempt, but only by imposing a fine.[79] The committee took account of art 6(1) of the European Convention on Human Rights (the right to a fair hearing by an independent tribunal on any criminal charge) which, at least in respect of someone who is not an MP, is difficult to reconcile with the exercise of penal jurisdiction by the House.[80]

The courts and parliamentary privilege[81]

Questions of privilege used to be a potential source of conflict between the Commons and the courts. The House claimed to be the absolute and sole judge of its own privileges, a claim that conflicted with the right of the courts, asserted in *Stockdale* v *Hansard*, to determine the nature and limit of parliamentary privilege in adjudicating on the rights of individuals outside the House. Another illustration of the relationship between courts and Parliament is provided by the complex Bradlaugh affair in the 1880s.

> Bradlaugh, an atheist, was elected as MP for Northampton on successive occasions. The House took the view that as an atheist he could not sit or vote, as he could not properly take the oath required by existing statute law. At one stage Bradlaugh was allowed by resolution of the House, subject to any legal penalties he might incur, to affirm instead of taking an oath. In an action brought against him by a common informer for penalties for sitting and voting without taking the oath, the Court of Appeal held that the Parliamentary Oaths Act 1866 and other statutes did not authorise him to affirm.[82]
>
> Later, following re-election to Parliament, Bradlaugh required the Speaker to call on him to take the oath. The Speaker refusing to do so, the House authorised the Serjeant at Arms to exclude Bradlaugh from the House. Bradlaugh sought an injunction against the Serjeant at Arms to restrain him from carrying out this resolution. In *Bradlaugh* v *Gossett*, it was held

---

[76] (1704) 2 Lord Raymond 1105.
[77] *Burdett* v *Abbot* (1811) 14 East 1.
[78] (1840) 11 A & E 273. And see E Stockdale [1990] PL 30.
[79] Nicholls report, paras 271–314.
[80] And see *Demicoli* v *Malta* (1992) 14 EHRR 47.
[81] Erskine May, ch 11.
[82] *Clarke* v *Bradlaugh* (1881) 7 QBD 38. And see Arnstein, *The Bradlaugh Case*.

that, this being a matter relating to the internal management of the procedure of the House, the court had no power to interfere. As Lord Coleridge CJ said, 'If injustice has been done, it is injustice for which the courts of law afford no remedy.'[83] The Act of 1866 permitted certain persons to affirm instead of taking an oath; any person making an affirmation otherwise than as authorised by the Act could be sued for certain penalties. Stephen J emphasised that, if the House had by resolution stated that Bradlaugh was entitled to make the affirmation, the resolution would not have protected him against an action for penalties: concerning a right to be exercised within the House itself, only the House could interpret the statute; but 'as regarded rights to be exercised out of and independently of the House, such as a right of suing for a penalty for having sat and voted, the statute must be interpreted by this court independently of the House.'[84]

It has been said that, 'there may be at any given moment two doctrines of privilege, the one held by the courts, the other by either House, the one to be found in the Law Reports, the other in Hansard'.[85] But this dualism must not be exaggerated. On the one hand, new privileges, for example, the absolute privilege which an MP has in forwarding a citizen's complaint to the Parliamentary Ombudsman,[86] must be created by statute and not by resolution of the House. On the other hand, the courts recognise the control which the House has over its own proceedings. Today it is not conceivable that the House would use its power to commit for contempt so as indirectly to create a new privilege when it was not willing to do this by process of legislation.[87]

In 1999, the Nicholls committee examined possible problems for parliamentary privilege arising from the increased use of judicial review, but it concluded that privilege was not a reason for restricting judicial review of executive decisions.[88] In 1993, a warning was given by Speaker Boothroyd that the parties to an application for judicial review of the government's decision to ratify the Treaty on European Union should respect art 9 of the Bill of Rights; in the event, court proceedings dealt solely with issues affecting the legality of the decision.[89]

The House today is likely to make a restrained use of its powers, especially when a minor breach of privilege or contempt is committed by a non-member. However, most MPs are vigilant to protect the right of a select committee to deliberate in private: it has repeatedly been emphasised that disclosure of the draft of a committee report and its unauthorised use or retention are contempts of the House.[90]

Procedure

How does the House exercise its power when a complaint of breach of privilege or contempt is raised? Before 1978, members were expected to bring a privilege complaint to the notice of the whole House at the earliest opportunity. Today the procedure operates under less pressure and enables trivial complaints to receive less publicity.[91] A member must give written notice of a privilege complaint to the Speaker as soon as is reasonably practicable. If the Speaker decides that the complaint should not have

---

[83] (1884) 12 QBD 271, 277.
[84] Ibid, 282.
[85] Keir and Lawson, *Cases in Constitutional Law*, p 255.
[86] Parliamentary Commissioner Act 1967, s 10(5); ch 29 D.
[87] Cf G F Lock [1985] PL 64 and (same author) in Oliver and Drewry, op cit, ch 4.
[88] Nicholls report, paras 46–55.
[89] See HC Deb, 21 July 1993, col 353; R Rawlings [1994] PL 367, 377–81; and *R v Foreign Secretary, ex p Rees-Mogg* [1994] QB 552.
[90] HC 607 (1998–99) (draft report of foreign affairs committee); HC 747 (1998–99) (social security committee). Also HC 376 (1985–86) and HC Deb, 20 May 1986, cols 293–332. And see Griffith and Ryle, *Parliament*, pp 98–104. See also n 36 above.
[91] HC 417 (1976–77); HC Deb, 6 February 1978, col 1155; and HC Deb, 29 April 1981, col 789.

precedence over other Commons business, the MP is told by letter and he or she may bring the matter to the House by other means. If the Speaker decides that the complaint should have priority over other business, this decision is announced to the House, whereupon the member may table a motion for the next day proposing that the matter be referred to the Committee on Standards and Privileges. The motion is then debated and voted on by the House. The committee, which has 11 members, was created in 1995 in place of the former Committee of Privileges. It is for the committee to decide on the procedure for investigating the complaint. It is not the practice of the House to authorise the person complained against to be represented by counsel. After examining witnesses and being advised by the Clerk of the House on relevant precedents, and if necessary by the Attorney-General on matters of law, the committee reports to the House and may recommend action that the House should take. The House need accept neither the conclusions nor the recommendations. The party whips are not applied on privilege issues.[92]

This procedure has often been criticised, in particular because the individual complained against has inadequate procedural safeguards. Improvements to meet these criticisms were recommended in 1967 but never implemented.[93] In 1999, the Nicholls committee set out what procedural fairness requires, referred to the right to a fair hearing under art 6 ECHR, and urged that the Committee on Standards and Privileges should devise an appropriate procedure.[94] One solution to the need for fair procedure would be for the House to vest the power to decide questions of privilege in an independent and impartial body outside the House, but the House is unlikely to accept this solution. Nicholls advised against such a solution, but stated that the role of the House should be limited to endorsing the report of the Privileges and Standards Committee or reducing a proposed penalty.[95] We shall see in the next section that similar procedural questions arise in regard to enforcement of the rules on MPs' interests.

B. Financial interests of members

It is one thing to assert the principle that MPs should have complete freedom of speech in Parliament, but another to ensure that they are, in fact, free of undue influence from financial and business interests outside the House and do not abuse their public office for private gain.

This is not a new problem, and perceptions of what is acceptable behaviour by politicians are likely to change. In the 18th century, the use of patronage enabled control over the House to be maintained. Today every MP is expected to take an active interest in questions that directly affect his or her constituency, such as the closure of a hospital or factory or issues which affect local businesses. At the national level, numerous interest groups (trade unions, professional associations, employers, manufacturers, environmental, charitable and social organisations) seek from widely varied motives to influence decisions and to win support in Parliament.

Many such groups consider it worthwhile to obtain political advice from MPs and to ensure that opportunities of promoting their cause in Parliament are taken. Where an MP gives time and effort to helping a constituent, no question of additional remuneration arises. But where an MP takes an interest in other matters, may he or she expect

---

[92] In 1996, a junior whip had to resign for having sought to exercise improper pressure on the former Committee on Members' Interests: HC 88 (1996–97).
[93] HC 34 (1967–68); and HC 417 (1976–77).
[94] Nicholls report, paras 280–92, citing *Demicoli* v *Malta* (see n 80 above).
[95] Nicholls report, para 294. See also text at pp 230–1 below.

to be remunerated for such efforts? In 1994, after press allegations that some MPs would ask questions of ministers in return for payment, the issue was examined by the Nolan committee on standards in public life and by the House itself.

This was not the first time that concern about the conduct of MPs had arisen. After the business network associated with the architect John Poulson collapsed on his bankruptcy in 1972, it was found that his influence had extended to central and local government, police committees and health authorities and also to three MPs, including a senior member of the shadow Cabinet, who had used their position as MPs to promote Poulson's business without disclosing benefits which they were receiving from him; the conduct of one of those MPs, who had raised matters in the House for reward, was a contempt of the House.[96] This affair caused the House in 1975 to create the first register of members' interests.

During the 1980s, a commercialised form of political lobbying developed which proved very lucrative for some MPs. The 'cash for questions' scandal in 1994 made it clear that, despite earlier attempts to regulate members' interests, the services of some MPs were in fact available for hire in one form or another.

Payments and rewards to members of Parliament

It was only in 1911 that MPs not holding ministerial office first received a salary. Payment of salaries became essential after the House of Lords had held that the use of trade union funds for political purposes was ultra vires and illegal,[97] thus preventing unions from paying salaries to the Labour MPs whom they supported. Today, in addition to a salary, members receive allowances for office costs, travel between Westminster and their constituencies, necessary overnight stays away from home, the benefit of a contributory pension scheme and an allowance when they cease to be members.[98] It is difficult to keep members' salaries and allowances fairly related to salaries outside the House; since 1987, these have been linked by means of a formula to civil service pay scales.[99] Since July 1996 these salaries are paid in full to members who also receive salaries as ministers.

Apart from public offices which disqualify from membership,[100] members may take paid employment outside the House, practise in their professions, and act as advisers or consultants to commercial or other organisations. Many members regard their public duties as occupying all their time, some regard them as the background to a successful career outside Parliament. Problems arise when payments or benefits from outside sources relate not to advice given outside the House but to acts of the member in Parliament.[101]

As long ago as 1695 the House resolved that 'the offer of any money, or other advantage, to any member of Parliament for the promoting of any matter whatsoever depending or to be transacted in Parliament is a high crime and misdemeanour.' In 1858, the House resolved that it was improper for a member to promote or advocate

---

[96] See HC 490 (1976–77); HC Deb, 26 July 1977, col 332; and G J Zellick [1978] PL 133.

[97] *Amalgamated Society of Railway Servants v Osborne* [1910] AC 87. Under the Trade Union and Labour Relations (Consolidation) Act 1992, unions may contribute to the expenses of parliamentary candidates from separate political funds, p 157 above.

[98] For the history of members' salaries, see Erskine May, ch 1.

[99] See HC Deb, 3 November 1993, col 455; 13 July 1994, col 1105; and 26 October 1995, col 1191.

[100] Ch 9 G.

[101] See generally HC 57 (1969–70); First Report of the (Nolan) Committee on Standards in Public Life, Cm 2850–I (1995); and HC 637 (1994–95).

in the House any proceeding or measure in which he had acted or was acting for pecuniary reward. In 1945, it was considered that, in accordance with the resolution of 1695, it would be a breach of privilege for an offer of money or other advantage to be made to a member, or to a local party or a charity, to induce him or her to take up a question with a minister.[102]

In 1947, the case of W J Brown MP, who had agreed with a civil service union to be their 'parliamentary general secretary', raised two questions: (1) Was the contract proper or did it improperly restrict the MP's freedom of action in Parliament? (2) If it were proper, were the union improperly restricting Brown's freedom if they sought to terminate the contract?

> The agreement, which provided Brown with valuable benefits, stated that (*a*) he was entitled to engage in his political activities with complete freedom, and (*b*) he should deal with all questions relating to the union which required parliamentary action. Disagreements having arisen between Brown and the union, the union's executive proposed to end the appointment on terms to be agreed. The Committee of Privileges reported that (i) it would be improper for an MP to enter any arrangement fettering his independence as a member; and (ii) no organisation should seek to punish an MP pecuniarily because of his actions in Parliament. However, (iii) Brown's contract was not improper; an MP who entered into such a contract must have accepted that its termination would not influence him in his parliamentary duties.

Accepting this ambivalent report, the House resolved that it was improper for an MP 'to enter into any contractual agreement with any outside body, controlling or limiting the Member's complete independence and freedom of action in Parliament or stipulating that he shall act in any way as the representative of such outside body in regard to any matters to be transacted in Parliament; the duty of a Member being to his constituents and to the country as a whole, rather than to any particular section thereof'.[103]

This is an important statement of principle, but why was the principle not breached by Brown's contract, which in return for payment envisaged action being taken by him in Parliament? The view taken in 1947 and later was that the contract did not in terms *require* Brown to take any specific action in Parliament – so that (in one sense) he was free to decide what issues to raise and what action to take. This view created uncertainty as to what was acceptable and left the door wide open for the growth of what came to be called 'parliamentary consultancies' – a door which in 1995 the Nolan committee said must be closed.[104] The register of members' interests in 1975 had compounded the uncertainty, since some MPs acted on the incorrect belief that registration of an interest was enough to legitimise it.[105]

The relationship between trade unions and Labour MPs in the House today bears no resemblance at all to the contractual arrangements in the *Brown* case. Following a revision of the arrangements in 1995 to coincide with the adoption of a code of conduct for Members of Parliament (on which see below), no money is now paid directly to an MP but to constituency funds under a constituency development plan agreement.[106] In the past, there were several occasions when questions of privilege were raised when branches of a union became dissatisfied with the political work of MPs whom they were sponsoring.[107]

---

[102] *Henderson*'s case, HC 63 (1944–45). See also *Robinson*'s case HC 85 (1943–44).
[103] HC Deb, 15 July 1947, col 284; HC 118 (1946–47).
[104] Cm 2850–I, pp 24–32.
[105] See the statement by Speaker Boothroyd in HC Deb, 12 July 1994, col 829.
[106] Ewing, *The Funding of Political Parties in Britain*, p 56. And see HC 57 (1969–70), app III.
[107] See e.g. HC 50 (1971–72), HC 634 (1974–75) and HC 512 (1976–77).

Voting and declarations of interest

By an old rule of the House, no member who has a direct pecuniary interest in a question may vote upon it. But this rule has been narrowly interpreted, Speaker Abbot declaring in 1811 that the rule applied only where the interest was a 'direct pecuniary interest and separately belonging to the persons . . . and not in common with the rest of His Majesty's subjects, or on a matter of State policy'. The rule was applied only to private legislation and a vote on a public Bill has never been disallowed.[108] By custom of the House, members had to declare their direct pecuniary interest when speaking in a debate, but the custom did not apply to question time or to letters which a member sent in his capacity as a member.[109] The duty to disclose private interests was given the authority of a rule of the House on 25 May 1974, when the House resolved:

> That in any debate or proceedings of the House or its committees or transactions or communications which a member may have with other members or with Ministers or servants of the Crown, he shall disclose any relevant pecuniary interest or benefit of whatever nature, whether direct or indirect, that he may have had, may have or may be expecting to have.

This resolution governs all parliamentary proceedings, but it does not in terms apply to dealings which MPs have with local councils, public corporations or foreign governments.

Register of members' interests

The House was slow to accept the need for a systematic method of making members' interests public, but in 1975 the Poulson affair caused the House to establish a compulsory register of members' interests.[110] The aim was to provide public information of any pecuniary interest or material benefit which might affect the conduct of members as such, or influence their actions, speeches or vote in Parliament. The register was maintained by a senior clerk of the House and supervised by a select committee. The initial criteria for registration were not always clear, yet in 1990 an MP who failed to register his financial interests was suspended from the House for 20 days.[111]

In 1995, the Committee of Privileges criticised two MPs who had been prepared to accept £1,000 from a *Sunday Times* reporter posing as a businessman, in return for asking a parliamentary question. The committee found that the reporter had committed a contempt of the House by secretly recording his conversations at Westminster with the MPs. The two MPs were suspended from the House, for 10 and 20 days respectively.[112]

The 'cash for questions' affair was one reason for the government's decision to appoint the Nolan committee on standards in public life. In its first report,[113] the committee restated seven key principles of conduct in public life (stressing such qualities as integrity, accountability and openness) and examined their application to MPs. MPs could properly be employed outside the House, but they should be barred from selling their services to firms engaged in lobbying on behalf of clients. Although deeply concerned by the nature of some parliamentary consultancies, the committee was against placing the rules of conduct for MPs on a statutory basis, and proposed new arrangements to enable the House to enforce the rules of conduct.

---

[108] HC 57 (1969–70), p xii; Erskine May, pp 361–5.

[109] See *Boothby*'s case, HC 5 (1940–41).

[110] See HC 57 (1969–70); and HC 102 (1974–75).

[111] See HC 135 (1989–90) and HC Deb, 7 March 1990, col 889. Also M Ryle [1990] PL 313; Griffith and Ryle, *Parliament*, pp 55–68.

[112] HC 351–I (1994–95) and HC Deb, 20 April 1995, col 350.

[113] Cm 2850–I, 1995. And see ch 14 B.

With the backing of a select committee on standards and conduct,[114] the House in 1995 adopted the following measures.

(i) A new officer of the House was appointed, the Parliamentary Commissioner for Standards, to maintain the Register of Members' Interests, to advise MPs on what to register, and to receive and investigate specific complaints about registration and the propriety of MPs' conduct.[115]

(ii) The Committee of Standards and Privileges was created, replacing the committees on registration of interests and on privileges, to oversee the work of the Commissioner for Standards, to consider matters relating to the conduct of members referred to it by the Commissioner, and to consider other matters relating to privileges referred to it by the House.[116]

(iii) Stricter rules for the register were adopted. There are ten categories of interest, including company directorships, employment, trade, profession and vocation; services to clients which arise from the member's position as MP; financial sponsorships, whether as a candidate (i.e. election expenses) or as a member; gifts, benefits and hospitality relating in any way to membership; overseas visits relating to membership; land and property of substantial value; certain shareholdings; and a residual category of any interest or benefit received which might reasonably be thought by others to influence the member's actions in Parliament.[117]

(iv) An MP who has entered into an employment agreement to provide services as a member must register a full copy of the agreement with the Commissioner and state the fees payable in specified bands.[118]

(v) The 1947 resolution[119] was restated by the House, with the addition of the following:

in particular, no Members . . . shall, in consideration of any remuneration, fee, payment, or reward or benefit in kind, direct or indirect . . .
(*a*)   advocate or initiate any cause or matter on behalf of any outside body or individual, or
(*b*)   urge any other Member of either House . . . including Ministers, to do so, by means of any speech, Question, Motion, introduction of a Bill or amendment to a Motion or Bill.[120]

(vi) A code of conduct for members was adopted, together with a guide to the rules.[121]

These measures have governed the conduct of MPs since 1995. Between 1997 and 2001, the Committee on Standards and Privileges issued some 70 reports, many of which concerned alleged failure by MPs to register relevant interests. Many complaints bordered on the trivial or were rejected, but the most serious led to a recommendation by the Committee that the MP in question be suspended by the House for a stated period.[122] The most substantial inquiry made by the first Commissioner, Sir Gordon Downey, was into allegations that, while an MP, Neil Hamilton had received undisclosed cash

---

[114] HC 637 and 816 (1994–95); HC Deb, 18 May 1995, col 481.

[115] See HC SO 150.

[116] See HC SO 149.

[117] The register is regularly updated and may be read on the Commons website. For what must be registered, see *The Code of Conduct together with the Rules Relating to the Conduct of Members*, HC 688 (1995–96), s 1, paras 1–34. A revised form of the Code was issued on 14 May 2002.

[118] Ibid, paras 35–36.

[119] See text at n 103 above.

[120] HC Deb, 6 November 1995, cols 604, 661.

[121] HC 688 (1995–96); and HC Deb, 24 July 1996, col 392. And see n [117].

[122] See HC 260 (1999–2000) (untruthful denial of connections with offshore companies, intended to deceive Committee); and HC 297 (2001–02) (inadequate replies to questions from Commissioner and Committee).

payments from Mr Al Fayed for lobbying services and undisclosed hospitality, including a stay at the Ritz Hotel in Paris. Mr Hamilton's appeal to the Committee against the Commissioner's findings did not succeed.[123] When necessary, the Committee considers questions as to the rules for registration of interests and may propose amendments to them.[124] Since the Commissioner plays a key role in enforcing the disclosure rules, it was unfortunate for the reputation of the House that in 2001 the appointment of the second Commissioner (Ms Elizabeth Filkin) was not renewed. MPs must also disclose certain donations received to the Electoral Commission, and donations may not be received from certain impermissible sources.[125]

Procedure for enforcing rules on members' interests

We have already considered the procedure followed concerning an alleged contempt or breach of privilege. Complaints about the Code of Conduct and the Register of Interests are made to the Parliamentary Commissioner for Standards, who has a discretion to investigate and report on them to the Committee.[126] The form of an investigation is decided by the Commissioner. The system was put to an arduous test with the inquiry into the Hamilton allegations. When Mr Hamilton appealed, the Committee decided that he had shown no grounds to justify any departure from the Commissioner's findings. As with complaints of breach of privilege, it would be possible to create an independent and impartial tribunal for deciding disputed questions regarding disclosure of MPs' interests, but this would mean removing responsibility from the House itself.[127]

MPs and the criminal law of corruption[128]

We have seen that MPs have no immunities from criminal law, except for the protection afforded by Art 9 of the Bill of Rights in respect of proceedings in Parliament. But the position in law of an MP who improperly provides services in return for payment is uncertain. In 1976, a royal commission chaired by Lord Salmon considered that neither statute law nor the common law on corruption applied where an MP was involved and recommended that the criminal law be strengthened.[129] Another view is that the existing law does apply to MPs, except that it is not permissible to rely on what has been said in Parliament to prove commission of an offence.[130] However, there should be no uncertainty in this area of the law, neither should the Bill of Rights be a shield against conviction for corrupt conduct. Legislation to remove the uncertainty and to

---

[123] See HC 30, 261 (1997–98); and HC Deb, 17 November 1997, cols 81–121. Mr Hamilton later sued Mr Al Fayed for libel without success (see n 26 above). Other reports include HC 240 (1997–98) (complaints against 25 MPs and former MPs); HC 611 (1998–99) (late registration of loan from fellow MP to buy house); HC 342 (1999–2000) (inadequate registration of lecture fees etc.).

[124] See HC 928 (1998–99) (membership of other elected bodies) and HC 267 (2000–01) (proposed amendments to Code of Conduct).

[125] Political Parties, Elections and Referendums Act 2000, Sch 7.

[126] HC SO 150(2)(e). For the investigation process, see HC 403 (1999–2000). The Commissioner's findings are not subject to judicial review: *R v Parliamentary Commissioner for Standards, ex p Al Fayed* [1998] 1 All ER 93.

[127] Nicholls report, pp 77–8. See also HC 633 and 1191 (1997–98).

[128] See P M Leopold, in Oliver and Drewry (eds), *The Law and Parliament*, ch 5; D Oliver (1997) 45 Political Studies 539.

[129] Cmnd 6524, 1976.

[130] G J Zellick [1979] PL 31. The common law of corruption applies to MPs in Canada (*R v Bunting* (1885) 7 OR 524) and Australia (*R v Boston* (1923) 33 CLR 386). See also *A-G of Ceylon v de Livera* [1963] AC 103, *US v Johnson* 383 US 169 (1966) and (in English law) *R v Greenway* (1992), reported at [1998] PL 356.

make a limited amendment to the Bill of Rights is necessary. The House of Commons has hitherto relied on self-regulation for maintaining adequate standards of conduct. In respect of allegations of corruption, self-regulation should now give way to the ordinary process of criminal law.[131] Practical considerations support this view, since the House is unable to conduct a criminal investigation and could not in a serious case impose appropriate penalties.

C. House of Lords

Questions of privilege rarely arise in relation to the House of Lords.

Privileges of the House and of peers

1 *Freedom from civil arrest for peers.*   In *Stourton* v *Stourton*[132] a peer was held to be privileged from a writ of attachment for civil contempt following his failure to send his wife her property under a court order. The judge found that arrest was being sought to compel performance of a civil obligation. This privilege may be claimed by an individual peer at any time, but the House claims privilege only 'within the usual times of privilege of Parliament'.[133] Freedom from arrest should be abolished for members of the House of Lords as well as for MPs.[134]

2 *Freedom of speech.*   Article 9 of the Bill of Rights applies to the Lords as it does to the Commons; a speech made in the House is not privileged if published separately from the rest of the debate.[135]

3 *The right to commit for contempt.*   The Lords can commit a person for a definite term and the imprisonment is not terminated by prorogation of Parliament. The Lords also have power to impose fines and to order security to be given for good conduct.

4 *The right to exclude disqualified persons from the proceedings of the House.*   The House itself decides, through the Committee for Privileges, the right of newly created peers to sit and vote. Claims to old peerages are referred by the Crown to the House and are also decided by the Committee for Privileges.[136] Following the removal of all but 92 hereditary peers from the House of Lords in 1999, this is an aspect of privilege that is likely to be of little practical importance in future.

Financial interests of peers

The House of Lords has not been under the same pressure as the Commons concerning the disclosure of interests. Formerly the view was held that peers ought not to be required to account publicly for their interests in the same manner as elected MPs. Yet many peers take an influential part in the legislative process and have access to government and they cannot expect to observe lower standards of public conduct than

---

[131] Nicholls report, paras 135–42. Also Nolan report (Cm 2850–I, 1995), paras 103–4.
[132] [1963] P 302.
[133] HL SO 78. Regarding the Mental Health Act 1983, see HL 254 (1983–84). Also P M Leopold [1985] PL 9 (on the 1983 Act) and [1989] PL 398 (on peers' freedom from arrest); and Nicholls report, para 336.
[134] Nicholls report, paras 325–8.
[135] *R v Lord Abingdon* (1795) 1 Esp 226.
[136] See e.g. *The Ampthill Peerage* [1977] AC 547.

MPs. In 1995, the House resolved that its members should act always on their personal honour and should never accept a financial benefit in return for exercising parliamentary influence; peers who have a direct interest in lobbying ought not to speak, vote or otherwise use their office on behalf of clients. The House created a register of peers' consultancies and similar financial interests in lobbying for clients. The register was of much narrower scope than the Commons register, but peers might register other matters 'which they consider may affect public perception of the way in which they discharge their parliamentary duties'.[137]

The scheme adopted in 1995 was limited in scope, especially in relation to the discretionary registration of other forms of interest. In 2000, the (Neill) committee on standards in public life recommended that the House should adopt a Code of Conduct, extending the register of interests, requiring the declaration of a wider range of interests and continuing to restrict members in parliamentary lobbying. The Code was adopted in July 2001, to come into effect on 31 March 2002.[138] Complaints of failure to register an interest would be heard by a sub-committee on the registration of interests, with a right of appeal to the House's Committee for Privileges, a committee that includes at least three law lords.

---

[137] See HL 90 and 98 (1994–95); HL Deb, 1 November 1995, col 1428, and 7 November 1995, col 1631.
[138] Cm 4903, 2000; HL 68 (2000–01); HL Deb, 2 July 2001, col 630 and 24 July 2001, col 1849.

Chapter 12

THE CROWN AND THE ROYAL PREROGATIVE

We have already seen that the functions of the executive are more diverse than those of the legislature and judiciary, having acquired a residual character after legislature and judiciary had become separated from the main work of governing.[1] The functions of the executive have been said to include 'the execution of law and policy, the maintenance of public order, the management of Crown property . . . the direction of foreign policy, the conduct of military operations, and the provision, regulation, financing, or supervision of such services as education, public health, transport and national insurance'.[2] Today such a catalogue is far from complete. To perform all the tasks of government the executive must comprise a wide array of officials and agencies. These include the Prime Minister and other ministers, government departments, the civil service, the armed forces and also the police, who are outside the direct hierarchy of central government but exercise a vital executive function. Outside central government, but closely linked to it, are local authorities and many public boards and regulatory agencies, which may be considered to perform executive functions, albeit confined to one locality or one economic activity.

Unlike the work of Parliament and the courts, much of the work of the executive is carried on behind closed doors. Although there is now much more openness and transparency than in the past, government still seeks to maintain secrecy on matters which it believes affect its own vital interests.[3] This secrecy often masks a divergence between the legal form and the political substance. Thus in exercising some of the Crown's powers, the Sovereign may exercise a personal discretion; others are exercised by the Sovereign on the advice of ministers; and many powers are exercised directly by ministers and civil servants. Whether a statutory power is conferred on the Queen in Council or directly on a named minister, the government is responsible to Parliament for the decisions taken. Since it is unusual for statutory powers to be vested in the Cabinet or the Prime Minister,[4] decisions taken in Cabinet or by the Prime Minister have to be translated into the appropriate legal form before they can take full effect. In view of this interplay of legal form and conventional practice, study of the executive in the United Kingdom must begin with the legal position of the Sovereign.

It is still formally the case that executive power in the United Kingdom is vested in the Crown, however little this may reflect the reality of modern government. The Sovereign may reign, but it is the Prime Minister and other ministers who rule. Yet within the executive in Britain, it is not possible to dismiss the position of the Sovereign as an anachronism since the Sovereign as head of state performs some essential functions. The fact that central government is carried on in the name of the Crown has left its mark on the law. Our law has never developed a notion of 'the state': the judges have been opposed to the idea of allowing interests of the state to override common law

---

[1] Ch 5.
[2] HLE, vol 8(2), para 9.
[3] See ch 25 below.
[4] But see Regulation of Investigatory Powers Act 2000, ss 57–63.

rights.[5] Although it is common to speak of state schools, state ownership and so on, legislation rarely refers to the state as such.[6] Instead, the Crown has developed as 'a convenient symbol for the State'.[7] It is usual to refer to 'the Sovereign' in matters concerning the personal conduct or decisions of the monarch and to 'the Crown' as the collective entity which in law may stand for central government.

A. The Sovereign[8]

Title to the Crown

In 1689, the Convention Parliament (that had been summoned by Prince William of Orange at the request of an improvised assembly of notables) filled the constitutional vacuum which arose on the departure of James II by declaring the throne vacant and inviting William of Orange and his wife Mary jointly to accept the throne.[9] These events finally confirmed the power of Parliament to regulate the succession to the Crown as it should think fit.[10] Today title to the Crown is derived from the Act of Settlement 1700, subsequently extended to Scotland in 1707 and to Ireland in 1800 by the Acts of Union. By the Act of Settlement, the Crown shall 'be remain and continue to the said most excellent Princess Sophia' (the Electress of Hanover, granddaughter of James I) 'and the heirs of her body being Protestant'.[11] The limitation to the heirs of the body, which has been described as a parliamentary entail, means that the Crown descends in principle as did real property under the law of inheritance before 1926.[12] That law inter alia gave preference to males over females and recognised the right of primogeniture. The major exception to the common law rules of inheritance is that for practical reasons the right of two or more sisters to succeed to real property as co-parceners does not apply: as between sisters, the Crown passes to the firstborn.[13] The Act of Settlement disqualifies from the succession Roman Catholics and those who marry Roman Catholics; the Sovereign must swear to maintain the Churches of England and Scotland and must join in communion with the former Church. This is a restriction which has been questioned in recent years as being not easily justifiable in an increasingly multi-cultural and secular society. Since 1714, when the Hanoverian succession took effect under the Act of Settlement, the line of hereditary succession has been altered only once: it was provided by His Majesty's Declaration of Abdication Act 1936 that the declaration of abdication by Edward VIII should have effect; that the member of the royal family then next in succession to the throne should succeed (thus Edward VIII's brother became King George VI); and that Edward VIII, his issue, if any, and the descendants of that issue should not thereafter have any right to the succession.

---

[5] *Entick v Carrington* (1765)19 St Tr 1030. But cf *Council of Civil Service Unions v Minister of State for Civil Service* [1985] AC 374. See p 256 below.

[6] Cf *Chandler v DPP* [1964] AC 763.

[7] G Sawer's phrase, quoted in Hogg, *Liability of the Crown* (1st edn), p 10; and see Marshall, *Constitutional Theory*, ch 2.

[8] For a fuller account of the law relating to the monarchy (dealing with styles and titles, royal marriages, accession and coronation, minority and incapacity and illness and incapacity), see the 12th edition of this work, pp 255–8.

[9] Maitland, *Constitutional History*, pp 283–5; Taswell-Langmead, *English Constitutional History*, pp 443–8.

[10] Taswell-Langmead, p 504.

[11] See *A-G v Prince Ernest Augustus of Hanover* [1957] AC 436, for construction of Princess Sophia Naturalization Act 1705 (repealed by British Nationality Act 1948) which entitled to British nationality all non-Catholic lineal descendants of Princess Sophia.

[12] On which, see Megarry and Wade, *The Law of Real Property*, ch 11 and HLE, vol 8(2), paras 34–40.

[13] Blackstone, *Commentaries*, I, p 193; Chitty, *Prerogatives of the Crown*, p 10.

The eldest son of a reigning monarch is the heir apparent to the throne; he is Duke of Cornwall by inheritance and is invariably created Prince of Wales.[14]

Financing the monarchy[15]

In the 17th century, when the Sovereign personally carried out the functions of government, the revenue from the taxes which Parliament authorised was paid over to the Sovereign and merged with the hereditary revenues already available to him. Today a separation is made between the expenses of government and the expenses of maintaining the monarchy. Since the time of George III, it has been customary at the beginning of each reign for the Sovereign to surrender to Parliament for his or her life the ancient hereditary revenues of the Crown, including the income from Crown lands.[16] Provision is then made by Parliament for meeting the salaries and other expenses of the royal household. This provision, known as the Civil List, was granted to the Queen for her reign and six months after, by the Civil List Act 1952. In 1952, the total annual amount paid was £475,000 but following an inquiry into the financial position of the monarchy by a select committee of the House of Commons,[17] the amount was raised to £980,000 by the Civil List Act 1972. The 1972 Act also provided that the annual sum might be increased by means of a Treasury Order subject to annulment by the House of Commons.

The idea behind the Civil List used to be that Parliament should not be asked to vote money for the expenses of the royal household each year and the 1972 Act provided for a periodic report from the Royal Trustees on the state of the royal finances. But because of continuing inflation, the Civil List Act 1975 empowered the Treasury to make payments to the Royal Trustees for supplementing sums payable under the Queen's Civil List and abolished the procedure of periodic reports. The select committee of the Commons in 1971 had rejected a proposal that the royal household should be placed on the footing of a government department to receive an annual payment voted by normal budgetary procedures, but the 1975 Act was a step in that direction. In 1990, however, the Prime Minister announced that as from 1991, the arrangements would return to those provided for in the 1972 Act and that a fixed annual payment of £7.9 million from the Consolidated Fund would be made.[18] The Queen's official expenses thus reverted to a standing service on the Consolidated Fund and the financial arrangements were such that it was hoped that the need for annual supplements voted by Parliament under the Civil List Act 1975 would cease. But the 1975 Act was left in place 'as a means of financing of last resort'.[19]

The Civil List, which is used 'to meet official expenditure necessarily incurred through [the Sovereign's] duties as head of state',[20] 'accounts for only a small percentage of government expenditure on the monarchy'.[21] Thus certain expenses in connection with the maintenance of the royal palaces and royal travel are now met by separate grants in aid voted annually by Parliament. The total head of state expenditure from public funds for 2000–2001 was £34,984,000, which included the Queen's Civil List

[14] On the constitutional role of the Prince of Wales, see R Brazier [1995] PL 401.

[15] For a good account, see Bogdanor, *The Monarchy and the Constitution*, ch 7.

[16] Under the Crown Estate Act 1961, the Crown Estate Commissioners are responsible for administering the Crown Estate: for the history, see HC 29 (1971–72), app 18. The Commissioners have wide powers under the Act. See *Walford* v *Crown Estate Commissioners* 1988 SLT 377.

[17] HC 29 (1971–72).

[18] Civil List (Increase of Financial Provision) Order 1990, SI 1990/2018. See also HC Deb, 4 July 2000, col 161.

[19] HC Deb, 24 July 1990, cols 299–306. See Hall, *Royal Fortune: Tax, Money and the Monarchy*.

[20] Bogdanor, p 186.

[21] Ibid, p 187.

payment. The Prince of Wales enjoys separate provision out of the Duchy of Cornwall to meet official and personal expenses, although he receives no parliamentary annuity. The Act of 1952, as amended in 1972, also makes provision for the Duke of Edinburgh, the Queen's younger children and other members of the royal family. Since 1975, however, the Queen has reimbursed the Treasury for the annuities paid to three members of her extended family and since 1993 she has reimbursed all but those paid to herself, the Duke of Edinburgh and the late Queen Mother.[22]

The Sovereign also holds property in a personal capacity and derives income from this. In 1971 the Commons Select Committee was assured that suggestions that the Queen owned private funds in the region of £50 million were 'wildly exaggerated' but no estimate of their actual value was given to the committee. In 1996 the Press Complaints Commission upheld a complaint from the Press Secretary to the Queen about an article in *Business Age* magazine which claimed that the Queen was the wealthiest person in Britain with an estimated wealth of £2.2 billion. In the view of the Commission 'the article presented speculation as established fact', 'failed adequately to check its facts' and 'made a number of errors which were not properly addressed'.[23] One matter of concern was the failure to distinguish private wealth from that held in trust by the Queen as Sovereign and Head of State and not as an individual.[24] Unlike other members of the Royal family, the Queen benefits from the principle that the Crown is not liable to pay taxes unless Parliament says so either expressly or by necessary implication.[25] In 1992, however, it was announced that the Queen had undertaken to pay tax on her private income with effect from 1993,[26] but this does not extend to inheritance tax. The Prince of Wales has also agreed to pay tax on income derived from the Duchy of Cornwall.[27]

Duties of the Sovereign

No attempt can be made to list the full duties which fall to the Sovereign to perform in person.[28] Many formal acts of government require her participation. Many state documents require her signature, and she receives copies of all major government papers, including reports from ambassadors abroad and their instructions from the Foreign Office, as well as minutes of Cabinet meetings and other Cabinet papers. 'There is therefore a continuing burden of unseen work involving some hours reading of papers each day in addition to Her Majesty's more public duties.'[29] She gives frequent audiences to the Prime Minister and visiting ministers from the Commonwealth, receives foreign diplomatic representatives, holds investitures and personally confers honours and decorations. She receives visits to this country by the heads of foreign states and makes state visits overseas. She attends numerous state occasions, for example to deliver the Queen's Speech at the opening of each session of Parliament. Her formal consent is needed for appointments made by the Crown on the advice of the Prime Minister, the Lord Chancellor and other ministers.

A catalogue of official duties does not reveal what influence, if any, the Sovereign has on the political direction of the country's affairs. In general, the Sovereign is bound

---

[22] HC 29 (1971–72), para 31.
[23] Press Complaints Commission, Report No 34 (1996), pp 5–8.
[24] Similar points are made also on the royal website: www.royal.gov.uk/today/personal.
[25] HC 29 (1971–72), app 12; and ch 12 D.
[26] HC Deb, 26 November 1992, col 982.
[27] HC 464 (1992–93).
[28] See HC 29 (1971–72), paras 16–17 and evidence by the Queen's Private Secretary, pp 30–41 and app 13. See also generally Pimlott, *The Queen: A Biography of Elizabeth II*.
[29] HC 29 (1971–72), para 17.

to act on the advice of the Prime Minister or other appropriate minister, for example, the Home Secretary in respect of the prerogative of mercy. The Sovereign cannot reject the final advice that ministers offer to her without the probable consequence of bringing about their resignation and their replacement by other ministers, thereby bringing the future of the monarchy into controversy. But to what extent may the Queen offer them guidance from her own fund of experience in public affairs? Bagehot described the Sovereign's rights as being the right to be consulted, the right to encourage and the right to warn.[30] While this may entitle the monarch to express personal views on political events to the Prime Minister, these views may have little influence over the whole range of the government's work.[31] This was so even in relation to the later years of Queen Victoria, whose attitude to Gladstone was, by the standards of her successors, not that of a constitutional monarch.

Much light was thrown upon the role of the Sovereign in the 20th century by Sir Harold Nicolson's biography of George V and by Sir John Wheeler-Bennett's biography of George VI. Thus it appears that the Sovereign, even before the days when Cabinet conclusions were regularly recorded by the Cabinet secretariat, could insist on the advice of the Cabinet being given in written form, if he felt that it was dangerous or opposed to the wishes of the people. This was so that the King could record in writing the misgivings and reluctance with which he followed the advice of his Cabinet.[32] The clear impression is given in these two biographies that the monarch is far from being a mere mouthpiece of his constitutional advisers. But it would be wrong to suppose that the right to be consulted, to encourage and to warn applies to all areas of policy-making, in many of which the Sovereign will have had no relevant experience. Such rights can be understood better in relation to those powers of the Sovereign where she may be required to exercise a personal discretion; they will be discussed in the next section.

The Private Secretary to the Sovereign plays a significant role in conducting communications between the Sovereign and her ministers and, in exceptional circumstances where this is constitutionally proper, between the Sovereign and other political leaders. Occasionally, the Sovereign's Private Secretary may be drawn into public controversies. In 1950 Sir Alan Lascelles, Private Secretary to George VI, wrote to *The Times* under a pseudonym, to outline the circumstances in which he believed the monarch could properly refuse a dissolution when requested by the Prime Minister.[33] In 1986, Sir William Heseltine, the Queen's Private Secretary, wrote to *The Times* following alleged disagreements between the Prime Minister (Mrs Thatcher) and the Queen on policy matters. Sir William made three points which he considered axiomatic:

1   The Sovereign has the right – indeed the duty – to counsel, encourage and warn her government. She is thus entitled to have opinions on government policy and to express them to her chief minister.
2   Whatever personal opinions the Sovereign may hold or may have expressed to her government, she is bound to accept and act on the advice of her ministers.
3   The Sovereign is obliged to treat her communications with the Prime Minister as entirely confidential between the two of them.[34]

Sir William asserted that it was preposterous to suggest that the Queen would suddenly depart from these principles.

---

[30] *The English Constitution*, p 111. See also Brazier, *Constitutional Practice*, p 185.
[31] Although it has been said as a result that 'the Sovereign may have a marginal but beneficial influence on governmental decisions' (Brazier, ibid, p 185).
[32] Nicolson, *George V*, p 115.
[33] See p 241 below.
[34] *The Times*, 29 July 1986. See G Marshall [1986] PL 505.

Reform of the monarchy

Unlike many of the other parts of the constitution, the monarchy has survived the reforming and modernising zeal of the 1990s. Indeed, in its election manifesto of 1997, which was the basis of much of the contemporary constitutional reform, the Labour Party announced: 'We have no plans to replace the monarchy.'[35] Although this 'fell considerably short of a ringing endorsement of the institution of monarchy',[36] it remains the case that there has been little serious debate about the desirability of retaining a hereditary monarch as Head of State in a modern democracy. In the 1990s, the Monarchy weathered a lot of unwanted publicity about the private lives and business activities of some of its senior figures, and was subject to public criticism following the premature death of the Princess of Wales in 1997.[37] But greater public exposure and a less deferential media have at best ignited concerns for a more responsive monarchy, not its replacement. The difficulties of reform of the latter kind were highlighted by the referendum in Australia in 1999 where the people voted to retain the monarchy when given the option of a republic instead. (The Queen is also the Head of State in Australia and indeed in a number of other prominent Commonwealth countries.) One of the problems facing the republican campaigners in Australia was the division among the anti-monarchists about how the Head of State in a republic should be chosen. Those who favoured a directly elected President (on the Irish model) were unhappy with the choice in the referendum between retaining the monarchy or moving to a President elected by Parliament.[38]

B. Personal prerogatives of the Sovereign

The appointment of a Prime Minister[39]

In appointing a Prime Minister the Sovereign must appoint that person who is in the best position to receive the support of the majority in the House of Commons. This does not involve the Sovereign in making a personal assessment of leading politicians since no major party could fight a general election without a recognised leader. Where an election produces an absolute majority in the Commons for one party, the leader of that party will be invited to become Prime Minister or, if already Prime Minister, he or she will continue in office. In these circumstances, 'the Sovereign has no choice whom he or she should appoint as Prime Minister, and it is obvious who should be called to the Palace.'[40]

By modern practice, a defeated Prime Minister resigns from office as soon as a decisive result of the election is known. Where after an election no one party has an absolute majority in the House (as in 1923, 1929 and February 1974), the Prime Minister in office may decide to wait until Parliament resumes to see whether he or she can obtain a majority in the new House with support from another party (as Baldwin did after the 1923 election, only to find that he could not) or he may resign without waiting for Parliament to meet (as Baldwin did in 1929 and Heath in 1974). When he or she has resigned, the Queen will send for the leader of the party with the largest number

---

[35] Labour Party, *New Labour: Because Britain Deserves Better* (1997), p 33.
[36] Blackburn and Plant (eds), *Constitutional Reform*, p 139.
[37] On which see Barnett, *This Time: Our Constitutional Revolution*.
[38] See C Munro [2000] PL 3. Also J Uhr [2000] 11 Public Law Review 7. See further, Winterton, *Monarchy to Republic*.
[39] See Jennings, *Cabinet Government*, ch 2; Brazier, chs 2, 3; and Bogdanor, ch 6.
[40] Bogdanor, p 84.

of seats (as in 1929 and 1974) or with the next largest number of seats (as in January 1924 after Baldwin had been defeated by combined Labour and Liberal votes).[41] Thus, where the election produces a clear majority for one party, the Sovereign has no discretion to exercise. Where an election does not produce a conclusive result, the Sovereign has no discretion except where the procedure described still fails to establish a government in office; in this case, the Sovereign would have to initiate discussions with and between the parties to discover, for example, whether a government could be formed by a politician who was not a party leader or whether a coalition government could be formed.[42]

Where a Prime Minister resigns because of ill-health or old age or dies while in office, a new leader of the governing party must be found. Formerly, in the case of the Liberal and Conservative parties, this was a situation in which the Sovereign was required to exercise a discretion, namely to invite a person to be Prime Minister who would command general support within the governing party. The parties now choose their own leader in accordance with their own rules. It was initially the case that the leader of the Conservative party was chosen by the party's MPs. It was under these rules that Mr Major replaced Mrs Thatcher as leader of the party in 1990,[43] following which Mrs Thatcher resigned as Prime Minister and 'arrangements' were made for Mr Major 'to see the Queen the next morning'.[44] The current leadership rules of the Conservative Party provide for the leader to be elected by the members of the party in a postal ballot.[45] The rules provide, however, that the candidates for election are to be chosen by the 1922 Committee, which is a committee of Conservative MPs. It is also provided that 'the procedure by which the 1922 Committee selects candidates for submission for election shall be determined by the Executive Committee of the 1922 Committee'. It was under these procedures that Mr Ian Duncan Smith was elected party leader in 2001. Both he and Mr Kenneth Clarke were presented for election by Conservative MPs after a number of votes in which other potential candidates were eliminated.

In the case of the Labour party, the right to vote in the election of leader was formerly confined to Labour MPs, but in 1981 the party changed its constitution and standing orders to provide for the leader and deputy leader to be elected at a party conference.[46] The electoral college is in three sections, Labour MPs and constituency parties each having one-third of the votes and affiliated organisations also having one-third. Successive ballots are held until one candidate has more than half the votes so apportioned. When Labour is in opposition, an election shall be held at each annual conference. When Labour is in government and the party leader is Prime Minister, an election takes place only if required by a majority of the conference on a card vote. While both parties have used these procedures to elect leaders while in opposition (the Conservatives in 1965 and 1975; Labour in 1983, 1992 and 1994), new ground was broken in 1976, again in 1990, and yet again in 1995. In 1976, when Harold Wilson announced his intention of resigning as Prime Minister, he remained in office until (under the party's former rules) Labour MPs elected their new leader, Mr Callaghan. Mr Wilson then resigned and Mr Callaghan became Prime Minister. In 1990, the Conservative party removed Mrs Thatcher as party leader against her wishes while she was also Prime Minister. Although Mrs Thatcher's leadership had previously been challenged by using

---

[41] The precedents thus show a preference for 'minority government' rather than 'majority coalition' (Bogdanor, p 253).
[42] See Brazier, ch 3; Butler, *Governing without a Majority: Dilemmas for Hung Parliaments in Britain*, ch 5; and Bogdanor, *Multi-party Politics and the Constitution*, chs 5, 6.
[43] See R K Alderman [1992] PL 30.
[44] Major, *The Autobiography*, p 199.
[45] For background, see K Alderman (1999) 52 Parliamentary Affairs 260.
[46] The rules were revised again in 1993: see R K Alderman [1994] PL 24.

the leadership procedures, her replacement by Mr Major in 1990 represents the first occasion in modern times that a serving peacetime Prime Minister has been forcibly removed from office. And in 1995 Mr Major resigned as leader of the Conservative party, thereby forcing an election for party leader, in which he was a candidate. He did not, resign as Prime Minister, though presumably he would have done so had he not succeeded in being re-elected as party leader.

Thus the Labour and Conservative parties have their own procedures for electing a new leader, as do the Liberal Democrats.[47] Does this mean that the Sovereign has no residual discretion to exercise in appointing a Prime Minister? First, since the election of a new leader may take some weeks, the appointment of an acting Prime Minister might well be needed if, unlike the position in 1976, the outgoing Prime Minister had died or was too ill to continue in office. Presumably a senior member of the Cabinet would be so appointed.[48] Moreover, there could well be circumstances in which reliance on normal party procedures would not produce an immediate solution: for example, where a party holding office broke up after serious internal dissensions; or where no party had a majority in the House and there was a deadlock between the parties as to who should form a government; or where a coalition agreement had broken down.[49] In such situations, the Sovereign could not avoid taking initiatives to enable a new government to be formed, for example by initiating inter-party discussions. In 1931, when Ramsay MacDonald and the Labour Cabinet resigned because of serious disagreement within the Cabinet over the steps that should be taken to deal with the financial crisis, George V, after consulting with Conservative and Liberal leaders, invited MacDonald to form a 'National Government' with Liberal and Conservative support. The extreme bitterness which MacDonald's defection caused in the Labour party led to criticism of George V's conduct as unconstitutional, but such criticism seems unjustified.[50] While therefore under stable political conditions the Sovereign will not need to exercise a personal discretion in selecting a Prime Minister, circumstances could arise in which it might become necessary for the Sovereign to do so.

Dissolution of Parliament[51]

In the absence of a regular term for the life of Parliament fixed by statute, the Sovereign may by the prerogative dissolve Parliament and cause a general election to be held. The Sovereign normally accepts the advice of the Prime Minister and grants a dissolution when this is requested. Since 1918, it has become established practice that a Cabinet decision is not necessary before the Prime Minister may seek a dissolution, although members of the Cabinet may be consulted before the Prime Minister makes a decision.[52] The refusal of a dissolution when the Prime Minister had requested it would probably be treated by him as tantamount to a dismissal. Are there circumstances in which the Sovereign would be justified in refusing a dissolution or is it automatic that the Sovereign should grant a dissolution when requested?

---

[47] See K Alderman and N Carter (2000) 53 Parliamentary Affairs 311.

[48] Cf Brazier, p 17. Under the Labour party rules, when the party is in government and the leader becomes 'permanently unavailable', 'the Cabinet shall in consultation with the National Executive Committee appoint one of its members to serve as party leader until a ballot . . . can be carried out'.

[49] See R Brazier [1986] PL 387.

[50] A full account is in Bassett, *1931: Political Crisis*. See also Mackintosh, *British Cabinet*, pp 419–20 and Middlemas and Barnes, *Baldwin*, ch 23.

[51] Forsey, *The Royal Power of Dissolution in the British Commonwealth*; Markesinis, *The Theory and Practice of Dissolution of Parliament*; Marshall, *Constitutional Conventions*, ch 3.

[52] Jennings, pp 417–19; Mackintosh, pp 453–5; Markesinis, ch 5 A.

It is doubtful whether there can be grounds for the refusal of a dissolution to a Prime Minister who commands a clear majority in the Commons.[53] Political practice accepts that a Prime Minister may choose the time for a general election within the five-year life of Parliament prescribed by the Parliament Act 1911. If a Sovereign did refuse dissolution to a Prime Minister who commanded a majority in the House and the Prime Minister then resigned from office with the other ministers, any other politician invited to be Prime Minister (for example, the Leader of the Opposition) would presumably have no prospect of a majority at Westminster until an election had been held. The Sovereign would therefore be faced with an early request for a dissolution from the new Prime Minister and with inevitable criticism of political bias if the request were granted. Where a minority government holds office, the position is more complicated but here again it is essential for the Prime Minister to choose the time for an election. Much would depend on the circumstances in which the minority government had come about and on how recently a general election had been held. Thus a Prime Minister who had been granted one dissolution and failed to get a majority at the ensuing election could not request a second dissolution immediately. There would be a duty to resign and to give the leader of another party the opportunity of forming a government. Where a Prime Minister had been in office for a considerable period (for example, some months) since the previous election and was then defeated on an issue of confidence in the House, he would then have a choice between resigning or, as MacDonald did in 1924, seeking a dissolution.

In 1950, during discussion of the problems caused by the Labour government's small majority after the election of that year, it was submitted by the Private Secretary to George VI that the Sovereign could properly refuse a dissolution if he were satisfied that (a) the existing Parliament was still 'vital, viable, and capable of doing its job', (b) a general election would be detrimental to the national economy and (c) he could rely on finding another Prime Minister who could carry on his government for a reasonable period with a working majority.[54] It will be seldom that all these conditions can be satisfied and it might even be argued that these are eminently matters for the Prime Minister in office to decide. It might be particularly difficult for the Sovereign to be reasonably certain that another Prime Minister could command a working majority in the House. Yet the Sovereign would be strongly criticised if, having refused a dissolution to one Prime Minister, he or she were faced with an early request from the new Prime Minister for dissolution.

In the last 100 years there are no instances of the Sovereign having refused a dissolution in the United Kingdom, but there are two leading illustrations of the problem from the former Dominions where the prerogative was exercisable by the Governor-General. In 1939, the Governor-General of South Africa refused a dissolution to the Prime Minister, General Hertzog, whose proposal that South Africa should be neutral in the Second World War had been defeated in Parliament and he invited General Smuts to form a government which remained in power thereafter. But in 1926, the Governor-General of Canada, Lord Byng, refused a dissolution to the Liberal leader, Mackenzie King, and instead invited Meighen, the Conservative leader, to form a government believing that Meighen would be supported by a third party which held the balance of power. When that support failed within a matter of days, Meighen sought a dissolution of Parliament which was granted by Lord Byng: the ensuing

---

[53] Markesinis, pp 84–6; Forsey, p 269. If an opportunist Prime Minister decided to take advantage of the death of the leader of the Opposition to seek an immediate dissolution, knowing that the rules of the opposition party required the election of a new leader to take a month, could the Sovereign insist on delaying the election so that the parties could campaign on more equal terms?

[54] For his pseudonymous letter to *The Times*, see Markesinis, pp 87–8 and app 4.

election was won by the Liberals and the Governor-General was much criticised for his decisions.[55]

The controversy between the 'automatic' and 'discretionary' views of the prerogative of dissolution arose again in 1969. Although Labour had a clear majority in the Commons, there were press reports of dissension within the party. The question was raised whether a Prime Minister could use the weapon of dissolution to defend his own position against attempts within the party to dislodge him.[56] In 1974, after the election in February of that year, when no party had an absolute majority, it was asked whether Mr Wilson as Prime Minister was entitled to a dissolution if his government were defeated in the Commons by a combined opposition vote. Certain Labour MPs, who feared that a Liberal–Conservative coalition might be formed to govern the country, urged that the Sovereign was both constitutionally and morally bound to grant dissolution whenever the Prime Minister requested it. In reply, the Lord President of the Council, Mr Short, told them: 'Constitutional lawyers of the highest authority are of the clear opinion that the Sovereign is not in all circumstances bound to grant a Prime Minister's request for dissolution'; it was impossible to define in advance the circumstances in which the Sovereign's discretion to refuse a request for a dissolution might be exercised.[57] The government refused to allow the matter to be debated in the Commons. In the event, when Mr Wilson sought a dissolution in September 1974, this was granted without question by the Sovereign.

That the Sovereign should not refuse a Prime Minister's request for dissolution except for very strong reason is obvious. In practice, the political significance of the Prime Minister's power to decide when Parliament should be dissolved is much greater than the possibility of the Sovereign's refusal of a dissolution. But the view that the Sovereign's reserve power may serve to restrain a Prime Minister who otherwise might be tempted to abuse his or her position is an argument for maintaining the reserve power as a potential weapon, not for abolishing it.

The dismissal of ministers

The refusal of a Prime Minister's request for a dissolution is one aspect of a larger question, namely whether the Sovereign may ever reject the advice of the Prime Minister on a major issue, for example, by refusing to make an appointment to ministerial office which the Prime Minister had recommended, by refusing to give the royal assent to a Bill which has passed through both Houses, or by insisting that a general election is held before the royal assent is given. In 1910 George V insisted that a general election be held on the Liberal proposal to remove the veto of the House of Lords, before he would create enough new Liberal peers to pass the Parliament Bill through the Lords against Conservative opposition; this decision was accepted by the Prime Minister, Asquith. But in other situations a refusal by the Sovereign to accept advice could be seen as a direct challenge to the authority of the Prime Minister and might mean his immediate resignation. The underlying question is whether the Sovereign is merely part of the formal apparatus of government and thus incapable of taking an independent position on a point of constitutional principle, or whether the monarchy provides some kind of safeguard against potential abuses of power by the Prime Minister and Cabinet.

[55] Forsey, above gives a detailed commentary.
[56] Markesinis, app 4. Earlier in 1969, Captain O'Neill, Prime Minister of Northern Ireland, had been granted a dissolution of the Northern Ireland Parliament at a time when members of the Unionist party were growing restive at O'Neill's measures of reform.
[57] *The Times*, 11 May 1974.

The last occasion on which it was seriously urged that the Sovereign should intervene to ensure that a general election should be held against the wishes of the government was during the crisis over Home Rule for Ireland between 1912 and 1914.[58] After the Parliament Act 1911 had become law, the Liberal government intended that the Government of Ireland Bill should be passed under the Parliament Act procedure. Opposition leaders regarded the relationship between the Liberal party and the Irish Nationalists as 'a corrupt parliamentary bargain'. They urged George V to insist that an election be held before the Bill became law or to withhold the royal assent. Asquith, the Prime Minister, reminded George V of the constitutional limitations on the Sovereign, of the principle of ministerial responsibility and of the value for the Sovereign of having no personal responsibility for the acts of executive and Parliament. The King concluded that he should not adopt the extreme course of withholding the royal assent from the Bill 'unless there is convincing evidence that it would avert a national disaster, or at least have a tranquillizing effect on the distracting conditions of the time'.[59]

Where the question is that of assent to a Bill which has passed through Parliament, it would not be prudent for the Sovereign to challenge the wishes of a majority in the House of Commons. Yet the relationship between Sovereign and Prime Minister is bilateral in the sense that both persons hold office subject to some principles of constitutional behaviour, however vague these principles often appear to be. If the Prime Minister steps outside those principles (as, for example, Ian Smith, Prime Minister of Rhodesia, did in 1965 when with his Cabinet he unilaterally declared Rhodesia independent of the United Kingdom), the Sovereign may respond by dismissing his or her ministers and by seeking to ensure the maintenance of constitutional government. In 1975, the Labor government of Australia was failing to get essential financial legislation through the Canberra Parliament because of opposition from the Senate, whose approval to the legislation was required. When Sir John Kerr, the Governor-General, had satisfied himself that Prime Minister Whitlam was not willing to hold a general election to resolve the deadlock, he dismissed Whitlam and invited the Opposition leader, Malcolm Fraser, to form an interim government and hold an election. The election was won by Fraser, but the acts of the Governor-General gave rise to controversy of a kind which would be more damaging to a hereditary monarchy than to a Governor-General with a limited tenure of office.[60]

British government depends to a large extent on implicit agreement between the parties and their leaders about the rules and understandings of the political contest. If, in a particular situation, it were clear that one party or its leader had seriously departed from the accepted rules, personal intervention by the Sovereign could be justified on constitutional grounds. But a plain instance of flagrant abuse is less likely than a situation which is not covered by existing rules and understandings and in which it may be difficult to determine what are the constitutional requirements.[61] While the Sovereign may have a sensitive role to play in enabling a constitutional deadlock to be resolved, one lesson of British history is that personal government by the Sovereign is excluded. Indeed, the Sovereign needs the cooperation of ministers even for the purpose of dissolving Parliament and causing a new general election to be held.[62] The political impotence of a monarch who cannot find ministers willing to hold office explains why,

---

[58] See Nicolson, ch 14; Jennings, ch 13.
[59] Draft letter by George V, 31 July 1914.
[60] The literature includes Evans (ed), *Labor and the Constitution 1972–5*; Kerr, *Matters for Judgment*; Sawer, *Federation under Strain*; and Whitlam, *The Truth of the Matter*. For a retrospective account, see M Coper [2000] 11 Public Law Review 251.
[61] Ch 2 B.
[62] Jennings, pp 412–17; Markesinis, p 56.

as a 'far-sighted precaution' at an early stage of the abdication crisis in 1936, Prime Minister Baldwin ensured that other political leaders would not be willing to form a government if he were forced to resign.[63]

C. The Queen in Council

The Tudor monarchs governed mainly through the Privy Council, a select group of royal officials and advisers, having recourse to Parliament only when legislative authority was considered necessary for matters of taxation or to give effect to royal policies. The Privy Council survived the 17th-century conflicts, although its judicial arm, the Court of Star Chamber, was abolished in 1641. But in the 50 years after the restoration of the monarchy in 1660, the Privy Council lost its position as the main political executive and its numbers grew, many becoming members because of other offices which they held. As the Cabinet system developed, so did the English Privy Council lose its policy-making and deliberative role.[64] Soon after the union of England and Scotland in 1707, the Scottish Privy Council was abolished and its functions were assumed by the Privy Council for Great Britain.[65] In a formal sense the Council remained at the centre of the administrative machinery of government, but despite an attempt by Parliament in the Act of Settlement to insist that the Privy Council should exercise its former functions, the Council had lost its political authority. Significantly, politicians began to remain members of the Council after they had ceased to be ministers, a practice which has continued until today.

Membership of the Privy Council is today a titular honour. Appointments are made by the Sovereign on ministerial advice. By convention all Cabinet ministers become Privy Councillors. Members of the royal family and holders of certain high offices of a non-political character, such as archbishops and Lords Justices of Appeal, are appointed members of the Council. So in recent years have the leaders of the Opposition parties 'so that they can be given classified information on "Privy Counsellor terms" should the need arise on a matter affecting national security'. In the 1970s, Len Murray, general secretary of the TUC, was made a Privy Councillor to facilitate consultation on government policy.[66] The office is a recognised reward for public and political service and appointments to it figure in the honours lists. The Council now numbers about 400 members. Members are entitled to the prefix, 'Right Honourable'. They take an oath on appointment which binds them not to disclose anything said or done 'in Council' without the consent of the Sovereign. As all members of the Cabinet are also Privy Councillors, it has been considered that it is this oath which, in addition to their obligations under the Official Secrets Acts 1911–89, binds to secrecy all present and past Cabinet ministers, who may disclose Cabinet proceedings and other confidential discussions only if so authorised by the Sovereign; but little reliance was placed on this oath in the *Crossman Diaries* case[67] and its wording does not seem apt to include Cabinet proceedings. Aliens are disqualified, but on naturalisation an alien becomes qualified for membership.[68]

Despite the many powers conferred by statutes on individual ministers, the Order in Council remains a principal method of giving the force of law to acts of the

[63] Middlemas and Barnes, p 999.
[64] For the history of this period, see Mackintosh, ch 2.
[65] See Devine, *The Scottish Nation*, pp 18, 21.
[66] Hennessy, *Whitehall*, pp 350–1.
[67] *A-G v Jonathan Cape Ltd* [1976] QB 752; for the oath, see HLE, vol 8(2), p 523.
[68] *R v Speyer* [1916] 2 KB 858.

government, especially the more important executive orders. A royal proclamation is issued when it is desired to give wide publicity to the action of the Queen in Council, as for the purpose of dissolving a Parliament and summoning its successor. Orders in Council are approved by the Sovereign at a meeting of the Council to which only four or five members are summoned. No discussion takes place and the acts of the Council are purely formal. Orders are made either under the prerogative, as for the dissolution of Parliament, or under an Act of Parliament, for example, orders which make regulations under the Emergency Powers Act 1920 after a state of emergency has been proclaimed.[69] Statutory Orders in Council are generally subject to the Statutory Instruments Act 1946.[70] A few traces remain of the Council's former advisory functions: the Committee for Channel Islands business is a survivor of the old standing committees appointed by the King at the beginning or in the course of his reign. Other committees are the Judicial Committee of the Privy Council,[71] and a committee to consider grants of charters to universities.

Issues of constitutional importance are sometimes referred to ad hoc committees of the Privy Council, as, for example, the legal basis of the practice of telephone tapping and matters affecting state security.[72] A committee of six Privy Councillors reviewed British policy towards the Falkland Islands leading up to Argentina's invasion in 1982; after the Prime Minister had consulted with five former Prime Ministers to secure their consent, the committee had access to the papers of previous governments and secret intelligence assessments.[73] The functions of the Privy Council are quite distinct from those of the Cabinet. The first gives legal form to certain decisions of the government; the second exercises the policy-making function of the executive in major matters. The Cabinet is summoned by the Prime Minister; the Council is convened by the Clerk of the Council, whose office dates back to the 16th century. The Lord President of the Council is usually a senior member of the Cabinet. He or she in the past has acted as chairman of Cabinet committees and as Leader of the House of Commons supervises the government's legislative programme. Where Privy Council business concerns the activities of a department, responsibility for that business is borne by the minister of that department; thus the Secretary of State for Education and Skills is responsible for decisions of the Privy Council regarding university charters, although this responsibility is obscured by the dignified facade of Privy Council formality.

D. The royal prerogative

Both the Sovereign, as head of state, and the government, as personified for many purposes by the Crown, need powers to be able to perform their constitutional functions. The rule of law requires that these powers are grounded in law and are not outside or above the system of law which the courts administer. In Britain the powers of the Sovereign and the Crown must either be derived from Act of Parliament or must be recognised as a matter of common law, for there is no written constitution to confer powers on the executive. In the 17th-century constitutional settlement, it was established that the powers of the Crown were subject to law and that there were no powers of the Crown which could not be taken away or controlled by statute. Once that position had been achieved against the claims of the Stuarts, the courts thereafter

---

[69] Ch 26 D.
[70] Ch 28.
[71] Ch 18 A.
[72] Ch 22.
[73] HC Deb, 1 July 1982, col 1039, and 8 July 1982, col 469; Cmnd 8787, 1983; and ch 13 B.

accepted that the Sovereign and the Crown enjoyed certain powers, rights, immunities and privileges which were necessary to the maintenance of government and which were not shared with private citizens. The term prerogative is used as a collective description of these matters. Blackstone referred to prerogative as 'that special pre-eminence which the King hath, over and above all other persons, and out of the ordinary course of the common law, in right of his royal dignity'.[74] A modern definition would stress that the prerogative has been maintained not for the benefit of the Sovereign but to enable the government to function, and that prerogative is a matter of common law and does not derive from statute. Thus Parliament may not create a new prerogative, although it may confer on the Crown new rights or powers which may be very similar in character to prerogative power, for example, the statutory power to deport aliens from the United Kingdom whose further presence is considered undesirable,[75] or the statutory power to create life peerages.

History of the prerogative[76]

The medieval King was both feudal lord and head of the kingdom. He thus had all the rights of a feudal lord and certain exceptional rights above those of other lords. Like other lords the King could not be sued in his own courts; as there was no lord superior to the King, there was no court in which the King could be sued. In addition, the King had powers accounted for by the need to preserve the realm against external foes and an 'undefined residue of power which he might use for the public good'.[77] We have already seen that medieval lawyers did not regard the King as being above the law.[78] Moreover certain royal functions could be exercised only in certain ways. The common law courts were the King's courts and only through them could the King decide questions of title to land and punish felonies. Yet the King possessed a residuary power of doing justice through his Council where the courts of common law were inadequate. In the 17th century, the main disputes arose over the undefined residue of prerogative power claimed by the Stuart kings.[79] Those common lawyers who allied with Parliament in resisting the Stuart claims asserted that there was a fundamental distinction between what was called the ordinary as opposed to the absolute prerogative. The ordinary prerogative meant those royal functions which could only be exercised in defined ways and involved no element of royal discretion. Thus the King could not himself act as a judge; he must dispense justice through his judges.[80] And he could make laws only through Parliament.[81] By contrast, the absolute or extraordinary prerogative meant those powers which the King could exercise in his discretion. They included not only such powers as the right to pardon a criminal or grant a peerage, but also the King's undoubted powers to exercise discretion in the interest of the realm, especially in times of emergency.

It was these powers on which Charles I relied in seeking to govern without Parliament. The conflict was resolved only after the execution of one King and the expulsion of another. But the particular disputes often gave rise to cases in the courts, in which the rival political theories were expressed in legal argument. Where the judges

---

[74] Blackstone, *Commentaries*, I, p 239. Cf Wade, *Constitutional Fundamentals*, pp 45–53.
[75] Ch 20 B.
[76] A valuable account is in Keir and Lawson, *Cases in Constitutional Law*, part II. See also Heuston, *Essays*, ch 3.
[77] Keir and Lawson, p 70.
[78] Ch 6.
[79] Ch 4 A.
[80] *Prohibitions del Roy* (1607) 12 Co Rep 63; ch 18 C.
[81] *The Case of Proclamations* (1611) 12 Co Rep 74; ch 4 A.

accepted the Crown's more extreme claims, their decisions had subsequently to be reversed by Parliament. As well as the cases on taxation and the dispensing power,[82] another outstanding case was *Darnel's* or *The Five Knights* case,[83] where it was held that it was a sufficient answer to a writ of habeas corpus to state that a prisoner was detained *per speciale mandatum regis* (by special order of the King). Thus the King was entrusted with a power of preventive arrest which could not be questioned by the courts and which in *Darnel's* case was used to enforce taxation levied without the consent of Parliament. This arbitrary power of committal was declared illegal by the Petition of Right 1628 and in 1640 the subject's right to habeas corpus against the King and his Council was guaranteed by statute.[84] The problem of the prerogative was confronted in two stages. The first was that of the 17th-century struggle culminating in the Bill of Rights 1689, which declared illegal certain specific uses and abuses of the prerogative.[85] The second stage was the growth of responsible government and the establishment of a constitutional monarchy.[86] It became established that prerogative powers could be exercised only through and on the advice of ministers responsible to Parliament. Nonetheless, the ability of ministers to rely on prerogative powers gives rise to continuing problems of accountability.

The prerogative today

Today the greater part of government depends on statute. But certain powers, rights, immunities and privileges of the Sovereign and of the Crown, which vary widely in importance, continue to have their legal source in the common law. Where these powers or rights are common to all persons, including the Crown (for example, the power to own property or enter into contracts), they are not described as matters of prerogative;[87] but the term royal prerogative is properly applied to those legal attributes of the Crown which the common law recognises as differing significantly from those of private persons. Thus the legal relationship between the Crown and Crown servants is an aspect of the prerogative since it differs markedly from the normal contractual relationship between employer and employee; the same applies to the power of the Crown in certain circumstances to override contracts to which it is a party.[88] Although it is true that Crown servants are now typically employed under contracts of employment, the Crown nevertheless retains a prerogative power to terminate them at pleasure.[89] Except in those special instances where prerogative powers involve the personal discretion of the Sovereign, prerogative powers are exercised by or on behalf of the government of the day. For their exercise, just as for the use of statutory powers, ministers are responsible to Parliament.

Thus questions may be asked of ministers about the exercise of prerogative power. Where a matter does not fall within the province of a departmental minister, questions may be addressed to the Prime Minister. To this rule there are certain exceptions: thus the Prime Minister may not be questioned in the Commons as to the advice that may have been given to the Sovereign regarding the grant of honours or the ecclesiastical patronage of the Crown.[90] Although an Act of Parliament may abolish or curtail the

---

[82] Ch 4 A.
[83] (1627) 3 St Tr 1.
[84] Habeas Corpus Act 1640. And see ch 31.
[85] Ch 2 A.
[86] Ch 7.
[87] And see B V Harris (1992) 108 LQR 626.
[88] Ch 32 B.
[89] See ch 13 D.
[90] Erskine May, *Parliamentary Practice*, p 298.

prerogative, the prior authority of Parliament is not required for the exercise of a prerogative power. For example, the Crown may recognise a new foreign government or enter into a treaty without first informing Parliament. Parliament may criticise ministers for their action and for the consequences; but Parliament has no right to be consulted in advance, except to the extent that a conventional practice has developed of assuring the opportunity for such consultation.[91] Certain prerogatives could be exercised only if the government were assured of subsequent support from Parliament. The Crown may declare war, but Parliament alone may vote the supplies which enable war to be waged. Again, where a treaty envisages changes in our domestic law, Parliament could frustrate the treaty made by the Crown if it subsequently refused to pass the necessary legislation. In the same way, although the authority of Parliament is required to maintain a standing army, the deployment of troops is a matter for the Defence Secretary under the royal prerogative.[92]

The extent of the prerogative today

Because of the diverse subjects covered by prerogative and because of the uncertainty of the law in many instances where an ancient power has not been used in modern times, it is not possible to give a comprehensive catalogue of prerogative powers.[93] Instead the main areas in which the prerogative is used today will be mentioned briefly; most of these are discussed more fully in other chapters.

1 *Powers relating to the legislature* By virtue of the prerogative the Sovereign summons, prorogues and dissolves Parliament. The prerogative power to create hereditary peers has been diminished in practice, first by the Life Peerages Act 1958 and then by the House of Lords Act 1999. But it is presumably possible in principle for the Queen to confer hereditary titles on her subjects (presumably also on the advice of her Prime Minister), who would not as a result be entitled to membership of the House of Lords.[94] It is under the prerogative that the Sovereign assents to Bills. The Crown retains certain powers to legislate under the prerogative by Order in Council or by letters patent. Formerly this was important in respect of the colonies,[95] but the power is still used in respect of the civil service.[96] While the Crown may not create new criminal offences or impose new obligations upon citizens,[97] it may under the prerogative create schemes for conferring benefits upon citizens provided that Parliament appropriates the necessary money to pay for these benefits; thus concerning the Criminal Injuries Compensation scheme, set up by means of a non-statutory document notified to Parliament, Diplock LJ said:

> It may be a novel development in constitutional practice to govern by public statement of intention made by the executive government instead of by legislation. This is no more, however, than a reversion to the ancient practice of government by royal proclamation, although it is

---

[91] For the 'Ponsonby rule' in relation to treaties, see ch 15 B.

[92] See ch 16 A and P Rowe, in Sunkin and Payne, *The Nature of the Crown*, ch 10.

[93] For a review of the scope of the prerogative, see HC Deb, 21 April 1993, col 490. For an account that was authoritative in its day, see Chitty, *Prerogatives of the Crown*; and see B S Markesinis [1973] CLJ 287, S Payne, in Sunkin and Payne, ch 4, and C Walker [1987] PL 62.

[94] House of Lords Act 1999, s 1.

[95] Roberts-Wray, *Commonwealth and Colonial Law*, ch 5. Cf Montserrat Constitution Order 1989, SI 1989 No 2401 and St Helena Constitution Order 1988, SI 1988 No 1842. The latter was made by Her Majesty in Council 'in exercise of the power conferred upon Her by section 112 of the Government of India Act 1833, the British Settlements Acts 1887 and 1945 *or otherwise in Her Majesty vested*'. Emphasis added.

[96] E.g. Civil Service Order in Council 1995. See ch 13 D.

[97] *The Case of Proclamations* (1611) 12 Co Rep 74.

now subject to the limitations imposed on that practice by the development of constitutional law in the 17th century.[98]

2 *Powers relating to the judicial system*[99]   While the Crown may still have a prerogative power to establish courts to administer the common law,[100] new courts are now established by statute. But the Crown nevertheless exercises many functions in relation to criminal justice. Thus in England prosecutions on indictment may be stopped by the Attorney-General entering a *nolle prosequi*, a power exercisable even in the case of those prosecutions over which he has no power of superintendence, as in the case of prosecutions by the Customs and Excise.[101] The Crown may pardon convicted offenders or remit or reduce a sentence on the advice of the Home Secretary. It is under the prerogative that the Crown grants special leave to appeal from colonial courts to the Judicial Committee of the Privy Council, where the right of appeal to the Privy Council has not been abolished.[102] In civil matters the Attorney-General represents the Crown as *parens patriae* to enforce matters of public right.[103] In 1991, the Court of Appeal held that the Crown, unlike ministers and servants of the Crown, was not subject to the contempt jurisdiction vested in the courts.[104]

3 *Powers relating to foreign affairs*[105]   The conduct of foreign affairs by the government is carried on mainly by reliance on the prerogative, for example, the making of treaties, the declaration of war and the making of peace. The prerogative includes power to acquire additional territory; thus by royal warrant in 1955, the Crown took possession of the island of Rockall, subsequently incorporated into the United Kingdom as part of Scotland by the Island of Rockall Act 1972. It is doubtful whether the Crown may by treaty cede British territory without the authority of Parliament and modern practice is to secure parliamentary approval,[106] but it seems that the prerogative includes power to declare or to alter the limits of British territorial waters.[107] The phrase 'act of state' is often used to refer to acts of the Crown in foreign affairs: while these acts would often fall within the scope of the prerogative, the concept of the prerogative is best confined to powers of the Crown exercised in relation to its own subjects and 'act of state' should apply only to a limited plea to the jurisdiction of the British courts, in respect of acts of the Crown performed in foreign territory in relation to aliens.[108]

The Crown has power under the prerogative to restrain aliens from entering the United Kingdom; but it is uncertain whether the Crown has a prerogative power to expel aliens who have been permitted to reside here. Today, powers over aliens are exercised under the Immigration Act 1971, although that Act expressly reserves such prerogative

---

[98] *R v Criminal Injuries Compensation Board, ex p Lain* [1967] 2 QB 864, 886; cf Wade, pp 47–8. See also *R v Home Secretary, ex p Harrison* [1988] 3 All ER 86, and *R v Home Secretary, ex p Fire Brigades Union* [1995] 2 AC 513.

[99] Ch 18.

[100] Ch 18 C.

[101] HC 115 (1995–96) (Scott Report), para C 3.10.

[102] Chs 15 C, 18 A.

[103] *Gouriet v Union of Post Office Workers* [1978] AC 435.

[104] *M v Home Office* [1992] QB 270. The House of Lords held the same, for other reasons: [1994] 1 AC 377.

[105] Ch 15.

[106] Anson, *Law and Custom of the Constitution*, II, ii, pp 137–42; and Roberts-Wray, ch 4. The Hong Kong Act 1985 provides that 'As from 1st July 1997 Her Majesty shall no longer have sovereignty or jurisdiction over any part of Hong Kong' (s 1(1)).

[107] *R v Kent JJ, ex p Lye* [1967] 2 QB 153; cf W R Edeson (1973) 89 LQR 364.

[108] See the varying opinions on the application of prerogative abroad in *Nissan v A-G* [1970] AC 179; and ch 15 A.

powers as the Crown may have (s 33(5)). The issue of passports to citizens is based on the prerogative.[109] At common law the Crown could restrain a person from leaving the realm when the interests of state demanded it by means of the writ *ne exeat regno*, but it is doubtful whether the power should today be exercised. In time of war the Crown may possibly under the prerogative restrain a British subject from leaving the realm or recall him from abroad, but during modern wars entry and exit have been controlled by statutory powers. The scope of the power to remove people from their surroundings was considered in a case dealing with the forcible removal of Indian Ocean islanders from the Chagos Archipelago to Mauritius to make way for a US military base. It was doubted whether the prerogative power of the Queen in Council extends so far as to permit the Queen in Council to exile her subjects from the territory where they belong. It was also said that 'it would be one thing to send [someone] to another part of the Queen's dominions, and quite another to send him out of the Queen's dominions altogether'.[110]

4 *Powers relating to the armed forces*[111]   Both by prerogative and by statute the Sovereign is commander-in-chief of the armed forces of the Crown. The Bill of Rights 1689 prohibited the keeping of a standing army within the realm in time of peace without the consent of Parliament; thus the authority of Parliament is required for the maintenance of the army, the Royal Air Force and other forces serving on land. Although many matters regarding the armed forces are regulated by statute, their control, organisation and disposition are within the prerogative and cannot be questioned in a court.[112] But members of the armed forces and the Ministry of Defence may be held liable for unlawful acts which infringe the rights of individuals.[113]

5 *Appointments and honours*[114]   On the advice of the Prime Minister or other ministers, the Sovereign appoints ministers, judges and many other holders of public office, including the members of royal commissions to inquire into matters of controversy. Appointments to the civil service are appointments to the service of the Crown. The Sovereign is the sole fountain of honour and alone can create peers, confer honours and decorations,[115] grant arms and regulate matters of precedence.[116] Honours are generally conferred by the Sovereign on the advice of the Prime Minister. In the case of peerages, the formal position is that the House of Lords Appointments Commission advises the Prime Minister about the non-political nominations and the Prime Minister passes these on to the Queen. The Commission also advises the Prime Minister about party political nominees, performing a task which was previously performed by the Political Honours Scrutiny Committee which is to vet all nominations on grounds of propriety. The Political Honours Scrutiny Committee (a committee of three Privy Councillors) still advises on the suitability of those who are recommended for other political honours (such as knighthoods and the like).[117] Certain honours, namely

---

[109] Ch 20 A.
[110] *R (Bancoult)* v *Foreign and Commonwealth Secretary* [2001] QB 1067 (S Palmer [2001] CLJ 234; A Tomkins [2001] PL 571).
[111] Ch 16 A.
[112] *China Navigation Co Ltd* v *A-G* [1932] 2 KB 197; *Chandler* v *DPP* [1964] AC 763; Crown Proceedings Act 1947, s 11.
[113] See ch 32 A.
[114] Jennings, ch 14; Richards, *Patronage in British Government*, ch 10; Walker, *The Queen Has Been Pleased*.
[115] On which see Cm 1627, 1991 (the Gulf Medal); and Cm 2447, 1994 (the Accumulated Campaign Service Medal).
[116] A Wagner and G D Squibb (1973) 80 LQR 352.
[117] See Cmd 1789, 1922; and Cm 4057-1, 1998. It is an offence to trade in honours: Honours (Prevention of Abuses) Act 1925.

the Order of the Garter, the Order of the Thistle, the Royal Victoria Order (for personal services to the Sovereign) and the Order of Merit are in the personal gift of the Sovereign.

6 *Immunities and privileges* It is a principle of interpretation that statutes do not bind the Crown except by express statement or necessary implication.

> In *Lord Advocate* v *Dumbarton Council*, the Ministry of Defence decided to erect an improved security fence at its submarine base at Faslane, Dunbartonshire. Part of the fence ran alongside the A814 road and when the roads authority (Strathclyde Council) discovered that the Ministry intended to place temporary works on part of the road, they notified the Ministry that it would require their consent under the Roads (Scotland) Act 1984. The Ministry replied that these provisions did not bind the Crown and contractors took possession of a one-mile stretch of part of the road by erecting a temporary fence. Thereupon the roads authority (Strathclyde) and the planning authority (Dumbarton) gave various notices under statutes to stop the work. The Lord Advocate sought judicial review of the councils' conduct, alleging that the statutes in question did not bind the Crown. Although the Crown's immunity was restricted by the Inner House of the Court of Session, the wider immunity was restored by the House of Lords. In the view of Lord Keith, 'the Crown is not bound by any statutory provision unless there can somehow be gathered from the terms of the relevant Act an intention to that effect. The Crown can be bound only by express words or necessary implication'. At the same time, Lord Keith rejected as no longer tenable the view that 'the Crown is in terms bound by general words in a statute but that the prerogative enables it to override the statute'.[118]

Tax is not payable on income received by the Sovereign as such, neither in respect of Crown property, nor on income received on behalf of the Crown by a servant of the Crown in the course of official duties.[119] But as we have seen, the Queen has undertaken to pay tax on her private income from 1993 and it is claimed on the official royal website that her private income is taxable 'as for any taxpayer'.[120] Many of the immunities of the Crown in civil litigation were removed by the Crown Proceedings Act 1947, but the Crown and government departments still have certain privileges. The 1947 Act preserved the personal immunity of the Sovereign from being sued.[121] The question has arisen whether the Crown enjoys immunity from criminal liability. During the Spycatcher affair in the mid-1980s, a retired MI5 officer, Mr Peter Wright, alleged that members of the Security Service had been engaged in surveillance operations which included burgling premises in London. The Home Secretary announced that the government had never asserted that actions 'could lawfully be done under the prerogative when they would otherwise be criminal offences'.[122]

7 *The prerogative in time of emergency* The extent of the prerogative in times of grave emergency cannot be precisely stated. That prerogative powers were wide was admitted by Hampden's counsel in the *Case of Ship Money*. Save in regard to taxation, they were not abridged by the Bill of Rights. In 1964, Lord Reid said: 'The prerogative certainly covers doing all those things in an emergency which are necessary for the conduct of war'; but he added that there was difficulty in relating the prerogative to modern conditions since no modern war had been waged without statutory powers:

---

[118] [1990] 2 AC 580; and ch 32 C.
[119] *Bank voor Handel en Scheepvaart NV* v *Administrator of Hungarian Property* [1954] AC 584.
[120] www.royal.gov.uk/today/finance. See also on royal finances, pp 235–6.
[121] Ch 32 C.
[122] HC Deb, 29 January 1988, col 397 (WA). Cf *A-G* v *Guardian Newspapers Ltd (No 2)* [1990] 1 AC 109, 190.

The mobilisation of the industrial and financial resources of the country could not be done without statutory emergency powers. The prerogative is really a relic of a past age, not lost by disuse but only available for a case not covered by statute.[123]

According to the old law, in time of sudden invasion or insurrection, the King might demand personal service within the realm.[124] Either the Crown or a subject might invade the land of another to erect fortifications for the defence of the realm.[125] But it is not certain whether this should be regarded as an aspect of the prerogative since it was a duty shared by the Crown with all its subjects.

The difficulty of applying the old common law in modern circumstances was evident in *Burmah Oil Company* v *Lord Advocate*.[126]

> In 1942 extensive oil installations were destroyed by British troops in Rangoon, not accidentally as a result of fighting but deliberately so as to prevent the installations falling into enemy hands. One day later, the Japanese army entered Rangoon. After receiving some £4 million from the British government as an ex gratia payment, the company sued the Lord Advocate representing the Crown in Scotland for over £31 million. It was agreed that the destruction had not been ordered under statutory authority and the company claimed compensation for the lawful exercise of prerogative power. The House of Lords held (*a*) that, as a general rule, compensation was payable by the Crown to the subject who was deprived of property for the benefit of the state, by prerogative act in relation to war and (*b*) that the destruction of the refineries did not fall within the 'battle damage' exception to the general rule. But the House left open the basis on which compensation should be assessed.

This decision established that where private property was taken under the prerogative, the owner was entitled at common law to compensation from the Crown; but the War Damage Act 1965 retrospectively provided that no person should be entitled at common law to receive compensation in respect of damage to or destruction of property caused by lawful acts of the Crown 'during, or in contemplation of the outbreak of, a war in which the Sovereign is or was engaged'. This Act prevented the Burmah Oil Company's claim from succeeding but its effect was limited to acts of the Crown which destroyed property during or in contemplation of a war; the principle that the Crown is obliged to pay compensation for property taken under the prerogative for use of the armed forces still seems to apply.[127]

The principle that compensation may be payable for lawful acts of the prerogative was already known before the *Burmah Oil* case. Thus the Crown may under prerogative requisition British ships in time of urgent national necessity, but compensation is payable, as it was in 1982 when British ships were requisitioned for use in the recapture of the Falkland Islands.[128] By the right of angary, the Crown may in time of war appropriate the property of a neutral which is within the realm where necessity requires, but compensation must be paid.[129] In both world wars, statutory powers of requisitioning property have been conferred on the Crown and compensation has been paid. But if, for example, an emergency arose in which it was necessary for the Armed Forces to take immediate steps against terrorist action within the United Kingdom, it is possible both that private property needed for this purpose could be

---

[123] *Burmah Oil Co Ltd* v *Lord Advocate* [1965] AC 75, 101; and see ch 26 D.
[124] Chitty, p 49.
[125] *The Case of the King's Prerogative in Saltpetre* (1607) 12 Co Rep 12.
[126] [1965] AC 75, discussed by A L Goodhart (1966) 82 LQR 97; T C Daintith (1965) 14 ICLQ 1000; and in (1966) 79 Harv LR 614.
[127] E.g. *Nissan* v *A-G* [1970] AC 179, 229 (Lord Pearce).
[128] Requisitioning of Ships Order 1982. And see *Crown of Leon* v *Admiralty Commissioners* [1921] 1 KB 595; W S Holdsworth (1919) 35 LQR 12.
[129] *Commercial and Estates Co of Egypt* v *Board of Trade* [1925] 1 KB 271. And see W I Jennings (1927) 3 CLJ 1.

occupied under prerogative and that compensation would at common law be payable to the owners.

8 *Miscellaneous prerogatives.*   Other historic prerogative powers concerning matters which are today largely regulated by statute relate to: the creation of corporations by royal charter; the right to mine precious metals; coinage; the grant of franchises, for example, markets,[130] ferries and fisheries; the right to treasure trove;[131] the sole right of printing or licensing others to print the Authorised Version of the Bible,[132] the Book of Common Prayer and state papers;[133] and the guardianship of infants (a prerogative jurisdiction exercised through the High Court and not excluded by the statutory powers of local authorities).[134] It has been said that the courts may 'interfere for the protection of infants, qua infants, by virtue of the prerogative which belongs to the Crown as *parens patriae*'.[135] When a court is exercising this paternal jurisdiction it is empowered to exclude the public where it is necessary to do so.[136] In *R v Central Television plc*,[137] however, it was held that the power could not be invoked to obscure the pictures of a man in a television programme imprisoned for indecency with young boys, on the ground that his identification would cause harm to his child: the programme had nothing to do with the care or upbringing of the child.

E. The royal prerogative and the courts

Some prerogative acts are unlikely to give rise to the possibility of challenge in the courts, for example the conferment of an honour or the dissolution of Parliament. But where an act purporting to be done under the prerogative directly affects the rights of an individual, the courts may be asked to determine a number of issues.

The existence and extent of a prerogative power

In principle the courts will not recognise the existence of new prerogative powers. In *Entick* v *Carrington*, in which the court held that the mere plea of state necessity would not protect anyone accused of an unlawful act, Lord Camden CJ said, 'If it is law, it will be found in our books. If it is not to be found there, it is not law.'[138] And in 1964 Diplock LJ said,

> It is 350 years and a civil war too late for the Queen's courts to broaden the prerogative. The limits within which the executive government may impose obligations or restraints on citizens of the United Kingdom without any statutory authority are now well settled and incapable of extension.[139]

---

[130] Cf *Spook Erection Ltd* v *Environment Secretary* [1989] QB 300 (beneficiary of market franchise not entitled to Crown's exemption from planning control).

[131] Treasure trove, i.e. gold or silver objects that have been hidden and of which no owner can be traced, is the property of the Crown; *A-G of Duchy of Lancaster* v *G E Overton (Farms) Ltd* [1982] Ch 277. See now Treasure Act 1996.

[132] *Universities of Oxford and Cambridge* v *Eyre & Spottiswoode Ltd* [1964] Ch 736 (royal prerogative did not extend to New English Bible).

[133] Copyright, Designs and Patents Act 1988, s 163.

[134] *Re M* [1961] Ch 328. But see now Children Act 1989, s 100.

[135] *Barnardo* v *McHugh* [1891] AC 388, 395.

[136] *Scott* v *Scott* [1913] AC 417.

[137] [1994] Fam 192.

[138] (1765) 19 St Tr 1030, 1066: ch 6 A. *Entick*'s case was distinguished in *Malone* v *Metropolitan Police Commissioner* [1979] Ch 344 (no evidence of unlawful act in tapping telephones); ch 22.

[139] *BBC* v *Johns* [1965] Ch 32, 79.

But some prerogative powers are very wide and difficulties arise when the courts are asked to decide whether an ancient power applies in a new situation; for example, whether the Crown's power to act in situations of grave national emergency justifies action to deal with a wholly new form of terrorist activity which threatens the nation or whether the prerogative right to intercept postal communications justifies the tapping of telephones.[140] In these situations, it may be difficult to distinguish between creating a new prerogative and applying an old prerogative to new circumstances.

In *R v Home Secretary, ex p Northumbria Police Authority*,[141] the Home Secretary made available CS gas and baton rounds to the police to deal with situations of serious public disorder, notwithstanding the objections of the local police authority. The police authority sought a declaration that the Home Secretary had no power to provide the equipment without their consent, save in a situation of grave emergency. The Court of Appeal held that the provision of the equipment was authorised by the Police Act 1964, but also by the royal prerogative. In so concluding, the court had first to determine that there did in fact exist a 'prerogative to enforce the keeping of what is popularly called the Queen's peace within the realm'. Although the court had difficulty in finding authority for such a power, Croom-Johnson LJ nevertheless concluded that such a general power is bound up with the Crown's 'undoubted right to see that crime is prevented and justice administered'. The supply of baton rounds and CS gas was held to fall within the scope of the prerogative, since it is open to the Home Secretary 'to supply equipment reasonably required by police forces to discharge their functions'.

A related question is whether the courts have power to rule that an ancient prerogative has become so unsuited to modern conditions that it can no longer be relied on by the Crown. In general, rules of common law do not lapse through desuetude.[142] But it is difficult to see why a court should be required to give new life to an archaic power which offends modern constitutional principles, merely because its existence had been recognised several centuries ago.

The effect of statutes upon prerogative powers

Parliament may abolish or restrict prerogative powers expressly or by necessary implication, whether or not coupling this with the grant of statutory powers in the same area of government. But often Parliament has not expressly abolished prerogative powers and has merely created a statutory scheme dealing with the same subject. Where this is the case, as a general principle must the Crown proceed under the statutory powers or may it rely instead upon the prerogative?

In *Attorney-General v De Keyser's Royal Hotel*[143] an hotel was required for housing the administrative staff of the Royal Flying Corps during the First World War. The Army Council offered to hire the hotel at a rent but, negotiations having broken down, a letter was sent on the instruction of the Army Council stating that possession was being taken under the Defence of the Realm Acts and Regulations. A petition of right was later brought against the Crown claiming compensation as of right for the use of the hotel by the authorities.

It was argued for the Crown that there was a prerogative power to take the land of the subject in case of emergency in time of war; that no compensation was payable as of right for

---

[140] Cf Cmd 283, 1957. In *Malone's* case, no claim of prerogative power was made.
[141] [1989] QB 26, criticised by A W Bradley [1988] PL 297.
[142] Maitland, *Constitutional History*, p 418; cf *Nyali Ltd v A-G* [1956] 1 QB 1, and *McKendrick v Sinclair* 1972 SC (HL) 25, 60–1.
[143] [1920] AC 508.

land so taken; and that this power could be exercised, notwithstanding provisions of the Defence Act 1842 which had been incorporated into the Defence of the Realm Acts and provided for statutory compensation as of right to the owners. The argument for the owners of the hotel was that the Crown had taken possession under the statutes and so could not fall back on the prerogative.

The House of Lords rejected the argument of the Crown, holding that on the facts the Crown had taken possession under statutory powers. The House also held that the prerogative had been superseded for the time being by the statute. The Crown could not revert to prerogative powers when the legislature had given to the Crown statutory powers which covered all that could be necessary for the defence of the nation, and which were accompanied by important safeguards to the individual. Thus for the duration of the statutory powers, the prerogative was in abeyance. The House therefore did not have to decide whether the Crown had a prerogative power to requisition land in time of war without paying compensation, but serious doubts were expressed about this claim.[144]

The principle in this case, that the 'executive cannot exercise the prerogative in a way which would derogate from the due fulfilment of a statutory duty',[145] is subject to a number of refinements. First, it applies only when Parliament has not given an express indication of its intention. Thus the Immigration Act 1971 provided that the powers which it conferred should be additional to any prerogative powers (s 33(5)), as did the Emergency Powers (Defence) Act 1939.[146] Secondly, there are suggestions that it may apply only where the statute confers rights or benefits on the citizen which would be undermined were the Crown to retain the right to use the prerogative power. In the *Northumbria Police* case, the Court of Appeal held that the supply of baton rounds and CS gas was authorised by the Police Act 1964, s 41, but also by the prerogative power to maintain the peace. Was the prerogative power displaced by the statute or could both exist and operate simultaneously? In opting for the latter position, Purchas LJ said:

> It is well established that the courts will intervene to prevent executive action under prerogative powers in violation of property or other rights of the individual where this is inconsistent with statutory provisions providing for the same executive action. Where the executive action is directed towards the benefit or protection of the individual, it is unlikely that its use will attract the intervention of the courts . . . [B]efore the courts will hold that such executive action is contrary to legislation, express and unequivocal terms must be found in the statute which deprive the individual from receiving the benefit or protection intended by the exercise of prerogative power.[147]

In the *Northumbria Police* case, even if the statute had not provided the necessary authority, the court was unable to find 'an express and unequivocal inhibition sufficient to abridge the prerogative powers, otherwise available to the Secretary of State, to do all that is reasonably necessary to preserve the peace of the realm'. Thirdly, where the statute restricting the prerogative is repealed, 'the prerogative power would apparently re-emerge as it existed before the statute'.[148] This is subject to 'words in the repealing statute which make it clear that the prerogative power is not intended by Parliament to be revived or again brought into use'.[149]

---

144 See the *Burmah Oil* case, p 252 above. See also *C O Williams Construction Ltd v Blackman* [1995] 1 WLR 102, 108; and *R v Home Secretary, ex p Fire Brigades Union* [1995] 2 AC 513.
145 *R v Home Secretary, ex p Fire Brigades Union* [1995] 2 AC 513.
146 Ch 26 D.
147 [1989] QB 26, 53.
148 *Burmah Oil Co Ltd v Lord Advocate* [1965] AC 75, Lord Pearce at 143.
149 *R v Foreign Secretary, ex p CCSU* [1984] IRLR 309, at 321 (Glidewell J).

The manner of exercise of a prerogative power

Although the courts have long had the power to determine the existence and extent of a prerogative power, traditionally they have had no power to regulate the manner of its exercise. This contrasts with statutory powers of the executive, which the courts have held must generally be exercised in accordance with the rules of natural justice and in accordance with the so-called *Wednesbury* principles.[150] Thus, the courts have held that the courts cannot question whether the Crown has wisely exercised its discretionary power regarding the disposition of the armed forces;[151] neither could the courts say whether the government should enter into a particular treaty;[152] nor whether the Home Secretary had properly advised the Sovereign regarding the prerogative of mercy.[153] In *Gouriet v Union of Post Office Workers*[154] the House of Lords held that the exercise of the Attorney-General's discretion in giving consent to the bringing of relator actions could not be reviewed by the courts. But even as this decision was being given, there were already some indications of a more flexible approach by the courts. In *Chandler v DPP*,[155] Lord Devlin said in the context of a discussion of the prerogative that: 'The courts will not review the proper exercise of discretionary power but they will intervene to correct excess or abuse.' 'Excess' means action which exceeds the limits of the prerogative and although the point was never developed, 'abuse' suggests the unreasonable use of an established power. Although it may not have been fully appreciated at the time,[156] *R v Criminal Injuries Compensation Board, ex p Lain*[157] was to prove an important breakthrough, where it was held that the High Court had the power to review the activities of the board, a body set up under the royal prerogative to administer benefits for the victims of criminal injury. Lord Parker CJ could see no reason why a body set up by prerogative rather than by statute should be any less amenable to judicial review for that reason alone. In *Laker Airways Ltd v Department of Trade and Industry*,[158] Lord Denning MR went further, saying that the use of prerogative power could be examined by the courts just as any other power that is vested in the executive. The position is now governed by the landmark decision of the House of Lords in *Council of Civil Service Unions v Minister of State for Civil Service*.[159]

In January 1984, the Foreign Secretary announced the government's decision to exclude trade unions from Government Communications' Headquarters (GCHQ). This would be done under an Order in Council of 1982 authorising the Minister for the Civil Service to give instructions regulating the terms and conditions of civil service employment. The instructions given directed that staff at GCHQ would no longer be permitted to be members of the civil service unions, but only to join an officially approved staff association. These steps had been taken because of earlier industrial action at GCHQ.

In deciding whether the government's decision was reviewable by the courts, a majority in the House of Lords held that the courts could review the manner of exercise of discretionary powers conferred by the prerogative just as they could review the manner of exercise of discretionary powers conferred by statute. Lord Diplock could 'see no reason why simply because

---

[150] See ch 30 A.
[151] *China Navigation Co Ltd v A-G* [1932] 2 KB 197; *Chandler v DPP* [1964] AC 763; Crown Proceedings Act 1947, s 11.
[152] *Blackburn v A-G* [1971] 2 All ER 1380. Also *R v Foreign Secretary, ex p Rees-Mogg* [1994] QB 552.
[153] *Hanratty v Lord Butler* (1971) 115 SJ 386, discussed by A T H Smith [1983] PL 398, 432. Cf B V Harris [1991] PL 386. But see *R v Home Secretary, ex p Bentley* (note 164 below).
[154] [1978] AC 435.
[155] [1964] AC 763, 810.
[156] See C P Walker [1987] PL 62.
[157] [1967] 2 QB 864.
[158] [1977] QB 643.
[159] [1985] AC 374. See H W R Wade (1985) 101 LQR 180.

a decision-making power is derived from a common law and not a statutory source, it should for that reason only be immune from judicial review'. It does not follow, however, that all prerogative powers would be subject to review in this way. According to the House of Lords, it depends on the nature of the power, and in particular whether the power in question is justiciable, i.e. whether it gives rise to questions which are capable of adjudication in a court of law. It is not clear which powers are justiciable, though Lord Roskill gave many examples of those which are not, including the making of treaties, the disposition of the armed forces, the granting of honours and the dissolution of Parliament.

Where a prerogative power is justiciable and subject to review, it may be challenged on the same grounds as statutory powers.[160] There are suggestions in Lord Diplock's speech that as far as the prerogative is concerned, the scope for judicial review is limited to matters of illegality and procedural impropriety. In the *CCSU* case there appeared to have been a procedural impropriety (the unions should have been consulted in advance) but nevertheless the unions failed on the ground that the government had acted in the interests of national security (the evidence of which was in an affidavit from the Cabinet Secretary). Despite subsequent decisions, the scope of the *CCSU* decision remains unclear,[161] particularly regarding the distinction between justiciable and non-justiciable powers though it has been said that the concept of justiciability has been interpreted expansively.[162] It may be presumed that the prerogative power to regulate terms of employment in the civil service is subject to review, although the impact of this is to some extent replaced by the willingness of the courts to accept that civil servants are employed under contract, with an expectation that they should seek a remedy in private law.[163] However, a number of other challenges have been made to the exercise of powers conferred by the royal prerogative including *R v Home Secretary, ex p Bentley*,[164] where it was held that 'some aspects of the exercise of the Royal Prerogative [of mercy] are amenable to the judicial process', notwithstanding authority to the contrary[165] and the suggestion of Lord Roskill in the *CCSU* case that the exercise of the prerogative of mercy was not justiciable.[166] In other cases, largely unsuccessful challenges have been made to the exercise of powers conferred by the royal prerogative regarding the employment of civil servants, while the power to issue a passport is now subject to judicial review.[167] But the most important case since *CCSU* is *R v Home Secretary, ex p Fire Brigades Union*.[168]

> The Criminal Justice Act 1988 provided for a new statutory scheme to compensate the victims of criminal injury, replacing the one which had been introduced in 1964 under the royal prerogative.[169] Under the Act the statutory scheme was to come into force on such day as the Secretary of State might by order appoint. But before bringing the Act into force, the government changed its mind and announced the introduction of a new tariff scheme; the 1988 Act would 'not now be implemented' but would be repealed 'when a suitable legislative opportunity occurs'. The effect of the new scheme was that 'particularly in relation to very serious injuries involving prolonged loss of earnings' the amount payable to the victim would be

---

[160] See ch 30.
[161] See C P Walker [1987] PL 62.
[162] B Hadfield, in Sunkin and Payne, ch 8, at p 230.
[163] See ch 13 D.
[164] [1994] QB 349. See subsequently, *R v Bentley* (2001) 1 Cr App Rep 307.
[165] *Hanratty v Lord Butler* (1971) 115 SJ 386 and *de Freitas v Benny* [1976] AC 239.
[166] [1985] AC 374 at p 418.
[167] *R v Foreign Secretary, ex p Everett* [1989] QB 811. Cf *R v Home Secretary, ex p Harrison* [1988] 3 All ER 86 where the court dismissed an application for judicial review of the Home Secretary's decision not to make an ex gratia payment of public funds from a non-statutory scheme to a person who had been improperly convicted and imprisoned.
[168] [1995] 2 AC 513; T R S Allan [1995] CLJ 489.
[169] See p 256 above.

'substantially less than the amount he would have received under the old scheme or the statutory scheme'.

The government's decision not to implement the statutory scheme and to introduce under prerogative the tariff scheme was challenged in an application for judicial review. The application succeeded in the House of Lords, which by a majority upheld what was in turn a majority decision of the Court of Appeal. Although under no duty to bring the statute into force, the Home Secretary could not 'lawfully surrender or release the power contained [in the Act] so as to purport to exclude its future exercise'. Nor could the Home Secretary lawfully use the prerogative power to replace the old scheme with the tariff scheme: by introducing the tariff scheme, the Home Secretary had debarred himself from exercising his statutory power for the purposes and on the basis which Parliament intended. The decision to introduce the tariff scheme was an abuse of the prerogative, but this did not involve application of the *De Keyser* principle: since 'the statutory provisions had not been brought into force, they had no legal significance of any kind'.

This decision confirms the present willingness of the courts to examine the legality and propriety of executive decisions, whether the powers in question are derived from statute or from the prerogative powers of the Crown.

The prerogative and the Human Rights Act

The growing willingness of the courts to review the exercise of prerogative powers is reinforced by the enactment of the Human Rights Act 1998 which gives the courts even greater powers of review. Under the Human Rights Act, Orders in Council made under the authority of the royal prerogative are deemed to be primary legislation[170] and must be read and given effect to in a way which is compatible with Convention rights (s 3).[171] Where the terms of such an Order in Council breach Convention rights, the courts are empowered to declare the Order in Council incompatible with Convention rights, although they are bound to continue to apply it until it is revoked or revised (s 4). A more likely source of challenge to the exercise of prerogative powers arises as a result of s 6 of the Human Rights Act 1998, which provides that it is unlawful for a public authority to act in a way which is incompatible with Convention rights. This means that public authorities must exercise any discretionary powers in a manner which is compatible with Convention rights, and they may be restrained by a 'victim' of any breach where they do not. The right to enforce Convention rights against an exercise of prerogative power does not formally depend on the power in question being justiciable. But in view of the fact that many prerogative powers deal with issues such as defence of the realm and national security, it may be expected that the courts would exercise caution in response to any claim under the Human Rights Act.

---

[170] On which see P Billings and B Pontin [2001] PL 21.
[171] For a full account of the Act, see ch 19 C below.

Chapter 13

THE CABINET, GOVERNMENT DEPARTMENTS AND THE CIVIL SERVICE

As organs of government, the Cabinet and the office of Prime Minister have evolved together since the 18th century. Their existence is recognised in occasional statutes (for example, the Ministerial and other Salaries Act 1975) but their powers of government derive neither from statute nor from common law administered in the courts. Parliament could confer powers directly on the Prime Minister or on the Cabinet. In practice this rarely happens, statutory powers being conferred either on named ministers or on the Queen in Council. Yet the Prime Minister and the Cabinet occupy key places at the heart of the political and governmental system.[1] As the Prime Minister provides the individual leadership of the majority party in the House of Commons, so the Cabinet provides the collective leadership of that party.[2] If national affairs are to be directed in any systematic way, if deliberate choices in government between competing political priorities are to be made, these decisions can be made only by the Prime Minister and the Cabinet. In the past, descriptions of the British system of government often labelled it Cabinet government. As L S Amery wrote:

> The central directing instrument of government, in legislation as well as in administration, is the Cabinet. It is in Cabinet that administrative action is co-ordinated and that legislative proposals are sanctioned. It is the Cabinet which controls Parliament and governs the country.[3]

Recently more emphasis has been placed on the role of the Prime Minister and less on the Cabinet itself. In 1963, when he had not yet served as a Cabinet minister, Richard Crossman wrote: 'The post-war epoch has seen the final transformation of Cabinet government into Prime Ministerial government', arguing that the Cabinet had joined the Crown and the House of Lords as one of the 'dignified' elements in the constitution.[4] This judgment appears to have been reinforced in the 1980s when it is claimed that 'members of Mrs Thatcher's Cabinets had allowed the usual forms of Cabinet government to be displaced by imperious prime ministerial rule'.[5] Although Mrs Thatcher's successor as Prime Minister promoted a more consensual approach to policy making,[6] a 'presidential' style of government is associated with Mr Blair.[7] It is claimed that the role of Cabinet as a forum for the discussion of policy has been significantly reduced: meetings are shorter and major decisions are taken by the Prime Minister in consultation with a small group of senior colleagues. There seems

---

[1] Bagehot's celebrated description of the Cabinet in *The English Constitution*, pp 65–9, must still be read, though his definition of the Cabinet as 'a committee of the legislative body selected to be the executive body' is misleading. For general accounts, see Jennings, *Cabinet Government*; Mackintosh, *The British Cabinet*; Gordon Walker, *The Cabinet*; Wilson, *The Governance of Britain*; Hennessy, *Cabinet*; Hennessy, *The Prime Minister*; and James, *British Cabinet Government*.

[2] Gordon Walker, p 56.

[3] *Thoughts on the Constitution*, p 70.

[4] Introduction to Bagehot, pp 51, 54. See also Berkeley, *The Power of the Prime Minister* and Mackintosh, ch 24; cf A H Brown [1968] PL 28, 96.

[5] R Brazier (1991) 54 MLR 471, 476.

[6] Major, *The Autobiography*, p 209.

[7] See Foley, *The British Presidency*.

little doubt that the grip of the Prime Minister has tightened since 1997, but it is also the case that Mr Blair was blessed with a very large parliamentary majority, a well-disciplined government and a relatively united party. A smaller majority in Parliament and internal party division might lead to a rather different style of management, which some Prime Ministers in the future may in any event prefer. Yet, although talk of imperious prime ministerial rule and presidential government is now commonplace, Mrs Thatcher's own experience should serve as a warning to others. As Brazier points out, her removal by her party in 1990 demonstrated that, 'there is clearly a point beyond which a Cabinet will not go in tolerating a Prime Minister who persists in clinging to electorally damaging policies and who sets the whole government's attitude on crucial questions in a fashion which is unsupported by the Cabinet and administration as a whole.'[8]

A. The Prime Minister[9]

The nature of the office

Like the Cabinet, the office of Prime Minister has evolved as a matter of political expediency and constitutional practice rather than of law. Although he did not recognise the title, Robert Walpole is now regarded as having been the first Prime Minister when he was First Lord of the Treasury, from 1721 to 1742. William Pitt the Younger did much to create the modern office of Prime Minister in the years after 1784. In fact the post acquired its present form only with the advent of the modern party system and the creation of the present machinery of government. For most of its history, the office of Prime Minister has been held together with a recognised post, usually that of First Lord of the Treasury. Between 1895 and 1900 Lord Salisbury was both Prime Minister and Foreign Secretary, and between 1900 and 1902 he was Prime Minister and Lord Privy Seal; during these years A J Balfour was First Lord of the Treasury and Leader of the Commons. Since 1902, the offices of Prime Minister and First Lord of the Treasury have always been held together by a member of the Commons.

In 1905, by act of the prerogative, the Prime Minister was given precedence next after the Archbishop of York[10] and the existence of the office is recognised by occasional statutes.[11] Since 1937 statutory provision of a salary and a pension has assumed that the Prime Minister is also First Lord of the Treasury. In the latter capacity, the Prime Minister is one of the Treasury ministers, although the financial and economic duties of the Treasury are borne primarily by the Chancellor of the Exchequer. Exceptionally, the Prime Minister may decide also to hold another office: Ramsay MacDonald was both Prime Minister and Foreign Secretary in the first Labour government in 1924. During the Second World War, Churchill assumed the title of Minister of Defence, although without a separate ministry and without his duties being defined. When the Civil Service Department was established in 1968,[12] the Prime Minister became the minister for the department, although another Cabinet minister undertook the regular administration of the department on the Prime Minister's behalf. The Prime Minister is also minister for the civil service.

---

[8] Brazier, above, p 476. And see G Marshall [1991] PL 1.
[9] For a good account of the office and recent incumbents, see Hennessy, *The Prime Minister*.
[10] *London Gazette*, 5 December 1905.
[11] E.g. Chequers Estate Act 1917; Chevening Estate Act 1959; Ministerial and other Pensions and Salaries Act 1991; and Regulation of Investigatory Powers Act 2000.
[12] The Department was abolished in 1981 and its functions transferred.

The Prime Minister is responsible for the appointment of commissioners to oversee the interception of communications and the work of the intelligence services.[13] The approval of the Prime Minister is also required for appointment of the most senior civil servants. The most important Crown appointments are filled on his or her nomination, for example, the senior judges, the bishops, the chairman of the BBC and the Parliamentary Ombudsman. The Prime Minister also still advises the Sovereign on new peerages,[14] on appointments to the Privy Council and the grant of honours[15] and the filling of those chairs in English universities which are in the gift of the Crown. In these appointments, the Prime Minister's freedom of action may to a greater or lesser extent be restricted by conventions requiring prior consultation with the interests affected. Nonetheless, the Prime Minister's extensive patronage gives rise at least to the possibility that non-political appointments could be used for political purposes.[16]

Powers of the Prime Minister in relation to the Cabinet

Although each Prime Minister must adopt his or her own style of leadership, the Prime Minister is in a position to exercise a dominant influence over the Cabinet, having powers which other ministers do not have, however senior and experienced they may be. A sense of perspective is, however, needed, for the point should not be exaggerated. As one commentator wrote following the removal of Mrs Thatcher, 'a Prime Minister's main political strength comes from the Cabinet and . . . from the parliamentary party'.[17] A Prime Minister who loses the confidence of both will be in a very vulnerable position, even though he or she may be the choice of the electorate. On the other hand, for the following reasons we should not underestimate the political power of the Prime Minister where such confidence does exist:

1   The Prime Minister effectively makes all appointments to ministerial office, whether within or outside the Cabinet. He or she may ask ministers to resign, recommend the Sovereign to dismiss them or, with their consent, move them to other offices. The Prime Minister settles the order of precedence in the Cabinet, and may name one of the Cabinet to be Deputy Prime Minister.[18] In forming his or her first Cabinet, a new Prime Minister will be expected to appoint from the senior members of the party; and a leading politician may be able to stipulate the Cabinet post which he or she is prepared to accept. In the case of the Labour party, the standing orders of the parliamentary party provide that on taking office as Prime Minister, the leader must appoint as members of his Cabinet those who were elected members of the Shadow Cabinet before the general election, provided that they have retained their seats in the new Parliament. Although there are no similar constraints on Conservative leaders, they too will normally rely on an established team when assuming the responsibilities of office.[19] But as the tenure of the Prime Minister extends, constraints of this kind will begin to wane: only nine members of Mr Blair's first Cabinet (including Mr Blair himself) were still Cabinet ministers in 2001.

---

[13] Regulation of Investigatory Powers Act 2000, ss 57, 59. For details, see ch 25.
[14] See ch 9 H.
[15] Some honours are granted on the advice of other ministers, e.g. the Foreign Secretary and the Defence Secretary. Some appointments are made on the recommendation of other ministers, e.g. High Court judgeships on the recommendation of the Lord Chancellor.
[16] Cf T Benn (1980) 33 Parliamentary Affairs 7.
[17] R Brazier (1991) 54 MLR 471, 477. For an assessment of the relationship between Prime Ministers and their Cabinets, see S James (1994) 47 Parliamentary Affairs 613, and Hennessy, *The Prime Minister*.
[18] In 1951, George VI refused to appoint Eden to this 'non-existent' office: Wheeler-Bennett, *King George VI*, p 797. But see Brazier *Constitutional Practice*, pp 78–81.
[19] See Brazier, ibid, pp 61–7.

2   The Prime Minister controls the machinery of central government in that he or she decides how the tasks of government should be allocated to departments and whether departments should be created, amalgamated or abolished. In 2001 a major reorganisation was undertaken by Mr Blair, with the abolition of three departments (Agriculture; Education and Employment; and Social Security), and their replacement with new departments for Environment, Food and Rural Affairs; Education and Skills; and Work and Pensions respectively.[20] The Prime Minister may take an interest in different areas of government from time to time and may indeed carry out policy in close co-operation with a minister whom he or she has appointed. Most Prime Ministers must take a special interest in foreign affairs, the economy and defence. The Prime Minister may intervene personally in crises, such as the foot and mouth epidemic which swept the UK in 2001. In consultation with individual ministers, he or she may take decisions or authorise them to be taken without waiting for a Cabinet meeting. When a Cabinet committee is dealing with a problem, the Prime Minister may take the chair and report on action taken to a later Cabinet meeting.

3   By presiding at Cabinet meetings, the Prime Minister is able to control Cabinet discussions and the process of decision-making by settling the order of business, deciding which items are to be discussed,[21] and by taking the sense of the meeting rather than by counting the votes of Cabinet members. While the Cabinet Secretariat provides services for the whole Cabinet, it owes a special responsibility to the Prime Minister, who, if necessary, settles disputes over the minutes. Lord Wilson has said, 'the writing of the Conclusions is a unique responsibility of the Secretary of the Cabinet . . . The Conclusions are circulated very promptly after Cabinet, and up to that time, no minister, certainly not the Prime Minister, asks to see them or conditions them in any way.'[22] By way of contrast, Mr Michael Heseltine was concerned about the minutes of a Cabinet meeting before his resignation in 1986, in particular the failure to record his protest about the Prime Minister's refusal to allow discussion on competing plans to rescue Westland, a helicopter manufacturing company.[23]

4   The doctrine of collective responsibility helps to reinforce the powers of the Prime Minister. The effect of the doctrine is that ministers must not criticise government policy in public and if necessary must be prepared to defend it. This means that if the firm hand of the Prime Minister is guiding that policy, there will be no public criticism from the most influential and informed people in the government. The importance of the doctrine for silencing potential criticism is underlined by the fact that many decisions of government are not taken by the Cabinet as a whole, but by the Prime Minister in consultation with a few key colleagues. This was true, for example, of an important decision such as transferring to the Bank of England in 1997 the responsibility for the setting of interest rates.[24] On one interpretation of the events, it was the attempt to control Cabinet colleagues by the doctrine of collective responsibility for decisions which had not been taken by the Cabinet which led to Mr Heseltine's resignation as Secretary of State for Defence in January 1986.

---

[20] Other departments had some of their responsibilities redistributed: one example is the Home Office which lost constitutional reform to an expanded Lord Chancellor's Department and electoral law to the Department for Transport, Local Government and the Regions.

[21] Mackintosh, p 449, asserts that the Prime Minister can keep any item off the agenda indefinitely but the examples he gives do not support this. Cf Wilson, p 47.

[22] Wilson, p 56.

[23] Cf the *Ministerial Code*, which provides that 'The Cabinet Office are instructed to avoid, so far as practicable, recording the opinions expressed by particular Ministers' (para 13).

[24] See Hennessy, *The Prime Minister*, pp 480–1.

5   Compared to other ministers, the Prime Minister has a more regular opportunity to present and defend the government's policies in Parliament and elsewhere.[25] He or she is available for questioning in the Commons on Wednesdays and may choose when to intervene in debates.[26] The Prime Minister is also in a position to control the government's communications to the press and to disclose information about government decisions and Cabinet business.[27] Alone among Cabinet ministers, he or she has regular meetings with the Sovereign and is responsible for keeping the Sovereign informed of the Cabinet's handling of affairs. In particular, he or she may recommend to the Sovereign that a general election be held and in doing so is not required to discuss this first with the Cabinet.[28] It is sometimes argued that the threat of a dissolution is a device whereby a Prime Minister may exercise authority over colleagues in government and Parliament. But this may not always be an option. Why would a Prime Minister wish to recommend that a general election be called if the party were weakened by internal dissension, particularly when the dissidents may not be among those most likely to lose their seats?

B. The Cabinet

Composition of the Cabinet

A modern Cabinet usually consists of 22 members (including the Prime Minister). No statute regulates the composition of the Cabinet, but there are both administrative and political constraints on the Prime Minister's freedom of choice. Thus in peacetime it is impossible to exclude certain offices, such as the Home Secretary, the Foreign Secretary, the Lord Chancellor and the Chancellor of the Exchequer. In addition to the Secretaries of State and ministers in charge of the major departments, every Cabinet includes two or three members with few if any departmental responsibilities, for example, the Lord President of the Council, also Leader of the House of Commons; the Lord Privy Seal, also Leader of the House of Lords; and a Minister without Portfolio with responsibility for Party rather than government affairs. Since 1951 the government chief whip in the Commons, whose formal title is Parliamentary Secretary to the Treasury, has regularly attended Cabinet and is now a member of it; the chief whip in the Lords attends Cabinet but is not a member. The Law Officers of the Crown[29] are not appointed to the Cabinet but, like other ministers outside the Cabinet, the Attorney-General may attend Cabinet meetings for particular matters.

The size of the Cabinet is primarily determined by practical and political considerations. But the number of salaried Cabinet posts is limited by statute: apart from the Prime Minister and the Lord Chancellor, not more than 20 salaries may be paid to Cabinet ministers at one time.[30] Political necessity requires that all members of the Cabinet are members of the Commons or the Lords, unless a minister is actively seeking election to the Commons at a by-election or is to be created a life peer.[31] In practice at least

---

[25] But see P Dunleavy, G W Jones et al. (1993) 23 British Journal of Political Science 267 on the declining accountability of the Prime Minister to Parliament. This is a process which has continued since 1997.

[26] Prime Ministers were previously available for questioning twice a week (Tuesdays and Thursdays). On Prime Minister's question time, see R K Alderman (1992) 45 Parliamentary Affairs 66.

[27] See Margach, *The Abuse of Power*.

[28] Ch 12 B.

[29] Ch 18 E.

[30] Ministerial and other Salaries Act 1975. See ch 9 G.

[31] Ch 2 B.

two Cabinet offices (Lord Chancellor and Leader of the House of Lords) will be held by peers but more may be appointed. In all modern governments there have been some ministers with departmental responsibilities who are outside the Cabinet. They may serve on Cabinet committees, will see Cabinet papers relating to their departments, and may be asked to attend Cabinet meetings. The amalgamation of departments to form larger departments which took place during the 1960s[32] meant that all major departments were placed under the supervision of a Cabinet minister and this continues to be the case. In wartime the normal Cabinet may be superseded by a small War Cabinet to take charge of the conduct of the war. In 1916 the War Cabinet consisted of five, later six, senior ministers, of whom only the Chancellor of the Exchequer had departmental duties. The War Cabinet of 1939–45 was larger, varying between seven and ten, including several senior departmental ministers.[33]

Cabinet committees[34]

The increase in the scale of government since 1900 has not been accompanied by a corresponding increase in the size of the Cabinet. Few problems of government can be solved by a single department acting on its own, if only because most policy decisions have expenditure and personnel implications (hence the interest of the Treasury in all new policies). The Cabinet could not have kept abreast of its work had there not developed under its umbrella a complicated structure of committees. In the 19th century, Cabinet committees were appointed for particular purposes (for example, to keep under review the conduct of the Crimean War). They were used much more frequently after 1918. Two main factors led to the appointment of a system of permanent committees. The first was the creation of the Committee of Imperial Defence in 1903, which showed the value of a permanent committee charged with a major policy area;[35] the second was the experience in two world wars of a system of specialised committees to deal with defined policy areas which operated under the authority of a small War Cabinet. In 1945, the Labour government decided to adapt the wartime system to the problems of peace. Since then, a structure of standing committees has remained an important feature of the Cabinet system.

An account of the Cabinet committee system is provided in the *Ministerial Code*, which contains the rules governing Cabinet ministers. The Code states that Cabinet committees have two purposes. The first is to relieve pressure on the Cabinet itself by settling as much business as possible at lower level; and the second is to 'support the principle of collective responsibility by ensuring that, even though an important question may never reach the Cabinet itself, the decision will be fully considered and the final judgment will be sufficiently authoritative to ensure that the Government as a whole can be properly expected to accept responsibility for it'.[36] It is thus clear that decisions reached by Cabinet committees are 'binding on all members of the Government', although they are 'normally announced and explained as the decision of the Minister concerned'. Because of the doctrine of collective responsibility, 'the privacy of opinions' expressed in Cabinet committee, as in the Cabinet itself, should be maintained.[37] Details of the Cabinet Committee structure are now published on the Cabinet Office website.

---

[32] Section C.
[33] For the War Cabinet, see 8th edn of this book, 1970, pp 201, 203–7; Jennings, ch 10; and Mackintosh, ch 14 and pp 490–9.
[34] Jennings, pp 255–61; Mackintosh, pp 521–9; Gordon Walker, pp 38–47; Wilson, pp 62–8.
[35] Jennings, ch 10.
[36] The *Ministerial Code*, para 4.
[37] Ibid, paras 16–17.

This reveals 44 ministerial committees dealing with a wide range of matters in four categories: economic and domestic, constitution, defence and overseas, and Europe. By far the largest category is the first. In addition to the ministerial committees, there are also official committees (of civil servants) to investigate issues, assemble material and present options for ministerial decisions.[38]

The Cabinet Office[39]

In 1917, to enable the War Cabinet and its system of committees to function efficiently, a Secretary to the Cabinet was appointed to be present at meetings of the Cabinet and its committees, to circulate minutes of the conclusions reached, to communicate decisions rapidly to those who had to act on them and also to circulate papers before meetings. Today the Secretary of the Cabinet is also Head of the Home Civil Service. The conclusions prepared by the Secretary to the Cabinet and circulated to the Sovereign and Cabinet ministers are the only official record of Cabinet meetings. This account is designed to record agreement and not controversy. Differences of opinion in discussion are not attributed to individuals, although the arguments for and against a decision may be summarised: 'behind many of the decisions lay tensions and influences which are not reflected in the official records.'[40] However, if a minister expressly wishes his or her dissent to be recorded, then this will be done.[41] The Cabinet Secretary is based in the Cabinet Office which plays a key role at the heart of government. The Cabinet Office is a department with 1,600 core staff, its primary responsibility being to coordinate the work of different government departments – to ensure that the government's programme is implemented. Day-to-day direction of the department is led by the Deputy Prime Minister, but the Cabinet Office reports to the Prime Minister as head of the government and Minister for the Civil Service.[42]

There are several different secretariats within the Cabinet Office, each with different areas of responsibility, as well as a number of units which have been established to tackle issues which cut across departmental boundaries. These include the social exclusion unit, the performance and innovation unit, the women's unit, and the anti-drugs coordination unit. The Cabinet Office – which also has responsibility for the programme of civil service reform – continues to grow and strengthen and is thought to be the Prime Minister's Department 'in all but name'. But although expanding the Cabinet Office, Mr Blair has resisted formally setting up such a department 'in order to avoid charges of presidentialism'.[43] In addition to the growing responsibilities of the Cabinet Office (which is located in Whitehall very close to Downing Street), a new administrative framework introduced in No 10 Downing Street after the June 2001 general election is said to be 'similar to the White House'. There had previously been a Downing Street policy unit which had been established by Mr Wilson in 1974, retained and strengthened by his successors.[44] The unit was absorbed into the new arrangements

---

[38] See Hennessy, *Cabinet*, pp 26–31.

[39] Jennings, pp 242–5; Gordon Walker, pp 47–55; Mosley, *The Story of the Cabinet Office*; Wilson, *The Cabinet Office to 1945*.

[40] Wilson, *The Cabinet Office to 1945*, p 4. At p 142 are printed instructions on minute-taking current in 1936. Crossman's comment 30 years later was that the minutes 'do not pretend to be an account of what actually takes place in the Cabinet' (p 198).

[41] It was the alleged failure to follow this convention which added to the drama surrounding the resignation of Mr Michael Heseltine in the so-called Westland affair in 1986.

[42] See Cabinet Office, *An Introduction to the Cabinet Office*, http://www.cabinet-office.gov.uk/organisation/introleaflet.htm.

[43] *The Times*, 13 June 2001.

[44] See D Willetts (1987) 65 Public Administration 443.

introduced in 2001 following its merger with the Prime Minister's Private Office and the introduction of a new 'tripartite' structure. This is part of a determined desire to strengthen the centre of government, ostensibly to concentrate 'relentlessly on delivery'. There is now in Downing Street a government and policy section (which includes the old policy unit), a communications and strategy section, and a government relations section to oversee relations with ministers, the devolved administrations, the Labour party and others.

Cabinet secrecy

The operation of the Cabinet system is surrounded by considerable secrecy.[45] Most Cabinet papers are made available for public inspection in the Public Record Office after 30 years or such other period as the Lord Chancellor may direct.[46] Many Cabinet decisions are notified to Parliament or otherwise made public, but the doctrine of collective responsibility throws a heavy veil over decision-making in Cabinet. It is inevitable that ministers often disagree as to the right course of action before a decision is made. One justification for Cabinet secrecy commonly supported by those with experience of the system is the view that anything which damages the collective unity and integrity of the Cabinet damages the good government of the country.[47] Certainly the public interest in national security requires that some information about defence and external relations must be kept secret by those in government. But the 'good government' argument goes very much further than national security since it seeks to preserve the process of decision-making within government from scrutiny by those outside. Some critics argue, to the contrary, that 'good government' in a democracy requires that more light be thrown on political decision-making and that government be more open. In fact the media frequently contain speculation about the Cabinet's deliberations, some of which may be based on unauthorised disclosures of Cabinet proceedings by ministers who wish to make their points of view known.

One important practice is that the ministers in one government do not have access to the papers of an earlier government of a different political party. On a change of government the outgoing Prime Minister issues special instructions about the disposal of the Cabinet papers of the outgoing administration. The practice applies to papers of the Cabinet and ministerial committees, as well as departmental papers that contain the private views of ministers and advice given by officials. The main reason for the practice is to prevent a minister from one party having access to 'matters that the previous administration had been most anxious to keep quiet'.[48] Former ministers retain the right of access to documents that they saw in office. Before access to Cabinet papers or other ministerial documents of a former government can be given to third persons, the present Prime Minister must seek the agreement of the former Prime Minister concerned or the current leader of his or her party. Thus, when a committee of privy councillors was appointed to review British policy towards the Falkland Islands before the Argentine invasion, five former Prime Ministers agreed to the relevant documents being seen by the committee.[49] Ministers relinquishing office without a change of government 'should hand over to their successors those Cabinet documents required for the current administration and should ensure that all others have been destroyed'.[50]

---

[45] Williams, *Not in the Public Interest*, ch 2; Gordon Walker, pp 26–33, 164–8; Report on Section 2 of Official Secrets Act 1911, Cmnd 5104, 1972, ch 11; Report on Ministerial Memoirs, Cmnd 6386, 1976.
[46] Public Records Act 1958, s 5 (amended by Public Records Act 1967).
[47] Cmnd 5104, 1972, p 68.
[48] HC Deb, 8 July 1982, col 474 (Mr M Foot).
[49] HC Deb, 1 July 1982, col 1039; 8 July 1982, col 469. See Lord Hunt [1982] PL 514.
[50] *Ministerial Code*, para 19. And see R Brazier [1996] CLJ 65, on the sale of the Churchill papers in 1995.

Cabinet secrecy and the courts

In law, Cabinet documents are protected to some extent from production as evidence in litigation by public interest immunity which authorises non-disclosure of documents which it would be injurious to the public interest to disclose[51] and from examination by the Parliamentary Ombudsman;[52] they may also be protected by the Official Secrets Acts[53] and be exempt from disclosure under the Freedom of Information Act 2000 when it is brought into force.[54] Political sanctions also operate: a serving Cabinet minister would be liable to lose office if he or she could be shown improperly to have revealed the details of Cabinet discussions. But is a former Cabinet minister, who may be subject to no political sanction, under a legal obligation not to reveal such secrets? The question arose for decision in *Attorney-General* v *Jonathan Cape Ltd*.[55]

> Richard Crossman kept a political diary between 1964 and 1970 while a Labour Cabinet minister. After his death in 1974, his diary for 1964–66 was edited for publication and, as was customary, submitted to the Secretary to the Cabinet. He refused to consent to publication, since the diary contained detailed accounts of Cabinet discussions, reports of the advice given to ministers by civil servants and comments about the suitability of senior civil servants for promotion. When Crossman's literary executors decided to publish the diary, the Attorney-General sought an injunction to stop them. Lord Widgery CJ held that the court had power to restrain the improper publication of information which had been received by a Cabinet minister in confidence, and that the doctrine of collective responsibility justified the court in restraining the disclosures of Cabinet discussions; but that the court should act only where continuing confidentiality of the material could clearly be shown. On the facts, he held that publication in 1975 of Cabinet discussions during the period 1964–66 should not be restrained. In this decision, no reliance was placed either upon the Privy Councillor's oath of secrecy or upon the Official Secrets Acts.

This decision established the power of the court to restrain publication of Cabinet secrets but gave no clear guidance as to when the power should be exercised. The problems of memoirs of ex-Cabinet ministers were subsequently considered by a committee of Privy Councillors.[56] The committee distinguished between secret information relating to national security and international relations, on which an ex-minister must accept the decision of the Cabinet Secretary, and other confidential material about relationships between ministers or between ministers and civil servants. In the latter case there should be no publication within 15 years, except with clearance from the Cabinet Secretary, but in the event of a dispute it must in the last resort be for ex-ministers themselves to decide what to publish. Advice given by a civil servant to a minister should not be revealed while the adviser is still a civil servant. The committee recommended against legislation, preferring to suggest a clear working procedure which would be brought to the attention of every minister on assuming office. The committee's recommendations were accepted by the government in 1976 and have been maintained by subsequent governments. There has since been a spate of ministerial memoirs.[57]

---

[51] Ch 32 C. On the relationship between the Cabinet and the courts, see M C Harris [1989] PL 251.
[52] Parliamentary Commissioner Act 1967, s 8(4); ch 29 D.
[53] Ch 25.
[54] Ch 13 E.
[55] [1976] QB 752; Young, *The Crossman Affair*.
[56] Cmnd 6386, 1976 (Radcliffe Report).
[57] The *Ministerial Code* requires former ministers to submit their manuscript to the Cabinet Secretary and to conform to the principles set out in the Radcliffe Report.

C. Ministers and departments

Ministerial offices

Some ministerial offices have a much longer history than the office of Prime Minister, others have been created more recently. The office of Lord Chancellor goes back to the reign of Edward the Confessor and was of great political and judicial significance for several centuries after the Norman conquest. The office of Lord Privy Seal dates from the 14th century and in a later period was often held by leading statesmen; but the historic duties in respect of the Privy Seal were abolished in 1884 and the office now carries no departmental responsibilities. The office of Lord President of the Council was created in 1497 and became important during the period of government through the Council under the Stuarts. The office of Secretary of State has almost as long a history, acquiring its political significance in the Tudor period, particularly during the tenure of the Cecils under Elizabeth I. It came to be recognised as the means by which communications could take place between citizen and Sovereign.[58] From the 17th century, two and sometimes three Secretaries of State were appointed who divided national and foreign affairs between them.

In 1782 a different division of functions vested in one Secretary of State responsibility for domestic affairs and the colonies and in the other Secretary responsibility for foreign affairs. Thus were created the offices of Home Secretary and Foreign Secretary. In 1794 a Secretary of State for War was appointed and thereafter, from time to time, additional Secretaryships (for example, for the colonies, for India, for Scotland) were created and abolished as need arose. In 2001 there were 15 Secretaries of State who between them headed nearly all the major departments. When statutory powers are conferred on a Secretary of State, it is usual for the statute to designate him or her as 'the Secretary of State' but it will be obvious from the context which Secretary of State is intended to exercise the new functions.[59] In law the duties of Secretaries of State are interchangeable, but in practice each Secretary's functions are limited to those related to his or her own department. One Secretary of State may be named by the Prime Minister as First Secretary; while this makes no legal difference to the office, it determines precedence in the Cabinet and the First Secretary may deputise for the Prime Minister in the latter's absence. In 2001 the position as First Secretary of State was combined with the office of Deputy Prime Minister.

Government departments

While the term 'government department' has no precise meaning in law, it usually refers to those branches of the central administration which are staffed by civil servants, paid for out of exchequer funds and headed by a minister responsible to Parliament. A single minister may be responsible for more than one department: thus the Chancellor of the Exchequer is responsible for the Treasury and the two revenue departments (Inland Revenue; and Customs and Excise), as well as the Office of Government Commerce which was established in 2000. Exceptionally, there are departments which for constitutional reasons do not have a ministerial head: thus the National Audit Office is headed by the Comptroller and Auditor-General.[60] For the purposes of legal proceedings against the Crown, a list of departments is maintained under the Crown Proceedings Act 1947.[61]

---

[58] For the history of the Secretaries of State, see Anson, *The Law and Custom of the Constitution*, vol II, i, pp 172–84.

[59] By the Interpretation Act 1978, unless the contrary intention appears, 'Secretary of State' means 'one of Her Majesty's Principal Secretaries of State'. See *Agee v Lord Advocate* 1977 SLT (Notes) 54.

[60] Ch 17 D.

[61] Ch 32 C.

For the purposes of investigation by the Parliamentary Ombudsman, a statutory list of departments is maintained and this is revised as new departments are established.[62] There are many public bodies with governmental functions which are not regarded as government departments. They include local authorities; regulatory bodies such as the Commission for Racial Equality and the Equal Opportunities Commission; grant-giving bodies such as the Arts Councils and the Higher Education Funding Council; advisory councils and committees, such as the Council on Tribunals, and other bodies which may report to ministers but are not directly controlled by them (for example, the English and Scottish Law Commissions).[63] Often such bodies are financed from central Exchequer funds.[64]

To enable changes in the structure of government to be carried out quickly, there have been statutory powers since 1946 by which new needs can be met without recourse to Acts of Parliament. The Ministers of the Crown Act 1975 now authorises the Crown, by Order in Council, to transfer to any minister functions previously exercised by another minister; to provide for the dissolution of a government department and for the transfer to other departments of the functions previously exercised by that department; and to direct that functions shall be exercised concurrently by two ministers. Consequential steps may also be authorised, such as the transfer of property from one department to another and changes in the title of ministers. Orders in Council under the 1975 Act are subject to parliamentary scrutiny. The powers conferred by the 1975 Act are in addition to the Crown's prerogative powers, which may still be exercised to make some governmental changes.[65] Although the Foreign and Commonwealth Office, the Department of Trade and Industry and the Ministry of Defence have remained intact since 1970, there are many changes elsewhere. Most recently new departments have been created for Transport, Local Government and the Regions; and the Environment, Food and Rural Affairs. There are also now separate departments for Health on the one hand and Work and Pensions on the other. Departmental structure will continue to change in response to political judgments made by Prime Ministers and in response to the changing political circumstances of contemporary government.

Ministers of the Crown[66]

According to one statutory definition, minister of the Crown means 'the holder of any office in Her Majesty's Government in the United Kingdom, and includes the Treasury . . . and the Defence Council'.[67] In a less technical sense, ministers are those members or supporters of the party in power who hold political office in the government. They are all appointed by the Crown on the advice of the Prime Minister and their offices are at the disposal of an incoming Prime Minister. They do not include members of the civil service or the armed forces, who continue in office despite a change of government; or special advisers to ministers, who may be paid salaries and are temporarily attached to departments but who lose their position when a minister leaves office; or members of public boards, regulatory bodies and so on. Unlike many of these other office-holders, ministers are not disqualified from membership of the House of

---

[62] Ch 29 D.

[63] See the government publication, *Public Bodies*; and ch 14 B.

[64] See also the peculiar position of the public utility regulators: ch 14 C.

[65] 1975 Act, s 5; see above, p 262; and The Secretaries of State for Transport, Local Government and the Regions and for Environment, Food and Rural Affairs Order 2001, SI 2001, No 2568; and the Transfer of Functions (Miscellaneous) Order 2001, SI 2001 No 3500 (transferring human rights and data protection from the Home Secretary to the Lord Chancellor). There have been many applications of this power.

[66] See Brazier, *Ministers of the Crown*, for a full account.

[67] Ministers of the Crown Act 1975, s 8(1).

Commons. Indeed it is a convention that ministerial office-holders should be members of one or other House of Parliament. Such membership is essential to the maintenance of ministerial responsibility. There is, however, no law that a minister must be in Parliament. But if a Prime Minister wishes to appoint to ministerial office someone who is not already in Parliament, it will be necessary for a life peerage to be conferred on the individual in question.

There are various grades of ministerial appointment today, but they may be grouped into three broad categories: (a) Cabinet ministers, who may or may not have departmental responsibilities; (b) departmental ministers and ministers of state who are outside the Cabinet, the duty of a minister of state being to share in the administration of a department headed by a Cabinet minister; and (c) parliamentary secretaries, whose duty it is to assist in the parliamentary work of a department and who may also have some administrative responsibility. The two Law Officers of the Crown for England and Wales are within category (b) but the government whips, who have no departmental responsibilities, may be allotted among the categories according to their status and seniority. By exercise of the prerogative, new posts in the Crown's service can be created, for example, extra Secretaries of State. But when a new ministry is formed, there is often secondary legislation to create the minister a corporation sole, thus giving him or her legal capacity, and providing in broad terms for his or her functions.[68] There are no legal limits on the number of ministers which the Crown may appoint, assuming that they are not to receive a salary and do not sit in the House of Commons, but as already pointed out there are statutory limits on the number of ministers who may be members of the Commons and on the number of salaries payable to holders of ministerial office.[69] Ministerial salaries are now governed by a formula set out in the Ministerial and Other Salaries Act 1975, as amended by the Ministerial and Other Salaries Act 1997.[70]

The *Ministerial Code*

The conduct of ministers is governed by the *Ministerial Code*. This was first compiled by Attlee in 1945, although some of its provisions go back further.[71] It deals with a range of matters relating to the relationship between ministers and the government, Parliament and the civil service. It also deals with ministers' private interests. Previously known as *Questions of Procedure for Ministers* (QPM), the Code was first made public by Mr Major in 1992 and was revised following the recommendations of the Committee on Standards in Public Life,[72] before being reissued by Mr Blair in 1997.[73] Section 1 reminds ministers that they are 'expected to behave according to the highest standards of constitutional and personal conduct in the performance of their duties'. In particular, they are required to observe the nine principles of ministerial conduct that are set out in the Code. These include a duty to uphold the principle of collective responsibility; a requirement to account for the activities of their departments and executive agencies; and an obligation to 'give accurate and truthful information to

---

[68] E.g. SI 2001 No 2568, note 65 above.

[69] Ch 9 G.

[70] The salary of the Lord Chancellor is governed by the Ministerial and other Pensions and Salaries Act 1991, by which his salary is '£2,000 a year more than the salary for the time being payable to the Lord Chief Justice' (s 3).

[71] HC 235 (2000–01).

[72] Cm 2850-I, 1995.

[73] The Code is set out in full at http://www.cabinet-office.gov.uk/central/1997/mcode. Section 1 is reproduced in the Sixth Report of the Committee on Standards in Public Life, Reinforcing Standards, Cm 4557-I, 2000, App VI.

Parliament, correcting any inadvertent error at the earliest opportunity'. Ministers who 'knowingly mislead Parliament will be expected to offer their resignation to the Prime Minister'. There are those who feel that the word 'knowingly' should be removed from the text.[74]

In addition to the duty not to mislead Parliament, the Code also advises ministers of the need to be 'as open as possible with Parliament and the public, refusing to provide information only when disclosure would not be in the public interest'. This should be determined in accordance with relevant statutes (which are not specified) and the Code of Practice on Access to Government Information (which is to be superseded by the Freedom of Information Act 2000). One of the other key principles provides that ministers should require civil servants who give evidence before Select Committees 'on their behalf and under their direction', to be as 'helpful as possible in providing accurate, truthful and full information in accordance with the duties and responsibilities of civil servants as set out in the Civil Service Code'. Other principles in the Code deal with ministerial conflicts of interest (on which see below) and a prohibition on using government resources for party political purposes. Ministers are also required to uphold the political impartiality of the civil service, and they are reminded of their responsibility 'for justifying their conduct to Parliament' and perhaps ominously that 'they can remain in office only for so long as they retain the Prime Minister's confidence'. The Code is 'not a legal document but a set of guidelines', although now 'an integral part of the new constitutional architecture'.[75]

Financial interests of ministers

Because of their office, many ministers take decisions which have a direct financial effect on particular businesses, sections of industry and land values. They also have access to confidential information about future decisions which could be put to financial profit. The Marconi affair of 1912 involved three leading members of the Liberal government who were alleged to have made use of secret information about an impending government contract to make an investment in Marconi shares: an inquiry by a parliamentary committee established that they had bought shares not in the company to which the contract was about to be awarded, but in a sister company.[76] In 1948 the Lynskey Tribunal of Inquiry reported on allegations that ministers and other public servants had been bribed in connection with the grant of licences by the Board of Trade; a junior minister, who later resigned from Parliament, was found to have received presents of wine and spirits and other gifts, knowing that they had been made to secure favourable treatment by the department of applications for licences.[77] While such conduct could give rise to criminal proceedings, additional safeguards are required if ministers are to avoid suspicion.

In 1952 the rules then in force were published in a parliamentary written answer.[78] They still remain in operation, although they have been amended and are now to be found in the *Ministerial Code*.[79] The overriding principle is that ministers must ensure that no conflict arises, or appears to arise, between their private interests and their public duties. This conflict could arise if a minister took any active part or had a financial interest in any undertaking which had contractual or other relations (for example,

[74] See A Tomkins [1996] PL 484. Cf HC 115 (1995–96), para K8.5.
[75] HC 235 (2000–01), para 15.
[76] See Donaldson, *The Marconi Scandal*.
[77] Cmd 7616, 1949.
[78] HC Deb, 25 February 1952, col 701; and 20 March 1980, col 293 (WA).
[79] Paras 113–40.

receiving a licence or a subsidy) with his or her department. Under the current rules in force, ministers should, on assuming office, resign any directorships which they hold and should dispose of controlling interests in any company which could give rise to a conflict of interest. In cases of doubt, for example as to the propriety of retaining certain shares in a company, the Prime Minister must be informed and is the final judge. Ministers are also reminded by the Code of legal obligations relating to conflicts of interest. These are said to be the rule against bias in administrative law (where the 'courts interpret conflict of interest increasingly tightly') and the Criminal Justice Act 1993, Part V, which relates to 'the use or transmission of unpublished price-sensitive information' obtained by ministers by virtue of their ministerial office. The *Ministerial Code* now provides that on leaving office ministers should seek advice from the Advisory Committee on Business Appointments about any appointments they wish to take up within two years of leaving office, other than unpaid appointments in non-commercial organisations or 'appointments in the gift of the government, such as Prime Ministerial appointments to international organisations'.[80]

D. Civil service: organisation and accountability

What is a civil servant?

The departments of central government are staffed by administrative, professional, technical and other officials who constitute the civil service. Civil servants perform many functions, from the development to the implementation of government policy. It has been said to be 'common ground that the civil service defies an easy universally applicable definition' and that 'a civil servant has no specific legal status'. A civil servant has been defined as 'a servant of the Crown working in a civil capacity who is not: the holder of a political (or judicial) office; the holder of certain other offices in respect of whose tenure of office special provision has been made; a servant of the Crown in a personal capacity paid from the Civil List'.[81] This definition excludes ministers of the Crown, members of the armed forces (who are Crown servants but are not employed in a civil capacity), the police and those employed in local government and the National Health Service, even though they are all engaged in public services. A somewhat similar definition is contained in s 2(6) of the Crown Proceedings Act 1947, which limits proceedings against the Crown in tort (or in Scots law, delict) to the act, neglect or default of an officer who 'has been directly or indirectly appointed by the Crown and was at the material time paid in respect of his duties as an officer of the Crown' wholly out of the national exchequer.[82] Whatever the precise legal nature of the civil servant's relationship with the Crown, it is an important constitutional principle that those concerned with the administration of government departments should, in fact, enjoy a tenure of office by which they may serve successive ministers of different political parties. Particularly since 1979, the size, expense and organisation of the civil service have become a matter of political controversy. But without the service, the achievements of modern government would have been impossible.

There are now approximately 450,000 civil servants. As far as their employment position is concerned, there is a sharp contrast between legal doctrine and practical reality. It is true that although civil servants traditionally have been regarded as appointed under the royal prerogative, the courts have recently recognised that they

---

[80] Ibid, para 129.
[81] HC 390–II (1992–93), p 261.
[82] Ch 32 A.

may have terms of service 'which are contractually enforceable'.[83] Nevertheless, the courts seem unwilling to challenge the traditional rule that civil servants are employed at the pleasure of the Crown, which means that they may be dismissed with no common law remedy for wrongful dismissal.[84] So if civil servants are to be regarded as being employed under a contract, its terms will be limited by the prerogative power of the Crown to dismiss without notice for any reason. Civil servants are deemed by statute to be employed under contracts of service for some employment protection purposes and will normally be able to bring an action for unfair dismissal.[85] There are also internal procedures which apply in the event of dismissal, with a final appeal to the Civil Service Appeals Board which is independent of the departments concerned. The decisions of the Board are subject to judicial review.[86]

Civil service structure

The structure of the civil service has undergone a great deal of change since the 1980s, reflecting growing Treasury concerns about cost and efficiency.[87] The starting point is the publication in 1988 of a report to the Prime Minister drawn up by Sir Robin Ibbs, entitled *Improving Management in Government: The Next Steps*.[88] This is the most far-reaching and fundamental review of the civil service since 1968 and has led to the most radical changes since 1854.[89] The report expressed concern that the civil service (then with over 600,000 staff) was too big and too diverse to be managed as a single organisation and that attempts should be made to establish a different way of conducting the business of government. It was suggested that the central civil service should consist of a relatively small core engaged in the function of servicing ministers and managing departments which would be the main sponsors of particular government policies and services. Responding to these departments would be a range of agencies employing their own staff, concentrating on the delivery of their particular service with responsibilities clearly defined between the Secretary of State and the permanent secretary, on the one hand, and the chairman and chief executive of the agencies, on the other.[90] These proposals reflected a perceived need to give greater priority to organising government so that its service delivery operations function effectively.

The proposals were largely accepted by the government and by 2000 137 agencies had been created (accounting for some 80% of the civil service), with another 12 on the way (covering another 7,000 civil servants). Spanning a wide range and diversity of functions, they vary enormously in size, from the National Weights and Measures Laboratory (45 staff) to the Employment Service (45,000 staff). Each agency has a defined task, or range of tasks, which are set out in its published framework document. In addition, 'key performance targets – covering financial performance, efficiency and

---

[83] *McLaren v Home Office* [1990] IRLR 338, 341; *R v Lord Chancellor's Department, ex p Nangle* [1992] 1 All ER 897. And see S Fredman and G Morris [1991] PL 485; and ch 32 B.

[84] *Dunn v R* [1896] 1 QB 116; *Riordan v War Office* [1959] 1 WLR 1046. And see ch 32 B.

[85] Employment Rights Act 1996, s 191.

[86] See *R v Civil Service Appeal Board, ex p Bruce* [1988] 3 All ER 686; *R v Civil Service Appeal Board, ex p Cunningham* [1991] 4 All ER 310.

[87] For a full and comprehensive account, see HL 55 (1998). See also G Drewry, in Jowell and Oliver (eds), *The Changing Constitution*, ch 7.

[88] The report had been commissioned in 1986. For the reaction to it, see Hennessy, *Whitehall*, pp 620–1, and Lawson, *The View from No 11*, pp 391–3. See also Woodhouse, *Ministers and Parliament*, chs 11, 12.

[89] See respectively Cmnd 3638, 1968 (Fulton Committee) and Northcote–Trevelyan Report (reprinted in app B of the Fulton Report).

[90] For the previous consideration of this option with reference particularly to Sweden, see Cmnd 3638, 1968, paras 188–91.

service to the customer – are set out by ministers annually. Each agency has a chief executive, normally directly accountable to ministers and with personal responsibility for the success of the agency in meeting its targets.'[91] Alongside the delegation of tasks to the agencies has been the delegation to the agencies and departments of responsibility for the pay and working conditions of staff. The process of delegation in the setting of working conditions (with an emphasis on performance-related incentives) was facilitated by the Civil Service (Management of Functions) Act 1992. In 1996 the long-established central pay bargaining arrangements were entirely replaced by a system which delegated to the departments and agencies the authority to make their own pay arrangements, 'albeit within the overall Treasury limits on running costs'.[92] Further steps in the direction of pay decentralisation were announced in 1999.[93]

The civil servant within the department

The senior civil servant within a department is the Permanent Secretary.[94] Beneath the Permanent Secretary, the affairs of the department will be handled by a number of divisions or branches, controlled (in descending order of seniority) by deputy secretaries, under-secretaries and assistant secretaries. These posts together form what is known as the 'Senior Civil Service', an entity created in 1996.[95] A key role is also played by special advisers to ministers, a position which has grown in numbers since 1997.[96] Where schemes of delegation exist within a department, they do not generally affect the legal position of the department or of outsiders dealing with it. Where the power to make a discretionary decision affecting an individual is vested in a minister, an official within the department may in general take that decision on behalf of the minister (the *Carltona* principle),[97] unless there are express or implied limitations in the statute conferring the power.[98] In a criminal case in which it was claimed that the Home Secretary had never approved a breathalyser device as required by the Road Safety Act 1973, Widgery LJ said: 'The minister is not expected personally to take every decision entrusted to him by Parliament. If a decision is made on his behalf by one of his officials, then that constitutionally is the minister's decision.'[99] In regard to the Secretary of State's powers under the Immigration Act 1971, it was held that immigration officers (in whom certain functions are expressly vested by the Act) were also entitled by virtue of the *Carltona* principle to exercise decision-making powers in regard to deportation on behalf of the Secretary of State.[100]

New questions about departmental delegation arise following the introduction of the executive agencies. Indeed, it has been suggested that the principle in the *Carltona* case is not strong enough to permit the delegation of ministerial authority to the agencies: 'the application of the *Carltona* principle was heavily contingent upon a certain structure of civil service administration which assumed and depended upon a very active notion of ministerial responsibility to Parliament, a principle which has been seriously eroded.' It has been argued further that there may therefore be no power for ministers

---

[91] Cm 2750, 1994, p ii.
[92] HL 55 (1997–98), para 94.
[93] Cm 4310, 1999, p 58.
[94] For a study of permanent secretaries, see K Theakston and G K Fry (1989) 67 Public Administration 129.
[95] HL 55 (1997–98).
[96] See HC 238 (1999–2000).
[97] *Carltona Ltd* v *Commissioners of Works* [1943] 2 All ER 560. See ch 7.
[98] *R* v *Home Secretary, ex p Oladehinde* [1991] 1 AC 254, at p 282.
[99] *R* v *Skinner* [1968] 2 QB 700, 707. See also *R* v *Home Secretary, ex p Doody* [1994] 1 AC 531, at p 566. And see ch 7.
[100] *R* v *Home Secretary, ex p Oladehinde* [1991] 1 AC 254.

to delegate to agencies, which 'cannot be seen as part of an integrated departmental structure, a departmental unity', such as the *Carltona* principle demands and that, as a result, legislation is necessary if powers conferred on ministers are to be delegated by them to agencies.[101] It is thus far from clear whether the case law which permits delegation by ministers to departmental officials for whom they are responsible would also permit delegation to members of executive agencies (even though they may be civil servants) for the operational activities of which the minister has disclaimed responsibility. It can hardly be said in these circumstances that the member of agency staff is a member of the minister's department 'for whom he accepts responsibility'. Neither is it clear whether it can be said that the minister must now 'answer before Parliament for anything that his officials have done under his authority'.[102] At the very least it may be that the *Carltona* principle will require a degree of refinement and flexibility in operation if it is to facilitate delegation of the type required by the creation of the agencies, although legislation would be a more appropriate form of regulation.[103]

Civil servants and ministerial responsibility

The principle of responsibility through ministers to Parliament is one of the most essential characteristics of the civil service. In a memorandum to the Treasury and Civil Service Committee, the Cabinet Office asserted that,

> The Minister in charge of a department is the only person who may be said to be ultimately accountable for the work of his department. It is usually on the Secretary of State as minister that Parliament has conferred powers, and Parliament calls on ministers to be accountable for the policy, actions and resources of their departments and the use of those powers. While ministers may delegate much of the day to day work of their departments, often now to agencies, they remain ultimately accountable to Parliament for all that is done under their power. Civil servants, except in those particular cases where statute confers powers on them directly, cannot take decisions or actions except insofar as they act on behalf of ministers. Civil servants are accountable to ministers, ministers are accountable to Parliament.[104]

According to the Cabinet Office, ministerial responsibility has often been used to describe this process. In recent years, however, there has been a significant refinement of the principle, the government taking the view that ministers are 'accountable' to Parliament for the work of their department, but are not 'responsible' for all the actions of civil servants in the sense of being blameworthy. There appears as a result to be a greater willingness to attribute responsibility for operational matters to individual civil servants. Although the distinction has been strenuously defended, there are those who remain sceptical, yet it remains unclear how far the distinction expresses anything which is qualitatively different from what was expressed by Sir David Maxwell-Fyfe in the aftermath of the Crichel Down affair in the 1950s.[105]

This is a question which has been brought sharply into focus as a result of the creation of the executive agencies. There is concern that there is now an 'accountability gap' whereby ministers have distanced themselves from the traditional full accountability for their departments.[106] These concerns were highlighted following difficulties in the Prison Service which led to the dismissal in October 1995 of its chief executive,

---

[101] M R Freedland [1996] PL 19. Also M R Freedland, in Sunkin and Payne (eds), *The Nature of the Crown*, ch 5.
[102] HL 55 (1997–98), para 459.
[103] See also HC 55 (1997–98).
[104] HC 27–II (1993–94), p 188.
[105] HC Deb, 20 July 1954, cols 1285–7. And see ch 7.
[106] HC 27–II (1993–94), p 189.

Mr Derek Lewis, by the Home Secretary, Mr Michael Howard. This followed the report of a review of security procedures in prisons by General Sir John Learmont, conducted after the escape of three prisoners from Parkhurst Jail on the Isle of Wight. The report made a number of criticisms of Parkhurst and its security, but also claimed that some of the problems could be 'traced along the lines of communication to Prison Service headquarters'.[107] In the words of the Home Secretary, Learmont did not find that 'any policy decision of [his], directly or indirectly, caused the escape'.[108] Mr Lewis was dismissed, although not without complaining of ministerial interference in operational matters and not without a substantial settlement being made in his favour for the premature termination of his appointment.[109] In the controversy that followed this dismissal, the Home Secretary declined to accept responsibility for the agency failures. In his view there was a distinction between policy and operations, a distinction said to be 'reflected in the framework document that established the Prison Service as an Executive Agency'.[110]

Civil servants and select committees

According to the government guidance on departmental evidence to select committees,[111] civil servants who give evidence to select committees do so on behalf of their ministers and under their directions.[112] One problem which has arisen is whether select committees can summon named individuals. During the Westland affair in 1985–6, the Defence Committee wished to examine five named officials, three from the Department of Trade and Industry and two from the Prime Minister's Office. The government took the view, however, that because these officials had participated in an internal departmental inquiry, it would be neither fair nor reasonable to expect them to submit to a second round of detailed questioning. The Defence Committee nevertheless asserted that 'its power to secure the attendance of an individual *named* civil servant is unqualified',[113] and that it was unacceptable for the government to prevent these officials from attending, a power which the same committee reasserted in 1994.[114] Although such instances are rare, Westland is not unique: in 1992, the Ministry of Defence frustrated efforts by the Trade and Industry Committee's inquiry into arms to Iraq which had wished to take evidence from recently retired officials.[115] In a decision which was subsequently criticised by Sir Richard Scott, the Ministry refused to help contact the officials in question on the ground that 'retired officials are not normally given access to departmental papers'.[116]

Sir Richard, in fact, proposed that in the interests of full and effective accountability select committees should not be hindered by the government in summoning named officials to appear before them, as did the Public Service Committee in 1996 which proposed that 'there should be a presumption that Ministers accept requests by Committees that named individual civil servants give evidence to them'.[117] The

---

[107] HC Deb, 16 October 1995, col 31.
[108] Ibid.
[109] *The Times*, 17 October 1995.
[110] HC Deb, 19 October 1995, col 519.
[111] Cabinet Office, *Departmental Evidence and Response to Select Committees*.
[112] But see HC Deb, 19 March 1997, cols 1046–7 and HL Deb, 20 March 1997, col 1057. See ch 7.
[113] HC 519 (1985–86).
[114] HC 27–I (1993–94). But this was contested by the government which pointed out that it was ministers who were ultimately accountable to Parliament 'for the whole range of a department's business', even though this did not mean that 'Ministers must be expected to be personally responsible, in the sense of being creditworthy or blameworthy, for every act of their department' (Cm 2627, 1994, p 28).
[115] HC 86 (1991–92).
[116] HC 115 (1995–96), para F4.64.
[117] HC 313–I (1995–96), para 83.

government agreed that 'where a Select Committee indicates that it wishes to hear evidence from named civil servants, Ministers should normally accept such a request',[118] and the rules have been amended accordingly.[119] But ministers retain the right to suggest an alternative official to that named by the committee if they feel that the former is better placed to represent them. Ministers may also wish to suggest someone else where the named official is likely to be exposed 'to questioning about their personal responsibility or the allocation of blame as between them and others'. But as the amended rules also make clear:

> If a Committee nonetheless insists on a particular official appearing before them, contrary to the Minister's wishes, the formal position remains that it could issue an order for attendance, and request the House to enforce it. In such an event (so far unprecedented) the official, as any other citizen, would have to appear before the Committee but, in all circumstances, would remain subject to Ministerial guidance.[120]

The Government also continues to be cautious about the position of retired officials who 'cannot be said to represent the Minister and hence cannot contribute directly to his accountability before the House'.[121]

E. Civil service: ethics and standards

The Civil Service Code

A statement of the ethical standards by which the civil service should be bound is to be found in the Civil Service Code which was brought into operation in 1996. Now formally incorporated into the Civil Service Management Code, it declares that: 'The constitutional and practical role of the Civil Service is, with integrity, honesty, impartiality and objectivity, to assist the duly constituted Government of the United Kingdom, the Scottish Executive or the National Assembly for Wales constituted in accordance with the Scotland and Government of Wales Acts 1998, whatever their political complexion, in formulating their policies, carrying out decisions and in administering public services for which they are responsible.' As such, civil servants are required to give 'honest and impartial advice' to ministers, assembly secretaries and the National Assembly as a body, and 'endeavour to deal with the affairs of the public sympathetically, effectively, promptly and without bias or maladministration'. They should endeavour to ensure the proper, effective and efficient use of public money. Civil servants are also required not to misuse their official position to further their own private interests (or those of others),[122] and they must conduct themselves in such a way as 'to deserve and retain the confidence of [the Administrations in which they serve] and to be able to establish the same relationship with those whom they may be required to serve in some future Administration'. So far as official information is concerned, this should not be disclosed without authority where it 'has been communicated in confidence within the Administration, or received in confidence from others'.

Apart from reminding officials of their duty to be impartial, the Code also provides that they 'should not seek to frustrate or influence the policies, decisions or actions of [the Administration] by the unauthorised, improper or premature disclosure outside the Administration of any information to which they have had access as civil servants'. There is no qualification that such information should be confidential. The emphasis

---

[118] HC 67 (1996–97), p x.
[119] Cabinet Office, *Departmental Evidence and Response to Select Committees*, para 41.
[120] Ibid, para 42.
[121] Ibid, para 44.
[122] See N Lewis and D Longley [1994] PL 596.

of the Code is on the responsibility of civil servants as servants of the Crown who 'owe their loyalty to the Administration in which they serve'. The extent to which the Code recognises that civil servants may have other obligations is controversial and at best constrained. Thus the duty to serve an administration is qualified by a recognition that all public officials must 'discharge public functions reasonably and according to the law' and that there is a 'duty to comply with the law, including international law and treaty obligations, and to uphold the administration of justice'. But there is no right, far less any obligation, to bring wrongdoing to public notice.[123] The civil servant may in certain circumstances report any impropriety 'in accordance with procedures laid down in [departmental] guidance or rules of conduct'. This applies where the civil servant is being required to act in a way which is 'illegal, improper or unethical', in 'breach of a constitutional convention or a professional code', or may involve possible maladministration or is otherwise inconsistent with the Code. Where a matter has been reported and the civil servant is dissatisfied with the response, it may be taken further by way of a complaint to the Civil Service Commissioners, a body set up in 1870 with the rather different task of promoting competitive entry into the civil service on the principle of intellectual merit. The Code is silent on the powers of the Civil Service Commissioners in this new capacity.[124]

Financial interests of civil servants

We have seen that ministers are subject to rules enforced by the Prime Minister that are intended inter alia to ensure that they do not profit improperly from their public position.[125] Civil servants are fully subject to the criminal law, including the Prevention of Corruption Acts 1906 and 1916. Internal rules of the service provide that no civil servant may engage in any occupation which might conflict with the interests of his or her department or with his or her position as a public servant; neither must they put themselves in a position (for example, by dealing in shares or land) where their duty to the public service might conflict with their private interests. Moreover, there are strict rules about the acceptance of gifts or hospitality which might compromise the civil servant's judgement or integrity.[126] The Civil Service Code also reminds civil servants that they 'should not misuse their official position or information acquired in the course of their official duties to further their private interests or those of others'. Nor should they place themselves in a position which 'might reasonably be seen to compromise their personal judgement or integrity'. The integrity of the civil service is protected further by established procedures for the awarding of contracts and the disposal of surplus property, breaches of which are subject to investigation by the Comptroller and Auditor-General.[127] Complaints of bias in the use of discretionary powers may be investigated by the Parliamentary Ombudsman.[128]

The public interest in integrity is not confined to what civil servants do while in post, but may extend to their actions after leaving the service. The rules that govern the taking up of private business appointments by former civil servants recognise the desirability of experienced administrators entering the private sector; but they also reflect

---

[123] The issue was considered inconclusively by the Public Service Committee in HC 313–I (1995–96).

[124] Civil servants should also report to 'the appropriate authorities' evidence of criminal or unlawful activity by others and may also report in accordance with the relevant procedures if he or she 'becomes aware of other breaches' of the Code or is required 'to act in a way which, for him or her, raises a fundamental issue of conscience'. See also Public Interest Disclosure Act 1998, which applies to civil servants.

[125] Section C in this chapter.

[126] *Civil Service Management Code*, para 4.1.3. Cf Cmd 3037, 1928.

[127] Ch 17 D.

[128] Ch 28 D.

a concern that there should be no cause for suspicion of impropriety about such an appointment. The Business Appointment Rules provide for the scrutiny of appointments which former civil servants propose to accept in the first two years after they leave the service. The aim of the rules is to 'avoid any suspicion that the advice and decisions of a serving officer might be influenced by the hope or expectation of future employment with a particular firm or organisation'; or 'to avoid the risk that a particular firm might gain an improper advantage over its competitors by employing someone who, in the course of their official duties, has had access to technical or other information which those competitors might legitimately regard as their own trade secrets or to information relating to proposed developments in government policy which may affect that firm or its competitors'. Most applications submitted under the rules are approved without condition, although in some cases a waiting period or other conditions may be imposed. The process is supervised by the Advisory Committee on Business Appointments, an independent body appointed by the Prime Minister whose members have experience of the relationship between the civil service and the private sector. There have been calls in the past for the rules to be made yet tighter.[129]

Political activities of civil servants

Servants of the Crown are prohibited from parliamentary candidature and disqualified from membership of the Commons. But should civil servants be subject to additional limitations, to secure the political impartiality of the civil service as a whole? The Civil Service Management Code 'points out that from the nature of the work which a civil servant is required to do and the context in which he has to do it, there must be certain restrictions on the type of political activities in which a civil servant is allowed to participate and the extent to which he may do so will of course depend on his position and seniority'.[130] The present scheme, first brought into force in 1954,[131] recognises that the political neutrality of the civil service is fundamental, but that the rules need not be the same for all members of the service. The scheme was fully reviewed by the Armitage Committee in 1978, in response to requests from the civil service unions for greater political freedom for civil servants. The committee reasserted the constitutional importance of the political neutrality of the civil service. It recommended that the scheme then in force should continue subject to substantial changes in its operation, the effect of which would be to reduce the number of civil servants in the 'restricted' category.[132] In 1984 these recommendations were adopted after extensive discussion between government and the civil service unions.[133]

Three categories exist. Participation in national political activities (for example, holding office in a political party; expressing public views on matters of national political controversy) is barred to the Senior Civil Service and other senior grades. This category must seek permission to take part in local political activities and must comply with any conditions laid down by their department or agency. A second 'intermediate' category may, with the leave of their departments, take part in national or local activities, although some grades have a mandate to take part in such activities without the need for permission. In cases where there is no mandate, permission will normally be refused only where civil servants are employed in sensitive areas where the impartiality

---

[129] HC 302 (1983–84); HC 392 (1987–88); and HC 622 (1987–88).
[130] R v *Civil Service Appeal Board, ex p Bruce* [1988] 3 All ER 686, at p 690 (May LJ). The arrangements are dealt with in *Civil Service Management Code*, para 4.4.
[131] See Cmd 7718, 1949, and Cmd 8783, 1953.
[132] Cmnd 7057, 1978.
[133] HC Deb, 26 March 1981, col 1186; 4 March 1982, col 503; 19 July 1984, col 272 (WA).

of the civil service is most at risk. A post is regarded as sensitive if: it is closely engaged in policy assistance to ministers; it is in the private office of a minister; it requires the postholder to speak regularly for the government; the postholder represents the government in dealing with overseas governments; or the postholder is involved in regular face-to-face contact with the public. The third 'politically free' category combines industrial staff and the non-industrial staff in minor and manipulative grades: they are free to engage in all political activities, national and local, except when on duty or on official premises or while wearing their uniform. But like all civil servants they are subject to the rules of the Official Secrets Acts on unauthorised disclosure of information gained from official sources.[134]

Civil servants and lobbyists

In 1998 new guidelines about contacts with lobbyists were issued to civil servants. These followed a press report that a journalist posing as an American businessman had been introduced by a lobbyist to a senior Downing Street official. In a disputed remark the official is reported to have said to the putative businessman: 'Just tell me what you want, who you want to meet and . . . I will make the call for you.'[135] As we have seen in chapter 11 B, the Cash for Questions affair in the 1990s led to the creation of the Committee on Standards in Public Life and tight rules to regulate the relationship between MPs and lobbyists. But at the time of 'Lobbygate', as this incident was known, there was no regulation of civil service contact with lobbyists. The new rules adopt what might best be referred to as a minimalist approach and reflect the view in the first report of the Committee on Standards in Public Life that 'it is the right of everyone to lobby parliament and Ministers, and it is for public institutions to develop ways of controlling the reaction to approaches from professional lobbyists in such a way as to give due weight to their case while always taking care to consider the public interest.'[136] The government's approach in the guidelines then is not to ban contacts between civil servants and lobbyists, but 'to insist that wherever and whenever they take place they should be conducted in accordance with Civil Service Code, and the principles of public life set out by the Nolan Committee' which are considered in chapter 14 E. Indeed, the guidelines acknowledge that lobbyists are 'a feature of our democratic system'.

The guidelines are drawn from the principle in the Civil Service Code that civil servants should conduct themselves with honesty and integrity. Some activities are said to be 'completely unacceptable' and to be serious disciplinary offences which could lead to dismissal. These are the leaking of confidential or sensitive material, especially market-sensitive material, to a lobbyist and deliberately helping a lobbyist to attract business by arranging for clients to have privileged access to a minister or undue influence over policy. Other situations are to be handled with care, although again any misjudgment could lead to disciplinary action. Ten basic rules are set out. These provide that the civil servants should not: grant a lobbyist preferential or premature access to information; meet one group making representations on a particular issue without offering other groups a similar opportunity; accept gifts from a lobbyist; do anything which might breach parliamentary privilege (for example by revealing the contents of a

---

[134] Ch 25. Apart from personal involvement in political activities, civil servants may wish to participate in political action through their trade unions. Several civil service unions have established political funds under what is now the Trade Union and Labour Relations (Consolidation) Act 1992 to enable them more effectively to represent their members. None is affiliated to any political party (although there are no legal restrictions on such affiliation), but several are affiliated to the TUC. See further ch 24 A.

[135] *The Observer*, 5 July 1998. The allegations were strongly denied: HC Deb, 8 July 1998, col 1065.

[136] Cm 280-I, 1995, para 72.

report not yet published); use knowledge of the workings of government to impress a lobbyist; help a lobbyist to obtain a benefit to which he or she is not entitled; or give the impression of offering a lobbyist preferential access to ministers. Civil servants should also declare to their department any family or business interests which may create a conflict of interest with departmental work; and take care in accepting hospitality from a lobbyist. The Committee on Standards in Public Life has recommended that the guidelines should be strengthened to ensure that a record is kept of any contact between civil servants and lobbyists.[137]

Future prospects: a Civil Service Act?

The large-scale changes to the civil service since 1988 have given rise to a great deal of analysis and assessment. In a major report in 1998, the House of Lords Select Committee on Public Service concluded that the changes represented a 'radical' and 'fundamental revolution' in public administration. But the Committee accepted that there had been 'little open or public debate about the extent of the structural changes being made to the Civil Service', and expressed itself as being not satisfied that 'the constitutional implications of the changes were fully thought through' before they were introduced. There was a tension between the (economic) justification for change based on efficiency, effectiveness and value for money, on the one hand, and traditional (political) concerns based on responsibility and accountability, on the other. The creation of the executive agencies was not thought, in a constitutional sense, to 'recast the architecture of the state', 'but only so long as accountability of Ministers to Parliament for the work of executive agencies remains the same as their accountability for any other aspect of their Department's work'. But the committee was concerned that 'the devolution to executive agencies was contributing to a sense of disunity in the Civil Service' although not yet to fragmentation. There was a need to determine how far this process of reducing the role of the core civil service should go and a need for 'open and public debate' about the irreducible nucleus of functions which must be carried out by the core civil service: this is as much 'a matter for the governed as for the governors'.

The process of civil service reform has continued under the Labour government elected in 1997 and has taken on a new dimension.[138] In the white paper, Modernising Government, it was announced in 1999 that permanent secretaries and heads of department will have performance targets 'for taking forward the government's modernisation agenda and ensuring delivery of the government's key targets'.[139] There is now great emphasis not only on the public service values of impartiality, objectivity and integrity, but also on the need for 'greater creativity, radical thinking, and collaborative working'. A central function of the Cabinet Office is to lead and support the process of reform, which is based around six themes set out in *Civil Service Reform*, a report of December 1999 to the Prime Minister by Sir Richard Wilson, the Head of the Home Civil Service. These developments have reinforced calls for a Civil Service Act to replace the current regulation of the civil service by royal prerogative which enables changes to be made without any parliamentary or public debate. A recommendation to this effect was made by the House of Lords Public Service Committee and was endorsed by the Committee on Standards in Public Life which regretted that

---

[137] Cm 4557-I (2000), R 28.
[138] On the implementation of these reforms, see C D Foster (2001) 79 Public Administration 725. For further analysis, see Hennessy, *The Prime Minister*, ch 18.
[139] See Cm 4310, 1999.

the commitment to an Act did not form part of the *Modernising Government* white paper. Although unwilling to comment at length on the scope and structure of such an Act, the Neill Committee accepted that it should be 'flexible so that the government could respond sufficiently quickly to changing circumstances'.[140] The government has indicated a commitment to such a measure. A more prescriptive and detailed position was adopted by the Lords' Public Service Committee in 1998.

F. Open government and freedom of information

Discussion of the structure of the civil service leads directly to a consideration of the question of open government and the public right of access to official information.[141] Historically there was no such right in the United Kingdom, in contrast to the position in other parliamentary democracies (notably Australia, Canada and New Zealand) where the right of access to information was introduced much earlier than in Britain.[142] Indeed it was often complained that it was easier to obtain information about the British government by using the US Freedom of Information Act than by making a direct request to a department in Whitehall. In 1979 a green paper on Open Government was published by the then Labour Government offering modestly a non-binding code of practice on access to official information.[143] But electoral defeat meant that these proposals were never implemented. Although campaigners for open government were thus disappointed, important initiatives in the direction of reform were nevertheless taken in the 1980s and 1990s. Apart from a number of specific statutory provisions,[144] these included the *Citizen's Charter* introduced in 1991 which provides that every citizen is entitled to expect openness and which states unequivocally that there should be no secrecy about how public services are run, how much they cost, who is in charge and whether or not they are meeting their standards.[145] This was followed in 1993 by the white paper, *Open Government*, which revived the idea of a non-binding code of practice. Such a code was, in fact, introduced in 1994 and revised in 1997,[146] allowing for complaints to be made to the Ombudsman (through the medium of a member of Parliament) that information had been unreasonably withheld.[147]

Background and scope

It was the Labour government's turn to publish a White Paper ('with green edges') on freedom of information in 1997.[148] The original plan was to replace existing open government initiatives (including the Code of Practice) 'with clear and consistent

---

[140] Cm 4557-I, para 5.50.

[141] For a full account, see Birkinshaw, *Freedom of Information*.

[142] Open government was actively discouraged by the Official Secrets Act 1911, esp s 2 by which it was an offence for a civil servant to communicate any information to a member of the public without authorisation. There was no right to information and no right to disclose it. Section 2 of the 1911 Act was repealed by the Official Secrets Act 1989. See ch 25.

[143] Cmnd 7520, 1979.

[144] Access to Personal Files Act 1987, Access to Medical Reports Act 1988, Access to Health Records Act 1990, Environmental Information Regulations 1992, SI 1992 No 3240. Also important was the Data Protection Act 1984 (now Data Protection Act 1998). See ch 22.

[145] Cm 1588, 1991. See C Scott [1999] PL 595.

[146] Cm 2290, 1993.

[147] See Parliamentary Ombudsman Annual Report 2000–01 (HC 5, 2001) pp 11–12, 51–7; also Birkinshaw, pp 238–50.

[148] *Your Right to Know: Freedom of Information*, Cm 3818, 1997. For comment, see P Birkinshaw [1998] PL 176.

requirements which would apply across government'.[149] The white paper proposed the introduction of 'a right, exercisable by any individual, company or other body to records or information of any date held by the public authority concerned in connection with its public functions'.[150] The presumption would be that information should be released unless disclosure would cause harm to one or more specified interests or would be contrary to the public interest. But these original proposals were abandoned and responsibility for open government transferred from the Cabinet Office to the Home Office (said to be 'one of the most overworked and accident-prone departments of government').[151] A diluted measure was subsequently introduced, this forming the basis of what is now the Freedom of Information Act 2000, which by the end of 2001 had not been brought into force. Although the Act will eventually give a legal right of access to official information, it was nevertheless criticised for being too restrictive in a number of key respects, these criticisms being voiced on two occasions by the Public Administration Committee of the House of Commons.[152] The Government openly acknowledged some of these criticisms[153] and responded by having 'some of that diluting removed'.[154]

Under the Act, any person making a request for information to a public authority will be entitled (a) to be told in writing by the authority whether it holds information of the type specified in the request, and if so (b) to have that information communicated to him or her (s 1). The public authorities to which the Act applies are listed in Schedule 1: there are over 400 such bodies, a list which may be added to by order of the Lord Chancellor (now the minister responsible for freedom of information) (s 4).[155] The list includes central government departments, local authorities, national health service bodies, schools and educational institutions, and the police. There is then an extensive list of other public bodies and offices (beginning with the Adjudicator for the Inland Revenue and Customs and Excise, and ending with the Zoos Forum). In this respect the Act contrasts sharply with the Human Rights Act 1998, which also applies to public authorities. But there is no definition of a public authority in the Human Rights Act (save to make clear that a court is a public authority), the scope of the Act being left to the courts to determine.[156] There is thus less room for uncertainty about the application of the Freedom of Information Act 2000.[157]

A request for information is to be made in writing to the relevant public authority (s 8), which may (but need not) charge a fee for the information in accordance with regulations (s 9). Requests are to be dealt with promptly and within 20 working days of receipt (s 10). There will be a right only to have access to information: there is no right to have access to documents.[158] The authority will be able to refuse to comply with a request for information where the cost would be excessive (s 12), or where the application is vexatious (s 14). The public authorities to which the Act applies will be required to provide advice and assistance to persons who propose to make or who have

---

[149] Cm 3818, 1997, para 1.6.

[150] Ibid, para 2.6.

[151] HL Deb, 20 April 2000, col 836.

[152] HC 570-I (1998–99); HC 78 (1999–2000).

[153] HL Deb, 20 April 2000, col 824.

[154] Ibid, col 831.

[155] The Act also allows an order to be made bringing in private bodies exercising public functions, such as companies running prisons and the British Board of Film Classification: HL Deb, 20 April 2000, col 825.

[156] See ch 19 C.

[157] For a valuable account, see S Palmer, in Beatson and Cripps (eds), *Freedom of Expression and Freedom of Information*, ch 15.

[158] The position was the same under the Code of Practice introduced in 1994.

made requests under the Act (s 16). Where an application for information is refused, the public authority will have to issue the applicant with a notice explaining the grounds for the refusal (s 17). Public authorities will also have to adopt and maintain a scheme which relates to the publication of information by the authority (s 19)[159] and model publication schemes will have to be produced by the Information Commissioner for which the Act provides (s 20).[160] The publication scheme should specify the classes of information which the authority in question publishes or intends to publish, specifying the manner in which information of each class is to be published, indicating whether a charge is made. It has been said that:

> the requirement for all public authorities to apply a scheme for publication – in effect to say what, when and how information will be published – is probably the most powerful push to openness in the [Act]. Authorities will not be able to get away with weak or self-serving publication schemes. They will all have to be approved by the Commissioner and she will ensure that they are strong and meaningful.[161]

Exemptions and enforcement

Just as there are a large number of authorities to which the Act applies, so there are a large number of categories of exempted information. There are 24 sections of exempt information (ss 21–44), many of which are wholly predictable. Exemptions fall into two categories: those which carry absolute exemption and those which do not (s 2). In the latter case, the exemption applies only where,

> in all the circumstances of the case, the public interest in maintaining the exclusion of the duty to confirm or deny outweighs the public interest in disclosing whether the public authority holds the information. (s 2(1)(b))

Information which will be absolutely exempt includes that which is reasonably accessible to the public by other means (s 21), information which relates to bodies dealing with security matters (s 23), information relating to court records (s 32), information which consists of personal data of which the applicant is the data subject (s 40), information obtained in confidence (s 41) and information the disclosure of which is prohibited by statute, is incompatible with an EC obligation or would constitute a contempt of court (s 44).

The larger category of information to which an absolute exemption will not apply includes information which is held by the authority with a view to its future publication (s 22), information required for the purpose of safeguarding national security (s 24), information relating to defence (s 26), information the disclosure of which would prejudice international relations (s 27), information the disclosure of which would prejudice relations between Whitehall and the devolved administrations or between the devolved administrations (s 28), and so on at some length. Among the other noteworthy exemptions are information which if disclosed would or would be likely to prejudice the economic interests of the United Kingdom or any part thereof or any administration in the United Kingdom (s 29);[162] information which relates to criminal investigations conducted by a wide range of statutory agencies (s 30) or law enforcement (s 31); information which relates to the formulation or development of government policy (s 35); as well as an exemption for information held by a government department which if disclosed could prejudice the effective conduct of public affairs (s 36).

---

[159] On the definition of public authority, see p 283 above.
[160] See ch 22 below.
[161] HL Deb, 20 April 2000, col 826 (Lord Falconer).
[162] On the purpose of this exemption, see HL Deb, 19 October 2000, col 1287.

Turning from exemption to enforcement, this is the responsibility of the new Information Commissioner and the new Information Tribunal (s 18).[163] A complaint may be made to the Commissioner that a public authority has failed to comply with the requirements of Part I of the Act and if the complaint is upheld the Commissioner may issue a decision notice specifying steps to be taken to comply with the Act (s 50). The Commissioner is also empowered to issue an enforcement notice (s 52), failure to comply with which may lead to the matter being referred to the High Court or Court of Session to be punished as a contempt of court (s 54). There is a right of appeal to the Information Tribunal against a decision of the Commissioner (s 57), with a further appeal on a point of law to the High Court or the Court of Session (s 59). Under s 60 the Tribunal has been given powers to quash a ministerial certificate protecting national security information from disclosure.[164] The Commissioner will also be required to promote good practice and to make recommendations to public authorities about good practice (ss 44–9).[165] It is an offence to destroy or tamper with information, but only if this is done after a request for disclosure has been made (s 77).

Criticisms of the Act

Some draw a distinction between open government and freedom of information and claim that the Act is an example of the former rather than the latter. Whether this is a distinction of substance or not, it remains the case that the Freedom of Information Act 2000 has not met all expectations,[166] although it has been claimed that 'probably no legislation which any responsible government could introduce would completely satisfy [the more ardent advocates of freedom of information]'.[167] In the first place, there is no statutory presumption in favour of disclosure as had been promised in the White Paper, the government taking the view at one stage that the 'right of access to information must be balanced against . . . other competing rights to privacy, confidentiality and so on'.[168] Concerns were allayed to some extent by what is now s 2(1)(b). The effect of this – a Liberal Democrat amendment at a late stage – is that: 'The starting point [for the public authority, the Information Commissioner and ultimately the courts] is the public right of access and the public interest in disclosure, and it is for the public authority to justify non-disclosure on the basis that public disclosure is outweighed in the circumstances of the case by the public interest in non-disclosure.'[169]

A second concern relates to the number of exclusions and, in particular, the number of class exclusions, that is to say the exclusion from the duty to disclose information because it belongs to a particular class of material, regardless of content. But this too is addressed to some extent by the fact that in most cases these class-based exemptions are subject to s 2(1)(b) which means that disclosure must be considered

---

[163] The Information Commissioner was previously the Data Protection Commissioner under the Data Protection Act 1998. The Freedom of Information Act 2000 extends the functions of and renames the latter.

[164] In introducing the Bill into the House of Commons the Home Secretary celebrated the fact that the Commissioner and the Tribunal will have 'clear powers to override the decisions of Ministers or any other public authority as to whether public information shall be released': HC Deb, 7 December 1999, col 714.

[165] The Act also requires the Secretary of State to issue a code of practice providing guidance to public authorities about good practice under the Act (s 45).

[166] For a stinging attack, see *The Guardian*, 14 November 2000 (Hugo Young).

[167] HL Deb, 20 April 2000, col 863.

[168] HL Deb, 17 October 2000, cols 888–9. But it was also said that information must be disclosed unless there is an overriding public interest in keeping specific information confidential' (HL Deb, 14 November 2000, col 143).

[169] HL Deb, 14 November 2000, col 137 (Lord Lester of Herne Hill).

on a case-by-case basis and ordered where the circumstances require. Other criticisms relate to the substance of some of the exclusions, with particular concern being expressed about the fact that confidential information is subject to an absolute exemption.[170] A more general criticism is that the exemptions typically apply where the disclosure would 'prejudice' a particular interest. It was felt by some that the higher standard of 'substantial prejudice' or 'necessity' would be more appropriate. There was criticism also of the wide exclusion of information relating to investigations relating to proceedings conducted by local authorities,[171] as well as information relating to the formulation of government policy and information which if disclosed would prejudice the effective conduct of public affairs.[172]

It was thought that these restrictions could prevent much information which ought to be in the public domain from being withheld, although again public authority objections can be overruled by s 2(1)(b) where the exemption is not absolute:[173] much will depend on the vigour of the Commissioner and the Tribunal.[174] Otherwise, s 53 proved to be controversial. This is the so-called 'executive override', a 'kind of nuclear option for the Government',[175] which allows a minister in some limited circumstances to override a decision notice (under s 50) or an enforcement notice (under s 52) of the Commissioner which has been served on a government department.[176] This power – to be exercised by means of a ministerial certificate which must be laid before Parliament – reflects the government's belief that 'there will be certain cases dealing with the most sensitive issues where a senior member of the Government, able to seek advice from his Cabinet colleagues, should decide on the final question of public interest in relation to disclosure'.[177] It is not easy to fathom the claim of a Home Office minister that it would be 'profoundly undemocratic' to permit the Commissioner to have the final say on what should be disclosed.

---

[170] See HL Deb, 14 November 2000, cols 176–7; HL Deb, 17 October 2000, col 905.

[171] HL Deb, 19 October 2000, col 1289.

[172] The former were said to be 'investigations of precisely the kind where the public wants to know the facts because they relate to matters which concern the public', with investigations into BSE, railway accidents, and food poisoning being cited, along with the investigation into the death of Stephen Lawrence: HL Deb, 19 October 2000, col 1289. Also cols 1295–6. But for a robust defence of these latter measures by a former Cabinet Secretary (Lord Armstrong), see HL Deb, 20 April 2000, col 861.

[173] HL Deb, 24 October 2000, col 297 where the minister gave the prescient example of broken rail beside the track.

[174] But even if these bodies rise to the challenge there is still concern that much of the information yielded in investigations of this kind will be excluded by the exemption in s 41 for information which is supplied to the public authority in confidence: HL Deb, 14 November 2000, col 174. The government undertook to ensure that the code of practice (see note 165) to be issued under the Act 'must be so constructed that information is genuinely obtained in confidence only when it is necessary to obtain the information and that that is appropriate' (ibid, col 177).

[175] HL Deb, 22 November 2000, col 843.

[176] The power applies only to decisions taken in relation to exempt information.

[177] HL Deb, 14 November 2000, col 258.

Chapter 14

PUBLIC BODIES AND REGULATORY AGENCIES

We have already considered the constitutional position of government departments and have seen that they are staffed by civil servants and headed by ministers who are responsible to Parliament for their activities. When functions are entrusted to local authorities, the administrative structure is very different from that in central government and political responsibility for the policies and decisions of local councils is borne by the elected councillors. Today many public tasks are entrusted not to central or local government, but to a wide variety of official boards, commissions and other agencies. Some are well known, such as the BBC, the Commission for Racial Equality and ACAS. Many of them operate in obscurity, known only to a few civil servants and specialists in the area concerned. It is difficult to generalise about such diversity, but these bodies have one feature in common, namely that the members of the boards and agencies are not publicly elected. Instead, these members have all been appointed to their posts, in the vast majority of cases by central government (that is, by the minister of the department concerned with the activity in question). Thus, while ministers do not directly administer the affairs of these bodies, ministers have an underlying but indirect responsibility to Parliament for their efficiency and effectiveness. Many of these bodies were created by legislation and many are wholly or mainly supported by public funds. If one of these bodies antagonises public opinion, overspends the funds available to it, is badly administered or has outlived its usefulness, the minister can be asked in Parliament to introduce legislation abolishing the body or reforming its powers, to appoint a new governing body or to take other steps for improving the position.[1] Moreover, because of the economic, financial and social significance of some agencies, strategic decisions concerning their activities are inevitably affected by government policies.

The proliferation of these bodies in recent years is not something about which constitutional lawyers can be sanguine. There are serious concerns that so much activity of government is conducted in this way: questions arise about the system of appointment to the bodies in question and the amount of patronage vested in ministers; and about the accountability of the bodies for the decisions which they make and the activities which they pursue. Political scientists have raised other questions about the effectiveness of some of these bodies and the dangers of 'capture' by the interests they are designed to regulate.[2] Indeed, the utilities regulators have been criticised particularly for failing to respond adequately to consumer interests,[3] although there is no suggestion that they have been 'captured' by the utility companies. Within government such bodies are described by such terms as 'fringe bodies' and 'non-departmental public bodies' (NDPBs). One unofficial term applied to them was 'quangos', that

---

[1] For an outstanding example, see the ill-fated Crown Agents, whose affairs led to the Fay committee of inquiry (HC 48 (1977–78)), a judicial tribunal of inquiry (HC 364 (1981–82)), and the Crown Agents Act 1979; and see G Ganz [1980] PL 454.

[2] M Moran (2000) 54 Parliamentary Affairs 19.

[3] HC 193-i (1999–2000), Appendix 14 (memorandum submitted by the Public Utilities Access Forum), para 3.

originally stood for 'quasi-non-governmental organisations',[4] although to confuse matters still more, it was used by the Committee on Standards in Public Life – itself a public body – to refer to the narrower group of NDPBs.[5] Mainly because there is no single agreed definition of the bodies concerned, it is not possible to state accurately how many exist. According to one official but incomplete list,[6] in 1996 there were 1,194. But in 1999 there were 1,057 non-departmental public bodies. These were of three kinds: executive bodies, which normally employ staff and have their own budgets; advisory bodies, set up by the minister to advise on a particular area or issue; and tribunals, including licensing and appeal bodies. The figure of 1,057 (which compares with 2,167 in 1979) does not include other important public bodies such as the surviving nationalised industries, the utility regulators, national health service bodies, agencies set up under the 'next steps' initiative, or task forces.

A. Origins and purpose

History

The creation of specialised public agencies that are not government departments is not new. In the 18th century, there were innumerable bodies of commissioners created by private Acts, which exercised limited powers for such purposes as police, paving, lighting, turnpikes and local improvements. Through the curtailment of the powers of the Privy Council in the previous century, they were free from administrative control by central government, but in England they were subject to legal control by means of the prerogative writs issued by the Court of King's Bench. These bodies were essentially local in character. In the period of social and administrative reform that followed the reform of Parliament in 1832, experiments were made in setting up national agencies with powers covering the whole country. One of the most notable experiments occurred in 1834 when the English Poor Law was reformed. The Poor Law Commissioners enforced strict central control on the local administration of poor relief, by means of rules, orders and inspection. Yet no minister answered for the commissioners in Parliament, to defend them against political attack or to control their decisions. In 1847, the experiment gave way to a system based on a minister responsible to Parliament but similar experiments occurred, such as the General Board of Health in 1848. Administration by the board system was much used in Scotland and in Ireland. By the late 19th century, it was accepted that the vesting of public powers in departments of central government had the great constitutional advantage of securing political control through ministerial responsibility.[7] As Chester remarked, the House of Commons has never found a way of making anybody other than ministers accountable to it.[8]

In the 20th century, the state acquired vast new social and economic powers. Particularly as a result of the nationalisation programme followed by the Labour government from 1945 to 1951, the United Kingdom became a mixed economy, in which privately owned and publicly owned industrial enterprises co-existed. Moreover, extensive schemes of social regulation and welfare have been and continue to be accepted by all political parties, although there is now perhaps sharper disagreement about the

---

[4] See Hague, Mackenzie and Barker (eds), *Public Policy and Private Interests*; and Barker (ed), *Quangos in Britain*.

[5] Cm 2850-I, 1995, p 65. See also e.g. Holland, *The Governance of Quangos*, and G Drewry [1982] PL 384.

[6] *Public Bodies* (Stationery Office, 1996).

[7] See also ch 7 above and, for rise and fall of the board system, F M G Willson (1955) 33 Public Administration 43 and Parris, *Constitutional Bureaucracy*, ch 3.

[8] D N Chester (1979) 57 Public Administration 51, 54.

nature and scope of these schemes. These developments not only meant an increase in the tasks entrusted to government departments. There was also a widespread creation of public boards and other agencies that are classifiable neither as government departments nor as local authorities. Reacting to these trends, the Conservative government after 1979 sought both to abolish unnecessary public agencies and through privatisation to return profitable public undertakings to private ownership, either wholly or in part. By 1997 major and possibly irreversible changes in the boundary between the public and private sectors had occurred. Indeed, quite apart from any other consideration, because of the costs involved it is likely that future concerns will be confined to questions of regulation rather than the public ownership of the industries in question. It has been suggested that because of the policy of privatisation pursued by Conservative governments since 1979 (on which see below) Britain is no longer a mixed economy.[9] But there is still a considerable amount of regulation of social and economic affairs by the state and, indeed, new agencies continue to be created.[10]

Reasons for the creation of public corporations and non-governmental bodies[11]

In theory, the tasks entrusted to public boards and agencies could be undertaken directly by civil servants working in government departments, although this would mean a vast increase in the civil service and the adoption by it of new methods. Indeed, before the Post Office was established in 1969 as a public corporation, postal and telephone services had been for very many years provided by the Post Office as a government department.[12] But the existence of public corporations affords strong evidence for the view that departmental administration of major industries is likely to be less efficient and less flexible than management by a public board. The post-war nationalisation legislation sought to apply the concept of the public corporation associated with the late Herbert Morrison.[13] This aimed at a combination of vigorous and efficient business management with an appropriate measure of public control and accountability. Civil service methods, Treasury control and complete accountability to Parliament were considered unsuited to the successful running of a large industry. In the 1945–51 period, when major public utilities, transport and energy undertakings were acquired by the state, they were entrusted not to departments but to new statutory boards. The relevant ministers were given important powers relating to the boards but were not expected to become concerned with day-to-day management of the industries. Similar reasoning led to the creation of public corporations to take over certain activities formerly performed by departments, for example the Atomic Energy Authority (1954) and the British Airports Authority (1965).

Another reason for establishing public corporations is to entrust an activity to an autonomous body and thereby reduce the scope for direct political control or interference. The existence of the BBC and the Independent Television Commission separate from the government is necessary if ministers are not to be responsible for every programme broadcast. The same reason explains why many grant-giving bodies have been established to distribute funds provided by Parliament. The government is

---

[9] D Marsh (1991) 69 Public Administration 459.

[10] For an account of developments since the election of the Labour government in 1997, see C Hood, O James and C Scott (2000) 78 Public Administration 283.

[11] The extensive literature includes: Chester, *The Nationalisation of British Industry 1945–51*; Robson, *Nationalised Industries and Public Ownership*; Friedmann and Garner (eds), *Government Enterprise*; Prosser, *Nationalised Industries and Public Control*.

[12] See now Postal Services Act 2000.

[13] See his book, *Government and Parliament*, ch 12.

responsible for the total grants made to such bodies as research councils, arts councils and the Higher Education Funding Councils, but not for the detailed allocation of these funds. The aim of enabling discretionary decisions to be made by an agency without regard to short-term political considerations explains also the existence of the Commission for Racial Equality and the Equal Opportunities Commission, which enforce social legislation designed to reduce discrimination. However, ministers may not absolve themselves of broad responsibility for the existence, activities, funding and composition of such agencies. Neither have all attempts to take a sensitive area of administration 'out of politics' by entrusting it to an appointed board been successful.[14]

Privatisation

After 1979 successive Conservative governments operated a policy of privatisation of public corporations, whereby the ownership of many state-controlled enterprises was returned to the private sector. In an important report by the Public Accounts Committee published in 1998, it was stated that:

> During that time over 150 United Kingdom businesses have been privatised, ranging from major undertakings with billions of pounds to small loss-making enterprises. In the process, the proportion of Gross Domestic Product accounted for by state-owned businesses has fallen from 11 per cent to 2 per cent. These privatisations have shared a number of overall objectives, including improving the efficiency of the business concerned, promoting the development of a market economy, reducing state debt and increasing state revenues.[15]

The programme has taken several forms, including the denationalisation of state corporations such as British Gas, British Telecom, British Airways, British Coal and British Rail;[16] the disposal of shares in companies previously owned by the government (such as Jaguar, Rolls-Royce, Amersham International, British Nuclear Fuels Ltd, and Cable and Wireless);[17] and the sale of government holdings in companies such as British Petroleum.[18] Two hotly contested privatisations, for different reasons, were of the water supply industry in England and Wales and the Trustee Savings Bank,[19] while two highly symbolic privatisations were those of the coal industry and the railways, both of which had been nationalised by the post-war Labour government. The process of offloading state enterprises nevertheless continues under Labour governments,[20] with the future of the Post Office in particular likely to be controversial.[21]

But although public ownership retreated in this period, it would be premature to see this as the end of the public body, as that term is used generically in this chapter. New public bodies have been created to regulate the privatised utilities. These include the Gas and Electricity Markets Authority and the Gas and Electricity Consumer Council, established under the Utilities Act 2000 to replace the separate regulatory and consumer bodies which had been established following the privatisation of these industries. Similar bodies have been created by the legislation privatising telecommunications, water

---

[14] As with financial relief for the unemployed in 1934: see Millett, *The Unemployment Assistance Board*.

[15] HC 992 (1997–98).

[16] See Gas Act 1986, Civil Aviation Act 1980, Telecommunications Act 1984, Railways Act 1993 and Coal Industry Act 1994. Other major privatisations included water (Water Act 1989) and electricity (Electricity Act 1989).

[17] See Atomic Energy (Miscellaneous Provisions) Act 1981 (Amersham, BNFL); British Telecommunications Act 1981, s 79 (Cable and Wireless). See also Atomic Energy Authority Act 1995. For the developments in the motor industry, see A A McLaughlin and W A Maloney (1996) 74 Public Administration 435.

[18] On this form of state intervention (the mixed enterprise), see pp 309–10 of the 10th edn of this book.

[19] See *Ross v Lord Advocate* [1986] 1 WLR 1077; and M Percival (1987) 50 MLR 231.

[20] See for example Commonwealth Development Corporation Act 1999.

[21] See Postal Services Act 2000. Also HC 170 (1994–95).

and the railways.[22] Regulatory agencies have also been established in a number of other fields, sometimes to administer newly created statutory rights and sometimes to replace an existing agency. Examples include, in broadcasting, the Independent Television Commission, the Broadcasting Standards Commission and the Radio Authority; in respect of the police and the security service, the Police Complaints Authority, the Interception of Communications Commissioner and the Intelligence Services Commissioner; and in legal services and the administration of justice, the Legal Services Commission.[23] Other important public bodies created since 1990 include the Higher Education Funding Councils, the Occupational Pensions Regulatory Authority, the Low Pay Commission, the National Lottery Commission, the Competition Commission, the Electoral Commission, and the Financial Services Authority.[24] A number of self-regulatory bodies have also been created under government pressure or with government encouragement. These include the Press Complaints Commission and the City Panel on Take-Overs and Mergers, the latter being used by the government as the 'centrepiece' of its policy of regulation in the field.[25] Also important are the bodies established to regulate the delivery of public services.[26]

B. Classification, status and composition of public bodies

Classification

The wide range of activities exercised by public bodies and the fact that they have nearly all been created under different Acts of Parliament make it difficult to classify them. One possible approach, that adopted by the government, is helpful, although not without its limitations.[27] According to the government's classification, there are three groups of public bodies.

1   Public corporations and nationalised industries, with the former being defined as corporate enterprises which are publicly owned and controlled but which, at the same time, have substantial freedom to conduct their affairs along business lines. The latter were said to be a 'group of particularly large and important public corporations':
(a)   There were only 12 public corporations listed in 1999, these including the Covent Garden Market Authority at one end of the scale and the Bank of England at the other. Other bodies in this group include a number which are prominent in the broadcasting sphere, including the BBC (incorporated under royal charter and operating under a licence from the government), Channel 4 Television Corporation, the Independent Television Commission, and the Radio Authority (the last three being established under the Broadcasting Act 1990).[28]
(b)   There are now very few nationalised industries of any consequence. Ten were listed in 1999, these being Highlands and Islands Airports, Caledonian MacBrayne, British Nuclear Fuels, Civil Aviation Authority, London Regional Transport, the Post Office,

---

[22] See section D below.
[23] See Broadcasting Act 1990, Police and Criminal Evidence Act 1984, Regulation of Investigatory Powers Act 2000 and Access to Justice Act 1999.
[24] See Further and Higher Education Act 1992, Pensions Act 1995, National Minimum Wage Act 1998, National Lottery Act 1998, Competition Act 1998, Political Parties, Elections and Referendums Act 2000 and Financial Services and Markets Act 2000.
[25] R v Panel on Take-Overs and Mergers, ex p Datafin [1987] 2 QB 815, at p 838. See *Weinberg and Blank on Take-overs and Mergers*, part 9.
[26] C Hood, O James and C Scott (2000) 78 Public Administration 283.
[27] See *Public Bodies* (Stationery Office 1999).
[28] Ch 23 C.

British Coal, British Shipbuilders, British Railways Board and the Scottish Transport Group. But the last four are merely residual authorities dealing with residual matters following privatisation – matters such as litigation, insurance claims and the like. Several other bodies are moving in the direction of full or partial privatisation.[29]

2   National Health Service bodies, including health authorities, special health authorities and NHS trusts, of which there were 417 in 1999. These bodies are all established under the authority of the National Health Service Act 1977[30] and the National Health Service and Community Care Act 1990. Other NHS authorities include the National Blood Authority and the Microbiological Research Authority.

3   Non-departmental public bodies, a huge classification of 1,057 bodies in 1999 which is in turn classified to include as follows:

(*a*)   Executive bodies (of which there were 306) which 'carry a wide range of administrative, regulatory, executive or commercial functions on behalf of government'. Examples of such bodies include the Advisory Conciliation and Arbitration Service (ACAS), the Commission for Racial Equality (CRE), the Equal Opportunities Commission (EOC), the Countryside Agency, the Higher Education Funding Council and the Teacher Training Agency.

(*b*)   Advisory bodies (of which there were 544) 'set up to provide independent, expert advice to ministers and officials'. Included in this category are the Advisory Committee on Pesticides, the Advisory Committee on NHS Drugs, the Council on Tribunals, the Law Commission, the Arts Council of England, the Broadcasting Standards Commission and the Football Licensing Authority.

(*c*)   Tribunals (of which there were 69 species) with jurisdiction in specialist fields of law, generally serviced by staff from the sponsoring department. They include both standing tribunals (with a permanent membership) and those covered from panels so that the actual number of tribunals sitting varies. Examples include the Dairy Produce Quota Tribunal, rent assessment panels, the Foreign Compensation Commission, the Mental Health Review Tribunal, and employment tribunals.[31]

The category of NDPBs also includes other bodies, most notably boards of visitors to penal establishments, but it excludes a large number of other bodies, including central government departments, local authorities and the civil and criminal courts (although it does include bodies like the tribunal established by the Regulation of Investigatory Powers Act 2000 whose membership includes senior members of the judiciary). More controversially, however, it also excludes what are referred to as non-ministerial government departments, on the one hand, and the next steps agencies, on the other.[32] The former includes the utility regulators, that is to say the Director General of Telecommunications (OFTEL), the Gas and Electricity Markets Authority, and the Director General of Water Supply (OFWAT).[33] Although the regulators are not treated as 'public bodies' for these purposes, their advisory bodies (such as the consumer councils) are included.

Legal status

Except where statutes provide otherwise, departments of central government share in the legal status of the Crown and may benefit from certain privileges and immunities

---

[29] See Postal Services Act 2000, s 62.
[30] As amended by the Health Authorities Act 1995.
[31] Ch 29 A.
[32] Ch 13 D. See Cabinet Office, *Executive NDPBs: 1999 Report* (2000); and *Executive Agencies: 1999 Report* (2000).
[33] See p 298 below.

which are peculiar to the Crown.[34] But local authorities, statutory bodies set up for local commercial purposes and privately owned companies do not benefit from Crown status.[35] Into which category do other public bodies fall?

> In *Tamlin* v *Hannaford*, it had to be decided whether, after nationalisation of the railways, a dwelling-house owned by the British Transport Commission was subject to the Rent Restriction Acts or was exempted from them by virtue of being Crown property. After examining the Transport Act 1947, the Court of Appeal rejected the view that the Commission was the servant or agent of the Crown, even though the Ministry of Transport had wide statutory powers of control over the Commission. 'In the eye of the law, the corporation is its own master and is answerable as fully as any other person or corporation. It is not the Crown and has none of the immunities or privileges of the Crown. Its servants are not civil servants and its property is not Crown property . . . It is, of course, a public authority and its purposes, no doubt, are public purposes, but it is not a government department nor do its powers fall within the province of government.'[36]

It would seem that this decision governs the status of other public corporations, unless they are expressly made to act by and on behalf of the Crown or are directly placed under a minister of the Crown. In *Pfizer Corpn* v *Ministry of Health*, it was held that, since a hospital board was acting on behalf of the then Minister of Health, the treatment of patients in NHS hospitals was a government function and thus the use of drugs was use 'for the services of the Crown'; the Crown could therefore make use of its special rights under patent law for importing drugs.[37] By contrast, in *BBC* v *Johns*, the BBC were held not to be entitled to benefit from the Crown's immunity from taxation since broadcasting had not become a function of the central government.[38] It was strange that financial considerations led the BBC in this case to argue its close dependence upon the Crown and central government, whereas usually the BBC is anxious to stress its independence. The immunities of many NHS bodies were later removed by the National Health Service and Community Care Act 1990.

It is today common for the statute which creates a new public corporation to make express provision for its status. Thus the Health and Safety Commission and the Health and Safety Executive, created in 1974 to exercise functions previously exercised by departments, are stated to perform their functions on behalf of the Crown.[39] The National Audit Act 1983 provides that the staff of the National Audit Office are not to be regarded as holding office under Her Majesty or as discharging any functions on behalf of the Crown. The Utilities Act 2000 provides that the Gas and Electricity Consumer Council shall not be regarded as a servant or agent of the Crown or as enjoying any status, immunity or privilege of the Crown (although it is curiously silent on the position of the regulator). A similar form of words is used, for example, in the case of the Higher Education Funding Councils, the National Rivers Authority, the Occupational Pensions Regulatory Authority and the Electoral Commission.[40] Where a public body does not benefit from Crown immunities, it is subject to the criminal law.[41] For the purposes of the law relating to corruption, the boards of nationalised industries are

---

[34] Chs 12 D and 32 C.
[35] *Mersey Docks and Harbour Trustees* v *Gibbs* (1866) LR 1 HL 93; ch 32 A.
[36] [1950] 1 KB 18, 24 (Denning LJ).
[37] [1965] AC 512. Cf *BMA* v *Greater Glasgow Health Board* [1989] AC 1211 and, from a different point of view, *Norweb plc* v *Dixon* [1995] 3 All ER 952.
[38] [1965] Ch 32.
[39] Health and Safety at Work etc. Act 1974, s 10(7).
[40] See Further and Higher Education Act 1992, Water Act 1989, Pensions Act 1995 and Political Parties, Elections and Referendums Act 2000.
[41] Some of the difficulties in particularly serious cases (such as those involving Railtrack) are explored in B Sullivan [2001] Crim LR 31. See also J Gobert (2002) 118 LQR 72.

'public bodies', since they have public duties to perform which they carry out for the benefit of the public and not for private profit.[42]

Appointments to public bodies

NDPBs are bodies which exercise a government function, but which are appointed rather than elected, whether directly or indirectly. Not surprisingly ministerial patronage of this kind has given rise to concern and was fully addressed by the Committee on Standards in Public Life.[43] In its first report the committee found no evidence of political bias in public appointments and rejected calls for an impartial and independent body to be given the responsibility for making appointments, recommending that 'ultimate responsibility for appointments should remain with ministers'. But it did not follow that ministers 'should act with unfettered discretion', and it was proposed that existing procedures should be 'substantially improved' in order to ensure that they were 'sufficiently robust'. The two safeguards proposed were first 'the establishment of clear published principles governing selections for appointment' and secondly more effective external scrutiny of appointments. So far as the former is concerned, this was to include the principle of appointment on merit; the principle that 'selection on merit should take account of the need to appoint boards which include a balance of skills and backgrounds'; and that appointments should be made only after advice from a panel or committee which includes independent members, who should normally account for at least one-third of the membership. So far as external scrutiny is concerned, this was to be achieved principally by the appointment of a Commissioner for Public Appointments to 'monitor, regulate and approve departmental appointments procedures' and to draw up a Code of Practice for public appointments procedures.

These recommendations were accepted by the government and a Commissioner of Public Appointments was appointed by Order in Council in November 1995 to oversee the way public appointments are made to the executive departmental bodies, a term defined to include only 274 NDPBs and executive NHS bodies. The jurisdiction of the Commissioner was extended in 1998 to include the nationalised industries, public corporations, the utility regulators and advisory NDPBs as well (but not tribunals).[44] The Commissioner is under a duty 'in the manner he considers best calculated to promote economy, efficiency and effectiveness in the procedures for making public appointments, [to] exercise his functions with the object of maintaining the principle of selection on merit in relation to public appointments'. The Commissioner is also required to 'prescribe and publish a code of practice on the interpretation and application' of the principle of appointment on merit and is expressly empowered to adopt and publish from time to time such additional guidance to appointing authorities as he thinks fit. In order to ensure that any procedures are duly followed, the Commissioner must 'audit appointment policies and practices pursued by appointing authorities to establish whether the code of practice is being observed' and may, from time to time, conduct an inquiry into the policies and practices followed by any authority in relation to any appointment or description of appointment. As well as the Code of Practice, the Commissioner is required to publish an annual report.

The Code of Practice is based on seven principles.[45] While recognising that 'the ultimate responsibility for appointment rests with ministers', the Code emphasises that

---

[42] *R v Manners* [1978] AC 43.

[43] Cm 2850-I, 1995. One complaint was that public bodies were ceasing to be representative and were increasingly dominated by businessmen. On developments in the health service, see L Ashburner and L Cairncross (1993) 71 Public Administration 357.

[44] Commissioner for Public Appointments, Fifth Report 1999–2000 (2000), p 27.

[45] The code can be found at http://www.ocpa.gov.uk/leaflets/code.htm.

'all public appointments should be governed by the overriding principle of selection based on merit'. Provision is made for independent scrutiny in all appointments to which the Code applies, as well as the need to promote equal opportunities. There is also a recognition of the need for openness and transparency to be applied to the appointments process, as well as proportionality in the appointments procedures. This means that these procedures should be 'appropriate for the nature of the post and the size and weight of its responsibilities' and there is a concern that some of the procedures are too elaborate.[46] The Code of Practice is accompanied by the Commissioner's more detailed guidance on appointments to public bodies which now requires candidates for public appointment to indicate involvement in political activities in the immediately preceding five years.[47] Complaints about public appointments may be made to the Commissioner,[48] who in 1999 conducted a review of procedures for appointment to NHS bodies.[49] The Commissioner is subject to scrutiny by the Public Administration Committee which has conducted two inquiries into different aspects of the work of the office,[50] in addition to the earlier examination by the Public Service Committee.[51]

C. Public utilities: the general framework

From public to private ownership

There was and is no uniform legislative framework for the nationalised industries. The structure of the British Gas Corporation is, however, typical. The corporation was established after a reorganisation of the industry by the Gas Act 1972, replacing the Gas Council established by the Gas Act 1948. It 'provided a public service, the supply of gas, to citizens of the state generally under the control of the state which could dictate its policies and retain its surplus revenue'.[52] The chairman and between ten and 20 other members of the corporation were appointed by the Secretary of State (s 1(2)), and were paid salaries and allowances determined by the Secretary of State with the consent of the Minister for the Civil Service. It was the duty of the corporation, which had a 'special monopoly power for the supply of gas',[53] to develop and maintain an efficient, coordinated and economical system of gas supply and to satisfy so far as economical to do so all reasonable demands for gas (s 2). The minister was authorised to give to the corporation such directions as he considered appropriate for securing that it was managed efficiently (s 4), and was empowered to give 'directions of a general character as to the exercise and performance by the Corporation of their functions . . . in relation to matters which appear to him to affect the national interest' (s 7).[54] Certain broad financial duties were laid upon the corporation (including a duty to ensure that revenues were 'not less than sufficient' to meet outgoings)

[46] See Sixth Report of the Committee on Standards in Public Life, *Reinforcing Standards* (Cm 4557-I, 2000), ch 9.
[47] For background to this, see HC 327 (1997–98), paras 36–43; Commissioner for Public Appointments, Third Report 1997–1998 (1998). See also Commissioner for Public Appointments, Fourth Report 1998–1999 (1999); and Cm 4557-I, 2000, pp 118–120.
[48] See Commissioner for Public Appointments, Fifth Report 1999–2000 (2000), pp 16–17.
[49] Commissioner for Public Appointments, *Public Appointments to NHS Trusts and Health Authorities* (2000); available at www.ocpa.gov.uk.
[50] HC 327 (1997–98); HC 723 (1997–98); HC 410 (1999–2000).
[51] HC 168 (1995–96).
[52] *Foster v British Gas plc* [1991] 2 AC 306, 316.
[53] *Foster v British Gas plc*, ibid. On the monopoly, see Gas Act 1972, s 29.
[54] See SI 1981, No 1459.

(s 14), but many of its financial powers (for example to borrow money) required the consent of the minister given with the approval of the Treasury (s 17). The corporation was required to keep proper accounts which had to be audited by a person approved by the Secretary of State, to whom a copy of the accounts had to be sent (s 23). The corporation was also required to give such information to the Secretary of State about its activities as he might require and to report annually to the minister, the report being laid before Parliament.

The difficulty in privatising nationalised industries with this structure is that the corporations had no share capital which could be sold to private investors.[55] Although privatisation has been secured by a number of different techniques,[56] the difficulty was overcome in some cases by providing that on a day appointed by the Secretary of State all the property, rights and liabilities of the corporation would be transferred to a company nominated by the minister, the company in question being limited by shares wholly owned by the Crown. The government is empowered to retain a holding in this successor company, with the proceeds of the sale of the rest being paid into the Consolidated Fund. The Secretary of State may by order dissolve the old corporation as soon as he is satisfied that its affairs have been wound up and nothing remains to be done. This technique has been used in the case of British Aerospace, the British Transport Docks Board, British Airways, British Telecom, British Gas and the water and electricity companies.[57] Each statute is 'very much a skeleton' with little provision being made with regard to the design of the privatised company.[58] These are matters dealt with in the articles of association of the companies, which are now governed by the Companies Act 1985 in terms of their legal structure, although the public utilities in particular are subject to specific regulation of their activities on a number of grounds discussed below. It is not to be assumed from this transfer to private ownership that the government has relinquished any interest in the way these businesses are conducted. 'Indeed, in an economy as complex and interdependent as that of modern Britain, it should not surprise us that no government can stand aloof from strategic industrial decisions.'[59] The removal of the companies from the public sector has thus been accompanied by a degree of statutory regulation in which, as we shall see, the Secretary of State plays an important part.

The legal structure of the privatised utility

A study by the Comptroller and Auditor-General in 1996 of the four main public utilities (water, gas, electricity and telecommunications) pointed out that they are 'large and economically significant' and together served some 25 million customers, in the process employing assets with a value of some £240 billion. Their total annual turnover of £51 billion represented roughly 8% of annual GDP of the UK.[60] These considerations alone make it inevitable that they should be subject to some form of

---

[55] For a full account of the issues raised in this paragraph, see C Graham and T Prosser (1987) 50 MLR 16.
[56] See e.g. Coal Industry Act 1994, Atomic Energy Authority Act 1995 and, in the case of HMSO, see HC Deb, 18 December 1995, col 1272.
[57] See British Aerospace Act 1980, Transport Act 1984, Civil Aviation Act 1980, Telecommunications Act 1984, Gas Act 1986, Water Act 1989 and Electricity Act 1989. See also Postal Services Act 2000. For an earlier approach, see Iron and Steel Act 1953.
[58] C Graham and T Prosser, p 22.
[59] C Graham and T Prosser, in Graham and Prosser (eds), *Waiving the Rules: The Constitution under Thatcherism*, p 73, at 88. See p 290 above.
[60] HC 645 (1995–96), p 2.

regulation, as does the fact that each of the industries contains an important element of monopoly or dominance by a small number of firms. An example of the statutory model of regulation is found in the Gas Act 1986, which abolished the statutory monopoly of British Gas.[61] Since heavily amended in crucial respects by the Gas Act 1995, the Competition Act 1998 and the Utilities Act 2000, the Gas Act 1986 provides that the principal objective of both the Secretary of State and the regulator (now the Gas and Electricity Markets Authority) is to protect the interests of consumers 'by promoting effective competition between persons engaged in, or in commercial activities connected with, the shipping, transportation or supply of gas'.[62] But although this is the principal objective, both the minister and the regulator are required to carry out their functions in a manner which will secure, 'so far as it is economical to meet them', that 'all reasonable demands' for gas are met and that licence holders are able to finance their activities. Both the minister and the regulator are also specifically directed to have regard to the interests of individuals who are disabled or chronically sick, as well as those who are of pensionable age, who have low incomes or who live in rural areas.[63] Licences for the supply of gas were issued originally by the Secretary of State in consultation with the regulator, but as a result of amendments in the Gas Act 1995 are now issued by the regulator alone.

Under the Gas Act 1986, licences – which will include a formula for prices – were issued for periods of 25 years. The terms of the licence could be varied only with the consent of the licence holder (s 23), failing which a reference could be made by the regulator to the Competition Commission to investigate and report on whether any matter relating to the supply of gas by a public gas supplier to tariff customers operated against the public interest (s 24); if the Commission reached adverse conclusions about the public interest, the regulator was required to make the necessary modifications to the licence conditions.[64] Complaints were previously made to the Monopolies and Mergers Commission, which, in a major review of the gas industry in 1993, concluded that British Gas should be required to separate its transportation and storage business from its trading business and that the tariff formula in the licence should be modified to permit a lower price increase.[65] Following amendments in 1995 and 2000, in some circumstances licences may now be varied by the regulator without consent and without the need for a reference to the Competition Commission. Although it was expected that the role of the regulator in the fixing of prices would become much less important with the introduction of full competition for gas supply under the Gas Act 1995, additional powers were conferred by the Competition Act 1998.[66] This provides that the Gas and Electricity Markets Authority is entitled to exercise concurrently with the Director General of Fair Trading powers under the Competition Act 1998 relating to agreements, decisions or concerted practices which distort competition, or conduct which represents an abuse of a dominant position.[67] Licence holders may also be subject to a number of statutory duties under the 1986 Act,[68] as amended.[69]

---

[61] Gas Act 1986, s 3.
[62] Gas Act 1986, s 4AA (as substituted by the Utilities Act 2000, s 9).
[63] Ibid.
[64] On the requirements of the regulator following a Competition Commission report, see *Re Northern Ireland plc's Application for Judicial Review* [1998] NI 300. See now Utilities Act 2000, s 83, amending Gas Act 1986.
[65] Cm 2315, 1993.
[66] On the changing role of the regulators, see McCrudden, ch 13.
[67] Competition Act 1998, Sch 10(3). See Rodger and McCulloch (eds), *The UK Competition Act*, ch 10.
[68] Gas Act 1986, s 9.
[69] Gas Act 1995, Utilities Act 2000.

The role of the regulator

The regulation of public utilities has generated a large body of academic and non-academic literature.[70] The key to the regulatory model initially adopted is based on the idea of 'a single independent regulator for each industry, operating without undue bureaucracy and supported by a small staff', the government rejecting regulatory systems found overseas, particularly the United States, 'in favour of a quicker and less bureaucratic system of regulation'.[71] But this model was strongly criticised by the Comptroller and Auditor-General, who raised questions about 'the over-concentration of power in one pair of hands', leading him to consider whether there might be a case for 'possible alternatives to the current system of industry-specific regulation by single regulators'. The gas and electricity regulators – OFGAS and OFFER – were merged in 1999, to become OFGEM (the Office of Gas and Electricity Markets) which operates under the direction and governance of the Gas and Electricity Markets Authority following the introduction of the Utilities Act 2000.[72] In making this move, the government explained that the task of regulation was becoming increasingly complex, with the interests of what are now hundreds of licensees to be considered and balanced. It is thus accepted that regulatory responsibilities can best be undertaken by a regulatory authority, to ensure that regulatory decisions are 'less dependent on the personality of a single regulator', thereby ensuring in turn greater continuity and consistency in decision-making.[73] But it remains the case that there are single regulators rather than regulatory authorities in the other utilities.

The regulators are a constitutional curiosity, bodies sui generis, sometimes described as 'a non-ministerial government department',[74] a phrase which contrasts with other descriptions of regulators as being 'independent of government', albeit with 'strong powers'.[75] Interesting questions also arise about their functions, the regulators exercising a blend of the legislative, executive and judicial powers. In the case of the gas industry, the Gas and Electricity Markets Authority has the power to make statutory instruments (a legislative power), to issue licences, vary the terms of licences and regulate the activities of licence holders (an executive power) and deal with complaints from consumers (a quasi-judicial power). Under the Utilities Act 2000, the regulator also has the power to impose financial penalties on licence holders who have breached a licence condition, a power which has given rise to questions about compliance with article 6 of the ECHR which guarantees the right to a fair trial in the determination of civil rights and obligations:

> How can the regulator, who determines the penalty, be an independent and impartial tribunal? The regulator decides whether he will pursue the licensee. He assesses whether the licensee has broken the terms of his licence. He then decides what the penalty is. He is an individual appointed by the executive. . . . he is legislator, prosecutor and judge, all rolled into one.[76]

Concern about the lack of accountability of the regulators has led to calls in the past from the regulated community for a right of appeal against their decisions, although these have so far gone unheeded. But the need for greater transparency on the part of

---

[70] Important contributions are Graham, *Regulating Public Utilities*; McCrudden (ed); MacGregor, Prosser and Villiers (eds), *Regulation and Markets Beyond 2000*; and Prosser, *Laws and the Regulators*, which give a good insight into the sheer scale of and scope of regulatory activity in contemporary Britain.

[71] A Carlsberg (1992) 37 New York Law School Law Rev 285.

[72] For background see Cm 3898, 1998; Prosser (1999) 62 MLR 196.

[73] HL Deb, 4 May 2000, col 1141.

[74] HL Deb, 5 July 1989, col 1201 (Baroness Hooper).

[75] HL Deb, 18 July 1983, col 36 (Mr Cecil Parkinson).

[76] HL Deb, 4 May 2000, col 1171 (Lord Kingsland).

the regulators has led to the introduction of a requirement that the Gas and Electricity Markets Authority must give reasons for its decisions.[77]

D. The accountability of public utilities and public utility regulators

Accountability to government

1 *Public corporations.*   Public ownership of an industry usually came about because of the need for greater public control than could be obtained by means of legal restrictions imposed on privately owned undertakings. If there is to be public control of a corporation, this must be achieved primarily through the relevant minister, who appoints the chairman and members of the board, who has power to call for information and give directions to the board, who approves the board's external financing limits and who receives the board's accounts and annual report. This does not mean that ministers should be responsible for every act of day-to-day administration, but they must at least have power to intervene on strategic matters which by the legislation are subject to their approval. In turn, ministerial responsibility to Parliament requires that ministers should account to Parliament for the use that they make of their statutory powers.

Whatever the framers of the nationalisation Acts in 1945–50 may have intended, ministers, in fact, exercised very considerable control over the industries and often intervened in their affairs. One reason for this was that while for some periods some nationalised industries were financially profitable, many went through periods when they made heavy losses and needed financial support from the government. Another reason was that the industries played a substantial part in the national economy, as employers, as providers of basic means of communication and energy, and in their investment programmes: management of the industries became an aspect of the management of the economy. Many of the industries' decisions had widespread social and economic repercussions, for example the level of prices charged to the consumer, wage rates for their employees, purchasing decisions (for example, whether British Airways should buy British aeroplanes) and the closure of unprofitable activities (for example, railway lines and coalmines). It was impossible to insulate such decisions from the political process, but it was extremely difficult to strike the right balance. A Commons select committee in 1968 advocated an 'arm's length' relationship between boards and ministers, with political intervention being confined to a few key points.[78]

2 *Privatised utilities.*   Privatisation has not removed the scope for ministerial intervention in the activities of the former nationalised industries. As the Comptroller and Auditor-General pointed out: 'The Government determined the initial position in which the industries would begin their life following privatisation. In particular they laid down the licences issued to companies, determined the capital structure of those companies that were formerly public owned, and set initial price controls for those which were monopolies or had a dominant position.'[79] The government also has a role in promoting competition, where the industry in question contains what is a 'natural monopoly' and for this purpose legislation may be necessary, as for example in the case of the Gas Act 1995 which extended competition in gas supply. On the other hand, the government has a role to play in protecting consumers from the unfair practices of the utility

---

[77] Utilities Act 2000, s 87.
[78] HC 371–I (1967–68), p 3.
[79] HC 645 (1995–96), p 7.

companies and to this end the legislation makes provision for the appointment by ministers of a regulator in each of the industries in question, with responsibilities determined by the government and Parliament. In some cases the legislation will address specific abuses, such as the provisions of the Utilities Act 2000 which deal with concerns about the large salaries which the directors of some of the utility companies were paying themselves. The companies must report annually to the Gas and Electricity Markets Authority whether there is in force an arrangement linking directors' remuneration to levels of performance regarding service standards. Where such an arrangement is in force, the report must also describe the arrangements and the remuneration and the details must be published by the company in a manner which will 'secure adequate publicity for it'. The report may also be published by the Authority.

Together with the regulator, ministers generally have prescribed statutory duties, as we have seen. Ministers are also empowered in some cases to give directions to the regulator in determining the allocation of priorities in the performance of his or her duties. Under the Gas Act 1986, the Secretary of State is required to issue guidance to the regulator about social and environmental policies.[80] Otherwise, the legislation empowers the minister to make regulations, although in the case of the gas industry the effect of the Gas Act 1995 has been to transfer much of this power to the regulator. Nevertheless, the power to make regulations can generally be exercised only with the consent of the minister, who in any event retains some powers, for example in the case of public safety. Thus the Secretary of State may make regulations empowering an officer to (i) enter premises in which there is a gas service pipe for the purpose of inspecting gas fittings on the premises; (ii) examine and test any such fittings or other related equipment; and (iii) disconnect or seal off any gas system on the premises, where 'in his opinion it is necessary to do so for the purpose of averting danger to life or property'. New powers under the Utilities Act 2000 give the Secretary of State the authority to introduce regulations requiring the adjustment of charges where he or she considers that any group of customers of authorised suppliers are treated less favourably than other customers. Regulations may also be made under the Utilities Act 2000 imposing energy efficiency targets on gas suppliers.

Select committees and accountability

1 *Public corporations.*   The difficulties encountered by MPs in obtaining information about the nationalised industries, together with the lack of adequate procedures for dealing with the reports and accounts laid annually before Parliament, led in the early 1950s to various attempts to use committees of the Commons to establish greater parliamentary control. In 1954–5, the House appointed a committee to inform Parliament about the current policy and practice of the industries, but excluded from its remit matters which involved a minister's responsibility to Parliament or were matters of day-to-day administration.[81] In 1956, there was set up a select committee with the duty of examining the reports and accounts of the nationalised industries.[82] The committee was regularly reappointed until 1979. By then its terms of reference had been widened to include powers in respect of other public undertakings, such as the Independent Broadcasting Authority and the Bank of England, except for certain of the Bank's activities which were reserved from inquiry. Between 1956 and 1979 this all-party committee made a series of searching and sometimes highly critical inquiries

[80] Gas Act 1986, s 4AB (as inserted by the Utilities Act 2000, s 10).
[81] HC 120 (1955–56).
[82] Coombes, *The Member of Parliament and the Administration.*

into the industries and their relationships with the government. The inquiries started from the published reports and accounts of the industry under review but evidence was taken from the industry, the department concerned and other interested parties.

The committee sought to discover how far the industries were subject to informal ministerial control and to ensure that ministers were responsible to Parliament for the influence which they in fact exercised, especially when ministerial pressure had prevailed against the commercial judgment of the boards. The committee's reports on topics of general concern, for example, ministerial control of the industries (in 1968), contributed much to the development of policies relating to the nationalised industries. The success of the committee on a non-partisan basis also contributed to the spread of specialised parliamentary committees into other areas of governmental activity.[83] When in 1979 the present scheme of select committees was set up, each committee was empowered to examine the expenditure, administration and policy of the principal departments and their 'associated public bodies'.[84] This was considered to leave no place for the nationalised industries committee. Certain industries have been reviewed by the resulting committees such as the Treasury Committee, the Trade and Industry Committee and the Transport Committee.[85] Some aspects of the industries' finances have been considered by the Public Accounts Committee, but although the accounts of the industries were laid annually in Parliament, the Comptroller and Auditor-General had no power to inspect the books of the industries themselves.[86] The National Audit Act 1983 extended the Auditor-General's power to examine the economy, efficiency and effectiveness of government departments and related bodies, but the nationalised industries and other public authorities, such as the BBC, were expressly excluded from the scope of the Act.[87]

2 *Privatisation.*   Although privatisation has reduced the scope for scrutiny of nationalised industries by the select committees, it has by no means disappeared. Investigations of different kinds have been conducted mainly by the Public Accounts Committee and the Trade and Industry Committee, although others also play a part. The Public Accounts Committee has been concerned mainly to investigate the process by which state enterprises have been sold, with a view to establishing whether value for money has been secured for the taxpayer.[88] Many of its reports have in fact included stinging criticism of government failure to raise more money from the sales or to pay too large a subsidy to purchasers.[89] The Stationery Office was sold for less than 'the most pessimistic pre-sale valuation',[90] the (Railway) Rolling Stock Leasing Companies were sold for £1.5 billion and then sold on for £2.7 billion,[91] and the share price of AEA Technology, British Energy plc and Railtrack respectively rose sharply after the sales.[92] Both of the latter two failures were said to demonstrate 'the merits of selling only part of the government's shareholding in a company on initial flotation'.[93] Other criticisms have related to the consequences of the sales, with the privatisation of the Rolling Stock Leasing Companies being condemned for having been conducted in a way which 'enabled

[83] Ch 10 D.
[84] HC SO 152(1); ch 10 D.
[85] See e.g. HC 597 (1988–89), HC 141 (1990–91).
[86] HC 115(1980–81).
[87] National Audit Act 1983, s 7(4) and Sch 4; ch 17 D.
[88] See generally HC 992 (1997–98).
[89] For an example of the latter, see HC 601 (1998–99).
[90] HC 599 (1997–98).
[91] HC 782 (1997–98).
[92] HC 749 (1997–98), HC 242 (1998–99), HC 256 (1998–99).
[93] HC 242 (1998–99), p vii.

a small number of former British Rail managers to become millionaires, with windfall gains ranging from £15 million to £33 million'. 'Such large payments', complained the Committee, 'risk discrediting privatisation as a whole'.[94]

Both the Public Accounts Committee and the Trade and Industry Committee have conducted a number of enquiries into the work of the regulators, who have been 'fairly regular witnesses' before select committees.[95] The Public Accounts Committee has been concerned to ensure that OFGEM maintained pressure on the gas companies to reduce their prices,[96] while the Trade and Industry Committee has in the past examined the annual reports of OFGAS (the former gas regulator)[97] and investigated the work of OFGAS and more recently OFGEM.[98] These investigations have dealt with a range of issues, although a constant refrain has been the role of the regulator in promoting price competition, on the one hand, and protecting the 'fuel poor', on the other.[99] The select committees have also examined the work of other regulators, including OFFER (the former electricity regulator), OFTEL and the Rail Regulator,[100] while the investigation by the Culture, Media and Sport Committee into the National Lottery included an examination of the work of the National Lottery Commission.[101] A number of important reforms to the regulatory framework have been proposed by the select committees,[102] and reforms have also been proposed by both witnesses and the committees in relation to the structure and powers of the select committees.[103] Many of the former (regulatory framework reforms) have been implemented by the Utilities Act 2000.[104] Otherwise the select committees have examined the utility companies themselves, and their practices. A particularly notable example of this is the Employment Committee's enquiry in 1994, following some controversial increases in executive pay.[105]

Judicial review

1 *Public corporations.*   As public corporations do not generally benefit from immunities of the Crown, in carrying out their operations they are fully subject to the law as are industrial enterprises in private ownership. In fact, many corporations provide public utility services which were subject to statutory control long before the era of nationalisation. So far as the principal powers and duties of the nationalised corporations were concerned, these were usually expressed in such general terms in the parent Acts that it was doubtful whether they could be enforced by legal process:

---

[94] HC 782 (1997–98).
[95] HC 193-i (1999–2000), p i.
[96] HC 171 (1999–2000).
[97] HC 646 (1994–95).
[98] HC 185 (1993–94); HC 193-i, ii (1999–2000).
[99] HC 174 (1998–99); HC 171 (1999–2000); HC 193-ii (1999–2000).
[100] HC 174 (1998–99), HC 93-i (1999–2000); HC 536 (1999–2000). In the case of the last it was claimed that the haste to privatise had led to weaknesses in the regulatory regime.
[101] HC 56, 57 (2000–2001). The committee lamented the lack of 'relevant skills or experience on the part of the Commission' and questioned whether the body selecting the licence holder should also be the regulator.
[102] HC 481 (1994–95).
[103] HC 646 (1994–95) (calls from gas regulator for separate select committee for the 'regulation and regulators'); HC 536 (1999–2000) (need for committee to take evidence from previous regulators where incumbent unable to explain decisions of predecessor).
[104] Notably the duty of the Gas and Electricity Markets Authority to give reasons for decisions: Utilities Act 2000, s 87.
[105] HC 159 (1994–95). See now Utilities Act 2000, ss 61, 97.

In *Charles Roberts and Co Ltd v British Railways Board*[106] a company which manufactured railway tank wagons sought a declaration that the board were not authorised to manufacture such wagons for sale to an oil company for use on railways in Britain. *Held* that the court should not interfere with the board's bona fide decision that such manufacture was an efficient way of carrying out the board's business within its statutory powers and duties; the judge declined to consider the economic effect which the board's policies might have on private manufacturers.

It would similarly be difficult by action in the courts to enforce the general duties of a board, as this seems to be left by the statutes to the minister concerned.[107] But public corporations are subject to the jurisdiction of the courts if they commit a tort or a breach of contract, if they exceed their powers or if they fail to observe statutory procedures or to perform specific statutory duties.[108] Questions have arisen as to the extent to which the BBC is subject to judicial review. Although it has been held that the corporation's duty of political impartiality is not enforceable in the courts,[109] it is not now possible to argue that judicial review does not apply at all on the ground that the BBC is a creature of prerogative.[110] Judicial review casts a long shadow and even regulatory bodies that do not exercise statutory functions may be subject to judicial review.[111]

2 *Privatisation.* So far as the privatised utilities are concerned, it is unclear whether the companies themselves would be subject to judicial review, although it has been held that a privatised water and sewerage undertaker is a public body for the purposes of the Human Rights Act.[112] Privatised utilities may also be regarded as authorities of the state for the purposes of the direct effect of EC directives, as were the nationalised industries after the House of Lords decision in *Foster v British Gas plc.*[113] In *Griffin v South West Water Services Ltd*[114] it was held that a privatised water company satisfied the test laid down in the *Foster* case for the purposes of direct effect to the extent that it was a body which (i) provided a public service, (ii) under the control of the state, for the purposes of which (iii) it had special powers. It was the second of these three conditions which gave rise to most difficulty, but the fact that the court was prepared to acknowledge such a degree of state control is an interesting reflection on the public nature of the activities of the privatised companies. Indeed Blackburne J went so far as to say that the extent of control by the state under legislation and licence was 'at least as great' as that exercised in relation to the nationalised industries, although this alone is not enough to make these companies subject to judicial review. The fact that the water company operated in what was described as 'a business environment in compliance with legislation but driven by economic criteria' did not detract from the conclusion of the court, although on the facts the point was academic for it was also held that the directive in question (75/129/EC) was not sufficiently

---

[106] [1964] 3 All ER 651.
[107] Cf *British Oxygen Co Ltd v South West Scotland Electricity Board* 1956 SC (HL) 112, 1959 SC (HL) 17.
[108] *Warwickshire CC v British Railways Board* [1969] 3 All ER 631; *Booth & Co (International) Ltd v National Enterprise Board* [1978] 3 All ER 624; *Grunwick Processing Laboratories Ltd v ACAS* [1978] AC 655; *Home Office v Commission for Racial Equality* [1982] QB 385; *R v Radio Authority, ex p Bull* [1997] 2 All ER 561.
[109] *Lynch v BBC* [1983] NILR 193.
[110] Cf *R v BBC, ex p Lavelle* [1983] ICR 99. See also *CCSU v Minister of State for the Civil Service* [1985] AC 374.
[111] *R v Panel on Take-Overs and Mergers, ex p Datafin plc* [1987] QB 815; ch 31.
[112] *Marcic v Thames Water Utilities Ltd* [2001] 4 All ER 326; [2002] 2 All ER 55. On the implication of the Human Rights Act, see Graham, pp 136–42.
[113] [1991] 2 AC 306.
[114] [1995] IRLR 15.

precise and unconditional to give rise to obligations which could be enforced directly in the domestic courts.

Different considerations apply in the case of the minister (exercising powers under the relevant regulatory legislation) and the regulators. There is perhaps more scope for review of the regulator than of anyone else in the process, either because of a failure to comply with ministerial directions or because of decisions which have been taken under the authority of the Act.[115] But because judicial review may be available in principle, it does not follow that it is 'always appropriate' or 'a substitute for proper political supervision and well thought-out decision-making procedures'.[116] Indeed, it has been suggested that judicial review offers no meaningful protection to a party that feels it has been wronged by a regulator's decision, on the ground that the courts are unprepared 'to question the quality of the regulator's decision or require that the evidence underpinning the decision be examined'.[117] By way of contrast, however, there is evidence that at least one regulator (OFGAS) has gone to considerable lengths to avoid judicial review by adopting a 'deliberate policy' of refusing to give reasons for decisions and by failing to keep adequate records of reasons for decisions (in this case relating to the adoption of a particular price control). This was strongly deprecated by the Public Accounts Committee, which considered it 'essential that public bodies keep adequate records of the reasons for their decisions, to help ensure the proper conduct of public business and accountability'.[118] The Utilities Act 2000 now requires reasons to be given for a wide range of decisions taken by both the Gas and Electricity Markets Authority and the Secretary of State.[119] Although judicial review could be proper and important in some cases, there may be cases where it is appropriate to seek declaratory relief by way of originating summons.[120]

Consumer consultation

The legislation has often provided formal machinery for consultation between the industries themselves and the consumers and users of their services. Consumer councils and consultative committees were created at different times for electricity, gas, coal, rail and air transport and the Post Office. Such consultative committees provided a means for the expression of the views of consumers, including opinions on the quality of services. They also provided a channel by which dissatisfied consumers might seek redress for grievances regarding the services they had received. But the existence of these consultative bodies was not widely known and in 1976 it was suggested that an Ombudsman be established for the industries to be an impartial investigator of consumer complaints.[121] Privatisation has seen the abolition of the existing consultative committees and consumer councils, although somewhat similar bodies have been established in the newly privatised utilities. Under the Utilities Act 2000, for example, the Gas and Electricity Consumer Council appointed by the Secretary of State has a number of wide-ranging responsibilities. These include providing advice and information and the investigation of consumer complaints. The Council is empowered to direct

---

[115] *R v Director of Passenger Rail Franchising, ex p Save our Railways*, *The Times*, 18 December 1995; *Re Northern Ireland Electricity plc's Application for Judicial Review* [1998] NI 300.

[116] A McHarg [1995] PL 539, at p 550.

[117] HC 481-iii (1994–95), p 77 (memorandum submitted by National Power plc). For fuller treatment of judicial review in this context, see McCrudden (ed), ch 7; and Graham, pp 68–75.

[118] HC 37 (1996–97).

[119] Utilities Act 2000, s 87, amending Gas Act 1986, s 38A.

[120] *Mercury Communications Ltd v Director General of Telecommunications* [1996] 1 WLR 48.

[121] Report by Justice, *The Citizen and Public Agencies: Remedying Grievances*. See also Robson, ch 10; HC 514 (1970–71) and Cmnd 5067, 1972; and HC 334 (1978–79).

both the regulator and any licence holder to supply it with information which it needs to carry out its functions.[122] The Council – which is designed to act as a 'powerful consumer champion, operating independently of the regulator'[123] – is required to report annually to the Secretary of State on its activities during the year.[124] A Consumer Council for Postal Services is established by the Postal Services Act 2000, an Act which paves the way for the dissolution of the Post Office.

E. Advisory bodies

While public boards may provide services or manage undertakings themselves, subject to a degree of control by ministers and departments, where a department wishes to retain all decision-making and management in its own hands, it may seek through advisory bodies to receive expert advice and assistance from persons outside government. Such advisory bodies can take many different forms. Some are primarily concerned with considering the need for fresh legislation; others are concerned with the choice of policies under existing laws. Some are appointed because an Act of Parliament says that they must be; others are appointed simply because the government wishes to seek information and advice from wherever it can find it. Some are appointed for a particular purpose and have a temporary existence. We now consider briefly some of the main kinds of advisory body.

Royal commissions and departmental committees

The appointment of a royal commission or a departmental committee is an act of the executive which requires no specific parliamentary approval, although often it may be a response to political demands. When an issue of public policy or a possible change in the law requires thorough examination and the government is not already politically committed to a definite policy, the task may be entrusted to an invited group of persons from outside the relevant departments. A departmental committee is appointed by one minister or by several ministers acting jointly. For substantial matters where greater formality is considered appropriate and where time is not of the essence, a royal commission may be appointed instead. This requires a royal warrant to be issued to the commissioners by the Sovereign on the advice of a Secretary of State. Apart from the formality and greater prestige of a royal commission, both commissions and departmental committees carry out their inquiries in a similar manner. The commission or committee will usually call for evidence from individuals and organisations outside government as well as from public authorities and it may undertake its own programme of research. Usually a royal commission hears the main evidence in public and copies of the oral and written evidence received are published; the commission's report is invariably published and laid before Parliament. A departmental committee is more likely to receive evidence in private and it is less common for its evidence to be published. But both the Committee on Ministers' Powers (1929–32) and the Committee on Administrative Tribunals and Inquiries (1955–7) took evidence in public and this was later published.[125] The reports of departmental committees are usually but not always published.[126]

---

[122] See Utilities Act 2000, Part III.
[123] HL Deb, 4 May 2000, col 1134.
[124] Utilities Act 2000, Sch 2(6).
[125] Ch 27.
[126] For the use of commissions and committees in 1945–69, see Cartwright, *Royal Commissions and Departmental Committees in Britain*.

Neither royal commissions nor departmental committees have power to compel the attendance of witnesses, unlike tribunals of inquiry appointed under the Tribunals of Inquiry (Evidence) Act 1921 by authority of Parliament.[127] The choice of the chairperson to a commission or committee is important since he or she must ensure that the commission or committee carries through its work efficiently and will seek to achieve a unanimous report where possible.[128] Usually the commission or committee disbands when it has reported but committees or commissions may be appointed on a more permanent basis and will produce a series of reports (for example, the Committee on Standards in Public Life, first appointed in 1994). When the investigating body has delivered its report, it is for the minister or the government to decide how far its recommendations are acceptable and if so in what form they should be carried out, for example by the preparation of a Bill to amend the law. In the 1980s and 1990s, royal commissions and departmental committees were much less conspicuous than they had been in the 1970s when a number of important reports were published (on matters such as official secrecy, obscenity and film censorship, and financial aid to political parties).[129] However, these forms of advisory body are far from dead. A royal commission under the chairmanship of Lord Wakeham was appointed in 1999 to consider the reform of the House of Lords.[130] Some of the work which in the past might have been undertaken by such bodies is now conducted by bodies such as the Committee on Standards in Public Life and by task forces.

The Committee on Standards in Public Life

A particularly important and effective advisory committee in recent years has been the Committee on Standards in Public Life. The Committee was established initially in 1994 by Mr John Major when he was Prime Minister, following allegations that some members of Parliament had accepted payments from a businessman for asking questions in Parliament on his behalf.[131] Chaired initially by Lord Nolan, the Committee included members who had political experience and those who were independent of party. Whatever the original intention of Mr Major, the Committee has become a standing body and as such is regarded as a genuinely independent body. Its members are appointed by the Prime Minister and formally it is an advisory NDPB sponsored by the Cabinet Office. Lord Nolan was replaced as the Committee's chairman by Lord Neill of Bladen in 1997 and in turn by Sir Nigel Wicks in 2001. In its first report the Committee developed a series of seven principles for the conduct of public life (selflessness, integrity, objectivity, accountability, openness, honesty and leadership). The first report is important also for applying these principles to guide the behaviour of MPs, ministers and civil servants, as well as appointments to public bodies.[132]

Many of the recommendations of the first report have been dealt with at different points in this book: these include the new rules relating to the conduct of MPs; the revision of the rules relating to the conduct of ministers and civil servants; and the creation of a Public Appointments Commissioner.[133] Other reports have dealt with

[127] Ch 29 C; cf Cartwright, pp 142–5.
[128] Report of Balfour Committee on Procedure of Royal Commissions, Cd 5235, 1910; and see Lords Benson and Rothschild (1982) 60 Public Administration 339.
[129] Cmnd 5104, 1972; Cmnd 7772, 1979; Cmnd 6601, 1976.
[130] Cm 4534, 2000. See chs 9 I and 10 B.
[131] See Major, *The Autobiography*, pp 567, 572–7. For the terms of reference, see HC Deb, 25 October 1994, col 758.
[132] Cm 2850, 1995.
[133] See chs 11, 13 E, 13 D and 14 B respectively.

the government of local funding bodies, standards of conduct in local government, NDPBs and NHS trusts, the funding of political parties and the standards of conduct in the House of Lords.[134] In its sixth report the Committee also undertook a review of the implementation of the first report, and in the course of doing so made a number of additional recommendations.[135] For the purposes of the inquiry into the funding of political parties, the terms of reference of the Committee had formally to be extended by the Prime Minister. The Committee's far-reaching recommendations led to the Political Parties, Elections and Referendums Act 2000 which requires the disclosure of contributions to political parties; restricts the foreign funding of political parties; and introduces expenditure limits for political parties and others during general elections.[136] The Act also imposes spending limits in referendums, contrary to the recommendations of the Committee.

Consultative committees

The practice of consultation between government departments and organisations outside government is a widespread phenomenon of British government even today. Consultation serves to meet the needs of the administrator for expert information and advice on scientific, technical or industrial matters. It also is an important means by which those in government seek to maintain the continuing consent of the governed and it thus serves important political purposes. Where consultative committees and advisory councils exist, they enable the practice of consultation to be placed on a regular and structured footing. Consultative committees are used over the whole range of government. They have proved particularly useful in the process by which new delegated legislation is prepared, but their use is not confined to projected legislation. In some cases there is a statutory obligation on a minister to consult a standing committee or named association, although the advisory body may be unable to take the initiative in discussing a subject without the matter being referred to it by the minister. Many advisory bodies are appointed and consulted at the discretion of the minister or department concerned and their discussions are often regarded as confidential, even where a more open approach to government would promote administrative fairness.[137]

An illustration of a statutory body which ministers must consult is the Police Negotiating Board for the United Kingdom. Regulations relating to the government, administration and conditions of service in police forces can be made under the Police Act 1996 and the equivalent Acts for Scotland and Northern Ireland only after the Secretary of State has consulted the Board, on which sit representatives of local police authorities and of all ranks of the police.[138] The Social Security Advisory Committee gives advice and reports to the Secretary of State for Social Security on his or her functions under the Social Security Acts. In particular, where the Secretary of State proposes to make regulations about social security benefits the proposal must be referred to the committee; when the regulations are laid before Parliament, the Secretary of State must inform Parliament of the committee's views and, if effect is not to be given to the committee's recommendations, of the reasons for this.[139] The Council on Tribunals, appointed to oversee the operation of tribunals and inquiries, is essentially a body which advises and is consulted by government departments; like most advisory

---

[134] Cm 3557, 1996; Cm 3702, 1997; Cm 4057, 1998; and Cm 4903, 2000.
[135] Cm 4557, 2000.
[136] See ch 9 C, E.
[137] *R v Secretary of State for Health, ex p US Tobacco Inc* [1992] QB 353.
[138] Police Act 1996, s 61.
[139] See now Social Security Administration Act 1992, Part XIII.

bodies it has no executive functions, but its watchdog role includes consideration of complaints about particular tribunals and inquiries.[140]

Task forces

A type of advisory body which has grown up since 1997 is the task force, described by one commentator as a 'surrogate for old Royal Commissions or departmental committees'.[141] A parliamentary written answer in November 1999 revealed a list of 148 review groups and task forces, established in many departments and covering a wide range of issues. They included the Modernising Government Quality Schemes Task Force (Cabinet Office), the Creative Industries Task Force (Department for Culture, Media and Sport), the School Standards Task Force (Department for Education and Employment), the Human Rights Task Force (Home Office) and the Coronary Disease Task Force (Scottish Executive).[142] Not all included ministers, but most had civil servants and people from the private sector among their members. Indeed some were chaired by corporate executives. Quite how many such task forces there are at any one time is controversial, as was pointed out in the Sixth Report of the Committee on Standards in Public Life, which revealed estimates of between 30 and 295, the latter in an academic study entitled Ruling by Task Force.[143] The Committee echoed the concern of others that task forces fall outside the scope of the procedures relating to public appointments, even though their purpose may be to bring 'external advice to bear on specific policy issues'.[144]

Part of the difficulty associated with regulating appointments to task forces is the want of an agreed definition about the term: it could mean anything from a royal commission to an internal working group. The Committee on Standards in Public Life has recommended that an agreed definition should be established by the Cabinet Office, in which the key elements should be a significant outside membership, operating within a time frame of less than two years.[145] One of the current concerns is that task forces can be established without any limit of time and in the process become in effect advisory NDPBs, but without any supervision of their appointments: this is an area in which the writ of the Commissioner for Public Appointments does not run.[146] The Committee on Standards in Public Life recommended that there is a need for a thorough review of the present position to address concerns about unregulated growth of task forces, the secret nature of their appointments, and their lack of accountability. The Committee also recommended that any task force which has been in existence for more than two years should be disbanded or reclassified as an advisory NDPB.[147] A worrying variation on this theme was the introduction of arrangements in late 2001 for leading businessmen to join the strategy board of the Department of Trade and Industry.[148]

---

[140] Ch 29 A.
[141] Peter Hennessy, as quoted in Cm 4557-I, 2000, para 10.1.
[142] HL Deb, 11 November 1999, WA 242.
[143] Barker, Byrne and Veall, Ruling by Task Force.
[144] Cm 4557-I, 2000, para 10.6.
[145] Ibid, paras 10.14–10.15.
[146] HC 327 (1997–98), para 7.
[147] Ibid, para 10.16.
[148] Financial Times, 22 November 2001. This was designed to make Whitehall 'more business friendly'. See HC 454-I (2001–2).

Chapter 15

FOREIGN AFFAIRS AND THE COMMONWEALTH

This chapter outlines the law relating to the conduct of the United Kingdom's foreign relations. International law has the primary function of regulating the relations of independent, sovereign states with one another.[1] For this purpose the United Kingdom of Great Britain and Northern Ireland is the state, with authority to act also for its dependent possessions, such as the Channel Islands, the Isle of Man and the surviving colonies, such as Gibraltar, none of which is a state at international law. But political groupings and national boundaries seldom last for all time. Thus the Empire gave way to the Commonwealth, whose members are now all independent states. In the development of the European Union, organs of the Union have acquired capacity on behalf of the member states to conduct relations on economic and commercial matters between the Union and non-member states.[2]

This chapter considers (a) the executive's power to conduct foreign affairs; (b) aspects of the making of treaties; and (c) in outline, the development and nature of the Commonwealth. It does not, however, outline the whole of what can be called foreign relations law.[3]

A. The foreign affairs prerogative, international law and the courts

In 1820, Chitty believed it essential for the conduct of foreign affairs that 'the exclusive power of managing and executing state measures' should be vested in one individual, as it was not practical for an assembly of people to decide what action should be taken by the state. The constitution, said Chitty, had vested in the King the supreme and exclusive power of managing the country's foreign affairs.[4] At common law, this power, like control of the armed forces,[5] is still vested in the Crown, although many aspects of foreign relations law are the subject of legislation (for example, the Diplomatic Privileges Act 1964 and the State Immunity Act 1978).[6] As a prerogative power, the foreign affairs power is exercised on the authority of the Cabinet or of ministers, in particular the Prime Minister and the Secretary of State for Foreign and Commonwealth Affairs. While parliamentary approval is not generally needed before action is taken, ministers are responsible to Parliament for their policies and decisions.[7]

The Foreign Secretary is responsible for the Foreign and Commonwealth Office, which includes the diplomatic service that represents British interests abroad. Other ministers and departments deal as required with international aspects of their work. These include

---

[1] Page 10 above. And see Brownlie, *Principles of Public International Law*, and Jennings and Watts, *Oppenheim's International Law: the Law of Peace*.
[2] Ch 8 A and p 318 below.
[3] See HLE, vol 18, title *Foreign Relations Law*.
[4] Chitty, *Prerogatives of the Crown*, ch 4.
[5] Ch 16.
[6] Pages 311–12 below.
[7] HLE, vol 8(2), pp 310–15.

the Ministry of Defence, the Treasury, the Home Office (especially immigration control), the Department of Trade and Industry (international trade) and the departments of Inland Revenue and Work and Pensions, concerned with British citizens who work abroad and foreigners who work in the United Kingdom.

The prerogative extends to the 'whole catalogue of relations with foreign nations',[8] such as making treaties, declaring war and making peace, instituting hostilities that fall short of war (as with the Falkland Islands, the Gulf campaign and Afghanistan), the recognition of foreign states, sending and receiving ambassadors, issuing passports[9] and granting diplomatic protection to British citizens abroad.[10]

But Crown prerogative does not include everything that is needed to carry out the government's foreign policies. Except in wartime, the prerogative does not extend to controlling trade between the United Kingdom and foreign countries. Thus import and export controls are authorised by statute.[11] Although some prerogative power exists to control the movement of aliens to and from the United Kingdom, immigration control is essentially derived from statute.[12] The prerogative does not include power to impose taxes for regulating foreign trade,[13] and the power to make treaties does not include power to change the law of the United Kingdom.[14]

The fact that the government may take action in foreign affairs without the prior consent of Parliament does not allow it to dispense with political support. Foreign affairs are the subject of debate and questions in Parliament; and the Foreign Affairs Committee of the House of Commons examines 'the expenditure, administration and policy of the Foreign and Commonwealth Office and of associated public bodies'.[15] Since 1979 the committee has reviewed many areas of foreign policy, sometimes in very critical terms.[16]

The relationship between national and international law[17]

The relationship between national and international law raises difficult questions in both theory and practice. By art 25 of the German Constitution, the general rules of public international law are declared to be an integral part of German law; they take precedence over other German laws and create rights and duties for the people. By contrast with this instance of 'monism', English law in general favours 'dualism', that is, a position in which the two systems of law (national and international) co-exist, but function separately: each has distinct purposes and the subjects of international law are typically sovereign states, not individual persons. This co-existence does not guarantee harmony between the two systems. Thus an executive act in foreign affairs which is lawful in national law – under the prerogative or by statute – may be a breach of international law for which the United Kingdom is responsible.[18] Conversely, an executive act which seeks to perform an international obligation may be unlawful in national law.[19] This dualism is best seen in respect of treaties.

---

[8] Mann, *Foreign Affairs in English Courts*, p 4.
[9] *R v Foreign Secretary, ex p Everett* [1989] QB 811; p 432 below.
[10] Cf *Mutasa v A-G* [1980] QB 114; *China Navigation Co Ltd v A-G* [1932] 2 KB 197.
[11] Import, Export and Customs Powers (Defence) Act 1939, made permanent by the Import and Export Control Act 1990: see (Scott Report) HC 115 (1995–96), vol I, pp 49–105; vol IV, pp 1759–66.
[12] Ch 20 B; cf Immigration Act 1971, s 33(5).
[13] Bill of Rights, art 4 (pp 14 and 56 above).
[14] See section B.
[15] And see ch 10 D.
[16] C Y Carstairs, in Drewry (ed), *The New Select Committees*, ch 9.
[17] Mann, chs 6–8; Brownlie, ch 2; Jennings and Watts, pp 56–63.
[18] E.g. *Mortensen v Peters* (1908) 8 F(J) 93; p 56 below.
[19] E.g. *Walker v Baird* [1892] AC 491; p 314 below.

It is axiomatic that municipal courts have not . . . the competence to adjudicate upon or to enforce the rights arising out of transactions entered into by independent sovereign states between themselves on the plane of international law.[20]

When new obligations are created by treaty, legislation is needed for them to become rules of national law.[21]

In respect of customary international law (the 'common law' of inter-state relations), English courts at one time stated that international law was part of the common law of England. Blackstone declared: 'the law of nations (wherever any question arises which is properly the object of its jurisdiction) is here adopted to its full extent by the common law, and is held to be a part of the law of the land.'[22] On this approach, by which international law may be said to be 'incorporated' in national law,[23] no specific act of 'transformation' is needed: a national court may directly apply the customary international rule, provided that this would not be contrary to statute or a prior decision binding on the court.[24] For the courts to apply such a rule of international law, it must have 'attained the position of general acceptance by civilised nations as a rule of international conduct, evidenced by international treaties and conventions, authoritative textbooks, practice and judicial decision'.[25] The difficulties in this process of recognition include the task of deciding whether a new rule of international law has emerged or whether an established international rule has changed. They are illustrated by the two following decisions.

In *R v Home Secretary, ex p Thakrar*,[26] arising from the expulsion of Asians from Uganda in 1972, the applicant, Thakrar (born in Uganda), claimed to be entitled to enter the United Kingdom on the basis of a rule of customary international law to the effect that a British protected person expelled from the country in which he was resident (here, Uganda) was entitled to enter British territory. The Court of Appeal held that no such rule of international law existed, nor (if it did) could it prevail against the Immigration Act 1971; in any event such a rule could not be enforced against the United Kingdom by a private individual, only by other states.

By contrast, in *Trendtex Trading Corpn v Central Bank of Nigeria*[27] a majority in the Court of Appeal held that because of changing practice in international law restricting sovereign immunity, the Central Bank of Nigeria was not immune from the jurisdiction of British courts. Since the rules of international law were changing to a narrower view of sovereign immunity, the court did not follow an earlier decision on the basis of which the bank would have been immune from being sued in British courts.

In fact, the adoption of customary international law by national courts in this manner is limited. One reason for this is that many matters such as state and diplomatic immunity are subject to legislation that is enacted in response to multilateral agreements.[28] The State Immunity Act 1978, enacted in part to give effect to the European Convention on State Immunity,[29] takes a narrower view of sovereign immunity than did the common law. Immunity from the jurisdiction of UK courts is enjoyed only by foreign states, governments and other entities exercising sovereign authority.[30] Exceptions from immunity arise in relation to commercial transactions, contracts to be

---

[20] *Rayner (Mincing Lane) Ltd v Dept of Trade* [1990] 2 AC 418, at 499 (Lord Oliver).

[21] Section B.

[22] *Commentaries*, iv, 67. And see e.g. *Triquet v Bath* (1764) 3 Burr 1478.

[23] See Brownlie, pp 42–47.

[24] *Chung Chi Cheung v R* [1939] AC 160, at 168 (Lord Atkin).

[25] *The Christina* [1938] AC 485, at 497 (Lord Macmillan).

[26] [1974] QB 684, criticised by M B Akehurst (1975) 38 MLR 72.

[27] [1977] QB 529, criticised by Mann, pp 124–5. See now State Immunity Act 1978, s 3.

[28] See e.g. Consular Relations Act 1968 and International Organisations Act 1968.

[29] Cmnd 5081, 1972.

[30] See e.g. *Kuwait Airways Corpn v Iraqi Airways Co* [1995] 3 All ER 694. The 1978 Act does not apply to visiting forces in the UK: see *Holland v Lampen-Wolfe* [2000] 3 All ER 833 (and p 316 below).

performed in the United Kingdom, the ownership or possession of land in the United Kingdom and death or personal injury arising from acts in the United Kingdom (ss 3–5). The Diplomatic Privileges Act 1964 gave effect within the United Kingdom to provisions of the Vienna Convention on Diplomatic Relations.[31] As well as categorising the diplomats and others entitled to claim immunity from legal process and the relevant immunities in each category, the Act authorises such immunities to be restricted by Order in Council for persons from a particular state if the privileges of the United Kingdom mission in that state are curtailed.[32] It was an obscure section of the State Immunity Act 1978 which the House of Lords had to interpret in deciding whether the former military ruler of Chile could be liable to extradition to Spain because of crimes of torture committed while he was in office.[33]

Executive evidence and 'facts of state'[34]

One problem for the courts in dealing with disputes relating to international events is that these are often the subject of conflicting opinions and are particularly within the experience and knowledge of the executive; and it has been considered expedient that the judiciary and the executive should speak with one voice on these matters.[35] Rather than calling for proof of the relevant issues by evidence, the courts have evolved a practice by which certain matters are proved by a certificate from the Foreign Secretary or by a statement of the Attorney-General. These matters include such questions as whether the United Kingdom is still at war with another state,[36] the extent of British territorial jurisdiction,[37] whether the status of a person gives rise to immunity from jurisdiction[38] and whether the existence of a state has been recognised.[39] An example of the last kind arose in *Carl Zeiss Stiftung* v *Rayner & Keeler Ltd*,[40] where the Foreign Office certificate stated that what was then East Germany was not an independent state but was subordinate to, and governed by, the Soviet Union. The court had therefore to determine the legal effect of decrees in East Germany on this basis. Such certificates state what the Foreign Office recognises, not necessarily what other states or persons would accept.[41]

Before 1980, these certificates might state whether the United Kingdom had recognised the new government of a state (after a coup or other such change of government). In 1980, the Foreign Office abandoned its practice of recognising governments where a new regime came to power unconstitutionally.[42] If necessary, the courts must now decide whether a foreign entity exists as a government. The following criteria are applied: (a) whether it is the constitutional government of the state; (b) the degree, nature and stability of the administrative control, if any, that it exercises over the territory; (c) whether the British government has had relations with it and, if so, their nature; and (d) in marginal cases, the extent of international recognition that it has as government

---

[31] Cmnd 1368, 1964; s 2 of and Sch 1 to the 1964 Act.

[32] 1964 Act, s 3(1).

[33] *R v Bow Street Magistrate, ex p Pinochet Ugarte (No 3)* [2000] 1 AC 147.

[34] Mann, ch 2.

[35] E.g. *The Arantzazu Mendi* [1939] AC 256, at 264 (Lord Atkin); *Carl Zeiss Stiftung* v *Rayner & Keeler Ltd (No 2)* [1967] 1 AC 853, at 961 (Lord Wilberforce).

[36] *R v Bottrill, ex p Kuechenmeister* [1947] KB 41; cf *Willcock v Muckle* [1951] 2 KB 844.

[37] *The Fagernes* [1927] P 311, approved in *Post Office v Estuary Radio Ltd* [1968] 2 QB 740.

[38] *Mighell v Sultan of Johore* [1894] 1 QB 149. Even without a certificate, material before a court may establish sovereign immunity: e.g. *Mellenger v New Brunswick Development Corpn* [1971] 2 All ER 593.

[39] For such a certificate, see *Buttes Gas & Oil Co v Hammer* [1982] AC 888, 927–8.

[40] [1967] 1 AC 853.

[41] Mann, p 24.

[42] Ibid, pp 42–6; Brownlie, p 104. Also C R Symmons [1981] PL 249.

of the state.[43] Criterion (c) requires evidence in the form of a Foreign Office certificate as to the dealings, if any, that Britain has had with the entity in question.

By judicial practice, the statement of facts contained in such a certificate is conclusive: as Lord Reid said, 'no evidence is admissible to contradict that information.'[44] Several statutes now provide for certificates to be given on particular matters within the knowledge of the executive.[45] Thus a certificate issued under the State Immunity Act 1978 provides conclusive evidence of the facts that it states.[46] Despite the conclusive effect of such a certificate in national law, a litigant might be able to show that the certificate is in breach of an overriding rule of Community law.[47]

Moreover, a certificate stating the facts (as perceived by the Foreign Office) is not conclusive as to the legal inferences that may be drawn. It is for the court to decide the legal consequences of a certificate declaring that a state has been recognised.[48] The court should not seek an executive certificate as a means of obtaining guidance as to the principles of international law to be applied.[49]

Judicial review of decisions under the prerogative

As we have seen,[50] the House of Lords in *CCSU* v *Minister for the Civil Service* opened up the possibility that decisions under the prerogative are subject to judicial review. As Lord Scarman said, 'the controlling factor in deciding whether the exercise of prerogative power is subject to judicial review is not its source but its subject matter.'[51] However, in the *CCSU* case it was envisaged that many prerogative powers would not be justiciable, including the making of treaties.[52] More generally, it has been stated that 'the conduct of foreign affairs cannot attract judicial review'.[53] Whether the government should make a treaty with country A,[54] or take proceedings in an international court against country B,[55] are plainly not matters for the judiciary to decide. But not all powers relating to foreign affairs are of the same kind. Even before *CCSU*, the Court of Appeal reviewed the legality of action taken by the government under a treaty with the United States concerning airline routes.[56] Since *CCSU*, a Foreign Office decision as to the issue of a passport has been held subject to review, on the basis that it 'is a matter of administrative decision, affecting the rights of individuals and their freedom of travel. It raises issues which are just as justiciable as . . . the issues arising in immigration cases'.[57] The courts may also rule on the legality of action taken in the course of foreign policy. In 1993, an application for judicial review of the government's decision to ratify the Treaty on European Union was rejected on the merits of the issues

---

[43] See *Republic of Somalia* v *Woodhouse Drake & Carey (Suisse) SA* [1993] 1 QB 54; *Sierra Leone Telecommunications Co Ltd* v *Barclays Bank plc* [1998] 2 All ER 821.

[44] *Carl Zeiss Stiftung*, note 35 above, at 901.

[45] E.g. Foreign Jurisdiction Act 1890, s 4 (extent of British jurisdiction in foreign country); Crown Proceedings Act 1947, s 40(3) (and see *Trawnik* v *Lennox* [1985] 2 All ER 368); Diplomatic Privileges Act 1964, s 4.

[46] Section 21. And see *R* v *Foreign Secretary, ex p Trawnik*, *The Times*, 21 February 1986; Mann, p 19.

[47] By analogy with *Johnston* v *Chief Constable, RUC* [1987] QB 129.

[48] *Carl Zeiss Stiftung*, note 35 above, at 950 (Lord Upjohn).

[49] Cf *The Philippine Admiral* [1977] AC 373, 399.

[50] Ch 12 E.

[51] [1985] AC 374, at 407 (Lord Scarman).

[52] Ibid, at 418 (Lord Roskill).

[53] Mann, p 50.

[54] *Rustomjee* v *R* (1876) 2 QBD 69; *Blackburn* v *A-G* [1971] 2 All ER 1380.

[55] *R* v *Foreign Secretary, ex p Pirbai*, *The Times*, 17 October 1985; Mann, p 20.

[56] *Laker Airways* v *Department of Trade* [1977] QB 643.

[57] *R* v *Foreign Secretary, ex p Everett* [1989] QB 811, at 820 (Taylor LJ).

argued before it. The court held (inter alia) that by entering the Union's common security and foreign policy the government was exercising prerogative power, not relinquishing it.[58] In 1994, the court declared unlawful the government's decision to fund the Pergau Dam project, since the statutory conditions for granting foreign aid had not been met.[59]

Acts of state[60]

The Crown's prerogative in foreign affairs does not include power to change the law. But the Crown's actions may nonetheless have legal effects for individuals; for example, a government decision to take hostile action against another state (for instance, the campaign against Argentina to regain possession of the Falkland Islands in 1982) may adversely affect British citizens or the citizens of third countries who reside in that state, or may prevent certain companies from doing business there. Those affected by the action taken may wish to obtain compensation for loss that they have suffered. For two reasons, the British courts are unlikely to afford such relief. First, the acts of the Crown are likely to be within the prerogative; lawful acts in general do not give rise to a duty to compensate. (In exceptional cases there may be a duty to compensate if the prerogative act amounts to a taking of private property for public use.)[61] Second, the international element in a dispute may lead the court to conclude that, whether or not a claim is well founded in international law, it is outside the jurisdiction of national courts: if so, the court turns the claimant away without deciding the legal merits of the claim.

Although it is applied confusingly to different situations,[62] the term 'act of state' is used in this context. One definition of act of state is that it is 'an act of the Executive as a matter of policy performed in the course of its relations with another state, including its relations with subjects of that state, unless they are temporarily within the allegiance of the Crown'.[63] This is not a wholly satisfactory definition,[64] and different legal inferences may be drawn from it. But some propositions may be stated briefly:

1   In general a plea of state necessity is not a justification for acts of the executive that are otherwise unlawful.[65]
2   The fact that the Crown has acquired territory or concluded a treaty does not in itself give rise to new rights enforceable against the Crown.[66]
3   In narrowly defined circumstances, a plea of act of state may be a reason why a claim for damages in tort or for compensation brought in the British courts may be held to be outside their jurisdiction. Such a plea is available to the Crown or an agent of the Crown when an alien who is resident abroad sues in respect of acts committed abroad.[67] In these circumstances, 'act of state' is a plea to the jurisdiction of the courts

---

[58] *R v Foreign Secretary, ex p Rees-Mogg* [1994] QB 552; see G Marshall [1993] PL 402; R Rawlings [1994] PL 254, 367.
[59] *R v Foreign Secretary, ex p World Development Movement* [1995] 1 All ER 611. And see *R v Foreign Secretary, ex p Bancoult* [2001] QB 1067 (unlawful removal of population from Chagos Islands).
[60] See Harrison Moore, *Act of State in English Law*; J G Collier [1968] CLJ 102; D R Gilmour [1970] PL 120; Mann, note 8 above, chs 9, 10; P Wesley-Smith (1986) 6 LS 325.
[61] *Burmah Oil Co v Lord Advocate* ([1965] AC 75; ch 12 D).
[62] *Buttes Gas & Oil Co v Hammer* [1982] AC 888, at 930 (Lord Wilberforce).
[63] E C S Wade (1934) 15 BYIL 98, 103.
[64] *Nissan v A-G* [1970] AC 179, at 212 (Lord Reid); and cf P J Allott [1977] CLJ 255, 270.
[65] *Entick v Carrington*, (1765) 19 St Tr 1030; ch 6 A.
[66] *Civilian War Claimants Association v R* [1932] AC 14.
[67] *Buron v Denman* (1848) 2 Ex 167; *Walker v Baird* [1892] AC 491. Cf *Johnstone v Pedlar* [1921] 2 AC 262 (no act of state when US citizen arrested in the United Kingdom). And see 10th edn of this work, pp 316–20.

and is not to be confused with a defence that the Crown was acting lawfully under the prerogative. Whether such a defence is valid needs to be decided by the courts only if the claim is (apart from the plea) within their jurisdiction. It is, however, for a court to decide whether the executive acts in question are 'acts of state' for this purpose.

> In *Nissan v Attorney-General*, a United Kingdom citizen who owned a hotel in Cyprus sued the Crown for compensation in respect of the occupation of the hotel by British troops; they had first entered Cyprus by agreement with the Cyprus government, and later remained there as part of a United Nations peace-keeping force. The House of Lords held that the Crown could not rely on the plea of 'act of state' as a bar to a claim based on these acts of the Crown. The House took the view that, while the agreement between the British and Cyprus governments might well have been an 'act of state', acts of the British forces in occupying the hotel did not constitute such an act of state: the plaintiff's claim was accordingly justiciable in the British courts.[68]

Among the difficult points of law left open by the House of Lords in *Nissan* was whether the plea of act of state can ever be raised to bar a claim brought against the Crown by a British citizen. Nor did the House resolve the question of whether prerogative power is being exercised by the Crown when its agents are carrying out its policy abroad.[69]
4 In the event of war being declared against a foreign state,[70] citizens of that state who are within the United Kingdom are liable to be detained as enemy aliens and an attempt to secure their release in the British courts may be met by a plea of act of state (or, as seems more satisfactory, by the defence of lawful action under the prerogative).[71] Where war has not been declared by the United Kingdom against a foreign state, but military action is undertaken, as was the case during the Gulf hostilities involving Iraq in 1991, nationals of that state resident in the United Kingdom are entitled to the protection of the courts against unlawful detention,[72] just as other friendly aliens within the jurisdiction are entitled to be protected against unlawful action.[73]
5 The plea of a 'foreign act of state' may arise where an action is brought in a British court in respect of the executive acts of foreign states, for example the making of a treaty; here too, the court declines jurisdiction, giving as a reason that such an act between states cannot be adjudicated upon in municipal courts. In this sense, 'act of state' reflects a general principle of non-justiciability, namely 'that the courts will not adjudicate on the transactions of foreign sovereign states'.[74] Thus British courts have no jurisdiction to rule on the validity of the constitution of a foreign state.[75]

The term 'act of state' is evidently not a far-reaching bar to legal claims arising from government action with a foreign element. The term came into use in a period when the doctrine of national sovereignty was at its most absolute. However, the doctrine

---

[68] *Nissan v A-G* [1970] AC 179.
[69] Ibid, at 213 (Lord Reid), 236 (Lord Wilberforce) and cf 227 (Lord Pearce). If a British citizen resident in Kuwait had been injured through action by British forces during the Gulf hostilities and sued the soldiers and the Crown in a British court, the best analysis would seem to be that (*a*) no act of state can be pleaded against a British citizen; (*b*) the soldiers were acting under the prerogative (preserved by the Crown Proceedings Act 1947, s 11; ch 32 A); (*c*) no duty to compensate arises for battle damage (cf *Burmah Oil Co v Lord Advocate*, ch 12 D). If a Kuwaiti or Iraqi citizen sued in a British court for such an injury, the plea of act of state would succeed.
[70] As to why a formal declaration of war is unlikely today, see C J Greenwood (1987) 36 ICLQ 283.
[71] *R v Vine Street Police Station, ex p Liebmann* [1916] 1 KB 268; *Netz v Ede* [1946] Ch 224.
[72] See e.g. *R v Home Secretary, ex p Cheblak* [1991] 2 All ER 319; also I Leigh [1991] PL 331 and F Hampson [1991] PL 507. But see now the detention provisions in the Anti-terrorism, Crime and Security Act 2001, Part IV.
[73] *Johnstone v Pedlar* [1921] 2 AC 262.
[74] See *Buttes Gas & Oil v Hammer* [1982] AC 888, at 931–4. And see *R v Bow Street Magistrate, ex p Pinochet Ugarte (No 3)* [2000] 1 AC 147, 201.
[75] *Buck v A-G* [1965] Ch 745.

does not require the courts to recognise foreign legislation that is contrary to British public policy.[76] Today its use is diminishing since, at least in Europe, the barriers between international and national law are being eroded. The claim that acts of 'foreign policy' affecting individuals should be beyond judicial scrutiny is unlikely to be welcomed today, whether in administrative law, Community law[77] or in European human rights law.

B. Treaties[78]

By the Vienna Convention on the Law of Treaties, a treaty is defined as an international agreement concluded between states in written form and governed by international law, whether embodied in a single instrument or in two or more related instruments and whatever its particular designation.[79] Whatever name may be given to it (convention, covenant, protocol, charter, exchange of notes etc.), a treaty is an agreement between two or more sovereign states which creates rights and obligations for the parties. A country's constitutional law determines who can exercise the treaty-making power. By the US Constitution, this power is vested in the President, 'by and with the advice of the Senate', provided that two-thirds of the Senate concur; treaties so approved have a status equal to that of legislation by Congress.[80]

By contrast, in the United Kingdom there is no direct parliamentary involvement in the making of treaties. To this, three qualifications must be made. First, under the so-called Ponsonby rule, which applies to treaties that have been negotiated and signed but have not come into effect because they have not (in international law) been ratified by the parties, the government notifies Parliament of the treaty and must not ratify it (save in cases of urgency) until 21 parliamentary days have elapsed.[81] This both informs Parliament of the treaty and enables it to be debated. Second, Parliament may restrict the ability of the executive to conclude or ratify treaties by imposing an express requirement of parliamentary consent.[82] Third, a treaty which is entered into by the government does not alter the law in the United Kingdom: 'the making of a treaty is an executive act, while the performance of its obligations, if they entail alteration of the existing domestic law, requires legislative action.'[83] Further: 'Except to the extent that a treaty becomes incorporated into the laws of the United Kingdom by statute, the courts . . . have no power to enforce treaty rights and obligations at the behest of a sovereign government or at the behest of a private individual.'[84] If the objects of a treaty require national law to be changed, this must be done by legislation. Often an Act of Parliament is necessary, but a minister may be able to make the required changes in national law by exercising existing powers of delegated legislation.[85] To avoid a situation in which a treaty has become binding but the necessary changes in national law have not been made, the implementing legislation may need to be enacted before

---

[76] *Kuwait Airways Corporation v Iraqi Airways Co* [2001] 1 All ER (Comm) 557.

[77] *Bourgoin SA v Ministry of Agriculture* [1986] QB 716; *Van Duyn v Home Office* [1975] Ch 358.

[78] See McNair, *Law of Treaties*; Brownlie, note 1 above, ch 26; Jennings and Watts, note 1 above, ch 14; Aust, *Modern Treaty Law and Practice*.

[79] Cmnd 4848, 1969, art 2, para 1.

[80] US Constitution, art II(2), art IV; *Whitney v Robertson* 124 US 190 (1888).

[81] HC Deb, 1 April 1924, cols 2001–4; Erskine May, *Parliamentary Practice*, pp 215, 549–50; HLE, vol 8(2), pp 465–9.

[82] See European Parliamentary Elections Act 1978, s 6(1) (no treaty increasing powers of European Parliament to be ratified unless approved by Act); *R v Foreign Secretary, ex p Rees-Mogg* [1994] QB 552.

[83] *A-G for Canada v A-G for Ontario* [1937] AC 326, at 347 (Lord Atkin).

[84] *Rayner (Mincing Lane) Ltd v Department of Trade* [1990] 2 AC 418, at 477 (Lord Templeman); *Littrell v USA (No 2)* [1994] 4 All ER 203.

[85] See ch 28.

the government ratifies the treaty. In general, a state cannot rely on defects in its own law as a defence to a claim in international law.[86]

Where a treaty has not been incorporated in national law by legislation, the courts may not directly enforce the treaty. Thus in 1991 the House of Lords held that the European Convention on Human Rights, ratified in 1951 but not the subject of legislation, could not be a source of rights and obligations.[87] In 1995, the High Court of Australia held that an unincorporated treaty could give rise to a 'legitimate expectation' that executive decision makers would act in accordance with the treaty.[88] Although the Australian government took prompt steps to prevent such an expectation arising, the principle was endorsed in 1998 by the Court of Appeal in London.[89]

Even where a treaty seeks to benefit a definite class of persons (for example, where a foreign government provides funds to compensate British citizens who have suffered at that government's hands), such persons do not acquire rights of enforcing the treaty against the British government.[90] The money received under such treaties may be distributed in accordance with a statutory scheme by the Foreign Compensation Commission, whose decisions are now subject to an appeal to the courts.[91] In the Sachsenhausen case, this procedure was not followed: a shortcut taken by the Foreign Office proved unsatisfactory, mainly because of an erroneous view that the Office had formed of the so-called Butler rules.[92] Were this to occur today, someone who claimed that the Foreign Office was not correctly applying the rules of distribution could seek judicial review.[93] Such an application might be strengthened if the treaty in question declared that the government was acting as agent or trustee for its subjects.[94] But this would not necessarily be decisive, since not all governmental obligations in the nature of a trust are justiciable.[95]

Interpretation of legislation giving effect to treaties

The methods by which Parliament may give effect in national law to obligations arising under a treaty include the following.[96] First, the statute may enact the substance of the treaty in its own words without referring to the treaty.[97] Second, the statute may name the treaty (for example, in the title of the Act) and then either enact all or part of the substance of the treaty in its own words.[98] Third, the statute may set out the text of the treaty in a schedule, while giving legal effect either to part of the treaty[99] or to the whole text.[100]

---

[86] Brownlie, p 34.

[87] *R v Home Secretary, ex p Brind* [1991] 1 AC 696. See ch 19 B. For ways in which, apart from incorporation, the courts could take account of the ECHR, see Hunt, *Using Human Rights Law in English Courts*.

[88] *Minister of State for Immigration v Teoh* (1995) 128 ALR 353. See R Piotrowicz [1996] PL 190 and Lord Lester [1996] PL 187. Also ch 30 C.

[89] *R v Home Secretary, ex p Ahmed* [1998] INLR 570. See also *Tavita v Minister for Immigration* [1994] NZLR 257.

[90] *Civilian War Claimants Association v R* [1932] AC 14; *Lonrho Exports Ltd v Export Credits Guarantee Dept* [1999] ch 158, 178–9.

[91] Foreign Compensation Act 1969, s 3 (enacted after *Anisminic Ltd v Foreign Compensation Commission*, ch 30 A).

[92] Ch 29 D.

[93] *R v Criminal Injuries Compensation Board, ex p Lain* [1967] 2 QB 864; see ch 12 D, E.

[94] *Civilian War Claimants Association* (note 90) at 26–7 (Lord Atkin).

[95] *Tito v Waddell (No 2)* [1977] Ch 106; cf *Mutasa v A-G* [1980] QB 114.

[96] Mann, *Foreign Affairs in English Courts*, pp 97–102.

[97] E.g. Evidence (Proceedings in other Jurisdictions) Act 1975, considered in *Re Westinghouse* [1978] AC 547.

[98] E.g. Arbitration Act 1975.

[99] E.g. Geneva Conventions Act 1957 (F Hampson [1991] PL 507); and Diplomatic Privileges Act 1964.

[100] E.g. Carriage of Goods by Road Act 1965; and *Buchanan & Co v Babco Ltd* [1978] AC 141.

The choice between these various methods might be thought to affect the manner in which the courts should seek to resolve problems of interpretation that arise, for example from a discrepancy between the statutory words and the treaty. However, the courts' approach does not turn on the precise method of incorporation, provided it appears, if necessary from extrinsic evidence, that a statute was enacted in pursuance of an international obligation. If Parliament uses express and unambiguous language, this must be given effect by the courts even if the result of so doing departs from what was intended by the treaty.[101] However,

> it is a principle of construction of United Kingdom statutes, now too well established to call for citation of authority, that the words of a statute passed after the treaty has been signed and dealing with the subject matter of the international obligation of the United Kingdom, are to be construed, if they are reasonably capable of bearing such a meaning, as intended to carry out the obligation and not to be inconsistent with it.[102]

The law may be developing even beyond this so that, whether the court is construing statutory words or resolving a disputed question of common law in an area where the United Kingdom has international obligations, the court may have regard to the treaty 'as part of the full content or background of the law'.[103] Before the Human Rights Act 1998 came into force, this doctrine had the effect of enabling the courts to take some account of the European Convention on Human Rights.

When a court does need to consider a treaty,[104] further questions may arise as to how that text should be interpreted. According to Lord Wilberforce, the approach 'must be appropriate for the interpretation of an international convention, unconstrained by technical rules of English law, or by English legal precedent, but on broad principles of general acceptance'.[105] In a case on political asylum where a UK statute excluded the removal of any person in breach of the Geneva Convention on the Status of Refugees, the House of Lords held that British courts must determine and apply the true meaning of the Convention, 'approached as an international instrument created by the agreement of contracting states as opposed to regulatory regimes established by national institutions', even if a different meaning were applied by French and German courts.[106]

The European Union and the law on treaties

The European Union, and the Communities within the Union, were created and enlarged by successive treaties.[107] The new legal order brought about by those treaties, as interpreted by the European Court of Justice, has consequences that go far beyond the general law of treaties. First, in giving effect to Community law, the European Communities Act 1972 provides a further variant to the methods of treaty implementation described earlier. The existing European Treaties were listed in a schedule to the Act but their texts were not set out. Those rights, obligations and other matters arising from the treaties that were to have legal effect without further enactment within the United Kingdom were declared to have that effect (s 2(1)).[108] Future European Treaties may be designated by Order in Council and thus brought within the scope of the Act (s 1(3)). While such an Order in Council is delegated legislation, and could be

---

[101] *Salomon v Commissioners of Customs & Excise* [1967] 2 QB 116.
[102] *Garland v British Rail Engineering Ltd* [1983] 2 AC 751, at 771 (Lord Diplock).
[103] *Pan-American World Airways v Department of Trade* [1976] 1 Lloyd's Rep 257.
[104] See e.g. *Derbyshire CC v Times Newspapers Ltd* [1993] AC 534.
[105] *Buchanan & Co v Babco Ltd* (note 100) at 152 (Lord Wilberforce).
[106] *R v Home Secretary, ex p Adan* [2001] 2 AC 474, 515 (Lord Steyn) And see ch 20 B.
[107] Ch 8 A.
[108] Ch 8 C.

challenged as ultra vires if the treaty which it named could not properly be regarded as a European Treaty,[109] such a challenge would be unlikely to succeed. The Treaty on European Union and the Treaty of Amsterdam were designated European Treaties not by Orders in Council but by the European Communities (Amendment) Acts of, respectively, 1993 and 1998. Through the doctrines of direct applicability and direct effect, no transformation or re-enactment is needed before many Community measures are enforceable in national courts.[110]

The European Community's powers include the making of international agreements with states outside the Union and with other international organisations.[111] New treaties are negotiated by the Commission in consultation with special committees appointed by the Council of Ministers and are concluded by the Council, generally after consulting the European Parliament (art 300, ex 228, EC Treaty). They are binding upon all member states and may contain provisions that are directly effective.[112] One consequence is that 'each time the Community, with a view to implementing a common policy envisaged by the Treaty, adopts provisions laying down common rules, . . . the Member States no longer have the right, acting individually or even collectively, to undertake obligations with third countries which affect those rules.'[113] Thus in these situations there is a transfer of treaty-making power from member states to the Community. Unlike treaties made by the British government, treaties concluded by the Communities may have direct domestic effect without legislative implementation.[114] The competence of the Community to enter into treaties does not include power to sub-scribe to the European Convention on Human Rights in its own right; in the opinion of the European Court of Justice, this would require an amendment to the EC Treaty.[115]

C. The United Kingdom and the Commonwealth[116]

In the heyday of empire, the imperial Crown, government and Parliament were at the apex of an impressive network of power that extended to many countries. Legal power was exercised through legislation and executive decision in London; and the Judicial Committee of the Privy Council heard appeals from national courts across the world.[117] Imperial rule was often indirect rule, since many territories within the sovereignty or protection of the Crown had their own forms of government, possibly involving elected assemblies; other territories kept in place rulers already in power when they came within British influence.[118] Within a territory, the form of government might be laid down in a constitutional instrument, enacted by the imperial Parliament or issued by the Crown, whether under prerogative powers or under powers delegated by statute (for example, the Foreign Jurisdiction Acts 1890 and 1913). For some countries that

---

[109] *R v HM Treasury, ex p Smedley* [1985] QB 657.

[110] Ch 8 B.

[111] EC Treaty, arts 133 (ex 113) (trade and commercial agreements), 310 (ex 238) (association agreements with states and international organisations) and 302–304 (ex 229–231) (relations with international organisations).

[112] E.g. *Case 104/81, Hauptzollamt Mainz v Kupferberg & cie KG* [1982] ECR 3641.

[113] *Case 22/70*, the ERTA case [1971] ECR 263, 274.

[114] See generally Hartley, *The Foundations of European Community Law*, ch 6; Mann, pp 113–19.

[115] *Re the Accession of the Community to the European Human Rights Convention (Opinion 2/94)* [1996] 2 CMLR 265; P Beaumont (1997) 1 Edin LR 235; and ch 19 B.

[116] See Roberts-Wray, *Commonwealth and Colonial Law*, and Dale, *The Modern Commonwealth*. Also Wheare, *The Constitutional Structure of the Commonwealth*, and de Smith, *The New Commonwealth and its Constitutions*.

[117] Pages 325–7 below and ch 18 A.

[118] Morris and Read, *Indirect Rule and the Search for Justice*.

had been settled from Britain, British forms of government developed by or during the 19th century: the need for responsible government in Canada was recognised in 1838.[119] While government within a territory might be subject to a constitution, the imperial authorities could always override this, if not by executive action then by recourse to the sovereignty of the Westminster Parliament; no written constitution restricted the imperial powers.[120]

Today, the former constitutional law of the colonies and the Empire is primarily of historic interest, except in the case of the few surviving overseas possessions of the United Kingdom.[121] The structure of the Commonwealth is scarcely a matter of law at all: the informality of the Commonwealth contrasts with the emphasis on law and legal form in the European Union. For the Commonwealth, there is no written constitution, nor, unlike most international organisations, was it created by treaty; it is 'a community of states in which the absence of a rigid legal basis of association is compensated by the bonds of common origin, history and legal tradition'.[122]

Dependence and independence[123]

The evolution of the Commonwealth involved a protracted process in which the United Kingdom's dependent territories first received some kind of representative legislature; then acquired responsible self-government in domestic affairs while still subject to imperial control in matters of defence and external relations; and later achieved full independence. By this last step, the territory became a separate state in international law, having its own organs of government and power to determine its own policies. Where British influence was felt, the English common law was often received into the legal system; and colonial government generated its own body of law relating to the powers and duties of colonial authorities. A notable contribution to colonial law was the Colonial Laws Validity Act 1865.[124] The Act was passed to confirm, subject to certain limits, the authority of colonial legislatures to make laws that departed from the English common law or from imperial statutes of general application. The Act also authorised a colonial legislature, at least half of whose members were democratically elected in the colony, to make laws respecting its own constitution, powers and procedure, provided that such laws were passed in such manner and form as might be required by any Act of Parliament or other law applying to the colony.[125] This Act reinforced the ability of colonial legislatures to act within their powers, but confirmed that their powers were limited and subject to imperial control.[126] What became known as Dominion status developed in the late 19th century as certain colonies (particularly Australia, Canada, New Zealand and South Africa) moved towards full statehood.[127] By the mid-1920s, the Dominions had full internal autonomy in accordance with their constitutions (contained in Acts of the imperial Parliament: for example, the British North America

---

[119] See the Earl of Durham's *Report on the Affairs of British North America*.
[120] In the leading case on colonial law, *Campbell* v *Hall* (1774) 1 Cowp 204, the dispute involved the Crown's power to legislate, not the authority of the British Parliament.
[121] In 2002 the 14 overseas territories included Anguilla, Bermuda, British Antarctic Territory, British Virgin Islands, Cayman Islands, Falkland Islands, Gibraltar, Montserrat, Pitcairn Islands and Turks and Caicos Islands. See Cm 4264, 1999 and the British Overseas Territories Act 2002.
[122] Jennings and Watts, p 266.
[123] See Roberts-Wray, chs 5, 6.
[124] Roberts-Wray, pp 396–409. For the background to the Act, see O'Connell and Riordan, *Opinions on Imperial Constitutional Law*, pp 60–74.
[125] This was the background to *A-G for New South Wales* v *Trethowan* [1932] AC 526; p 66 above.
[126] See *R* v *Foreign Secretary, ex p Bancoult* [2001] QB 1067.
[127] The older meaning of 'dominion' in the phrase 'Her Majesty's dominions', denotes all territories belonging to the Crown: Roberts-Wray, pp 23–9.

Act 1867 in the case of Canada, and the Commonwealth of Australia Act 1900) and had acquired the right to conduct their own foreign relations. The imperial conference in 1926 declared that Great Britain and the Dominions were:

> autonomous Communities within the British Empire, equal in status, in no way subordinate to another in any aspect of their domestic or external status, though united by a common allegiance to the Crown, and freely associated as members of the British Commonwealth of Nations.[128]

This important statement of equal status reflected the changing conventional relationship between the United Kingdom and the Dominions, but in law the Dominions still had the status of colonies and were subject to the Colonial Laws Validity Act 1865. Thus even in 1926 the Canadian Parliament had no power to abolish certain criminal appeals from Canadian courts to the Privy Council.[129]

To deal with these limitations on Dominion authority, and to implement resolutions of imperial conferences in 1926, 1929 and 1930,[130] the Statute of Westminster was enacted by the British Parliament in 1931.[131] The preamble to the Statute described the Crown as the symbol of the free association of the members of the British Commonwealth of Nations, united by a common allegiance to the Crown; and referred to the 'established constitutional position' that changes in the law relating to the succession to the throne and the royal style and titles should receive the assent of the Dominion parliaments as well as of the United Kingdom Parliament.[132] The Statute broadened the powers of the Dominion legislatures by, for instance, authorising them to amend or repeal Acts of the United Kingdom Parliament applying to the Dominion (s 2). However, this did not authorise a legislature to ignore limits on its powers laid down in the Act containing the country's constitution.[133]

Section 4 of the Statute stated that no future Act of the British Parliament would extend to the Dominion as part of its law 'unless it is expressly declared in that Act that that Dominion has requested, and consented, to the enactment thereof'. The effect of this on the sovereignty of the Westminster Parliament was considered in the *British Coal Corporation* case, when Lord Sankey said that the power of the imperial Parliament to legislate for Canada on its own initiative remained unimpaired, adding: 'But that is theory and has no relation to realities.'[134] A more decisive note was struck by the Supreme Court of South Africa: 'freedom once conferred cannot be revoked.'[135] It is unlikely that Parliament would ever have wished to disregard s 4 of the Statute of Westminster. Had it done so, the Australian, Canadian or New Zealand courts would have acted properly if they had taken no notice of the attempt to legislate. But British courts would have been bound by the legislation.[136]

The ability of Westminster to legislate for Canada remained important long after the Statute of Westminster. This was because the British North America Act 1867, which contained Canada's constitution, included no amendment power: therefore legislation at Westminster was required to amend the Canadian constitution. This anomaly was

---

[128] Cmd 2768, 1926, p 14; Dale, p 21.
[129] *Nadan v R* [1926] AC 482; and see p 326 below.
[130] Cmd 2768, 1926; Cmd 3479, 1930; and Cmd 3717, 1930.
[131] Wheare, *The Statute of Westminster and Dominion Status*; Marshall, *Parliamentary Sovereignty and the Commonwealth*; Dale, part 1.
[132] On the accession of Elizabeth II, see Wheare, *Constitutional Structure of the Commonwealth*, pp 164–8.
[133] See s 7(1) (Canada) and ss 8, 9(1) (Australia). For South Africa, see *Harris v Minister of the Interior* 1952 (2) SA 428 and also D V Cowan (1952) 15 MLR 282, (1953) 16 MLR 273.
[134] *British Coal Corporation v R* [1935] AC 500, 520.
[135] *Ndlwana v Hofmeyr* 1937 AD 229, 237. And see *Blackburn v A-G* [1971] 2 All ER 1380.
[136] See ch 4 B.

removed when the Canada Act 1982 was enacted at Westminster to bring about the 'patriation' of the constitution to Canada. The 1982 Act, whose text had been prepared in Canada after a most controversial process,[137] gave the force of law to a Constitution Act which provided for its own future amendment; and it was declared that no future Act of the United Kingdom Parliament should extend to Canada as part of its law.[138] When the validity of the Canada Act 1982 was challenged by indigenous peoples in Canada who claimed that their consent was needed to the legislation, the English Court of Appeal held that it was sufficient compliance with the Statute of Westminster that the 1982 Act declared that 'Canada' had requested and consented to its enactment; the court could not go behind this declaration.[139]

A less controversial change took place in 1986 with the passing of the Australia Act at Westminster, together with related legislation by the parliaments of the Commonwealth of Australia and the Australian States. One effect was to sever the remaining legislative links between the United Kingdom and Australia; another was to terminate appeals to the Privy Council from any Australian court.[140]

In 1931, as we have seen, it was envisaged that there might be subjects on which the United Kingdom would continue to legislate on behalf of one or more Dominions. When after 1945 independence was granted to India, Pakistan, Ceylon, Ghana and many other countries, it was seen to be anomalous for Westminster to retain any power to legislate for independent states, even with their consent. Thereafter, it was provided for a country at independence that the United Kingdom government should have no responsibility for the country's government; that the Colonial Laws Validity Act 1865 should cease to apply; and that no future Act of the United Kingdom Parliament should extend to the country as part of its law.[141]

Although the political campaign for independence was often very turbulent, for the most part the actual conferring of independence took place in a lawful manner. One exception to this occurred in 1965 when Mr Ian Smith and other Cabinet ministers of the self-governing colony of Rhodesia, impatient with waiting for independence, unilaterally declared Rhodesia to be independent of the United Kingdom. The consequences of this unlawful declaration were complex[142] and for some years it seemed that this revolution had been successful. But internal and international pressure continued and in 1979 a constitutional conference in London laid the basis for a return to legality. In April 1980, under the authority of the Westminster Parliament, independence was conferred on the new state of Zimbabwe.[143]

The divisibility of the Crown

At one time the British Crown was considered in law to be a single, ubiquitous entity in the many territories under British sovereignty. Thus in 1919 the Privy Council referred to the Crown as 'one and indivisible throughout the Empire'.[144] But this unity could not be maintained given the growth of responsible government in many colonies, the

---

[137] See *Re Amendment of the Constitution of Canada* (1981) 125 DLR (3d) 1; and Marshall, *Constitutional Conventions*, ch 11 (and app A, 10th edn of this work).

[138] Canada Act 1982, s 2.

[139] *Manuel v A-G* [1983] Ch 77 (and Marshall, *Constitutional Conventions*, ch 12); also *R v Foreign Secretary, ex p Indian Association of Alberta* [1982] QB 892.

[140] See J Goldring [1986] PL 192.

[141] See e.g. Nigeria Independence Act 1960, s 1(2) and Sch 1.

[142] They included the Southern Rhodesia Act 1965 and, in the Privy Council, *Madzimbamuto v Lardner-Burke* [1969] 1 AC 645. (And see the 10th edn of this work, pp 430–2.)

[143] See the Southern Rhodesia Act 1979, the Zimbabwe Act 1979 and SI 1979 No 1600.

[144] *Theodore v Duncan* [1919] AC 696, at 706 (Lord Haldane).

creation of federal constitutions in Canada and Australia and (later) with the conferment of independence on former colonies. As separate governments came into being, the Crown in one sense comprehended them all; in reality the legal concept began to fragment. Moreover, when independence was conferred, obligations of the British government in relation to a particular territory passed by succession to that country's government.[145] Thus the Crown 'in right of the United Kingdom' (i.e. the British government) was held to have no continuing liability in respect of a royal proclamation of 1763 that reserved certain land in Canada for the Indian peoples; any liability arising from that proclamation was enforceable, if at all, against the Crown in right of Canada (i.e. the Canadian government).[146] While the transfer of responsibilities is an inevitable consequence of a country's independence, the divisibility of the Crown could arise at an earlier stage of development.[147] Thus the Court of Appeal held that passports issued to citizens of Mauritius by the governor of the colony were not United Kingdom passports, even though their holders were 'citizens of the United Kingdom and Colonies'.[148] However, this decision did not take full account of the fact that the United Kingdom government *was* responsible for a colony's international relations; and it was 'the Crown in right of the Government of the United Kingdom'[149] which had full control over the actions of such a subordinate government.[150]

Membership of the Commonwealth

Independence of the United Kingdom and membership of the Commonwealth are not the same. The granting of independence to a dependent territory of the United Kingdom is a matter for the British government and the territory concerned. But the admission of a new member to the Commonwealth requires the agreement of existing members. In 1971, it was declared by the heads of Commonwealth governments meeting at Singapore that the Commonwealth

> is a voluntary association of independent sovereign states, each responsible for its own policies, consulting and co-operating in the common interests of their peoples and in the promotion of international understanding and world peace.[151]

There are no written rules of membership.[152] Possibly the most significant change in the basis of membership occurred in 1949 when India announced its intention of becoming a republic. Before then, all members owed common allegiance to the Crown. In 1949, the response of other governments was to note India's desire to continue its full membership of the Commonwealth and its acceptance of the British Sovereign 'as the symbol of the free association of its independent member nations and as such the Head of the Commonwealth'. Since 1949, while some states adopted republican status after becoming independent, others became republics at the moment of independence or became monarchies with their own royal head of state. In 2002, only some 16 out of 54 Commonwealth states owed allegiance to the Crown, but all states recognised the Queen

[145] Cf *A-G v Great Southern and Western Rly* [1925] AC 754.
[146] *R v Foreign Secretary, ex p Indian Association of Alberta* [1982] QB 892.
[147] The judgments in *Ex p Indian Association* offer three different explanations of the date of the 'division' of the Crown.
[148] *R v Home Secretary, ex p Bhurosah* [1968] 1 QB 266.
[149] Crown Proceedings Act 1947, s 40(2) (b) and (c).
[150] But cf *Tito v Waddell (No 2)* [1977] Ch 106, 254; and *Trawnik v Lennox* [1985] 2 All ER 368, at 357 (Browne-Wilkinson LJ).
[151] Commonwealth Declaration, 22 January 1971 (Dale, p 41).
[152] For the practice, see Dale, ch 3.

in the symbolic role of Head of the Commonwealth, a role that involves her in no specific governmental functions.

Most states that became independent of the United Kingdom after 1945 considered it worthwhile to become members of the Commonwealth. In 1961, when South Africa decided to become a republic, the government withdrew its application to remain in membership rather than have it rejected; with the ending of apartheid-based government 30 years later, South Africa was welcomed back to membership.[153] A member state may leave the Commonwealth at any time (secession is too strong a word for the act of withdrawal) and it seems likely that a member could be expelled against its wishes; in 1995, because of the lack of democracy and disregard for human rights, the membership of Nigeria was suspended. The category of Special Member has been devised for certain very small territories (including Nauru and Tuvalu) which have the right to participate in activities of the Commonwealth but not to attend meetings of heads of Commonwealth governments.[154] Membership is reserved for independent states. Thus territories such as Bermuda and Gibraltar are not members of the Commonwealth in their own right. In 1995 membership was extended to Mozambique, although this had never been a dependency of the United Kingdom.

Meetings of heads of Commonwealth governments

After 1944, meetings of Commonwealth Prime Ministers were held in London and were presided over by the British Prime Minister; the secretariat for the meetings was provided by the British government. The meetings gave way to what are now biennial meetings of heads of Commonwealth governments, over which the head of government of the host country has presided. In 1965, the Commonwealth Secretariat was established, headed by a Secretary-General. The headquarters are in London, but the Secretariat is responsible for servicing Commonwealth conferences wherever they may be held. The Secretariat has oversight of many forms of practical Commonwealth cooperation. The Secretary-General has an important diplomatic role on international issues that directly affect the Commonwealth. Under the Commonwealth Secretariat Act 1966, an Act of the Westminster Parliament, the secretariat is a body corporate and its members, from many Commonwealth countries, are entitled to diplomatic immunities and privileges.

Since the enlargement of the Commonwealth, the nature of the heads of government meetings has changed. While they provide an umbrella for various forms of practical cooperation, the meetings themselves are mainly concerned with contentious issues of world politics, such as economic development and the global environment. In 1971, the Singapore conference produced the Commonwealth Declaration, which defined the nature of the Commonwealth, stressed the diversity of its membership and stated the principles which were held in common by the members. In 1991, the meeting at Harare reaffirmed the Singapore Declaration and renewed its support for the 'fundamental political values' of the Commonwealth (including democracy and the rule of law) and for the promotion of sustainable economic development within a framework of respect for human rights and the protection of the global environment.[155] In 1995 the Commonwealth Ministerial Action Group on the Harare Declaration was created to assess and respond to serious departures from the Harare principles in Commonwealth countries.[156]

---

[153] And see the South Africa Act 1995.
[154] Dale, p 62.
[155] And see A W Bradley [1991] PL 477.
[156] For the Group's meetings, see the *Commonwealth Yearbook 2000*, pp 39–50.

Other aspects of Commonwealth membership

As independent sovereign states, members of the Commonwealth do not observe any uniform pattern in their own systems of government. While most of them entered on independence with constitutions drafted under the guiding influence of Westminster and Whitehall, many of these gave way to new constitutions after independence or were pushed aside by political or military coups and civil war. In the case of members which are monarchies and owe allegiance to the Queen, a Governor-General is appointed by the Queen, on the advice of the government of the state in question, to act as head of state. To resolve uncertainty about the position of a Dominion's Governor-General, the imperial conference laid down in 1926 that the Governor-General held the same position in relation to the affairs of the Dominion as the Sovereign did in the United Kingdom and that he was not the representative or agent of the United Kingdom government.[157] However, depending on the constitution of the country concerned, the Governor-General may have to consider exercising a personal discretion which could not arise in the same form in the United Kingdom.[158] Where a Governor-General is appointed by the Queen on the advice of the government concerned, questions may arise as to her duties if thereafter she receives advice from that government to dismiss the Governor-General.[159] Answers to these questions depend on the constitution of the country in question: the British Prime Minister does not advise the Queen in the matter.

The United Kingdom's relations with other Commonwealth members are carried on by the Secretary of State for Foreign and Commonwealth Affairs. Members are represented in other member states by high commissioners; they do not have the title of ambassador but are members of the diplomatic service of their own state and are equal in rank and status to ambassadors. Members of the Commonwealth conduct their own defence and foreign policies and have their own treaty-making capacity. By comparison with the European Community, which exists as an entity in international law, the position of the Commonwealth in international law is uncertain.[160]

Appeals to the Privy Council

In deciding appeals from the overseas territories of the United Kingdom, the Judicial Committee of the Privy Council exercises the ancient jurisdiction of the King in Council to hear appeals from the overseas dependencies of the Crown.[161] This jurisdiction was based on 'the inherent prerogative right and, on all proper occasions, the duty of the King in Council to exercise an appellate jurisdiction, with a view not only to ensure . . . the due administration of justice in the individual case, but also to preserve the due course of procedure generally'.[162] This jurisdiction was given statutory form by the Judicial Committee Acts of 1833 and 1844.

Where the jurisdiction survives, appeals may be brought without special leave of the Privy Council or with special leave. Appeals without special leave, available mainly in civil cases, are regulated by legislation applying to the territory in question. This legislation lays down the requirements for appealing and states whether there is a full

[157] Cmd 2768, 1926, p 7. And see Evatt, *The King and his Dominion Governors*.
[158] As in Australia in 1975, when the Governor-General, Sir John Kerr, amid fierce controversy, dismissed the Labor Prime Minister; ch 12 B.
[159] V Bogdanor and G Marshall [1996] PL 205.
[160] Fawcett, *The British Commonwealth in International Law*; Dale, note 116 above, ch 6; Jennings and Watts, note 1 above, pp 263–5.
[161] Ch 18 A; Roberts-Wray, note 116 above, pp 433–63; Dale, p 128.
[162] *R v Bertrand* (1867) LR 1 PC 520, 530.

right of appeal or whether leave to appeal is needed; these provisions may if necessary be interpreted by the Judicial Committee.[163]

Appeals with special leave of the Privy Council apply mainly in criminal cases: special leave may be granted by the Judicial Committee where the local court has no power to grant an appeal or, exceptionally, has in the exercise of discretion decided not to grant it.[164] The Judicial Committee is not a court of criminal appeal in the usual sense of the term. Appeals are allowed with special leave only where there has been a clear departure from the requirements of justice and it is shown that by a disregard of the forms of legal process or by some violation of the principles of natural justice, or otherwise, substantial and grave injustice has been done.[165]

It is only when a territory becomes independent that its legislature acquires the power, subject to the national constitution,[166] to abolish or curtail appeals to the Privy Council.[167] Most Commonwealth states have in fact abolished appeals to the Privy Council, but those states that have not done so include Antigua, the Bahamas, Barbados, Belize, Dominica, Jamaica, Kiribati, Mauritius, New Zealand and Trinidad and Tobago. In Singapore, the right to appeal to the Judicial Committee (except by consent of both parties) was taken away in 1989, the evident aim of the government being to prevent an appeal to London about freedom of the press.[168]

It is evident that the legal link between Commonwealth states which arises from appeals to the Judicial Committee is less substantial than in the past. At one time, the Committee played an important if controversial role as a constitutional court, especially in regard to Canada; it helped to develop the common law in jurisdictions outside the United Kingdom, but without excluding autonomous developments in the law;[169] and it still seeks to preserve certain fundamentals of criminal justice.[170] From time to time proposals were made for reconstituting the Judicial Committee as a travelling Commonwealth court of appeal, but these never attracted much support.[171] The Committee's role is significant in relation to those constitutions that include protection for fundamental human rights, but the degree of protection which the Committee has given in this role has been very uneven. In particular, the Committee has fluctuated between adopting a strict and legalistic approach to fundamental rights provisions and a broader, more purposive approach that recognises the constitution as a living instrument.[172]

The most recent decisions made by the Privy Council in death penalty cases have done much to temper the harshness and injustice of 'death row' conditions in the

---

[163] *Davis* v *Shaughnessy* [1932] AC 106.

[164] Cf *Thomas* v *R* [1980] AC 125.

[165] *Ibrahim* v *R* [1914] AC 599; *Prasad* v *R* [1981] 1 All ER 319. And see e.g. *Knowles* v *R* [1930] AC 366, and *Taito and Bennett* v *R* [2002] UK PC 15.

[166] Colonial Laws Validity Act 1865, s 2.

[167] *Moore* v *A-G of Irish Free State* [1935] AC 484; *British Coal Corporation* v *R* [1935] AC 500; *A-G for Ontario* v *A-G for Canada* [1947] AC 127.

[168] See *Dow Jones Publishing Co (Asia) Inc* v *A-G of Singapore* [1989] 1 WLR 1308 (and [1990] PL 453).

[169] See e.g. *Invercargill City Council* v *Hamlin* [1996] 1 All ER 756.

[170] E.g. *Dunkley* v *R* [1995] 1 AC 419 (withdrawal of counsel during murder trial); *Burut* v *Public Prosecutor* [1995] 2 AC 579 (confession obtained by oppression).

[171] Roberts-Wray, pp 461–3; J E S Fawcett, in Miller (ed.), *Survey of Commonwealth Affairs: Problems of Expansion and Attrition 1953–1969*, p 429. And see Swinfen, *Imperial Appeal*, for an excellent historical account; and Stevens, *The Independence of the Judiciary*, chs 4 and 8.

[172] See K D Ewing, in Finnie, Himsworth and Walker (eds), *Edinburgh Essays in Public Law*, at 231. For the broader approach, see *Minister of Home Affairs* v *Fisher* [1980] AC 319 and *A-G of Trinidad and Tobago* v *Whiteman* [1991] 2 AC 240; and *Maharaj* v *A-G of Trinidad and Tobago (No 2)* [1979] AC 385. See also note 173 below. For the least liberal decision, see *Ong Ah Chuan* v *Public Prosecutor* [1981] AC 648 (criticised in Pannick, *Judicial Review of the Death Penalty*).

Caribbean, but they are marked by many differences of judicial opinion as to the appropriate outcome.[173] Significant decisions have also been made in respect of freedom of expression,[174] a human right that will give rise to many questions under the Human Rights Act 1998.

---

[173] See e.g. *Pratt v A-G of Jamaica* [1994] 2 AC 1 (reversing *Riley v A-G of Jamaica* [1983] AC 719); *Henfield v A-G of Bahamas* [1997] AC 413 (distinguishing *Reckley v Minister of Public Safety and Immigration* [1995] 2 AC 491); *Fisher v Minister of Public Safety and Immigration* [1998] AC 673; *Thomas v Baptiste* [2000] 2 AC 1; and *Lewis v A-G of Jamaica* [2001] 2 AC 50 (overruling *Reckley v Minister of Public Safety and Immigration (No 2)* [1996] AC 527, *Fisher v Minister of Public Safety and Immigration (No 2)* [2000] 1 AC 434, and *Higgs v Minister of National Security* [2000] 2 AC 228).

[174] See e.g. *De Freitas v Permanent Secretary of Ministry of Agriculture* [1999] 1 AC 69; *Cable and Wireless (Dominica) Ltd v Marpin Telecoms Ltd* (2000) 9 BHRC 486; *Benjamin v Minister of Information and Broadcasting* (2001) 10 BHRC 237; *Observer Publications Ltd v Matthew* (2001) 10 BHRC 252.

Chapter 16

THE ARMED FORCES

In the interests of constitutional government and the rule of law, the exercise of the physical might of the modern state must be subject to democratic control. Experience of government at the hands of Cromwell's army led after the restoration of the monarchy in 1660 to a declaration by Parliament in the Militia Act 1661 that:

> the sole supreme government, command and disposition of the militia and of all forces by sea and land is, and by the laws of England ever was, the undoubted right of the Crown.

Subsequent attempts by Charles II and James II against parliamentary opposition to maintain their own armies led to the declaration in the Bill of Rights that:

> the raising or keeping of a standing army within the Kingdom in time of peace, unless it be with consent of Parliament, is against law.

This declaration remains important not because there is now any possibility that Parliament would withdraw authority for the continued maintenance of an army but because it asserts that the armed forces are constitutionally subordinate to Parliament.

From the earliest times the armed forces have thus raised important constitutional issues and that legacy continues to determine the constitutional position of the army, navy and Air Force today. In this chapter we concentrate on three such issues, with a full account of military law being beyond the scope of a work such as this. The first issue relates to the constitutional structure within which the armed forces operate: the nature of legislative authority and parliamentary scrutiny. The second issue concerns aspects of military law and, in particular, the extent to which military law complies with the European Convention on Human Rights. Here we find that a number of important changes have taken place in recent years as a result of decisions of the European Court of Human Rights. The third issue raises questions about the rule of law and the extent to which the military authorities and military law are subject to the ordinary law of the land. The need for military effectiveness in the defence of the realm does not mean that the armed forces should be immune from criminal or civil liability in appropriate cases, or indeed that the law of judicial review has no role to play in this as in other areas of governmental activity.

A. The constitutional structure

Legislative authority for the armed forces[1]

After the Bill of Rights, it became the custom of Parliament each year to pass a Mutiny Act, giving authority for one year to the Crown to maintain armed forces up to the

---

[1] For the history of the legal position of the armed forces, see Maitland, *Constitutional History*, pp 275–80, 324–9, 447–62; Anson, *Law and Custom of the Constitution*, vol II (2), ch 10. For the current position, see Rowe, *Defence: The Legal Implications*; and Rowe, *The Gulf War 1990–91*.

limit of manpower stated in the Act and to enforce rules of discipline. Eventually what had become a lengthy and detailed collection of rules of military law was codified in the Army Act 1881. This code was until 1955 continued in force from year to year by the passing of an Act known after 1917 as the Army and Air Force (Annual) Act. Amendments to the 1881 Act were made when necessary by the annual act. When a separate Air Force was constituted in 1917, its discipline was governed by the Army Act 1881 with modifications. By 1955, it had come to be accepted that approval of the size of the Armed Forces was granted through parliamentary consideration of the defence estimates and the formal procedure for appropriating supply to the armed forces. Following a series of reports from select committees of the Commons,[2] there was enacted the Army Act 1955 and the Air Force Act 1955. Each Act was in the first instance limited to a duration of 12 months, but for a period of five years it could be continued in force from year to year by resolution of each House of Parliament. At the end of the five years a further Act would be needed.[3]

The effect of this has been to use the requirement for regular approval of the armed forces as a device whereby the Commons may scrutinise periodically the rules and procedures of service discipline. Thus the Armed Forces Acts from 1966 to 2001 have revised the disciplinary codes of the forces and related legislation. One feature of the procedure has been that each Armed Forces Bill has, after second reading, been referred to a select committee of the Commons, which has examined the Bill thoroughly, a process which is now a procedural rarity.[4] In 1971, the Naval Discipline Act 1957 was brought within the same system. There has been a tendency to make similar provision for the main matters of discipline in each armed force. But although statutory authority is necessary to maintain the armed forces, it is important to emphasise that statutory authority is not required before they are deployed. This is a matter for the royal prerogative: 'In constitutional theory no consent of Parliament is required to send the British armed forces abroad to take part in an armed conflict, or to take part in a United Nations force or for humanitarian purposes.'[5] But in constitutional practice, no government could contemplate such action without the support – if not the prior approval – of Parliament.

Legislative authority for maintaining the armed forces does not confer power on the executive to conscript citizens into the forces. Recruitment for the navy by impressment under the prerogative is now only a matter of history. In both world wars conscription was authorised by Parliament. After the Second World War, conscription was continued under the National Service Act 1948 until its operation was brought to an end in 1960. Like earlier legislation, the 1948 Act made provision for conscientious objectors to military service.[6] As well as the full-time regular forces of the Crown, the reserve forces are maintained under statutory authority. The legislation makes provision for the recall of the reserve forces, in some circumstances by notice from the Secretary of State for Defence, but in the case of imminent national danger or great emergency by an order of the Sovereign, signified by the Secretary of State and notified to

---

[2] HC 244 and 331 (1951–52), 289 (1952–53) and 223 (1953–54).

[3] See Armed Forces Act 2001, s 1. Although a 'relatively short maximum period' compared to other countries (P Rowe, in Sunkin and Payne (eds), *The Nature of the Crown*, p 270), it has been argued that these arrangements do not overcome the Bill of Rights prohibition on a standing army: see (1981) 4 State Research 149.

[4] See e.g. HC 170 (1985–86), HC 179 (1990–91), HC 143 (1995–96).

[5] P Rowe, note 3 above, p 270.

[6] For details, see 8th edn of this work, pp 394–6. See also Loveland (ed), *Frontiers of Criminality*, ch 3, where it is pointed out that in the First World War objectors found themselves exposed to punishment 'without receiving the benefit of the procedural due process protection traditionally associated with the criminal trial'.

Parliament; if Parliament is not sitting at the time, it must meet within five days.[7] It is an offence for a member of the reserve forces to fail to respond to a call out, unless he or she has leave or reasonable excuse. The power to recall was used (selectively) during the Gulf hostilities when those with 'medical qualifications were called out to supplement volunteers with relevant military and medical experience';[8] and again in 2001 during the hostilities in Afghanistan. Under the Reserve Forces (Safeguarding of Employment) Act 1985 (as amended), an employer must reinstate a reservist at the end of his or her period of service.[9]

Central organisation for defence

Like other branches of central government, the armed forces are placed under the control of ministers of the Crown, who are in turn responsible to Parliament. Formerly each of the main services had its own ministerial head. Today the responsibility for a unified defence policy rests on the Secretary of State for Defence, whose office has undergone several changes since the post of Minister of Defence was created and occupied by Winston Churchill in the Second World War. In 1964, the Ministry of Defence became a unified ministry for the three services and absorbed the Admiralty, the War Office and the Air Ministry.[10] The present ministerial structure dates from May 1981, when the junior minister for the navy was dismissed after publicly criticising proposed reductions in Britain's naval strength. The Prime Minister promptly abolished the separate junior ministerial posts for the three services. The Ministry was in 2001 headed by the Secretary of State for Defence, with (a) a minister of state responsible for all the armed forces, (b) a minister of state responsible for defence procurement and equipment, and (c) a parliamentary under-secretary responsible for a range of matters.

All statutory powers for the defence of the realm which formerly were vested in the separate service ministers were in 1964 vested in the Secretary of State.[11] The creation of a unified Ministry of Defence was necessary because it had been found inadequate for a Minister of Defence to seek to control defence policy by coordinating the policies of three departments responsible to separate ministers. A unified ministry was also essential if the defence budget were to strike a proper balance between the commitments, resources and roles of the three services. Within the Ministry of Defence, there is a Defence Council, whose members include the defence ministers, the Chief of the Defence Staff, the three service chiefs of staff and the Vice-Chief of the Defence Staff. Beneath the Defence Council there are separate boards for the navy, the army and the Air Force, to whom is delegated management of the three services, including formal powers in relation to the regulation and discipline of each service.[12] The chiefs of staff are the professional heads of the armed forces; they give professional advice to the government on strategy and military operations and on the military implications of defence policy.

The collective responsibility of the government for defence is exercised primarily through the Cabinet's Committee on Defence and Overseas Policy under the chairmanship of the Prime Minister. Its terms of reference are simply to keep under review the government's defence and overseas policy and, in 2001, the members of the committee were the Deputy Prime Minister, the Foreign Secretary, the Chancellor of the

---

[7] Reserve Forces Act 1996, ss 52–4.
[8] P Rowe [1991] PL 170, 173.
[9] See *Slaven v Thermo Engineers Ltd* [1992] ICR 295.
[10] Cmnd 2097, 1963.
[11] Defence (Transfer of Functions) Act 1964.
[12] The boards also deal with grievances of service personnel. See Army Act 1955, s 180 and Armed Forces Act 1996, s 20. Also Employment Rights Act 1996, s 193; ch 32 B below.

Exchequer, the Secretary of State for Defence, the Secretary of State for Trade and Industry and the Secretary of State for International Development. In attendance on this committee are the Chief of the Defence Staff and the chiefs of staff of each of the three services if the business so requires. Major questions of defence policy which were set out in the Defence Review White Paper[13] cannot be decided in purely military terms without reference to the government's financial and economic policies, which affect the size, disposition and equipment of the armed forces.

Parliamentary control of the armed forces

As we shall see in chapter 21, the chain of command within the police stops with the chief constable and neither local police authorities nor central government may give him or her instructions on the operational use of the police. This is not the case with the armed forces. In the case of the army, for example, the line of command runs upwards from the private soldier, through his or her commanding officer and higher levels of command to the Chief of the Defence Staff and the Secretary of State for Defence. During active operations many immediate decisions have to be taken by soldiers in the field. But the tasks which are undertaken by the armed forces, the objectives which they are set and the manner in which they carry out these tasks are matters for which the government is accountable to Parliament – whether it be the activities of the troops in Northern Ireland, the use of the army to empty dustbins during a prolonged strike by local authority workers (as in Glasgow in 1975), the making of a controversial public speech by a high-ranking army officer, the sinking of the Argentinian ship *General Belgrano* during the Falklands conflict in 1982, or the conduct of the Armed Forces during the Gulf hostilities or while performing peace-keeping duties in what was once Yugoslavia. The full range of parliamentary procedures which are available in respect of other branches of central government may be used in respect of defence and the armed forces. Thus the Public Accounts Committee has often investigated cases of spending by the services.

Since 1979 the Defence Committee of the House of Commons has conducted major inquiries into strategic nuclear weapons policy, the handling of press and public information during the Falklands conflict and the future defence of the Falkland Islands.[14] The committee played an important part in the Westland affair and in the process did much to raise the profile and highlight the value of select committees generally.[15] The committee has subsequently examined ethnic monitoring and the armed forces[16] and business appointments taken by service personnel and Ministry of Defence officials.[17] In 1988–89 the committee expressed concern about the lack of availability of merchant shipping for defence purposes[18] and in 1994–95 it delivered a strong rebuke to the Ministry of Defence for its response to allegations of a 'Gulf War syndrome' afflicting those who had served in the conflict, as well as their families. The Ministry was said to have been 'reactive rather than proactive' and to have behaved with 'scepticism, defensiveness and general torpor'.[19] More recently the committee has examined matters such as the future of NATO, military action in Kosovo, and major procurement projects.[20]

---

[13] Cm 3999, 1998. See HC 138 (1997–98); HC 29 (2000–01).
[14] See respectively HC 35, 130 (1980–81), HC 17-I (1982–83) and HC 154 (1982–83).
[15] See HC 518 and 519 (1985–86). Also ch 10 D.
[16] HC 391 (1987–88).
[17] HC 392 (1987–88).
[18] HC 495 (1988–89).
[19] HC 197 (1994–95), para 60. See also HC 125, 753 (1999–2000); 517-1 (2001–02).
[20] HC 459 (1998–99), 347 (1999–2000) and 463 (2000–01).

Defence policies and expenditure are often matters of keen political debate in the House. As mentioned earlier, military law has received close scrutiny from select committees appointed to consider the Armed Forces Bills. Members of the forces are entitled under service regulations to communicate with MPs on all matters, including service matters, so long as they do not disclose secret information, but it is the policy of the Ministry of Defence that wherever possible servicemen and women should pursue the normal channels of complaint open to them through superior officers.[21] While allegations of maladministration on the part of the Ministry of Defence may be referred by MPs for investigation by the Parliamentary Ombudsman, it is outside his jurisdiction to investigate action relating to appointments, pay, discipline, pension, or other personnel matters affecting service in the armed forces; neither may he investigate complaints relating to the conduct of judicial proceedings under military law.[22] A proposal for a Military Ombudsman has not received very much support.[23]

B. Military law and human rights

The nature and scope of military law[24]

Military law is the internal law of the armed forces, administered by officers with appropriate authority, by courts-martial and on appeal by the Courts-Martial Appeal Court. It is made by Parliament and, under the authority of Parliament, by the defence authorities by means of Queen's Regulations. There is also power to make rules of procedure for the administration of military law. Military law must be distinguished from 'martial law', a term used to describe the situation which arises when the normal processes of law and justice have broken down and the military exercise de facto authority over the public at large.[25] Strictly speaking, military law applies to the army alone. Air Force law was founded on the army's scheme of discipline and closely resembles it. Discipline within the navy derived from separate statutes but is today being brought closer to army and Air Force law.[26] Because of the loss of freedom involved in military service, it is important that, in the absence of conscription, enlistments into the forces are voluntary. The formal process of enlistment is laid down by the Army Act. The terms of engagement on which members of the forces are enlisted are governed by regulations made by the Defence Council; it is provided that the statutory rights of existing members of the forces are not to be varied or revoked by a change of regulations except with their consent.[27]

The Army Act 1955, and its counterparts for the Air Force and the navy, create a large number of offences, including mutiny, insubordination, disobedience to orders, desertion, absence without leave, malingering and, by s 69 (as amended by the Armed Forces Act 1986), a residual offence of any act or omission to 'the prejudice of good order and military discipline'.[28] It is also an offence against the Army Act, s 70, for

---

[21] Army Act 1955, ss 180 and 181. Cf the Stevenson case, HC 112 (1954–55).

[22] Parliamentary Commissioner Act 1967, Sch 3, paras 6, 10.

[23] Cmnd 4509, 1971, app 5.

[24] See the Manual of Military Law for a complete account, and J Stuart-Smith (1969) 85 LQR 478 for a lucid introduction. For a full account of recent developments, see G R Rubin (2002) 65 MLR 36.

[25] Ch 26 C.

[26] The law is currently a mess: the 1955 Acts have been regularly amended not only by the quinquennial service legislation, but also on many other occasions as well. The need for review and consolidation is overwhelming.

[27] Armed Forces Act 1966, s 2 as subsequently amended by the Army Act 1992 and the Armed Forces Act 1996.

[28] On which, see R v Dodman [1998] 2 Cr App R 338.

any person subject to military law to commit, whether in the United Kingdom or else-where, a civil offence, i.e. an offence punishable by English criminal law or which, if committed in England, would be so punishable. It is not only serving members of the armed forces and reservists undergoing training who are subject to military law. Various classes of civilians are also subject to military law. As well as civilian employees of the Ministry of Defence who accompany the armed forces when they are on active service, the Army Act 1955 makes subject to military law, albeit with modifications, civilians who are employed outside the United Kingdom within the limits of the com-mand of any officer commanding a body of the regular forces. Also subject to military law are the families of members of the armed forces who are residing with them outside the United Kingdom and even relatives merely staying with a service family on holiday.[29]

The main effect of this is to make the families of British servicemen and women overseas subject to be tried under military law for 'civil offences', defined by s 70 of the 1955 Act as acts or omissions punishable under English law or which, if committed in England, would be so punishable. In *Cox* v *Army Council*,[30] it was held that a 'civil offence' for this purpose included the offence of careless driving on a public road in Germany.[31] In view of difficulties encountered in entrusting such extensive jurisdiction over civilians to courts-martial, the Armed Forces Act 1976 authorised the Secretary of State for Defence with the approval of the Lord Chancellor to specify areas abroad to be served by a Standing Civilian Court. The court deals with the less serious offences committed by civilians in the area concerned. It consists of a legally qualified magis-trate, appointed by the Lord Chancellor to the staff of the Judge Advocate General (on which see below); for dealing with juvenile offenders, he or she sits with two other persons. As in the case of courts-martial, the sentencing powers of the Standing Civilian Court were extended by the Armed Forces Acts 1986 and 1991 and a number of other reforms were introduced in 1996.[32] Nevertheless concerns were expressed in one case where the son of a serving soldier who had returned to England was sent back to Germany to stand trial by court-martial for murder, thereby deprived of the right to trial by jury.[33]

Military law and police powers

There are a number of different police forces in the armed forces: these are the Royal Navy Regulating Branch, the Royal Marines Police, the Royal Military Police and the RAF Police. These bodies (which have a fearsome reputation) come to public promin-ence from time to time and are not to be confused with the Ministry of Defence Police.[34] New powers of the service police (which do not apply to the MOD Police) were intro-duced by the Armed Forces Act 2001. These are very similar to the powers contained in the Police and Criminal Evidence Act 1984 and relate to powers of stop and search, the search of persons following arrest, as well as powers of entry, search and seizure of property. There is a power to stop and search service personnel (or anyone 'the service policeman has reasonable grounds for believing to be subject to service law') for stolen or prohibited articles, drugs or Her Majesty's stores (s 2). The power may only be exercised on reasonable suspicion and may be exercised in a public place

---

[29] Army Act 1955, s 209 and Sch 5 (as subsequently amended in 1976, 1981, 1986, 1996 and 2001). And see G J Borrie (1969) 32 MLR 35.
[30] [1963] AC 48.
[31] See also HC 143 (1995–96), p 169.
[32] Armed Forces Act 1966, s 2 as subsequently amended by the Army Act 1992 and the Armed Forces Act 1996.
[33] *R* v *Martin* [1998] AC 917, at p 923.
[34] On which, see p 334 below.

or on property occupied or controlled by the armed forces; but not in a dwelling or service living accommodation. In some cases these powers may also be exercised by the commanding officer of a member of the armed forces (s 4).

The Armed Forces Act 2001 now requires a warrant to be obtained before residential premises are searched for evidence relating to a number of specified offences under the service Acts (or any other offence specified in a ministerial order). The warrant must be issued by a judicial officer (on whom see later) on an application by a service police officer; and the residential premises to which it applies are accommodation for military personnel or other premises 'occupied as a residence (alone or with other persons) by (i) a person who is subject to service law, or (ii) a person who is suspected of having committed while subject to service law an offence in relation to which the warrant is sought' (s 5). In some circumstances a search may be authorised by a commanding officer (s 7), although in these circumstances the search and any subsequent seizure must be reviewed by a judicial officer as soon as practicable (s 8). Provision is made for access to excluded or special procedure material.[35] Service police officers may enter residential premises to arrest a person under any of the service Acts or to save life or limb or prevent serious damage to property (s 9). They may also search a person who has been arrested (s 10), while the Police and Criminal Evidence Act 1984, ss 18–22 have been adapted for application by the service police (s 11).[36]

As already indicated, these provisions of the Armed Forces Act 2001 do not apply to the Ministry of Defence Police. This is a civilian force of some 3,500 dedicated to meeting the policing requirements of the MOD.[37] Proposals to extend the role of the MOD police to include general policing duties were excluded from the Armed Forces Bill in 2001 in the face of parliamentary opposition and the need to ensure that the Bill was not delayed before the expected general election. The Anti-terrorism, Crime and Security Act 2001 provided another opportunity for these measures to be introduced in what is in fact a wide-ranging measure. The latter Act amends the Ministry of Defence Police Act 1987 so that members of the MOD police may assist on request the members of another police force in the execution of their duties in relation to a particular incident, investigation or operation.[38] When performing any such role, the members of the MOD police have the powers and privileges of constables for the purposes of the incident, investigation or operation. There is also provision for the chief officer of any police force to request the Chief Constable of the MOD police to provide constables or other assistance 'for the purpose of enabling that force to meet any special demand on its resources'.[39]

Military law and human rights

Military law is the basis of discipline in the armed forces, for a disciplined force could not be run on the ordinary law applicable to civilians. But it does not follow from this that those who join the armed forces should be required to surrender the right to be treated fairly or that they should be expected to waive their human rights. In 1994 (as a result of the requirements of EC law), the Sex Discrimination Act 1975 was extended to members of the forces[40] and there have been many cases, some highly controversial, involving servicewomen who were discharged because of their pregnancy and who have

---

[35] For the meaning of these terms, see ch 21.
[36] See ch 21.
[37] Ministry of Defence Police Act 1997.
[38] 1987 Act, s 2(3A), inserted by Anti-terrorism, Crime and Security Act 2001, s 98.
[39] 1987 Act, s 2A, inserted by Anti-terrorism, Crime and Security Act 2001, s 99.
[40] SI 1994 No 3276.

been able successfully to seek compensation as a result.[41] The regulations extending the 1975 Act provide that nothing is to render unlawful an act done for the purpose of ensuring the combat effectiveness of the naval, military or air forces of the Crown.[42] The Race Relations Act 1976 applied to the armed forces from the time of enactment,[43] although initially enforcement was by way of a complaint to the Defence Council under the Army Act 1955.[44] Following the Armed Forces Act 1996, complaints relating to race discrimination, sex discrimination and equal pay may now be made to employment tribunals, although in all cases complainants are required to submit their case for consideration under the services' internal grievance procedures, a requirement which at least in sex discrimination complaints involves a qualification rather than an extension of an existing right.

Particularly controversial has been the policy of the armed forces towards homosexual men and women. Although homosexual acts in the armed forces were not unlawful,[45] homosexual activity or orientation was an absolute bar to membership of the Armed Forces and could lead to discharge. It was held by the Court of Appeal in 1994 that the policy was not irrational, although the view was also expressed that 'so far as this country's international obligations are concerned, the days of this policy are numbered'.[46] The European Court of Human Rights held the practice to breach article 8 of the ECHR,[47] and on 12 January 2000 the government announced that the ban had been lifted. No primary or secondary legislation was necessary for this purpose, although a new Code of Social Conduct was introduced at the same time to deal with the personal relationships of those serving in the armed forces. The code is designed to 'apply across the forces, regardless of service, rank, gender or sexual orientation' and to 'complement existing policies' such as those dealing with bullying, harassment and discrimination. At the heart of the code is what is referred to as the service test whereby people are judged not on the basis of their sexuality but on whether their 'actions or behaviour' have 'adversely impacted or are likely to impact on the efficiency or operational effectiveness of the service'.[48]

Military discipline and human rights

Offences against military discipline are governed by the service discipline Acts,[49] the Queen's Regulations and procedural regulations. The arrangements have been significantly revised on a number of occasions since 1996 in order to comply with the ECHR, the Strasbourg court having held on a number of occasions that military law failed to comply with articles 5 (right to liberty) and 6 (right to a fair trial) of the Convention. The Convention has had an impact on the earliest stages of military discipline procedure, including the decision whether a suspect should be detained pending trial by court-martial. This obviously raises article 5 issues and the European Court of Human Rights held that the role of the applicant's commanding officer in authorising his pre-trial detention violated article 5(3) which calls for detained persons to be 'brought promptly before

---

[41] For background to this issue, see *Ministry of Defence* v *Cannock* [1994] ICR 918.

[42] See *Sidar* v *Secretary of State for Defence* [1999] All ER (EC) 928.

[43] But for allegations of serious racism in the armed forces, see J Mackenzie, NLJ, 14 June 1996. Also HC 143 (1995–96), pp 209–15.

[44] *R* v *Army Board, ex p Anderson* [1992] QB 169.

[45] Criminal Justice and Public Order Act 1994, s 146.

[46] *R* v *Ministry of Defence, ex p Smith* [1996] QB 517. For the views of the Defence Committee, see HC 143 (1995–96), para 34.

[47] *Lustig-Prean* v *UK* (1999) 29 EHRR 548.

[48] HC Deb, 12 January 2000, cols 287 et seq. For the code see www.mod.uk.

[49] Army Act 1955, Air Force Act 1955 and Naval Discipline Act 1957.

a judge or other officer authorised by law to exercise judicial power'.[50] There are now detailed statutory procedures for dealing with detention before charge, after charge and during the conduct of court-martial proceedings. In the case of detention before charge, the procedure is now similar to that operating in civil law under the Police and Criminal Evidence Act 1984. In particular, any detention beyond 48 hours requires the authority of a judicial officer and may not extend beyond 96 hours.[51] Judicial officers are appointed for this purpose by the Judge Advocate-General; as we have seen, they now have other responsibilities in the sphere of military law.

A person charged with an offence against military discipline may be dealt with in one of two ways. Under the Army Act 1955, s 76 (and the comparable provisions of the other service Acts) certain alleged breaches of military discipline may be dealt with summarily by a commanding officer. But concerns that this may not be compatible with the ECHR led in 1996 to the introduction of a new procedure (revised in 2000) whereby the accused could elect trial by court-martial. Where the accused is content to be dealt with by his or her commanding officer, there were still concerns that there was no appeal to 'a judicial process'.[52] Consequently, the Armed Forces Discipline Act 2000 created a new summary appeal court to hear appeals from the findings or sentence imposed by the commanding officer, or both (s 14). This court consists of a judge advocate appointed by the Judge Advocate-General, and two other serving officers who will be 'generally from the appellant's service', but 'from outside his chain of command'.[53] The procedure in the summary appeal court is designed to mirror the procedure of the Crown Court when dealing with appeals from the magistrates' court. The appeal takes the form of a rehearing, but the summary appeal court may not impose a punishment more severe than that imposed by the commanding officer. Proceedings are to be held in public except in cases prescribed.

There are thus two types of case which may be dealt with by court-martial: summary cases where this is elected by the accused person; and non-summary cases.[54] A pivotal position was occupied in the past by the Convening Officer, who determined the charges and appointed the court-martial; the decision of the latter would not take effect until confirmed by the Convening Officer. In *Findlay* v *United Kingdom*[55] these arrangements were found to be in breach of article 6 of the ECHR and the procedures have been overhauled as a result. In 1995, the governmenat undertook to establish new prosecuting authorities staffed by legal officers, with the responsibility to decide whether to prosecute, what charges should be brought and to conduct the prosecutions. Moreover: '[T]he administrative arrangements for courts-martial will be in the hands of cells independent of both higher authorities and the prosecuting authorities. These cells will be responsible for selecting court-martial members, who will be officers who are not in the same command as the accused.'[56] It is no longer the case that the decisions of the court-martial must be confirmed by the Convening Officer. This means that they take immediate effect, although there is a right of appeal to the Courts-Martial Appeal Court, in accordance with procedures in the Courts-Martial (Appeals) Act 1968.[57]

---

[50] *Hood* v *UK* (1999) 29 EHRR 365. And see *Findlay* v *UK* (1997) 24 EHRR 221.
[51] Armed Forces Discipline Act 2000, ss 1–11, amending the service discipline Acts.
[52] HC Deb, 17 February 2000, col 1129.
[53] HC Deb, 17 February 2000, col 1129.
[54] For an account of military discipline in practice, see HC 253 (1999–2000).
[55] (1997) 24 EHRR 221.
[56] HC Deb, 13 December 1995, col 1028.
[57] See esp s 8.

Courts-martial, the Judge Advocate-General and the Courts-Martial Appeal Court

Apart from field general courts-martial (which are only assembled on active service),[58] courts-martial are of two different kinds: general courts-martial and district courts-martial; the latter try less serious cases and have no authority to try officers.[59] Amendments to the composition of these bodies were introduced by the Armed Forces Act 2001. A general court-martial consists of a president (who is a military officer), a judge advocate (who is legally qualified) and at least four other members who must be military officers, of whom up to two may be warrant officers. A district court-martial consists of a president (who is a military officer), a judge advocate, and at least two other members who must be military officers, one of whom may be a warrant officer. Field general courts-martial consist only of three members and may but need not include a judge advocate.[60] Courts-martial have the power to require the attendance of witnesses (under arrest if necessary) and to award costs.[61] The new procedures have so far withstood challenge under the Human Rights Act, though fresh uncertainty has been caused by yet another decision of the European Court of Human Rights.[62] But the other major impact of the human rights movement on military law has been the removal of capital punishment as a possible sentence for breach of military law. This change was introduced by the Human Rights Act 1998 in response to backbench pressure.[63]

A key actor in the court-martial procedure is the Judge Advocate-General, who appoints the judge advocates to be members of courts-martial. The office of Judge Advocate-General has been in continuous existence since it was created in 1666. The incumbent must have a ten-year qualification within the meaning of the Courts and Legal Services Act 1990 and is appointed by the Crown on the advice of the Lord Chancellor. He or she may be removed from office only for inability or misbehaviour.[64] The Judge Advocate-General has an overall responsibility to monitor the criminal justice system of the army and the RAF, in order to ensure that it works properly and efficiently. (There is a separate Judge Advocate of the Fleet for the Royal Navy.) The office is not governed by statute but by the incumbent's letters patent which provide that all members of both the army and the RAF are subject to his or her authority. It is thought important that the office is purely a civilian one and that the Judge Advocate-General is separate and independent from the forces it is his or her duty to serve. The office was in 2001 held by a circuit judge.

An important link between military courts and the ordinary judicial system is provided by the Courts-Martial Appeal Court, which is governed by the Courts-Martial (Appeals) Act 1968. The judges of the court are the Lord Chief Justice, the judges of the Court of Appeal and such of the judges of the Queen's Bench Division of the High Court and corresponding judges for Scotland and Northern Ireland as may be nominated, together with such other persons of legal experience as the Lord Chancellor may appoint.[65] A person convicted by a court-martial may appeal to the court against both conviction and sentence, which means that all court-martial decisions are subject to scrutiny by a civilian court. But leave to appeal must be obtained from the court itself

---

[58] See *Manning's Military Law*, p 131.

[59] Army Act 1955, ss 84–85.

[60] Armed Forces Act 2001, s 19, Sch 2.

[61] Armed Forces Act 2001, ss 25, 26.

[62] See *R v Spear* [2001] QB 804, and *Morris v UK* (2002) 34 EHRR 1253.

[63] Human Rights Act 1998, s 21.

[64] Courts-Martial (Appeals) Act 1951, ss 29–32 (as amended by the Courts and Legal Services Act 1990, Sch 10). See ch 18. For the history of the Judge Advocate-General, see Stuart-Smith (above).

[65] A judge is not disqualified because he may previously have acted for the Ministry of Defence before elevation to the Bench: *R v Spear* [2001] QB 804.

and only one application for leave to appeal may be made.[66] In deciding an appeal, the court must consider whether a conviction is in all the circumstances unsafe; otherwise the appeal must be dismissed.[67] A further appeal to the House of Lords lies by leave of the court or of the House on a point of law of general public importance.[68] The High Court has no power to make orders of mandamus, prohibition or certiorari 'in relation to the jurisdiction of a court-martial' under the three service Acts, a restriction which applies to matters relating to trial by court-martial for an offence or appeals from a Standing Civilian Court.[69] This is an important change introduced by the Armed Forces Act 2001 to bring court-martial procedure into line with the Crown Court in non-military cases. Where cases are tried on indictment, there is no right to seek judicial review, there being a right to appeal if the defence is unhappy with the way a trial is conducted. The Courts-Martial Appeal Court performs the same function in military law.[70]

C. The armed forces and the ordinary law

Dual jurisdiction

To what extent are the military subject to the ordinary law? We have already seen that the role of the ordinary law by way of judicial review has been removed from the area of military discipline, but that the judges of the Courts-Martial Appeal Court are the senior judges from the civil courts. It does not follow, however, that those who are subject to the military law are not also subject to the ordinary criminal law and to the jurisdiction of the criminal courts in the United Kingdom. In the context of military law, by a somewhat confusing usage which will be followed here, the ordinary criminal courts are referred to as 'civil courts' to distinguish them from military courts. Except so far as Parliament provides otherwise, the soldier's obligations under the Army Act and Queen's Regulations are in addition to his or her duties as a citizen. As we have seen, s 70 of the Army Act provides that a civil offence committed by a person subject to military law may be dealt with as an offence against military law; but certain serious crimes (including treason, murder, manslaughter and rape) must, if committed in the United Kingdom, be tried by the competent civil court.

Does the dual jurisdiction of the military and civil courts lead to a possible conflict of duty for the soldier? In theory there is no conflict since military law is part of the law of the land and a soldier is only required to obey orders which are lawful.[71] If an order involves a breach of the general law, a soldier is not only under no obligation to obey it but is under an obligation not to obey it. In practice, particularly when troops are operating in a peace-keeping role within the United Kingdom at a time when the civil courts are functioning, as in Northern Ireland, soldiers may be placed in an awkward position. They are not trained, neither may they have time, to assess the legality of an order. But if, for example, unlawful injuries are inflicted on a citizen as the result of compliance, the soldier may be liable to an action for damages or to a criminal prosecution. In principle, the defence of obedience to the order of a superior is not accepted by the civil courts if the order is unlawful. But if a soldier disobeys an order

---

[66] *R v Grantham* [1969] 2 QB 574.
[67] Courts-Martial (Appeals) Act 1968, s 12 (as amended by the Criminal Appeal Act 1995, Sch 2, para 5). See *R v Dodman* [1998] 2 Cr App Rep 338.
[68] E.g. *Cox v Army Council* [1963] AC 48, *R v Warn* [1970] AC 394, and *R v Martin* [1998] AC 917.
[69] Armed Forces Act 2001, s 23. See p 333 above.
[70] HL Deb, 23 April 2001, cols 1151–2.
[71] Army Act 1955, s 34 (as amended by Armed Forces Act 1971, s 8(2)). Also Armed Forces Act 1996, s 32(1).

claiming that it is unlawful, a court-martial may hold that it was lawful. The practical difficulty for the soldier is only partially eased by the possibility of an appeal to the Courts-Martial Appeal Court, whose judges are in a position to ensure that military law and the ordinary law do not conflict; indeed, their duty is to use their powers 'so far as they think it necessary or expedient in the interests of justice'.[72] But it may be better to leave the soldier in a position of some difficulty and for the circumstances to be relied on in mitigation of a criminal offence, than to place him or her and thus the army outside the ordinary law.

There is little direct authority on the matter. In *Keighley* v *Bell*, Willes J expressed the opinion that if a prosecution results from obedience to an order, the soldier who obeys it is not criminally liable unless the order was necessarily or manifestly illegal.[73] This opinion was followed during the Boer War by a special court in South Africa which acquitted of murder a soldier who had shot a civilian in obedience to an unlawful order given to him by his officer,[74] a decision which today seems an alarming one in view of the facts. It would seem that for the defence to succeed the mistaken belief in the legality of the order must be reasonable and this would be a matter for the jury to decide. In a Scottish case, *Her Majesty's Advocate* v *Hawton and Parker*, when a naval officer and a marine were charged with killing a fisherman on a trawler which was being intercepted by a naval vessel, Lord Justice General McNeill said: 'It was the duty of the subordinate to obey his superior officer, unless the order given by his superior was so flagrantly and violently wrong that no citizen could be expected to obey it.'[75] This test is materially different from that proposed by Willes J but there was in the Scottish case no order to kill. In the circumstances in which British troops have been used in Northern Ireland, the question of criminal liability for the death or injury of a civilian will normally depend not on the legality of army orders but on whether a soldier's use of firearms is reasonably justifiable in the immediate circumstances.[76] It was held in *R* v *Clegg*[77] that a soldier who killed a person by discharging a firearm in self-defence was guilty of murder rather than manslaughter where the force used was excessive and unreasonable.

Criminal offences and civil liability

In practice, most criminal offences committed by members of the armed forces in the United Kingdom are dealt with in peacetime by the civil courts. The decision rests with the civil prosecutor: but offences affecting the person or property of a civilian will usually be prosecuted in the civil courts.[78] Even alleged breaches of the Official Secrets Acts may be dealt with in civil rather than military courts, as with the prosecution of eight signals personnel based in Cyprus who were prosecuted unsuccessfully in 1986 under the 1911 Act for allegedly passing intelligence information to enemy agents in return for sexual favours.[79] Where a person subject to military law has been tried for

---

[72] Courts-Martial (Appeals) Act 1968, s 1(3).

[73] (1866) 4 F & F 763, 790.

[74] *R* v *Smith* (1900) 17 Cape of Good Hope SCR 561.

[75] (1861) 4 Irvine 58, 69.

[76] The case of Marine Bek, *The Times*, 31 March 1971; *A-G for Northern Ireland's Reference (No 1 of 1975)* [1977] AC 105; *Farrell* v *Secretary of State for Defence* [1980] 1 All ER 166; *R* v *Thain* (1985) 11 NIJB 31. And see ch 26.

[77] [1995] 1 AC 482. See Cm 2706, 1995, p 52.

[78] Stuart-Smith, note 24 above, p 492.

[79] A subsequent inquiry found the pre-trial detention and questioning of the suspects to be unlawful, in the sense that the 'procedures in RAF and military law intended to protect individuals against oppressive treatment and arbitrary detention had been honoured more in the breach than in the observance'. The government undertook to make ex gratia payments to those involved. See Cmnd 9781, 1986 (Calcutt Report); A W Bradley [1986] PL 363.

an offence by court-martial or has been dealt with summarily by his or her commanding officer, a civil court may not try him or her subsequently for the same or substantially the same offence.[80] Apart from this there is no restriction on a civil court trying a member of the armed forces for an offence under criminal law. A person tried by a civil court in the United Kingdom or elsewhere is not liable to be tried again under military law in respect of the same or substantially the same offence.[81] In general, a person who is no longer subject to military law is liable to be tried under military law for offences committed while he or she was so subject, but only within prescribed time limits after he or she ceased to be subject to military law (three months in the case of summary proceedings and six months in the case of trial by court-martial).[82]

Apart from the criminal liability of service personnel, questions also arise as to whether the Crown can be vicariously liable in tort or delict for the acts or omissions of members of the armed forces. The problem could arise in the event of a member of the armed forces negligently causing damage to another member of the services or to a third party; and such a case could arise either in wartime or in peace. Before the Crown Proceedings Act 1947 difficulties would have been faced by some plaintiffs (particularly those who were themselves members of the armed forces) by virtue of the Crown's immunity from liability. But even with the passing of the Act difficulties would still be encountered by a member of the armed forces who was injured by the negligence of another, if the Secretary of State issued a certificate under s 10 of the 1947 Act that the (death or) injury of the plaintiff was attributable to service for the purposes of a war pension. However, s 10 was repealed in 1987[83] though the 1987 Act provides a complex provision for the revival of s 10 of the 1947 Act in response to any 'imminent national danger or of any great emergency' or 'for the purposes of any warlike operations in any part of the world outside the United Kingdom'. The order must be made by the Secretary of State, the power being exercisable by statutory instrument which is subject to annulment by Parliament. As a result of the 1987 Act, it is thus possible for a member of the armed forces to sue the Ministry of Defence, not only in respect of injuries sustained by the negligence of another as a result of military operations in peacetime (as in Northern Ireland), but also in times of war or other hostilities (as in the case of the Gulf campaign in 1991, and the campaign in Afghanistan in 2001–2002).

For reasons explained this is a matter about which there is not a great deal of authority.[84] There is, however, authority for the view that the Crown could be vicariously liable for injuries sustained by a member of the armed forces as a result of the negligence of another in peacetime[85] and by third parties as a result of negligence by a member of the armed forces who was not engaged at the time in operations against the enemy.[86] But there is also authority for the view that there is no liability to a third party where the injury is sustained by the negligence of a member of the armed forces while in the course of an actual engagement with the enemy.[87]

---

[80] Army Act 1955, s 133 (as amended).

[81] Army Act 1955, s 134, as amended by Armed Forces Act 1991, s 26.

[82] Army Act 1955, s 132(3), amended by Armed Forces Act 1981, s 6 and Armed Forces Act 1986, s 8. The time limit does not apply to mutiny, desertion or, with the consent of the Attorney-General, offences committed outside the UK.

[83] See Crown Proceedings (Armed Forces) Act 1987; and ch 32 A.

[84] For an account of some of the issues, see Z Cowan (1950) 66 LQR 478.

[85] *Groves v Commonwealth of Australia* (1982) 150 CLR 113. See also *Barrett v Ministry of Defence* [1995] 3 All ER 87 and *Jebson v Ministry of Defence* [2000] 1 WLR 2055 (scope of liability where a soldier off duty dies or is injured because of over-indulgence in alcohol).

[86] *Shaw, Savill and Albion Co Ltd v The Commonwealth* (1940) 66 CLR 344.

[87] *Shaw, Savill and Albion*, ibid.

In *Mulcahy* v *Ministry of Defence*[88] a soldier deployed in Saudi Arabia during the Gulf conflict was injured as a result of a fellow soldier negligently causing a howitzer to fire while the plaintiff was fetching water from the front of the gun. An action for damages for negligence, claiming that the Ministry was vicariously liable, was struck out by the Court of Appeal on the ground that it disclosed no cause of action. Although no order had been made under s 2 of the 1987 Act to revive s 10 of the Crown Proceedings Act 1947, it was nevertheless held that (adopting a dictum of the High Court of Australia)[89] there is no civil liability for injury caused by the negligence of persons in the course of an actual engagement with the enemy, in accordance with 'common sense and sound policy'. In the view of Sir Iain Glidewell, 'it could be highly detrimental to the conduct of military operations if each soldier had to be conscious that, even in the heat of battle, he owed [a duty of care] to his comrade'.

Visiting Forces Act 1952

Just as it is necessary for British military jurisdiction to be exercised when British forces are stationed abroad, so it is necessary that foreign troops stationed in the United Kingdom should be able to enforce their own military law. This would be unlawful without the authority of Parliament. The Visiting Forces Act 1952 gave effect to an agreement reached between parties to the North Atlantic Treaty on the legal status of the armed forces of one state when stationed in the territory of another.[90] It also applies to forces from member states of the Commonwealth which are stationed in the United Kingdom and it may be extended to forces from other countries by Order in Council. The Act was extended by the Armed Forces Act 1996 to apply also to countries with which this country has 'arrangements for defence cooperation', to accommodate the possibility of military personnel from the countries of central and eastern Europe exercising in the UK.

Under Part I of the Act, the service courts and service authorities of visiting forces may exercise in the United Kingdom all the jurisdiction given to them by their own national law over all persons (including civilians accompanying the visiting forces) who may be subject to their jurisdiction; the death penalty may not, however, be carried out in the United Kingdom unless under United Kingdom law the death sentence could have been passed (s 2). The Act excludes the jurisdiction of criminal courts in the United Kingdom over members of visiting forces only if the alleged offence (*a*) arises out of and in the course of military duty; or (*b*) is one against the person or a member of the same or another visiting force, for example, murder or assault; or (*c*) is committed against property of the visiting force or of a member thereof (s 3). The service authorities of the visiting force may, however, waive jurisdiction over such an offence. A member of a visiting force who has been tried by his or her own service court cannot be put on trial in a United Kingdom court for the same offence (s 4). Police powers of arrest and search in respect of offences against United Kingdom law may still be exercised notwithstanding the jurisdiction of the visiting service authorities, but the police may deliver an arrested member of a visiting force into the custody of that force (s 5). The 1952 Act also makes provision for the settlement by the Secretary of State for Defence of certain civil claims in respect of acts or omissions of members of visiting forces (s 9).

In Part II of the 1952 Act, s 13 confers important powers on the police and on United Kingdom courts to arrest and hand over into the custody of the appropriate visiting force persons who are deserters or absentees without leave from the forces of any country to which the Act applies. In *R* v *Thames Justices, ex p Brindle*,[91] the Court of Appeal

---

[88] [1996] QB 732.
[89] *Groves* v *Commonwealth of Australia*, in note 85.
[90] Cmd 8279, 1951.
[91] [1975] 3 All ER 941. And see *R* v *Tottenham Magistrates' Court, ex p Williams* [1982] 2 All ER 705.

held that this power could be exercised in respect of any person who had deserted from any of the forces of a country to which the Act applied and was not restricted to persons who had deserted from visiting forces while they were serving in the United Kingdom; thus a United States citizen who deserted from a unit of the US army in Germany and came to England could be handed over to the US authorities in England, who might then return him in custody to the United States. A British civilian, or a member of the British armed forces, may be required to appear before a service court of visiting forces in order to give evidence. In such cases the summons must be issued by 'an officer of any of the home forces'.[92] Difficulties of a different kind arose in relation to the community charge; although visiting forces were exempt, British wives of US service personnel were not.[93]

---

[92] Visiting Forces and International Headquarters (Application of Law) Order 1999, SI 1999 No 1736, article 16 and Sch 7. The Order also confers other immunities and privileges on visiting forces, similar to those enjoyed by UK forces. For background, see HC 521 (1998–99).

[93] *Tatum* v *Cherwell DC* [1992] 1 WLR 1261 and *Earl* v *Huntingdonshire DC* [1994] CLYB 2936.

Chapter 17

THE TREASURY, PUBLIC EXPENDITURE
AND THE ECONOMY

Government policies for taxation and public expenditure have long been liable to give rise to legal and constitutional disputes. In the 20th century, the responsibilities of central government widened to include not just raising and spending the proceeds of taxation to meet the costs of government but also the tasks of overseeing the national economy, maintaining policies on employment and the social services, and securing a sound external balance of payments. These responsibilities will continue long into the 21st century. In chapter 10 C, an account was given of the financial procedures of Parliament. The present chapter deals in outline with the main financial procedures of government. These matters are mostly the responsibility of the Treasury which, with the Cabinet Office, is at the centre of government. We also deal with the institutional structures which have evolved for the purpose of management of the economy, a Treasury responsibility.

A. The Treasury[1]

Since 1714 the ancient office of Lord High Treasurer has been in commission; that is, its duties have been entrusted to a board of commissioners. Today the commissioners are the First Lord of the Treasury, an office held by the Prime Minister; the Chancellor of the Exchequer; and the Junior Lords of the Treasury, who are the assistant government whips in the House of Commons. The Treasury Board never meets, individual members of the board being responsible for the Treasury's business. The Chancellor of the Exchequer's responsibilities cover the whole range of Treasury business, including the control of public expenditure and the direction of economic and financial policy. The other Treasury ministers include the Chief Secretary to the Treasury, who is often a member of the Cabinet and deals with public expenditure planning and control, public sector pay, export credit and value for money in the public services. The Financial Secretary to the Treasury is responsible for procurement policy, competition and deregulation policy, export credit, HM Customs and Excise and parliamentary financial business. The Economic Secretary to the Treasury deals with National Surveys, the Debt Management Office, the Office for National Statistics and the Royal Mint. The Parliamentary Secretary to the Treasury acts as the government's chief whip in the Commons and has had no connection with Treasury business since political patronage in the civil service disappeared in the 19th century.[2]

---

[1] See Beer, *Treasury Control*; Bridges, *The Treasury*; Heclo and Wildavsky, *The Private Government of Public Money*; Roseveare, *The Treasury*; and Thain and Wright, *The Treasury and Whitehall*. For the views of insiders, see Barnett, *Inside the Treasury*; Healey, *The Time of My Life*, chs 18–22; and Lawson, *The View from No 11*. For a detailed textbook-style description of some of the matters raised in this chapter, see Daintith and Page, *The Executive in the Constitution*, chs 4–6.

[2] The duties of Paymaster General are purely formal: payments on account of the public service are made to the Paymaster General by the Bank of England and the money is then paid out in his or her name to the departments and other persons authorised to receive it. In practice the Paymaster General may

Functions of the Treasury

The Treasury's functions were formerly concerned primarily with financial matters, including the imposition and regulation of taxation, the control of expenditure and the management of the government's funds and accounts. But in the 20th century, except for two periods when a separate department for economic affairs was established (for some months in 1947 and between 1964 and 1969), the Treasury also became an economic policy department. Since a review of senior management structures in 1995, its work is organised into a number of directorates. These deal with matters such as macroeconomic policy and international finance; budget and public finances; finance regulation and industry; financial management and reporting; and public services. The Treasury has a strong complement of the most senior civil servants, who include the Permanent Secretary to the Treasury. There are also a number of executive agencies within the Treasury, including the Office for National Statistics and the Royal Mint. Moreover, both the Inland Revenue and Customs and Excise operate fully on agency lines. The former was established in 1849[3] and the latter in 1909 following a merger of the separate boards of customs and excise, each of which was founded in the 17th century. The Inland Revenue is responsible for the administration of income and corporation tax, while the Customs and Excise is responsible for VAT and excise duty as well as the problem of drug trafficking. Both come under the general direction of the Chancellor of the Exchequer, who is responsible to Parliament for their work. Although Customs and Excise have a number of responsibilities unrelated to fiscal matters (such as enforcing export controls) it is their traditional role of collecting customs duties on imported goods which explains why departmentally they fall under the aegis of the Treasury.[4]

The economic functions of the Treasury, together with its control over spending, give the Department a uniquely powerful position in government. Responsibility for monetary policy has been devolved to the Monetary Policy Committee of the Bank of England (see below), at the same time as other initiatives (such as public service agreements) (see below) have tightened the Treasury's grip on the activities of other departments. It is inevitable that the Treasury's pursuit of its published objectives will mean that it develops close working relationships with other departments. These objectives include improving the quality and cost effectiveness of public services; increasing the productivity of the economy; expanding economic and employment opportunities for all; and promoting a fair and efficient tax and benefit system with incentives to work, save and invest.[5] Concern has been expressed that the Treasury has become more powerful in recent years, that its influence over the strategic direction of the government has grown, and that it is exercising too much influence on policy making.[6] According to the House of Commons Treasury Committee, 'in the case of the DSS, the impression is given that the Treasury has taken charge of the welfare reform process' and that 'in the case of the DTI, the Treasury gives the impression of having taken charge of microeconomic policy'.[7] But complaints about the power of the Treasury are as old as government itself, although they do appear to be made now with greater intensity.

---

serve as a minister without portfolio or may be assigned ministerial duties in the Treasury or in another department.

[3] Inland Revenue Board Act 1849.
[4] HC 115 (1995–96) (Scott Report), para C 3.3.
[5] www.hm-treasury.gov.uk/docs/1999/aims.html.
[6] See Hennessy, *The Prime Minister*, pp 513–14.
[7] HC 73 (2000–2001), para 25.

Statutory powers of the Treasury

Novel powers of the Treasury were introduced by the Anti-terrorism, Crime and Security Act 2001, replacing narrower powers contained in the Emergency Law (Re-enactments and Repeals) Act 1964. These new measures are designed to enable the Treasury to freeze the assets of terrorist suspects,[8] although as we shall see the powers range much more widely. Under s 4 of the 2001 Act, the Treasury may make a freezing order if two conditions are satisfied. The first is that the Treasury reasonably believe that (a) action to the detriment of the United Kingdom economy (or part of it) has been or is likely to be taken by a person or persons; or (b) action constituting a threat to the life or property of one or more United Kingdom nationals has been or is likely to be taken by a person or persons. The second condition is that the person who has taken or who is likely to take the action is (a) the government of a country or territory outside the United Kingdom, or (b) a resident of a country or territory outside the United Kingdom.[9] Concern was expressed in Parliament that these measures were 'extraordinarily wide' and would allow the freezing of assets of persons other than suspected terrorists, a feature of the Act openly acknowledged by the government. The example was given of the Swiss government inducing a Japanese company to invest in Switzerland rather than the United Kingdom:

> That 'is plainly action to the detriment of the United Kingdom', with the result that at least in theory, the Treasury could make a freezing order stopping anyone in the United Kingdom, or United Kingdom nationals resident abroad, from making payments to the Swiss government.[10]

Under s 5 of the 2001 Act, the effect of a freezing order is to prohibit anyone from making funds available to or for the benefit of the person specified in the order. Detailed provision is made for the content of freezing orders (preventing funds being made available to the target of the order and requiring documents and information to be made available). Apart from the scope of the power (which the government claims will be regulated in its operation by EU law, international trade law and the Human Rights Act 1998),[11] the other notable feature of this provision is the procedure for making a freezing order. Curiously, the order is made not on an application to a court, but by statutory instrument. The order is valid once made and, although it has to be laid before Parliament, it may be effective without the consent of Parliament which must be given within 28 days of the order being made. No explanation was given as to why a court was an inappropriate venue for restraints of this nature or why it was thought appropriate that the statutory instrument procedure was thought appropriate for ad hominem measures designed to target individuals as well as governments. Freezing orders will, however, be subject to judicial review, although given the nature of their subject matter it is likely that the courts would apply a light standard of review in any such case. Provision is made for the amendment and revocation of orders.[12]

---

[8] HC Deb, 19 November 2001, col 34.
[9] On definitions, see 2001 Act, s 9.
[10] HL Deb, 28 November 2001, col 348 (Lord Goodhart). For the government's response, see col 353 (Lord McIntosh).
[11] Ibid.
[12] 2001 Act, ss 11 and 12.

B. The Bank of England

The Bank of England was first established in 1694, mainly to provide loans to meet the needs of the Crown; it eventually became the government's bankers for all purposes. It was taken into public ownership under the Bank of England Act 1946, although the Treasury had for many years been able to control its policies. Under the 1946 Act, the Bank of England remains a separate institution from the Treasury and it is not a government department, although the Governor and directors of the Bank are appointed by the Crown[13] and the Treasury may issue formal directions to the Bank;[14] not now, however, in relation to monetary policy.[15] But it has been pointed out that 'unlike the detailed constitutions of some of the other central banks', the 1946 Act 'did not accord the Bank stated duties and responsibilities'.[16] Instead it was an 'apparently simple Act by which the Treasury merely acquired stock from the Bank's proprietors, made arrangements for the Crown to appoint the Governors and directors, and gave legal support firstly to the ultimate authority of the Treasury over the Bank in matters of policy and secondly to the authority of the Bank over the banks'.[17] The position of the Bank has been substantially reformed by the Bank of England Act 1998.

Constitution and functions

The constitution of the Bank of England is now governed by the Bank of England Act 1998, which makes a number of radical changes to the functions performed by the Bank. The Bank continues to be governed by a court of directors, which consists of the governor, two deputy governors and 16 directors, all appointed by the Crown. It was the optimistic intention of the government that the directors would be representative of the nation as a whole.[18] The governor and deputy governors are appointed for renewable periods of five years; and the directors for three. Members of the court may be removed from office by the Bank for a number of prescribed reasons, with the consent of the Chancellor of the Exchequer (Sch 1). The functions of the court of directors as set out in the 1998 Act are to 'manage the Bank's affairs, other than the formulation of monetary policy' (which is the responsibility of the Monetary Policy Committee) (s 2(1)). These functions include in particular 'determining the Bank's objectives (including objectives for its financial management) and strategy' (s 2(2)). Provision is also made in s 3 to give an 'enhanced role to the non-executive directors of the Bank, who [are to] ensure that the bank performs its functions effectively and manages its resources efficiently'.[19] The Bank must report annually to the Chancellor of the Exchequer, who must lay the report before Parliament (s 4).

The Bank has a number of responsibilities which have evolved over its long history: these include acting as banker to the government and to the clearing banks; the implementation of monetary policy; the issue of currency.[20] A major initiative introduced in 1997 was to give the Bank operational responsibility to set interest rates.[21] This step

---

[13] The Governor, Deputy Governor and directors are known as the Court of Directors: Bank of England Act 1998, s 1.

[14] Bank of England Act 1964, s 4.

[15] Bank of England Act 1998, s 10. But see 1998 Act, s 19 (Treasury reserve powers), discussed below.

[16] HC 98–I (1993–94), para 13.

[17] Fforde, *The Bank of England and Public Policy 1941–1958*, p 5.

[18] HC Deb, 20 May 1997, col 509.

[19] HC Deb, 11 November 1997, col 719.

[20] Responsibilities for the management of government debt were transferred to the Treasury (HC Deb, 20 May 1997, col 509) and for the supervision of other banks and financial institutions to the Financial Services Authority (Bank of England Act 1998, s 21).

[21] HC Deb, 6 May 1997, col 509; also HC Deb, 20 May 1997, col 507 et seq.

was taken by the Prime Minister and the Chancellor of the Exchequer, without consulting the Cabinet, in order 'to ensure that decision-making on monetary policy was more effective, open, accountable, and free from short term political manipulation'.[22] Under the 1998 Act the Bank is responsible for monetary policy within the objectives set out in the Act: these are to maintain price stability and to support the economic policy of the government, 'including its objectives for growth and employment' (s 11). Provision is also made for the government to set the inflation target for the bank, which is reviewed annually and announced in the Budget; it is the operational responsibility of the bank to achieve that target (s 12).[23] It is the specific responsibility of the Monetary Policy Committee of the Bank of England to formulate monetary policy. The committee consists of the governor and the deputy governor, two senior Bank officials with responsibility for monetary policy and market operations, but also 'four other expert members appointed from outside the Bank by the government'.[24] The Treasury has reserve powers to give the Bank directions relating to monetary policy in 'extreme economic circumstances' (s 19).[25]

Transparency and accountability

A great deal of secrecy has traditionally surrounded matters of national finance and it remains the case that there are still restrictions on access to banking and financial information. Public interest immunity applies to documents 'which cover discussions and communications between the bank and the government', as well as to financial information communicated to the government and to the Bank by major businesses.[26] It is also the case that the Freedom of Information Act 2000 has an exemption for information the disclosure of which would or would be likely to prejudice the financial interests of any administration in the United Kingdom (s 29).[27] But for all that, important steps in the direction of greater transparency were taken in 1997 and contained in the Bank of England Act 1998. We have already referred to the requirement that the Bank publish an annual report. Perhaps more importantly, the interest rate decisions of the Monetary Policy Committee must be published immediately (s 14), and minutes of the meetings of the Committee must be published within six weeks (s 15). The Bank must (now by statute) also prepare a quarterly inflation report, which must also be published (subject to the approval of the Monetary Policy Committee) (s 18).

Transparency of decisions and decision-making is itself a form of accountability and will enhance the scrutiny which Parliament can provide. Between 1969 and 1979 the Bank was, in some of its activities, subject to investigation by the select committee on the nationalised industries.[28] Since 1979, the Bank has come within the sphere of the Treasury and Civil Service Committee and now the Treasury Committee, as one of the 'associated public bodies' related to the Treasury.[29] A major study of the Bank was conducted by the Treasury and Civil Service Committee in 1993,[30] which is said to have influenced the reforms introduced in 1997.[31] As part of that process of reform, it was

---

[22] HC Deb, 20 May 1997, col 508 (Gordon Brown).
[23] Ibid.
[24] Ibid.
[25] The government expects this power to be used 'rarely, if at all' (HC Deb, 20 May 1997, col 509).
[26] *Burmah Oil Co* v *Bank of England* [1980] AC 1090. See ch 32 C below.
[27] Also Bank of England Act 1998, Sch 7.
[28] Ch 14 D. See HC 258 (1969–70).
[29] Ch 10 D.
[30] HC 98–I (1993–94).
[31] HC Deb, 20 May 1997, col 508.

anticipated that the Bank's annual report would be debated in the House of Commons each year and that the Bank would appear before the Treasury Committee four times a year to answer questions on its inflation reports.[32] The Treasury Committee has shown considerable interest in the work of the Monetary Policy Committee: in addition to examining the work of the MPC,[33] it also holds confirmation hearings to see whether those nominated to the MPC are adequately qualified,[34] a power which the Treasury Committee asserted in 1997.[35] Valuable scrutiny work is also undertaken by a House of Lords select committee.[36]

C. Public finance

The annual cycle of revenue and expenditure that was established in the 19th century depended on a highly centralised system of financial procedure built up by a combination of statutory and parliamentary rules, Cabinet conventions and administrative practices. In chapter 10 C we saw that without the formal authority of Parliament the Crown could neither raise money by taxation nor incur expenditure. While permanent authority was given by statute for some forms of expenditure and revenue, authority for much expenditure and taxation was given by Parliament strictly on an annual basis. This led to the system by which each year the Treasury coordinated the expenditure needs of the departments. While the annual cycle ensured that Parliament should regularly approve the government's financial proposals, the government in fact retained a firm control over the House; thus by a standing order of the House dating from 1713, the House could not consider new charges on the public revenue or new taxes except on the recommendation of the Crown signified by a minister.[37] This emphasised that the government bore responsibility for all taxation and expenditure. In this section we consider three issues which relate to that responsibility: the legal authority for the raising of money by taxation; the funds into which tax and other revenues are paid and from which expenditure is made; and the procedures – recently reformed – for accounting for government finance.[38]

Authority for taxation

Permanent authority for tax collection is contained in such Acts as the Income and Corporation Taxes Act 1988 and the Taxation of Chargeable Gains Act 1992. These Acts provide for the appointment of the Commissioners of Inland Revenue,[39] who are all civil servants: under their direction, a citizen's liability to tax is assessed by inspectors of taxes and the assessed tax is collected by collectors of taxes. In performing their duties, the Commissioners of Inland Revenue are subject to the authority, direction and control of the Treasury.[40] Where a taxpayer does not accept that he or she has been correctly assessed for income tax, he or she has a right of appeal to an

---

[32] Ibid, col 509. Although the Bank appears regularly, it is not clear that this particular expectation has been met.

[33] HC 42 (2000–01).

[34] For example, HC 449 (2000–01); HC 940 (1999–2000).

[35] HC 282 (1997–98).

[36] See HL 34 (2000–01) and HL 96 (1998–99) (House of Lords Select Committee on the Monetary Policy Committee of the Bank of England).

[37] Ch 10 C.

[38] For the comparable arrangements relating to Scotland, see Public Finance and Accountability (Scotland) Act 2000.

[39] See Johnston, *The Inland Revenue*, and annual reports of the Commissioners.

[40] Inland Revenue Regulation Act 1890, s 2. Cf *IRC v Nuttal* [1990] 1 WLR 631.

independent tribunal which may be either the General Commissioners of Income Tax or the Special Commissioners of Income Tax. From these tribunals, appeals on points of law lie to the High Court in England or to the Court of Session in Scotland; further appeals may reach the House of Lords.[41] The principal forms of indirect taxation, such as value added tax and customs and excise duties, are administered by the second revenue department, the Commissioners of Customs and Excise,[42] whose position closely resembles that of the Inland Revenue Commissioners. As with income tax, VAT and customs and excise duties must be collected in accordance with the law and assessments are subject to an appeal to the VAT and Duties Tribunal and thence to the court. The detailed rules of these forms of taxation are contained in continuing Acts of Parliament, but the rates of duty may be subject to variation from time to time by the Treasury or by a Secretary of State under statutory authority.[43] Many duties administered by the Commissioners of Customs and Excise are directly affected by obligations which arise from British membership of the EU.

Whenever a department demands payment of a tax or other charge from the citizen, the citizen may challenge the legality of the demand in the courts but he or she may first be required to appeal to the relevant tribunal. When such a dispute reaches the court, the court may take into account the ancient principle in the Bill of Rights that the authority of Parliament must be shown to exist if any charge on the citizen is to be lawful.[44] Thus a tax may not be imposed in reliance on a resolution of the House of Commons alone, in the absence of a statute giving legal effect to the resolution.[45] Subordinate legislation which infringes the Bill of Rights principle may be declared invalid by the courts.[46] When in 1975 the television licence fee was increased, it was held unlawful for the Home Office to use a discretionary power to revoke licences so as to prevent viewers from receiving the benefit of an overlapping licence bought at the lower rate just before the increased fee became operative.[47] The courts control the legality not only of the taxes which may be demanded but also of administrative steps leading to a tax assessment: thus in *Dyson* v *Attorney-General*[48] the court declared that certain information demanded by the Commissioners of Inland Revenue on threat of a £50 penalty could not lawfully be required. Money which has been paid to a public authority under tax regulations which are ultra vires is recoverable by the taxpayer as of right and with interest.[49] The implications of the Human Rights Act 1998 for taxation (and for other areas of the Treasury's work) have yet to be fully tested, although article 6 of the ECHR (right to a fair trial) and article 1 of the First Protocol (peaceful enjoyment of possessions) are clearly relevant.[50] But the European Court of Human Rights has emphasised 'a Contracting State's margin of appreciation in the tax field'.[51]

Although the assessment of tax is governed by law, some areas of tax administration tend to escape judicial control. Thus the revenue authorities may exercise their

---

[41] See Tiley, *Revenue Law*, pp 68–73.
[42] Customs and Excise Management Act 1979; Value Added Tax Act 1994. Crombie, *Her Majesty's Customs and Excise*. See HC 115 (1995–96) (Scott Report), para C 3.11–3.65, for an account of the work of customs and excise on matters relating to export control.
[43] E.g. Excise Duties (Surcharges or Rebates) Act 1979.
[44] Ch 2 A.
[45] *Bowles* v *Bank of England* [1913] 1 Ch 57; ch 10 C.
[46] *Commissioners of Customs and Excise* v *Cure and Deeley Ltd* [1962] 1 QB 340.
[47] *Congreve* v *Home Office* [1976] QB 629.
[48] [1912] 1 Ch 158.
[49] *Woolwich Building Society* v *IRC (No 2)* [1993] AC 70. See J Beatson (1993) 109 LQR 401; and ch 32 A.
[50] The Human Rights Act 1998 presented a number of difficulties during the passage of the Financial Services and Markets Act 2000. See Financial Services and Markets Bill. Memorandum from HM Treasury to the Joint Committee on Parts V, VI and XII of the Bill in relation to the ECHR, www.treasury.gov.uk/docs/1999/fsmbmemo175.
[51] *National and Provincial Building Society* v *UK* (1997) 25 EHRR 127, at p 169.

discretion not to enforce payment against an individual taxpayer or a class of taxpayers; only in very exceptional circumstances could another taxpayer complain of such a decision to the courts.[52] Although they have been criticised for doing so, the revenue authorities may also issue extra-statutory concessions by which they announce that tax due will be waived in certain circumstances[53] and in other cases may agree a settlement which is not a true estimate of liability, a feature of the investigation of wealthy tax avoiders carried out by the Inland Revenue which was exposed by the prosecution of a senior tax inspector for corruption in 1997.[54] These concessions may come under the scrutiny of the Comptroller and Auditor-General. An individual's complaint about the refusal of a concession in his or her case may be investigated by the Parliamentary Ombudsman on a complaint of maladministration causing injustice to the citizen.[55] The Inland Revenue Commissioners are subject to judicial review. Although it would not normally be proper for the Commissioners to absolve a taxpayer from an undisclosed tax liability of which the Commissioners were unaware, in principle it may be possible successfully to challenge a decision by the Commissioners assessing liability to pay tax if it is unfair to the taxpayer because the later conduct of the Commissioners is similar to a breach of contract or a breach of a representation in view of earlier events.[56] This principle does not enable a taxpayer to avoid payment of tax where a full disclosure of the facts has not been made to the Inland Revenue.[57]

Consolidated Fund and other funds

With certain exceptions, all revenue derived from taxation is paid into the Consolidated Fund.[58] In the case of receipts which arise in the course of a department's business (for example, sales or fees for services provided) these may be appropriated in aid of the department's estimate of the resources which it will need, thereby reducing the provision which would otherwise have to be made by Parliament. Formerly, all money lent by the government came from the Consolidated Fund but in 1968 a separate account with the Bank of England was established, named the National Loans Fund, through which all borrowing by central government and most domestic lending transactions now pass. The operations of the two funds are very closely linked: thus sums needed to meet charges on the National Loans Fund must be paid into it from the Consolidated Fund and a process of daily balancing takes place between the funds.[59]

The annual cycle of financial provision by Parliament proved unsuitable as a means of financing activities of government which were in the nature of trading or business undertakings. In 1973, it was provided that certain services (for example, the Royal Mint and Her Majesty's Stationery Office)[60] could be financed by means of a trading fund established with public money, instead of by means of annual votes and appropriations from Parliament.[61] The enabling powers in the Act were extended in the Government Trading Act 1990 as part of civil service management changes. The 1990

[52] R v IRC, ex p National Federation of Self-Employed [1982] AC 617; and ch 31.
[53] Vestey v IRC [1980] AC 1148; ch 28.
[54] Guardian, 19, 20 February 1997.
[55] Ch 29 D.
[56] R v IRC, ex p Preston [1985] AC 835; and ch 30 C.
[57] R v IRC, ex p Matrix-Securities Ltd [1994] 1 All ER 769.
[58] Consolidated Fund Act 1816 and Exchequer and Audit Departments Act 1866, s 10. Certain payments are made to special funds, e.g. the National Insurance Fund in the case of social security contributions (Social Security Administration Act 1992, s 162).
[59] National Loans Act 1968, s 18.
[60] HMSO was privatised in 1996 and most of its functions were transferred to the Stationery Office Ltd. The Royal Mint became a next steps agency in 1990. And see ch 13 D.
[61] Government Trading Funds Act 1973.

Act 'somewhat elaborated the 1973 regime, but did not change its general principles'.[62] If it appears to a minister that any operations of a department are suitable to be financed by a trading fund and that such a fund would be in the interests of improved efficiency and effectiveness of the management of these operations, he or she may by order, with Treasury concurrence, establish such a fund. The order may designate a person other than the minister to control and manage the fund and it should also designate either the National Loans Fund or the minister as the source of loans to the trading fund, which in the first instance must come from money provided by Parliament.

These initiatives were designed to encourage the civil service to take a more business-like approach to the efficiency and quality of the delivery of government services, by introducing greater financial discipline akin to that under which private sector organisations operate.[63] Trading funds 'remain government departments or parts of government departments and, like other public bodies, are bound by the normal considerations of regularity and propriety'.[64] Most trading funds are likely to be established in agencies created under the 'next steps' programme (which is considered more fully in chapter 13 D) although agencies which are not trading funds can now be required by the Treasury to produce commercial-style accounts to be audited by the Comptroller and Auditor-General and laid before Parliament.[65] Where a fund is established the staff remain members of the civil service.[66] An example of many such funds is the Land Registry Trading Fund, which was established in 1993 under the control and management of the Chief Land Registrar with designated assets, liabilities and public dividend capital. Assets include freehold and leasehold land used or allocated for use in the funded operations as well as plant and equipment and computer hardware and software. The fund is empowered to borrow up to a statutory limit, with the National Loans Fund being designated as the authorised lender.[67]

Consolidated Fund and supply services

The expenditure of central departments may be classified under two heads, namely Consolidated Fund services and supply services. The Consolidated Fund services are payments under statutes which provide continuing authority for the payments in question: the customary statutory phrase is that such payments 'shall be charged on and paid out of the Consolidated Fund'. As this authority continues from year to year, it is not necessary for the payments to be voted each year by the Commons. A principal expenditure under this heading has been the provision which is made via the National Loans Fund for paying the interest on the national debt. There are also charged on the Consolidated Fund other payments which for constitutional reasons are considered inappropriate for annual authorisation by Parliament. These include the Civil List[68] and the salaries of the Speaker, the judiciary, the Comptroller and Auditor-General, the Parliamentary Ombudsman, and the members of the Electoral Commission. This means that there is no regular annual opportunity of discussing in Parliament the work of these officers. This practice tends purposely to preserve their independence, but the justification for it loses some of its force during rapid inflation when the Civil List and public salaries may need to be increased or supplemented annually.

---

[62] Daintith and Page, p 136.
[63] See HC Deb, 8 January 1990, cols 726–9.
[64] HM Treasury, *Government Accounting*, para 7.2.2.
[65] Government Resources and Accounts Act 2000, s 7: this enables the Treasury to direct a government department to prepare for each financial year accounts in relation to any specified matter.
[66] HM Treasury, *Government Accounting*, para 1.3.8.
[67] SI 1993 No 938.
[68] Ch 12 A.

A different example of a charge on the Consolidated Fund was created by the European Communities Act 1972: s 2(3) gives continuing authority for payment from the Consolidated Fund or National Loans Fund of any amounts required to meet Community obligations.[69] While it was argued by the government in 1972 that such continuing authority was an essential feature of British membership of the EEC,[70] it is politically convenient for the government to have continuing authority to pay over the sums concerned, without seeking fresh approval from Parliament each year. By contrast, supply services involve charges for purposes stated by the statutes which authorise them to be payable 'out of money to be provided by Parliament'. Following the introduction of new accounting arrangements by the Government Resources and Accounts Act 2000, the form in which the appropriation is presented in the Appropriation Acts has changed: the Appropriation Acts (which indicate the purposes for which supply may be spent by each department) now indicate the resources as well as the cash which is to be made available for these purposes. The great bulk of departmental expenditure is voted annually on this basis, through the procedure of supply already described.[71]

Questions arise, however, about how far the annual Appropriation Act can be regarded as sufficient authority for the exercise of functions by a government department in cases where no other statutory authority exists. In a Treasury-Public Accounts Committee Concordat of 1932, it was accepted that there should be both statutory authority for the expenditure and a vote of supply to meet it. Although 'it is usually legal for departments to commit resources or incur expenditure on the sole authority of the Appropriation Act, it may not be proper for them to do so'.[72] For expenditure to be properly incurred, 'there should therefore normally be specific statutory authority for the activity or service as well as authority through estimates for the related expenditure'.[73] By the same token, although it is possible for the Appropriation Act to 'override express provisions of other statutes which may impose limits on the amounts of the same grants' (in effect override powers specifically set by statute),[74] the PAC has taken the view that 'constitutional propriety requires that such extensions should be regularised at the earliest possible date by amending legislation, unless they are of a purely emergency or non-continuing character'.[75]

Government accounting practices

The Government Resources and Accounts Act 2000 introduced important changes to the way in which government accounts are managed and presented.[76] The Act is said to go 'to the heart of Parliament's role in holding government to account' and to mark 'a milestone on the way to full implementation of the biggest reform and modernisation of the country's public finances since the time of Gladstone'.[77] As such it was the first major piece of legislation since 1921 to deal with government accounting and the main purpose of the Act attracted all-party support. Indeed the preparatory work for what was to become the 2000 Act had been undertaken in the Treasury when the

---

[69] See *Monckton* v *Lord Advocate* 1995 SLT 1201.
[70] HC Deb, 22 February 1972, col 1137, and 8 June 1972, col 813. Cf *R* v *HM Treasury, ex p Smedley* [1985] QB 657.
[71] Ch 10 C.
[72] *Government Accounting*, para 2.2.2.
[73] Ibid, para 2.2.4.
[74] Ibid, para 2.2.8.
[75] Ibid, annex 2.1. And see p 204 above.
[76] See F White and K Hollingsworth [2001] PL 50; also White and Hollingsworth, *Audit, Accountability and Government*, esp ch 2, and Daintith and Page, pp 164–8.
[77] HL Deb, 10 April 2000, col 11.

Conservatives were in government. This is not to say that the 2000 Act was wholly uncontroversial, with a number of criticisms being made by the House of Commons Public Accounts Committee in particular,[78] as well as by a number of prominent parliamentarians experienced in the field of government accounting.[79] But these criticisms were of a practical nature: concerned more with a failure fully to consult with the Public Accounts Committee in good time about the legislation and about the difficulties encountered in the move to a new accounting system than by the principles embraced by the Act.

The main purpose of the Act is to replace the existing cash-based system of accounting and budgeting with what accountants refer to as resource accounting and resource-based supply. This is secured by s 5(1) which requires government departments for which an estimate is approved by the House of Commons to prepare accounts detailing (a) resources acquired, held or disposed of by the department during the year; and (b) the use by the department of resources during the year. The accounts are to be prepared in accordance with directions issued by the Treasury (s 5(2)), although these should seek to ensure that the resource accounts conform to 'generally accepted accounting practice' (s 5(3)). Resource accounting is explained by the Public Accounts Committee as a 'commercial-style accrual accounting for central Government departments'.[80] It was also explained that accounts 'will include for the first time a balance sheet to show a department's assets and liabilities'; that departments will 'provide an analysis of expenditure by aims and objectives'; and that 'Parliament will authorise the resources, rather than the cash, that departments can use'.[81] The Public Accounts Committee endorsed the introduction of resource accounting on the ground that 'it should lead to greater clarity and improved financial information to Parliament'.[82] The new resource-based financial management system was fully implemented in April 2001.[83]

The other major accounting initiative introduced by the Government Resources and Accounts Act 2000 deals with 'whole of government accounts', said by one leading Opposition member in the Lords to be 'accounts which are broadly in line with the private sector, both with regard to the profit and loss account and with regard to balance sheets'.[84] This is dealt with in s 9 of the Act which requires the Treasury to prepare annual accounts to cover bodies which exercise functions of a public nature or which are entirely or substantially funded from public money. Bodies which are designated by order of the Treasury to fall within the scope of the Act must provide financial information to the Treasury as requested, in the form directed by the Treasury (s 10). This initiative is said by ministers to have three overlapping aims. First, it is designed to improve the information available to support the conduct and monitoring of fiscal policy; second, to improve the accountability of the government to Parliament; and third, to provide greater transparency to taxpayers.[85] It is realised, however, that 'full audited whole of government accounts' will need 'greater conformity of accounting

---

[78] HC 127 (1999–2000) (4th Report), and HC 159 (1999–2000) (9th Report).

[79] As is so often the case, the most effective contributions were made in the House of Lords: see HL Deb, 10 April 2000, col 16 et seq.

[80] HC 159 (1999–2000) (9th Report), para 7. The difference between cash and accrual accounting was explained by the Treasury in 1995: 'Cash accounts record payments and income as they are actually made and received, regardless of when the obligation to pay arises and of the period over which it may extend, whereas accruals accounts record current expenditure and income in the year to which that obligation relates, even if the cash was not paid or received in that year, also recording the difference between the accruals measure and the actual cash paid or received, usually as a creditor or debtor' (Cm 2929 (1995), p 5).

[81] 9th Report, ibid.

[82] Ibid, para 11.

[83] HM Treasury, *Managing Resources: Full Implementation of Resource Accounting and Budgeting* (2001), p 2.

[84] HL Deb, 10 April 2000, col 19 (Lord Higgins).

[85] HL Deb, 10 April 2000, cols 13–14 (Lord McIntosh).

policies, systems and procedures' and that as a result it will be necessary to develop this initiative on a staged basis.[86]

D. Public expenditure control and accountability

The raising of income and accounting for its use are only one part of the Treasury's responsibilities for public finance. Also of critical importance is the role of the Treasury in controlling public expenditure: the prior authority of the Treasury is required for such expenditure. The context within which public expenditure is now incurred is determined by the government's fiscal rules and its Code of Fiscal Stability which was introduced in 1998. So far as the former are concerned, the first is the so-called Golden Rule by which the government will borrow only to invest but not to fund current spending; and the second is the Sustainable Investment Rule by which borrowing to fund investment will be set at a stable and prudent level (related to GDP). As far as the Code of Fiscal Stability is concerned, this is based on the 'key principles of transparency, stability, responsibility, fairness and efficiency' in fiscal policy and national debt management policy.[87] Within this context new procedures have been introduced for dealing with public expenditure, with the role of the Treasury – in setting targets and in ensuring that they are met – ever more prominent. In this section we consider these procedures for the control of public expenditure and the arrangements in place for departmental accountability and the audit of government expenditure.

Public expenditure limits

In 1961 the Plowden report recommended that regular surveys should be made of public expenditure as a whole, over a period of years ahead and in relation to prospective resources; and that decisions involving substantial future expenditure should be taken in the light of those surveys.[88] This influential report led to the creation of a new system of public expenditure control,[89] but changes in that system became necessary in the 1970s as economic growth declined and the control of expenditure broke down during the period of rapid inflation in 1973–5. Further changes were made in the 1980s to accommodate the new policy of government to reduce public expenditure in real terms.[90] Under current arrangements (which have no statutory authority) there has evolved a practice of regular review of government spending, known previously as the Public Expenditure Survey and now referred to as the spending review (see below). The effect of this process is to plan government spending as far as possible on the basis of three-year cycles.

The most significant change made during the 1970s was probably the introduction of cash limits in 1976.[91] Before then, public expenditure was essentially planned in

---

[86] It is intended initially to concentrate on central government, executive agencies and non-departmental public bodies, before making any decisions about extending the coverage to the rest of the public sector: ibid, col 14.

[87] Finance Act 1998, s 155. Also Daintith and Page, p 166.

[88] Cmnd 1432, 1961.

[89] For early accounts of PESC, see Cmnd 4071, 1969, and HC 549 (1970–71); Clarke, *New Trends in Government*, ch 2; and Heclo and Wildavsky, ch 5.

[90] See generally, Harrison, *The Control of Public Expenditure 1979–89*. See *Autumn Statement 1992* (Cm 2096, 1992), paras 2.01–02. It was also announced that new ways would be found to mobilise 'the private sector to meet needs which have traditionally been met only by the public sector'. See also HC 508 (1992–93).

[91] Cmnd 6440, 1976; HC 274 (1977–78); M Elliott (1977) 49 MLR 569; and Likierman, *Cash Limits and External Financing Limits*.

'volume terms'; that is, it was based on the volume of approved programmes (for example, so many new miles of motorway). As wages and prices of material increased with inflation, the programmes were not themselves affected and the cash requirement was automatically increased. In 1976, cash limits were applied by the Labour government to counter this automatic increase in cash provision. The method was extended by the Conservative government after 1979 as a primary means of restraining public expenditure and of managing the economy. Thus, cash limits have been used to limit pay increases within the public sector and to control the numbers of those so employed.[92] Cash limits are applied to as many spending programmes as possible, including the revenue support grant paid to local authorities, but they do not apply to programmes which are 'demand determined', such as social security payments, which must be paid to every person who becomes entitled to them (although from 1988 cash limits were imposed on payments from the Social Fund).[93] Since 1979, cash limits have been related directly to the supply estimates and as such are approved by Parliament.

In 1992, new arrangements were introduced for the distribution of public expenditure. Concern had been expressed about earlier procedures and the dominant role played by bilateral discussions between the Chief Secretary and individual ministers, it being argued that this arrangement left insufficient room for consideration of priorities in the government's overall spending plans.[94] Limits were set on each department rather than particular programmes being considered on their merits. The drawbacks of this arrangement led to reforms and in particular to 'a more explicitly top-down approach'[95] to the distribution of public expenditure, with the government agreeing to what was referred to as the new control total (NCT) for each of the three planning years. Under these arrangements expenditure was measured against a new spending aggregate (the NCT), which was to be constrained to a rate that ensured that total public spending grew by less than the economy as a whole over the economic cycle.[96] A new Cabinet committee prepared options for particular programmes for the Cabinet to consider. This was followed by the bilateral discussions between the Chief Secretary and the individual ministers in which the Chief Secretary's role was similar to that in the past, except that there was now no need for him or her to reach an agreement with the ministers in question. Rather, he or she reported back to the Cabinet committee which was able to make an informed decision on the basis of the Chief Secretary's discussions.

The spending review and public service agreements

Yet further changes for the planning and control of public expenditure were introduced with effect from 1999–2000, following a comprehensive spending review which examined the most effective use of public money across and within each department. Under the new arrangements, the former annual Public Expenditure Survey has been replaced by biennial reviews which set firm plans for three years ahead in spending reviews. In the course of a spending review,[97] each department is set a resource and capital budget and they must meet objectives set out in public service agreements concluded between each department and the Treasury.[98] The process is supervised

---

[92] See P K Else and G P Marshall (1981) 59 Public Administration 253, and G Bevan, K Sisson and P Way (1981) 59 Public Administration 379.
[93] See Social Security Contributions and Benefits Act 1992, s 168, and e.g. *R v Social Fund Inspector, ex p Stitt* [1990] COD 288.
[94] HC 20 (1989–90).
[95] HC 201 (1992–93), para 174.
[96] *Autumn Statement 1992* (Cm 2096, 1992), para 2.02.
[97] On which see HM Treasury, *Spending Review 2000*, www.hm-treasury.gov.uk/sr/2000.
[98] On which see Cm 4315, 1999.

by a Cabinet committee chaired by the Chancellor of the Exchequer (the Public Services and Public Expenditure Committee, replacing similar committees of previous administrations). It has been emphasised that it is now the Treasury which is the key source of decision-making about the allocation of resources rather than the committee, which principally has an oversight function.[99] But not all expenditure can be subject to firm limits extending over three years. These cases are referred to as annually managed expenditure and fall outside departmental expenditure limits for which the three-year plans are made. This category is subject to annual review in the Budget process.

Public service agreements between the Treasury and individual departments are said to be 'essentially a contract with the Treasury for the renewal of public services' and a contract that in each service area 'requires reform in return for investment'.[100] The use of the language of contract in this context has been said to be a 'remarkable tribute to the current dominance of market-based thought and discourse in public administration'.[101] Nevertheless, in announcing these arrangements, the Chancellor of the Exchequer said that the contract sets down the new departmental objectives and targets that have to be met over a three-year period, the stages by which they will be met, how departments intend to allocate resources to achieve these targets and the process that will monitor results. Departmental performance is scrutinised by the Public Services and Public Expenditure Committee and money is released only if departments keep to their plans: 'Money, but only in return for modernisation.'[102] These measures are designed in part to allow for the targeting of public money on priority areas (such as education and health) within the context of the new framework of financial discipline. It remains the case, nevertheless, that the new procedures have drawn strong criticism from the House of Commons Treasury Committee, concerned about the commanding influence of the Treasury in the affairs of other departments.

The tentacles of the Treasury have been said to exert 'an unprecedented sway within departments'.[103] The Treasury Committee was particularly critical about the fact that the Treasury both 'set the framework within which departments should operate, using the Spending Review and PSA process' and also acted as 'the sole assessor of whether or not departments are achieving their objectives'.[104] Concerns about this lack of independence in monitoring departmental targets could be addressed in the committee's view by a body accountable to Parliament, such as the National Audit Office or the Audit Commission. In this way there would be some role – albeit weak and indirect – for Parliament in the process of review. Concern about the powerful role in government of the Treasury in particular led to parallel proposals for the Public Services and Public Expenditure Committee of the Cabinet to be reconstituted, 'so that its dominance by Treasury ministers is reduced'. This could be done by a sub-committee for performance monitoring being chaired by a non-Treasury minister in order to 'demonstrate that PSAs are not simply tools of the Treasury and that the priorities enshrined in them serve the Government as a whole, rather than just the Exchequer'.[105] Yet despite these concerns about PSAs as a symptom of growing Treasury power, it has been claimed by one study that these agreements do not 'reflect a fundamental shift in the nature of relationships within the executive', so much as 'express an enlargement of the

[99]   Daintith and Page, p 150.
[100] HC Deb, 14 July 1998, col 188 (statement by the Chancellor of the Exchequer on the Comprehensive Spending Review).
[101] Daintith and Page, p 192.
[102] HC Deb, 14 July 1998, col 187.
[103] Hennessy, p 513.
[104] HC 73 (2001), para 32.
[105] Ibid, para 38.

ambitions of central control, and an executive-led attempt to enhance accountability by specification of expected performance'.[106]

Departmental accountability for public expenditure

For each department the Treasury appoints an Accounting Officer (AO) who, by long-standing practice approved by the Public Accounts Committee, is the permanent secretary of the department, although in the case of the executive agencies the chief executive may be designated the AO. According to a Treasury memorandum of 2001, the AO has the personal duty of signing the accounts described in his or her letter of appointment and of being a witness to the Public Accounts Committee to deal with questions arising from the accounts or from reports made to Parliament by the Comptroller and Auditor-General under the National Audit Act 1983. Officials are expected to combine their role as AO with their 'duty to serve the minister in charge of their department, to whom they are responsible and from whom they derive authority' (para 2). Under the terms of the memorandum, the AO must 'ensure that there is a high standard of financial management in the department as a whole; that financial systems and procedures promote the efficient and economical conduct of business and safeguard financial propriety and regularity throughout the department; and that financial considerations are fully taken into account in decisions on policy proposals' (para 5). The AO has particular responsibility for ensuring compliance with parliamentary requirements in the control of expenditure and in particular to ensure that funds for which he or she is responsible are used 'only to the extent and for the purposes authorised by Parliament' (para 12). He or she must also ensure that appropriate advice is tendered to ministers on all matters of financial propriety and regularity, and more broadly as to all considerations of 'prudent and economical administration, efficiency and effectiveness' (para 14).[107]

But what happens if the minister is 'contemplating a course of action involving a transaction which an AO considers would infringe the requirements of propriety or regularity' (para 15)? In these cases the Treasury memorandum provides that the AO should set out in writing his or her objection to the proposals, the reasons for the objection and his or her duty to notify the Comptroller and Auditor-General (C&AG) should the AO's advice be overruled. If the minister proceeds, the AO should seek written instructions to make the payment and must then comply, but should also inform the Treasury of what has happened and pass the papers to the C&AG 'without delay', in which case the AO will bear no 'personal responsibility' for what happens (para 15). If this procedure is adopted, the Public Accounts Committee can be expected to recognise that the AO 'bears no responsibility for the transaction' (para 15). Following an important case in 1991 (when the Foreign Secretary overruled the AO in the Overseas Development Administration about expenditure of £234 million on the Pergau Dam project in Malaysia) the AO must now send the C&AG 'without undue delay' the papers relating to all cases where the AO has been overruled on matters relating to economy, efficiency and effectiveness, as well as impropriety or irregularity.[108] It has been said that the 'incidence of ministers overruling their accounting officers on matters of value for money appears to be on the increase, but remains rare'.[109] These arrangements have implications for appearances before the Public Accounts Committee where 'in general,

[106] Daintith and Page, p 192.
[107] See HM Treasury, *The Responsibilities of an Accounting Officer* (2001). See also, *Ministerial Code*, paras 59–61.
[108] See HC 271 (1993–94), Cm 2602, 1993–94. See also F White, I Harden and K Donnelly [1994] PL 526. See further *R v Foreign Secretary, ex p World Development Movement* [1995] 1 All ER 611.
[109] White, Harden and Donnelly, where 15 such instances since 1979 are noted.

the rules and conventions governing appearances of officials before parliamentary committees apply' (para 29).

In the case of NDPBs, the chief executive is normally designated as the accounting officer.[110] In this case the departmental AO has responsibilities to ensure that proper financial and management systems are in place and that the standards adopted by the NDPB 'conform with the requirements both of propriety and of good financial management' (para 6). The NDPB AO also has a number of responsibilities relating to financial management within the framework set by the sponsoring department (paras 8–11). There is again a particular responsibility to ensure that any requirements are met for the control of expenditure imposed by Parliament or the sponsor department (para 12) and an obligation to seek approval for any expenditure which falls outside the scope of delegated authority. Delegation 'does not remove the obligation to submit to its sponsor department proposals which are novel or contentious' (para 13). Provisions similar to those operating for departmental AOs apply in the case of NDPB AOs where the board of an NDPB is proposing a course of action which would infringe the requirements of propriety or regularity: apart from giving due advice to the board and the duty to notify the C&AG should the advice be ignored, the NDPB AO should also notify the sponsoring department which may intervene (para 15). The NDPB AO may be called before the Public Accounts Committee, normally with the AO of the sponsoring department, to give evidence relating to any audit or inspection by the C&AG (paras 19–23). Controversially, however, the C&AG does not have authority in relation to all executive agencies, but only those established since 1997.[111]

Comptroller and Auditor-General[112]

An essential aspect of parliamentary control of expenditure is that the House of Commons should be able to ensure that public money is used for the purposes for which it has been voted. The Comptroller and Auditor-General is head of the National Audit Office, known before 1984 as the Exchequer and Audit Department.[113] Like senior judges, he holds office during good behaviour, subject to a power of removal by the Crown on an address from both Houses of Parliament. His duties are twofold. First, as Comptroller, he ensures that all revenue is duly paid into the Consolidated Fund and the National Loans Fund, and his authority to the Bank of England is required before the Treasury may withdraw money from the Funds; in this capacity, he must see that the total limits of expenditure authorised by Parliament are not exceeded. Second, as Auditor-General, he is responsible for examining the resource accounts of departments annually, to ensure that money had been spent only for the purpose intended by Parliament.[114] In practice, from the 19th century the audit also sought to discover instances of waste and extravagance. Express authority for 'value for money' and 'efficiency' auditing was given by the National Audit Act 1983.[115] The Comptroller and Auditor-General may under that Act carry out examinations into the economy, efficiency and effectiveness with which a department has used its resources in discharging its functions; but he may

[110] HM Treasury, *The Responsibilities of a NDPB Accounting Officer* (2001).
[111] This is a matter which drew strong criticism from the House of Commons Treasury Committee: HC 159 (1999–2000) (9th Report). See also, F White and K Hollingsworth [2001] PL 50.
[112] Normanton, *The Accountability and Audit of Governments*; Henley (and others), *Public Sector Accounting and Financial Control*, chs 2, 7; White and Hollingsworth, esp chs 3–6.
[113] Exchequer and Audit Departments Act 1866.
[114] Exchequer and Audit Departments Act 1921, s 1, now Government Resources and Accounts Act 2000, s 6.
[115] For the background, see Cmnd 7845, 1980; HC 115 (1980–81), discussed by G Drewry [1981] PL 304; and Cmnd 8323, 1981. See White and Hollingsworth, ch 3.

not question the merits of the policy objectives set for a department. His powers extend not only to central departments but also to the National Health Service, and to other bodies or institutions (such as the universities) which are wholly or mainly supported from public funds and to whose records and accounts he has access for inspection purposes.[116] Since 1994, the Comptroller and Auditor-General may examine records relating to expenditure by the Security Service under the intelligence vote. The Public Accounts Commission examines the annual accounts of the National Audit Office.[117]

The Comptroller and Auditor-General reports on his investigations to the Public Accounts Committee of the Commons, said to be the 'doyen' of select committees,[118] with no other select committee having the 'same authority, clarity of remit and breadth and depth of advice available to it'.[119] This committee has 15 members and its chairman by tradition is always a senior Opposition MP.[120] The practice of the committee is to follow up selected audit reports by calling the departmental accounting officer before it to explain publicly the actions of the department. In exceptional circumstances, as described earlier, the minister may have to account to the committee for a particular item of expenditure. The committee's work depends essentially on the investigations made by the staff of the Comptroller and Auditor-General. This may reveal misuse of funds that was unknown to the department concerned, as in 1963 when serious over-charging by contractors in the Bloodhound missile contracts was discovered.[121]

In Session 2000–01, matters examined by the Committee included the Millennium Dome; Inland Revenue Appropriation Accounts; the National Audit Office Resource Estimate; the Channel Tunnel Rail Link; the Private Finance Initiative; Inland Flood Defence; Educating and Training Health Professionals; the National Blood Service; the Strategic Rail Authority; Maintaining the Royal Palaces; Emergency Aid and Kosovo; and Draft Social Security (Inherited SERPS) Regulations 2001.

The reports made to the Commons by the Public Accounts Committee are debated annually by the House.[122] The government is expected to reply to criticisms and to act on them. The published rulings made by the committee and the related Treasury Minutes are an authoritative guide to the main rules of financial accountability.

Important changes in the status of the Comptroller and Auditor-General were made by the National Audit Act 1983. Appointments to the office are no longer made by the Crown on the advice of the Prime Minister, but by the Crown on a resolution of the House of Commons, moved by the Prime Minister with the approval of the chairman of the Public Accounts Committee (s 1(1)). The Comptroller and Auditor-General is declared to be an officer of the House of Commons (s 1(2)), a statutory change which confirmed the assumption made since 1866 that he exercises his powers on behalf of the House. While he has complete discretion in exercising his functions, he must take into account proposals regarding his investigations that may be made by the Public Accounts Committee (s 1(3)). The staff of the Comptroller are no longer civil servants:

[116] National Audit Act 1983, ss 6–8.
[117] National Audit Act 1983, s 2. The Commission consists of the chairman of the Commons Public Accounts Committee, the Leader of the House and seven other MPs appointed by the House, none of whom is a minister.
[118] J F McEldowney, in Jowell and Oliver (eds), *The Changing Constitution* (3rd edn), ch 7. The same author's contribution to the 4th edition of *The Changing Constitution* (Ch 8) contains a valuable account of the issues discussed in this chapter.
[119] A Robinson, in Drewry (ed), *The New Select Committees*.
[120] Erskine May, *Parliamentary Practice*, p 677. On the Public Accounts Committee, see also Griffith and Ryle, *Parliament*, pp 441–4; and White and Hollingsworth, pp 122–5.
[121] HC 183 (1963–64) and HC Deb, 19 April 1964, col 408.
[122] See Erskine May, pp 684–5.

they are appointed by and are answerable to him.[123] The aim behind these reforms was to strengthen still further the authority and independence of the audit system and to improve the ability of the Commons to ensure the proper use of public funds. But no system of public audit can guarantee that controversial political decisions involving heavy expenditure will not be made (for example, the costly development of the Concorde aircraft)[124] and economies for their own sake are not always popular, either with politicians or civil servants.[125]

E. Management of the economy

Power to control public expenditure and the imposition of taxes are only two of the means by which governments seek to manage the economy. In a vast area of governmental power, which public lawyers now explore,[126] other means include monetary policy and control of borrowing, financial assistance to business and industry and 'partnership' with the private sector in the provision and delivery of public services through measures such as the Private Finance Initiative.[127] These different techniques of economic management have been accompanied by the emergence of new structures and methods of government.

Tripartism and the Social Contract[128]

So far as the former is concerned, perhaps the most significant development in the post-war period was the emergence of systematic consultation between government and the leaders of the trade union and business communities. Important symbols of this phenomenon (which is common practice in other European countries and which was not confined to Labour governments) were the wage restraint bargain of 1948, the creation of the National Economic Development Council in 1962 and the 'social contract' of 1974–6. The first two initiatives were tripartite and in terms of institutional innovation the creation of the NEDC is perhaps the most significant. Designed to be a national planning body which 'established a permanent niche for itself in the machinery of economic policy making', it did not, however, have any executive power and hardly evolved beyond being 'a useful framework for the exchange of different views'.[129] It was chaired by the Chancellor of the Exchequer and included senior trade and industry ministers as well as senior representatives of the trade union and business communities.[130] Yet despite its symbolic and practical importance, the NEDC was not the creature of statute, but a product of the relative informality of much of the British administrative state, which could easily be sidelined and eventually abolished (in 1992) when it no longer suited government strategy in terms of the content or method of economic policy-making.[131]

---

[123] See I Harden (1993) 13 LS 16, at p 23.

[124] See HC 335 (1972–73) and generally, Turpin, *Government Procurement and Contracts*.

[125] Cf Chapman, *Your Disobedient Servant*. For the cautionary tale of the Crown Agents, see G Ganz [1980] PL 454.

[126] E.g. V Korah (1976) 92 LQR 42; T C Daintith (1976) 92 LQR 62, (1979) 32 CLP 41, (1982) 9 Jl of Law and Society 191 and in Jowell and Oliver, *The Changing Constitution* (3rd edn), ch 8; and A C Page (1982) 9 Jl of Law and Society 225.

[127] On which see J F McEldowney, in Jowell and Oliver (4th edn), pp 214–15.

[128] See K D Ewing [2000] PL 405.

[129] Grant and Marsh, *The Confederation of British Industry*, p 141.

[130] See National Economic Development Council, Annual Report 1978–79, for an account of membership and terms of reference, as well as the activities of the NEDC.

[131] See Davies and Freedland, *Labour Legislation and Public Policy*, p 439.

The special powers which economic difficulties during the 1970s forced governments to take to deal with inflation were usually limited in duration; they enabled governments to intervene more extensively in private economic transactions than had previously been possible in peacetime. This legislation (long since repealed) had a number of novel aspects. Thus the Price Commission, a regulatory body set up under the Counter-inflation Act 1973, could issue orders or notices to employers and businesses. Breach of these could create criminal liability, yet the orders or notices themselves might define expressions used in the Act under which they were issued.[132] The Remuneration, Charges and Grants Act 1975 was notable for the manner in which the 'social contract' approved by the trade unions as a basis for voluntary wage restraint was given a measure of statutory effect and provision made for a new policy document to take its place.[133] One consequence of the need to continue an incomes policy after the 1975 'social contract' expired came in the Chancellor of the Exchequer's 1976 Budget: certain increases in personal tax allowances were made conditional on the agreement of the trade unions being obtained to an incomes policy. This agreement was duly obtained and the allowances were included in the Finance Act 1976, but some considered that this development diminished the authority of both government and Parliament.[134]

Between 1979 and 1997, Conservative governments adopted a wholly different approach to economic management, emphasising the importance of a market economy and the need to remove perceived barriers to the free functioning of the market. Financial and economic policy was directed mainly at the control of inflation, the restraining of public expenditure and the lifting of bureaucratic controls on pay, prices, dividends, credit and foreign exchange. Industrial policy was directed mainly at the encouragement of small firms, the break-up of monopolies, the fostering of competition and the releasing of business from public sector constraints. In the labour market, policy was directed at encouraging flexibility, a goal reflected in the spate of legislation since 1980 designed to limit the power of trade unions and reduce the scope of employment protection legislation.[135] One consequence of viewing trade unions as an obstacle to the free functioning of the market was to deny them any role in economic policy-making.[136] While in the 1970s trade unions reached the zenith of their power in a quasi-corporatist state, by 1997 they had little if any political influence on a government which repudiated the very idea that they had a role to play in the formulation of economic policy.

Trade unions which had been drawn into the process of economic management were now pushed to the margins of government, there being no doubt that until 1979 trade unions had an important constitutional role. It is true that, as already indicated, this did not crystallise in any formal legal sense, but this did not make it any less real, for as Beer has pointed out in relation to the wage restraint bargain of 1948 (which was not embodied in any legislative instrument), it 'achieved a regulation of an important aspect of the British economy that no such legislative instrument by itself could have done. Indeed, one may think of it as a kind of extra-governmental legislation'.[137] With the abolition of the NEDC and the retreat of dialogue between government and the social partners, it is seriously open to question how much of the 'constitutional

---

[132] Counter-inflation Act 1973, Sch 3, para 1(1), discussed by Korah, p 44.

[133] Remuneration, Charges and Grants Act 1975, s 1.

[134] E.g. *The Times*, 7 April 1976 (editorial). See also the Labour government's efforts to enforce non-statutory guidelines on pay by means that included the boycotting of companies which breached the guidelines. See R B Ferguson and A C Page (1978) 128 NLJ 515; G Ganz [1978] PL 333; HC Deb, 13 December 1978, col 673, and 14 December 1978, col 920.

[135] See Cmnd 9474, 1985.

[136] See K D Ewing, in Graham and Prosser (eds), *Waiving the Rules: The Constitution under Thatcherism*, ch 8.

[137] Beer, *Modern British Politics*, p 205.

architecture of the Keynesian State', built with 'no formal constitutional changes', remains intact, as has been suggested.[138] It could, however, be rebuilt just as quickly as it has been demolished. Although regulatory informality has not been removed altogether with the reshuffling of the pack of constitutional players, there is a sense in which it is in retreat having been displaced to some extent by a greater emphasis on regulatory instruments, including contracts and licences.[139]

Regional development agencies

Since the general election in 1997, a number of steps have been taken to extend the scope of the decision-making process. In chapter 14 E, reference was made to the growth in the number of task forces with members recruited from outside government, often from the business community. It is true that there has been no return to the corporatist strategies of earlier times (partly because the direction of economic policy no longer requires it). Yet there are examples in action of what the government refers to as 'partnership' with trade unions and business leaders. An outstanding example of this is the Low Pay Commission, a body which includes representatives of trade unions and employers with the task of advising the government on the level at which the national minimum wage should be set.[140] Also significant is the creation of TUC/CBI working groups on productivity established at the initiative of the Chancellor of the Exchequer.[141] But these developments are eclipsed by the establishment of regional development agencies to 'provide for effective and properly coordinated regional economic development' and to 'enable the English regions to improve their competitiveness'.[142] The Regional Development Agencies Act 1998 divides England into nine regions, with a development agency appointed for each (s 1). Some see the agencies not only as instruments of economic regeneration, but also a scheme for English devolution in embryo.

The regional development agencies, established as non-departmental public bodies,[143] have from 8 to 15 members, all appointed by the Secretary of State.[144] Members should have some experience which is relative to the functions of the agency; and the minister must consult representatives of local authorities, businesses, trade unions and the rural economy, as well as others, before making an appointment (s 2). The functions of an agency are set out in s 4 of the 1998 Act: to further the economic development and the regeneration of its area; to promote business efficiency and competitiveness; to promote employment; to enhance the development and application of skills relevant to employment in its area; and to contribute to the achievement of sustainable development in the United Kingdom. To perform these functions, powers set out in s 5 enable the agencies to provide financial assistance, dispose of land at below market value and form or acquire an interest in a body corporate, although in all cases the consent of the minister is required. Ministers may delegate additional functions to the agencies (although not functions of a legislative character or functions which involve the fixing of fees or charges) (s 6), and may direct the agency to designate 'a body which is representative of those in a regional development agency's area with an interest in its work' to be the regional chamber for the agency (s 8). But it is important to stress that the

---

[138] I Harden [1994] PL 609, at p 616.
[139] See N Deakin and K Walsh (1996) 74 Public Administration 33.
[140] National Minimum Wage Act 1998, s 8.
[141] www.treasury.gov.uk/press/2001/p 116.
[142] HC Deb, 14 January 1998, col 372. Also Cm 3814, 1997.
[143] See ch 14.
[144] The government anticipated that there would be 12 members in each board, which would be 'business-led', but which would also include people with experience in education, the trade unions, rural interests and the voluntary sector (HC Deb, 14 January 1998, col 378).

Act does not provide for the creation of regional assemblies, which can be designated only where they emerge on a voluntary basis.[145]

The regional development agencies are thus subject to a great deal of ministerial control; in terms of their membership and in the exercise of their functions. This is maintained in the arrangements for their financing, with the Act providing that the minister is to 'determine the financial duties of the agency', albeit after consultation with the agency and the approval of the Treasury (s 9). Moreover, it is for the minister with the approval of the Treasury, to make 'to a regional development agency grants of such amount, and on such terms, as he thinks fit' (s 10). The power of the agencies also depends on the consent of the minister who in turn must have the approval of the Treasury (s 11). Ministerial control can also be detected in s 16 which imposes a duty on an agency to provide the minister with 'such information, advice and assistance as he may require', and in s 17, which requires the agencies to report to the minister on an annual basis; the reports must be laid before Parliament and are published. Where there is a regional chamber (as provided for by s 8), the minister may direct an agency to supply the chamber with specified information, to answer questions put by the chamber and to take other steps 'for the purpose of accounting to the chamber for the exercise of its functions as may be so specified' (s 18).[146] Other ministerial powers include an authority to alter regional boundaries (s 25), and to issue guidance or directions to an agency (s 27).

It is perhaps paradoxical that regional development agencies should be the subject of so much central control. It is true that they are designed principally as instruments of economic policy rather than a devolution of political power. This was made clear by ministers,[147] who also drew attention to the poor economic performance of many regions and the need for regional measures to integrate the government's policies for 'jobs, growth and social cohesion'.[148] Nevertheless the lack of democratic accountability to the communities they serve was seen by many as a key weakness of the agencies. The current arrangements were criticised as being 'constitutionally objectionable', not only because of the 'enormous increase in ministerial power bestowed by [the Act]',[149] but also because none of the board members would be directly elected.[150] The agencies have been described as 'the most powerful quangos ever seen in this country'.[151] It is little consolation to those concerned by the democratic deficit that 'partnership' is to be one of the government's guiding principles of the agencies. This includes partnerships with local authorities, training and enterprise councils, industry and voluntary groups; but although admirable only one category of these potential partners is directly elected.[152] Neither were critics consoled by the representative nature of the (voluntary) regional chambers.[153]

---

[145] Regional chambers have been described as 'a voluntary grouping of interested parties in each region': they are not statutory bodies; and they are not elected: M Grant, *Current Law Statutes 1998*, 45-14. They may in due course form the basis for directly elected bodies. The essential minimum requirements of a voluntary regional chamber under s 8 are set out in the white paper, Cm 3814, 1997. A prominent theme is that the chambers should be representative of local political opinion, but that about 30% of places should be reserved for other interests. Attention should also be paid to the gender, ethnic and disability composition of the membership.

[146] Agencies must hold a public meeting following the publication of their annual reports, subject to the guidance and directions as to the conduct of the meeting which may be issued by the minister (s 18).

[147] 'The main purpose of the RDAs is to address the economic deficit that has bedevilled the English regions for many years' (HC Deb, 14 January 1998, col 377).

[148] Ibid, col 374.

[149] Ibid, col 381.

[150] Ibid, col 385.

[151] Ibid.

[152] Ibid, col 376.

[153] On which see note 145 above.

Chapter 18

THE COURTS AND THE MACHINERY OF JUSTICE

In chapter 5 the broad relationship between the judiciary, the legislature and the executive was examined. If a strict separation of powers is not a necessary precondition of constitutional government, the same cannot be said about an independent judiciary, an issue which also raises questions fundamental to the discussion of the rule of law in chapter 6. If government is to be conducted in accordance with the law, the law must be administered by as independent a judiciary as possible, otherwise there is a danger that the law will serve the ends of government rather than the interests of justice: the two may not always be synonymous. In this chapter we address the major constitutional aspects of the judiciary and the machinery of justice, but in doing so we are concerned principally with three broad themes. After the barest outline of the structure of the courts, we examine (i) the manner of appointment of the judges and the measures designed to protect their independence, as well as measures which might be seen to compromise that independence; (ii) the steps taken to ensure that litigants have a right to a fair trial and how that right is balanced with the right to freedom of expression mainly through the law of contempt of court; and (iii) the role of the executive in the administration of justice, concentrating on the role of the Lord Chancellor and the procedures for the prosecution of offenders and miscarriages of justice.

A. The courts

There are in the United Kingdom three distinct court systems: in England and Wales, in Scotland, and in Northern Ireland.[1] The judiciaries in the three systems are separate from each other, except that judges and senior practitioners in each system are eligible for appointment to the House of Lords as Lords of Appeal in Ordinary. They are also eligible for appointment to the Court of Justice and to the Court of First Instance of the European Communities and to the European Court of Human Rights.[2] But it is to be noted that the judicial system is not confined to the courts of general civil and criminal jurisdiction.[3] The numerous administrative tribunals, in whose proceedings judges of the civil and criminal courts rarely play a part, will be examined in chapter 29 A. Rather than creating such tribunals, Parliament has sometimes created specialised courts which are solely composed of judges of the superior courts (for example, the election court[4] or the Patents Court) or which include both judges and lay members. The Employment Appeal Tribunal is a prominent example of the latter, being established in 1975 to hear appeals on points of law from employment tribunals, for example on claims by employees against employers for unfair dismissal.[5]

---

[1] For accounts of the English legal system, see Ingman, *The English Legal Process*; Partington, *Introduction to the English Legal System*; Spencer, *Jackson's Machinery of Justice*; and Zander, *Cases and Materials on the English Legal System*. For Scotland, see White and Willock, *The Scottish Legal System*.
[2] Human Rights Act 1998, s 18.
[3] *R v Home Secretary, ex p Cheblak* [1991] 2 All ER 319, at 333 (Lord Donaldson MR).
[4] Ch 9 E.
[5] Employment Tribunals Act 1996.

Courts of civil and criminal jurisdiction

In England and Wales, civil jurisdiction is exercised by the High Court, the judges of which sit in three divisions (Queen's Bench, Chancery and Family) and, on appeal, by the Court of Appeal, Civil Division. Together the High Court, the Court of Appeal and the Crown Court form the Supreme Court. It is the High Court in England and Wales which deals with applications for judicial review, the procedure normally followed for actions against public bodies. These cases are now dealt with by specially assigned judges in what is now called the Administrative Court and the procedure is considered in chapter 31. From the Court of Appeal, and in some cases direct from the High Court, appeals lie with leave to the House of Lords, sitting as a court. A limited civil jurisdiction is exercised by the county courts and on a few subjects (for example, certain matrimonial disputes) by the magistrates' courts, though the jurisdiction of the former may be extended by the Lord Chancellor exercising powers contained in the Courts and Legal Services Act 1990, which authorises the transfer of business from the High Court to the county courts.[6] Criminal jurisdiction is exercised at first instance in summary trials by the magistrates' courts and in jury trials by the Crown Court, created by the Courts Act 1971, which sits in London and in over 90 provincial centres. In the Crown Court the judge may be a High Court judge, a circuit judge or a recorder. Criminal appeals lie, depending on the nature and grounds of the appeal, to the Queen's Bench Divisional Court of the High Court (composed of two or three judges sitting together) or to the Court of Appeal, Criminal Division. A further appeal in criminal cases on matters of law may lie, with leave, to the House of Lords.

In Scotland, civil jurisdiction is exercised by the ancient Court of Session.[7] Single judges sit in the Outer House for trials at first instance; eight senior judges form the Inner House, sitting in two divisions for mainly appellate purposes. A wide civil jurisdiction is exercised by the sheriff court, from which appeals may lie to the Inner House of the Court of Session. Criminal jurisdiction, for jury trials and appeals, is exercised by the High Court of Justiciary, which comprises the same judges as sit in the Court of Session; and also by the sheriff court, both for summary trials and jury trials. The district courts, established by the District Courts (Scotland) Act 1975, have a summary criminal jurisdiction. Appeals from Scotland in civil cases, but not in criminal cases, lie to the House of Lords. In Northern Ireland, jurisdiction is exercised by the High Court, the Crown Court and the Court of Appeal, forming the Supreme Court of Northern Ireland. Civil jurisdiction is exercised by the High Court (with Queen's Bench, Chancery and Family divisions) and the Court of Appeal. At an intermediate level, civil jurisdiction is exercised by the county courts. At a local level, civil and criminal jurisdiction is exercised by magistrates' courts, presided over by resident magistrates who are legally qualified. Civil and criminal appeals from the Court of Appeal and, in specified cases, from the High Court lie to the House of Lords.

The House of Lords

For practical purposes, the House of Lords sitting as the final court of appeal is distinct from the House in its legislative capacity, although judicial business is governed by standing orders of the House. The sittings of the House for judicial business used to be ordinary sittings of the House. After *O'Connell*'s case,[8] in which the presence of lay peers was ignored by the Lord Chancellor, it was a conventional rule that no lay

---

[6] SI 1991 No 724.

[7] The constitution and administration of the Court of Session are now governed by the Court of Session Act 1988, as amended by the Bail, Judicial Appointments etc. (Scotland) Act 2000.

[8] *O'Connell* v R (1844) 11 Cl & Fin 155, 421–6.

peer should take part in appellate work. Because of a shortage of peers who held judicial office, the Appellate Jurisdiction Act 1876 provided for the appointment of two Lords of Appeal in Ordinary, for whom the statutory qualification was to have held high judicial office in the United Kingdom or to have been a practising barrister (or advocate in Scotland) for 15 years. The Act declared that appeals should not be heard unless there were present at least three from the following: the Lord Chancellor, the Lords of Appeal in Ordinary and such peers as held or had previously held high judicial office (i.e. in a superior court in the United Kingdom). The Lords of Appeal in Ordinary, of whom up to 12 may now be appointed,[9] are salaried and under an obligation to sit for appellate work; the other qualified peers serve voluntarily. Usually appeals are heard by five judges but in exceptional cases seven judges may sit.[10]

In 1948, as a temporary measure, the House of Lords authorised the hearing of appeals by an appellate committee. This practice became permanent: appeals are now heard by the Law Lords sitting as one or two appellate committees of the House. Judgment is still delivered by members of a committee in the full Chamber; the speeches of the individual members are not delivered orally but are handed to the parties and their counsel already printed. The Lord Chancellor may sit (as may previous Lord Chancellors, even though not appointed under the 1876 Act): the Lord Chancellor is entitled to preside on such occasions. The appellate committees may sit to hear appeals when Parliament has been prorogued, or dissolved, or during an adjournment of the House. Standing orders also provide for two appeals committees which consider and report to the House on petitions for leave to appeal. Being at the apex of the hierarchy of courts in the United Kingdom, except that it has no jurisdiction in Scottish criminal cases, the House of Lords has great authority in influencing the development of the law through the system of precedent.[11] For many years the House regarded itself as bound by its own previous decisions,[12] but in 1966 the Lords of Appeal in Ordinary made through the Lord Chancellor a statement modifying that doctrine and accepting that too rigid adherence to precedent might lead to injustice in a particular case and unduly restrict the proper development of the law.[13] The House of Lords now treats its former decisions as normally binding but is prepared to depart from a previous decision when it appears right to do so.[14]

Judicial Committee of the Privy Council

Although in 1640 the Long Parliament abolished the jurisdiction of the King in Council at home, the power of the Council to receive petitions from the Channel Islands and the Isle of Man survived. From the late 17th century onwards, an increasing number of petitions by way of appeal were brought from the colonies and other overseas possessions of the Crown. In 1833, the Judicial Committee of the Privy Council was set up by statute to exercise the jurisdiction of the Council in deciding appeals from colonial, ecclesiastical and admiralty courts. In the heyday of the British Empire,

---

[9] Maximum Number of Judges Order 1994, SI 1994 No 3217.

[10] E.g. *Murphy v Brentwood DC* [1991] 1 AC 398; *Pepper v Hart* [1993] AC 593; and *R v Bow Street Metropolitan Stipendiary Magistrate, ex p Pinochet Ugarte (No 3)* [2000] 1 AC 147.

[11] For studies of its work, see Blom-Cooper and Drewry, *Final Appeal*; Paterson, *The Law Lords*; Stevens, *Law and Politics*; and B Dickson, in Carmichael and Dickson, *The House of Lords*, ch 7.

[12] *London Street Tramways Co v LCC* [1898] AC 375.

[13] Practice Statement [1966] 3 All ER 77; and see Paterson, *The Law Lords*, ch 6. But see *R v Kansal* [2001] 3 WLR 1562.

[14] For use made of this freedom in public law cases, see e.g. *Conway v Rimmer* [1968] AC 910, *Knuller Ltd v DPP* [1973] AC 435, *R v Home Secretary, ex p Khawaja* [1984] AC 74, and *Murphy v Brentwood DC* [1991] 1 AC 398. For exercise of the power in criminal law, see *R v Shivpuri* [1987] AC 1. On judicial law-making in the House of Lords, see Ingham, pp 299–309.

the Judicial Committee was indeed an imperial court exercising what was potentially a vast jurisdiction over much of the globe. Today its role as an appeal court within the Commonwealth has much declined, although a steady flow of cases continues to be heard.[15] The role and status of the Privy Council have been revived by the devolution legislation which provides that the Privy Council is the final court of appeal for deciding what falls within the jurisdiction of the Scottish Parliament or the Welsh and Northern Ireland assemblies.[16] It is the Privy Council which thus must 'achieve uniformity in the determination of these issues throughout all parts of the United Kingdom'.[17] A similar role was performed under the Government of Ireland Act 1920 in relation to the now defunct Stormont Parliament, but this led to only one decision of the Judicial Committee in 50 years.[18]

In addition to these functions in relation to devolution, the Privy Council performs a miscellany of other judicial activities: it is for example the final court of appeal from the Channel Islands and the Isle of Man. A matter may also be referred to the Privy Council by the Crown for an advisory opinion, an interesting but infrequently used procedure established by s 4 of the 1833 Act.[19] The composition of the Judicial Committee is governed by the 1833 Act: usually three or five Lords of Appeal in Ordinary sit but the committee also includes the Lord Chancellor, the Lord Justices of Appeal, such members of the Privy Council as hold or have held high judicial office in the United Kingdom, or have been judges in the superior courts of the Commonwealth states from which appeals still lie to the Committee, or of any colony that may be determined by Order in Council. In cases arising under the modern devolution legislation, however, composition is limited to Lords of Appeal in Ordinary or others who hold or have held high judicial office in the United Kingdom. In theory the Judicial Committee does not deliver judgment, but merely advises the government, which by convention acts on its report and issues an Order in Council to give effect to the advice. Until 1966 the opinion of the majority alone was given but dissenting opinions are now permissible.[20] Although the committee in form gives advice to the Crown, 'in substance, what takes place is a strictly judicial proceeding'.[21]

B. The judiciary and judicial appointments

Judicial appointments in the United Kingdom are a matter for the executive. The Queen's judges are appointed on the advice of the Queen's ministers. There is no formal machinery, such as a Judicial Service Commission, to insulate judicial appointments from executive control, although there is now a Judicial Appointments Commission to monitor appointments. Neither is there, as in the United States, any requirement that the executive's nominees be subject to scrutiny and confirmation by the legislature. Appointments to the House of Lords and to the most senior judicial posts in England (including Lord Justice of Appeal, Master of the Rolls, President of the Family Division and Lord Chief Justice) are made by the Queen on the advice of the Prime Minister. High Court judges, circuit judges, recorders and district judges are appointed by the

---

[15] Chs 15 C, 18 A. For the background, see L P Beth [1975] PL 219. See also Swinfen, *Imperial Appeal*.

[16] See *Montgomery* v *HM Adv* 2001 SC (PC) 1; and *Hoekstra* v *HM Adv (No 3)* 2001 SLT 28. For background, see D Oliver [1999] PL 1; Lord Bingham, HL 66-iii/HC 332-iii (2000–01), Q 110.

[17] *Brown* v *Stott* [2001] 2 All ER 97, 125 (Lord Hope).

[18] *Reference under the Government of Ireland Act 1920* [1936] AC 353; Calvert, *Constitutional Law in Northern Ireland*, pp 298–301.

[19] See *Re MacManaway* [1951] AC 161; *Re Parliamentary Privilege Act 1770* [1958] AC 331.

[20] Judicial Committee (Dissenting Opinions) Order 1966.

[21] *Hull* v *McKenna* [1926] IR 402.

Queen on the advice of the Lord Chancellor.[22] Magistrates are appointed to the commission of the peace by the Lord Chancellor. Judges of the Court of Session (as well as sheriffs principal and sheriffs) are now appointed by the Queen on the recommendation of the First Minister, who must consult the Lord President before making a recommendation. The Lord President and the Lord Justice Clerk are appointed by the Queen on the recommendation of the Prime Minister, who in turn must recommend the persons nominated by the First Minister. The First Minister must consult the Lord President and the Lord Justice Clerk (unless in either case the office is vacant) before making a nomination.[23]

Qualifications for appointment

By statute, minimum qualifications for appointments must be observed. Before the Courts and Legal Services Act 1990 judges of the High Court had to be of at least ten years' standing as a barrister. Since the 1990 Act, however, it is now possible for solicitors with rights of audience in the High Court and for circuit judges of at least two years' standing to be appointed.[24] As far as the Court of Appeal is concerned, candidates for appointment as a Lord Justice of Appeal had previously to be of at least 15 years' standing as a barrister or already have been a High Court judge.[25] Since the 1990 Act, however, this has been reduced to ten years and extended to include solicitors with rights of audience in the High Court, as well as anyone who is already a member of the High Court[26] (which in principle would allow someone appointed to the Circuit Bench to move quickly through the system). In Scotland, membership of the Court of Session is regulated by a rule of five years' standing as a member of the Faculty of Advocates.[27] In 1990, however, the rules were liberalised, with eligibility being extended to sheriffs principal and sheriffs (who must have held office for at least five years) and solicitors, who must have had a right of audience in the Court of Session for at least five years.[28] There are also rules of standing for members of the inferior judiciary.

In practice, appointments to the superior courts are made only from successful legal practitioners and the average experience of those appointed is well above the legal minimum. The Lord Chancellor reports that he is committed to 'ensure that the best candidates are appointed to judicial office, regardless of gender, ethnic origin, marital status, sexual orientation, political affiliation, religion or disability', except in the last case where 'the disability prevents the fulfilment of the physical requirements of the office'.[29] It has been said that the Lord Chancellor 'seeks to appoint candidates of the highest integrity and judicial quality, looking in particular for the good judgement once described by Lord Devlin as the first quality of a good judge'.[30] But it has also been said that the Lord Chancellor now aims 'to ensure and oversee appointments processes that recognise diversity and promote equality',[31] although, as we shall see, there is still some way to go if these aims are to be achieved. A major innovation in recent years has been to advertise vacancies up to the level of the High Court. Appointment to the more senior positions (Court of Appeal and House of Lords) is by way of promotion

---

[22] Supreme Court Act 1981, s 10; Justices of the Peace Act 1997, s 10A, inserted by the Access to Justice Act 1999.
[23] Scotland Act 1998, s 95.
[24] Courts and Legal Services Act 1990, s 71.
[25] Supreme Court Act 1981, s 10(3).
[26] Courts and Legal Services Act 1990, s 71.
[27] Treaty of Union 1706, art 19.
[28] Law Reform (Miscellaneous Provisions) (Scotland) Act 1990, s 35.
[29] Lord Chancellor's Department, *Judicial Appointments Annual Report 1999–2000*, Cm 4783, 2000, p 6.
[30] HC 52-II (1995–96), p 129.
[31] Lord Chancellor's Department, *Judicial Appointments Annual Report 1999–2000*, p 6.

and follows 'regular consultation' which is undertaken with senior members of the judiciary about these appointments.[32] Not all High Court positions are filled following advertising: some are still appointed following an invitation by the Lord Chancellor.

The appointment process

In making judicial appointments, the Lord Chancellor 'attaches significant weight to the independent views of members of the professional legal community'.[33] The Lord Chancellor's Department disputes (repeatedly) the description of this process as being one of 'secret soundings'. It is said that candidates 'are generally told which judges and members of the profession will be consulted and asked to name people who can assess their suitability'. The consultees (as they are referred to) are then required to assess each candidate's suitability against published criteria for appointment. It remains the case, however, that none of this applies to the senior judicial appointments, that the assessments provided during the consultation process remain confidential, and that the process is likely to be dominated by the judgments of existing or former members of the judiciary, although a lay person may be involved at the interview stage. A review of the process was conducted by Sir Leonard Peach in 1999 with terms of reference which required him to report on the selection procedures and the extent to which candidates were assessed objectively in accordance with the procedures.

Sir Leonard seemed broadly satisfied with the procedures, although a number of changes were recommended, including the introduction of a Judicial Appointments Commission to provide an independent review of the way in which the procedures operate in practice.[34] This recommendation was accepted by the government which was careful to point out that the Commission 'will not advise on the appointments to be made', although the Lord Chancellor claimed to have an open mind on whether further reform may be required in the future.[35] It is already the case that the Scottish Executive has announced the establishment of a non-statutory Judicial Appointments Board, as an advisory non-departmental public body to advise on judicial appointments. The proposed Board is to advise on the appointment of Court of Session judges as well as sheriffs, although not the Lord President or the Lord Justice Clerk. It is also proposed that the Board shall have ten members, five of whom will be lay members and the other five lawyers from both branches of the profession. Although it is anticipated that the membership of the Board will include judges, it is also proposed that it will be chaired by one of the lay members. There has not been any change to the Scotland Act 1998 to accommodate this development.

Composition of the judiciary

Should the judiciary be 'representative' and, if so, what does this mean? The idea that the judiciary should be 'representative of the community' was repudiated by the Home Affairs Committee and by the Lord Chancellor's Department, on behalf of which it was asserted that:

> It is not the function of the judiciary to reflect particular sections of the community, as it is of the democratically elected legislature. The judges' role is to administer justice in accordance

---

[32] Lord Chancellor's Department, *Judicial Appointments Annual Report 1999–2000*, p 8.

[33] Ibid, p 7.

[34] L Peach, *An Independent Scrutiny of the Appointment Processes of Judges and Queen's Counsel in England and Wales*, http://www.opengov.uk/lcd/judicial/peach/report.htm. See K D Ewing (2000) 38 Alta LR 708.

[35] Lord Chancellor's Department, *Judicial Appointments Annual Report 1999–2000*, p 19. The appointment of the first commissioner was announced on 15 March 2001.

with the laws of England and Wales. This requires above all professional legal knowledge and competence. Any litigant or defendant will usually appear before a single judge and it is of paramount importance that the judge is fully qualified for the office he or she holds, and is able to discharge his or her functions to the highest standards. Social or other considerations are not relevant for this purpose; the Lord Chancellor accordingly seeks to appoint, or recommend for appointment, those who are the best qualified candidates available and willing to serve at the time.[36]

On the other hand, however, there is recognition of the principle that the judiciary should 'more closely' reflect the make-up of society as a whole, which should tend over time to emerge by 'ensuring the fullest possible equality of opportunity for persons in all sections of society who wish to enter the legal profession and who aspire to sit judicially'. But as was pointed out, this will require 'equality of opportunity at all levels of the educational system and the legal system as well as in the appointments system itself', a sentiment that it is perhaps easier to identify than implement.[37] More recently the Lord Chancellor has expressed a desire to 'promote equality' while still maintaining that 'it is not the purpose of the judiciary to be representative of society'.[38]

Although there has been some improvement in recent years, women and members of the ethnic minority communities remain poorly represented on the bench, particularly at its highest levels. Information provided by the Lord Chancellor's Department shows that in December 2001 none of the 12 Lords of Appeal in Ordinary is a woman; only two of the 35 members of the Court of Appeal are women; and only six of 107 High Court judges are women. But if women are poorly represented, the position of ethnic minority communities is even worse: there is not a single black or Asian member of the High Court, Court of Appeal or House of Lords (Appellate Committee). Indeed out of a total of 3,792 judges (from deputy district judges to Lords of Appeal) no fewer than 3,280 are men and 3,633 are white. The Race Relations Act 1976 (as amended in 2000) now applies to judicial appointments and like other public bodies, those responsible for judicial appointments are under a duty to promote equality of opportunity between persons of different racial groups. Both the Sex Discrimination Act 1975 and the Race Relations Act 1976 apply to the legal profession in the sense that it is unlawful for a barrister or a barrister's clerk to discriminate on the grounds of sex or race in relation to pupillage or tenancy.[39] This is clearly important if there is to be a pool of eligible candidates for appointment to the highest positions, although it is open to question whether unequal representation can be promoted by anti-discrimination measures alone: there is no evidence of discrimination being an issue in judicial appointments in recent years.

C. Independence of the judiciary

Like many other constitutional principles, judicial independence has many facets.[40] Judges should be independent of government; but also independent of the parties appearing

---

[36] HC 52-II (1995–96), p 130.

[37] Contrast the policy as to the representativeness of the magistracy which should 'broadly [reflect] the communities which they serve' (HC 52-II (1995–96)) and the view that 'the aim of balancing the bench to take account of the age, employment background and political leanings of magistrates has not, as yet, been achieved' (HC 52-I (1995–96)). See also *Arthur* v *Attorney-General* [1999] IRC 631.

[38] Lord Chancellor's Department, *Equality and Diversity* (2001), p 9.

[39] Courts and Legal Services Act 1990, s 64, amending the Sex Discrimination Act 1975 and the Race Relations Act 1976.

[40] See N Browne-Wilkinson [1998] PL 44.

before them. The principle also raises questions about judicial salaries.[41] Judges need to be protected from the threat of government cuts to their salary (lest they be penalised for unpopular decisions). Salaries are now governed by statute),[42] and reviewed by the Senior Salaries Review Body. Judges also need to have security of tenure (lest they be removed for an unpopular decision); to be protected from political pressure and intimidation (but not necessarily popular criticism); and to be immune from liability – whether criminal or civil – for the manner in which they discharge the responsibilities of office. Before considering these matters, it is to be noted that the principle of judicial independence has been reinvigorated by the Human Rights Act 1998, with article 6 of the ECHR guaranteeing a right to a fair and public hearing 'by an independent and impartial tribunal'. In *Starrs v Ruxton*,[43] the High Court of Justiciary held that temporary sheriffs were not independent and impartial because, under the terms of their appointment, such judges could be recalled by the minister before the end of their appointment which was for a renewable period of only one year. Different questions relating to judicial independence may arise as a result of the growing tendency of some judges to court media attention, as in December 2001 when the Lord Chief Justice 'sparked a row over civil liberties when he suggested that the law could be changed to allow paedophiles not yet convicted of a crime to be locked up to protect the public'.[44]

The Sovereign and the courts

According to Blackstone, 'All jurisdiction of courts are either indirectly or immediately derived from the Crown. Their proceedings are generally in the King's name; they pass under his seal, and are executed by his office', but it is 'impossible as well as improper that the King personally should carry into execution this great and extensive trust'.[45] The notion of the Sovereign as the fountain of justice was important in feudal times in helping to ensure that a single system of justice prevailed over competing jurisdictions. The early kings delivered justice in their own courts. But the delegation of this duty to judges was an inevitable result of the growth of the business of government and the development of a system of law requiring specialised knowledge. In England, it was enacted in 1328 by the Statute of Northampton that the royal command should not disturb or delay common justice and that, although such commands had been given, the judges were not therefore to cease to do right in any point. In Scotland, the Court of Session, which was placed on a permanent basis in 1532, more than once had to resist royal interference in the course of justice and issued a notable rebuff to King James VI in 1599.[46]

---

[41] See W S Holdsworth (1932) 48 LQR 25; Heuston, *Lives of the Lord Chancellors 1885–1940*, pp 513–19.

[42] Judges' Remuneration Act 1965. The Act of Settlement provided that judicial salaries should be 'ascertained and established', suggesting that judicial salaries should be fixed by statute and not left to executive discretion.

[43] 2000 JC 208; A O'Neill (2000) 63 MLR 429. See further ch 19 C below. See now Bail, Judicial Appointments etc. (Scotland) Act 2000. For consequential changes in England and Wales, see Lord Chancellor's Department, *Judicial Appointments Annual Report 1999–2000*, pp 21–2.

[44] *The Guardian*, 27 December, and 31 December 2001. Similar issues may arise from the growing practice of judges contributing to law journals. The Lord Chancellor's Department advises judges that 'it may sometimes be advisable for a judge to avoid writing on a subject of wider or more general public interest' (Lord Chancellor's Department, *Judges and QCs* (2000)). The same document also gives advice to judges on financial interests, non-commercial directorships, charitable, political and business contacts and the misuse of office. See further ch 30 B.

[45] I *Commentaries*, Book 1, ch VII.

[46] *Bruce v Hamilton*, recounted in (1946) 58 JR 83; and see *Earl of Morton v Fleming* (1569) Morison 7325.

In 1607 James, who had by then also become King James I of England, claimed the right in England to determine judicially a dispute between the common law courts and the ecclesiastical courts. In the case of *Prohibitions del Roy*, it was decided by all the common law judges headed by Coke that the right of the King to administer justice no longer existed.[47] In a famous passage, Coke declared:

> that the King in his own person cannot adjudge any case, either criminal, as treason, felony, etc, or betwixt a party and party, concerning his inheritance, chattels or goods, etc, but this ought to be determined and adjudged in some Court of Justice, according to the law and custom of England; . . . true it was, that God had endowed His Majesty with excellent science, and great endowments of nature; but His Majesty was not learned in the laws of his realm of England, and causes which concern the life, or inheritance, or goods, or fortunes of his subjects, are not to be decided by natural reason, but by the artificial reason and judgment of law, which law is an act which requires long study and experience, before that a man can attain to the cognizance of it: that the law was the golden met-wand and measure to try the causes of the subjects; and which protected His Majesty in safety and peace.

This declaration may not have been supported by all Coke's precedents[48] but it served to establish a fundamental constitutional principle. This principle was reinforced by provisions in the Bill of Rights 1689 and the Scottish Claim of Right which restricted royal interference in the course of justice. Certain prerogative powers in relation to the administration of justice have survived and will be examined later in this chapter. But the Crown can no longer by the prerogative create courts to administer any system of law other than the common law.[49] This restriction had its roots in the common lawyers' distrust of the prerogative courts of the Star Chamber and the High Commission. Its effect today is that new courts and tribunals may be created only by Act of Parliament, but this does not prevent the Crown under prerogative power from establishing a body to administer a scheme for conferring financial benefits on individuals.[50]

Security of tenure

Today one of the most important ways by which judicial independence is preserved is by the security of tenure of judicial office-holders: they cannot be dismissed because they are unpopular with government. Judges of the High Court and Court of Appeal hold office during good behaviour, subject to a power of removal by the Queen on an address presented by both Houses of Parliament.[51] A similar provision applies to Lords of Appeal in Ordinary.[52] These statutory rules clearly prevent a judge being removed at the pleasure of the Crown, but their meaning is not wholly certain. The wording of the provision in the Act of Settlement from which these rules derived,[53] suggests that the intention of Parliament was that, while a judge should hold office during good behaviour, Parliament itself should enjoy an unqualified power of removal. Assuming that there was no intention to alter the effect of the Act of Settlement by the revised wording now contained in the Supreme Court Act 1981, it is theoretically possible for a judge to be dismissed not only for misconduct but for any other reason which might induce both Houses to pass the necessary address to the Crown. It is, however, extremely unlikely that Parliament would be willing to pass an address from any motive other than to remove a judge who had been guilty of misconduct. The judicial

---

47 (1607) 12 Co Rep 63.
48 Cf Dicey, *The Law of the Constitution*, p 18.
49 *Re Lord Bishop of Natal* (1864) 3 Moo PC (NS) 115.
50 *R v Criminal Injuries Compensation Board, ex p Lain* [1967] 2 QB 864; ch 12 E.
51 Supreme Court Act 1981, s 11(3).
52 Appellate Jurisdiction Act 1876, s 6.
53 Ch 2 A.

retirement age is 70, although this may be extended to 75.[54] Inferior judges receive a lesser degree of protection. Circuit judges and district judges may be removed from office by the Lord Chancellor, if he thinks fit, for incapacity or misbehaviour.[55]

In Scotland, the historic tenure on which judges hold office is *ad vitam aut culpam*, i.e. they cannot be removed except on grounds of misconduct.[56] Judges of the Court of Session now hold office subject to the retiring age of 75. Judges of the Court of Session may be removed by Her Majesty following a recommendation by the First Minister, who may make a recommendation only with the authority of the Scottish Parliament.[57] Provision is to be made for a tribunal (to be chaired by a judicial member of the Privy Council) to be established by the First Minister to investigate whether a Court of Session judge is unfit for office by reason of 'inability, neglect of duty or misbehaviour'.[58] This must be done before the First Minister seeks parliamentary approval to recommend the removal of a judge. A sheriff may be removed from office only after an inquiry, conducted jointly by the Lord President of the Court of Session and the Lord Justice-Clerk, has established unfitness for office by reason of inability, neglect of duty or misbehaviour, and only by means of an order of removal made by the First Minister and laid before the Scottish Parliament.[59]

Use of judges for extra-judicial purposes

Judges have often been called on by the government to preside over royal commissions, departmental committees and inquiries conducted under the Tribunals of Inquiry (Evidence) Act 1921. From 1953 to 1973, not including judges who served on permanent committees for law reform, 79 such appointments were made.[60] More recent figures are not easily available, although in the 1980s and 1990s judges continued to be used by government for a wide range of extra-judicial purposes, including safety at sports grounds, prison riots, the collapse of an international bank, the so-called Arms for Iraq affair, the future of legislation against terrorism, BSE and the Bloody Sunday killings in 1972. An emerging theme of some significance is the appointment of senior judges as commissioners to oversee and to report annually to the Prime Minister about the operation of surveillance powers created by legislation such as the Regulation of Investigatory Powers Act 2000.[61] This is based on the earlier arrangements which saw Lord Diplock accept appointment as a commissioner to review the operation of the practice of telephone tapping before it was placed on a statutory basis.[62] Also important is the appointment of Lord Nolan in 1994 to examine concerns about standards of conduct in public life.[63] Many judges are well suited to this work but there are potential dangers to judicial independence in the practice, especially when matters of acute political controversy are referred to a judge for an impartial opinion.

---

[54] Judicial Pensions Act 1981, Sch 2, para 1(1) and Judicial Pensions and Retirement Act 1993, s 26(7).

[55] Courts Act 1971, s 17(4). Lay magistrates may be removed from the commission of the peace at the discretion of the Lord Chancellor, although in practice a magistrate is not removed unless he or she has been arrested for a criminal offence of some gravity or for persistent minor offences or has in some other way ceased to uphold the law, for example, by taking part in a civil disobedience campaign.

[56] Claim of Right 1689, art 13; *Mackay and Esslemont v Lord Advocate* 1937 SC 860.

[57] Scotland Act 1998, s 95.

[58] Ibid, s 95(8).

[59] Sheriff Courts (Scotland) Act 1971, s 12. See *Stewart v Secretary of State for Scotland* 1998 SC (HL) 81.

[60] HC Deb, 7 December 1973, col 478 (WA). And see Griffith, *Politics of the Judiciary*, and G Zellick [1972] PL 1.

[61] See ch 22 D.

[62] See ch 22 D.

[63] HC Deb, 25 October 1994, col 757. Lord Nolan was also a commissioner under the Interception of Communications Act 1985. And see ch 22 D.

Particularly controversial references were the investigations conducted by Lord Denning on the request of the Prime Minister into the security aspects arising out of the resignation of a minister (J Profumo) in 1963; by the Lord Chief Justice, Lord Widgery, in 1972 into deaths in Londonderry; and by Lord Bridge in 1985 into allegations of improper telephone tapping of trade unionists and peace activists by members of the security service.[64] Such references may give rise to allegations that the government is using the judiciary for its own ends; and they may expose the judge in question, particularly if he or she is the sole member of the inquiry, to political criticism by those who disagree with his or her report. It needs to be stressed that such work is not the primary task of the judges and that the government cannot assume that the services of a judge will be available whenever an awkward political situation might be eased by an impartial inquiry. There may also be concerns about judges being too intimately involved with the operation and needs of government, particularly in cases where they are drawn on to give advice on a matter about which they are subsequently called upon to adjudicate, albeit in a different context. There is a strong convention that judges should not become involved in party political activities.[65]

Political and parliamentary criticism of the judiciary

The work of the courts should not be outside the scope of political discussion. There is, however, a convention that members of the executive, whether ministers or civil servants, do not criticise the judiciary or judicial decisions. The government may say that a judicial decision differs from the legal advice on which it had acted or that it proposes to bring in amending legislation, but ministers are not expected to state that a court's decision is wrong. Nonetheless in 1977 Mr Michael Foot, while holding a senior Cabinet post, told a trade union rally that the British people, especially trade unionists, would have 'precious few' freedoms if these had been left to the good sense and fair-mindedness of the judges.[66] In 1982 the Prime Minister stated that she found the decision of a judge to impose a suspended prison sentence for rape of a six-year-old girl incomprehensible and informed the House of Commons of action taken by the Lord Chancellor requiring trials for rape to be conducted by senior judges.[67] In 1987 when the Prime Minister said at question time that she was unable to comment on a particular sentence, the Speaker subsequently ruled: 'It is perfectly in order to criticise or to question a sentence: but it is not in order to criticise a judge. That has to be done by motion.'[68] As individuals, backbench MPs are also subject to restraints in their criticism of judges, although not to the same degree as are members of the executive. There is a long-standing rule of the House that unless the discussion is based on a substantive motion, reflections must not be cast on the conduct of judges or upon judges generally.[69]

Another parliamentary rule seeks to protect the principle of a fair trial rather than the status of the judges: by the *sub judice* rule, matters awaiting the adjudication of a court may not be raised in debate. The rule applies to matters pending decision both in criminal and civil cases; but in regard to civil cases, the Speaker has a discretion to permit reference to matters awaiting adjudication where they relate to ministerial decisions which can be challenged in court only on grounds of misdirection or bad faith or to issues of national importance, such as the national economy, the essentials

---

[64] See respectively Cmnd 2152, 1963; HC 220 (1971–72); and *The Times*, 7 March 1985.
[65] See ch 2 B. See now Lord Chancellor's Department, *Judges and QCs* (note 44 above).
[66] *The Times*, 16 May 1977.
[67] HC Deb, 14 December 1982, col 123; 15 December 1982, col 285.
[68] HC Deb, 2 July 1987, col 641.
[69] Erskine May, *Parliamentary Practice*, pp 332–3 and 384–5.

of life or public order.[70] The reason for this relaxation is to permit some parliamentary discussion of ministerial decisions or other major issues of public concern, notwithstanding the fact that a civil action may have been instituted.[71] The operation of the rule arose for consideration in 1987 when the British government was seeking to restrain the publication of Mr Peter Wright's book, *Spycatcher*. At a time when proceedings had been instituted against the publishers in Australia, the Speaker ruled: 'It is legitimate to raise anything that has come out in the Australian courts, but what should not be raised under our *sub judice* rule is the action that is pending before the British courts . . . anything that has come out in the Australian courts is fair game.'[72] The *sub judice* rule has been described as a self-denying ordinance, created by the Commons so that Parliament should not influence or seem to be influencing the administration of justice.[73] It does not affect the power of Parliament to legislate: thus the War Damage Act 1965 altered the law retrospectively while litigation against the government was in process. A similar rule applies in the Scottish Parliament.[74]

Judicial membership of the House of Lords

The standing orders of the House of Commons and other principles and rules of the constitution thus protect the judges from political pressures of various kinds. But how far can it be said that judicial independence is compromised by judicial membership of the House of Lords? How far is it possible for judges to take part in the work of Parliament, in its legislative and scrutiny roles, in a manner which is consistent with judicial independence? As full members of the House of Lords, the Lords of Appeal are entitled to take part in the debates of the House. But to do so could present difficulties if the judge is later required to hear a case on a piece of legislation in the making of which the judge has played a part. In a statement issued in 2000, Lord Bingham (as the Senior Law Lord) drew attention to two principles by which the judges considered themselves bound 'when deciding whether to participate in a particular matter or to vote'. The first is that 'they do not think it appropriate to engage in matters where there is a strong element of party political controversy'; and the second is that they 'bear in mind that they might render themselves ineligible to sit judicially if they were to express an opinion on a matter which might later go to an appeal to the House'.[75] The contribution made by the Law Lords to the work of the House of Lords was recognised by the Royal Commission on Lords Reform in 2000 which (possibly without fully considering all the issues) recommended that they should continue to be ex officio members of the reformed Second Chamber.[76]

The other question which arises in this context is whether judges may (or should) appear before select committees to give an account of themselves to Parliament. An event of considerable constitutional significance occurred on 26 March 2001 when Lord Bingham appeared before the Joint Committee on Human Rights, together with Lord Woolf (the Lord Chief Justice) and Lord Phillips (the Master of the Rolls) to discuss the implementation of the Human Rights Act. The uniqueness of the occasion was matched only by the uncertainty of both sides. In a letter to the Committee Lord Bingham was unsure how much help he would be able to give, for in his view 'the

---

[70] Ibid, p 383; HC Deb, 23 July 1963, col 1417; 28 June 1972, col 1589.
[71] See e.g. debate on the thalidomide cases, HC Deb, 29 November 1972, col 432.
[72] HC Deb, 13 July 1987, col 710. And see ch 23 G.
[73] HC Deb, 29 July 1976, col 882; and see HC 222 (1978–79).
[74] Scottish Parliament Standing Orders, Rule 7.5.
[75] As explained by Lord Bingham HL 66-iii/HC 332-iii (2000–01), Q 105. This statement followed a recommendation by the Royal Commission on the Reform of the House of Lords, Cm 4534, 2000, para 9.10.
[76] Ibid, paras 9.6–9.7.

separation of powers as between the legislature and the judiciary is an important constitutional principle, neither being accountable to the other' and he would 'feel inhibited in answering any question which relates not just to individual cases but to past or likely future trends of decision-making'. For its part the committee had no wish to place the witnesses 'in an awkward or invidious position' and would expect it to be known if their questions pushed the judges 'up against the constitutional boundaries between the roles of the legislature and the judiciary'.[77] The occasion passed without incident, but the interesting exchanges which took place on a range of issues raise questions about whether this can be seen as a precedent for structured dialogue between legislature and judiciary in the future.

Judicial immunity from civil action

Just as the public interest in free debate in Parliament justifies the rule of absolute privilege for things said in the course of parliamentary debates, so the public interest in the administration of justice justifies similar protection for judicial proceedings. At common law no action will lie against a judge for any acts done or words spoken in his or her judicial capacity in a court of justice.

> It is essential in all courts that the judges who are appointed to administer the law should be permitted to administer it under the protection of the law independently and freely, without favour and without fear. This provision of the law is not for the protection or benefit of a malicious or corrupt judge, but for the benefit of the public, whose interest it is that the judges should be at liberty to exercise their functions with independence and without fear of consequences.[78]

The judge of a superior court is not liable for anything done or said in the exercise of judicial functions, however malicious, corrupt or oppressive are the acts or words complained of.[79] A similar immunity attaches to the verdict of juries[80] and to words spoken by parties, counsel and witnesses in the course of judicial proceedings.[81] But barristers no longer enjoy immunity for the negligent conduct of a client's case in court.[82] The immunity of judges is reinforced by the Crown Proceedings Act 1947, s 2(5), which absolves the Crown from liability for any person 'while discharging or purporting to discharge any responsibilities of a judicial nature vested in him' or in the execution of judicial process. But immunity does not extend to the acts or words of a judge in his or her private capacity.

Judicial immunity also applies to the work of inferior courts, for example county courts and magistrates' courts. But the immunity is narrower than in the case of the superior courts. In *Sirros v Moore*,[83] the Court of Appeal appeared to assimilate the position of judges in inferior courts to that of judges in superior courts when it held that a circuit court judge was immune from liability for damages after he had by a wholly erroneous procedure ordered a Turkish citizen to be detained by the police. The Court of Appeal considered that no distinction should be drawn in principle between the protection given to superior court judges and that given to inferior courts. According to Lord Denning and Ormrod LJ, every judge, including a justice of the peace, was entitled to be protected from liability in respect of what he did while acting judicially and in the honest belief that his acts were within jurisdiction. But the scope

---

[77] HL 66-iii/HC 332-iii (2000–01), Q 77.
[78] *Scott v Stansfield* (1868) LR 3 Ex 220, 223 per Kelly CB.
[79] *Anderson v Gorrie* [1895] 1 QB 668. And see generally Olowofoyeku, *Suing Judges*.
[80] *Bushell's case* (1670) 6 St Tr 999.
[81] *Munster v Lamb* (1883) 11 QBD 588.
[82] *Hall (Arthur JS) & Co v Simons* [2000] 3 WLR 543.
[83] [1975] QB 118, discussed by M Brazier [1976] PL 397.

of this decision was doubted, at least as far as justices of the peace are concerned. They are now protected by legislation for acts done within their jurisdiction and for acts outside their jurisdiction unless, in the latter case, the plaintiff can show bad faith.[84] Despite their immunities, it would be wrong to suppose that professional judges are uncontrolled despots. For one thing, lay persons make a significant contribution to the administration of justice: the role of the jury in major criminal trials is an important constitutional safeguard against an oppressive judiciary; removal of the right to trial by jury is a matter of grave concern.[85] So too is interference with the freedom of the jury, whether it takes the form of criminal conduct or 'jury vetting'.[86] Lay magistrates in England and Wales discharge a heavy burden of adjudication. Non-lawyers have a significant role to play in courts of specialised jurisdiction and in tribunals.

D. Contempt of court and safeguards for the administration of justice

As we have seen, article 6 of the ECHR provides that the individual has the right to a fair and public hearing within a reasonable time by an independent and impartial tribunal. There are a number of legal rules which are designed to maintain the quality of justice in the courts. In principle all trials are conducted in open court,[87] although, exceptionally, cases may be heard in camera;[88] witnesses may be permitted to give evidence anonymously;[89] and limits may be imposed on reporting legal proceedings.[90] The written rules of court procedure as well as the unwritten rules of natural justice seek to ensure for each litigant a fair and orderly hearing.[91] The rules of evidence, particularly in criminal trials before a jury,[92] exclude material which might be unfairly prejudicial to an accused. To the extent that legal representation contributes to the quality of justice, there are also schemes to enable people with limited means to be defended by a lawyer in criminal proceedings and to seek redress through the civil courts.[93] It is important to note, however, that the right to a fair and public hearing has to be balanced against other Convention rights, most notably the right to freedom of expression in article 10 of the ECHR. There is a difficult tension between the right to a fair trial and the right to freedom of expression when newspapers publish material which might prejudice the position of an accused person by influencing a jury. One of the functions of the law of contempt of court is to manage this tension, although it also has other functions; these include protecting the dignity of the court and generally safeguarding the administration of justice.

The nature of contempt

Contempt of court, broadly speaking, takes two forms. Civil contempt is the failure to obey the order of a superior court of record which prescribes certain conduct upon

---

[84] Justices of the Peace Act 1997, ss 51, 52, 53A (as inserted by the Access to Justice Act 1999). See also Human Rights Act 1998, s 9.

[85] 'The constitutional law of England requires that a man accused of a serious crime should be tried by Judge and Jury': Lord Denning [1990] Crim LR 536.

[86] See ch 25.

[87] See *Scott* v *Scott* [1913] AC 417. Also *Clibbery* v *Allan* [2002] 1 All ER 865 for a review of the issues.

[88] Official Secrets Act 1911, s 8(4); Children and Young Persons Act 1933, s 37.

[89] *R* v *Murphy* [1990] NI 306; *R* v *Lord Saville of Newgate ex p A* [1999] 4 All ER 860 (B Hadfield [1999] PL 633).

[90] For example Judicial Proceedings (Regulation of Reports) Act 1926, on which see *Gilchrist* v *Scott* 2000 SCCR 28; and Employment Tribunals Act 1996, ss 11, 31.

[91] Ch 30 B.

[92] On which, see ch 21 E.

[93] See now Access to Justice Act 1999.

a party to a civil action. A civil judge may commit to prison anyone who disregards an order addressed to him or her. In this way, decrees of specific performance and injunctions, as well as the writ of habeas corpus and other judicial orders, may be enforced by the High Court. The power of courts to enforce their orders against litigants is not available against the Crown, but ministers of the Crown and civil servants are liable to be proceeded against for contempt of court in respect of acts or omissions by them personally and it is no defence that what would otherwise constitute a contempt of court was committed in the discharge or purported discharge of official duties.[94] Although a civil contempt is not a criminal offence or a misdemeanor,[95] the court may nevertheless commit a wrongdoer to prison for a fixed period,[96] may fine him or her or may order his or her property to be sequestrated. The Official Solicitor to the Supreme Court is required to review all cases of persons committed to prison for contempt and may intervene to secure their release.[97] The Crown may not grant a pardon in cases of civil contempt since this would be to intervene in litigation between parties.

Conduct which is calculated to interfere with the due administration of justice or to bring the courts into disrepute gives rise to proceedings which are in the nature of criminal proceedings, and both civil and criminal courts may exercise the jurisdiction. Although criminal contempt takes various forms and although it is necessary to protect the workings of the courts, nevertheless judges should seek to ensure, in the words of Lord President Normand,

> that the greatest restraint and discrimination should be used by the court in dealing with contempt of court, lest a process, the purpose of which is to prevent interference with the administration of justice, should degenerate into an oppressive or vindictive abuse of the court's powers.[98]

The need for restraint is all the greater since one of the consequences of contempt of court is to restrict freedom of expression. But not all judges are so sanguine, with concern being expressed in one case that the Contempt of Court Act 1981 may have tilted the balance too much in favour of freedom of expression: 'Parliament may have redrawn the boundary at a point which would not have been chosen by those people looking at the matter primarily from the standpoint of the administration of justice.'[99] The main categories of contempt will now be outlined.

Scandalising the court[100]

The law protects courts and judges from criticism which might undermine public confidence in the judiciary, in particular scurrilous abuse and attacks on the integrity or impartiality of a judge. Proceedings on this ground are rare: 'More than fifty years have passed since the last successful prosecution in England and Wales for scandalising the court.'[101] Nevertheless, criticism of a court's decision may be a contempt if it imputes unfairness and partiality to a judge in the discharge of his or her duties.

---

[94] *M v Home Office* [1994] 1 AC 377. And see *R v City of London Magistrates' Court, ex p Green* [1997] 3 All ER 551.

[95] *Cobra Golf Ltd v Rata* [1998] ch 29.

[96] On which see *Nicholls v Nicholls* [1997] 2 All ER 97; and *Taylor v Ribby Hall Leisure Ltd* [1997] 4 All ER 760.

[97] *Churchman v Joint Shop Stewards' Committee* [1972] 3 All ER 603; *Enfield BC v Mahoney* [1983] 2 All ER 901.

[98] *Milburn, Petitioner* 1946 SC 301, 315.

[99] *Cox and Griffiths, Petitioners* 1998 SCCR 561.

[100] See D Hay (1987) 25 Osgoode Hall LJ 431.

[101] C Walker (1985) 101 LQR 359.

In 1928, the *New Statesman*, commenting on a judgment in a libel action against Dr Marie Stopes, a known advocate of birth control, concluded, 'an individual owning to such views as those of Dr Stopes cannot apparently hope for a fair hearing in a court presided over by Mr Justice Avory and there are so many Avorys'. Three colleagues of the judge in question, though they imposed no fine on the editor, adjudged him guilty of contempt.[102]

Yet it is clearly in the public interest that there should be public discussion and criticism of judicial decisions and the work of the courts. When a colonial newspaper had discussed a variation in sentence in two apparently similar cases, suggesting that this was due to the personal attitudes of the judge, the Privy Council set aside the conviction for contempt. The judgment of the Judicial Committee was given by Lord Atkin, who said:

> But whether the authority and position of an individual judge, or the due administration of justice, is concerned, no wrong is committed by any member of the public who exercises the ordinary right of criticising, in good faith, in private or public, the public act done in the seat of justice. The path of criticism is a public way: the wrongheaded are permitted to err therein: provided that members of the public abstain from imputing improper motives to those taking part in the administration of justice, and are genuinely exercising a right of criticism, and not acting in malice or attempting to impair the administration of justice, they are immune. Justice is not a cloistered virtue: she must be allowed to suffer the scrutiny and respectful, even though outspoken, comments of ordinary men.[103]

Discussion of the legal merits or social implications of judicial decisions is therefore not contempt, even where a Queen's Counsel chooses to make sweeping and inaccurate criticism of the Court of Appeal in the columns of *Punch*.[104] This aspect of the law has the potential to deter a critic who sought to show that the judges were biased politically or socially or that a particular court was failing to administer justice. But today the scope of permissible criticism has widened, to judge by the sharp controversy over the National Industrial Relations Court between 1971 and 1974, by the attacks made on some of Lord Denning's decisions before his retirement in 1982 and by some of the criticisms of the Law Lords after the first *Spycatcher* case in 1987. The Phillimore committee recommended that this branch of contempt should be replaced by an offence of publishing matter which imputes improper judicial conduct with the intention of impairing confidence in the administration of justice,[105] but this recommendation has wisely not been adopted.

Contempt in the face of the court

All superior courts have power to punish summarily by fine or imprisonment violence committed or threats uttered in face of the court. Thus the judge may punish an attack on anyone in court or restrain the use of threatening words or scurrilous abuse. The issue whether an act constitutes a contempt is for the judge alone. If the act is committed in court, the judge is in a sense prosecutor, chief witness, judge and jury.

In *Morris v Crown Office*,[106] a group of students demonstrated in support of the Welsh language by interrupting a sitting of the High Court in London, where they sang, shouted slogans and scattered pamphlets. After order was restored, the trial judge sentenced some of the students to prison for three months and fined others £50 each. On appeal, the Court of

---

[102] *R v New Statesman (Editor), ex p DPP* (1928) 44 TLR 301.
[103] *Ambard v A-G for Trinidad and Tobago* [1936] AC 322, 335.
[104] *R v Metropolitan Police Commissioner, ex p Blackburn (No 2)* [1968] 2 QB 150. Probably the most savage criticism of a British court ever published was N J D Kennedy (1896) 8 JR 268.
[105] Cmnd 5794, 1974, pp 69–71.
[106] [1970] 2 QB 114.

Appeal, Civil Division, held that a High Court judge still had power at common law to commit instantly to prison for criminal contempt; and that the requirement under the Criminal Justice Act 1967 that prison sentences under six months be suspended did not apply to committal for contempt. The court did not consider the prison sentences to be excessive, but, having regard to all the circumstances, allowed the appeal against sentence and bound over the appellants to be of good behaviour for one year.

Contempt in the face of the court includes insulting behaviour,[107] disregard of a judge's ruling and refusal by a witness to give evidence or to answer questions which he or she is required to answer.[108]

In *Attorney-General v Mulholland and Foster*,[109] two journalists refused to disclose their sources of information to a tribunal of inquiry appointed after an Admiralty clerk, Vassall, had been convicted of espionage. The tribunal had by statute the powers of the High Court in examining witnesses.[110] On appeal against a prison sentence imposed by the High Court, to whom the tribunal had reported the journalists, it was held that journalists had no legal privilege to refuse to disclose sources of information given to them in confidence, where the information was relevant and necessary to the trial or inquiry.

So too, in *British Steel Corpn v Granada Television Ltd*,[111] the House of Lords ordered the Granada company to reveal the name of an employee of the corporation who had passed secret documents to Granada that were then used in a programme about the corporation. Although failure by Granada to comply with this order would have constituted contempt, the matter was resolved when the employee concerned made his identity known. In the Contempt of Court Act 1981, the power of the court to demand information was limited by s 10 Parliament. The court may not now request a person to disclose the source of information contained in a publication for which he or she is responsible, unless the court is satisfied that disclosure is necessary in the interests of justice or national security or for the prevention of disorder or crime.[112] If cases such as *Mulholland* and *British Steel Corpn* were to occur today, the statutory test of necessity would have to be applied before the court decided to require disclosure, but the outcome might still be the same.

In *Secretary of State for Defence v Guardian Newspapers Ltd*[113] a junior civil servant delivered anonymously to the *Guardian* newspaper confidential documents addressed to Cabinet ministers by the Secretary of State for Defence. The documents related to the arrival of US cruise missiles at Greenham Common airbase. The Ministry of Defence sought to recover the documents to help them to identify the person responsible for the leak. The House of Lords held that s 10 of the 1981 Act was a valid defence not only where a journalist was asked a direct question in court, but also in an action for recovery of property where the property once recovered would help to reveal the newspaper's source. But the House also held (Lords Fraser and Scarman dissenting) that it was necessary to recover the documents and identify the source of the leak in the interests of national security. The minister had expressed concern that a significant document relating to the defence of Britain had found its way to a national newspaper. This was of grave importance for national security, since Britain's allies could not be expected to continue to entrust the government with secret information if it was liable to unauthorised disclosure.

Guardian Newspapers is only one of a number of cases in which the courts at the highest levels have been willing to order the disclosure of journalists' sources by

[107] See *R v Powell* (1994) 98 Cr App R 224.
[108] *R v Montgomery*, [1995] 2 Cr App R 23.
[109] [1963] 2 QB 477. And see *Senior v Holdsworth* [1976] QB 23.
[110] Ch 29 C.
[111] [1981] AC 1096.
[112] Contempt of Court Act 1981, s 10.
[113] [1985] AC 339.

applying a low threshold which applicants need cross.[114] The more robust view of the European Court of Human Rights on this issue has led to conflict between that body and the House of Lords.[115] The domestic courts nevertheless appear willing to require the disclosure of sources where this will help an employer to identify an employee within an organisation who has leaked commercial information or confidential medical information about a patient.[116] But the courts may refuse to order the disclosure of sources where the applicant's interests will be adequately protected by an injunction[117] or where in the circumstances the applicant has not tried to find the source of the disclosure by other means first.[118]

The strict liability rule

Until the Contempt of Court Act 1981, it was on the basis of the common law that penalties were imposed on those whose publications were prejudicial to a fair trial or to civil proceedings.[119] The law was reformed in 1981, following recommendations of the Phillimore committee,[120] and the decision of the European Court of Human Rights in the *Sunday Times* case.

> Nearly 400 claims against Distillers Ltd, the manufacturers of thalidomide, were pending when the *Sunday Times* published an article which inter alia urged the company to make a generous settlement. Later it proposed to publish an article examining the precautions taken by the company before the drug was sold. On the Attorney-General's request, the Divisional Court granted an injunction to restrain publication of the article, holding that it would create a serious risk of interference with the company's freedom of action in the litigation. The Court of Appeal discharged the injunction, on the grounds that the article commented in good faith on matters of outstanding public importance and did not prejudice pending litigation since the litigation had been dormant for some years.
>
> The House of Lords restored the injunction, holding that it was a contempt to publish an article prejudging the merits of an issue before the court where this created a real risk that a fair trial of the action would be prejudiced; the thalidomide actions were not dormant, since active negotiations for a settlement were going on. It was a contempt to use improper pressure to induce a litigant to settle a case on terms to which he or she did not wish to agree, or to hold a litigant up to public obloquy for exercising his or her rights in the courts.[121] Thereafter the *Sunday Times* claimed that the decision of the House of Lords infringed the freedom of expression protected by art 10 of the European Convention on Human Rights. Before the European Court of Human Rights, the main issue was whether, under art 10, the ban on publication was 'necessary in a democratic society . . . for maintaining the authority and impartiality of the judiciary'. By 11 to 9 votes, the court held that the ban had not been shown to be necessary for this purpose.[122]

---

[114] *Maxwell v Pressdram Ltd* [1987] 1 All ER 656, *Re an Inquiry under the Company Securities (Insider Dealing) Act 1985* [1988] AC 660, and *X v Morgan Grampian (Publishers) Ltd* [1991] 1 AC 1. See T R S Allan [1991] CLJ 131; S Palmer [1992] PL 61.

[115] *Goodwin v UK* (1996) 22 EHRR 123, concluding that the decision in *Morgan Grampian* contravened article 10 of the ECHR.

[116] See *Camelot Group v Centaur Ltd* [1999] QB 124, and *Ashworth Hospital Authority v MGN* [2001] 1 WLR 515.

[117] See *Saunders v Punch Ltd* [1998] 1 WLR 986.

[118] *John v Express Newspapers* [2000] 1 WLR 1931, and *Broadmoor Hospital v Hyde*, *The Independent*, 4 March 1994.

[119] Leading cases arising out of criminal litigation before 1981 include *R v Bolam, ex p Haigh* (1949) 93 SJ 220; *R v Evening Standard Co Ltd* [1954] 1 QB 578; *R v Thomson Newspapers Ltd, ex p A-G* [1968] 1 All ER 268; and *Stirling v Associated Newspapers Ltd* 1960 JC 5. And in relation to civil litigation, see *Vine Products Ltd v Green* [1966] Ch 484.

[120] Cmnd 5794, 1974.

[121] *A-G v Times Newspapers Ltd* [1974] AC 273.

[122] *Sunday Times v UK* (1979) 2 EHRR 245.

The Contempt of Court Act 1981 was designed to bring British law into line with the requirements of the *Sunday Times* decision, although there is much scope for argument about whether it does so fully.[123]

Liability for contempt under the 1981 Act is based on the strict liability rule, defined to mean 'the rule of law whereby conduct may be treated as a contempt of court as tending to interfere with the course of justice in particular legal proceedings regardless of intent to do so' (s 1). By s 2, the strict liability rule applies to any publication which creates 'a substantial risk that the course of justice in the proceedings in question will be seriously impeded or prejudiced'. This applies to both civil and criminal proceedings. The other requirement of s 2 is that the proceedings in question must be 'active', governed by Sch 1, which lays down in detail when civil or criminal proceedings begin to be active. Criminal proceedings become active when an individual is arrested or orally charged or when an arrest warrant is issued (whereas at common law liability for contempt could arise where legal proceedings were imminent).[124] Civil proceedings become active not when the writ is served but when the action is set down for trial. In some cases, proceedings may be instituted at common law to deal with publications which are likely to prejudice the outcome of proceedings not yet active within the statutory definition.[125] Proceedings remain active in criminal cases until concluded by acquittal, sentence or discontinuance, and in other cases until the proceedings are disposed of, discontinued or withdrawn.[126]

Application of the strict liability rule

The question whether there is a substantial risk that the course of justice in particular legal proceedings will be seriously impeded or prejudiced is ultimately one of fact; this will depend primarily on whether the publication will bring influence to bear which is likely to direct the proceedings in some way from the course which they would otherwise have followed.[127] Many of the cases on contempt of court, both before and after 1981, are concerned with pre-trial publicity which may influence the jury. Thus *Attorney-General* v *Times Newspapers Ltd*[128] concerned reports carried by newspapers about a man who had intruded into the Queen's bedroom at Buckingham Palace. The man in question was awaiting trial on a number of counts, including the theft of a bottle of wine. It was held that a newspaper report that he had admitted the theft was a contempt, since it was difficult to see how an assertion that an accused person had admitted the very fact which was in issue could do otherwise than cause a very substantial risk that the trial might be prejudiced. The leading case on s 2(2) is *Re Lonrho plc*,[129] an extraordinary case which arose out of a battle for control of the London department store, Harrods.

---

[123] See S Bailey (1982) 45 MLR 301.
[124] *R v Savundranayagan* [1968] 3 All ER 439; *R v Beaverbrook Newspapers Ltd* [1962] NI 15.
[125] *A-G v News Group Newspapers* [1989] QB 110. Cf *A-G v Sport Newspapers Ltd* [1991] 1 WLR 1194.
[126] On the question of appeals against sentence and 'misguided' press campaigns, see *R v Vano, The Times*, 29 December 1994.
[127] *Re Lonrho* [1990] 2 AC 154.
[128] *The Times*, 12 February 1983. See also *A-G v News Group Newspapers Ltd* [1986] 2 All ER 833; *A-G v ITN Ltd* [1995] 2 All ER 370; *A-G v BBC* [1997] EMLR 76; *A-G v MGN Ltd* [1997] 1 All ER 456 (no contempt where trial would not take place for several months and where already saturation coverage); *A-G v Birmingham Post and Mail Ltd* [1999] 1 WLR 361. For Scotland, see *Robb v Caledonian Newspapers Ltd* 1994 SCCR 659; *HM Advocate v Caledonian Newspapers Ltd* 1995 SCCR 330; *Cox and Griffiths, Petitioners* 1998 SCCR 561; *Al Megrahi v Times Newspapers Ltd* 1999 SCCR 824; *Galbraith v HM Advocate* 2000 SCCR 935.
[129] [1990] 2 AC 154.

In 1987 the Secretary of State for Trade and Industry appointed inspectors to investigate the affairs of the company which owned the store. The inspectors submitted their report in 1988, but the Secretary of State refused to publish it and he also refused to refer the matter to the Monopolies and Mergers Commission. Lonrho instituted two applications for judicial review, designed to compel the minister to publish the inspectors' report and to refer the matter to the Commission. While appeals on both applications were pending before the House of Lords, Lonrho acquired a copy of the inspectors' report, which the *Observer* agreed to publish in a special issue of the newspaper. Some copies of the issue were sent to persons on a mailing list to whom Lonrho had been regularly sending propaganda literature. These people included four of the five Lords of Appeal in Ordinary who were to hear the appeals. These circumstances were referred to three other members of the House of Lords. They held that the special issue (which contained extensive extracts from the inspectors' report as well as editorial comment accusing the Secretary of State of bad faith) did not create a substantial risk that the course of justice in Lonrho's appeals would be seriously impeded or prejudiced. 'So far as the appellate tribunal is concerned, it is difficult to visualise circumstances in which any court in the United Kingdom exercising appellate jurisdiction would be in the least likely to be influenced by public discussion of the merits of a decision appealed against or of the parties' conduct in the proceedings.'

A number of defences are provided in the 1981 Act. The first of these is the defence of innocent publication (s 3), where the person responsible for the publication can prove that, having taken all reasonable care, he or she did not know that relevant legal proceedings were active.[130] The second is the contemporary reporting of legal proceedings in respect of 'a fair and accurate report of legal proceedings held in public, published contemporaneously and in good faith' (s 4(1)). However, a court may order that publication of reports be delayed where necessary to avoid a substantial risk of prejudice to the administration of justice (s 4(2)).[131] 'In forming a view whether it is necessary to make an order for avoiding such a risk a court will inevitably have regard to the competing public interest considerations of ensuring a fair trial and of open justice.'[132] The power was used at the trial of Clive Ponting under the Official Secrets Act 1911 to prevent a television company from recreating the court proceedings as a drama documentary at the end of each day.[133] Before granting an order under s 4(2), the magistrates are entitled to hear representations from the press that the order should not be granted.[134] The third defence is where the publication contains a good faith discussion of public affairs if the risk of prejudice to particular legal proceedings is merely incidental to the discussion (s 5). In *Attorney-General* v *English* Lord Diplock noted that s 5 does not take the form of an exception to s 2, but stands on an equal footing with it: 'It does not set out exculpatory matter. Like s 2(2) it states what publications shall *not* amount to contempt of court despite their tendency to interfere with the course of justice in particular legal proceedings'.[135]

In *Attorney-General* v *English* the *Daily Mail* published an article in support of a woman standing for election to Parliament as an independent pro-life candidate, one of her aims being to stop the alleged practice in hospitals whereby newly-born handicapped babies were allowed to die. At the time the article was published a well-known paediatrician was standing trial, accused of murdering a three-day-old boy with Down's syndrome, by allowing him to die of

---

[130] See also *HM Advocate* v *Express Newspapers plc* 1998 SCCR 471.

[131] For the approach which the courts should adopt in such cases, see *MGN Pension Trustees Ltd* v *Bank of America* [1995] 2 All ER 355. On the right of appeal against an order issued under s 4(2), see Criminal Justice Act 1988, s 159. For Scotland, see *The Scottish Daily Record, Petitioner* 1998 SCCR 626.

[132] *Ex p The Telegraph plc* [1993] 2 All ER 971, at 975. See *R* v *Horsham Justices, ex p Farquharson* [1982] QB 762; M J Beloff [1992] PL 92.

[133] Ewing and Gearty, *Freedom under Thatcher*, p 145.

[134] *R* v *Clerkenwell Metropolitan Magistrate, ex p The Telegraph plc* [1993] QB 462.

[135] [1983] 1 AC 116, 141.

starvation. The House of Lords held that this did not amount to a contempt of court; although the publication of the article on the third day of the trial was capable of prejudicing the jury, the publication was a discussion in good faith on a matter of wide public interest and the risk of prejudice was incidental to the discussion. To hold otherwise 'would have prevented [the candidate] from . . . obtaining publicity for what was a main plank in her election programme and would have stifled all discussion in the press . . . about mercy killing from the time that [the doctor] was charged in the magistrates' court in February 1981 until the date of his acquittal [in] November of that year.'[136]

The strict liability rule does not apply to the good faith reporting of proceedings of the Scottish Parliament or Welsh Assembly.[137]

Other acts interfering with the course of justice

Nothing in the Contempt of Court Act 1981 is designed to restrict liability for contempt of court in respect of conduct intended to impede or prejudice the administration of justice (s 6(2)). Many other acts are punishable as contempts, some of them also being criminal offences in their own right, for example attempts to pervert the course of justice or interference with witnesses.[138] A prison governor who, acting under prison rules, obstructed a prisoner's communication with the High Court was held to be in contempt.[139] It is a contempt to punish or victimise a witness for evidence which has already been given, even in proceedings which have concluded, since this might deter potential witnesses in future cases.[140] It may be a contempt of court for a solicitor to disclose to a journalist documents relating to litigation.

> A prisoner challenged the legality of a Home Office decision to set up a 'control unit' for prisoners considered to be troublemakers. An order for discovery of documents being made against the Home Office, a large number of official documents were made available to the prisoner's solicitor. She undertook that the documents would be used only for the case in hand, but she later allowed a journalist to see documents which had been read out in open court. The journalist published an article based on these documents. The House of Lords held (by three to two) that although the documents had been read in court, and could have been reported by journalists present, the solicitor was guilty of contempt since she had used the documents for a purpose which was not necessary for the conduct of her client's case, and had broken her implied undertaking to the court that had ordered discovery.[141]

Interference with the work of a jury may constitute contempt, whether before, during or after a trial. By s 8 of the Contempt of Court Act 1981, it is a contempt of court to solicit, obtain or disclose details of any statements made or votes cast by jurors during their deliberations in any legal proceedings. This reversed a decision in 1980 that a magazine article disclosing aspects of the jury's deliberations during the trial of Mr Jeremy Thorpe was not a contempt of court.[142] It is an offence under s 8 for a newspaper to publish information disclosed to it by a jury member, but the section

---

[136] [1983] 1 AC 116, at 144 (Lord Diplock).
[137] Scotland Act 1998, s 42; and Government of Wales Act 1998, s 78.
[138] See *Peach Grey & Co v Sommers* [1995] 2 All ER 513.
[139] *Raymond v Honey* [1983] AC 1.
[140] *A-G v Butterworth* [1963] 1 QB 696; *Moore v Clerk of Assize, Bristol* [1973] 1 All ER 58.
[141] *Home Office v Harman* [1983] AC 280. Subsequent proceedings under the European Convention on Human Rights were the subject of a friendly settlement. In 1987 the decision was largely reversed by an amendment to the Rules of the Supreme Court, which released parties from any undertaking once the material has been read in open court. See *Apple Corp v Apple Computer Inc, The Times*, 10 April 1991, and now *Lilly Icos Ltd v Pfizer Ltd* [2002] 1 All ER 842.
[142] *A-G v New Statesman Publishing Co* [1981] QB 1.

applies only to 'what passes among the jurors while they are considering their verdict after the judge has directed them to retire to do so'.[143]

The dynamic nature of the law of contempt has been well demonstrated by decisions arising out of important disputes between the courts and the press. It is a contempt for a newspaper to disregard a judge's directions that the names of prosecution witnesses in blackmail cases should not be published.[144] But the power to issue such directions is not limited to blackmail cases.

> In *Attorney-General* v *Leveller Magazine Ltd* a magazine published the name of a prosecution witness at an official secrets trial, who had been described in court as Colonel B. The House of Lords held that it was contempt of court to publish a witness's name if this interfered with the administration of justice. But on the facts no contempt had occurred, since inter alia, no clear direction against publication had been given by the magistrates; and Colonel B's identity could have been discovered from evidence given in open court.[145]

The uncertainties left by this decision were lessened by the Contempt of Court Act 1981. By s 11, where a court has the power to withhold evidence from the public (although the court is sitting in public) and allows the name of a witness or other matter to be withheld, it may restrict publication accordingly.[146] Thus it would be a contempt of court to publish such information, even though the identity of the witness could be discovered from evidence given in open court, as in the *Leveller Magazine* case. However, a court cannot prohibit the press from reporting names which are mentioned in court unless there has first been a direction that these names should be withheld from the public.[147] And it has been said that the courts should be careful about exercising this power, which should not be used simply to protect privacy or avoid embarrassment.[148] This applies particularly where anonymity is sought by one of the parties to litigation rather than by a witness.[149]

It may also be contempt to publish material which has been the subject of an injunction against another party.[150] A third party who knowingly acts in breach of the terms of the injunction may be in contempt even though he or she is not a party to the proceedings and indeed may not have had an opportunity to make representations in these proceedings:

> In 1986 interlocutory injunctions were granted against two newspapers, the *Guardian* and the *Observer*, restraining them from publishing material from the book *Spycatcher*, by Mr Peter Wright, pending a full trial of the action in which the Attorney-General sought permanent injunctions on the ground that the information was confidential. While interlocutory injunctions were still in force, extensive extracts from the book were published in other newspapers, including the *Sunday Times*. The House of Lords held that these publications amounted to a contempt of court, even though the injunctions had not been issued against these newspapers in the first place. In the view of the House, where a party (C) knowingly does something which would if done by B be a breach of an injunction obtained by A against B, C is guilty of contempt of court if this conduct interferes with the administration of justice between A and B. In this case the publication by C (the *Sunday Times*) did interfere with proceedings between

---

[143] *Scottish Criminal Cases Review Commission, Petitioners*, 2001 SLT 1198, at p 1200, and *A-G* v *Associated Newspapers* [1994] 2 AC 238 respectively.

[144] *R* v *Socialist Worker Ltd, ex p A-G* [1975] QB 637. But magistrates cannot withhold their identity from the public or the press: *R* v *Felixstowe JJ, ex p Leigh* [1987] QB 582.

[145] [1979] AC 440.

[146] The exercise of this power is also governed by the *Practice Note* [1983] 1 All ER 64.

[147] *R* v *Arundel Justices, ex p Westminster Press* [1985] 2 All ER 390.

[148] *R* v *Westminster City Council, ex p Castelli, The Times*, 14 August 1995. Also *Trustor AB* v *Smallbone* [2000] 1 All ER 811.

[149] *R* v *Legal Aid Board, ex p Kaim Todner* [1999] QB 966.

[150] *A-G* v *Times Newspapers Ltd* [1992] 1 AC 191. See also *A-G* v *Observer* [1988] 1 All ER 385.

A (the Attorney-General) and B (the *Guardian* and the *Observer*). The consequence of the publication by the *Sunday Times* before the main *Spycatcher* trial was to nullify, in part at least, the purpose of such trial, because it put into the public domain part of the material which the Attorney-General claimed should remain confidential.

The principle in this case is sometimes referred to as the 'Spycatcher principle', for obvious reasons. The Court of Appeal has since been unwilling to accept that 'conduct by a third party which is inconsistent with a court order in only a trivial or technical way should expose a party to conviction for contempt'.[151] It has also been held that the publication by a third party of material which was already in the public domain was not a contempt and that the publication of fresh material would be a contempt only if the necessary *mens rea* could be established: this requires knowledge on the part of the defendant that the publication would interfere with the course of justice by defeating the purpose underlying the injunctions.[152]

> In *AG v Punch Ltd*[153] an injunction was granted to restrain Associated Newspapers Ltd (proprietors of the *Mail on Sunday*) from publishing any information obtained from Mr David Shaylor which was obtained by him in the course of or as a result of his employment in the security service. Mr Shaylor subsequently started to write a weekly column for *Punch*, the aim of the column being to criticise the performance of the security service. Following the publication of an article about an IRA bombing in London, the Attorney-General brought contempt proceedings against *Punch*. The Court of Appeal overturned the first instance decision that there had been a contempt, the appeal court accepting that the editor 'thought that the purpose of the [injunction] was to restrain material dangerous to national security' which it was not his intention to publish. The court also rejected the remarkable submission for the Attorney-General that no newspaper could knowingly publish any matter which fell within the wide terms of the injunction without first obtaining clearance from himself or the court. This would subject the press to the censorship of the Attorney-General and would extend the law of contempt beyond the principle that it is an offence intentionally to interfere with the course of justice.

Procedure in contempt cases

Many legal disputes are determined not by the civil and criminal courts but by administrative tribunals.[154] These bodies have no inherent power to deal with conduct which prejudices their proceedings, but the High Court has power to punish conduct that is in contempt of inferior courts.[155] Are tribunals to be classified as inferior courts for this purpose? In 1980 the House of Lords held that, despite its name, a local valuation court that hears appeals against rating valuations was not a court, since its functions were essentially administrative; it was thus not protected by the law of contempt.[156] The government's response to this decision was to propose that contempt of court be extended to all tribunals, but neither this nor a proposal to list tribunals for this purpose was accepted in Parliament.[157] The Contempt of Court Act 1981 thus does not deal with the matter, although s 19 defines 'court' as including 'any tribunal or body exercising the judicial power of the state'. The effect of this definition in the framework

---

[151] *A-G v Newspaper Publishing plc* [1997] 1 WLR 926 (Lord Bingham CJ). Also *Harrow LBC v Johnstone* [1997] 1 WLR 459.
[152] *A-G v Punch Ltd* [2001] QB 1028.
[153] Ibid.
[154] Ch 29 A.
[155] RSC Ord 52, r 1.
[156] *A-G v BBC* [1981] AC 303. See *Badry v DPP of Mauritius* [1982] 3 All ER 973 and N V Lowe and H F Rawlings [1982] PL 418.
[157] HL Deb, 9 February 1981, col 163; HC Deb, 16 June 1981, col 917. Cf Tribunals and Inquiries Act 1992, Sch 1.

of the Act is far from clear, though it has been held that a mental health review tribunal is a court for this purpose, and as a result its proceedings are subject to the law of contempt.[158] The same is true of employment tribunals which have 'many of the characteristics to which the authorities refer as being those of a court of law'.[159] But it has also been held that the Professional Conduct Committee of the General Medical Council is not part of the judicial system of the state, when exercising (with statutory sanction) 'the self-regulatory power and duty of the medical profession to monitor and maintain standards of professional conduct'.[160]

In English law contempt is treated as a common law misdemeanour. Unlike other crimes it may be dealt with by a superior court in summary proceedings and without a jury. An indictment before judge and jury is possible but unusual. Criminal contempts may be punished by a fine or by a prison sentence. A two-year prison sentence is now the maximum that may be imposed by a superior court.[161] Inferior courts may imprison for up to one month or impose a fine. All orders for committal must now be for a fixed term, but the court may order release at an earlier date.[162] While the superior courts need to be able to exercise summary powers, the normal safeguards of criminal process should not be absent from contempt proceedings. In 1960 a general right of appeal was provided in cases of criminal contempt[163] and legal aid became available in 1981.[164] In appropriate cases it may be possible to obtain an injunction to restrain a publication which creates a substantial risk of serious prejudice to the trial of the action.[165] For although the courts are rightly concerned to protect freedom of expression, they are equally anxious to protect the right to a fair trial. Prejudicial publicity may also lead to a conviction being quashed.[166]

The law of contempt of court serves the same broad purposes in both England and Scotland. But the law is distinct and there are many procedural differences. Thus Scots law does not recognise the distinction between civil and criminal contempts and the law of contempt is regarded as 'sui generis'.[167] The contempt jurisdiction may be exercised by the Court of Session, the High Court of Justiciary and the sheriff court. Reliance is placed for some purposes upon the residual authority, or nobile officium, of the Court of Session and the High Court, to whom a petition and complaint alleging a contempt may be presented with the consent of the Lord Advocate. Appeal lies either by normal channels of appeal or through a petition to the nobile officium. Before 1981 the law was more strictly applied in Scotland than in England[168] and it is perceived that the 1981 Act is more strictly construed in Scotland than England.[169] The Phillimore committee considered that the law applying to the press and broadcasting should be the same in the two jurisdictions; consequently the Contempt of Court Act 1981 for the most part applies both in England and Scotland, including the reforms in the strict liability rule discussed earlier.[170]

---

[158] *Pickering* v *Liverpool Daily Post plc* [1991] 2 AC 370.
[159] *Peach Grey and Co* v *Sommers* [1995] 2 All ER 513, at p 519.
[160] *General Medical Council* v *BBC* [1998] 1 WLR 1573.
[161] The county court ranks as a superior court for this purpose: County Courts (Penalties for Contempt) Act 1983, overruling *Peart* v *Stewart* [1983] 2 AC 109. On the principles applicable to sentencing, see *R* v *Montgomery* [1995] 2 All ER 28.
[162] See e.g. *Enfield BC* v *Mahoney* [1983] 2 All ER 901.
[163] Administration of Justice Act 1960, s 13. See *A-G* v *Hislop* [1991] 1 QB 514.
[164] Contempt of Court Act 1981, s 13.
[165] See *A-G* v *News Group Newspapers* [1987] QB 1.
[166] *R* v *McCann* (1991) 92 Cr App R 239. See also *R* v *Wood* [1996] 1 Cr App R 207.
[167] Gordon, *Criminal Law*, ch 51.
[168] E.g. *Stirling* v *Associated Newspapers Ltd* 1960 JC 5.
[169] On the position in Scotland, see the cases in note 131 above.
[170] See pp 381–4 above.

E. The executive and the machinery of justice[171]

The court system is part of the framework by which our society is governed and it cannot be totally separated from the executive. Such questions as what courts we should have, in what buildings they should be housed, and how the court system should be paid for, are questions that cannot be decided by the judges and the legal profession. Many countries have a Ministry of Justice to administer the court system. This was proposed for the United Kingdom in 1918 by the Haldane committee on the machinery of government,[172] but a Ministry of Justice by that name has never been established for England and Wales. Instead the duties that would fall to such a ministry are exercised principally by the Lord Chancellor and the Home Secretary. The conflicting responsibilities of the Lord Chancellor sometimes cause difficulties, as we shall see later. But it has been said that although the office is 'a difficult one', it is not easy 'to work out, against the background of our system, a good alternative that would protect . . . the independence of the judiciary'. Having the head of the judiciary accountable to Parliament for the administration of the courts is said by one Lord Chancellor to be 'probably as good an arrangement as we can achieve'.[173] Others have argued that the position is unsustainable and that the office should be abolished.[174] The position is different in Scotland, where there is now a Department of Justice in the Scottish Executive.

Role of the Lord Chancellor[175]

The Lord Chancellor is concerned with virtually all judicial appointments in England and Wales, appointing to the magistracy himself, formally advising the Crown on new circuit and High Court judges and informally advising the Prime Minister on the most senior judicial appointments. He is titular head of the Supreme Court; within the High Court, he is president of the Chancery Division, although the duties of this office are performed by the Vice-Chancellor. It is the responsibility of the Court Service – an executive agency of the Lord Chancellor's Department – to provide administrative support to the Court of Appeal, the High Court and the Crown Court, as well as the county courts. HM Magistrates' Courts Service Inspectorate reports to the Lord Chancellor on the administration and management of the Magistrates' Court Service, but not on the decisions of magistrates' courts. Other responsibilities of the Lord Chancellor include civil law reform (he appoints the members of the Law Commission);[176] legal services and criminal defence;[177] administrative tribunals; and the rules of procedure in the civil courts. Already described as 'increasingly powerful',[178] the responsibilities of the Lord Chancellor's Department were extended in 2001 formally to include human rights, freedom of information, data protection and constitutional reform; these previously had been the responsibility of the Home Office.[179]

---

[171] See Brazier, *Constitutional Practice*, ch 12.
[172] Cd 9230, 1918.
[173] HL Deb, 27 April 1994, col 804 (Lord Mackay). See also the comments by Lord Bingham, as reported in *The Times*, 17 July 2001.
[174] Woodhouse, *The Office of the Lord Chancellor*, p 212.
[175] See Haldane Report, Cd 9320, ch 10; Schuster (1949) 10 CLJ 175; Heuston, *Lives of the Lord Chancellors 1885–1940*; Spencer, *Jackson's Machinery of Justice*, pp 497–9. See also Stevens, *The Independence of the Judiciary, The View from the Lord Chancellor's Office*.
[176] Law Commissions Act 1965. There is a separate Scottish Law Commission.
[177] See now Access to Justice Act 1999.
[178] Cm 4534, 2000, para 9.11 (Royal Commission on the Reform of the House of Lords).
[179] See p 269 above.

The Lord Chancellor is also Speaker of the House of Lords (on which 'he spends a significant proportion of his time' and for which 14% of his salary is paid by the House of Lords)[180] and a member of the Cabinet (which together with his duties as head of the judiciary consumes most of his time). He has no greater security of tenure than any other minister, although the post is in fact less vulnerable to Cabinet reshuffles and Lord Chancellors tend to remain in post longer than other Cabinet ministers. The office is a bridge between the judicial and the political worlds. Despite its judicial responsibilities, the office must be classed as political, although some controversy was created in 2001 when the Lord Chancellor hosted a Labour party fund-raising dinner attended by lawyers. A previous political career is not an essential qualification, but (until the appointment of Lord Mackay of Clashfern in 1987) all modern Lord Chancellors have had extensive and successful experience of practice at the English bar; some before becoming Lord Chancellor have already held judicial appointments, others have been law officers of the Crown. Despite the heavy departmental duties of the Lord Chancellor, it was only in 1992 that a junior minister was appointed to his department, able to act for him if required in the House of Commons; there are now two parliamentary secretaries. When in 1979 the present scheme of select committees related to government departments was created by the Commons, neither the Lord Chancellor's department nor the Law Officers' departments were brought within it, although this would have been a valuable means of informing MPs about the problems of administering the system of justice.[181] In 1991 the government agreed to extend the select committee system to include the Lord Chancellor's and Law Officers' departments, but excluding individual cases and judicial appointments, the advice of the Law Officers to the government and prosecution policy.[182]

The Lord Chancellor and the separation of powers

The Lord Chancellor is entitled to preside over the House of Lords in its judicial work and the Judicial Committee of the Privy Council. Lord Mackay sat on 67 occasions (House of Lords and Privy Council) between 1987 and 1994, while Lord Hailsham sat 68 times as Lord Chancellor between 1979 and 1987.[183] This means that in the period between 1979 and 1994 the Lord Chancellor sat in only about one-tenth of cases in the House of Lords and Privy Council. Lord Irvine has also taken part in a number of cases.[184] Although their predecessors sat less frequently, it is thus the case that the Lord Chancellor sits only infrequently.[185] Questions nevertheless arise about whether it is appropriate that he should sit at all in view of his role as a member of the Cabinet. In response to concerns about the separation of powers, Lord Irvine claimed in 1998 that discretion is exercised in determining the cases in which the Lord Chancellor sits, 'as a safeguard against any perception of partiality or conflict of interest'.[186] But he refused to give an undertaking not to sit in cases where constitutional or political issues are involved or cases arising under the Human Rights Act 1998 and the devolution legislation.[187] However, where cases arise in which 'the government

---

[180] HL Deb, 20 October 1992, col 82 (WA).
[181] See ch 10 D; HC 588–1 (1977–78), p lv; and HC Deb, 25 June 1979, cols 118, 230. See also A W Bradley [1988] PL 163.
[182] HC Deb, 1 May 1991, col 183 (WA). See Woodhouse, pp 176–81.
[183] HL Deb, 24 October 1994, col 395 (WA). Also HL Deb, 20 October 1992, col 82 (WA).
[184] See for example *DPP* v *Jones* [1999] 2 AC 240 (ch 24); and *National Power plc* v *Carmichael* [1999] ICR 1227.
[185] Compare A Bradney, in Carmichael and Dickson (eds), *The House of Lords*, ch 8.
[186] HL Deb, 20 October 1998, WA 137.
[187] HL Deb, 20 October 1998, WA 137 and 138.

or a minister has an interest as a party litigant', he would not sit where it was 'inappropriate or improper to do so'.[188]

The role of the Lord Chancellor as judge was brought into sharp focus following the decision of the European Court of Human Rights in *McGonnell* v *United Kingdom*:[189]

> In that case it was held that the applicant was denied a fair trial under article 6 of the Convention in the determination of a planning appeal. The latter decision had been taken by the Bailiff, a judicial officer who also performed both legislative and judicial functions. In particular, the Bailiff who heard the appeal had also presided over the States of Deliberation when the development plan was adopted, 'the very act which was at issue' in the applicant's later appeal. These circumstances were held to give rise to enough doubt about the impartiality of the Bailiff as to constitute a breach of the Convention.

The implications of the case were not lost on critics of the dual role of the Lord Chancellor. However, it is not clear whether the *McGonnell* case has any practical implications for the work of the Lord Chancellor. The Court made clear that 'neither Article 6 nor any other provision of the Convention requires States to comply with any theoretical constitutional concepts as such' (such as the separation of powers) and 'the question is always whether, in a given case, the requirements of the Convention are met'. Responding to the decision, Lord Irvine said that he would 'never sit in any case concerning legislation in the passage of which he had been directly involved nor in any case where the interests of the executive were directly engaged'.[190] But not everyone is so sanguine: even if the Lord Chancellor does not sit as a judge, 'questions must be asked about a minister appointing judges who will hear cases against the Government'.[191]

The Lord Chancellor and judicial independence

In his Holdsworth Club address in 1950, Lord Justice Denning, as he then was, stoutly defended the independence of the judiciary, reminding his audience that: 'No member of the Government, no member of Parliament, and no official of any Government department has any right whatever to direct or influence or to interfere with the decisions of any of the judges.'[192] In a speech which repays reading to this day, he went on to say that the critical test which judges must pass 'if they are to receive the confidence of the people' is that 'they must be independent of the executive'. The difficulty, however, is that government criticism is unlikely to be publicly expressed (although this may happen), but is more likely to take more insidious forms of pressure which are unlikely to come to public attention. One such case, however, involved an exchange of correspondence between the President of the Employment Appeal Tribunal (Mr Justice Wood) and the Lord Chancellor in 1994. The details were disclosed in the *Observer*[193] newspaper and the matter was the subject of a robust article in the *New Law Journal*[194] by Sir Francis Purchas, who had recently retired from the Court of Appeal. The correspondence, which was deposited in the House of Lords library, tended to show that the Lord Chancellor had put pressure on the President to speed up the backlog of appeals and 'to ensure that public money is not wasted on preliminary hearings in cases where there is no point of law shown in the notice of appeal'. After consulting senior judicial colleagues, Sir John Wood replied in terms which Lord Mackay thought 'frankly disappointing'. Lord Mackay sought in turn an 'immediate assurance' that

---

[188] Ibid, WA 137.
[189] (2000) 30 EHRR 289.
[190] HL Deb, 23 February 2000, WA 34.
[191] Woodhouse, p 212.
[192] Denning, 'The Independence of the Judges', in Harvey (ed), *The Lawyer and Justice*, p 53, at p 57.
[193] *The Observer*, 6 March 1994.
[194] 'The Constitution, Lord Mackay and the Judges', 22 April 1994.

preliminary hearings would not be used where 'no jurisdiction is shown in a notice of appeal', the letter concluding 'If you do not feel that you can give me that assurance, I must ask you to consider your position'. The matter was raised in a House of Lords debate,[195] in the course of which several speakers not only defended the propriety of Sir John Wood's interpretation of his legal responsibilities, but also criticised the Lord Chancellor for the manner of his intervention.

The debate in the House of Lords raised important questions about the relationship between the executive (in the form of the Lord Chancellor) and the judges and indeed also about the relationship between judges. In the first place, it highlights the practical problems caused by the anomalous position occupied by the office of Lord Chancellor ('a standing violation of the pure constitutional doctrine of the separation of public powers'). Thus as Lord Lester of Herne Hill pointed out, the Lord Chancellor will command the confidence of his judicial colleagues only if he 'will protect the judges' independence from any improper interference'; but he will enjoy the confidence of his political colleagues only by giving effect to 'the government's political programme while remaining democratically responsible to Parliament, administratively as well as financially, for the proper functioning of the courts and the proper performance by the judges of their duties'. There can be no doubt, however, that in the hierarchy of obligations it is the former which must prevail, and must be defended if government is to be conducted according to the law. In this affair a number of senior judges expressed strongly the view that the Lord Chancellor had applied pressure to a judge in an 'unconstitutional way'. Lord Oliver thought the matter to be one of 'very grave public concern', on the ground that, 'the pressure which was applied in this case, for whatever reason, constituted an attempt by the Executive – no doubt in the praiseworthy interests of economy and expedition – to overbear the conscience of a judge in the way in which he was to exercise his judicial duty and his judicial discretion.' For his part, however, the Lord Chancellor denied that his conduct was in any way 'prejudicial to the proper independence of the judge', although he regretted not having expressed himself more plainly.

The Law Officers of the Crown[196]

The Law Officers of the Crown in respect of England and Wales are the Attorney-General and Solicitor-General. Their historic role is to represent the Crown in the courts. They now act as legal advisers to the government on important matters which cannot be left to the lawyers in the civil service who advise the departments on day-to-day matters. The Treasury Solicitor's Department – an executive agency responsible to the Law Officers – provides litigation services and legal advice to government departments. The English Law Officers are today invariably members of either the House of Commons or the House of Lords, and are usually also members of the English bar; as ministers they support the government of the day. Their duties require them to fill a wide variety of roles, which include leading for the Crown in major prosecutions (especially in trials involving state security) or in major civil actions to which the Crown is a party. They are assisted by junior counsel to the Treasury, who are practising barristers and hold no political office. Representing the Crown, the Law Officers take part in many judicial or quasi-judicial proceedings relating to the public interest, such as statutory tribunals of inquiry[197] and contempt of court proceedings.[198] The Attorney-General's consent is

---

[195] HL Deb, 27 April 1994, cols 751–804.
[196] Edwards, *The Law Officers of the Crown* and *The Attorney-General, Politics and the Public Interest*.
[197] Ch 29 C.
[198] Section D above.

needed for relator actions: his decisions granting or refusing consent are not subject to review by the courts.[199]

The Law Officers also have parliamentary responsibilities, helping to see legal and fiscal Bills through the Commons and giving advice to the Committee on Privileges and Standards. The Attorney-General is leader of the English bar. He has sometimes been a member of the Cabinet but in view of his duties in connection with prosecutions, it is regarded as preferable that he should remain outside the Cabinet as the government's chief legal adviser, attending particular Cabinet meetings only when summoned. Many Law Officers receive further advancement to judicial or political posts, but today the Attorney-General has no claim to become Lord Chief Justice when a vacancy in that office occurs: the development of any such claim was effectively stifled by the disastrous elevation of Sir Gordon Hewart as Lord Chief Justice in 1922.[200] In 1974 the Labour Law Officers declined the knighthoods that have customarily gone with their jobs.[201] Where a Law Officer has given advice to a minister on a matter on which the minister has subsequently acted, the opinion is treated as confidential and not laid before Parliament or quoted from in debate; but if a minister considers it expedient to do so, he or she may make the advice known to Parliament and there is no absolute rule of confidentiality.[202]

The machinery of justice in Scotland

The procedures relating to the machinery of justice in Scotland were transformed by the Scotland Act 1998. The Scottish Parliament has responsibility for such matters and within the Scottish Executive they are administered by the Justice Department which deals with a range of matters: these include the police, criminal justice and the early release of offenders, civil law (such as family law), courts administration, legal aid, liaison with the legal profession and electoral procedures (including the registration of electors). The Justice Department also plays a part in judicial appointments (other than to the District Court), and provides a base for two executive agencies – the Scottish Court Service and the Scottish Prison Service. The Minister of Justice is responsible to the Scottish Parliament for the affairs of the department. The Scottish Courts Service is an executive agency within the Justice Department responsible for providing and maintaining the court houses and 'for ensuring the supply of well-trained staff and of administrative and organisational services', to support the Scottish judges, including sheriffs.[203] Also located in the Justice Department is the Central Advisory Committee on Justices of the Peace (Scotland), to advise about problems relating to the appointment and distribution of justices of the peace. The Scottish Law Commission is classified as an advisory non-departmental public body.

The law officers for Scotland are the Lord Advocate and the Solicitor-General for Scotland. They represent the Crown's interests before the Scottish courts, advise the Scottish executive on legal matters, and control public prosecutions in Scotland. Before devolution both the Lord Advocate and the Solicitor-General were ministers in the United Kingdom government and as such the Lord Advocate at least would normally be a member of the Westminster Parliament (if necessary by means of a

---

[199] *Gouriet* v *Union of Post Office Workers* [1978] AC 435; chs 12 E and 31.

[200] Edwards, *The Law Officers of the Crown*, ch 15.

[201] Cf Edwards, ibid, pp 282–5.

[202] Erskine May, p 389; Edwards, ibid, pp 256–61. In the Westland affair in 1985–6, a Cabinet minister resigned because he had authorised civil servants to leak to the media a confidential letter of advice from the Solicitor-General to other ministers.

[203] Convery, *The Governance of Scotland*, p 333.

peerage).[204] Under the Scotland Act 1998, however, the Scottish Law Officers are now members of the Scottish Executive and as such are appointed and may be removed by the Queen on the recommendation of the First Minister, whose recommendation must have the prior agreement of the Scottish Parliament.[205] The Lord Advocate at the time of writing is not a member of the Scottish Parliament. The Scotland Act 1998 created a new position in the United Kingdom government to fill some of the space left by the transfer of the Lord Advocate and the Solicitor-General for Scotland. The function of the Advocate General for Scotland is to advise the United Kingdom government on questions of Scots law. There are no statutory qualifications for appointment to the office and although the first holder of the office was a Member of Parliament this is not required by law.[206]

F. Prosecution of offenders and miscarriages of justice

In principle, private persons may institute prosecutions in English law for any criminal offence unless by statute this has been excluded.[207] In practice, the great majority of criminal prosecutions are initiated by the police; others are instituted by government departments (for example, revenue departments for evasion of tax) or local authorities (for example, for breach of byelaws). Certain prosecutions may by statute be instituted only with the consent of the Attorney-General, for example, for certain offences against the state or public order, under the Official Secrets Acts 1911–89 or the Public Order Act 1986 and for obscenity in dramatic productions under the Theatres Act 1968. The position regarding criminal prosecutions in England and Wales was overhauled by the Prosecution of Offences Act 1985, which introduced a public prosecution service.[208] The philosophy of the Act was 'to separate the functions of the investigation of crime, that being the responsibility of the police, and the prosecution of offences, that being the prosecution of a single national prosecution service'.[209] The position is very different in Scotland where prosecutions are under the control of the Lord Advocate and where private prosecutions are extremely rare.[210]

The Crown Prosecution Service

The Crown Prosecution Service, 'an autonomous and independent agency' though 'not a body corporate but a collection of individuals with statutory functions to perform',[211] is under the central direction of the Director of Public Prosecutions, an office created in 1879. Until 1983 the DPP, a barrister or solicitor of not fewer than ten years' standing, was appointed by the Home Secretary, but is now appointed by the Attorney-General to work under his general supervision. Apart from the DPP, other key personnel in the Crown Prosecution Service are the Chief Crown Prosecutors (appointed by the DPP to supervise the work of the CPS in geographical areas) and

---

[204] For difficulties of the first Labour government, see J P Casey (1975) 26 NILQ 18.

[205] Scotland Act 1998, s 48. On the Lord Advocate's obligations and the Human Rights Act, see *Montgomery v HM Advocate* 2001 SC (PC) 1.

[206] See generally Convery, pp 301–3; and Scotland Act 1998, s 87.

[207] For the procedural rights of a private prosecutor, see *R v George Maxwell (Developments) Ltd* [1980] 2 All ER 99; *R v DPP, ex p Hallas* (1988) 87 Cr App Rep 340.

[208] See Report of Royal Commission on Criminal Procedure, Cmnd 8092, 1981, part II.

[209] *Elguzouli-Daf v Metropolitan Police Commissioner* [1995] QB 335, at p 346.

[210] See Renton and Brown, *Criminal Procedure in Scotland*, paras 3.09–3.15.

[211] *Elguzouli-Daf*, at pp 346, 351. On the work of the CPS, see HC 193-i (1993–94). See also HC 425 (1995–96). See now Crown Prosecution Service Inspectorate Act 2000 (Chief Inspector of CPS to be appointed by Attorney-General).

Crown Prosecutors (barristers or solicitors who conduct proceedings under the direction of the DPP). Perhaps surprisingly, the dismissal of a Crown Prosecutor from his or her employment is not normally subject to judicial review.[212] The Prosecution of Offences Act 1985 requires the DPP to issue a Code for Crown Prosecutors.[213] This makes it clear that there is no duty to bring criminal proceedings against a person suspected of having committed an offence:[214] the general rule is that proceedings will be brought only when (a) there is enough evidence to provide a realistic prospect of conviction, and (b) it is in the public interest to prosecute; the Code gives guidance on the factors to be weighed in making this judgment.[215] A decision not to prosecute is subject to judicial review,[216] although the power is 'sparingly exercised' in such cases.[217] Where it is decided not to proceed against a police officer following the death of a person in custody, reasons for not doing so should normally be given.[218] But although there is no duty to prosecute in every case, equally the DPP does not have the power to grant an immunity from prosecution: 'The power to dispense with and suspend laws and the execution of laws without the consent of Parliament was denied to the Crown and its servants by the Bill of Rights 1688.'[219]

The CPS reviews police decisions to prosecute and conducts prosecutions on behalf of the Crown. The Service also institutes proceedings in difficult or important cases and gives advice to the police on all matters relating to criminal offences. Although the CPS is under a duty to take over all legal proceedings instituted by the police, it is not required to but may take over proceedings begun by others (such as private prosecutions). Having taken over such proceedings the CPS may discontinue them if the evidence is insufficient, if the proceedings would be contrary to the public interest, to avoid duplication, or for any other good reason.[220] If it is too late to discontinue, the prosecutor may offer no evidence, so that an acquittal automatically follows. The Attorney-General may, however, exercise the prerogative power to stop a prosecution on indictment by issuing a nolle prosequi.[221] This power is rarely used today: abuse of the power would be subject to criticism in Parliament, but may not be reviewed by the courts. The Attorney-General, and through him the DPP, are accountable to Parliament for what they do in relation to criminal proceedings. It has been said that the 1985 Act creates 'a coherent and consistent framework in which the right of the private citizen to bring a prosecution is preserved but subject always to the Director's right to intervene at any stage'. The Act thereby 'provides a useful and effective safeguard' against the danger of any 'improper inaction'.[222] The Director's decision to intervene (or not) is subject to judicial review.[223]

---

[212] R v Crown Prosecution Service, ex p Hogg, The Times, 14 April 1994.

[213] www.cps.gov.uk. The DPP may also have the power to make a public statement on his or her prosecuting policy other than in the Code for Crown Prosecutors: R (Pretty) v DPP [2002] 1 All ER 1, at p 21. The Lord Advocate exercises such a power in Scotland: ibid, esp Lord Hope at pp 34–5.

[214] As explained by Hartley Shawcross QC when Attorney-General: 'It has never been the rule in this country – I hope it never will be – that suspected criminal offences must automatically be the subject of prosecution' (HC Deb, 29 January 1951, col 681).

[215] The Code for Crown Prosecutors, para 6.

[216] R v DPP, ex p C [1995] 1 Cr App R 136. But the decision to prosecute is not, 'absent dishonesty, mala fides or an exceptional circumstance': R (Pretty) v DPP [2002] 1 All ER 1, at p 31; applying R v DPP, ex p Kebeline [2000] 2 AC 326.

[217] R v DPP, ex p Manning [2001] QB 330, at p 343.

[218] Ibid. See also Inquiry into Crown Prosecution Service Decision-Making in Relation to Deaths in Custody and Related Matters (Report by His Hon Gerald Butler QC, 1999).

[219] R (Pretty) v DPP [2002] 1 All ER 1, at p 21 (Lord Bingham).

[220] See R v DPP, ex p Duckenfield [2000] 1 WLR 55.

[221] For examples of its use in relation to customs prosecutions (where the Attorney-General had no duty of superintendence), see HC 115 (1995–96) (Scott Report), para C 3.10.

[222] R v Bow Street Magistrate, ex p South Coast Shipping [1993] 1 All ER 219, at p 222.

[223] DPP v Duckenfield, above note 220.

The Attorney-General

In the case of prosecutions instituted by the DPP or the Attorney-General, what political control is there over the discretion that may have been exercised? Can the Prime Minister or the Cabinet control or influence the Attorney-General's decision? What is the Attorney-General's responsibility to Parliament for prosecution decisions? These questions were raised by the Campbell case in 1924, which brought down the first Labour government.[224] In brief, the Attorney-General, Sir Patrick Hastings, who was experienced in advocacy but not in ministerial work, authorised the prosecution of J R Campbell, acting editor of a Communist weekly, for having published an article which apparently sought to seduce members of the Armed Forces from their allegiance to the Crown. A few days later, the prosecution was withdrawn in circumstances which suggested that improper political pressure had been brought to bear on the Attorney-General. The true facts are not easy to establish but the Cabinet minutes record a decision by the Cabinet on 6 August 1924 that '*no public prosecution of a political character should be undertaken without the prior sanction of the Cabinet being obtained*'; the Cabinet also agreed to adopt the course indicated by the Attorney-General, i.e. to withdraw the Campbell prosecution.[225]

Whatever the faults of the different actors in the Campbell affair (and the precedents were less clear than the critics of the Labour government stated) there can be no doubt that the Cabinet decision in the words italicised was asserting a right to interfere in prosecuting decisions which was constitutionally improper, as well as being seriously vague.[226] The decision was promptly rescinded by the next Cabinet. The present doctrine is something like this: the Attorney-General is required to take his own prosecuting decisions and must not receive directions from the Cabinet or any ministerial colleague; in his decisions he must not be influenced by considerations of party advantage or disadvantage; but if he considers that a particular case involves wider questions of public interest or state policy, he may seek information from ministerial colleagues and also their opinions.[227] It is not possible to know whether it is present-day practice for such information or opinions to be sought at meetings of the Cabinet, but this seems unlikely. Since current practice emphasises that the Attorney-General must make his decisions personally, it follows that he bears personal responsibility to Parliament for these decisions; and that there is no collective responsibility for his decisions, except to the extent that the Prime Minister could be criticised for allowing an incompetent Attorney-General to remain in office. It is in order for questions to be asked in the Commons about particular decisions made by the Attorney-General: how much information the Attorney-General gives in reply is a matter for his own discretion.[228]

Accountability of the Crown Prosecution Service

The creation of the Crown Prosecution Service in 1988 brought into prominence both the scope for central influence over the criminal justice system, which had previously

---

[224] Edwards, *Law Officers of the Crown*, chs 10 and 11; Edwards, *The Attorney-General, Politics and the Public Interest*, pp 310–17; F H Newark (1969) 20 NILQ 19; Ewing and Gearty, *The Struggle for Civil Liberties*, ch 3. For the censure debate, see HC Deb, 8 October 1924, col 581.

[225] Ewing and Gearty, *The Struggle for Civil Liberties*, ch 3, for a full account of this episode.

[226] What *is* a public prosecution of a political character? It might refer to (*a*) prosecution of a politician for an ordinary criminal offence, (*b*) prosecution of a politician for offences related to political activities, e.g. corruption or election offences, (*c*) prosecution of an individual for political beliefs, (*d*) prosecution for criminal conduct committed in the course of a strike or political demonstration, (*e*) prosecution for offences against the security of the state, etc.

[227] See the Shawcross statement in the debate on the gas strikers, HC Deb, 29 January 1951, col 681; and HC Deb, 16 February 1959, col 31. See also p 394 above.

[228] Cf Edwards, *Law Officers of the Crown*, p 261.

been exercised without publicity,[229] and the question of accountability for the abuse of power by public prosecutors. It is true that 'by convention the Attorney-General is answerable to Parliament for general prosecution policy and for specific cases where the Attorney-General and the Director of Public Prosecutions intervenes'. But, as has been pointed out, 'Parliament can usually only call the Attorney-General to account after a prosecution has run its course.'[230] And Parliament will not give directions to the Attorney-General. The House of Commons thus has no effective machinery for ensuring due accountability to the House for the Attorney-General's decisions, the assumption being that both he and the DPP should be free from extraneous political interference in their work. So far as accountability to the courts is concerned, the scope for judicial review appears to be very limited, although there may be remedies in private law for malicious prosecution or misfeasance in public office. The CPS will not, however, normally be liable in negligence, as in one case where the plaintiff had been detained for 85 days before proceedings were discontinued, the plaintiff alleging that it should not have taken this long to conclude that the case against him was bound to fail. Although it was 'always tempting to yield to an argument based on the protection of civil liberties', the Court of Appeal concluded on contestable grounds that 'the interests of the whole community are better served by not imposing a duty of care on the CPS'.[231]

However, it may not always be possible for prosecutors to escape detailed scrutiny. The role of the Attorney-General in the Matrix Churchill affair was closely reviewed and sharply criticised by Sir Richard Scott's inquiry into the export of arms for Iraq. Sir Richard found in his report that the decision to prosecute three executives of the company was taken by the Commissioners of Customs and Excise following the advice of Treasury counsel. In this decision the Attorney-General was not consulted and indeed he was not necessarily or usually kept informed of important Customs prosecutions, having no duty of superintendence of such prosecutions, although he did have 'an overall purview of prosecutions brought by the Crown by any authority'. His position was called into question nevertheless, as a result of his conduct in relation to public interest immunity (PII) certificates dealing with the development of government policies over exports to Iraq, the granting of export licences to Matrix Churchill and other companies and certain security operations. Although a number of ministers had signed such certificates, the President of the Board of Trade (Mr Heseltine) refused to do so, on the ground that the interests of justice required the disclosure of many of the documents in question. Yet although he had not read them, the Attorney-General informed Mr Heseltine that he was under a duty to sign the certificates (as a result of the case-law)[232] but that his reservations could be put to the judge. In the event Mr Heseltine's reservations were not even disclosed to the prosecution legal team, despite the fact that Mr Heseltine's position was well known in government, an omission which drew a strong rebuke from Sir Richard Scott. Sir Richard also repudiated the belief of the Attorney-General that he was personally as opposed to constitutionally blameless for the inadequacy of the instructions sent to prosecuting counsel, in relation particularly to the position of Mr Heseltine.[233]

---

[229] See the controversy over jury-vetting in 1978–80: HC Deb, 1 August 1980, col 1929. M D A Freeman [1981] CLP 650; Harman and Griffith, *Justice Deserted*. Also *Practice Note* [1980] 3 All ER 785.

[230] *Elguzouli-Daf* v *Metropolitan Police Commissioner* [1995] QB 335, at p 346.

[231] Ibid at p 349. See also *Olotu* v *Home Office* [1997] 1 WLR 328.

[232] *Makanjuola* v *Metropolitan Police Commissioner* [1992] 3 All ER 617. On the law of public interest immunity, see ch 32 C and especially *R* v *Chief Constable of the West Midlands Police, ex p Wiley* [1995] 1 AC 274, where the House of Lords over-ruled *Makanjuola*. Compare HC 115 (1995–96) (Scott Report), para G 59.

[233] See further A W Bradley [1996] PL 373.

Miscarriages of justice

One of the most regrettable features of the criminal justice system in the 1970s and 1980s was the number of miscarriages of justice, particularly the number of people who were wrongly convicted for offences which they did not commit.[234] Some of these cases arose out of terrorist incidents, most notably the pub bombings at Guildford and Birmingham in 1974,[235] although there were many other cases unrelated to acts of terrorism, including that of the so-called 'Bridgewater 3'.[236] A number of different factors were responsible for these events, not the least significant of which were the serious shortcomings of the police and the prosecuting authorities.[237] The matter was reviewed by the Royal Commission on Criminal Justice appointed in 1991 with terms of reference which included 'whether changes were needed in the arrangements for considering and investigating allegations of miscarriages of justice when appeal rights have been exhausted'.[238] The procedures then in force were governed by the Criminal Appeal Act 1968, s 17, which authorised a reference to the Court of Appeal by the Home Secretary. Although this provided 'the mechanism for unlocking the door back to the criminal justice system',[239] the royal commission pointed out that the Home Secretary and the civil servants advising him operated within 'strict self-imposed limits', which rested 'both upon constitutional considerations and upon the approach of the Court of Appeal itself to its own powers'. The Home Secretary would not refer cases to the Court of Appeal merely to enable it to reconsider matters that it had already considered, but would 'normally only refer a conviction if there is new evidence or some other consideration of substance which was not before the trial court'. The Home Office adopted this approach 'not only because they have thought that it would be wrong for Ministers to suggest to the Court of Appeal that a different decision should have been reached by the courts on the same facts', but also because there was 'no purpose' in referring a case where there was 'no real possibility of the Court of Appeal taking a different view than it did on the original appeal because of the lack of fresh evidence or some other new consideration of substance'.[240]

These arrangements were criticised both by Sir John May (who had been asked to inquire into the cases of the Guildford Four and the Maguire Seven)[241] and by the Royal Commission on Criminal Justice[242] and a new procedure was proposed for the referral of cases. This would require the creation of a new body, independent of both the government and the courts, for dealing with allegations that a miscarriage of justice had occurred, reflecting concern that the Home Secretary should not be 'directly responsible for the consideration and investigation of alleged miscarriages of justice as well as being responsible for law and order and for the police'.[243] The Criminal Appeal Act 1995 addresses the incompatibility of these procedures 'with the constitutional

---

[234] For a wider definition of the term, see HC 419 (1993–94). For a detailed examination of miscarriages of justice, see Nobles and Schiff, *Understanding Miscarriages of Justice*. See also Whitty et al., *Civil Liberties Law*, ch 3.

[235] See *R v Richardson, The Times*, 20 October 1989; *R v McIlkenny* [1992] 2 All ER 417; *R v Maguire* [1992] QB 936. And note the case of Judith Ward: *R v Ward* [1993] 1 WLR 619.

[236] See *The Times*, 21–22 February 1997.

[237] See on specific aspects, I H Dennis [1993] PL 291.

[238] Cm 2263, 1993.

[239] *R v Home Secretary, ex p Hickey (No 2)* [1995] 1 All ER 490, at p 494.

[240] Cm 2263, 1993, pp 181–2. The propriety of this approach was called into question in *R v Home Secretary, ex p Hickey (No 2)* [1995] 1 All ER 490 where it was suggested that the Secretary of State should ask another question: could the new material reasonably cause the Court of Appeal to regard the verdict as unsafe? If it could, the matter should then have been referred without more ado.

[241] HC 296 (1992), pp 93–4.

[242] Cm 2263, 1993, pp 181–2.

[243] Ibid, p 182.

separation of powers as between the courts and the executive',[244] and makes provision for the appointment by the Queen (on the advice of the Prime Minister) of a Criminal Cases Review Commission (s 9). The Commission is empowered to refer to the Court of Appeal (following the conviction of an offence on indictment) any conviction or sentence where it considers that 'there is a real possibility that the conviction, verdict, finding or sentence would not be upheld were the reference to be made' (s 13): this is a 'judgment entrusted to the Commission and to no one else'.[245] The Act also introduces for the first time a power (on the part of the Commission) to refer convictions or sentences arising from cases tried summarily (s 11), in this case to the Crown Court, subject to the same conditions as apply in the case of references to the Court of Appeal following a conviction on indictment. The Commission has wide powers to obtain documents and to appoint investigating officers to carry out inquiries in relation to a case under review, although these will generally be carried out by the police rather than by the Commission's own officers (ss 17–20).[246]

It has been said that a miscarriage of justice by which a man or woman has lost his or her liberty is one of the gravest matters which can occupy the attention of a civilised society.[247] Although it is important that a procedure should exist to enable such miscarriages to be rectified when they do occur, it is also important that they do not happen in the first place. It is expected that the many changes of police procedure introduced since the Police and Criminal Evidence Act 1984 will go a long way towards preventing such incidents,[248] although it is to be noted that not all cases that gave rise to concern, including that of Stefan Kiszko, occurred before the implementation of the Act and its related codes of practice. It is also the case that 'a number of safeguards provided by PACE [i.e. the 1984 Act] in the interests of fairness are denied in terrorist cases',[249] which, as already noted, have contributed significantly to the number of miscarriages of justice.[250] Yet apart from seeking to prevent miscarriages of justice, it is clearly important to ensure that victims are properly compensated, to the extent that this is possible, for their loss of liberty. The Criminal Justice Act 1988, s 133, applies where a conviction has been reversed on a reference under the Criminal Appeal Act 1995 or a convicted person has been pardoned 'on the ground that a new or newly discovered fact shows beyond reasonable doubt that there has been a miscarriage of justice'.[251] In such cases the Home Secretary must pay compensation to the person concerned or his or her personal representative, the amount to be determined by an assessor appointed by the minister.[252] But it is often complained that there is excessive delay in making payments.

---

[244] Ibid. And see HC Deb, 6 March 1995, col 32.

[245] *R v Criminal Cases Review Commission, ex p Pearson* [1999] 3 All ER 498, at p 505. For concerns that the Commission may be applying the test too strictly, see HC 106 (1998–99), para 30. For clarification of the powers of the Commission, see Criminal Cases Review (Insanity) Act 1999.

[246] Leading cases include *R v Bentley* [2001] 1 Cr App R 307; *R v Johnson* [2001] 1 Cr App R 408; and *R v Kansal* [2001] 3 WLR 1562. For similar, although not identical provisions in Scotland, see *Scottish Criminal Cases Review Commission, Petitioners*, 2001 SLT 1198.

[247] See also *R v Criminal Cases Review Commission, ex p Pearson* [1999] 3 All ER 498, at p 502 (Lord Bingham).

[248] See also HC 449 (1993–94).

[249] Ibid, p 300.

[250] 'If all the safeguards of PACE are necessary to avoid miscarriages of justice then it must be recognised that in terrorist cases greater risks of injustice are accepted than in the ordinary course of criminal cases', ibid, p 300.

[251] Cf *Maharaj v A-G of Trinidad (No 2)* [1979] AC 385 (right to compensation for judicial error derived from constitutional guarantee of remedy for infringement of fundamental rights).

[252] See now Criminal Appeal Act 1995, s 28.

The prerogative of pardon[253]

The royal prerogative of pardon is exercised by the Crown on the advice of the Home Secretary in cases from England and Wales and, in cases from Scotland, by the Scottish ministers. Each minister acts on his individual responsibility in giving his advice to the Crown. A royal pardon could in law be used as a bar to criminal prosecution being brought (as was the effect of the blanket pardon given by President Ford to ex-President Nixon in 1974). But in British practice, a pardon is granted only after conviction when there is some special reason why a sentence should not be carried out or why the effects of a conviction should be expunged. Now that the right of an appeal in criminal cases is recognised, a pardon is not normally granted in respect of matters that could be raised on an appeal. Pardons under the prerogative are of three kinds: (*a*) an absolute or free pardon, which sets aside the sentence but not the conviction;[254] (*b*) a conditional pardon, which substitutes one form of punishment for another (for example, the substitution of life imprisonment for the death penalty, which occurred when the prerogative of mercy was exercised in the days of capital punishment);[255] and (*c*) a remission, which reduces the amount of a sentence without changing its character and has been used to enable a convicted spy to be exchanged for a British subject imprisoned abroad or to reward prisoners who have given exceptional assistance to prison staff, the police or the prosecuting authorities.

The prerogative power of pardon may not be used to vary the judgment of the court in matters of civil dispute between citizens. Under the Act of Settlement 1700, a pardon may not be pleaded in bar of an impeachment by the Commons, nor under the Habeas Corpus Act 1679 may the unlawful committal of any person to prison outside the realm be pardoned. Extensive use of the power of pardon could come close to being an attempt to exercise the royal power to dispense with laws which was declared illegal in the Bill of Rights 1689. The Home Secretary is answerable to Parliament for the advice which he or she gives to the Queen. Before the abolition of the death penalty, questions could not be raised in the House of Commons regarding a case while it was still pending.[256] The question arises whether the power of pardon is now needed following the reforms introduced by the Criminal Appeal Act 1995. In the view of the government, however, it is thought still to be necessary but only for 'the very exceptional case' where there is new evidence which for some reason is inadmissible.[257] In these cases the Home Secretary may refer to the Criminal Cases Review Commission 'any matter which arises in the consideration of whether to recommend the exercise of Her Majesty's prerogative of mercy in relation to the conviction' (s 16). The Commission is required to give reasons where it is of the opinion that the minister should recommend the exercise of the prerogative, but strangely is not required to do so where it makes no such recommendation, even though it is in the latter type of case that the need for judicial review is likely to be greater.[258]

---

[253] See A T H Smith [1983] PL 398; also the report 'Miscarriages of Justice', HC 421 (1981–82) and, for the position in Scots law, C H W Gane 1980 JR 18.

[254] *R v Foster* [1985] QB 115.

[255] P Brett (1957) 20 MLR 131.

[256] G Marshall [1961] PL 8.

[257] HC Deb, 6 March 1995, col 26.

[258] See *R v Home Secretary, ex p Bentley* [1994] QB 349. See, further, ch 12 E.

Part III

THE CITIZEN AND THE STATE

Chapter 19

THE NATURE AND PROTECTION
OF HUMAN RIGHTS

This chapter is concerned with the protection of human rights. The first task is to determine what is meant by human rights: there is a great deal of terminological inconsistency in this area, with a number of terms frequently used – human rights, civil liberties, fundamental rights – often referring to the same thing. For our purposes, human rights take two forms. On the one hand, there are social and economic rights – the right to employment, health care, housing and income maintenance during periods of ill-health, unemployment or old age. On the other hand, there are the classical civil and political rights – the right to liberty of the person, the right to form political parties and to participate in elections, and the rights to freedom of conscience, religion and expression. Traditionally, human rights lawyers have confined their concerns to this latter category, to the exclusion of the former even though social and economic security are indispensable to effective participation in the civil and political life of the community. Yet although there are several international treaties promoting social and economic security,[1] the boldness of their aspirations is generally matched only by the difficulties in their enforcement, while few democracies in the common law tradition take them seriously as fundamental rights. The position is different with regard to so-called civil and political rights. One international treaty in particular – the European Convention on Human Rights[2] – has had a significant influence on British law and practice, with the British government having been held in violation of its terms on an increasing number of occasions and having introduced legislation on several occasions to give effect to rulings of the European Court of Human Rights.[3] Many countries give constitutional protection to civil and political rights, often in a Bill of Rights with which in some cases both executive and legislative measures must comply, failing which they may be struck down by the courts. Legal protection of human rights in Britain is now to be found in the Human Rights Act 1998 which enables the Convention rights to be enforced in the British Courts.[4]

---

[1] These include the Conventions of the International Labour Organisation, a United Nations agency based in Geneva, set up to promote the interests of working people. Also important is the Council of Europe's Social Charter of 1961 and the Revised Social Charter of 1996, while the EC Charter of the Fundamental Social Rights of Workers of 1989 has contributed to the development of social law. There is also the EU Charter of Fundamental Rights, adopted at Nice in December 2000. See ch 8 above. On the Council of Europe's Social Charter, see Harris and Darcy, *The European Social Charter*. On the EC Charter, see Bercusson, *European Labour Law*.

[2] Cmd 8969, 1953.

[3] See A W Bradley, 'The United Kingdom before the Strasbourg Court 1975–1990', in Finnie, Himsworth and Walker (eds), *Edinburgh Essays in Public Law*.

[4] See section C.

A. The British approach

The common law

The traditional British approach to the protection of civil liberties and human rights has been greatly influenced by Dicey.[5] For him there was no need for any statement of fundamental principles operating as a kind of higher law, because political freedom was adequately protected by the common law and by an independent Parliament acting as a watchdog against any excess of zeal by the executive.[6] Under the common law, a wide measure of individual liberty was guaranteed by the principle that citizens are free to do as they like unless expressly prohibited by law. So people already enjoy the freedom of religion, the freedom of expression and the freedom of assembly, and may be restrained from exercising these freedoms only if there are clear common law or statutory restrictions. This approach is illustrated by a number of classical decisions, the first of which is *Entick* v *Carrington*[7] where the Secretary of State issued a warrant to search the premises of John Entick and to seize any seditious literature. When the legality of the conduct was challenged, the minister claimed that the existence and exercise of such a power were necessary in the interests of the state. But the court upheld the challenge on the ground that there was no authority in the common law or in statute for warrants to be issued in this way. A second example is *Beatty* v *Gillbanks*,[8] where members of the Salvation Army in Weston-super-Mare were forbidden to march on Sundays because their presence attracted a large hostile crowd of people, thereby causing a breach of the peace. When the Salvationists ignored the order not to assemble, they were bound over to keep the peace for having committed the crime of unlawful assembly. The order binding them over was set aside on appeal because they had done nothing wrong. In the view of the court, they could not be prohibited from assembling merely because their lawful conduct might induce others to act unlawfully.

Although there are thus important illustrations of the principle, it is open to question whether this approach is an adequate basis for the protection of liberty. In the first place, the common law rule that people are free to do anything which is not prohibited by law applies (it would seem) equally to the government. As a result, the government may violate individual freedom even though it is not formally empowered to do so, on the ground that it is doing nothing which is prohibited by law. So in *Malone* v *Metropolitan Police Commissioner*[9] the practice of telephone tapping was exposed as being done by the executive without any clear lawful authority. But when Mr Malone sought a declaration that the tapping of his telephone was unlawful, he failed because he could not point to any legal right of his which it was the duty of the government not to invade. There was no violation of his property rights, no breach of confidence and no invasion of any right to privacy recognised by the law. A second difficulty with the British approach is that liberty is particularly vulnerable to erosion. The common law merely recognises that people are free to do anything which is not unlawful, but is powerless to prevent new restrictions from being enacted by the legislature. Paradoxically, many restrictions on liberty are imposed by the common law, for it is sometimes convenient for the executive to avoid seeking new powers from Parliament.[10] In this way the authorities may seek a decision of the courts which will

---

[5] Dicey, *The Law of the Constitution*. And see ch 6.

[6] For a vivid expression of this view, see *Wheeler* v *Leicester City Council* [1985] AC 1054, at p 1065 (Browne-Wilkinson LJ). For a powerful critique, see Craig, *Public Law and Democracy*.

[7] (1765) 19 St Tr 1030; ch 6.

[8] (1882) 9 QBD 308.

[9] [1979] Ch 344.

[10] Cf Lord Browne-Wilkinson [1992] PL 397, and Sir J Laws [1993] PL 59.

develop the law restrictively and create a precedent of general application. As a source of restraint of individual liberty, rules of this kind can be as effective as legislation by Parliament. Thus in *Moss* v *McLachlan*[11] the Divisional Court created, from the common law powers of the police to control and regulate public assemblies, an extended right to prevent people from assembling in the first place. And in the *Spycatcher* and other cases, it was held that injunctions could be granted to the Attorney-General to restrain the publication of confidential government secrets.[12]

The role of Parliament

Another weakness of the traditional British approach relates to the decline in the power of Parliament. The late 19th century, when Dicey was writing, was in many ways the high-water mark of an independent Parliament acting as a watchdog of the executive.[13] This was the time when Parliament was 'a body which chose the government, maintained it and could reject it' and which 'operated as an intermediary between the electorate and the executive'.[14] Since then, however, the inexorable growth of the party system and its attendant discipline has seen the executive increasingly gain control of the House of Commons. As a result, the government in the early 21st century, unlike the position in the late 19th century, can now expect its Bills to be passed by a largely quiescent House of Commons. To put the matter into perspective, in the 1980s only one government Bill was defeated on its second reading in the House, a rare and exceptional occurrence for a government with a working majority.[15] Modern governments have tended to take advantage of this development, resulting in statutory initiatives which it is said are corrosive of individual freedom.[16] These measures having been passed by Parliament, there is little that the courts can do to deny effect to these measures. As a result the residue of liberty, the freedom to do that which is not unlawful, becomes conspicuously less extensive. Such measures include the Police and Criminal Evidence Act 1984 (extending police powers of arrest and detention), the Public Order Act 1986 and the Criminal Justice and Public Order Act 1994 (extending police powers to prohibit and regulate public meetings and assemblies) and the Regulation of Investigatory Powers Act 2000 (extending the legal powers of the police and security service, particularly in relation to the surveillance of individuals).

On the other hand, however, steps have been taken to ensure that government is more open than in the past. Important measures in this respect include the Local Government (Access to Information) Act 1985 (giving rights of access to local authority meetings and to documents and records), the Access to Personal Files Act 1987 (giving individuals the right of access to manual records containing personal information for the purposes of housing and social services) and the Data Protection Acts of 1984 and 1998 (introducing general rights of individuals to personal data held by third parties). The Freedom of Information Act 2000 must now be added to this list, although it is not yet in force. Legislation has also strengthened the rights of those who have grievances against agencies of the state. Thus, a new Police Complaints Authority was set up and, despite the concerns about the Regulation of Investigatory Powers Act 2000,[17] new tribunals have been created for those who claim that a warrant has been

---

[11] [1985] IRLR 76. See ch 24 below.
[12] *A-G* v *Guardian Newspapers Ltd* [1987] 1 WLR 1248; [1990] 1 AC 109.
[13] See Mackintosh, *The British Cabinet.*
[14] Mackintosh, *The Government and Politics of Britain.*
[15] See Brazier, *Constitutional Practice*, pp 219–20. See also ch 10 A.
[16] See, e.g., Ewing and Gearty, *Freedom under Thatcher.*
[17] See ch 22 C and D below.

improperly issued to intercept their communications or gain access to their home for the purposes of surveillance. The Public Order Act 1986, although restricting freedom of assembly, also strengthened the law on incitement to racial hatred, thereby promoting the rights of racial minorities in particular.[18] And partly as a result of EC initiatives, the statutory rights for women at work have been extended in a number of directions, while the Disability Discrimination Act 1995 – strengthened in 1999 – was an important 'concession of the facts of social exclusion and marginalisation of a sizeable minority' of British citizens.[19]

Race Relations Act 1976

The British principle of liberty – that people are free to do anything which is not prohibited by law – is open to criticism because it fails to acknowledge that unrestrained liberty, particularly of private as opposed to public power, can be the antithesis of the liberty of others. For that reason Parliament may need to intervene to restrain that power and to regulate competing interests of liberty and freedom. Thus in the fields of race and sex discrimination, common law rules relating to freedom of contract permitted the most egregious forms of racist and sexist behaviour by those in positions of power and authority – employers, landlords and traders – over others.[20] If a policy commitment to equality of opportunity were to be implemented, this could be done only by legislation. So in this way Parliament needs to act as a watchdog, not only to restrain the possibility of abuse by the executive, but also to initiate measures to revise common law rules which in a changing social climate are seen to be oppressive.

In the field of race relations Parliament first intervened with the Race Relations Act 1965, strengthened and extended by the Race Relations Act 1968.[21] The law is now found in the Race Relations Act 1976 which was improved in a number of important respects by the Race Relations (Amendment) Act 2000. The 1976 Act – which has been described judicially as 'pioneering legislation designed to produce a social, as much as a legal, change'[22] – applies to discrimination on grounds of race, defined to mean colour, race, nationality or ethnic or national origins.[23] It seeks to outlaw both direct and indirect discrimination.[24] The former occurs where the discriminator treats one person less favourably on racial grounds than he or she would treat another.[25] The latter – introduced in 1976 and based on US case law[26] – occurs where a person acts in a manner not in itself overtly discriminatory but where the effect of that action, intentional or not, is to discriminate. Thus, in terms of the 1976 Act, a person may apply

---

[18] Patten, *Political Culture, Conservatism and Rolling Constitutional Change.*
[19] B Doyle (1997) 60 MLR 64, at p 64. See also Doyle, *Disability, Discrimination and Equal Opportunities.*
[20] Only exceptionally did the common law provide protection for members of minority racial groups: *Constantine* v *Imperial Hotels Ltd* [1944] KB 693; *Scala Ballroom* v *Ratcliffe* [1958] 3 All ER 220.
[21] For good accounts of these measures, see Lester and Bindman, *Race and Law,* and Hepple, *Race, Jobs and the Law in Britain.* See also Lester McColgan, *Discrimination Law.*
[22] *Nagarajan* v *London Regional Transport* [2000] 1 AC 501, at p 509 (Lord Browne-Wilkinson).
[23] Problems have arisen as to whether Jews (*Seide* v *Gillette Industries* [1980] IRLR 427), Sikhs (*Mandla* v *Dowell Lee* [1983] 2 AC 548), gypsies (*CRE* v *Dutton* [1989] IRLR 8) and Rastafarians (*Crown Suppliers PSA* v *Dawkins* [1993] ICR 517) are covered by the Act. Discrimination against someone because he or she is English is unlawful: *BBC Scotland* v *Souster* [2001] IRLR 151.
[24] It is also unlawful to discriminate against someone who has made a complaint of race discrimination or commenced legal proceedings (s 2). But see *Chief Constable of West Yorkshire* v *Khan* [2001] 1 WLR 1947.
[25] The fact that less favourable treatment took place without a racial motive is irrelevant: *R* v *CRE, ex p Westminster City Council* [1984] ICR 770 and *James* v *Eastleigh BC* [1990] 2 AC 751. See also *Dhatt* v *McDonald's Hamburgers Ltd* [1991] IRLR 130, and *Nagarajan* v *London Regional Transport* (note 22 above).
[26] *Griggs* v *Duke Power Co* 401 US 424 (1971). See Lustgarten, *Legal Control of Racial Discrimination.*

to another a requirement or condition,[27] which he or she applies or would apply equally to persons of different racial groups (defined by reference to colour, race, nationality or ethnic or national origins) and which therefore does not directly or overtly discriminate. Such action becomes discrimination, however, when the condition imposed is such that the proportion of persons of the same racial group who can comply with it is considerably smaller than the proportion of other persons who can comply; and when the condition is not justifiable irrespective of racial considerations[28] and has a detrimental effect on those who cannot comply. *Mandla* v *Dowell Lee* concerned the question whether the headmaster of a private school discriminated against a Sikh boy by enforcing rules on school uniform which forbade the wearing of headgear. This was a requirement with which the plaintiff could not comply because of the practice of his religion. Holding the rules to be discriminatory, the House of Lords interpreted the words 'can comply' to mean not 'can physically comply', but 'can in practice comply' or 'can consistently with the customs and cultural conditions of the racial group comply'.[29]

Discrimination is unlawful in the field of employment,[30] except where being of a particular racial group is a genuine qualification for stated jobs (for example, the theatre) and except for employment in a private household (ss 4, 5).[31] It is, further, unlawful to discriminate in the choice of partners for partnerships of six or more persons, admission to trade unions and professional organisations, granting of licences and qualifications for trades or vocations, vocational training and employment agency services (ss 10–14). Discrimination is also unlawful in education and in the provision of goods, services and facilities to the public or a section of the public. There are exceptions for residential accommodation in small premises and for the fostering or care of children in a person's home (s 23(2)). Associations which have more than 25 members may not discriminate as respects admission to membership or the treatment of associate members (s 25)[32] but an association whose main aim is to provide benefits to persons of a particular racial group may discriminate on grounds of race, nationality or ethnic or national origin but not as regards colour (s 26). Advertising in terms which suggest an intention to discriminate is unlawful, but it is permissible to state that a job requires a member of a particular racial group (for example, a Chinese waiter for a Chinese restaurant) (s 29). Other conduct declared unlawful includes the adoption of discriminatory requirements or conditions (s 28), and instructing, inducing or aiding persons to commit unlawful discrimination (ss 30, 31, 33).[33]

The Commission for Racial Equality replaced both the former Race Relations Board and the Community Relations Commission. Its chair and members are appointed by the Home Secretary and its annual report is laid before Parliament.[34] Unlike the former Board, the Commission has power on its own initiative or when directed by the Home Secretary to carry out formal investigations and, for this purpose, it may

---

[27] On the meaning of 'requirement or condition', see *Perera* v *Civil Service Commission* [1983] ICR 428 and *Meer* v *London Borough of Tower Hamlets* [1988] IRLR 399.

[28] See *Hampson* v *Department of Education and Science* [1991] 1 AC 171, and *Webb* v *EMO Air Cargo* [1992] 4 All ER 929.

[29] [1983] 2 AC 548, at 565–6 (Lord Fraser). This test was derived from that applied in the sex discrimination case, *Price* v *Civil Service Commission* [1978] 1 All ER 1228.

[30] See *Glasgow City Council* v *Zafar* [1998] ICR 120.

[31] See *Lambeth London Borough Council* v *CRE* [1990] ICR 768.

[32] On the law before 1976, see *Charter* v *Race Relations Board* [1973] AC 868 and *Race Relations Board* v *Dockers' Labour Club* [1976] AC 285.

[33] See *Hallani* v *Avery* [2001] 1 WLR 655; *Anyanwu* v *South Bank Student Union* [2001] 1 WLR 638.

[34] The Commission also conducts valuable periodic reviews of the legislation. See most recently CRE, *Reform of the Race Relations Act 1976: Proposals from the CRE – Third Review* (1998). For a comprehensive review of the anti-discrimination legislation with proposals for reform, see Hepple et al., *Equality: A New Framework* (2000).

require evidence to be given to it (ss 48–52). Such investigations must not, however, be lightly undertaken. The Commission may not embark on an investigation unless it has a reasonable suspicion that acts of discrimination have occurred.[35] If discrimination is established, the Commission has power to issue a non-discrimination notice (against which there is a right of appeal)[36] and may within five years follow up such a notice by seeking an injunction from the county court or, in Scotland, an interdict from the sheriff court (ss 57–61). Enforcement in the employment field by individuals takes the form of a complaint by the victim of discrimination to an employment tribunal, from which an appeal on a point of law lies to the Employment Appeal Tribunal.[37] When such a complaint is brought to a tribunal, the services of a conciliation officer are available. The tribunal may declare the rights of the parties in regard to the alleged discrimination, order compensation to be paid or recommend other steps to be taken by way of a remedy (ss 53–5).[38] Complaints of discrimination outside employment may be brought by the victim before designated county courts. The court may award damages,[39] including compensation for injury to feelings, but it is a defence to an action for damages based on indirect discrimination if the alleged discriminator proves that he or she did not intend to discriminate against the claimant on racial grounds (s 57(3)).[40] By virtue of the Race Relations (Remedies) Act 1994 there is no limit on the amount of compensation that may be awarded.[41] The Commission for Racial Equality has power to assist complainants in pursuing their remedies in difficult or important cases (s 66).[42] The Act applies to service under the Crown (including the armed forces)[43] and to the police.

The scope of the Act was extended in a number of key directions by the Race Relations (Amendment) Act 2000.[44] A new s 19B inserted into the 1976 Act provides that it is unlawful for a public authority 'to do any act which constitutes discrimination'. A public authority includes any person certain of whose functions are functions of a public nature (s 19B(2)(a)), although in relation 'to a particular act', a person is not a public body 'by virtue only' of s 19B(2)(a) 'if the nature of the act is private'. There are also a number of exceptions relating to Parliament and the security and intelligence services. Although the Act appears to apply to judicial appointments,[45] it does not apply to judicial or legislative acts; neither does it apply to discrimination on grounds of nationality or ethnic or national origins in carrying out immigration and nationality functions.[46] Also important is the new s 71 of the 1976 Act which previously applied only to local authorities.[47] Now there is a duty on a large number of specified public

---

[35] R v Commission for Racial Equality, ex p Hillingdon Council [1982] AC 779, applied in Re Prestige Group [1984] 1 WLR 335; and see Home Office v CRE [1982] QB 385.

[36] CRE v Amari Plastics Ltd [1982] QB 265.

[37] Ch 18 A.

[38] Problems may arise in discrimination cases in relation to the disclosure of confidential documents. See Science Research Council v Nassé [1980] AC 1028 and, as to public interest immunity, Halford v Sharples [1992] 3 All ER 624 (see also ch 32 C).

[39] On damages, see Alexander v Home Office [1988] 2 All ER 118. On exemplary damages, see Kuddus v Chief Constable of Leicestershire [2001] 3 All ER 193, and ch 32 A below.

[40] See J H Walker Ltd v Hussain [1996] ICR 291.

[41] See Racial Equality Council Cleveland v Widlinski [1998] ICR 1124, Prison Service v Johnson [1997] ICR 275.

[42] As it did in Mandla v Dowell Lee [1983] 2 AC 548.

[43] See R v Army Board of Defence Council, ex p Anderson [1992] QB 169; Armed Forces Act 1996, s 23.

[44] See C O'Cinneide [2001] PL 220.

[45] Cf Arthur v Attorney-General [1999] ICR 631.

[46] Race Relations Act 1976, ss 19C–19D, inserted by Race Relations (Amendment) Act 2000, s 1. Cf Re Admin [1983] 2 AC 818.

[47] See Wheeler v Leicester City Council [1985] AC 1054; R v Lewisham London BC, ex p Shell UK Ltd [1988] 1 All ER 938; R v London Borough of Tower Hamlets, ex p Mohib Ali (1993) 25 HLR 218. See also Local Government Act 1988, s 18.

bodies to carry out their functions in a way which has due regard to the need to eliminate unlawful racial discrimination and to promote equality of opportunity and good relations between persons of different racial groups.[48] The duty applies by no means to all public bodies, but only to central and local government, the armed forces, the national health service, educational bodies, housing bodies and the police. Nevertheless, where there is a failure to comply with this duty, the CRE may issue a compliance notice which may be enforced by the Commission in a designated county or sheriff court. The 2000 Act also provides that police officers are to be treated as being in the employment of the chief officer of police, who will be vicariously liable for any discriminatory acts of their officers.[49]

B. European Convention on Human Rights[50]

The protection of human rights, which is primarily a matter for the state in whose territory the rights may be enjoyed, cannot today be confined within national boundaries. The European Convention on Human Rights was signed at Rome in 1950, was ratified by the United Kingdom in 1951, and came into force among those states which had ratified it in 1953. The Convention is a treaty under international law and its authority derives solely from the consent of those states who have become parties to it. It was a direct result of the movement for cooperation in Western Europe which in 1949 created the Council of Europe. Inspiration for the Convention came from the wide principles declared in the United Nations Universal Declaration of Human Rights in 1948.[51] The Convention declares certain human rights which are or should be protected by law in each state. It also provides political and judicial procedures by which alleged infringements of these rights may be examined at an international level. In particular, the acts of public authorities may be challenged even though they are in accordance with national law. The Convention thus provides a constraint on the legislative authority of national parliaments, including that at Westminster.[52]

The scope of the Convention

The Convention does not cover the whole field of human rights. It omits economic and social rights and is confined to certain basic rights and liberties which the framers of the Convention considered would be generally accepted in the liberal democracies of Western Europe. These rights and liberties include:

---

[48] The obligation to promote equality of opportunity does not apply to the carrying out of immigration and nationality functions (Race Relations Act 1976, s 71A; inserted by Race Relations (Amendment) Act 2000, s 2).

[49] Race Relations (Amendment) Act 2000, s 4, inserting new Race Relations Act 1976, s 76A; reversing *Farah v Metropolitan Police Commissioner* [1998] QB 65.

[50] The extensive literature includes Beddard, *Human Rights and Europe*; Jacobs and White, *The European Convention on Human Rights*; Harris, O'Boyle and Warbrick, *Law of the European Convention on Human Rights*; Janis, Kay and Bradley, *European Human Rights Law: Text and Materials*; Jowell and Cooper, *Understanding Human Rights Principles*; Mowbray, *Cases and Materials on the European Convention on Human Rights*; Robertson and Merrills, *Human Rights in Europe*. For valuable comparative studies of the operation of the Convention in a number of jurisdictions, see Blackburn and Polakiewicz (eds), *Fundamental Rights in Europe* and Gearty (ed), *European Civil Liberties*. Also important is Simpson, *Human Rights and the End of Empire*.

[51] See Brownlie, *Basic Documents on Human Rights*.

[52] Ch 4 C.

the right to life (art 2);

freedom from torture, or inhuman or degrading treatment or punishment (art 3);

freedom from slavery or forced labour (art 4);

the right to liberty and security of the person (art 5), including the right of one who is arrested to be informed promptly of the reasons for his or her arrest and of any charge against him or her;

the right to a fair trial by an impartial tribunal of a person's civil rights and obligations and of criminal charges against him or her (art 6), including the right to be presumed innocent of a criminal charge until proved guilty and the right to be defended by a lawyer and to have free legal assistance 'when the interests of justice so require';

the prohibition of retroactive criminal laws (art 7);

the right to respect for a person's private and family life, his home and correspondence (art 8);

freedom of thought, conscience and religion (art 9) and freedom of expression (art 10);

freedom of peaceful assembly and of association with others, including the right to form and join trade unions (art 11);

the right to marry and found a family (art 12).

By art 14, the rights declared in the Convention are to be enjoyed

> without discrimination on any ground such as sex, race, colour, language, religion, political or other opinion, national or social origin, association with a national minority, property, birth or other status.

All persons within the jurisdiction of the member states benefit from the Convention regardless of citizenship, although a state may restrict the political activities of aliens.

Many of these rights are subject to exceptions or qualifications. Thus art 5 sets out the grounds on which a person may lawfully be deprived of his or her liberty; these include the lawful arrest of a person to prevent his or her entering the country without authority and the lawful detention 'of persons of unsound mind, alcoholics or drug addicts or vagrants' (art 5(1)(f)). So too the right to respect for private and family life under art 8 is protected from interference by a public authority

> except such interference as is in accordance with the law and is necessary in a democratic society in the interests of national security, public safety or the economic well-being of the country, for the prevention of disorder or crime, for the protection of health or morals, or for the protection of the rights and freedoms of others.

Clearly, it is essential that such restrictions should not be interpreted so widely that the protected right becomes illusory. Member states may derogate from most but not all of their obligations under the Convention in time of war or other public emergency (and the United Kingdom has done so in respect of Northern Ireland), but they must inform the Secretary-General of the Council of Europe of the measures taken and the reasons (art 15).[53]

The scope of the Convention was extended by the First Protocol concluded as an addendum to the Convention in 1952 and ratified by the United Kingdom. By this protocol, every person is entitled to the peaceful enjoyment of his possessions (art 1); the right to education is protected and states must respect the right of parents to ensure

---

[53] See *Lawless* v *Ireland* (1961) 1 EHRR 15; *Brannigan* v *UK* (1993) 17 EHRR 539; and *Arksoy* v *Turkey* (1996) 23 EHRR 396.

education of their children in conformity with their own religious and philosophical convictions (art 2);[54] and the right to take part in free elections by secret ballot is declared (art 3).[55] The Fourth Protocol to the Convention, concluded in 1963, guarantees freedom of movement within a state and freedom to leave any country; it also precludes a state from expelling or refusing to admit its own nationals. This protocol has not been ratified by the United Kingdom because our citizenship and immigration laws are not guaranteed to all citizens the right to enter the United Kingdom.[56] The Sixth Protocol provides for the abolition of the death penalty thereby qualifying the terms of art 2 of the Convention itself. Under the terms of the protocol, which is now ratified by the United Kingdom, no one is to be condemned to death or executed, with the only exception being made for times of war when the penalty could be imposed only 'in the instances laid down in the law and in accordance with its provisions'. The Seventh Protocol (not ratified by the UK) deals mainly with appeals procedures in criminal cases, although it also provides (in art 5) for 'equality of rights and responsibilities of a private law character' between spouses. Of the remaining protocols, the Eleventh and Twelfth are by far the most significant. The former is dealt with below and the latter (which has not been ratified by the United Kingdom) contains a general prohibition against discrimination.[57]

Institutions and procedure

One novel feature of the Convention was the right which it gave to individuals to complain of breaches of the Convention by the states party to it. The enforcement procedure has been changed; but initially it made use both of the Committee of Ministers of the Council of Europe (a committee of political representatives of the member states) and of two institutions created by the Convention: (*a*) the European Commission of Human Rights, which comprised individual members, elected by the Committee of Ministers but in office acting independently; and (*b*) the European Court of Human Rights, comprising judges elected by the Consultative Assembly of the Council of Europe. No two members of the Commission or the Court respectively could be citizens of the same state. The function of the Commission was to receive and inquire into alleged breaches of the Convention either (*a*) at the request of any state party to the Convention which alleged that another state had breached the Convention (known as inter-state cases); or (*b*) where a state had recognised the competence of the Commission to receive such petitions, on the receipt of a petition from an individual or a non-governmental organisation alleging a violation of rights by the state in question.

Although not all states recognised the right of individuals to petition to the Commission, very many more individual petitions came to the Commission than inter-state cases. When an individual petition was received, the Commission had first to decide whether it was admissible under the Convention. If a petition cleared the hurdle of admissibility, the Commission had then to investigate the facts fully and offer its services to the parties with a view to securing a friendly settlement of the dispute. If

---

[54] The United Kingdom accepted the latter principle 'only so far as is compatible with provision of efficient instruction and training, and the avoidance of unreasonable public expenditure'; see *Campbell and Cosans* v *UK* (1982) 4 EHRR 293.
[55] See *Liberal Party* v *UK* (1982) 4 EHRR 106 (simple majority electoral system not a breach of Convention), and *Matthews* v *UK* (1999) 28 EHRR 361.
[56] Ch 20.
[57] See U Khaliq [2001] PL 457 on the Twelfth Protocol.

such a settlement was not arranged, a secret report on the dispute was sent by the Commission to the state or states concerned and to the Committee of Ministers. Thereafter the matter might be dealt with finally by the Committee of Ministers, deciding by a two-thirds majority, or it could be brought within three months before the European Court of Human Rights. A case could be at that time brought before the Court only where the states concerned had accepted the compulsory jurisdiction of the Court or expressly consented to the case coming to the Court. Only the Commission or a state concerned could refer a case to the Court: the individual applicant had only a limited right to refer their case to the Court.[58]

New procedures for dealing with complaints were introduced by the Eleventh Protocol which abolished the Commission and created a new full-time court. Although it has the same title as the old court which it replaced, 'it is an entirely different body with new functions, powers and composition'.[59] Under the new arrangements, the court consists of a number of judges equal to the number of states which are party to the Convention (art 20), with a judge from each country, although they are to be elected by the Parliamentary Assembly of the Council of Europe by a majority of the votes cast from a list of three candidates nominated by the country in question (art 22). The judges serve for renewable periods of six years. The protocol had the effect of radically pruning the existing text of the Convention, replacing arts 19–56 with new arts 19–51. The main effect of the changes, however, is to enable applicants complaining of a breach of the Convention to apply directly to the Court. For this purpose the new court operates through a number of bodies, the judges sitting in committees, chambers and the Grand Chamber (art 27). Applications may continue to be made by one state against another (art 33) or by 'any person, non-governmental organisation or group of individuals claiming to be the victim of a violation' (art 34).

There is still a requirement that an applicant should have exhausted all domestic remedies and have brought the complaint within six months of the final decision of the domestic authorities. There is no jurisdiction to deal with complaints which are anonymous or substantially the same as any already examined by the Court, which is required to declare inadmissible any application submitted under art 34 considered to be incompatible with the terms of the Convention, manifestly ill-founded or an abuse of the right to petition (art 35). Under the present procedures, cases are dealt with initially by a committee of three judges who determine whether the complaint is admissible. A complaint may be ruled inadmissible only by a unanimous vote (art 28), failing which the decision on admissibility must be taken by a chamber of seven judges (who must also decide on the admissibility of inter-state applications), which also deals with the merits of the case (art 29). In some cases, however, the chamber may relinquish jurisdiction in favour of a Grand Chamber of 17 judges, an option which is available where the case 'raises a serious question affecting the interpretation of the Convention or the protocols thereto, or where the resolution of a question before it might have a result inconsistent with a judgment previously delivered by the Court' (art 30). Provision is made for disposing of an application by means of a friendly settlement, where it has been ruled admissible, for which purpose the Court will place itself at the disposal of the parties (art 38). Decisions of committees are final (art 29), as are decisions of chambers and Grand Chambers (art 44). The convention retains the power of the Court to afford just satisfaction to the injured party (art 41).

---

[58] See A R Mowbray [1991] PL 353. See also Harris, Boyle and Warbrick, pp 661–3. For a valuable review of the work of the court, see C A Gearty [1993] 45 CLJ 89.
[59] A R Mowbray [1994] PL 540 (and [1993] PL 419). See also Harris, Boyle and Warbrick, ch 26; Janis, Kay and Bradley, ch 3; H Schermers (1994) 19 Eur Law Rev 367.

Cases involving the United Kingdom[60]

Under the original scheme of the Convention, enforcement depended essentially on a state recognising both the right of individuals to apply to Strasbourg and the compulsory jurisdiction of the court. In 1966, the British government first made the two optional declarations for which the Convention provided[61] and these declarations were renewed at intervals.[62] One result of the changes in 1998 is that member states today have no choice in these fundamental matters and must accept the right of individuals to apply to the Court. Since 1966 a wide variety of individual petitions have been brought against the UK government and there have also been inter-state references to the Commission by the Republic of Ireland. In addition to the innumerable decisions and opinions being given by the Commission, the Court between 1975 and April 1990 decided 30 cases involving the United Kingdom, with a number of others awaiting decision. In 21 of the 30 cases the Court found breaches of the Convention, whereas the other nine were dismissed. This ratio of 70:30 in the success rate for cases brought against the United Kingdom was very nearly the same as for the Court's record as a whole between 1960 and 1987. During that period 108 principal decisions of the Court were made and breaches were found to have occurred in 75 cases, a 'success' ratio of 69:31.[63] More recent information shows that as of 3 April 1995, the Court had found at least one breach of the Convention on 35 occasions in the case of the UK. This compared with 82 in the case of Italy, 29 in the case of France, 27 in the case of Austria, 23 in the case of the Netherlands, 21 in the case of Sweden and 11 in the case of Germany.[64] Many countries recognised the right of individual petition later than Britain, so it is not possible to conclude from these statistics that the requirements of the Convention are (in relation to population) more liable to be infringed in the UK than in any other country. Indeed it was suggested in 1995 that Britain came 14th out of 30 Council of Europe states (the first being Italy with the poorest record) in a comparison based on population and the number of years the right of individual petition had been recognised.[65]

The British cases before the Court have spanned a wide range of subjects. In *McCann* v *United Kingdom*[66] it was held that art 2 (protecting the right to life) had been violated following the use of lethal force by members of the security forces in Gibraltar. Questions concerning the interpretation of art 3 (protection against torture and inhuman or degrading treatment or punishment) arose in *Republic of Ireland* v *United Kingdom*[67] in relation to the interrogation of IRA suspects, in *Tyrer* v *United Kingdom*[68] in relation to the corporal punishment of juveniles in the Isle of Man and in *Soering* v *United Kingdom*[69] in relation to the request for the extradition of a German citizen to the USA to stand trial for murder with the risk of being sentenced to capital punishment and being kept on Death Row. In *X* v *United Kingdom*[70] the Court held

---

[60] The account draws heavily on A W Bradley, note 3 above. See also R R Churchill and J R Young [1991] BYIL 283.

[61] For the making of the decisions involved, see A Lester [1984] PL 46 and [1998] PL 237.

[62] See HC Deb, 13 December 1995, col 647.

[63] Bradley, note 3, at p 188.

[64] HL Deb, 18 April 1995, col 44 (WA).

[65] HL Deb, 5 June 1995, col 86 (WA).

[66] (1996) 21 EHRR 97.

[67] (1978) 2 EHRR 25.

[68] (1978) 2 EHRR 1. See also *Costello-Roberts* v *UK* (1995) 19 EHRR 112, and *A* v *UK* (1998) 27 EHRR 611 (child severely beaten by stepfather).

[69] (1989) 11 EHRR 439. See also *D* v *UK* (1997) 24 EHRR 423 (proposed removal of drug smuggler to St Kitts under the Immigration Act 1971. Applicant had AIDS and proposed removal found to be in breach of art 3).

[70] (1981) 4 EHRR 188.

certain procedures for the compulsory detention of mental patients to infringe art 5, a similar conclusion being reached in *Brogan* v *United Kingdom*[71] in relation to the provisions of the Prevention of Terrorism (Temporary Provisions) Act 1984 authorising the detention of suspects for up to seven days without judicial authority. The automatic denial of bail for certain offences in the Criminal Justice and Public Order Act 1994 was found to breach art 5 in *Caballero* v *United Kingdom*.[72] Article 6 has been found to have been violated in a number of cases, including *Murray* v *United Kingdom*[73] where the applicant was denied access to a solicitor for 48 hours while in police detention. Similarly in *Benham* v *United Kingdom*[74] a complaint was upheld in a case brought by a person denied legal aid and imprisoned for failure to pay the community charge (poll tax) without the benefit of legal representation. In *McMichael* v *United Kingdom*[75] a breach was found to have taken place where the natural parents of a child were denied access to relevant confidential reports in child care proceedings. A series of cases have found the courts-martial system for dealing with offences against military discipline to breach art 6 on the ground that the court-martial was not an independent and impartial tribunal.[76] Article 6 was also found to have been breached in *V* v *United Kingdom*[77] following the conviction of two minors (for a notorious murder of a child) after a trial conducted in the full glare of highly charged media publicity. A number of cases have also concentrated on the withholding of evidence by the prosecution and the use of public interest immunity.[78]

In *Dudgeon* v *United Kingdom*,[79] legislation in Northern Ireland making homosexual conduct between adult males a crime was held to infringe the individual's right to respect for his private life under art 8. The practice of telephone tapping was held to infringe art 8 in *Malone* v *United Kingdom*[80] and in *Halford* v *United Kingdom*.[81] The law of contempt of court was held to infringe freedom of expression under art 10 in *Sunday Times Ltd* v *United Kingdom*,[82] but the English law on obscene publications survived scrutiny in *Handyside* v *United Kingdom*.[83] In three other important cases it was held that art 10 had been violated by (i) restraints on the publication by newspapers (the *Observer, Guardian* and *Sunday Times*) of the contents of a book (*Spycatcher*) by a retired security service officer;[84] (ii) a requirement imposed by a court that a journalist should disclose the confidential sources of an article he had written, publication of which had been restrained by the courts;[85] and (iii) the award of £1.5m damages to Lord Aldington for defamatory remarks contained in a pamphlet written by a historian.[86]

---

[71] (1988) 11 EHRR 117; and see ch 26 E.
[72] (2000) 30 EHRR 643.
[73] (1996) 22 EHRR 29.
[74] (1996) 22 EHRR 293. See also *Perks* v *UK* (2000) 30 EHRR 33 (applicant imprisoned by magistrates for non-payment of the community charge, without the benefit of legal representation at her trial).
[75] (1995) 20 EHRR 205.
[76] *Findlay* v *UK* (1997) 24 EHRR 221; *Moore* v *UK* (2000) 29 EHRR 728; and *Hood* v *UK* (2000) 29 EHRR 365. See ch 16.
[77] (2000) 30 EHRR 121.
[78] See *Rowe* v *UK* (2000) 30 EHRR 1; *Jasper* v *UK* (2000) 30 EHRR 441; and *Fitt* v *UK* (2000) 30 EHRR 480 (all were unsuccessful).
[79] (1981) 4 EHRR 149. See also *Smith* v *UK* (2000) 29 EHRR 493 (discharge of military personnel because they were homosexual found to be a breach of art 8). But compare *Laskey* v *UK* (1997) 24 EHRR 39 (conviction of homosexual men for sado-masochistic practices conducted in private not a breach of art 8).
[80] (1984) 7 EHRR 14.
[81] (1997) 24 EHRR 523.
[82] (1979) 2 EHRR 245; and see ch 18 D.
[83] (1976) 1 EHRR 737. See also *Wingrove* v *UK* (1997) 24 EHRR 1.
[84] (1991) 14 EHRR 153, 229.
[85] *Goodwin* v *UK* (1996) 22 EHRR 123.
[86] *Tolstoy Miloslavsky* v *UK* (1995) 20 EHRR 442.

Cases under art 10 have also called into question restrictions in electoral law[87] and on the freedom of peaceful protest.[88] In *Young, James and Webster v United Kingdom*[89] three former employees of British Railways, dismissed for refusing to join a trade union, established that their freedom of association had been infringed as a result of legislation on the closed shop initiated by a Labour government in 1974 and 1976: they were awarded substantial compensation.[90] But in *Lithgow v United Kingdom*[91] it was held that the compensation arrangements following the nationalisation of the shipbuilding industry did not breach the protection for private property in art 1 of the First Protocol. And in *Air Canada v United Kingdom* it was held that there was no breach of art 1 of the First Protocol where an aeroplane was seized by customs officers after it was found to be carrying cannabis.[92] But in *Matthews v United Kingdom*[93] the denial of British citizens resident in Gibralter from voting in elections for the European Parliament was found to breach article 3 of the First Protocol, this guaranteeing the right to take part in free elections.

These decisions have often led to changes in the law intended to prevent future infringements of the Convention. Such legislative changes include the Contempt of Court Act 1981 (regulating more clearly the circumstances in which pre-trial publicity is unlawful), the Interception of Communications Act 1985 and the Regulation of Investigatory Powers Act 2000 (regulating the circumstances in which telephone tapping may take place and giving individuals a right of redress against improper use) and the Homosexual Offences (Northern Ireland) Order 1982 (changing the law on homosexual conduct in Northern Ireland). Other significant consequences of Court decisions include the introduction of amendments to the procedures for detention and release of mental patients following the decision in *X v United Kingdom*[94] and the issuing of new prison rules and changing practices in prisons following decisions on prisoners' correspondence. In at least two cases, however, the government has been unwilling to give effect to decisions of the European Court and has taken steps to avoid doing so. In *Abdulaziz v United Kingdom*[95] the Court held that British immigration rules discriminated against women permanently settled in the United Kingdom because their husbands and fiancées were not entitled to enter, whereas the wives and fiancées of men settled here were entitled to enter. The government responded to this decision by amending the Immigration Rules to remove the entitlement of wives and fiancées to enter, thereby removing the source of discrimination. More recently, in *Brogan v United Kingdom*[96] the government responded to the Court's decision, that the detention powers of the Prevention of Terrorism (Temporary Provisions) Act 1984 violated art 5, by declaring that the power was necessary on security grounds and by depositing at Strasbourg a limited derogation from the Convention to the extent that the legislation violated art 5. Although the practice of birching offenders on the Isle of Man was held to violate art 3,[97] the law on the island was not immediately altered to give effect to the Court's ruling.

[87] *Bowman* v UK (1998) 28 EHRR 1; C Gearty (2000) 51 NILQ 381.
[88] *Steel* v UK (1999) 28 EHRR 603; and *Hashman* v UK (2000) 30 EHRR 241.
[89] (1981) 4 EHRR 38.
[90] See K D Ewing and W M Rees (1983) 12 ILJ 148.
[91] (1986) 8 EHRR 329.
[92] (1995) 20 EHRR 150.
[93] (1998) 28 EHRR 361.
[94] (1981) 4 EHRR 188.
[95] (1985) 7 EHRR 471.
[96] (1988) 11 EHRR 117. See now ch 26 E.
[97] *Tyrer* v UK (1978) 2 EHRR 1.

C. The Human Rights Act 1998[98]

The Human Rights Act 1998 provides that Convention rights may now be enforced in the domestic courts. Described as 'a constitutional instrument introducing into domestic law the relevant articles of the Convention',[99] the Act is a culmination of a long campaign for the incorporation of the Convention in which senior judges played a leading part.[100] Although the United Kingdom was the first country to ratify the ECHR[101] and allowed individuals to petition Strasbourg as long ago as 1966,[102] the ECHR nevertheless could not be enforced in the British courts.[103] This gave rise to concern about the fact that people had to take the long road to Strasbourg to enforce their rights, a concern which was fuelled by the delays in the Strasbourg system. There were also concerns that human rights were not adequately protected in British law, concerns which were vindicated for some by Britain's poor record before the Strasbourg court (on which see earlier). Successive governments were nevertheless opposed to incorporation, although it was supported by the Liberal Democrats.[104] It was not until 1996 that the cause was adopted by the Labour party which – while in Opposition – issued a consultation paper proposing incorporation to 'enable British people to enforce their rights in UK courts and enable our own judges to apply the ECHR in their jurisdictions'.[105]

The cause of those who campaigned vigorously for incorporation of the ECHR into domestic law was strengthened by the fact that several other countries in the common law tradition had adopted measures for the better protection of human rights. Two particularly influential but very different measures are the Canadian Charter of Rights and Freedoms 1982[106] and the New Zealand Bill of Rights Act 1990. The former empowers the courts to strike down legislation which conflicts with the Charter and generally to ensure that the administrative activities of public authorities comply with Charter rights and freedoms. It does not, however, apply to the common law and is not enforceable between private parties.[107] The latter in contrast is an altogether weaker measure, imposing a duty on the courts only to interpret legislation consistently with its terms. The New Zealand courts have no power to strike down an Act of Parliament, although the Bill of Rights nevertheless has been particularly influential in the developing field of police powers.[108] Apart from Canada and New Zealand, other

---

[98] There is a very full literature on the Act. See e.g. Clayton and Tomlinson, *The Law of Human Rights*; Lester and Pannick, *Human Rights Law and Practice*; and Wadham and Mountfield, *Guide to the Human Rights Act 1998*. Also K D Ewing (1999) 62 MLR 79; and D Feldman [1999] LS 165.

[99] *R v Offen* [2001] 1 WLR 253, per Lord Woolf, CJ.

[100] See HL Deb, 25 January 1995, col 1136 (Lord Taylor, LCJ, Lord Browne-Wilkinson, Lord Lloyd of Berwick, Lord Woolf (by proxy)). See also T Bingham (1993) 109 LQR 390; Lord Woolf [1995] PL 57; J Laws [1993] PL 59 and [1995] PL 72. See also S Sedley [1995] PL 386. For comment on some of this, see J A G Griffith (2000) 63 MLR 159; (2001) 117 LQR 42.

[101] See A Lester [1984] PL 46.

[102] See A Lester [1998] PL 237.

[103] *Malone v Metropolitan Police Commissioner* [1979] Ch 244; *R v Home Secretary, ex parte Brind* [1991] 1 AC 696; and *R v Ministry of Defence, ex p Smith* [1996] QB 517. But the courts might rely on it to construe ambiguous legislation (*Waddington v Miah* [1974] 1 WLR 683) or to resolve any uncertainties in the common law (*Derbyshire County Council v Times Newspapers Ltd* [1992] 1 QB 770 (CA); [1993] AC 534. In *Rantzen v Mirror Group Newspapers Ltd* [1994] QB 670 the Court of Appeal took into account guidance from the Strasbourg court in determining the level of damages in libel cases.

[104] See also J A G Griffith (1979) 42 MLR 1; T G Ison (1985) 10 Adelaide LR 1.

[105] J Straw and P Boateng, *Bringing Rights Home* (1996). See K D Ewing and C A Gearty [1997] EHRLR 146.

[106] The literature on the Charter is vast. See Hogg, *Constitutional Law of Canada*; also D Beatty (1997) 60 MLR 481; T Ison (1999) 60 MLR 499; and R Penner [1996] PL 104.

[107] *Retail, Wholesale and Department Store Union v Dolphin Delivery* (1986) 33 DLR (4th) 174.

[108] See J Allan (2000) 9 Otago LR 613.

jurisdictions which have recently moved to embrace the constitutional protection of human rights include Hong Kong and South Africa.[109]

The Convention rights

For the purposes of the Human Rights Act 1998, Convention rights are defined to mean arts 2–12 and 14 of the ECHR, arts 1–3 of the First Protocol and arts 1 and 2 of the Sixth Protocol (s 1(1)). These are to be read with arts 16 and 17 of the Convention: the former permits the imposition of restrictions on the political activities of aliens; while the latter deals with the abuse of rights by providing that no state, group or person has any right to engage in any activity or perform any act aimed at the destruction of any of the Convention rights. The main exclusions are thus arts 1 and 13. Article 1 imposes a duty on the 'High Contracting Parties' to 'secure to everyone within their jurisdiction' the rights and freedoms set out in the Convention, an obligation which the government considers to have been met by the enactment of the Human Rights Act. The exclusion of art 13 in contrast is more controversial, this providing that everyone whose Convention rights and freedoms are violated 'shall have an effective remedy before a national court'. Not everyone is prepared to accept that the contents of the Act fully satisfy this requirement, as the government also claimed.[110]

Section 1 also provides that the Convention rights are to have effect for the purposes of the Act subject to any derogation or reservation. At the time the Human Rights Act 1998 was passed, a derogation had been made to protect the detention provisions of the terrorism legislation which had been found to breach the right to liberty as protected by art 5(3).[111] There was also a reservation in place relating to art 2 of the First Protocol (dealing with education). Additional derogations or reservations may be made by ministerial order, subject to renewal every five years.[112] It is this power which was used in November 2001 to derogate in order to protect the Anti-Terrorism, Crime and Security Act 2001 which provides for the detention without trial of persons suspected by the Home Secretary of being international terrorists whose presence in the United Kingdom is a risk to national security, again in possible breach of art 5.[113] There is no reason in principle why a derogation order should not be subject to judicial review as going beyond the grounds for which derogation is permitted by art 15 of the Convention; but it seems unlikely that the courts will wish to second-guess ministers on what national security requires.[114] Nevertheless the Joint Committee on Human Rights

---

[109] On South Africa, see H Corder [1996] PL 291 and S Kentridge (1996) 112 LQR 257. Australia also appeared to take an important step in this direction when the High Court of Australia implied freedom of expression restrictions into the federal constitution. But the step has faltered in recent years. See *Australian Capital Television Pty Ltd* v *Commonwealth of Australia* (1992) 66 AJLR 695. See K D Ewing [1993] PL 256 and H P Lee [1993] PL 606. The case spawned a voluminous literature in the Australian law reviews, of which the (1994) 16 *Sydney Law Review* 145–305 is particularly interesting and in which the piece by T D Campbell, p 195, is most valuable for a British audience. See generally, Alston (ed), *Promoting Human Rights through Bills of Rights.*

[110] See HL Deb, 18 November 1997, cols 475–7. For a fuller discussion of points raised during the passing of the Act, see K D Ewing (1999) 62 MLR 79.

[111] During the Second Reading debates on the Terrorism Act 2000, the Home Secretary announced that the government hoped that this derogation could be withdrawn following enactment. See SI 2001 No 1216.

[112] Human Rights Act 1998, ss 14–16.

[113] SI 2001 No 3644. The order was made on 11 November, laid before Parliament on 12 November, and brought into force on 13 November. It was not debated until 19 November. See HC Deb, 19 November 2001. The Joint Committee on Human Rights report on the Bill was published on the 14th and the Home Affairs Committee report on the 19th.

[114] See *Home Secretary* v *Rehman* [2002] All ER 122.

(on which see later) was not convinced that the derogation of November 2001 could be justified.[115]

The Human Rights Act and parliamentary sovereignty

The structure of the Human Rights Act reflects the government's desire that 'courts should not have the power to set aside primary legislation, past or future, on the ground of incompatibility with the Convention'. This reflects the importance 'which the government attaches to parliamentary sovereignty'.[116] In practice this is not a major qualification, given that many of the cases which have gone to Strasbourg in the past have not been concerned with legislative action, so much as with executive or administrative action, and in some cases judicial action (relating to the operation of the common law). But it does not follow from this that the courts have no powers in relation to legislation. In the first place, they are required to interpret legislation (primary and secondary) where possible in a manner consistent with the Convention (s 3(1)).[117] This is in effect 'a new rule of construction',[118] which applies if the court has decided that there would otherwise be a breach of Convention rights.[119] The duty operates where the construction in favour of Convention rights may not be the most obvious or the most reasonable construction:

> the interpretative obligation under s 3 of the 1998 Act is a strong one. It applies even if there is no ambiguity in the language in the sense of the language being capable of two different meanings. It is an emphatic adjuration by the legislature. . . . The White Paper made clear that the obligation goes far beyond the rule which enabled the courts to take the Convention into account in resolving any ambiguity in a legislative provision.[120]

Section 3 has been said by some to be a 'radical tool';[121] but by others to contain a power which is a significant limitation of Parliament's sovereign will.[122] This latter is a conclusion reinforced by Lord Steyn's observation that '[i]n accordance with the will of Parliament as reflected in s 3 it will sometimes be necessary to adopt an interpretation which linguistically may appear strained'.[123] Where it is not possible to construe legislation in a manner which is consistent with Convention rights, the High Court and superior courts (but not tribunals or inferior courts), after giving the Crown an opportunity to take part in the proceedings (s 5),[124] may make a declaration of incompatibility (s 4(2)). But this is a 'measure of last resort' which 'must be avoided unless it is plainly impossible to do so', as in the case where 'a clear limitation on convention rights is stated in terms' or where a contradiction arises by 'necessary implication'.[125] Such a

---

[115] HL 37; HC 372 (2001–02). Compare the Home Affairs Committee (HC 351 (2001–02)).

[116] Cm 3782, 1997, para 2.13. See A W Bradley, in Jowell and Oliver (eds), *The Changing Constitution*, ch 2; and A Lester, in the same volume, ch 4; also Allan, *Constitutional Justice*, pp 225–8.

[117] See A Lester [1998] EHRLR 520 and F Bennion [2000] PL 77. On the exercise of this obligation, see *R v A* [2001] 3 All ER 1 (Youth Justice and Criminal Evidence Act 1999, s 41 – sexual history evidence in rape cases); *R v Lambert* [2001] 3 WLR 206 (Misuse of Drugs Act 1971, s 28 – burden of proof on the accused); and *R v Offen* [2001] 1 WLR 253 (Crime Sentences Act 1997, s 2 (now Powers of Criminal Courts Sentencing Act 2000, s 109) – automatic life sentences for previous offenders).

[118] *R v Leeds Crown Court, ex p Wardle* [2001] 2 All ER 1.

[119] See Lord Lester [1998] EHRLR 665.

[120] *R v A* (note 117 above), at p 17 (Lord Steyn).

[121] F Klug and K Starmer [2001] PL 654, at p 664.

[122] T Campbell, in Campbell, Ewing and Tomkins (eds), *Sceptical Essays on Human Rights*, ch 2.

[123] *R v A*, at p 17.

[124] *Wilson v First County Trust (No 2)* [2001] 3 WLR 42 (intervention by the Secretary of State for Trade and Industry).

[125] *R v A* (note 117 above), pp 17 and 35 (Lords Steyn and Hope respectively).

declaration is stated not to be binding on the parties and does not affect the validity or operation of primary legislation (s 4(6)).

> The first statutory provision was found incompatible with Convention rights is the Mental Health Act 1983, s 73, in *R(H)* v *London North and East Region Mental Health Review Tribunal*.[126] The Act placed the burden of proof on the patient – who in this case had been convicted of manslaughter and was being detained at Broadmoor – to show that he was no longer suffering from a disorder to warrant his continued detention.

If a declaration of incompatibility is made, it is for the government and Parliament to decide how to proceed – whether to amend the legislation or not. Such a device goes as far as possible without undermining Parliament's sovereignty and, in introducing the Human Rights Bill, the Home Secretary indicated that there were circumstances where the government would be unwilling to bring forward amending legislation, citing the area of abortion as an example.[127] Nevertheless an Act of Parliament which carries a declaration of incompatibility is likely to be badly wounded and some confusion may arise as a result. The first of two consequences which flow from a declaration is that it may be very difficult for any public authority to apply the provision that has been declared incompatible with Convention rights, since both the individual who obtained the declaration of incompatibility and the others affected by the incompatible provision will be encouraged by the declaration to apply to Strasbourg for a ruling on the matter. But a public authority may be bound to apply the law until it is repealed and may be challenged for not doing so. This dilemma of whether to apply legislation or not after a declaration of incompatibility seems destined for the courts at the highest level.

The second consequence of a declaration of incompatibility is that it may lead to a new 'fast-track' form of remedial action by means of delegated legislation. If a declaration of incompatibility is made, the government will normally be expected to respond by introducing primary legislation to remove the incompatibility. But where the minister considers that there are 'compelling reasons' for doing so, the Act empowers the government to make a 'remedial order' for amending primary legislation so as to remove the incompatibility (s 10 and Sch 2). A remedial order may also be made after a decision by the Strasbourg court in proceedings against the United Kingdom has indicated that primary legislation is incompatible with the Convention (s 10(1)(b)), although again only if there are compelling reasons for doing so.[128] The stated purpose of this procedure (which has been criticised as being a new Henry VIII clause) is to enable incompatibility with a Convention right to be removed from the statute book more quickly than if an amending Act of Parliament were needed.

The Human Rights Act and public authorities

Sections 6 and 7 of the Human Rights Act are particularly important for the enforcement of Convention rights in the courts. The Act makes it unlawful for public authorities (including courts and tribunals) to act in a way which is incompatible with Convention rights, unless primary legislation permits no other cause of action (s 6). This also applies to acts of persons other than public authorities, where those acts are done in exercise of 'functions of a public nature' but not if the 'nature of the act' is

---

[126] [2001] 3 WLR 553. A declaration of incompatibility was also issued in *Wilson* v *First County Trust (No 2)* [2001] 3 WLR 42 (Consumer Credit Act 1974, s 127).

[127] HC Deb, 21 October 1998, col 1301.

[128] For the view that 'exceptional' in this context should be read widely, see Loveland, *Constitutional Law – A Critical Introduction*, p 607.

private (s 6(3)(b), (5)). It is seen by some as a major problem and by others as a great strength that there is no definition or list of public authorities for this purpose. Although some bodies define themselves obviously as public authorities (the police, the security service, government departments, local authorities, the Crown Prosecution Service, the Electoral Commission and the immigration authorities), there is uncertainty about others (the BBC, the Press Complaints Commission, the Advertising Standards Authority, the Jockey Club and the privatised utilities). Cases decided in European law (on the meaning of the state for the purposes of the direct effect of directives) and administrative law (on the scope of judicial review) may give some guidance.[129] But although the definition of public authority and public function should be given a 'generous interpretation',[130] it is clear that the courts 'will need to weigh up a number of factors' to determine whether a body is a public authority for the purposes of the Human Rights Act.[131]

By virtue of s 7, an actual or potential victim of an unlawful act may bring proceedings in respect of the unlawful act or may rely on Convention rights as a defence in legal proceedings (for example, as a defence to a prosecution). In particular the actual or potential victim may apply for judicial review of the public authority's decision (s 7(3), (4)). By restricting applications to victims or potential victims, the Act effectively bars some public interest groups and others with standing (a 'sufficient interest') in judicial review proceedings from bringing claims that public authorities are violating Convention rights. A court or tribunal may provide 'such relief or remedy or make such order within its jurisdiction as it considers just and appropriate' (s 8(1)). However, damages for breach of Convention rights are available only in a civil court which otherwise has the power to award damages; and, in assessing damages, the civil court must take account of Strasbourg decisions awarding 'just satisfaction' under the Convention (s 8(2), (3)).[132] The Act preserves the immunity of holders of judicial office from any liability in respect of judicial acts done in good faith, except to the extent that individuals who have been unlawfully detained have a Convention right under art 5(5) to be compensated (s 9(3), (4)).

Uncertainty is likely to be fuelled by the fact that courts and tribunals are expressly stated to be public authorities. This means that courts and tribunals must conduct their affairs in a way which is consistent with Convention rights (such as the right to a fair trial (art 6) and the right to freedom of expression (art 10)). But it means much more, for it applies also to the remedies which a court may order. So it would not be possible for a court to issue an injunction if to do so would violate the Convention rights of the defendant; or to fail to issue an injunction if to do so would violate the Convention rights of the applicant. In this way the Act may have implications for the common law and indeed for litigation between private parties. So although Convention rights are directly enforceable against only public authorities, it is impossible to rule out the likelihood that they could be enforced indirectly by one private party against another.[133] This question – the so-called horizontal status of the Convention – has

---

[129] *Aston Cantlow PCC v Wallbank* [2001] 3 WLR 1323.

[130] *Poplar Housing Association Ltd v Donoghue* [2001] 3 WLR 183, at p 199 (Lord Woolf MR).

[131] D Oliver [2000] PL 476. See *Poplar Housing Association Ltd v Donoghue* (housing association a functional public authority); *Marcic v Thames Water Utilities Ltd* [2001] 3 All ER 698, [2002] 2 All ER 55 (privatised water company a public body); and *Aston Cantlow PCC v Wallbank* (Parochial Parish Council a public authority, because 'it possesses powers which private individuals do not possess to determine how others should act' (p 402). But compare *RSPCA v Attorney-General* [2001] 3 All ER 530 (RSPCA not a public authority).

[132] See A R Mowbray [1997] PL 647.

[133] Cf *RSPCA v Attorney-General* [2001] 3 All ER 530, at p 547 (Lightman J).

given rise to a great deal of analysis in the literature.[134] The better view appears to be that (i) Convention rights may not be directly enforced by one private party against another, but that (ii) Convention rights may be relied on in an established cause of action to extend the rights of either party. An example would be where the applicant brings an action against the defendant for breach of confidence and relies in the course of these proceedings on the art 8 right to privacy in order to extend the boundaries of the protection which the common law otherwise provides.[135]

Concerns that the Act might be used to extend existing or develop new causes of action in litigation between private parties gave rise to special measures relating to freedom of expression. There was concern in particular from the newspaper industry and its self-regulators (the Press Complaints Commission) about the possible implications of the right to privacy in art 8. These and other concerns led to s 12 which applies where a court is considering whether to grant any relief which might affect the exercise of the Convention right to freedom of expression. In these cases, s 12 limits the circumstances in which a court may make interim injunctions, though in view of the inclusion of the courts as public authorities it may be questioned whether these special measures are strictly necessary. Unless there are compelling circumstances, no interim injunction is to be granted without the respondent having been notified (s 12(2)); moreover, no interim relief is to be granted unless the court is satisfied that the applicant is likely to succeed at the full trial (s 12(3)).[136] Section 12(4) addresses in particular the threat to freedom of expression created by the right to privacy and is a remarkable testament to concerns about the latter. Thus a court is to have particular regard to the importance of the Convention right to freedom of expression and in proceedings relating to journalistic material to 'any relevant privacy code'. The idea here is that no injunction should be granted to restrain a publication on the ground that it violates the privacy of the applicant if the respondent can show that it complies with the Codes of Practice of the Press Complaints Commission or the Broadcasting Standards Commission respectively.[137] Section 13 contains special protection for religious bodies from the application of Convention rights which might undermine their doctrine and practices.[138]

The Human Rights Act in practice

The Human Rights Act came fully into force on 2 October 2000, although it was in force in Scotland and Wales before then in relation to devolution issues.[139] The experience in Scotland in particular is that the Act is most likely to be felt in the field of criminal justice. A spate of cases have raised questions about the extent to which

---

[134] See M Hunt [1998] PL 423; G Phillipson (1999) 62 MLR 824; R Buxton (2000) 116 LQR 48; W Wade (2000) 116 LQR 217.

[135] *Douglas v Hello!* [2001] QB 967; *Venables v News Group Newspapers Ltd* [2001] Fam 430. See ch 22 F.

[136] This qualifies the normal rules relating to interim injunctions as set out in *American Cyanamid Ltd v Ethicon Co* [1975] AC 396 where the House of Lords held that in order to obtain interim relief the applicant need only show a serious issue to be tried and that the balance of convenience lies in favour of granting the injunction sought. The interim injunction holds the ring until the full trial of the action, which may not take place until some considerable time in the future. There is no need to show that a court is likely to grant the remedy sought at the trial of the action, with questions of legality being weighed against other factors in the balance of convenience. Such a procedure gives rise to interesting questions about the compatibility of procedural law with the principle of the rule of law, quite apart from its implication for human rights. Section 12(3) has been diminished in at least one case: *Imutran Ltd v Uncaged Campaigns Ltd* [2001] 2 All ER 385, at p 391. See also *Douglas v Hello!* (note 135 above).

[137] See further ch 23 B and C.

[138] See P Cumper [2000] PL 254.

[139] The Act has a limited retrospective effect. See s 22(4) and *R v Lambert* [2001] 3 WLR 206, *R v Kansal* [2001] 3 WLR 1562, and *R v Saunders, The Times*, 1 February 2002.

Scottish criminal procedure complied in particular with the right to a fair trial as guaranteed by art 6 of the ECHR.[140]

> In *Starrs* v *Ruxton*[141] the accused raised as a devolution issue the question of whether their rights under art 6 were infringed by being tried by a temporary sheriff. They contended that a temporary sheriff was not independent and impartial on two grounds: under the Sheriff Courts (Scotland) Act 1971 temporary sheriffs could be recalled by the Secretary of State before the end of their appointments; and appointments were made for renewable periods of one year only. In accepting these contentions, the Lord Justice-Clerk (Cullen) said that 'there is a real risk that a well-informed observer might think that a temporary sheriff might be influenced by his hopes and fears as to his prospective advancement'.[142]

Other cases (also under art 6) have challenged: (i) delay in the prosecution of offences; (ii) police questioning of a suspect in the absence of a solicitor; (iii) statutory violations of the right against self-incrimination; (iv) lack of sufficient information in the charge; and (v) the admission of evidence said to be prejudicial and the implications of extensive pre-trial publicity. In most (but not all) of these cases, the points relating to Convention rights did not succeed.[143]

The Human Rights Act has already generated a huge literature, as practitioners and others assess its impact. Much of the literature has been concerned with the implications of the Act for specific subjects, such as administrative law, criminal law, commercial law, company law, insolvency law, land law, family law, employment law, social security law, planning law, tort law, and so on.[144] But it is clear that many of the early predictions about the likely impact of the Human Rights Act have been exaggerated,[145] although it will take some time for its true impact to be fully clarified. Much will depend on how interventionist or restrained the courts choose to be. It is true that the first declaration of incompatibility was made within six months of the Act coming into force, but it is also the case that in *Brown* v *Stott*[146] Lord Bingham indicated that the courts will defer to 'the decisions of a representative legislature and a democratic government within the discretionary area of judgment accorded to those bodies'.[147] He has also emphasised that the Convention is concerned with 'rights and freedoms which are of real importance in a modern democracy governed by the rule of law'. It does not, as is sometimes mistakenly thought, offer relief from 'the heart-ache and the thousand natural shocks that flesh is heir to'.[148]

These observations of the senior law lord are a revealing insight into how the courts may see the role and function of the Convention: principally as an instrument in promoting rather than frustrating the principles and practices of representative government.[149] In the same case, Lord Steyn referred to the ECHR as representing 'our Bill of Rights' but compared it to Bills of Rights in other constitutional systems, most notably the

---

[140] Questions have also been raised about other Convention rights: *Burn (Petitioner)* 2000 JC 403 and *Smith* v *Donnelly* 2001 SLT 1007. For an assessment, see S Tierney [2001] PL 38 and C M G Himsworth, in Campbell, Ewing and Tomkins (eds), *Sceptical Essays on Human Rights*, ch 8.

[141] 2000 JC 208. See A O'Neill (2000) 63 MLR 429. On a different point, see *Hoekstra* v *HM Advocate* 2001 SLT 28.

[142] See subsequently *Gibbs* v *Ruxton* 2000 JC 403, *Clancy* v *Caird* 2000 SLT 546 and *Millar* v *Dickson* 2001 SLT 988. See also *Crummock (Scotland) Ltd* v *HM Advocate* 2000 JC 408 (on the independence of the jury).

[143] Those which did include *HM Advocate* v *Little* 1999 SLT 1145, *Docherty* v *HM Advocate* 2000 JC 307 and *HM Advocate* v *P* 2001 SLT 924.

[144] See D McGoldrick (2001) 50 ICLQ 901 for a comprehensive review.

[145] See J Wadham [2001] EHRLR 620 for a review of the case law in the first year of the Act's operation.

[146] *Brown* v *Stott* [2001] 2 All ER 97.

[147] Ibid, at p 114 (Lord Bingham). See also *McIntosh, Petitioner* 2001 SC (PC) 89, at p 102.

[148] Ibid.

[149] See also *R* v *DPP, ex p Kebeline* [2000] 2 AC 326, at p 380 (Lord Hope).

American where some of the rights (including in particular the right to freedom of expression) are drafted in categorical terms. In his view, the framers of the Convention

> realised only too well that a single-minded concentration on the pursuit of fundamental rights of individuals to the exclusion of the interests of the wider public might be subversive of the ideal of tolerant European democracies. The fundamental rights of individuals are of supreme importance but those rights are not unlimited: we live in communities of individuals who also have rights. The direct lineage of this ancient idea is clear: the convention is the direct descendant of the Universal Declaration of Human Rights which in art 29 expressly recognised the duties of everyone to the community and the limitation on rights in order to secure and protect respect for the rights of others.[150]

These considerations also point in the direction of judicial restraint in the application of Convention rights:[151] they emphasise the view that individuals have responsibilities as well as rights; that rights are to be constrained by the interests of the community as a whole; and that 'where difficult questions arise' in the event of a clash of rights (such as privacy and expression), 'a balance is to be struck'.[152] But the point perhaps ought not to be pushed too far: it will be for the courts to determine the boundaries of Parliament's 'discretionary area of judgment', in the same way that it will be for the courts to determine the circumstances in which it is 'appropriate' to 'defer, on democratic grounds, to the considered opinion of the elected body as to where the balance is to be struck between the rights of the individual and the needs of society'.[153]

One likely effect of the Act in practice is that it will lead to a greater assessment of the human rights implications by the government in the drafting of legislation and by Parliament in considering government bills.[154] This is a process which is formally encouraged by s 19 of the Human Rights Act which provides that a minister in charge of a Bill must make a statement to the effect that the Bill is either (i) in his or her view compatible with Convention rights; or (ii) the government wishes the Bill to proceed even though he or she is unable to make a statement of compatibility.[155] In practice Bills contain such a statement on their face and by 2002 no Bill had been introduced without bearing a statement of compatibility, although in some cases the statement seemed optimistic. Also important in terms of parliamentary oversight is the creation of the Joint Committee on Human Rights, which came into operation in February 2001. This is an all-party committee with terms of reference which include (i) an examination of ministerial statements of compatibility and (ii) remedial orders made under s 10. There is also a power to consider human rights issues generally, including human rights treaties other than the ECHR. The Committee has addressed a number of issues, including the implementation of the Human Rights Act and a number of bills to determine whether they are compatible with human rights obligations.[156] The Committee has not

---

[150] *Brown* v *Stott* (note 146 above), at p 118 (Lord Steyn). See also *R (Alconbury Ltd)* v *Environment Secretary* [2001] 2 WLR 1389, esp Lords Nolan and Hoffmann. See further the remarkably robust position adopted by Laws LJ in *R (Mahmood)* v *Home Secretary* [2001] UKHRR 307, at p 323.

[151] A point reinforced in *McIntosh, Petitioner*, at p 102 where Lord Bingham referred to the legislation which was being challenged in that case as being a statutory scheme which had been 'approved by a democratically elected Parliament and [which] should not be at all readily rejected'.

[152] It is an approach which also emphasises the practical importance of the different drafting of different Bills of Rights. Given the 'categorical language' of the US Bill of Rights, it must be open to question whether the decisions of the US Supreme Court ought to be of much value in the construction of the Human Rights Act.

[153] *R* v *A* [2001] 3 All ER 1, at p 21.

[154] On parliamentary scrutiny, see M Ryle [1994] PL 192; Kinley, *The European Convention on Human Rights*.

[155] The *Ministerial Code* already required ministers to consider the impact of the ECHR in preparing business for Cabinet.

[156] See HL 66; HC 332 (2000–01); HL 69; HC 448 (2001–02).

been unwilling to challenge ministers' claims that bills are compatible with the ECHR;[157] neither has it been reluctant to test proposed legislation for compatibility with other international instruments.[158]

D. Conclusion

The Human Rights Act has been said to weave Convention rights 'into the warp and woof of the common law and statute law'.[159] While this is true, the impact of the Act should not be overestimated. Following the general deference of the House of Lords and Privy Council to the principles of representative government, and a recognition that 'decisions as to what the general interest requires are made by democratically elected bodies or persons accountable to them',[160] existing law has proved to be very robust and not easy successfully to challenge. Even in the field of criminal justice, some controversial practices and procedures have been upheld, including (i) a statutory breach of the rule against self-incrimination;[161] (ii) property confiscation orders under the Drug Trafficking Act 1994 and subsequent legislation;[162] (iii) measures which placed the burden of proof on the defendant in criminal proceedings;[163] and (iv) the use of illegally obtained evidence in such proceedings.[164] There is also a realisation that in many cases the same result will be achieved by applying the normal principles of judicial review as may be achieved by applying the Human Rights Act,[165] and indeed that in many cases these principles already provide protection where Convention rights overlap with the traditional principles of judicial review.[166] It will not, of course, always necessarily be like this and different patterns of judicial involvement may emerge as new governments are elected and different generations of judges occupy senior judicial office. Nor should it be overlooked that the boundaries of existing causes of action – in both public and private law – will be stretched by the need to comply with Convention rights.[167] Yet the enactment of the Human Rights Act now raises questions about the incorporation of other human rights treaties, not the least of which is its sibling, the Council of Europe's Social Charter of 18 October 1961, in relation to which the United Kingdom has a very poor record of compliance.[168]

---

[157] See HL 37; HC 372 (2001–02) (Anti-terrorism, Crime and Security Bill).
[158] See HL 30; HC 314 (2001–02) (Homelessness Bill: consideration given to compatibility with International Covenant on the Elimination of Racial Discrimination, and International Covenant on Economic, Social and Cultural Rights).
[159] Lord Lester, in Jowell and Oliver (eds), *The Changing Constitution*, ch 4.
[160] *R (Alconbury Ltd) v Environment Secretary* [2001] 2 WLR 1389, per Lord Hoffmann.
[161] *Brown v Stott* [2001] 2 All ER 97.
[162] *R v Benjafield* [2001] 3 WLR 75; *McIntosh, Petitioner* 2001 SC (PC) 89.
[163] *R v Lambert* [2001] 3 WLR 206; also *R v Forbes* [2001] 1 AC 473.
[164] *Attorney-General's Reference (No 3 of 1999)* [2001] AC 91.
[165] See *R (Daly) v Home Secretary* [2001] 3 All ER 433.
[166] *R (Alconbury Ltd) v Environment Secretary* (note 160 above).
[167] See *Douglas v Hello!* (note 135 above); *R v Home Secretary, ex p Daly* (doctrine of proportionality in judicial review); and *Director General of Financial Trading v Proprietary Association of Great Britain* [2001] UKHR 429 (the rule against bias modified to meet Convention standards; see ch 30 B.
[168] For the position in 2000, see K D Ewing (2001) 30 ILJ 409.

Chapter 20

CITIZENSHIP, IMMIGRATION
AND EXTRADITION

A. Citizenship

Nationality in international law

It is impossible to use a passport in travelling from one country to another without being aware of the significance of the national status which the passport gives to its holder. Both in international and national law, the nationality or citizenship of an individual determines many aspects of the relationship which a person has with the state of which he or she is a national, and with other states. As has been said,

> To the extent to which individuals are not directly subjects of international law, nationality is the link between them and international law. It is through the medium of their nationality that individuals can normally enjoy benefits from international law.[1]

By an established principle of international law, each state is entitled (subject to treaty obligations which it may have) to determine, through its constitution and other laws, who are its subjects or nationals.[2] The fact that states enact their own rules on nationality may cause some persons to have dual or multiple nationality, or (more seriously) may cause others to have no nationality, i.e. to be stateless.

Upon an individual's nationality, other rights and duties may depend – not only the right to hold a passport, but also liability to military service, political rights and possibly the right to seek employment, own land or enter the civil service. In general, most national law (the ordinary civil and criminal law, access to the legal system) applies to all those within a country, regardless of nationality. Where a state is party to the European Convention on Human Rights, it must respect the human rights of all persons within its jurisdiction, whatever their nationality.[3] But some areas of national law, notably freedom of movement and its control by immigration law, may depend crucially on one's national status.

In general, and in the absence of treaty obligations to the contrary, a state is under no duty in international law to admit citizens of foreign states (aliens) to its territory. A state's immigration law lays down admission procedures, determines whether aliens will be admitted, regulates their status after entry and when they may be required to leave the country. Usually immigration law does not regulate the admission and removal of the state's own citizens, for the reason that a state has a duty in international law to admit to its territory such of its nationals as are not allowed to remain in the territory of other states and no other state is obliged to admit them.[4]

---

[1] Jennings and Watts, *Oppenheim's International Law*, p 849.
[2] Ibid, p 852; and Brownlie, *Principles of Public International Law*, ch 19, esp pp 385–9.
[3] Ch 19 B. By customary international law, every state must observe minimum standards of treatment in respect of aliens in its territory: Jennings and Watts, p 903.
[4] Jennings and Watts, p 857. For an ordinance that sought unlawfully to remove the entire population of a British colony, see *R v Foreign Secretary, ex p Bancoult* [2001] QB 1067.

Because of the importance of nationality for the individual and the state, the basic rules which determine who are citizens are often in the constitution,[5] amplified if necessary by other legislation. In the United Kingdom, nationality developed from the allegiance to the King which subjects owed at common law; and powers under the prerogative could be exercised over aliens who wished to enter or leave the jurisdiction. Only in the 20th century were nationality and immigration control placed on a statutory basis.

Today these matters are governed primarily by the British Nationality Act 1981 and the Immigration Act 1971 (as amended subsequently). Particularly between 1962 and 1982, the broad categories of British citizenship defined by the British Nationality Act 1948 contained many more citizens of Commonwealth countries than successive governments were willing to admit to the United Kingdom as a matter of public policy. During these years, immigration law was used to prevent certain classes of British subject from exercising their right at common law to enter the United Kingdom. To distinguish between British subjects who had the right of abode and those who did not, the Immigration Act 1971 created the concept of 'patriality'.[6] The Act of 1981 recast the law of nationality to take account of immigration policy, converting the criteria for 'patriality' into the criteria for citizenship. This enabled 'patriality' as such to disappear from immigration law.

In this chapter, this section mentions the main features of nationality law; section B describes the system of immigration control; section C outlines the law of extradition, which (inter alia) enables those in the United Kingdom who are charged with or convicted of serious crimes in another country to be removed there in the interests of justice.

The rules of nationality and immigration law are complex. Technicalities abound and may have crucial significance for individuals they affect. It must be emphasised that the present account is not comprehensive and detailed exceptions are not always mentioned.

The development of nationality law[7]

The development of nationality from the common law to the British Nationality Act 1981 has been shaped by the growth of the United Kingdom, by the transition from the Empire to today's Commonwealth,[8] and most recently by European integration. The subjects of the English king were at first all those who owed allegiance to the Crown. The primary means of becoming a subject was by the 'ius soli': a person born within the King's dominions became a subject regardless of the status of the parents.[9] As early as 1350, the English statute *De natis ultra mare* applied the 'ius sanguinis' (i.e. birth by descent, regardless of the place of birth) so that certain persons born abroad whose fathers (or in some cases both parents) were subjects would also be subjects. In *Calvin*'s case,[10] those born in Scotland after James VI of Scotland had become James I of England were held not to be aliens in England, since they owed allegiance to the

---

[5] See e.g. Constitution of the USA, 14th Amendment (1868), s 1: 'All persons born or naturalized in the US . . . are citizens of the US and of the State wherein they reside.'

[6] See section B.

[7] For the current law, see Fransman, *British Nationality Law*; Macdonald and Webber, *Immigration Law and Practice in the United Kingdom*, ch 2. For the history, see Dummett and Nicol, *Subjects, Citizens, Aliens and Others*; also Parry, *Nationality and Citizenship Laws of the Commonwealth*.

[8] Ch 15 C.

[9] An early exception to the 'ius soli' was made for those born within the territory to a foreign envoy or diplomat, or to enemy aliens.

[10] (1608) 7 Co Rep 1a. And see *Stair Memorial Encyclopedia: the Laws of Scotland*, vol 14, pp 743–4.

same king. In 1707, English and Scottish citizens became British subjects by reason of the Treaty of Union; and they were joined by the Irish in 1800. Although citizenship was generally acquired on birth, it could also be conferred by law, when individuals or defined classes were 'naturalised' by Parliament; from 1870, the power of naturalisation was exercised by the executive.[11]

As the Empire grew, the status of 'British subject' became a common citizenship throughout most of the Empire. The British Nationality and Status of Aliens Act 1914 declared that all persons born within the King's dominions were British subjects.[12] Some territories (mainly in Africa and India) under British control were never possessions of the Crown, but were only in the protection of the Crown: persons born there became 'British protected persons', not British subjects.

At common law, those who were not British subjects were regarded as aliens. Aliens within the King's territory owed local allegiance to the monarch, and were entitled to protection of their person and property in the courts.[13] In the event of war being declared upon a foreign state, citizens of that state became enemy aliens; if they were in Britain, they lost their right to protection of the courts.[14] In 1698, Parliament had declared that aliens were not to be permitted to vote,[15] but it was not until 1905 that legislation restricted the entry of some aliens into the United Kingdom. In 1914, further measures for controlling the entry and presence of aliens were authorised.[16]

Until 1948 the status of British subject applied across the Commonwealth. The entry of British subjects into the United Kingdom was not restricted by law. Neither was there power for the executive to distinguish between British subjects present in the United Kingdom according to their place of origin. However, the dominion and colonial legislatures often restricted entry to their territories;[17] and there was no universal freedom of movement throughout the Commonwealth.

The British Nationality Act 1948

The desire of countries such as Canada and Australia to have their own citizenship laws led to the British Nationality Act 1948, enacted after a Commonwealth conference.[18] The 1948 Act assumed that each independent state would provide its own scheme of citizenship,[19] and on this basis created a common citizenship for the Commonwealth. The Act used the terms *British subject* and *Commonwealth citizen* with the same meaning, namely a person who was a citizen of the United Kingdom and colonies or of an independent state in the Commonwealth.

For the United Kingdom and its dependencies, the 1948 Act created the term *Citizen of the United Kingdom and Colonies* (CUKC). The Act did not change the common law right of all British subjects (both CUKCs and citizens of other Commonwealth states) to enter and reside in the United Kingdom; no distinction was made for this purpose between persons having a close connection with the United Kingdom, those whose home was in a colony and those who were citizens of independent Commonwealth states.

---

[11] See Dummett and Nicol, pp 71–7.
[12] Subject to the exception of those born to foreign diplomats and to enemy aliens.
[13] A person who owes allegiance to the Crown is subject to the law of treason (*R v Casement* [1917] 1 KB 98; *Joyce v DPP* [1946] AC 347). The Crown's duty to provide protection in return for allegiance is not enforceable by judicial process: *China Navigation Co v A-G* [1932] 2 KB 197; *Mutasa v A-G* [1980] QB 114.
[14] See p 431 below.
[15] Dummett and Nicol, p 73.
[16] British Nationality and Status of Aliens Act 1914; and see the Aliens Order 1953.
[17] Dummett and Nicol, pp 115–25.
[18] See Cmd 7326, 1948.
[19] Hence in the 1948 Act, s 32(7). And see *R v Foreign Secretary, ex p Ross-Clunis* [1991] 2 AC 439.

After 1948, when a dependent territory gained independence, the legislation conferring independence generally provided that the population of the territory would cease to be CUKCs and would become citizens of the new state. By virtue of that new citizenship, they would remain 'Commonwealth citizens' under the 1948 Act if the new state chose to remain in the Commonwealth.[20] However, some residents in the territory might be permitted to remain as CUKCs rather than take up the new state's citizenship, as were the Asian minorities in the East African countries. The independence legislation also sought to ensure that no one became stateless by losing one citizenship and gaining nothing in its place.[21]

The 1948 Act provided for a residual category of *British subjects without any other citizenship*. It also recognised the status of *British protected persons*. Irish citizens did not qualify to be Commonwealth citizens (Ireland left the Commonwealth on becoming a republic in 1949). However, the Ireland Act 1949 declared that they were not aliens and that Ireland was not a foreign country; while in the United Kingdom, Irish citizens may, like British subjects, exercise political rights.

The British Nationality Act 1981

Section B will describe how British subjects under the 1948 Act were affected by immigration policy between 1962 and 1982. The British Nationality Act 1981 created categories of citizenship that were narrower than under the 1948 Act and were intended to fit the United Kingdom's immigration policies. The Act also changed the old rule conferring citizenship on all those born in the United Kingdom, to a more complex rule by which a child born in the United Kingdom during or after 1983 becomes a British citizen only if his or her parents satisfy conditions as regards their immigration status.

Categories of citizenship

Under the 1981 Act, which came into effect on 1 January 1983 (as modified subsequently),[22] there are, including Irish citizens and aliens, nine main categories of citizenship:

(1) Virtually all those who before 1983 were citizens of the United Kingdom and Colonies (CUKCs) and were patrials under the Immigration Act 1971 became *British citizens*.[23]
(2) Those who before 1983 were CUKCs by reason of their connection with a dependent territory but did not have a sufficient connection with the United Kingdom to be patrials became *British Dependent Territories citizens*.[24]
(3) Those who before 1983 were CUKCs and did not come within the first two previous categories formed a residual category, *British Overseas citizens*.[25]

---

[20] They would however owe allegiance to the British Crown only if their state recognised the Queen as head of state; most Commonwealth states are republics and recognise the Queen only as titular head of the Commonwealth; ch 15 C.

[21] The United Kingdom is a party to the UN Convention on the Reduction of Statelessness, 1961. See now the British Nationality Act 1981, s 36 and Sch 2.

[22] By the British Nationality (Falkland Islands) Act 1983; the Hong Kong Act 1985; and the British Nationality (Hong Kong) Act 1990; and the British Overseas Territories Act 2002.

[23] See Immigration Act 1971, s 1(1) (section B below); British Nationality Act 1981, s 11(1). And see s 11(2), (3).

[24] 1981 Act, s 23. Under the British Nationality (Falkland Islands) Act 1983, those BDT citizens whose connection was with the Falkland Islands were declared retrospectively to have become *British citizens* on 1 January 1983. By the British Overseas Territories Act 2002, British Dependent Territories citizens are renamed *British Overseas Territories citizens*. They are to receive full British citizenship (carrying with it the right of abode in the United Kingdom), except if their connection is with the Sovereign Base Areas of Akrotiri and Dhekelia in Cyprus.

[25] 1981 Act, s 26.

(4) Because of the ending of British rule over Hong Kong in 1997, a new form of British nationality, *British Nationals (Overseas)*, was created by the Hong Kong Act 1985. British Dependent Territories citizens whose local connection was with Hong Kong could between 1987 and 1997 apply for registration as British Nationals (Overseas).[26]

(5) The term *British subject* lost the meaning which it had under the 1948 Act. It now denotes only persons who under the 1948 Act were 'British subjects without citizenship'; this included persons who were born in an independent Commonwealth country before 1949 and who neither had citizenship of that country nor became CUKCs. Some older citizens of Ireland are also British subjects.[27]

(6) The term *Commonwealth citizen* retains the broad meaning that it had under the 1948 Act. It comprises citizens of the 50 or so states of the Commonwealth, as well as all persons with British citizenship or nationality (i.e. categories 1–5).[28]

(7) *British protected persons* continue under the 1981 Act with no material change from their status under the 1948 Act.[29]

(8) *Citizens of the Republic of Ireland* (unless they have a second nationality) are neither Commonwealth citizens nor aliens.

(9) The status of *alien* denotes a person who is outside categories 1–8.[30]

Under the Treaty on European Union, those who for this purpose are nationals of one of the 15 member states of the Union enjoy the status of *citizen of the Union*, and thus the rights conferred by arts 8–8e of the European Community Treaty.[31] This class comprises British citizens (category 1), British Overseas Territories citizens from Gibraltar,[32] Irish citizens (category 8) as well as the citizens of all other EU states (who, unless they have dual nationality, are aliens in United Kingdom law). Except for the Gibraltarians, those in categories 2–7 above are not European Union citizens.

Acquisition of British citizenship after 1 January 1983

Under the 1981 Act, there are five ways by which British citizenship may be acquired where this did not occur by operation of law on 1 January 1983.

1 *Birth in the United Kingdom.* A person born in the United Kingdom (in which the 1981 Act includes the Channel Islands and the Isle of Man)[33] on or after 1 January 1983 acquires British citizenship only (*a*) if his or her parents are married and at least one of them is a British citizen or is settled in the United Kingdom; or (*b*) if his or her parents are not married and the mother is a British citizen or is settled in the United Kingdom. To be 'settled' in the United Kingdom, a parent must be 'ordinarily resident' there without being subject under the Immigration Act 1971 to any restriction on the period for which one may remain.[34] No one is 'ordinarily resident' who is in the United Kingdom 'in breach of the immigration laws'.[35] A woman is taken to be the mother

---

[26] Hong Kong (British Nationality) Order 1986, SI 1986 No 948.
[27] 1981 Act, ss 30–31. And see Macdonald and Webber, p 50.
[28] 1981 Act, s 37 and Sch 3.
[29] Ibid, ss 38 and 50(1). And see SI 1982 No 1070, as amended. Under the 1948 Act, a person could be both a British protected person and a CUKC: *Motala v A-G* [1992] 1 AC 281.
[30] 1981 Act, s 50(1).
[31] Such rights include the right to move and reside freely in the territory of member states, subject to limitations deriving from the EC Treaty; and the right to vote and stand in local and European elections in other member states. See ch 8 above and section B below.
[32] Gibraltar is the only British overseas territory within Europe. On the UK declaration for EU purposes, see p 446 below.
[33] 1981 Act, s 50(1).
[34] Ibid, s 50(2); see also s 50(3), (4); and section B.
[35] 1981 Act, s 50(5).

of any child born to her; a man is taken to be the father only of a legitimate child born to him.[36]

2 *Adoption in the United Kingdom.*   A minor (i.e. a person under 18) who is not a British citizen and is adopted in the United Kingdom on or after 1 January 1983 becomes a British citizen on adoption if the adopter or one of joint adopters is a British citizen.[37]

3 *Citizenship by descent.*   A person born outside the United Kingdom on or after 1 January 1983 acquires British citizenship by descent if at least one of the parents (*a*) is a British citizen otherwise than by descent;[38] or (*b*) is abroad in Crown service under the UK government or (on certain conditions) is working for the European Community or for certain public services.[39]

4 *Registration.*   There are various grounds on which one who does not qualify under these rules may be registered by the Home Secretary as a British citizen. Registration is an entitlement for someone born in the United Kingdom who did not become a British citizen at birth (*a*) if, while he or she is still a minor, a parent becomes a British citizen or settled in the United Kingdom and an application is made for registration;[40] or (*b*) if he or she, during the first ten years of his or her life, has not been absent from the United Kingdom for more than 90 days each year.[41] The Home Secretary also has a general power to register any minor as a British citizen.[42] Registration as a British citizen is an entitlement for British Overseas Territories citizens and other categories, including British protected persons, who meet certain requirements as to being settled or present in the United Kingdom.[43]

5 *Naturalisation.*   The Home Secretary may grant naturalisation as a British citizen to any person who is of full age and capacity and satisfies certain requirements as to residence, character, language and future intentions.[44]

The departure made by the 1981 Act from the rule that birth in the United Kingdom qualifies the child for British citizenship means that a child's citizenship depends on the citizenship or immigration status of the parents. The complex rules as to registration mitigate some of the adverse effects of the new rule.

Where the Home Secretary has discretion in registration or naturalisation, it must be exercised without regard to the race, colour or religion of persons affected.[45] The Home Secretary is not required to assign any reason for granting or refusing applications which are at his or her discretion, nor are these decisions 'subject to appeal to, or review in, any court'.[46] Yet the 1981 Act also states that the court has jurisdiction

---

[36] Ibid, s 50(9). The father's position is subject to the legitimation of the child by subsequent marriage: s 47. For birth on ships or aircraft outside the United Kingdom, s 50(7).

[37] 1981 Act, s 1(5).

[38] For the meaning of British citizen by descent, see 1981 Act, s 14.

[39] Ibid, s 2.

[40] Ibid, s 1(3).

[41] Ibid, s 1(4). The Home Secretary has discretion to dispense with the 90-day rule: s 1(7). Under s 3, certain minors born abroad to a British citizen by descent are entitled to be registered as British citizens.

[42] Ibid, s 3(1).

[43] Ibid, s 4. British Overseas Territories citizens from Gibraltar have an absolute right to be registered as British citizens: s 5. And see the British Overseas Territories Act 2002 (note 24 above).

[44] Ibid, s 6 and Sch 1. The requirements are less onerous where the applicant is married to a British citizen: s 6(2).

[45] Ibid, s 44(1).

[46] Ibid, s 44(2).

concerning the rights of any person under the Act; accordingly, where an individual claims to be entitled to be registered as a British citizen, he or she may seek judicial review of a decision rejecting such an entitlement.[47] However, since the relief obtained by judicial review is itself discretionary, the court may refuse relief on public policy grounds to an applicant guilty of criminal deception in obtaining citizenship.[48] In 1996, the Court of Appeal held that, although the Home Secretary was under no duty to give reasons for refusing naturalisation, he must act fairly; he must give sufficient indication about the subject matter of his concern as to whether the criteria for naturalisation are met to enable the applicant to make submissions to him.[49]

Termination of British citizenship

A British citizen may renounce that citizenship to acquire another nationality, but the renunciation does not take effect until it has been registered by the Home Secretary, who may on various grounds withhold registration.[50] The Home Secretary may deprive a British citizen of citizenship acquired by registration or naturalisation,[51] but only on certain grounds, including the use of fraud, false statements or concealment to obtain citizenship,[52] disloyalty or disaffection towards the Queen, trading or communicating with the enemy and (within 5 years of becoming a British citizen) receiving a sentence of imprisonment for not less than 12 months. The Home Secretary must also be satisfied that it is 'not conducive to the public good' that the person should continue to be a British citizen.[53] Notice of the grounds must be given and the citizen may apply for a formal inquiry to be held.[54]

Aliens

The class of aliens was defined by the British Nationality Act 1981.[55] Aliens present in the United Kingdom are subject to the general law and are entitled to the protection of the courts.[56] They are also subject to common law and statutory rules affecting aliens except, in the case of European citizens, where those rules are inconsistent with EU law. Another exception applies to members of foreign armed forces visiting the United Kingdom.[57] Aliens are subject to some political disabilities: they have no right to vote (European citizens may vote in local and European elections);[58] they may not be members of the Privy Council or either House of Parliament;[59] and certain restrictions

---

[47] Ibid, s 44(3).

[48] R v Home Secretary, ex p Puttick [1981] QB 767.

[49] R v Home Secretary, ex p Fayed [1997] 1 All ER 228, applying A-G v Ryan [1980] AC 718. For earlier comment on s 44, see T St J N Bates [1982] PL 179.

[50] The Home Secretary must be satisfied that the individual will acquire some other nationality and may refuse to register a renunciation in time of war: 1981 Act, s 12. For resumption of citizenship after renunciation, see s 13.

[51] 1981 Act, s 40.

[52] This is the sole ground for deprivation in respect of citizens who became CUKCs by registration or naturalisation before 1983: 1981 Act, s 40(2) (b), (c). And see R v Home Secretary, ex p Parvaz Akhtar [1981] QB 46.

[53] 1981 Act, s 40(5) (a). Cf the 'not conducive' ground for deportation, section B.

[54] See also 1981 Act, s 40(6)–(8).

[55] Page 428 above.

[56] See e.g. Kuchenmeister v Home Office [1958] 1 QB 496 and R v Home Secretary, ex p Cheblak [1991] 2 All ER 319.

[57] See the Visiting Forces Act 1952; ch 16 C.

[58] Ch 9 A.

[59] Act of Settlement, s 3.

exist as to their appointment to civil or military office under the Crown.[60] Other restrictions affect the ownership by aliens of British ships and of aircraft registered in the United Kingdom.[61] Aliens benefit from the European Convention on Human Rights, the rights under which extend to all persons within national jurisdiction[62] and from the Race Relations Act 1976, which outlaws discrimination on grounds (inter alia) of nationality and national origin.[63] The EC Treaty excludes discrimination against nationals of member states.[64] If aliens are ill treated while in the United Kingdom, they may seek consular or diplomatic protection from their own state.

In the event of war being declared between the United Kingdom and a foreign state, they may be interned or expelled by the Crown[65] and are subject to other disabilities.[66] In neither the Falkland Islands campaign in 1982 nor the Gulf hostilities in 1991 was there a declaration of war; thus citizens of Argentina and Iraq did not become enemy aliens. In 1991, when the government detained certain Iraqi citizens in Britain, the power used was that of detention with a view to deportation under the Immigration Act 1971, a power that was not wholly appropriate.[67]

The right to travel

Under art 12(2) of the International Covenant on Civil and Political Rights, to which the United Kingdom is a party: 'Everyone shall be free to leave any country, including his own.' Since Magna Carta in 1215, it has been recognised that citizens ought to be free to enter and leave the realm. But the right to travel abroad is not protected in law as it is under the USA and Irish Constitutions.[68] The old common law writ *ne exeat regno* originally enabled the Crown for reasons of state to prevent a subject from leaving the realm; it now merely prevents a wealthy defendant from leaving the jurisdiction to frustrate a lawful claim before the court and does not enable the government to prevent a citizen from travelling abroad.[69] Despite the virtual necessity today of having a passport if one wishes to travel abroad, the issue of passports is a matter for the Crown, acting through the UK Passport Agency under authority emanating from the royal prerogative, not from an Act of Parliament. Decisions to refuse or revoke a passport are subject not to appeal but to judicial review; while the Foreign Secretary may have a policy for refusing a passport abroad to someone accused of serious crime in the United Kingdom, reasons must be given for the refusal and the citizen must have a chance to show that an exception should be made.[70]

---

[60] Aliens Employment Act 1955, s 1, modifying the Aliens Restriction (Amendment) Act 1919, and modified by the EC (Employment in the Civil Service) Order, SI 1991 No 1221. See also Army Act 1955, s 21.

[61] Status of Aliens Act 1914, s 17; UK (Air Navigation) Order 1980, SI 1980 No 1965.

[62] E.g. *Soering v UK* (1989) 11 EHRR 439; and ch 19 B.

[63] Ch 19 A.

[64] EC Treaty, art 6 (formerly art 7). And see *Case C-221/89, R v Transport Secretary, ex p Factortame Ltd (No 3)* [1992] QB 680.

[65] See *Netz v Ede* [1946] Ch 244; *R v Bottrill, ex p Kuechenmeister* [1947] KB 41.

[66] See Jennings and Watts, pp 904–910; McNair and Watts, *The Legal Effects of War*, chs 2 and 3.

[67] *R v Home Secretary, ex p Cheblak* [1991] 2 All ER 319; I Leigh [1991] PL 331 and F Hampson [1991] PL 507. See now the Anti-terrorism, Crime and Security Act 2001, Part IV.

[68] See respectively *Kent v Dulles* 357 US 116 (1958) and *A-G v X* [1992] 2 CMLR 277, 303 (Finlay CJ).

[69] See *Felton v Callis* [1969] 1 QB 200 and *Al Nahkel for Contracting Ltd v Lowe* [1986] QB 235.

[70] *R v Foreign Secretary, ex p Everett* [1989] QB 811. Passports are also withheld (*a*) to prevent a minor going abroad contrary to a court order or the wishes of the parent with custody; (*b*) until a citizen repays the cost of repatriation to the United Kingdom at public expense; and (*c*) most rarely, to protect the public interest against travel by a person whose activities are demonstrably undesirable. And see *Going Abroad: A Report on Passports* (Justice, 1974); HC Deb, 15 November 1974, col 265 (WA); HL Deb, 22 January 1981, col 558.

The rights of British citizens (as European citizens) to travel within European Union states may require national courts to protect them against improper refusal of a passport. The Immigration (European Economic Area) Regulations 2000[71] sought to incorporate in national law free movement directives issued under the EC Treaty, but did not deal with a British citizen's right under EU law to be issued with a travel document to facilitate movement within Europe. There is a case to be made for placing the system of passports upon a firm legislative base, but until that is done the freedom of movement within Europe may if necessary be protected by means of judicial review.

B. Immigration and deportation[72]

Background to the Immigration Act 1971

In section A, we saw that at international law, and apart from any treaty obligations, a state is entitled to control entry into its territory by citizens of other states. At common law, the Crown had power under the prerogative to prevent aliens from entering the United Kingdom.[73] As Widgery LJ said in *Schmidt v Home Secretary*:

> when an alien approaching this country is refused leave to land, he has no right capable of being infringed in such a way as to enable him to come to this court for the purpose of assistance . . . In such a situation the alien's desire to land can be rejected for good reason or bad, for sensible reason or fanciful or for no reason at all.[74]

At common law, although no definite authority existed, it was possible that the Crown had power to expel friendly aliens who had been previously admitted into the United Kingdom.[75] Such prerogative powers as the Crown may have in respect of aliens have been expressly preserved in being.[76] But for virtually all purposes today, the executive relies on statutory powers for controlling the entry of aliens and for enabling aliens here to be deported.

By contrast with aliens, British subjects before and after the British Nationality Act 1948 could enter and remain in the United Kingdom without restriction and the Crown had no power to prevent their admission, to deport them or to prevent their departure.[77] These rights were available to the citizens of all member states of the Commonwealth.

The right of British subjects (within the meaning of the 1948 Act) to enter the United Kingdom was severely restricted by the Commonwealth Immigrants Acts of 1962 and 1968. The 1962 Act, passed to check immigration from the Caribbean, India and Pakistan, subjected all British subjects to immigration control, except for those born in the United Kingdom and those who were citizens of the United Kingdom and Colonies (CUKCs) and held passports issued by the United Kingdom government.[78] The 1962 Act also

---

[71] SI 2000 No 2326, which replaced SI 1994 No 1895 (discussed by C Vincenzi [1995] PL 259).

[72] The leading text is Macdonald and Webber, *Immigration Law and Practice*. See also Dummett and Nicol, *Subjects, Citizens, Aliens and Others*; Legomsky, *Immigration and the Judiciary*.

[73] *Musgrove v Chun Teeong Toy* [1891] AC 272; cf *Poll v Lord Advocate* (1899) 1 F 823.

[74] [1969] 2 Ch 149, 172. In 2001, despite humanitarian considerations, the Australian government successfully prevented a ship laden with Afghans from landing in Australian territory: see *Ruddock v Vadarlis* (2001) 183 ALR 1.

[75] See Parry (ed.), *British Digest of International Law*, vol 6, pp 83–98; *A-G for Canada v Cain* [1906] AC 542, 547; Dicey, *Law of the Constitution*, pp 224–7; and C L Vincenzi [1985] PL 93.

[76] Immigration Act 1971, s 33(5), which ousts the principle in *A-G v De Keyser's Royal Hotel Ltd* [1920] AC 208 (ch 12 E).

[77] Cf D W Williams (1974) 23 ICLQ 642.

[78] Passports issued by colonial governments did not entitle holders to enter the United Kingdom: *R v Home Secretary, ex p Bhurosah* [1968] 1 QB 266.

authorised the deportation of Commonwealth citizens (but not holders of United Kingdom passports) who had been convicted of offences punishable with imprisonment and recommended by a court for deportation.

The Commonwealth Immigrants Act 1968 was passed in great haste to forestall what was feared might be a mass exodus to Britain from Kenya of persons of Asian origin who, when Kenya had become independent in 1963, had chosen to continue as CUKCs rather than become citizens of Kenya. Since they held passports issued by the British government, they were not subject to the controls established by the 1962 Act.[79] The 1968 Act was notable because it took away from a non-resident CUKC the right of entry into the United Kingdom unless he or she, or at least one of his or her parents or grandparents, had a prior United Kingdom connection (for example, through having been born, adopted or naturalised in the United Kingdom). The 1968 Act thereby prevented CUKCs from entering the United Kingdom, even though they were subject to expulsion from the state in which they had been residing and were entitled to enter no other country. The UK government subsequently came under great pressure to admit other UK citizens in similar circumstances and, notwithstanding the 1968 Act, did admit many of the Asians expelled from Uganda in 1972.[80]

The Immigration Act 1971 and after

The 1971 Act provided a new and extensive code for the control of immigration. On 1 January 1973 when it came into operation, the legal distinction between aliens and Commonwealth citizens lost much of its significance for purposes of immigration control, but this did not mean a relaxation in the system of control. Since it was in 1973 that the United Kingdom joined the European Communities, a new distinction arose between citizens of Community countries and those from non-Community countries.

Under the 1971 Act, the most important distinction was between those who had the right of abode in the United Kingdom and those (whether aliens or Commonwealth immigrants) who were subject to immigration control and needed permission to enter and reside in the United Kingdom. The fact that an intending immigrant might be a CUKC or a citizen of a Commonwealth country did not confer the right of entry. The 1971 Act created the concept of patriality to identify those British subjects who were considered to have a sufficient connection with the United Kingdom to entitle them to the right of abode there. The class of patrials included (i) those who were CUKCs by reason of birth, adoption, naturalisation or registration in the United Kingdom or in the Islands (i.e. the Isle of Man and the Channel Islands); (ii) citizens of other Commonwealth countries who were born to or adopted by a parent who at the time of the birth or adoption was a United Kingdom citizen by virtue of his or her birth in the United Kingdom or Islands; and (iii) women who were Commonwealth citizens and married to patrials. Those claiming to be patrial could prove their status by obtaining a certificate of patriality. In *R v Home Secretary, ex p Phansopkar*, the court ordered the Home Secretary to hear and determine an application for such a certificate made by an Indian woman, married to a man who had become a United Kingdom citizen by registration; the woman's right to a certificate could not be withheld by arbitrary delay on the part of the Home Office.[81]

---

[79] For the controversy over the government's intentions towards the Kenyan Asians in 1963, see HC Deb, 27–28 February 1968; HL Deb, 29 February 1968; Steel, *No Entry*; Dummett and Nicol, ch 11; and Evans, *Immigration Law*, pp 64–8.

[80] Cf *R v Home Secretary, ex p Thakrar* [1974] QB 684. And see *East African Asians v UK* (1973) 3 EHRR 76.

[81] [1976] QB 606. See now Immigration Act 1971, s 3(9) (b), as amended in 1988 (certificate of entitlement to right of abode). And see *R v Home Secretary, ex p Mersin* [2000] INLR 511.

The elaborate concept of patriality was subject to much criticism. Foremost was the criticism that patriality did not extend to persons who, like the East African Asians, were CUKCs but had no country to which they might go other than the United Kingdom. For this reason the United Kingdom government could not ratify the fourth protocol to the European Convention on Human Rights, which declares that 'on one shall be denied the right to enter the territory of which he is a national'.[82] Patriality was also criticised for including citizens of other Commonwealth countries at least one of whose parents had been born in the United Kingdom; this rule favoured those of British origin from countries such as Australia, Canada and New Zealand, exposing the 1971 Act to the charge that it was racially motivated.

The desire to bring the law of nationality into conformity with immigration policy and to take account of changes in the Commonwealth since 1948 was the main reason for the British Nationality Act 1981. As we saw in section A, the 1981 Act created a new category of British citizen, the rules defining which were derived from the rules of patriality. Some criticisms of the 1971 scheme remain applicable to the 1981 Act.

Immigration law has been modified many times since 1971. The Immigration Act 1988 tightened up aspects of the law, cutting down rights of appeal against deportation orders and making it a continuing offence to overstay leave to enter. Since 1988, the most pressing problems in immigration control have arisen in relation to the large number of claims from very diverse countries for admission as refugees.[83] There have been three major responses to these problems: the Asylum and Immigration Appeals Act 1993, the Asylum and Immigration Act 1996 and the Immigration and Asylum Act 1999.[84] The last of these amended the Immigration Act 1971 and dealt with such topics as carriers' liability, bail, support for asylum seekers and the appeals system. What follows is no more than a selective outline of aspects of a complex and imperfect body of legislation.

Immigration control

In broad terms, the following are the main categories for purposes of immigration control. They mostly derive from the British Nationality Act 1981 and were explained in section A.

(a) *British citizens.* They have the right of abode in the United Kingdom and do not need leave to enter or reside there.

(b) *British overseas territories citizens, British overseas citizens, British subjects and citizens of other Commonwealth countries.* In general, they do not have the right of abode in the United Kingdom and are subject to immigration control. But some Commonwealth citizens, who as patrials under the 1971 Act had the right of abode in the United Kingdom, continue to have that right.[85] In 2002, the British Overseas Territories Act conferred the right of abode on British overseas territories citizens.

(c) *Citizens of the Republic of Ireland.* They benefit from the 'common travel area' for immigration purposes formed by the United Kingdom, the Isle of Man, the Channel Islands and the Republic of Ireland, travel within which is in principle not subject to immigration control.[86] Irish residents enter the United Kingdom from Ireland without passing through immigration control, but they are subject to deportation from the United

---

[82] See ch 19 B and cf *R v Home Secretary, ex p Thakrar* (above).
[83] Pages 505–7 in this chapter.
[84] The 1999 Act was based on Cm 4018, 1998.
[85] 1971 Act, s 2(1) (b) and (2), as amended by British Nationality Act 1981.
[86] 1971 Act, s 1(3). And see s 9 and Sch 4.

Kingdom under the 1971 Act. Under the Terrorism Act 2000, port and border controls may be exercised on travel to and from Northern Ireland by police, immigration and customs officers.[87]

(d) *Aliens who are nationals of other EU countries.* They benefit from the right to freedom of movement within the EU conferred by Community law, which necessarily restricts the powers of the UK authorities over them. When such persons are exercising an enforceable Community right to enter or remain in the United Kingdom, they do not require leave under the 1971 Act to do so.[88] To this category may be added the nationals of Iceland, Norway and Liechtenstein, which are outside the EU but are parties to the Agreement on the European Economic Area. The area comprises all EU states together with the additional countries. The agreement provides freedom of movement within the area for all qualified nationals of the states concerned.[89]

(e) *Other aliens* (i.e. those outside category (d)). As nationals of non-EEA countries, they are subject to immigration control. Similarly placed are British protected persons, who do not come within category (b).

An important practical distinction is between visa nationals (i.e. those from countries requiring a visa to enter the United Kingdom, which includes several Commonwealth countries) and nationals of other countries.[90]

Under the 1971 Act, as amended, those who have the right of abode in the United Kingdom 'shall be free to live in, and to come and go into and from, the United Kingdom without let or hindrance', except such as may be required under the Act to enable their right to be established (s 1(1)). Those who are not British citizens and do not have the right of abode may not enter or remain in the United Kingdom unless leave is given to them in accordance with the Act. Such leave may be given for a limited or an indefinite period. Where a person is given a limited leave to enter or remain, this leave may be given subject to conditions restricting employment or occupation in the United Kingdom, requiring him to maintain himself and his dependants without recourse to public funds, or requiring him to register with the police (s 3(1)); where indefinite leave to remain is given, no such conditions may be imposed (s 3(3)). Even if a non-British citizen has indefinite leave to remain, he or she may be deported if the Home Secretary deems that this would be 'conducive to the public good' (s 3(5)).[91] A person's leave to enter or remain may lapse when he or she goes outside the common travel area and fresh leave will be needed on return (s 3(4)).

The 1971 Act exempts certain groups of non-British citizens from the need to get individual leave to enter and remain. These groups include non-British citizens who were settled in the United Kingdom on 1 January 1983; that is, they were ordinarily resident in the country and were not subject to any restriction on the period for which they might remain.[92]

Other groups exempted from the need to get individual leave to enter and remain include crew members of a ship or aircraft coming temporarily to the United Kingdom,

---

[87] Ch 26 E. Under earlier legislation, exclusion orders could prevent individuals moving between Great Britain and Northern Ireland: see e.g. *R v Home Secretary, ex p Adams* [1995] 3 CMLR 476.

[88] Immigration Act 1988, s 7; and p 446 below.

[89] European Economic Area Act 1993; Immigration (European Economic Area) Regulations 2000, SI 2000 No 2326.

[90] Immigration Rules, rr 24–30C; and Immigration (Leave to Enter and Remain) Regulations Order 2000, SI 2000 No 1161. On the application of visa requirements to Commonwealth countries, see R M White [1987] PL 350.

[91] Immigration Rules, Part 10 and app 2.

[92] 1971 Act, ss 1(2) and 33(2A); *R v Home Secretary, ex p Mughal* [1974] QB 313. See s 1(5) of the 1971 Act, for an assurance of freedom of movement given to Commonwealth citizens settled in the United Kingdom in 1971 but revoked by the Immigration Act 1988.

diplomats and others entitled to diplomatic privilege, and members of certain military forces.[93]

The 1971 Act, as amended, equips the Home Secretary and immigration officers with a wide range of powers considered necessary for immigration control. These include power to grant or refuse leave for entry before an individual arrives in the United Kingdom, to examine persons arriving or leaving the United Kingdom, to remove persons who are refused leave to enter, have entered unlawfully or have outstayed a limited leave to remain and to detain persons pending examination or removal. Many powers of control on entry are vested directly in immigration officers. Other powers (for example, the decision to deport someone without the right of abode) are vested in the Home Secretary. A few powers must be exercised by the Home Secretary personally,[94] but most of them may be exercised on his or her behalf by officials in the Home Office (including members of the immigration service).[95]

Part III of the Act, as extended by later Acts, created many criminal offences including illegal entry,[96] overstaying a limited leave to enter or remain, failure to observe a condition of a limited leave, assisting or harbouring illegal entrants, failure without reasonable excuse to submit to examination on arrival into the United Kingdom, securing or facilitating the entry of illegal entrants or the obtaining of leave to remain by deception and (for one who is not a British citizen) using deception to enter the United Kingdom. It is an offence for anyone to facilitate the entry of illegal entrants, but in relation to asylum claimants this does not apply to acts that are not done for gain or to acts done by staff of a bona fide organisation that assists asylum claimants.[97] Because of the Geneva Convention on the status of refugees, a refugee has a defence to the offence of entry by deception if he or she can show good cause for the illegal entry and asylum was claimed as soon as practicable.[98] The offence of remaining in the United Kingdom beyond the time limit for which leave to enter was granted is a continuing offence, but not more than one prosecution may be brought in respect of the same limited leave.[99] Immigration authorities and police may exercise wide powers of enforcement, including arrest, search and entry.[100] A registrar of marriages who suspects that a marriage between two persons will be a sham marriage must report the suspicion to the Home Secretary.[101] Onerous duties are laid on airlines and other carriers by Part II of the 1999 Act, which imposes penalties for carrying clandestine entrants.[102]

Immigration rules[103]

The policies of the immigration authorities may derive from primary legislation, but they are mainly contained in immigration rules which the Home Secretary lays down as the practice to be followed in the administration of the Act (1971 Act, s 3(2)). Statements of the rules must be laid before Parliament. If such a statement is disapproved

---

[93] 1971 Act, s 8; Macdonald and Webber, ch 6.
[94] E.g. Immigration and Asylum Act 1999, ss 62(4), 64(2).
[95] *R v Home Secretary, ex p Oladehinde* [1991] 1 AC 254, applying the so-called *Carltona* principle, ch 13 D above.
[96] See *R v Naillie* [1993] AC 674 and *R v Home Secretary, ex p Ku* [1995] QB 364.
[97] Immigration Act 1971, ss 24A, 25(1).
[98] Immigration and Asylum Act 1999, s 31 (and see *R v Uxbridge Magistrates' Court, ex p Adimi* [2001] QB 667).
[99] 1971 Act, s 24(1) (b), (1A).
[100] Immigration and Asylum Act 1999, Part VII.
[101] Immigration and Asylum Act 1999, s 24. And see Part IX.
[102] And see Carriers' Liability (Clandestine Entrants) (Code of Practice) Order 2000, SI 2000 No 684. On the earlier law, see A Ruff [1989] PL 222.
[103] See Macdonald and Webber, pp 21–24; Legomsky, pp 50–72.

by resolution of either House passed within 40 days, the Home Secretary shall 'as soon as may be' make such changes in the rules as appear to him to be required.[104] The status of the rules is difficult to define. They are not statutory instruments[105] but, as they are binding on those who decide immigration appeals, they are akin to delegated legislation and they are far from being mere circulars or guidance.[106] They must be interpreted sensibly, according to the natural meaning of the words used,[107] and may be declared ultra vires if they conflict with a statutory provision or on other grounds.[108] The present rules, dating from 1994 and often amended since,[109] are much fuller than earlier versions of the rules. Some passages merely refer to requirements in the parent legislation; some contain procedural rules; many state the policies which are to be applied or list the factors to be taken into account in the exercise of discretion. As we shall see, the rules have a crucial effect when appeals are brought.[110]

The rules provide that immigration control is to be exercised without regard to a person's race, colour or religion (r 2). The rules do not apply to those who are entitled to enter the United Kingdom as EEA nationals (r 5). As far as entry is concerned, a person arriving in the United Kingdom must produce a valid passport or other document establishing his or her identity and nationality (r 11) and also, if this is claimed, the right of abode (r 12); prior entry clearance is required of many persons wishing to enter, in the form of a visa or an entry certificate (rr 24, 25). Certain persons are admitted for short-term visits or other temporary purposes, for example as students (rr 57–87) or for au pair placements (rr 88–94). A person arriving for employment must normally hold a work permit issued by the Department of Employment (r 128), but work permits are not needed for certain occupations, for example ministers of religion (rr 169–177) and overseas journalists (rr 136–43). Subject to conditions, admission is granted to persons intending to establish themselves in business (rr 200–23) or, if they own at least £1 million, as investors (rr 224–31). A Commonwealth citizen who can show that one grandparent was born in the United Kingdom does not need a work permit and will be admitted for four years (rr 186–93). Children born in the United Kingdom who are not British citizens because of the status of their parents,[111] have left the country and later wish to return, will in general be given leave to return on the same basis as their parents (rr 304–9). The rules apply to the granting of leave to enter or remain and to the variation of such leave (rr 31–33A), for example where a person admitted as a visitor seeks leave to remain in another capacity.

Important changes of policy can be made by alteration of the immigration rules, subject only to the parent legislation or (where applicable) to Community law. The Acts and the rules leave many difficult decisions of law, fact and discretion to be made by the immigration authorities. The rights of individuals thus depend a great deal upon the scope for appealing against decisions by immigration officials. In addition to the immigration rules, the Home Office issues internal guidance and direction for immigration and nationality staff, which are kept constantly under review and are often amended. Many of these directions are published under the 'open government' policy.[112]

---

[104] New rules made by the government were disapproved by the Commons on 22 November 1972 and 15 December 1982; in each case revised rules were later approved by the Commons. And see ch 28.

[105] Ch 28.

[106] *R v Chief Immigration Officer, ex p Salamat Bibi* [1976] 3 All ER 843, 848; *R v Home Secretary, ex p Hosenball* [1977] 3 All ER 452, 459, 463; *Pearson v Immigration Appeal Tribunal* [1978] Imm AR 212, 224.

[107] *Alexander v IAT* [1982] 2 All ER 766.

[108] E.g. *R v IAT, ex p Begum* [1986] Imm AR 385.

[109] HC 395 (1994–95) (as amended); and see Macdonald and Webber, pp 1283–1382.

[110] Page 440 below.

[111] Section A above.

[112] These can be seen on *www.homeoffice.gov.uk*. See also ch 13 F.

Immigration appeals[113]

Before 1969 there was no right of appeal against decisions refusing admission to the United Kingdom, although they were subject to review by the courts on grounds of legality. The Immigration Act 1971 provides a two-tier system of appeals.[114] The lower tier consists of adjudicators, who since 1987 have been appointed by the Lord Chancellor. The upper tier is the Immigration Appeal Tribunal, appointed by the Lord Chancellor, whose president must be a lawyer of not less than seven years' standing and in 2001 was a High Court judge. Both adjudicators and the tribunal are subject to the supervision of the Council on Tribunals. In 2000–2001, a total of 413 adjudicators (including both full-time and part-time adjudicators) decided some 32,900 appeals and the tribunal (comprising 88 full-time and part-time members, sitting in panels of three members) decided some 11,400 appeals, but the appeals system continued to be under great pressure.[115]

While these bodies hear appeals against many immigration decisions, some appeals are entrusted to other tribunals. In cases where the Home Secretary decides to deport a person in the public interest and on national security grounds, appeals are decided by the Special Immigration Appeals Commission.[116] By Part V of the 1999 Act, the Immigration Services Commissioner regulates immigration advisers and immigration services providers; appeals from the Commissioner's decisions lie to the Immigration Services Tribunal. By Part VI, asylum support adjudicators hear appeals relating to the scheme of support for asylum seekers.

The right of appeal against immigration decisions applies to such matters as the refusal of leave to enter the United Kingdom, a refusal to vary limited leave that has been granted, a decision by the Secretary of State to make a deportation order or to refuse to revoke such an order, the giving of directions for a person's removal and the refusal of a claim for asylum. But these rights are subject to closely defined limitations and restrictions.[117] Thus a person may not appeal against a refusal of leave to enter while in the United Kingdom, unless he/she is claiming asylum or was refused such leave at a port of entry while holding a current entry clearance or work permit.[118] The 1999 Act created a right of appeal against any decision relating to the right to enter or remain in the United Kingdom where the ground of appeal is that the decision maker acted in breach of the appellant's human rights or was affected by racial discrimination, but the Home Secretary may in some circumstances issue a certificate that bars such an appeal.[119] In response to the repeated use of rights of appeal as a delaying tactic, the 1999 Act enables there to be a 'one-stop' procedure, imposing a duty on the applicant to disclose all available grounds for seeking asylum.[120] Operation of the appeal system is governed by procedural rules made under the 1999 Act.[121]

---

[113] Macdonald and Webber, ch 18.

[114] See previously the Immigration Appeals Act 1969 and the Wilson report on immigration appeals (Cmnd 3387, 1967).

[115] Annual Report of Council on Tribunals, 2000–2001; and ch 29 A.

[116] See the Special Immigration Appeals Commission Act 1997 as amended in 2001 (p 626 below). Also *Chahal* v *UK* (1996) 23 EHRR 413 and *Secretary of State* v *Rehman* [2002] 1 All ER 122.

[117] Immigration and Asylum Act 1999, Part IV and Schs 2–4.

[118] Ibid, s 60(3).

[119] Ibid, s 65 (amended by the Race Relations (Amendment) Act 2000); and s 73(2).

[120] Ibid, ss 74–77.

[121] Immigration and Asylum Appeal (Procedure) Rules 2000, SI 2000 No 2333. Other procedure rules are SI 1998 No 1881 (special immigration appeals commission), SI 2000 No 541 (asylum support), SI 2000 No 2244 (one-stop appeals), SI 2000 No 2739 (immigration services).

Where an individual exercises a right of appeal, what are the powers of the adjudicator over the decision appealed against? An adjudicator must allow an appeal in two situations: (i) if he or she considers that the decision was not in accordance with the law[122] or with the relevant immigration rules (for this purpose he or she may review questions of fact); (ii) if he or she considers, where the decision involved the exercise of discretion, that the discretion should have been exercised differently. Otherwise the appeal must be dismissed. No decision in accordance with the immigration rules is to be treated as having involved the exercise of discretion merely because the Home Secretary was asked to depart from the rules and refused to do so.[123] These rules also bind the Immigration Appeal Tribunal, to whom an appeal may lie with leave from the adjudicator's decision. A refusal of leave to appeal is subject to judicial review. Selected decisions by the tribunal are published and bind adjudicators. Given this framework of rules and an independent hierarchy to administer them, decisions that involve the exercise of discretion may be reviewed by adjudicators without, from the Home Office point of view, creating too great a risk of decisions on appeal that cut across the regular pattern of administration. The system has at times been criticised for being unduly influenced by the Home Office[124] and in some areas of law for the fact that the decisions of some adjudicators reflect a 'culture of disbelief'. However, many steps to foster the independence of the appeals system have been taken since 1987 and the right to appeal continues to be a vital aspect of immigration control.

Before 1993 there was no further appeal from decisions of the Immigration Appeal Tribunal, but these were subject to judicial review in the High Court.[125] Since 1993, there has been an appeal on law (from final determinations made by the tribunal) with leave to the Court of Appeal or (where the adjudicator's decision was made in Scotland) to the Court of Session.[126]

Apart from the appeal process, the Home Secretary exercises an exceptional discretion[127] to permit individuals to enter or remain in the United Kingdom even though the adjudication authorities cannot do so. In asylum cases, exceptional leave to remain may be granted on humanitarian or other grounds where the case for asylum status is not made out.

Refugees and asylum status

The most difficult branch of immigration law is that which gives effect to international norms relating to refugees and asylum.[128] By customary international law, it was for each sovereign state to decide whether to admit those who sought refuge. The United Kingdom has a long history of admitting political and other refugees when this seemed justified in the national interest.[129] The migration of human beings in pursuit of survival or a more tolerable existence may occur for many reasons, including civil war and other disasters, whether natural or man-made. The Geneva Convention of 1951 defines a refugee rather narrowly, as being one who:

---

122 Which includes the principles of administrative law: *Singh* v *IAT* [1986] 2 All ER 721, 728. Cf *R* v *IAT, ex p Home Secretary* [1992] IAR 554; and Macdonald and Webber, 837, 840.
123 Immigration and Asylum Act 1999, Sch 4, para 21.
124 E.g. Evans, note 79 above, pp 362–74 (written in 1983).
125 Chs 30, 31.
126 Immigration and Asylum Act 1999, Sch 4, para 23.
127 The legal basis for which is uncertain: C Vincenzi [1992] PL 300.
128 See Goodwin-Gill, *The Refugee in International Law*; Hathaway, *The Law of Refugee Status*; Harvey, *Seeking Asylum in the UK*; Macdonald and Webber, ch 12.
129 See Dummett and Nichol, ch 8.

owing to well-founded fear of being persecuted *for reasons of race, religion, nationality, membership of a particular social group or political opinion*, is outside the country of his nationality and is unable, or owing to such fear, is unwilling to avail himself of the protection of that country.[130] (italics supplied)

The words italicised are often called 'the Convention reasons'. At the heart of the Convention is the duty of states under art 32 not to 'expel or return (*refouler*) a refugee in any manner whatsoever to the frontiers of territories where his life or freedom would be threatened' for a Convention reason. Moreover, art 3 of the European Convention on Human Rights obliges states not to return someone to a country where there are substantial grounds for believing that he/she faces a real risk of being subjected to torture or to inhuman or degrading treatment or punishment.[131]

These duties are not breached if, instead of being returned to the country where they fear persecution, asylum seekers are sent to a 'safe third country', which normally will be one through which they passed in reaching the country in which asylum is sought. Whether in a particular case a third country can be regarded as 'safe' is often a difficult question.[132] The 1999 Act now authorises asylum seekers to be removed to another EU country under standing arrangements, the country being deemed to be safe; the Home Secretary may designate other countries for the same purpose.[133] Under former legislation, it was held that the United Kingdom could not return Somali and Algerian asylum seekers to Germany and France respectively, since courts in those countries did not on the issue of responsibility for persecution by non-state agents apply the 'true and autonomous meaning' of the Convention;[134] removal of the asylum seekers to Germany and France would have created a real risk of their being sent back to countries in which they had a well-founded fear of persecution.

The Geneva Convention provides no permanent judicial mechanism for supervising observance of the Convention. Divergent national decisions are likely because of the abundant case law from many countries interpreting the elements in the Convention definition of 'refugee'. In one leading British decision, two Pakistani women, forced to leave their homes after allegations of adultery and at risk of draconian criminal proceedings if they returned, were held to have a well-founded fear of persecution; women in Pakistan were held to be a 'particular social group' for Convention purposes as they lived in a society which discriminated against them on grounds of their sex, and the state denied them protection from violence which it gave to men.[135] That decision binds decision-makers in the United Kingdom but not elsewhere.

Persecution for a Convention reason may arise where the home state is directly persecuting the refugees itself or fails to protect them against abusive treatment by others. When a Roma in Slovakia claimed to be at risk of attacks by neo-Nazi skinheads, it was held that 'persecution' implied a failure by the state to provide due protection against the attacks; protection under the Convention was said to be a surrogate for the protection that the home state should provide for vulnerable individuals.[136]

---

[130] Geneva Convention on the Status of Refugees, 1951, art 1A(2) amended by the 1967 Protocol.
[131] E.g. *Chahal* v *UK* (1996) 23 EHRR 413; *Ahmed* v *Austria* (1996) 24 EHRR 278; cf *Vilvarajah* v *UK* (1991) 14 EHRR 248.
[132] E.g. *R* v *Home Secretary, ex p Bugdaycay* [1987] AC 514; *R* v *Home Secretary, ex p Abdi* [1996] 1 All ER 641 (HL) (Somalis staying briefly in Spain on way to UK).
[133] Immigration and Asylum Act 1999, ss 11–12. In 2001, the designated countries were Canada, Norway, Switzerland and USA: SI 2000 No 2245. For the Dublin Convention 1990 which has effect under the 1999 Act, s 11, see Macdonald and Webber, pp 557–64.
[134] *R* v *Home Secretary, ex p Adan* [2001] 2 AC 477 applying the Convention as interpreted in *Adan* v *Home Secretary* [1999] 1 AC 293.
[135] *R* v *Immigration Appeal Tribunal, ex p Shah* [1999] 2 AC 629.
[136] *Horvath* v *Home Secretary* [2001] 1 AC 489.

However, the evidence in that case was held insufficient to show that the Roma was suffering from a 'sustained or systemic violation of basic human rights demonstrative of a failure of state protection'.[137]

The overriding approach of the courts in asylum cases was indicated in 1988 by Lord Bridge:

> The most fundamental of all human rights is the individual's right to life and, when an administrative decision under challenge is said to be one which may put the applicant's life at risk, the basis of the decision must surely call for the most anxious scrutiny.[138]

The decision of whether there is a well-founded fear of persecution for a Convention reason involves both subjective and objective factors; the test is whether there is a real risk or likelihood of persecution if the applicant is returned,[139] not whether it is more probable than not that such persecution will occur. The fear must be well founded at the time when the request for asylum is decided. An historic fear of persecution is not sufficient, but may support a present fear.[140]

Even if an applicant faces a real risk of persecution if returned, he is not protected by the Convention where there are serious reasons indicating that he has committed a crime against humanity, a war crime or a serious non-political crime.[141] Difficult questions arise where the Home Secretary considers for reasons of national security that someone's presence in the United Kingdom is 'not conducive to the public good', but the applicant can show that there is a risk of persecution or treatment in breach of art 3, ECHR, if he/she is returned to the home country. As a matter of asylum law, a balancing exercise may be necessary,[142] but the European Court of Human Rights has held that national security considerations must be excluded in applying art 3.[143] The national security of the United Kingdom may be endangered even though an individual's activities are targeted solely against foreign governments.[144]

The narrow scope of the 1951 Convention is illustrated by the ruling that the risk to security and liberty created by a civil war is not enough to ground a claim to asylum, unless the individual can show fear of persecution for Convention reasons beyond the ordinary risks of civil war.[145] In many cases, failure to gain asylum under the Convention does not mean that the applicant will be removed from the United Kingdom (or that the claim was 'bogus'). In a civil war situation, and in other situations where it would be harsh or inhuman to compel individuals to return, the Home Secretary is likely to exercise discretion outside the immigration rules by granting the individual 'exceptional leave to remain'. Such decisions must take account of the individual's rights under the European Convention on Human Rights.[146]

Many asylum seekers cannot leave their countries without using false documents and on arrival in the country of destination are at risk of being treated as illegal entrants. Under the 1951 Convention, art 31, a receiving state must not impose penalties for

---

[137] Ibid, at 498 (Lord Hope) quoting from Hathaway, op cit, pp 104–5.
[138] *R v Home Secretary, ex p Bugdaycay* [1987] AC 514, 531 (whether Ugandan at risk of being sent on to Uganda if he were returned to Kenya).
[139] *R v Home Secretary, ex p Sivakumaran* [1988] AC 958.
[140] *Adan v Home Secretary* [1999] 1 AC 293. On the burden of proof in respect of past or present facts, see *Karanakaran v Home Secretary* [2000] 3 All ER 449.
[141] Geneva Convention, art 1 F. See *T v Home Secretary* [1996] AC 742 (airport explosion killing innocent civilians); and section C in this chapter.
[142] *R v Home Secretary, ex p Chahal* [1995] 1 All ER 658.
[143] *Chahal v UK* (1996) 23 EHRR 413 (and see the Special Appeals Commission Act 1997).
[144] *Home Secretary v Rehman* [2002] 1 All ER 122.
[145] *Adan v Home Secretary* [1999] 1 AC 293.
[146] A refusal of exceptional leave to remain may now give rise to an appeal under the Immigration and Asylum Act 1999, s 65.

illegal entry on refugees who claim asylum without delay and show good cause for the entry. Remarkably, the authorities in Britain regularly conducted prosecutions without regard for art 31, until in 1999 the Divisional Court ruled that asylum seekers had a legitimate expectation that executive authorities would observe the duties imposed by the Convention.[147]

The question of procedures for dealing with increased numbers of asylum seekers became controversial during the 1990s, and the government tried various measures to cut back support for them. In 1996, the Court of Appeal declared unlawful social security regulations that deprived asylum seekers of the right to receive benefits if they had claimed asylum after entering the country and not at the port of entry, but the regulations were hastily validated by Parliament.[148] The 1999 Act authorised a new national scheme of support for asylum seekers, enabling them to be dispersed to areas of Great Britain away from the south-east and, if they appeared destitute, to receive vouchers for essential living needs in place of cash payments. In 2001, the Court of Appeal upheld the government's policy of detaining all asylum seekers at a former RAF base for an initial period of seven to ten days to enable their claims to be processed speedily.[149] Further legislation on asylum matters was before Parliament in 2002.

Deportation and removal from the United Kingdom[150]

The power to deport or to remove a person is a drastic power that must be subject to political and judicial safeguards. Before 1971, an alien could be deported *either* where a criminal court recommended deportation after his/her conviction for a crime punishable with imprisonment *or* if the Home Secretary deemed it 'conducive to the public good' that he/she should be deported. The latter power proved highly resistant to judicial review.[151] Indeed, deportation could at that time be used as 'disguised extradition' since, although the Home Secretary could not name the country to which the alien must go, the same result could be achieved by placing him/her on a specified ship or aircraft.[152]

Today there is no power to deport British citizens but most non-British citizens are, in principle, subject to powers of removal and deportation. Thus a non-British citizen who has or had limited leave to remain may be removed for having breached conditions of leave or overstayed the limit, for having obtained leave to remain by deception or in certain circumstances where a member of his/her family is removed.[153] There are also powers for the summary removal of illegal entrants and others refused leave to enter.[154] A non-British citizen may be deported if the Home Secretary considers that this would be 'conducive to the public good', if (in certain circumstances) a member of his/her family is being deported, or if he/she has been convicted of an offence punishable with imprisonment and is recommended for deportation by the trial court.[155] Certain

---

[147] *R v Uxbridge Magistrates' Court, ex p Adimi* [2001] QB 667. See now Immigration and Asylum Act 1999, s 31.

[148] *R v Social Security Secretary, ex p JCWI* [1996] 4 All ER 385; Asylum and Immigration Act 1996, s 11. See CJ Harvey [1997] PL 394. Cf *R v Wandsworth Borough Council, ex p O* [2000] 4 All ER 590, 599: 'If there are to be immigration beggars on our streets, then let them at least not be old, ill or disabled' (Simon Brown LJ).

[149] *R (Saadi) v Home Secretary* [2001] 4 All ER 961.

[150] Macdonald and Webber, chs 15, 16; Immigration Rules 1994, Part 13.

[151] See e.g. *R v Governor of Brixton Prison, ex p Soblen* [1963] 2 QB 243; and P O'Higgins (1964) 27 MLR 521.

[152] *R v Home Secretary, ex p Chateau Thierry* [1917] 1 KB 922. And see section C in this chapter.

[153] Immigration and Asylum Act 1999, ss 9–15.

[154] Immigration Act 1971, Sch 2, paras 8–10 (as amended).

[155] Immigration Act 1971, s 3(5), (6) (as amended).

exemptions from deportation were given to Commonwealth citizens and Irish citizens who were ordinarily resident in the United Kingdom on 1 January 1973.[156] EU citizens are not exempt from deportation, but exercise of the power must have regard to their rights under Community law.[157]

The decision of whether an individual should be deported or removed may involve the exercise of a broad discretion,[158] particularly if the issue is whether deportation would be 'conducive to the public good'. The individual will generally have a right of appeal to an adjudicator against a decision to deport or against a refusal to revoke a deportation order, with a further appeal to the Immigration Appeal Tribunal. In some circumstances, the right of appeal and/or the powers of the adjudicating authority are restricted. Where it is decided that a deportation is conducive to the public good in the interests of national security, the deportee's appeal is to a three-person tribunal known as the Special Immigration Appeals Commission.[159] The Commission comprises a person who has held high judicial office, a senior immigration adjudicator and a person with experience of national security. The Commission may for reasons of national security hear part of the appeal in closed session, during which the appellant is represented by a special advocate appointed by the Commission, both the appellant and his/her ordinary representative being excluded. Against the decision of the Commission, either the individual or the Home Secretary may with leave appeal on a question of law to the Court of Appeal.[160]

This procedure seeks 'to deal with the tension which will inevitably arise in cases involving national security between the rights of the individual and the need to maintain the confidentiality of security information'.[161] It was created because the Strasbourg Court had held that the former procedure under the Immigration Act 1971 (involving a limited right to be heard before three advisers to the Home Secretary)[162] breached Art 5(4), ECHR, since it did not give a detainee the right to have the lawfulness of the detention decided by a court.[163]

If it is claimed that a decision by an immigration authority relating to entitlement to enter or remain in the United Kingdom was taken in breach of an individual's Convention rights or was racially discriminatory, a right of appeal lies to an adjudicator.[164] The adjudicator (or the appeal tribunal) may allow the appeal if the breach of Convention rights or the discriminatory act is established (for example, if deportation would have a disproportionate effect on the right of those concerned to respect for their family life).[165] Where such an appeal is pending, no order or directions for the individual's deportation or removal may have effect.[166]

---

[156] Immigration Act 1971, s 7.
[157] See e.g. *R v Home Secretary, ex p Santillo* [1981] QB 778; *R v Home Secretary, ex p Dannenberg* [1984] QB 766.
[158] Immigration Rules, paras 364–380.
[159] Special Immigration Appeals Commission Act 1997; Special Immigration Appeals Commission (Procedure) Rules 1998, SI 1998 No 1881.
[160] 1997 Act, s 7. And see *Home Secretary v Rehman* [2002] 1 All ER 122 (deportation of member of Islamic terrorist organisation).
[161] *Home Secretary v Rehman* [2000] 3 All ER 778, 783 (Lord Woolf MR).
[162] See *R v Home Secretary, ex p Hosenball* [1977] 3 All ER 452 and *R v Home Secretary, ex p Cheblak* [1991] 2 All ER 319. And I Leigh [1991] PL 331 and F Hampson [1991] PL 506. The advisory procedure under the 1971 Act replaced a right of appeal created in 1969: see B A Hepple (1971) 34 MLR 501.
[163] *Chahal v UK* (1996) 23 EHRR 413.
[164] Immigration and Asylum Act 1999, s 65 (as amended). But see also s 72.
[165] See e.g. *R v Home Secretary, ex p Mahmood* [2001] ACD 38; *R v Home Secretary, ex p Isiko* [2001] ACD 39. Cf *Berrehab v Netherlands* (1988) 11 EHRR 322; *Beljoudi v France* (1992) 14 EHRR 801.
[166] Immigration and Asylum Act 1999, Sch 4, para 20.

If an EEA citizen is excluded or deported on grounds relating to public policy, public security and public health,[167] questions as to the compatibility of UK law with Community law may arise as regards both substance and procedure.[168]

Formerly a deportee could not challenge the choice by the Home Secretary of the country to which he/she was to be sent. Today a person who is ordered to be deported or removed to one country may generally appeal to an adjudicator on the ground that he/she ought to be removed (if at all) to a different country; the appellant must produce evidence that that country will admit him or her.[169]

Judicial review of immigration decisions[170]

In principle, all decisions under the immigration legislation are within the jurisdiction of the Administrative Court and potentially subject to judicial review. But if an immigration decision is subject to appeal, the individual will be expected to appeal rather than to have recourse to judicial review. Asylum decisions were brought within the appeal system in 1993. Since then, decisions of the Immigration Appeal Tribunal have been subject to an appeal on law (with leave) to the Court of Appeal.[171] Particularly in the case of asylum seekers, several legislative attempts have been made to restrict the scope for repeated appeals and the concept of a 'one-stop' appeal was introduced in 1999.[172] However, decisions that are not subject to appeal (for example a decision by the Immigration Appeal Tribunal refusing leave to appeal from an adjudicator) are subject to judicial review. In practice, immigration law generates much of the judicial review caseload of the Administrative Court. Habeas corpus, that enables the legality of a person's detention to be determined, may sometimes be available when detention occurs under immigration law.[173]

The grounds on which immigration decisions may be reviewed include breach of duty by the Home Office,[174] failure to take account of relevant considerations[175] and errors in the interpretation of statutory provisions and the Immigration Rules. It is not the function of the court to substitute itself for the immigration authorities.[176] The court may not take a fresh decision on the merits of an individual case; however, in the absence of any specific defect in the decision-making process, the court may intervene when there are no grounds upon which the decision-maker could reasonably have come to a particular conclusion (applying what is called the *Wednesbury* test of unreasonableness).[177] In 1983, the House of Lords held in *Khawaja*'s case that the question whether someone was an illegal entrant was a 'precedent fact', the correctness of which had to be established to the satisfaction of the court.[178] Only if that fact can be established

---

[167] Immigration (European Economic Area) Regulations 2000, SI 2000 No 2326, regs 21–23, 29, 31.

[168] See e.g. *R v Home Secretary, ex p McQuillan* [1995] 4 All ER 400.

[169] Immigration and Asylum Act 1999, ss 59(4), 63(4), 67–68.

[170] Macdonald and Webber, op cit, pp 918–25; Legomsky, op cit, ch 1. For judicial review, see chs 30, 31 below.

[171] Asylum and Immigration Appeals Act 1993, s 9.

[172] Immigration and Asylum Act 1999, ss 74–77.

[173] See *R v Governor of Durham Prison, ex p Hardial Singh* [1984] 1 All ER 983 and *R v Home Secretary, ex p Muboyayi* [1992] QB 244. But see S Brown [2000] PL 31 and *Sheikh v Home Secretary* [2001] ACD 33. And see pp 750–3 below.

[174] E.g. *Phansopkar*'s case, note 81 above.

[175] E.g. *Bugdaycay*'s case, notes 132 and 138 above.

[176] Particularly not in respect of national security: *Home Secretary v Rehman* [2002] 1 All ER 122.

[177] See *Associated Provincial Picture Houses Ltd v Wednesbury Corporation* [1948] 1 KB 233; ch 30 A.

[178] *R v Home Secretary, ex p Khawaja* [1984] AC 74, reversing on this point *R v Home Secretary, ex p Zamir* [1980] AC 930.

on the evidence does the Home Secretary have power to remove the individual as an illegal entrant.[179]

When judicial review is sought of decisions affecting an asylum claim, it was held in *Bugdaycay*'s case that the test of *Wednesbury* unreasonableness (not the precedent fact test) applies. However, as we have seen, that test must be applied with 'the most anxious scrutiny' since the decision in question might affect the individual's fundamental right to life.[180]

Immigration decisions may also be challenged on grounds of natural justice (the right to a fair hearing and the rule against bias) and fairness.[181] Before the present system of immigration appeals was established, the Home Secretary was not even required to give a hearing to an alien before deciding that he/she should leave the United Kingdom.[182] Thus in *Re H K*, decided in 1967, when an immigration officer had to decide whether an immigrant was under 16 and the son of a Commonwealth citizen settled in England, the officer was held bound to act impartially and fairly, but need not hold any full-scale inquiry nor adopt judicial procedure.[183] Since then, the extension of immigration control to all non-British citizens and the creation of an appeals system have caused a marked broadening in the scope for natural justice and fairness. One stimulus for this came from EC law, where in 1981 the European Court of Justice held that Community law, in cases involving citizens from EC countries, might impose procedural requirements (including the right of representation before an independent authority) greater than those imposed by national law.[184] Moreover, under the European Convention on Human Rights, the Strasbourg Court has power to decide whether judicial review in national law provides effective control of immigration decisions that raise Convention issues.[185] The expanding scope of judicial review together with the perceived need for due process in immigration decision making caused Hale LJ in 2000 to say:

> [Today] a right of access to a tribunal or other adjudicative mechanism established by the state is just as important and fundamental as a right of access to the ordinary courts.[186]

Immigration law and the European Union

A primary aim of the Treaty of Rome 1957 in establishing the European Economic Community was to abolish, as between member states, 'obstacles to the free movement of persons, services and capital'.[187] This aim was achieved primarily by creating freedom of movement for workers, the right of establishment (namely the right of individuals and companies to set up undertakings) and the freedom to supply services within member states.[188] Discrimination on grounds of nationality within the scope of the Treaty was prohibited (EC Treaty, art 12 (ex 6)). Discrimination based on nationality between workers of member states as regards employment, remuneration and other

---

[179] For the purposes of detention, it is now sufficient that there are reasonable grounds for suspecting someone of being an illegal entrant: Immigration Act 1971, Sch 2, para 16(2) (as amended).

[180] See note 138 above. See also *R v Minister of Defence, ex p Smith* [1996] QB 517, stressing the significance for judicial review of the human rights context of a decision.

[181] Ch 30 B.

[182] See *R v Leman Street Police Inspector, ex p Venicoff* [1920] 3 KB 72 and *Schmidt v Home Secretary* [1969] 2 Ch 149.

[183] [1967] 2 QB 617.

[184] *Case 131/79 R v Home Secretary, ex p Santillo* [1981] QB 778.

[185] See e.g. *Vilvarajah v UK* (1991) 14 EHRR 248 and *Chahal v UK* (1996) 23 EHRR 413.

[186] *R v Home Secretary, ex p Saleem* [2001] 1 WLR 443, 458 (procedural rule held ultra vires because its effect would in some situations be to deny an asylum seeker the chance to appeal).

[187] Art 3(1)(c) (ex 3(c)) EC Treaty. And see Macdonald and Webber, ch 7.

[188] EC Treaty, respectively arts 39 (ex 48), 43 (ex 52), 49 (ex 59).

labour conditions was prohibited; for employment purposes, workers might move between member states, 'subject to limitations justified on grounds of public policy, public security or public health' (EC Treaty, art 39 (ex 48)). Detailed provision was made by EC regulations and directives for the freedom of movement of workers and their families, defining who their families were for this purpose, requiring equal treatment by national authorities without discrimination as regards nationality and providing for matters like the issue of residence permits.[189]

In this sensitive area, the scope of the Treaty of Rome was extended by subsequent treaties, in particular the Single European Act 1986, the Treaty on European Union 1992 and the Treaty of Amsterdam 1997. As we saw in section A, the Treaty on European Union provides for every national of a member state to be a citizen of the Union, having the right to move and reside freely within member states, subject to limitations and conditions in the Treaty and in implementing measures. These European measures are reflected in national immigration law: thus persons exercising their Community rights do not require leave under the Immigration Act 1971 to enter and remain in the United Kingdom.[190]

The apparent breadth of these rights of movement within Europe is both enhanced and limited by the context of European law. First, the provisions of Community law which govern the free movement of persons have direct effect within national law, thus modifying powers which could otherwise be exercised under UK legislation.[191] Second, Community law leaves each member state to decide who are its nationals that may enjoy the right of free movement. When the British Nationality Act 1981 came into effect, the British government made a declaration recognising three categories of persons for this purpose: (*a*) British citizens; (*b*) British subjects with the right of abode in the United Kingdom; and (*c*) British Dependent Territory citizens from Gibraltar.[192] Other categories of British nationals were excluded from the benefits of Community law. Thus the policy of free movement of persons was limited to those whom member states accepted as their own nationals; the policy did not directly benefit the citizens of non-member states, whether in seeking admission to a member state or in seeking to move freely within Europe.

These limitations in the original framework are being addressed in a complex chapter of European integration that is still being written. By the time of the Single European Act, the broad aim of creating an internal market was considered by most member states to create the need for a common external frontier that would replace internal frontiers. In 1985, the Schengen Agreement was created (outside the framework of the European Treaties) with the aim of abolishing immigration controls at the common borders of the participating European states and this was reinforced in 1990 by the Schengen Implementation Convention. The United Kingdom and Ireland were in 2001 the only EU states that remained outside the Schengen Agreement.

The Treaty on European Union in 1992 provided in Title VI for member states to cooperate (outside the Community structure) in matters of justice and home affairs. These matters included asylum policy, control over the external border of states, immigration policy and policy regarding nationals of third countries (including conditions

---

189 Including EC Regulations 1612/68 and 1251/70, and Directives 64/221, 68/360, 72/194, 73/148, 75/34, 77/486, 90/364, 90/365 and 93/96. And see Craig and de Burca, *EU Law*, ch 16; Wyatt and Dashwood, *European Community Law*, ch 14; Burrows, *Free Movement in Community Law*. Also Macdonald and Webber, materials at pp 1589–1643.

190 Immigration Act 1988, s 7; and see Immigration (European Economic Area) Regulations 2000, SI 2000 No 2326. On the former Immigration (EEA) Order 1994, see C Vincenzi [1995] PL 259.

191 See ch 8 B; and e.g. *Case 41/74, Van Duyn v Home Office* [1975] Ch 358 (exclusion of Dutch scientologist). Also *Case C-370/90, R v IAT, ex p Home Secretary* [1992] 3 All ER 798.

192 Cmnd 9062, 1983; Macdonald and Webber, pp 193–5.

of entry, residence and movement by such nationals within member states). Such co-operation was to be in compliance with the European Convention on Human Rights and the Convention on the Status of Refugees, but the cooperation was not to affect the responsibility of states for law and order and internal security.[193] In 1997, by a protocol to the Treaty of Amsterdam, the Schengen Agreement and Implementation Convention, with related decisions and declarations (collectively referred to as 'the Schengen *acquis*') were brought directly within the EU framework.[194] The protocol envisaged that closer measures of cooperation in such matters as asylum and immigration policy would be established between the Schengen states; it provided that the United Kingdom and Ireland would not be bound by the Schengen *acquis* but could request to participate in some or all of the Schengen provisions. A request of this kind (relating inter alia to police cooperation in respect of immigrant trafficking) was granted by the EU Council in 2000.[195] However, in 2001 the UK government was not prepared to take part in Schengen measures relating to frontier controls.

The Treaty of Amsterdam 1997 further extended the scope of the EC Treaty by providing under Title IV (ex Title IIIa) that the Council of Ministers must within five years take measures to ensure not only the free movement of persons in conjunction with related measures on external border controls, asylum and immigration, but also the observance of minimum standards relating to the reception of asylum seekers, procedures for granting or withdrawing refugee status and temporary protection for displaced persons from third countries. Measures would also be taken in regard to aspects of immigration policy such as residence permits and the repatriation of illegal entrants.[196] However, in an important recognition of the separate positions of the United Kingdom, Ireland and Denmark, the provisions of Title IV and measures thereunder are not binding on those countries unless they notify the Council that they wish to accept the measure.[197] The effect of these and other provisions is that the United Kingdom can continue to exercise frontier controls and to apply immigration policies under the powers granted by the Immigration Act 1971 and later Acts.

C. Extradition

The statutory background[198]

The object of extradition is to ensure that those accused or convicted of serious crime do not escape from justice by crossing international boundaries. Extradition is the procedure by which a person present in state A may be arrested by the authorities of that state and handed over to state B, for the reason either that he or she is wanted to stand trial for a criminal offence in state B or that he or she has been convicted in state B of an offence and is wanted back to serve the lawful punishment. This procedure gives rise to questions both of international and national law. Requests for extradition may also raise issues which are politically sensitive within a state or internationally. Sometimes, an alternative to extradition may be for state A, in which the requested person is found, to place that person on trial in its own courts rather than return him or her

---

[193] Treaty on European Union, arts 29, 30 (ex K.1, K.2).
[194] But only so far as the Schengen provisions were compatible with EU and Community law: see Council Decisions 1999/435 and 1999/436.
[195] See Council Decision 2000/365 (OJ 2000, L131/43).
[196] Art 63, EC Treaty (ex Art 73k).
[197] Art 69, EC Treaty (ex Art 73q). See generally Peers, *EU Justice and Home Affairs Law*.
[198] See Jones, *Extradition and Mutual Assistance*; Stanbrook, *Extradition Law and Practice* and Gilbert, *Aspects of Extradition Law*.

to stand trial in state B. This is possible where the law of state A permits extraterritorial jurisdiction to be exercised over the alleged offences.[199]

In the United Kingdom, extradition procedures are statutory and the police have no common law powers to arrest anyone with a view to his or her extradition.[200] Before the Extradition Act 1989, there were three main forms of extradition. First, extradition to and from some 50 foreign states (not including Ireland or states in the Commonwealth) was governed by the Extradition Acts 1870–35 and by bilateral treaties entered into between the United Kingdom and each of the states. Second, extradition between Commonwealth states was governed by the Fugitive Offenders Act 1967. Third, and not directly affected by the 1989 Act, the return of escaping wrongdoers between the United Kingdom and the Republic of Ireland was (and continues to be) undertaken not by extradition but by a simple procedure authorised in UK law by the Backing of Warrants (Republic of Ireland) Act 1965. In brief, arrest warrants issued in the Republic may be endorsed by a justice of the peace in the United Kingdom; if the named person is arrested by the British police, the justice may be required to order his delivery to the Irish authorities. Some of the safeguards that exist in extradition law apply to the procedure; in particular, offences of a political character are excluded.[201]

During the 1980s it became evident that aspects of the first two forms of extradition made it too difficult for criminals to be extradited from the United Kingdom, and extensive changes were made by the Criminal Justice Act 1988.[202] The Extradition Act 1989 was enacted to consolidate the legislation. One aim of the new law was to harmonise the procedures for extradition to and from foreign states with those for extradition to and from Commonwealth countries. Its enactment enabled the United Kingdom to ratify the European Convention on Extradition,[203] so that extradition to and from most European states (including Cyprus) is now conducted on the basis of that Convention.

As far as extradition to and from non-European states is concerned, the United Kingdom could not by its own act alter the treaties with those states which had effect under the former Extradition Acts. Accordingly, those treaties remain in force; the machinery by which they apply, derived from the 1870 Act, is now found in Sch 1 to the 1989 Act.[204] However, all new treaties will operate under the 1989 Act, and existing bilateral treaties are being renegotiated for this purpose.

As far as Commonwealth countries are concerned, the Fugitive Offenders Act 1967 had operated by the mutual agreement of Commonwealth states and without a structure of formal treaties; in 1990, an amended scheme for dealing with fugitive offenders was adopted by Commonwealth states and this enabled the Extradition Act 1989 to be applied.[205]

In the outline that follows, emphasis is given to the law enacted in the 1989 Act (section references in the text are to that Act). Some reference will be made to case-law under the earlier legislation, much of which is still relevant. It must not be assumed,

---

[199] See e.g. Suppression of Terrorism Act 1978, s 4 (giving effect to the European Convention on the Suppression of Terrorism, 1977); and Criminal Justice Act 1988, s 134, incorporating the UN Torture Convention (1984) into UK law.

[200] *Diamond* v *Winter* [1941] 1 KB 656.

[201] The UK case-law includes *Keane* v *Governor of Brixton Prison* [1972] AC 204 and *R* v *Governor of Winson Green Prison, ex p Littlejohn* [1975] 3 All ER 208. For the Irish case-law, see H Delany and G Hogan [1993] PL 93. See also the 11th edn of this work, pp 465–7.

[202] See *A Review of the Law and Practice of Extradition in the United Kingdom* (Home Office, 1982); Cmnd 9421, 1985; and Cmnd 9658, 1986. Also C Warbrick [1989] Crim LR 4.

[203] SI 1990 No 1507.

[204] This applies, in particular, to the USA.

[205] Commonwealth Scheme for the Rendition of Fugitive Offenders, as amended in 1990. For designation of the states, see SI 1991 No 1700.

however, in any particular instance that the general provisions in the 1989 Act necessarily apply, since (except within the Commonwealth) the procedure may still be governed by Sch 1 to the Act.

Availability of extradition procedures

For extradition between the United Kingdom and a foreign state to occur, there must usually be in place 'general extradition arrangements'. These will often take the form of a bilateral treaty between the two states made in accordance with the Act of 1989 (or the Extradition Acts 1870–1935) and to which the relevant legislation has been applied, with any necessary exceptions or qualifications, by Order in Council (1989 Act, ss 3, 4). Such 'general extradition arrangements' may also be created by a multilateral treaty such as the European Convention on Extradition 1957, which the United Kingdom ratified in 1990.

In the absence of general extradition arrangements with a foreign state, the United Kingdom and that state may agree to operate 'special extradition arrangements' in the case of a particular individual (ss 3(3) (b), 15). The existence of general extradition arrangements is proved conclusively by the relevant Order in Council and the existence of special extradition arrangements by a certificate from the Foreign Secretary (ss 4(3), 15(2)).

In the case of extradition to and from Commonwealth states, the 1989 Act applies to every such state which has been designated for the purpose by Order in Council, and it also applies to every colony (ss 1(2), 5).[206]

Definition of extradition crime

Formerly, under the Extradition Acts 1870–1935, a crime giving rise to extradition existed where the conduct charged if committed within English jurisdiction would have been within the classes of crimes listed in Sch 1 to the 1870 Act. This list has been added to and varied from time to time: for example, the Criminal Justice (International Cooperation) Act 1990 provided that offences contrary to the Drug Trafficking Offences Act 1986 are to be extraditable offences. However, an extradition treaty might contain a list of offences narrower than that in the 1870 Act, impose restrictions on the 1870 Act list or might impose a rule of double criminality, i.e. requiring exact equivalence between the definition of the crime in the two states concerned. After many years in which a different view of the law was taken, it was held by the House of Lords that, apart from specific treaty provisions to the contrary, there was no general rule of double criminality.[207] The House also held that the English magistrate considering a request for extradition ought not to hear evidence as to foreign law or consider the terms of the treaty and should consider only whether the conduct alleged was an offence in English law.[208] In respect of Commonwealth states, a double criminality test was imposed under the Fugitive Offenders Act 1967.[209]

Under the 1989 Act, there is no list of extradition offences. Instead, an extradition crime means primarily conduct in the territory of the requesting state which is punishable under the law of that state with imprisonment for a term of 12 months or more,

---

[206] See also ss 32–4 (special provision for colonies) and *R v Governor of Brixton Prison, ex p Kahan* [1989] QB 716 (Fiji's designation not affected by departure from Commonwealth).

[207] *Re Nielsen* [1984] AC 606, disapproving *Re Arton* [1896] 1 QB 108; see also *United States of America v McCaffery* [1984] 2 All ER 570.

[208] *R v Governor of Pentonville Prison, ex p Sinclair* [1991] 2 AC 64.

[209] *Government of Canada v Aronson* [1990] 1 AC 579. And see Cmnd 3008, 1966, para 10, cited in [1990] 1 AC at 592.

and which would be so punishable if it occurred in the United Kingdom (s 2(1) (a)). The effect of this change was to bring more offences within the scope of extradition.

> When Spain sought the extradition from Britain of General Pinochet, for serious crimes that he was alleged to have committed from 1972 to 1990 while President of Chile, the House of Lords by 6–1 held (Lord Millett dissenting) that the double criminality rule must be satisfied at the time of the alleged crimes, not at the date on which extradition was sought. Thus, Pinochet could not be extradited for acts of torture and conspiracy to commit torture committed before 29 September 1988, when the international crime of torture became an offence in UK law by incorporation of the Torture Convention, but only for allegations of torture relating to events between then and 11 March 1990 when he resigned as president.[210] It was also held by 6–1 (Lord Goff dissenting) that under the State Immunity Act 1978, s 20, Pinochet as ex-head of state had no immunity for the offences charged; the international crime of torture was not a 'head of state' function for which immunity continued once he had left that position.

The Extradition Act 1989 extends the purposes of extradition to include a number of offences (such as unlawful seizure of aircraft, the taking of hostages and unlawful acts in relation to nuclear material) which are the subject of international multilateral conventions. Such offences may be the basis of requests for extradition from states that are parties to those conventions but do not have general extradition arrangements with the United Kingdom (s 22).

Offsetting the wider scope of extraditable offences, there continue to be many restrictions on the return of individuals and an elaborate procedure must be observed before extradition takes effect.

General restrictions on return of individuals

Under the 1989 Act, Part II, the same general restrictions on the return of individuals apply whether the requesting state is a foreign state or a member of the Commonwealth. However, in the case of a particular foreign state, additional restrictions can be imposed by conditions in the extradition treaty.

Of primary importance is the rule that no person shall be returned if it appears 'that the offence of which that person is accused or was convicted is an offence of a political character' (s 6(1) (a)). Since a similar rule has applied to extradition since 1870, the earlier case-law may still be relevant. In regard to those who seek asylum, as we have already seen, the 1951 Convention does not apply to a person where there are reasons for considering that he or she 'has committed a serious non-political crime' before seeking admission as a refugee.[211] Thus someone who has committed a 'serious non-political crime' is denied refugee status and may be subject to extradition; but someone who has committed an 'offence of a political nature' is not subject to extradition for that act and may claim asylum.

The phrase 'offence of a political character', used in the Extradition Act 1870 and now in the 1989 Act, has been found difficult to interpret. In 1996, the English decisions were reviewed by the House of Lords in a case arising from a claim for asylum.

> In *T v Home Secretary*, the asylum seeker was an Algerian who belonged to a revolutionary movement in Algeria and had been involved in two terrorist incidents: one was the planting of a bomb at a civilian airport in which ten members of the public were killed; the other was an attempt to steal arms from army barracks, during which one person was killed.

---

[210] *R v Bow Street Magistrate, ex p Pinochet Ugarte (No 3)* [2000] 1 AC 147. This reasoning differed from that in *Pinochet Ugarte (No 1)* [2000] 1 AC 61.
[211] Convention relating to the Status of Refugees, 1951, art 1F(b); p 442 above.

Lord Lloyd (Lords Keith and Browne-Wilkinson concurring) defined a crime as a 'political crime' for the purposes of the 1951 Convention if: '(1) it is committed for a political purpose, i.e. with the object of overthrowing or subverting or changing the government of a state or inducing it to change its policy; and (2) there is a sufficiently close and direct link between the crime and the alleged political purpose. In determining whether such a link exists, the court will bear in mind the means used to achieve the political end and will have particular regard to whether the crime was aimed at a military or governmental target, on the one hand, or a civilian target, on the other, and in either event whether it was likely to involve the indiscriminate killing or injuring of members of the public.'[212] On the facts, the two crimes in which T was involved satisfied condition (1) but not condition (2) and could not be regarded as political. The Home Secretary's decision not to grant T asylum was upheld.

Lord Mustill agreed with the result, but not with the test of 'sufficiently close and direct link' between the crime and the alleged purpose. He would exclude from the concept of political crimes acts of terrorism, which he held to be criminal acts directed against a state ('depersonalised and abstract violence') and intended to create terror in the minds of a group of persons or the public.[213] Lord Slynn took a similar approach, holding that 'serious non-political crime' included acts of violence which were intended or likely to create a state of terror in the minds of individuals or the public and which caused, or were likely to cause, injury to persons who had no connection with the government of the state.[214]

Since the House in this case accepted that the same basis for defining political offences would apply both to asylum and extradition, it is not necessary here to review the earlier extradition decisions in any detail. However, they are generally consistent with the new definition.[215] Thus, in 1891, the killing of a municipal guard in the course of an armed uprising against the cantonal government in Switzerland was held to be an offence of a political character.[216] In 1894, anarchist explosions in Paris were held to be directed against the public at large, not against the government, and were not political offences.[217] In *Schtraks v Government of Israel*,[218] offences of child stealing and perjury were committed in the course of a family dispute over the religious upbringing of a young boy. The subject of the dispute was a matter of political controversy in Israel, but the offences were held not to be of a political character: the fugitive was (in Lord Radcliffe's words) not at odds with the Israeli government on any issue connected with the political control or government of the country;[219] moreover, the Israeli government was concerned only to enforce the criminal law and did not have ulterior political motives for seeking Schtraks' extradition. The requirement of a political conflict between the fugitive and the state requesting extradition was applied by the House of Lords when a Taiwanese citizen, while in the USA, took part in the attempted murder of a Taiwanese political leader hoping to bring about a change in the Taiwan government. The US government obtained the fugitive's return to serve his sentence in the USA. Lord Diplock confined the 'political offence' exception to offences in which the offender's political purpose was directed against the government of the state requesting his surrender and not against a third state.[220]

The decision in *T v Home Secretary* must be seen against the background of increasing concern about terrorism and the necessity for securing international

---

[212] [1996] AC 742, 786–7. And see *R v Home Secretary, ex p Fininvest SpA* [1997] 1 All ER 942.
[213] [1996] AC at 773.
[214] Ibid at 776.
[215] The decisions are summarised in Jones, note 198 above, ch 3.
[216] *Re Castioni* [1891] QB 149.
[217] *Re Meunier* [1894] 2 QB 415. And see *Re Arton (No 1)* [1896] 1 QB 108.
[218] [1964] AC 556.
[219] Cf *R v Governor of Brixton Prison, ex p Kolczynski* [1955] 1 QB 540.
[220] *Cheng v Governor of Pentonville Prison* [1973] AC 931.

cooperation to deal with terrorists[221] and for outlawing crimes against humanity such as genocide.[222]

Another general restriction on the return of offenders is that a person may not be extradited if the request for the return is in fact made 'for the purpose of prosecuting or punishing him on account of his race, religion, nationality or political opinions' or, if returned, he or she might be prejudiced at the trial or be punished, detained or restricted by reason of such opinions (s 6(1) (c), (d)). This restriction broadly corresponds to the test applied under immigration law to claims for refugee status.[223]

Other restrictions come into play where someone was convicted in his/her absence or seeks to rely on the 'double jeopardy' rule through having previously been tried for the offence (s 6(2), (3)). The Act seeks to prevent abuse of the procedure by requiring that before an individual is extradited, arrangements must exist to ensure that after the return he or she will be tried only for the offences for which the extradition was sought and that he or she must be given an opportunity to leave the country again before being tried for other offences, save with the consent of the Secretary of State (s 6(4)–(7)). That consent can be given only if the additional offences were themselves extraditable (s 6(6)).

Extradition procedure[224]

In general, proceedings under Part III of the 1989 Act are commenced by a request being made to the UK government by a diplomatic or consular representative of a foreign state or by a Commonwealth government (s 7(1)). On receiving a request containing the requisite information (s 7(2)), the Home Secretary[225] may issue an authority to proceed, unless it appears that an order for extradition could not lawfully be made or would in fact not be made (s 7(4)). When authority to proceed is given, a warrant for the arrest of the individual to be extradited may be issued by the chief metropolitan magistrate (in Scotland, by the sheriff of Lothian and Borders) (s 8(1) (a)). In case of urgency, a provisional warrant may be issued by any magistrate, justice of the peace or sheriff and the Home Secretary may thereafter issue an authority to proceed or may cancel the provisional warrant (s 8(1)(b), (4)).

When an individual is arrested on a warrant issued under the Act, he or she must be brought before either a metropolitan magistrate (in London) or the sheriff of Lothian and Borders (in Edinburgh), sitting as a court of committal (s 9(1)).[226] The court of committal must be satisfied that the offence in question is an extradition crime and may in some cases need to decide whether there is sufficient evidence to make a case requiring an answer by the individual if the proceedings had been a summary trial of an information against him or her.[227] Under the 1989 Act, s 9(4), the need for the magistrate to consider the sufficiency of the evidence arises less frequently than under the Extradition Acts 1870–1935.

---

[221] See especially the Suppression of Terrorism Act 1978, s 1 (certain offences not to be regarded as of a political character when requesting state is a party to the European Convention on the Suppression of Terrorism), and Extradition Act 1989, s 24.

[222] See Extradition Act 1989, s 23(1).

[223] Note 130 above.

[224] This account deals only with procedure on extradition under Part III of the Act, not on extradition under Sch 1.

[225] Or a Minister of State or an Under-Secretary of State: s 28(1).

[226] On the duties of the magistrate as court of committal, see *In re Evans* [1994] 3 All ER 449.

[227] 1989 Act, s 9(8), amended by Criminal Justice and Public Order Act 1994, s 148(5). See *R v Governor of Brixton Prison, ex p Levin* [1997] AC 741 (ordinary rules of criminal evidence apply); *R v Governor of Brixton Prison, ex p Gross* [1999] QB 538 (individual entitled to give and call evidence before magistrate).

If the court refuses to commit the individual to custody or on bail, the requesting state may challenge the refusal in law by requiring the court to state a case for the opinion of the High Court (in Scotland, the High Court of Justiciary) on the question of law involved (s 10). This procedure was not available before the 1989 Act.[228]

If the court makes a committal order, the individual has the right to apply to the High Court for a writ of habeas corpus within 15 days: he or she cannot be extradited during that time and until the habeas corpus proceedings are settled (s 11).[229] On such an application, the High Court may order discharge if it seems to the court (by reason of the trivial nature of the offence or of the passage of time since it was committed[230] or because the accusation is not made in good faith in the interests of justice) that in all the circumstances extradition would be unjust or oppressive (s 11(3)).[231] The High Court will consider matters such as whether the magistrate had jurisdiction to order the committal or whether there was material on which the order could properly have been made. But the High Court will not re-examine facts which were before the magistrate or generally admit fresh evidence. However, additional evidence may be received that is relevant to the court's power to decide whether it would be unjust or oppressive to extradite the applicant, or that relates to the power of the court to apply the general restrictions on return (including the exception for offences of a political character) already summarised.[232] There is an appeal, with leave, to the House of Lords from the High Court.[233]

If the application for habeas corpus does not succeed, the Home Secretary may by warrant order the individual to be returned to the requesting state, unless that return is prohibited by the Act or the Home Secretary decides to make no such order (s 12(1)). The Home Secretary has a general discretion as to whether to make an order (s 12(2)), but no order must be made if, having regard to the same grounds as the High Court could consider on habeas corpus, it would be unjust or oppressive to do so. He may also decide not to order the return if the person could be or has been sentenced to death for the offence for which return is sought (s 12(2) (b)).[234] No order may be made for return of a person who is serving a prison sentence or is facing charges for an offence in the United Kingdom (s 12(3)). Moreover, the Home Secretary must at this stage consider whether any of the general restrictions on return[235] are applicable.

If the Home Secretary is minded to order extradition, notice of this must be given and the individual then has 15 days in which to make representations as to why he or she should not be extradited (s 13). When the Home Secretary orders the return to take place, the individual has at least seven days within which to seek judicial review of the Home Secretary's decision and may not be removed while review proceedings are pending (s 13(6), (7)). Time limits apply to the validity of the committal order and on the warrant for extradition and, if these are not observed, the individual may be discharged by the court (s 16). A much simpler procedure applies if he or she decides not to challenge the extradition (s 14).

The general restrictions on return which were described earlier apply at almost every stage of this procedure, since they must be taken into account by the Home Secretary,

---

[228] *Atkinson v United States* [1971] AC 197.

[229] An equivalent to habeas corpus is available in Scotland: s 11(6).

[230] On delay, see e.g. *Oskar v Government of Australia* [1988] AC 366.

[231] See *Re Schmidt* [1995] 1 AC 339 (no discretion in court to stay proceedings for abuse of process) and *Cornelius v Government of Sweden* (Divisional Court, 17 June 1998: absence of key witness more significant than delay).

[232] Text at notes 211–23 above.

[233] Administration of Justice Act 1960, s 15.

[234] Cf *Soering v United Kingdom* (1989) 11 EHRR 439.

[235] Text at notes 211–23 above.

the court of committal and the High Court, whether on an application for habeas corpus or for review of an order of committal (s 6(1), (9)).

Despite the reforms made in the Extradition Act 1989, the procedure is still elaborate and sets many obstacles in the way of achieving criminal justice when a suspect or offender has moved to another jurisdiction. In 1998, Lord Steyn referred to the 'transnational interest' in bringing to justice those accused of serious crimes and said that extradition treaties and statutes ought where possible to be given 'a broad and generous construction'.[236] In this situation, some states (including the United States)[237] have resorted to self-help by kidnapping wanted offenders who have taken refuge abroad. Within Europe, such events would be in breach of the European Convention on Human Rights, which permits the lawful exercise of powers of extradition.[238] In 1993, the House of Lords held that the power of the High Court to stay a prosecution on the grounds of abuse of process could be exercised where an accused person had been brought to England from South Africa by an irregular procedure.[239] In 2001, the Home Office initiated a review of extradition law that envisaged the extension to countries within the European Union of a fast-track procedure based on the system of backing warrants that applies between the United Kingdom and Ireland, supplemented by more elaborate procedures for countries with a less close relationship with the United Kingdom.[240] One week after the terrorist attacks on New York and Washington in September 2001, the EC Commission issued a detailed proposal for European arrest warrants and for the mutual recognition of legal decisions and verdicts. This proposal built on earlier steps taken within the European Union for closer legal integration, arguing that procedures for extradition constituted 'a heavy and obsolete mechanism' and that the political discretion inherent in extradition procedure should be abolished.[241]

Enacted in response to the terrorist attacks in September 2001, the Anti-terrorism, Crime and Security Act 2001, s 111, enabled certain amendments to the Extradition Act 1989 to be made by regulations rather than by Act. Made under this power, the European Union Extradtion Regulations 2002[242] came into effect on 20 March 2002 as between the United Kingdom and those EU states which were parties to two conventions, the Convention on Simplified Extradition Procedure between member states of the Union (signed on 10 March 1995) and the Convention on Extradition between states of the Union (27 September 1996). The Regulations amend sections 2, 6, 18 and 26 of the Extradition Act 1989 (most notably, removing the political offence exception to extradition) and make other changes to the European Convention on Extradition affecting future requests for extradition between the states concerned. The account of extradition given in the preceding pages must be read subject to the 2002 Regulations.

---

[236] *In re Ismail* [1999] 1 AC 320, 327.
[237] *US v Alvarez-Machain* 119 L Ed 2d 441 (1992).
[238] See European Convention on Human Rights, art 5(1) (f) and e.g. *Bozano v France* (1987) 9 EHRR 297 (disguised extradition held to be unlawful deportation).
[239] *R v Horseferry Road Magistrates' Court, ex p Bennett* [1994] 1 AC 42. Cf *In re Schmidt* (note 231 above).
[240] *The Law on Extradition: A Review* (March 2001).
[241] *Proposal for a Council Framework Decision* (Brussels, COM (2001) 522 final).
[242] SI 2002, No 419. See also HC Deb, 19 December 2001, col 326, and Home Office Circular 10/2002.

Chapter 21

THE POLICE AND PERSONAL LIBERTY

The preservation of law and order and the prevention and detection of crime are matters of great importance to the maintenance of organised government. But it is equally important that these concerns should not be used to justify equipping the police with more power than is absolutely necessary, for every power conferred on police officers inevitably means a corresponding reduction in the liberty of the individual. It is difficult to exaggerate the central importance of personal liberty in a free and democratic society. As the European Court of Human Rights reminded us, protection from arbitrary interference by the state with an individual's liberty is 'a fundamental human right' and as such it is protected by art 5 of the ECHR.[1] This is a measure which assumes greater significance with the enactment of the Human Rights Act 1998, although it is by no means the only Convention right which will have a bearing on police conduct. As we shall see, arts 3 (inhuman and degrading treatment), 6 (fair trial) and 8 (respect for private life, home and correspondence) also have a role to play. There is thus a need to ensure that the police have adequate measures to protect the public without at the same time conferring powers that undermine the very freedom which the police are employed to defend. This chapter considers how this problem of modern democracy is resolved in English law.

A. Organisation of the police[2]

While the executive has a strong interest in maintaining an effective police system, the central government does not itself undertake the policing of the country. In 1962 a royal commission which inquired into the constitutional position of the police in Great Britain examined the arguments for and against establishing a national police force. The commission rejected the view that a national force would lead to a totalitarian 'police state', considering that a national force in Britain would be subject to the law and to the authority of Parliament. But, except for an incisive dissenting opinion from Dr A L Goodhart, the commission concluded that the police should not be brought under the direct central control of government and that the police should continue to be linked with local government; provided that the responsibilities of central government and the controls from the centre were made more explicit, a system of local police forces should be continued.[3] The commission's report led to the Police Act 1964 which, as amended subsequently, contained the main legal framework of the police system in England and Wales until 1994. As such it provided a structure of the police which is 'sui generis': while police forces have connections with local government, the police

---

[1] *Brogan v UK* (1989) 11 EHRR 117, at 134.
[2] For stimulating accounts of the issues, see Lustgarten, *The Governance of Police*, and Walker, *Policing in a Changing Constitutional Order*.
[3] Cmnd 1728, 1962, ch 5; cf memorandum of dissent by A L Goodhart. And see Marshall, *Police and Government*, and J Hart [1963] PL 283.

system is not a typical local government service; neither is it in form a central government service, although its operation is supervised by central government.

Within this framework there are signs of a growing centralisation of policing activity and a tendency towards the concentration of power in the hands of the Home Office.
As we shall see, the Home Secretary has always had extensive supervisory powers in
respect of local policing and indeed could, on occasion, assert some degree of supervision over operational matters. A major step in this direction was taken in the Police
and Magistrates' Courts Act 1994 which conferred a number of additional powers on
the Home Secretary and indeed gave him powers in respect of the membership of local
police authorities, although the latter proved much less directly intrusive than had
originally been proposed. Part II of the consolidating Police Act 1996 (headed 'Central
Supervision, Direction and Facilities') gives the Home Secretary powers to set objectives for police authorities and to direct police authorities to set performance targets,
as well as powers to give directions as to minimum budgets. A further step in the direction of the greater centralisation of police activity is to be seen in the Police Act
1997 and the provision which it makes in Part I for the National Criminal Intelligence
Service and in Part II for the National Crime Squad.[4] The function of the former is to
acquire and provide criminal intelligence for police forces (s 2), while the function of
the latter is to prevent and detect serious crime which is of relevance to more than one
police area in England and Wales (s 48). According to the government, 'the arrangements for both services will be firmly rooted in our structure of local policing'.[5]

Local police authorities

Under the Police Act 1996, England and Wales are divided into police areas, of which
there are three kinds: the Metropolitan Police district, the City of London police, and
those listed in Sch 1 to the Act. The Metropolitan Police was created in 1829 as the
first modern British force: it is the only police force for which the Home Secretary was
directly responsible as the police authority, though that responsibility has now passed
to the Metropolitan Police Authority under the Greater London Authority Act 1999.[6]
As a result the rules relating to the structure and organisation of the metropolitan police
have been broadly assimilated to those relating to other police forces. The chief officer
is the Commissioner of Police for the Metropolis, who is appointed by the Crown on
the advice of the Home Secretary, who must take into account the views of the
Metropolitan Police Authority and the London Mayor. The City of London Police is
a separate force; the chief officer, the Commissioner, is appointed by the police authority, the Court of Common Council, subject to the approval of the Home Secretary.
Outside London there are 41 police areas listed in the Schedule to the 1996 Act,
giving a total of 43, the same number as before the 1994 reforms. In the white paper
preceding the 1994 Act, the government did announce, however, that it intended to
implement a programme of police force amalgamation in the future and powers to alter
police areas are now found in s 32 of the Police Act 1996, to be exercised by the Home
Secretary where it appears expedient 'in the interests of efficiency or effectiveness'. The
Act also provides that for each police area there shall be a police authority (which in
turn shall be a body corporate), but as a result of controversial measures introduced
in 1994, the composition of these authorities has changed, most notably by the reduction in the number of local authority councillors. Although local authority representatives will still be in the majority (with nine out of the standard membership of 17),

---

[4] See also the amending Greater London Authority Act 1999, and the Criminal Justice and Police Act 2001.
[5] HC Deb, 12 February 1997, col 345.
[6] 1999 Act, s 319, amending Police Act 1996, s 101.

five of the members are to be appointed from a short-list prepared by the Home Secretary. The remaining members are appointed by local magistrates from among their number, whereas, before the 1994 changes, one-third of the membership of the committee was appointed in this way.[7]

The 1996 Act retains the duty whereby each police authority must secure the maintenance of an effective and efficient police force for its area (s 6). But in discharging this duty police authorities are required to have regard to any objectives which may be set by the Home Secretary; the local policing objectives and performance targets set by the police authority; and any local policing plan, local policing authorities now being required to issue such plans on an annual basis (s 6). Subject to the approval of the Home Secretary, the police authority appoints the chief constable, as well as assistant chief constables (although in this latter case after consultation with both the chief constable and the Home Secretary). But a police force is under the direction and control of the chief constable, who must have regard to the local policing plan.[8] It is true that the police authority has power to require the chief constable and any assistant chief constable to retire in the interests of efficiency or effectiveness (ss 11, 12). But in exercising this power the police authority must act with the approval of the Home Secretary, who may take the initiative by requiring the police authority to retire the chief constable (s 42). The chief constable must be given an opportunity to make representations to the police authority or the Home Secretary before he or she can be required to retire (ss 11, 42). The police authority may institute disciplinary proceedings against the chief constable.[9] The police authority is the paymaster for local police expenditure,[10] although salaries are fixed according to national scales.

The Home Secretary

The Home Secretary has many statutory powers affecting the police, the provisions which follow applying also to the metropolitan police, with modifications in some cases. These powers were extended in 1994 so that he may (by order) determine policy objectives for police authorities, after consultation with persons representative of the police authorities as well as chief constables (s 37). Where objectives have been set in this way, the Home Secretary may direct police authorities to establish performance targets, the minister having a wide discretion to issue a direction to one or more or to all police authorities, and a power to impose different conditions on different authorities (s 38). He may also issue codes of practice relating to the discharge by police authorities of any of their functions (s 39). Otherwise the Home Secretary may require a police authority to report on any matter relating to the discharge of its functions (s 43) and may require chief constables to do the same (s 44). Still further powers enable the Home Secretary to cause a local inquiry to be held into any matter connected with the policing of any area (s 49) and to provide and maintain 'such organisations, facilities and

---

[7] For the composition of police authorities, see Police Act 1996, Sch 2. On the need for a representative political balance on police authorities, see Criminal Justice and Police Act 2001, s 105, amending 1996 Act, Sch 2. For the Metropolitan Police Authority, see Greater London Authority Act 1999, Sch 26, inserting a new Sch 2A to the Police Act 1996.

[8] For similar arrangements in London, see Greater London Authority Act 1999, s 314, inserting new Police Act 1996, s 59A.

[9] Cf *Ridge* v *Baldwin* [1964] AC 40, ch 30 B below, which concerned the dismissal of a chief constable under the pre-1964 legislation. The arrangements for disciplining senior officers were reviewed in 1987, 'in the light of concern expressed about the investigation of allegations against the former deputy chief constable of Greater Manchester, Mr John Stalker': HC Deb, 22 July 1987, col 200 (WA). Cf Stalker, *Stalker*.

[10] On the financial powers of police authorities, see *R* v *DPP, ex p Duckenfield* [2000] 1 WLR 55.

services as he considers necessary or expedient for promoting the efficiency and effectiveness of the police' (s 57). This extends powers previously contained in the Police Act 1964, s 41, which were nevertheless held to be wide enough to enable the Home Secretary to make available from a central store baton rounds and CS gas to be used in the event of serious public disorder.[11] By s 50 of the 1996 Act, the Home Secretary may make regulations for the government, administration and conditions of service of police forces, in particular with respect to ranks, qualifications for appointment and promotion, probationary service, voluntary retirement, discipline, duties, pay, allowances, clothing and equipment.

In addition to these wide statutory powers, the Home Secretary has always exercised considerable financial control. Since 1856, a grant has been made from the exchequer towards the police expenses of local authorities. Payment of the grant, formerly 51% of all approved expenses, is now determined annually by the Home Secretary with the approval of the Treasury. In determining how much any one authority receives, the Home Secretary 'may exercise his discretion by applying such formulae or other rules as he considers appropriate' (s 46). Her Majesty's Inspectors of Constabulary have proved powerful instruments in maintaining the efficiency and effectiveness of police forces: they are appointed by and report to the Home Secretary (s 54). The Inspectorate of Constabulary must submit an annual report to the Home Secretary (s 54) and may be directed by him to carry out an inspection of any force. Where a report states that the force is not efficient or not effective, or will cease to be efficient or effective unless remedial measures are taken, the Home Secretary may direct the police authority to take prescribed measures (s 40), a power which further reinforces the power of central government. This includes a power specifically to give directions as to the minimum level of the annual budget to be provided by the authority (s 41). But despite these 'wide and diverse' powers of the Home Secretary, it has been thought necessary to emphasise that they 'do not extend to operational matters'.[12]

B. Personal liberty and police powers

In 1929 a royal commission on police powers and procedure, reviewing the practice of the police in searching the dwelling of a person for whose arrest a warrant had been issued, expressed the concern that police 'in the discharge of their essential duties, should have to rely on powers of which the legality seems doubtful'.[13] But the law was not reformed and in 1960 an eminent judge wrote: 'The police power of search under English law is haphazard and ill-defined.'[14] The comment was almost equally true of the law of arrest. In 1978 a royal commission was set up by the Labour government to review the powers and duties of the police in the investigation of offences and the prosecution of crime. The commission was required to have regard 'both to the interests of the community in bringing offenders to justice and to the rights and liberties of persons suspected or accused of crime'. Its report sought within the criminal justice system 'to define a balance between the rights of individuals and the security of society and the state'. Many of the changes recommended by the report were controversial, but there could be little disagreement with the commission's main finding that there

---

[11] *R v Home Secretary, ex p Northumbria Police Authority* [1989] QB 26; and see A W Bradley [1988] PL 298.
[12] Bailey, Harris and Jones, *Civil Liberties Cases and Materials*, ch 2.
[13] Cmd 3297, 1929, p 45.
[14] Devlin, *The Criminal Prosecution in England*, p 53.

was a strong need to bring the law up to date. Existing police powers were 'found in (or extracted with difficulty from) a mixture of statute law, common law, evidential law, and guidance to the police from the judges and the Home Office'; the law regulating police investigation needed 'to be reformulated and restated in clear and coherent terms that have regard to contemporary circumstances'.[15]

This broad conclusion was accepted by the Conservative government, which introduced what was to become the Police and Criminal Evidence Act 1984, 'an important reforming statute'[16] usually referred to by its acronym PACE.[17] Together with codes of practice[18] issued under the authority of the Act,[19] this measure provided a very extensive (although not comprehensive) code of police powers, which both conferred new powers on the police and introduced new safeguards for the citizen. However, the Act tilted the scales of justice very firmly in favour of the police and it is seriously open to question whether the safeguards for individual liberty that the Act provided are adequate. Before turning to these questions, we may note that deprivation of personal liberty may take place by means other than arrest and detention by police officers in the exercise of their duties to investigate and prevent crime. One important measure relates to the compulsory admission to hospital of those suffering from acute mental disorder.[20] Under statute, compulsory admission generally requires an application to have been made by the nearest relative of the patient or an approved social worker, and to be supported by the recommendation of two medical practitioners, one of whom must have had special experience in the diagnosis or treatment of mental disorder. In an acute emergency, admission for up to 72 hours may be based on only one medical recommendation. Voluntary patients already in hospital may be detained from leaving for up to six hours on the decision of a mental nurse and for up to 72 hours on the decision of a hospital doctor.[21] The criminal courts may make hospital and restriction orders for the compulsory admission of those suffering from mental disorder who have been convicted of, or in some cases merely charged with, criminal offences.[22] Since 1959 compulsorily detained patients have been able to seek release by applying to a mental health review tribunal.[23]

Police powers short of arrest

Most police powers affecting the individual's liberty depend on an arrest having been made. At common law, the pre-arrest powers of the police are very limited, a point

---

[15] Cmnd 8092, 1981 (the Philips report on criminal procedure), pp 8 and 110. For comment, see M Inman [1981] Crim LR 469; K W Lidstone [1981] Crim LR 454; D McBarnet [1981] Crim LR 445; and B Smythe [1981] PL 184, 481.

[16] Vince v Chief Constable of Dorset [1993] 2 All ER 321, at p 335.

[17] See Zander, The Police and Criminal Evidence Act 1984. See also articles at [1985] PL 388 and (1989) 40 NILQ 319.

[18] There are five codes of practice: Code A: Code of Practice for the Exercise by Police Officers of Statutory Powers of Stop and Search; Code B: Code of Practice for the Searching of Premises by Police Officers and the Seizure of Property Found by Police Officers on Persons or Premises; Code C: Code of Practice for the Detention, Treatment and Questioning of Persons by Police Officers; Code D: Code of Practice for the Identification of Persons by Police Officers; and Code E: Code of Practice on Tape Recording of Interviews with Suspects. The codes were revised in 1995 and amended in 1999 and 2001.

[19] Police and Criminal Evidence Act 1984, ss 66, 67.

[20] For full accounts, see Hoggett, Mental Health Law, and Jones, Mental Health Act Manual. See also Unsworth, The Politics of Mental Health Legislation.

[21] Mental Health Act 1983, Part II.

[22] Mental Health Act 1983, Part III. Separate legislation exists for Scotland.

[23] Now constituted under Mental Health Act 1983, s 65 as amended. See R (H) v London North and East Region Mental Health Review Tribunal [2001] 3 WLR 512.

illustrated in different ways by three cases. In *Jackson* v *Stevenson*,[24] it was held to be contrary to constitutional principle and illegal to search someone to establish whether there are grounds for an arrest. In *Kenlin* v *Gardiner*,[25] it was held that the police had no right physically to detain someone for questioning without first arresting the person concerned. Anyone who resists such detention cannot be guilty of obstructing a police officer in the execution of his duty. And in *R* v *Lemsatef*[26] it was held that the police cannot require individuals to accompany them to the police station in order to help the police with their inquiries. In a forceful judgment, Lawton LJ said that if the idea 'is getting around' that the police could detain suspects for this purpose, the sooner people disabuse themselves of the idea, the better. But although the police have no common law right to stop and search, no right to detain for questioning, and no right to require assistance with their inquiries,[27] these common law rules may be modified by statute. An early example is the Metropolitan Police Act 1839, which by s 66 gave to the police in London the power to stop and search persons and vehicles reasonably suspected of having stolen property on or in them. The same power was adopted in local Acts applying to urban areas outside London. There are clearly potential dangers in granting wide stop and search powers to the police for there is a possibility that the power will be abused,[28] with harassment of ethnic minority groups being a particular concern. Nevertheless, in his report on the Brixton disorders, Lord Scarman thought such powers necessary to combat street crime, provided that the safeguard of 'reasonable suspicion' was properly and objectively applied.[29]

Stop and search powers are now found in a number of statutes. By s 23 of the Misuse of Drugs Act 1971, a constable may search (and detain for the purpose of the search) anyone who is suspected on reasonable grounds to be in unlawful possession of a controlled drug.[30] Similar powers apply in relation to vehicles. Powers to stop and search are also found in Part I of PACE.[31] Thus a constable may search a person or vehicle, or anything which is in or on the vehicle, for stolen or prohibited articles, a term defined to include an offensive weapon or an article used for the purpose of burglary or related crimes (s 1). The power may be so exercised only if the constable 'has reasonable grounds for suspecting that he will find stolen or prohibited articles' (s 1(3)), or that someone is carrying a knife or other sharp implement in a public place.[32] Code of Practice A (on the Exercise by Police Officers of Statutory Powers of Stop and Search) gives some guidance as to reasonable grounds for suspicion. Paragraph 1.7 provides:

> Reasonable suspicion can never be supported on the basis of personal factors alone without supporting intelligence or information. For example, a person's colour, age, hairstyle or manner of dress, or the fact that he is known to have a previous conviction for possession of an unlawful article, cannot be used alone or in combination with each other as the sole basis on which to search that person. Nor may it be founded on the basis of stereotyped images of certain persons or groups as more likely to be committing offences.[33]

---

[24] (1879) 2 Adam 255. Cf *Lodwick* v *Sanders* [1985] 1 All ER 577.
[25] [1967] 2 QB 510.
[26] [1977] 2 All ER 835.
[27] See also *Rice* v *Connolly* [1966] 2 QB 414, and *O'Loughlin* v *Chief Constable of Essex* [1998] 1 WLR 374.
[28] See Home Office Advisory Committee on Drug Dependence, Powers of Arrest and Search in Relation to Drug Offences, 1970.
[29] Cmnd 8427, 1981, para 7.2.
[30] See *Wither* v *Reid* 1979 SLT 192 (on the distinction between (*a*) arrest and (*b*) detention for search).
[31] Note that they are powers of 'stop and search' not 'stop and question'. See Zander, p 10.
[32] See Criminal Justice Act 1988, s 139.
[33] But compare paragraph 1.7AA: 'Where there is reliable information or intelligence that members of a group or gang who habitually carry knives unlawfully or weapons or controlled drugs, and wear a distinctive item of clothing or other means of identification to indicate membership of it, the members may be identified by means of that distinctive item of clothing or other means of identification.'

If during a search a constable discovers stolen or prohibited articles, they may be seized (s 1(6)). But before exercising these powers, a constable must (inter alia) inform the person to be searched of his or her name and police station and of the grounds for the search. The Act also requires a police officer to provide documentary evidence that he or she is a police officer if he or she is not in uniform (s 2). Details of the search must be recorded and if requested a copy must be supplied to the person searched (s 3). Failure to do so could render the action unlawful.[34] Reasonable force may be used by the police (s 117) but during any search made before an arrest a person may not be required to remove any clothing in public except for an outer coat, jacket or gloves (s 2(9)).[35] Stop and search powers were extended in 1988 to knives[36] and again in the Criminal Justice and Public Order Act 1994 (s 60) to prevent incidents of serious violence which it is reasonably anticipated may take place.

Under the Road Traffic Act 1988, s 163, a constable in uniform may require a person driving a vehicle or a cyclist to stop. Failure to do so is an offence. It has been held that in exercising this power the police may immobilise a vehicle by removing the keys. Where a police officer has required a vehicle to stop, he 'is entitled to take reasonable steps to detain it for such reasonable time as will enable him, if he suspects it to have been stolen, to effect an arrest and to explain to the driver the reason for the arrest'.[37] In some circumstances, a police officer can require the driver to produce his or her driving licence and his or her name, address and date of birth.[38] But otherwise the driver is under no duty to answer any questions which the police may ask: 'the right to silence in such a circumstance is predominant.'[39] In addition to powers conferred by the Road Traffic Act 1988, s 4 of PACE authorises the police to set up road checks when it is believed that there is or about to be in the locality during the period of the check someone who has committed or witnessed a serious arrestable offence, someone who is intending to commit such an offence, or an escaped prisoner. In view of the wide definition of serious arrestable offence (which includes serious harm to public order)[40] this is a considerable power, though it can be used only for the purpose of determining whether the vehicle is carrying any of the categories of person referred to. It confers no power on the police to question the driver or occupants of a vehicle and imposes no duty on such people to respond to police questions. Additional powers are found in the Terrorism Act 2000.[41] In addition to these statutory provisions, a common law power to stop vehicles appears to have been recognised by the Divisional Court in *Moss* v *McLachlan*.[42] We consider this case more fully in chapter 24.

Police powers of arrest

1 *The grounds for arrest.* Powers of arrest are not exclusive to the police and some may be exercised by any person. But today the very great majority of arrests are undertaken by the police. The significance of the act of arrest is that it is at that moment that an individual loses his or her liberty and, if the arrest is lawful, becomes subject

---

[34] *Osman* v *DPP* (1999) 163 JP 725.
[35] See further Code of Practice A, para 3. On the use of the s 1 power see Bailey, Harris and Jones, p 219. Figures produced there indicate that the power was used on 714,100 occasions in 2000–01, representing a fall of 17% on the previous year; 13% of the cases led to an arrest.
[36] Criminal Justice Act 1988, s 140.
[37] *Lodwick* v *Sanders* [1985] 1 All ER 577.
[38] Road Traffic Act 1988, s 163.
[39] *Lodwick* v *Sanders* [1985] 1 All ER 577, 581. But see later on the 'right to silence'.
[40] Police and Criminal Evidence Act 1984, s 116.
[41] See ch 26 E below.
[42] [1985] IRLR 76. See G S Morris (1985) 14 ILJ 109.

to lawful detention. Arrests are of two kinds: (*a*) with a warrant and (*b*) without a warrant.

(*a*) *Arrest with a warrant.*   Most arrests relate to the initiation of proceedings in the criminal courts. Under the Magistrates' Courts Act 1980, s 1, proceedings may be initiated either by the issue of a summons, requiring the accused to attend court on a certain day, or, in more serious cases, by a warrant of arrest, naming the accused and the offence with which he or she is charged. A warrant is obtained from a magistrate after a written application (information) has been substantiated on oath.[43] In issuing a warrant for arrest, the magistrate may endorse it for bail.[44] A warrant may be executed anywhere in England or Wales by a police constable.[45] If the warrant is to arrest a person charged with an offence, it may be executed even when a constable does not have it in his or her possession, but the warrant must be shown on demand to the arrested person as soon as possible.[46] Despite judicial dicta to the contrary,[47] a person arrested would seem entitled to know that he or she is being arrested under a warrant (for if not, how can he or she demand to see it?). Where a constable in good faith executes a warrant that seems valid on its face, he or she is protected from liability for the arrest by the Constables' Protection Act 1750 if it should turn out that the warrant was beyond the jurisdiction of the magistrate who issued it.[48] The requirement that the warrant be issued by a magistrate is thus as much a safeguard for the police as it is for the person named on it. When an arrest warrant has been issued, a constable may enter and search premises to make the arrest, using such reasonable force as is necessary.[49]

(*b*) *Arrest without a warrant under PACE.*   The law on arrest without a warrant was formerly a complicated mixture of common law and statutory powers.[50] The Police and Criminal Evidence Act 1984 made further reform of the law which was begun when the Criminal Law Act 1967, s 2, abolished the distinction between felonies and misdemeanours, and created a new category of arrestable offences. This initially comprised: (*a*) all offences for which the sentence is fixed by law (for example, life imprisonment in the case of murder); (*b*) all offences for which a first offender over 18 may be sentenced to five years' imprisonment or more; and (*c*) certain other specified offences (under such legislation as the Official Secrets Acts 1911–89, the Sexual Offences Act 1956, and the Customs and Excise Acts), even though they may not carry prison sentences of five years or longer.[51] Other offences (dealing, for example, with obscene publications, publications intended or likely to stir up racial hatred and kerb crawling) have been added by subsequent legislation.[52]

Any person (whether a constable or not) may arrest without a warrant anyone who is, or whom he or she reasonably suspects to be, in the act of committing an arrestable

---

[43] The exercise of the power may not be delegated: *R v Manchester Stipendiary Magistrate, ex p Hill* [1983] 1 AC 328.

[44] Magistrates' Courts Act 1980, s 17.

[45] They may now be executed in Scotland: Criminal Justice and Public Order Act 1994, s 136. For the cross-border execution of warrants in the UK, see C Walker [1997] 56 CLJ 114.

[46] Magistrates' Courts Act 1980, s 125(3); and cf *R v Purdy* [1975] QB 288. And see Police and Criminal Evidence Act 1984, s 33.

[47] *R v Kulynycz* [1971] 1 QB 367, 372.

[48] See also *McGrath v RUC* [2001] 2 AC 731.

[49] Police and Criminal Evidence Act 1984, ss 17, 117.

[50] For the position in Scots law, see Renton and Brown's, *Criminal Procedure.*

[51] Police and Criminal Evidence Act 1984, s 24, replacing Criminal Law Act 1967, s 2.

[52] See Football (Offences) Act 1991, s 5(1) Criminal Justice and Public Order Act 1994, ss 85(2), 155, 166(4), and 167(7), and Criminal Justice and Police Act 2001, s 71.

offence. Where such an offence has actually been committed, any person may arrest anyone who is with reasonable cause suspected to be guilty of the offence or is guilty of it. Where there is merely reasonable cause to suspect that an arrestable offence has been committed, a constable has the additional power of arresting any person whom he or she reasonably suspects of having committed it: but a private person does not have this additional power and may be liable in damages to the person arrested if it should turn out that no arrestable offence has been committed by anyone.[53] A constable may also arrest any person whom with reasonable cause he or she suspects to be about to commit an arrestable offence.

> In *O'Hara v Chief Constable of the RUC*[54] the appellant had been arrested under the Prevention of Terrorism (Temporary Provisions) Act 1984, which provided by s 12 that a constable may arrest without a warrant anyone whom 'he has reasonable grounds for suspecting' to be involved with acts of terrorism, a form of words similar to that used in PACE, s 24. At issue was whether the police officer could arrest a suspect (who in this case was detained for 15 days without any explanation, before being released without charge) after a briefing from other colleagues, in the course of which he was told that the appellant had been involved in a murder. It was held by the House of Lords that in order for there to be a reasonable suspicion 'the information which causes the constable to be suspicious of the individual must be in existence to the knowledge of the police officer at the time he makes the arrest'. The power is vested in the constable, and cannot be exercised simply on the request or instruction of another officer, though the information which causes the arresting officer to be suspicious of the individual 'may come from other officers'. On the facts of this case, however, the appeal failed and the arrest was held to have been lawful, even though the trial court had 'scanty evidence' of the matters disclosed to the arresting officer at the briefing.

In addition to the power to arrest without a warrant for an arrestable offence, s 25 of PACE applies to any other offence which has been or is being committed or attempted, and it seems to a constable impracticable or inappropriate to rely on the service of a summons at a later date. Such an arrest may be made when any of the 'general arrest conditions' is satisfied. These conditions include situations in which the constable does not know and cannot ascertain the name of the relevant person; where the constable reasonably doubts whether the name given by the person is his or her real name; where the person has not provided a satisfactory address for the service of a summons; and where the constable reasonably believes that an arrest is necessary to prevent the person causing physical harm to another, damage to property, an offence against public decency, or obstruction of the highway.[55]

(c) Other powers of arrest without warrant.   In addition to the powers of arrest without a warrant under ss 24 and 25 of PACE, other specific statutory powers of arrest continue in force, while there remain some residual common law powers. The former include the power to arrest someone apparently driving a car while unfit through drink or drugs, and persons reasonably suspected of various offences, including absence without leave from the armed forces, entering and remaining on property under the Criminal Law Act 1977, illegal entry under the Immigration Act 1971 and offences under the Public Order Act 1936. The police may also arrest and detain prisoners who

---

[53] Police and Criminal Evidence Act 1984, s 24(4)–(6), which maintains the rule in *Walters v W H Smith & Son Ltd* [1914] 1 KB 595. See *R v Self* (1992) 95 Cr App R 42.

[54] [1997] AC 286.

[55] The general arrest conditions are not satisfied where the arresting officer doubts the veracity of the arrested person's name and address, and these doubts are 'based solely on his experience that people who commit offences did not give their correct name and address': *G v DPP* [1989] Crim LR 150. Failure to give a name and address is not in itself a ground for arrest. See *Nicholas v Parsonage* [1987] RTR 199.

are unlawfully at large; children who are neglected, exposed to moral danger or absent without authority from a place of safety; and persons liable to be examined or removed from the United Kingdom under the Immigration Act 1971. New specific statutory powers of arrest without a warrant have also been introduced since 1984. For example, under the Public Order Act 1986, a police officer may arrest without warrant anyone he or she reasonably suspects is committing an affray, or who is reasonably suspected of using threatening, abusive or insulting words or behaviour towards another person, with intent to cause that person to believe that immediate unlawful violence will be used against him or her or another. The same Act also confers a power to arrest a person without a warrant for disorderly conduct which a constable has warned the person in question to stop and he or she fails to do so.[56]

At common law, a police officer has a power to arrest without warrant anyone who commits a breach of the peace. The important decision in *R* v *Howell*[57] established that there is a power of arrest where a breach of the peace was committed in the presence of the person making the arrest; or if the person making the arrest reasonably believed that such a breach would be committed in the immediate future by the person arrested, even though at the time of the arrest he or she had not committed the breach; or if a breach of the peace has been committed and it is reasonably believed that a renewal of it is threatened. *Howell* also established that there can be no breach of the peace unless an act was done or threatened to be done which actually either harmed a person or his or her property, was likely to cause such harm, or put someone in fear of such harm being done.[58] An apprehended breach of the peace is an essential ingredient in the power to arrest without a warrant for obstructing a police officer in the execution of his duty.

In *Wershof* v *Metropolitan Police Commissioner*[59] a young solicitor was telephoned by his brother and asked to come to the family jewellery shop where the brother was engaged in a dispute with a police officer about a ring which the officer thought had been stolen. When the solicitor arrived, he told the police officer that he could take the ring only if he produced a receipt for it. The officer refused to provide a receipt, the solicitor refused to let him have the ring and after an argument the solicitor was arrested for obstructing a police officer in the execution of his duty. The police officer thereupon put a tight and painful grip on the solicitor's right arm and frog-marched him down the road. In a successful action by the solicitor for damages for assault, the court held that a police officer has power to arrest without a warrant a person who wilfully obstructs him in the execution of his duty only if the obstruction was such that an offender actually caused or was likely to cause a breach of the peace. In this case the solicitor would not have physically resisted a seizure of the ring by force and this should have been apparent to the police officer.

2 *The manner of arrest.*   Although the first ingredient of a proper arrest is the existence of lawful authority to make the arrest, it is not the only one. The arrest must also be executed in a proper manner, which means that the arrested person must be told of the fact of arrest (i.e. that he or she is under arrest) and also of the reasons for the arrest (PACE, s 28), measures 'laid down by Parliament to protect the individual against the excess or abuse of the power of arrest'.[60] The origin of the latter rule

---

[56] See Public Order Act 1986, s 5. See also Protection from Harassment Act 1997.
[57] [1982] QB 416. See also *Albert* v *Lavin* [1982] AC 546, and *Foulkes* v *Merseyside Chief Constable* [1998] 3 All ER 705.
[58] A breach of the peace may occur in private premises: *McConnell* v *Chief Constable of Greater Manchester* [1990] 1 All ER 423.
[59] [1978] 3 All ER 540.
[60] *Hill* v *Chief Constable of South Yorkshire* [1990] 1 All ER 1046.

(requiring reasons to be given for the arrest) may be found in *Christie* v *Leachinsky*,[61] where the Liverpool police had purported to exercise a power of arrest contained in a local Act when they knew that the conditions for this were not met. When the officers concerned were later sued for wrongful arrest and false imprisonment, it was argued that the arrest was lawful because at the time they had information about Leachinsky which would have justified his arrest for another offence. The House of Lords held that the arrest was unlawful, since it was a condition of a lawful arrest that the person arrested should be entitled to know the reason for it. An actual charge need not be formulated at the time of arrest, but 'the arrested man is entitled to be told what is the act for which he is arrested'. Indeed it has been said that 'giving the correct information of the reasons for an arrest was of the utmost constitutional significance'.[62]

This information must be given at the time of arrest or as soon as practicable thereafter.[63] Otherwise the arrest is unlawful (PACE, s 28(1), (3)) although there is nothing laid down in the Act specifying how the information should be communicated to an arrested person.[64] A duty to inform people of the fact of arrest is also recognised by the common law. In *Alderson* v *Booth*,[65] the accused had given a positive breath-alyser test to a police officer who then said to the accused: 'I shall have to ask you to come to the police station for further tests.' He went and subsequently was acquitted at his trial for drunk driving on the ground that he had not been arrested before going to the police station, a lawful arrest being a condition precedent to a conviction under the drink/driving legislation. On appeal the acquittal was upheld, the court taking the view that compulsion is a necessary element of arrest and that police officers should use clear words to bring home to a person that he or she is under arrest, such as the words, 'I arrest you'. However, in *R* v *Inwood*,[66] it was made clear that there is no single magic formula for this purpose and that different procedures may have to be followed with different people, depending on age, ethnic origins, knowledge of English, intellectual qualities and mental disabilities.[67] The common law may be relevant in other respects too. Unlike the police stop and search powers, there is no statutory duty on police officers (even if not in uniform) to identify themselves as such to an arrested person. *Abbassy* v *Metropolitan Police Commissioner*[68] suggests, however, that there may be a common law obligation to this effect.

In relation to the requirements of s 28 of PACE, two interesting questions have arisen. The first is, what happens if the police are unable to inform the arrested person of the fact and reasons at the time of arrest and then fail to do so as soon as it becomes practicable? Does this subsequent failure mean that the earlier arrest is unlawful? In *DPP* v *Hawkins*,[69] the court's answer was no:

---

[61] [1947] AC 573, 593 (Lord Simonds). And see *Pedro* v *Diss* [1981] 2 All ER 59. But note that the 1984 Act goes beyond the common law position: see *Hill* v *Chief Constable of South Yorkshire* (note 60 above). On the continuing importance of *Christie* v *Leachinsky*, see *O'Loughlin* v *Chief Constable of Essex* [1998] 1 WLR 374, and *R* v *Chalkley* [1998] QB 848.

[62] *Edwards* v *DPP* (1993) 97 Cr App R 301. In the case of someone arrested under s 14(1)(b) of the Prevention of Terrorism (Temporary Provisions) Act 1989 (power to arrest on reasonable suspicion of involvement in terrorism rather than a specific crime), it is not necessary to specify the crime alleged: *Oscar* v *Chief Constable of RUC* (1993) 2 BNIL 52. See now the differently worded provisions of the Terrorism Act 2000, ss 40 and 41.

[63] See *Dawes* v *DPP* [1995] 1 Cr App R 65.

[64] See *Nicholas* v *Parsonage* [1987] RTR 199.

[65] [1969] 2 QB 216. Cf *Nichols* v *Bulman* [1985] RTR 236.

[66] [1973] 2 All ER 645.

[67] On the continuing importance of *Booth* and *Inwood*, see *R* v *Brosch* [1988] Crim LR 743.

[68] [1990] 1 All ER 193, 202 (citing Burn's *Justice of the Peace*, 1755).

[69] [1988] 3 All ER 673.

When a police officer makes an arrest which he is lawfully entitled to make but is unable at the time to state the ground because it is impracticable to do so, . . . it is his duty to maintain the arrest until it is practicable to inform the arrested person of that ground. If, when it does become practicable, he fails to do so, then the arrest is unlawful, but that does not mean that acts, which were previously done and were, when done, done in the execution of duty, become, retrospectively, acts which were not done in the execution of duty.[70]

The second question relates to the position where the police have no reason to delay informing an arrested person of the fact and reasons for the arrest. Does this initial failure, rendering the arrest therefore unlawful, vitiate all the subsequent proceedings? Again, it seems not.

In *Lewis v Chief Constable of South Wales*[71] two women were arrested for burglary but were not told why they were being arrested. They were then taken to a police station where they were informed of the reasons for the arrest, within (respectively) 10 minutes and 23 minutes after the time of arrest. Some five hours later both were released. They subsequently sued for wrongful arrest and false imprisonment and the question which arose was whether they were entitled to be compensated for 10 and 23 minutes respectively or for the entire five-hour period. The Court of Appeal agreed with the first instance decision that, although the initial arrest had been unlawful because the women had not been given the reasons for it, it ceased being unlawful when this was done. The court did not consider this result to be inconsistent with s 28(3) of PACE.

While a police officer may use reasonable force to make the arrest,[72] the use of un-reasonable force does not necessarily make the arrest unlawful.[73]

3 *Invoking the power of arrest.* Although the police must thus have grounds for arrest and must exercise these powers in a proper manner, it does not follow that an arrest will necessarily be lawful where these conditions have been met. The power of arrest is a discretionary power, and like other discretionary powers of public officials, it is subject to review by the courts to ensure that it is not exercised improperly.

In *Holgate-Mohammed v Duke*[74] the appellant was arrested without a warrant and taken to a police station where she was questioned in connection with the theft of jewellery. The arrest was made under the Criminal Law Act 1967, s 2(4) (now PACE, s 24(6)) which permitted a constable to arrest without warrant anyone whom he, with reasonable cause, suspected to be guilty of an offence which he, with reasonable cause, suspected to have been committed. The appellant was later released without charge, whereupon she brought proceedings for wrongful imprisonment. In dismissing her appeal, the House of Lords held that the statutory power of arrest must be exercised in accordance with the so-called *Wednesbury* principles, meaning in essence that the discretion so conferred should not be abused. There was no such abuse in this case when the police officer arrested the appellant in the belief that she would be more likely to respond truthfully to his questions if she were questioned under arrest at the police station than if she were questioned at her own home, 'from which she could peremptorily order him to depart at any moment'.

Although this decision establishes a crucially important point of principle, in practice the courts are unlikely very often to say that the power of arrest has been unreasonably exercised in the *Wednesbury* sense. Although the court stressed that this was

---

[70] At 674.
[71] [1991] 1 All ER 206.
[72] Police and Criminal Evidence Act 1984, s 117.
[73] *Simpson v Chief Constable of South Yorkshire Police*, *The Times*, 7 March 1991. Cf *Hill v Chief Constable of South Yorkshire* (note 60 above).
[74] [1984] AC 437.

likely to happen only exceptionally, nevertheless *Plange* v *Chief Constable of South Humberside*[75] is one such case.

> The plaintiff had allegedly assaulted a third party, who had reported it to the police. Knowing that the complaint had subsequently been withdrawn and having no intention of charging the plaintiff, a police officer nevertheless proceeded to arrest him and detained him for four hours. It was conceded for the plaintiff that at the time of arrest there were reasonable grounds for suspecting that an arrestable offence had been committed by the person arrested. But it was held albeit on the 'special facts' of the case that 'there was sufficient evidence to go to the jury that notwithstanding that the condition precedent in section 24(6) [of PACE] was satisfied the arrest was nevertheless unlawful'.

Plange was distinguished in *R* v *Chalkley*[76] where the police arrested the defendants without a warrant (under PACE, s 24(6)) in connection with credit card frauds. This was done to gain access to the home of the accused so that a listening device could be placed in the hope that this would provide evidence about even more serious crimes of which they were suspected. After being arrested for the frauds, the defendants were released and tape recordings of conversations picked up by the listening devices were used in evidence against them in proceedings for armed robbery. The Court of Appeal held that they had not been unlawfully arrested on the ground that 'a collateral motive for an arrest on otherwise good and stated grounds does not necessarily make it unlawful'.

C. Police powers of detention and questioning of suspects

The detention of suspects

Apart from powers given by anti-terrorism legislation,[77] the police in England and Wales did not before 1984 have express power to detain suspects for further investigations to be carried out; neither did they have a general power to detain individuals for questioning, whether as suspects or potential witnesses.[78] In practice, the police sometimes acted as if they had such powers.[79] The royal commission on Criminal Procedure recommended in 1981 that extra powers to detain suspects for questioning should be given to the police, with safeguards to ensure that those powers were not abused.[80] These extra powers were granted by PACE, which provides that an arrested person must be brought to a police station as soon as practicable after the arrest (s 30), although this may be delayed if his or her presence elsewhere is necessary for immediate investigation (s 30(10)). At every police station that is designated for such detention,[81] there must be a custody officer of the rank of sergeant or above (s 36).[82] It is the duty of the custody officer to authorise the detention of suspects if this is necessary to secure or preserve evidence relating to an offence or 'to obtain such evidence by questioning' the suspect (s 37). The custody officer is required to ensure that the detention is carried out in accordance with the 1984 Act and the Code of Practice on the Detention, Treatment

---

[75] *The Times*, 23 March 1992.
[76] [1998] QB 848. Compare *R* v *Kirk* [1999] 4 All ER 698. See also *Henderson* v *Chief Constable of Cleveland Police* [2001] 1 WLR 1103.
[77] See ch 26 E.
[78] But cf *Holgate-Mohammed* v *Duke* [1984] AC 437.
[79] See the condemnation of this practice by Lawton LJ in *R* v *Lemsatef* [1977] 2 All ER 835.
[80] Cmnd 8092, 1981, ch 4.
[81] See 1984 Act, s 35.
[82] On the limitations of this crucial measure designed 'to ensure that the welfare and interests of detained subjects are properly protected', see *Vince* v *Chief Constable of Dorset* (note 16 above).

and Questioning of Persons by Police Officers (Code C) (s 39).[83] In addition to the custody officer, the other intermediary between the arrested person and the investigating team is the review officer, who in the case of someone who has not been charged is an officer of the rank of inspector or above who has not been involved in the investigation. The review officer is required by the Act to conduct regular reviews of detention. The first review should take place not later than six hours after the detention was first authorised and subsequent reviews should take place at intervals of no more than nine hours. The review may be postponed if the review officer is not available or if it would prejudice the investigation, although in either case it should be carried out as soon as practicable (s 40).[84]

At common law someone arrested on the authority of a warrant had to be brought before the magistrates immediately, while someone arrested without a warrant had to be brought before the magistrates as soon as possible. In practice, however, people were detained for questioning, often euphemistically 'helping the police with their enquiries'. In *R v Holmes, ex p Sherman*,[85] it was held that 48 hours was the maximum period someone could be detained without being brought before magistrates. Detention for police questioning was first authorised by the Prevention of Terrorism (Temporary Provisions) Act 1974[86] which permitted detention for up to seven days. It was introduced as a general power in Scotland by the Criminal Justice (Scotland) Act 1980, which authorised detention (without arrest) for up to six hours.[87] PACE now allows the police to detain people who have been arrested for up to 24 hours without being released or charged in the first instance (s 41). This may be extended to 36 hours by an officer of the rank of superintendent or above where the offence is a 'serious arrestable offence' (s 42), a term defined to include murder, manslaughter, rape, kidnapping and other arrestable offences which are likely to have consequences such as serious harm to state security or public order, or death, serious injury or serious financial loss to any person.[88] When serious arrestable offences are concerned, the period of 36 hours may be extended for up to 96 hours in total, if a magistrates' court (defined as a court of *two or more* justices of the peace, a potentially important safeguard) on application by the police is satisfied that further detention is justified to secure or preserve evidence by questioning the detainee (s 43). The detainee must be notified of the application to the magistrates and may be legally represented at the hearing. If the court does not authorise further detention, the detainee must be released or charged. Thus, from the time an arrested person reaches the police station, he or she may be detained for questioning by the police in connection with a serious arrestable offence for up to 96 hours.

Arrested persons brought to a police station may be searched, examined, fingerprinted and have samples taken of an intimate and non-intimate nature.[89] The search of arrested or detained persons is authorised by s 54 of PACE which requires the custody

---

[83] For the duties of the custody officer in respect of arrested juveniles, see Criminal Justice Act 1991, s 59.

[84] Failure to conduct a review at the proper time could render detention unlawful: *Roberts v Chief Constable of Cheshire* [1999] 1 WLR 662. The review may be conducted by telephone if the appropriate officer is not present at the police station at the relevant time: 1984 Act, s 40A; also s 45A (video links), both provisions inserted by the Criminal Justice and Police Act 2001, s 73. The new s 45A reverses the decision in *R v Kent Chief Constable, ex p Kent Police Federation* [2000] 2 Cr App R 196.

[85] [1981] 2 All ER 612.

[86] See ch 26 E.

[87] Now Criminal Procedure (Scotland) Act 1995, s 14. See Renton and Brown, *Criminal Procedure*, and Ashton and Finch, *Constitutional Law in Scotland*, ch 17.

[88] For the definition of a serious arrestable offence, see 1984 Act, s 116.

[89] Suspects (and others) may also be photographed (with or without their consent), although unlike searches, fingerprints and samples, the practice is not regulated by statute, subject to the exception in note 91 below. The practice is authorised by Code D. See note 105 below.

officer to ascertain and record everything which the person has in his or her possession.[90] Any item may be seized and retained except for clothing and personal effects, which may be seized only if the custody officer has reasonable grounds to believe the item is evidence relating to the offence; or believes that the arrested person may use the items in question to cause physical injury personally or to another, damage property, interfere with evidence, or assist him or her to escape. Under section 54A, an officer of the rank of inspector may authorise that a person detained in a police station be searched or examined to establish whether he or she has any mark that would tend to identify him or her as a person involved in the commission of an offence.[91] Section 55 authorises intimate searches, i.e. the physical examination of a person's body orifices other than the mouth.[92] But this may be done only if it has been authorised by an officer of the rank of inspector or above and there are reasonable grounds for believing that the person may have concealed on him or her either a Class A drug or an article which could be used to cause physical injury to himself or herself or others. In the course of such an examination, the police may 'seize' any material where there is cause to believe that it could be used to cause physical injury, damage property, interfere with evidence, or assist an escape. An intimate search for drugs should be conducted by a medical practitioner or nurse at a hospital or surgery. Otherwise the search may be conducted at a police station and the requirement that it should normally be by a doctor or nurse can be dispensed with if none is available. If anything is seized, the person is to be told of this unless incapable of understanding what is said to him or her. Both a non-intimate and an intimate search must be carried out by a police officer of the same sex as the detainee (ss 54(9), 55(7)). It is open to question whether these formidable powers should be exercisable at the discretion of the police alone or whether magistrates or some other third party should be required to authorise what could be a monstrous invasion of privacy, particularly in the case of an innocent person.[93]

It was formerly the law that fingerprints could be taken only with the consent of the arrested person. Otherwise a magistrates' court order was required and even this could be granted only in the case of a person who was not less than 14 years old and who had been charged with a criminal offence.[94] So there was no power to fingerprint anyone without their consent before charge. The position was different in Scotland[95] and it changed in England and Wales as a result of PACE. Section 61 allows fingerprints to be taken without consent with the authority of a police inspector in an expanding range of circumstances.[96] These include the situation where there are reasonable grounds both to suspect the individual's involvement in a recordable offence and to believe that the prints will tend to prove or disprove guilt; as well as where the individual has been charged with a recordable offence.[97] By s 62, intimate samples may

---

[90] For the position at common law, see *Lindley* v *Rutter* [1981] QB 128; *Brazil* v *Chief Constable of Surrey* [1983] 3 All ER 537.

[91] Introduced by the Anti-terrorism, Crime and Security Act 2001, s 90. The new section permits any such mark to be photographed without the consent of the detainee.

[92] See *R* v *Hughes* [1994] 1 WLR 876 (an intimate search requires physical intrusion, not visual examination).

[93] See further Code C: Code of Practice for the Detention, Treatment and Questioning of Persons by Police Officers, especially para 4 and annex A.

[94] Magistrates' Courts Act 1980, s 49.

[95] *Adair* v *McGarry* 1933 SLT 482.

[96] The circumstances in which prints may be taken and the nature of the prints which may be taken were extended by amendments introduced by the Criminal Justice and Police Act 2001, s 78. Fingerprints are defined to include palmprints.

[97] The definition of 'recordable' offence is wider than 'arrestable' offence and includes any offence punishable with imprisonment as well as others: see SI 2000 No 1139.

also be required in more limited circumstances, an intimate sample being defined to include various bodily fluids, including blood and swabs from intimate parts of the anatomy (s 65), but not now swabs taken from the mouth.[98] Apart from urine and saliva, such samples must be taken by a doctor or a nurse and dental impressions by a dentist. Unlike fingerprints, however, intimate samples may be taken only with the consent of the detainee. It is indeed difficult to imagine how some such samples could be taken without consent. However, a refusal without good cause to consent may lead a court to 'draw such inferences from the refusal as appear proper' (s 62(10)). A non-intimate sample (e.g. hair, a sample from under a nail, or a swab taken from the mouth) may, in contrast, be taken without consent, if authorised by an officer of the rank of inspector or above, if the offence for which the arrested person is being detained is a recordable offence (s 63). A non-intimate sample may also be taken without consent from a person who has been charged with or convicted of a recordable offence.[99] In some cases those in police detention may also be tested for drugs.[100]

An important question which has arisen in the light of scientific developments relates to the possibility that information obtained from samples (intimate and non-intimate) can be used by the police to compile a DNA register of individuals, on a national scale. Indeed, one of the aims of the 1994 reforms to PACE was to allow samples to be taken for DNA testing, a process which is to be a major weapon of the police, the intention being that this country would have the most comprehensive DNA database in the world. The implications of this for personal privacy are obvious, and although the prevention and detection of crime are important counterweights,[101] there is clearly the need for safeguards in the way in which any information may be used by the police. It is for consideration whether any such information should be stored by the police rather than by an independent public agency,[102] and it is open to question whether the existing legal framework strikes the appropriate balance between two competing public interest concerns. The Police and Criminal Evidence Act 1984 expressly authorises the police to check information derived from samples obtained under the Act against other information or samples which are held by or on behalf of the police.[103] In addition, the circumstances in which such material can be retained and used for the purposes of 'speculative searches' – even where it relates to people who have not been suspected, charged, or convicted of any offence – has been greatly increased by a number of changes to PACE in recent years.[104] The original obligation in PACE to destroy prints and samples has been significantly diluted to enable the database to be compiled.[105]

---

[98] Criminal Justice and Public Order Act 1994, s 58, amending PACE, s 65.

[99] PACE, s 63(3A), (3B), inserted by Criminal Justice and Public Order Act 1994, s 55. See now Criminal Evidence (Amendment) Act 1997.

[100] 1984 Act, s 63B, inserted by Criminal Justice and Court Services Act 2000, s 57.

[101] See *Attorney-General's Reference (No 3 of 1999)* [2001] 2 AC 91.

[102] See Royal Commission on Criminal Justice, Cm 2263, 1993, pp 14–16.

[103] PACE, s 63A, amended by Criminal Justice and Police Act 2001, s 81.

[104] See Criminal Justice and Police Act 2001, ss 80–82, introducing a number of changes to PACE, ss 62–64.

[105] So far as photographs are concerned, Code D requires the destruction of photographs and negatives if the suspect is prosecuted and cleared or is not prosecuted (unless he or she admits the offence and is cautioned). But destruction is not required where someone has been convicted. In such cases, the use of a photograph taken without consent may be protected by the law of confidence, although this does not prevent the release of a photograph (in the public interest, for the purposes of identification) by the police to shopkeepers who had been subjected to a 'sustained campaign of harassment, vile language and general mayhem': *Hellewell* v *Chief Constable of Derbyshire* [1995] 1 WLR 804 (Laws J).

The rights of suspects

1 *The right to silence.*[106]   An important principle in criminal procedure is the right of a suspected or accused person to remain silent; it is for the police to obtain evidence of guilt, not for a suspect to clear himself or herself, strengthened now by art 6 of the ECHR which provides for the right to a fair trial.[107] The main control over abuse at the stage of questioning is exercised by the criminal courts.[108] It has long been established that a confession or statement by an accused person is not admissible in evidence at the trial unless it is voluntary, in the sense that it has not been obtained by fear of prejudice or hope of advantage, exercised or held out by a person in authority, or by oppression.[109] Moreover, in 1912, and again in 1964,[110] the judges of the Queen's Bench Division drew up rules to govern the taking of statements from those being questioned by the police. The Judges' Rules did not have the force of law, but voluntary statements taken in accordance with the rules were usually admitted in evidence at a trial and statements taken in serious breach of the rules might be excluded.[111] The 1964 Judges' Rules required that a person being questioned should be cautioned as soon as a police officer had evidence which afforded reasonable grounds for suspecting that he or she had committed an offence. When a person was charged with an offence, he or she had again to be cautioned; thereafter only for special reasons might further questions be put to him or her. In issuing the rules, the judges emphasised that the rules were not to affect certain principles, including the principle that every person at any state of an investigation should be able to consult privately with a solicitor (provided that no unreasonable hindrance was thereby caused to the investigation); and that a person should be charged with an offence as soon as there was enough evidence to do this.[112]

The 1984 Act did not directly affect the right to silence. From time immemorial it has been accepted that the burden is on the police to obtain evidence of guilt, not on the suspect to prove innocence. As we have seen, however, the principle was eroded by the provisions of the 1984 Act which permit negative inferences to be drawn from an accused's failure to provide an intimate sample. More seriously, this was extended by the Criminal Justice and Public Order Act 1994, which permits the court in criminal proceedings to draw such inferences as appear to it to be proper where the accused failed to mention 'any fact relied on in his defence in these proceedings' when questioned by the police or on being charged with an offence, where the fact was one which in the circumstances 'the accused could reasonably have been expected to mention' (s 34).[113] The Act also permits a court or jury 'to draw such inferences as appear proper' from the failure of the accused to give evidence at his or her trial or without good cause to answer any question. The court or jury may, moreover, draw

---

[106] On the different meanings of the right to silence, see *R v Director of Serious Fraud Office, ex p Smith* [1993] AC 1, per Lord Roskill. See generally Zander, pp 303–23. See also Cmnd 4991, 1972; and S Greer (1990) 53 MLR 709.

[107] Although 'not an absolute right', the right to silence is said by the European Court of Human Rights to lie 'at the heart of the notion of a fair procedure under article 6': see *Condron v UK* (2000) 31 EHRR 1, at p 20. Also *Murray v UK* (1996) 22 EHRR 29.

[108] See *Lodwick v Sanders* [1985] 1 All ER 577, at pp 580–1 (Watkins LJ).

[109] *Ibrahim v R* [1914] AC 599.

[110] *Judges' Rules and Administrative Directions to the Police*, Home Office Circular No 89/1978; Cmnd 8092–1, app 12.

[111] See e.g. *R v Prager* [1972] 1 All ER 1114.

[112] See *R v Holmes, ex p Sherman* [1981] 2 All ER 612.

[113] For background to the changes, see Royal Commission on Criminal Justice (note 102), which argued in favour of the right to silence. On their application, see *R v Argent* [1997] 2 Cr App R 27; *R v McGarry* [1999] 1 WLR 1500; *R v Condron* [1997] 1 Cr App R 185; and *Condron v UK* (2000) 31 EHRR 1.

such inferences as appear proper in such circumstances in determining whether the accused is guilty of the offence charged. The accused is not, however, required to give evidence on his or her own behalf and is not guilty of contempt of court for failing to do so (s 35).[114] Subsequent amendments have confined the operation of these measures to situations where the accused has enjoyed the benefit of legal representation before remaining silent.[115] Although the drawing of adverse inferences is not per se a breach of the ECHR,[116] the operation of these measures in particular cases has been found to breach art 6 of the Convention.[117] But it is not yet generally an offence to refuse to answer questions put by the police.[118]

2 *Detention and questioning.*   PACE allows people to be detained for questioning, in extreme cases for up to 96 hours. In order to help reduce the risk of this power being abused, the detention and questioning of suspects should be carried out in accordance with the safeguards laid down in the Act and in Code of Practice C. The Act itself provides two safeguards. The first is the right not to be held incommunicado. A person who has been arrested and is held in custody in a police station is entitled on request to have a friend or relative (or some other person who is known to him or her) informed of the arrest, as soon as reasonably practicable (s 56).[119] The other safeguard provided by the Act is that arrested persons held in custody in a police station are entitled on request to consult a solicitor privately at any time (s 58).[120] It is for the person detained and not the police to decide who would be an appropriate solicitor for the purposes of giving advice.[121] In some cases the exercise of these rights may be delayed for up to 36 hours, where the arrest is for a serious arrestable offence and where the delay has been authorised by an officer at least of the rank of inspector. This applies particularly where there is a risk of danger to evidence or witnesses; or where the detained person has benefited from drug trafficking. Neither of the rights in ss 56 or 58 applies to persons arrested or detained under the Terrorism Act 2000, s 41 or Sch 8. The former gives a general arrest power without a warrant for offenders under the Act; and the latter deals with detention at ports and borders. Separate provision is made in the Terrorism Act 2000 for informing third parties and securing legal representation.[122] Both rights can be delayed for up to 48 hours and in some circumstances the right to consult a solicitor may be subject to the condition that it is conducted within 'the sight and hearing' of a uniformed officer.[123]

---

[114] See *R v Cowan* [1996] QB 373.

[115] Youth Justice and Criminal Evidence Act 1999, s 58; enacted in the light of *Murray v UK* (1996) 22 EHRR 29.

[116] *Averill v UK* (2001) 31 EHRR 839.

[117] *Condron v UK* note 113 above. See generally, A Jennings, A Ashworth and B Emmerson [2000] Crim L R 879.

[118] But there may be a duty in some circumstances to answer questions put by those investigating offences: see Financial Services and Markets Act 2000, s 171. Because of the guarantees in art 6 of the ECHR, any information obtained in this way may not be used in evidence against a person subsequently charged (s 174). For background, see *Saunders v UK* (1997) 23 EHRR 313 (Companies Act 1985, s 436), and subsequently *IJL et al. v UK* (2000) 33 EHRR 225.

[119] See *R v Kerawalla* [1991] Crim LR 451.

[120] See *R v Samuel* [1988] QB 615; *R v Alladice* (1988) 87 Cr App R 380. In *R v South Wales Chief Constable, ex p Merrick* [1994] 2 All ER 560 it was held that s 58 does not apply to give the accused the right of access to a solicitor where he is in custody in a magistrates' court following the denial of bail. But it was also held that there is a common law right to this effect 'which preceded the Act of 1984 and which [was] not abrogated by that Act' (p 572). This apparent common law right does not extend to having the solicitor present during police interviews: *R v Chief Constable of the RUC, ex p Begley* [1997] 1 WLR 1475. On the role of the solicitor, see *R v Paris* (1993) 97 Cr App R 99.

[121] *R (Thompson) v Chief Constable of Northumbria* [2001] 1 WLR 1342.

[122] See ch 26 E below.

[123] Terrorism Act 2000, Sch 8, para 9.

The statutory rights not to be held incommunicado and to consult privately with a solicitor are supplemented by the Code of Practice for the Detention, Treatment and Questioning of Persons by Police Officers (Code C).[124] So far as the right not to be held incommunicado is concerned, detained persons may receive visits at the custody officer's discretion and may speak on the telephone for a reasonable time to one person, although the call (other than to a solicitor) may be listened to and anything said used in evidence in any subsequent criminal proceedings (para 5). As far as the right to legal advice is concerned, a person must be permitted to have his or her solicitor present while being questioned by the police. The solicitor may be required to leave the interview only if his or her conduct is such that the investigating officer is unable properly to put questions to the suspect (para 6). The code also deals with such matters as the conditions of detention (para 8), the giving of cautions to detained persons (para 10), and the conduct of interviews (para 11). Regarding cautions, a suspected person 'must be cautioned before any questions about [the suspected offence] . . . are put to him'. The effect of the 1994 Act is that the caution should be in the following terms: 'You do not have to say anything. But it may harm your defence if you do not mention when questioned something which you later rely on in court. Anything you do say may be given in evidence.' In conducting interviews, officers should neither try 'to obtain answers to questions or to elicit a statement by the use of oppression' nor 'indicate, except in answer to a direct question, what action will be taken on the part of the police if the person being interviewed answers questions, makes a statement or refuses to do either' (para 11). In any period of 24 hours, a detained person normally should be allowed a continuous period of at least eight hours for rest, free from questioning, travel or other interruption arising out of the investigation (para 12).

3 *Miscarriages of justice.* Despite these safeguards, concern continues to be expressed about miscarriages of justice arising largely from convictions based on evidence given by suspects in police stations.[125] Apart from the cases of the Bridgewater Three, the Guildford Four and the Birmingham Six, who were convicted before the 1984 Act came into operation, the most notorious is the case of the Tottenham Three. Three men were convicted for offences in connection with the murder of a police officer during a riot at Broadwater Farm, North London, in 1985. The men's convictions were overturned by the Court of Appeal in 1991[126] (following a Home Secretary's reference under the Criminal Appeal Act 1968, s 17)[127] when it became clear that the confession evidence which led to their convictions had been fabricated. Steps have now been taken to require the tape-recording of interviews at police stations,[128] though, remarkably, these did not apply to terrorist offences. As a result there would have been no obligation to tape-record the interviews of the Birmingham Six, the injustice visited on whom by false confession evidence is one of the greatest ever perpetrated in Britain. The Terrorism Act 2000 now makes provision for similar arrangements to apply to detentions in such cases.[129] The Home Secretary may now issue an order to require the video recording of police interviews with suspects and may issue guidance on video recording in a code of practice.[130]

---

[124] See D Wolchover and A Heaton-Armstrong [1991] Crim LR 232.
[125] See Walker and Starmer, *Justice in Error*, and Nobles and Schiff, *Understanding Miscarriages of Justice*. See also ch 18 F.
[126] *R v Silcott, Braithwaite and Raghip, The Times*, 9 December 1991.
[127] See ch 18 F.
[128] SI 1991 No 2687; SI 1992 No 2803.
[129] Terrorism Act 2000, Sch 8, para 3.
[130] Criminal Justice and Police Act 2001, s 76, inserting new 1984 Act, s 60A. Similar provision for video recording in terrorism cases is made in the Terrorism Act 2000, Sch 8, para 3.

D. Police powers of entry, search and seizure[131]

Police powers of entry

'By the law of England', said Lord Camden in *Entick v Carrington*,[132] 'every invasion of private property, be it ever so minute, is a trespass. No man can set foot upon my ground without my licence, but he is liable to an action though the damage be nothing.' This principle was applied in *Davis v Lisle*[133] where it was held that two police officers, who had entered a garage to make inquiries about a lorry which had been obstructing the highway, became trespassers when the occupier told them to leave. There are, however, three circumstances in which the police may lawfully enter private property. One, as Lord Camden suggests, is with the consent of the owner or occupier.[134] Indeed, in *Robson v Hallett*[135] it was held that a police officer, like other members of the public coming to a house on lawful business, has an implied licence from the householder to walk to the front door and to ask whether he can come inside; and that he must be allowed a reasonable time to leave the premises before he becomes a trespasser. Otherwise, the police may have statutory authority to enter private property even without the consent of the owner. Under the Police and Criminal Evidence Act 1984, a police officer may enter private premises to execute a search warrant (s 8); and to execute an arrest warrant; arrest a person for an arrestable offence;[136] arrest a person for certain public order offences; recapture a person who is unlawfully at large;[137] save life and limb, or prevent serious damage to property (s 17).[138]

These powers under s 17 are generally exercisable only if the officer has reasonable grounds for believing that the person whom he or she is seeking is on the premises. There is a power to search the premises entered, but only a search that is reasonably required for the purpose for which the power to enter was exercised. So if the officer enters premises under s 17 to arrest a person, he or she may search the premises to find that person, but may not under s 17 search for evidence relating to the offence. Other provisions of PACE confer this power.[139] Before exercising these powers the police should normally inform the occupant of the reasons.[140] Additional powers of entry were conferred by the Police Act 1997, Part III, which empowered senior police officers to authorise entry to and interference with property, mainly for the purposes of surveillance, as in the placing of listening devices. These controversial provisions were heavily amended as a result of opposition in the House of Lords to the government's proposals, so that in many instances (for example, in respect of domestic or office premises) the authorisation will not take effect until approved by a judicial commissioner.[141]

Apart from entry with consent or under statutory authority, a power of entry may arise from common law. Although s 17(5) abolishes all common law rules authorising the entry of private premises by the police, it is expressly provided that this does

---

[131] See Stone, *Entry, Search and Seizure: A Guide to Civil and Criminal Powers of Entry*. Also Polyviou, *Entry, Search and Seizure: Constitutional and Common Law*.
[132] (1765) 19 St Tr 1030, 1066; ch 6.
[133] [1936] 2 KB 434.
[134] See Code of Practice B, para 4.
[135] [1967] 2 QB 939.
[136] *Chapman v DPP* [1988] Crim LR 842.
[137] See *D'Souza v DPP* [1992] 4 All ER 545 (no right of entry unless *in pursuit* of someone unlawfully at large).
[138] As amended by the Prisoners (Return to Custody) Act 1995 and Powers of Criminal Courts (Sentencing) Act 2000.
[139] Police and Criminal Evidence Act 1984, s 32(2)(b). For an example of other powers of entry without a warrant, see *Whitelaw v Haining* 1992 SLT 956.
[140] *O'Loughlin v Chief Constable of Essex* [1998] 1 WLR 374.
[141] See further ch 22 C below.

not affect any power of entry to deal with or prevent a breach of the peace. The existence of such a power appears to have been recognised in *Thomas* v *Sawkins*,[142] although the ratio of that case is controversial.[143] The existence of the common law power was recognised by the European Court of Human Rights in *McLeod* v *United Kingdom*.[144] In that case the complainant argued that by forcibly entering her house, ostensibly to prevent a breach of peace, the police had violated her right to respect for her home and private life in art 8 of the ECHR. The police had entered to help the complainant's former husband to recover property while the complainant was absent. The domestic courts held the entry to be lawful,[145] but the European Court of Human Rights upheld the complaint. The government argued that the entry could be justified under art 8(2). But although the Court accepted that the common law power of entry was a power 'prescribed by law' for the purposes of art 8(2), it was held that the exercise of the power in this case could not be justified.

Police powers of search

1 *Search with a warrant.*   The effect of decisions such as *Entick* v *Carrington* was that, except for the power to search for stolen goods, for which a warrant could be obtained at common law from a magistrate,[146] statutory powers were needed if the police were lawfully to search private premises. Before the Police and Criminal Evidence Act 1984, the law was haphazard and irrational. Although there were about 50 statutes conferring the power to issue search warrants, as Lord Denning pointed out in *Ghani* v *Jones*,[147] none gave power to a magistrate or a judge to issue a search warrant for evidence of murder. Included among these statutes are powers conferred upon Inland Revenue officials to obtain a search warrant from a circuit judge if there is reasonable ground to suspect that a serious tax fraud is being, has been or is about to be committed, and evidence of it is to be found on the premises specified in the application.[148] These powers were described by Lord Scarman as 'a breathtaking inroad on the individual's right of privacy and right of property',[149] before they were modified in 1989. By the Misuse of Drugs Act 1971, s 23(3), a search warrant may be obtained if a constable satisfies a magistrate that there are reasonable grounds for suspecting that controlled drugs are in the unlawful possession of a person on any premises. Very wide powers of search are conferred by the Official Secrets Act 1911, s 9: a magistrate may issue a warrant authorising the search of named premises and persons found there and the 'seizure of anything which is evidence of an offence under this Act having been or about to be committed'; where the interests of the state require immediate action, a police superintendent may authorise such a search. These powers were used to search the premises of BBC Scotland in Glasgow following government concern about the proposed broadcast of a television programme about a British spy satellite.[150]

---

[142] [1935] 2 KB 249; and see ch 24.
[143] See A L Goodhart (1936) 6 CLJ 22, and Ewing and Gearty, *The Struggle for Civil Liberties*, ch 6. The power is not confined to meetings. See *McLeod* v *Metropolitan Police Commissioner* [1994] 4 All ER 553.
[144] (1998) 27 EHRR 493.
[145] *McLeod* v *Metropolitan Police Commissioner* [1994] 4 All ER 553.
[146] See now Theft Act 1968, s 26.
[147] [1970] 1 QB 693.
[148] Taxes Management Act 1970, s 20C, as amended. See *R* v *Inland Revenue Commissioners, ex p Tamosius & Partners* [2000] Crim LR 390.
[149] *R* v *IRC, ex p Rossminster Ltd* [1980] AC 952, 1022; and see Cmnd 8822, 1983. Customs officers have long exercised similar powers without warrants in respect of smuggled goods under the so-called 'writ of assistance'. See Customs and Excise Management Act 1979, s 161; and [1983] PL 345.
[150] See Ewing and Gearty, *Freedom under Thatcher*, pp 147–52.

General powers for the granting of search warrants are now found in s 8 of PACE.[151] A search warrant may be granted by a justice of the peace on an application by a police constable where there are reasonable grounds for believing that a serious arrestable offence has been committed and that there is material on the premises which is likely to be of substantial value in the police investigation.[152] This power of magistrates to grant a warrant does not apply, however, to material which consists of or includes items subject to legal privilege, 'excluded material' or 'special procedure material'. Items subject to legal privilege include communications between a lawyer and his or her client (s 10),[153] while excluded material is defined to cover confidential personal records,[154] human tissue or tissue fluid taken for purposes of medical treatment and held in confidence, and journalistic material which is held in confidence (s 11).[155] Special procedure material refers to other forms of journalistic material,[156] and also other material that is held in confidence or subject to an obligation of secrecy and has been acquired in the course of any business, profession or other occupation (s 14). No warrant can be issued in relation to material subject to legal privilege, but orders may be issued by a circuit judge under Sch 1, para 4, following an *inter partes* hearing requiring excluded material or special procedure material to be delivered to a police constable within seven days.[157] If this is not complied with, a circuit judge may issue a warrant authorising a police officer to enter and search premises and seize the material in question (Sch 1, para 12). In some circumstances, a warrant may be secured under para 12 without first seeking an order under para 4. This practice was, however, strongly deprecated in R v *Maidstone Crown Court, ex p Waitt*,[158] where it was said:

> The special procedure under section 9 and schedule 1 is a serious inroad upon the liberty of the subject. The responsibility for ensuring that the procedure is not abused lies with circuit judges . . . The responsibility is greatest when the circuit judge is asked to issue a search warrant under paragraph 12. It is essential that the reason for authorising the seizure is made clear. The preferred method of obtaining material for a police investigation should always be by way of an *inter partes* order under paragraph 4, after notice of application has been served under paragraph 8. An *ex parte* application under paragraph 12 must never become a matter of common form and satisfaction as to the fulfilment of the conditions is an important matter of substance.

Apart from thus extending the grounds for granting search warrants, the 1984 Act also introduced new safeguards.[159] These are found in ss 15 and 16 and they apply not only to search warrants issued under PACE, but also to warrants issued to a constable 'under any enactment, including an enactment contained in an Act passed after

---

[151] K W Lidstone (1989) 40 NILQ 333. See also Code of Practice B, esp paras 2 and 5.

[152] See also PACE 1984, s 8(3), and R v *Reading JJ, ex p South West Meat Ltd* [1992] Crim LR 672.

[153] Cf R v *Central Criminal Court, ex p Francis and Francis* [1989] AC 346. See R v R [1994] 4 All ER 260, and R v *Manchester Crown Court, ex p Rogers* [1999] 4 All ER 35.

[154] On confidential material, see Zuckerman [1990] Crim LR 472.

[155] Hospital records of patient admission and discharge are excluded material: see R v *Cardiff Crown Court, ex p Kellam, The Times*, 3 May 1993.

[156] On journalistic material, see s 13. Also R v *Bristol Crown Court, ex p Bristol Press Agency Ltd* (1987) 85 Cr App R 190; R v *Middlesex Crown Court, ex p Salinger* [1993] QB 564; R v *Manchester Stipendiary Magistrate, ex p Granada Television Ltd* [1999] QB 1202; and R v *Central Criminal Court, ex p Bright* [2001] 2 All ER 244.

[157] The material may be surrendered voluntarily by the person who holds it without the consent of the person to whom it relates: R v *Singleton* [1995] 1 Cr App R 431. Powers of circuit judges to grant production orders are also in the Criminal Justice Act 1988, s 93H, and the Drug Trafficking Act 1994. On the relationship between these measures and PACE, see R v *Guildford Crown Court, ex p DPP* [1998] QB 243, and R v *Southwark Crown Court, ex p Bowles* [1998] 2 All ER 193 which deals also with the purpose for which an order may be obtained.

[158] [1988] Crim LR 384.

[159] Further safeguards are in Code of Practice B, paras 2 and 5.

this Act'.[160] An application, which is made ex parte, must be in writing and must explain the grounds for the application and the premises to be searched. The constable must answer on oath any question put by the justice of the peace or the circuit judge. The warrant authorises only one search, and unlike an arrest warrant must be executed within one month from the date of its issue. Entry and search must be at a reasonable hour. Where the occupier of the premises is present, the police officers must identify themselves, produce the warrant, and supply a copy to the occupier.[161] If there is no person present, a copy of the warrant should be left in a prominent place on the premises. A search under the warrant does not authorise a general search of the premises, but only a search to the extent required for the purpose for which the warrant was issued (s 16).

> In R v Longman,[162] police officers with a search warrant effected entry to a house by deception, as a result of difficulties they had encountered in the past. A woman police officer in plain clothes pretended to deliver flowers. When the door was opened to her, other officers in plain clothes immediately entered the house, with one shouting 'Police, got a warrant' which he held in his hand. The Court of Appeal held that this procedure complied with ss 15 and 16 of PACE. The court rejected the contention that 'before entering the premises a police officer must not only identify himself but must produce his warrant card and . . . also the search warrant and serve a copy of the search warrant on the householder'. It is enough that these things are done after entry to the premises. To hold otherwise, said Lord Lane CJ, would mean that the whole object of the more important type of search would be stultified.

2 Search without a warrant.   Police powers to search without a warrant arise in three circumstances. The first is the power to search a person following arrest. At common law such a power was recognised, as also was the power of the police to take possession of articles which might be evidence connected with the offence or which might help the arrested person to escape or cause harm.[163] However, the police had a discretion to exercise and could not apply an automatic rule of searching every arrested person.[164] These powers are extended by PACE. Section 32 allows a constable to search an arrested person, at a place other than a police station, 'if the constable has reasonable grounds for believing that the arrested person may present a danger to himself or others'. A constable may search an arrested person for anything which might be used to escape from lawful custody, or for anything which might be evidence relating to an offence (s 32(2)), although in both these cases the power to search is a power to search only to the extent that is reasonably required for the purpose of discovering 'any such thing or any such evidence' (s 32(3)). Moreover, the power to search does not authorise the police to require a person to remove any clothing in public, except an outer coat, jacket or gloves (s 32(4)), but it does authorise the search of a person's mouth.[165] A police officer conducting such a search may seize any item which may cause physical injury, might assist in an escape from lawful custody, or is evidence relating to any offence (s 32(8)). The only items which may not be seized in this way are those which are subject to legal privilege (although no such exception applies to excluded material or to special procedure material) (s 32(9)). An arrested person should be taken directly to a police station (s 30). Once there he or she may be searched again. Depending

---

[160]   Police and Criminal Evidence Act 1984, s 15(1).
[161]   See R v Chief Constable of Lancashire, ex p Parker [1993] QB 577 (the warrant and any schedule must be shown; an uncertified photocopy is impermissible, rendering the search unlawful and requiring the return of any seized documents).
[162]   [1988] 1 WLR 619.
[163]   Dillon v O'Brien (1887) 16 Cox CC 245.
[164]   Lindley v Rutter [1981] QB 128; Brazil v Chief Constable of Surrey [1983] 3 All ER 537.
[165]   Criminal Justice and Public Order Act 1994, s 59.

on the circumstances, this may be a strip search and/or an intimate search of body orifices.[166]

The second power of search without a warrant is a power to search premises ancillary to arrest. In the Irish case, *Dillon v O'Brien*,[167] the existence of a common law power to search property following an arrest was recognised in order to preserve material evidence of guilt. Not only was the right to take evidence admitted, but there was a right to take it by force if necessary. This position was confirmed by *Ghani v Jones*:[168] where police officers arrest a man lawfully, with or without a warrant, for a serious offence, they are entitled to take away goods which they find in his possession or in his house which they reasonably believe to be material evidence. The position is governed now by PACE, s 32, whereby following the arrest of a person, a constable may enter any premises in which the person was when arrested or immediately before he or she was arrested. The constable may search the premises for evidence relating to the offence for which the person was arrested (s 32 (2)(b)). At common law, the power to search premises incidental to arrest was a power to search at the time of the arrest. So in *McLorie v Oxford*[169] it was held that after having arrested a suspect and detained him in custody, the police had no right to return to the house to search for the instruments of crime, even of serious crime; that is to say, no right to do so unless they could get a search warrant, although (as we have seen) that would not have been available in all circumstances where it might have been necessary. Yet although the police powers to secure search warrants are now much wider, so too are their powers of search ancillary to arrest without a warrant. Section 32 is at least open to the interpretation that the power to search the premises where the person was when arrested may be, but need not be, contemporaneous with the arrest. The only safeguard is that the power can be used only if the police officer has reasonable grounds for believing that there is evidence on the premises for which a search is permitted, and this must be the genuine reason for the entry.[170]

The third power of search without a warrant is a power to search the home of the arrested person, even though he or she was not arrested there and even though he or she was not there immediately before arrest. At common law, the courts seemed reluctant to recognise any such power.

> In *Jeffrey v Black*,[171] the accused was arrested for stealing a sandwich from a public house. He was taken to a police station and charged, and was told that police officers intended to search his house. The accused went to the house in the presence of officers, who did not have a search warrant, and let them in, though he did not consent to the search; cannabis being found, charges were brought under the Misuse of Drugs Act 1971. It was held that the search was unlawful, the court refusing to accept that there was a common law right to search a person's premises without a warrant in circumstances where the person was arrested elsewhere.[172]

There were suggestions, however, that such a search might be permitted where the house search was concerned with securing evidence relating to the offence for which the person had been arrested. But that was not the case in *Jeffrey v Black*, with the police using the alleged theft of a sandwich as an excuse to look for drugs. Section 18 of PACE now permits a constable to enter and search any premises occupied or controlled by any person who is under arrest for an arrestable offence if there are

---

[166] See section C above.
[167] (1887) 16 Cox CC 245.
[168] [1970] 1 QB 693.
[169] [1982] QB 1290.
[170] *R v Beckford* (1992) 94 Cr App R 43.
[171] [1978] QB 490.
[172] But the cannabis found at the flat was held to be admissible as evidence. See section E below.

reasonable grounds to suspect that there is on the premises evidence (other than items subject to legal privilege) relating to that offence or to a related arrestable offence. So *Jeffrey* v *Black* should be decided the same way today, though s 18 removes the doubt about the existence of the power in appropriate cases. The exercise of the power should normally be authorised in writing by an inspector or an officer of a higher rank, although the power can be used without first taking a suspect to the police station and securing authorisation, if this is necessary for the effective investigation of the offence.

Police powers of seizure

The powers of search which we have discussed are generally also associated with a power of seizure. However, the nature of that power varies from case to case. In the case of entry to search for an escaped person or to make an arrest (s 17), there is no power to seize and retain property. In the case of search with a search warrant (s 8), there is a power only to seize and retain 'anything for which a search has been authorised'. The same is true of the power to enter and search an arrested person's premises after arrest (s 18). In the case of a search of premises where the arrested person was at or immediately before the arrest (s 32), there is no power of seizure in the section itself, although in the case of a personal search there is a right to retain anything reasonably believed to be evidence of any offence, including an offence unrelated to the grounds for the arrest. What is the position if the police are on property for any of these purposes or if they are present with the consent of the owner or occupier and they stumble across something which may suggest that an offence has been committed? In what circumstances, if any, can the police seize that evidence? Clearly, they can do so if they are present with a search warrant and the material relates to the offence for which the warrant was granted. But what if it relates to some wholly unconnected offence? Similarly, what is the position if the police enter under s 17 to make an arrest and stumble across incriminating evidence? Difficult questions arose at common law as to the police power to seize and retain private property.

> In *Elias* v *Pasmore*[173] the police raided the premises of the National Unemployed Workers' Movement to execute a warrant for the arrest of Wal Hannington for sedition. The police arrested Hannington and also took away a large quantity of documents, though they did not have a search warrant. The documents were later used as evidence in proceedings against Syd Elias for inciting Hannington to commit the sedition. Horridge J held that the 'interests of the State' justified the police in seizing material that was relevant to the prosecution for any crime of any person, not only of the person being arrested.

In this poorly reasoned judgment, Horridge J argued that although it may at the time have been improper to seize the material, its later use as evidence justified the seizure. These views were disapproved by the Court of Appeal in *Ghani* v *Jones*,[174] a case arising out of an investigation of a suspected murder in the course of which police officers wished to retain the passports of the victim's close relatives and some letters belonging to them. The Court of Appeal ordered the police to return the passports and letters to the relatives, since it had not been shown that they were material evidence to prove the commission of the murder, nor that the police had reasonable grounds for believing that the relatives were in any way implicated in a crime. The court laid down certain principles which it considered to apply when the police need to take private property in the course of an investigation: the police must have reasonable grounds

---

[173] [1934] 2 KB 164. See E C S Wade (1934) 50 LQR 354, and Ewing and Gearty, *The Struggle for Civil Liberties*, ch 5.
[174] [1970] 1 QB 693.

for believing (*a*) that a serious crime has been committed; (*b*) that the article is the instrument by which the crime was committed or is material evidence to prove commission of the crime; and (*c*) that the person in possession of the article is implicated in the crime 'or at any rate his refusal (of consent to the police) must be quite unreasonable'; moreover (*d*) the police must not keep the article longer than is reasonably necessary; and (*e*) the lawfulness of the conduct of the police must be judged at the time and not (as in *Elias* v *Pasmore*) by what happens afterwards.[175]

Additional powers of seizure and retention are in PACE, ss 19–22, and now the Criminal Justice and Police Act 2001, ss 50–70. These powers supplement but do not replace the common law powers (s 19(5)). So to the extent that the statute is less extensive, the police may continue to rely on their common law powers as recognised by *Ghani* v *Jones*[176] and in subsequent cases.[177] The powers conferred by s 19 apply where a constable is lawfully on any premises, whether by invitation, to make an arrest, or to conduct a search with or without a warrant. In such circumstances material may be seized where the constable has reasonable grounds to believe *either* that it has been obtained as a result of the commission of any offence (s 19(2)); *or* that it is evidence in relation to an offence which he or she is investigating, or any other offence (s 19(3)). In either case, seizure is permitted only where this is necessary to prevent the items from being concealed, lost, damaged, altered or destroyed. The only restriction on what may be seized relates to items reasonably believed to be subject to legal privilege (s 19(6)). By s 21, a constable who seizes anything is required, if requested, to provide a record of what is seized to the occupier of the premises or the person who had custody of it immediately before the seizure. In addition, the person who had custody or control of the item seized has a right of access to it under the supervision of a police officer, although this may be refused if the officer in charge of the investigation reasonably believes that access would prejudice the investigation.[178] The effect of the changes introduced in 2001 is to enable the police to seize material so that it can be sifted elsewhere. That which cannot lawfully be retained must be returned, as must any material which is subject to legal privilege, as well as excluded and special procedure material, though there are circumstances in which such material may be retained.[179]

E. Remedies for abuse of police powers

Having examined the rights and duties of the police in respect of the citizen, we now turn to consider the remedies available when the police overstep the mark. We consider five possible remedies or consequences of unlawful police conduct:

1   the right to resist the police in self-defence;
2   the writ of habeas corpus;
3   the right to initiate legal proceedings to recover damages for any loss suffered;
4   the right to complain to the Police Complaints Authority;
5   in the event of criminal proceedings being brought against the victim of police misconduct, the possibility that evidence improperly obtained may be excluded.

---

[175] Cf *Frank Truman (Export) Ltd* v *Metropolitan Police Commissioner* [1977] QB 952; *Wershof* v *Metropolitan Police Commissioner* [1978] 3 All ER 540.
[176] [1970] 1 QB 693.
[177] See, e.g., *Garfunkel* v *Metropolitan Police Commissioner* [1972] Crim LR 44.
[178] It has been said that these provisions 'vest in the police no title to the property seized but only a temporary right to retain property for the specified statutory purposes': *Costello* v *Chief Constable of Derbyshire* [2001] 1 WLR 1437 at p 1441 (Lightman J).
[179] Criminal Justice and Police Act 2001, ss 50–70. For the position before the Act, see *R* v *Chesterfield JJ, ex p Bramley* [2000] QB 576.

Self-defence[180]

At the time of interference with person or property, the citizen may have some right of self-defence and this can affect both civil and criminal liability. The point is acknowledged in the leading case, *Christie v Leachinsky*,[181] the ratio of which (as we have seen) forms the basis of what is now s 28 of PACE. There Lord Simonds said that 'it is the corollary of the right of every citizen to be thus free from arrest that he should be entitled to resist arrest unless that arrest is lawful'.[182] In *Abbassy v Metropolitan Police Commissioner*,[183] Woolf LJ acknowledged that one of the reasons for the rule that a person is to be told the reason for his arrest is so that if what he is told is not a reason which justifies his arrest he can exercise 'his right to resist arrest'.[184] On the other hand, under the Police Act 1996, s 89, it is an offence to assault, resist or wilfully obstruct a constable in the execution of his or her duty. There are therefore hazards in the way of a citizen who uses force to resist what he or she believes to be an unlawful arrest by police, whether of himself or herself or of a close relation.[185] 'The law does not encourage the subject to resist the authority of one whom he knows to be an officer of the law'.[186] Although in *Kenlin v Gardiner* two boys were entitled to use reasonable force to escape from two constables who were seeking to question them,[187] in general it is inexpedient by self-defence to resist arrest by a police officer: if the arrest is lawful, the assault on the constable is aggravated because he or she is in execution of duty. But if a defendant 'applies force to a police or court officer which would be reasonable if that person were not a police or court officer, and the defendant believes that he is not, then even if his belief is unreasonable he has a good plea of self-defence'.[188] The offence of obstructing a constable in execution of his duty has been widely interpreted in English law;[189] the equivalent offence in Scotland has been interpreted as limited to some physical interference with the police.[190]

Habeas corpus[191]

If an individual is wrongfully deprived of liberty, it is not sufficient that he or she should be able to sue the gaoler for damages under the ordinary civil law. Whether detained by an official or by a private individual, it would be wrong that the detention should continue while the process of civil litigation takes its normal lengthy course. English law provides in the writ of habeas corpus a means by which a person detained without legal justification may secure prompt release. The person responsible for the detention is not thereby punished, but the person imprisoned is set free and may pursue such further remedies for compensation or punishment as may be available. Habeas corpus may be sought by convicted prisoners, those detained in custody pending trial, and those held by the police during criminal investigations;[192] those awaiting deportation or

---

[180] See C Harlow [1974] Crim LR 528.
[181] [1947] AC 573.
[182] At 591.
[183] [1990] 1 All ER 193.
[184] And see *Edwards v DPP* (1993) 97 Cr App R 301.
[185] *R v Fennell* [1971] QB 428.
[186] *Christie v Leachinsky* [1947] AC 573, 599 (Lord du Parcq).
[187] [1967] 2 QB 510. And see *Lindley v Rutter* [1981] QB 128; *Pedro v Diss* [1981] 2 All ER 59; and *Dawes v DPP* [1995] 1 Cr App R 65.
[188] *Blackburn v Bowering* [1994] 3 All ER 380, at 384.
[189] R C Austin [1982] CLP 187; Smith, *Criminal Law* pp 416–19.
[190] *Curlett v McKechnie* 1938 JC 176.
[191] And see ch 31 below.
[192] See, e.g., *R v Holmes, ex p Sherman* [1981] 2 All ER 612.

otherwise detained under the Immigration Act 1971; those awaiting extradition; and mental patients. We have seen that the Bill of Rights declared that excessive bail ought not to be required: legislation today encourages magistrates to give bail to persons awaiting trial whenever possible,[193] although this presumption has been seriously eroded by the Criminal Justice and Public Order Act 1994 in respect of serious offences (s 25) and offences committed while on bail (s 26).

Habeas corpus has often been described as 'the most important writ known to the constitutional law of England, affording as it does a swift and imperative remedy in all cases of illegal restraint or confinement'.[194] Its scope is potentially very wide. Suffice to say for present purposes that it is available to anyone who is illegally detained by the police. In 1981 Donaldson LJ pointed out that, 'all should know that the writ of habeas corpus has not fallen into disuse, but is . . . a real and available remedy.'[195] On that occasion, before the passing of PACE, the writ was issued in the case of a man who had been in police detention for two days without being charged or brought before magistrates. However, now that 'strict time limits apply to detention, with provision for magistrates' court warrants to extend detention periods, there should be very little scope for habeas corpus applications in relation to suspects in police custody'.[196] But an action would lie if someone were detained for more than 36 hours without a warrant or, as shown in *Re Gillen's Application*,[197] where there is evidence that the police are physically maltreating a suspect. It has been said that:

> Habeas corpus is probably the oldest of the prerogative writs. Authorising its issue in appropriate cases is regarded by all judges as their first duty, because we have all been brought up to believe, and do believe, that the liberty of the citizen under the law is the most fundamental of all freedoms. Consistently with this, an application for a writ of habeas corpus has virtually absolute priority over all other court business.[198]

The duty to make the remedy available as a means of testing the legality of any contested detention is imposed on the United Kingdom by the European Convention on Human Rights, art 5(4).[199]

Legal proceedings against the police

A person who claims to be the victim of unlawful police conduct may be able to bring an action for damages against the chief constable, who is vicariously liable for the torts committed by his or her officers.[200] An action may be for assault, wrongful arrest, false imprisonment, trespass to property or goods[201] or may take the form of an action for

---

[193] Bail Act 1976.
[194] *Home Secretary* v *O'Brien* [1923] AC 603, 609 (Lord Birkenhead). And see ch 31.
[195] *R v Holmes, ex p Sherman* [1981] 2 All ER 612, 616.
[196] Robertson, *Freedom, the Individual and the Law*, p 43. But cf *Re Maychell*, *The Independent*, 26 February 1993 (territorial army officer detained under close arrest by military authorities for 75 days following a charge under the Official Secrets Act 1911, s 1. Habeas corpus refused because delay was not excessive in the circumstances).
[197] [1988] NILR 40.
[198] *R v Home Secretary, ex p Cheblak* [1991] 2 All ER 319, 322.
[199] On the continuing significance of habeas corpus, see *R v Oldham Justices, ex p Cawley* [1996] 1 All ER 464. See also R Epstein, NLJ, 8 November 1996 (on its application to people under 21 who are unlawfully imprisoned for fine default) and Sir William Wade (1997) 113 LQR 55. See further ch 31.
[200] Police Act 1996, s 88. See Lustgarten, pp 136–8. See also Clayton and Tomlinson, *Civil Actions against the Police*.
[201] See *O'Loughlin* v *Chief Constable of Essex* (note 140 above); and *Abraham* v *Metropolitan Police Commissioner* [2001] 1 WLR 1257.

the return of property which has been improperly seized.[202] An action for malicious prosecution may be maintained by any person who is prosecuted for a criminal offence maliciously and without reasonable and probable cause; but it is difficult to win such an action against the police.[203] In principle, public officials are personally liable for their own wrongful acts. But special protection is given to some officials against certain liabilities.[204] Many of the cases discussed earlier in this chapter relate to civil proceedings brought by aggrieved individuals. So in *Wershof* v *Metropolitan Police Commissioner*[205] the plaintiff was awarded £1,000 for his wrongful arrest. Exemplary damages may be awarded against the police, even though there has been no oppressive behaviour or other aggravating circumstances.[206]

Civil liability may arise even where an arrest is lawful, for subsequent detention as well as the initial arrest must be in accordance with law.[207] In *Kirkham* v *Chief Constable of Greater Manchester*[208] it was held that the police owe a duty of care towards prisoners in their custody and that the widow of a man who had committed suicide while in police custody was entitled to damages in circumstances where there had been negligence by the police. And in *Treadaway* v *Chief Constable of West Midlands*,[209] £2,500, £7,500 aggravated and £40,000 exemplary damages were awarded to a plaintiff who had signed a confession 'only after he had been handcuffed behind his back and a succession of plastic bags had been placed over his head with the ends bunched up behind his neck causing him to struggle and pass out'. Many of the actions which are initiated against the police are settled before they reach the court. One of the most widely publicised was the settlement by the South Yorkshire police in favour of 39 former striking miners in connection with incidents arising from clashes between police and demonstrators at Orgreave coking plant in June 1984. The police force is reported to have paid a total of £425,000 in favour of the plaintiffs who had sued for assault, wrongful arrest, malicious prosecution and false imprisonment.[210]

In 1997 concern about the size of damages awards in civil actions against the police led to the Court of Appeal issuing guidelines for juries on the level of exemplary damages in which an 'absolute maximum' of £50,000 should be awarded for particularly bad conduct by officers of at least the rank of superintendent.[211] This followed two cases in which awards of £302,000 and £220,000 respectively had been awarded to victims of police brutality.[212] Quite apart from civil proceedings, a criminal prosecution may be instituted against the police for unlawful conduct such as an assault. In England, the possibility of a private prosecution of a police officer is sometimes a valuable means of legal protection: in 1963 it was a private prosecution of police officers in Sheffield which led to an official inquiry into the 'rhino tail' assaults,[213] and in 1998 private prosecutions were brought against senior police officers for alleged

---

[202] *Webb* v *Chief Constable of Merseyside Police* [2000] QB 427; *Costello* v *Chief Constable of Derbyshire* [2001] 1 WLR 1437. See now Criminal Justice and Police Act 2001, s 57.

[203] See *Glinski* v *McIver* [1962] AC 726; *Wershof* v *Metropolitan Police Commissioner* [1978] 3 All ER 540. Cf *Hunter* v *Chief Constable of West Midlands Police* [1982] AC 529.

[204] See, e.g., Constables' Protection Act 1750, s 6.

[205] [1978] 3 All ER 540.

[206] See also *Kuddus* v *Chief Constable of Leicestershire* [2001] 3 All ER 193; and ch 32 A.

[207] *Re Gillen's Application* [1988] NILR 40.

[208] [1990] 2 QB 283. See also *Reeves* v *Metropolitan Police Commissioner* [2001] 1 AC 360 – House of Lords reduced damages by half on account of contributory negligence.

[209] *The Times*, 25 October 1994.

[210] *The Guardian*, 20 June 1991.

[211] *Thompson* v *Metropolitan Police Commissioner* [1998] QB 498; and see ch 32 A.

[212] *The Guardian*, 20 February 1997.

[213] Cmnd 2176, 1963.

manslaughter and neglect of duty following the Hillsborough football tragedy.[214] There are, however, serious difficulties in practice with private prosecutions or indeed any criminal prosecution against the police, even in cases following serious miscarriages of justice to which the actions of the police were alleged to contribute.[215] It may be possible also to challenge some decisions of police officers in judicial review proceedings.[216]

Complaints against the police

Police complaints are supervised by the Police Complaints Authority, an independent body appointed by the government.[217] Under the Police Act 1996, complaints made by or on behalf of a member of the public against a police officer are submitted to the chief officer of the force concerned. It is his or her first duty to take steps to obtain or preserve relevant evidence.[218] The procedure thereafter depends on whether or not the complaint concerns a senior officer (that is, above the rank of chief superintendent). The main difference is that investigation of complaints about senior officers is the duty of the police authority, while other complaints are handled by the chief officer. What follows outlines the standard procedure to be adopted by a chief officer. Having established that he or she rather than the police authority is responsible, the chief officer must record the complaint. Thereafter three levels of complaint are distinguished and treated differently.

(a)   At the lowest level is a category of complaint suitable for informal resolution: it is the chief officer's duty to decide whether a complaint falls into this category. The complaint cannot be dealt with informally unless the complainant consents and the chief officer is satisfied that the conduct complained of, even if proved, would not justify a criminal or disciplinary charge.[219] The actual arrangements for informal resolution may vary but will include discussion with the complainant and, in some cases, a meeting between the complainant and the accused officer. Most recorded complaints are informally resolved, withdrawn or not proceeded with.

(b)   If a complaint is not suitable for informal resolution or if it is incapable of being resolved informally, the chief officer must arrange for it to be investigated either by an officer from his or her own force or from another area. When the report of the investigation is received, the chief officer must send a copy to the Director of Public Prosecutions in all cases where there is an indication that a criminal offence may have been committed and the officer ought to be charged with it. The Director then decides whether criminal proceedings should be taken against the officer concerned.[220] Consideration will also have to be given to the possibility of disciplinary proceedings being initiated against a police officer, a possibility which may arise both where there is and is not an indication that a criminal offence has been committed.[221] In some cases the chief officer of police must notify the Police Complaints Authority whether disciplinary

---

[214] See *R v DPP, ex p Duckenfield* [2000] 1 WLR 55.

[215] Cf *R v Bow Street Magistrates, ex p DPP* (1992) 95 Cr App R 9.

[216] See *R (Thompson) v Chief Constable of Northumbria* [2001] 1 WLR 1342.

[217] Police Act 1996, Part IV; Sch 5. For the background, see Cmnd 8681, 1982; and Cmnd 9072, 1983.

[218] 1996 Act, s 67(1). On the question of public interest immunity for material obtained in the course of police complaints proceedings, see *R v Chief Constable of West Midlands, ex p Wiley* [1995] 1 AC 274, on which see ch 32 C. See also Cm 396, 1994, p 13. See now 1996 Act, s 80.

[219] 1996 Act, s 69.

[220] 1996 Act, s 75.

[221] Ibid.

proceedings have been initiated,[222] and in some cases the PCA may direct such action to be taken.[223] Disciplinary proceedings are conducted by the chief constable and must allow a fair hearing. If an officer is found guilty of an offence, penalties range from dismissal to a caution. The more serious penalties of dismissal, requirement to resign or reduction in rank may not, however, be awarded unless the officer has been given the prior opportunity of electing to be legally represented at the hearing.[224] There is a right of appeal to a police appeals tribunal.[225]

(c)   The role of the Police Complaints Authority is much stronger in relation to the third category of complaint. If a complainant alleges that the conduct of a police officer has been the cause of a death or serious injury, the complaint must be referred to the Authority before the investigation begins.[226] In addition to these mandatory references, the Authority itself may require a complaint to be referred to it where there is otherwise no obligation on the police to do so.[227] A chief officer may refer to the Authority other complaints and other matters which are not the subject of a complaint but which indicate a criminal or disciplinary offence and, by reason of their gravity or exceptional circumstances, ought to be so referred.[228] In the cases which must be referred to it, as well as others where it is deemed desirable in the public interest,[229] the Authority does not merely monitor the outcome of an investigation but supervises the investigation itself. The Authority has to approve the appointment of the investigating officer and it may thereafter give instructions on the conduct of the investigations. Once the investigation is complete, however, the outcome is processed as in other cases.

The admissibility of evidence

If the police act unlawfully by denying a citizen any rights provided by PACE; or if they secure evidence by unlawful means, as by an illegal search; or if they extract a confession from a suspect in breach of the code of practice, what is the position regarding the evidence which has been obtained in this way? Can it be used in legal proceedings against the accused? In the United States, unlawfully obtained evidence has been excluded by the Supreme Court, which has argued that constitutional rights to liberty and privacy should not be 'revocable at the whim of any police officer who, in the name of law enforcement itself, chooses to suspend [their] enjoyment'.[230] But in truth this is not an easy matter to resolve, for a difficult conflict of principle arises. On the one hand, there is a clear public interest in protecting the citizen against the unlawful invasion of his or her liberties by the police; on the other hand, there is an equally clear public interest in ensuring that those who commit serious criminal offences should not escape the consequences of their actions on what may be merely formal or technical grounds.[231] At common law in Scotland, irregularity in the obtaining of evidence does not necessarily render it inadmissible, but it may do so; and whether unlawfully obtained evidence is admitted is a matter for the trial judge, who may

---

[222] 1996 Act, s 75(4), (5).
[223] 1996 Act, s 76.
[224] 1996 Act, s 84. For the previous exclusion of legal representation, see *Maynard* v *Osmond* [1977] QB 240.
[225] 1996 Act, s 85.
[226] 1996 Act, s 70.
[227] Ibid.
[228] 1996 Act, s 71.
[229] 1996 Act, s 72.
[230] *Mapp* v *Ohio* 367 US 643 (1961) (Clark J). See also *Miranda* v *Arizona* 389 US 436 (1966).
[231] See *Lawrie* v *Muir* 1950 JC 19, 26 (Lord Cooper).

deem it inadmissible if it has been obtained in circumstances of unfairness to the accused.[232]

The position in England and Wales is now governed by ss 76 and 78 of PACE.[233] Section 76 provides that a confession made by an accused person may be given in evidence against him or her so far as it is relevant and is not excluded by the court exercising powers contained in s 76(2). This requires the court to exclude evidence obtained by oppression of the person who made it,[234] or 'in consequence of anything said or done which was likely, in the circumstances existing at the time, to render unreliable any confession which might be made in consequence thereof'.[235] Where a representation has been made to the court that a confession may have been secured in either of these ways, the onus is on the prosecution to establish otherwise (s 76(1)). The term oppression is defined 'to include torture, inhuman or degrading treatment, and the use or threat of violence (whether or not amounting to torture)' (s 76(8)).[236] In *R v Fulling*[237] the court said that otherwise 'oppression' should be given its ordinary meaning, that is to say, the exercise of authority or power in a burdensome, harsh or wrongful manner or giving rise to unjust or cruel treatment. In that case it was held that there was no oppression where a confession had been made by a woman after being told by police of her lover's affair with another woman.[238] But although oppressive conduct by the police is thus discouraged by s 76, much of the impact of this is lost by s 76(4), which provides that the exclusion of a confession does not affect the admissibility in evidence of any facts discovered as a result of the confession, or 'where the confession is relevant as showing that the accused speaks, writes or expresses himself in a particular way, of so much of the confession as is necessary to show that he does so'. The fruit of the poison tree thus appears to be edible in English law.

Section 78, introduced as a result of pressure in the Lords from Lord Scarman and others, provides that in any proceedings the court may refuse to allow evidence on which the prosecution proposes to rely 'if it appears to the court that, having regard to all the circumstances, including the circumstances in which the evidence was obtained, the admission of the evidence would have such an adverse effect on the fairness of the proceedings that the court ought not to admit it'.[239] Despite the lack of clarity in its drafting, there is evidence to suggest that, together with s 76, this provision has helped to induce the judges to take a more assertive approach when faced with improper police practice. Thus in *R v Canale*,[240] the Court of Appeal held that the trial judge should not have admitted evidence of interviews which had not been contemporaneously recorded by the police officers conducting the interviews: they had been

---

[232] *HM Advocate v Turnbull* 1951 JC 96; *Fairley v Fishmongers of London* 1951 JC 14; *HM Advocate v Hepper* 1958 JC 39; *Leckie v Miln* 1982 SLT 177; *HM Advocate v Graham* 1991 SLT 416; *Drummond v HM Advocate* 1994 SCCR 789; and *Wilson v Brown* 1996 SCCR 470.

[233] For background, see Cmnd 8092, 1981, pp 112–18. Section 78 is qualified by the Criminal Procedure and Investigations Act 1996, Sch 1, para 26, in respect of proceedings before examining magistrates.

[234] On oppression, see *R v Fulling* [1987] QB 426. See also *R v Ismail* [1990] Crim LR 109.

[235] On unreliability, see *R v Goldenberg* (1988) 88 Cr App Rep 285, *R v Silcott, Braithwaite and Raghip, The Times*, 9 December 1991 and *R v Walker* [1998] Crim LR 211.

[236] Confession evidence may also be excluded under s 78 (see below). See *R v Mason* [1987] 3 All ER 481.

[237] [1987] QB 426.

[238] For a disturbing example of oppression which 'horrified' the Court of Appeal, and in which the accused was 'bullied and hectored', see *R v Paris* (1993) 97 Cr App R 99. ('The officers . . . were not questioning him so much as shouting at him what they wanted him to say. Short of physical violence, it is difficult to conceive of a more hostile and intimidatory approach by officers to a suspect'.)

[239] See K Grevling (1997) 113 LQR 667 for a full account. Also *Cross and Tapper on Evidence*, pp 187–91; 633–6.

[240] [1990] 2 All ER 187.

written up afterwards.[241] These breaches of Code of Practice C, as it was then drafted, were described as 'flagrant', 'deliberate' and 'cynical'. In so holding the Lord Chief Justice sharply observed:

> This case is the latest of a number of decisions emphasising the importance of the 1984 Act. If, which we find it hard to believe, police officers still do not appreciate the importance of that Act and the accompanying Codes, then it is time that they did.[242]

Another area where s 78 has been invoked successfully by defendants relates to the denial of access to a solicitor,[243] though it has been said not to be possible 'to give general guidance as to how a judge should exercise his discretion under section 78' on the ground that 'each case had to be determined on its own facts'.[244]

It does not follow that evidence obtained in breach of the codes of practice or in breach of the defendant's statutory rights will always be held to be inadmissible. In more recent cases the courts have taken a more cautious approach to s 78 and the Court of Appeal in particular has been criticised for its willingness to admit improperly obtained evidence.[245] In R v *Chalkley* the Court of Appeal emphasised that the test to be applied in determining whether to admit evidence is not whether the evidence has been obtained illegally or oppressively, but one of fairness: neither the 'labelling of conduct as unlawful' nor the 'application to it of the epithet oppressive' 'automatically overrides the fundamental test of fairness in admission of evidence'.[246] Particular difficulties have arisen with police undercover work, it having been held that obtaining evidence by entrapment, by an agent provocateur, or by a trick did not of itself require the judge to exclude it, although it may be excluded if the circumstances so require in the interests of fairness.[247] The House of Lords has held that evidence obtained by means of an illegally placed surveillance device is admissible:[248] the fact that the conduct of the police amounted to an apparent or probable breach of the ECHR, art 8, was simply 'a consideration which may be taken into account for what it is worth'.[249] Questions arise about the implications of art 6 of the ECHR for the admissibility of evidence, particularly since the Human Rights Act. But the European Court of Human Rights has also held that irregularly obtained evidence may be admitted[250] and the view of the English courts is that the requirements of s 78 of the 1984 Act and art 6 are the same in this respect.[251]

---

[241] See also R v *Keenan* [1990] 2 QB 54.

[242] [1990] 2 All ER 187, 190 (Lord Lane CJ).

[243] R v *Samuel* [1988] QB 615; R v *Absolam* (1989) 88 Cr App R 332; R v *Beylan* [1990] Crim LR 185. Cf R v *Alladice* (1988) 87 Cr App R 380.

[244] R v *Smurthwaite* [1994] 1 All ER 898.

[245] A Choo and S Nash [1999] Crim LR 929.

[246] [1998] QB 848, at p 874 (Auld LJ). Also R v *Smurthwaite* (note 244 above) and R v *Cooke* [1995] 1 Cr App R 318.

[247] R v *Smurthwaite* (note 244 above). Also R v *Sang* [1980] AC 402, R v *Christou* [1992] QB 979, R v *Latif* [1996] 1 All ER 353 and *Nottingham City Council* v *Amin* [2000] 1 WLR 1071. For comment, see A J Ashworth (1998) 114 LQR 108. See now Regulation of Investigatory Powers Act 2000.

[248] R v *Khan* [1997] AC 558. See now Police Act 1997, Part III. See ch 22 below. On the approach of the House of Lords to s 78, see also R v *Southwark Crown Court, ex p Bowles* [1998] AC 641, and R v *P* [2001] 2 All ER 58.

[249] At p 582 (Lord Nolan).

[250] *Schenck* v *Switzerland* (1988) 13 EHRR 242. In *Teixeira de Castro* v *Portugal* (1998) 28 EHRR 101 the Court said that 'the admissibility of evidence is primarily a matter for regulation by national law and as a general rule it is for the national courts to assess the evidence before them. The Court's task under the Convention is not to give a ruling as to whether statements of witnesses were properly admitted as evidence, but rather to ascertain whether the proceedings as a whole, including the way in which evidence was taken, were fair' (pp 114–15).

[251] R v *P* [2001] note 248 above. See also *Attorney-General's Reference (No 3 of 1999)* [2001] AC 91.

F. Accountability and control of the police[252]

Whether in the field of maintaining public order or in the work of detecting and prosecuting crime, police decisions constantly involve the exercise of discretion, choice between alternative courses of action, and the setting of priorities for the use of limited resources. In a stable society it is easier for the police to seek to play an impartial and a non-political role, but even this role has latent political significance. In less stable conditions, issues of law and order acquire a more immediate political content. In the sometimes troubled 1980s, questions were often raised about the procedures for police accountability. Problems about police reaction to racial violence, to public demonstrations, and to the events surrounding the miners' strike in particular all contributed to the concern. A complicating dimension is what some see as the movement towards greater centralisation of police work. There are many forms of cooperation between forces, but there is also now the potential for the development of common policies, informally through the activities of bodies such as the Association of Chief Police Officers (ACPO).[253] This emerging centralisation raises new questions about police accountability which the existing institutional structure may not be well suited to answer. But it should not be overlooked that police investigation of individual incidents can have national implications of the greatest significance. The circumstances surrounding the police response to the murder of the London teenager Stephen Lawrence raised a number of different questions of police accountability, and to a finding of institutional racism in aspects of the police service.[254]

Local police authorities

The police authority is responsible for ensuring an efficient and effective force[255] and it exercises a measure of supervision over the chief constable. In practice, however, the changes introduced by the Police and Magistrates' Courts Act 1994 have gone some way to diminish further the already limited scope for local control of the police. As we have seen, the objectives for police authorities are set by the Home Secretary,[256] while the representation of elected representatives on police authorities has been reduced, with each authority now containing members appointed by the Home Secretary, their legitimacy and authority perhaps being no more than the fact that they are 'people with management or financial experience'.[257] The police authority has no power to give instructions to the chief constable about the deployment of the police or to interfere with the chief officer's overall operational control. A measure of the diminishing role of police authorities as agents of accountability is reflected in rather startling terms in the white paper, *Police Reform*, which preceded the changes introduced by the 1994 Act. There it is said that in future police authorities would 'act on behalf of local people as the "customer" of the service which the police force provides',[258] a role which not all will find beyond question. It is true that police authorities are now required to determine local policing objectives on an annual basis and that in doing so they must

---

[252] On police accountability see Baldwin and Kinsey, *Police Powers and Politics*; Jefferson and Grimshaw, *Controlling the Constable*; Morgan and Newburn, *The Future of Policing*; Reiner, *The Politics of the Police*; Spencer, *Called to Account*; Uglow, *Policing Liberal Society*; Walker, *Policing in a Changing Constitutional Order*.

[253] For statutory recognition of ACPO, see Criminal Justice and Police Act 2001, s 127.

[254] The Stephen Lawrence Inquiry (Cm 4262, 1999).

[255] Police Act 1996, s 6. And see section A above.

[256] Ibid, s 37.

[257] Cm 2281, 1994, p 21. See Jones and Newburn, *Policing After the Act*.

[258] Ibid, p 20.

not only consult the chief constable, but also consider any views obtained in accordance with arrangements made under s 96 of the 1996 Act. This requires the police authority to make arrangements to obtain the views of the local population about local policing arrangements. But the Act does not prescribe what arrangements should be made for this purpose and so far as it gives any guidance the white paper suggested that the duty might be discharged through the medium of local consultative groups (not necessarily elected) and by canvassing local views in a variety of ways, for example by public opinion surveys.[259]

In addition to the statement of policing objectives, the police authority is required to produce an annual policing plan, which must give particulars, inter alia, of local policing objectives (s 7). The plan is in fact drafted by the chief constable and submitted for consideration by the police authority, which in turn must consult with the chief constable before any amendments are made to his or her draft (s 8). Even then the chief constable is not bound by the plan, but is required in the discharge of his or her duties simply to 'have regard to it' (s 10). Chief constables are, however, required to report annually to the police authority and (subject to a power of the chief constable with the support of the Home Secretary to withhold information which in the public interest ought not to be disclosed), the authority may require the chief constable to report on specific matters connected with the policing of the area (s 22). This is a power (previously contained in the Police Act 1964) to which Lord Scarman attached some importance in his inquiry into the Brixton riots in 1981. The breakdown of order in the social, and particularly racial, conditions of Brixton led Lord Scarman to make substantial criticisms of the police and their relations with the community. He recommended that, without the sacrifice of independence, police accountability should be improved and argued that police authorities should take more seriously their existing powers under the Police Act 1964 to require reports from the chief constable and to ensure close cooperation between police authority and chief officer.[260] Questions continue to arise about the political accountability of the police authority, which is advanced only by the terms of s 20 of the 1996 Act that arrangements should be made by local authorities to enable questions on the discharge of the functions of a police authority to be put by members of the local council.[261] Local authorities are now required to formulate and implement 'a strategy for the reduction of crime and disorder' in their area.[262]

Accountability to Parliament and the courts

It is both inevitable and desirable that there should be parliamentary interest in the work of the police. One problem which has often faced MPs wishing to raise police subjects in Parliament has been that there is no direct ministerial responsibility either for the acts of the police or for the decisions of police authorities. The position of London has always been exceptional since it has long been recognised in the Commons that the Home Secretary accepts what has been described as an extremely wide and detailed responsibility for the metropolitan police.[263] The royal commission in 1962 proposed additional powers for the central government which, the commission considered, would make the Home Secretary accountable to Parliament for the efficient

---

[259] Ibid.
[260] Cmnd 8427, 1981.
[261] Cf R v *Lancashire Police Authority, ex p Hook* [1980] QB 603. Similar arrangements now exist for the Greater London Assembly and the metropolitan police authority: Police Act 1996, s 20A, as inserted by the Greater London Authority Act 1999, Sch 27, para 78.
[262] Crime and Disorder Act 1998, s 6.
[263] Marshall, *Police and Government*.

policing of the whole country. The Police Act 1964 did not go as far as the royal commission recommended, but the extent of ministerial responsibility for police outside London was undoubtedly widened by the Act. Thus MPs who wish to raise a matter of local policing may now ask the appropriate Secretary of State whether he or she proposes to call for a report on the matter from the chief constable, institute an inquiry into the matter, to require the chief constable to resign in the interests of efficiency and so on. But the fact that such a question may be asked does not mean that as full an answer will be given as the MP would like. The Home Secretary will not give to Parliament details of police work which he or she considers should not be publicly disclosed. Neither does the jurisdiction of the Parliamentary Ombudsman include power to investigate complaints against the police.[264] On specific matters of great political concern, however, the Secretary of State may be willing to order an inquiry to be held[265] or to lay before Parliament the report received from a chief officer of police.[266] More general police subjects are suitable for examination by the Home Affairs Committee of the House of Commons.[267]

Relying on the time-worn but seriously inaccurate sentiment that a policeman possesses few powers not enjoyed by the ordinary citizen and is only 'a person paid to perform, as a matter of duty, acts which if he were so minded he might have done voluntarily', the royal commission in 1962 came to an astonishing conclusion: 'The relation of the police to the courts is not . . . of any greater constitutional significance than the relation of any other citizen to the courts.'[268] The corrective was supplied in *R v Metropolitan Police Commissioner, ex p Blackburn*.[269]

> Under the Betting, Gaming and Lotteries Act 1963, certain forms of gaming were unlawful, and gaming clubs in London sought to avoid the Act. After legal difficulties in enforcing the Act had arisen, the Commissioner issued a secret circular to senior officers giving effect to a policy decision that no proceedings were to be taken against a gaming club for breach of the law, unless there were complaints of cheating or it had become the haunt of criminals. Blackburn sought an order of mandamus against the Commissioner which in effect ordered him to reverse that policy decision. The circular was withdrawn before the case was concluded, but the Court of Appeal held that every chief constable owed a duty to the public to enforce the law. That duty could if necessary be enforced by the courts. Although chief officers had a wide discretion with which the courts would not interfere, the courts would control a policy decision which amounted to a failure of duty to enforce the law. The court in this case left open whether Blackburn had a sufficient interest in the matter to ask for mandamus. In a later case brought by Blackburn to enforce the obscenity laws, the court held on the merits that the Commissioner was doing what he could to enforce the existing laws with the available manpower and no more could reasonably be expected.[270]

Further consideration was given to the 'clear legal duty'[271] which the police owe to the public to enforce the law in *Hill v Chief Constable of West Yorkshire*, where it was

---

[264] See ch 29 D.

[265] See the reports by Lord Scarman into the Red Lion Square disorders, Cmnd 5919, 1975, and into the Brixton disorders, Cmnd 8427, 1981.

[266] E.g. HC 351 (1974), report from Metropolitan Police Commissioner on the Lennon case.

[267] E.g. Race relations and the 'sus' law (HC 559 (1979–80)); Deaths in police custody (HC 631 (1979–80)); Special Branch (HC 71 (1984–85)); Metropolitan Police Service responding to calls from the public (HC 33 (1995–96)); Police discipline and complaints procedures (HC 258, 1997–98); and Police training and recruitment (HC 81, 1999–2000).

[268] Cmnd 1728, p 34.

[269] [1968] 2 QB 118.

[270] *R v Metropolitan Police Commissioner, ex p Blackburn (No 3)* [1973] QB 241. See also *R v Chief Constable of Devon and Cornwall, ex p CEGB* [1982] QB 458, and *R v Oxford, ex p Levey*, *The Times*, 1 November 1986.

[271] *R v Metropolitan Police Commissioner, ex p Blackburn* [1968] 2 QB 118, at 138 (Salmon LJ).

held that the existence of a general duty in the police to suppress crime does not carry with it a liability to individuals for damage caused to them by criminals whom the police have failed to apprehend in circumstances when it was possible to do so.[272] In a controversial decision of the European Court of Human Rights, questions were raised about the compatibility of this police immunity with art 6 of the ECHR,[273] although the court has since emphasised that it is not the immunity with which it is concerned, so much as the right of individuals to test the scope of the immunity in litigation.[274] Obvious difficulties are presented by the proposal that a court should direct a chief constable in the performance of his or her duties at the instance of a member of the public. It is one thing for a court to strike down instructions by a chief constable which are plainly illegal; it is another for the court to impose its own views on the priorities for the use of police resources.[275] Given that the courts must allow the police discretion in carrying out their work, a capable chief constable with some appreciation of the law should have little difficulty in keeping within the permissible bounds. Rather than relying to the extent that we have come to do on the autonomy and professional judgment of the chief officer to solve difficult questions of social policy for us and then looking to the courts to control their decisions, it might be better to reassess the proper scope for political direction and parliamentary discussion of police policies.

---

[272] [1989] AC 53 (unsuccessful action in negligence brought by mother of a victim of Sutcliffe, the Yorkshire Ripper). See also *Osman v Ferguson* [1993] 4 All ER 344 ([1994] PL 4), and *Ancell v McDermott* [1993] 4 All ER 355.

[273] *Osman v UK* (2000) 29 EHRR 245. See C A Gearty (2000) 64 MLR 179; T Weir [1999] CLJ 4.

[274] *Z v UK* (2002) 34 EHRR 97.

[275] See *R v Chief Constable of Sussex, ex p International Trader's Ferry Ltd* [1999] 2 AC 418.

Chapter 22

THE PROTECTION OF PRIVACY

There has for some time now been a great debate about whether the right to privacy should be protected by the British legal systems. Part of the trouble with privacy is that it is notoriously difficult to define and it is largely for this reason that the Younger Committee on Privacy recommended against the introduction of any such right in 1972, although the Committee was agreed that 'privacy requires additional protection'.[1] This was an influential report which was to structure the debate for almost a generation. A second difficulty with the protection of privacy is in determining from whom the protection is needed. Many are agreed that the intrusive tendencies of the state – which for some has lurid Orwellian tendencies – needs to be contained. But many of the problems associated with the violation of privacy are perpetrated not by the state, but by other private parties – newspapers engaged in a never-ending circulation war or employers checking on employees (in one famous case to monitor calls to a solicitor by an employee who was suing her employer for sex discrimination).[2] A third difficulty is that the invasion of personal privacy by a range of devices is now seen to be a necessary weapon in the fight against organised crime and other unlawful acts which threaten public safety and national security.[3]

A. The case for protection

But although these are persuasive concerns, they are not compelling. It is true that privacy is a concept of indeterminate scope and that it is closely related to concepts that might be encountered in the law of tort (trespass), equity (breach of confidence) or intellectual property (copyright).[4] But it is important also for the public lawyer. Privacy is closely associated with liberty and with ideas about freedom from interference by the state.[5] As a principle, privacy is important also as a way of reinforcing other constitutional liberties – most notably the right to freedom of association and assembly. One of the principal means of violating the liberty of those individuals and organisations who support unpopular causes is to monitor them, to keep them under surveillance, to maintain records about their members, and to circulate information about them – to provide the fuel for oppression and discrimination.[6] It is true – as we shall see in section B – that the concept of privacy as protected by the ECHR and now the Human Rights Act 1998 extends some way beyond concerns of this kind. But for the

---

[1] Cmnd 5012, 1972, esp paras 651–2. See also for a valuable yet sceptical account, Wacks, *The Protection of Privacy*. Also, Wacks, *Personal Information*, especially ch 1.

[2] *Halford v UK* (1997) 24 EHRR 523.

[3] HC Deb, 6 March 2000, col 768 (Mr Jack Straw). These powers are now justified as being directed mainly at 'drug, terrorist, paedophilia and money-laundering crimes': ibid, col 834 (Mr Charles Clarke).

[4] See Bailey, Harris and Jones, *Civil Liberties Cases and Materials*, ch 9.

[5] See Lustgarten and Leigh, *In From the Cold*, p 40. See also D Feldman [2000] PL 61.

[6] For the surveillance of the Communist Party of Great Britain, see Ewing and Gearty, *The Struggle for Civil Liberties*, ch 3.

public lawyer the foregoing are core concerns which address fundamental issues about the political freedom of the individual in a democratic society.

New technologies which allow for even greater forms of surveillance make the case for some form of protection irresistible. But there can be no case for an unqualified or an unlimited right to privacy. Privacy is a restraint on freedom of expression and as such gives rise to concerns when relied on by public officials and politicians who have something to hide, and who wish to prevent the disclosure of information which may expose hypocrisy or worse. It is also a restraint on the activities of the police and other authorities in the criminal justice system who are engaged in legitimate activities in the public interest to detect the drug dealers and other traffickers in human misery. This is not to say, of course, that there should be no right to privacy: it is a case for balancing competing rights and interests. But where rights of privacy are restricted, there is a case for doing so only with clear legal authority and only where necessary for a legitimate purpose. And while it might be expected that the state would refrain from violating the privacy of the individual except where there is good cause to do so, equally it might be expected that the state would intervene to take steps to protect the privacy, particularly of the weak and vulnerable, from commercial exploitation and other forms of abuse by global corporations and other powerful organisations.[7]

We have already encountered in chapter 21 one of the most invasive violations of privacy in the form of police entry and search of domestic premises. In this chapter we address other forms of infringement, as well as some of the different ways by which privacy is regulated and protected. We have identified privacy for the purposes of this chapter as being concerned with four principal matters. These are (i) surveillance in the sense of gathering of information about an individual; (ii) the interception of communications, an activity which is a particular form of surveillance, though it may be used also for other purposes, such as criminal investigation; (iii) the storage and use of information about the individual, a matter of acute concern in the computer era, though trade unionists and others will be aware of blacklisting from the earliest times;[8] and (iv) the unwanted publication of confidential or personal information about an individual. We consider threats to privacy from both public authorities and private bodies (mainly the press), but begin with an account of how the principle is protected by the wide terms of the ECHR and conclude by assessing the implications of the Human Rights Act 1998.

B. Privacy and the ECHR

It is well established that there is no general right to privacy as such in English common law,[9] although privacy has been described judicially as 'fundamental',[10] and there are many who have argued for the introduction of such a right. In contrast, a right to privacy is to be found in the ECHR, art 8.[11] This provides:

---

[7] So much is required by the ECHR: see *Spencer* v *UK* (1998) 25 EHRR CD105; and by the Human Rights Act: see *Venables* v *News Group Newspapers Ltd* [2001] Fam 430.

[8] See *McKenzie* v *Iron Trades Employers' Insurance Association* 1910 SC 79. See now Data Protection Act 1998 and Employment Relations Act 1999, s 3.

[9] See *Kaye* v *Robertson* [1991] FSR 62. But this not the same as saying that privacy is wholly unprotected by English law: see *Hellewell* v *Derbyshire Chief Constable* [1995] 1 WLR 804, where it was said by Laws J that there are circumstances where the law may 'protect what might reasonably be called a right to privacy', although it might attach a different name to the cause of action.

[10] *Morris* v *Beardmore* [1981] AC 446, at p 464 (Lord Scarman); *Schering Chemicals Ltd* v *Falkman Ltd* [1982] QB 1, at p 21 (Lord Denning).

[11] See Mowbray, *Cases and Materials on the European Convention on Human Rights*, ch 8.

1 Everyone has the right to respect for his private and family life, his home and his correspondence.

2 There shall be no interference by a public authority with the exercise of this right except such as is in accordance with the law and is necessary in a democratic society in the interests of national security, public safety or the economic well-being of the country, for the prevention of disorder or crime, for the protection of health or morals, or for the protection of the rights and freedoms of others.

The ECHR has been a major source in the development of the patchwork protection of privacy in British law. Many of the cases have been concerned with the police and the security services and with various practices such as telephone tapping, surveillance and the use of bugging devices.[12] In all these cases it was held by the European Court of Human Rights that British practice violated art 8(1) of the Convention and could not be saved by art 8(2), because in each case there was no legal authority for the practices in question. It thus could not be said that the restrictions on the private life of the complainants were in accordance with law, the Court insisting that in order to justify any restraint under art 8, it was necessary to have regard to the quality of the law.

It has been said by the Strasbourg court that private life is a 'concept which covers the physical and moral integrity of the person, including his or her sexual life.'[13] There are five major issues which have been raised under the Convention, the first of which relates to what might be referred to as the sexual identity of the individual. In *Rees v United Kingdom*,[14] the Court appeared to accept that the claims of transsexuals were legitimate concerns for the purposes of art 8. But it was held that member states were to be accorded a wide margin of appreciation in dealing with the legal status of those who had undergone a sex-change operation. In this case it was held that there was no breach of art 8 where the authorities refused to permit the applicant – who had been registered at birth as a female – to alter his birth certificate to show him as a male, which is how he appeared on all other official documents. The matter was re-examined in *Cossey v United Kingdom*[15] but the Court saw no reason to depart from the position which it adopted in *Rees*. The Court did, however, acknowledge the 'seriousness of the problems facing transsexuals and the distress they suffer'.[16]

The second group of cases deal with sexuality and sexual activities. In *Dudgeon v United Kingdom*,[17] it was held that the law in force in Northern Ireland whereby homosexual activity was a criminal offence, was a breach of the applicant's rights under art 8. The very existence of such legislation was said 'continuously and directly' to affect the applicant's 'private life': 'Either he respects the law and refrains from engaging (even in private with consenting male partners) in prohibited sexual acts to which he is disposed by reason of his homosexual tendencies, or he commits such acts and becomes liable to criminal prosecution.' In *Lustig-Prean v United Kingdom*,[18] it was not disputed that sexuality fell within the scope of art 8: it had been acknowledged earlier by Sir Thomas Bingham MR when the circumstances giving rise to that case were before the Court of Appeal that 'to dismiss a person from his or her employment on the

---

[12] *Malone v UK* (1985) 7 EHRR 14; *Hewitt and Harman v UK* (1992) 14 EHRR 657; *Khan v UK* (2001) 31 EHRR 1016.

[13] *X and Y v Netherlands* (1985) 8 EHRR 235.

[14] (1986) 9 EHRR 56.

[15] (1990) 13 EHRR 622.

[16] Ibid, p 641. See also *Sheffield and Horsham v UK* (1998) 27 EHRR 163.

[17] (1981) 4 EHRR 149. See also *Norris v Ireland* (1988) 13 EHRR 186.

[18] (1999) 29 EHRR 548; (2001) 31 EHRR 601. Also *ADT v UK* (2001) 31 EHRR 803.

grounds of a private sexual preference, and to interrogate him or her about private sexual behaviour, would not appear to me to show respect for that person's private and family life'.[19] But doubts have been expressed about whether the sado-masochistic sexual practices of consenting adults in private constitutes private life for the purposes of art 8.[20]

The third and fourth issues considered by the Court bring us back to state surveillance and interference with one's home and other premises. So far as the former (surveillance) is concerned, it is accepted that surveillance by the security services falls within art 8, which applies also to practices such as telephone tapping. But although such surveillance by the state is covered by art 8, it may easily be justified under art 8(2).[21] The same is true of telephone tapping.[22] The Court has also held, however, that the right to privacy in art 8 applies to the interception and monitoring of private phone calls by employers. In *Halford* v *United Kingdom*,[23] the government argued unsuccessfully that such communications were excluded from the protection of art 8 because there was 'no reasonable expectation of privacy in relation to them'.[24] So far as the latter (violation of the home) is concerned, an important issue has been the right of the police to enter domestic premises without the consent of the householder ostensibly to prevent a breach of the peace. In *McLeod* v *United Kingdom*,[25] it was not disputed that such conduct was covered by art 8. But although the existence of this common law power of entry was saved by art 8(2), it is clear that care has to be taken before it is exercised.[26]

The fifth category of cases deals with the disclosure or transmission of confidential personal information about the individual. In *MS* v *Sweden*,[27] the applicant's confidential medical records were disclosed by her doctor to the social security authorities without her knowledge or consent. Despite remaining confidential once transmitted to the social security authorities, the Court held that the disclosure of the information entailed an interference with art 8 rights. While accepting that the records remained confidential, 'they had been disclosed to another public authority and therefore to a wider circle of public servants'. The Court was also concerned that the information had been collected and stored at the clinic in connection with medical treatment, but that its subsequent communication had served a different purpose, which was to enable the social security authorities to assess a claim the applicant had made for compensation for an industrial injury. In an earlier case, it was held that art 8 had been breached by a court order which would allow legal proceedings containing confidential medical information of the applicant to be reported publicly after a period of ten years. But there was no breach where the applicant's medical records were ordered to be disclosed in legal proceedings against her husband for a number of sexual offences.[28]

---

[19] *R* v *Ministry of Defence, ex p Smith* [1996] QB 517, at p 558.

[20] *R* v *Brown* [1994] 1 AC 212, per Lords Templeman and Lowry; and *Laskey, Jaggard and Brown* v *UK* (1997) 24 EHRR 39, at pp 56–7. But compare Lords Mustill and Slynn in *R* v *Brown*, and see now *ADT* v *UK* (note 18 above).

[21] *Leander* v *Sweden* (1987) 9 EHRR 433; *Christie* v *United Kingdom* (1994) 78A DR 119 (E Com HR). But cf *Foxley* v *UK* (2001) 31 EHRR 637.

[22] *Malone* v *UK* (note 12 above). Also *Camenzind* v *Switzerland* (1999) 28 EHRR 458, and *Valenzuela Contreras* v *Spain* (1999) 28 EHRR 483.

[23] (1997) 24 EHRR 523.

[24] At p 453.

[25] (1998) 27 EHRR 493. See also *Niemietz* v *Germany* (1992) 16 EHRR 97.

[26] See ch 21 E above.

[27] (1997) 28 EHRR 313.

[28] *Z* v *Finland* (1997) 25 EHRR 371.

C. Surveillance: acquiring information

The first way in which the privacy of the individual may be undermined is by different techniques of surveillance in order to obtain information about him or her.[29] This may be done in a number of ways – by the state, by the press and by others: it may involve breaking into his or her home and rifling through personal effects, it may involve the use of bugging devices or it may involve the interception of communications of various kinds. As far as the common law is concerned, the placing of someone under surveillance is not in itself unlawful. But there are circumstances where various types of surveillance may be unlawful, although only where the surveillance involves an interference with existing rights already recognised by the law. The invasion of someone's privacy has not by itself given cause for the courts to intervene in the past.

Trespass

Perhaps the best known example of common law protection for privacy is *Entick* v *Carrington*,[30] where John Entick's home was the subject of an illegal entry and his possessions the subject of an illegal search. Although clearly a violation of his home and his private life, his action for damages succeeded because it was also a trespass to his property rights. In the memorable words of Lord Camden CJ, in one of the great judgments of the common law:

> No man can set his foot upon my ground without my licence, but he is liable for an action, though damage be nothing; . . . If he admits the fact, he is bound to show by way of justification, that some positive law has empowered or excused him.

In that case there was no power or excuse. It is true that the officers conducting the search were armed with a warrant issued by the Home Secretary. But this was no defence, because the Home Secretary had no legal authority to issue the warrant in the first place: such authority could be provided only by Parliament, save exceptionally in the case of warrants issued in relation to stolen goods.

The value of trespass as a means of protecting privacy in modern times was highlighted in *Morris* v *Beardmore*,[31] where the defendant was suspected of being involved in a road accident. He left the scene and was followed to his house by the police who entered with the permission of the defendant's son. Despite being told to leave the house, the police entered the bedroom of the defendant in order to take a breath specimen. He refused to provide the specimen and was arrested. It was held by the House of Lords that the requirement to undergo a breath test is unlawful if made as a result of a trespass to land committed against the person to whom the requirement is addressed. But an attempt to extend the law of trespass to cover surveillance by means of telephone tapping was made unsuccessfully in the *Malone* case.[32] In that case there were striking similarities with *Entick* v *Carrington*, in the sense that the interception was done under the authority of a warrant issued by the Home Secretary, who again had not been empowered by Parliament to issue such warrants. Nevertheless the application failed: the key difference with *Entick* v *Carrington* was that there was no violation of the applicant's property rights and no trespass. It was not necessary to enter the applicant's home to place the interception device which in this case had been done at the telephone exchange.

---

[29] See *Robertson* v *Keith* 1936 SLT 9.
[30] (1765) 19 St Tr 1030; and see ch 6 A.
[31] [1981] AC 446.
[32] *Malone* v *Metropolitan Police Commissioner* [1979] Ch 344.

Interference with property

The law of trespass took on a new role in relation to the use of listening devices by the police to record conversations involving people who were suspected of involvement in criminal activity.

In R v Khan,[33] the accused was suspected in being involved in the importation of illegal drugs. The police placed a listening device on the outside of a house which he was visiting. This was done without any statutory authority, though in accordance with Home Office guidelines relating to the use of such devices. Nevertheless it was accepted by the Crown that the conduct of the police involved both a trespass and damage to the property on which the device was placed. Khan was found guilty on charges relating to the importation of drugs, the evidence against him being found mainly in tape recordings acquired as a result of the listening device. He appealed against conviction and argued that the evidence should not have been admitted because it had been illegally obtained and had been obtained in breach of the ECHR, art 8. The appeal failed: in determining whether evidence should be admitted, the illegality of the means used is not decisive. The question was whether it was secured in circumstances which tainted the fairness of the proceedings. But although the House of Lords thought not, the case nevertheless exposed the illegality of this particular practice.[34]

The 'lack of a statutory system regulating the use of surveillance devices' by the police led to an expression of astonishment from the bench.[35] It was all the more remarkable for the fact that similar activity by the security service required the authority of a warrant from the Home Secretary under the Security Service Act 1989. (The position relating to the security services is now governed by the Regulation of Investigatory Powers Act 2000, which is considered in section D.)

English law and practice relating to the use of listening devices by the police was found by the European Court of Human Rights to breach art 8 of the ECHR.[36] The use of bugging devices by the police is now governed by the Police Act 1997, Part III,[37] which proved to be extremely controversial at the time it was passed.[38] It provides that '[n]o entry on or interference with property or with wireless telegraphy shall be unlawful if it is authorised by an authorisation having effect under this Part' (s 92). Authorisation may be given to take action in respect of private property as may be specified in the authorisation, where the authorising officer believes that the action is necessary on the ground that it is likely to be of 'substantial value in the prevention or detection of serious crime'. It must also be shown that 'the taking of the action is proportionate to what the action seeks to achieve' (s 93).[39] For these purposes, conduct is to be regarded as serious crime only if (a) 'it involves the use of violence, results in substantial financial gain or is conducted by a large number of persons in pursuit of a common purpose', or (b) the offence is one for which a person over the age of 18 with no previous convictions could reasonably be expected to be jailed for at least three years.[40]

Authorisation may be given by a chief constable; or by the directors general of the National Criminal Intelligence Service and the National Crime Squad (or his or

---

[33] [1997] AC 558. See now Khan v UK (2001) 31 EHRR 1016.

[34] See also R v Loveridge [2001] 2 Cr App R 591 and Teixeira de Castro v Portugal (1998) 28 EHRR 101.

[35] [1997] AC 558, at p 582 (Lord Nolan).

[36] Khan v UK, note 12 above.

[37] For a good account, see Fenwick, Civil Rights: New Labour, Freedom and the Human Rights Act, pp 372–7.

[38] See Ewing and Gearty, A Law Too Far: Part III of the Police Bill 1997 (1997).

[39] Police Act 1997, s 75(2)(b), as amended by the Regulation of Investigatory Powers Act 2000, s 75.

[40] As amended by the Criminal Justice and Court Services Act 2000, Sch 7.

her designate) respectively; or by any customs officer specially designated by the Commissioners of Customs and Excise (s 93). Under the Regulation of Investigatory Powers Act 2000, the authorisation may also be given by the chief constables of the Ministry of Defence Police and the British Transport Police, as well as the three provosts marshal.[41] The authorisation should normally be given in writing, although in urgent cases it may be given orally (s 95).[42] In some cases, the authorisation will not take effect until approved by a surveillance commissioner appointed under s 91 of the Act.[43] Approval by a commissioner is required where any property specified in the authorisation is used as a dwelling or as a bedroom in a hotel or constitutes office premises. Approval is also required if it is likely to yield matters subject to legal privilege, confidential personal information or confidential journalistic material (s 97).[44] If approval is refused by a commissioner or if an authorisation is quashed, the authorising officer may appeal to the chief surveillance commissioner (s 104). The chief surveillance commissioner has a duty to keep the operation of these measures under review and to report annually to the Prime Minister (s 107).[45] Complaints by persons who are the subject of an authorisation under s 93 may be made to the Investigatory Powers Tribunal established under the Regulation of Investigatory Powers Act 2000.

Surveillance and undercover operations

Additional measures relating to surveillance are to be found in the Regulation of Investigatory Powers Act 2000, Part II.[46] This applies to surveillance activities not only by the police but by a number of other agencies which now play a part in law enforcement, including the intelligence services and Customs and Excise. But the Act does not by any means apply to all surveillance.[47] Although the RIPA 2000 deals with a wider range of activities than the use of bugging devices, it applies to this form of surveillance as well, and thus adds what is at times a confusing layer of regulation on top of the Police Act 1997, Part III, which remains in place, subject to a number of amendments. The RIPA 2000 deals with what are referred to as *directed surveillance, intrusive surveillance* and *the conduct and use of covert human intelligence sources*.[48] Surveillance is *directed* if it is covert but not intrusive and undertaken for the purposes of a specific operation to obtain private information about a person.[49] Surveillance is *intrusive* if covert and (*a*) carried out in relation to anything taking place on any residential premises or in a private vehicle, and (*b*) involves the presence of an individual on the premises (such as a paid informer or someone who is concealed) or is

---

[41] 41 RIPA 2000, s 75.

[42] An oral authorisation lapses after 72 hours, while written authorisations lapse after 3 months, although they may be renewed.

[43] This provides for the appointment of a chief commissioner and other commissioners to be appointed by the Prime Minister after consultation with the Scottish ministers (SI 1999 No 1747). The persons appointed must be people who hold or have held senior judicial office.

[44] These terms are defined in ss 98–100.

[45] S 107(5A), as inserted by RIPA 2000, Sch 4(1).

[46] For a fuller treatment, see Fenwick, pp 377–85. For the comparable provisions in Scotland, see Regulation of Investigatory Powers (Scotland) Act 2000.

[47] See page 511 below. It is also the case that the use of CCTV cameras is largely unregulated. Legal authority for use by local authorities is provided by the Criminal Justice and Public Order Act 1994, s 163.

[48] Regulation of Investigatory Powers Act 2000, s 26.

[49] Private information is defined to include any information relating to a person's private or family life: s 26(10). There will be circumstances where surveillance does not require authorisation: see Official Report, Standing Committee F, 30 March 2000, col 274.

carried out by means of a surveillance device. *Covert human intelligence* sources may be 'informants, agents [or] undercover officers'.[50]

These different forms of activity appear from time to time in the reported cases.[51] But until the RIPA 2000 they were conducted without formal legal authority (with the exception of intrusive surveillance conducted under the Police Act 1997). The Act is designed to ensure that practice in this area is brought into line with the ECHR by requiring that the different kinds of surveillance to which it applies are authorised in advance.[52] There is also a right to complain to the tribunal established under the Act against any authorisation.[53] *Directed* surveillance may be authorised if necessary on one of seven grounds specified in the Act (which include national security, the prevention or detection of crime, and the prevention of disorder) provided that the authorised surveillance is proportionate to the end to be achieved (s 28). A similar regime operates for the authorisation of *covert human intelligence* sources (s 29). In the case of directed surveillance, authorisation may be given by a designated person in one of 23 specified public authorities.[54] Predictably, these include the police and the intelligence services, but also various government departments, local authorities and other public bodies such as the Post Office. In the case of surveillance by covert human intelligence sources, authorisation may be given by an additional five public authorities including the Health and Safety Executive.

Intrusive surveillance is different. This may be authorised only on one of three grounds: where necessary in the interests of national security; for the purpose of preventing or detecting serious crime; or the interests of the economic well-being of the United Kingdom. Again the authorisation must be proportionate to the end to be achieved by carrying it out (s 32). Authorising officers are chief constables, commissioners of police, provosts marshal, persons designated by the Commissioners of Customs and Excise and the directors general of NCIS and the National Crime Squad (s 32). In the case of intrusive surveillance by the police and customs, an authorisation does not take effect unless approved by a surveillance commissioner (s 36).[55] Provision is made for intrusive surveillance to begin in cases of urgency. An appeal lies to the chief surveillance commissioner by an authorising officer against any refusal by a surveillance commissioner to approve an authorisation. In the case of intrusive surveillance by the intelligence services, the Ministry of Defence and the Armed Forces, authorisation must be given by the Home Secretary, whose decision does not need to be approved and from whose decision there is no appeal by the person seeking the authorisation. A person who is the subject of a surveillance authorisation may make a complaint to the Investigatory Powers Tribunal.

---

[50] Official Report, Standing Committee F, 30 March 2000, col 274 (Mr Charles Clarke). See *Teixeira de Castro* v *Portugal* (1998) 28 EHRR 101.

[51] See *R* v *Smurthwaite* [1994] 1 All ER 898; *R* v *Latif* [1996] 1 WLR 104; and *R* v *Khan* [1997] AC 558. Also the notorious case of Colin Stagg, *The Times*, 15–19 September 1994.

[52] HC Deb, 6 March 2000, col 767 (Mr Jack Straw).

[53] Regulation of Investigatory Powers Act 2000, s 65.

[54] Regulation of Investigatory Powers (Prescription of Offices, Ranks and Position) Order 2000, SI 2000 No 2417. See also Regulation of Investigatory Powers (Source Records) Regulations 2000, SI 2000 No 2725.

[55] The reason why prior approval is not required in the case of the other forms of surveillance relates to the volume of such activity. Although no records are kept of the number of covert surveillance operations annually, the police estimate that they alone carry out more than 60,000 across a range of activities. Other agencies also carry out surveillance operations. According to the government: 'To expect many of these cases to require prior approval would bring the statutory functions to a standstill, significantly restricting the activities of the police and others' (Official Report, Standing Committee F, 30 March 2000, cols 276–7).

Overlapping regimes

A great deal of the activity which is authorised by the Police Act 1997, Part III, would now fall within the definition of intrusive surveillance in the RIPA 2000 and is presumably now subject to the tighter restrictions which the latter imposes. So while the Police Act 1997 allows the use of surveillance devices in vehicles on the authorisation of the police alone, the RIPA 2000 would require such activity to be approved by a commissioner. In fact, the combined effect of the two regimes is that prior approval would normally be required for most forms of surveillance: in the case of dwellings, hotel bedrooms and offices it would be required by the Police Act; and in the case of vehicles it would be required by RIPA. Only exceptionally could bugging devices be used on the word of the police alone: one example would be the bugging of a known meeting place of suspected criminals (such as a warehouse or a pub). The chief surveillance commissioner has been given additional duties to keep under review the operation of RIPA, Part II (and Part III on which see later).[56] In addition to the ordinary surveillance commissioners for which provision is made in the 1997 Act, the RIPA provides for the appointment by the Prime Minister of assistant surveillance commissioners, for purposes which are obvious from their title.[57]

D. Interception of communications

The interception of communications has been recognised by government as a 'patent invasion of individuals' privacy, and it should occur only when it is properly justified within the law'.[58] It involves the interception of both post and telephone communications and, as technology has advanced, now includes matters such as faxes, email and mobile phones. It has long been an offence to intercept the mail without the authority of a warrant granted by the Home Secretary.[59] In 1937, the practice was adopted whereby telephone calls would be intercepted under the authority of a warrant granted to the police or the security service by the Home Secretary.[60] But the legal basis for the practice remained obscure.[61] A legal challenge to the procedure in *Malone v Metropolitan Police Commissioner*[62] was unsuccessful on the ground that the interception of communications did not involve the violation of any of the rights of the applicant. There was no trespass, there was no breach of confidence, and he had no enforceable right to privacy in English law. The matter was said by Sir Robert Megarry V-C to be one which 'cries out for legislation'.[63] As we have seen, the practice was, however, found to breach art 8 of the ECHR: although art 8(2) permits limitations on a person's art 8(1) rights, these must be prescribed by law, a requirement which was not met by the British practice of interception at the time.[64]

---

[56] Regulation of Investigatory Powers Act 2000, s 62.
[57] If the foregoing formalities are not complied with, it will still be possible to admit evidence obtained from an unauthorised interception in criminal proceedings. The matter would fall to be governed by PACE 1984, s 78. See ch 21.
[58] HC Deb, 6 March 2000, col 771 (Mr Jack Straw).
[59] Post Office Act 1953, s 58. But see now Postal Services Act 2000, ss 83 and 84.
[60] Cmnd 283, 1957. Since 1966 it has been the practice of successive governments that the telephones of MPs are not to be tapped: HC Deb, 30 October 1997, col 861 (WA).
[61] Ibid, p 15.
[62] [1979] Ch 344; C P Walker [1980] PL 184; V Bevan [1980] PL 431.
[63] [1979] Ch at p 380.
[64] *Malone v UK* (1985) 7 EHRR 14.

The statutory framework

The European Court of Human Rights did not comment on the substance of the procedures then in place for the granting of warrants by the Home Secretary to intercept communications. In effect, it merely invited the British government to introduce legislation to give these procedures statutory force. This is largely what happened, although the Interception of Communications Act 1985 also introduced a number of new safeguards to restrain any possible misuse of the new statutory procedures, addressing concerns that the practice of telephone tapping had been abused in the past.[65] But the 1985 Act has had to be substantially revised, for two reasons. The first is in response to another decision of the European Court of Human Rights, *Halford* v *United Kingdom*:[66] in that case it was held that the UK was in breach of art 8 for failing to regulate the interception of communications by employers. The second is in response to new technology and new means of communication. In particular, the 1985 Act did not apply to the use of cordless phones.[67] These and other issues have been addressed in the Regulation of Investigatory Powers Act 2000, Part I, although doubts were expressed shortly after its enactment about whether even these new provisions were sufficiently comprehensive.[68]

The RIPA 2000 repeals much of the 1985 Act, but the structure of the new regulatory framework remains largely the same.[69] This means that it is a criminal offence 'intentionally and without lawful authority' to intercept a communication transmitted by post or by means of a public telecommunication system (s 1(1)).[70] It is now also an offence intentionally and without lawful authority to intercept a communication being transmitted on a private communications system unless liability is excluded by s 1(6). Section 1(6) excludes criminal liability where the interception is conducted by the operator of a private telecommunications system with the express or implied consent of the person whose communication has been intercepted. Apart from criminal liability, an innovation of the RIPA 2000 is the introduction of civil liability for employers and other operators of private telecommunications systems for an interception which takes place without consent: in this case there is liability to either the sender or the recipient of the message or both.

Lawful authority

Lawful authority under the Regulation of Investigatory Powers Act 2000 will arise in one of three circumstances. The first is where both the sender and the recipient consent to the interception or where either has consented and the interception takes place by an undercover agent whose activities have been authorised under Part II of the Act (s 3).[71] The second is on one of the grounds specified in s 4 which gives statutory

---

[65] On which see *R* v *Home Secretary, ex p Ruddock* [1987] 2 All ER 518.

[66] (1997) 24 EHRR 523.

[67] *R* v *Effik* [1995] 1 AC 309.

[68] See Y Akdeniz, N Taylor and C Walker [2001] Crim LR 73.

[69] For a full account, see Fenwick, pp 345–70.

[70] On the meaning of a public telecommunications system, see *Morgans* v *DPP* [2001] 1 AC 315 where it was held that call-logging devices were covered. But in *R* v *Effik* [1995] 1 AC 309 it was held that a cordless phone was not covered; and in *R* v *Taylor-Sabori* [1999] 1 WLR 858 it was held that pager messages were not covered. Both would be regarded as private communications. This means that under the 1985 Act any interception would not require a warrant and that evidence of the interceptions would be admissible in legal proceedings. A warrant is now required for the interception of private communications. The drafting of the RIPA 2000, s 1 is slightly different from the drafting of s 1 of the 1985 Act on which it is based. On the implications, see *R* v *Sargent* [2002] 1 All ER 161.

[71] The government gives the example of the situation where a kidnapper is telephoning the relatives of a hostage and the police wish to record the call in order to identify or trace the kidnapper. The operation

authority for interception without a warrant and without any additional formality. This applies to certain communications intercepted for certain business practices in accordance with rules made by the Secretary of State;[72] under prison rules;[73] in high-security psychiatric hospitals; and in state hospitals in Scotland. Third, authority may be provided by a warrant issued by the Secretary of State (s 5). No judicial authorisation is required before a warrant is granted.[74] There are now four grounds for the issuing of a warrant: the interests of national security, the prevention or detection of serious crime, safeguarding the economic well-being of the United Kingdom, and to give effect to an international mutual assistance agreement (s 5(3)).[75] The conduct authorised by the warrant must be proportionate to the end to be achieved, and before a warrant is granted consideration should be given to the possibility of the information being obtained by other means (s 5(4)).

There is no definition of national security in the Act, although it is now 'generally understood to refer to the survival and well-being of the state and community and includes such matters as threats to the security of the nation by terrorism, espionage and major subversive activity but is not confined to these matters'.[76] Serious crime is widely defined to mean either (a) a crime which could reasonably lead to imprisonment for at least three years if committed by someone over the age of 18 convicted of a first offence; or (b) conduct that 'involves the use of violence, results in substantial financial gain or is conduct by a large number of persons in pursuit of a common purpose' (s 81(3)). An application for a warrant may be made by one of ten people specified in s 6(2): these include chief constables and the directors general of the Security Service and the National Criminal Intelligence Service (NCIS), as well as the director of GCHQ, the Commissioners of Customs and Excise, and the Chief of Defence Intelligence. This represents an extension of the previous practice under the 1985 Act,[77] in relation to which it was reported that warrants were obtained only by NCIS, the Special Branch, Customs and Excise, the RUC, the Scottish police, the security service, SIS and GCHQ, but 'no other agencies'.[78]

The application will be made to an appropriate minister, although in the past the burden has been carried mainly by the Home Secretary and the Secretary of State for Scotland (whose functions in this field are now exercised by the First Minister).[79] The only other ministers who by 2000 had signed warrants are the Foreign Secretary and the Secretary of State for Northern Ireland.[80] Applications are normally granted,

---

[72] Telecommunications (Lawful Business Practice) (Interception of Communications) Regulations 2000, SI 2000 No 2699. These have been controversial in a number of respects, not least because they allow interception without consent 'to investigate or detect the unauthorised use of telecommunications systems'. This would allow the monitoring of telephone calls and emails. But the Human Rights Act 1998 is lurking in the background and any exercise of power under the Act (at least by a public authority) would have to meet the standards set by art 8 of the ECHR, which in 2000 were unknown in the absence of litigation on the point.

will be authorised as surveillance rather than by means of an interception warrant: RIPA 2000, Explanatory Notes. See also *R* v *Rasool* [1997] 1 WLR 1092, which presumably would be decided differently today, for a number of reasons.

[73] Cf *R* v *Owen* [1999] 1 WLR 949.

[74] See HC Deb, 6 March 2000, col 770 (Mr Jack Straw) for an explanation.

[75] According to the government the request 'would have to satisfy the law of the requesting country as well as UK interception law': HC Deb, 6 March 2000, col 832 (Mr Charles Clarke).

[76] Cm 4364, 1999, para 14. It has also been said that the 'normal object of a national security warrant is to assist in the build up of an intelligence picture, for example about a suspected terrorist or terrorist group' (ibid).

[77] Despite the government's concern that 'it should be used only by a narrow and tight range of agencies': HC Deb, 6 March 2000, col 831 (Mr Charles Clarke).

[78] Cm 4778, 2000. No warrant had ever been issued to anyone else: Cm 4364, 1999.

[79] See ch 3 B. See also Cm 4778, 2000, paras 28–30.

[80] Cm 4778, 2000, para 7.

although there are rare cases where despite being 'reasonably and responsibly made', an application is refused because the minister has decided that it does not satisfy the statutory criteria. The fact that applications are normally but not always granted is not thought to be a problem: it shows that the Secretary of State is not a 'rubber stamp'.[81] There has been a sharp increase in the number of warrants issued, from a total of 519 to the Home Secretary and the Secretary of State for Scotland in 1988 to 2,022 in 1999 (with a steady increase in between).[82] This substantial increase is not 'a cause for concern' and is due to the 'continuing incidence of serious and organised crime and an increased facility to counter it'.[83] Most warrants relate to the prevention and detection of serious crime and it appears that there are now very few warrants in force relating to counter-subversion: in 1997 no warrants were in force or were issued on this ground.[84] No figures are given for the warrants issued by the Foreign Secretary or the Secretary of State for Northern Ireland.[85]

Safeguards and supervision

The Regulation of Investigatory Powers Act 2000, Part I, contains a number of different safeguards designed to ensure that there is no abuse of the powers which it authorises. The first is the provision for a body of commissioners to exercise oversight in relation to these different powers. The Interception of Communications Commissioner was established under the Interception of Communications Act 1985 and the office is continued by virtue of s 57 of the RIPA. The Commissioner is a senior judicial figure and is appointed by the Prime Minister. The first holder of the office was Lord Justice Lloyd who was succeeded by Sir Thomas Bingham, in turn succeeded by Lord Nolan. The Commissioner has a number of duties to review the operation of powers under the Act and he or she must report annually to the Prime Minister regarding the discharge of his or her duties. The report must then be laid before Parliament, although parts of it may be excluded in the public interest. The procedures adopted by the Commissioner are described in these reports. Lord Nolan's practice was to make two 'warranty' visits annually to each of the departments and agencies concerned with interceptions and to examine a sample of warrants to determine whether the issuing of a warrant was justified.[86] There has been no case of a warrant being unjustified, although a number of 'errors' have been acknowledged.[87]

The second safeguard against abuse is the provision for a tribunal to deal with a wide range of complaints that may be made about the exercise of powers under the Act. Tribunals of this kind were previously established under the Interception of Communications Act 1985, the Security Service Act 1989 and the Intelligence Services Act 1994. These different tribunals are now combined into a single tribunal; the Investigatory Powers Tribunal; with Lord Justice Mummery as its president in 2001, the tribunal has extended powers to reflect the wider range of issues dealt with in RIPA

---

[81] Cm 4001, 1998, paras 10, 11.

[82] Cm 4778, 2000.

[83] Ibid, para 14.

[84] Cm 4001, 1998, para 15. In 1994, it was said that in 1993 there were 'no warrants currently in force against individual subversives on the ground that they represent a threat to parliamentary democracy and so to national security' and that only 'a few organisations are currently the subject of interception on that ground' (Cm 2522, 1994). It is to be assumed from the silence that in every other year (but 1997) warrants have been issued on these grounds.

[85] It has been said that while the numbers have declined in the former case (but from what to what?), in the latter case they have 'increased substantially': Cm 2522, 1994.

[86] Cm 4778, 2000, paras 10–12. In his last report Lord Nolan praised successive Home Secretaries in particular for their 'exemplary thoroughness' (ibid, para 12).

[87] On which see Fenwick, p 354.

2000. However, the model for the new tribunal is that which was established in the 1985 Act which authorised the Interception of Communications Tribunal to deal with complaints about the improper issuing of warrants under that Act. Although the tribunal had a limited jurisdiction, it received a considerable number of applications. Between the time it was established in 1986 and 1999, it dealt with 712 complaints, not one of which was found to have breached the Act. As Lord Nolan pointed out in his 1997 report, the fact that not a single case succeeded 'led to a measure of suspicion as to the effectiveness of the Tribunal's work'.[88] But, as was pointed out, in only eight of the then 568 cases dealt with by the Tribunal was an interception carried out with the authority of a warrant and in each case the warrant had been properly issued.

In many countries judicial intervention takes place at the point of granting the warrant: it is common practice for warrants to be granted by judges rather than by politicians.[89] The enactment of the RIPA provided an opportunity to consider adopting judicial authorisation rather than judicial supervision. But the Home Secretary expressed the view that 'it does not necessarily follow that, just because a judicial warrant is required, there is a greater safeguard for the individual'.[90] It is important to note, however, that the role of the Commissioner is not confined to safeguarding the rights of the individual. One reason for the increase in the number of Home Office and (what was then) Scottish Office warrants is the revocation in 1992 of the quota system which had been in operation for many years whereby a restriction was imposed on the number of warrants issued to the Customs and Excise on the one hand and the police on the other. The quota system was considered by the then Commissioner (Sir Thomas Bingham) who questioned whether 'the Secretary of State should circumscribe his discretion to authorise the issue of warrants by reference to an arithmetical norm'. There was 'much to be said for dealing with applications . . . very strictly on their merits and without reference to numerical constraints beyond those necessarily imposed by the existence of limited facilities'.[91]

The exclusion of the courts

Although senior judges are thus involved as commissioners and as President of the Tribunal, there is little role for the courts in the operation of the Act. The Tribunal is protected by a statutory provision which precludes judicial review of its decisions, including decisions as to jurisdiction.[92] Moreover, no evidence may be adduced in legal proceedings which tends to suggest that a warrant has been issued under the Act; or that an offence has been committed by a servant of the Crown, a police officer, a person providing a postal service or a public telecommunications operator (s 17).[93] This is designed to prevent 'the asking of questions suggesting that a warrant to intercept communications has been or is to be issued':[94] 'neither the existence of a telephone intercept under warrant nor the result thereof are to be disclosed in evidence'.[95] The

---

[88] Cm 4001, 1998, para 31.
[89] For Opposition proposals for the same in this country, see HC Deb, 6 March 2000, col 688.
[90] Ibid, col 770.
[91] Cm 2173, 1993, paras 14–16. Other reasons for the increase is that there are more phones and more crime: HC Deb, 6 March 2000, col 830 (Mr Charles Clarke).
[92] Regulation of Investigatory Powers Act 2000, s 67(8).
[93] Interception evidence obtained by an unlawful interception is not admissible any more than interception evidence obtained by lawful interception. There would otherwise be 'a remarkable and unacceptable anomaly' (*Morgans* v *DPP* [2001] AC 315). See also *R* v *Sargent* [2002] 1 All ER 161.
[94] *R* v *Preston* [1994] 2 AC 130, at p 144 (Lord Jauncey). There are, however, qualifications in s 18 whereby a trial judge may order material to be disclosed for exceptional purposes in exceptional circumstances. See generally, Standing Committee F, 28 March 2000, cols 228–39.
[95] *R* v *Preston*, ibid.

position compares with evidence obtained from listening devices and other forms of surveillance by the intelligence services and the police which may be disclosed not only for the purpose of preventing or detecting serious crime, but also for the purpose of criminal proceedings.[96] Although it might be thought that the total exclusion of interception evidence would normally benefit the defence, there may be circumstances where the accused is precluded from relying on evidence of the interception to rebut the case against him or her.[97]

E. Storing and processing information

The storage and use of information about individuals is an issue which has assumed much greater significance as a result of the computer revolution and the greater capacity now to store and process personal information. But we should not overlook the fact that the storage and use of personal information in different forms had occurred for many years before the invention of the computer. Obvious examples include the files maintained by the intelligence services about people deemed to be politically subversive;[98] the disclosure of medical information to insurance companies and employers;[99] and the blacklisting of trade unionists which was conducted by organisations sympathetic to employers. It goes without saying that the common law proved of little value to regulate this activity and indeed failed to develop any tools to deal with it. The use of this material did not did attract liability for conspiracy to injure,[100] although there might be liability in defamation if the information were distributed – but only if it were untrue. The Security Service Act 1989 provided a limited opportunity for individuals to complain to the tribunal established by that Act about inquiries conducted about them by the security service, and about the disclosure of information 'for use in determining whether [they] should be employed'.[101] At the time of writing no application has ever succeeded under the Act, although no breakdown was given by the tribunal about the type of cases coming before it, and in particular about how many related to surveillance and vetting by the security service.[102]

The Data Protection Act 1998

The important protection of this aspect of privacy is to be found in the Data Protection Act 1998. Designed to give effect to Council Directive 95/46/EC, this replaces the 1984 Act of the same name which applied only to computer-related data.[103] Data for the purposes of the 1998 Act are defined as 'information' which is recorded or processed by computer; as well as any other information which is recorded as part of a relevant filing system.[104] The Act also applies to certain health records, educational records,

---

[96]   R v Khan [1997] AC 558, at p 576 (Lord Nolan).
[97]   R v Preston (note 94 above).
[98]   See L Lustgarten and I Leigh, In From the Cold, ch 5.
[99]   See Access to Medical Records Act 1990 by which the practice is now regulated, although in a manner which arguably permits access to too much information by employers and insurance companies, albeit with the 'consent' of the individual.
[100]   McKenzie v Iron Trades Employers' Insurance Association 1910 SC 79.
[101]   Security Service Act 1989, Sch 1 (2) and (3): see Leigh and Lustgarten, pp 153–6.
[102]   The work of the tribunal under the 1989 Act has been merged with that of the tribunal under the Interception of Communications Act 1985 by the RIPA 2000.
[103]   The following is a necessarily condensed account of the Act which highlights the main features. For a more detailed account, see Banbridge, Data Protection Law; and Carey, Data Protection in the UK.
[104]   A relevant filing system is defined to mean 'any set of information relating to individuals to the extent that, although the information is not processed by means of equipment operating automatically in response to instructions given for that purpose, the set is structured, either by reference to individuals or by

local authority records, and other information held by a public authority (s 1).[105] Some data are described as being 'sensitive personal data', a term which is defined to mean personal data consisting of any of the following information about the data subject: racial or ethnic origin, political opinions, religious belief, trade union status, physical or mental health or condition, sexual life, the commission or alleged commission of an offence, and any criminal proceedings brought against him or her (s 2).[106] The other key concept in the Act is 'the special purposes'. This is a term which is defined to mean journalism, artistic purposes or literary purposes (s 3).

Underpinning the Act are the eight data protection principles, with which data controllers must comply (s 4). These are set out in Sch 1 as follows: (i) personal data shall be fairly and lawfully processed; (ii) they shall be obtained only for a specified and lawful purpose; (iii) they shall be 'adequate, relevant and not excessive' in relation to the purposes for which they are processed; (iv) they shall be accurate and kept up to date; (v) they shall not be kept longer than necessary for the purpose for which the data are processed; (vi) they shall be processed in accordance with the rights of the data subject; (vii) appropriate measures are to be taken against unauthorised or unlawful processing of personal data; and (viii) they shall not be transferred outside the European Economic Area. These principles are subject to detailed interpretation in the Act itself and, in the case of the first, it is provided additionally that at least one of the six conditions in Sch 2 must be met. This provides that data are to be processed only if the data subject consents, or if the processing is necessary for one of a number of purposes which include the administration of justice and the exercise of any functions of the Crown, a minister of the Crown or a government department.[107] Where the data are sensitive personal data, at least one of the ten conditions in Sch 3 must also be met.[108]

Data subjects and data controllers

The first of two key substantive aspects of the Act relate to the rights of the data subject, that is to say the person whose personal data are being stored and used by another. Under the Act the data subject is entitled on request and in writing to be (*a*) informed by any data controller whether any personal data are being processed by the data controller; (*b*) given a description of the personal data and the purposes for which they are being used, as well as the people to whom they may be disclosed; (*c*) supplied with the information which is being processed and informed of the logic of any decision

---

reference to criteria relating to individuals, in such a way that specific information relating to a particular individual is readily accessible': Data Protection Act 1998, s 1(1).

[105] Public authority for this purpose has the same meaning as in the Freedom of Information Act 2000.

[106] See *R (A) v Chief Constable of C* [2001] 1 WLR 461.

[107] The other conditions specified are that the processing is necessary for the purposes of a contract to which the data subject is a party; to comply with any legal obligation to which the data controller is subject; to protect the vital interests of the data subject; or for 'the purposes of legitimate interests pursued by the data controller or by the third party or parties to whom the data are disclosed'.

[108] These are (i) the data subject has given 'his explicit consent'; (ii) the processing is necessary for the purposes of exercising any right or duty of the data controller in connection with employment; (iii) the processing is necessary to protect the vital interests of the data subject; (iv) the processing is carried out in the course of the legitimate activities of a non-profit making association; (v) the information contained in the personal data has been made public as a result of steps deliberately taken by the data subject; (vi) the processing is necessary for purposes relating to legal proceedings; (vii) the processing is necessary for the administration of justice, the exercise of a statutory duty or the exercise of any functions of the Crown, a minister or a government department; (viii) the processing is necessary for medical purposes and is undertaken by a health professional or another person who owes an equivalent duty of confidentiality; (ix) the processing is undertaken for the purpose of ethnic monitoring; and (x) any other circumstances specified in an order made by the Secretary of State. On the last, see Data Protection (Processing of Sensitive Personal Data) Order 2000, SI 2000 No 417.

taken in relation to him or her (such as performance at work) which is based solely on the 'processing by automatic means of personal data' (s 7). This last would be designed to protect people excluded credit because of their postal code or workers refused employment or promotion because of psychometric testing. There are a number of exceptions to the right of access (particularly where it would necessarily involve disclosing confidential information about another person), and provision is made as to the manner in which the information should be disclosed. In some circumstances, the data subject is entitled by giving notice in writing to require the data controller to stop processing the personal data of the data subject in question, and an application may be made to court for an order to the data controller to correct or destroy any inaccurate personal data being stored or processed by the data controller.

The second of the two main substantive provisions of the Data Protection Act 1998 relates to the responsibilities of data controllers. Personal data are not to be processed unless the data controller has first registered with the Information Commissioner (s 17), a post which is created by the Act (s 6). Those applying for registration must describe the personal data to be processed, the purposes for which they are to be processed and the persons to whom the data controller intends to disclose the data (s 16). They must also provide a 'general description of measures to be taken for the purpose of complying with the seventh data protection principle' (s 18(2)(b)). There is in addition a duty to notify the Commissioner of any material changes to the practice of the data controller with regard to personal data (s 20). It is an offence to process data without being registered and to fail to notify any relevant changes (s 21). The Lord Chancellor is empowered to make regulations to provide for the appointment of data protection supervisors by data controllers: the role of the supervisor would be to monitor 'in an independent manner the data controller's compliance with the provisions of [the] Act' (s 23). One of the most important provisions of the Act is s 4(4) which, as we have seen, imposes a duty on data controllers 'to comply with the data protection principles in relation to all personal data with respect to which he is the data controller'.

Perhaps predictably there are a number of situations where the Act does not apply or where its application is diluted. There are at least ten such general categories of exempt data, the first of which are data where exemption is required for the purpose of safeguarding national security (s 28). These are exempt from all the data protection principles. A ministerial certificate stating that the exemption is required is enough for this purpose, though any person affected by the issuing of the certificate may appeal to the Information Tribunal against the certificate (s 28(4)).

> In an important decision, the Information Tribunal – sitting to deal with national security appeals – overruled a blanket certificate of the Home Secretary exempting the Security Service from much of the Act. The Liberal Democrat MP Norman Baker wrote to the Service asking if it is processing personal data of his and if so what such data are. The Service could neither confirm nor deny. The decision of the Tribunal was confined to the duty of a data controller under s 7(1)(a) of the 1998 Act to inform people from whom a request is made whether or not their personal data are being processed. The Tribunal held that the ministerial certificate was too wide because it would 'exempt the Service from the obligation to respond positively to any request made to it under section 7(1)(a) of the Act, regardless of whether national security would be harmed by a positive response in a particular case'.[109] Following this decision the Home Secretary issued a fresh certificate under s 28 of the 1998 Act which removes the blanket exemption of the Security Service. Individuals may now make an application to the Service which may now be refused on the grounds of national security only on a case-by-case basis.

---

[109] *Baker v Home Secretary*, www.dataprotection.gov.uk.

There is also an exemption from aspects of the first data protection principle for data processed for the prevention or detection of crime or for the assessment or collection of tax (s 29). There is then power vested in the Lord Chancellor to exempt by order from other aspects of the first data protection principle personal data relating to the physical or mental health of the data subject (s 30). Other exemptions relate to the activities of regulatory bodies (s 31), personal data which are processed with a view to publication as journalism, literature or art (s 32), personal data which are processed for research purposes (including historical and statistical research) (s 33), manual data held by local authorities (s 33A),[110] personal data which the data controller is obliged to make available to the public by statute (s 34), or otherwise disclose by virtue of any legal obligation or court order (s 35). An exemption is also made to avoid infringing parliamentary privilege (s 35A),[111] for personal data processed for domestic purposes (s 36) and for a number of other miscellaneous purposes (s 37).

The Information Commissioner

Enforcement of the Act is principally by means of the Information Commissioner and the Information Tribunal (s 6). The Commissioner is a continuation of the office of Data Protection Registrar under the Data Protection Act 1984, and is appointed by the government ('Her Majesty by Letters Patent' according to the statutory form) (s 6); but neither the Commissioner nor his or her staff are to be regarded as Crown servants. Appointments are for renewable fixed terms of up to five years each, though the same person may not hold office for more than two terms save in exceptional circumstances where the public interest so requires. But once appointed a Commissioner can be removed within the term only after an address from both Houses of Parliament. The Tribunal in contrast is appointed by the Lord Chancellor, to include a legally qualified chairman and deputy chairmen, as well as persons to represent the interests of data subjects and data controllers respectively. The Tribunal is a tripartite body except in national security cases when all three members are legally qualified and in these cases the Tribunal sits in private.[112] Unlike the Tribunal appointed under the RIPA 2000, both the Information Commissioner and the Information Tribunal are subject to judicial review: there is no statutory exclusion clause ousting the courts.

The Commissioner may issue an enforcement notice to a data controller if the Commissioner is satisfied that the data controller is breaching the data protection principles (s 40). The notice may require the data controller to take steps specified in the notice or to refrain from conduct specified in the notice. This might include the erasing of inaccurate data. Under s 42, any person directly affected by the processing of any data may seek an assessment from the Commissioner as to whether the processing is being carried out in accordance with the Act. Where such a request has been made, the Commissioner may serve the data controller with an information notice requiring the data controller to supply the specified information within a specified time (s 43). In the case of special purposes data, a special information notice may be issued to ascertain whether data are being processed only for the special purposes (s 44). If they are not, a determination may be made by the Commissioner (s 45). It is only if a determination under s 45 has been made that an enforcement notice may be issued in relation to special purposes data and even then normally only with the leave of a court (s 46). It is an offence to fail to comply with an enforcement, information or special

110 As inserted by the Freedom of Information Act 2000, s 70.
111 As inserted by the Freedom of Information Act 2000, Sch 6(2).
112 Data Protection Tribunal (National Security Appeals) Rules 2000, SI 2000 No 206, reg 23.

information notice (s 47), although anyone who has been served with such a notice may appeal to the Tribunal against the notice.[113]

Apart from the power to issue these various notices, the Commissioner may also apply to a circuit judge for a warrant where there are reasonable grounds to suspect that a data controller is contravening the data protection principles or that an offence against the Act has been committed.[114] The warrant will authorise the entry and search of premises and the inspection, examination, operation and testing of any equipment which is found there, and which is used for the processing of personal data. The warrant also author- ises the seizure of any material which may be evidence that the data principles have been violated or an offence committed. No warrant is to be issued in respect of any personal data processed for 'special purposes' unless a s 45 determination has first been made by the Commissioner. Otherwise, the Commissioner has the general duty under the Act to promote good practice by data controllers, and also has the power to issue codes of practice 'for guidance as to good practice' (s 51).[115] The Commissioner is required to report annually to Parliament and any codes of practice are to be laid before Parliament (s 52). The Commissioner is also empowered in some cases to provide assistance to applicants in legal proceedings, which may include bearing the legal costs (s 53).[116]

Data protection and the RIPA 2000

Provision is made in the RIPA 2000 to deal with the situation where it is deemed necessary for public authorities to secure access to communications data. Before the Act came into force, this was done under a voluntary regime set up under the Telecommunications Act 1984 and the Data Protection Act 1998. It was thought that this 'loosely regulated' regime was 'unacceptable in terms of human rights and because, in certain cases, it has led to unacceptably high demands on the public telecommunications operators'.[117] As a result Chapter II of Part I of the RIPA intro- duces a statutory procedure whereby the law enforcement and other agencies can require service providers to supply communications data in defined circumstances.[118] Com- munications data are data about the use which the individual has made of a postal service or telecommunications system.[119] Any request for such data must now be made by an authorised officer within a relevant public authority (such as a police force or the intelligence services). The RIPA also contains controversial provisions whereby the police, the intelligence services and other public authorities are empowered to require a person in possession of encrypted information to supply the key to the relevant information (s 49).[120] This power may be exercised where the information has come into the possession of the authorities as a result of statutory powers of search and seizure, interception of communications, surveillance or by other lawful means.[121] Under the

---

[113] An appeal lies from the Tribunal to the High Court or the Court of Session (s 49).

[114] Data Protection Act 1998, Sch 9.

[115] See Draft Code of Practice, The Use of Personal Data in Employer/Employee Relationships (2002).

[116] See also, Data Protection Act 1998, Sch 10.

[117] HC Deb, 6 March 2000, col 773 (Mr Jack Straw).

[118] These are that it is necessary to obtain the data in the interests of national security, for the purpose of preventing or detecting crime, or preventing disorder, in the interests of the economic well-being of the UK, in the interests of public safety, for the purpose of assessing or collecting taxes, in an emergency to prevent death or injury, or any other purpose specified in a ministerial order: RIPA 2000, s 22.

[119] RIPA 2000, s 21 (4) and (6). It has been said to cover 'billing data, subscriber data, details of numbers dialled or internet sites accessed by a given subscriber,' but not 'for example, the content of voice calls'. W Malcom and D Barker, NLJ, 25 January 2002.

[120] For the government's response to claims that these procedures violate art 6 of the ECHR, see HC Deb, 6 March 2000, col 833.

[121] The Explanatory Notes to the Act give the example of material which has been voluntarily handed over (p 41).

Anti-Terrorism, Crime and Security Act 2001, s 102 the Home Secretary is to issue a code of practice which will provide for the retention of communications data by communications providers (defined to include telephone companies and internet service providers). This is designed to facilitate access to such data for the purposes of preserving national security and preventing or detecting crime.[122]

F. Privacy and the press

The emphasis in this chapter so far has been on restraints on privacy by the state. But, as already pointed out, private parties may also be responsible for infringing the privacy of individuals. These private parties may include employers and newspaper proprietors. It is true that some of the antics of the press will be caught by some of the measures already discussed, most notably telephone tapping, which will be an offence unless there is consent under s 3 of the RIPA 2000. The use of surveillance devices by journalists will not require authorisation under the RIPA 2000 and may be unlawful if a trespass is involved. But a 'sting' operation – in a hotel bedroom, for example – may take place with the consent of the owner of the property.[123] And as far as data protection is concerned, we have seen that the 1998 Act expressly excludes journalistic material. Yet the invasion of privacy by the press has given rise to great concern in recent years. Paradoxically, indeed, it is the infringement of privacy by the newspapers rather than by public authorities which has been primarily responsible for the growing demands for a legally enforceable right to privacy. There is a duty under the ECHR to take positive steps to ensure that Convention rights are observed, a duty which 'may involve the adoption of measures even in the sphere of relations between individuals'.[124] In this section we consider the evolution of such a right to protect individuals from what is in effect the violation of their privacy by unwanted publicity.[125]

Breach of confidence

The starting point is the equitable doctrine of breach of confidence.[126] The genesis of the modern action is *Prince Albert* v *Strange*[127] which related to a number of etchings which the Prince had made of close members of his family. The defendant had obtained a copy of the etchings from an employee of a printer to whom they had been given by the Prince so that they could be reproduced. The Prince secured an injunction to restrain the defendant from exhibiting the etchings. In somewhat tendentious terms, the Lord Chancellor rejected the claim of the defendant that he was 'entitled to publish a catalogue of the etchings, that is to say, to publish a description or list of works or compositions of another, made and kept for the private use of that other, the publication of which was never authorised, and the possession of copies of which

---

[122] For a good account of this provision and some of the concerns which it raises, see Malcolm and Barker, above.

[123] *Grobbelaar* v *News Group Newspapers Ltd* [2001] 2 All ER 437.

[124] *Spencer* v *UK* (1998) 25 EHRR CD 105, at p 112, citing *Plattform 'Ärtze für das Leben'* v *Austria* (1988) 13 EHRR 204. Also *X* v *Netherlands* (1985) 8 EHRR 235.

[125] There are a number of miscellaneous statutory provisions which offer protection of the same kind. These are designed to prevent the publication of confidential or highly personal information which is disclosed in legal proceedings from being published. See Judicial Proceedings (Regulation of Reports) Act 1926 and the Children and Young Persons Act 1933, s 39.

[126] See Gurry, *Breach of Confidence*, H Fenwick and G Phillipson [1996] CLJ 447, and H Fenwick and G Phillipson (2000) 63 MLR 660.

[127] (1849) 1 Mac&G 25. See also *Pollard* v *Photographic Co* (1888) 40 Ch D 345.

could only have been obtained by surreptitious and improper means'.[128] It was held that an injunction could lie in property, trust, confidence or contract. In *Argyll v Argyll*,[129] the court restrained the publication of confidential marital secrets and in doing so made clear that 'the court in the exercise of its equitable jurisdiction will restrain a breach of confidence independently of any right of law'. The publication of confidential information can thus be restrained, even though there is no breach of contract or any violation of property rights.[130]

Actions for breach of confidence have been brought on a number of occasions since *Argyll v Argyll* to restrain confidential information of a wide and varied kind.[131] In one case, it was held that an action could be brought where the defendant disclosed the existence of a sexual relationship between the applicant and another woman (a murder victim) which the applicant had told the defendant in confidence.[132] In another it was held that a newspaper could be restrained from publishing a story to the effect that two unnamed doctors with AIDS were employed by a particular health authority and were continuing to practise despite their condition.[133] It has also been held that there was a breach of confidence involved in the tapping of the applicant's telephone by a newspaper;[134] but that there was no breach of confidence when it was done by the police investigating criminal offences.[135] As one judge has said, 'there is no confidence as to the disclosure of iniquity' and the cases show that such publications will not be restrained, even if the information was originally given in confidence.[136] It has also been said that, 'Although the basis of the law's protection of confidence is that there is a public interest that confidences should be preserved and protected by the law, nevertheless that public interest may be outweighed by some other counter-vailing public interest which favours disclosure.'[137]

In *Spencer v United Kingdom*[138] the European Commission of Human Rights found that breach of confidence was an adequate and sufficient basis for the alleged violation of privacy in that case. The applicants had claimed that their privacy had been violated by a series of newspaper articles which had reported an extra-marital affair by the Earl and an eating disorder on the part of his wife. The application was ruled inadmissible for a failure to exhaust domestic remedies. The case has been said to have 'given a boost' to claims that 'a development of the present frontiers of a breach of confidence action could fill the gap in English law which is filled by privacy law in other developed countries'.[139]

---

[128] At p 42.

[129] [1967] Ch 302. The protection of confidentiality does not apply to sexual relationships outside marriage in the same way: *A v B (a company)* [2002] 2 All ER 545.

[130] The ingredients required to establish a breach of confidence are set out in *Coco v A N Clark Engineers Ltd* [1969] RPC 41, at p 47, and in *Attorney-General v Guardian Newspapers (No 2)* [1990] AC 109, at p 281.

[131] See *Saltman Engineering Co Ltd v Campbell Engineering Co Ltd* [1963] 3 All ER 413; *Fraser v Evans* [1969] 1 QB 349; *Lion Laboratories Ltd v Evans* [1985] QB 526.

[132] *Stephens v Avery* [1988] Ch 449. Also *Barrymore v News Group Newspapers Ltd* [1997] FSR 600.

[133] *X v Y* [1988] 2 All ER 648.

[134] *Francome v Mirror Group Newspapers Ltd* [1984] 2 All ER 408.

[135] *Malone v Metropolitan Police Commissioner* [1979] Ch 344.

[136] *Fraser v Evans* (note 131 above) and *Hubbard v Vosper* [1972] 1 All ER 1023.

[137] *Attorney-General v Guardian Newspapers Ltd (No 2)* [1990] AC 109, at p 282. See *Initial Services Ltd v Putterill* [1968] 1 QB 396; *Lion Laboratories Ltd v Evans* (note 131 above); *Woolgar v Chief Constable of Sussex Police* [2001] 1 WLR 25. For full consideration of this aspect, Cripps, *The Legal Implications of Disclosure in the Public Interest*. Also ch 23. There are statutory provisions which exceptionally allow for the disclosure of confidential information and the protection of those who do disclose: see Public Interest Disclosure Act 1998 (J Gobert and M Punch (2000) 63 MLR 25).

[138] (1998) 25 EHRR CD 105.

[139] *Douglas v Hello! Ltd* [2001] QB 967, at p 985 (Brooke LJ).

Limits of the common law

The reported cases indicate that it is almost impossible for the individual successfully to rely on the doctrine of breach of confidence when privacy has been violated by the police.[140] There will normally be a compelling public interest consideration which will take priority and, for this purpose, the bar is set at a low level.[141] The position is different where the violation of privacy is by the press. Here the doctrine of breach of confidence has proved to be more robust and has been successfully relied on in a number of different situations. But even here there are limits to just how far the common law could protect the individual even from what have been described judicially as the most 'monstrous' invasions of privacy.[142] A clear example is *Kaye* v *Robertson*,[143] where a famous actor was in hospital after having been injured in an accident. Journalists from a tabloid newspaper made their way into the hospital and interviewed and took photographs of the applicant which they then published, announcing untruthfully that the applicant had agreed to the publication. The applicant sought an interlocutory injunction to restrain the publication, his case being based on malicious falsehood, libel, battery and passing off.[144]

The application succeeded on the ground of malicious falsehood alone, with the nature of the protection offered by this particular tort being felt by the court to fall some way short of what justice required. The question of a privacy law was considered by the Calcutt committee on privacy and related matters which was set up in 1989, 'following a number of striking instances in which sections of the press had been severely criticised for intruding upon accident victims and other patients in hospital, for using stolen private correspondence or photographs and for publishing scurrilous (and sometimes false) details of individuals' private lives'.[145] In *Kaye* v *Robertson*,[146] Glidewell LJ thought the facts of that case were 'a graphic illustration of the desirability of Parliament considering whether and in what circumstances statutory provision can be made to protect the privacy of individuals'.[147] But Calcutt recommended against the introduction of a new tort of privacy, as many had recommended, citing 'arguments of principle, practical concerns and the availability of other options for tackling the problems'.[148] Calcutt pinned his sails to the mast of self-regulation and proposed that the press should be given one last chance to prove that self-regulation could work. To this end he recommended the introduction of a new Press Complaints Commission – modelled on the Broadcasting Complaints Commission[149] – to replace the existing Press Council.[150] Funded by the newspaper and magazine publishing industry,[151] the PCC has produced a Code of Practice which deals with privacy.[152]

---

[140] See pp 516–17 below.

[141] *Hellewell* v *Chief Constable of Derbyshire* [1985] 1 WLR 804. See p 516 below.

[142] *Kaye* v *Robertson* [1991] FSR 62, at p 70 (Bingham, LCJ).

[143] [1991] FSR 62.

[144] There was no claim for breach of confidence: 'No cases derived from the law of confidence were cited to the court during the one-day hearing': *Douglas* v *Hello! Ltd* (note 139 above). Quaere whether such an action would now lie, following Laws J's remarks about photography in *Hellewell*.

[145] Cm 1102, 1990.

[146] [1991] FSR 62.

[147] At p 66.

[148] Cm 1102, 1990.

[149] The Broadcasting Complaints Commission is a statutory body (Broadcasting Act 1990) and has the power to investigate complaints relating to privacy. See ch 23 C.

[150] On which, see Robertson, *The People against the Press*.

[151] Press Complaints Commission, Annual Report (2000). The Commission has an independent chair as well as independent members and representatives of the national and regional press.

[152] But with other matters as well, relating to various questions of journalistic ethics.

In 1993 Sir David Calcutt concluded that the PCC had not been effective and that a new statutory press complaints tribunal should be established. He repeated the earlier recommendation for the introduction of a number of offences (such as un-authorised entry onto private property with intent to obtain personal information with a view to its publication) subject to a number of public interest defences and that the government should give full consideration to the introduction of a new tort of infringement of privacy.[153] Further support for a statutory right to privacy was provided by the National Heritage Committee of the House of Commons, which accepted that 'a free society requires the freedom to say or print things that are inconvenient to those in authority', but argued forcefully that 'in a democratic society there must be a right to privacy as well', a right which must not be 'ignored by those who claim that everything that everybody does is fair game, so long as it provides a saucy story'.[154] The Committee rejected Calcutt's recommendation for a statutory press complaints tribunal on the ground that it was not in favour of legislation which applied to the media exclusively and, in practice, to the press alone.[155] Instead the committee proposed the introduction of a Protection of Privacy Bill, which would provide protection for all citizens and contain 'both a new tort of infringement of privacy and criminal offences resulting from unauthorised use of invasive technology and harassment'.[156]

The Press Complaints Commission

There now seems little prospect of such legislation, with the preferred route for the legal protection of privacy being through the medium of the Human Rights Act 1998. Indeed, as we shall see, the Human Rights Bill was amended so as not to undermine the work of the PCC which would like to continue to play a prominent part in the protection of privacy. But it will do so in the shadow of the art 8 right which is now enforceable in the British courts and under a cloud following its handling of the press coverage of the business interests of the Countess of Wessex in 2001: the PCC was thought by some to be acting too much in the interests of the royal family. Its Code of Practice covers a wide range of issues. Privacy is dealt with in clause 3 of the revised code in the following terms:

> 3 Privacy
> (i) Everyone is entitled to respect for his or her private and family life, home, health and correspondence. A publication will be expected to justify intrusions into any individual's private life without consent;
> (ii) The use of long-lens photography to take pictures of people in private places without their consent is unacceptable.

Private places are defined to mean 'public or private property where there is a reasonable expectation of privacy'. The PCC hears complaints about breaches of the Code of Practice and a newspaper is required to print any PCC adjudication to which it is a party 'in full and with due prominence'. But 'the PCC has no legal power to prevent publication of material, to enforce its rulings or to grant any legal remedy against the newspaper in favour of the victim'.[157]

---

[153] Cm 2135, 1993.
[154] HC 294-I (1992–93).
[155] But it was later to deliver a stinging rebuke to the PCC on the ground that 'time and time again' its 'reaction to criticism is to offer half measures when radical change is called for' (HC 86 (1996–97)).
[156] See also HC 38 (1993–94).
[157] *Spencer* v *UK* (1998) 25 EHRR CD 105. For an account of some of the privacy issues with which the Commission was concerned in 2000 (including the 'naming and shaming' of paedophiles by the *News of the World*), see http://www.pcc.org.uk/2000/statistics_review.asp.

Although the PCC is not a statutory body and its code of practice not legally enforceable, there was concern during the enactment of the Human Rights Act 1998 that it might nevertheless be a public body for the purposes of that Act.[158] This means that it will be required to act in such a way as not to violate Convention rights and that it could be restrained in legal proceedings should it do so, either in the way in which it conducts its proceedings or in the adjudications which it gives. This would mean in particular that it would have to give due weight to the right to freedom of expression. Concerns expressed in Parliament by Lord Wakeham (the chairman of the PCC) led to an amendment to the Human Rights Bill and the introduction of what is now s 12 – a solution which emphasises that unlike in some countries, in this country freedom of expression is 'not in every case the ace of trumps' and must be qualified by other societal values, even though 'it is a powerful card' to which the courts must always pay proper respect.[159] The amendment provides that courts are required to give due weight to freedom of expression (s 12(4)) – which they would surely be required to do anyway.[160] But it also provides that in proceedings which relate to journalistic, literary or artistic material, the court is to have regard – among other matters – to whether it would be in the public interest for the material to be published, as well as 'any relevant privacy code'.

What this seems designed to achieve is that if proceedings are brought to restrain a publication which relates to the private life of the applicant, the courts must take into account two questions: (i) is publication in the public interest, and (ii) has the newspaper complied with the PCC code? If the answer to both is 'yes', then the courts are less likely to restrain publication than if the answer is 'no'. In this way the PCC Code of Practice has an indirect legal effect: it is still not legally enforceable as such, but failure by a newspaper to comply with it could lead to a publication being restrained. In the words of Brooke LJ in *Douglas* v *Hello! Ltd*: 'A newspaper which flouts cl 3 of the code is likely in those circumstances to have its claim to an entitlement to freedom of expression trumped by article 10(2) considerations of privacy.'[161] Compliance with the code is, of course, not conclusive: the fact that a newspaper has complied with the Code will not be a decisive factor if, for example, the courts take the view that the code or the way in which it is applied falls short of Convention rights as protected by art 8.[162] So in this way the PCC itself will need to ensure that its code is applied in a manner which reflects the requirements of art 8, though there was little jurisprudence in 2001 by which it can be guided. But s 12 has proved to be a very flimsy protection against a spate of injunctions by media celebrities concerned to protect their privacy, and there is some anxiety that the emergence of a legal right to privacy in the slip-stream of the Human Rights Act will inevitably diminish the role of the PCC.

G. Privacy and the Human Rights Act

By virtue of the Human Rights Act, article 8 is now enforceable in the domestic courts against public authorities.[163] This means that the exercise of different powers referred to in sections C and D of this chapter may now be challenged under the Human Rights

---

[158] See HL Deb, 24 November 1997, col 772 (Lord Wakeham). On a judicial review of the Commission, see *R (Ford)* v *Press Complaints Commission* [2002] EMLR 5.
[159] *Douglas* v *Hello! Ltd* [2001] QB 967, at p 982 (Brooke LJ).
[160] Cf *Douglas* v *Hello! Ltd*, ibid, at p 1004 (Sedley LJ).
[161] Ibid, at p 994. See also *A* v *B* (*a company*) [2002] 2 All ER 545.
[162] See *Venables* v *News Group Newspapers Ltd* [2001] 2 WLR 1038 Fam 430.
[163] See ch 19 C.

Act and indeed that it may be possible to challenge some of the statutory provisions as being incompatible with Convention rights. But although none of the legislation can be presumed to be watertight, it is most unlikely that many challenges will succeed. There are also unlikely to be many cases where the Human Rights Act will add much in practice to the legal armoury of the individual concerned that powers of surveillance and interception have been improperly exercised. By virtue of their different supervisory roles, senior judges are now directly involved in the supervision and management of the different schemes, with the substance of which they seem broadly content, failing to uphold a single complaint in over 15 years in which the exercise of a power to infringe privacy has been improperly authorised. Paradoxically (again) the weight of any right to privacy derived from the Human Rights Act is likely to be felt most acutely in the field of private law, to protect the individual's right to privacy from the exercise of private rather than state power, particularly that exercised by the press.

Privacy, the Human Rights Act and the police

The issues considered in earlier parts of this chapter by no means exhaust the different ways by which the police and other public authorities might invade personal liberty. Another obvious way by which privacy may be infringed is by the search of premises,[164] although as discussed in chapter 21 this is a form of infringement which is the subject of statutory regulation. The same is true of other forms of violation such as the taking of samples and the requirement that doctors and others hand over intimate personal details to the police. But there remain forms of police conduct which do not require statutory authority and which are not formally regulated.[165] Apart from non-directed surveillance, the keeping of files about individuals and entry on a DNA database, other practices which infringe personal privacy include the photographing of demonstrators and the publishing of suspects' photographs.[166] There can be no objection to the latter course of action when a crime has been committed and the police are looking for a suspect. But different considerations apply when the police publish the photograph of someone whom they believe may commit a crime in the future – as in the case of the political activists who were believed to be likely to cause trouble at the May Day protests in London in 2001.[167] Yet it is unclear whether the Human Rights Act will add significantly to the protection of individuals distressed by these various infringements.

It was held in *Hellewell* v *Chief Constable of Derbyshire*[168] that 'disclosure of a photograph may, in some circumstances, be actionable as a breach of confidence'.[169] Where the police take a photograph of a suspect at the police station in circumstances where the suspect's consent is not required, 'they are not, by law, free to make whatever use they will of the picture so obtained'. Such a photograph will convey to anyone looking at it that the subject is known to the police and is a piece of confidential information which imposes legal obligations on the police, 'breach of which may sound

---

[164] *McLeod* v *UK* (1998) 27 EHRR 493.

[165] See *R* v *Loveridge* [2001] 2 Cr App R 591.

[166] On the taking of photographs, see *Bernstein* v *Skyviews Ltd* [1978] 1 QB 479 – there is no law against taking a photograph. See also *Stewart-Brady* v *UK* (1999) 27 EHRR 284. But there are exceptions, where the photograph is taken of an individual where privacy might be expected: *Shelley Films Ltd* v *Rex Features Ltd* [1994] EMLR 134, *Hellewell* v *Derbyshire Chief Constable* [1995] 1 WLR 804, at p 807 (Laws J), and *Creation Records Ltd* v *News Group Newspapers Ltd* [1997] EMLR 444. On the position of suspects in police custody, see Code of Practice for the Identification of Persons by Police Officers (Code D), para 4.

[167] *Evening Standard*, 24 April 2001; *The Times*, 25 April 2001.

[168] [1995] 1 WLR 804.

[169] At p 807. See *Pollard* v *Photographic Co* (1889) 40 Ch D 345.

in an action at private law'. But 'common sense and law alike dictate that the police should be subject to no legal sanctions if they make honest and reasonable use of a suspect's photograph in the fight against crime'. In such cases the police have a public interest defence to any action brought against them for breach of confidence. *Hellewell* was approved by the Court of Appeal in *R v Chief Constable of the North Wales Police, ex p Thorpe*[170] in which an attempt was made to challenge the disclosure of information by the police by using public law rather than private law. This was the case where in the exercise of a policy to disclose details of the identity of convicted paedophiles, the police revealed the convictions of the applicants to the owners of a caravan site where they lived. The disclosure was made in advance of school holidays which would bring a large number of children to the site.

One reason why it was necessary to proceed in *Thorpe* by way of judicial review rather than by way of an action for breach of confidence was simply because the fact of the convictions was already in the public domain, even though it may not have been known to the people to whom it was disclosed: it was therefore not confidential. This 'did not mean that the police as a public authority were free to publish information about [the applicants'] previous offending absent any public interest in this being done'. But in dismissing the application, it was held that as a matter of administrative law 'the police are entitled to use information when they reasonably conclude this is what is required (after taking into account the interests of the applicants), in order to protect the public and in particular children'.[171] So far as Convention rights are concerned, it is true that the Human Rights Act had not been passed when *Thorpe* was decided. Nevertheless, it will not encourage those who might look to the Act that Lord Bingham CJ should have concluded at first instance that the disclosure was justified under art 8(2), 'provided that the disclosure was made in good faith and in the exercise of a careful professional judgment, and provided that the disclosure was limited to that reasonably judged necessary for the public purpose which the [North Wales Police] sought to protect'.[172] These conditions were held to have been met.[173]

Privacy, the Human Rights Act and the press

Although the Human Rights Act does not permit an individual to sue a newspaper for a violation of privacy, the Act has nevertheless significantly advanced the cause of those who have argued that self-regulation of the newspaper industry is not a secure enough basis for the protection of privacy. It is true that there is no duty on the part of the court to 'create a free standing cause of action based on the Convention', but there is nevertheless a duty 'to act compatibly with convention rights in adjudicating upon existing common law causes of action'.[174] The jurisprudence of the Strasbourg court led the Employment Appeal Tribunal to construe the Sex Discrimination Act 1975 to apply to discrimination on the grounds of sexuality as well as sex.[175] But this was reversed by the Court of Session.[176] In cases where there is no legislation on which the courts can bite, the position is much more difficult where an individual has claimed that his or her Convention rights have been infringed by the actions of a private party and not

---

[170] [1999] QB 396.
[171] At p 429 (Lord Woolf MR).
[172] *R v Chief Constable of the North Wales Police, ex p AB* [1997] 4 All ER 691, at p 702.
[173] See also *R v Chief Constable of C* [2001] 1 WLR 461. See now Sexual Offenders Act 1997, authorising the disclosure of details of convictions of sex offences; and Protection of Children Act 1999, requiring the Secretary of State to keep lists of people deemed unsuitable to work with children.
[174] *Venables v News Group Newspapers Ltd*, (note 162 above), p 446.
[175] *MacDonald v Ministry of Defence* [2000] IRLR 748.
[176] *Ministry of Defence v MacDonald* [2001] IRLR 431.

a public authority. The scope of application of convention rights is unclear in such a case.[177] In the view of the Lord Chancellor when the Human Rights Bill was in the House of Lords:

> the court is not obliged to remedy the failure by legislating via the common law either where a convention right is infringed by incompatible legislation or where, because of the absence of legislation – say, privacy legislation – a convention right is left unprotected. In my view, the courts may not act as legislators and grant new remedies for infringement of convention rights unless the common law itself enables them to develop new rights or remedies.[178]

Yet it remains the case that even before the enactment of the Human Rights Act 1998, the judges were 'pen-poised, regardless of incorporation of the Convention, to develop a right to privacy to be protected by the common law'.[179] Since the enactment of the Human Rights Act, two major decisions have advanced the law relating to privacy significantly, although the main point to emerge from this continuing incremental development is that breach of confidence continues to bear the burden of this load as the action around which these developments continue to evolve.[180] Only Sedley LJ has so far been able to say that 'we have reached a point at which it can be said with confidence that the law recognises and will appropriately protect a right of personal privacy';[181] the other judges in these cases have been much more circumspect.[182] In the first of these cases – *Douglas v Hello! Ltd*[183] – the claimants had entered into an arrangement with a magazine to publish their wedding photographs. A rival magazine was about to publish unauthorised photographs of the wedding and the claimants moved to have them stopped. It was accepted by Brooke LJ that

> equity may intervene to prevent the publication of photographic images taken in breach of an obligation of confidence. In other words, if on some private occasion the prospective claimants make it clear, expressly or impliedly, that no photographic images are to be taken of them, then all those who are present will be bound by the obligations of confidence created by their knowledge (or imputed knowledge) of this restriction. English law, however, has not yet been willing to recognise that an obligation of confidence may be relied on to preclude such unwarranted intrusion into people's privacy when those conditions do not exist.

In rejecting the claim for an interlocutory injunction, Brooke LJ also considered the effect of s 12 of the Human Rights Act, which required him to balance 'the competing considerations of freedom of expression on the one hand and privacy on the other'.[184] But he held that this did not help the applicants, on the ground that their case based on privacy was not a strong one. Although they tried to stop guests and others from taking photographs at the wedding, they 'did not choose to have a private wedding'. In the other case, however, an injunction was granted to restrain a publication which would seriously affect the privacy of the applicants, although the court in this case also hesitated in restraining freedom of expression for that reason alone. In *Venables v News Group Newspapers Ltd*,[185] the applicants had been convicted as youths for the notorious killing of a child. They sought an injunction, based on breach of confidence, to restrain newspapers from publishing information about their identity after their release

---

[177] *Douglas v Hello! Ltd* (note 159 above), at p 1001–2 (Sedley LJ).
[178] HL Deb, 24 November 1997, col 785.
[179] Ibid, col 784 (Lord Chancellor).
[180] See also *A v B (a company)* [2002] 2 All ER 545. For an earlier crafting of a right to privacy at common law, see the seminal article by S D Warren and L D Brandeis (1890) 4 Harv LR 193.
[181] *Douglas v Hello! Ltd* [2001] QB 967, at p 997.
[182] See also *A v B* [2002] 1 All ER 499.
[183] [2001] QB 967.
[184] Ibid, p 995.
[185] [2001] Fam 430.

from detention. This unprecedented application succeeded, despite the fact that it would restrain the freedom of the press, as protected by art 10. It was feared that if their identity were revealed following their release from detention, the applicants would be subject to the risk of serious physical injury or even death. An injunction was therefore granted 'against the whole world', the court holding that in such exceptional circumstances, it was necessary to place the applicants' right to confidentiality above the right of the media to publish information about them. In applying s 12 of the Human Rights Act, the court took into account arts 2 and 3 of the Convention: having regard to art 10(2) it was held that these rights of the applicants took priority over art 10(1), freedom of the press. So the privacy of the applicants was protected because of fears for their safety.

Chapter 23

FREEDOM OF EXPRESSION

The right to freedom of expression in the words of art 10 of the European Convention on Human Rights, includes freedom to hold opinions 'and to receive and impart information and ideas without interference by public authority and regardless of frontiers'. This freedom is fundamental to the individual's life in a democratic society. In the first place, it has a specific political content. The freedom to receive and express political opinions, both publicly and privately, is linked closely with the freedom to organise for political purposes and to take part in free elections:

> Without free elections the people cannot make a choice of policies. Without freedom of speech the appeal to reason which is the basis of democracy cannot be made. Without freedom of association, electors and elected representatives cannot bind themselves into parties for the formulation of common policies and the attainment of common ends.[1]

So does freedom of expression closely affect freedom of religion. Lawyers remember *Bushell*'s case in 1670 as having established the right of the jury to acquit an accused 'against full and manifest evidence' and against the direction of the judge: they should also remember that Bushell was foreman of the jury which acquitted the Quakers William Penn and William Mead on charges of having preached to a large crowd in a London street contrary to the Conventicle Act.[2] Moreover, liberty of expression is an integral part of artistic, cultural and intellectual freedom – the freedom to publish books or produce works of art, however disconcerting they may be to the prevailing orthodoxy.[3]

A. The Nature of Legal Protection

The Human Rights Act

The right to freedom of expression has been formally strengthened by the Human Rights Act 1998, although even before the enactment and coming into force of this measure, the right to freedom of expression was winning a new prominence in the case law, being supported by a number of powerful judicial dicta and extrajudicial statements.[4] It is true that the bold assertion of freedom of expression in art 10 of the ECHR is subject

> to such formalities, conditions, restrictions or penalties as are prescribed by law and are necessary in a democratic society, in the interests of national security, territorial integrity or public safety, for the prevention of disorder or crime, for the protection of health or morals, for the protection of the reputation or rights of others, for preventing the disclosure of information received in confidence, or for maintaining the authority and impartiality of the judiciary.

---

[1] Jennings, *Cabinet Government*, p 14. See also Laski, *A Grammar of Politics*, ch 3.
[2] *R v Penn and Mead* (1670) 6 St Tr 951.
[3] See also *R v Home Secretary, ex p Simms* [2000] 2 AC 115, at p 126, per Lord Steyn. For a good account of some of the issues discussed in this chapter, see Barendt, *Freedom of Speech*.
[4] See *Reynolds v Times Newspapers Ltd* [2001] 2 AC 127, *McCartan Turkington Breen v Times Newspapers Ltd* [2001] 2 AC 277 and *Loutchansky v Times Newspapers Ltd* [2001] 3 WLR 404.

In this sense it is the most heavily qualified of all the Convention rights, paradoxically perhaps in light of Lord Steyn's acknowledgement of freedom of expression as 'the lifeblood of democracy'.[5] Nevertheless, the Human Rights Act contains special protection in the sense that no remedy is to be granted which affects the exercise of the Convention right to freedom of expression without ensuring that the respondent has been notified of the proceedings and given an opportunity to apply (s 12(2)). This is particularly important in the context of an application for an interim injunction to restrain a publication. So too is the parallel requirement that interim relief is not to be granted before a trial 'unless the court is satisfied that the applicant is likely to establish that publication should not be allowed' (s 12(3)). In all cases 'the court must have particular regard to the importance of the Convention right to freedom of expression' (s 12(4)).

But the courts seem poised to take a cautious approach to these provisions, which are said not to require them 'to treat freedom of expression as paramount' and are not 'intended to direct the court to place even greater weight on the importance of freedom of expression than it already does'.[6] In fact the Human Rights Act has made only a limited impact in the field of freedom of expression, despite the very robust judicial dicta in its defence to which we have already referred. Part of the reason for this limited impact is that 'the courts emphasised the importance of freedom of expression or speech long before the enactment of the 1998 Act'.[7] Indeed a number of important decisions have been taken in recent years to extend the boundaries of free speech quite independently of the Human Rights Act (although clearly within its shadow),[8] but perhaps not as far as many would like. Another reason for this limited impact of art 10 has been the willingness on the part of the courts to have the fullest regard for the rights and freedoms of others. So we find that the rights of the press have been subordinated to the demands of copyright,[9] defamation[10] and confidentiality.[11] Indeed in the last case the Act may have helped fashion a new restraint on press freedom by encouraging the development of an enforceable right to privacy on the back of the equitable doctrine of breach of confidence. These developments reflect an appreciation on the part of the judges that large newspapers can be engines of oppression and that newspaper proprietors, editors and journalists can trespass on the rights of others while exercising their own.

Freedom of expression: rights and restraints

The Human Rights Act is not the only source of protection for freedom of expression. It has been said that freedom of expression is a 'sinew of the common law'.[12] Individuals are thus free to speak and write what they like, provided that what they say is not otherwise unlawful. Protection is provided by the law of parliamentary privilege for proceedings in Parliament[13] and there is now a growing body of legislation which

---

[5] *R v Home Secretary, ex p Simms* [2000] 2 AC 115, at p 126.
[6] *Imutran Ltd v Uncaged Campaigns Ltd* [2001] 2 All ER 385, at p 391. Also *Douglas v Hello!* [2001] QB 967.
[7] *Imutran Ltd v Uncaged Campaigns Ltd*, note 6 above, at p 391.
[8] For example, *Reynolds v Times Newspapers Ltd* [2001] AC 127.
[9] *Hyde Park Residence Ltd v Yelland* [2001] Ch 143; *Ashdown v Telegraph Group* [2001] 3 WLR 1368; and *Imutran Ltd v Uncaged Campaigns Ltd*, note 6 above.
[10] *Loutchansky v Times Newspapers Ltd*, note 4 above.
[11] *Douglas v Hello*, note 6 above; *Imutran Ltd v Uncaged Campaigns Ltd*, note 6 above.
[12] *R v Advertising Standards Authority, ex p Vernons* [1993] 2 All ER 202 (Laws J).
[13] See ch 11A.

in different ways promotes and protects freedom of expression. There is now a statutory right to information under both the Data Protection Act 1998, which will be reinforced by the Freedom of Information Act 2000.[14] Both of these measures will aid the work of the investigative journalist, whose role has been celebrated judicially.[15] Also important in this respect is the Contempt of Court Act 1981, s 10, which protects the journalist from having to reveal his or her sources, although as discussed in chapter 18, this provision has been narrowly construed against the journalists by the courts. Apart from these measures facilitating access and protecting the sources of information, the Public Interest Disclosure Act 1998 provides a limited protection for 'whistleblowers', that is to say workers who bring into the public domain serious concerns about the conduct of their employer's business.[16] It remains the case nevertheless that freedom of expression is subject to a wide range of restrictions, many of which are longstanding and most of which are likely to withstand challenge under the Human Rights Act 1998.

Restrictions are of two kinds: the first is censorship of material by state authorities before it is published or displayed, and the second is the imposition of penalties or the granting of redress in the case of someone specifically harmed by the material, after the event. Restrictions of the first kind have often been viewed with great suspicion, and have been strongly deprecated by the US Supreme Court in cases arising under the free speech guarantee in the First Amendment. Yet despite Blackstone's insistence that free speech meant 'laying no previous restraints upon publication',[17] there is still some censorship in Britain, particularly of films and video recordings, though there are also restrictions imposed by Parliament and by governments on what may be broadcast on television and radio.[18] Thus, in 1988, the Home Secretary instructed the BBC and the IBA not to broadcast interviews with members or supporters of named organisations which included terrorist groups and also Sinn Fein, a lawful political party.[19] Although there is now no prior censorship of the press, there are important rules on newspaper ownership which are designed to ensure that transfers operate in the public interest. So far as other restrictions are concerned, there is a wide range of criminal offences which restrict free speech. These offences exist to protect the security of the state and public order; to protect public morality by punishing the publication of obscene material; and by virtue of the law on contempt of court, to maintain the authority and impartiality of the judiciary. Restrictions imposed by the law of defamation exist to protect the rights and reputations of others, while the developing law on breach of confidence may help to prevent the disclosure of information received in confidence.[20] These different restrictions will now be examined in turn, with the exception of the law relating to contempt of court which was dealt with in chapter 18. Limits on free speech which relate to public meetings and demonstrations will be considered in chapter 24 and the Official Secrets Acts and other national security restraints in chapter 25.

---

[14] See chs 22 E and 13 F respectively.
[15] *Loutchansky* v *Times Newspapers Ltd*, note 4 above.
[16] See J Gobert and M Punch (2000) 63 MLR 25; and Hobby, *Whistleblowing and the Public Interest Disclosure Act 1998*.
[17] *Commentaries*, 9th edn, IV, p 151.
[18] The classic legal study of censorship is O'Higgins, *Censorship in Britain*.
[19] See *R* v *Home Secretary, ex p Brind* [1991] 1 AC 696.
[20] It is important also not to lose sight of the possible limits arising under the law of copyright: see *Hyde Park Residence Ltd* v *Yelland*, note 9 above, *Imutran Ltd* v *Uncaged Campaigns Ltd*, note 6 above, and *Ashdown* v *Telegraph Group*, note 9 above.

B. Censorship and prior restraints

Theatres[21]

For many years dramatic and operatic performances in Great Britain were subject to the prior censorship of the Lord Chamberlain, an officer of the royal household. The Theatres Act 1968 abolished the requirement that plays should receive a licence before being performed.[22] Theatres are now licensed by local authorities, but only in regard to such matters as public health and safety. In place of censorship, rules against obscenity similar to those in the Obscene Publications Act 1959 are applied to the performance of plays, subject to a defence of public good. Other criminal restraints placed on theatrical performances are in respect of the use of threatening, abusive or insulting words or behaviour intended or likely to stir up racial hatred[23] or occasion a breach of the peace.[24] Prosecutions for these various offences, including obscenity, require the consent of the Attorney-General in England and Wales. There may be no prosecution at common law for any offence the essence of which is that a performance of a play is 'obscene, indecent, offensive, disgusting or injurious to morality' neither may there be prosecutions under various statutes relating to indecency (1968 Act, s 2(4)), an important safeguard against moral censorship. However, in 1982 a private prosecution of the director of the National Theatre's production of *The Romans in Britain* was withdrawn after the judge had decided that the Sexual Offences Act 1956, s 13 (relating to gross indecency between males) could apply to simulated homosexual acts on stage.[25]

Cinemas[26]

Censorship of films originated unintentionally with the Cinematograph Act 1909, which authorised local authorities to license cinemas in the interests of public safety, mainly against fire. In fact, with the approval of the courts,[27] local authorities extended the scope of licensing to other matters to include the approval of the films shown in licensed cinemas. In the Cinematograph Act 1952, and more recently in the Cinemas Act 1985, Parliament confirmed the power of licensing the films shown and required licensing authorities to impose conditions restricting children from seeing unsuitable films. Licensing authorities are now the district councils and the London borough councils: they may delegate their powers to a committee or to the local magistrates. The main work of censorship of films is undertaken by the British Board of Film Classification (previously the British Board of Film Censors), a non-statutory body set up by the film industry, with the approval of central and local government. The board is responsible for the classification of films with special reference to the admission of young children and others under 18. Although a licensing authority normally allows the showing of films which have been classified by the board, the authority may not transfer its functions to the board and must retain power to review decisions of the board.[28] Thus it may refuse a local showing to a film classified by the board; it may vary the board's classification; or it may grant permission to a film refused a certificate by the board.

---

[21] On theatrical censorship, see Findlater, *Banned!*
[22] For the background, see HC 503 (1966–67).
[23] Public Order Act 1986, s 20.
[24] Theatres Act 1968, s 6.
[25] *The Times*, 19 March 1982.
[26] Hunnings, *Film Censors and the Law*; Williams report on obscenity and film censorship, Cmnd 7772, 1979; Robertson, *Freedom, the Individual and the Law*, pp 238–41.
[27] E.g. *LCC v Bermondsey Bioscope Ltd* [1911] 1 KB 445.
[28] *Ellis v Dubowski* [1921] 3 KB 621; *Mills v LCC* [1925] 1 KB 213.

Powers of local censorship are not popular with the film industry, but a case can be made for maintaining some local option in issues of public morality.

The relationship between the system of film censorship and the law of obscenity and public indecency has caused many difficulties. By the Criminal Law Act 1977, s 53, the public showing of films was brought within the Obscene Publications Act, subject to a defence that showing a film is for the public good in the interests of drama, opera, ballet, or any other art, or of literature or learning. The consent of the Director of Public Prosecutions is required for a prosecution, and forfeiture of films of not less than 16 millimetres in width. The Video Recordings Act 1984 (as amended)[29] established a scheme for the censorship of video recordings, under which it is an offence to supply (whether or not for reward) any recording for which no classification certificate has been issued. Certain recordings are exempt from this requirement (such as those concerned with sport, religion or music and those designed to be educational) and so are certain kinds of supply. A video work may not, however, be an exempted work if to any extent it depicts or is designed to encourage such matters as 'human sexual activity or acts of force or restraint' (s 2(2)(a)).[30] Neither is it exempt if to any extent it depicts criminal activity which is likely to any significant extent to stimulate or encourage the commission of an offence.[31] Classification is conducted by the British Board of Film Classification, which may certify that a video work is suitable for general viewing, suitable only for persons over the age of 18,[32] or that it is to be supplied only in a licensed sex shop.[33]

The press: ownership and self-regulation

The historic freedom of the press means that, subject to the civil and criminal restraints on publication which will be considered later, any person or company may publish a newspaper or magazine without getting official approval in advance. For economic reasons, this liberty is unlikely to be exercised effectively on a national scale except by a very few newspaper publishers. Fears of a movement towards monopoly conditions in sectors of the press led to the enactment in what is now the Fair Trading Act 1973, ss 57–62 (as amended), of provisions to ensure that newspaper mergers above a certain scale do not take place in a manner contrary to the public interest. By s 58, it is an offence for one newspaper to be transferred to the proprietor of another without the consent of the Secretary of State for Trade and Industry where the joint circulation of the two newspapers is 500,000 or more. Consent should not normally be given until the matter has been investigated by the Competition Commission following a reference to it by the minister. The duty of the Commission is to consider 'whether the transfer in question may be expected to operate against the public interest, taking into account all matters which appear in the circumstances to be relevant and, in particular, the need for accurate presentation of news and free expression of opinion'.[34] One case which was opposed on these grounds was the proposed transfer of the *Bristol Evening Post* to Mr David Sullivan who held a 50% interest in the company publishing the *Sunday Sport* and *The Sport*, both of which are said to operate at the lower end of the tabloid market.[35] In some cases, the Trade and Industry

---

[29] By the Video Recordings Act 1993, and the Criminal Justice and Public Order Act 1994.
[30] See *Kent CC v Multi Media Marketing*, The Times, 9 May 1995.
[31] Criminal Justice and Public Order Act 1994, s 89. And see s 88, increasing the penalties for breach.
[32] On which, see *Tesco Stores Ltd v Brent London Borough Council* [1993] 1 WLR 1037.
[33] For the procedures adopted by the Board, see *Wingrove v UK* (1996) 24 EHRR 1. For appeals to the Video Appeals Committee, see S Edwards [2001] Crim LR 305.
[34] See Fair Trading Act 1973, s 59(3).
[35] Cm 1083, 1990.

Secretary may approve a transfer without first referring the matter to the Commission; but in such cases he or she must be satisfied that the newspaper which is the subject of the proposed transfer is not economic as a going concern and that the transfer is urgent if the newspaper is to survive.[36] One controversial acquisition which was not referred for investigation took place in 1981 when Rupert Murdoch bought *The Times* and *Sunday Times*, thereby giving him 30% of the national daily circulation and 36% of the national Sunday circulation.[37] Even where a reference has been made, the Trade and Industry Secretary is probably not bound by the report of the Competition Commission and could thus reject the recommendations, although he or she would clearly be required to take them into account in reaching a decision.[38] These measures appear to have done little to prevent the growing concentration of newspaper titles in the hands of a few proprietors. Indeed, in 1995–96 the four principal newspaper publishers – News International, Mirror Group, United Newspapers, and Associated Newspapers – controlled between them 85% of the national daily and 88.7% of national Sunday circulation.[39]

Freedom of expression is capable of being abused: 'Newspapers are sometimes irresponsible and their motives in a market economy cannot be expected to be unalloyed by considerations of commercial advantage.'[40] Sensational reporting, intrusive investigations and careless editing may cause unjustified distress to private individuals. As we saw in chapter 22, the Press Complaints Commission was created in 1991. Established as an alternative to a statutory tort of privacy, it replaced the Press Council which had been formed by the newspaper industry in 1953,[41] and was seen as a last chance for the proprietors to show that self-regulation could work. There are 16 members of the Commission, which, as we have also seen, is funded by a voluntary levy of newspaper and magazine publishers: apart from the independent chair, there are eight independent members with no press connections and seven senior editors drawn from the national and regional newspapers and magazines. Its primary responsibilities include the handling of complaints of alleged violations of the Code of Practice which was published in 1991 (by the newspaper industry) to regulate its conduct on a range of matters dealing mainly with accuracy and privacy. The Code is kept under scrutiny and has been amended on a number of occasions since, as in 1993 when a new clause was inserted on the use of listening devices, and in 1999 when a new clause was introduced in anticipation of the Human Rights Act 1998. Where there is a breach of the Code leading to a formal adjudication by the commission, the publication concerned must publish the critical adjudication 'in full and with due prominence', but the commission does not award compensation to successful complainants, neither does it fine publications. The commission received 2,225 complaints in 2000, which is broadly in line with the recent average. Most of the complaints were about accuracy, with only one in eight dealing with privacy. The commission adjudicated in only 57 complaints, of which 24 were upheld. Most complaints were thus settled or fall outside the commission's remit.[42] The

---

[36] Fair Trading Act 1973, s 58(3).
[37] Curran and Seaton, *Power without Responsibility*, ch 7.
[38] Cf *R v Trade and Industry Secretary, ex p Anderson Strathclyde plc* [1983] 2 All ER 233. Cf *Pepper v Hart* [1993] AC 593.
[39] Williams, *Media Ownership and Democracy*, p 39. And see T Gibbons [1992] PL 279 and Gibbons, *Regulating the Media*, pp 207–11.
[40] *R v Central Independent Television plc* [1994] Fam 192, at p 202. See also *Reynolds v Times Newspapers Ltd* [2001] 2 AC 277, at p 202 (Lord Nicholls).
[41] See Robertson, *People Against the Press*.
[42] See generally www.pcc.org.uk.

Code of Practice is not legally enforceable:[43] but it has been given statutory recognition and an indirect legal effect by the Human Rights Act 1998.[44]

C. Regulation of television and radio[45]

The BBC

In the case of broadcasting, technical reasons have so far prevented access to the medium being open to all comers as in the case of the press. Even if all broadcasting were to be provided by privately owned companies, it would still be necessary for a regulatory agency to allocate channels and wavelengths to them. Until 1954, the British Broadcasting Corporation enjoyed a public monopoly of all broadcasting in the United Kingdom and it still provides a large share of broadcasting services. The BBC is a corporation set up by royal charter and its chairman and governors are appointed by the Crown on the advice of the Prime Minister. It transmits broadcasts throughout the United Kingdom under licence from the government issued under the Wireless Telegraphy Acts.[46] Although the BBC is mainly financed by a grant from the exchequer, equivalent to the net revenue of television licence fees, the structure of the BBC seeks to maintain its independence of the government of the day. The BBC's charter was renewed in 1996 for a period of ten years,[47] together with a new agreement between the corporation and the government whereby the broadcaster is subject to a number of duties. These are similar in terms to those imposed on the commercial broadcasters by legislation. Questions have been raised whether the BBC should be regulated by legislation rather than royal prerogative, but this was rejected by the National Heritage Committee in 1993 on the ground that the present arrangements 'gave the BBC flexibility and that it helped its independence'.[48] But although the charter is debated by both Houses of Parliament before it is granted by the Queen in Council,[49] this is a poor substitute for legislation which would give MPs 'the opportunity to debate the substance of the statutes and to move detailed amendments'.[50] This issue was not revisited when the Culture Media and Sport Committee reviewed the BBC in 1999.[51]

Certain duties are imposed on the BBC: it must broadcast a daily account of the proceedings in Parliament and any minister of the Crown may require announcements to be broadcast. The minister responsible for broadcasting (in 2001 Secretary of State for Culture, Media and Sport) may require the BBC not to broadcast certain matters. The BBC may not broadcast its own opinions about current affairs or matters of public policy, being under a duty to do all it can to treat controversial subjects with due accuracy and impartiality, 'both in the Corporation's news services and in the more general field of programmes dealing with matters of public policy, or of political or industrial controversy'. But 'due impartiality does not require absolute neutrality on every issue or detachment from fundamental democratic principles', the meaning of which is not specified. The BBC should also seek to ensure that programmes do not

---

[43] On the possibility of judicial review, see *R (Ford) v Press Complaints Commission* [2002] EMLR 545.
[44] See ch 22 E.
[45] Barendt, *Broadcasting Law*; Craufurd Smith, *Broadcasting Law and Fundamental Rights*.
[46] For the charter, see Cm 3248, 1996, and for the licence and agreement, Cm 3152, 1996. And see *BBC v Johns* [1965] Ch 32.
[47] Cm 3248, 1996. See HL Deb, 9 January 1996, col 13.
[48] HC 77–I (1993–94), para 51.
[49] *The Future of the BBC*, Cm 2621, 1994, p 53.
[50] HC 77–I (1993–94), para 50.
[51] HC 25 (1999–2000).

include 'anything which offends against good taste or decency or is likely to encourage or incite to crime or lead to disorder or to be offensive to public feeling'.[52] In an emergency the government may take over the BBC's broadcasting facilities. Apart from these specific powers, the government may not control the BBC's programmes, although it may bring great pressure to bear, particularly at a time of emergency such as the Falklands campaign,[53] or in respect of terrorism in Northern Ireland.[54] The government is responsible for the structure of broadcasting as well as for financing the BBC.

Commercial television and radio

Television and radio services financed by advertising are now regulated by the Broadcasting Acts 1990 and 1996, the latter responding to demands presented by new technology in the form of digital television. The Independent Television Commission is a body corporate, whose members are appointed by the Secretary of State to regulate the provision of television services which are provided within the UK other than by the BBC and by the Welsh Fourth Channel Authority. By virtue of amendments introduced in 1996, its regulatory duties extend to what are referred to as 'multiplex services' and 'digital additional services'. The Commission is under a duty to provide both a wide range of services and fair and effective competition in the provision of services, a duty which applies also in respect of their licensing activities under Part I of the 1996 Act. Provided that certain quality thresholds laid down in the 1990 Act are met, the licences for Channel 3 television must be awarded to the highest bidder, although there are several restrictions as to who may be a licence holder (political organisations are barred). Restrictions also apply to newspaper proprietors, although these were amended by the 1996 Act to 'prevent those groups having 20% or more of national newspaper circulation from acquiring Channel 3 [and Channel 5] licences'.[55] Controversially, however, 'this restriction does not apply to the emerging markets of cable, satellite and digital terrestrial broadcasting'.[56] Licences issued under the 1996 Act are not issued to the highest cash bidders, but by having regard to the extent to which 'the award of the licence to each applicant would be calculated to promote the development of digital television broadcasting in the United Kingdom otherwise than by satellite'.[57]

Important restrictions on what may be broadcast are contained in s 6 of the 1990 Act. This requires the ITC to be satisfied that (a) nothing is included in the programmes which offends against good taste or decency, or is likely to encourage or incite to crime, or to lead to disorder, or be offensive to public feeling; (b) all news is presented with due accuracy and impartiality; (c) due impartiality is preserved in respect of matters of political or industrial controversy or relating to current public policy; and (d) due responsibility is exercised with respect to the content of any religious programmes and in particular that any such programmes do not involve any improper exploitation of any susceptibilities of those watching the programmes.[58] Regarding (c) (due impartiality),

[52] Cm 3152, 1996.
[53] On the handling of press and public information during the Falklands conflict, see HC 17 (1982–83) and Cmnd 8820, 1983. On the protection of military information in general, see Cmnd 9112, 1983.
[54] See Windlesham and Rampton, *Report on 'Death on the Rock'* (government pressure on the Independent Broadcasting Authority).
[55] HL Deb, 16 January 1996, col 473.
[56] Ibid. See Gibbons, pp 204–26.
[57] Broadcasting Act 1996, s 8.
[58] Cf Broadcasting Act 1990, s 47(4), (5).

the ITC is to draw up a code giving guidance as to the rules to be observed. The code will indicate to such extent as the Commission considers appropriate what due impartiality does and does not require, as well as ways in which due impartiality may be achieved in connection with particular kinds of programmes. The rules are also to specify that due impartiality does not require absolute neutrality on every issue or detachment from fundamental democratic principles (whatever that may mean). Presumably this is designed to ensure that due impartiality is not used to prevent controversial programmes about extremist organisations. The 1990 Act also contains strict rules on advertising: no advertisements may be directed to political ends or relate to any industrial dispute. In the latter case an exception is made if the advertisement is by the government. One effect of these rules is that there can be no television advertising by political parties during general election campaigns, unlike in many other countries.

The Broadcasting Standards Commission[59]

The Broadcasting Act 1996 established the Broadcasting Standards Commission (BSC) which replaced two different bodies which had been regulated by the Broadcasting Act 1990, these being the Broadcasting Complaints Commission (BCC) and the Broadcasting Standards Council. Appointed by the Secretary of State for Culture, Media and Sport, the Commission has two principal tasks, the first of which is regulatory or standard setting, the second being the adjudication of complaints. So far as the first is concerned, the Commission is required to draw up a code for dealing with unjust or unfair treatment in programmes as well as the unwarranted infringement of privacy in, or in connection with, the obtaining of material included in such programmes. It is also under a duty to draw up a code of practice giving guidance on practices to be followed in connection with the portrayal of sex and violence and on standards of taste and decency generally. So far as the Commission's second task is concerned, it must consider and adjudicate on complaints which relate either to unjust or unfair treatment on the one hand,[60] or to the unwarranted invasion of privacy on the other.[61] It may also deal with complaints about the portrayal of sex and violence or alleged failures of programmes to attain standards of taste and decency. The former are referred to in the Act as 'fairness complaints', the latter as 'standards complaints'.[62]

The Commission is authorised to deal with fairness complaints only if made by the individual affected or by someone authorised by him or her,[63] and it may refuse to entertain a fairness complaint relating to unjust or unfair treatment if the person

---

[59] For a good account, see Gibbons, pp 264–74.

[60] Cf *R v Broadcasting Complaints Commission, ex p BBC, The Times*, 26 May 1994 (a complaint could not be made by a researcher on a programme complaining of unfair treatment. The complainant's interest had to be in the subject matter of the programme).

[61] Cf *R v Broadcasting Complaints Commission, ex p BBC, The Times*, 16 October 1992 (the right to complain about invasion of privacy applies not only to the broadcast itself but also to the techniques used to collect information for a programme). Cf also *R v Broadcasting Complaints Commission, ex p Granada Television Ltd, The Times*, 16 December 1994 (a broadcast may invade privacy even though the matter had previously been reported and the matter was already in the public domain).

[62] As was pointed out in relation to one of the Commission's predecessor bodies (the Broadcasting Standards Council) this is 'an extremely interesting body from the public perspective' in that it performs 'the legislative power to make a binding Code of Practice, the executive power to monitor programmes and make complaints concerning them, and the judicial power to hold hearings and make findings on complaints about breaches of the Code' (F Coleman [1993] PL 488, at p 512). But as we saw in ch 14 it is not the only regulatory body of this kind.

[63] A complaint may be made by a company alleging an infringment of its privacy: 'A company does have activities of a private nature which need protection from unwarranted intrusion.' See *R v Broadcasting Standards Commission, ex p BBC* [2001] QB 885.

making the complaint does not have a sufficient interest to justify making the complaint.[64] A fairness complaint may also be refused if it is not made in good time, while a standards complaint must normally be made within two weeks in the case of a television programme and three weeks in the case of radio. Other restrictions on complaints mean that they cannot be considered where the matter complained of is the subject of court proceedings, while in the case of a fairness complaint jurisdiction may be denied if it appears to the Commission that the person affected has a remedy by way of legal action in a court of law. The Commission sits in private to hear complaints, although it has a discretion in the case of standards complaints to hear these in public. It may direct the broadcasting authority to publish a summary of the complaint together with the Commission's findings or observations. The Commission does not, however, have the power to order any compensation to be paid to the victim of unfair or unjust treatment, although its intervention may help to prevent any continuation or recurrence of the offending conduct. At least one half of the costs of the Commission are met by the industry itself, which is under a duty to arrange for the publication of regular announcements publicising the BSC. It is proposed that the work of the BSC will be transferred to OFCOM, a new communications regulator announced by the government, which will also assume the responsibilities of a number of other regulatory bodies in the broadcasting field.

The role of the courts

A few attempts have been made to challenge broadcasting content in the Courts. A difficulty with the BBC, however, is that it was established under the prerogative and, at least until the *CCSU* case,[65] it was unclear to what extent those exercising power under the prerogative were subject to judicial review. As late as 1983, the High Court in Northern Ireland was unwilling to enforce the BBC's policy of political impartiality in an action brought by the Workers' Party contesting election broadcasting.[66] It now appears to be accepted, however, that the BBC is subject to judicial review.[67] So in *Houston v BBC*,[68] an interim interdict was granted to restrain the corporation from broadcasting in Scotland an extended interview with the Prime Minister three days before the local government elections. It was accepted that the pursuers had established a prima facie case that the broadcast would violate the BBC's duty, under the terms of its licence, to treat controversial subjects with due impartiality and that the balance of convenience favoured the granting of relief to prevent the programme being broadcast until after the close of the poll.

The former IBA, a statutory body, was thus an easier target in legal proceedings.

> In *Attorney-General, ex rel McWhirter v IBA*, McWhirter, a member of the public, sought an injunction against the IBA to stop a film being shown about Andy Warhol which according to press reports contained matter offending against good taste and decency. An interim injunction was granted by the Court of Appeal at a time when members of the IBA had not seen the film. Some days later, the injunction was lifted since the court was then satisfied that the

---

[64] Cf *R v Broadcasting Complaints Commission, ex p Channel Four Television*, *The Times*, 6 January 1995 (the term 'direct interest' had to be broadly construed, even if it meant that 'too many complaints' would be made). But cf *R v Broadcasting Complaints Commission, ex p BBC*, *The Times*, 24 February 1995 (complaint by National Council for One Parent Families refused on the ground that it did not have a sufficiently direct interest in a 'Panorama' programme which was said to build up a false picture of lone parents by using misleading and false information).

[65] *Council of Civil Service Unions v Minister for the Civil Service* [1985] AC 374.

[66] *Lynch v BBC* [1983] NILR 193.

[67] See C Munro, NLJ, 14 April 1995, p 518, NLJ, 4 October 1996, p 1433.

[68] 1995 SLT 1305. See also *R v BBC, ex p Referendum Party*, *The Times*, 29 April 1997.

IBA had performed its statutory duty and there were no grounds on which the court should interfere with the IBA's decision. Lawton LJ said, 'In the realm of good taste and decency, whose frontiers are ill-defined, I find it impossible to say that the (IBA) have crossed from the permissible into the unlawful.' Although the interim injunction had been sought by McWhirter in his own name, the court ruled that such proceedings required the consent of the Attorney-General, since the individual had no locus standi to apply for the injunction himself.[69]

While this case lays down the admirable principle that the IBA like everyone else is required to observe the law and that the IBA's decisions are subject to judicial review, the court did not show a desire to assume the role of censor, nor indeed would such a role be desirable. A similar restraint has been shown in the cases which have been brought to challenge party election broadcasts (more fully explained in chapter 9 D) and now the operation of the statutory restrictions on political advertising,[70] although there are exceptions.[71] There are also cases where the television or radio company itself may be the subject of legal proceedings.

In *R v Central Independent Television plc*[72] the respondents were due to broadcast a programme on the work of the obscene publications squad of Scotland Yard and in particular about the work of detectives engaged in tracing a man who was imprisoned on two charges of indecency. The man had previously been married to Mrs R who was the mother of his child and there was concern that the programme contained scenes which would identify the mother and the child, causing the latter distress. Invoking the parental jurisdiction of the court, the mother moved successfully to have the moving pictures of the father obscured, a decision reversed by the Court of Appeal which held that the press and broadcasters were entitled to publish the results of criminal proceedings, even though 'the families of those convicted had a heavy burden to bear and the effect of publicity on small children might be very serious'.

In a robust defence of freedom of expression, in a case where it was perhaps unnecessary, Hoffmann LJ said:

Publication may cause needless pain, distress and damage to individuals or harm to other aspects of the public interest. But a freedom which is restricted to what judges think to be responsible or in the public interest is no freedom. Freedom means the right to publish things which government and judges, however well motivated, think should not be published. It means the right to say things which 'right-thinking people' regard as dangerous or irresponsible. This freedom is subject only to clearly defined exceptions laid down by common law or statute.

It is to a consideration of some of these exceptions that we now turn.

D. Offences against the state and public order

Sedition

It is an offence at common law to publish a seditious libel or to utter seditious words. In 1886, at a trial of Socialist leaders for speeches made at a demonstration in Trafalgar Square which had been followed by disorder, a seditious intention was defined very widely as:

---

[69] [1973] QB 629.
[70] *R v Radio Authority, ex p Bull* [1997] 2 All ER 561.
[71] *Wilson v Independent Broadcasting Authority* 1979 SLT 279. Cf *Wilson v Independent Broadcasting Authority* 1988 SLT 276. Also C Munro NLJ, 4 October 1996, p 1433, and NLJ, 11 April 1997, p 528.
[72] [1994] Fam 192.

an intention to bring into hatred or contempt, or to excite disaffection against the person of, Her Majesty . . . or the government and constitution of the United Kingdom, as by law established, or either House of Parliament, or the administration of justice, or to excite Her Majesty's subjects to attempt, otherwise than by lawful means, the alteration of any matter in Church or State by law established, or to raise discontent or disaffection amongst Her Majesty's subjects, or to promote feelings of ill-will and hostility between different classes of such subjects.[73]

But at the same time it was explained that it is not seditious to point out errors or defects in the government or constitution of the United Kingdom, to seek to bring about changes in Church or State by lawful means or, with a view to their removal, to draw attention to matters which were tending to produce ill-will or hostility between classes of Her Majesty's subjects. In prosecutions for seditious libel, the element of incitement to violence was stressed. In *R v Aldred*, a journal advocating independence for India published articles which commended political assassination soon after an assassination by an Indian nationalist had occurred in London; Coleridge J told the jury that sedition implied violence or lawlessness in some form and said, 'the test is this: was the language used calculated, or was it not, to promote public disorder or physical force or violence in a matter of State?' Aldred, editor of the journal, was convicted.[74]

The test of whether the words were *calculated* (that is, likely) to promote violence was not followed in *R v Caunt*, where Birkett J directed the jury that proof of *intention* to promote violence was an essential part of the offence:

At a time shortly before the creation of the state of Israel, when British troops in Palestine were being subjected to terrorist atrocities and soldiers had been murdered, the editor of the *Morecambe and Heysham Visitor* published a leading article attacking British Jews in virulent terms and calling for Jews to be ostracised. The article ended with a suggestion that violence might be the only way to bring British Jews to the sense of their responsibility to the country in which they lived. Notwithstanding these words, the jury acquitted the editor of having published a seditious libel.[75]

Such a case provided a severe test for the principle of free speech. A possible comment on the outcome is that the jury shared the editor's views or at least did not find his anti-Semitism so abhorrent to them that he should be punished for having published them. On the other hand, given the judge's direction on the law of seditious libel, the jury may not have been satisfied beyond reasonable doubt that the editor was intending to incite his readers to violence: in evidence he had denied any such intention, while adhering to the words of his article. It is fundamental in such a case that a jury does not give reasons for its verdict, nor need the jurors each come to their decision by the same route. Nevertheless, the scope of sedition has appeared to change in the sense that the prosecution must now show an intention to promote violence and disorder over and above the strong criticism of public affairs.[76] Further developments took place in *R v Chief Metropolitan Stipendiary Magistrate, ex p Choudhury*.[77]

This case concerned an attempt to bring criminal charges against Mr Salman Rushdie, author of *The Satanic Verses*. It was alleged that publication constituted seditious libel on the ground that 'it raised widespread discontent and disaffection among Her Majesty's subjects, contrary

---

[73] *R v Burns* (1886) 16 Cox CC 355, citing Stephen's *Digest of Criminal Law*. And see Williams, *Keeping the Peace*, ch 8.
[74] (1909) 22 Cox CC 1.
[75] See *An Editor on Trial*, 1948; and E C S Wade (1948) 64 LQR 203.
[76] Smith and Hogan, *Criminal Law*, p 740; cf *Boucher v R* [1951] SCR 265.
[77] [1991] 1 QB 429.

to common law'. When the magistrate refused to issue the summons, the applicants sought judicial review of his decision, thereby providing an opportunity for reconsideration of the scope of seditious libel. Agreeing with the magistrate, the Divisional Court followed the Supreme Court of Canada in *Boucher* v R,[78] where it was held that 'the seditious intention on which a prosecution for seditious libel must be founded is an intention to incite to violence or to create public disturbance or disorder against His Majesty or the institutions of government'. Apart from thus reinforcing the requirement of an intention to promote violence, this indicates a further qualification: namely that sedition can no longer be constituted by an intention to promote feelings of ill-will and hostility between different classes of subjects. According to Watkins LJ, not only must there be proof of an incitement to violence in such cases, 'but it must be violence or resistance or defiance for the purpose of disturbing constituted authority'. In this case, given the absence of any element of attacking, obstructing, or undermining public authority, the court held that the magistrate was bound not to issue the summonses.

It would thus appear that there is no basis in the future for prosecution for sedition in cases such as *Caunt*.

Incitement to disaffection[79]

Parliament has on several occasions legislated to prevent the spread of disaffection, mainly to protect members of the armed forces, who might otherwise be exposed to attempts to persuade them to disobey their orders. The Incitement to Mutiny Act 1797, passed following the Nore mutiny, made it a felony maliciously and advisedly to endeavour to seduce members of the armed forces from their duty and allegiance to the Crown or to incite members to commit any act of mutiny. Although the 1797 Act has been repealed, the Aliens Restriction (Amendment) Act 1919, s 3, still prohibits an alien from causing sedition or disaffection among the civil population as well as among the armed forces; and it is an offence for any alien to promote or interfere in an industrial dispute in any industry in which he or she has not been bona fide engaged in the United Kingdom for at least two years preceding an alleged offence. The Police Act 1996, s 91, replacing legislation first passed in 1919 at a time of serious unrest within the police, prohibits acts calculated to cause disaffection among police officers or to induce them to withhold their services or commit breaches of discipline. Under the Incitement to Disaffection Act 1934, which passed through Parliament against severe criticism from a variety of quarters,[80] it is an offence maliciously and advisedly to endeavour to seduce a member of the armed forces from his duty or allegiance.

The 1934 Act contains stringent provisions for the prevention and detection of the offence, including wide powers of search on reasonable suspicion, but a warrant may be issued only by a High Court judge. Moreover, it is an offence for any person, with intent to commit or to aid, counsel or procure commission of the main offence, to have in his possession or under his control any document of such a nature that the distribution of copies among members of the forces would constitute that offence. Notwithstanding the safeguards in the Act, it does restrain certain forms of political propaganda; and it could be used to suppress or interfere with the distribution of pacifist literature. Prosecutions under the Act in England require the consent of the Director of Public Prosecutions. This consent was given between 1973 and 1975 for prosecution

---

[78] [1951] SCR 265.
[79] Bunyan, *The Political Police in Britain*, pp 28–36; Ewing and Gearty, *The Struggle for Civil Liberties*, chs 2–5.
[80] See Ewing and Gearty, ch 5.

of members of a campaign for the withdrawal of British troops from Northern Ireland in respect of leaflets which they had prepared. One conviction was upheld by the Court of Appeal.[81] The accused has a right to jury trial: it would be a matter for the jury to decide whether a leaflet which gave information to a soldier about procedures for leaving the army and his or her rights as a soldier was an attempt to seduce him or her from duty or allegiance to the Crown.

Blasphemy

While it continues to be a common law offence to utter or publish blasphemous words and writings, the old precedents which held that it is blasphemy to deny the truth of the Christian religion or the existence of God have ceased to be helpful. 'If the decencies of controversy are observed, even the fundamentals of religion may be attacked without the writer being guilty of blasphemy.'[82] In the absence of modern authorities, it became unclear what the essentials of the offence were. But in *R v Lemon*, the publishers of *Gay News* were in 1977 convicted by a jury of publishing a blasphemous libel, in the form of a poem by James Kirkup that linked homosexual practices with the life and crucifixion of Christ. The House of Lords held by three to two that it was sufficient for the prosecution to prove that blasphemous material had been published and not necessary to prove that the defendants intended to blaspheme. In the view of the House, a blasphemous libel was material calculated to outrage and insult a Christian's religious feelings; it is not an element of the offence that the publication must tend to lead to a breach of the peace.[83] More recently, in *Ex p Choudhury*,[84] a Divisional Court confirmed that the offence is limited to Christianity and does not extend to other religions, in this case Islam. Although prosecutions for blasphemy are now largely unknown, the law is by no means yet redundant.

The continuing significance of blasphemy was revealed in *Wingrove v United Kingdom*[85] where the British Board of Film Classification (designated for this purpose by the Video Recordings Act 1984) refused to issue a classification certificate for a film entitled 'Visions of Ecstasy' which included an 'intense erotic' moment between St Teresa and Jesus Christ. The decision was taken on the ground that the film was blasphemous, and the decision was upheld by the Video Appeals Committee. In rejecting a complaint that this censorship violated the right to freedom of expression, the European Court of Human Rights held that it could be justified under art 10(2) of the Convention; this permits a wide margin of appreciation to contracting states 'when regulating freedom of expression in relation to matters liable to offend intimate personal convictions within the sphere of morals or, especially, religion'. Although the law continues to attract criticism, in 2002 there were no serious plans to abolish the offence, as the Law Commission proposed as long ago as 1985.[86] Government proposals to introduce an offence of incitement to religious hatred in the Anti-Terrorism, Crime and Security Bill 2001 had to be dropped in the face of political opposition, although religiously

---

[81] *R v Arrowsmith* [1975] QB 678; and see *Arrowsmith v UK* (1978) 3 EHRR 218 (no infringement of European Convention on Human Rights).

[82] *R v Ramsay and Foote* (1883) 15 Cox CC 231, 238 (Coleridge CJ). See also *Bowman v Secular Society* [1917] AC 406; and *R v Gott* (1922) 16 Cr App R 87.

[83] *R v Lemon* [1979] AC 617. And see *Gay News Ltd v UK* (1982) 5 EHRR 123.

[84] [1991] 1 QB 429; Poulter, *Ethnicity, Law and Human Rights*, pp 98–106.

[85] (1996) 24 EHRR 1.

[86] Law Commission No 145 (HC 442 (1985)). See also Law Commission's Working Paper No 79, Offences Against Religion and Public Worship. See further St J Robilliard (1981) 44 MLR 556.

aggravated offences now attract higher sentences along with racially motivated offences.[87]

Incitement to racial hatred

It has long been recognised that the preservation of public order justifies the imposition of criminal sanctions on those who utter threats, abuse or insults in public places which are likely to give rise to a breach of the peace.[88] In 1965, when Parliament first created machinery to deal with racial discrimination,[89] an offence of incitement to racial hatred was created which was not dependent on proof of an immediate threat to public order. The reason for this was the belief that racial hatred itself contains the seeds of violence.[90] The position is now governed by the Public Order Act 1986, which deals specifically with 'racial hatred', taken to mean 'hatred against a group of persons defined by reference to colour, race, nationality (including citizenship) or ethnic or national origins' (s 17).[91] This replaces measures enacted in the Race Relations Act 1976 and previously in the Race Relations Act 1965.[92] By s 18 of the 1986 Act, it is an offence for a person to use threatening, abusive or insulting words or behaviour or to display any material which is threatening, abusive or insulting if he does so with intent to stir up racial hatred or if in the circumstances racial hatred is likely to be stirred up.[93] The Act applies to publicising or distributing such material (s 19),[94] theatrical performances (s 20), the distribution, showing or playing of a recording of visual images or sounds (s 21), and television and radio broadcasts (s 22).

A new offence in s 23 of the Act relates to the possession of material which if published or displayed would amount to an offence under the Act. Where there are reasonable grounds for suspecting that a person has possession of such material, a justice of the peace may grant a warrant to a police constable authorising the entry and search of premises for such material. It is not an offence to publish a fair and accurate report of proceedings in Parliament, or of proceedings publicly heard before a tribunal or court where the report is published contemporaneously with the proceedings (s 26). No prosecution in England and Wales may occur without the consent of the Attorney-General (s 27). Although these are wide-ranging restrictions, they are justifiable primarily because a serious threat to personal security and dignity, not to mention public order, is inherent in certain forms of political and social expression. Sadly, legislation of this kind will not in itself necessarily reduce the occurrence of racial violence and harassment in the streets. But it may help, as in a more specific context may the Football (Offences) Act 1991 (as amended), which by s 3 makes indecent or 'racialist' chanting at football matches a criminal offence.[95]

---

[87] Anti-terrorism, Crime and Security Act 2001, s 39.
[88] Ch 24.
[89] Ch 19 A.
[90] See D G T Williams [1966] Crim LR 320; Lester and Bindman, *Race and Law*, ch 10; and P M Leopold [1977] PL 389.
[91] As amended by the Anti-terrorism, Crime and Security Act 2001, s 37.
[92] *R v Britton* [1967] 2 QB 51; *R v Malik* [1968] 1 All ER 582. See also A Dickey [1968] Crim LR 48.
[93] It is not now necessary, as it was under the 1965 Act, to prove that the accused intended to stir up racial hatred: in practice, such proof had been too stringent a requirement for the law to be an effective restraint on racist propaganda. See also W J Wolffe [1987] PL 85 and S Poulter [1991] PL 371.
[94] The offence under s 19 is an arrestable offence for the purposes of the Police and Criminal Evidence Act 1984 (Criminal Justice and Public Order Act 1994, s 155).
[95] See also Football (Disorder) Act 2000, Sch 1, amending Football Spectators Act 1989.

E. Obscene publications

Before the Act of 1959

It resulted from the development of the law concerning the printing of books that, as with seditious, blasphemous and other libels, it became an offence punishable by the common law courts to publish obscene material. This jurisdiction was exercised for the first time in *Curl's* case when the court held that it was an offence to publish a book which tended to corrupt morals and was against the King's peace.[96] The flourishing business of pornography in the Victorian underworld led to the Obscene Publications Act 1857. This Act gave the police power to search premises, seize obscene publications kept for sale, and bring them before a magistrates' court for destruction. The Act did not define 'obscene' but its sponsor, Lord Campbell, stated that it was to apply 'exclusively to works written for the single purpose of corrupting the morals of youth, and of a nature calculated to shock the common feelings of decency in any well regulated mind.'[97] In 1868, in *R v Hicklin*, Cockburn CJ declared the test for obscenity to be

> whether the tendency of the matter charged as obscenity is to deprave and corrupt those whose minds are open to such immoral influences and into whose hands a publication of this sort may fall.[98]

This test came to dominate the English law of obscenity. It required account to be taken of the circumstances of publication: in *Hicklin's* case, Cockburn CJ said that immunity for a medical treatise depended on the circumstances, since the publication of some medical details would not be fit for boys and girls to see. But the test did not permit the author's intention to be taken into account. Although the tendency to deprave and corrupt was often assumed from the character of a book, who might the potential readers be? In 1954, in *R v Reiter*, the Court of Criminal Appeal took the view that a jury should direct their attention to the result of a book falling into the hands of young people.[99] But a few months later, in *R v Secker Warburg Ltd*, Stable J asked: 'Are we to take our literary standards as being the level of something that is suitable for the decently brought up young female aged 14?' He continued:

> A mass of literature, great literature from many angles, is wholly unsuitable for reading by the adolescent, but that does not mean that the publisher is guilty of a criminal offence for making those works available to the general public.[100]

Other difficulties in the law included the lack of authority establishing that the publication of matter prima facie obscene might nonetheless be for the public good; the use of the 1857 Act against serious literature; the failure of the 1857 Act to enable a publisher or author to defend a work against destruction; and the tendency of prosecutors to take selected passages of a book out of context. A lengthy campaign by publishers and authors led to the Obscene Publications Act 1959.[101]

---

[96] (1727) 17 St Tr 153; Robertson, *Obscenity*, ch 2.
[97] HL Deb, 25 June 1857, col 329.
[98] (1868) LR 3 QB 360, 371.
[99] [1954] 2 QB 16.
[100] [1954] 2 All ER 683, 686 (Kauffman's *The Philanderer*).
[101] See HC 123 (1957–58); and Robertson, *Obscenity*, pp 40–4.

The Obscene Publications Acts 1959 and 1964

The 1959 Act, which does not apply to Scotland, sought both to provide for the protection of literature and to strengthen the law against pornography. For the purposes of the 1959 Act (but not of other Acts in which the word 'obscene' is used):[102]

> an article shall be deemed to be obscene if its effect or (where the article comprises two or more distinct items) the effect of any one of its items[103] is, if taken as a whole, such as to tend to deprave and corrupt persons who are likely, having regard to all relevant circumstances, to read, see or hear the matter contained or embodied in it (s 1(1)).

A wide definition of 'article' (s 1(2)) includes books, pictures, films, records and such things as film negatives used in producing obscene articles[104] and video cassettes.[105] It is an offence to publish an obscene article, whether for gain or not, or to have obscene articles in one's possession, ownership or control for the purpose of publication for gain or with a view to such publication,[106] whether for sale within Britain or abroad.[107] The definition of 'publishing' includes distributing, circulating, selling, hiring and, for example, showing pictures or playing records; since 1991 it includes television and sound broadcasting.[108] No person may be prosecuted for an offence at common law consisting of the publication of an article when the essence of the offence is that the matter is obscene.[109] It is a defence to prove that publication of an obscene article is justified 'as being for the public good on the ground that it is in the interests of science, literature, art or learning or other objects of general concern'. Expert evidence on the literary, artistic, scientific or other merits of an article is admissible to establish or negative the defence of public good.[110]

The 1959 Act, s 3, confers search, seizure and forfeiture powers similar to those in the 1857 Act. A warrant may be obtained by a constable (or the Director of Public Prosecutions)[111] from a magistrate for the search of specified premises, stalls or vehicles, where there is reasonable suspicion that obscene articles are kept for publication for gain. When a search is made, articles believed to be obscene and also documents relating to a trade or business may be seized. The seized articles must be brought before a magistrate. When notice has been given to the occupier of the premises to show cause why the articles should not be forfeited, the magistrates' court may order forfeiture if satisfied that the articles are obscene and were kept for publication for gain. The owner, author or maker of the articles may also appear to defend them against forfeiture. The defence that publication is for the public good is available and expert evidence relating to the merits of the articles may be called. In these proceedings there is no right to the decision of a jury, but there are rights of appeal to the Crown Court or the High Court. Because of certain defects in the 1959 Act, the Act of 1964 was passed to strengthen the law against publishing obscene matter. Inter alia, the Act made it an offence to have an obscene article for publication for the purposes of gain[112] and authorised a forfeiture order to be made following a conviction under the 1959 Act.

---

[102] *R v Anderson* [1972] 1 QB 304, 317 (*Oz, School Kids Issue*).

[103] On the item by item test, see *R v Anderson*, ibid, at 312.

[104] 1964 Act, s 2, the sequel to *Straker v DPP* [1963] 1 QB 926.

[105] *A-G's Reference (No 5 of 1980)* [1980] 3 All ER 816.

[106] 1959 Act, s 2(1), as amended in 1964. See *R v Taylor* [1995] 1 Cr App R 131 (publication where films depicting obscene acts are developed, printed and returned to the owner).

[107] *Gold Star Publications Ltd v DPP* [1981] 2 All ER 257; and see (1983) 5 EHRR 591.

[108] Broadcasting Act 1990, s 162, amending 1959 Act, s 1(3).

[109] 1959 Act, s 2(4). This does not prevent a prosecution for conspiracy to corrupt public morals: see later. In the case of cinema performances, such prosecution is excluded by 1959 Act, s 2(4A), inserted by Criminal Law Act 1977, s 53.

[110] 1959 Act, s 4.

[111] Criminal Justice Act 1967, s 25.

[112] Cf *Mella v Monahan* [1961] Crim LR 175.

One difficulty is the 1959 Act's definition of obscenity as 'a tendency to deprave and corrupt'. The definition makes it impossible to rely on such synonyms as 'repulsive', 'filthy', 'loathsome' or 'lewd'[113] and requires the jury to consider whether the effect of a book is to tend to deprave and corrupt a significant proportion of those likely to read it. 'What is a significant proportion is entirely for the jury to decide.'[114] Lord Wilberforce has said: 'An article cannot be considered as obscene in itself: it can only be so in relation to its likely readers.'[115] Experienced police officers may for practical purposes not be susceptible to being depraved and corrupted,[116] but it seems that a man may be corrupted more than once.[117] Although the circumstances in which articles are sold are relevant, it is no defence for booksellers to prove that most of their sales are made to middle-aged men who are already addicted to pornography; articles may 'deprave and corrupt' the mind without any overt sexual activity by the reader resulting.[118] Obscenity is not confined to sexual matters: a book dealing with the effects of drug taking may be obscene,[119] and so may cards depicting scenes of violence when sold with chewing gum to children.[120] Other difficulties have been caused by the defence of public good. Expert evidence relating to literary and other merits may not deal with the issue of whether the article is obscene,[121] except when the jury needs to be informed of the likely effect of an article on children; it is not admissible to establish that obscene articles may have a therapeutic effect on some individuals.[122]

Other legislation on indecency and pornography

Fewer legal difficulties arise in the exercise of other powers of restriction on moral grounds. Under the Customs Consolidation Act 1876, s 42, and the Customs and Excise Management Act 1979, s 49, customs officers may seize and destroy 'indecent or obscene' books and other articles being imported into the United Kingdom;[123] and the Postal Services Act 2000, s 85, seeks to prevent the postal services being used for the dispatch of 'indecent or obscene' articles. These statutes do not provide a defence of publication for the public good, and the test appears to be whether an article offends current standards of propriety.[124] The concept of indecency is no doubt as subjective as obscenity, but implies a less serious judgment and in practice is easier to apply than obscenity.[125] A difficulty with the customs restrictions has arisen in the context of EC law. Article 28 of the EC Treaty facilitates the free movement of goods by prohibiting restrictions on imports from other EC countries. Although art 30 allows import restrictions on the grounds of public morality, in Case 121/85 *Conegate Ltd* v *Customs and Excise Commissioners*[126] it was held that this cannot be used to restrict the import of indecent material which may be manufactured and sold in Britain, but it can be used

[113] *R v Anderson* [1972] 1 QB 304; cf the perceptive analysis by Windeyer J in *Crowe v Grahame* (1968) 41 AJLR 402, 409.
[114] *R v Calder & Boyars Ltd* [1969] 1 QB 151, 168. But it is 'more than a negligible number' (*R v O'Sullivan* [1995] 1 Cr App R 455).
[115] *DPP v Whyte* [1972] AC 849, 860.
[116] *R v Clayton and Halsey* [1963] 1 QB 163.
[117] *Shaw v DPP* [1962] AC 220, 228 (CCA).
[118] *DPP v Whyte* [1972] AC 849, 867.
[119] *Calder (Publications) Ltd v Powell* [1965] 1 QB 509; *R v Skirving* [1985] QB 819.
[120] *DPP v A & BC Chewing Gum Ltd* [1968] 1 QB 159.
[121] *R v Anderson*, note 113 above. And see *R v Stamford* [1972] 2 QB 391.
[122] *DPP v Jordan* [1977] AC 699; and see *A-G's Reference (No 3 of 1977)* [1978] 3 All ER 1166.
[123] See *Derrick v Commissioners of Customs and Excise* [1972] 2 QB 28; C Manchester [1981] Crim LR 531, [1983] Crim LR 64.
[124] *R v Stamford* [1972] 2 QB 391.
[125] See *McGowan v Langmuir* 1931 JC 10 (Lord Sands).
[126] [1987] QB 254.

to restrict the import of obscene material.[127] There is no breach of art 28 where legal products may only be sold in licensed premises.[128]

The Protection of Children Act 1978[129] tightened up the law with regard to indecent photographs (including films and video recordings) involving children under 16. Offences under the Act include the taking and distribution of indecent photographs of children and the distribution, showing or advertisement of such photographs. Prosecutions require the consent of the Director of Public Prosecutions. By the Criminal Justice Act 1988,[130] it is an offence for a person to have any indecent photograph of a child in his or her possession. The Indecent Displays (Control) Act 1981 deals with the public nuisance aspects of pornography, making it an offence to display publicly any indecent matter, where the display is visible from a public place.[131] A public place is a place to which the public have access, except either on payment for the display or within a shop where the public have passed a warning notice, provided in each case that entry is limited to persons over 18. The exceptions to the Act include television broadcasts, displays in art galleries or museums that are not visible from outside the premises, and matter contained within the performance of plays and films. Since the Act contains no definition of indecency, 'indecent' will probably receive the same interpretation as in the Customs and Post Office legislation.[132] In 1982, district councils were authorised to license sex shops and sex cinemas, by resolving to introduce a licensing scheme.[133] The grounds on which a council may refuse a licence include the reason that the existing number of such establishments in the area is equal to or exceeds the number which the council considers to be appropriate.

Common law offences

The specific objectives of these recent Acts prevent them from being a grave restriction on the liberty of expression. The same cannot be said of the common law offence of conspiracy to corrupt public morals. In *Shaw* v *DPP*, the appellant had published the *Ladies' Directory*, an illustrated magazine containing names, addresses and other details of prostitutes and their services. The House of Lords upheld Shaw's conviction for the offence of conspiracy to corrupt public morals. Lord Simonds accepted that the law must be related to the changing standards of life, having regard to fundamental human values and the purposes of society; he said that 'there remains in the courts of law a residual power to enforce the supreme and fundamental purpose of the law, to conserve not only the safety and order but also the moral welfare of the State'.[134] It was the jury which provided a safeguard against the launching of prosecutions to suppress unpopular or unorthodox views. Lord Reid, dissenting, rejected the view that the court was guardian of public morals. This controversial decision derived in part

---

[127] On which see *Henn* v *DPP* [1981] AC 850. Cf *R* v *Bow Street Metropolitan Stipendiary Magistrate, ex p Noncyp Ltd* [1990] 1 QB 123 (obscene articles imported from EC countries may be seized under customs legislation even although publication under the 1959 Act would not be an offence because of the public good defence in s 4). See also *Wright* v *Commissioners of Customs and Excise* [1999] 1 Cr App R 69 and *R* v *Forbes* [2001] 3 WLR 428. For a good discussion, see Weatherill and Beaumont, *EU Law*, pp 528–30.

[128] *Case C-28/79, Quietlynn Ltd* v *Southend-on-Sea BC* [1991] 1 QB 454.

[129] As amended by the Criminal Justice and Public Order Act 1994.

[130] Section 160.

[131] See K D Ewing [1982] SLT (News) 55.

[132] See J L Lambert [1982] PL 226 and R T H Stone (1982) 45 MLR 62.

[133] Local Government (Miscellaneous Provisions) Act 1982, s 2 and Sch 3. The numerous cases include *Quietlynn Ltd* v *Plymouth City Council* [1988] QB 114.

[134] [1962] AC 220, 268. See D Seaborne Davies (1962) 6 JSPTL 104, J E Hall Williams (1961) 24 MLR 626 and Robertson, *Obscenity*, ch 8.

from the supposed offence of conspiracy to effect a public mischief, which was later held not to be part of criminal law.[135]

Although Shaw was also convicted for having published an obscene book, contrary to the 1959 Act, *Shaw*'s case enabled prosecutions to be brought at common law for conspiracy rather than for breaches of the 1959 Act. Thereafter the Law Officers assured the House of Commons that a conspiracy to corrupt public morals would not be charged so as to circumvent the 'public good' defence in the 1959 Act.[136] In *Knuller Ltd v DPP*, the House of Lords reaffirmed the decision in *Shaw*'s case. The appellants had published a magazine which contained advertisements by male homosexuals seeking to meet other homosexuals. The Lords upheld a conviction of the appellants for conspiracy to corrupt public morals, rejecting a defence based on the Sexual Offences Act 1967 by which homosexual acts between adult males in private had ceased to be an offence. A second conviction for conspiracy 'to outrage public decency' was quashed on the ground of misdirection, but a majority of the House held that at common law it was an offence to outrage public decency and also to conspire to outrage public decency; and that such a conspiracy could take the form of an agreement to insert outrageously indecent matter on the inside pages of a magazine sold in public.[137] Lords Reid and Diplock did not agree that 'outraging public decency' was an offence; Lord Reid said, 'To recognise this new crime would go contrary to the whole trend of public policy followed by Parliament in recent times.'[138]

The common law of conspiracy was reformed by the Criminal Law Act 1977, which created a new statutory offence of conspiracy. But the abolition of common law conspiracy is not to affect a conspiracy that involves an agreement to engage in conduct which tends to corrupt public morals or outrages public decency.[139] However, few prosecutions for conspiracy to corrupt public morals or to outrage public decency have been brought since *Knuller*. But one such case is *R v Gibson*,[140] in which both the owner of an art gallery and an artist were convicted for exhibiting a model's head to the ears of which were attached earrings made out of a freeze-dried human foetus of three or four months' gestation. The case raised the question whether a prosecution at common law to outrage public decency was precluded by s 2(4) of the Obscene Publications Act 1959, whereby common law proceedings are not to be brought where 'it is of the essence of the offence that the matter is obscene'. The Court of Appeal held that there are two broad types of offence involving obscenity and that the 1959 Act applied only in respect of one (those involving the corruption of public morals) but not the other (those which involve an outrage on public decency, whether or not public morals are involved). This decision may make it easier for the Crown to bring prosecutions at common law, thereby circumventing the defences which would otherwise be available in a prosecution brought under the Act. Of these, the most important is undoubtedly the public good defence in s 4.

Reform of the law

The law of obscenity and indecency was reviewed by a Home Office committee (chairman, Professor Bernard Williams) which reported in 1979.[141] The committee analysed the purposes for which regulation of obscenity was justified. It considered that the

---

[135] *DPP v Withers* [1975] AC 842.
[136] HC Deb, 3 June 1964, col 1212.
[137] See now *R v Walker* [1996] 1 Cr App R 111.
[138] *Knuller Ltd v DPP* [1973] AC 435, 459.
[139] Criminal Law Act 1977, s 5(3); cf s 53(3).
[140] [1990] 2 QB 619; M Childs [1991] PL 20.
[141] Cmnd 7772, 1979. See Simpson, *Pornography and Politics – the Williams Report in Retrospect*.

existing law should be scrapped and a fresh start made with a comprehensive new statute. In particular, terms such as 'obscene', 'indecency', 'deprave and corrupt' should be abandoned as having outlived their usefulness. The government did not accept these recommendations and developing technology has subsequently presented more new challenges for the legislation.[142] Since 1979, as we have seen, Parliament has legislated in a piecemeal manner that in important respects runs contrary to the Williams report. Further evidence of the tendency towards greater restriction is reflected by the provisions of the Criminal Justice and Public Order Act 1994 whereby offences under the Obscene Publications Acts 1959–64 are deemed to be serious arrestable offences for the purposes of the Police and Criminal Evidence Act 1984. It may be reflected also in the expressions of frustration by the courts in whose judgment 'the only way of stamping out this filthy trade is by imposing sentences of imprisonment on first offenders and all connected with the commercial exploitation of pornography'.[143] Judges continue to express difficulty with the compexity of the legislation[144] and a study published in 1998 doubted its efficacy in preventing the publication of pornography.[145]

But there was in 2002 no prospect of another governmental attempt to review the law with a view to its reform. On the contrary, one of the main challenges in this area in the immediate future relates to the internet, where there is a real concern about child pornography and the sexual solicitation of children, as well as problems of access by children to unsuitable material. Unlike other forms of electronic media there is no statutory regulation of the internet to regulate access to sexually explicit or other material (although internet service providers and internet users will be subject to ordinary civil and criminal liabilities, such as defamation and incitement to racial hatred).[146] In the UK, the matter is addressed by a further example of self-regulation, in the form of the Internet Watch Foundation which was established in 1996 by United Kingdom internet service providers to advise internet users about how best to restrict access to harmful or offensive content on the internet generally.[147] The Foundation is independent of government and, although it works very closely with government, the Foundation has no statutory powers. Internet users report material to the Foundation which they believe to be criminal: this can be for any reason, although complaints are overwhelmingly about child pornography. If on investigation the material is thought to be criminal, the internet service provider will be asked to remove it and the information will be passed to the police. The government has announced that the proposed new broadcasting regulator (OFCOM) will work with the IWF to strengthen ways of identifying suitable and unsuitable content on the internet.

F. Defamation

Criminal libel[148]

To publish defamatory material in writing became a criminal offence punishable by the common law courts after the abolition of Star Chamber in 1640. The justification

---

[142] On computer pornography, see HC 126 (1993–94).

[143] *R v Holloway* (1982) 4 Cr App R (S) 128. The Court of Appeal expressly repudiated the Williams committee: 'There is an evil in this kind of pornography. It is an evil which in our opinion has to be stopped.' But for evidence of serious problems in the enforcement of the law, see NLJ, 9 August 1996, p 1179.

[144] *R v O'Sullivan*, note 114 above.

[145] S Edwards [1998] Crim LR 843.

[146] See *Godfrey v Demon Internet Ltd* [2001] QB 201 (defamation). See generally on this hugely controversial issue, Akdeniz, Walker and Wall (eds), *The Internet, Law and Society*.

[147] Internet Watch Foundation, Annual Report (2001).

[148] J R Spencer [1977] Crim LR 383 and [1979] CLJ 60.

for treating libel as a criminal offence was considered to be the threat to the preservation of the peace which some libels presented. Today criminal proceedings are rarely instituted for libel. If they are, it is not necessary to prove that the libel was likely to cause a breach of the peace,[149] but a criminal libel must be a serious libel to justify invoking the criminal law. At common law, truth was no defence to a prosecution for libel but by the Libel Act 1843, truth is a defence if the accused also proves that the publication was for the public benefit. By the Law of Libel Amendment Act 1888, s 8, no prosecution may be commenced in respect of a libel in a newspaper without the order of a High Court judge. Prosecutions are rare but in 1976, Wien J gave an order enabling a private prosecution to be brought by Sir James Goldsmith against the publishers of *Private Eye* in respect of repeated allegations that Goldsmith was the ringleader of a conspiracy to obstruct the course of justice; the judge said that the press does not have licence to publish scandalous or scurrilous matter which is wholly without foundation.[150] In 1982, the Law Commission's provisional view was that criminal libel at common law should be abolished and replaced by a much narrower statutory offence, aimed at a person who publishes a deliberately defamatory statement which he or she knows or believes to be untrue, and is likely to cause the victim significant harm.[151] But it has been argued that the criminal law should be excluded from the area of defamation.[152]

Civil liability

The law of defamation seeks to resolve the conflict between the freedom of speech and publication and the right of the individual to maintain his or her reputation against improper attack.[153] Possibly because of this, defamation law is one of the most complex branches of civil liability. In principle, the law provides a remedy for false statements which expose a person to 'hatred, ridicule or contempt' or which tend to lower him or her 'in the estimation of right-thinking members of society generally'.[154] Defamation takes two main forms: (*a*) slander (defamation in a transitory form by spoken word or gesture) and (*b*) libel (defamation in a permanent form such as the written or printed word). By statute, words used in the course of broadcasting and of public performances in a theatre are treated as publication in permanent form.[155] With certain exceptions, slander is actionable only when the plaintiff can prove special damage as a result of the slander, whereas libel is actionable without such proof. Actions for defamation are one of the few surviving forms of civil action where either party has a right to insist on trial by jury.[156] When the judge rules that a statement is capable of being regarded as defamatory, it is the jury which decides whether the plaintiff has been defamed and if so the damages that he or she should recover. Substantial damages may be awarded for injury to reputation and may include exemplary damages[157]

---

[149] *R v Wicks* [1936] 1 All ER 384; *Gleaves v Deakin* [1980] AC 477.

[150] *Goldsmith v Pressdram Ltd* [1977] QB 83. And see *Desmond v Thorne* [1982] 3 All ER 268.

[151] Law Commission, Working Paper No 84, Criminal Libel. See also J R Spencer [1983] Crim LR 524 and Cmnd 5909, 1975, ch 16.

[152] G Robertson [1983] PL 208.

[153] For fuller accounts of the law of defamation, see textbooks on the law of tort and also Robertson, *Freedom, the Individual and the Law*, ch 7 and Report of Committee on Defamation, Cmnd 5909, 1975.

[154] *Sim v Stretch* (1936) 52 TLR 669, 671 (Lord Atkin). For an action to succeed, the publication must be read as a whole, rather than one or more isolated passages. See *Charleston v News Group Newspapers Ltd* [1995] 2 AC 65. But liability is strict: *E Hulton & Co v Jones* [1910] AC 20.

[155] Broadcasting Act 1990, s 166; and Theatres Act 1968, s 4.

[156] Supreme Court Act 1981, s 69. See *Alexander v Arts Council of Wales* [2001] 1 WLR 1840. There are exceptions, for example where the court is of the opinion that the trial will require a prolonged examination of documents.

[157] *Broome v Cassell and Co Ltd* [1972] AC 1027; *Riches v News Group Newspapers Ltd* [1986] QB 256. Cf *John v Mirror Group Newspapers* [1997] QB 586.

– designed 'to prevent a newspaper profiting from the libel by increasing its circulation'.[158] In fact many claims are settled out of court and newspapers often publish notes of correction or apology to persons whom they have unintentionally defamed.

The law of libel has undergone a number of important changes in recent years, with major revisions being made both by statute and the courts. So far as legislation is concerned, the major source of change has been the Defamation Act 1996 which expands the defences available in defamation cases; reduces the limitation period for actions to be brought to one year; introduces measures to eradicate delaying tactics by the parties; introduces a new 'fast-track' procedure to provide a prompt and inexpensive remedy for less serious cases; and amends the law relating to absolute and qualified privilege. The Act also contains controversial measures designed to overcome obstacles presented by the 1689 Bill of Rights to actions for defamation brought by members of Parliament. But in addition to these wide-ranging statutory reforms, important initiatives have been taken by the Court of Appeal, reflecting public concern about the amount of damages which were being awarded by libel juries. So in *John* v *Mirror Group Newspapers*,[159] steps were taken in an important judgment to propose that judges give greater guidance to libel juries, this following the decision of the European Court of Human Rights in the *Tolstoy* case in which it was held that a libel award of £1.5 million in favour of Lord Aldington was a violation of the applicant's right to freedom of expression under art 10 of the ECHR.[160] Also in the interests of free speech, it has been held that neither local authorities (and by inference central government departments), nor political parties may sue in libel.[161]

Absolute and qualified privilege

Publication of statements that would otherwise be defamatory may be protected if made in circumstances of absolute or qualified privilege. Many, though not all, of the common law categories of privilege are now the subject of statutory privilege.[162] The Defamation Act 1996 is the most recent legislation on this issue, though as was suggested by the House of Lords in *Reynolds* v *Times Newspapers Ltd*[163] the categories of privilege are not closed. Absolute privilege applies to, inter alia, (*a*) statements made during parliamentary proceedings and statements in the official reports of debates or in other papers published by order of either House of Parliament;[164] (*b*) statements made by one officer of state to another in the course of his or her official duty, a privilege which in absolute form applies only to certain communications at a high level;[165] (*c*) reports by and statements to the Parliamentary Ombudsman;[166] (*d*) the internal documents of a foreign embassy;[167] and (*e*) the fair and accurate report of proceedings in public before a court in the UK if published contemporaneously with the proceedings. For this purpose a court includes any tribunal or body exercising the judicial power of the state.[168]

---

[158] *Thompson* v *Metropolitan Police Commissioner* [1998] QB 498, at p 512.
[159] [1997] QB 586.
[160] *Tolstoy Miloslavsky* v *UK* (1995) 20 EHRR 442. See also *Rantzen* v *Mirror Group Newspapers* [1994] QB 670.
[161] See respectively *Derbyshire County Council* v *Times Newspapers Ltd* [1993] AC 534 and *Goldsmith* v *Bhoyrul* [1998] QB 459; E Barendt [1993] PL 449.
[162] *Reynolds* v *Times Newspapers Ltd* [2001] 2 AC 127, at p 197 (Lord Nicholls).
[163] Ibid.
[164] Ch 11 A.
[165] E.g. *Chatterton* v *Secretary of State of India* [1895] 2 QB 189.
[166] Parliamentary Commissioner Act 1967, s 10(5); ch 29 D.
[167] *Al-Fayed* v *Al-Tajir* [1988] QB 712.
[168] Defamation Act 1996, s 14(3)(a). And see *Trapp* v *Mackie* [1979] 1 All ER 489, and *Mahon* v *Rahn (No 2)* [2000] 1 WLR 2150.

Absolute privilege also applies to the fair and accurate report of public proceedings of the European Court of Justice and the European Court of Human Rights.[169]

Qualified privilege, unlike absolute privilege, is destroyed as a defence if the plaintiff proves malice on the part of the defendant.[170] Under the Defamation Act 1996, Sch 1, such privilege arises in two types of case. The first comprises reports privileged without 'explanation or contradiction', a category which applies to the fair and accurate report of public proceedings by a legislature or international organisation anywhere in the world;[171] a court anywhere in the world;[172] or a person appointed to hold a public inquiry by a government or legislature anywhere in the world.[173] It also applies to the fair and accurate report of any public document and of any material published by or on the authority of a government or legislature anywhere in the world, as well as to any matter published anywhere in the world by an international organisation or conference.[174] The second category comprises reports privileged subject to explanation or contradiction, in the sense that there is no defence if the plaintiff shows that the defendant failed following a request, 'to publish in a suitable manner a reasonable letter or statement by way of explanation or contradiction'.[175] This latter category includes 'a notice or other matter issued for the information of the public' by the legislature, government or any authority carrying out governmental functions (expressly defined to include police functions) of any member state of the EU; and a fair and accurate report of proceedings at any public meeting in the UK of (*a*) a local authority or local authority committee; (*b*) a justice of the peace acting otherwise than as a court exercising judicial functions; (*c*) a commission or tribunal; (*d*) a local authority inquiry; or (*e*) any other statutory tribunal, board or inquiry. The second category also includes the fair and accurate reports or copies of (*a*) public meetings, (*b*) a general meeting of a UK public company, (*c*) documents circulated to members of UK public companies, (*d*) the findings of one of a number of regulatory bodies of a voluntary nature and (*e*) any adjudication or report by a body or person designated by the Lord Chancellor.[176] A press conference has been held to be a public meeting the reporting of which attracts qualified privilege, and this extends to written press releases distributed but not necessarily read out at the meeting.[177] Defamatory statements at an election meeting are not covered by qualified privilege, although fair and accurate reports of them by a newspaper may be.[178]

Other defences in defamation law

Certain other defences are also available. The defendant may seek to justify the defamatory statement, that is, to prove at the trial that what he or she said was true. Not every detail of the statement need be shown to be literally true, provided that the

---

[169] Defamation Act 1996, s 14(3)(b)–(d).
[170] Ibid, s 15(1). But carelessness, impulsiveness or irrationality do not amount to malice: *Horrocks* v *Lowe* [1975] AC 135.
[171] See also ch 11 A.
[172] See also ch 18 D and *Webb* v *Times Publishing Co* [1960] 2 QB 535.
[173] See *Tsikata* v *Newspaper Publishing plc* [1997] 1 All ER 655 (report need not be a contemporary report).
[174] Defamation Act 1996, Sch 1, Part 1.
[175] Ibid, s 15(2)(a).
[176] Ibid, Sch 1, Part II. The protection does not apply to the publication of a matter which is not of public concern or the publication of which is not for the public benefit (s 15(3)): see *Kingshott* v *Associated Kent Newspapers* [1991] 1 QB 88.
[177] *McCartan Turkington Breen* v *Times Newspapers Ltd* [2001] 2 AC 277.
[178] Defamation Act 1952, s 10, reversing *Braddock* v *Bevins* [1948] 1 KB 580.

defendant shows it to be true in substance.[179] The defence of 'fair comment' protects expressions of opinion on matters of public interest. The comment itself can be quite outspoken, and even unfair, provided that the comment could have been made by an honest person holding strong, exaggerated or even prejudiced views. It is also important that the comment does not contain any incorrect allegations of fact,[180] that the subject of the comment is a matter of public interest, and that malice on the part of the defendant is not shown.[181] The policies and acts of politicians are clearly of public interest. In *Silkin v Beaverbrook Newspapers Ltd*, described by Diplock J as an important case since it concerned 'the right to discuss and criticise the utterances and actions of public men', a former Cabinet minister sued the *Sunday Express* over remarks by a political columnist which pointed to inconsistencies between the plaintiff's speeches in Parliament and his business interests: the jury decided that the defence of fair comment had been established.[182] In *Slim v Daily Telegraph Ltd*, fair comment was a defence to an action brought concerning two letters which criticised a company and its legal adviser over the use of cars on a riverside footpath; Lord Denning MR said, 'When a citizen is troubled by things going wrong, he should be free to "write to the newspaper": and the newspaper should be free to publish his letter. It is often the only way to get things put right.'[183] In both these cases, the court stressed that the facts on which the comment was based were correctly stated.

Two other defences are to be found in the Defamation Act 1996. The first, in s 1, is a defence of 'innocent dissemination' which is intended to supersede the common law defence which was thought to be too uncertain. The statutory defence applies to anyone other than the author, editor or publisher of the statement complained of; it is available where he or she took 'reasonable care' in relation to the publication and 'did not know, and had no reason to believe, that what he or she did caused or contributed to the publication of a defamatory statement'.[184] The other defence is the defence of 'unintentional defamation' which replaces the more complex (and consequently little used) provision of the Defamation Act 1952, s 4, a change recommended on a number of occasions. Under s 2 of the 1996 Act, a person who has published a statement alleged to be defamatory may offer to make amends, either generally or 'in relation to a specific defamatory meaning which the person making the offer accepts that the statement conveys' ('a qualified offer'). An offer to make amends is an offer to make a suitable correction and apology and to pay to the aggrieved party agreed compensation and costs. The failure of the plaintiff to accept an offer which has not been withdrawn is a defence, either generally, or in the case of a qualified offer 'in respect of the meaning to which the offer related'. The defence does not, however, apply where the statement complained of (*a*) refers to the aggrieved party or was likely to be understood as so referring, and (*b*) was both false and defamatory of that party. However, the onus is on the plaintiff to show that the defendant knew that the statement referred to him or her, and also that the defendant knew it to be both false and defamatory. The offer may be relied on in mitigation of damages whether or not it was relied on as a defence.

---

[179] See *Polly Peck (Holdings) plc v Trelford* [1986] QB 1000; *Prager v Times Newspapers* [1988] 1 All ER 300; *Bookbinder v Tebbit* [1989] 1 All ER 1169; and *Cruise v Express Newspapers plc* [1999] QB 931.
[180] See Defamation Act 1952, s 6.
[181] See *Telnikoff v Matusevitch* [1992] 2 AC 343.
[182] [1958] 2 All ER 516, discussed in *Reynolds v Times Newspapers Ltd* [1998] 3 WLR 862 (CA).
[183] [1968] 2 QB 157.
[184] See *Godfrey v Demon Internet Ltd* [2001] QB 201 (liability of internet service provider).

The press and the law of defamation

There is no doubt that the press and the broadcasting authorities have constantly to be aware of the law of defamation. The position of the press is very different in the United States, where, by the First Amendment to the Constitution, 'Congress shall make no law . . . abridging the freedom of speech, or of the press' and, by the Fourteenth Amendment, 'No State shall make or enforce any law which shall abridge the privileges or immunities of citizens of the United States'. The effect of Supreme Court decisions on the freedom of the press, particularly *New York Times* v *Sullivan*,[185] has been to create a new law of libel concerning matters of public or general interest under which the press has much greater freedom to publish information and comment than under English law. Thus in an action brought by a public figure, the plaintiff must prove that the publication was false and that it was published either with knowledge of its falsity or with serious doubts as to its truth. It has been said in the High Court of Australia that the great virtue of the American approach is that 'it offers some protection to the reputation of the individual who is defamed and at the same time offers a large measure of protection to the publisher'.[186] This is an issue which has given rise to a lively body of jurisprudence in a number of Commonwealth countries in recent years, the law moving in the direction of *Sullivan* in Australia and South Africa,[187] but not Canada or New Zealand.[188]

The adoption of an approach somewhat similar to *Sullivan* was rejected by the House of Lords in *Reynolds* v *Times Newspapers Ltd*,[189] where the newspaper sought 'the incremental development of the common law' by the recognition of a new category of qualified privilege. This was the category of 'political information' broadly defined to mean 'information, opinion and arguments concerning government and political matters that affect the people of the United Kingdom'. It was argued that 'malice apart', the publication of such information should be privileged 'regardless of the status and source of the material and the circumstances of publication'. Although very sensitive of the need to protect freedom of expression, in a persuasive judgment the House of Lords nevertheless concluded that this approach did not go far enough to protect the reputation of the individual from being besmirched without foundation; it was also thought to be 'unsound in principle to distinguish political discussion from discussion of other matters of serious public concern'. The House of Lords preferred a solution that 'enables freedom of speech to be confined to what is necessary in the circumstances of the case', and one in which 'having regard to the admitted or proved facts', the question whether the publication was subject to qualified privilege 'is a matter for the judge'.[190] It has since been held that there is no qualified privilege in a newspaper report alleging corruption by a sports personality,[191] and that the defence

---

[185] 376 US 254 (1964). See Lewis, *Make No Law*, where it is argued that without this decision it is questionable whether the press could have done as much as it has to penetrate the power and secrecy of modern government or to inform the public of the reality of policy issues. Some may see this as unduly hyperbolic: just how effective is the American press in penetrating public or private power? And just how ineffective is its British counterpart? See *Loutchansky* v *Times Newspapers Ltd* [2001] 3 WLR 404, at p 426.

[186] *Theophanos* v *Herald and Weekly Times* (1994) 68 ALJR 713 (I Loveland [1996] PL 126).

[187] See *Lange* v *Australian Broadcasting Corp* (1997) 145 ALR 96 and *National Media Ltd* v *Bogoshi* 1998 (4) SA 1196.

[188] See *Hill* v *Church of Scientology of Toronto* (1995) 126 DLR (4th) 129 and *Lange* v *Atkinson* [1998] 3 NZLR 424.

[189] [2000] 2 AC 127.

[190] For a full discussion expressing disappointment at the approach, see I Loveland [2000] PL 351. And for a general review of this area of the law, see Loveland, *Political Libels*.

[191] *Grobbelaar* v *News Group Newspapers Ltd* [2001] 2 All ER 437.

must be established on the basis of information known to the defendant at the time of publication, thereby excluding information which may be discovered subsequently.[192]

The press, the law of defamation and parliamentary privilege

A rather paradoxical and unanticipated protection for the press emerged as a result of the operation of art 9 of the Bill of Rights of 1689, which precludes any court from impeaching or questioning the freedom of speech and debates or proceedings in Parliament. In the decision of the Privy Council in *Prebble* v *Television New Zealand Ltd*,[193] the plaintiff was a Cabinet minister in the New Zealand government who claimed that he had been defamed by the television company. The defendants wished to demonstrate the truth of the allegations by relying on things said or done in Parliament, but were confronted by the Bill of Rights. In upholding the lower courts on the first point to arise, the Privy Council held that: 'Parties to litigation, by whomsoever commenced, cannot bring into question anything said or done in the House (whether by direct evidence, cross-examination, inference or submission) that the actions or words were inspired by improper motives or were untrue or misleading.' But on a second point, the Privy Council reversed a decision of the lower court to stay the proceedings in the light of the disability under which the defendant laboured, on the ground that although there 'may be cases in which the exclusion of material on the grounds of parliamentary privilege makes it quite impossible fairly to determine the issues between the parties', on the facts this was not one of them. Where, however, 'the whole subject matter of the alleged libel relates to the plaintiff's conduct in the House so that the effect of parliamentary privilege is to exclude virtually all the evidence necessary to justify the libel', the proceedings should be stayed not only to prevent an injustice to the defendant, but also to avoid the 'real danger' that 'the media would be forced to abstain from the truthful disclosure of a member's misbehaviour in Parliament'.

> Although the plaintiff was permitted to proceed with his action on the facts, the impact of the *Prebble* decision was immediately felt in this country by two Conservative members of Parliament. In the case of Rupert Allason,[194] an action against *Today* newspaper was stayed, the defendant seeking to show that which was prohibited, namely that 'early day motions were at least inspired by improper motives'. To enforce parliamentary privilege but to refuse a stay would be unjust to the defendant, who would be deprived of their only defence 'while allowing the plaintiff to continue on an unsatisfactory and unfair basis'. In the view of Owen J, MPs 'had to take the ill consequences together with the good consequences' of parliamentary privilege. In the case of Neil Hamilton, it was claimed by the plaintiff that he had been libelled by the *Guardian* which alleged that he had received money from a businessman in return for asking ministers questions which were intended to further that businessman's interests. On this basis it was ruled by May J that the case could not proceed as the evidence directly involved proceedings in Parliament.[195]

The *Prebble* case and its progeny were thought to create a real injustice and in the House of Lords an amendment to the Defamation Bill was introduced by Lord Hoffmann.[196] It was pointed out, however, that it would be unfortunate if the amendment 'were seen in some way to be especially for the protection of the rights of Mr Hamilton or any other MP currently engaged in legal proceedings'. The issue was therefore dealt with as a 'matter of principle'; it was enacted that any person might

---

[192] *Loutchansky* v *Times Newspapers Ltd* [2001] 3 WLR 404; also *Bradshaw* v *Lord* [1984] QB 1.
[193] [1995] 1 AC 321. G Marshall [1994] PL 509, M Harris (1996) 8 Auckland UL Rev 45.
[194] *Allason* v *Haines, The Times*, 25 July 1995.
[195] For details, see HL Deb, 7 May 1996, cols 24–5. See also cols 42–3 (regarding Mr Ian Greer).
[196] Ibid, col 24.

waive the protection of any rule of law which prevented proceedings in Parliament being impeached or questioned in any court or place out of Parliament. This allows the individual to overcome the problem presented by art 9 of the Bill of Rights in the following way: a claimant may bring an action in defamation to vindicate his or her reputation provided he or she is willing to permit the defence to refer to proceedings in Parliament in order to justify what it had written. On the other hand, if the claimant is not prepared to waive the protection of art 9 then *Prebble* will continue to apply and the action may be stayed, on the ground that the newspaper must be allowed in defamation proceedings to prove that what it said was true. Newspapers would otherwise be 'extremely reluctant to criticise what anyone said in Parliament if it meant that they could be sued while they had to stand with their hands tied behind their backs'.[197] But although s 13 'deals specifically with the circumstances raised by Mr Hamilton's case against the *Guardian*',[198] Mr Hamilton dropped his action against the newspaper. He was subsequently found by the House of Commons Committee on Standards and Privileges to have received money from Mr Al Fayed for lobbying services. In a second libel case, this time against Mr Al Fayed about allegations made by him on television, Mr Hamilton invoked s 13 of the 1996 Act to waive parliamentary privilege. This would allow his parliamentary conduct to be challenged and was found by the House of Lords to provide a complete answer to the attempt by the defence to have the action stayed because of parliamentary privilege.[199] The libel action failed.

G. Breach of confidence

In the law of defamation, the courts are reluctant to ban publication of a book or article before trial of the action; in particular, the courts do not restrain publication of a work, even though it is defamatory, when the defendant intends to plead justification or fair comment on a matter of public interest and it is not manifest that such a defence is bound to fail.[200] According to Griffiths LJ in *Herbage v Pressdram Ltd*, this is because of 'the value the court has placed on freedom of speech and . . . also on freedom of the press, when balancing it against the reputation of a single individual, who . . . can be compensated in damages'.[201] In actions for breach of confidence, however, damages may be recovered but emphasis is laid on the power of the court by an injunction to prohibit publication which would be in breach of confidence. We have already seen in chapter 22 how the action for breach of confidence has provided the basis for the emerging right to privacy. But the law relating to confidentiality does not apply only to protect information relating to the private life of the individual. The same action was invoked in 1975 by the Attorney-General in his attempt to restrain publication of the Crossman diaries. While in that case an injunction was not granted, Lord Widgery CJ ruled that publication of information received by a Cabinet minister prejudicial to the collective responsibility of the Cabinet would be restrained if the public interest clearly required this.[202] It must be emphasised that the label of 'confidential' applied to a document, whether by a public authority or not, does not mean that the court will restrain publication of it should a copy reach a newspaper. In *Fraser v Evans*,

---

[197] Ibid, col 251.
[198] *Hamilton v Al Fayed* [2001] 1 AC 395, Lord Browne-Wilkinson. See A Sharland and I Loveland [1997] PL 113, and K Williams (1997) 60 MLR 388.
[199] *Hamilton v Al Fayed*, ibid. See A W Bradley [2000] PL 556.
[200] *Fraser v Evans* [1969] 1 QB 349.
[201] [1984] 2 All ER 769, 771.
[202] *A-G v Jonathan Cape Ltd* [1976] QB 752. See also *Commonwealth of Australia v John Fairfax and Sons Ltd* (1980) 147 CLR 39.

the court refused to ban publication of a confidential report which Fraser, a public relations consultant, had prepared for the Greek government, when the *Sunday Times* had obtained a copy of it from Greek sources: Fraser's contract with the Greek government required him but not the government to keep it confidential.[203]

It is nevertheless clear that an action for breach of confidence may be brought to restrain the publication of government secrets. In this respect, the action acquired considerable prominence as a tool for restraining the disclosure of secret information by disaffected members of the security services. At this point severe difficulties are encountered in defining the relationship between a private duty of confidence, the public interest in the protection of confidence, and the public interest in information being made known.[204] The most sensational case to raise these difficulties was the so-called *Spycatcher* case.

Mr Peter Wright, a retired security service officer, wrote a book, *Spycatcher*, in which he claimed to reveal secrets relating to activities of the British security service. The book was due to be published initially in Australia, which the British government sought an injunction to restrain. Two British newspapers (the *Guardian* and the *Observer*) carried accounts of what the book was said to contain, at which point the Attorney-General moved for an injunction to restrain the newspapers from carrying any such reports. An interim injunction was granted on the ground that publication would be a breach of confidence. Legal proceedings to restrain publication in Australia failed,[205] and the book was also published in the United States. When copies of the book began freely to enter the United Kingdom, the *Guardian* and the *Observer* moved to have the interim injunctions discharged, on the ground that there was now no public interest in maintaining the injunctions in view of the fact that the contents of the book were widely known and freely available throughout the world. The House of Lords (by a majority of three to two) refused the application on the ground that the restrictions remained necessary in the public interest (for reasons that were neither clear nor convincing).[206]

However, the Attorney-General's application for permanent injunctions against the newspapers failed.[207] The House of Lords agreed that security service personnel owe a life-long duty of confidence and that they may be restrained by injunction from disclosing any information which they obtain in the service of the Crown, as may any third party to whom such information is improperly conveyed. However, the availability of the book in the United States fatally undermined the government's claim that the maintenance of the injunctions was necessary in the public interest. In the opinion of Lord Keith, 'general publication in this country would not bring about any significant damage to the public interest beyond what has already been done. All such secrets as the book may contain have been revealed to any intelligence service whose interests are opposed to those of the United Kingdom'.[208] But although the actions for permanent injunctions failed, the conviction of several newspapers for contempt of court was subsequently upheld by the House of Lords. The appellants had published material which breached the terms of the injunctions against the *Observer* and the *Guardian*, and it was held that in their conduct they had interfered with the administration of justice.[209]

It was subsequently held by the European Court of Human Rights that the refusal of the House of Lords in 1987 to discharge the injunctions violated art 10 of the European Convention on Human Rights on the ground that, after publication of the book in

---

[203] [1969] 1 QB 349.
[204] X v Y [1988] 2 All ER 648. Other difficult cases include *Schering Chemicals v Falkman Ltd* [1982] QB 1. And see Cripps, *The Legal Implications of Disclosure in the Public Interest*.
[205] (1987) 8 NSWLR 341 (Powell J); (1987) 75 ALR 353 (NSW Court of Appeal); (1988) 78 ALR 449 (High Court of Australia). See Turnbull, *The Spycatcher Trial*.
[206] *A-G v Guardian Newspapers Ltd* [1987] 3 All ER 316.
[207] *(The same) (No 2)* [1990] 1 AC 109.
[208] For a fuller treatment of this intricate affair, see Ewing and Gearty, *Freedom under Thatcher*, pp 152–69. See also Bailey, Harris and Jones, *Civil Liberties Cases and Materials*, pp 848–68; D G T Williams (1989) 12 Dalhousie LJ 209; and A W Bradley [1988] All ER Rev 55.
[209] *A-G v Times Newspapers Ltd* [1992] 1 AC 191.

the United States, the material in question was no longer confidential.[210] Breach of confidence has nevertheless become an established basis for regulating the publication of material about the security service,[211] and continues in this role the Human Rights Act notwithstanding.

> In *Attorney-General* v *Times Newspapers Ltd*[212] the newspaper gave an undertaking to the Attorney-General not to publish information about the secret service (SIS) which had been given to them by Richard Tomlinson, a former agent. When his book was subsequently published in Russia, *The Times* successfully applied to the court to have the undertaking varied, to allow them to publish any of Tomlinson's material which was 'generally accessible to the public at large'. The Attorney-General thought that this variation was too wide, but the Court of Appeal overruled his objections and also rejected his claim that any publication should be approved in advance either by himself or by the court. Having regard to the Human Rights Act the court did not think it right that the newspaper 'should seek confirmation from the Attorney-General or the court that facts that they intend to republish have been sufficiently brought into the public domain by prior publication so as to remove from them the cloak of confidentiality'. But the court emphasised that the newspaper was bound by confidentiality, the effect of the decision being that the newspaper alone should be responsible for determining when it thought the boundaries had been reached. Should it break the obligation, it would be 'subject to the sanctions that exist for contempt of court'.

So although Times Newspapers succeeded in having the undertaking varied, the result was hardly a ringing endorsement of freedom of expression, despite the Human Rights Act. The court also stated 'It is desirable that there should usually be consultation between a newspaper and representatives of SIS before the newspaper published information that may include matters capable of damaging the service or endangering those who serve in it.' Such consultation does, in fact, take place. Where a publication is made in breach of confidence, the agent may be required to account for his or her profits.[213]

---

[210] *The Observer* v *UK* (1992) 14 EHRR 153. And see I Leigh [1992] PL 200.
[211] See *Lord Advocate* v *Scotsman Publications Ltd* [1990] 1 AC 812; N Walker [1990] PL 354.
[212] [2001] 1 WLR 885.
[213] *Attorney-General* v *Blake* [2001] AC 268.

Chapter 24

FREEDOM OF ASSOCIATION AND ASSEMBLY

This chapter examines the principal features of the law relating to freedom of association and assembly.[1] These freedoms traditionally were protected in the same way as other freedoms and liberties in English law. That is to say, people are free to associate and assemble to the extent that their conduct is not otherwise unlawful. The principle is best illustrated in this context, in the case of freedom of assembly, by the seminal decision in *Beatty* v *Gillbanks*,[2] one of the few cases in this area where, until recently, the court appeared sensitive to the constitutional significance of the issues raised.

> The case arose out of opposition to the Salvation Army in its early days, members of which insisted in marching through the streets of Weston-super-Mare despite violent opposition from the 'Skeleton Army' and despite an order from the magistrates that they should not march. In an attempt to stop the Salvationist marches, the police sought to have their leaders bound over to keep the peace on the ground that they had committed an unlawful assembly. If the Salvationists had not marched there would clearly have been no disturbance of the peace. As previous processions had led to disorder, the Salvationists knew that similar consequences were likely to ensue. The Divisional Court held that the acts of the Salvation Army were lawful and that it was not a necessary and natural consequence of these acts that disorder should have occurred. The court did not accept that a man might be punished for acting lawfully if he knew that his doing so might lead another man to act unlawfully.

This approach does not recognise a guaranteed right of collective protest, but it does ensure that civil or criminal restrictions on the freedom of people to meet together must be shown to derive from existing law. It may be debated, however, whether the approach provides a firm enough foundation for such freedom, at a time when it is under heavy pressure from competing interests and is subject now to a wide range of statutory and common law restrictions. Indeed, it is possible that on similar facts to those in *Beatty* v *Gillbanks*, the police could today lawfully arrest those taking part in the procession. As we shall see, the subsequent decision in *Duncan* v *Jones*[3] did much damage to the principle in *Beatty* v *Gillbanks*.

The rights to freedom of association and assembly are protected by art 11 of the European Convention on Human Rights and in domestic law now by the Human Rights Act 1998.[4] But it should not be overlooked that these rights are subject to important qualifications which permit extensive regulation. Limits may have to be imposed to respect

---

[1] See Bailey, Harris and Jones, *Civil Liberties Cases and Materials*, ch 4; Robertson, *Freedom, the Individual and the Law*, ch 2; Ewing and Gearty, *Freedom under Thatcher*, ch 4; Ewing and Gearty, *The Struggle for Civil Liberties*, chs 5 and 6; Feldman, *Civil Liberties and Human Rights*, ch 18; C A Gearty, in McCrudden and Chambers (eds), *Individual Rights and the Law in Britain*, ch 2; Fenwick, *Civil Rights*, ch 4. See also Morgan, *Conflict and Order*, and Townshend, *Making the Peace*.

[2] (1882) 9 QBD 308. And see Hart and Honoré, *Causation in the Law*, pp 333–5. Cf *Deakin* v *Milne* (1882) 10 R(J) 22.

[3] [1936] 1 KB 218.

[4] For a full discussion of the implications of the Human Rights Act in this area, in the light of contemporary developments, see H Fenwick and G Phillipson (2001) 21 LS 535.

the rights and interests of others, and someone must ultimately have the responsibility for enforcing these limits. Recent events in Northern Ireland provide a timely reminder of the need to accommodate competing interests, and also a novel example of how they might be accommodated. Under the Public Processions (Northern Ireland) Act 1998 a Parades Commission has been established to regulate the circumstances in which public processions may go ahead. The Commission is designed to be representative of the community in Northern Ireland and has a wide range of responsibilities which include a duty to promote greater understanding by the general public of issues concerning public processions, as well as a duty to promote the mediation of disputes about public processions (s 2). It must also issue a code of conduct relating to public processions (s 3) and, ultimately, has the power to impose conditions on the conduct of public processions, having regard to a number of statutory guidelines (s 8). Decisions of the Commission are subject to judicial review.[5] There is no comparable body in Britain.

A. Freedom of association[6]

In principle, the law imposes no restrictions on the freedom of individuals to associate together for political purposes. Thus people are free to form themselves into political parties, action groups, campaign committees, and so on, without any official approval. People are generally also free to determine with whom they will associate: organisations cannot normally be expected to accept into membership or to retain individuals whose membership is not wanted.[7] There are, however, restrictions on the right to freedom of association, which fall broadly into two categories, in addition to the various restrictions imposed on associations such as trade unions, charities and political parties by the state. In the first place, freedom of association is denied to some individuals, principally in order to promote the need for a politically neutral public service. Police officers may not take any active part in politics,[8] a rule designed 'to prevent a police officer doing anything which affects his impartiality or his appearance of impartiality'.[9] Local government officers in politically restricted posts may not actively engage in party politics, although there appears to be no restriction on membership of a political party.[10] The position of civil servants is dealt with in chapter 13 D. The threat of subversion and fears for external security led to a purge of communist and fascist (but mainly the former) sympathisers from the civil service under a procedure introduced in 1948. The other measure directed at the threat of subversion is the security vetting procedure, which seeks to exclude the members or supporters of disapproved organisations from entry to 'all posts which are considered to be vital to the security of the state, and is invoked when the reliability of a public servant is thought to be in doubt

---

[5] See *Re Faulkner's Application* [1999] NIJB 151; *Re McConnell's Application* [2000] NIJB 116; and *Re Tweed's Application* [2001] NILR 165.

[6] See K D Ewing, in McCrudden and Chambers (eds), *Individual Rights and the Law in Britain*.

[7] See *RSPCA v Attorney-General* [2001] 3 All ER 530. But compare Trade Union and Labour Relations (Consolidation) Act 1992, ss 64–7, 174.

[8] Police Regulations 1995, SI 1995 No 215, Sch 2. See also Police Act 1996, s 64(1), restrictions on freedom of police officers to join trade unions.

[9] *Champion v Chief Constable of Gwent* [1990] 1 All ER 116.

[10] Local Government and Housing Act 1989, ss 1, 2; Local Government Officers (Political Restrictions) Regulations 1990, SI 1990 No 851. Also SI 1990 No 1447. See K D Ewing (1990) 19 ILJ 111, 192; *NALGO v Environment Secretary*, *The Times*, 2 December 1992; and *Darroch v Strathclyde Regional Council* 1993 SLT 1111. These arrangements have been found not to violate the ECHR, art 10: see *Ahmed v UK* (2000) 29 EHRR 1. See G Morris [1998] PL 25; [1999] PL 211.

on security grounds'.[11] With the end of the Cold War many of these restrictions have become redundant, although vetting in the civil service continues particularly to avoid infiltration by members and supporters of terrorist organisations. The concern about external security also led to the controversial banning of trade union membership at Government Communications Headquarters (GCHQ) in 1984. This was in response to fears about the threat to national security by industrial action organised by trade unions. The ban was revoked in 1997, but restraints were imposed on trade union freedom at GCHQ.

Secondly, some forms of association are forbidden. Under the Public Order Act 1936, s 1, it is an offence for any person in a public place or at a public meeting to wear a uniform signifying association with a political organisation or with the promotion of any political object.[12] Passed in response to the conduct of fascists in the 1930s, s 2 of the same Act makes it an offence (*a*) to organise or train the members or supporters of any association for the purpose of enabling them to be used in usurping the functions of the police or the armed forces, or (*b*) to organise and train (or equip) them, either for enabling them to be employed for the use or display of physical force in promoting any political object, 'or in such manner as to arouse reasonable apprehension that they are organised and either trained or equipped for that purpose'. In 1963 the leaders of a movement known as Spearhead, whose members wore uniforms and exchanged Nazi salutes, were convicted under this section, even though there was no evidence of specific training for attacks on opponents.[13] The organisers of a volunteer force intended to be available for maintaining order in emergencies would run some risk of contravening this section, even if their avowed aim were to lend support when needed to the police or armed forces.[14] In 1974, several organisations of this kind started by former army officers were severely criticised on such grounds. More recently, the Terrorism Act 2000 re-enacted wide-ranging restrictions on membership and participation in the activities of terrorist organisations.[15] This Act contains what appears to be the only example of British legislation which makes it an offence simply to be a member of a specific organisation;[16] the proscribed organisations include the Irish Republican Army and the Irish National Liberation Army.[17]

B. The right of public meeting

Meetings or assemblies may be private or public and the protection of art 11 of the ECHR covers meetings and assemblies of a wide and varied kind. Public meetings may be held in the open air in places to which the public have free access. Here, however, it is usually necessary to get the prior consent of the owners of the land. Many local authorities have made byelaws governing the use of parks, beaches etc. for various purposes, including public meetings; breach of these byelaws is a criminal offence, unless the court is prepared to hold the byelaw to be ultra vires,[18] and a civil remedy may

---

[11] Fredman and Morris, *The State as Employer*, p 23.
[12] See *O'Moran v DPP* [1975] QB 864. See now Terrorism Act 2000, s 13.
[13] *R v Jordan and Tyndall* [1963] Crim LR 124; D G T Williams [1970] CLJ 96, 102–4.
[14] Supperstone, *Brownlie's Law of Public Order and National Secretary*, p 185.
[15] Terrorism Act 2000. Part II.
[16] K D Ewing, note 6 above.
[17] There are, in fact, 14 proscribed organisations listed in the Terrorism Act 2000, Sch 2; the Act contains a power for more to be added (s 3), on which see SI 2001 No 1261 which includes another 21.
[18] *De Morgan v Metropolitan Board of Works* (1880) 5 QBD 155; *Aldred v Miller* 1925 JC 21. And see *R v Barnet Council, ex p Johnson* (1990) 89 LGR 581 (condition excluding 'political activity' at community festival held invalid).

also be available to restrain persistent breach of the law.[19] In the case of Trafalgar Square in London, statutory regulations have been made under which application for the holding of any assembly had to be made to what was the Department of National Heritage;[20] but this is a responsibility which has now been transferred to the Greater London Authority and the Mayor acting on its behalf.[21] Similarly, in the case of Hyde Park, no meetings may be held as of right:[22] although Speaker's Corner is available for any who wish to speak, the law is applied there 'as fully as anywhere else'.[23] Following an important decision of the House of Lords in 1999.[24] It may now be possible to hold an assembly on the highway without the need for prior consent. But the scope of this right is not to be exaggerated: the assembly must be 'reasonable and non-obstructive, taking into account its size, duration and the nature of the highway'. It must, moreover, be 'not inconsistent with the primary right of the public to pass and repass'.[25]

For meetings, rallies or assemblies which are not held in the open air, a major practical restriction is the need to find premises for them, to say nothing of the cost of hiring a hall and dealing with security.[26] The organisers of an unpopular cause may find it difficult to hire suitable halls, whether these are owned by private individuals or by public authorities such as a local council. However, candidates at local, parliamentary and assembly elections are entitled to the use of schools and other public rooms for the purpose of holding election meetings.[27] Otherwise local authorities appear to have a wide discretion in deciding to whom to let their halls, although this discretion is subject to law and may now be open to challenge on the ground of illegality under the Human Rights Act 1998.[28] But not even the Human Rights Act 1998 has fully met the argument that local authorities in particular should be under a general duty to make their halls available to all groups, whether popular or unpopular, without discriminating between them on political or other grounds.[29] Indeed, such a duty applies to universities, polytechnics and colleges under the Education (No 2) Act 1986. By s 43, the governing bodies of such establishments must 'take such steps as are reasonably practicable to ensure that freedom of speech within the law is secured for members, students and employees of the establishment and for visiting speakers'. This includes an obligation 'to ensure, so far as is reasonably practicable, that the use of any premises of the establishment is not denied to any individual or body of persons on any ground connected with (*a*) the beliefs or views of that individual or of any member of that body; or (*b*) the policy or objectives of that body'. Governing bodies must issue and keep up to date a code of practice to facilitate the discharge of these duties.[30]

---

[19] Cf *Llandudno UDC v Woods* [1899] 2 Ch 705.

[20] SI 1997 No 1639. See *Ex p Lewis* (1888) 21 QBD 191, discussed in *DPP v Jones* [1999] 2 AC 240.

[21] Greater London Authority Act 1999, s 383; SI 2000 No 801.

[22] *Bailey v Williamson* (1873) 8 QBD 118; Royal and Other Open Spaces Regulations 1997, SI 1997 No 1639.

[23] *Redmond-Bate v DPP* [2000] HRLR 249.

[24] *DPP v Jones* [1999] 2 AC 240. See p 577 below.

[25] Ibid, per Lord Irvine (Lord Chancellor).

[26] Under the Criminal Justice and Public Order Act 1994, s 170, the security costs of political party conferences may be met by the Treasury.

[27] Representation of the People Act 1983, ss 95, 96. See *Webster v Southwark Council* [1983] QB 698; *Ettridge v Morrell* (1986) 85 LGR 100. Also SI 1999 No 450 (Welsh Assembly); SI 1999 No 787 (Scottish Parliament).

[28] Such decisions may also be open to challenge if the refusal to let a hall is unreasonable in the *Wednesbury* sense: *Wheeler v Leicester City Council* [1985] AC 1054. Cf *Verrall v Great Yarmouth BC* [1981] QB 202.

[29] Street, *Freedom, the Individual and the Law* (5th edn), p 56.

[30] See E Barendt [1987] PL 344.

In *R* v *University of Liverpool, ex p Caesar-Gordon*,[31] the university authorities refused permission for a meeting at the university to be addressed by two first secretaries from the South African Embassy. This was done because of fear that in the event of the meeting taking place public violence would erupt in Toxteth, the residential area adjacent to the university. In an application for judicial review by the chairman of the student Conservative Association, the Divisional Court held that, on a true construction of s 43(1), the duty imposed on the university is local to the members of the university and its premises. Its duty is to ensure, so far as is reasonably practical, that those whom it may control, that is to say its members, students and employees, do not prevent the exercise of freedom of speech within the law by other members, students and employees and by visiting speakers in places under its control. But under s 43(1), the university was not entitled to take into account threats of 'public disorder' outside the confines of the university by persons not within its control. A declaration was granted that the university acted ultra vires in denying permission to hold the meeting. The court suggested, however, that had the university authorities confined their reasons when refusing permission 'to the risk of disorder on university premises and among university members', then no objection could have been taken to their decisions.

C. Public processions and assemblies

Public processions

By contrast with static meetings on the highway, at common law a procession in the streets is prima facie lawful, being no more than the collective exercise of the public right to use the highway for its primary purpose.[32] This does not mean that it would be a reasonable use of the highway for a dozen demonstrators to link arms and proceed down a street so as to interfere with the right of others to use the highway or for a large group of demonstrators to decide to obstruct a street: a procession would become a nuisance 'if the right was exercised unreasonably or with reckless regard of the rights of others'.[33] Because processions were prima facie lawful, statutory powers were needed if the police were to control them. General powers were contained in the Public Order Act 1936, passed at a time when fascist marches in the East End of London were a serious threat to order. By s 3 of the Act, if a chief officer of police, having regard to the time, place and route of an actual or proposed procession, had reasonable ground for apprehending that the procession might occasion serious public disorder, he could issue directions imposing on the persons organising or taking part in the procession such conditions as appeared to him to be necessary for the preservation of public order, including conditions prescribing the route of the procession and prohibiting it from entering any public place specified; but he could not restrict the display of flags, banners or emblems unless this was reasonably necessary to prevent a breach of the peace. Breach of the conditions was an offence against the 1936 Act.[34] If these powers were insufficient to prevent serious public disorder being occasioned by the holding of processions in any urban area, the chief officer of police could apply to the local authority for an order prohibiting all or any class of public processions for a period not exceeding three months; such an order could be made by the council only with the approval of the Secretary of State. In the case of London, the Commissioner of the Metropolitan Police could himself, with the approval of the Home Secretary, issue a prohibition order. The need for the approval of the Secretary of State made it likely that the matter would be raised in Parliament if MPs disagreed with the ban.

---

[31] [1991] 1 QB 124.
[32] A Goodhart (1937) 6 CLJ 161, 169.
[33] *Lowdens* v *Keaveney* [1903] 2 IR 82, 90 (Gibson J); and see *R* v *Clark (No 2)* [1964] 2 QB 315.
[34] See *Flockhart* v *Robinson* [1950] 2 KB 498.

These powers were extended by the Public Order Act 1986. The first major change is the introduction of a requirement that the organisers of a public procession should give advance notice to the police (s 11). The duty applies in respect of processions designed (*a*) to demonstrate support for or opposition to the views or actions of any person or body of persons; (*b*) to publicise a cause or campaign; or (*c*) to mark or commemorate an event. There are a few exclusions from the duty to notify,[35] but most processions for political purposes will be caught by these requirements. The notice, which must specify the proposed time, date and route, must be delivered to a police station (in the area where the procession is to start) at least six clear days in advance. In addition to this notice requirement, the 1986 Act extends the grounds for which conditions can be imposed on public processions, as well as the circumstances whereby such processions may be banned. So even if serious public disorder is not likely, a senior police officer may impose conditions where he or she reasonably believes that the procession may result in serious damage to property or serious disruption to the life of the community. He or she may also impose conditions where the purpose of the organisers of the procession is to intimidate others (s 12). The directions may be such as appear necessary to prevent disorder, damage, disruption or intimidation, including conditions prescribing the route and prohibiting entry to a specified public place. Unlike the 1936 Act, there is now no restriction on the giving of directions relating to the display of flags, banners or emblems. If these powers to impose conditions are not enough to prevent serious public disorder, the chief officer of police may apply for a banning order under what is now s 13 of the 1986 Act. The procedure here is similar to that in s 3(2) of the 1936 Act, and the power to apply for a banning order is restricted to serious public disorder; the section does not permit a banning order to be made on the wider grounds on which conditions may now be imposed.

Similar powers in Scotland are in the Civic Government (Scotland) Act 1982 (as amended by the Local Government etc. (Scotland) Act 1994).[36] By s 62, the organisers of a public procession must notify (at least seven days in advance) both the police and the local authority in whose area the procession is to be held. After consulting the chief constable, the local authority may then prohibit the holding of the procession or impose conditions upon it. These measures are additional to the Public Order Act 1986, s 12, which extends to Scotland.[37] It thus appears that a local authority in Scotland could ban a specific march, whereas in England and Wales the ban must be on the holding of all public processions or of any class of public processions specified in the order. Another important difference between Scots law and the 1986 Act is the appeal procedure in s 64 of the Civic Government (Scotland) Act. A person who has given notice of a procession under s 62 may appeal within 14 days to the sheriff against an order prohibiting or imposing conditions on the procession. The grounds of appeal are limited by the statute to error of law, mistake of fact, unreasonable exercise of discretion or that the local authority have 'otherwise acted beyond their powers'. There is no comparable provision in the Public Order Act 1986. It is true that the organiser of a procession could seek judicial review of a banning order or of an order to impose conditions.[38]

---

[35] By s 11(2), there is no duty to notify where 'the procession is one commonly or customarily held in the police area (or areas) in which it is proposed to be held or is a funeral procession organised by a funeral director acting in the normal course of his business'.

[36] See Ewing and Finnie, *Civil Liberties in Scotland: Cases and Materials*, ch 8. See also W Finnie, in Finnie, Himsworth and Walker (eds), *Edinburgh Essays in Public Law*, pp 251–77.

[37] The Public Order Act 1986, ss 11 and 13, do not extend to Scotland.

[38] Judicial review was also available in principle to challenge banning orders under s 3(2) of the Public Order Act 1936. See *Kent* v *Metropolitan Police Commissioner*, *The Times*, 15 May 1981. For the position under the European Convention on Human Rights, see *Plattform 'Ärzte für das Leben'* v *Austria* (19) 13 EHRR 204.

But, unlike in Scotland, this would be review and not an appeal; it would be in the High Court under the judicial review procedure and not in the local sheriff court; and in any event the Court of Appeal has made it clear, in a case involving a banning order under s 3(2) of the 1936 Act, that it is not willing to encourage such applications.[39] There is also the practical problem of securing judicial review in enough time before the procession is due to be held. There is no duty on the police to give notice of the conditions 'as early as possible', as there is on the local authority in Scotland.[40] If the police exercise their powers unreasonably, it may be possible for anyone arrested for violating the conditions to challenge their legality as a defence in criminal proceedings. But this will not restore their right to participate in the procession, or the right to conduct the procession as initially conceived.

Public assemblies

Police powers specifically to regulate public assemblies were introduced in the Public Order Act 1986 (s 14). The senior police officer present at an assembly (or the chief constable in the case of an assembly intended to be held) may impose conditions as to its location and duration, as well as the number of people who may be present. These conditions may be issued where it is reasonably believed (*a*) that the assembly may result in serious public disorder, serious damage to property, or serious disruption to the life of the community; or (*b*) that the purpose of organising the assembly is to intimidate others. A public assembly is defined to mean an assembly of 20 or more people in a public place which is wholly or partly open to the air (s 16). (In imposing conditions, could the police limit the presence to a smaller number than 20?) There is no procedure in the Act for challenging instructions issued under this power, although if they are issued long enough in advance, judicial review is available in principle, subject to the reluctance of the courts to encourage review of such decisions. The only other means of challenging any directions would be collaterally, as a defence in criminal proceedings for violating a direction given under the Act. It could be argued that the police had exceeded their powers, for example, because the purpose of an assembly was to cause inconvenience and embarrassment to third parties, rather than to intimidate them.[41] Nevertheless, the section gives the police wide powers to control public assemblies and by the power to issue directions to frustrate the purpose of the assembly.

The Criminal Justice and Public Order Act 1994 added new powers in respect of public assemblies, corresponding to the powers relating to public processions in s 13 of the 1986 Act.[42] These new powers apply to 'trespassory assemblies', that is to say an assembly 'on land to which the public has no right of access or only a limited right of access', a definition wide enough to include the public highway. The power of the police – in what is now Public Order Act 1986, s 14A – is activated where a chief officer 'reasonably believes' that such an assembly (*a*) is likely to be held without the permission of the occupier of the land, and (*b*) may result in serious disruption to the life of the community or significant damage to land, a building or monument of historical, architectural, archaeological or scientific importance. If these conditions are met the chief officer of police may apply to the local authority for an order prohibiting all 'trespassory assemblies' in the district or part of it, for a specified period of up to four days

---

[39] *Kent v Metropolitan Police Commissioner* (note 38 above).
[40] Civic Government (Scotland) Act 1982, s 63.
[41] *Police v Lorna Reid* [1987] Crim LR 702.
[42] On the 1994 Act, see M J Allen and S Cooper (1995) 59 MLR 364.

to an area within five miles radius of a specified centre. The order, which may be varied or revoked before it expires, may be made after consulting the Secretary of State who must give consent and the order may be made as requested, or with modifications. In Scotland there is no need for ministerial approval to the making of the order (or in granting it with varied terms) while in London the order may be issued by the Metropolitan Police Commissioner with the consent of the Home Secretary.

It is an offence to organise or take part in an assembly which is known to be prohibited and a constable in uniform may (*a*) arrest without a warrant anyone committing an offence and (*b*) stop any person reasonably believed to be on the way to an assembly 'likely to be an assembly which is prohibited', and 'direct him [or her] not to proceed in the direction of the assembly'. It is an offence to fail to comply with a direction.

> In *DPP* v *Jones*[43] an order had been made prohibiting the holding of assemblies within a four-mile radius of Stonehenge from 29 May to 1 June 1995. While the order was in force, a peaceful assembly was held within the area covered by the order. When those present refused to disperse, they were arrested and convicted of trespassory assembly. The conviction was overturned by the Crown Court, and on an appeal by way of case stated it was held that conduct could constitute a trespassory assembly even though the conduct complained of was peaceful and did not obstruct the highway. The question was whether the assembly exceeded the public's right of access to the highway for the purposes of the definition of a 'trespassory assembly': if the public had the right to use the highway in this way, there would be no 'trespass' under the 1986 Act as amended. The House of Lords (dividing 3:2) reversed and reinstated the decision of the Crown Court. The Lord Chancellor said that the right to use the highway was not limited to passage and repassage: 'the public highway is a public place which the public may enjoy for any reasonable purpose, provided the activity in question does not amount to a public or private nuisance and does not obstruct the highway by unreasonably impeding the primary right of the public to pass and repass: within these qualifications there is a public right of peaceful assembly on the highway'.[44]

Although s 14 of the Public Order Act 1986 appears to be the first police power specifically to regulate public assemblies, there are a number of general police powers which have been available for this purpose. The first of these is the statutory offence of obstructing a police officer in the execution of his or her duty.[45] We deal with this later, but in practice this would give to the police powers perhaps as great as those to be found in s 14 of the 1986 Act, but which may be used even when the assembly does not include 20 or more. This offence remains unaffected by the 1986 Act and it is strongly arguable that in practice s 14 adds little to the existing law.

D. Freedom of assembly and private property rights

Picketing

The purpose of picketing is to enable pickets to impart information or opinions to those entering or leaving premises or in some cases to seek to persuade them not to enter in the first place. Those who picket may be subject to directions issued by the police under s 14 of the Public Order Act 1986 if there are 20 or more of them. The police may also issue directions to prevent a breach of the peace; failure to comply with such directions may lead to an arrest for obstructing a police officer.[46] But even if a picket is perfectly

---

[43] [1999] 2 AC 240; G Clayton (2000) 63 MLR 252.
[44] Ibid, at p 257.
[45] Police Act 1996, s 89(2).
[46] Ibid.

peaceful and is not subject to regulation by the police in these ways, those who participate may in law be committing offences for which they can be arrested without a warrant. Under the Trade Union and Labour Relations (Consolidation) Act 1992, s 241, it is an offence for a person 'wrongfully and without legal authority' to 'watch and beset' premises where a person works or happens to be with a view to compelling him or her to abstain from doing something which he or she is entitled to do. Although this offence had fallen into disuse, it was revived during the miners' strike of 1984/85 as one of the weapons in the police armoury for dealing with the large-scale picketing which then took place.[47] More usually perhaps, picketing may lead to an arrest for obstructing the highway under the Highways Act 1980, s 137. A picket is no more a lawful use of the highway than is any other kind of assembly.[48]

Apart from possible criminal liability, those who organise a picket may also face civil liability. There is authority for the view that picketing premises may constitute a private nuisance against the owner or occupier of these premises. At least the law is sufficiently unclear that an interlocutory injunction is likely to be granted in an application by such a plaintiff.

> In *Hubbard* v *Pitt*, a community action group organised a peaceful picket outside the offices of estate agents in Islington, distributing leaflets and displaying placards to protest against the firm's part in improving property at the expense of working-class residents. On the issue of whether an interim injunction should be issued to the firm against the pickets, Forbes J held that the picketing was unlawful since it was not in contemplation or furtherance of a trade dispute (on the significance of which, see below) and was inconsistent with the public right to use the highway for passage and repassage. But in the Court of Appeal, the majority upheld the interim injunction on quite different grounds, holding only that the plaintiffs had a real prospect of establishing at the eventual trial that the protesters were committing a private nuisance against them and that the balance of convenience lay in favour of the picketing being stopped until the main hearing of the action. Lord Denning MR dissented, holding that the use of the highway for the picket was not unreasonable and did not constitute a nuisance at common law; he considered that picketing other than for trade disputes was lawful so long as it was done merely to obtain or communicate information or for peaceful persuasion.[49]

During the miners' strike of 1984/85 an attempt was made – successfully in the short term – to extend the tort of private nuisance. So in *Thomas* v *NUM (South Wales Area)*,[50] Scott J held that pickets would be liable not only to the owner or occupier of the premises being picketed, but also to workers (and presumably others) who were 'unreasonably harassed' in entering the premises. This extension of tortious liability was subsequently disapproved by Stuart-Smith J, in relation to an industrial dispute at Wapping in 1985/86.[51]

Special rules govern picketing in the case of trade disputes. As now provided by statute:

> It shall be lawful for a person in contemplation or furtherance of a trade dispute[52] to attend
> (*a*) at or near his own place of work; or
> (*b*) if he is an official of a trade union, at or near the place of work of a member of that union whom he is accompanying and whom he represents

---

[47] See P Wallington (1985) 14 ILJ 145.

[48] See *Broome* v *DPP* [1974] AC 587; *Kavanagh* v *Hiscock* [1974] QB 600; and *Hirst* v *Chief Constable of West Yorkshire* (1987) 85 Cr App R 143.

[49] [1976] QB 142. See P Wallington [1976] CLJ 82. But picketing is not necessarily a nuisance: see K Miller and C Woolfson (1994) 23 ILJ 209, at pp 216–17.

[50] [1986] Ch 20. See K D Ewing [1985] CLJ 374. See now Protection from Harassment Act 1997, and *Hunter* v *Canary Wharf* [1997] AC 655.

[51] *News Group Newspapers Ltd* v *SOGAT 1982 (No 2)* [1987] ICR 181.

[52] For the meaning of the term 'trade dispute', see Trade Union and Labour Relations (Consolidation) Act 1992, s 244.

for the purpose only of peacefully obtaining or communicating information or peacefully persuading any person to work or abstain from working.[53]

This provision, unlike its predecessors, restricts the freedom to picket in a trade dispute to one's own place of work. Secondary picketing – the picketing of other workplaces – is thus excluded.[54] There is no restriction in the Act on the number of people who may picket in this way, but a Code of Practice on Picketing issued by the then Department of Employment (with parliamentary approval)[55] recommends no more than six people at any particular site, although this could be reduced if the police are of the view that, to prevent a breach of the peace, a smaller number is necessary.[56] Even if these requirements are met, there is no right on the part of pickets to stop vehicles and to compel drivers and their occupants to listen to what they have to say. In *Broome v DPP*,[57] the House of Lords refused to read such a right into a statutory predecessor of the current law on the ground that it would involve reading into the Act words which would seriously diminish the liberty of the subject. Everyone has the right to use the highway free from the risk of being compulsorily stopped by any private citizen and compelled to listen to what he or she does not want to hear.[58] Pickets thus have a right to seek to communicate information or to seek peacefully to persuade, but not to stop persons or vehicles.

The purpose of these provisions is to give workers and trade union officials a limited protection from both criminal and civil liability. So far as the criminal law is concerned, those who picket peacefully for the permitted purposes will not be liable under either the Highways Act 1980, s 137, or the Trade Union and Labour Relations (Consolidation) Act 1992, s 241. This is because the latter, by s 220 (providing that picketing 'shall be lawful'), gives legal authority to obstruct the highway and to watch and beset. If, however, the purpose of the picket is deemed to be the causing of an obstruction rather than the peaceful communication of information, then s 220 of the 1992 Act will not prevent those involved from being arrested and convicted. So far as civil liability is concerned, s 220 provides an immunity from liability for private nuisance where the pickets are acting peacefully.[59] But it does not provide immunity where the purpose of the picket is adjudged to be to harass others, as in *Thomas v NUM (South Wales Area)*.[60] Together with s 219 of the 1992 Act, s 220 also gives pickets immunity in tort for conspiracy, inducing breach of contract, and intimidation.[61] In this case, however, the protection is of qualified value, for it applies only where the increasingly tight restrictions on the conduct of industrial action have been complied with, including the holding of a secret ballot and the giving of appropriate notice to employers. But there may be circumstances where picketing in the course of a trade dispute does not involve the commission of a tort and where as a result the immunity is unnecessary. Although such cases are rare, they are not unknown.

---

[53] Trade Union and Labour Relations (Consolidation) Act 1992, s 220. And see the Code of Practice on Picketing issued under the 1992 Act (note 55 below).

[54] As to secondary action under the old law, see *Duport Steels Ltd v Sirs* [1980] 1 All ER 529.

[55] SI 1992 No 476. Failure to comply with the code does not render any person liable to proceedings, but it may be taken into account by a court or tribunal. See, e.g., *Thomas v NUM (South Wales Area)* (note 50 above).

[56] Code of Practice on Picketing, para 51.

[57] [1974] AC 587. Also *Kavanagh v Hiscock* [1974] QB 600.

[58] [1974] AC 587, 603.

[59] *Hubbard v Pitt* [1976] QB 142.

[60] [1986] Ch 20.

[61] For full consideration of these questions, reference should be made to the labour law texts, e.g. Collins, Ewing and McColgan, *Labour Law Text and Materials*; Deakin and Morris, *Labour Law*; and Smith and Thomas, *Industrial Law*.

In *Middlebrook Mushrooms Ltd v Transport and General Workers' Union*[62] the plaintiff employers were in dispute with some of their employees who went on strike and were subsequently dismissed. The employees then organised a campaign to distribute leaflets outside supermarkets to persuade shoppers not to buy the plaintiff's mushrooms. An injunction was granted at first instance to restrain the defendants from directly interfering with the employer's contracts, but was discharged on appeal. Neither party relied on the 1992 Act and it was held that in order for the defendant's action to be tortious, the persuasion had to be directed at one of the parties to the contracts allegedly interfered with (in this case between the supermarket and the employers). Here the 'suggested influence was exerted, if at all, through the actions or the anticipated actions of third parties who were free to make up their own minds'. The leaflets were directed at customers and contained no message which was directed at the supermarket managers.

But for all practical purposes the freedom conferred by the 1992 Act is very narrow and does not address the crucial problem of the extraordinarily wide discretionary powers vested in the police to regulate the competing claims of pickets and others.

Sit-ins, squatting and forcible entry

In recent years the expression of protest has often taken the form of entry onto private land, most notably by animal rights protesters and environmental activists, the former protesting about field sports in particular, and the latter about the building of new motorways which in the process spoil or destroy the natural or built environment. Other groups to engage in this type of activity in the past were workers protesting about the threat of job losses, and peace campaigners anxious about nuclear weapons. This form of protest action may fall foul of some of the measures already discussed, although there are other provisions which may be relevant. So in *Chandler v DPP*,[63] an attempt by nuclear disarmers to enter and sit down on an RAF base was held to be a conspiracy to commit a breach of the Official Secrets Act 1911, s 1(1), which makes it an offence for any purpose prejudicial to the safety of the state to approach or enter 'any prohibited place'. In *Galt v Philp*,[64] a sit-in at a hospital laboratory by scientific officers was held to be a breach of s 7 of the Conspiracy and Protection of Property Act 1875 (now s 241 of the Trade Union and Labour Relations (Consolidation) Act 1992).

Action of this type is also governed to some extent by the Criminal Law Act 1977, which extensively reformed the law following the recommendation of the Law Commission.[65] The old offences of forcible entry and forcible detainer were abolished and conspiracy to commit a civil trespass, as in *Kamara v DPP*,[66] ceased to be a criminal offence (ss 1(1), 5(1), 13). Part II of the 1977 Act created various offences relating to entering and remaining on property. These include (*a*) without lawful authority, to use or threaten violence for the purpose of securing entry into any premises on which another person is present and against the will of that person (s 6); (*b*) to remain on residential premises as a trespasser after being required to leave by or on behalf of a displaced residential occupier of the premises (s 7); (*c*) without lawful authority, to have offensive weapons on premises after having entered them as a trespasser (s 8); (*d*) to enter as a trespasser any foreign embassies and other diplomatic premises (s 9); and (*e*) to resist or obstruct a sheriff or bailiff seeking to enforce a court order for possession (s 10). Additional measures directed at trespassing on private land 'with the

---

[62] [1993] ICR 612.
[63] [1964] AC 763.
[64] [1984] IRLR 156. See K Miller (1984) 13 ILJ 111. For the offence under the 1992 Act, see p 558 above.
[65] HC 176 (1975–76).
[66] [1974] AC 104.

common purpose of residing there for any period' were introduced by the Public Order Act 1986.[67]

Yet further restrictions were introduced by the Criminal Justice and Public Order Act 1994. Indeed, Part V of the Act is entitled 'Public Order: Collective Trespass or Nuisance on Land', but deals with a wide range of different issues, not all of which are concerned with freedom of assembly. This part of the Act deals, for example, with people trespassing on land, 'with the common purpose of residing there for any period' (s 61), gatherings on land in the open air of 100 or more persons (whether or not trespassers) at which amplified music is played during the night (so-called raves) (s 63), the removal of squatters (ss 75–6) and unauthorised campers residing on land, without the consent of the occupier (s 77). The Act does, however, deal expressly with questions of freedom of assembly and public protest, not least in the provision which it makes for 'trespassory assemblies', the terms of which we have already encountered. Otherwise s 68 deals with what are referred to as 'disruptive trespassers', the main targets being apparently animal rights activists who trespass on land to disrupt fox-hunting events in particular. But s 68 is not confined to such activity, the government declining to accept an Opposition amendment to limit its scope to country sports, on the ground that there is no reason why events such as church fêtes, public race meetings or open-air political meetings 'should suffer the invasion of others who intend to intimidate, obstruct or disrupt these proceedings'.[68] Thus it is an offence (of aggravated trespass) for any person to trespass on land in the open air to intimidate persons taking part in lawful activities or to obstruct or disrupt such activity.[69] Anyone suspected of committing such an offence may be arrested without a warrant by a constable in uniform and the senior police officer present at the scene is em-powered to require anyone committing or participating in aggravated trespass to leave the land in question; failure to do so is also an offence.[70]

As in the case of picketing,[71] liability in civil law has an important role to play here too.

In *Department of Transport v Williams*,[72] an application was made for injunctions to restrain protesters from action designed to disrupt the building of the M3 extension over Twyford Down. Interim injunctions were granted by Alliott J to restrain the defendants from (i) entering upon land specified in the order, (ii) interfering with the use of the highway specified in the order, and (iii) restraining them from interfering with the carrying on of work authorised by the M3 Motorway Scheme (SI 1990 No 463). In the case of the first injunctions, it was held that these could be granted on the ground of trespass, but that the second should be set aside because they added nothing to the first. The third required there to be a basis in law for holding that it was tortious to prevent or interfere with the department's carrying out of works under the authorisation in the statutory instrument. It was held that in such a case an injunction could be grounded in the tort of wrongful interference with business; the unlawful means for the pur-poses of establishing this was found in the Highways Act 1980, which provides by s 303 that it is an offence wilfully to obstruct any person carrying out his lawful duties under the Act.[73]

---

[67] See *Krumpa v DPP* [1989] Crim LR 295.

[68] Official Report, Standing Committee B, 8 February 1994, col 614.

[69] See *Winder v DPP*, *The Times*, 14 August 1996 (Schiemann LJ), and *DPP v Barnard*, *The Times*, 9 November 1999 (Laws LJ). In the latter case the offence was not made out where there was a trespass onto the site of an opencast mine to stop the mining: a bare allegation of occupation was not enough – it had to be supported by allegations of what the defendant was actually doing.

[70] See D Mead [1998] Crim LR 870 and Fenwick and Phillipson (note 4 above). These measures are largely unaffected by the Countryside and Wildlife Act 2000, which introduces a limited right of access to pri-vate land for recreational purposes.

[71] *Hubbard v Pitt* [1976] QB 142 (p 558 above).

[72] *The Times*, 7 December 1993.

[73] See also *CIN Properties Ltd v Rawlins*, *The Times*, 9 February 1995.

The risk of civil liability is particularly serious in view of the principle in *American Cyanamid Co* v *Ethicon Ltd*[74] that an interim injunction may be granted on the ground that there is a serious issue to be tried and that the balance of convenience is in favour of relief, pending the trial of the action. The defendant thus need not be acting unlawfully to be restrained, it being possible and indeed likely that the balance of convenience will lie in favour of the plaintiff where disorder is threatened. On the other hand, it has been held that *American Cyanamid Co* does not deal with the situation where the granting or otherwise of the interim injunction is likely to dispose finally of the matter,[75] as in the case of a protest, the cause of which may well have passed before the matter comes to trial. In these cases, it has been held that 'the degree of likelihood the plaintiff would have succeeded in establishing his right to an injunction if the action had gone to trial, is a factor to be brought into the balance'.[76] It has also been held, however, that interim proceedings are not the place to decide difficult questions of fact and law.[77]

E. Public order offences

Riot and violent disorder

As well as the rules relating to assemblies and processions, there are several ways in which breaches of public order constitute offences. Such offences were initially developed through the common law, but following Law Commission recommendations in 1983[78] these common law offences were abolished and replaced with new offences in the Public Order Act 1986.[79] The first of these is *riot*, now defined by s 1 of the 1986 Act to apply where 12 or more persons who are present together use or threaten unlawful violence for a common purpose in circumstances where their conduct 'would cause a person of reasonable firmness present at the scene to fear for his personal safety'.[80] The scope of the offence is widened considerably, since no person of reasonable firmness need actually be present at the scene and since, unlike at common law, a riot may be committed in private as well as in a public place.[81] Although charges of riot are unusual today,[82] they were brought during the miners' strike of 1984/85, although many of the prosecutions collapsed in controversial circumstances.[83] When a riot is in progress, the police and other citizens may use such force as is reasonable in the circumstances to suppress it.[84] Anyone convicted of riot is liable to imprisonment of up to ten years or a fine, or both,[85] while anyone who suffers property damage in a

---

[74] [1975] AC 396.

[75] *NWL Ltd* v *Woods* [1979] ICR 867 (a trade dispute case, where the *American Cyanamid Co* rule was modified by statute).

[76] Ibid, at p 881 (Lord Diplock).

[77] *Series 5 Software Ltd* v *Clarke* [1996] 1 All ER 853. Also *Department of Transport* v *Williams*.

[78] Criminal Law: Offences Relating to Public Order (Law Commission 123).

[79] 1986 Act, Part I. For the background to the 1986 Act, see Cmnd 7891, 1980; HC 756 (1978–80); Cmnd 9510, 1985. Also Law Commission, Criminal Law: Offences Relating to Public Order (above).

[80] For the common law definition, see *Field* v *Metropolitan Police Receiver* [1907] 2 KB 853. At common law riot could be committed by three or more people. For a general account of the law in practice, see Vogler, *Reading the Riot Act*.

[81] Public Order Act 1986, s 1(5).

[82] Charges of mobbing and rioting were unsuccessfully brought in Scotland during the miners' strike in 1972, when strikers used force to prevent supplies of coal reaching a power station. See P Wallington (1972) 1 ILJ 219.

[83] See McCabe and Wallington, *The Police, Public Order and Civil Liberties*, p 163.

[84] Criminal Law Act 1967, s 3. The Riot Act 1714 has now been repealed, both for England and Wales, and Scotland.

[85] Public Order Act 1986, s 1(6).

riot may bring a claim for compensation against the police authority under the Riot
(Damages) Act 1886.[86] Compensation has been paid for damage done by those celeb-
rating the end of the First World War[87] and by football fans seeking to climb into Stamford
Bridge football ground to watch Chelsea play Moscow Dynamo during their post-war
British tour.[88]

Section 2 of the Public Order Act 1986 replaces the old common law offence of
unlawful assembly with a new offence of *violent disorder*. The history of unlawful
assembly is an important part of the history of the law of public order. After the lapse
of the Seditious Meetings Act 1817, it fell to the courts to develop the definition of
an unlawful assembly, upon which depended the powers of the police to control and
disperse such assemblies.[89] The new statutory offence clears up some of the confusion
of the old law.[90] Violent disorder is committed where three or more persons who are
present together use or threaten unlawful violence and their conduct (taken together)
is such as would cause a person of reasonable firmness present at the scene to fear for
his or her personal safety. As with riot, no person of reasonable firmness need
actually be present, and the offence may be committed in private as well as in public
places. As with the old common law rules, a meeting which begins as a lawful
gathering may become an unlawful assembly if disorder takes place, weapons are produced or if language inciting an offence is used by speakers. But unlike the common
law, under the new statutory offence, when this transformation occurs persons present who do not share the unlawful purpose are not guilty of violent disorder. A
person is guilty of violent disorder only if he or she intends to use or threaten violence
or is aware that his or her conduct may be violent or threaten violence.[91] Such a
person is liable on conviction on indictment to imprisonment for up to five years and
on summary conviction to imprisonment for up to six months.[92] In both cases a fine
may be imposed rather than or as well as imprisonment. At common law when an
unlawful assembly was in progress, it was the duty of every citizen to assist in restoring order, for example by dispersing or by going to the assistance of the police.[93]
Presumably the duty survives the abolition of the common law offence and its replacement with violent disorder.[94]

Prosecutions for unlawful assembly and violent disorder are not unknown in
modern times. When serious disorder occurred at a demonstration protesting against
a Greek dinner at the Garden House Hotel in Cambridge (at a time when the Greek
government was unpopular in radical circles) students in the forefront of the disorder
were convicted of riot and unlawful assembly.[95] In *Kamara v DPP*,[96] students from
Sierra Leone occupied the Sierra Leone High Commission in London, locking the staff

[86] *Field v Metropolitan Police Receiver*, note 80 above; *Munday v Metropolitan Police Receiver* [1949]
1 All ER 337. In Scotland, compensation is payable under the Riotous Assemblies (Scotland) Act 1822,
s 10 (as amended by the Local Government etc (Scotland) Act 1994).

[87] *Ford v Metropolitan Police Receiver* [1921] 2 KB 344.

[88] *Munday v Metropolitan Police Receiver* [1949] 1 All ER 337.

[89] Leading cases included *R v Vincent* (1839) 9 C & P 91, and *R v Fursey* (1833) 6 C & P 80. See also
Hawkins, *Pleas of the Crown*, c 63, s 9.

[90] See *R v Chief Constable of Devon and Cornwall, ex p CEGB* [1982] QB 458. See also HC 85 (1983–84),
p 38.

[91] Public Order Act 1986, s 6(2). The same is true for riot, see s 6(1).

[92] Ibid, s 2(5).

[93] Charge to the Bristol Grand Jury (1832) 5 C & P 261; *R v Brown* (1841) Car & M 314. And see *Devlin
v Armstrong* [1971] NILR 13.

[94] Cf *A-G for Northern Ireland's Reference (No 1 of 1975)* [1977] AC 105.

[95] *R v Caird* (1970) 54 Cr App R 499. And see *The Listener*, 8 October (S Sedley) and 26 November 1970
(A W Bradley).

[96] [1974] AC 104. For unlawful assembly during an industrial dispute, see *R v Jones* (1974) 59 Cr App R
120.

in a room and threatening them with an imitation gun. Their conviction for, inter alia, unlawful assembly was upheld by the House of Lords, which ruled that it was not necessary to show that an unlawful assembly had occurred in a public place. As we have seen, this ruling has been given statutory force for the purposes of violent disorder.[97] Unlawful assembly charges were brought during the miners' strike of 1984/85, reflecting 'a specific prosecution policy intended to have a deterrent effect even before charges were proved and sentence pronounced'. However, many charges were dropped before the first hearing and, of those which did proceed, only 'a few indictments for unlawful assembly resulted in conviction'.[98] A few charges of affray were also brought during the strike. This ancient offence consists of unlawful fighting or a display of force by one or more persons in a public place or on private premises, involving a degree of violence calculated to terrify persons present who are of reasonably firm character.[99] The Public Order Act 1986 placed this offence on a statutory footing (s 3).[100]

Threatening, abusive and insulting behaviour

Apart from riot, violent disorder and affray, the other category of offences dealt with by the Public Order Act 1986 relates to threatening, abusive and insulting behaviour. This offence – which appears to correspond to the Scottish common law offence of breach of the peace – was originally enacted in the Public Order Act 1936, s 5. This provided that it was an offence to use threatening, abusive or insulting words or behaviour with intent to provoke a breach of the peace or whereby a breach of the peace was likely to be occasioned. If the purpose of ss 1–4 of the 1936 Act was to regulate the conduct of fascist demonstrators in the 1930s, the purpose of s 5 was, it seems, to deal with communist counter-demonstrators who would disrupt fascist rallies. Section 5 of the 1936 Act has been replaced by ss 4 and 5 of the Public Order Act 1986. By s 4:

> A person is guilty of an offence if he –
> (*a*) uses towards another person threatening, abusive or insulting words or behaviour, or
> (*b*) distributes or displays to another person any writing, sign or other visible representation which is threatening, abusive or insulting,
> with intent to cause that person to believe that immediate unlawful violence will be used against him or another by any person, or to provoke the immediate use of unlawful violence by that person or another, or whereby that person is likely to believe that such violence will be used or it is likely that such violence will be provoked.

This provision of the 1986 Act was supplemented by a new s 4A inserted by the Criminal Justice and Public Order Act 1994. This provides that it is an offence for a person with intent to cause a person harassment, alarm or distress to (*a*) use 'threatening, abusive or insulting words or behaviour, or disorderly behaviour' or (*b*) display any writing, sign or other visible representation which is threatening, abusive or insulting, thereby causing that person or another person (who need not be the intended target of the conduct) 'harassment, alarm or distress'. This complements s 5 of the 1986

---

[97] Public Order Act 1986, s 2(4).
[98] McCabe and Wallington, *The Police, Public Order and Civil Liberties*, pp 99–100.
[99] *Button* v *DPP* [1966] AC 591; *Taylor* v *DPP* [1973] AC 964.
[100] By s 3 of the 1986 Act, a person is guilty of *affray* if he uses or threatens unlawful violence towards another and his conduct is such as would cause a person of reasonable firmness present at the scene to fear for his personal safety. Where two or more persons use or threaten the unlawful violence, it is their conduct taken together that must be considered. See *I* v *DPP* [2002] AC 285 (brandishing petrol bombs constitutes an offence; but it must be directed towards a person or persons present at the scene).

Act by which it is an offence for any person to use the words or behaviour in s 4 (*a*) or display material referred to in s 4 (*b*) within the hearing of any person 'likely to be caused harassment, alarm or distress thereby'.[101] All three offences may be committed in a public or private place, although no offence is committed in a private place where the words or behaviour are used by a person within a dwelling and the person harassed, alarmed or distressed is also inside the dwelling. It is a defence under ss 4A and 5 that the accused's conduct took place inside a dwelling and that he or she had no reason to believe that it would be seen or heard outside. It is also a defence under ss 4A and 5 that the accused's conduct was reasonable, and additionally under s 5 that he or she had no reason to believe that there was any person within hearing or sight who was likely to be caused harassment, alarm or distress.[102] Moreover, a person is guilty of an offence under ss 4 and 5 only if he or she intends or is aware that the conduct is threatening, abusive, insulting or disorderly.[103] A constable may arrest without a warrant under ss 4 and 4A, but may do so under s 5 only after the person to be arrested fails to heed a warning to stop the offending conduct; the arrest need not be by the same police officer who gave the warning.[104]

As with s 5 of the 1936 Act, the crucial words 'threatening, abusive or insulting' are not defined, although a person is guilty of an offence under ss 4 and 5 (but not under s 4A) only if he or she intends the conduct to be threatening, abusive or insulting or, in the case of s 5 only, disorderly (s 6). Decisions under s 5 of the 1936 Act may thus be helpful in the construction of ss 4, 4A and 5 of the 1986 Act. On what is meant by insulting, the leading case is *Brutus* v *Cozens*.[105]

> During a Wimbledon tennis match, Brutus and other anti-apartheid protesters went on to the court, distributed leaflets and sat down. The spectators strongly resented the interruption of play. Brutus was prosecuted for using insulting behaviour whereby a breach of the peace was likely to be occasioned. The justices dismissed the charge, finding that the conduct was not insulting. On appeal by the prosecutor, the Divisional Court directed the justices that behaviour was insulting if it affronted other people and evidenced a disrespect or contempt for their rights, and thereby was likely to cause the resentment which the spectators had expressed at Wimbledon. The House of Lords unanimously allowed an appeal by Brutus against this direction, holding that 'insulting' was to be given its ordinary meaning and that the question of whether certain behaviour had been insulting was one of fact for the justices to determine. Lord Reid pointed out that s 5 of the 1936 Act did not prohibit *all* speech or conduct likely to occasion a breach of the peace. Vigorous, distasteful and unmannerly speech was not prohibited. There could be no definition of insult: 'an ordinary sensible man knows an insult when he sees or hears it.'

It is not enough that the accused's conduct is insulting. Under the Act it must, for example in the case of s 4, be likely to provoke violence. This corresponds with the requirement in s 5 of the 1936 Act that the accused's conduct be likely to provoke a breach of the peace. In *Jordan* v *Burgoyne*,[106] the accused was convicted under s 5 because

---

[101] The threat of violence is not a requirement of s 5 (nor indeed of s 4A), and 'a police officer can be a person who is likely to be caused harassment and so on' (*DPP* v *Orum* [1988] 3 All ER 449).

[102] See *Morrow, Geach and Thomas* v *DPP* [1994] Crim LR 58 (defence not made out in a case of a protest outside an abortion clinic – 'shouting slogans, waving banners, and preventing staff and patients from entering' thereby causing distress to patients).

[103] See *DPP* v *Clarke* (1992) 94 Cr App R 359 (defendants displaying pictures outside an abortion clinic: even though the defendants must have been aware that pictures might cause alarm or distress, it did not follow that they intended them to be threatening, abusive or insulting or were aware that they might be so).

[104] The effect of an amendment to s 5 by the Public Order (Amendment) Act 1996. See K Reid [1998] Crim LR 864.

[105] [1973] AC 854.

[106] [1963] 2 QB 744.

a speech he made in Trafalgar Square was provocative 'beyond endurance' to Jews, blacks and ex-servicemen in the crowd. It was held that the words used were insulting, and the Divisional Court rejected the interpretation of the court below that the words used by the defendant were not likely to lead ordinary, reasonable persons to commit breaches of the peace. In the view of the court the defendant must 'take his audience as he finds them, and if those words to that audience or that part of the audience are likely to provoke a breach of the peace, then the speaker is guilty of an offence'.[107] A similar conclusion would be reached under the 1986 Act.

An important issue under s 4 of the 1986 Act relates to the question of how soon after insulting conduct must the violence be likely to take place. Section 5 of the 1936 Act 'did not require that the breach of the peace which was either intended or likely to be occasioned should follow immediately upon the actions of the defendant.' The question whether such a requirement now exists was considered in *R v Horseferry Road Magistrate, ex p Siadatan*.[108]

> The applicant laid an information against Penguin Books and Mr Salman Rushdie, the publishers and author of *The Satanic Verses*, which many devout Muslims found offensive. It was alleged that the respondents had distributed copies contrary to s 4(1) of the 1986 Act on the ground that the book contained abusive and insulting writing whereby it was likely that unlawful violence would be provoked. On a strict construction of the Act, the Divisional Court held that the magistrate was correct in refusing to issue a summons. In the view of the court, the requirement in the Act that the insulted person should be 'likely to believe that such violence will be used' means that the insulted person is likely to believe that the violence will be used immediately. Watkins LJ observed: 'A consequence of construing the words "such violence" in s 4(1) as meaning "immediate unlawful violence" will be that leaders of an extremist movement who prepare pamphlets or banners to be distributed or carried in public places by adherents to that movement will not be committing any offence under s 4(1) albeit that they intend the words in the pamphlet or on the banners to be threatening, abusive and insulting and it is likely that unlawful violence will be provoked by the words in the pamphlet or on the banner'.[109]

Although s 4 of the 1986 Act thus appears to be narrower than the corresponding provisions of the 1936 Act, the police have other powers which may go some way towards closing any 'gap in the law which did not exist under the 1936 Act'.[110] These include the powers conferred by the Police Act 1996, s 89(2). It is a separate offence if any of the foregoing offences under ss 4, 4A or 5 of the 1986 Act are racially or religiously aggravated.[111]

Other offences

1 *Obstruction of the highway.* We have already encountered this offence in this chapter. Under the Highways Act 1980, s 137, it is an offence 'if a person without lawful authority or excuse in any way wilfully obstructs the free passage along a highway'. An obstruction in this sense is caused when a meeting or assembly is held on the highway (which for this purpose includes the pavement as well as the road). It is no defence that the obstruction affected only part of the highway leaving the other part

---

[107] Ibid, at 749.
[108] [1991] 1 QB 260.
[109] Compare *DPP v Ramos* [2000] Crim LR 768.
[110] [1991] 1 QB 260, at 266.
[111] Crime and Disorder Act 1998, s 31, as amended by Anti-terrorism, Crime and Security Act 2001, s 39. On the meaning of racially or religiously aggravated: s 28. Indecent or racialist chanting at designated football matches is also an offence: Football (Offences and Disorder) Act 1999, s 9.

clear.[112] Nor is it a degree that the arrested person was only one of a number of people causing the obstruction,[113] or that the defendant believed that she was entitled to hold meetings at the place in question or that other meetings had been held there.[114] The offence thus gives wide powers to the police to disperse what may be a peaceful assembly and it has been widely used. Following *DPP v Jones*,[115] however, it is now recognised that the highway may be lawfully used for some political purposes where this does not interfere with the primary purpose of the highway which is passage and repassage. Such use will provide a lawful excuse to any charge of obstruction. This is a conclusion which had been reached already in *Hirst v Chief Constable of West Yorkshire*[116] by the Divisional Court in relation to the Highways Act 1980, a decision which was expressly approved in *Jones*.

> A group of animal rights supporters were demonstrating outside a furrier's shop, and handing out leaflets. They were convicted of obstruction of the highway, contrary to the Highways Act 1980, s 137. In reversing the convictions Glidewell LJ said that the question whether someone was causing an obstruction without lawful excuse was to be answered by deciding whether the activity in which the defendant was engaged was or was not a reasonable user of the highway. This would be for the magistrates to decide, but it was clearly anticipated that the distribution of handbills could be a reasonable user.

Apart from the Highways Act 1980, obstruction of the highway is a public nuisance, which may be prosecuted as an indictable offence at common law.[117]

2 *Protection from harassment.*   Closely associated with the Public Order Act 1986, ss 4, 4A and 5 is the Protection from Harassment Act 1997, which has been said to target 'anti-social behaviour which had previously been viewed as too trivial or too imprecise to attract criminal or . . . civil liability'.[118] The Act is considered briefly in this chapter because it has been used against protestors (particularly animal rights protestors), and as a way of regulating the exercise of the right to freedom of assembly. It is unlawful to pursue a course of conduct which amounts to the harassment of another and which the person pursuing the conduct knows or ought to know amounts to harassment (s 1). It is a defence that the course of conduct was reasonable in the circumstances (s 1(3)).[119] A course of conduct must involve conduct on at least two occasions and conduct includes speech (s 7). It is an arrestable offence to pursue a course of conduct in breach of s 1 (s 2), and civil proceedings may be brought by a victim for an injunction to restrain an unlawful course of conduct and for damages suffered as a result (s 3).[120] Where an injunction is granted, the victim may apply to the court to issue a warrant for the arrest of the respondent (s 3(2)). It is also an offence under s 4 to engage in a course of conduct which causes another person to fear on at least two occasions that violence will be used against him or her. A court may issue a restraining order against a person convicted under section 2 or 4 prohibiting the defendant from doing anything specified in the order which amounts to harassment or which will

---

[112] *Homer v Cadman* (1886) 16 Cox CC 51.
[113] *Arrowsmith v Jenkins* [1963] 2 QB 561.
[114] Ibid. Cf *Cambs CC v Rust* [1972] 2 QB 426.
[115] [1999] AC 240; p 557 above.
[116] (1987) 85 Cr App R 143. See S Bailey [1987] PL 495.
[117] *R v Clark (No 2)* [1964] 2 QB 315. See also *News Group Newspapers Ltd v SOGAT 82 (No 2)* [1987] ICR 181.
[118] Fenwick, *Civil Rights*, p 162.
[119] See *DPP v Selvanayagam*, *The Times*, 23 June 1999 (conduct cannot be reasonable if in breach of a court injunction).
[120] See *Huntingdon Life Sciences Ltd v Curtin*, *The Times*, 11 December 1997; and *Thomas v News Group Newspapers Ltd* [2002] EMLR 78.

cause a fear of violence (s 5). The Act is adapted for application to Scotland (s 8). Additional restraints on demonstrating outside someone's home were introduced by the Criminal Justice and Police Act 2001 in response to the activities of animal rights protestors who picketed the homes of directors and employees of companies said to be engaged in vivisection.[121]

3 *Breach of the peace.* The apprehension of a breach of the peace is important in the law of arrest and for the purpose of binding over, but the concept of breach of the peace at common law is not clear-cut.[122] English law does not recognise a substantive offence of breach of the peace. By contrast, in Scots law there is a very broad common law offence of breach of the peace,[123] which includes the use of violent and threatening language in public, breaches of public order and decorum, and even the making of indecent suggestions in private to young persons, but not the peaceful singing of hymns at a prayer meeting in the street.[124] The offence has more recently been adapted for use against excited football fans,[125] and against an individual selling a National Front newspaper outside a football ground.[126] The broad nature of this offence probably explains why, on facts very similar to those in *Beatty* v *Gillbanks*, the Scottish courts convicted the local leaders of a Salvation Army procession of breach of the peace.[127] Breach of the peace is commonly used by the police in public order situations. During the miners' strike of 1984/85, of the 1,046 charges brought in Scotland, no fewer than 678 of these were for breach of the peace.[128] Although used to deal with a wide range of anti-social behaviour, this offence may serve as a flexible and adaptable restraint on different forms of public protest.

> *Colhoun* v *Friel*[129] concerned the protest against the M77 motorway, in the course of which the appellant sat astride a felled tree which a workman was cutting up with a chainsaw. When he refused to comply with a request to move, the appellant was arrested for breach of the peace and convicted, the conviction being upheld on appeal on the ground that 'it is well settled that the test to be applied is whether the proved conduct may reasonably expect to cause any person who observed it to be alarmed, upset or annoyed or to provoke a disturbance'. The appellant had 'placed himself and the workman in a position of danger by his refusal to move as the workman proceeded in the task of cutting the tree up with the power-operated saw. This was disorderly conduct which might reasonably have caused a person to be alarmed by virtue of what might ensue if the appellant was to remain in that position as the work proceeded.'

F. Preventive powers of the police and courts

Entry into meetings

In a public place like Trafalgar Square, there can be no doubt of the power of the police to be present and to deal with outbreaks of disorder if they occur. Where a public

---

[121] Criminal Justice and Police Act 2001, s 42. The same Act also permits directors of such companies not to publish their home addresses.
[122] See *R* v *Howell* [1982] QB 416; *R* v *Chief Constable of Devon and Cornwall, ex p CEGB* [1982] QB 458; *McConnell* v *Chief Constable of Greater Manchester* [1990] 1 All ER 423.
[123] See Christie, *Breach of the Peace.*
[124] *Ferguson* v *Carnochan* (1880) 2 White 278; *Dougall* v *Dykes* (1861) 4 Irv 101; *Young* v *Heatly* 1959 JC 66; *MacKay* v *Heywood* 1998 SCCR 210.
[125] *McGivern* v *Jessop* 1988 SCCR 511.
[126] *Alexander* v *Smith* 1984 SLT 176.
[127] *Deakin* v *Milne* (1882) 10 R(J) 22.
[128] McCabe and Wallington, p 164.
[129] 1996 SCCR 497. But see now *Steel* v *UK* (1998) 28 EHRR 603.

meeting is held on private premises, the power of the police to attend is less certain. At one time the official view of the Home Office was that except when the promoters of a meeting asked the police to be present in the meeting, they could not go in, unless they had reason to believe that an actual breach of the peace was being committed in the meeting.[130] This view was stated after disorder occurred at a fascist meeting at Olympia in London, when the stewards inflicted physical violence on dissentients in the audience. No police were stationed on the premises, although large numbers had been assembled in nearby streets. Within a year, the court disapproved of the Home Office view of the law.

> In *Thomas* v *Sawkins*[131] a meeting had been advertised in a Welsh town (*a*) to protest against the Incitement to Disaffection Bill which was then before Parliament, and (*b*) to demand the dismissal of the Chief Constable of Glamorgan. The meeting was open to the public without payment, and the police arranged for some of their number to attend. The promoter requested the police officers to leave. A constable committed a technical assault on the promoter thinking that the promoter was on the point of employing force to remove a police officer from the room. There was no allegation that any criminal offence had been committed at the meeting or that any breach of the peace had occurred. When the promoter prosecuted the constable for assault, the magistrates' court found that the police had reasonable grounds for believing that if they were not present there would be seditious speeches and other incitement to violence, and that breaches of the peace would occur; that the police were entitled to enter and remain in the hall throughout the meeting; and that consequently the constable did not unlawfully assault the promoter. In the Divisional Court these findings were upheld. Lord Hewart CJ was of opinion that the police have powers to enter and to remain on private premises when they have reasonable grounds for believing that an offence is imminent or likely to be committed; nor did he limit this statement to offences involving a breach of the peace. In the opinion of Avory J, 'the justices had before them material on which they could probably hold that the police officers in question had reasonable grounds for believing that, if they were not present, seditious speeches would be made and/or that a breach of the peace would take place. To prevent any such offence or a breach of the peace the police were entitled to enter and remain on the premises'.[132]

Although the second objective of the meeting in *Thomas* v *Sawkins* was admittedly provocative to the local police, it did not suggest an incitement to violence, which is a necessary element in the offence of sedition. Neither does protest against a Bill involve a breach of the peace. It is unclear whether Lord Hewart's opinion is confined to public meetings on private premises or whether it also applies to private meetings and other activities on private premises. May the police enter any private premises if they reasonably believe that any offence is imminent or is likely to be committed? The judgments in the case gave scant consideration to the argument that as soon as the promoter asked the police to withdraw from the premises, this rescinded the open invitation given to the public (including the police) to attend. Did this not make the officers trespassers on private premises from that point onwards?[133] It may be that it is in the public interest that the police should be entitled to enter and remain in any public meeting: but why should a similar right apply to private meetings? Doubts as to the width of *Thomas* v *Sawkins* are resolved by the Police and Criminal Evidence Act 1984, which preserves the power of the police to enter premises to deal with or prevent a breach of the peace, but otherwise abolishes all common law powers of the police to enter premises without a warrant.[134]

---

[130] HC Deb, 14 June 1934, col 1968.
[131] [1935] 2 KB 249. See Ewing and Gearty, *The Struggle for Civil Liberties*, ch 6.
[132] [1935] 2 KB 249, at 256.
[133] *Davis* v *Lisle* [1936] 2 KB 434, *Robson* v *Hallett* [1967] 2 QB 939.
[134] 1984 Act, s 17(5), (6); ch 21 D.

Obstruction of the police

The statutory offence of obstructing the police in the execution of their duty has already been considered in relation to the law of arrest.[135] It is no less important in the law of public order. The leading case is *Duncan* v *Jones*[136] in 1936, which gave rise to fears about the uses to which the offence could be put.

Mrs Duncan was forbidden by Jones, a police officer, to hold a street meeting at a place opposite a training centre for the unemployed. She refused to hold the meeting in another street 175 yards away. Fourteen months previously, Mrs Duncan had held a meeting at the same spot, which had been followed by a disturbance in the centre attributed by the superintendent of the centre to the meeting. Mrs Duncan mounted a box on the highway to start the meeting but was arrested and charged with obstructing a police officer in the execution of his duty. There was no allegation of obstruction of the highway or of inciting any breach of the peace. The lower court found (*a*) that Mrs Duncan must have known of the probable consequences of her holding the meeting, viz, a disturbance and possibly a breach of the peace, and was not unwilling that such consequences should ensue, (*b*) that Jones reasonably apprehended a breach of the peace, (*c*) that in law it therefore became his duty to prevent the holding of the meeting, (*d*) that by attempting to hold the meeting Mrs Duncan obstructed Jones when in the execution of his duty. The Divisional Court upheld the conviction. Humphreys J remarked that on the facts as found, Jones reasonably apprehended a breach of the peace: it then became his duty 'to prevent anything which in his view would cause that breach of the peace.'

The decision has been strongly criticised on several grounds. First, for reasons of principle. Goodhart remarked:

At first sight it may seem unreasonable to say that a police officer cannot take steps to prevent an act which, when committed becomes a punishable offence. But it is on this distinction between prevention and punishment that freedom of speech, freedom of public meeting and freedom of the press are founded.[137]

Secondly, the decision gave rise to concern about the nature of the power extended to police officers. On one view, it would give a police officer power to prevent the holding of a lawful meeting if he or she suspected not that the meeting itself might be disorderly but that breaches of the peace might occur as a result of the meeting, whether committed by supporters or opponents of the speakers at the meeting. The reasoning of Humphreys J brings forward in time and widens the preventive powers of the police to a degree that could lead to intolerable restrictions on the liberty of meeting. On this basis the police could forbid a meeting in the students' union of a college from taking place merely because a 'disturbance' had previously occurred in the college after a similar meeting.

Yet despite this criticism and concern, the offence of obstructing a police officer is now an important weapon in the armoury of police powers for controlling public protest. It would appear to give to the police much wider powers than those contained in the Public Order Act 1986, s 14. Thus, it applies to all public order policing situations, not just assemblies, and the power to issue directions can be exercised even though fewer than 20 people may be present. For although *Duncan* v *Jones* illustrates the power to issue directions as to location where this is considered necessary to maintain the peace, other cases illustrate that the power may be used to issue directions as to numbers. In *Piddington* v *Bates*,[138] a police officer gave instructions that during a trade dispute at a factory in North London only two pickets would be permitted outside each entrance.

---

135   Police Act 1996, s 89(2). See ch 21 B.
136   [1936] 1 KB 218; Ewing and Gearty, *The Struggle for Civil Liberties*, ch 5.
137   (1937) 6 CLJ 22, 30. See also E C S Wade (1937) 6 CLJ 175, and T C Daintith [1966] PL 248.
138   [1960] 3 All ER 660.

When the appellant insisted on joining the pickets, despite a police officer's instructions not to do so, he was arrested for obstruction. The Divisional Court dismissed his appeal against the conviction, in which it was argued that a restriction to two pickets was arbitrary and unlawful. In the view of Lord Parker CJ, 'a police officer charged with the duty of preserving the Queen's peace must be left to take such steps as, on the evidence before him, he thinks are proper'.[139] But apart from this wide power to give directions as to how a demonstration or picket is conducted, more recent developments indicate that the power permits the police to give directions not only to disperse a demonstration but effectively to ban or to prevent one from being held in the first place.

> In *Moss* v *McLachlan*[140] the defendants were stopped during the miners' strike at a motorway exit by police officers who suspected that they were travelling to attend a picket line at one of a number of collieries several miles away. When they refused to turn back, they were arrested for obstructing a police officer in the execution of his duty. Their appeals against conviction were dismissed, with Skinner J observing that 'The situation has to be assessed by the senior police officers present. Provided they honestly and reasonably form the opinion that there is a real risk of a breach of the peace in the sense that it is in close proximity both in place and time, then the conditions exist for reasonable preventive action including, if necessary, the measures taken in this case'.[141]

The cases suggest that the courts have not been anxious to scrutinise the exercise of the power very closely, willing too readily perhaps to defer to the police constable on the spot; a more rigorous approach is suggested by *Redmond-Bate* v *DPP*[142] which will require the police to have more regard to the rights to freedom of expression and assembly of the protestor or picket than is evident in *Duncan* v *Jones* and its progeny to date.

> The appellant was arrested for refusing to comply with an instruction to stop preaching outside Wakefield Cathedral. A crowd in excess of 100 people had gathered, some of whom were hostile. In reversing the convictions, it was held by the Divisional Court that the test of reasonableness of the constable's action was objective in the sense that it was for the court to decide whether in the light of what he knew and perceived at the time it was reasonable to fear an imminent breach of the peace. According to Sedley LJ, the situation perceived by the constable in which three women were preaching about morality and religion 'did not justify him apprehending a breach of the peace, much less a breach of the peace for which the three women would be responsible'.

Binding over to keep the peace[143]

Magistrates in England and Wales have a wide power to order any person to enter into a recognisance (undertaking), with or without sureties, to keep the peace or to be of good behaviour, either in general or towards a particular person.

> At a time of suffragette militancy, when many acts of damage to property were being committed, George Lansbury made speeches encouraging the women to continue. The magistrate required him to give undertakings to be of good behaviour in the sum of £1,000 and to find sureties for his good behaviour, or in default to go to prison for three months. The Divisional Court upheld the order, holding that a person could be bound over for inciting breaches of the peace even though no particular person was threatened.[144]

---

[139] Ibid, at 663.
[140] [1985] IRLR 76. See G S Morris (1983) 14 ILJ 109. Also *O'Kelly v Harvey* (1883) 15 Cox CC 435.
[141] [1985] IRLR 76, at 78. For evidence of the practice being adopted by the Scottish police (although inevitably on a different legal base, possibly breach of the peace), see Miller and Woolfson, n 49 above, at pp 220–1.
[142] [2000] HRLR 249.
[143] Williams, *Keeping the Peace*, ch 4, and [1977] Crim LR 703; A D Grunis [1976] PL 16; D Feldman [1988] CLJ 101.
[144] *Lansbury v Riley* [1914] 3 KB 229. See also *Wise v Dunning* [1902] 1 KB 167.

The origin of this power is obscure: it may rest upon the Justices of the Peace Act 1361 or it may be inherent in the commission of the peace held by magistrates. Although controversial, the power has been found not to contravene the ECHR in a case where the order was imposed after a finding that the respondent had committed a breach of the peace.[145] But a breach of art 10 was found in a subsequent case involving anti-hunt protestors where there had been no breach of peace and where the order directed the respondents not to commit a breach of the peace, or to act *contra bonos mores* in the future.[146]

Subject to this uncertainty about the state of the law, a magistrate may bind over a person when it is apprehended that he or she is likely to commit a breach of the peace, or do something *contra bonos mores* or contrary to law, a wider power still.[147] But in the case of breach of the peace it may now be necessary to show that something has been done calculated to lead to acts of personal violence.[148] In *Percy* v *DPP*[149] it was held, in a successful appeal against a binding-over order, that a non-violent protest in an RAF base could not constitute a breach of the peace. 'A civil trespass itself cannot amount to a breach of the peace' and 'although circumstances can easily be imagined in which trespass may produce violence as its natural consequence', it was highly improbable that non-violent acts of trespass 'would provoke trained personnel to violent reaction'. Moreover, it has been held that conduct capable of provoking violence (so as to be a breach of the peace) must also be unreasonable, which would exclude cases where 'the defendant was properly exercising his own basic rights, whether of assembly, demonstration or free speech'.[150] Where an order is made by the magistrates, a person who refuses to give an undertaking to be of good behaviour may be committed to prison for a term not exceeding six months.[151] There is a right of appeal to the Crown Court against an order binding a person over, although the making of an order does not constitute a conviction.[152] Natural justice requires that a person may not be bound over until he or she has been at least told what is passing through the magistrate's mind and given a chance of answering.[153] Nevertheless it has been argued that the power is 'open to serious objection when one considers the principles which ought to underpin sound modern domestic English law'.[154]

Binding-over orders were used extensively during the miners' strike of 1984/85[155] and they are in fact routinely used on a surprisingly extensive scale.[156] The strike also saw the emergence of a new and closely related preventive power, the use of bail conditions as a means of keeping people away from picket lines or other areas of protest. In some areas striking miners charged with public order offences were routinely

---

[145] *Steel* v *UK* (1998) 28 EHRR 603.

[146] *Hashman* v *UK* (1999) 30 EHRR 241.

[147] *Hughes* v *Holley* (1986) 86 Cr App R 130.

[148] *R* v *Sandbach, ex p Williams* [1935] 2 KB 192; cf *R* v *Aubrey-Fletcher, ex p Thompson* [1969] 2 All ER 846.

[149] [1995] 3 All ER 124. And see *Steel* v *UK* (note 145 above).

[150] *Nicol* v *DPP* (1996) 160 JP 155, at p 163.

[151] Magistrates' Courts Act 1980, s 115.

[152] Magistrates' Courts (Appeals from Binding Over Orders) Act 1956 (amended by Courts Act 1971); *Shaw* v *Hamilton* [1982] 2 All ER 718. See Law Commission, Working Paper 103, pp 26–8 which also deals with the possibility of judicial review. In *Percy* it was thought that the proceedings were criminal rather than civil.

[153] *Sheldon* v *Bromfield JJ* [1964] 2 QB 573. Also *R* v *South Molton JJ, ex p Ankerson* [1988] 3 All ER 989. But see now *R* v *Lincoln Crown Court, ex p Jude* [1998] 1 WLR 24.

[154] Law Commission Report 222, Binding Over, Cm 2439, 1994, para 4.34. The Law Commission recommended the abolition of the power.

[155] P Wallington (1985) 14 ILJ 145.

[156] Cm 2439, 1994, para 2.19 ('a crude extrapolation of a month's returns produced an annual figure of 34,000 binding over orders made in magistrates' courts' alone').

remanded on bail by the justices subject to the conditions that they should not 'visit any premises or place for the purpose of picketing or demonstrating in connection with the current trade dispute between the NUM and NCB other than peacefully to picket or demonstrate at their usual place of employment'. The conditions were imposed under the Bail Act 1976, which by s 3(6) provides that a person granted bail must comply 'with such requirements as appear to the court to be necessary to secure that . . . he does not commit an offence while on bail'. In R v *Mansfield Justices, ex p Sharkey*,[157] the imposition of such conditions was upheld to prevent defendants from resuming intimidatory picketing, which, in the view of Lane LCJ, would almost certainly have been an offence under s 5 of the Public Order Act 1936. The decision has, however, been strongly criticised for authorising what was merely a pretext to stop secondary picketing, which was not then and is not now per se a criminal offence.[158]

G. Freedom of assembly and the Human Rights Act 1998

In recent years there has been a growing recognition on the part of the courts of the importance of freedom of assembly,[159] and there have been a number of cases which have made bold claims about its value.[160] These cases reflect a significant change in judicial attitude which previously had been concerned in a rather one-dimensional way with public order to the neglect of other considerations. The developments in the English courts are reflected to some extent by developments in the European Court of Human Rights,[161] but it appears that the growing liberalisation has arisen quite independently of the Human Rights Act 1998,[162] although obviously within its shadow. It is perhaps premature to draw too many conclusions from the emerging trends,[163] which in any event are not necessarily reflected in the decisions of the lower courts or in the practice of the police.[164] But the appreciation of the importance of freedom of assembly parallels the growing appreciation of freedom of expression which is to be found in some of the contemporary case law,[165] and may be explained to some extent by the willingness on the part of some judges to see freedom of assembly as, in effect, an instrument of freedom of expression.[166] It is particularly important that, in the leading case on freedom of assembly, the Lord Chancellor should consider the 'public's rights of access to the public highway' as 'an issue of fundamental constitutional importance'.[167]

Changing judicial attitudes are demonstrated in a number of ways. In the first place there is now a recognition that passage and repassage are not the only lawful uses of the highway. As we have seen it was acknowledged in *DPP* v *Jones* that 'the holding of a public assembly on a highway can constitute a reasonable user of the highway and accordingly will not constitute a trespass', even if it did not follow that 'a peaceful and non-obstructive public assembly on a highway is always a reasonable user

---

[157] [1984] IRLR 496.

[158] McCabe and Wallington, pp 145–6. For the use of bail conditions in this way during the Timex dispute in Dundee in 1994, see Miller and Woolfson, note 49 above.

[159] On which see the valuable article by H Fenwick (1999) 62 MLR 491, esp pp 492–5.

[160] *Redmond-Bate* v *DPP* [2000] HRLR 249 and *DPP* v *Jones* [1999] 2 AC 240.

[161] *Steel* v *UK* (1998) 28 EHRR 603; *Hashman* v *UK* (1999) 30 EHRR 241.

[162] See esp *DPP* v *Jones* [1999] 2 AC 240.

[163] See D Mead [1998] J Civ Lib 206.

[164] Fenwick, ch 4.

[165] See ch 23.

[166] For a valuable account of the link between these two different freedoms, with a full analysis of *DPP* v *Jones*, see H Fenwick and G Phillipson [2000] PL 627.

[167] *DPP* v *Jones*, note 162 above, at p 251.

and is therefore not a trespass'.[168] This recognition at the highest level of the right of lawful assembly on the highway is accompanied by an emerging preparedness on the part of the courts to read down legislation which is being used to impose an unwarranted restraint on freedom of assembly:

> In *Huntingdon Life Sciences Ltd v Curtin*[169] the court allowed the British Union for the Abolition of Vivisection to be removed from an injunction (granted ex parte) to restrain three defendants from harassing the plaintiffs, a company which undertook research on animals and which had complained of a sustained and menacing campaign against it and its employees. The injunction had been issued under the Protection from Harassment Act 1997. In granting the request to vary the injunction, Eady J said that the 1997 Act 'was clearly not intended by Parliament to be used to clamp down on the discussion of matters of public interest or upon the rights of political protest and public demonstration which was so much part of our democratic tradition'. He had 'little doubt that the courts would resist any wide interpretation of the Act as and when the occasion arose' and thought it 'unfortunate that the terms in which the provisions of the Act were couched were seen to sanction any such restrictions'.[170]

There also appears to be a greater willingness on the part of at least some judges to challenge the exercise of discretion by police officers who take steps, including arrest, to disperse an assembly in order to prevent a breach of the peace. In the *Redmond-Bate* case, it was said:

> Free speech includes not only the inoffensive but the irritating, the contentious, the eccentric, the heretical, the unwelcome and the provocative provided it does not tend to provoke violence. Freedom only to speak inoffensively is not worth having.[171]

But it should not be overlooked that this last passage is from a case concerned with individuals who had been arrested for refusing to stop preaching on the steps of Wakefield Cathedral when instructed to do so by the police. It remains to be seen whether the same vigorous approach to freedom of assembly will be adopted in other cases – perhaps involving noisy anti-globalisation or angry anti-fascist protestors. It is in such cases that the right to freedom of assembly under the Human Rights Act 1998 will be most sternly tested.[172] The law discussed here was made before the coming into force of the Human Rights Act 1998, so some of it may well be open to challenge as violating Convention rights.[173] There have in fact been a number of cases before the Strasbourg authorities concerning public order restraints on freedom of assembly, which, as we have seen, have thrown the law on binding over into some confusion.[174] Nevertheless it seems likely that the main impact of Convention rights in this area will not be to call into question the substantive law, but to constrain the manner of its exercise. This means that the public authorities – local authorities and the police – will be bound to have regard to arts 10 and 11 when exercising discretionary powers, such as the power to arrest in the case of the police. Criticism of the policing of May Day demonstrations in London in 2001 – when protestors complained that they had been herded and detained by the police for up to eight hours[175] – suggest that the Act is only slowly

---

[168] Ibid, per Lord Hutton, at p 293.

[169] *The Times*, 11 December 1997.

[170] But see *DPP v Selvanayagam, The Times*, 23 June 1999.

[171] *Redmond-Bate v DPP*, note 160 above (Sedley LJ).

[172] In one case the Court of Appeal has reversed a conviction under the Public Order Act 1986 for disorderly behaviour likely to cause harassment, alarm or distress where the appellant argued that her defacing of the US flag was protected by art 10 of the ECHR: the *Guardian*, 22 December 2001.

[173] For an account of the potential significance of the ECHR in this area and of the potential implications of the Human Rights Act, see D Mead [1998] J Civ Lib 206 and H Fenwick (1999) 62 MLR 491.

[174] *Steel v UK* (1998) 28 EHRR 603, *Hashman v UK* (1999) 30 EHRR 241.

[175] *The Times*, 2 May 2001.

having an effect and that there is some way to go before it can be said to have led to practical change on the ground.

The courts will likewise be required to have regard to Convention rights, when for example called on to issue an injunction to prevent or disperse an assembly. It is in relation to the granting of injunctive relief in civil proceedings that the Human Rights Act could make a particularly important contribution to the protection of freedom of assembly. The procedural rules whereby injunctive relief can be granted simply where there is a serious question to be tried and the balance of convenience lies in favour of relief look particularly ripe for review. It was on this ground that the interlocutory injunction was granted in *Hubbard* v *Pitt*:[176] the pickets were restrained not because they were doing anything unlawful, but because they *might* be doing something unlawful. The courts will now be required to ensure that any remedy does not trespass on the respondent's Convention rights. An injunction to restrain peaceful picketing would almost certainly constitute a breach of arts 10 and 11 of the ECHR. It will be for the courts to consider whether the injunction can be justified as being necessary for any of the reasons permitted in arts 10 and 11. But for this purpose the courts may have to give more weight to the legal rights of the parties than is currently required by the existing procedural rules. It will be difficult to justify a violation of the rights to freedom of expression and assembly on the ground only that the applicant's legal rights may be breached by the action of the pickets. A firmer basis for interfering with Convention rights will surely be necessary.[177]

---

[176] [1976] QB 142, above, p 558.

[177] Compare Human Rights Act 1998, s 12(3) which provides that no relief is to be granted 'to restrain publication before trial unless the court is satisfied that the applicant is likely to establish that publication should not be allowed'. This does not appear to apply to restraints on freedom of expression which do not take the form of a publication. See also *NWL Ltd* v *Woods* [1979] ICR 867 (p 562 above), and now *Douglas* v *Hello!* [2001] QB 967, ch 22 F.

Chapter 25

STATE SECURITY AND OFFICIAL SECRETS

The maintenance of the security of the state is a primary duty of the government. But in performing this duty, it is important that governments do so without trespassing on individual liberty any more than is reasonably necessary. Today state security, or more commonly national security, is mentioned in a large number of statutes, which will often make special provision for matters relating to national security. Thus the Parliamentary Ombudsman may not investigate action with the authority of the Secretary of State for the purposes of protecting the security of the state,[1] and rights under the Data Protection Act 1998 may be excluded for the purpose of safeguarding national security.[2] The right of journalists to protect their sources may have to yield to the interests of national security,[3] as may the right of access to official information even when the Freedom of Information Act 2000 is brought fully into force.[4] The common law may at first sight appear to take little account of state necessity.[5] However, national security is a matter to which the courts in fact attach considerable importance.[6] This does not mean that the judges should abandon all their power to decide at the mere mention by an official of national security,[7] but the terrorist attacks in the United States in September 2001 appear to have induced British judges to move further into the background when national security is raised.[8]

There is also the problem of how to secure effective political accountability for security measures. There has, however, been in recent years a welcome lifting of the veil of secrecy which has for so long surrounded the security and intelligence services. This is reflected most notably in the greater role of legislation in regulating their affairs, and in particular by the extension of the principle of judicial oversight and with it the publication of annual reports by the judicial commissioners. But it is reflected also in the slightly greater degree of openness and accountability in terms of their finances. Although there is still some way to go, since 1994 the government has brought forward in a single published vote the aggregate expenditure of all three agencies, this being 'fully open to scrutiny by the Comptroller and Auditor General, apart from limited restrictions to protect the identities of certain sources of information and the details of particularly sensitive operations'.[9] Perhaps less seriously, the lifting of the veil of secrecy is reflected further by steps such as the announcement of the names of the heads of the various security and intelligence services, and by the publication in 1993 of

---

[1] Parliamentary Commissioner Act 1967, Sch 3(5).
[2] See ch 22 E.
[3] Contempt of Court Act 1981, s 10; *Secretary of State for Defence* v *Guardian Newspapers Ltd* [1985] AC 339.
[4] See ch 13 F.
[5] *Entick* v *Carrington* (1765) 19 St Tr 1030.
[6] E.g. *Conway* v *Rimmer* [1968] AC 910, at 955, 993; *A-G* v *Jonathan Cape Ltd* [1976] QB 752, 768.
[7] *Chandler* v *DPP* [1964] AC 763, 811, and *R* v *Central Criminal Court, ex p Bright* [2001] 2 All ER 244.
[8] *Home Secretary* v *Rehman* [2002] 1 All ER 122; A Tomkins (2002) 118 LQR 200. Compare S Brown [1994] PL 579, at pp 589–90.
[9] HC Deb, 24 November 1993, col 52 (WA). The vote for 2001–2002 was £747,000,000.

a booklet by MI5 outlining its activities, together with the delivery of the Dimbleby lecture by the Director-General of the Security Service in the following year[10] and the publication of her memoirs in 2001.[11] The security service website also provides some basic information about activities and funding.[12]

Many of the reforms which have taken place in recent years have been driven by the European Convention on Human Rights and, more recently, by the requirements thought likely to arise under the Human Rights Act 1998. As we have seen,[13] many of the provisions of the Convention allow for exceptions and these generally include national security, provided that the restriction can be shown to be prescribed by law and necessary in a democratic society. This is true, for example, of arts 8, 9, 10 and 11. One of the difficulties with the procedures and practices operating in this country was their relative informality and the lack of clear legal rules setting out the functions and powers of the security and intelligence services.[14] So to the extent that the activities of the security services violate the private life of the individual, it could not be said until recently that the restrictions were prescribed by law. But of course it is not enough that there should be legal authority for such restrictions. Also important is the nature and quality of the law: to satisfy the Convention any restriction on Convention rights must be proportionate to the objective which it is sought to be achieved. Restrictions on the rights of the individual in the interests of national security must be proportionate.

The security service

The security service was created in the War Office in 1909 to deal with the fears about German espionage in the period immediately before the First World War. The unit was called MO5, and later MI5. In 1935, MI5 was amalgamated with the section of the Metropolitan Police dealing with counter-subversion and in that year it changed its name to the security service.[15] The domestic security service is, however, still referred to as MI5. A remarkable feature of these developments is that they took place without statutory authority. The service was set up by executive decision (presumably under the royal prerogative) with functions determined by the executive and accountable only to the executive. In his report on the security service following the Profumo scandal in 1963, Lord Denning wrote:

> The Security Service in this country is not established by Statute nor is it recognised by Common Law. Even the Official Secrets Acts do not acknowledge its existence. The members of the Service are, in the eye of the law, ordinary citizens with no powers greater than anyone else. They have no special powers of arrest such as the police have. No special powers of search are given to them. They cannot enter premises without the consent of the householder, even though they may suspect a spy is there. If a spy is fleeing the country, they cannot tap him on the shoulder and say he is not to go. They have, in short, no executive powers. They have managed very well without them. We would rather have it so, than have anything in the nature of a 'secret police'.[16]

---

[10] See respectively *MI5, The Security Service* and Rimington, *Security and Democracy – Is there a Conflict?*

[11] Rimington, *Open Secret*.

[12] www.securityservice.gov.uk.

[13] See ch 19 B.

[14] *Malone* v *UK* (1984) 7 EHRR 14; *Hewitt and Harman* v *UK* (1992) 14 EHRR 657; and *Khan* v *UK* (2001) 31 EHRR 1016.

[15] For a full account of its origins, see Andrew, *Secret Service*. See also West, *MI5: British Security Service Operations 1909–45*; and *A Matter of Trust: MI5. 1945–72*. For further analyses, see Ewing and Gearty, *The Struggle for Civil Liberties*, ch 2; Gill, *Policing Politics*; Lustgarten and Leigh, *In from the Cold*; Williams, *Not in the Public Interest*, part 2; and Bunyan, *The Political Police in Britain*, chs 3, 4.

[16] Cmnd 2152, 1963.

According to Lord Denning, this absence of legal powers was made up for by the close cooperation between the security service and the police, particularly the Special Branch.[17] The security service would make all the initial investigations relying on its technical resources and specialised field force. But as soon as an arrest was possible, the police were called into consultation and from that point onwards both forces worked as a team. Because of the lack of executive power of the security service, an arrest would be made by the police and if a search warrant were sought, this too would be done by the police.[18]

Before the Security Service Act 1989 (on which see below), the operation of the service was governed by a directive issued by the Home Secretary in 1952 (Sir David Maxwell Fyffe) to the Director-General.[19] This provided that, although the security service was not a part of the Home Office, the Director-General would be responsible to the Home Secretary personally, with a right on appropriate occasions of direct access to the Prime Minister. The directive also stated that the service 'is part of the Defence Forces of the country' and that 'its task is the Defence of the Realm as a whole, from external and internal dangers arising from attempts at espionage and sabotage, or from actions of persons and organisations whether directed from within or without the country, which may be judged to be subversive of the State'. The work of the service was to be strictly limited to what is necessary for these purposes and was expressly required to be kept absolutely free from any political bias or influence. Questions of political responsibilities of the service were clarified by Lord Denning in his 1963 report.[20] Although the function of the service is the defence of the realm, political responsibility does not lie with the Secretary of State for Defence, but with the Home Secretary and the Prime Minister, who is advised on security matters by the Cabinet Secretary.[21] This confused chain of responsibility is reinforced by the Security Service Act 1989. It is, however, an open question just what degree of political responsibility does exist, particularly in view of the convention that ministers 'do not concern themselves with the detailed information which may be obtained by the Security Services in particular cases, but are furnished with such information only as may be necessary for the determination of any issue on which guidance is sought.'[22]

Since 1989 the work of the service has changed in response to the new and evolving international position, with the events of 11 September 2001 likely to have major implications for its future work. During the Cold War the service was concerned to a large extent with counter-subversion and counter-espionage. So far as the former is concerned, it was reported in 1995 that the threat from subversive organisations had decreased to the point where it was assessed as being 'low'. The Communist Party of Great Britain (CPGB) no longer existed, while the main surviving organisation (the Communist Party of Britain) was assessed to be only about 1,100 strong, compared to 25,000–30,000 in the CPGB in the 1970s and 56,000 at its peak in 1942.[23] According to the Security Commission, it had been agreed inter-departmentally that the investigation of subversive organisations should be reduced[24] and in 1992 the service assumed a new responsibility in the form of 'Irish republican terrorism' which was transferred from the Special Branch. Although this step seems clearly to have been inspired

---

[17] See p 586 below.
[18] Cmnd 2152, 1963, para 273.
[19] Reproduced in R v Home Secretary, ex p Hosenball [1977] 3 All ER 452 in the judgment of Lord Denning MR.
[20] See also Wilson, The Labour Government 1964–70, p 481.
[21] Cmnd 2152, 1963, para 238.
[22] Ibid.
[23] Pelling, The British Communist Party, p 192.
[24] Cm 2930, 1995.

by the need to fill the gap in the work of the service caused by the end of the Cold War, it was explained in Parliament that the service already had responsibility for Irish loyalist and international terrorism and for Irish republican terrorism overseas.[25] Indeed, it was only the accident of history which had given the police the leading responsibility for Irish republican terrorism, a decision which had been taken in 1883 when the Special Irish Branch was formed to track down Fenians who at the time were placing bombs in London. The Home Affairs Committee of the House of Commons expressed anxiety in 1992 that 'intelligence gathering in terrorism will be followed by work in other areas previously within the control of the police', in which case there was a need for 'effective scrutiny'.[26] The role of the service has in fact been extended by the Security Service Act 1996 so that it now has duties in respect of serious crime.

The Secret Intelligence Service, GCHQ and the Defence Intelligence Staff

The existence of the Secret Intelligence Service (SIS or MI6 as it is more commonly known) was first officially acknowledged in May 1992, although it is thought to have been founded in 1909, but not in its modern form. Despite the ending of the Cold War, the government is nevertheless of the view that there is a role for the security and intelligence services 'alongside the armed services and diplomatic services in protecting and furthering the interests of Britain and its citizens at home and abroad'.[27] The threats which are said to make the continued existence of these agencies necessary 'include nuclear, chemical, biological and conventional proliferation of weapons', as well as 'terrorism and the threat to our armed forces in times of conflict, serious crime, espionage and sabotage'.[28] Officially, MI6 produces secret intelligence in support of the government's security, defence, foreign and economic policies as laid down by the Joint Intelligence Committee, an official committee now chaired by an official in the Cabinet Office with direct access to the Prime Minister. The members of the committee include senior officials in the Foreign Office, Ministry of Defence and the Treasury, as well as the heads of the three security and intelligence agencies. Its responsibilities include giving directions to and keeping under review the organisation and working of British intelligence activity at home and overseas. It also submits requirements and priorities for intelligence gathering, and coordinates interdepartmental plans for intelligence activity.

Although it had been operating at least since 1947, Government Communications Headquarters (GCHQ) was not publicly acknowledged to exist until the trial of Geoffrey Prime, an official who was convicted under s 1 of the Official Secrets Act 1911 in 1982 for passing information to the Soviet Union. This was followed by a report of the Security Commission which not only revealed the existence of the centre but also gave an account of the security procedures in operation there, including those for physical and document security.[29] It came more prominently to the fore in 1984 when controversially the government announced a trade union ban,[30] one irony of which is that as a result GCHQ 'has become as well known in political circles as MI5 and MI6'.[31] Officially, the centre provides government departments and military commands with signals intelligence in support of the government's security, defence, foreign and

---

[25] HC Deb, 8 May 1992, cols 297–306.
[26] HC 265 (1992–93).
[27] HC Deb, 22 February 1994, col 155 (Mr Douglas Hurd).
[28] Ibid (giving examples of the work of MI6 in the contemporary world).
[29] Cmnd 8876, 1983.
[30] See p 589 below.
[31] Official Report, Standing Committee E, 15 March 1994, col 115.

economic policies, again in accordance with requirements laid down by the Joint Intelligence Committee. It also produces advice and assistance to government departments and the armed forces on the security of their communications and information technology systems, a task undertaken by the Communication Electronics Security Group. The Director of GCHQ, like the Chief of SIS, is personally responsible to the Foreign Secretary, subject to the overall responsibility of the Prime Minister for intelligence and security matters. Both GCHQ and SIS have been placed on a statutory footing by the Intelligence Services Act 1994 (on which see below): like the security service before them, they have come in from the cold.

Although not formally a security and intelligence agency, mention might nevertheless be made of the Defence Intelligence Staff. Established in 1964, it is run by the Chief of Defence Intelligence. Much of its work is said to be devoted exclusively to military subjects and it is also concerned with weapons proliferation, arms sales and control, as well as defence industries.[32] It serves the Ministry of Defence, the armed forces and other government departments and analyses information from a wide variety of sources, both overt and covert. The Chief of Defence Intelligence is responsible to the Secretary of State for Defence, subject to the overall responsibility of the Prime Minister. But although it appears in official accounts of the security and intelligence services, the work of DIS is not subject to any statutory regulation or independent oversight in the manner of the other agencies. The DIS is, however, recognised by statute: under the Regulation of Investigatory Powers Act 2000, the Chief of Defence Intelligence may apply for an interception warrant.[33] But the DIS does not fall within the definition of the intelligence services in the Act (which is confined to the Security Service, the Secret Intelligence Service and GCHQ). Neither is the DIS the only part of the Ministry of Defence intelligence activity, which includes 'intelligence elements throughout the armed forces and within the single Service Commands'.[34] It is funded from the Defence Votes.[35]

The Security Service Act 1989[36]

The security service is now governed to some extent by the Security Service Act 1989.[37] In providing for the continuation of the service, the Act defines its function to be 'the protection of national security and, in particular, its protection against threats from espionage, terrorism and sabotage, from the activities of agents of foreign powers and from actions intended to overthrow or undermine parliamentary democracy by political, industrial or violent means' (s 1(2)). The term 'national security' is not defined, although it has been said to be wider than the particular heads specified in the Act.[38] The service also has the task of safeguarding the economic well-being of the country against threats posed by the actions or intentions of persons outside the United Kingdom (s 1(3)). By an amendment to the 1989 Act introduced by the Security Service Act 1996, it is also the function of the service to act in support of the

---

[32] See HC 115 (1995–96) (Scott Report), para C 2.26.

[33] Regulation of Investigatory Powers Act 2000, s 6.

[34] Statement on the Defence Estimates 1994, Cm 2550, 1994, p 41.

[35] For a brief account, see Cabinet Office, *National Intelligence Machinery* (2000).

[36] See I Leigh and L Lustgarten (1989) 52 MLR 801; also Ewing and Gearty, *Freedom under Thatcher*, pp 175–88.

[37] For arrangements in other countries, see S Farson [1992] PL 377 (Canada), and Lee, Hanks and Morabito, *In the Name of National Security* (Australia). See also Lustgarten and Leigh, note 15 above, which is strong on Australian and Canadian developments.

[38] Cm 1480, 1991. Although not 'easily defined', it 'includes the defence of the realm and the government's defence and foreign policies involving the protection of vital national interests at home and abroad'. What is a vital national interest is 'a question of fact and degree', more 'easily recognised when being considered than defined in advance'.

activities of police forces and other law enforcement agencies (such as the National Criminal Intelligence Service, and the National Crime Squad) in the prevention and detection of serious crime. According to the government, this last provision reflects 'the firm intention' that the service 'should be deployed against organised crime' and that the 'drug traffickers, the money launderers and the racketeers' are to become the service's new targets. The role of the service is to be 'a supporting one' in this capacity, the legislation reflecting fully 'the principle that the public and the law enforcement agencies will retain the primary responsibility'.[39] Nevertheless, these provisions were extremely controversial and gave rise to concern in Parliament and elsewhere. There is no definition of 'serious crime' and no guarantee that the work of the service will be confined to organised crime, the search for a definition of which was dismissed, as it would 'distract us from our task', and could create 'loopholes that could be exploited by unscrupulous defence lawyers to challenge the legality of the security service's involvement in a case'.[40] Admittedly, the executive powers of the service are restricted by a definition of serious crime which restrains the circumstances in which a warrant may be issued to interfere with property, but even this is extremely wide, as was pointed out during the committee stage in the House of Lords.[41] Apart from the absence of effective legal boundaries, concerns were also expressed about the lack of accountability of the service when performing its new function in assisting the police: there will be no accountability to local police authorities and no supervision by the Police Complaints Authority.[42]

In exercising these wide powers, the service continues to be under the operational control of the Director-General, who is appointed by the Home Secretary (s 2(4)). The duties of the Director-General, who must make an annual report to the Prime Minister and the Home Secretary (s 2), include taking steps to ensure that the service does not take any action to further the interests of any political party (s 2(2)(b)). This is narrower than the rule contained in the Maxwell Fyffe directive which required the service to be kept free from 'any political bias or influence', a rule which allegedly did not prevent the surveillance of the Campaign for Nuclear Disarmament or trade unions involved in pay disputes.[43] The 1989 Act also conferred a new power on the service. This is the power to apply to the Home Secretary for a warrant authorising 'entry on or interference with property' (s 3).[44] Hitherto there was no power to grant any warrant, but it appears that the service may not have been unduly impeded in the absence of such power. Indeed, in *Attorney-General v Guardian Newspapers (No 2)* Lord Donaldson MR appeared willing to turn a blind eye to the unauthorised entry of private property by the security services, referring to it as a 'covert invasion of privacy' which might be considered excusable in the defence of the realm.[45] Section 3 has been replaced by ss 5 and 6 of the Intelligence Services Act 1994 (see below), but was not repealed, though it ceased to have effect.[46]

The 1989 Act is significant also for having introduced new procedures for the supervision of the service. These are modelled on procedures introduced in the Interception

[39] HL Deb, 14 May 1996, cols 398–9 (Baroness Blatch). The meaning of detection for these purposes is widely defined: s 1(5), as inserted by the Regulation of Investigatory Powers Act 2000, s 82(1).
[40] HL Deb, 14 May 1996, cols 398–9 (Baroness Blatch).
[41] HL Deb, 10 June 1996, col 1495 (Lord Williams of Mostyn).
[42] This point is considered in some detail at HL Deb, 10 June 1996, cols 1500–20. For a particularly powerful critique, see the *Guardian*, 10 June 1996 (editorial).
[43] Allegations to this effect were made by a retired MI5 officer, Cathy Massiter, in a Channel 4 television programme. For the unsuccessful challenge to the legality of this activity, see *R v Home Secretary, ex p Ruddock* [1987] 2 All ER 518.
[44] On the way this power is exercised, see Cm 1480, 1991, para 3.
[45] [1990] AC 109, at 190. Cf *Entick v Carrington* (1765) 19 St Tr 1030.
[46] See Cm 3253, 1996.

of Communications Act 1985, which was discussed in chapter 22. The 1989 Act made provision for the appointment of a Security Service Commissioner, being someone who holds or has held high judicial office (s 4); and also a Security Service Tribunal to hear complaints against the service (s 5). The Commissioner was required to keep under review the power of the Home Secretary to issue warrants to the service. The office of Commissioner was held from its inception by Lord Justice Stuart-Smith. But unlike the Commissioner appointed under the Interception of Communications Act 1985, the Security Service Commissioner did not provide details of the number of warrants issued under s 3 in any one year, explaining that this is because of the 'comparatively small number of warrants issued under the 1989 Act and the fact that the purpose for which they can be granted is more restricted than under the 1985 Act'.[47] The practice of the Commissioner was to review all the warrants issued, reviewed and cancelled,[48] and in some cases the products obtained by the operation.[49] He always found the procedures in good order and warrants to have been properly issued. An exception was in 1999 when in one case an application was said to be 'thin and lacking in particularity'. After interviewing the responsible officers, he was able to conclude that the application had been properly made and the officers in question were asked to make a supplementary written statement to the Secretary of State to clarify the position. Notwithstanding this apparent irregularity, the Commissioner was nevertheless able to report that the 'Secretaries of State have been properly advised' and that they 'have exercised their powers under the Act correctly'.[50]

The office of Security Service Commissioner has been abolished by the Regulation of Investigatory Powers Act 2000, with the Intelligence Services Commissioner appointed under the Intelligence Services Act 1994 now having oversight for all the intelligence services (including in some cases those attached to the Ministry of Defence).[51] The Intelligence Services Commissioner is required to keep under review the way in which both ministers and members of the intelligence services exercise their powers under Parts II and III of the Regulation of Investigatory Powers Act 2000, insofar as these powers relate to the intelligence services. These include powers connected with surveillance. In addition to oversight by the Commissioner (who must report annually to the Prime Minister), the Regulation of Investigatory Powers Act 2000 provides that the investigatory powers tribunal established by s 65 of the Act may hear complaints against any of the intelligence services,[52] this replacing the jurisdiction of the tribunal created by the 1989 Act which has been abolished. The tribunal is the appropriate forum for dealing with such complaints concerned with conduct by the intelligence services which relate to the complainant, his or her property or his or her communications. This means that the tribunal is not confined to bugging or phone tapping, but could conceivably cover all forms of conduct targeted at an individual, including security vetting. In the unlikely event of a complaint being upheld (none of the complaints to the security service tribunal under the 1989 Act was upheld), the tribunal may make an award of compensation or other order as it thinks fit, including the cancelling of any warrant or authorisation and the destruction of any records held about the complainant. The Secretary of State is empowered to make regulations providing for an appeal from a tribunal's decision.

[47] Cm 1480, 1991. And see Cm 3253, 1996.
[48] Cm 4002, 1998, para 5; Cm 4365, 1999, para 7; and Cm 4779, 2000, para 15.
[49] Cm 4365, 1999, para 7.
[50] Cm 4779, 2000, paras 16 and 17.
[51] Regulation of Investigatory Powers Act 2000, s 59.
[52] A total of 338 complaints were made to the 1989 Act tribunal between 1989 and 1999: Cm 4779, 2000, para 37. In 42 of these cases it appears that the complainant was the subject of a personal file kept by the security service.

The Intelligence Services Act 1994

So far as the Secret Intelligence Service is concerned, its activities are governed by the Intelligence Services Act 1994, which also applies to GCHQ. The functions of SIS are stated by s 1(1) to be (*a*) the obtaining and providing information relating to the actions or intentions of persons outside the British Islands, and (*b*) the performing of 'other tasks relating to the actions or intentions of such persons'. These extraordinarily wide provisions are constrained by s 1(2) which provides that the statutory functions are exercisable only (*a*) in the interests of national security (with 'particular reference to the defence and foreign policies of Her Majesty's Government'), (*b*) in the interests of the economic well-being of the United Kingdom, or (*c*) in support of the prevention or detection of serious crime.[53] The 'interests of national security' are not otherwise defined, neither (more surprisingly) is what constitutes 'serious crime'.[54] And although 'a well-worn provision', it was acknowledged that a power to take action 'in the interests of the economic well-being' of the UK 'sometimes causes puzzlement as to what it can mean'.[55] It was explained, however, that the power 'might be useful' where 'substantial British economic interests were at stake or where there was a crisis or a huge difficulty about the continued supply of a commodity on which our economy depended'.[56] Under the Act the agencies are not permitted to become involved in domestic economic, commercial or financial affairs, although they may acquire information that has a bearing on domestic issues.[57]

The Act also places GCHQ on a statutory footing, under the authority of the Foreign Secretary. By virtue of s 3, its functions are twofold: the first being 'to monitor or interfere with electromagnetic, acoustic and other emissions and any equipment producing such emissions' (and 'to obtain and provide information derived from or related to such emissions or equipment'). The second duty is to provide advice and assistance about language and cryptology, this information to be provided to the armed forces, government departments or any other organisation approved by the Prime Minister. As in the case of SIS these functions are exercisable only in the interests of national security (with particular reference to the defence and foreign policies of the government); or the interests of the economic well-being of the United Kingdom 'in relation to the actions or intentions of persons outside the British Islands; or in support of the prevention and detection of serious crime'. These measures were strongly criticised in standing committee as providing a mandate which is 'wide and sweeping', inadequately constrained by the 'partial stricture' that it be exercised in the interests of national security.[58] It was pointed out in reply, however, that there were a number of safeguards in the Act to prevent the abuse of power (according to the minister there were 11 in total). So far as the duty of GCHQ to assist in the prevention and detection of crime is concerned, this was said not to be new, but had been going on for 'decades'. It appears that GCHQ intervenes when criminals use 'sophisticated communications devices to commit a crime' and assists in the deciphering of diaries and notebooks kept by criminals in sophisticated codes.[59]

The Act authorises 'entry on or interference with property or with wireless telegraphy' by each of the three security and intelligence agencies, provided that any

---

[53] The meaning of detection and prevention for these purposes is widely defined: s 11(1A), as inserted by the Regulation of Investigatory Powers Act 2000, s 82.
[54] See Cm 3288, 1996, para 8.
[55] HC Deb, 22 February 1994, col 157 (Mr Hurd).
[56] Ibid.
[57] See HC 115 (1995–96) (Scott Report).
[58] Official Report, Standing Committee E, 15 March 1994, col 117.
[59] Ibid, col 132.

such action is taken with the authority of a warrant issued by the Secretary of State (or in some cases the Scottish Ministers);[60] otherwise the action is 'unlawful', although unlike the unauthorised interception of communications it is not an offence. A warrant may be issued only if the Secretary of State 'thinks it necessary' for the purpose of assisting the agency making the application in carrying out any of its functions, provided that the taking of the action is proportionate to what the action seeks to achieve (s 5). A warrant issued on the application of either the SIS or GCHQ may not relate to British property, unlike warrants issued to the Security Service which may be issued for two such purposes. The first relates to the traditional functions of the Service, as defined in s 1(2) and (3) of the Security Service Act 1989, in which case it may relate to property in Britain, without further qualification. The second relates to the new function of the Service, added by the Security Service Act 1996, namely to act in support of the police and law enforcement agencies (such as the National Criminal Intelligence Service and the National Crime Squad) in the prevention and detection of serious crime. In this case the warrant may authorise action in respect of property in Britain, but only if the action is to be taken in relation to offences that involve violence, result in substantial financial gain, or constitute conduct by a large number of persons in pursuit of a common purpose, or if the offence is one which carries a term of three years' imprisonment on conviction for the first time.[61] Warrants are normally to be issued by a Secretary of State (or in some cases a member of the Scottish Executive)[62] and are valid for up to six months, although they may (but need not) be cancelled before the period of six months expires (s 6).

Apart from the power to interfere with property (albeit with the authority of a warrant), the 1994 Act also contains a remarkable power for the Secretary of State to authorise a person to commit an act 'outside the British Islands' which would be unlawful 'under the criminal or civil law of any part of the United Kingdom' (s 7). The effect of such authorisation is to give the individual committing an offence (or other unlawful act) immunity from legal liability in this country (but not in the country in which the crime or unlawful act may be committed), although authorisation should only be given where the acts to be done by the authorisation are 'necessary for the proper discharge of a function of the Intelligence Service'. Understandably these powers gave rise to some concern in Parliament, with one Opposition member pointing out that they grant 'the Secretary of State complete power to authorise activities that violate the law of other states as well as that of the United Kingdom. There is no limit on what can be authorised. In extreme cases the use of lethal force will be allowed'.[63] Ministers were, however, rather coy about the way in which these powers would be used, and appeared to think it enough to reassure the House that 'certain actions can be undertaken by the agencies under the specific authority of ministers only,'[64] and were unwilling to contemplate even an obligation to report annually to the Intelligence and Security Committee (on which see below) on the number and general description of all acts authorised under this section, on the ground that provision was made for the appointment of a judicial commissioner to ensure that the ministers' powers were exercised properly.[65]

Political responsibility for the agencies was said to be 'primarily' that of the Foreign Secretary 'under the Prime Minister'.[66] Under the Act, however, the operations of the

---

[60] See SI 1999 No 1750.
[61] 1994 Act, s 5, as amended by Security Service Act 1996.
[62] SI 1999 No 1750.
[63] Official Report, Standing Committee E, 17 March 1994, col 174.
[64] HC Deb, 22 February 1994, col 160.
[65] Official Report, Standing Committee E, 17 March 1994, col 175.
[66] HC Deb, 22 February 1994, col 154.

SIS continue to be under the control of the Chief of the Intelligence Service (s 2), while the operations of GCHQ continue to be under the control of the Director (s 4). Each is responsible for ensuring the efficiency of the respective services, and that no information is obtained by their organisations except so far as is necessary for the proper discharge of their functions. They must also ensure that information is not disclosed by their organisations except 'so far as necessary' for the proper discharge of their functions, and that the respective agencies do not take 'any action to further the interests of any United Kingdom political party' (ss 2(2)(b), 4(2)(b)). By a strange quirk of drafting (although it may not be unintended) either service may disclose information even though it is not necessary for it to do so in 'the proper discharge of its functions'. Thus the SIS may disclose material (without violating the duty of the Chief of the Intelligence Service) on the additional (but not necessarily consequential) ground that it is in the interests of national security, for the prevention or detection of serious crime, or for the purpose of any criminal proceedings (s 2(2)(a)). GCHQ may disclose information falling into the last of these three categories, even though, again, disclosure is not necessary for the proper discharge of its functions, a much narrower incidental power than that possessed by SIS. Both the Chief of Intelligence Service and the Director of GCHQ are required to make an annual report to the Prime Minister and the Foreign Secretary, and they may report to either 'at any time' on any matter relating to the work of their respective services (ss 2(4) and 4(4)).

Following the precedents established in 1985 and 1989, the 1994 Act made provision for the creation of an Intelligence Services Commissioner (appointed by the Prime Minister and being a person who holds or has held high judicial office) and a tribunal for the investigation of complaints about the SIS or GCHQ (the first President of which was Lord Justice Simon Brown). The decisions of both the Commissioner and the tribunal (including decisions as to jurisdiction) were not subject to appeal and were not liable to be questioned in any court of law. The first Commissioner under the Act was Lord Justice Stuart-Smith, who, as we have seen, was also the Security Service Commissioner. In his five annual reports the Commissioner was generally satisfied with the way in which ministers exercised their powers under the Act, although a number of problems were identified. In 1997, concern was expressed about errors which in one case led to five days' unauthorised interference with property taking place;[67] in 1998, a procedural error led to action taken by GCHQ being unlawful;[68] and in 1999, concern was expressed about warrants being issued by officials outside the relevant minister's department.[69] The Commissioner felt it appropriate to record in his fifth annual report that in some cases 'the application could have been presented in rather greater detail' and that 'the case for warranty could have been more convincingly made'.[70] The Commissioner did not feel it appropriate to disclose the number of warrants which had been issued or the number of authorisations granted. Although 35 complaints (some from people who clearly 'suffered from delusions') were referred to the tribunal, none was upheld. Lord Justice Stuart-Smith was replaced as Commissioner by Lord Justice Simon Brown and the jurisdiction of the office expanded to include that of the Security Service Commissioner, an office which no longer exists. The tribunal established under the 1994 Act has been abolished, its functions now performed by the investigatory powers tribunal established by the Regulation of Investigatory Powers Act 2000, s 65, with Lord Justice Mummery as its president in 2001.

---

[67] Cm 3677, 1997.
[68] Cm 3975, 1998.
[69] Cm 4361, 1999. See now Regulation of Investigatory Powers Act 2000, s 74(3).
[70] Cm 4777, 2000.

The Special Branch[71]

Another agency engaged in work related to state security is the police Special Branch, which as we have seen was formed in 1883 in response to a Fenian bombing campaign in London. After three years the word 'Irish' was dropped from the Branch's title and it was expanded to deal with other security problems. After 1945 provincial police forces established their own permanent Special Branch, and today each police force has a Special Branch under the direction of its chief constable. According to *Home Office Guidelines*, 'each Special Branch remains an integral part of the local police force, accountable to individual Chief Officers and available for them to deploy on any duties flowing from their responsibility for the preservation of the Queen's Peace, including the prevention and detection of crime'.[72] The size of each Branch and the rank of its Head depend on the size of the force as a whole and the nature and extent of the responsibilities given to the Branch in the force area.[73] There is no national Special Branch force, although 'the small size of most Special Branches, the specialised nature of their work and the potential for exceptional demands to arise from time to time in a particular locality have necessitated more extensive arrangements for cooperation between Special Branches within regions than was once the case'.[74] Moreover, there are a number of 'national policing arrangements' which affect Special Branch work, in the sense that much Special Branch activity is coordinated by the Metropolitan Police Special Branch (said to exercise a 'national role') which together with the Security Service also has responsibility for 'initial and continuation training'. Special Branch officers are bound by the same disciplinary code as other police officers, and have no additional powers by virtue of their employment in the Special Branch.

Although the organisation and functions of the Special Branches are neither prescribed nor directly regulated by statute, the *Home Office Guidelines* describe their role as being:

> primarily to acquire intelligence, to assess its potential operational value, and to contribute more generally to its interpretation. They do so both to meet local policing needs and also to assist the Security Service in carrying out its statutory duty under the Security Service Act 1989 – namely the protection of national security and, in particular, protection against threats from espionage, terrorism, and sabotage, from the activities of agents of foreign powers and from actions intended to overthrow or undermine parliamentary democracy by political, industrial or violent means.[75]

In practice, however, it is countering the threat of terrorism which is said to be the most important single function of the Special Branch, with any intelligence acquired being passed on to the Security Service, now the 'lead agency' since responsibility was transferred in 1992. As part of their counter-terrorist role, Special Branches provide armed personal protection for people at risk and keep watch at airports and seaports. So far as counter-subversion is concerned, this has been reduced in recent years, though the Special Branch continues to gather information about the public order implications of events such as marches and demonstrations,[76] particularly in cases where there is a possibility of 'politically motivated violence or subversive influence'; in other

---

[71] See Bunyan (note 15 above), and Allason, *The Branch: A History of the Metropolitan Police Special Branch 1883–1983*.

[72] *Home Office Guidelines on Special Branch Work in Great Britain* (1994), para 2. In December 2001 these were in the process of being revised.

[73] Ibid, para 16.

[74] Ibid, para 17. This is said to occur informally and on the basis of the mutual aid provisions in what is now the Police Act 1996.

[75] Ibid, para 3.

[76] It would also include picketing in the course of trade disputes: HC 71 (1984–85).

cases the police 'routinely look to other parts of their organisations to provide information on public order events'.[77] This enables measures to be taken to ensure the physical safety of participants and the public, and that proportionate and cost-effective policing arrangements are made to deal with any likely disorder or violence. Although not referred to in the *Home Office Guidelines*, Special Branches in the past have assisted in jury vetting in cases involving national security or terrorism, to exclude jurors with 'political beliefs so biased as to go beyond normally reflecting the broad spectrum of views and interests in the community to reflect the extreme views of sectarian interest or pressure group to a degree which might interfere with his fair assessment of the facts of the case or lead him to exert improper influence on his fellow jurors'.[78] In 1984, the Home Affairs Committee concluded that there was no cause for anxiety about the work of the Special Branches and that they were adequately controlled through chief constables.[79]

Security procedures in the civil service[80]

Since 1948 procedures have been in place to seek to exclude from sensitive positions in the civil service those who are perceived to be a threat to national security. The first of these, the so-called purge procedure, was thought to have been introduced (in 1948) as a result of American pressure following major spy scandals in the immediate post-war period. The aim was to ensure that 'no one who is known to be a member of the Communist Party, or to be associated with it in such a way as to raise legitimate doubts about his or her reliability, is employed in connection with work, the nature of which is vital to the security of the State'.[81] This was followed by the introduction of positive vetting in 1952, which had been on the agenda at least since the arrest and conviction of Klaus Fuchs in 1950 for communicating atomic secrets to the Soviet Union, for which he was sentenced to 14 years' imprisonment. Its implementation was a direct consequence of the defection of Donald MacLean and Guy Burgess to Moscow, in the aftermath of which the Foreign Secretary set up a committee under the chairmanship of Sir Alexander Cadogan to examine all aspects of the security arrangements in the Foreign Office. The committee reported in November 1951, approving plans for positive vetting which had already been prepared, and recommending that it should apply widely within the Foreign Service. The committee proposed that vetting should cover not only 'political unreliability' but also 'the problem of character defects, which might lay an officer open to blackmail, or otherwise undermine his loyalty and sense of responsibility'. The practice of positive vetting was thus introduced as a 'regular system' at the beginning of 1952, but without recourse to legislation, or without even informing or seeking the approval of Parliament.[82] It has since been extended well beyond the Foreign Service.

The procedures were revised in 1985, again in 1990 and, most recently, in 1994. In a statement on vetting policy,[83] it was announced that, '[in] the interests of national

---

[77] *Home Office Guidelines on Special Branch Work*, para 14.

[78] [1988] 3 All ER 1086, at 1087 (Attorney-General's guidelines).

[79] HC 71 (1984–85).

[80] See Fredman and Morris, *The State as Employer*, pp 232–6; Robertson, *Freedom, the Individual and the Law*, pp 148–52.

[81] HC Deb, 25 March 1948, cols 3417–26. See M L Joelson [1963] PL 51. The procedure was applied also to fascists, although communists were the real target.

[82] 'Not surprisingly the purge procedure has been regarded as of dwindling importance since Positive Vetting has been applied to new entrants to sensitive posts in the civil service for more than thirty years': Lustgarten and Leigh, p 131.

[83] HC Deb, 15 December 1994, col 765 (WA).

security, safeguarding Parliamentary democracy and maintaining the proper security of the Government's essential activities, it is the policy of HMG that no one should be employed in connection with work the nature of which is vital to the interests of the State', who fell within one of five categories. The first of these relates to those who are or who have been involved in or associated with espionage, terrorism, sabotage or actions intended to overthrow or undermine parliamentary democracy by political, industrial or violent means. The second category applies to anyone who is or has recently been a member of an organisation which has advocated such activities or associated with any such organisation or its members 'in such a way as to raise reasonable doubts about his or her reliability'. The third and fourth categories apply to those who are 'suscept-ible to pressure or improper influence', and to those who have shown 'dishonesty or lack of integrity which throws doubt upon their reliability', while the fifth applies in respect of those who have 'demonstrated behaviour' or are 'subject to circumstances which may otherwise indicate unreliability'. Less rigorous inquiries are made in the case of those who have frequent and uncontrolled access to SECRET information than in the case of those who deal with TOP SECRET information. In the former case individuals are subjected to a security check, whereas in the latter case the level of clear-ance to which the person is submitted is known as developed vetting and will involve inquiries being made of people familiar with the person concerned. Counter-terrorist checks (CTC) are also made in respect of a number of sensitive posts.

> A major change in recent years has been the relaxation of the rule whereby homosexuality was an automatic bar to security clearance for posts involving access to highly classified infor-mation. But the susceptibility of the subject to blackmail or pressure by a foreign intelligence service continues to be a factor in the vetting of all candidates for such positions.[84]

These non-statutory procedures are complemented by a new appeals mechanism which was announced in 1997.[85] The Security Vetting Appeals Panel (chaired by a High Court judge) now hears appeals against the refusal or withdrawal of security clearance at security check or developed vetting levels. The Panel has no jurisdiction in cases involving new recruits, nor does it apply to members of the security and intelligence services, but is otherwise available to 'all those . . . in the public and private sectors and in the armed forces' who are subject to security vetting, have 'exhausted existing appeals mechanisms within their own organisations and remain dissatisfied with the result'.[86] Members of the security and intelligence services who have a grievance about their security clearance could complain to the investigatory powers tribunal, as indeed could anyone else who believes that a refusal to grant them clearance was as a result of the actions of one of these services. Persons refused clearance are usually given reasons by the department in question, unless national security requires otherwise. A complaint may be made in writing to the Panel setting out the reasons; the respondent depart-ment will reply in writing; and an oral hearing may then be held. Neither departmen-tal officials nor their sources (for obvious reasons) are subject to cross-examination, with proceedings conducted through the chair. The appellant may be accompanied by a friend, who may be a lawyer. Proceedings of the Panel are in principle subject to judicial review, although in practice the courts have shown little stomach in the past for reviewing security vetting decisions.[87]

---

[84] HC Deb, 23 July 1991, col 476 (WA). Also HC Deb, 12 January 2000, col 287 et seq.
[85] For an account of the procedures operating before then, see Lustgarten and Leigh, pp 139–49; Fredman and Morris, p 233.
[86] HC Deb, 19 June 1997, col 243 (WA).
[87] R v Director of GCHQ, ex p Hodges, The Times, 26 July 1988. See also R v Home Secretary, ex p Hosenball [1977] 3 All ER 452, 460.

The security service and employment law

Staff employed by the security and intelligence services were traditionally denied the rights normally extended to other workers.[88] The Trade Union and Labour Relations (Consolidation) Act 1992 gives rights in relation to trade union membership, among other things; the Employment Rights Act 1996 covers a larger area, including rights relating to unfair dismissal. Both of these statutes apply to Crown servants,[89] but in both cases an exception was made for those in Crown employment in respect of whom there was a ministerial certificate exempting the employment from the protection of the legislation 'for the purpose of safeguarding national security'.[90] Certificates were issued excluding the members of the security services and subsequently the staff at GCHQ, where rights in respect of trade union membership were unilaterally withdrawn in controversial circumstances in 1984.[91] This rather foolish decision did more than anything to draw attention to GCHQ and the work which it does, as well as generating international condemnation for breaching the freedom of association guarantees in International Labour Organisation Convention 87, an international treaty to which the United Kingdom is a party.[92] Trade union rights at GCHQ were substantially (but not wholly) restored in 1997.[93]

The position under the Employment Relations Act 1999 is that almost all employment rights now apply to members of the security services, with a number of exceptions and qualifications.[94] It is expressly provided that the protections for whistleblowing extended by the Public Interest Disclosure Act 1998 do not apply in relation to employment in the Security Service, SIS or GCHQ. There are, however, procedures introduced after the Spycatcher affair designed to enable members of the security services to raise concerns internally.[95] But the right of workers to be accompanied by a trade union official in grievance or disciplinary matters at the workplace does not apply to the members of the intelligence services.[96] It is also provided that in some circumstances an employment-related complaint must be dismissed by the employment tribunal where it is shown that the action complained of was taken for the purpose of safeguarding national security. This applies specifically to cases where the complainant is alleging that he or she has been subjected to a detriment because of trade union membership or activities; or that he or she has been unfairly dismissed.[97] But it is not only where an individual has been dismissed for reasons of national security that sensitive security matters may be raised in tribunal proceedings. There is a fear that security matters could be ventilated in a hearing where someone has been dismissed because of misconduct, or alleges that she has been discriminated against on grounds of race or sex.

---

[88] For a full account of public service employment law generally, including the position of civil servants, see Fredman and Morris, note 85 above.

[89] Trade Union and Labour Relations (Consolidation) Act 1992, s 273; Employment Rights Act 1996, s 191. And see ch 32 B.

[90] Trade Union and Labour Relations (Consolidation) Act 1992, s 275; Employment Rights Act 1996, s 193.

[91] See *Council of Civil Service Unions* v *Minister for the Civil Service* [1985] AC 374; G S Morris [1985] PL 177.

[92] But it did not breach the ECHR, art 11: *CCSU v UK* (1988) 10 EHRR 269; S Fredman and G S Morris (1988) 17 ILJ 105.

[93] For a fuller account, see 12th edition of this work, pp 647–8; also Ewing, *Britain and the ILO*.

[94] See Employment Relations Act 1999, Sch 8, amending the 1992 and 1996 Acts respectively.

[95] See Rimington, *Open Secret*, pp 176–7.

[96] Employment Relations Act 1999, s 15. See HL Deb, 8 July 1999, col 1101. The government claimed that 'the security and intelligence services already have good grievance and disciplinary procedures in place' (col 1101).

[97] Employment Tribunals Act 1996, s 10(1), as inserted by the Employment Relations Act 1999, Sch 8. But see *Deulin v UK* (2002) 34 EHRR 1029.

The Employment Relations Act 1999 introduced a number of procedural changes to address such concerns, although the changes were mildly controversial and led to criticism of the government by the Intelligence and Security Committee (paradoxically for not going far enough to protect the officials).[98] These related first to the tripartite structure of the tribunal, with the Secretary of State empowered to make regulations to alter the normal composition of the employment tribunal (i) in cases relating to Crown employment proceedings, where (ii) it is expedient to do so in the interests of national security. Further, they relate to the procedure adopted by the tribunal, with the Secretary of State again empowered to make regulations authorising him or her to issue directions to an employment tribunal in Crown employment proceedings where it is expedient in the interests of national security to do so. The directions may require a tribunal to sit in private, to exclude the applicant or his or her representative from all or part of the proceedings, to take steps to conceal the identity of a particular witness, or to keep the reasons for its decision secret. If either of the last two directions is given, it is an offence to publish anything likely to lead to the identification of the witness, or the reasons for the tribunal's decision.[99]

The Official Secrets Acts 1911–89[100]

The Official Secrets Acts 1911–89 serve two distinct but related purposes:

(*a*) to protect the interests of the state against espionage and other activities which might be useful to an enemy and therefore injurious to state security;
(*b*) to guard against the unauthorised disclosure of information which is held by servants of the state in their official capacity, whether or not the information has any direct reference to state security as such.

The legal sanctions under (*b*) help to support the sanctions against espionage, since it may in a particular case be possible to prove unauthorised disclosure of information without being able to prove elements of espionage. But they may also serve to protect the corridors of power against disclosure of information and publicity which a government might find politically embarrassing or inconvenient. The Official Secrets Act 1911, on which later Acts have been built, was passed rapidly through Parliament in circumstances in which ministers emphasised purpose (*a*) as the primary object of the Act, and did not mention purpose (*b*). In 1972, the Franks committee on s 2 of the 1911 Act commented that new legislation should be introduced to separate the espionage laws from the general protection of official information.[101]

Section 1(1) of the 1911 Act creates a group of offences, mainly connected with espionage. It is an offence, punishable with 14 years' imprisonment:

if any person *for any purpose prejudicial to the safety of the State* –
(*a*) approaches, inspects, passes over or is in the neighbourhood of, or enters any prohibited place within the meaning of this Act; or
(*b*) makes any sketch, plan, model, or note which . . . might be or is intended to be directly or indirectly useful to an enemy; or
(*c*) obtains, collects, records, or publishes or communicates to any other person any secret official code word, or pass word, or any sketch, plan, model, article, or note, or other document or information which . . . might be or is intended to be directly or indirectly useful to an enemy.

---

[98] Cm 4532, 1999. Also Cm 4777, 2000.
[99] Employment Tribunals Act 1996, s 10B, as inserted by the Employment Relations Act 1999, Sch 8.
[100] Ewing and Gearty, *The Struggle for Civil Liberties*, ch 2; Bailey, Harris and Jones, *Civil Liberties Cases and Materials*, ch 8; Andrew, *Secret Service*; Williams, *Not in the Public Interest*, part 1.
[101] Cmnd 5104, 1972.

The italicised phrase caused difficulties when charges under s 1 were brought following a non-violent political demonstration against an RAF base, in *Chandler v DPP*.[102]

> Anti-nuclear demonstrators sought to immobilise an RAF bomber base by sitting down on the runway. They were arrested as they approached the base and charged with conspiring to enter a prohibited place for a purpose prejudicial to the safety or interests of the state, contrary to s 1 of the 1911 Act. The trial judge refused to allow the accused to bring evidence to show that it would be beneficial to the United Kingdom if the government's nuclear policy were abandoned. For a variety of interlocking reasons, the House of Lords unanimously upheld the conviction. The demonstrators admittedly wished to obstruct the use of the airbase and it was immaterial that they believed that such obstruction would ultimately benefit the country. The offences created by the 1911 Act, s 1 were not confined to spying but included sabotage and other acts of physical interference.

This decision was criticised,[103] but it seems impossible to argue that Parliament intended a spy who had passed military secrets to a foreign power to be able to establish as a defence that his or her purpose in so doing was to force the British government to change its policies. The outcome in *Chandler*'s case would have been different if the demonstrators' intention had merely been to hold a protest meeting on the road outside the airbase, since the prosecution would have had to establish that to protest about nuclear policy was itself an act prejudicial to the interests of the state. In *Chandler*'s case, Lord Devlin alone stressed that it was for the jury to decide all questions of fact, including the issue of the accused's purpose and its likely effect on the interests of the state. During an official secrets trial in 1978, Mars-Jones J indicated that the use of s 1 in situations that fell short of spying and sabotage could be oppressive.[104] Cases since then have been concerned mainly with spying, including the convictions of Geoffrey Prime in 1983,[105] Michael Bettaney in 1984[106] and Michael Smith in 1993,[107] all of whom had communicated secret information to the USSR. The other celebrated s 1 prosecution in the 1980s was that of eight signals intelligence officers based in Cyprus.[108] But unlike the cases of Prime, Bettaney and Smith, the prosecution failed. A subsequent inquiry by David Calcutt QC revealed that the accused had been unlawfully and oppressively detained while investigations were being conducted by the police and security service.[109]

Section 2 of the 1911 Act created a plethora of over 2,000 different offences related to the misuse of official information.[110] In particular, by s 2(1) it was an offence punishable by two years' imprisonment

> if any person having in his possession or control . . . any document or information . . . which has been entrusted in confidence to him by any person holding office under Her Majesty . . . communicates the . . . document or information to any person, other than a person to whom he is authorised to communicate it or a person to whom it is in the interests of the State his duty to communicate it.[111]

Other offences included the unauthorised retention of documents and failure to take reasonable care of documents. Section 2 plainly extended to the disclosure of information

---

[102] [1964] AC 763.
[103] D Thompson [1963] PL 201.
[104] A Nicol [1979] Crim LR 284; Aubrey, *Who's Watching You?*
[105] *R v Prime* (1983) 5 Cr App R (s) 127.
[106] *R v Bettaney* [1985] Crim LR 104.
[107] Cm 2903, 1995.
[108] See A W Bradley [1986] PL 363. See also Cmnd 9923, 1986.
[109] Cmnd 9781, 1986.
[110] Cmnd 5104, 1972, para 16.
[111] In *R v Ponting* [1985] Crim LR 318 it was held that the interests of the state are the interests of state as determined by the government of the day.

which bore no relation to national security.[112] An offence could be committed even though the information was not secret,[113] and even though it was disclosed in order to promote rather than undermine British interests abroad.[114] The scope of the section – well described as a 'catch all'[115] – was, however, mitigated in two ways. First, as with all offences under the Official Secrets Acts, the consent of the Attorney-General in England (or the Lord Advocate in Scotland) was necessary before any prosecution could be brought.[116] Second, the authorisation which prevented disclosure of information being an offence could be wholly informal and could be implicit in the circumstances of disclosure. Ministers and many senior civil servants, by what was known as the practice of self-authorisation, were able to decide for themselves how much information to disclose, at least in matters relating to their own duties.[117] Thus, when an off-the-record briefing was given to a journalist (for example, to enable him to 'leak' the contents of a Bill before it is published in Parliament) no breach of the Official Secrets Acts would have occurred. More than once it had been stressed that s 2 of the 1911 Act was not to be blamed for secrecy in government, since at any time ministers could adopt a more open approach.[118] Nonetheless, the form of the 1911 Act often presented journalists with a real difficulty in knowing what they might safely publish.

Other provisions of the Official Secrets Acts include s 7 of the 1920 Act, under which it is an offence to attempt to commit any offence under the Acts or to endeavour to persuade another person to commit such an offence, or to aid and abet or to do *any act preparatory* to the commission of such an offence. Under the 1920 Act, s 8, a court may exclude the public from the trial of an offence under the Acts if the prosecution applies for this on the ground that the publication of evidence would be prejudicial to national safety. This measure, which is employed in s 1 prosecutions[119] and which has also been employed in s 2 cases,[120] is an important departure from the general rule of 'the English system of administering justice' that 'it be done in public'.[121] For if 'the way the courts behave cannot be hidden from the public ear and eye this provides a safeguard against judicial arbitrariness or idiosyncrasy and maintains the public confidence in the administration of justice'.[122] Even if a prosecution is held behind closed doors, the accused and his or her lawyer may not be excluded and sentence must be delivered in open court.[123] Section 6 of the 1920 Act effectively removes a suspect's right of silence in a case brought under s 1 of the 1911 Act by providing that a Secretary of State may authorise the police to call a prospective witness for questioning about a s 1 offence and in this event refusal to attend or to give information constitutes an offence.[124] Moreover, s 9 of the 1911 Act confers wide powers of search and seizure, authorising a magistrate to grant a search warrant permitting the police to enter and search premises 'and every person found therein', and to seize anything which is evidence of an offence under the Act 'having been or being about to be committed'.

---

[112] See *Loat v James* [1986] Crim LR 744.
[113] *R v Crisp* (1919) 83 JP 121.
[114] *R v Fell* [1963] Crim LR 207.
[115] Cmnd 5104, 1972, para 17.
[116] Official Secrets Act 1911, s 8.
[117] Cmnd 5104, 1972, para 18.
[118] E.g. Cmnd 4089, 1969, p 11; Cmnd 5104, 1972, ch 5.
[119] E.g. in the cases of *Bettaney*, note 106 above, and the Cyprus intelligence personnel, p 591 above.
[120] E.g. in the *Ponting* case, note 133 below.
[121] *A-G v Leveller Magazine Ltd* [1979] AC 440, at 449–50.
[122] Ibid, at 450.
[123] Official Secrets Act 1920, s 8(2).
[124] Before the Official Secrets Act 1939 amended the 1920 Act, s 6, refusal on demand by a police inspector to disclose the source of information obtained in breach of the Acts was itself an offence (*Lewis v Cattle* [1938] 2 KB 454).

In cases of 'great emergency' where in the interests of the state immediate action is necessary, written authority for such a search may be granted by a superintendent of police.

> In January 1987 it was reported that the BBC had decided not to broadcast a programme about the Zircon spy satellite in the interests of national security. In so doing the Corporation denied that there had been any government pressure. Two days later, an injunction was obtained by the Attorney-General restraining the journalist responsible for the programme, Duncan Campbell, from talking or writing about the contents of the film. He could not be found, however, to be served with the injunction, whereupon the *New Statesman* published details about the contents of the film. This was followed by a Special Branch raid of the *New Statesman*'s offices, and subsequently of the BBC's premises in Glasgow. The latter raid – which lasted for 28 hours – was conducted under the authority of a warrant granted under s 9 of the 1911 Act.[125] The police filled several police vans with documents, discarded film clips and over 200 containers of film. It was never entirely clear what the police were looking for, and no prosecutions followed. The episode illustrates the extent to which the 1911 Act may be used oppressively, even without a prosecution taking place.[126]

The Official Secrets Act 1989

The operation of the Official Secrets Act 1911, s 2, was examined closely by a committee chaired by Lord Franks which reported in 1972.[127] The committee had been appointed after an unsuccessful prosecution of the *Sunday Telegraph* for publishing Foreign Office documents relating to the Labour government's policy towards the Nigerian civil war.[128] The committee reported that the law then in force was unsatisfactory and that there should be a new Official Information Act, to protect only certain forms of information, namely:

(*a*) classified information relating to defence or internal security, or to foreign relations, or to the currency or to the reserves, the unauthorised disclosure of which would cause serious injury to the interests of the nation;
(*b*) information likely to assist criminal activities or to impede law enforcement;
(*c*) Cabinet documents (in the interests of collective responsibility);[129]
(*d*) information which has been entrusted to the government by a private individual or concern (for example, for tax or social security purposes or in a census).

The requirement that information of the kind specified in (*a*) must be classified would make necessary a new system of classifying documents which, unlike the existing system, would have legal consequences. Offences under the proposed new Act were recommended to include the communication by a Crown servant, contrary to his or her official duty, of information subject to the Act; the communication by any person of information of the kinds set out in (*a*), (*b*) and (*c*) which he or she reasonably believed had reached him or her as a result of a breach of the Act; and the use of official information of any kind for purposes of private gain.

The Franks committee therefore recommended that protection of official information by criminal sanctions should continue only where the public interest clearly required this. But no reform of the Official Secrets Acts was forthcoming at that time,

---

[125] The warrant was arguably unlawful, having been issued by a sheriff, not by a justice of the peace: R Black (1987) J of the Law Society of Scotland 138.
[126] For fuller details, see Ewing and Gearty, *Freedom under Thatcher*, pp 147–52. See also A W Bradley [1987] PL 1, 488.
[127] Cmnd 5104, 1972.
[128] See Aitken, *Officially Secret*.
[129] Cf ch 13 B.

although other weaknesses in the law became evident during the so-called ABC trial in 1978.[130] In 1979 the Conservative government introduced not a Freedom of Information Bill but a Protection of Official Information Bill. This sought to give absolute protection to information regarding security and intelligence, regardless of whether that information was already available to the public.[131] But the Bill was abandoned by the government because of the severe political reaction to the disclosure that Anthony Blunt had been a Russian spy, a disclosure which could have been criminal if the Bill had been enacted. Pressure for reform was maintained in the 1980s, with interest fuelled by some controversial prosecutions. These included the cases of Sarah Tisdall, a Foreign Office clerk, who leaked to the *Guardian* a secret document relating to the delivery of cruise missiles to Greenham Common,[132] and Clive Ponting, a senior official in the Ministry of Defence, who leaked to an MP documents relating to the sinking of the Argentinian vessel, the *General Belgrano*, during the Falklands War.[133] Tisdall was convicted and Ponting was found not guilty, a verdict which ran counter to McCowan J's direction to the jury.[134]

The pressure for reform culminated in the Official Secrets Act 1989, which many would argue does not go far enough.[135] While repealing s 2 of the 1911 Act, the 1989 Act introduced new restrictions on the unauthorised disclosure of an admittedly narrower range of information. One category of information protected from disclosure relates to security and intelligence, in that s 1 of the Act distinguishes between disclosures without lawful authority by security and intelligence staff, on the one hand, and civil servants and government contractors, on the other.[136] So far as the former are concerned, it is an offence for any such person to disclose any information obtained in the course of employment in the service; in the case of the latter, the unauthorised disclosure is unlawful only if 'damaging' to the work of the security and intelligence services. Sections 2 and 3 make it an offence for a civil servant or government contractor, without lawful authority, to disclose any information relating to defence or international affairs if the disclosure is damaging. In the case of defence, disclosure is defined as being damaging if it damages the capability of the armed forces to carry out their tasks, while in both cases disclosure is damaging if it endangers the interests of the United Kingdom abroad or endangers the safety of British citizens abroad (s 2(2)). It is an offence by s 4 for a civil servant or a government contractor to disclose without lawful authority any information if this results in the commission of an offence, facilitates an escape from legal custody, or impedes the prevention or detection of offences or the apprehension or prosecution of suspects. Section 4 further provides that it is an offence to disclose information 'relating to the obtaining of information' (as well as any information obtained) as a result of warrants issued under the Interception of Communications Act 1985 or the Regulation of Investigatory Powers Act 2000, s 5 (phone tapping), the Security Services Act 1989 (interference with private property) or the Intelligence Services Act 1994 (interference with property or unlawful acts done outside the UK). It is thus not an offence under s 4 to disclose information obtained unlawfully without a warrant, although it might be an offence under s 1.

---

[130] A Nicol [1979] Crim LR 284.

[131] HL Deb, 5 November 1979, col 612; cf Cmnd 7285, 1978, para 31.

[132] For the circumstances, see *Secretary of State for Defence* v *Guardian Newspapers Ltd* [1985] AC 339.

[133] See Ponting, *The Right to Know: The Inside Story of the Belgrano Affair*. Also R Thomas [1986] Crim LR 318.

[134] *R* v *Ponting* [1985] Crim LR 318.

[135] For background, see Cm 408, 1988. For analyses, see S Palmer [1990] PL 243; Birkinshaw, *Reforming the Secret State*.

[136] See s 12 on the scope of the Act.

The offences under the Act are committed only where disclosure is made without lawful authority. This corresponds to the former s 2 of the 1911 Act, whereby the offence was committed only if the disclosure was unauthorised. The question of when a Crown servant was authorised to disclose information is, as we have seen, one which gave rise to considerable difficulty, particularly in the case of Cabinet ministers and senior officials.[137] By s 7 of the 1989 Act, a disclosure is authorised if it is made in accordance with the official duty of the minister or civil servant concerned. An offence may be committed not only by the official disclosing the information, but also by a third party, such as a newspaper, which reports it. Although it is no longer an offence to receive information protected against disclosure (as it was under s 2 of the 1911 Act), it is an offence for the recipient to disclose the information without lawful authority, knowing or having reasonable cause to believe that it is protected from disclosure (s 5). In effect, it is an offence for a newspaper to publish protected information which has been leaked without authority. Controversially, there is no public interest defence available in this or indeed in other cases, the government having rejected such a measure.[138] However, in these circumstances, a newspaper is liable only if the disclosure is damaging and is made knowing or having reasonable cause to believe that it is damaging. The 1911 Act is unaffected by the Freedom of Information Act 2000.

Official secrets and human rights

Many of the offences under the Official Secrets Acts are associated with the publication of information. Many prosecutions have been for the same reason. The question which now arises is whether these measures are consistent with the guarantees of free speech in the ECHR and whether the Human Rights Act provides a defence to anyone prosecuted under the Official Secrets Act 1911–1989. This is a question which has become more urgent in recent years following another spate of unauthorised disclosures by a number of former members of the security and intelligence services in the late 1990s. These include Richard Tomlinson, who published a book in Russia and also material on the internet identifying individuals who recruited for the security service. They also include David Shayler, who fled to France after a number of high-profile revelations about the activities of the Security Service. On his return from France, Mr Shayler faced charges under the Official Secrets Act 1989, which in December 2001 had yet to be heard. But in some of the preliminary litigation, the Court of Appeal held that although Mr Shayler was entitled to the protection of freedom of expression under the Human Rights Act, the Official Secrets Act was designed to protect national security and the restriction which it imposed on freedom of expression was justified.[139] No proceedings were brought against a former director of M15 who published her memoirs in 2001 in a blaze of publicity, the book also being serialised in the *Guardian* newspaper in the same year.

The question whether the Official Secrets Acts are compatible with the Human Rights Act was raised in *Attorney-General* v *Blake*[140] where it was held that the Attorney-General was entitled to an account of profits earned by a former member of the

---

[137] See Cmnd 5104, 1972, para 18. See also Bailey, Harris and Jones, *Civil Liberties Cases and Materials*, who contrast the prosecution of Tisdall and Ponting with the failure to prosecute two Cabinet ministers (p 831).

[138] Cm 408, 1988.

[139] *R v Shayler* [2001] 1 WLR 2206. The decision was upheld by the House of Lords: [2002] 2 All ER 477. The affair has generated a body of case law. See also *Attorney-General* v *Punch* [2001] QB 1028 (ch 19) and *R v Central Criminal Court, ex p Bright* [2001] 2 All ER 244.

[140] [2000] 3 WLR 625.

security services for a publication which was made in breach of a contractual obligation not to disclose material obtained as a result of his employment. In the course of the case it was argued that s 1 of the Official Secrets Act 1989 is 'drawn too widely' because it criminalises disclosure of information when no damage results, by focusing on the 'status of the individual who makes the disclosure, rather than on the nature of the information itself'. But although the House of Lords preferred not to deal with this point, Lord Nicholls drew attention to another factor which appears to be decisive in an action where the Human Rights Act is relied on by a member of the Security Service. This was the undertaking not to disclose information which Blake had voluntarily given when he joined the service. According to Lord Nicholls, neither Blake nor any other member of the service should have an incentive to break this undertaking. He continued:

> It is of paramount importance that members of the service should have complete confidence in all their dealings with each other, and that those recruited as informers should have the like confidence. Undermining the willingness of prospective informers to co-operate with the services, or undermining the morale and trust between members of the services when engaged on secret and dangerous operations, would jeopardise the effectiveness of the service. An absolute rule against disclosure, visible to all, makes good sense.[141]

It is unclear when – if ever – the prosecution of a disclosure in breach of the Official Secrets Act 1989 would be regarded as a disproportionate protection of national security. But the Human Rights Act must surely operate to protect the security service employee at least in cases where serious wrongdoing is revealed, which usurps the function of the service and the rule of law itself.

Defence advisory notices

The Official Secrets Acts impose important restrictions on press freedom in the sense that they effectively control the information which might be made available. And as we saw in chapter 23 G, the action in equity for breach of confidence has the capacity to do much the same. Indeed, it was this which formed the basis for controlling the press during the so-called Spycatcher affair in 1987. But there are other restrictions and fetters on press freedom which have been introduced in the interests of national security. One of these is the system of 'DA' notices (known previously as 'D' notices),[142] a form of extra-legal censorship in which the press cooperates with the government. A DA notice is a means of providing advice and guidance to the media about defence and counter-terrorist information, the publication of which would be damaging to national security. DA notices are issued by the Defence, Press and Broadcasting Advisory Committee (DPBAC), an advisory body composed of senior civil servants and editors from national and regional newspapers, periodicals, news agencies, television and radio. The committee is chaired by the Permanent Under-Secretary of State for Defence and although membership may be varied by agreement, in 2001 there were three members representing government departments (Home Office, Ministry of Defence and Foreign Office) and 12 members nominated by the media (only the Publishers' Association declined to nominate a representative). The committee normally meets twice a year to review the contents of existing notices and the advice and guidance given by its secretary over the course of the year.

The system was overhauled in 1993 (following a review by the committee itself) in the light of international changes (in particular the break-up of the Soviet Union and

---

[141] Ibid, at p 641.
[142] D Fairley (1990) 10 OJLS 430; Williams, *Not in the Public Interest*, ch 4.

Warsaw Pact) and the increased emphasis on openness in government. As a result the number of standing notices was reduced from eight to six (although from time to time it may be found necessary to issue a DA notice on a particular subject), and their content and style revised to make them 'more relevant and user-friendly'. It was as a result of this review that the name of the notices was changed from D to DA notices and that of the committee to Defence, Press and Broadcasting Advisory Committee, 'better to reflect the voluntary and advisory nature of the system'.[143] Further revision in May 2000 led to a reduction in the number of notices from six to five. The five DA notices are now published on the Committee's website,[144] and deal respectively with Military Operations, Plans and Capabilities (DA Notice 1); Nuclear and Non-Nuclear Weapons and Equipment (DA Notice 2); Ciphers and Secure Communications (DA Notice 3); Sensitive Installations and Home Addresses (DA Notice 4); and United Kingdom Security and Intelligence Services and Special Forces (DA Notice 5). Each of the notices gives details of the kind of information which editors are requested not to publish, usually information which relates to defence or anti-terrorist capabilities, or to individuals who might be a terrorist target. The notices also include a 'rationale' explaining their purpose.

The secretary of the committee plays a key role in advising the media on the interpretation of notices. The current incumbent is a retired rear-admiral employed as a civil servant on the budget of the Ministry of Defence. The secretary 'is available at all times to Government departments and the media to give advice on the system', and in September 2001 he advised the media to minimise speculation about imminent military action in Afghanistan for fear of helping the 'enemy'.[145] It is a problem that DA notices are inevitably drafted in general terms, although it is the application of a DA notice to a particular set of circumstances on which the secretary is expected to give guidance, 'after consultation with Government departments as appropriate'. The Ministry of Defence has pointed out that the secretary is not 'invested with the authority to give rulings nor to advise on considerations other than national security'; and, on the other hand, that 'compliance with the DA notice system does not relieve the editor of responsibilities under the Official Secrets Act'; nor indeed will it necessarily prevent legal proceedings being brought to restrain any publication or broadcast.[146] The importance of the secretary's role was shown in 1967 when the *Daily Express* published a report that copies of private cables and telegrams sent overseas from the United Kingdom were regularly made available to the security authorities, a practice authorised by the Official Secrets Act 1920, s 4. The Prime Minister, Mr Wilson, claimed that this article was a breach of a 'D' notice. An investigation by three privy councillors established that this was not the case but, that there had been misunderstandings to which the secretary of the committee had contributed.[147] The Defence Committee of the House of Commons reviewed the 'D' notice system in 1980 and concluded (with reservations) that 'D' notices should be maintained, despite sharp divisions within the press about the value of the scheme which, judged in legal terms, is manifestly imperfect and imprecise.[148]

---

[143] HC Deb, 23 July 1993, col 454 (WA).

[144] www.dnotice.org.uk.

[145] *The Independent*, 27 September 2001.

[146] See *A-G v BBC*, *The Times*, 18 December 1987 regarding the broadcast by the BBC of a radio series ('My Country Right or Wrong') about the security service.

[147] Cmnd 3309 and 3312, 1967; Hedley and Aynsley, *The D-notice Affair*. In 1967 Prime Minister Wilson rejected the finding that no breach of a 'D' notice had occurred but he later admitted that his handling of the affair was wrong: *The Labour Government 1964–70*, pp 478–82, 530–4.

[148] HC 773 (1979–80); J Jaconelli [1982] PL 37.

The Security Commission[149]

An initiative taken in 1964 as a result of the Profumo affair is designed to respond to breaches of security as they arise. The creation of the Security Commission was announced by the Prime Minister, Sir Alec Douglas-Home, on 23 January 1964 with the following terms of reference:

> If so requested by the Prime Minister, to investigate and report upon the circumstances in which a breach of security is known to have occurred in the public service, and upon any related failure of departmental security arrangements or neglect of duty; and, in the light of any such investigation, to advise whether any change in security arrangements is desirable.

The Prime Minister also stated that before asking the Security Commission to investigate a particular case, he would consult the Leader of the Opposition.[150] Normally the Commission sits in private and it is left to the Commission to determine whether legal representation of witnesses is necessary for the protection of their interests. The chairman of the Security Commission is a senior judge and it may also include members of the civil service, the armed forces and the diplomatic service. Recent chairmen have included Lord Diplock, Lord Bridge, Lord Griffiths, Lord Lloyd, and Dame Elizabeth Butler-Sloss.[151]

The Commission may be called upon to investigate in a wide range of circumstances. So, for example, after two ministers (Earl Jellicoe and Lord Lambton) resigned in 1973 because of sexual impropriety, the Commission considered whether security had been endangered by their conduct.[152] In 1982 the Commission completed a full review of security procedures in the civil service,[153] and in 1983 it reported on the security implications of the conviction for spying of Geoffrey Prime, a member of staff at GCHQ.[154] Since then it has reported on the security implications of the conviction under s 1 of the Official Secrets Act 1911 of Michael Bettaney, a member of the security services;[155] on security in signals intelligence following the (unsuccessful) prosecution of the 'Cyprus 8';[156] and the security implications of the case of Michael Smith, also convicted (in 1993) under s 1 of the 1911 Act.[157] The last mentioned report gives a remarkable and disarmingly frank assessment of the work of the Security Service, it being reported that 'Michael John Smith first came to the notice of the Security Service in November 1971 when a Michael Smith living in Birmingham applied to join the Communist Party of Great Britain (CPGB). Efforts were made at that stage by the Security Service and the police, at the former's request, to identify Smith but without result.' The Security Commission 'is not an oversight body, an inspectorate, or an appeal tribunal. It does not sit continuously, is not pro-active, has no links with any department or ministry, and has no adjudicative function'. By the same token, it 'may venture on any terrain where security may be said to be involved' and it may go wherever the Prime Minister directs.[158] But it is no substitute for effective parliamentary oversight of the security and intelligence services, and it is now largely overshadowed by the Intelligence and Security Committee established in 1994, although it continues to be asked by the Prime

---

[149] For a full account, see Lustgarten and Leigh, pp 476–92.
[150] HC Deb, 23 January 1964, cols 1271–5. The terms of reference were subsequently modified. The chairman of the Commission's view is also considered before any matter is referred to it.
[151] For details of composition and procedure, see Lustgarten and Leigh, pp 476–87.
[152] Cmnd 5367, 1973.
[153] Cmnd 8540, 1982.
[154] Cmnd 8876, 1983.
[155] Cmnd 9514, 1985.
[156] Cmnd 9923, 1986.
[157] Cm 2930, 1995.
[158] Lustgarten and Leigh, p 477.

Minister to inquire into sensitive matters, most recently in 1999 following the conviction of a naval officer under the Official Secrets Act 1911, s 1.

Parliamentary scrutiny

1 *The Home Affairs Committee.* In 1999 the Home Affairs Committee of the House of Commons concluded that 'the accountability of the security and intelligence services to Parliament ought to be a fundamental principle in a democracy'.[159] Yet there is some way to go before this principle is fully realised, with successive governments resisting the possibility of full parliamentary scrutiny of the security and intelligence services.[160] In 1992 the Home Affairs Committee invited the Director-General of the Security Service to appear before them, possibly in private. In a series of remarkable exchanges, the invitation was declined after consultation with the Home Secretary, who later said that he would consider whether the committee might meet her informally, 'perhaps over lunch'. This stance was adopted following the convention 'under which information on matters of security and intelligence is not placed before Parliament', which the Home Secretary regarded 'as binding in relation to Departmental Select Committees no less than in relation to Parliament itself'. In his view, the Security Service was not to be regarded as falling within the ambit of any select committee, although this need not 'prevent the Director-General from having a meeting with [the Chairman of the Committee] and one or two senior members on an informal basis to discuss the work of the Security Service in general terms providing that the Government's position is understood'. Mrs Rimington (the then Director-General) was said to share this view and would 'accordingly be in touch with [the Chairman] to invite [him] and a couple of [his] senior colleagues to lunch'. As the committee said, however, an informal lunch with Mrs Rimington (who was 'permitted to lunch with the press'), 'while a welcome move towards openness', was 'no substitute for formal parliamentary scrutiny of the Security Service'.

The Home Affairs Committee was of the view that the service fell within its terms of reference and that 'the value-for-money of the Security Service and its general policy are proper subjects for parliamentary scrutiny as long as such scrutiny does not damage the effectiveness of the Service'. The committee then reviewed the various options for enhanced accountability of the service by means of parliamentary scrutiny which in its view would meet 'an important public interest and help to protect against any possible future abuse of power'.[161] For its part, however, the government responded by saying that in 1989 Parliament had considered very carefully the question of oversight.[162] It had concluded in favour of preserving the existing approach to accountability, by which the Director-General of the Security Service is responsible to the Home Secretary of the day, who is himself accountable to Parliament for the work of the Security Service. (It is, however, a strange kind of accountability which labours under a convention which prevents matters relating to security and intelligence from being placed before Parliament.) The government also referred to the procedures for judicial oversight of the service by means of a commissioner and a tribunal under the Security Service Act 1989. In the government's view this system had worked well in the three and a half years since the 1989 Act had come into force, although, once again, it is a strange

---

[159] HC 291 (1998–99), para 48.
[160] HC Deb, 16 December 1989, col 36; also HC 773 (1979–80); HC 242 (1982–83); HC Deb, 12 May 1983, col 444 (WA).
[161] HC 265 (1992–93).
[162] Cm 2197, 1993.

kind of oversight which examines only the exercise of specific statutory powers rather than the work of the Service as a whole, and more importantly which has no base in Parliament itself. The government accepted that the position should be examined afresh and an opportunity to do so was provided by the Intelligence Services Act 1994 where important concessions in the direction of democratic accountability were made, although it is open to question whether they go far enough. In 1998 the then Home Secretary (Jack Straw) refused a request from the Home Affairs Committee to take evidence from the Director-General of the Security Service in a public session, offering instead a briefing from the Director-General.[163]

2 *The Intelligence and Security Committee.*[164]   One of the reasons given by Mr Straw for refusing the Home Affairs Committee's request was that Parliament had given responsibility for overseeing the Security Service to the Intelligence and Security Committee. Under the Intelligence Services Act 1994, this committee of parliamentarians (it is not a parliamentary committee) is charged with the responsibility of examining 'the expenditure, administration and policy' of the security service, the intelligence service and GCHQ (s 10(1)). It consists of nine members drawn from both the House of Commons and the House of Lords (although none may be a minister of the Crown) and is appointed by the Prime Minister after consulting the Leader of the Opposition. In 2001 the committee was chaired by a former Conservative Cabinet minister and included among its other eight members one member of the House of Lords, as well as MPs from the three major political parties. Under the Act the committee is required to make an annual report on the discharge of its functions to the Prime Minister, which must then be laid before Parliament, although parts of the report may be held back, after consultation with the committee, if it appears to the Prime Minister that the publication of any matter would be prejudicial to any of the agencies. Some of the reports are badly disfigured by omissions.[165]

In its first report, the committee commented that because of the nature of its work 'it must have access to national security information', with the result that committee members 'have all been notified under the Official Secrets Act 1989'. The constitutional position was that the committee was 'now operating within the "ring of secrecy"', reporting directly to the Prime Minister on its work and, through him, to Parliament. An important development reported in 1999 was the appointment of an investigator by the committee to enable it more fully to examine different aspects of agencies' activities.[166] The committee's annual reports reveal that it has examined a wide range of issues. These include the priorities and plans of the agencies, their financing, and personnel management issues. An interesting issue raised in the annual reports for 1997–98 and 1998–99 respectively relates to the destruction of security service files. It was noted in 1998 that 110,000 files had been destroyed since 1992, the vast majority of which related to subversion, on targets about whom the service was no longer conducting any investigations. Following concerns that the service was solely responsible for the review and destruction of files and that some form of 'independent check should be built into the process', it was agreed that Public Record Office officials should be involved in the examination of files identified by the security service for destruction.[167]

The committee has also issued specific reports on a number of contentious issues, including most notably the publication of the so-called Mitrokhin Archive. This

---

[163] HC 291 (1998–99), app 1.
[164] See M Supperstone [1994] PL 329.
[165] See Cm 4309, 1999 (Sierra Leone).
[166] Cm 4532, 1999; and see Cm 4073, 1998; also HC 291 (1998–99), para 14.
[167] Cm 4073, 1998, and Cm 4532, 1999.

consisted of material held by the KGB which Mr Mitrokhin had removed from Russia and which identified a number of British citizens as Soviet agents. A number of these individuals were subsequently named in public, although none was prosecuted, their identities having been known to or suspected by the authorities in this country for many years. The report of the Intelligence and Security Committee provides a fascinating insight into the working of the intelligence services at a number of levels. It was revealed, for example, that the security service had failed to consult the Law Officers about whether one of the alleged spies should be prosecuted, taking the view that prosecution would not be in the public interest, a decision which was for the Attorney-General to make. It was also revealed that a well-known Cambridge historian of the security services was 'security cleared and had signed the Official Secrets Act' and that he was a 'good choice' of person for SIS to have approached in 1995 to collaborate in the publication of the Archive, 'knowing that ministerial approval would be required before the book could be published'. It was also revealed that problems inadvertently arise following a change of government in ensuring that all relevant security information is passed to new ministers.[168] Whatever else it does, the Intelligence and Security Committee casts some light where there would otherwise be only darkness.

---

[168] Cm 4764, 2000. For the government's response, see Cm 4765, 2000.

Chapter 26

EMERGENCY POWERS AND TERRORISM

In times of grave national emergency, normal constitutional principles may have to give way to the overriding need to deal with the emergency. In Lord Pearce's words, 'the flame of individual right and justice must burn more palely when it is ringed by the more dramatic light of bombed buildings'.[1] The European Convention on Human Rights, art 15, permits a member state to take measures derogating from its obligations under the Convention 'in time of war or other public emergency threatening the life of the nation'. The United Kingdom government has exercised the right of derogation in respect of events in Northern Ireland and more recently in response to international terrorism in the aftermath of events in the United States on 11 September 2001.[2] But even under such circumstances no derogation is permitted from art 2 (which protects the right to life) except in the case of deaths resulting from lawful acts of war, art 3 (which prohibits the use of torture), art 4(1) (which prohibits slavery) and art 7 (which bars retrospective criminal laws). Thus even in grave emergencies there are limits beyond which a state may not go, and it is open to question whether and how far 'the desirability of an effective remedy for judicial review must yield to the higher interests of the State'.[3] This chapter examines the role of the armed forces and the use of statutory emergency powers during war and peace and includes an account of recent anti-terrorist legislation. Emphasis will be both on the increased powers of the state in emergencies and on the continuing limits on state action.

A. Use of troops in assisting the police

In chapter 24 we examined the main powers available to the police in maintaining public order. In the 20th century in Great Britain, the police, with greater or less difficulty depending on the circumstances, were able to control and contain public protest. For most of the century (with the notable exception of the period of strikes in South Wales in 1911), the armed forces have not been used to suppress unrest.[4] They have been required, however, to maintain essential services during strikes[5] and on occasion to deal with extreme terrorist action (for example, the occupation of the Iranian embassy in London in May 1980), as well as to assist with the disposal of carcasses during the

---

[1] *Conway v Rimmer* [1968] AC 910, 982.
[2] See ch 19 B.
[3] *R v Home Secretary, ex p Adams* [1995] All ER (EC) 177, at p 185 (Steyn LJ). See *R v Home Secretary, ex p Cheblak* [1991] 2 All ER 319 where judicial review yielded rather too easily. Compare the thoughtful discussion of this issue by Sedley J in *R v Home Secretary, ex p McQuillan* [1995] 4 All ER 400, at pp 420–1. But following the events in the United States on 11 September 2001, there are indications that the courts are now less likely to question executive judgments about what national security requires. See *R v Home Secretary, ex p Rehman* [2002] 1 All ER 122, esp Lord Hoffmann. See p 628 below.
[4] See Williams, *Keeping the Peace*, pp 32–5.
[5] Cm 3223, 1996, pp 27–8.

foot and mouth epidemic on British farms in 2001.[6] But in the 19th century and earlier, when there was less political freedom and police forces were weaker, the local magistrates were expected to call in detachments of soldiers to restore order when necessary. Today in Great Britain, conditions would indeed have the character of an emergency if it became necessary to call on the armed forces for this purpose.

As emphasised by events such as the miners' strike of 1984/85 and the fuel protests of September 2000,[7] it is increasingly unlikely that the military will be called on to maintain order. Despite large-scale public disturbances, national coordination of policing together with new training and operational methods meant that it was unnecessary to deploy the army in either of these situations.[8] A decision to call in the troops to restore order was, in the past at least, a decision enabling firearms to be used to repress the disturbances. This use of the troops may be illustrated by a rather late example, the Featherstone riots in 1893.[9] When the police were engaged elsewhere, a small detachment of soldiers was summoned to protect a colliery against a riotous crowd which broke windows and set buildings on fire. As darkness was falling, a magistrate called on the crowd to disperse and he read the proclamation from the Riot Act. When the crowd did not disperse, the magistrate authorised the soldiers to fire and their officer decided that the only way to protect the colliery was to fire on the crowd. Two members of the crowd were killed. A committee of inquiry held that the action of the troops was justified in law.

When troops are thus used, what is the basis of their authority? Whatever may be the rules today that govern the decision that the armed forces should be called in,[10] their legal authority to act in a situation of riot seems to rest on no statutory or prerogative powers of the Crown, but simply on the duty of all citizens to aid in the suppression of riot and on the duty of the armed forces to come to the aid of the civil authorities.[11] In place of the common law rules on the use of force in the prevention of crime, s 3 of the Criminal Law Act 1967 now provides:

> A person may use such force as is reasonable in the circumstances in the prevention of crime, or in effecting or assisting in the lawful arrest of offenders or suspected offenders or of persons unlawfully at large.

Thus, the use of firearms must be justified by the necessity of the situation and does not become legal by reason of the decision to call in the troops. Indeed, the use of excessive force or the premature use of firearms would render the officer in command and the individual soldiers personally responsible for death or injuries caused. Issues of liability are decided by the criminal or civil courts after the event.[12]

By contrast with 19th-century practice, the 'civil power' that may call in the armed forces appears no longer to be the local magistracy, but the Home Secretary, acting on a request from a chief officer of police.[13] It is then for the Secretary of State for Defence to respond to the call. In such a situation, conventions of individual and

---

[6] The Defence Review white paper anticipates that there 'may well be an increased requirement for some specialist support to civil authorities, for example in countering drug-related crime' (Cm 3999, 1998, para 46). It has also been pointed out that the armed forces provide assistance to other departments in a number of ways: apart from counter-drug activities, it includes fishing protection and assistance in natural emergencies: Cm 5109, 2001, p 3.

[7] On which see H Fenwick and G Phillipson (2001) 21 LS 535.

[8] See McCabe and Wallington, *The Police, Public Order and Civil Liberties*, pp 49–50.

[9] Report of the Committee on the Disturbances at Featherstone, C 7234, 1893. And see HC 236 (1908).

[10] See authorities cited in note 13 below.

[11] *Charge to Bristol Grand Jury* (1832) 5 C & P 261.

[12] See *R v Clegg* [1995] 1 AC 482.

[13] HC Deb, 8 April 1976, col 617. See also E Bramall (1980) 128 JL of Royal Society of Arts 480; S C Greer [1983] PL 573; and Evelegh, *Peace Keeping in a Democratic Society*, pp 11–21, 91–4.

collective responsibility of ministers must merge. It may be assumed that the decisions of both Cabinet ministers would be taken through machinery authorised by the Cabinet for dealing with civil emergencies, machinery serviced in previous cases by what was the Civil Contingencies Unit of the Cabinet Office.[14] In themselves, these arrangements for joint operations between police and army give no additional legal authority to police or army for interfering with the rights of citizens. In modern conditions, the proposition that to call in the troops makes possible the use of firearms needs to be qualified in two ways. First, the police have already had to train and equip themselves with firearms 'to deal with armed criminals and political terrorists not posing any extraordinary problem or capable of posing a limited threat'.[15] The occasions on which firearms may be carried are governed by police rules, but it has been argued that the discretion of the individual constable extends to cover the use of firearms: 'A jury or a police disciplinary inquiry may examine his actions but his use of a firearm does not differ in law from his use of a truncheon.'[16] Second, it is no longer correct, as was said in 1893, that a soldier can act only by using deadly weapons.[17] To call in the army to deal with civil unrest would indeed be of incalculable political significance. But the British army's experience in Northern Ireland suggests that there are many other ways of dealing with hostile crowds which are more effective and less deadly than firing into them – batons, riot shields, water cannon, rubber bullets and even CS gas[18] – and the armed forces do not have a monopoly of the use of CS gas.[19]

B. Use of troops in Northern Ireland

The nature and scale of military involvement

The use of troops in Northern Ireland and their potential use against political terrorists are of the kind which have been described by a military writer as low-intensity operations.[20] Such use gives rise to formidable political and constitutional problems, not least in the identification of political groups whose activities may be described as subversive.[21] In 1975 the Home Office defined subversion as comprising activities 'which threaten the safety or well-being of the State, and are intended to undermine or overthrow parliamentary democracy by political, industrial or violent means'.[22] On this basis, since 1969 the scale of subversive activities in Northern Ireland has required the armed forces to share with the police a difficult and unenviable role in maintaining internal security.[23] Reference has been made already to the grave errors made in the adoption of interrogation in depth against selected internees.[24] In 1972 the Northern Ireland Court of

---

[14] Now the Civil Contingencies Secretariat.

[15] Cmnd 6496, 1976, p 95.

[16] Ibid (Sir Robert Mark). Incidents involving the discharge of firearms by the police are supervised by the Police Complaints Authority. See HC 469 (1995–96), p 27, where it is reported that a police officer would be charged with murder as a result of a firearms incident.

[17] C 7234, pp 10, 12.

[18] See reports on medical and toxicological aspects of CS gas, Cmnd 4173, 1969; Cmnd 4775, 1975. On the use of CS incapacitants, see HC 469 (1995–96), p 39.

[19] On the power to make it available to the police, see R v Home Secretary, ex p Northumbria Police Authority [1989] QB 26. Also HC 469 (1995–96), p 39.

[20] Kitson, Low Intensity Operations.

[21] See e.g. Kitson's definition at p 3 of subversion as 'all illegal measures short of the use of armed force taken by one section of the people . . . to overthrow those governing the country . . . or to force them to do things which they do not want to do'; and note the reference to the role of the law at pp 69–70.

[22] HC Deb, 6 April 1978, col 618.

[23] See e.g. the critical study by Evelegh, note 13 above.

[24] Ch 6.

Appeal decided that the Northern Ireland Parliament under the Government of Ireland Act 1920 had no legal authority to confer powers of arrest on the armed forces; this decision led instantly to legislation which retrospectively conferred this power on the Stormont parliament.[25]

The nature and scale of military involvement in Northern Ireland have been outlined in some detail in the annual statement on the defence estimates. The General Officer Commanding Northern Ireland is responsible to the Secretary of State for Northern Ireland and the Chief Constable of the Royal Ulster Constabulary (now the Police Service of Northern Ireland)[26] for directing the military contribution to security policy and counter-terrorist operations, and is responsible to the Ministry of Defence for the conduct of operations by all elements of the armed forces in Northern Ireland.[27] In 1969 the normal peacetime garrison in Northern Ireland was about 3,000, but since then the number of military personnel has fluctuated from a high of over 30,000 in 1972 to 17,000 in 1983–85; in the first half of the 1990s, the military presence was typically in the region of 19,000.[28] But despite this heavy presence, it is said that the RUC took the lead in maintaining law and order and that the role of the army was 'to support the RUC in combatting terrorism'.[29] Moreover,

> Armed forces' operations are carried out to meet the requirements set by the RUC, and are agreed in advance with them. Most of these operations are carried out jointly. There is very close cooperation between RUC and military commanders, who often meet on a daily basis to plan operations, with the RUC chairing the meetings. At the highest operational level, the Province Executive Committee, which assists in the overall co-ordination of the counter-terrorist effort, is chaired by a Deputy Chief Constable.[30]

When first deployed in Northern Ireland in 1969, the army was used primarily to maintain public order. But since then the role has changed, with military operations now being intended to (i) deter terrorist activity, (ii) reassure the community by providing a visible armed presence, and (iii) reduce terrorist capability through the arrest of terrorists and the seizure of arms, explosives and other terrorist equipment.[31] The announcement of the republican and loyalist ceasefires in August 1994 enabled the military presence to be reduced in a 'cautious and carefully planned way',[32] with measures being taken to reduce the military profile and to extend the areas in Northern Ireland where the police operated without routine military support. This process has continued following the Belfast peace agreement in 1998 and the beginning of IRA decommissioning of its weapons in September 2001.[33] But public order (including the powers of the armed forces) is a 'reserved' rather than a 'transferred' matter under the Northern Ireland Act 1998.

Legal position of the soldier

The legal position of the soldier called to assist the civil authorities in Northern Ireland to contain terrorist or political violence may not be the same as that of his or her counterpart called to assist the civil authorities elsewhere for other purposes:

---

[25] *R (Hume et al.)* v *Londonderry Justices* [1972] NILR 91; Northern Ireland Act 1972.
[26] Police (Northern Ireland) Act 2000, s 1.
[27] Statement on the Defence Estimates 1994, Cm 2550, 1994, p 38.
[28] It was reduced to 17,500 in 1996: Statement on the Defence Estimates 1996, Cm 3223, 1996, p 24.
[29] Statement on the Defence Estimates 1994, p 36.
[30] Ibid.
[31] Ibid, p 37.
[32] Statement on the Defence Estimates 1995, Cm 2800, 1995, p 42.
[33] Cm 4208, 1999, para 8.

There is little authority in English law concerning the rights and duties of a member of the armed forces of the Crown when acting in aid of the civil power; and what little authority there is relates almost entirely to the duties of soldiers when troops are called upon to assist in controlling a riotous assembly. Where used for such temporary purposes it may not be inaccurate to describe the legal rights and duties of a soldier as being no more than those of an ordinary citizen in uniform. But such a description is in my view misleading in the circumstances in which the army is currently employed in aid of the civil power in Northern Ireland . . . In theory it may be the duty of every citizen when an arrestable offence is about to be committed in his presence to take whatever reasonable measures are available to him to prevent the commission of the crime; but the duty is one of imperfect obligation and does not place him under any obligation to do anything by which he would expose himself to the risk of personal injury . . . In contrast to this a soldier who is employed in aid of the civil power in Northern Ireland is under a duty, enforceable under military law, to search for criminals if so ordered by his superior officer and to risk his own life should this be necessary in preventing terrorist acts. For the performance of this duty he is armed with a firearm, a self-loading rifle, from which a bullet, if it hits the human body, is almost certain to cause serious injury if not death.[34]

It has been said by the government, however, that 'service personnel are given certain specific powers under the law (for example, to make arrests and carry out searches) in order to enable them to carry out effective support to the RUC. In exercising these powers and in seeking to uphold the law, service personnel remain accountable to the law at all times. They have no immunity, nor do they receive special treatment. If service personnel breach the law, they are liable to arrest and prosecution under the law. This applies equally to the use of force, including lethal force.'[35]

Considerable controversy has, nevertheless, arisen from time to time as a result of the use of firearms by the military, most notably on 30 January 1972 when 13 civilians were killed 'when the army opened fire during a demonstration in Derry'.[36] Between 1969 and 1994 the security forces are said to have been responsible for 357 deaths in Northern Ireland, of which 141 were republican 'military activists', 13 were loyalist equivalents and 194 were civilians. Eighteen of these deaths led to criminal charges, with a total of six convictions being secured, one for attempted murder, one for manslaughter and four for murder:[37]

In *Attorney-General for Northern Ireland's Reference (No 1 of 1975)*[38] the accused was a soldier on foot patrol who shot and killed a young man in an open field in a country area in daylight. The shot had not been preceded by a warning shot and the rifle was fired after the deceased ran off after having been told to halt. The area was one in which troops had been attacked and killed by the IRA and where a surprise attack was a real threat. When the accused fired, he believed that he was dealing with a member of the IRA, but he had no belief at all as to whether the deceased had been involved or was likely to be involved in any act of terrorism. In fact, the deceased was an 'entirely innocent person who was in no way involved in terrorist activity'. After the soldier's acquittal for murder, the House of Lords held that the stated circum-stances (where 'he fires to kill or seriously wound an unarmed person because he honestly and reasonably believes that person is a member of a proscribed organisation [in this case the Provisional IRA] who is seeking to run away, and the soldier's shot kills that person') raised an issue for the tribunal of fact as to whether the Crown had established beyond reasonable doubt that the shooting constituted unreasonable force. According to Lord

---

[34] *A-G for Northern Ireland's Reference (No 1 of 1975)* [1977] AC 105, at 136–7 (Lord Diplock).

[35] Statement on the Defence Estimates 1994, p 36.

[36] C A Gearty (1994) 47 CLP 19, at p 33. See HC 220 (1971–72) (Widgery Report). In 1998 a second inquiry into these events was appointed, but had not reported by December 2001. See p 683 below, and *R v Lord Saville of Newdigate, ex p A* [1999] 4 All ER 860.

[37] Gearty and Kimbell, *Terrorism and the Rule of Law*, pp 57–8.

[38] [1977] AC 105. See also *Farrell v Defence Secretary* [1980] 1 All ER 166; *R v Bohan and Temperley* (1979) (5) BNIL; *R v Robinson* (1984) (4) BNIL 34; *R v McAuley* (1985) (10) BNIL 14. See also R J Spjut [1986] PL 38 and [1987] PL 35.

Diplock (at p 138), 'there is material upon which a jury might take the view that the accused had reasonable grounds for apprehension of imminent danger to himself and other members of the patrol if the deceased were allowed to get away . . . , and that the time available to the accused to make up his mind was so short that even a reasonable man could only act intuitively'.

On the other hand, in *R v Clegg*[39] it was held that a soldier who used excessive force in self-defence leading to the death of the victim was guilty of murder rather than manslaughter. The use of firearms earlier gave rise to allegations of a shoot-to-kill policy, these being directed at both the RUC and the armed forces.[40] The allegations were sufficiently serious that an inquiry was appointed under the chairmanship of Mr John Stalker, the Deputy Chief Constable of Greater Manchester.[41] Following Mr Stalker's removal from the inquiry in controversial circumstances, it was completed by Mr Sampson, the Chief Constable of West Yorkshire. No evidence was published to substantiate the allegations,[42] although the controversy was revived following the decision of the European Court of Human Rights in *McCann v United Kingdom*,[43] which concerned the fatal shooting of three IRA activists in Gibraltar in 1987.

Three known IRA personnel were shot by four SAS officers while it was thought that they were about to detonate a bomb, to the danger of life on Gibraltar. It transpired that this belief was erroneous and that the suspects were not only unarmed, but that they also were not in possession of bomb equipment at the time of their deaths. They were nevertheless shot 29 times (one suspect being shot 16 times) in highly controversial circumstances. By a majority of 10 to 9, the Court held that there had been a breach of art 2 which in protecting the right to life was said to rank as 'one of the most fundamental provisions in the Convention'.[44] There was no evidence of 'an execution plot at the highest level of command in the Ministry of Defence or in the Government'; although 'all four soldiers shot to kill', on the facts and in the circumstances the actions of the soldiers did not in themselves give rise to a violation of art 2. But it was held that the operation as a whole was controlled and organised in a manner which failed to respect art 2, and that the information and instructions given to the soldiers rendered inevitable the use of lethal force in a manner which failed to take adequately into consideration the right to life of the three suspects. Having regard 'to the decision not to prevent the suspects from travelling into Gibraltar, to the failure of the authorities to make sufficient allowances for the possibility that their intelligence assessments might in some respects, at least, be erroneous, and to the automatic recourse to lethal force when the soldiers opened fire', the Court was not persuaded that 'the killing of the three terrorists constituted the force which was no more than absolutely necessary in defence of persons from unlawful violence.'[45]

C. Martial law

The meaning of martial law

The term martial law may be given a variety of meanings. In former times martial law included what is now called military law.[46] In international law, martial law refers

---

[39] [1995] 1 AC 482.
[40] For suggestions that such an alleged policy conflicts with the ECHR, see *Farrell v UK* (1983) 5 EHRR 466. See also *McCann v UK* (1995) 21 EHRR 97.
[41] See Stalker, *Stalker*.
[42] See HC Deb, 25 January 1988, cols 21–35.
[43] (1995) 21 EHRR 97.
[44] Art 2(1) provides that 'Everyone's life shall be protected by law', while art 2(2) provides by way of qualification that 'Deprivation of life shall not be regarded as inflicted in contravention of this Article when it results from the use of force which is no more than absolutely necessary: (a) in defence of any person from unlawful violence . . .'
[45] The political reaction to the decision was very critical of the Court: see e.g. HL Deb, 29 January 1996, col 1225. Compare C Gearty, 'After Gibraltar', *London Review of Books*, 16 November 1995.
[46] Ch 16 B.

to the powers exercised by a military commander in occupation of foreign territory. In the present context, martial law refers to an emergency amounting to a state of war when the military may impose restrictions and regulations on citizens in their own country.[47] In such a situation of civil war or insurrection, the ordinary functioning of the courts gives way before the tasks of the military in restoring the conditions which make normal government possible. Unlike the use of armed forces for restoring order during riots, when the military are subject to direction by the civil authorities and to control by the courts if excessive force is used, under martial law the military authorities are (for the time being) the sole judges of the steps that should be taken. These steps might involve taking drastic steps against civilians, for example, the removal of life, liberty or property without due process of law, but possibly accompanied by the creation of military tribunals to administer summary justice. Such tribunals are not to be confused with the courts-martial which regularly administer military law.

It would be wrong to state the principal aspects of martial law as if they were part of present-day law, if only for the reason that within Great Britain occasions for the exercise of martial law have not arisen since at least 1800. Moreover, the Petition of Right 1628 contains a prohibition against the issue by the Crown of commissions of martial law giving the army powers over civilians, at least in peace time, and the meaning of this prohibition is far from clear today.[48] In times of national emergency today, Parliament prefers to give the civil and military authorities wide powers of governing by means of temporary legislation. It is submitted, therefore, that any discussion of the possible operation of martial law in Great Britain must assume that Parliament itself is prevented by the urgency of events from giving the necessary powers to the military authorities. If Parliament is sitting but refuses to pass emergency legislation, there would seem to be great difficulty, from a constitutional standpoint, in accepting that extraordinary powers of the military arise by process of common law.[49] Moreover, short of a military coup or an extreme emergency in which human survival becomes the only criterion, it must be assumed that the government continues to control the armed forces and to be responsible for their use to Parliament. In Northern Ireland since 1969, at no time has the British government invoked the doctrine of martial law as a justification for exempting the actions of the forces from scrutiny in the courts; instead there has been reliance on statutory powers or on the use of common law powers falling far short of a martial law situation.

An attempt to describe the doctrine of martial law must be based on case law arising out of the Boer War, the civil war in Ireland early in the 1920s, and incidents in the earlier history of British colonies. But it would take an alarming deterioration in political stability for it to be necessary to determine whether this mingled case law is applicable in Great Britain.[50] During the two world wars, the civil and criminal courts continued to function in Great Britain although their operation was subject to statutory restrictions. No state of martial law was declared. The Defence of the Realm Act 1914 authorised for a few months the trial of civilians by court-martial for offences against defence regulations. The Emergency Powers (Defence) (No 2) Act 1940, passed under the threat of imminent invasion, gave authority for special war zone courts to exercise criminal jurisdiction if, on account of military action, criminal justice had to be more speedily administered than in the ordinary courts. Such courts were never required to sit. In Northern Ireland since 1969, the ordinary civil and criminal courts have

---

[47] Keir and Lawson, *Cases in Constitutional Law*, ch III C; Heuston, *Essays in Constitutional Law*, pp 150–62.
[48] Cf *Marais v General Officer Commanding* [1902] AC 109, 115.
[49] Cf *Egan v Macready* [1921] 1 IR 265, 274.
[50] Cf the argument in Dicey, *The Law of the Constitution*, ch 8, that martial law is unknown to the law of England.

continued to function, although in dealing with terrorist offences the powers and procedures of the criminal courts have been much amended.[51]

Position of the courts during martial law

If, in a state of civil war or insurrection, the administration of justice breaks down because the courts are unable to function, it follows as a matter of fact that the acts of the military in seeking to restore order cannot be called into question in the courts so long as this situation lasts. As the English Law Officers said in 1838 in relation to the power of the governor of Lower Canada to proclaim martial law, martial law 'can only be tolerated because, by reason of open rebellion, the enforcing of any other law has become impossible'.[52] If in such a situation the executive proclaims martial law, the proclamation does not increase the powers of the military but merely gives notice to the people of the course which the government must adopt to restore order. In 1838 the Law Officers considered that, when the regular courts were in operation, any persons arrested by the military must be delivered to the courts to be dealt with according to law: 'there is not, as we conceive, any right in the Crown to adopt any other course of proceeding.'[53]

In 1902, in the *Marais* case, the Privy Council significantly extended the doctrine of martial law by holding that a situation of martial law might exist although the civil courts were still sitting. During the Boer War martial law had been proclaimed over certain areas of Cape Colony: Marais, a civilian, sought in the Supreme Court at Cape Town to challenge the legality of his arrest and detention for breach of military rules in an area subject to martial law. Lord Halsbury, on behalf of the Judicial Committee, declared that where war actually exists, the ordinary courts have no jurisdiction over the military authorities, although there might often be doubt as to whether a situation of war existed, as opposed to a mere riot or other disturbance.[54] Once a war situation had been recognised to exist, the military would presumably be able to deal with the inhabitants of an area under martial law on the same footing as the population of a foreign territory occupied during a war between states, subject only to the possibility of being called to account for their acts in civil courts after the resumption of normal government at a later date.

Advantage of the *Marais* case was taken by the United Kingdom government during the serious disturbances in Ireland in 1920–21. Early in 1920 the Westminster Parliament passed the Restoration of Order in Ireland Act, which gave exceptional powers to the executive, created new offences, provided for civilians to be tried and sentenced by properly convened courts-martial and prescribed the maximum penalties that could be imposed. Yet, in December 1920, martial law was proclaimed in areas of Ireland and the general officer commanding the army declared inter alia that any unauthorised person found in possession of arms would be subject to the death penalty. The general also established informal military courts for administering summary justice to those alleged to have committed the prohibited acts. In *R v Allen*, the King's Bench Division in Ireland refused to intervene in the case of a death sentence imposed by such a military court on a civilian for possession of arms. The court held that a state of war existed in the area in question; that military acts could not therefore be questioned in the civil courts even though the latter were still operating; and that the army authorities could take the lives of civilians if they deemed it to be absolutely essential. It was immaterial

---

[51] Terrorism Act 2000, Part 7. See section E below.
[52] Opinion of J Campbell and R M Rolfe, 16 January 1838; Keir and Lawson, p 231.
[53] Ibid.
[54] *Marais* v *General Officer Commanding* [1902] AC 109. And see *Tilonko* v *A-G of Natal* [1907] AC 93.

that Parliament had not authorised the death penalty for unauthorised possession of arms.[55]

The decisions of other Irish courts were not all so favourable to the army. In *Egan* v *Macready*, O'Connor MR distinguished the *Marais* case, holding that the Restoration of Order in Ireland Act 1920 created a complete code for military control of the situation which excluded the power of the army to impose the death penalty where Parliament had not granted this; he ordered the prisoner to be released by issuing habeas corpus.[56] In *R (Garde)* v *Strickland*, the court in strong terms asserted its power and duty to decide whether or not a state of war existed which justified the application of martial law, holding also that, as long as that state existed, no court had jurisdiction to inquire into the conduct of the army commander in repressing rebellion.[57] In *Higgins* v *Willis*, in which an action was brought for wrongful destruction of a civilian's house, the court declared that the plaintiff had a right to have his case against the military decided by the courts as soon as the state of war had ceased.[58] In the only decision by the House of Lords, *Re Clifford and O'Sullivan*, on facts similar to those in *R v Allen* it was held that the courts could not, by issuing a writ of prohibition, review the proceedings of a military tribunal set up under a proclamation of martial law.[59] This decision turned on the technical scope of the writ of prohibition, at that time considered to be available only against inferior bodies exercising judicial functions.[60] The House of Lords regarded the military tribunal in question, which was not a regularly constituted court-martial, as merely an advisory committee of officers to assist the commander in chief; moreover its duties had already been completed. The House expressly refrained from discussing the merits of other remedies that might be available, for example, a writ of habeas corpus. It followed that the army's decision to take the life of a citizen did not become subject to judicial control merely because an informal hearing had been given to the civilian by a military tribunal.

Position of the courts after martial law ends

After termination of the state of martial law, the courts have jurisdiction to review the legality of acts committed during the period of martial law. It is not possible to state with any certainty what standards will be applied by the courts in respect either of criminal or civil liability. First, there is no doubt that at common law many acts of the army which are necessary for dealing with civil war and insurrection will be justified; neither would there be liability at common law for damage to person or property inflicted accidentally in the course of actual fighting.[61] But what is not clear is whether the test should be that of strict necessity or merely bona fide belief in the necessity of the action, whether a stricter standard may be required in the case of some acts than others nor where the burden of proof should lie. Secondly, there is some uncertainty as to the legal effect of superior orders.[62] Third, in the past it was usual after martial law for an Act of Indemnity to be passed giving retrospective protection to the armed forces. On the basis of *Wright* v *Fitzgerald*[63] it would seem that in interpreting an Indemnity

[55] [1921] 2 IR 241. See Campbell, *Emergency Law in Ireland 1918–1925*. For Cabinet discussion of martial law in Ireland, see Jones, *Whitehall Diary*, vol 3, part I.
[56] [1921] 1 IR 265, criticised in Heuston, p 158.
[57] [1921] 2 IR 317.
[58] [1921] 2 IR 386.
[59] [1921] 2 AC 570.
[60] Ch 31.
[61] *Burmah Oil Co* v *Lord Advocate* [1965] AC 75; and ch 12 D.
[62] Ch 16.
[63] (1798) 27 St Tr 765, discussed by P O'Higgins (1962) 25 MLR 413.

Act, the courts presume that Parliament does not intend to indemnify a defendant for merely wanton or cruel acts not justified by the necessities of the situation, but the extent of protection depends on the terms of the Indemnity Act, which may be both explicit and very wide.[64]

D. Emergency powers in peace and war

While the Crown has some emergency powers under the prerogative, particularly in time of war or invasion, these powers are generally too uncertain for the government to rely on them.[65] During the two world wars, Parliament conferred exceptional powers for the conduct of the war and the maintenance of civilian life. During time of peace there is permanent statutory authority by which a state of emergency may be declared and the Cabinet's Civil Contingencies Committee reviews the arrangements to ensure that supplies and services essential to the life of the community are in place in the event of an emergency. There is also machinery in the form of the Civil Contingencies Secretariat for enabling the government to respond rapidly in emergency situations.

Emergency powers in peacetime

By the Emergency Powers Act 1920, as amended in 1964, a wide power to govern in emergency by means of statutory regulations is conferred on the executive, subject to parliamentary control.[66] This power arises only when a state of emergency has been declared by royal proclamation. A proclamation of emergency may be issued if at any time it appears to the Crown that there have occurred, or are about to occur, events of such a nature as to be calculated to deprive the community, or any substantial part of it, of the essentials of life by interfering with the supply and distribution of food, water, fuel or light, or with the means of locomotion. Such events might in principle include include a strike in one or more major public utilities or industries, natural disasters or a serious nuclear accident.[67] A proclamation can remain in force only for one month, although the emergency may be prolonged by the issue of a fresh proclamation. The proclamation must be communicated forthwith to Parliament. If Parliament is not sitting, it must be summoned to meet within five days.

So long as a proclamation is in force, regulations may be made by Order in Council for securing the essentials of life to the community. Such powers may be conferred on government departments, the armed forces, and the police as may be deemed necessary for preserving peace, or for securing and regulating the supply and distribution of necessities for maintaining the means of transport, 'and for any other purposes essential to the public safety and the life of the community' (1920 Act, s 2(1)). But the regulations may not impose compulsory military service or industrial conscription or make it an offence for anyone to take part in a strike or peacefully persuade others to do so. Regulations may provide for the trial, by courts of summary jurisdiction, of persons guilty of offences against the regulations, subject to maximum penalties; but existing procedure in criminal cases may not be altered and no right to punish by fine or imprisonment without trial may be conferred. The regulations must be laid before Parliament and expire after seven days unless a resolution is passed by both Houses providing for their continuance.

---

[64] See the notorious example in *Phillips v Eyre* (1870) LR 6 QB 1 and cf Indemnity Act 1920.
[65] Ch 12 D.
[66] On the Act, see Ewing and Gearty, *The Struggle for Civil Liberties*, chs 2 and 4.
[67] But see HC Deb, 14 February 1996, col 629 (WA).

The 1920 Act has been used 12 times, to deal with strikes by coalminers, dockers, power workers, as well as others. Indeed, no fewer than five states of emergency were declared by the Conservative government between 1970 and 1974. However, the Act has not been used since then despite the fact that there have been major public-sector strikes, including the so-called winter of discontent of 1978/79 and the miners' strike of 1984/85. The Act thus appears to have fallen into disuse, with governments preferring to rely on other powers when faced with major conflict in the public services.[68] These include the Emergency Powers Act 1964, s 2 of which gave permanent force to defence regulations originating in the Second World War that enable members of the armed forces, by order of the Defence Council, to be temporarily employed in agriculture or in 'urgent work of national importance'.[69] This has enabled troops to be used to maintain essential services and utilities which have been interrupted by strikes;[70] it also provided the authority for the use of troops during the outbreak of foot and mouth disease in 2001.

Also potentially important in the context of some industrial action are the emergency powers provisions in the privatisation statutes. For example, the Electricity Act 1989 authorises the Secretary of State to give 'such directions of a general character as appear to the Secretary of State to be requisite or expedient for . . . mitigating the effects of any civil emergency which may occur' (s 96(1)). A civil emergency means 'any natural disaster or other emergency which, in the opinion of the Secretary of State, is or may be likely to disrupt electricity supplies' (s 96(7)). It has been claimed that an unpublished directive was issued by the Energy Secretary in 1990 to the electricity generating companies to hold £1 billion of coal stocks as insurance against a miners' strike.[71] The stockpiling of coal may have been a major factor in determining the outcome of the 1984/85 miners' strike.[72] Under the Railways Act 1993, s 118, powers are given to the Secretary of State to control the railways in times of hostility, severe international tension or great national emergency, the last being defined to mean 'any national disaster or other emergency which, in the opinion of the Secretary of State, is or may be likely to give rise to such disruption of the means of transport that the population, or a substantial part of the population, of Great Britain is or may be likely to be deprived of essential goods or services'. Owners or operators of services who suffer loss as a result of ministerial intervention are entitled to compensation, the amount to be determined by arbitration in default of an agreement.[73]

Emergency powers in time of war

Before the mid-19th century it was the practice in times of national danger to pass what were often known as Habeas Corpus Suspension Acts.[74] Such Acts took various forms. Some prevented the use of habeas corpus for securing speedy trial or the right to bail in the case of persons charged with treason or other offences. Others conferred wide powers of arrest and detention which would not normally have been acceptable. After the danger was over, it was often the practice to pass an Indemnity Act to

---

[68] For a full account, see Morris, *Strikes in Essential Services*; also G S Morris [1980] PL 317 and C Whelan (1979) 8 ILJ 222.

[69] For a full account of the 1964 Act, see Morris, pp 98–106, esp p 100.

[70] Cm 3223 (1996), pp 27–8. Note also the possibility of the police being used to maintain essential supplies during a strike: see G S Morris (1980) 9 ILJ 1.

[71] See G S Morris, 1991 20 ILJ 89, at p 98.

[72] For other strategies, see e.g. Imprisonment (Temporary Provisions) Act 1980.

[73] For further details of the emergency powers and industrial disputes, see Deakin and Morris, *Labour Law*, ch 11.10.

[74] Dicey, *The Law of the Constitution*, pp 229–37.

protect officials retrospectively from liability for illegal acts which they might have committed. During the two world wars, habeas corpus was not suspended but extremely wide powers were conferred on the executive. The Defence of the Realm Acts 1914–15 empowered the Crown to make regulations by Order in Council for securing public safety or for the defence of the realm.[75] In *R v Halliday, ex p Zadig* the House of Lords held that this general power was wide enough to support a regulation authorising the Secretary of State to detain persons without trial on the grounds of their hostile origins or associations.[76] In a powerful and memorable dissent, Lord Shaw of Dunfermline declined to infer from the delegation of a general power to make regulations for public safety and defence the right to authorise the detention of a man without trial and without being accused of any offence.

Although the powers of the executive were wide, it was still possible to challenge defence regulations in the courts.

In *Attorney-General v Wilts United Dairies Ltd*[77] an attempt by the Food Controller to impose a charge of two pence a gallon as a condition of issuing licences for the supply of milk was held invalid, on the ground that the Food Controller's power under defence regulations to regulate the supply of milk did not confer power to impose charges upon the subject. Doubt was also expressed whether a regulation conferring such a power would have been within the general power to make regulations for the public safety or the defence of the realm. In *Chester v Bateson*[78] a defence regulation empowered the Minister of Munitions to declare an area in which munitions were manufactured to be a special area. The intended effect of such a declaration was to prevent any person without the consent of the minister from taking proceedings to recover possession of any dwelling-house in the area, if a munitions worker was living in it and duly paying rent. It was held that Parliament had not deliberately deprived the citizen of access to the courts and that the regulation was invalid, since it could not be shown to be a necessary or even reasonable way of securing the public safety or the defence of the realm.

Such decisions explain the passing after the war of the wide Indemnity Act 1920 and a separate Act relating to illegal charges, the War Charges Validity Act 1925.

When war was declared in 1939 the Emergency Powers (Defence) Act 1939 empowered the making of regulations by Order in Council which appeared necessary or expedient for the public safety, the defence of the realm, the maintenance of public order, the efficient prosecution of any war in which His Majesty might be engaged and the maintenance of supplies and services essential for the life of the community. There followed a list of particular purposes for which regulations could be made, including the detention of persons in the interests of public safety or the defence of the realm. To avoid another *Wilts United Dairies* case, the Treasury was empowered to impose charges in connection with any scheme of control under Defence Regulations. Treasury regulations imposing charges required confirmation by an affirmative resolution of the House of Commons. Other regulations had to be laid before Parliament after they were made and could be annulled by negative resolution within 28 days.[79] Compulsory military service was imposed by separate National Service Acts and compulsory direction of labour to essential war work was authorised by the Emergency Powers (Defence) (No 2) Act 1940. Although access to the courts was not barred, the scope for judicial review of executive action was limited. Thus the courts could not consider

---

[75] For a fascinating account of these powers and their operation, see Rubin, *Private Property, Government Requisition and the Constitution, 1914–1927*. See also Ewing and Gearty, ch 2.

[76] [1917] AC 260.

[77] (1921) 37 TLR 884.

[78] [1920] 1 KB 829.

[79] Ch 28.

whether a particular regulation was necessary or expedient for the purposes of the Act which authorised it.[80] The courts could, however, hold an act to be illegal as being not authorised by the regulation relied on to justify it.[81]

Special problems of judicial control arose in relation to the power of the executive to authorise detention without trial in the interests of public safety or the defence of the realm. Under Defence Regulation 18 B, the Home Secretary was empowered to detain those whom he had reasonable cause to believe came within specified categories (including persons of hostile origin or association) and over whom it was necessary to exercise control. Persons detained could make objections to an advisory committee appointed by the Home Secretary. The Home Secretary had to report monthly to Parliament on the number of persons detained and the number of cases in which he had not followed the advice of the committee. It was open to a detainee to apply for habeas corpus, but such applications had little chance of success in view of the decision of the House of Lords in *Liversidge* v *Anderson*.[82] In spite of a powerful dissenting judgment by Lord Atkin, the House took the view that the power to detain could not be controlled by the courts, if only because considerations of security forbade proof of the evidence on which detention was ordered. The words 'had reasonable cause to believe' only meant that the Home Secretary must have a belief which in his mind was reasonable. The courts would not inquire into the grounds for his belief, although apparently they might examine positive evidence of mala fides or mistaken identity.[83] Stress was laid on the responsibility of the Home Secretary to Parliament. In only one case did a person who had been detained under the regulation secure his release by habeas corpus proceedings. His detention having been ordered on the ground that he was connected with a fascist organisation, he was wrongly informed that the order had been made on the ground of his being of hostile origins and association. The Divisional Court ordered his release, but the Home Secretary thereupon made a new order for his detention.[84]

E. Emergency powers and political violence[85]

Special legislation for dealing with terrorism was first introduced in Britain in 1974,[86] although special powers to deal with threats to security in Northern Ireland are almost as old as the Province itself[87] and indeed were to generate some controversial decisions

---

[80] *R* v *Comptroller-General of Patents, ex p Bayer Products* [1941] 2 KB 306. See also *Pollok School* v *Glasgow Town Clerk* 1946 SC 373.

[81] E.g. *Fowler & Co (Leeds) Ltd* v *Duncan* [1941] Ch 450.

[82] [1942] AC 206; and see C K Allen (1942) 58 LQR 232 and R F V Heuston (1970) 86 LQR 33.

[83] Lord Wright at p 261. The majority decision in *Liversidge* v *Anderson* cannot now be relied on as an authority, either on the point of construction or in its declaration of legal principle: *R* v *Home Secretary, ex p Khawaja* [1984] AC 74, at p 110 (Lord Scarman), and see e.g. *Ridge* v *Baldwin* [1964] AC 40, at p 73 (Lord Reid).

[84] *R* v *Home Secretary, ex p Budd* [1942] 2 KB 14; *The Times*, 28 May 1941. On Regulation 18 B generally, see Simpson, *In the Highest Degree Odious*.

[85] For background dealing with the issue from a number of perspectives, see Gearty, *Terror*.

[86] Prevention of Terrorism (Temporary Provisions) Act 1974, re-enacted in 1976; reviewed Cmnd 7324, 1978 (Lord Shackleton) and Cmnd 8803, 1983 (Lord Jellicoe); re-enacted again in 1984 and 1989. The 1984 Act was reviewed in Cm 264, 1987 (Viscount Colville).

[87] Civil Authorities (Special Powers) Act 1922, replaced by Northern Ireland (Temporary Provisions) Act 1973, amended in 1975 and 1977 and re-enacted in 1978, 1987, 1991 and 1996. On the 1922 Act, see Calvert, *Constitutional Law in Northern Ireland*, ch 20; Campbell, *Emergency Law in Ireland 1918–1925*; and Ewing and Gearty, *The Struggle for Civil Liberties*, ch 7. The 1973 Act was preceded by the Diplock Report, Cmnd 5185, 1972. For periodic reviews of the legislation, see Cmnd 5847, 1975 (Lord Gardiner); Cmnd 9222, 1984 (Sir George Baker); Cm 1115, 1990 (Viscount Colville); and Cm 2706, 1995 (J J Rowe QC). For a critique of the legislation and its operation, see Jennings (ed), *Justice under Fire*.

of the courts.[88] The position is now governed by the Terrorism Act 2000,[89] which replaces the Prevention of Terrorism (Temporary Provisions) Act 1989 and the Northern Ireland (Emergency Provisions) Act 1996, and brings the provisions of both together in a single text.[90] Both these measures were subject to the formality of annual renewal by Parliament and indeed the two predecessors to the 1989 Act were expressly provided to expire after five years: hence the reference to temporary provisions in their short title. Although there is a prospect of peace in Northern Ireland, the government took the view that the problem of terrorism generally was sufficiently important as to require permanent legislation: this is a judgment in which it no doubt felt vindicated by the bomb at Omagh in 1998 in which 29 people died. The Terrorism Act 2000 is in fact designed to implement the recommendations of an Inquiry into Legislation Against Terrorism conducted by Lord Lloyd of Berwick in 1996.[91] The Lloyd report proposed that legislation against terrorism should be based on a number of principles:

(i) Legislation against terrorism should approximate as closely as possible to the ordinary criminal law and procedure.
(ii) Additional statutory offences and powers may be justified, but only if they are necessary to meet the anticipated threat. They must then strike the right balance between the needs of security, and the rights and liberties of the individual.
(iii) The need for additional safeguards should be considered alongside any additional powers.
(iv) The law should comply with the UK's obligations in international law.

The Lloyd report led to the removal of some 'particularly controversial' powers,[92] such as internment without trial[93] and the Secretary of State's power to make exclusion orders prohibiting the movement of terrorist suspects from Northern Ireland to Great Britain and preventing non-British citizens from being in or entering the United Kingdom.[94] These latter provisions were criticised judicially (and otherwise) as violating freedom of movement, said to be 'a fundamental value of the common law', which exclusion orders compromised by effectively condemning 'a citizen of this country to what has become known in other parts of the world as internal exile or banishment'.[95] But the government did not accept all Lloyd's recommendations, a matter of particular controversy being the definition of terrorism which goes some way beyond that proposed by Lloyd,[96] so that the Act 'has a much wider application' than the measures

---

[88] See *McEldowney v Forde* [1971] AC 632.
[89] For an early account of the Act, see Fenwick, *Civil Rights*, ch 3. See also J J Rowe [2001] Crim LR 527. For a discussion of the broader context, see Whitty, Murphy and Livingstone, *Civil Liberties Law*, ch 3.
[90] The 1989 Act replaces the similarly worded Act of 1984 which in turn replaced the Act of 1976 which replaced the Act of 1974. The 1974 Act – passed in the immediate aftermath of the Birmingham pub bombs – was said by its author to be a 'drastic' measure: Jenkins, *A Life at the Centre*, p 394. For a discussion of the background to the Act, see Jenkins, pp 393–8. On the 1989 Act, see D Bonner [1989] PL 440; B Dickson (1989) 40 NILQ 250. Also Walker, *The Prevention of Terrorism in British Law*.
[91] Cm 3420, 1996. See also on reform the important study by Gearty and Kimbell, *Terrorism and the Rule of Law*.
[92] Cm 3420, 1996, para 16.3.
[93] Northern Ireland (Emergency Provisions) Act 1996, s 36. See Cm 1115, 1990 and for a full account of the procedures (which had been discontinued for some time despite their re-enactment in 1996 (HC Deb, 9 January 1996, col 37)), see *Ireland v United Kingdom* (1978) 2 EHRR 25.
[94] Prevention of Terrorism (Temporary Provisions) Act 1989, Part II.
[95] *R v Home Secretary, ex p Adams* [1995] All ER (EC) 177. The powers were defended by the government on the ground that they 'deter people from carrying out terrorist acts and deprive the groups to which they belong some of their experienced operators' (HC Deb, 14 March 1996, cols 1127–8). Other important litigation arising from the operation of the power includes *R v Home Secretary, ex p Gallagher* [1994] 3 CMLR 295 and *R v Home Secretary, ex p MacQuillan* [1995] 4 All ER 400.
[96] See HC Deb, 14 Dec 1999, col 186 (Mr Simon Hughes).

it replaced.[97] Neither is the Act the final word on the matter, with additional measures to be found in the Anti-Terrorism, Crime and Security Act 2001 which was passed in direct response to the terrorist attacks in the United States in September 2001. This extends by some way what were already wide and far-reaching powers, most controversially to allow for the detention without trial of suspected international terrorists.[98] It also reintroduced powers of detention without trial, though admittedly not for use in the specific context of Northern Ireland.

The definition of terrorism

One of the most controversial features of the Terrorism Act 2000 is the wide definition of terrorism in s 1 to mean action or the threat of action (including action outside the United Kingdom) which (a) falls within s 1(2); (b) is designed to influence the government or to intimidate the public or a section of the public; and (c) is made for the purpose of advancing an ideological cause. Much of the concern relates to the wide scope of the action falling within s 1(2), which applies not only to serious violence, serious damage to property and the endangering of human life, but also to creating 'a serious risk to the health or safety of the public or a section of the public', as well as seriously interfering with or seriously disrupting an electronic system.[99] Section 1 also makes it clear that the Act applies to terrorist activity overseas, as well as that directed at the British government. The action to which the section applies may be action outside the United Kingdom and the government which it is designed to influence may be the government of the United Kingdom (or a part thereof), or of a country other than the United Kingdom. The wide definition gave rise to a great deal of comment and a number of difficult questions were raised as the Bill was completing its journey through Parliament. A good example is the following:

> If someone decided to break into a mink farm in order to release the mink from their cages, or to break into a research station and destroy the animals' cages, that would clearly be an act of serious violence. It would be a criminal act – and one that I deplore. But why should such organisations be classified as terrorist under [section] 1?[100]

The Home Secretary conceded that this conduct might well fall under s 1, but felt that the answer to the potentially wide scope of the legislation lay in the self-restraint of the prosecuting authorities.[101] He also drew attention to the Human Rights Act 1998 – and in particular arts 5 and 6 – as a 'profound safeguard against the disproportionate use of the powers' in the Act.[102] But apart from the fact that the Human Rights

---

[97] J J Rowe [2001] Crim LR 527, at p 542.

[98] For an account of the position in other European countries, see Vercher, *Terrorism in Europe*.

[99] Lord Lloyd had proposed that terrorism should be defined as: 'the use of serious violence against persons or property, or the threat to use such violence, to intimidate or coerce a government, the public or any section of the public, in order to promote political, social or ideological objectives'.

[100] HC Deb, 14 Dec 1999, col 155 (Douglas Hogg). There was also the case of the women who attacked the Hawk aircraft with hammers, as well as the case of the Trident Ploughshares 2000 organisation, which attacked the Trident submarine – ibid, col 200.

[101] 'I believe that we must have some confidence in the law enforcement agencies and the courts. If we look back at the past 25 years, we can see that the powers have been used proportionately in the face of an horrific threat from terrorism in Ireland and from international terrorism' (HC Deb, 14 Dec 1999, col 155). See also at col 165 (independence of the police, the DPP and the Attorney-General). The consent of the DPP is necessary before any prosecution (s 117).

[102] Ibid, col 160. It was also claimed by a former minister from the Opposition benches that 'the integrity of Ministers is often bolstered by the knowledge of the existence of judicial review' (HC Deb, 14 Dec 1999, Mr Tom King).

Act safeguards ring rather hollow following the enactment of the Anti-Terrorism, Crime and Security Act 2001,[103] there was nevertheless still concern about the application of the definition to international terrorism. One recurring question was whether British-based support for the anti-apartheid activities of the ANC in South Africa before the end of apartheid would have been caught by the Act. Other concerns related to 'international campaigns, such as those that support, for example, the actions of the Kurds resisting being driven from their lands by the building of dams, the resistance of the Ogoni in Nigeria to the theft and pollution of their lands and the resistance of the Amazon Indians to the destruction of their rainforests. All those campaigns of resistance have involved incidents of violent collision with those who would destroy people's livelihoods and lives'.[104] The government has expressed the view, however, that support for such international causes 'will not even remotely come under the [Act]'.

Proscribed organisations and terrorist property

1 *Proscribed organisations.* Part II of the Terrorism Act 2000 restricts freedom of association in the United Kingdom by proscribing specified organisations. There are 14 bodies listed in Sch 2, all connected with events in Northern Ireland. The Secretary of State also has power to add to the list by order (s 3), a power which has been exercised in respect of another 21 organisations which are said to be involved in terrorist activities in different parts of the world but which are thought to operate in or from this country.[105] Before an organisation may be added to the list, the Secretary of State must believe that it is 'concerned in terrorism' (s 3(4)), which means not only that it commits or prepares acts of terrorism, but that it promotes or encourages terrorism or is 'otherwise concerned in terrorism' (s 3(5)). The Secretary of State also has the power to remove an organisation by order from the proscribed list, following an application by the organisation or any person affected by the organisation's proscription (s 4). Given that it is an offence to be a member of a proscribed organisation (on which see later), this could be a bold move, particularly if the application is refused. If the Secretary of State refuses the application, an appeal may be made to the Proscribed Organisations Appeal Commission, which is required to apply the principles of judicial review (s 5), with a right of appeal from the Commission on a point of law to the Court of Appeal, Court of Session or Court of Appeal in Northern Ireland, as appropriate (s 6).

As under the 1989 Act, it is an offence to be a member (or to profess membership) of a proscribed organisation (s 11); to invite support for such an organisation (s 12); or to organise a meeting (whether in public or private) in support of such an organisation. Breach of these provisions could lead to imprisonment of up to ten years or to a fine or both, if convicted on indictment (s 12(6)). It is also an offence under s 13 for a person in a public place to wear an item of clothing or wear, carry or display an article 'in such a way or in such circumstances as to arouse reasonable apprehension that he is a member or supporter of a proscribed organisation' (s 13(1)). Conduct violating s 13 may also be unlawful under s 1 of the Public Order Act 1936, which makes it an offence to wear a political uniform in public. Although the 1936 Act was designed initially for use against Oswald Mosley's fascists, this measure was used successfully in 1975 against IRA members who led funeral processions in England, dressed

---

[103] See pp 625–7 below.
[104] HC Deb, 14 December 1999, col 160 (Mr Alan Simpson). To this might be added the question of support for the people of Chechnya who are said by the Russian government to be terrorists (HC Deb, 14 Dec 1999, col 216).
[105] SI 2001 No 1261.

in dark pullovers, dark berets and dark glasses.[106] The restrictions in the Terrorism Act 2000 (and the 1989 Act which preceded it) are wider, there being no need to show that the demonstration of support amounts to the wearing of a uniform as such.

2 *Terrorist property.*   Part III of the Terrorism Act 2000 (as amended by the Anti-Terrorism, Crime and Security Act 2001) deals with terrorist property, defined to mean both money and property which is likely to be used for the purposes of terrorism and including any resources of a proscribed organisation (s 14). It is an offence to solicit, receive or give money or property for terrorist purposes (s 15). The Act also contains additional measures which were first introduced in 1989 'to strike at the financial roots of terrorism',[107] at a time when it was thought that the IRA (then the main target) had an annual income of £ 3–4 million, generated not only by robbery and extortion, but also by apparently legitimate business activity which gave the organisation 'an assured income and a firmer base'.[108] So apart from the direct financing of terrorism, it is an offence to use or possess money or property for terrorist purposes (s 16) and to be involved in 'an arrangement' whereby money or property is made available for terrorist purposes (s 17). This is intended to cover banking transactions involving payments to a customer's order and also an arrangement whereby money or other property is made available to a lawful business and either that money, or the profits of that activity, is 'intended to be used for terrorist purposes'. Section 18 contains the so-called laundering offence, making it unlawful to enter into an arrangement 'which facilitates the retention or control by or on behalf of another person of terrorist property', by concealment, removal from the jurisdiction, transfer to nominees or 'in any other way'.

Where someone suspects that another person has committed an offence under ss 15–18, it is an offence not to inform the police as soon as reasonably practicable (s 19). There is an exception for employees who have informed their employer in accordance with any procedure for reporting concerns of this kind (although if the employer has no procedure there would be no defence for failing to notify the police). There is also an exception for lawyers in relation to information obtained from a client in connection with the provision of legal advice. But there is no exception for journalists,[109] although there is a general defence of reasonableness from which journalists might benefit.[110] Section 21 deals with the position of police informers, so that it is not an offence for a person to withhold information under ss 15 to 18 if acting with the express consent of the police; neither is it an offence to be involved in a money-laundering arrangement after informing the police that the money or other property in question is terrorist property. The latter provision would protect the bank or other body which is the medium for the unlawful action and also give the police access to information about the arrangement. Where a person is convicted of an offence under ss 15–18, a court may make an order for the forfeiture of money or property destined for terrorist use or which was the subject of an arrangement for handling or laundering terrorist funds (s 23). There are also powers for the seizure, detention and forfeiture in civil proceedings of cash intended to be used for terrorist purposes, as well as cash which represents the resources of a proscribed organisation or property obtained through terrorism. The powers of forfeiture may be exercised even

---

[106] *O'Moran* v *DPP* [1975] QB 864.
[107] HC Deb, 6 Dec 1988, col 212 (Mr Douglas Hurd).
[108] Ibid, col 213.
[109] A point which was raised in Parliament at Second Reading in the Commons: HC Deb, 14 Dec 1999, col 181 (Fiona Mactaggart). See also J J Rowe [2001] Crim LR 527, at pp 537–8.
[110] HL Deb, 23 May 2000, col 653 (Lord Bassam).

though no criminal proceedings have previously been brought in connection with the cash.[111]

Terrorist investigations, police powers and terrorist offences

1 *Terrorist investigations.* A 'terrorist investigation' is defined to mean an investigation of one of five matters: the commission, preparation or instigation of acts of terrorism; an act which appears to have been done for the purposes of terrorism; the resources of a proscribed organisation; the possibility of making a proscription order under s 3; and the commission, preparation or instigation of an offence under the Terrorism Act itself (s 32). Sections 33–6 empower the police to impose cordons for up to 28 days in the course of terrorist investigations and to order people to leave the area, to leave premises in the cordoned area and to remove vehicles from the area. An order designating a cordoned area, may be made by a police officer of the rank of superintendent or above, although it may also be done by an officer of lesser rank where necessary 'by reason of urgency' (s 34(2)). There are few formalities associated with the exercise of this power: if made orally, the designation is to be confirmed in writing as soon as reasonably practicable; and it can only be made for 14 days in the first instance, to be renewed as necessary. There is no reporting to the Home Secretary or to anyone else on the exercise of this power and not even an annual reporting obligation on the number of times the power is exercised.[112]

There are also extensive powers conferred on the police to obtain information for the purposes of a terrorist investigation. By virtue of s 37 and Sch 5, a justice of the peace may issue a search warrant if there are reasonable grounds for believing that there is material on the premises which is likely to be of substantial value to the investigation (para 1(5)) and does not consist of items subject to legal privilege or excluded or special procedure material (as defined by PACE) (para 4).[113] In the case of excluded or special procedure material, a constable may apply to a circuit judge for an order requiring the person in possession to produce it for the constable to take away or have access to it (paras 5–10). Unlike PACE, there is no provision in the Terrorism Act 2000 requiring that the application for an order should be made *inter partes*.[114] Where an order is not complied with or where access to the material is needed more immediately, the constable may apply to the circuit judge for a warrant to search the premises for the excluded or special procedure material (paras 11 and 12). A circuit judge may also issue an order requiring a person to provide an explanation of any material which has been produced or seized under the foregoing provisions (para 13).[115] Amendments introduced in 2001 make it an offence to fail to provide information to the police if the person in question 'knows or believes' that the information 'might be

---

[111] Anti-terrorism, Crime and Security Act 2001, s 1 and Sch 1.

[112] These powers may also be exercised in some circumstances by the British Transport Police and by the Ministry of Defence Police following amendments introduced by the 2001 Act.

[113] Separate provisions deal with police access to confidential customer information held by banks, extended in 2001 to include a police power to monitor bank accounts (with the authority of a circuit judge or sheriff) and to freeze accounts (which curiously can be done only by statutory instrument). See Terrorism Act 2000, Sch 6 and Anti-terrorism, Crime and Security Act 2001, ss 4–16, and Schs 2 and 3.

[114] See ch 21 D. For the procedure to be followed in such cases see R v *Middlesex Guildhall Crown Court, ex p Salinger* [1993] QB 564.

[115] In urgent cases ('of great emergency'), a police officer of the rank of superintendent or above may by written order authorise conduct which would otherwise require a warrant from a justice of the peace or a circuit judge (para 15). In cases of great emergency, such a police officer may also require a person to provide an explanation of any material seized in pursuance of an order under para 15 (para 16).

of material assistance' in preventing the commission by another person of an act of terrorism.[116]

2 *Police powers.* Police powers of arrest, search, and stop and search are dealt with in Part V of the Terrorism Act 2000. They apply to someone who is a terrorist, defined to mean not only someone who has committed an offence under the Act, but also someone who has been 'concerned in the commission, preparation or instigation of acts of terrorism'. For this purpose terrorism carries the meaning set out in s 1 (s 40). Section 41 gives a power to a constable to 'arrest without a warrant a person whom he reasonably suspects to be a terrorist'.[117] A person so arrested may be detained for up to 48 hours, in contrast to the normal 24 hours (or 36 in the case of a serious arrestable offence). Further detention must be authorised by a warrant issued by a judicial authority (a district judge in England and Wales; a sheriff in Scotland; or a county court judge or resident magistrate in Northern Ireland). A person should not be detained for more than seven days in total from the time of arrest. Under the 1989 Act, a person could be detained for up to seven days with the authority of the Secretary of State, despite earlier legislation to the same effect being found in breach of art 5(3) of the ECHR. This provides that an arrested or detained person 'shall be brought promptly before a judge or other officer entitled to exercise judicial power'.[118] Provision is made in Sch 8 for the treatment of persons detained under these powers.[119]

In addition to powers of arrest, a police officer may apply to a justice of the peace for a warrant to enter and search any premises on reasonable suspicion that a person concerned with the commission, preparation or instigation of acts of terrorism will be found there (s 42). A police officer also has the power to stop and search a person whom 'he reasonably suspects to be a terrorist', in order 'to discover whether he has in his possession anything which may constitute evidence that he is a terrorist' (s 43(1)). A police officer may also search a person arrested under s 41 'to discover whether he has in his possession anything which may constitute evidence that he is a terrorist' (s 43(2)). There are also random stop and search powers in s 44,[120] which enable a senior police officer to grant an 'authorisation' for renewable periods of 28 days which in turn 'authorises' a constable in uniform in the area or place specified in the authorisation to stop and search vehicles and pedestrians.[121] An authorisation may only

---

[116] Anti-terrorism, Crime and Security Act 2001, s 117, inserting a new s 38 B into the Terrorism Act 2000.

[117] See *O'Hara* v *Chief Constable of the RUC* [1997] 1 All ER 129. This formulation of the power of arrest replaces the much criticised provisons in s 14 of the Prevention of Terrorism Act 1989. Cf Gearty and Kimbell, pp 18–19 and *Inquiry into Legislation Against Terrorism* (Lord Lloyd) (Cm 3420, 1996), pp 40–2. Section 41 does not appear to meet the objections raised about its predecessors, namely that they permitted the police to arrest and detain someone who has not and is not suspected of having committed an offence. This remains the case and doubt has been raised about whether this power is consistent with art 5 of the ECHR. See J J Rowe [2001] Crim LR 527, esp pp 532–3 where the author refers to concerns raised in Parliament by Lord Lloyd as the Bill was being enacted.

[118] See *Brogan* v *UK* (1989) 11 EHRR 117; *Brannigan* v *UK* (1993) 17 EHRR 539. See S Livingstone (1989) 40 NILQ 288.

[119] See also *Re Gillen's Application* [1988] NILR 40 (habeas corpus in the event of unlawful detention). On legal representation, see *Murray* v *UK* (1996) 22 EHRR 29; *Magee* v *UK* (2001) 31 EHRR 822, and *Averill* v *UK* (2001) 31 EHRR 36 (ECHR, art 6); and *R* v *Chief Constable of the RUC, ex p Begley* [1997] 1 WLR 1475 (no common law right).

[120] This provision has its origins in Prevention of Terrorism (Temporary Provisions) Act 1989, s 13A (inserted by the Criminal Justice and Public Order Act 1994, s 81); and s 13B (inserted by the Prevention of Terrorism (Additional Powers) Act 1996). For the frequency of the use of these powers, see Cm 3420, 1996, p 57. Between February and August 1996 the police in London carried out searches under ss 13A and 13B of 9,700 drivers and passengers and of 270 pedestrians.

[121] The authorisation ceases to have effect within 48 hours unless approved by the Secretary of State (s 46(4)).

be given if 'expedient for the prevention of acts of terrorism' and the power of stop
and search may be exercised 'whether or not the constable has grounds for suspecting
the presence' of articles of a kind which could be used in connection with terrorism.[122]
Unlike PACE where there are also stop and search powers,[123] there is no duty on the
part of chief constables to report annually on the exercise of these powers. There are
also powers for the police to impose parking restrictions.[124]

3 *Terrorist offences.* Part VI of the 2000 Act contains a number of terrorist offences.
Section 54 provides that it is an offence to provide or receive instruction or training
in the making or use of firearms, radioactive material, explosives, or chemical, biological or nuclear weapons. It is also an offence to direct the activities of an organisation which is concerned in the commission of acts of terrorism (s 56), and to possess
any article for a purpose connected with the commission, preparation or instigation
of acts of terrorism (s 57). It is a defence to prove that the article was not in the
possession of the individual for a terrorist purpose (and it appears that the onus is on
the defendant), although sufficient evidence of possession may be established where
the accused and the article in question were both present on the premises (s 57). This
is a provision which was first introduced in 1994 as s 16A of the Prevention of Terrorism
Act 1989,[125] and was considered by the House of Lords in *R v DPP, ex p Kebeline*[126]
where questions were raised about the compatibility of s 16A with art 6(2) of the ECHR.
This provides that everyone charged with a criminal offence 'shall be presumed innocent until proved guilty according to law'.

According to Lord Cooke it is 'at best doubtful whether article 6(2) can be watered
down to an extent that would leave [what was then s 16A] unscathed', although the
House of Lords in *Kebilene* seemed disinclined to press the matter. Lord Cooke did not
exclude the possibility that 'the European Court of Human Rights, whose jurisprudence in the field is not yet extensively developed, may be prepared to treat terrorism
as a special subject' for the purposes of art 6(2).[127] Nevertheless, the provisions of
s 57 have slightly diluted the original provisions in s 16A so that the burdens placed
on defendants are 'evidential rather than persuasive or legal burdens'.[128] Where an
article is found in the possession of the accused, it now gives rise only to an 'assumption' that the accused possessed it, which the accused may rebut. Under s 16A it gave
rise to 'sufficient evidence' of proof, although again rebuttable.[129] Also dating from 1994
is s 58 which makes it an offence for a person to collect or record any information
which is of such a nature as is likely to be useful to a person committing or preparing
an act of terrorism; it is a defence under s 58 for the person charged to prove that 'he
had a reasonable excuse for his action or possession'.[130] By virtue of s 59 it is an offence
to incite terrorism overseas, a measure designed to 'deter those who use the United
Kingdom as a base from which to promote terrorist acts abroad'.[131]

---

[122] On the extension of these powers to the British Transport Police and the Ministry of Defence Police, see
   Anti-terrorism, Crime and Security Act 2001, Sch 7.
[123] See ch 21 B.
[124] Terrorism Act 2000, s 50.
[125] Prevention of Terrorism Act 1989, s 16A, inserted by the Criminal Justice and Public Order Act 1994.
[126] [2000] 2 AC 326.
[127] Ibid, at p 373. Also Lord Hope at pp 385–6.
[128] See HL Deb, 23 May 2000, col 754 (Lord Bassam).
[129] For a full consideration see *R v DPP ex p Kebilene*, note 126 above.
[130] First introduced as Prevention of Terrorism Act 1989, s 16B, inserted by the Criminal Justice and Public
   Order Act 1994.
[131] HC Deb, 14 Dec 1999, col 162.

The Terrorism Act 2000 and Northern Ireland

1 *Scheduled offences.*   Although the separate emergency legislation for Northern Ireland has been repealed, Part VII of the Terrorism Act 2000 continues to make special provision for the Province, many of these provisions being carried over from the Northern Ireland (Emergency Provisions) Act 1996. Indeed, Part VII looks like diluted old wine in a new bottle. Diluted in the sense that some of the controversial provisions of the 1996 Act have now gone, most notably the provisions authorising internment, or detention without trial in its more sanitised form. Old wine in a new bottle, furthermore, in the sense that many of the other provisions remain and indeed Part VII – like the 1996 Act before it – expires after a year unless it is continued in force (either in whole or in part) by order of the Secretary of State (s 112). This power of annual renewal is itself subject to a five-year term, so that Part VII will cease to have effect five years from the date it is brought into force. If the powers which it contains are to be retained, Part VII will have to be re-enacted, with or without modifications. These powers include the steps to deal with what are referred to as scheduled offences, defined to include both common law offences (for example, murder, manslaughter, riot and kidnapping) and statutory offences (for example, under the Offences against the Person Act 1861, the Explosive Substances Act 1883, and the Firearms (NI) Order 1981).

Three points of particular note arise in relation to the scheduled offences. The first is that bail may not be granted by magistrates, but only by a judge of the High Court or Court of Appeal; and in determining whether to grant bail, the judge must take into account factors which include the character, antecedents, associations and community ties of the accused (s 67). Second, a trial on indictment for a scheduled offence is to be held only at the Crown Court in Belfast, unless the Lord Chancellor after consulting the Lord Chief Justice of Northern Ireland directs otherwise; or unless the latter alone directs otherwise (s 74). All such trials 'shall be conducted by the court without a jury' (s 75). These are the co-called Diplock courts, introduced following recommendations by Lord Diplock in 1972 to deal with the problem of intimidation of jurors.[132] Third, provision is also made about evidence and the onus of proof in scheduled offence prosecutions. Particularly important is s 77, which effectively transfers the onus of proof to the accused in cases relating to the possession of explosive substances, petrol bombs and firearms. Where it is proved that both the accused and any offending article were present on the same premises, 'the court may assume that the accused possessed (and if relevant, knowingly possessed) the article, unless he proves that he did not know of its presence on the premises or that he had no control over it' (s 77(2)).

2 *Powers of the police and armed forces.*   Part VII of the Terrorism Act 2000 includes additional wide powers for the police and the armed forces. Any member of the armed forces on duty, or any constable may stop any person 'so long as it is necessary in order to question him' for the purpose of ascertaining the person's identity and movements, and what he or she knows about a 'recent explosion or incident' which has endangered human life or in which someone has been killed (s 89). None of the safeguards laid down in Part I of PACE appears to apply here. A constable may arrest without a warrant any person whom he or she has reasonable grounds to suspect is committing, has committed or is about to commit a scheduled offence or any other offence under the Act (s 82).[133] A member of the armed forces on duty may

---

[132]   Cmnd 5185, 1972. For a consideration of this measure, see Cm 2706, 1995 and Cm 3420, 1996. Also, Gearty and Kimbell, pp 56–7. See also Jackson and Doran, *Judge without Jury.*

[133]   There is no longer a right, as there was in s 11 of the Northern Ireland (Emergency Provisions) Act 1978, for a constable to arrest without a warrant any person he or she suspects of being a terrorist. As interpreted by the House of Lords in *McKee* v *Chief Constable for Northern Ireland* [1985] 1 All ER 1 (the

also arrest without a warrant, and detain for up to four hours, a person whom he or she has reasonable grounds to suspect is committing, has committed, or is about to commit any offence (s 83). The power of arrest by the armed forces under the Act is thus wider than that of the police, while the requirements for executing a lawful arrest are also different. A member of the armed forces making an arrest 'complies with any rule of law requiring him to state the grounds of arrest if he states that he is effecting the arrest as a member of Her Majesty's forces' (s 83(2)).

In *Murray v Ministry of Defence*[134] the plaintiff had been suspected of the offence of collecting money for the purchase of arms for the IRA in the United States. At 7 am armed soldiers arrived at her house to arrest her and take her to a screening centre in Belfast. One of the soldiers told Mrs Murray to get dressed while the others searched every room in the house and asked all the occupants to assemble in one room downstairs. After the plaintiff had dressed and come downstairs, she was told by a soldier 'As a member of the armed forces I arrest you', and was taken to the screening centre where she was released several hours later. One issue in subsequent proceedings for wrongful imprisonment was whether the failure to tell the plaintiff that she was being arrested until the soldiers were about to leave the house rendered the arrest unlawful. The House of Lords held that the arrest was lawful and that it was proper to delay speaking the words of arrest until all reasonable precautions had been taken to minimise the risk of danger and distress. According to Lord Griffiths, 'If words of arrest are spoken as soon as the house is entered before any precautions have been taken to search the house and find the other occupants, . . . there is a real risk that the alarm may be raised and an attempt made to resist arrest, not only by those within the house but also by summoning assistance from those in the immediate neighbourhood.'[135]

Part VII also contains wide powers of entry, search and seizure. Thus, any member of the armed forces on duty, or a constable, may enter any premises 'if he considers it necessary to do so in the course of operations for the preservation of the peace or the maintenance of order' (s 90). This is in addition to powers to search for munitions and transmitters (s 84), explosives (s 85), and 'unlawfully detained persons' (s 86). But the Terrorism Act 2000 not only contains powers of entry, search and seizure, it also includes the power to take possession of land – where the Secretary of State considers it 'necessary for the preservation of the peace or the maintenance of order' (s 91). This may be done with a minimum of formality and without the need for a warrant. In addition a member of the armed forces or a constable may wholly or partly close a road or prohibit or restrict the exercise of a right of way, if 'he considers it immediately necessary for the preservation of the peace or the maintenance of order' (s 92). The Secretary of State also has powers to order roads to be closed entirely or to a specified extent, this time where it is considered 'necessary for the preservation of the peace or the maintenance of order' (s 94). Again there is no formality to be complied with, although in principle any decision would be subject to judicial review and in any prosecution for breach of the directions, the legality of the order may be challenged. The same is true of the Secretary of State's more general power by regulations to make provision 'for promoting the preservation of the peace and the maintenance of order' (s 96).

These are considerable powers which remain vested in the police and the military authorities. Questions inevitably arise about the safeguards against abuse, not trivial questions in the light of the difficulties which have occurred since the current troubles began in 1969. The safeguards include the power to appoint an Independent Assessor

---

suspicion need not be reasonable but must be honestly held), the power was held to violate art 5(1) of the ECHR (no one to be deprived of liberty except on *reasonable suspicion* of having committed an offence) in *Fox v UK* (1991) 13 EHRR 157.

[134] [1988] 2 All ER 521. See C A Gearty [1988] CLJ 332; C Walker (1989) 40 NILQ 1.

[135] [1988] 2 All ER 521 at 527. It was also held in *Murray* that the army could question a suspect about activities other than those in connection with which he or she had been arrested.

of Military Complaints Procedures in Northern Ireland (s 98). The function of the Independent Assessor is to keep under the review the procedures adopted by the General Officer Commanding Northern Ireland for dealing with complaints against the behaviour of the army in Northern Ireland. The Independent Assessor may make representations to the GOC about the inadequacies of the procedures, but appears to have no express power to make recommendations about how they might be improved. However, the GOC is under a duty to provide such information, disclose such documents, and provide such assistance as the Independent Assessor may reasonably require for the performance of his or her functions. Other safeguards for Northern Ireland include the power of the Secretary of State to issue codes of practice to deal with the exercise of various powers by the police and members of the armed forces under the Act (s 99). The Chief Constable of the Police Service of Northern Ireland must ensure that a record is made of each exercise by a constable of a power under the Act, so far as it is reasonably practicable to do so (s 104). There is an entitlement to compensation where under Part VII of the Act 'real or personal property is taken, occupied, destroyed or damaged', or 'any other act is done which interferes with private rights of property'.[136]

3 *Police evidence and the right to silence in Northern Ireland.*   Controversial provisions first introduced by the Criminal Justice (Terrorism and Conspiracy) Act 1998 are retained in ss 107–11 of the Terrorism Act 2000. These apply to offences under s 11 (membership and support of a proscribed organisation) in relation to organisations which are both proscribed and specified in the Northern Ireland (Sentences) Act 1998. This has the effect of confining these provisions to bodies which are based in Northern Ireland and which are not on ceasefire (such as the Continuity IRA).[137] Where someone is charged with an offence under s 11, it will be sufficient corroboration to secure a conviction that a police officer of at least the rank of superintendent has stated in oral evidence that 'in his opinion' the accused belongs to an organisation specified in the 1998 Act or did belong to such an organisation at a time when it was specified (s 108). Where someone is charged with an offence under s 11, adverse inferences may be drawn from the silence of the accused both under questioning before being charged and on being charged; provided that in both cases the accused has been permitted to consult a solicitor (s 109). A person convicted under s 11 – who at the time of the offence belonged to a specified organisation – may be the subject of a forfeiture order requiring him or her to surrender money or property which has been or may be used for the purposes of the organisation (s 111).

These provisions provoked a storm of parliamentary protest when they were first introduced,[138] and it is not easy to find a precedent on the statute book for this provision.[139] There are exceptional cases where someone's property may be violated on the authority of a police superintendent in an emergency;[140] but this is rather different from the deprivation of liberty for membership of an association. It is true that an accused 'shall not be committed for trial, be found to have a case to answer or be convicted solely on the basis' of the police officer's statement. Nevertheless, the opinion of the police officer is not qualified by a requirement that it should be a

---

[136] Terrorism Act 2000, Sch 12(1). The Schedule makes provision for applications for compensation to be determined by the Secretary of State, with a right of appeal to the county court.

[137] See for example SI 1998 No 488, subsequently amended. Bodies are specified under s 3 of the 1998 Act for other purposes (the release of prisoners).

[138] HC Deb, 2 September 1998, cols 736 et seq; also cols 848–88.

[139] On the 1998 Act, see C Campbell [1999] Crim LR 941, and C Walker (1999) 62 MLR 879.

[140] Official Secrets Act 1911, s 9. See ch 25.

'reasonable' opinion; neither is there any obligation on the part of the police officer to justify the opinion, which may be based on information from intelligence sources that the police are reluctant to disclose or discuss. Questions are bound to arise about whether this provision is compatible with the Human Rights Act 1998 and, in particular, with the right to a fair trial, even having regard to the possibility advanced in *Kebeline* that standards may have to be lowered in cases involving terrorism. The retention of this measure after the commencement of the Human Rights Act is therefore surprising.

International terrorism: additional powers

1 *Disclosure of information.*   As we have seen, much of the Terrorism Act 2000 applies to international terrorism.[141] Nevertheless additional powers addressed specifically to international terrorism in the aftermath of the attacks in the United States are to be found in the Anti-terrorism, Crime and Security Act 2001.[142] We have already considered those provisions which deal with the forfeiture of terrorist property (Part 1)[143] and the making of orders to freeze the assets of those reasonably believed by the Treasury to have taken action to the detriment of the United Kingdom or action constituting a threat to the life or property of nationals or residents of the United Kingdom (Part 2).[144] Particularly controversial is Part 3, which deals with the disclosure of information. Public authorities – such as National Health Service bodies and regulatory agencies (such as the EOC, the CRE and the utility regulators) – generally may not disclose information about individuals obtained in the course of their activities, unless there is statutory authority. In some cases legislation will authorise disclosure for the purpose of criminal proceedings.[145] The 2001 Act extends these powers of disclosure of such information 'for the purpose of any criminal investigation', including those which are not confined to terrorist activity or national security (s 17).

Wide powers have also been taken to allow the disclosure of confidential information held by the Inland Revenue and the Commissioners of Customs of Excise, powers which apply retrospectively to information obtained before the Act came into force. The effect is to allow the intelligence services and the police to have access to financial information about individuals held by the tax authorities where this is requested 'for the purpose of facilitating the carrying out by any of the intelligence services of any of that service's functions' or 'for the purpose of any criminal investigation whatever which is being or may be carried out, whether in the United Kingdom or otherwise' (s 19(2)).[146] There is no formality (in terms of a warrant or other judicial authorisation) to be complied with before these remarkable powers may be exercised; the only restraint is that in s 19(3) which provides that no disclosure is to take place 'unless the person by whom the disclosure is made is satisfied that the making of the disclosure is proportionate to what is sought to be achieved by it'. A similar qualification operates in relation to the narrower disclosure provisions in s 17, already referred to. There are also porous restraints on the further disclosure of information

---

[141] The definition of terrorism includes conduct designed to influence the government (s 1(1) and for this purpose government is defined to mean the government of the United Kingdom or a part of the United Kingdom, or of 'a country other than the United Kingdom' (s 1(4)(d)). It is also an offence under the 2000 Act to incite terrorism overseas (ss 59–61). See also Criminal Law Act 1977, s 1A (inserted by Criminal Justice (Terrorism and Conspiracy) Act 1998, s 5) (conspiracy to commit offences outside the United Kingdom).

[142] For a useful summary, see M Zander, NLJ, 21 December 2001.

[143] See pp 618–19 above.

[144] See ch 17.

[145] See e.g. Sex Discrimination Act 1975, s 61 and Race Relations Act 1976, s 52.

[146] Disclosure may also take place for a number of other purposes specified in s 19.

which has been secured under this provision: further disclosure by the person to whom the information has been disclosed may be authorised by the tax authorities (s 19(5)).

2 *Detention without trial.*   One of the most symbolically important provisions of the Terrorism Act 2000 was the repeal of the provisions in the Northern Ireland (Emergency Provisions) Act 1996 dealing with the detention without trial – or internment – of terrorist suspects. Although the power to intern was retained until the commencement of the 2000 Act,[147] it was in practice discontinued in 1975, having proved to be not only highly controversial but also of questionable effect.[148] In *Ireland v United Kingdom*,[149] the European Court of Human Rights held that these procedures violated art 5 of the ECHR, but that derogation could be justified under art 15.[150] A fresh derogation has been made to authorise new powers of detention without trial now contained in Part 4 of the Anti-terrorism, Crime and Disorder Act 2001. These highly contentious measures provide that the Secretary of State may issue a certificate in respect of an individual whose presence in the United Kingdom is reasonably believed to present a risk to national security and who is reasonably suspected of being a terrorist (s 21(1)). A terrorist for this purpose is defined with reference to international terrorism (s 21(2)), and terrorism carries the same meaning for this Act as it does for the Terrorism Act 2000.

Where a certificate is issued that someone is a suspected international terrorist, the individual may be refused leave to enter or remain in the United Kingdom, or deported or removed in accordance with immigration law (s 22).[151] But there may be circumstances where removal or deportation is prevented by 'a point of law which wholly or partly relates to an international agreement' or to 'a practical consideration' (s 23). An example of the former would be art 3 of the ECHR which – as construed by the Strasbourg court – prevents the deportation of individuals to countries where they might suffer inhuman or degrading treatment or punishment.[152] In these cases the suspected international terrorist may be detained indefinitely without trial (s 23), a measure which attracted fierce opposition. An appeal lies to the Special Immigration Appeals Commission by someone who has been certified as a suspected international terrorist (s 25) and the Commission must cancel a certificate if it concludes that there are no reasonable grounds for the suspicion. The Commission must also review any certificate after six months and at three-monthly intervals thereafter. A review may also be conducted at the request of the certified individual if the Commission considers that the review should be held because of a change of circumstances (s 26). There is an appeal on a point of law to the Court of Appeal or the Court of Session (s 27).[153]

3 *Terrorist methods.*   The concerns about international terrorism relate in part to the methods which it is anticipated that the terrorists might use. The events in the United States on 11 September 2001 raised fears about attacks other than the bombings and shootings which have been associated with events in Northern Ireland. As a result the Anti-Terrorism, Crime and Security Act 2001 contains yet further measures to

---

[147] See HC Deb, 9 January 1996, col 37. Cf Cm 2706, 1995, p 33.
[148] For background, see Cm 1115, 1990. A full account of the procedures is given in *Ireland v UK* (1978) 2 EHRR 25.
[149] (1978) 2 EHRR 25.
[150] It was also held, however, that the techniques employed to interrogate interned suspects violated art 3 as inhuman and degrading treatment.
[151] See ch 20 B.
[152] See e.g. *Chahal v UK* (1997) 23 EHRR 413.
[153] By virtue of an amendment made by the 2001 Act, the Special Immigration Appeals Commission is now a superior court of record (s 27). See ch 20.

deal with anticipated international terrorist attacks, measures which it could never have been contemplated would ever be found in British legislation. Part 6 of the Act deals with 'weapons of mass destruction', and is aimed at the use of biological and chemical weapons (ss 43–6) and nuclear weapons (ss 47–9). As far as the latter is concerned, it is an offence knowingly 'to cause a nuclear explosion' (s 47(1)(a)),[154] although anyone guilty of this offence would surely be guilty of other offences in any event, assuming that there was anyone left to bring a prosecution.[155] There is an exception for acts authorised by the Secretary of State and also for acts done in the course of armed conflict. It is for the Secretary of State to determine whether anything was done in the course of armed conflict (s 48).[156]

Other measures are directed at the security of pathogens, with Part 7 introducing a duty to notify the Secretary of State before any scheduled pathogens of toxins are kept or used on any premises.[157] Among the many other provisions relating to the storage and use of these substances, s 64 provides that the Secretary of State may by order give directions to the occupier of any premises that a named individual is not to have access to the premises or to any dangerous substance. This is a power which can be exercised only in the interests of national security and there is an appeal 'by any person aggrieved by directions given under s 64' to the newly created Pathogens Access Appeal Commission (s 70). Measures designed to enhance security in the nuclear industry are included in Part 8, with measures designed to enhance aviation security dealt with in Part 9.[158] One particularly important provision with wider implications is s 79 which makes it an offence to 'disclose any information or thing the disclosure of which might prejudice the security of any nuclear site or any nuclear material'. Apart from protecting the country from the risk of international terrorism, there are concerns that this widely drafted provision will frustrate legitimate public protest about the movement of nuclear waste material around the country.

F. Conclusion: terrorism and human rights

The nature of emergency powers in British law has changed radically over the course of the 20th century. Initially, special powers were taken to deal with the consequences of war (Defence of the Realm Act 1914) and then large-scale industrial unrest (Emergency Powers Act 1920). These measures tended to authorise the making of secondary legislation for a limited period and for a specific end, albeit secondary legislation of a far-reaching kind in some instances. In recent years the nature of the threat to stability has changed and so too have the techniques adopted in response. The threat of terrorism – both domestic and international – has seen the development of standing legislation replacing the original strategy for dealing with terrorism which was for legislation for fixed periods, also subject to annual renewal by Parliament: we now live in a state of 'permanent emergency'. The response to terrorism has been at a considerable cost to traditional liberties formally protected by the ECHR and the Human Rights Act, despite which there has been the introduction of measures which compromise

---

[154] It is also an offence to develop or produce a nuclear weapon, to possess a nuclear weapon, to participate in the transfer of a nuclear weapon or to engage in military preparations intending to use or threaten to use a nuclear weapon (s 47(1)(b)–(e)).

[155] The offence carries a sentence of life imprisonment on conviction (s 47(5)).

[156] The exception applies also to the offences in s 47(1)(b)–(e).

[157] The substances in question are listed in Sch 5 which the Secretary of State 'may by order modify' (s 58).

[158] Other parts of this wide-ranging Act are dealt with elsewhere in this volume. See chapters 16 (powers of the Ministry of Defence Police); 21 (police powers); 22 (retention of communications data; and 23 (race hatred).

in varying degrees of severity the right to liberty (art 5), the right to privacy (art 8) and the right to freedom of association (art 11), to say nothing of the right to private property (First Protocol, art 1). This tension between terrorist legislation and human rights has generated a remarkable amount of litigation before the Strasbourg court[159] and shows no signs of abating.[160]

While attempts can doubtless be made to justify the foregoing measures as being a necessary response to particular circumstances, there are concerns that many of the powers are overbroad and that terrorist activity has been used as a cover to take powers which bear little relationship to the public emergency which induced them. There are also concerns about the effectiveness of Parliament when faced by a government determined to have its way with measures of this kind. It is true that Parliament extracted some concessions from the government in the enactment of the 2001 Act: unusually, ss 22 and 23 expire after 15 months unless revived by order of the Secretary of State; and end on 10 November 2006 whatever happens.[161] Also, a committee of privy councillors is to conduct a review of the Act within two years and may specify provisions that are to cease to have effect unless Parliament decides otherwise.[162] Yet despite no fewer than five critical reports from parliamentary committees,[163] the substance of the core provisions of the Bill was enacted largely intact.[164] It is thus up to the courts to ensure that these wide powers are not misused. But concern about the unenviable role in which they have been cast is hardly eased by Lord Hoffmann's postcript in the *Rehman* case[165] where he said that the events of 11 September 2001 in Washington and New York were

a reminder that in matters of national security, the cost of failure can be high. This seems to me to underline the need for the judicial arm of government to respect the decisions of ministers of the Crown on the question of whether support for terrorist activities in a foreign country constitutes a threat to national security. It is not only that the executive has access to special information and expertise in these matters. It is also that such decisions, with serious potential results for the community, require a legitimacy which can be conferred only by entrusting them to persons responsible to the community through the democratic process. If the people are to accept the consequences of such decisions, they must be made by persons whom the people have elected and whom they can remove.[166]

---

[159] *Ireland* v *UK* (1978) 2 EHRR 25, *Farrell* v *UK* (1983) 5 EHRR 466, *McCann* v *UK* (1995) 21 EHRR 97 (art 2); *Brogan* v *UK* (1988) 11 EHRR 117, *Brannigan* v *UK* (1993) 17 EHRR 539, *Fox* v *UK* (1990) 13 EHRR 157, *Murray* v *UK* (1994) 19 EHRR 193 (art 5); *Murray* v *UK* (1996) 22 EHRR 29 (art 6); *Magee* v *UK* (2001) 31 EHRR 822; and *Averill* v *UK* (2001) 31 EHRR 839, *Brennan* v *UK* (2002) 34 EHRR 507 (art 6).

[160] C Gearty (1999) ALS 367; and J J Rowe [2001] Crim LR 527.

[161] Anti-terrorism, Crime and Security Act 2001, s 29.

[162] Ibid, ss 122, 123.

[163] See Zander (note 142 above), citing the Home Affairs Committee, the House of Lords Constitution Committee, the House of Lords Select Committee on Delegated Powers and Regulatory Reform, and two reports of the Joint Committee on Human Rights.

[164] The government did lose provisions dealing with incitement to religious hatred and had to concede a number of other points.

[165] *R* v *Home Secretary, ex p Rehman* [2002] 1 All ER 122.

[166] Ibid, p 142.

Part IV

ADMINISTRATIVE LAW

Chapter 27

THE NATURE AND DEVELOPMENT
OF ADMINISTRATIVE LAW

During the last 25 years, there has been, and continues to be, a remarkable growth in litigation seeking judicial review of the decisions of public authorities.[1] This may be why the law of judicial review is sometimes thought to be the only part of administrative law that lawyers need to know. But this is no more correct than to say that employment lawyers need study only the law of unfair dismissal or tort lawyers only the law of negligence. Certainly, the law of judicial review, outlined in chapters 30 and 31, is a vital part of administrative law, but the part must not be mistaken for the whole.

A formal definition of administrative law is that it is a branch of public law concerned with the composition, procedures, powers, duties, rights and liabilities of the various organs of government that are engaged in administering public policies.[2] These policies have been either laid down by Parliament in legislation or developed by the government and other authorities in the exercise of their executive powers. On this broad definition, administrative law includes at one extreme the general principles and institutions of constitutional law outlined in earlier chapters; and at the other the detailed rules contained in statutes and ministerial regulations that govern the provision of complex social services (such as social security), the regulation of economic activities (such as financial services), the control of immigration, and environmental law.

As we will see later, there is no 'bright line' demarcating constitutional and administrative law. Building on the account of the principles of constitutional government already given, this part of the book deals with aspects of administrative law relevant to all areas of government. These are the powers of the executive to make secondary, or delegated, legislation; the procedures whereby specialised tribunals and inquiries and the Parliamentary Ombudsman make decisions or provide redress for individual grievances; judicial review of public authorities; and the liability of public authorities, notably central government, to be sued for damages. The aim will be to identify the key institutions that help to ensure that lawful standards of public administration are observed.[3]

Functions of administrative law

One important function of the law is to enable the tasks of government to be performed. Administrative agencies are created by law and equipped with powers to carry out public policies on behalf of the state and in the general interest. A second function of the law is to govern the relations between various public agencies, for example, between

---

[1] In 1981, 533 applications for judicial review were made, of which 376 were allowed; in 1987, 1,529 were made and 767 allowed; in 1994, 3,208 were made and 1,260 allowed: Bridges, Meszaros and Sunkin, *Judicial Review in Perspective*, app 1. In 1997, 3,739 applications were made and in 1999, 4,437: *Review of the Crown Office List*, 2000, p 3. In 2001, 5,298 applications were made: [2002] All ER (D) 12 (Feb).

[2] For fuller accounts, see the textbooks on administrative law by (respectively) Cane, Craig, Foulkes, and Wade and Forsyth. See also Richardson and Genn (eds), *Administrative Law and Government Action*; Harlow and Rawlings, *Law and Administration* and Taggart (ed.), *The Province of Administrative Law*.

[3] Cf de Smith, Woolf and Jowell, *Judicial Review of Administrative Action*, ch 1.

a minister and a local authority[4] or between two local authorities.[5] A third function of the law is to govern the relations between a public agency and those individuals or private bodies over whose affairs the agency is entrusted with power. By providing a public agency or other body with legal powers to perform its tasks, the legislator also imposes a measure of control since an agency is not authorised to go outside its powers. The granting of powers may be subject both to express conditions or limitations and also to implied requirements, such as the duty to exercise powers in good faith and not corruptly. The extent of the powers granted will reflect the system of social, economic, and political values recognised in a given society.

Individuals are affected by administrative powers in many ways, sometimes to their benefit and sometimes to their detriment. An individual's rights are seldom absolute: thus a landowner whose farm is required for a new motorway does not have an absolute right to prevent the acquisition of that land for a purpose considered to be in the general interest of the community. Neither, to take a very difficult example, do parents with a seriously ill child have an absolute right to medical treatment for him or her in the NHS when this is not recommended on clinical grounds.[6] Conversely, the powers of public authorities should not themselves be regarded as absolute. Few would dispute that individuals, local communities and minority groups have a right to legal protection when confronted with the coercive powers of the state. The difficulty comes in determining the form and extent of that protection and the basis on which such disputes may be resolved. The more fundamental the rights of the individual affected, the greater ought to be the degree of protection.[7]

The constitutional background to administrative law

Earlier chapters described the structure of central government; the responsibility of ministers to Parliament; the use of public bodies to regulate public utilities and other services; and the effect of public powers on the individual's rights and liberties. The legislative supremacy of Parliament is relevant to administrative law, since (except where a conflict with rights in Community law arises) no court can hold that the powers of an agency created by Act of Parliament are invalid or inoperative. Whether or not the role of the courts in supervising executive acts is founded directly on the supremacy of Parliament,[8] there is no doubt that Parliament may, as it did in the Human Rights Act 1998, modify the judicial approach to the interpretation of legislation and extend the courts' powers in supervising the acts and decisions of public authorities.[9] Where an agency's powers do not come from primary legislation in the form of an Act of Parliament, but from other legislative measures (such as statutory instruments or legislation enacted in Northern Ireland, Scotland or Wales) the courts may review the legality of the agency's powers, as well as the decisions taken in reliance on those powers.

In a modern legal system, the way that disputes arising out of administration are handled is of constitutional significance. Where, as in Germany, there are separate

---

[4] E.g. *Education Secretary v Tameside MB* [1977] AC 1014; ch 30 A.
[5] E.g. *Bromley BC v Greater London Council* [1983] AC 768.
[6] *R v Cambridge Health Authority, ex p B* [1995] 2 All ER 129.
[7] See Lord Browne-Wilkinson [1992] PL 397; Sir J Laws [1993] PL 59 and [1998] PL 254. This principle was expressly approved in respect of judicial review in *R v Ministry of Defence, ex p Smith* [1996] QB 517, 554.
[8] See Forsyth (ed), *Judicial Review and the Constitution*; and p 696 below.
[9] Ch 19 C.

superior courts, one entrusted with interpreting the constitution and one dealing with disputes between the citizen and the administration, a distinction between constitutional and administrative law can be based on the actual work done by the two courts. In the United Kingdom, it is impossible to draw a hard and fast line between constitutional and administrative law.[10] In England and Wales, the section of the High Court dealing with judicial review and related appeals was in October 2000 named the Administrative Court, but this meant no change in the High Court's jurisdiction. Issues of constitutional significance arise from civil cases involving private litigants[11] as well as from cases involving criminal justice[12] and judicial review.[13] In 1985, in *Wheeler* v *Leicester City Council*,[14] a judicial review case, the House of Lords held that the council acted unlawfully in barring a rugby club from using public playing fields because club members had played rugby in South Africa during apartheid. The judgments turned primarily on aspects of local government and race relations law. Were similar facts to occur today, the Human Rights Act 1998 would cause the club members' right to freedom of expression to be at the heart of the case. Indeed, the fact that the 1998 Act makes it unlawful for public authorities to act inconsistently with the Convention rights is another reason why administrative cases cannot be separated from cases having a constitutional effect. The criminal law as such falls outside administrative law, but management of the police and the penal system often give rise to disputes about the exercise of official powers (for example, over the rights of convicted prisoners against the prison authorities).[15] The procedures of Parliament fall outside administrative law, but the rules of public audit affect the working of government departments[16] and so do parliamentary procedures for the scrutiny of delegated legislation.[17]

Administrative law and 'droit administratif'

The study of administrative law in Britain was formerly dominated by the comparison which Dicey drew between the system of administrative jurisdiction (*le contentieux administratif*) in France, under which a special hierarchy of administrative courts (headed by the Conseil d'Etat) deals with most disputes concerning the exercise of administrative power and the common law in England.[18] Dicey contrasted the disadvantages involved in a system of administrative courts handling disputes between officials and citizens with the advantages enjoyed in Britain through the absence of such a system. The common law, as Dicey saw it, subjected executive actions to control by the same courts and according to the same principles as governed the relationships between private citizens. Dicey concluded that the common law gave the citizen better protection against arbitrary action by the executive than the French system. Unfortunately, his denial that 'droit administratif' existed in England led many to suppose that there was no such thing as administrative law in the United Kingdom.

---

[10] And see Craig, *Public Law and Democracy*, ch 1.
[11] *Hamilton* v *Al Fayed* [2001] 1 AC 395.
[12] *Boddington* v *British Transport Police* [1999] 2 AC 143.
[13] E.g. *R* v *Home Secretary, ex p Fire Brigades Union* [1995] 2 AC 513 and *R* v *Foreign Secretary, ex p World Development Movement* [1995] 1 All ER 611.
[14] [1985] AC 1054.
[15] E.g. *R (Daly)* v *Home Secretary* [2001] 2 AC 532.
[16] See Turpin, *Government Procurement and Contracts* and ch 17 D.
[17] Ch 28.
[18] *The Law of the Constitution*, ch 12 and app 2. See F H Lawson (1959) 7 Political Studies 109, 207; Brown and Bell, *French Administrative Law*; and, for a critique of Dicey's approach to administrative law, H W Arthurs (1979) 17 Osgoode Hall LJ 1.

Old beliefs died hard[19] but today administrative law in Britain needs no proof of its existence. In 1987, the government circulated a booklet bringing to the notice of civil servants the existence of what it called 'The Judge Over Your Shoulder', accompanying it with a secret Cabinet memorandum entitled, 'Reducing the Risk of Legal Challenges'.[20] The judiciary in Britain are now well aware that their power to control the actions of public authorities is of constitutional significance. Lord Diplock described the rapid development of 'a rational and comprehensive system of administrative law' as having been 'the greatest achievement of the English courts' in his judicial lifetime.[21] One judge has written that in this area of common law, 'the judges have in the last 30 years changed the face of the United Kingdom's constitution'.[22]

Despite these developments, there are many differences between the English and French approaches to administrative law. The French system is founded on the use of separate administrative courts whereas the British system relies heavily on the superior civil courts. In both systems, the essential principles of judicial control are judge-made and do not derive from either codes or statutes. But in France, the price paid for a separate administrative jurisdiction is a complex body of law dividing jurisdiction between the civil and the administrative courts (that is, between private and public law); questions of conflict must be settled by the Tribunal des Conflits or by legislation. Where the French system gains is that administrative courts develop rules of procedure (for example, regarding the obtaining of evidence from government departments) and rules of substantive liability (for example, regarding administrative contracts or the state's liability for harm caused by official acts) which take account of the public setting of the disputes. These rules may confer special duties upon the administration (for example, liability without fault in certain circumstances),[23] not merely immunities.

By contrast, the British approach, seen both in case-law and in the Crown Proceedings Act 1947, has been to apply general principles of liability in contract and tort to public bodies as well as to private citizens. It was by application of the general law of negligence that the liability of the Home Office was decided in respect of harm done by escaping Borstal boys.[24] The position is different regarding judicial review of official decisions, since this jurisdiction has no direct counterpart in private law. We consider later in this chapter the extent to which a distinction between public and private law now exists. Whatever may have been the position in the past, judges in the United Kingdom now accept that one of their tasks is to adjudicate on disputes between the individual and government. While judicial review stops far short of enabling every problem of government to be solved, the courts today are capable of providing an effective, authoritative and timely remedy to individuals who challenge the legality of official acts.

Historical development

One effect of the constitutional settlement in 1689 was to restrict the power of the King's government in London to supervise the conduct of local administration by such

---

[19] Mr Maudling, when Home Secretary, said in debating a clause of the Immigration Bill 1971: 'I have never seen the sense of administrative law in our country, because it merely means someone else taking the Government's decisions for them' (Official Report, Standing Committee B, 25 May 1971, col 1508).

[20] See A W Bradley [1987] PL 485 and [1988] PL 1; and D Oliver [1994] PL 514.

[21] *Re Racal Communications Ltd* [1981] AC 374, 382; and *R v Inland Revenue Commissioners, ex p National Federation of Self-Employed* [1982] AC 617, 641. And see Lord Diplock [1974] CLJ 233; Lord Scarman [1990] PL 490.

[22] Sir S Sedley, in Richardson and Genn (note 2), p 36.

[23] R Errera [1986] CLP 157.

[24] *Dorset Yacht Co v Home Office* [1970] AC 1004; ch 32 A. And see Bell and Bradley (eds), *Governmental Liability: A Comparative Study*.

persons as justices of the peace for the counties, who met quarterly to dispense criminal justice and to govern their locality. The powers of the justices in such matters as the poor law, licensing and highways, were derived from Acts of Parliament. Although there was little, if any, central control over the activities of the justices, their exercise of power could be challenged in the Court of King's Bench on grounds of legality and jurisdiction by recourse to the prerogative writs.[25] Particularly after 1832, new bodies were established by Parliament such as the poor law guardians, public health boards and school boards. When modern local authorities were created and new departments of central government emerged, the Court of King's Bench extended its controlling jurisdiction to include all these bodies. In his lectures in 1887–88, the historian Maitland argued for a broad approach to constitutional law that would include these new organs of government:

> Year by year the subordinate government of England is becoming more and more important. The new movement set in with the Reform Bill of 1832: it has gone far already and assuredly it will go further. We are becoming a much governed nation, governed by all manner of councils and boards and officers, central and local, high and low, exercising the powers which have been committed to them by modern statutes.[26]

Since these bodies were exercising statutory powers, disputes about the limits of their power were settled by the courts, often by recourse to the prerogative writs. Thus the procedures of judicial control, which originally checked the powers of inferior courts, were used to review the exercise of powers, first by local authorities and then by ministers of the Crown.[27] It is a long step from reviewing the rate levied by county justices to pay for repairs to a bridge[28] to reviewing a decision by the Home Secretary to introduce a new and less costly scheme of compensation for criminal injuries.[29] Yet in both instances the court's role is to ensure that those who exercise executive power observe due standards of legality in doing so.

Inevitably, the supervisory role of the courts has developed as patterns of government have changed. Judicial control of central government is complementary to, not a substitute for, the responsibility of ministers to Parliament. The grounds of judicial control have never been defined in legislation. However, by the common law doctrine of precedent, unsystematic as its working may be, principles have developed both for policing the limits of powers and for reviewing the use of discretionary powers. In 1992, an eminent New Zealand judge summarised administrative law in this way: 'The administrator must act fairly, reasonably and according to law. That is the essence and the rest is mainly machinery.'[30] Such principles apply whenever public power is exercised, regardless of its legal source.[31]

In Scotland, the detailed history of the law is different but the general form of the development has been similar. After the abolition of the Privy Council for Scotland, following the Union with England in 1707, the Court of Session adopted a supervisory role comparable to that of the Court of King's Bench in England. Since the prerogative writs were never part of Scots law, and since a separate court of equity was never created, the remedies for controlling inferior tribunals and administrative agencies were

---

[25] See Henderson, *Foundations of English Administrative Law*; de Smith, Woolf and Jowell, *Judicial Review of Administrative Action*, ch 14.

[26] Maitland, *Constitutional History*, p 501.

[27] E.g. *Board of Education v Rice* [1911] AC 179 and *Local Government Board v Arlidge* [1915] AC 120, on which see Dicey, *The Law of the Constitution*, app 2.

[28] *R v Glamorganshire Inhabitants* (1700) 1 Ld Raym 580.

[29] *R v Home Secretary, ex p Fire Brigades Union* [1995] 2 AC 513.

[30] Sir Robin Cooke, quoted in *R v Devon CC, ex p Baker* [1995] 1 All ER 73, 88.

[31] E.g. *CCSU v Minister for Civil Service* [1985] AC 374.

obtained from the Court of Session by the procedures used for civil litigation between private parties. But the principles upon which judicial control was founded were remarkably similar to those developed in English law.[32] The sheriff court exercised an important role in enabling many local administrative disputes to be settled judicially.[33] Since 1900, much of the development in government has been by statute law applying both in England and Scotland and the response of the Scottish courts has been similar to that of the English courts.

In Scotland, as well as Northern Ireland and Wales, there is now a layer of devolved government to which administrative law applies. Apart from questions as to the extent of the devolved powers, which must be decided in accordance with the devolution legislation,[34] decisions by the devolved governments are subject to the same process of judicial review as are decisions of other public bodies.

Reform of administrative law

The explosion of government in the 20th century did not wait for lawyers and academic writers in Britain to acquire an understanding of administrative law. The first textbooks on the subject appeared in the late 1920s.[35] At first a narrow approach was taken to the subject, confining it to delegated legislation and the exercise of judicial powers by administrative bodies. Only later was a broader definition of administrative law adopted as covering all administrative powers and duties as well as judicial control of the administration.

The hesitant development of administrative law since the 1920s may be illustrated by reference to three committees appointed by the Lord Chancellor to inquire into aspects of the subject. The first, a committee that examined the archaic law protecting the Crown and government departments from being sued, made no effective progress.[36] The second, the Committee on Ministers' Powers, was appointed in 1929 at a time when a storm of criticism was directed against departments by some judges and barristers, by academic lawyers at Oxford and a small group of MPs. Indeed, the Lord Chief Justice (Lord Hewart) had just published a strident book, *The New Despotism*, in which he argued that Britain was experiencing administrative lawlessness rather than the rule of law. The terms of reference of the committee were:

> to consider the powers exercised by, or under the direction of (or by persons or bodies appointed specially by), Ministers of the Crown by way of (*a*) delegated legislation, and (*b*) judicial or quasi-judicial decision, and to report what safeguards were desirable or necessary to secure the constitutional principles of the sovereignty of Parliament and the supremacy of the law.

The committee vindicated the civil service from the charge of bureaucratic tyranny, analysed in terms of constitutional principle the legislative and judicial powers vested in ministers and made recommendations to improve delegated legislation and administrative justice.[37] No government adopted its recommendations and it was not until 1944 that the House of Commons established a select committee to scrutinise delegated legislation.[38]

---

[32] See e.g. *Moss Empires Ltd* v *Glasgow Assessor* 1917 SC (HL) 1. Also *Stair Memorial Encyclopaedia, The Laws of Scotland*, vol 1, title Administrative Law; Clyde and Edwards, *Judicial Review*.
[33] *Brown* v *Hamilton DC* 1983 SC (HL) 1.
[34] Ch 3 B.
[35] Robson, *Justice and Administrative Law*, and Port, *Administrative Law*.
[36] See Cmd 2842, 1927, discussed by J Jacob [1992] PL 452; and ch 32 A.
[37] Cmd 4060, 1932.
[38] Ch 28.

In 1955, when the government machine was again under attack from sections of political opinion,[39] the Committee on Administrative Tribunals and Inquiries was appointed to review:

(a) The constitution and working of tribunals other than the ordinary courts of law, constituted under any Act of Parliament by a Minister of the Crown or for the purposes of a Minister's functions.

(b) The working of such administrative procedures as include the holding of an inquiry or hearing by or on behalf of a Minister on an appeal or as the result of objections or representations, and in particular the procedure for the compulsory purchase of land.

This committee (the Franks committee) reported in 1957.[40] In examining tribunals and inquiries, it covered again ground which the Committee on Ministers' Powers had already reviewed (judicial and quasi-judicial decisions taken by or for ministers) but, unlike that committee, it found great difficulty in distinguishing between judicial and administrative decisions. Adopting a more pragmatic approach, it examined one by one the procedures within its terms of reference and inquired how far the characteristics of openness, fairness and impartiality applied to each. The committee concluded that judicial control, whether by direct appeal to the courts or by review through the prerogative orders, should be maintained and where necessary extended. These recommendations led directly to the Tribunals and Inquiries Act 1958, which set up the Council on Tribunals, and to other action implementing the committee's report.[41]

The Franks committee's attention was confined to areas where recourse to a tribunal or a public inquiry was already available. The committee could not consider those areas of governmental power where neither safeguard existed, nor could it consider the provision of redress for individuals suffering from maladministration. These two problems were examined in 1961 by a committee appointed by Justice.[42] The report, *The Citizen and the Administration*, recommended (a) that, except where there are overriding considerations of government policy, a citizen should be entitled to appeal from a departmental decision on a matter of discretion to an impartial tribunal; rather than the creation of many new tribunals, a general tribunal should be created to hear appeals against discretionary decisions and (b) that a Parliamentary Commissioner (Ombudsman) be appointed to investigate complaints of maladministration. Nothing came of the former recommendation, but the first appointment of a Parliamentary Ombudsman was made in 1967. The creation of an Ombudsman did not affect the rules of administrative law. In 1969, the government decided not to appoint a royal commission to examine the whole of administrative law and asked the English and Scottish Law Commissions to study the effectiveness of administrative law remedies in the English and Scottish courts. In 1976, the English Commission recommended important procedural reforms[43] and these were implemented between 1977 and 1981, creating the current procedure of application for judicial review.[44] A similarly named procedure was introduced into Scots law in 1985.[45]

The continuing refusal of governments to make a general inquiry into administrative law led in 1979 to a further initiative by Justice, with All Souls College Oxford, to

---

[39] The attack was intensified by the Crichel Down affair: ch 7.

[40] Cmnd 218, 1957.

[41] Ch 29 A and B, and see J A G Griffith (1959) 22 MLR 125.

[42] For comment, see I M Pedersen [1962] PL 15; J D B Mitchell [1962] PL 82; and A W Bradley [1962] CLJ 82. Justice is the British section of the International Commission of Jurists.

[43] Cmnd 6407, 1976; and see Scottish Law Commission, *Remedies in Administrative Law*, Memorandum No 14, 1971.

[44] Ch 31.

[45] See note 32 and T Mullen, K Pick and T Prosser [1995] PL 52.

create a committee to review administrative law in the United Kingdom, under the chairmanship of Sir Patrick Neill QC. But it took nine years for the committee to report and none of its recommendations (dealing with such matters as the duty to give reasons for decisions and the need for victims of maladministration to have a right to compensation) was adopted by the government.[46]

In 1994, the English Law Commission reported on the mechanism of judicial review and the statutory procedures for appeals to the High Court from inferior courts, tribunals and other bodies.[47] It proposed some limited changes in procedure and nomenclature, which (inter alia) would enable public interest challenges to official decisions to be made by interest groups. It was not until October 2000 that judicial review procedures were subject to limited changes (including the relabelling of historic remedies and the emergence of the Administrative Court under that name), following another survey of court practice.[48] At the same time, the Human Rights Act 1998 came into effect, with extensive implications for administrative law, since it introduced new rules of statutory interpretation, required public authorities to act consistently with Convention rights and thereby created new grounds of judicial review.[49] Except for the Human Rights Act and the creation of the procedure of judicial review in 1977, it remains the case that the development in the public law role of the courts in recent years owes more to changing attitudes on the part of the judges than it does to formal procedures of law reform.

Law and the administrative process

The principle that government must be conducted according to law means that for every act performed in the course of government there must be legal authority.[50] That authority is usually derived expressly or by implication from statute or sometimes from the royal prerogative. Moreover, the Crown has at common law the same capacity as any other person to make contracts, own property etc.[51] A public body must be able to show that it is acting in accordance with legal authority when its action (for example, the levying of a tax) adversely affects the rights or interests of a private individual. Exceptionally, the public interest may require the government to satisfy a court that its decisions are lawful even if no private individuals are affected except as members of the public at large.[52]

It is not possible to describe the administrative process in terms of law alone. There are many tasks (for example, budgeting, coordination and planning) to which law is not of primary relevance. Many politicians and administrators are likely to view law instrumentally as a means of achieving social or economic policies. In areas of government such as taxation, the detailed rules are found in statutes or in judicial decisions interpreting the statutes. Even so, those rules may not provide the complete

---

[46] *Administrative Justice: Some Necessary Reforms*, discussed by P McAuslan [1988] PL 402 and C T Emery [1988] PL 495.

[47] Law Com No 226; HC 669 (1993–94). See also Lord Woolf [1992] PL 221; R Gordon [1995] PL 11; and C T Emery [1995] PL 450.

[48] See *Review of the Crown Office List* (Bowman report), 2000; Civil Procedure Rules, Part 54. Also ch 30 and M Fordham [2001] PL 4.

[49] See chs 19 C and 30 A.

[50] The contrary view, expressed in *Malone* v *Metropolitan Police Commissioner* [1979] Ch 344, was disapproved in *R* v *Somerset CC, ex p Fewings* [1995] 3 All ER 20, and would conflict with the European Convention on Human Rights. See H Mountfield in Jowell and Cooper (eds), *Understanding Human Rights Principles*, p 5.

[51] B V Harris (1992) 108 LQR 626.

[52] See e.g. *R* v *Foreign Secretary, ex p Rees-Mogg* [1994] QB 552; *R* v *Foreign Secretary, ex p Worldwide Development Movement* [1995] 1 All ER 611; and ch 31.

picture since circumstances may arise in which the revenue authorities exercise an extra-statutory discretion not to enforce payment of tax in a situation which neither Parliament nor the government can have foreseen. But the practice of granting extra-statutory concessions would defeat the whole purpose of imposing taxes by law if it became widespread; by the nature of a tax concession, it may escape challenge in a court of law.[53]

By contrast with taxation, in many areas of government the nature of the legal framework is deliberately skeletonic, so as to allow for wide discretion on the part of the department concerned in promoting policies that are nowhere laid down in statutory rules. Thus an agency responsible for grants to industry may wish to make selective grants to certain forms of industry or to discriminate between areas of high and low unemployment.[54] Wide discretion is found in many other areas of government, such as the control of immigration or the granting of permission for the development of land. In principle, discretionary powers are subject to control by the courts. In practice, the exercise of discretion is often closely controlled through policy decisions taken by ministers or departmental rules which lay down how officials should exercise their powers.[55] At one time, such policies and rules were often protected from publication outside Whitehall, but the more open approach to government that now exists requires disclosure of all policies and rules that are relevant to decision-making in individual cases.

Many officials are therefore concerned with administering government policies rather than with administering the law as such. It is often difficult to separate the administration of an existing policy from the making of a new policy. When a department is exercising discretionary powers and a case arises that raises new features, a decision on the facts will serve as a precedent for future decisions of a similar kind. Thus the process gives rise to the formulation of a more detailed policy than had previously existed.

Decision-making within a department is very different from the process by which a court settles a dispute between two parties. A civil case, for example, is decided by the judge after hearing evidence and legal arguments brought before the court by the parties in an adversary procedure.[56] Oral proceedings take place in public before the judge, in the presence of the parties and their lawyers. A reasoned decision is announced in open court; when made it can be challenged only by appeal to a higher court. By contrast, a departmental decision is typically taken in secret, without an adversary procedure. Often it is not known at what level in the department the decision has been taken. Political pressure may be brought to bear on the department both before and after the decision. Except where a statute so requires, reasons for the decision need not be given.

Although the two processes of administrative and judicial decision-making are different, it would be wrong to assume that one method is superior to the other or to suppose that a department should always try to adopt the methods of a court. Everything depends on the type of decision to be made and on the results which it is desired to achieve from a particular scheme.[57] Where such decisions directly affect an individual's civil rights and obligations, as in the case of decisions granting or refusing planning permission, the right to a fair hearing under Art 6(1) ECHR arises, but this

---

[53] But not judicial criticism: *Vestey v IRC* [1980] AC 1148. And cf *R v IRC, ex p National Federation of Self-Employed* [1982] AC 617.

[54] See e.g. *British Oxygen Co v Board of Trade* [1971] AC 610.

[55] On departmental rules and 'quasi-legislation', see ch 28. For the relevance of policies in planning decisions, see *R (Alconbury Developments Ltd) v Environment Secretary* [2001] 2 All ER 929.

[56] Cf Art 6(1), ECHR (ch 19 B) by which everyone has a right to a fair and public hearing 'in the determination of his civil rights and obligations'.

[57] G Ganz [1972] PL 215, 229. Cf *Local Government Board v Arlidge* [1915] AC 120.

does not prevent ministers deciding such questions after a public inquiry procedure, provided that the decisions are themselves subject to a sufficient level of judicial review.[58] Decisions that are made on the basis of general rules and after a procedure that enables the specific facts to be ascertained and the competing considerations to be weighed up are likely to be fairer than if made without such aids to decision-making.[59] Thus many classes of decisions are taken not by civil servants in the department but by independent tribunals, which apply a modified form of judicial procedure in making decisions. In other cases, Parliament has provided that a stage of the administrative process should be exposed to view in the form of a public inquiry, while leaving the final decision in the hands of the minister or department.[60]

Powers, duties and discretion

A recurring feature in administrative law is the interplay between powers, duties and discretion. If someone satisfies the legal rules that govern who may vote in parliamentary elections, then she has a right to be entered on the electoral register and a right to vote in the area where she is registered. The relevant officials are under a correlative duty to give effect to her rights. Many situations that arise in the course of public administration are less clear-cut. Thus a minister may be under a duty to achieve certain broad policy objectives without in law being required to take action of any particular kind. Clearly, steps taken in the performance of such a duty involve the exercise of discretion. As Lord Diplock said:

> The very concept of administrative discretion involves a right to choose more than one possible course of action on which there is room for reasonable people to hold differing opinions as to which is to be preferred.[61]

Where an Act confers authority to administer a branch of government, it may confer a broad duty on the minister and other public authorities to fulfil certain policy objectives. It may impose specific duties on the minister to act when certain conditions exist and it will probably confer powers on the authorities concerned. In administrative law, 'power' has two meanings, which are not always distinguished: (*a*) the capacity to act in a certain way (for example, power to provide a library service or to purchase land by agreement for public recreation); and (*b*) authority to restrict or take away the rights of others (for example, power to regulate the mini-cab trade in a city or to buy land compulsorily that is needed for a public purpose, even though the owner does not wish to sell). Since it is inherent in the nature of a power that it may be exercised in various ways, use of a power invariably requires the exercise of discretion. Sometimes, there may be a duty to exercise a discretion. When an official decides to perform a duty or to exercise a power or discretion in a certain way, the decision may delight some persons and disappoint others. Within a democracy, choices of this kind should be made by those who bear political responsibility for them, not by judges.[62] Those whose rights or interests are adversely affected by an administrative decision may consider (or be advised) that the decision was not properly taken: in such a case, they may have recourse to any rights of appeal that exist or they may seek judicial review.

---

[58] *R (Alconbury Developments Ltd)* v *Environment Secretary* [2001] 2 All ER 929.
[59] See J Jowell [1973] PL 178 and (the same author) in Jowell and Oliver (eds), *The Changing Constitution*, ch 1.
[60] Ch 29 A and B.
[61] *Secretary of State for Education* v *Tameside MB* [1977] AC 1014, at p 1064. And see Davis, *Discretionary Justice*, and Galligan, *Discretionary Powers*.
[62] See the *Alconbury* case (above), esp paras 48 (Lord Slynn), 70 (Lord Hoffmann), 139–141 (Lord Clyde).

A difficult question arises when, under severe constraints on expenditure, a public authority takes its budgetary position into account in deciding whether it can provide a certain benefit to an individual or must, for example, close down valuable community services. Here the legal answer may depend on the exact terms of the legislation under which the service or benefit is provided.[63] The statute may impose a duty which must be performed in any event or confer a qualified duty or a discretion, whose exercise may depend on the individual's situation and other matters. In such cases, the court is not concerned with the political merits of the authority's policy, but it must protect individual rights where these are granted by statute. Questions inevitably arise as to where the dividing line comes between matters that a public authority should decide and those that should be decided by the judges.[64]

These matters will be considered more fully in later chapters. In the rest of this chapter, we consider two general matters, namely the classification of powers and the distinction between public and private law, which are relevant to the process of judicial control of government.

Classification of powers

Under a written constitution founded on the separation of powers, it may be necessary for a court to decide whether legislative or executive action has improperly infringed the judicial power.[65] Although this is not the case in the United Kingdom, there are several purposes in administrative law for which attempts have been made to classify the powers of government as being legislative, administrative or judicial in character. Thus under the Statutory Instruments Act 1946 in its application to earlier statutes, a distinction was drawn between instruments that were legislative and those which were executive in character.[66] The jurisdiction of the Parliamentary Ombudsman applies to 'action taken in the exercise of administrative functions' by a government department, which may mean that he is not concerned with the functions of departments which are legislative in character.[67] Under the Crown Proceedings Act 1947, s 2(5), the Crown is not liable for the acts of any person who is discharging responsibilities of a judicial nature.[68] However, by the Human Rights Act 1998, s 9, there are circumstances in which the Crown must compensate those who have been detained by reason of a judicial act.[69] It also may be necessary for other purposes to decide whether a particular procedure may be described as judicial. Thus, absolute privilege at common law protects a witness who gives evidence at a statutory inquiry into a teacher's dismissal.[70] The law of contempt of court extends to employment tribunals and mental health tribunals[71] but not to a local valuation court which decides disputes about the valuation of property under the rating system.[72] Under art 234 (ex 177) of the EC Treaty,

---

[63] *R v Gloucestershire CC, ex p Barry* [1997] AC 584; cf *R v Cambridge Health Authority, ex p B* [1995] 2 All ER 129 and *R v Sefton Council, ex p Help the Aged* [1997] 4 All ER 532.

[64] E.g. *Bromley BC v Greater London Council* [1983] AC 768 and the *Alconbury* case (above); and ch 30. Also Lord Devlin (1978) 41 MLR 501 and Lord Irvine [1996] PL 59.

[65] *Liyanage v R* [1967] 1 AC 259; *Shell Co of Australia Ltd v Federal Commissioner of Taxation* [1931] AC 275. And ch 5.

[66] SI 1948 No 1, reg 2(1); ch 28.

[67] Parliamentary Commissioner Act 1967, s 5(1); ch 29 D.

[68] Ch 32 A.

[69] The 'judicial act of a court' includes 'an act done on the instructions, or on behalf, of a judge' (Human Rights Act 1998, s 9(5)).

[70] *Trapp v Mackie* [1979] 1 All ER 489.

[71] *Peach Grey & Co v Sommers* [1995] 2 All ER 513; *P v Liverpool Daily Post plc* [1991] 2 AC 370.

[72] *AG v BBC* [1981] AC 303; ch 18 B.

only a court or a tribunal has power to refer questions for a preliminary ruling to the European Court of Justice and this would exclude an administrative body without judicial functions.[73]

There were formerly two reasons in administrative law why the classification of functions was emphasised. First, it was considered that the prerogative writs of prohibition and certiorari, which had long been available to control inferior courts and tribunals, could be used by the court of King's Bench to control administrative bodies only if these bodies were required to 'act judicially'. Second, it was at one time considered that administrative bodies had to observe the rules of natural justice only when they were performing judicial functions.[74]

While many powers may be described without difficulty as legislative (for example, the power to make statutory regulations), administrative (for example, the power to decide where a department's offices should be located) or judicial (for example, the determination of a disputed tax assessment), many powers are so classifiable only with difficulty and others defy such classification. Laws are not always general in application; legislative form may be used to apply government policy in an individual case.[75] Government departments exercise both formal and informal powers of rule-making: is the issue of a circular which delegates executive powers to be regarded as a legislative act?[76] How should we classify the decision to build a motorway,[77] the revocation of a licence[78] or the dismissal of a chief constable?[79] Does a decision change its character from being judicial to administrative if it is vested in a government department instead of a court?[80]

Particularly in the 1930s there was much dispute in the literature of public law over the nature of administrative and judicial functions.[81] The term 'quasi-judicial' came into vogue to describe a function which could not easily be classified as either judicial or administrative. It was used variously to describe judicial functions vested in a body which was not a court and also powers vested in a department which gave rise to a public inquiry. In the latter case, the term quasi-judicial was sometimes applied to the whole process of public inquiry and the resulting decision, and sometimes merely to the inquiry itself.[82] Fortunately, the expansion in the scope of judicial review now makes it unnecessary to enter into the earlier debate, which often led to circular argument and involved the court in the process of 'labelling' particular functions.[83]

The heresy that a public authority's powers had to be described as 'judicial' before its decisions could be subject to judicial review was dispelled by the House of Lords in *Ridge v Baldwin*. Lord Reid stated that where officials had power to make decisions affecting the rights of individuals, the duty to act judicially was readily inferred from the nature of the decision; it was not necessary to look for any express judicial elements, such as the duty to give a formal hearing.[84] In the light of *Ridge v Baldwin*, administrative functions are today subject to the controlling jurisdiction of the courts

---

[73] See Ellis and Tridimas, *Public Law of the European Community*, pp 471–8; and ch 8 A.

[74] Ch 30 B.

[75] *Hoffmann-La Roche & Co v Trade Secretary* [1975] AC 295.

[76] *Blackpool Corpn v Locker* [1948] 1 KB 349.

[77] *Bushell v Environment Secretary* [1981] AC 75.

[78] *Nakkuda Ali v Jayaratne* [1951] AC 66.

[79] *Ridge v Baldwin* [1964] AC 40.

[80] *Local Government Board v Arlidge* [1915] AC 120.

[81] See D M Gordon (1933) 49 LQR 94, 419; Robson, *Justice and Administrative Law*, ch 1; and Jennings, *Law and Constitution*, app 1.

[82] E.g. *Errington v Minister of Health* [1935] 1 KB 249, 273 (Maugham LJ).

[83] For an extreme example, see *Nakkuda Ali v Jayaratne* [1951] AC 66. See also *Franklin v Minister of Town Planning* [1948] AC 87, criticised by H W R Wade (1949) 10 CLJ 216; ch 30 B.

[84] [1964] AC 40; ch 30 B.

without it being necessary for a court first to apply the appropriate label:[85] 'It is the characteristics of the proceeding that matter, not the precise compartment or compartments into which it falls.'[86] The language of judicial, quasi-judicial and administrative functions may still be heard in some judgments[87] but the classification of functions has lost its earlier significance. Even where the rules of natural justice do not fully apply, administrative bodies are under a duty to act fairly.[88] The Human Rights Act 1998 will not revive out-moded debates as to the scope of judicial review, but may make necessary a new process of classification in order to determine when it is that an administrative function must be exercised subject to the right to a fair hearing required by Art 6(1) ECHR.[89]

Public and private law

A different classification problem comes from the tendency that the courts developed after 1980 of resolving questions about jurisdiction, liability and procedure by asking whether the matter was one of private or public law. This formal distinction is reflected in the structure of many European legal systems. Thus in France it determines whether a dispute is decided by the administrative courts or by the civil courts. By contrast, in Britain the superior civil courts exercise an undivided jurisdiction over all justiciable disputes, whether they concern private citizens or public authorities.[90]

Lord Woolf has described public law as 'the system which enforces the proper performance by public bodies of the duties which they owe to the public'; and private law as 'the system which protects the private rights of private individuals or the private rights of public bodies'.[91] This is a deceptively simple distinction. Even apart from the burgeoning effects of privatisation, there is no clear-cut line between public bodies and private persons; and many acts of public bodies are subject to private law.[92] Moreover, in the common law tradition the system which protects the private rights of private individuals *is* to an important extent the system which enforces the performance by public bodies of the duties which they owe to the public, at least if the public is regarded as comprising all private individuals.[93] To take personal liberty as an example, one's liberty is protected both by the law of habeas corpus[94] and by the law of tort (the action for false imprisonment): does the former remedy come within public law (as it may lead to an order against an official if the applicant's detention is unlawful) and the latter private law (as it may lead to damages being paid to the detained person)? In the area of property, many disputes (over compulsory purchase, for example)

---

[85] See e.g. *R v Hillingdon BC, ex p Royco Homes Ltd* [1974] QB 720; *R v Commission for Racial Equality, ex p Cottrell and Rothon* [1980] 3 All ER 265, 271.

[86] *Re Pergamon Press Ltd* [1971] Ch 388, 402 (Sachs LJ).

[87] E.g. *R v Home Secretary, ex p Tarrant* [1985] QB 251, 268. In *R v Army Board of Defence Council, ex p Anderson* [1992] QB 169, the Board's power to decide on a soldier's complaint of racial discrimination was held to be judicial; cf *R v Department of Health, ex p Gandhi* [1991] 4 All ER 547.

[88] *Re HK (an infant)* [1967] 2 QB 617; ch 30 B.

[89] Art 6(1) ECHR: 'In the determination of his civil rights and obligations . . . everyone is entitled to a fair and public hearing . . . by an independent and impartial tribunal . . .' For the application of Art 6(1) to town planning decisions, see *R (Alconbury Developments Ltd) v Environment Secretary* [2001] 2 All ER 929.

[90] Cf J D B Mitchell [1965] PL 95, advocating the creation of a new public law jurisdiction.

[91] [1986] PL 220, 221. Also Woolf [1995] PL 57, 60–5.

[92] See e.g. *R v Lord Chancellor, ex p Hibbit & Saunders* [1993] COD 326. Wade's argument in (1985) 101 LQR 180, 195–7, that *CCSU v Minister for the Civil Service* [1985] AC 374 concerned private law issues has not received support.

[93] E.g. *Entick v Carrington* (1765) 19 St Tr 1030, ch 6; and *Cooper v Wandsworth Board of Works* (1863) 14 CB (NS) 180. And see Allison, *A Continental Distinction in the Common Law*.

[94] See chs 21 E and 31.

arise exactly at the interface between a person's private rights and the powers and duties of the public authority.

In this difficult matter, it is worthwhile considering (1) the different levels of separation between public and private law that may arise, and applying this analysis to (2) the broad tasks of the courts in administrative law.[95] (*a*) The most extreme separation occurs where the two bodies of law are administered by separate courts and judges, according to separate rules of substance and procedure. (*b*) Separation is less marked when private law and public law are applied in different branches of a co-ordinated court system, by judges sharing the same training, but applying distinct rules of substance and procedure. (*c*) An even weaker form of separation exists when public law and private law are administered in the same courts, but *some* of the substantive and procedural rules depend on whether a dispute is between private persons or whether it raises questions of public power. (*d*) Finally, there may be no separation at all, regardless of who the parties to a dispute are and what it concerns.

There are two broad tasks that the courts perform within administrative law. The first (which we may call 'judicial review') arises when an individual seeks to review the legality of a decision taken by a public authority or a specialised tribunal and the court must in exercise of this supervisory jurisdiction decide whether to uphold or set aside the decision. This task has no exact equivalent in private law, although in areas of law such as trusts, company and trade union law, disputes may arise as to the validity of decisions taken by trustees, company directors and trade union committees and comparable supervisory principles may be applied in the process of review.[96] The second broad task ('governmental liability') arises when individuals seek compensation in the form of damages for loss caused by a public authority's unlawful acts (for example, a tort or a breach of contract). This task plainly has much in common with the general law of tort, contract and restitution.

To apply to these two tasks the analysis of levels of separation made earlier, France provides a strong example of (*a*), entrusting both 'judicial review' and most 'governmental liability' questions to separate administrative courts. Germany and Italy are examples of category (*b*): 'judicial review' is entrusted to the administrative courts, but all 'liability' questions are decided by the civil courts. The United Kingdom is an example of (*c*): governmental liability cases are decided by the ordinary civil courts and judicial review cases in the High Court (by judges designated for the purpose and sitting in what is now termed the Administrative Court). The process of judicial review is largely, but not wholly, distinct from ordinary civil procedure; and some governmental liability questions are decided by rules that do not apply to ordinary actions in tort or contract.[97] However, the liability of a public body, such as a social services authority, to compensate an individual for injury that she may have suffered while in the care of the authority, depends essentially not on public law rules that determine the authority's powers, but on the familiar test of whether reasonable care was exercised in exercise of the authority's discretion.[98]

Accordingly, the use of the public law/private law distinction emphasised by Lord Diplock in *O'Reilly* v *Mackman*[99] may be limited to indicating when it is that the

---

[95] This analysis draws on Craig, *Administrative Law* (1983), pp 11–21, a passage which does not appear in later editions.

[96] See Oliver, *Common Values and the Public–Private Divide*; and P Craig in Taggart (ed.), *The Province of Administrative Law*, ch 10.

[97] E.g. *Town Investments Ltd* v *Department of Environment* [1978] AC 359 (interpretation of lease of government offices governed by public law); C Harlow (1977) 40 MLR 728.

[98] *X (Minors)* v *Bedfordshire CC* [1995] 2 AC 633; *Barrett* v *Enfield Council* [2001] 2 AC 550; and ch 32 A.

[99] [1983] 2 AC 237; ch 31.

procedure of making an application for judicial review *must* be used and when it would be an abuse of process to sue by ordinary writ. That use of the distinction gave rise to the so-called exclusivity rule that for a time led to much complex and costly litigation caused by the procedural choices made by litigants. Eventually, the courts (without depreciating the value of judicial review procedure in cases that fell squarely within the scope of judicial review) adopted a more flexible approach to matters that were of an essentially procedural kind.[100]

The most difficult questions that arose in these cases concerned the choice of procedure when the same dispute raised questions of private law rights and public law duties. In *Davy v Spelthorne Borough Council*, the House of Lords held that an action in damages for negligence against a local council was 'an ordinary action for tort' which did not raise 'any issue of public law as a live issue'.[101] In a separate judgment, Lord Wilberforce urged caution in use of the public/private law distinction:

> Before the expression 'public law' can be used to deny a subject a right of action in the court of his choice it must be related to a positive prescription of law, by statute or by statutory rules. We have not yet reached the point at which mere characterisation of a claim as a claim in public law is sufficient to exclude it from consideration by the ordinary courts.[102]

In *Roy v Kensington Family Practitioner Committee*[103] the House of Lords allowed an NHS doctor to sue by ordinary action for statutory payments to which he claimed to be entitled, even though as a defence the NHS committee relied on a decision that it had taken under statutory powers reducing the amount of the payments. Consistently with this approach, the House of Lords has reaffirmed the right of someone accused of a byelaw offence to rely on the defence that the byelaw in question was invalid.[104]

The law in Scotland has escaped the difficulties discusssed in this section almost entirely, since the supervisory jurisdiction of the Court of Session does not depend on the private law/public law distinction.[105] However, the Human Rights Act 1998 may bring into focus in both English and Scots law other aspects of the private/public distinction. The duty under the Act to act compatibly with Convention rights binds every 'public authority'; a public authority includes both a body that is one for all of its functions (such as a government department) and one whose functions include some functions of a public nature and others of a private nature. A body with mixed public and private functions is regarded as a public authority only in relation to its functions that are of a public nature.[106] The importance of identifying public authorities under the 1998 Act is to an extent offset by the fact that courts and tribunals are public authorities for the purposes of the Act and will thus have a duty to act consistently with Convention rights in adjudicating on disputes that arise between private parties.[107] For this reason alone it would be wrong to suppose that areas of private law such as contract, tort, property and employment are unaffected by the Act.

---

[100] See e.g. *Rye Pension Fund Trustees v Sheffield Council* [1997] 4 All ER 747; *Clark v University of Lincolnshire* [2000] 3 All ER 752; and ch 31.

[101] [1984] AC 262; and see P Cane [1984] PL 16.

[102] [1984] AC at 276. And see *Mercury Communications Ltd v Director General of Telecommunications* [1996] 1 All ER 575, 581 (Lord Slynn).

[103] [1992] 1 AC 624; and see P Cane [1992] PL 193.

[104] *Boddington v British Transport Police* [1999] 2 AC 143.

[105] *West v Secretary of State for Scotland* 1992 SLT 636; and see W J Wolffe [1992] PL 625.

[106] Human Rights Act 1998, s 6(1), (2)(b) and (5). See ch 19 C; Clayton and Tomlinson, *The Law of Human Rights*, pp 186–204; and D Oliver [2000] PL 476.

[107] See e.g. *Douglas v Hello! Ltd* [2001] QB 967; and ch 19 C. Also M Hunt [1998] PL 423 and (the same) in Jowell and Cooper (eds), *Understanding Human Rights Principles*, p 161.

Local government – a note

The emphasis in this book is on the constitutional structures that underlie the democratic government of the United Kingdom. In the context of administrative law, we are concerned with how public bodies are providing services, exercising regulatory powers and so on. At a national level, the government undertakes such tasks as oversight of the economy, control of the physical environment, the provision or supervision of services such as the National Health Service and education, management of the state's revenues, the promotion of 'law and order' and the maintenance of the judicial system. As the example of the police shows, it is neither necessary nor desirable that all public services should be provided directly from Whitehall. Certainly, given the privatisation of the public utilities and the policy of involving private enterprise in many sectors of government, not all public services are provided directly by public authorities.

In the record of public administration in the United Kingdom, local authorities have played an important role, second in importance only to that of central government, and they have featured prominently in the development of administrative law. Since the 19th century, the operation of elected local councils has been affected by such fundamental doctrines of public law as the ultra vires rule, whereby a council, with power to levy local taxes and impose charges for services, and in receipt of grants from central government, may properly incur expenditure only for purposes authorised by statute.[108] However, since 1979, the structure and organisation of local government have been subjected to a bewildering quantity of legislative changes (including reorganisation of local government areas, new forms of local taxation and new methods of organisation and management within councils) which it is not possible to outline here.[109] The constitutional importance of elected councils continues to be that they promote local democracy, as well as providing or enabling social services (such as education) and administering regulatory systems (such as the control of land development under planning legislation, public health and licensing) at a local level.

It must be hoped that the essential qualities of local government will survive despite the pressures on them from central government and from local opinion in a changing society. A working relationship has to be rebuilt between central and local government, based in part on the unfashionable notion of partnership.[110]

In view of the conflicting demands being made on local authorities and on their limited resources, they are often involved in the contentious side of administrative law, whether seeking judicial review against central government[111] or other local authorities,[112] defending applications for judicial review brought by individuals,[113] regulatory agencies[114] or government departments[115] or resisting actions for damages in tort resulting from alleged failures of duty.[116] Local councils have never had the privileges and immunities that government departments enjoy because of their identification with

---

[108] Ch 30 A.

[109] For the law, see Bailey (ed.), *Cross on Local Government Law* and Himsworth, *Local Government in Scotland*. See also Loughlin, *Local Government in the Modern State*; Byrne, *Local Government in Britain*; and Stewart and Stoker (eds), *Local Government in the 1990s*.

[110] Works on central–local relations include M Loughlin, in Jowell and Oliver (eds), *The Changing Constitution*, ch 6; and (the same) *Legality and Locality: the Role of Law in Central–Local Government Relations*.

[111] E.g. *R v Environment Secretary, ex p Hammersmith BC* [1991] 1 AC 521.

[112] E.g. *Bromley Council v GLC* [1983] 1 AC 768.

[113] E.g. *Wheeler v Leicester Council* [1985] AC 1054; *R v Gloucestershire CC, ex p Barry* [1997] AC 584.

[114] E.g. *R v Birmingham Council, ex p EOC* [1989] AC 1155.

[115] E.g. *Lord Advocate v Dumbarton DC* [1990] 2 AC 580.

[116] *X (Minors) v Bedfordshire CC* [1995] 2 AC 633; *Barrett v Enfield Council* [2001] 2 AC 550.

the Crown.[117] Local government officers are not civil servants and local methods of management are usually very different from those in government departments.[118] Councillors operate in a political context and the legality of party groups has been recognised,[119] but this does not exclude the operation of mechanisms for securing public accountability and the maintenance of proper standards of conduct. Finally, local councils are 'public authorities' for the purposes of the Human Rights Act 1998. Every local authority is bound to exercise its functions in a way that is compatible with the Convention rights protected by the Act, except where, as a result of provisions of primary legislation, it is unable to act differently or has acted to give effect to primary legislation that could not be read in a manner compatible with the Convention rights.[120]

---

[117] E.g. *Mersey Docks Trustees* v *Gibbs* (1866) LR 1 HL 93; ch 32 A.
[118] The principle in *Carltona Ltd* v *Commissioners of Works* [1943] 2 All ER 560 (p 127 above) does not apply in local government.
[119] *R* v *Waltham Forest BC, ex p Baxter* [1988] QB 419; and see I Leigh [1988] PL 304.
[120] Human Rights Act 1998, s 6(1), (2)(a).

Chapter 28

DELEGATED LEGISLATION

We saw in chapter 27 that during the 20th century it came to be realised that the operation of government is carried on to a large extent not directly through laws made by Parliament, but by means of rules made by members of the Executive under powers delegated to them by Parliament. This vast body of rules is known as delegated legislation, but it may also be described as secondary (or subordinate) legislation, by comparison with the primary legislation found in Acts of Parliament. In a few instances (especially in the conduct of foreign policy) government still relies not on statutory powers, but on the royal prerogative, that is, the common law powers that are exclusive to the Crown. But reliance on prerogative powers has long been the exception not the rule, because of the restrictive view that the common law since the 17th century has taken to claims of prerogative power. In particular, the *Case of Proclamations*[1] held that the Crown had no residual power to legislate so as to impose obligations or restrictions on the people. Yet it was held over 300 years later that this fundamental principle did not prevent the Crown having power under the prerogative to confer financial benefits on the victims of criminal violence.[2]

The term statute law covers both Acts of Parliament and delegated legislation. The main distinction between the two levels of statute law is that delegated legislation, unlike an Act of Parliament, is not the work of a supreme Parliament and is subject to judicial review. Nevertheless, the combined effect of the two levels is to set up public bodies to perform the tasks of government, and to equip them with the detailed powers needed for operating public services. It is, in fact, very rare for an Act to contain all the provisions which are essential if a complex service is to be provided. An Act frequently does no more than outline the main features of the scheme, leaving the details to be filled in by subordinate legislation. In complex areas of government such as education, planning and immigration, a lawyer must have access to publications which bring together primary and subordinate legislation, along with codes of practice, ministerial circulars and often a digest of the case-law. The bulk of statutory instruments is formidable. In 1998, there were enacted 49 Public General Acts which were contained in 3,117 pages. In the same year the total of statutory instruments issued was over 3,300; although many of these were local in effect, the nine published volumes of general instruments amounted to some 7,400 pages.

Historical development

The formal process by which a Bill becomes an Act has never been the sole method of legislation. In the earliest years of Parliament, it was difficult to distinguish between enactment by King in Parliament and legislation by the King in Council. Even when legislation by Parliament had become a distinct process, broad power to legislate by

---

[1] (1611) 12 Co Rep 74, p 50 above; and ch 12 D.
[2] *R v Criminal Injuries Compensation Board, ex p Lain* [1967] 2 QB 864.

proclamation remained with the Crown. In 1539, by Henry VIII's Statute of Proclamations, royal power to issue proclamations 'for the good order and governance' of the country was recognised to exist and such proclamations were to be enforced as if made by Act of Parliament. One reason given for the Act was that sudden occasions might arise when speedy remedies were needed which could not wait for the meeting of Parliament; the Act contained saving words to protect the common law, life and property. The repeal of the statute in 1547 made little difference to the Tudor use of proclamations and Henry VIII's name remains associated with the controversial practice of delegating power to the executive to amend Acts of Parliament.

The practice of Parliament delegating power to make laws is of long standing. An instance of delegation to the Commissioners of Sewers in respect of rivers and land drainage dates back to 1531. After 1689, the annual Mutiny Acts delegated power to the Crown to make regulations for the better government of the army, but it was not until the 19th century that delegation of wide legislative power became common. The first modern Factories Act in 1833 conferred power on the inspectors appointed under the Act to make orders and regulations, breaches of which were punishable under the criminal law.[3] A very wide power that remained law for over a century was the power, first vested in the Poor Law Commissioners, 'to make and issue all such rules, orders and regulations for the management of the poor . . . and for carrying this Act into execution . . . as they shall think proper.'[4]

The late 19th century saw a great increase in the delegation of legislative power to government departments and other bodies, granted piecemeal as need arose. The Rules Publication Act 1893 sought to introduce order into the proliferation of powers in Whitehall, by creating a generic term, 'statutory rules and orders', and requiring that such measures be published. During both world wars, Parliament granted power in very wide terms to the government to make regulations for the conduct of the war.[5]

After 1918, many lawyers and politicians became concerned at the wide legislative powers of government departments. An inquiry by the Committee on Ministers' Powers[6] concluded that unless Parliament were willing to delegate law-making powers, it would be unable to pass the kind or quantity of legislation which modern public opinion required. The committee drew attention to certain dangers in delegated legislation and proposed greater safeguards against abuse. In 1946, the Statutory Instruments Act replaced the Rules Publication Act 1893 and promoted a greater uniformity of procedure. Since 1944, a scrutinising committee has been regularly appointed by Parliament, first by the Commons and today by the Commons and Lords jointly. The practice of delegated legislation has been reviewed by many parliamentary committees,[7] but the flood of subordinate legislation shows no sign of abating. Between 1981 and 1996 the number of instruments subject to parliamentary procedure increased by around 50 per cent, that is, from under 1,000 a year to around 1,500 a year; of these the number subject to the negative procedure in Parliament almost doubled, from some 700 in the early 1980s to around 1,300 in the period 1994–99.[8] During this period, the contents of

---

[3] Labour of Children etc. in Factories Act 1833. See now Health and Safety at Work etc. Act 1974, ss 15 and 80.

[4] Poor Law Amendment Act 1834, s 15.

[5] Ch 26 D. Defence of the Realm Act 1914; Emergency Powers (Defence) Act 1939. See Carr, *Concerning English Administrative Law*; Allen, *Law and Orders* and (written from a different standpoint) Ewing and Gearty, *The Struggle for Civil Liberties*.

[6] Ch 27.

[7] HC 310 (1952–53); HL 184, HC 475 (1971–72) and HL 204, HC 468 (1972–73); HC 588–1 (1977–78), ch 3; HC 152 (1995–96); and HC 48 (1999–2000).

[8] HC 152 (1995–96), para 10 and HC 48 (1999–2000), para 25. For the negative procedure, see p 656 below.

instruments may have changed. As one committee said in 1986, 'Instead of simply implementing the "nuts and bolts" of Government policy, statutory instruments have increasingly been used to change policy, sometimes in ways that were not envisaged when the enabling primary legislation was passed.'[9]

In 1996, another committee concluded that 'there is . . . too great a readiness in Parliament to delegate wide legislative powers to Ministers, and no lack of enthusiasm on their part to take such powers'.[10] Such committees have often criticised the way in which Parliament gives 'second-rate' consideration to secondary legislation.[11]

Justification of delegated legislation

Delegated legislation is an inevitable feature of modern government for several reasons.

Pressure on parliamentary time

If Parliament attempted to enact all legislation itself, the legislative machine would break down, unless there were a radical alteration in the procedure for considering Bills. The granting of legislative power to a department which is administering a public service may obviate the need for amending Bills. Although many statutory instruments are laid before Parliament, only a minority of them gives rise to matters which need the consideration of either House and Parliament spends a very small proportion of its time on business connected with them.[12]

Technicality of subject matter

Legislation on technical topics necessitates prior consultation with experts and interests concerned. The giving of legislative power to ministers facilitates such consultation. Draft Bills are often regarded as confidential documents and their text is not disclosed until they have been presented to Parliament and read a first time. No such secretive custom need impede the preparation of delegated legislation. There is also a good reason for keeping out of the statute book highly technical provisions which do not involve questions of principle and which only experts in the field concerned can readily understand.[13]

The need for flexibility

When a new public service is being established, it is not possible to foresee every administrative difficulty that may arise or to have frequent recourse to Parliament for amending Acts to make adjustments that may be called for after the scheme has begun to operate. Delegated legislation fills those needs. When the community charge, or poll tax, came into operation under the Local Government Finance Act 1988, as amended in 1989, no fewer than 47 sets of regulations were made in the years 1989–91. But even such extensive exercise of delegated powers could not prevent the tax from being a failure. A power commonly delegated to ministers is the power to make a commencement order,

---

[9] HC 31–xxxvii (1985–86), p 2.
[10] HC 152 (1995–96), para 14, endorsed in HC 48 (1999–2000), para 26.
[11] P Tudor (2000) 21 Statute Law Review 149, 150.
[12] In 1999–2000 and 2000–01, the House of Commons spent respectively 2.5% and 3.9% of its time considering statutory instruments, compared with 7% in 1994–95 and 10% in 1984–85 (*Sessional Returns* for these years). Not included is the time spent by Commons committees on statutory instruments.
[13] J A G Griffith (1951) 14 MLR 279, 425.

bringing into operation all or part of a statute. Often there are practical reasons why a new Act should not come into effect as soon as the royal assent is given. There is no duty on the minister to exercise a commencement power, but the minister must not act so as to defeat Parliament's expectation that the Act will come into operation.[14]

State of emergency

In times of emergency a government may need to take action quickly and in excess of its normal powers. Many written constitutions include provision in emergency for the suspension of formal guarantees of individual liberty. Although the Crown possesses an ill-defined residue of prerogative power capable of use in time of national danger, the Emergency Powers Act 1920 makes permanent provision enabling the executive to legislate subject to parliamentary safeguards in the event of certain emergencies.[15] On the return of Northern Ireland to direct rule by the British government in 1972, wide power to legislate for Northern Ireland was conferred on the Queen in Council.[16] This enabled laws to be made for Northern Ireland by Order in Council, a procedure which does not allow full scope for democratic discussion.[17]

Exceptional types of delegated legislation

While much delegated legislation is essential, governments are often tempted to obtain from Parliament greater powers than they should be given. Criticism centres on particular types of delegated legislation.

Matters of principle

There is a clear threat to parliamentary government if power is delegated to legislate on matters of general policy or if so wide a discretion is conferred that it is impossible to be sure what limit the legislature intended to impose. There is no formal limit to the delegation of legislative powers and Acts of Parliament frequently confer legislative powers in wide terms. One reason for this is that if powers are phrased more narrowly, this will make it more likely that the department will need to seek increased powers from Parliament in future. A proposal that Parliament should adopt a policy of passing framework legislation, with all details left to delegated legislation, was rightly rejected by the House of Commons Committee on Procedure in 1978, on the ground that this would further weaken parliamentary control.[18] Nonetheless, governments sometimes propose Bills that have been described as 'skeleton Bills', Bills that are 'little more than a licence to legislate'.[19] Such Bills can operate only when extensive regulations are made and MPs may require to see the regulations that are to be made before approving a Bill in this form. But there are few absolutes in this area and legislative practice is often a compromise between different attitudes to delegation.

---

[14] *R v Home Secretary, ex p Fire Brigades Union* [1995] 2 AC 513.
[15] Ch 26 D.
[16] Northern Ireland (Temporary Provisions) Act 1972, s 1(3) and Sch, para 4; Northern Ireland Act 1975, Sch 1, para 1.
[17] See Hadfield, *The Constitution of Northern Ireland*, ch 5; and HLE, vol 8(2), p 82.
[18] HC 588-I (1977–78), ch 2.
[19] See Tudor, p 152: in 1992–99 four Bills were described by the House of Lords Delegated Powers Committee as skeletal, two as near skeletal. The lack of flesh may apply only to one or two limbs of a Bill: HL 112 (1998–99), para 28.

Delegation of taxing power

We have seen how vital to the development of parliamentary government was the insistence that Parliament alone could authorise taxation.[20] This insistence survives in an attenuated form, but modern pressures, particularly associated with the economy, have made it necessary for Parliament to delegate certain powers in relation to taxation to the government. In particular, the working of a system of customs duties combined with the development of the European Union has made necessary delegation of the power to give exemptions and reliefs from such duties.[21] Since 1961, the government has also had power to vary certain classes of indirect taxation by order of the Treasury.[22] These powers are subject to parliamentary control in that orders imposing import duties or varying indirect taxation cease to have effect unless they are confirmed by a resolution of the House of Commons within a limited time.

Sub-delegation

When a statute delegates legislative power to a minister, exercisable by statutory instrument, it may be assumed that Parliament intends the statutory instrument itself to contain the rules. Is it a proper use of such powers for the instrument to subdelegate legislative power, by authorising rules to be made by another body or by another procedure? The legal maxim, *delegatus non potest delegare*, means that a delegate may not sub-delegate his or her power, but the parent Act may always override this by authorising sub-delegation, as did the Emergency Powers (Defence) Act 1939. Without express authority in the parent Act, it is doubtful whether sub-delegation of legislative powers is valid. Where sub-delegation occurs, control by Parliament becomes more difficult. In 1978, the Joint Committee on Statutory Instruments criticised the recurring tendency of departments to seek to bypass Parliament by omitting necessary detail from statutory instruments and vesting a wide discretion in ministers to vary the rules without making further statutory instruments.[23] Under the European Communities Act 1972, sub-delegation is prohibited except for rules of procedure for courts or tribunals.[24]

Retrospective operation

It follows from the supremacy of Parliament that Acts may have retrospective operation.[25] If on occasions retrospective legislation is considered necessary, this should be done by Parliament itself and not through delegated legislation.[26] By reason of Article 7, ECHR, applied by the Human Rights Act 1998, it is not possible that delegated legislation should retrospectively create new offences or impose additional penalties.

Exclusion of the jurisdiction of the courts

The power of the courts in reviewing delegated legislation is confined to declaring it ultra vires, whether on grounds of substance or procedure.[27] While control over the

---

[20] Ch 4 A.
[21] Customs and Excise Duties (General Reliefs) Act 1979.
[22] Excise Duties (Surcharges or Rebates) Act 1979.
[23] HL 51, HC 579 (1977–78), p 10; and see *Customs and Excise Commissioners* v *J H Corbitt (Numismatists) Ltd* [1981] AC 22.
[24] European Communities Act 1972, s 2(2) and Sch 2.
[25] Ch 4 B.
[26] The unsatisfactory decision in *R* v *Social Security Secretary, ex p Britnell* [1991] 2 All ER 726 upheld regulations that had been made as 'transitional provisions' and retrospectively modified an earlier Act.
[27] See p 661 below.

merits of delegated legislation is a matter for ministers and for Parliament, the possibility of control by the courts should not be excluded. It should never be for a minister to determine the limits of his or her own powers.[28]

Authority to modify an Act of Parliament

However undesirable this might appear in principle, Parliament frequently delegates to ministers power to amend Acts of Parliament.[29] The term 'Henry VIII clause' is given to such provisions and numerous examples may be found in the Scotland Act 1998 and the Government of Wales Act 1998.[30] When the power in a new Act is restricted to amending earlier Acts that are directly affected by the new reforms, the power is less objectionable than when it extends to amending the very Act that contains the power.[31] Yet some Acts dealing with schemes of social and industrial control empower a minister to broaden or narrow the scope of the schemes in the light of experience.[32]

Three instances of delegated power to modify Acts of Parliament may be given. The European Communities Act 1972, by s 2(2), authorises the making of Orders in Council and ministerial regulations to implement Community obligations of the United Kingdom, to enable rights under the European treaties to be exercised and 'for the purpose of dealing with matters arising out of or related to any such obligations or rights'. Schedule 2 to the Act excludes certain matters from the general power, including the imposition of taxes, retroactive legislation and the sub-delegation of legislative power (other than power to make rules of procedure for any court or tribunal). Subject to these limitations, measures made under s 2(2) may make 'any such provision (of any such extent) as might be made by Act of Parliament' (s 2(4)). The intention in using such wide language must have been to exclude the possibility of judicial review on grounds of vires in the case of instruments made under s 2(2).[33]

By the Regulatory Reform Act 2001, replacing Part I of the Deregulation and Contracting Out Act 1994, ministers may amend or repeal Acts passed at least two years previously which impose what are considered to be unjustifiable burdens on persons (such as companies, small businesses or voluntary organisations) in carrying on any activity, in so doing either to revoke the burden entirely or to replace it with a burden that is proportionate to the benefit of compliance. These powers, providing an alternative to legislation by Bill, have made necessary the creation of new procedures within Parliament for preventing their misuse.[34]

The third example of power to amend primary legislation is found in the Human Rights Act 1998, s 10.[35] This authorises ministers or the Queen in Council to make remedial orders when a superior court has declared primary legislation incompatible with a Convention right or the European Court of Human Rights has made a similar finding. The purpose of a remedial order is to amend the offending legislation so as to

---

[28] Yet under the Counter-Inflation Act 1973, Sch 3, para 1, an order made under part II of the Act could 'define any expressions used in the provisions under which it is made'. And see *Jackson* v *Hall* [1980] AC 854.

[29] MPR, pp 36–8; Carr, *Concerning English Administrative Law*, pp 41–7.

[30] See Scotland Act 1998, ss 30(2), 79, 89, 104–8, 113(5), 114, 124 and Sch 7; Government of Wales Act 1998, ss 22, 27(9), 28(7), 30(7), 117(2), 39(3), 143(4), 144(5), 146(3) and 151. These powers were considered necessary for implementing devolution; see HL 101, 124 and 146 (1997–98).

[31] See e.g. Freedom of Information Act 2000, s 75 (Secretary of State may by order repeal or amend any statutory provision which appears to him to be capable of preventing the disclosure of information).

[32] Health and Safety at Work etc. Act 1974, ss 15 and 80; Sex Discrimination Act 1975, s 80, esp sub-s (3).

[33] See HL Deb, 17 February 1976, cols 399–417, and HL 51, HC 169 (1977–78), pp 17–18. Cf *R* v *HM Treasury, ex p Smedley* [1985] QB 657. And see ch 8 E.

[34] See [1995] PL 21 (M Freedland) and 34 (C M G Himsworth); and pp 659–60 below.

[35] See ch 19 C.

remove the incompatibility and, like orders under the Regulatory Reform Act, the making of the order is subject to an unusually full degree of parliamentary supervision.[36]

Nomenclature

Despite the Statutory Instruments Act 1946, terminology is often confusing. The term 'statutory instrument' is a comprehensive expression to describe all forms of subordinate legislation subject to the 1946 Act.[37] Within the scope of the Act are many powers conferred on ministers by Acts passed before the 1946 Act came into operation. As regards Acts passed thereafter, there are two categories of statutory instrument: (*a*) legislative powers conferred on the Queen in Council and stated in the parent Act to be exercisable by Order in Council; (*b*) legislative powers conferred on a minister of the Crown and stated to be exercisable by statutory instrument. The first of these, the statutory Order in Council, must be distinguished from prerogative Orders in Council, which are not statutory instruments at all, though for convenience some are published in the annual volumes of statutory instruments. One reason why some legislative powers are vested in the Queen in Council and others are vested in a named minister is that some powers may need to be exercised by any department of the government whereas others concern only one department; also the greater formality of an Order in Council is thought appropriate to some classes of legislation. The expression 'statutory instrument' does not include local byelaws or such acts as the confirmation of compulsory purchase orders. Moreover, there are other kinds of rule made under statutory authority which are not statutory instruments, for example immigration rules under the Immigration Act 1971 and regulations made by the Electoral Commission under the Political Parties, Elections and Referendums Act 2000.

Although statutory instrument is the generic term, various names apply to different kinds of statutory instrument: rules, orders, regulations, warrants, schemes and even licences and directions. Several of these terms may be used in a single Act to distinguish different procedures applied to different powers. In practice, the term 'regulation' is used mainly for matters of wide general importance. Where the legislation deals with procedure, rules are generally enacted, for example, the Civil Procedure Rules. With the term 'order' there is less uniformity; thus an Order in Council may bring into effect all or part of an Act of Parliament and in town planning law a general development order contains detailed rules for the control of development.

To add to the scope for confusion, statutes may authorise the making of codes of practice, guidance and other forms of rules and provide sanctions of various kinds if they are not followed.[38] These measures must be distinguished from the informal administrative rules (guidelines, circulars, etc.), which are made without express statutory authority and are considered later in this chapter.

A distinction is drawn by the Human Rights Act 1998 between what the Act defines as 'primary legislation' and 'subordinate legislation'.[39] The reason for the distinction is to protect Acts of Parliament from being set aside or invalidated by the courts for inconsistency with Convention rights. However, the demarcation line drawn is awkward in that the Act includes in 'primary legislation' various measures that are not

---

[36] See HC 472 and 473 (2001–02) on the making of the first remedial order under the Human Rights Act, s 10.

[37] The official abbreviation for statutory instruments is SI followed by the year and number, e.g. SI 1998 No 252 (or SI 1998/252).

[38] E.g. School Standards and Framework Act 1998, s 84 (code of practice on school admissions).

[39] Human Rights Act 1998, ss 3(2), 4, 21 (1). And see ch 19 C.

Acts of Parliament. These include measures of the Church Assembly, instruments made under primary legislation that amend Acts of Parliament and also Orders in Council made under the Crown's prerogative.[40] It is difficult to see why, if a minister uses a Henry VIII clause to amend a statute, and thereby creates inconsistency with a Convention right, the minister's action should be treated as if it were an Act of Parliament.

If delegated legislation is a necessary phenomenon in the modern state, then it is essential (1) that the process by which it is made should include the consultation of interests; (2) that Parliament should oversee and supervise the exercise of delegated powers; (3) that the delegated legislation itself should be published; and (4) that it is subject to challenge in the courts should reasons for this arise. These matters will now be examined.

Consultation of interests

Unlike the process of legislation by Bill, which involves public debate of the Bill in principle and in detail as it passes through both Houses, most delegated legislation comes into force as soon as it is made public, either at once or after a short interval stated in the document itself. There is no general requirement of prior publicity, and an ordinary member of the public has little chance of getting to know about proposed statutory instruments. But the department proposing to make a new statutory instrument frequently takes steps to consult interests affected by the proposal. Some Acts make this obligatory. Many kinds of social security regulations must be submitted in draft to the Social Security Advisory Committee, whose disagreements, if any, with the Secretary of State must be reported to Parliament along with the regulations.[41] So too the Council on Tribunals must be consulted before rules of procedure for tribunals and inquiries are made.[42] Several Acts do not specify the bodies to be consulted, leaving it to the minister to consult with such associations and bodies as appear to him or her to be affected.[43] Where there is a duty to consult, either because of a statutory duty or a consistent practice of consultation,[44] the courts have laid down the criteria for proper consultation: the consultation must be undertaken when the proposal is at a formative stage; sufficient reasons must be given for the proposal to enable an informed response to be given; adequate time must be allowed for the response to the proposals; and the product of consultation must be conscientiously taken into account when the ultimate decision is made.[45] Where there is a duty to consult, fairness may require disclosure to an interested person of the scientific advice on which the minister is proposing to rely.[46] Even where there is no duty to consult before delegated legislation is made, departments can obtain much benefit from consulting organisations and interests likely to be affected, since genuine consultation may promote consensus and may bring in specialised knowledge from outside government.

---

[40] See P Billings and B Pontin [2001] PL 21.
[41] Social Security Administration Act 1992, ss 170, 172–4.
[42] Tribunals and Inquiries Act 1992, ss 8, 9. For the Cabinet Office's *Code of Practice in written consultation*, see [2002] Judicial Review 35.
[43] For the effect of a failure to consult, see *Agricultural Training Board v Aylesbury Mushrooms Ltd* [1972] 1 All ER 280; also *R v Social Services Secretary, ex p Association of Municipal Authorities* [1986] 1 All ER 164.
[44] See *Council of Civil Service Unions v Minister for the Civil Service* [1985] AC 374.
[45] *R v North Devon Health Authority, ex p Coughlan* [2001] QB 213, at [108].
[46] *R v Health Secretary, ex p US Tobacco International Inc* [1992] QB 353.

Control by Parliament

To what extent does Parliament control or supervise the making of delegated legislation? This difficult question raises various matters: (a) the nature of the powers conferred; (b) procedures for the making of statutory instruments; (c) the role of the House of Lords; (d) technical scrutiny of statutory instruments; and (e) considering the merits of statutory instruments.

The conferment of powers

Since all delegated legislative powers stem from statute, there is always, at least in theory, an opportunity at the committee stage of a Bill to examine clauses that seek to delegate legislative powers. As long ago as 1931, the Ministers' Powers Committee recommended that Bills conferring such powers should be referred to a standing committee in each House to report whether there were any objections of principle to them.[47] It was only in 1992 that the House of Lords appointed a committee (on the lines of a committee of the Australian Senate) to consider clauses in Bills proposing to delegate legislative powers and to receive for each Bill a government memorandum justifying the proposals. By reporting promptly on such proposals, the committee (renamed in 2001 the Committee on Delegated Powers and Regulatory Reform) aims to discourage the granting of excessive powers and ensure that appropriate safeguards are included in parent legislation. Its reports receive no media attention, but it has succeeded in persuading government to accept its views on such questions as the choice of procedure for parliamentary scrutiny in relation to a specific Bill.[48]

Procedures for the making of statutory instruments

In delegating legislative powers to government, Parliament typically provides for some parliamentary control or oversight to be built into the use of specific powers. However, two basic reasons for delegating legislative power are pressure on Parliament's time and the technical nature of the subjects; the very object of delegation would be frustrated if Parliament had to approve each instrument in detail. The procedure through which a statutory instrument must pass depends on the terms of the parent Act. The principal procedures are the following:

(*a*) laying of draft instrument before Parliament, and requiring affirmative resolution before instrument can be 'made';
(*b*) laying of instrument after it has been made, to come into effect only when approved by affirmative resolution;
(*c*) laying of instrument that takes immediate effect, but requires approval by affirmative resolution within a stated period as a condition of continuance;
(*d*) laying of instrument that takes immediate effect, subject to annulment by resolution of either House;
(*e*) laying in draft, subject to resolution that no further proceedings be taken – in effect a direction to the minister not to 'make' the instrument;
(*f*) laying before Parliament, with no further provision for control.

Finally, some statutory instruments are not required to be laid before Parliament at all.

---

[47] MPR, pp 67–8. Cf HC 310 (1952–53).
[48] See C M G Himsworth [1995] PL 34, HL 112 (1998–99), P Tudor (2000) 21 Statute Law Review 149 and see e.g. report on the Anti-terrorism, Crime and Security Bill HL 45 (2001–02).

In cases (*a*)–(*c*) (positive procedure), an affirmative resolution of each House (or in the case of financial instruments, of the Commons alone) is needed if the instrument is to come into force or to remain in operation. In cases (*d*) and (*e*) (negative procedure), no action need be taken in either House unless there is some opposition to the instrument.

Of these procedures, by far the most common is case (*d*) (subject to annulment); the most common of the positive procedures is case (*a*). Under the positive procedure, the minister concerned must secure the affirmative resolution and, if necessary, the government must allot time for the resolution to be discussed; current practice is for the instrument to be debated, however briefly, in a 'delegated legislation standing committee'. Under the negative procedure, it is for any member who so wishes to 'pray' that the instrument should be annulled. It has been impossible in recent years to ensure that time is found to debate all prayers for annulment which have been tabled.[49] The situation has been eased by the greater use of standing committees to debate statutory instruments and by changes in the timetabling of House of Commons business[50] but difficulties remain.[51]

A novel provision made by the European Communities Act 1972 was that a statutory instrument made under s 2(2) should be subject to annulment by a resolution of either House unless a draft of the instrument had been approved by each House before the instrument was made.[52] Thus the government may choose whether the negative or positive procedure should be used. Both Labour and Conservative governments have been criticised for choosing the negative procedure for important measures modifying Acts of Parliament.[53]

One feature common to all these procedures is that neither House may amend a statutory instrument, except for very rare instances where amendment is expressly authorised by the parent Act.[54] If this were possible, it might involve the House in detailed consideration of matters which Parliament had delegated to a minister. Where a House is not satisfied with an instrument as it stands, the minister must withdraw it and start again.

While an Act that delegates powers specifies its own procedures, the Statutory Instruments Acts 1946 contains some general requirements. By s 4, where an instrument must be laid in Parliament after being made, it must in general be laid before it comes into operation; every copy of such an instrument must show on its face three dates, showing when it was made, laid and came into operation respectively. What constitutes laying before Parliament is governed by the practice or direction of each House[55] and an instrument may be laid when Parliament is not sitting. The rule that an instrument be laid before it comes into operation is clear: although there is no binding judicial authority on the matter, it is submitted that failure to lay an instrument prevents it from coming into operation.[56] But the position is doubtful in the case of delegated legislation that is outside the 1946 Act. While under the 1946 Act an

---

[49] A Beith (1981) 34 Parliamentary Affairs 165; Griffith and Ryle, *Parliament*, pp 345–50.

[50] HC 20–I (1991–92), p xxii and HC 491 (1994–95), p xvi. Also HC Deb, 12 December 1994, col 1456 and 2 November 1995, col 405.

[51] See HC 152, 1995–96 and HC 48, 1999–2000.

[52] European Communities Act 1972, Sch 2, para 2.

[53] HL 51, HC 169 (1977–78), para 36; HC 15–viii (1981–82); and see Cmnd 8600, 1982.

[54] Emergency Powers Act 1920, s 2(4), and Census Act 1920, s 1(2).

[55] Laying of Documents before Parliament (Interpretation) Act 1948, and see *R v Immigration Appeal Tribunal, ex p Joyles* [1972] 3 All ER 213.

[56] Cf de Smith, Woolf and Jowell, *Judicial Review*, pp 274–5, and A I L Campbell [1983] PL 43. The point was assumed but not decided in *R v Social Services Secretary, ex p Camden BC* [1987] 2 All ER 560 (A I L Campbell [1987] PL 328).

interval of one day between laying and operation is sufficient, in practice departments should ensure that the interval is not less than 21 days.[57]

By s 5 of the 1946 Act, where an instrument is subject to annulment, as in procedure (d) earlier, there is a uniform period of 40 days during which a prayer for annulment may be moved, exclusive of any time during which Parliament is adjourned for more than four days or is prorogued or dissolved. Where, as in procedure (e), an instrument is laid in draft but subject to the negative procedure, a similar period of 40 days applies. In the case of instruments which need an affirmative resolution before they can come into operation (procedure (b)), no set period is provided as the government in each case must decide how urgently the instrument is needed. Under procedure (c) the length of time during which the affirmative resolution must be secured is stated in the parent Act.

The role of the House of Lords

Because of its majority in the House of Commons, the government can almost always win any vote taken on a statutory instrument. The position is different in the Lords and in 2000 the royal commission on House of Lords reform considered that a reformed upper house should make a strong contribution to enhanced scrutiny of secondary legislation.[58]

Although a parent Act may expressly confine control of statutory instruments to the Commons, the House of Lords is usually granted the same powers of control as the Commons. Moreover, the procedure under the Parliament Acts 1911 and 1949 for by-passing the Lords applies to Bills and not to statutory instruments. But it is extremely rare for the House of Lords to exercise its veto over subordinate legislation. When on 18 June 1968 the House rejected an order containing sanctions against the Rhodesian government made under the Southern Rhodesia Act 1965,[59] this caused the Labour government to propose to abolish the power of the Lords to veto statutory instruments.[60] The proposal did not succeed and in 1994 the House of Lords declared that it was entitled to reject a statutory instrument and was not bound by a constitutional convention against doing so.[61] In 2000, the House exercised its power, rejecting the Greater London Election Rules and a related order on election expenses because of a disagreement over granting candidates a free postal delivery.[62] The Lords thus have a power to veto all instruments, except for financial instruments that are laid only in the Commons. There is a case to be made for converting the veto power into a delaying power that can be overridden by vote of the Commons, but the scrutiny of delegated legislation in both Houses must continue.

The technical scrutiny of statutory instruments

In the oversight of subordinate legislation, both Houses depend on the work of committees advised by qualified persons. All general statutory instruments laid before Parliament, as well as other statutory orders, come under scrutiny by the Joint Committee on Statutory Instruments, consisting of seven members appointed from each House.

---

[57] HL 51, HC 169 (1977–78), pp 11–12.
[58] Cm 4534, 2000, ch 7. See also Russell, *Reforming the House of Lords*, pp 269–270 and Shell, *The House of Lords*, ch 8.
[59] A month later, on 18 July 1968, an identical order was approved by the Lords.
[60] Cmnd 3799, 1969, pp 22–3; Parliament (No 2) Bill 1969, clauses 13–15. And see ch 10 B.
[61] HL Deb, 20 October 1994, col 356.
[62] HL Deb, 22 February 2000, cols 136 and 182. Equivalent rules were later approved: HL Deb, 6 March 2000, col 849.

The members from the Commons also meet separately to scrutinise those instruments which are laid only in the Commons. The joint committee is advised by the Speaker's Counsel and by Counsel to the Lord Chairman of committees.

The committee must consider whether the attention of the Houses should be drawn to an instrument on several legal and procedural grounds. In summary, these are:

(*a*)   that an instrument imposes a charge on public revenues or requires payments to be made to any government department or public authority or prescribes the amount of such charge or payments;

(*b*)   that it has been made under an Act that excludes it from challenge in the courts;

(*c*)   that it purports to have retrospective effect where the parent Act does not authorise this;

(*d*)   that there has been unjustifiable delay by the department (in publishing it, laying it in Parliament or in giving notice that it has come into operation before being laid);

(*e*)   that there is doubt as to whether it is intra vires or that it makes an unusual use of the delegated powers;

(*f*)   that for any reason its form or purport need to be elucidated; or

(*g*)   that its drafting is defective.

Relatively few instruments are reported to the two Houses.[63] Before such a report is made, the department concerned will have supplied an explanation of the position to the committee. An adverse report does not necessarily have any effect on the instrument; in particular, if the committee expresses doubts about the vires of an instrument, that is a question that only the courts may decide.

The grounds that arise most frequently are grounds (*g*), (*f*) and (*e*), in that order, and it is rare for other grounds to arise.

Considering the merits of statutory instruments

The Joint Committee on Statutory Instruments does not examine the merits or policy of an instrument. Occasionally, these matters may be discussed by the whole House if a debate is held on an affirmative resolution or on a prayer for annulment, but in general such debates are held in delegated legislation standing committees. Several such committees are regularly appointed, on the lines of the standing committees used for the committee stage of Bills.[64] In the committee, one and a half hours are allowed for considering each instrument.[65] After this consideration, a vote on the affirmative resolution or the prayer for annulment may be taken in the whole House without further debate. The standing committee debate enables important issues to be ventilated, but many such debates are no more than a formality. It has been proposed that the two Houses should appoint a 'sifting committee' to find out which instruments raise issues of policy that deserve the attention of Parliament[66] and that the most important instruments should be debated for two and a half hours.

The thrust of these proposals is that the resources of Parliament should be focused more sharply on certain instruments if the work of members is to be effective. One idea is that a new category of 'super-affirmative' instruments should be created to receive particularly close attention, including pre-legislative scrutiny by the relevant select committee of the Commons. Two types of such an instrument exist and were mentioned

---

[63]   In 1999–2000, the committee considered around 1,460 instruments and reported 90 instruments on ground (g) (defective drafting), 18 on ground (e), 13 (elucidation needed) and 4 (delay) (*Sessional Returns*).

[64]   Ch 10 A.

[65]   In the case of instruments concerning Northern Ireland, 2¹/₂ hours. HC SO 101(4).

[66]   See HC 152 (1995–96), para 33; HC 48 (1999–2000), paras 52–59; and Cm 4534, 2000, ch 7.

earlier. One, under the Human Rights Act 1998, s 10, is the 'remedial order' by which the government amends primary legislation to remove an inconsistency with a Convention right. The other, under the Regulatory Reform Act 2001, amends primary legislation to ease the burden of a regulatory scheme. The procedure required by each parent Act provides for greater scrutiny than is usual and the period for parliamentary action is 60 days rather than the usual 40. In the former case, the Joint Committee on Human Rights has the primary task of scrutiny. In the latter case, the Delegated Powers and Regulatory Reform Committee of the Lords and its counterpart in the Commons are concerned.

In order that each House may inform itself about EC secondary legislation, committees of the two Houses have been appointed which have functions comparable with those of the committees which deal with statutory instruments.[67]

This account of secondary legislation is confined to the Westminster Parliament. Under the Scotland Act 1998, on matters within the devolved competence of the Scottish Parliament, responsibility for making subordinate instruments is transferred to members of the Scottish Executive and the task of scrutinising such instruments to the Scottish Parliament.[68] By contrast, the National Assembly of Wales has no power to make primary legislation, but is itself responsible for making subordinate legislation affecting Wales that was previously the task of the Secretary of State for Wales and other ministers.[69]

Publication of statutory instruments

Although it is desirable that all legislation should be publicised before it takes effect, there are some matters, for example changes in indirect taxation, where the object of the legislation would be defeated if it had to be made known to the public in advance of enactment. The Statutory Instruments Act allows that for essential reasons a statutory instrument may come into operation even before it is laid before Parliament, with the safeguard that the Lord Chancellor and the Speaker must be provided with an immediate explanation. Further, a uniform procedure exists for numbering, printing, publishing and citing statutory instruments.[70] An instrument classified as local by reason of its subject-matter and certain classes of general instrument may be exempted from the requirements of printing and sale. Each year is published a collected edition of all general instruments made during the year which are still operative. It is a defence in proceedings for breach of a statutory instrument to prove that it had not been issued by the Stationery Office at the date of the alleged breach, unless it is shown by the prosecutor that reasonable steps had been taken to bring the purport of the instrument to the notice of the public, or of persons likely to be affected by it, or of the person charged.[71] Thus ignorance of a statutory instrument is no defence, but failure to issue it may in certain circumstances be a defence.

---

[67] Ch 8 C.

[68] Scotland Act 1998, ss 52, 117, 118, and Sch 4, para 11; Standing Orders of the Scottish Parliament, ch 10.

[69] Government of Wales Act 1998, ss 44, 58, 64–67. See J Osmond in Hazell (ed.), *The State and the Nations*, pp 55–58.

[70] Statutory Instruments Act 1946, s 2, amended by the Statutory Instruments (Production and Sale) Act 1996.

[71] Statutory Instruments Act 1946, s 3(2); *R v Sheer Metalcraft Ltd* [1954] 1 QB 586. For the argument that at common law delegated legislation must be published before it can come into force, see D J Lanham (1974) 37 MLR 510 and [1983] PL 395; for the contrary view, A I L Campbell [1982] PL 569.

Challenge in the courts

If made in accordance with the prescribed procedure, and within the powers conferred by the parent Act, a statutory instrument is as much part of the law as the statute itself. The essential difference between statute and statutory instrument is that, unlike Parliament, a minister's powers are limited. Consequently, if a department attempts to enforce a statutory instrument against an individual, the individual may as a defence question the validity of the instrument. The courts have power to decide this question even though the instrument has been approved by resolution of each House of Parliament.[72]

The validity of a statutory instrument may be challenged on two main grounds: (*a*) that the content or substance of the instrument is ultra vires the parent Act; (*b*) that the correct procedure has not been followed in making the instrument. The chances of success in such a challenge depend essentially on the terms of the parent Act, as interpreted by the court.[73] The duty under the Human Rights Act 1998, s 3(1), to interpret legislation consistently with the European Convention rights where it is possible to do so, significantly widens the scope for challenges to the validity of delegated legislation. To summarise a complex matter, except where the parent Act expressly or by necessary implication authorises regulations to be made that infringe Convention rights, a general power to make regulations on a given subject should be interpreted as excluding power to make regulations that infringe Convention rights.[74] The Human Rights Act thus widened the power of the courts to strike down a secondary instrument where it is not possible to interpret the instrument consistently with Convention rights, even though apart from the 1998 Act the regulation would be within the powers conferred by the parent Act. But the court may not strike down secondary legislation where primary legislation prevents the secondary legislation being made in any other terms.[75] In the latter case, the court may, under the 1998 Act, s 5, declare that the regulation is incompatible with a Convention right.

Quite apart from the Human Rights Act, there is a long-established presumption of interpretation that Parliament does not intend delegated powers to be exercised for certain purposes unless by express words or by necessary implication it has clearly authorised them. The principles that no one should be deprived of access to the courts except by clear words of Parliament and that there is no power to levy a tax without clear authority are illustrated in cases arising out of defence regulations made during the First World War.[76] The former principle was applied in 1997 when an order by the Lord Chancellor increasing the court fees payable for litigation and requiring them to be paid by someone on income support was held to deprive that person of the constitutional right of access to the courts.[77] That basic principles can cut down the width of even such expressions as 'power to make such regulations as seem to the minister to be necessary' was illustrated in *Commissioners of Customs and Excise v Cure and Deeley Ltd.*

---

[72] *Hoffmann-La Roche v Trade Secretary* [1975] AC 295.

[73] See *R v Environment Secretary, ex p Spath Holme Ltd* [2001] 2 AC 349.

[74] See A W Bradley, R Allen and P Sales [2000] PL 358. Also D Squires [2000] EHR LR 116.

[75] Human Rights Act 1998, s 3(2). And ch 19 C.

[76] *A-G v Wilts United Dairies Ltd* and *Chester v Bateson*, discussed in ch 26 D. And see *Kerr v Hood* 1907 SC 895.

[77] *R v Lord Chancellor, ex p Witham* [1998] QB 575; cf *R v Lord Chancellor, ex p Lightfoot* [2000] QB 597. Executive policies are subject to review on the same grounds: *R (Daly) v Home Secretary, ex p Daly* [2001] 2 AC 532.

The Finance (No 2) Act 1940 empowered the Commissioners to make regulations providing for any matter for which provision appeared to them to be necessary for giving effect to the statutory provisions relating to purchase tax. Regulations were made under which, if proper tax returns were not submitted by manufacturers, the Commissioners might determine the amount of tax due, 'which amount shall be deemed to be the proper tax due', unless within seven days the taxpayer satisfied the Commissioners that some other sum was due. *Held* that the regulation was invalid in that it purported to prevent the taxpayer proving in a court the amount of tax actually due, and substituted for the tax authorised by Parliament some other sum arbitrarily determined by the Commissioners.[78]

By similar reasoning a court might declare invalid a statutory instrument which purported to have retrospective effect in the absence of clear authority from Parliament. In 1973, the Court of Session declared ultra vires a regulation made by the Secretary of State for Scotland which sought to remove from qualified teachers the right to continue teaching without first registering with a statutory Teaching Council.[79] In 1982, the Home Secretary's power to make rules for the management of prisons was held not to permit him to make rules fettering a prisoner's right of access to the courts.[80] But in *McEldowney* v *Forde*, which concerned the freedom of association in Northern Ireland, the House of Lords by 3–2 upheld a remarkably phrased ban on republican clubs imposed by the Northern Ireland Minister for Home Affairs.[81] In 1990, byelaws made by the Defence Secretary barring access to Greenham Common, then a nuclear missile base, were held ultra vires because they ignored the provision in the Military Lands Act 1892 that such byelaws must not prejudicially affect the rights of the commoners.[82] Social security regulations which deprived an asylum seeker of all benefits while his or her appeal for asylum was pending were unlawful because their effect was to prevent the right to appeal from being exercised.[83]

In reviewing delegated legislation, the courts do not lightly strike down a statutory instrument, but if necessary they may apply a test of unreasonableness where a regulation is so unreasonable that Parliament cannot be taken as having authorised it to be made under the Act in question.[84] Where an order by the Environment Secretary 'capping' selected local councils' expenditure was subject to approval by resolution of the House of Commons, the House of Lords held that if the order came within the 'four corners' of the parent statute it was subject to review for unreasonableness only on the extreme grounds of bad faith, improper motive or manifest absurdity.[85]

A serious procedural error by the department concerned could lead to an instrument being declared invalid. Where there was a duty to consult interested organisations before regulations were made, it was held that the mere sending of a letter to an organisation did not amount to consultation;[86] and no effective consultation occurred when a department failed to allow sufficient time for this.[87] But not every procedural error vitiates the statutory instrument; some procedural requirements are held to be directory (that is, of such a kind that failure to comply with them does not invalidate the instrument) and not mandatory or imperative.[88]

---

[78] [1962] 1 QB 340. See also *R* v *IRC, ex p Woolwich Building Society* [1991] 4 All ER 92.
[79] *Malloch* v *Aberdeen Corpn* 1974 SLT 253; and see Education (Scotland) Act 1973.
[80] *Raymond* v *Honey* [1983] AC 1 and *R* v *Home Secretary, ex p Leech* [1994] QB 198.
[81] [1971] AC 632. And see D N MacCormick (1970) 86 LQR 171.
[82] *DPP* v *Hutchinson* [1990] 2 AC 783. And see n 93 below.
[83] *R* v *Social Security Secretary, ex p Joint Council for Welfare of Immigrants* [1996] 4 All ER 385.
[84] *Maynard* v *Osmond* [1977] QB 240; *Cinnamond* v *British Airports Authority* [1980] 2 All ER 368.
[85] *R* v *Environment Secretary, ex p Hammersmith BC* [1991] 1 AC 521, applying *Notts CC* v *Environment Secretary* [1986] AC 240 (C M G Himsworth [1986] PL 374, [1991] PL 76).
[86] The *Aylesbury Mushrooms* case, note 43 above.
[87] *R* v *Social Services Secretary, ex p Association of Metropolitan Authorities* [1986] 1 All ER 164.
[88] de Smith, Woolf and Jowell, *Judicial Review*, pp 265–74; and ch 30 B.

Where either on grounds of substance or procedure an instrument is to some extent defective, this does not necessarily mean that the whole instrument is a nullity; it may still be operative to its lawful extent or be binding upon persons not affected by the defect of procedure.[89] The decision of when such 'severance' is permissible may involve a textual, or 'blue pencil' test (does deletion of the offending phrase or sentence leave a grammatical and coherent text?) and also a test of whether after deletion of the unlawful part the substance of the provision remains essentially unchanged in purpose and effect from what had been intended.[90]

It was at one time believed that if the parent Act provided that regulations when made should have effect 'as if enacted in this Act', the courts were precluded from inquiring into the validity of the regulations; however, this expression in the parent Act adds nothing to the binding effect of a properly made instrument.[91] Where a tribunal must adjudicate on the rights of an individual and the extent of those rights is directly affected by a regulation the tribunal must if necessary decide whether the regulation is valid;[92] its decision on this issue will be subject to appeal or review. So too, if someone is prosecuted for breach of a regulation or byelaw, it is always a good defence in law for the defendant to show that the instrument in question is invalid.[93]

Byelaws are a form of delegated legislation that generally applies only in a particular locality or certain public places (for example, airports). They are usually made by a local council or a statutory undertaking and are subject to ministerial confirmation before they take effect. The courts formerly exercised greater control over byelaws than over departmental regulations.[94]

Administrative rule-making

Legislation by statutory instrument is more flexible than primary legislation, since the law can be changed without the need for a Bill to pass through Parliament. Nonetheless, statutory instrument procedures are complex and the instruments are expressed in formal language. In government today, many less formal methods of rule-making are used. Such methods are sometimes directly authorised by Act of Parliament, but rules so made may have an uncertain legal status (for example, immigration rules made under the Immigration Act 1971).[95] Two forms of rule-making that are often authorised by statute are codes of practice and administrative guidelines or notes of guidance.[96] They do not have the full force of delegated legislation and generally do not have a mandatory effect,[97] but a department may be expected either to observe them or take steps to change them.[98] A local authority must follow statutory guidance from central government except if it can state a good reason for not doing so.[99]

---

[89] *Dunkley* v *Evans* [1981] 3 All ER 285; the *Aylesbury Mushrooms* case, note 43 above.

[90] *DPP* v *Hutchinson* [1990] 2 AC 783 (A W Bradley [1990] PL 293); and *R* v *IRC, ex p Woolwich Building Society* [1991] 4 All ER 92.

[91] *Minister of Health* v *R* [1931] AC 494.

[92] *Chief Adjudication Officer* v *Foster* [1993] AC 754 (and see D Feldman (1992) 108 LQR 45; A W Bradley [1992] PL 185).

[93] E.g. *R* v *Reading Crown Court, ex p Hutchinson* [1988] QB 384 (A W Bradley [1988] PL 169); and *Boddington* v *British Transport Police* [1999] 2 AC 143.

[94] See *Kruse* v *Johnson* [1898] 2 QB 91; *Cinnamond* v *British Airports Authority* [1980] 2 All ER 368.

[95] See ch 20 B.

[96] See e.g. Police and Criminal Evidence Act 1984, Part VI; Freedom of Information Act 2000, ss 45 and 46.

[97] See e.g. *Laker Airways* v *Department of Trade* [1977] QB 643.

[98] *R* v *Home Secretary, ex p Khan* [1985] 1 All ER 40 (and A R Mowbray [1985] PL 558).

[99] *R* v *Islington Council, ex p Rixon* [1997] ELR 66.

Depending on the parent Act, these rules may totally evade the procedures for parliamentary control described earlier. In fact, many administrative rules are issued without direct statutory authority. This phenomenon was once described as 'administrative quasi-legislation',[100] when it was related to the practice of issuing the official interpretation of doubtful points in statutes and of stating concessions that would be made in individual cases. The practice has continued, for the revenue authorities often choose to waive the application of over-harsh laws rather than seek changes in the legislation. In 1979, the Inland Revenue's use of executive discretion rather than a statutory basis for assessing tax was described by the House of Lords as unconstitutional.[101] As Walton J had said: 'One should be taxed by law, and not be untaxed by concession.'[102]

In many areas of government, such as town planning, education and health, ministerial statements of policy and circulars to local authorities have a practical effect which falls little short of declaring or modifying the law. On matters of general policy where controversial issues are involved, government by circular is not a satisfactory substitute for legislation. Neither can such circulars require the performance of unlawful acts.[103]

Informal rule-making is frequently adopted by departments in order that wide discretion vested in public authorities may be exercised by officials in a reasonably uniform manner.[104] In the past, many authorities were reluctant to publish such rules, a stance which caused problems when a person affected by them had a right of appeal to a tribunal or wished to know the reasons for a decision. Secrecy has been maintained when changes have been made in published rules or policies and the government wishes to avoid being criticised for the changes. This occurred notably with the changed policies on the export of defence-related equipment to Iraq, which the Scott report found caused ministers repeatedly to give misleading answers to MPs.[105] Like any large organisation, a department may wish to give instructions to its staff on purely internal matters without publishing them. But rules which directly affect the individual should be published. Problems arising out of the use of departmental rules have frequently come before the Parliamentary Ombudsman, most notably in the Sachsenhausen case[106] and are also likely to arise in the context of European Convention rights.[107]

Steps to encourage greater openness in government have alleviated some of the problems relating to departmental rules. The non-statutory code of practice on access to government information, policed by the Parliamentary Ombudsman, obliged departments (inter alia):

> to publish or otherwise make available explanatory material on departments' dealing with the public (including such rules, procedures, internal guidance to officials, and similar administrative manuals as will assist better understanding of departmental action in dealing with the

[100] R E Megarry (1944) 60 LQR 125; Ganz, *Quasi-Legislation*; R Baldwin and J Houghton [1986] PL 239. Informal administrative rules may be termed 'tertiary rules' (Baldwin, *Rules and Government*, ch 4) or, in the European context, 'soft law': K Wellens and G Borchardt (1989) 14 EL Rev 267. Also Craig, *Administrative Law*, pp 392–399.

[101] *Vestey v IRC (No 2)* [1980] AC 1148.

[102] *Vestey v IRC* [1979] Ch 177, 197. And see D W Williams [1979] British Tax Review 137.

[103] *Royal College of Nursing v DHSS* [1981] AC 800; *Gillick v West Norfolk Health Authority* [1986] AC 112.

[104] E.g. Local Authority Social Services Act 1970, s 7 (guidance of Secretary of State) and s 7A (directions by Secretary of State) (added by NHS and Community Care Act 1990, s 50).

[105] See HC 115 (1995–96) (Scott Report) esp vol IV, para K.

[106] Ch 29 D, and see A R Mowbray [1987] PL 570.

[107] See e.g. *Silver v UK* (1983) 5 EHRR 347.

public) except where publication could prejudice any matter which should properly be kept confidential under Part II of the Code.[108]

Publication of administrative rules may lead to criticism in Parliament and the media or to judicial scrutiny, but a regular practice of publication should generally make it easier for departments to explain their decisions and to give reasons for those decisions.

---

[108] *Code of Practice on Access to Government Information* (2nd edn, 1997), para 3 (ii). See now the Freedom of Information Act 2000; and ch 13 F.

Chapter 29

ADMINISTRATIVE JUSTICE

The title of this chapter might seem a contradiction in terms: there are such marked differences between the way in which decisions are made by civil servants and ministers on the one hand, and by the courts on the other, that the two systems, administration and justice, should be kept quite separate. However, as we will see in relation to the judicial control of administrative action, there is a strong tendency in public law for principles derived from the courts, such as the doctrine of natural justice,[1] to be applied to administrative decisions. The same tendency applies to the development of institutions within government. In his seminal book, *Justice and Administrative Law*, first published in 1928, Robson described the extent to which 'trial by Whitehall' had developed in the British constitution. He argued that the judicial powers given to administrative bodies served to promote the welfare of society and that administrative justice could become 'as well-founded and broad-based as any other kind of justice now known to us and embodied in human institutions'.[2] Today, the significance of administrative justice is seen in the decisions of the European Court of Human Rights interpreting art 6 of the European Convention.[3]

In this chapter, we examine institutions and procedures concerned with an extensive area of decision-making that lies somewhere between the world of government departments on one hand and that of the law courts on the other. This territory is liable to become a battleground as competing interests from the administrative and legal worlds struggle to occupy it. In one sector of the territory that was formerly under strong departmental influence, namely administrative tribunals, the judicial model of decision-making now holds sway. The British system of tribunals, today best referred to without the adjective 'administrative', will be outlined in section A of this chapter. In another sector, that of public inquiries (considered in section B), government departments exercise the dominant influence over the procedures and the decisions that are made. Further, when things go wrong in government, impartial means are needed for discovering what happened so that those responsible may be called to account. In section C will be described one constitutional device, the 'tribunal of inquiry' appointed under the Tribunals of Inquiry (Evidence) Act 1921, that allows techniques of judicial investigation to be applied to scandals and disasters of special importance. Section D is concerned with the Ombudsman. The mission of this office is to investigate individual complaints about governmental action and to remedy injustice that official errors have caused, but the Ombudsman carries out this mission by investigatory means which owe little to traditional court procedures. Before we examine these sectors of administrative justice separately, a brief discussion of the role of tribunals and inquiries may be helpful.

---

[1] Ch 31 B.

[2] Robson, *Justice and Administrative Law*, p 515. And see W A Robson [1979] CLP 107.

[3] See A W Bradley (1995) 1 Euro Public Law Rev 347; C Harlow in Alston (ed.) *The EU and Human Rights*, ch 7. Also Harris and Partington (eds), *Administrative Justice in the 21st Century*.

When Parliament authorises new forms of public service or regulation, it is inevitable that questions and disputes will arise out of the application of the legislation. There are three main ways in which such questions and disputes may be settled: (*a*) by conferring new jurisdiction on the ordinary civil courts; (*b*) by creating new machinery in the form of special tribunals; (*c*) by leaving all decisions to the authority with primary responsibility for the scheme, whether it be local authority or central department. In case (*c*), the Act may create rights of appeal (for example, from a local council to a central department), or it may require a hearing or public inquiry to be held before certain decisions are made. If decisions are entrusted entirely to a public authority, it may be desirable for someone who is dissatisfied with a decision to be able to seek review at a higher level within the authority. In any event, the procedure of judicial review exists to supervise the legality of decisions. But reliance on judicial review, which should be an exceptional remedy, is not adequate to ensure the quality of numerous decisions at first instance. In such cases, there is likely to be a need for an appeal to a court or tribunal, possibly after the original decision has been reviewed administratively.[4]

There are important distinctions to be drawn between tribunal decisions and departmental decisions involving a public inquiry. The Franks report of 1957 made it clear that tribunals and inquiries differ in their constitutional status and functions. No tribunal should appear merely to be part of the departmental structure, for the typical tribunal exercises functions which are essentially judicial in character, although of a specialised nature. As the Franks committee stated:

> We consider that tribunals should properly be regarded as machinery provided by Parliament for adjudication rather than as part of the machinery of administration. The essential point is that in all these cases Parliament has deliberately provided for a decision outside and independent of the Department concerned.[5]

On the other hand, the public inquiry, while it grants citizens affected by official proposals some safeguard against ill informed and hasty decisions, is essentially a step in a complex process which leads to a departmental decision for which a minister is responsible to Parliament.

Structures of administrative justice are affected by changing pressures on government. As we saw in chapter 20 B, the system for immigration appeals was changed several times during the 1990s and so was the appeals structure in such fields as social security and education. An appeal structure must be able to cope with fluctuations in the caseload and also to stand scrutiny under art 6 of the European Convention on Human Rights. A large question examined in 2001 was whether a coordinated system of tribunals across the whole of government should be created to replace the existence of numerous piecemeal tribunals, each with its own jurisdiction.[6] Developments such as these reinforce the conclusion of the Franks committee in 1957 that internal administrative procedures are not enough to protect the individual's interests. All powers of government should be exercised fairly – but principles of openness, fairness and impartiality are more likely to be maintained when there are statutory procedures designed to promote these qualities.

---

[4] See e.g. Lord Woolf [1992] PL 221, 228–9; and Law Commission, *Administrative Law: Judicial Review and Statutory Appeals*, pp 14–15.
[5] Cmnd 218, 1957, p 9; ch 27.
[6] See pp 670–2 below.

A. Tribunals[7]

Reasons for creation of tribunals

For many centuries Britain has had specialised courts in addition to the courts of general jurisdiction. Medieval merchants had their courts of pie poudre; the tin miners of Devon and Cornwall had their courts of Stannaries.[8] The growth of the welfare state led to the creation of many procedures for the settlement of disputes. The National Insurance Act of 1911, which created the first British social insurance scheme, provided for the adjudication of disputes by new administrative agencies. The present social security scheme includes a complex structure for the settlement of disputes concerning the benefits or pension payable to claimants.

The creation of tribunals has sometimes been considered to endanger the position of the judiciary and the authority of the law administered in the ordinary courts.[9] The right of access to the courts is indeed an important safeguard for the citizen, but the machinery of the courts is not suited for settling every dispute which may arise out of the work of government. One reason for this is the need for specialised knowledge if certain disputes are to be resolved fairly and economically. Areas such as taxation, social security or immigration embody complex systems of regulation which require innumerable decisions to be made by officials trained in what is required. The ordinary courts could not deal with the mass of appeals from such decisions unless they, the legal profession and legal aid were organised quite differently. While policy decisions and oversight of a department's work are entrusted to ministers, most schemes require a structure of rules which officials may apply without constant recourse to the minister, a fact which underlies the present use in Whitehall of executive agencies.[10] In such schemes, individuals are likely to need a right of appeal from official decisions to a tribunal designed with a particular area of government in mind. This is a better remedy against poor decisions than the principle of ministerial responsibility.

In other areas of government, there may be more need to retain power to decide in the hands of the department and the minister. In some fields, notably the regulation of civil aviation, a special agency such as the Civil Aviation Authority exists with power to develop policies through the mechanism of licensing, but with ultimate control being retained by the minister, to whom appeals against the Authority's decisions may be brought.[11] In other fields, such as social security, the rules applicable are laid down in statutes or statutory instruments, and the duty of applying them is vested in a hierarchy of tribunals, for whose decisions no minister is responsible and which the government can control only by amending the statutory rules. Here the relationship between minister and tribunal approaches that which exists between the government and the judiciary. Such tribunals exist not because they exercise a political discretion which it would be inappropriate to confer on the judges, but because they do the work of adjudication required more efficiently than the courts.[12]

---

[7] See report of the Franks committee, Cmnd 218, 1957, parts II and III; Wraith and Hutchesson, *Administrative Tribunals*; Farmer, *Tribunals and Government*; Richardson and Genn (eds), *Administrative Law and Government Action*, part II; Harlow and Rawlings, *Law and Administration*, ch 14; Leggatt, *Tribunals for Users*.

[8] See *R v East Powder Justices, ex p Lampshire* [1979] QB 616.

[9] See e.g. Lord Scarman, *English Law – the New Dimension*, part III. For an historical critique, see Arthurs, *Without the Law: Administrative Justice and Legal Pluralism in the 19th Century*.

[10] See ch 13 D.

[11] See *Laker Airways Ltd* v *Department of Trade* [1997] QB 643; G R Baldwin [1978] PL 57 and (the same) *Regulating the Airlines*.

[12] Cf the distinction between 'policy-oriented' and 'court-substitute' tribunals: Farmer, ch 8, and H Genn, in Richardson and Genn (eds), ch 11.

This approach can be justified on several grounds. As was said in relation to claims for social security, 'For these cases we do not want a Rolls-Royce system of justice.'[13] Practical factors that have favoured the setting up of tribunals include: the desire for a procedure which avoids the formality of the courts; the need, in implementing a new social policy, for the speedy, cheap and decentralised determination of many individual cases; and the need for expert and specialised knowledge on the part of the tribunal, which may include not only lawyers but also other professionals with relevant experience. Another important characteristic of tribunals is that the legal profession has no monopoly of the right to represent those appearing before tribunals. This fact alone makes tribunals more accessible to the public than the courts, since an individual's case may be presented effectively by a trade union official, an accountant, a surveyor, a social worker or a friend.

The need for securing administrative justice does not mean that tribunals should be created for their own sake when the decisions in question would be better taken by the courts. In the view of the Franks committee, 'a decision should be entrusted to a court rather than to a tribunal in the absence of special considerations which make a tribunal more suitable.'[14] However, in 1957 the comparison being made was between the ordinary courts and tribunals as they existed at that time. There have been many changes since then in the procedures and operation of both tribunals and courts. Today there is a striking overlap between the types of decision made by courts and tribunals and also the procedures by which they are made. For example, in deciding claims for unfair dismissal and discrimination brought by employees against employers, employment tribunals are making decisions that in other legal systems are entrusted to a specialised court. Conversely, under Part VII of the Housing Act 1996, if a homeless person is aggrieved by a local authority's decision, he/she must first ask for the decision to be reviewed and, if still dissatisfied, can appeal to the county court on a point of law. Jurisdiction in homelessness cases could well have been entrusted to a housing tribunal, had such a tribunal existed. In that event, the right of appeal need not have been confined to points of law.

In reality, the essential qualities of adjudication apply to both tribunals and courts. The right to a fair hearing before an independent and impartial court or tribunal that arises under art 6 ECHR does not depend on the name of the decision-maker. It is fundamental that neither judges nor tribunal members should be subject to dismissal when a government department is dissatisfied with their decisions. Procedures in a tribunal are often said to be informal. But informality is difficult to reconcile with the need for legal precision[15] and tribunal procedures are not always less formal than procedures in a comparable court. When a county court is dealing with a small claim through arbitration, it adopts very informal procedure. In general, tribunals are not bound by the rules of evidence observed in courts, but minimum standards of evidence and proof must be observed if justice is to be done.[16]

Some tribunals (for example, employment tribunals) differ from courts in that they are constituted not by a lawyer sitting as sole judge, but by a legal chairman sitting with two laypeople with relevant experience. However, in 2001 many tribunals (e.g. those dealing with immigration and many social security appeals) took the form of a lawyer sitting alone. A safeguard common to all tribunals is that it should be possible to challenge their decisions on points of law, whether by appeal to a higher court or tribunal or by way of judicial review. A related safeguard is that reasons should be

---

[13] Street, *Justice in the Welfare State*, p 3.
[14] Cmnd 218, 1957, p 9.
[15] See H Genn, note 12 above.
[16] See e.g. *R v Deputy Industrial Injuries Commissioner, ex p Moore* [1965] 1 QB 456.

given for their decisions. In 1957, many tribunals were perceived to provide 'second-class justice', using procedures that fell below those of the courts in their lack of openness and impartiality. Since then, standards and expectations have risen greatly. Today, leaving aside questions of organisation, it is impossible not to describe the functions of tribunals except in terms that also apply to courts.

Organisation and classification of tribunals

In 2001, for the first time since the Franks report of 1957, a review of all tribunals was conducted. It was undertaken for the Lord Chancellor by a retired Court of Appeal judge, Sir Andrew Leggatt, assisted by an expert panel.[17] He found that, leaving regulatory bodies to one side, there were some 70 different tribunals in England and Wales, between them disposing of nearly a million cases each year. But of the 70 tribunals, only 20 heard more than 500 cases a year: many of the tribunals were defunct and some had never met. Leggatt criticised the lack of system in tribunals, commenting that tribunals had grown up in a haphazard way, created piecemeal by legislation and separately administered by government departments with wide variations of approach, in a way that (in his view) took more account of departmental needs than the convenience of tribunal users. He proposed the creation of what would indeed be a system of administrative justice, 'a single, overarching structure' that would give the individual improved access to all tribunals. Although this would involve reorganising the structure and servicing of tribunals, many existing tribunals, particularly those with large caseloads, would continue to function with little practical change being necessary. Whether or not this scheme is adopted, an outline of the structure that Leggatt proposes will cast light on the scope and variety of existing tribunals.

There is certainly no need for there to be as many as 70 tribunal systems. The Leggatt review proposed that there should be a single tribunal system, administered by an integrated tribunal service, and operating in nine divisions according to subject-matter. The following summary mentions the principal tribunals that would fall within each division, together with some comments on them; the figure in square brackets shows the number of cases decided by the tribunals in 2000.[18]

(1) Immigration

This division would bring together three tribunals, the immigration adjudicators [32,875], the Special Immigration Appeals Commission and the Immigration Services Appeal Tribunal.[19]

(2) Social security and pensions

This division would include, as well as the pension appeal tribunals [3,416] and the Criminal Injuries Compensation Appeal Panel [8,109], the massive number of appeals determined by the Appeals Service [151,290]. In 2001, that Service (which had replaced the former Independent Tribunal Service) was responsible for tribunals sitting at over 140 local venues for appeals relating to social security benefits, child support, vaccine damage, tax credit, compensation recovery, council tax benefit and housing benefit.[20]

---

[17] Leggatt, *Tribunals for Users*, and see A W Bradley [2002] PL 200.
[18] The summary derives from Leggatt, ch 6. The statistics are for England and Wales and come from the report of the Council on Tribunals for 2000–2001, app A.
[19] And see ch 20 B.
[20] The relevant legislation includes the Social Security Act 1998, Part I and Schs 1–5; Child Support, Pension and Social Security Act 2000, ss 10, 11, 68 and Sch 7; Social Security and Child Support (Decisions and Appeals) Regulations 1999, SI No 991; and Housing Benefit and Council Tax Benefits (Decisions and Appeals) Regulations 2001, SI No 1002. See also Davis, Wikeley and Young, *Child Support in Action*;

The tribunals often consist of a lawyer sitting alone, but for complex cases of child support, housing benefit and council tax benefit, a lawyer may sit with an accountant; for appeals relating to incapacity benefits, a lawyer sits with a medical practitioner; for disability and attendance allowance appeals, a lawyer sits with a medical practitioner and a person with experience of disabilities; for disablement appeals relating to industrial accidents, the lawyer may sit with two medical consultants. The history of social security appeals could be said to be the history of tribunals in the 20th century, since a right of appeal to an independent panel was created in 1911 and the structure of appeals became a notable aspect of the welfare state after 1945.[21]

(3) *Land and valuation*
This division would include the valuation tribunals, concerned with the valuation of property for purposes of local taxation [36,199], rent assessment panels, primarily charged with assessing a fair rent for certain rented dwellings [8,452], the Leasehold Valuation Tribunal, the Commons Commissioners [218] and the Agricultural Lands Tribunal [74].

(4) *Financial*
This division would include the authorities that adjudicate on tax disputes (in particular the general commissioners of income tax [13,154], the special commissioners of income tax [174] and the VAT and Duties Tribunal [604]). These would be grouped with the Financial Services and Markets Tribunal, created by the Financial Services and Markets Act 2000 to hear appeals concerning financial services regulation.

(5) *Transport*
This would include the Parking and Traffic Appeals Service for London [30,472] and the National Parking Adjudication Service [1,461].

(6) *Health and social services*
This division would include the Mental Health Review Tribunal, which reviews the legality of a patient's compulsory detention in hospital for assessment or treatment for mental disorder [11,833],[22] the Family Health Service Appeal Authority and the tribunal set up by the Protection of Children Act 1999.[23]

(7) *Education*
This would include the independent panels set up under the School Standards and Framework Act 1998 to hear appeals in respect of school admissions [62,655]; panels under the same Act that hear appeals about the permanent exclusion of pupils from school [863];[24] and the Special Educational Needs and Disability Tribunal [1,143]. The main function of this Tribunal is to determine disputes between a local education authority and a parent as to the provision to be made for a child with special educational

---

R Young, N Wikeley and G Davis in Harris and Partington (eds) *Administrative Justice in the 21st Century*, ch 13; N Wikeley, (1998) 5 JSSL 104 and (1999) 6 JSSL 155; S Rahilly, (2001) 8 JSSL 57 and R Sainsbury in Harris (ed.) *Social Security Law in Context*, ch 7. See also HC 581 (1998–99) and HC 263 (1999–2000).

[21] On the earlier tribunals, see e.g. Baldwin, Wikeley and Young, *Judging Social Security*; Fullbrook, *Administrative Justice and the Unemployed*; and Adler and Bradley (eds) *Justice, Discretion and Poverty*.

[22] See the special report of the Council on Tribunals on these tribunals, Cm 4740, 2000. Also G Richardson and D Machin [2000] PL 494.

[23] The Care Standards Act 2000 requires this tribunal also to decide appeals concerning the registration of children's, nursing and care homes.

[24] See N Harris and K Eden, *Challenges to School Exclusions*.

needs.[25] One feature of this division is that it would hear appeals from local education authorities and from the governing bodies of schools, not from a department or agency of central government.

(8) Regulatory

This division would bring together a wide range of procedures for hearing appeals involving such matters as consumer credit licensing under the Consumer Credit Act 1974, licensing of estate agents, insolvency practitioners and conveyancers, intellectual property (the Copyright Tribunal and the Registered Designs Appeal Tribunal), claims for foreign compensation (the Foreign Compensation Commission), data protection (the Information Tribunal) and betting levy. Despite the diverse subject-matter, its caseload would be smaller than any other division.

(9) Employment

This division would comprise the employment tribunals (formerly known as industrial tribunals), which decide disputes arising in respect of unfair dismissal, unlawful discrimination (sex, race and disability), equal pay, breach of contract and redundancy.[26] In 2000, no fewer than 107,357 new cases were received in England and Wales: 28,808 cases were decided by tribunals; 57,593 cases were withdrawn, in many of which the parties would have agreed to settle the dispute.

These tribunals are distinct from most tribunals in that they are predominantly deciding disputes between two private parties, an employee and his/her employer (who may be a public authority, a commercial undertaking or a private person). Some tribunals concerned with the valuation of land also resolve disputes between private parties. But most tribunals decide disputes between a citizen and a public authority, whether a government department, local authority or other public agency.

The above scheme is extensive, but does not include all tribunals and related procedures. Thus, the Leggatt review concluded that the Investigatory Powers Tribunal, created by the Regulation of Investigatory Powers Act 2000 to replace earlier tribunals such as the Interception of Communications Tribunal, should be excluded from the general structure, because its concern is with national security and its membership would not be interchangeable with other tribunals.[27] Also outside the general scheme are cases in which legislation provides no right of appeal to a tribunal, but lays down procedures involving administrative review: if such procedures are pursued without success, the individual's remedy is to apply for judicial review. This applies to discretionary payments from the Social Fund, that are intended to be a residual way of meeting acute hardship: the original decision, made by a designated officer of the Benefits Agency, is subject to an elaborate procedure of review by another officer and then by a social fund inspector, acting under the guidance of the Social Fund Commissioner.[28] Not included in the Leggatt scheme are professional regulatory bodies, such as the Disciplinary Committee of the Law Society. These bodies are tribunals in all but name and exercise statutory powers of adjudication. It is in the public interest that they should

---

[25] See the Special Educational Needs and Disability Act 2001. Also Harris, *Special Educational Needs and Access to Justice*; and N Harris, in Harris and Partington (eds), *Administrative Justice in the 21st Century*, chap 14.

[26] See the Employment Rights Act 1996, the Employment Tribunals Act 1996, and the Employment Tribunals (Constitution and Rules of Procedure) Regulations 2001, SI 2001 No 1171.

[27] Leggatt, *Tribunals for Users*, para 3.11. See ch 25. See also the Proscribed Organisations Appeal Commission, that hears appeals under the Terrorism Act 2000, s 5 and Sch 3, against refusals by the Home Secretary to deproscribe organisations.

[28] Buck, *The Social Fund: Law and Practice*; M Sunkin and K Pick [2001] PL 736; HC 232 (2000–01).

function properly, but they are not within the direct responsibility of a government department.

'First instance' decisions and appeals

The tribunals so far mentioned may loosely be said to be exercising jurisdiction at first instance, but if we consider how cases reach tribunals, we will see that this statement is potentially misleading. So far as the tribunals in divisions (1)–(8) are concerned, the right of appeal to the tribunal arises only where a public body or official (for example, a tax inspector or an immigration officer) has made a decision that the individual disputes. In many cases, whether or not it is required by law, the agency concerned may arrange for such a decision to be subject to internal review. Thus, these 'first instance' tribunals typically hear appeals brought against a prior administrative decision. By contrast, employment tribunals generally make the first instance decision in a dispute between two parties (employer and employee).

In respect of many but not all 'first instance' tribunals, the legislation provides a further appeal from their decisions. In 1957, the Franks committee considered that the ideal appeal structure took the form of a general appeal from the tribunal of first instance to an appellate tribunal and that all tribunal decisions should be subject to review by the courts on points of law.[29] That ideal structure has seldom been adopted. Indeed, the confusing complexity and lack of system in relation to tribunals generally extend to the piecemeal provision made for appeals.[30] In many cases, an appeal from the first tribunal lies to an appellate tribunal. This applies to immigration, where further appeals may go to the Immigration Appeal Tribunal [11,427]; social security and child support, where appeals lie to the Social Security and Child Support Commissioners [4,754];[31] valuation, where appeals go to the Land and Valuation Appeal Tribunal; and financial and revenue matters, where appeals go to the Income Tax, VAT and Duties Appeal Tribunal. In place of an appeal from a first instance tribunal to an appellate tribunal, legislation may provide for appeal to the High Court on a point of law, as with the Special Educational Needs Tribunal. From some appellate tribunals, there is a further appeal to the High Court or, from the Social Security and Child Support Commissioners and the Employment Appeal Tribunal, an appeal to the Court of Appeal. Where no right of appeal is provided in the legislation, the decisions and procedures of a tribunal are subject to judicial review.[32]

To rationalise provision for appeals, Leggatt proposed that the new tribunal structure should include an appeals division. This division would include existing appellate tribunals, such as the Immigration Appeal Tribunal and the Social Security and Child Support Commissioners. It would also provide a structure within which appeals might be brought from first instance tribunals where at present no such right exists. The Leggatt review envisaged that full-time judges, including some from the High Court, would preside over the divisions of the new structure, particularly the appeals division.

Some general considerations

As we have seen, tribunals cover a very wide range of activities extending across government, but they have been created by piecemeal legislation enacted at different

---

[29] Cmnd 218, 1957, p 25.
[30] See Lord Woolf (1988) 7 Civil Justice Quarterly 44; Law Commission, *Administrative Law: Judicial Review and Statutory Appeals* (HC 669, 1993–94), part XII.
[31] See D Bonner, T Buck and R Sainsbury (2001) 8 JSSL 9.
[32] See chs 30, 31.

dates. Since there is no single set of rules that tribunals must observe, countless variations in tribunal rules and procedures exist. Since its creation in 1958, the Council on Tribunals has endeavoured to develop general standards that apply to all tribunals,[33] but it has lacked the authority to require central government to adopt these standards in a uniform manner. Several general questions must be asked whenever the role of an existing tribunal is being assessed or the creation of a new tribunal is proposed. The importance of these questions is reinforced by the effect of art 6, ECHR, that guarantees the right to a fair hearing before a court or tribunal in the determination of one's civil rights and obligations.[34] (*a*) What is the composition of the tribunal? Tribunals are not composed of government officials. They may include lay members (as in the case of employment tribunals, where the wing members come from groups such as employers' organisations or trade unions), but will generally include a lawyer as chair or sole member. Certain tribunals regularly include those with specialist qualifications, for example in medicine or psychiatry, or with experience in the needs of disabled persons or in education. (*b*) Who appoints the members and who may dismiss them? Appointments are generally made for a fixed period of years, either by the minister concerned, by the Lord Chancellor (where legal qualifications are required) or jointly by the relevant minister and the Lord Chancellor. It would strengthen the independence of tribunals if all appointments were made by the Lord Chancellor, who is entrusted with making most judicial appointments. In general, dismissal is by the Lord Chancellor or at least requires his or her concurrence.[35] (*c*) What are the questions that the tribunal must decide? What statutory rules apply? Does the tribunal exercise a broad discretion or is it restricted to deciding the facts and applying precise rules to the facts? Most tribunals exercise functions that are similar to those of the courts and within the limits laid down by legislation they become aware of the legal, social and cultural factors that apply in their particular field. It is rare for tribunals to be appointed to decide what might loosely be called 'policy questions', at least without provision for statutory guidance or directions from the department concerned.[36] (*d*) What procedures are followed by the tribunal and how formal are they? Is the tribunal expected to act inquisitorially or by an adversary procedure? (*e*) What forms of representation, if any, occur in the tribunal and how are they financed? In 2001, publicly funded legal representation was available only in a few tribunals, including the Employment Appeal Tribunal, immigration adjudicators and the Immigration Appeal Tribunal, and mental health review tribunals.[37] Legal advice and assistance without representation could be obtained in connection with all tribunal proceedings. Those individuals who attend the hearing and are represented have a higher success rate than non-attenders or those who attend but without a representative.[38] (*f*) What rights of appeal, whether on law, on fact or on the merits, are there against the tribunal's decision? Is the appeal to an appellate tribunal or a court and is leave to appeal needed? Are the tribunal's decisions published and, if so, do they have authority as binding or

---

[33] See e.g. the Council's model rules for tribunals (Cm 1434, 1991) and the Council's report, *Tribunals – their Organisation and Independence* (Cm 3744, 1997).

[34] See ch 19 B.

[35] See p 675 below.

[36] For an example of a tribunal with 'policy' functions at a local level, see the 'adjudicators' created by the School Standards and Framework Act 1998 to decentralise local policy decisions about school admissions criteria: and see e.g. *R (Wirral Council)* v *Chief Schools Adjudicator* [2001] ELR 574.

[37] See the Access to Justice Act 1999, pt 1 and sch 2; also the Community Legal Service (Financial) Regulations 2000, SI No 516/2000, and the Legal Services Commission's Funding Code. On legal representation at tribunals, see Leggatt, *Tribunals for Users*, paras 4.21–28.

[38] In 1999, only 17% of social security appeals succeeded that were decided on the papers. The success rate rose to 45% if the appellant attended and to 63% if he/she was represented. See HC 581 (1998–99); and Genn, *The Effectiveness of Representation at Tribunals*.

persuasive precedents for future decisions? (*g*) What form does the administration of the tribunal take? Is it administered by the Lord Chancellor's Department or another government department? Is there a national president for the tribunal? Who is responsible for training the members? Is there a system for assessing the effectiveness of the tribunal – for instance, in monitoring the waiting time before appeals to the tribunal are heard? (*h*) Finally, a question made necessary by the Human Rights Act 1998, how is it ensured that the tribunal in its structure and procedure complies with the requirements of art 6, ECHR?

If an integrated structure for tribunals were to be created, the answers to these questions would be far less diverse than those that now apply to the range of existing tribunals.

Tribunals and Inquiries Act 1992

We have already seen that the Franks committee in 1957 concluded that tribunals should be regarded as machinery for adjudication and that their operation should be marked by fairness, openness and impartiality. As well as making detailed recommendations for improving existing tribunals, the committee proposed certain general reforms that were implemented by the Tribunals and Inquiries Act 1958, re-enacted in 1971 and again in 1992. By s 6 of the 1992 Act, chairmen of certain tribunals must be selected by the minister concerned from a panel of persons approved by the Lord Chancellor, but recent legislation often goes further and requires appointments of all tribunal members to be made by the Lord Chancellor. Even if a minister has power to terminate membership of a tribunal, this power can be exercised only with the concurrence in England and Wales of the Lord Chancellor, and in Scotland of the Lord President of the Court of Session (s 7). Appeals on points of law lie from certain tribunals to the High Court or the Court of Session (s 11). All tribunals are under a duty, if requested on or before the giving or notification of the decision, to give reasons for their decision (s 10).[39] In practice, many rules of procedure for particular tribunals require reasons to be given in every case.

Council on Tribunals[40]

The Tribunals and Inquiries Act 1992 continued in being the Council on Tribunals, first established under the 1958 Act. The members of the council (in number between 10 and 15) are appointed by the Lord Chancellor and the Scottish ministers (in respect of Scotland) and the council has a Scottish committee. The council is under a duty to keep under review the constitution and working of a large number of tribunals, both those named in the First Schedule to the 1992 Act and also those subsequently included by statutory instrument made by the Lord Chancellor and the Scottish ministers (s 13). The Lord Chancellor and the Scottish ministers may ask the council to consider and report on matters concerning any tribunal other than ordinary courts of law. Concerning those administrative procedures which involve a statutory inquiry, the council may itself take the initiative on a matter determined to be of special importance.[41] The council's functions are essentially advisory and consultative; it has no power to interfere with the decision of a tribunal, although it may comment on the way in which tribunals operate. The council has no executive powers: the council may make

---

[39] pp 721–2 below.
[40] Accounts of the Council include D G T Williams [1984] PL 73 and (1990) 9 CJQ 27; Harlow and Rawlings, *Law and Administration*, pp 467–71; D L Foulkes (1993) Eur Rev of Public Law (special issue) 262.
[41] Section B below.

general recommendations to the relevant minister on the appointment of tribunal members (s 5) but it has no power to make appointments.

The council makes an annual report to the Lord Chancellor and the Scottish ministers and other reports by the council may be made (s 4); the council's Scottish committee publishes an annual report. The council may take the initiative in reporting on any tribunal placed under its general supervision, but the departments concerned will not necessarily take action on its reports. The council has no rule-making powers, but it must be consulted before procedural rules are made for any tribunals subject to its supervision (s 8) or for any procedures involving a statutory inquiry (s 9). Often the council is consulted by the government on proposed legislation to create new tribunals and similar procedures,[42] but some departments are reluctant to accept the expert advice given or leave consultation until the last minute. In 1991, the Department of Health was criticised by the council, over the strange devolution of certain NHS appeals by the Health Secretary to the Yorkshire Health Authority, for 'a major failure to observe the basic principles advocated over 30 years ago by the Franks committee as to the . . . establishment of new tribunals and their procedures'.[43]

The council seeks to remind departments of the qualities of fairness, openness and impartiality which the Franks committee stressed that tribunals should possess.[44] It has neither the resources nor the power to investigate complaints about particular tribunals[45] but its members regularly visit tribunals and hearings. In 1994, the jurisdiction of the Parliamentary Ombudsman was extended to include complaints against the administrative staff of certain tribunals, but not against tribunal decisions.[46] The council has often drawn attention to excessive delays occurring in particular tribunals, for example in immigration and mental health appeals. Where a department does not accept the council's advice, the council can publish the fact in its annual report.

In 1988, the Justice/All Souls report recommended that an administrative review commission be created on the lines of the Administrative Review Council in Australia to provide independent scrutiny of all administrative procedures and to work alongside the Council on Tribunals.[47] No such commission was appointed. However, in the 1990s the council was prepared to advocate proper structures of administrative justice and to exceed its formal remit for good reason.[48]

Despite the council's efforts, it has not been able to resist the proliferation of tribunals and its work has not been brought sufficiently to the notice of Parliament. In 2001, Sir Andrew Leggatt was critical of the council's record, but he favoured its continued existence, since its primary role should be 'to act as the hub of the wheel of administrative justice, or at any rate tribunal justice'.[49] If an integrated tribunal structure were created, the council would retain oversight of decision-making by bodies that were outside that structure (such as the Civil Aviation Authority). In the longer term, the council's functions could broaden to include monitoring developments in administrative law generally.[50]

The council and its Scottish committee were created long before devolution. The Scotland Act 1998 has had a complex impact on these arrangements. The Scottish

---

[42] Report of Council on Tribunals for 1991–92, app H (Code for Consultation).

[43] Report of Council on Tribunals for 1990–91, pp 11–14. In 1995, the functions were transferred to the Family Health Service Appeal Authority.

[44] And see the model rules of tribunal procedure issued by the council in 1991: Cm 1434, 1991.

[45] See Cmnd 7805, 1980, ch 7.

[46] Parliamentary Commissioner Act 1994; and section D below.

[47] *Administrative Justice – Some Necessary Reforms*, ch 4; and cf A W Bradley [1991] PL 6.

[48] E.g. report of Council for 1995–96, pp 6–8 and app A (non-statutory inquiries); section C.

[49] *Tribunals for Users*, para 7.49.

[50] Ibid, paras 7.46–55 and 12.3. See also, on the role of the Council on Tribunals, Harris and Partington (eds), *Administrative Justice in the 21st Century*, chs 24–27.

Parliament has power to create a separate body with oversight of all tribunals and inquiries in Scotland that come within its devolved powers; a question that might then arise is whether the Scottish Ministry of Justice could also become responsible for tribunals in Scotland, including those concerned with taxation, social security, immigration and employment, that operated under legislation that was not devolved to Edinburgh. For the time being, the council and its Scottish committee are classed as 'cross-border public authorities', as their functions relate both to devolved and reserved matters.[51]

B. Public inquiries

We have seen that tribunals should be regarded as machinery for adjudication rather than as part of the machinery of administration. The same conclusion is not applicable to public inquiries, whose role is deeply embedded in the whole process of government and administration. Later we examine the attitude of the courts to inquiries in the context of natural justice.[52] Generalisation is difficult in view of the many purposes which inquiries serve, but two views on the nature of inquiries have often been expressed. As seen by the Franks committee in 1957, the 'administrative' view was to regard the inquiry as a step leading to a ministerial decision in the exercise of discretion, for which the minister was responsible only to Parliament. By contrast, on the 'judicial' view, the inquiry appeared 'to take on something of the nature of a trial and the inspector to assume the guise of a judge', so that the ensuing decision must be based directly on the evidence presented at the inquiry.[53]

The Franks committee rejected these two extreme interpretations. In the committee's view, the objects of the inquiry procedure were (a) to protect the interests of the citizens most directly affected by a governmental proposal by granting them a statutory right to be heard in support of their objections; and (b) to ensure that thereby the minister would be better informed of the whole facts of the case before the final decision was made.[54] To ensure a reasonable balance between the conflicting interests concerned, the committee recommended (1) that individuals should know in good time before the inquiry the case they would have to meet; (2) that any relevant lines of policy laid down by the government should be disclosed at the inquiry; (3) that the inspectors who conduct inquiries should be under the control of the Lord Chancellor, not of the minister directly concerned with the subject-matter of their work; (4) that the inspector's report should be published together with the letter from the minister announcing the final decision; (5) that the decision letter should contain full reasons for the decision, including reasons to explain why the minister had not accepted recommendations of the inspector; (6) that it should be possible to challenge a decision made after a public inquiry in the High Court, on the grounds of jurisdiction and procedure.[55]

With one exception, the Franks recommendations were accepted and this is reflected in the procedural rules that now apply to public inquiries. The exception was the recommendation that inspectors be transferred to the Lord Chancellor's department. This was not adopted, but the status of inspectors has changed since 1957, when

---

[51] See ch 3 B; *Tribunals for Users*, ch 11; and SI 1999 No 1319.
[52] Ch 30 B. And see generally Wraith and Lamb, *Public Inquiries as an Instrument of Government*.
[53] Cmnd 218, 1957, p 58.
[54] 'The purpose of an inquiry is two-fold: it is both to reach a rational planning decision and to allow the various parties to have their concerns heard': HC 364 (1999–2000), para 34 (Committee on Environment, Transport and Regional Affairs).
[55] Cmnd 218, 1957, part IV.

they worked in the department responsible for planning. Today, nearly 400 full-time and part-time inspectors form the Planning Inspectorate, an executive agency of the Department for Transport, Local Government and the Regions.[56]

Since its creation, the Council on Tribunals has had power to consider and report on matters arising out of the conduct of statutory inquiries. In this context, 'statutory inquiry' includes both an inquiry or hearing held by or on behalf of a minister in pursuance of a duty imposed by any statutory provision, and also what is known as a discretionary inquiry, that is, an inquiry initiated by a minister in exercise of a statutory discretion, where such an inquiry is designated for this purpose by statutory instrument.[57]

The inquiries examined by the Franks committee mostly concerned such matters as the compulsory purchase of land needed for public purposes (for example, the construction of a new town, a power station or a motorway), and disputes under planning law about the use and development of land. Inquiries and similar procedures serve many other purposes, for example to inquire into electoral boundaries[58] or to investigate the causes of a public disaster (such as a rail accident) or the failure by a local authority to maintain proper standards of care in relation to children.[59] Another form of procedure occurs when there is a right of appeal to a minister against certain decisions and the individuals concerned must be heard before the minister determines the appeal. Thus, the Director-General of Fair Trading may refuse to grant a consumer credit licence if the individual is not a fit person to hold the licence: if he or she appeals to the Secretary of State, the appeal will be heard by a panel of independent persons, but the minister retains the right to make the final decision.[60]

Rules of procedure for public inquiries

Under the Tribunals and Inquiries Act 1992, s 9, the Lord Chancellor (or the Scottish ministers, in the case of Scotland) may, after consulting the Council on Tribunals, make rules regulating the procedure at statutory inquiries. Rules have been made in respect of inquiries held for many purposes, including inquiries into compulsory purchase orders, both by ministers and by other public authorities; inquiries into the purchase of land for highway purposes; and appeals against the refusal of planning permission.[61] On a compulsory purchase of land by non-ministerial public authorities, if an inquiry is to be held the Secretary of State must give notice to the acquiring authority and those entitled to object, and may cause a pre-inquiry meeting to be held to discuss procedural matters. At least 42 days' notice of the inquiry must be given to the public authority and to every owner of an interest in the land affected who has objected to the making of the compulsory purchase order. At least 28 days before the inquiry, the public authority must send to every objector and to central departments a full statement of the reasons for the order. Both objectors and the public authority have a right to appear

---

[56] In 2000–01, the Inspectorate served English departments and the Welsh Assembly, using 70% of its resources in determining over 20,000 planning appeals. Forty-one inquiries were held by independent inspectors appointed by the Lord Chancellor. For assessment of the Inspectorate, see HC 364 (1999–2000) and, in response, Cm 4891, 2000.

[57] Tribunals and Inquiries Act 1992, s 16(1); and see SI 1975 No 1379, as amended by SI 1976 No 293, SI 1983 No 1287 and SI 1992 No 2171.

[58] Ch 9 B.

[59] See Justice/All Souls report, *Administrative Justice*, pp 312–27; S Sedley (1989) 52 MLR 469; L Blom-Cooper [1993] CLP 204 and e.g. the (Butler-Sloss) report of inquiry into child abuse, Cm 412, 1987; the report of the Ladbroke Grove rail enquiry (part 1) by Lord Cullen (June 2001); and section C.

[60] Consumer Credit Act 1974, Part III, esp ss 25, 32, 41. And see G Borrie [1982] JL of Business Law 91.

[61] See respectively SI 1994 No 3264 and SI 1990 No 512; SI 1994 No 3263; SI 2000 No 1624 and SI 2000 No 1625.

at the inquiry and to be represented, either by a lawyer or some other person. In advance of the inquiry, a written statement of evidence (and a summary) may be required from any person entitled to appear at the inquiry. Objectors must be informed of the views of any government departments which support the order, and departmental representatives are required to attend the inquiry in order that they may give evidence about departmental policy. However, the inspector may disallow a question put to such a representative if in the inspector's opinion it is 'directed to the merits of government policy'. Subject to the rules, procedure at the inquiry is determined by the inspector. The degree of formality depends on the circumstances of the inquiry, particularly the extent of legal representation. The inspector may visit the land alone before or during the inquiry, but if he or she makes a formal visit during or after the inquiry, notice must be given to the public authority and to the objectors, who have the right to be present. The inspector's report must include his or her conclusions and recommendations, if any; it will be sent to the parties when the minister's decision is notified to them.

One important rule deals with the situation where the minister, after considering the inspector's report, either differs from the inspector on a finding of fact or, after the close of the inquiry, 'takes into consideration any new evidence or new matter of fact (not being a matter of government policy)'. In such a case, if the minister proposes not to follow the inspector's recommendation because of this new material, the public authority and objectors must be informed and they have the right to require the inquiry to be reopened. The background to this lies in what was known as the chalk-pit affair:[62] after an inquiry into a controversial application to extract chalk in the Essex countryside, the department that conducted the inquiry consulted privately with the Ministry of Agriculture about a key issue, the harm that the chalk working would cause to neighbouring property. This secret consultation was defended at the time, but today such consultation would breach the inquiry rules.

In seeking to maintain the integrity of the inquiry process, the procedure rules protect all those affected by public inquiries, since the rules are enforceable in the courts and an objector is not restricted to relying on a breach of natural justice at common law.[63] But rules of natural justice, or fairness, apply to any inquiry not governed by statutory rules of procedure.[64] Although the rules define those who are entitled to statutory notice of an inquiry and to take part in it, they give the inspector a discretion to allow members of the public to appear at the inquiry. In practice, community associations and other interest groups are permitted to take part. By taking part in the inquiry such groups acquire a right to come to the court to enforce the rules of procedure.[65] Similar rules apply to many public inquiries in Scotland.[66]

Through consultation, the Council on Tribunals has taken an active part in the preparation of these rules and in seeking to secure the award of costs to those taking part in inquiries, at least for owners who successfully object to the compulsory purchase of their land. But in circumstances of serious abuse, the courts have power to give an effective remedy to an owner which the council lacks.[67] Moreover, the council has neither the powers nor the resources properly to investigate complaints about inquiries. If someone is aggrieved by the improper conduct of an inquiry, or by the

---

[62] See J A G Griffith (1961) 39 Public Administration 369; and *Buxton v Minister of Housing* [1961] 1 QB 278.

[63] Ch 30 B.

[64] *Fairmount Investments Ltd v Environment Secretary* [1976] 2 All ER 865; *Bushell*'s case, note 76 below.

[65] *Turner v Environment Secretary* (1973) 72 LGR 380.

[66] See SI 1997 No 796.

[67] For the rebuff suffered by the Council on Tribunals in the Packington Estate case, see [1966] PL 1 and Crossman, *Diaries of a Cabinet Minister*, I, pp 450–1, 456–7, 467–8, 528.

acts of the department related to the inquiry, he or she may take the complaint to the Parliamentary Ombudsman, who can conduct a full investigation into the matter.[68]

Developments in the use of public inquiries

The public inquiry continues to be part of the process by which certain decisions are made, especially those concerning the use of land for developments of environmental significance. A direct consequence of the Franks report was the greater legalisation of inquiries. Increased involvement of the legal profession in inquiries was one aspect of the pressure on the planning process that led to delays and over-centralisation of decisions on many local issues. It is not possible to summarise here the changing role of the local inquiry in the planning process under the Town and Country Planning Act 1990. One variant of the full-scale inquiry, used for examining proposed amendments to 'structure plans', is the *examination in public*, held by the planning authority before a panel appointed by the Secretary of State and which deals with such matters as the authority considers ought to be examined or as the Secretary of State directs.[69] By contrast, a district council's 'local plan' to which objections are received is subject to a public inquiry held before an inspector appointed by the Secretary of State.[70]

As regards the control of development, government policy has been to reduce delay by transferring the power to decide planning appeals from the Secretary of State to the inspectorate. All appeals in respect of applications for planning permission and all appeals against enforcement notices may be decided by an inspector;[71] however, the Secretary of State retains power to decide certain appeals and may 'call in' applications for decision.[72] An inspector's decision is subject to review in the courts, but the Secretary of State is not responsible to Parliament for it. In 2000–01, 73% of planning appeals were decided not after an inquiry but on the basis of written representations exchanged between the parties; 20% were decided after a hearing in private given to the parties; only 7% of appeals were decided after a public inquiry.[73] In making their decisions, the inspectors must take account of published ministerial policies, but it is less clear whether they should take account of government proposals to change these policies.[74]

While the transfer of power to decide planning appeals was possible because in most cases only local issues arose, the role of the inquiry in matters of national importance has often been controversial. During the 1970s, government policy in promoting motorways led to stormy scenes at inquiries, as objectors came to realise that proceedings at an inquiry might have little effect where the Department of Transport had already decided that a new motorway was needed. In 1978, a review of highway procedures made detailed proposals for improving the assessment of need for new trunk roads and for restoring public confidence in the inquiry system.[75] So far as the courts were concerned, the history of motorway inquiries culminated in *Bushell* v *Environment Secretary*.[76]

---

[68] Section D below.

[69] Town and Country Planning Act 1990 (as amended), ss 35, 35A and 35B.

[70] 1990 Act (as amended), ss 36–45. And see the Environment Department's circular 05/00.

[71] 1990 Act, Sch 6 and SI 1997 No 420.

[72] 1990 Act, s 77–79. And see the *Alconbury* case (note 78 below).

[73] For the procedure rules, see SI 2000 No 1265 (inquiries), SI 2000 No 1626 (hearings), SI 2000 No 1628 (written representations).

[74] See HC 364 (1999–2000), paras 22–25.

[75] Cmnd 7133, 1978; report of Council on Tribunals for 1977–78, p 25 and app C; also P H Levin (1979) 57 Public Administration 21.

[76] [1981] AC 75. And see *R* v *Transport Secretary, ex p Gwent CC* [1988] QB 429.

During a lengthy inquiry held concerning the M40 extension near Birmingham, the inspector allowed the objectors to bring evidence challenging estimates of future traffic growth, but refused to allow civil servants to be cross-examined on the matter. After the inquiry and before the minister took his decision, the department revised its traffic estimates, but the minister did not allow the inquiry to be reopened for examination of the new estimates. The objectors claimed that natural justice entitled them (*a*) to cross-examine officials on the traffic predictions and (*b*) to a re-opening of the inquiry. The House of Lords upheld the motorway orders, holding that natural justice had not been infringed. The judges stressed that an inquiry was quite unlike civil litigation. An inspector had wide discretion to disallow cross-examination if it would serve no relevant purpose. The methods of predicting future traffic growth were an essential element in national policy for motorways, and were not suitable for investigation at local inquiries. Lord Edmund-Davies, dissenting, held that the objectors had been denied 'a fair crack of the whip'.[77]

This decision was a reminder that a public inquiry into a controversial proposal put forward by a government department is only part of a broader political process in which the minister cannot be expected to assume a cloak of judicial impartiality. A similar reminder was given in *R (Alconbury Developments Ltd) v Environment Secretary*.[78]

A Human Rights Act challenge was made to the minister's power to determine planning appeals which, instead of being decided by an inspector, had been 'called in' to enable the minister to do so. Similar challenges were made to the minister's power to approve a compulsory purchase order under the Highways Act 1980 and a new rail link under the Transport and Works Act 1992. The claimants argued that (1) the decisions affected their civil rights; (2) by art 6(1) ECHR, such questions must be determined by an independent and impartial tribunal, failing which a decision must be subject to review by a court with full jurisdiction to consider its legality; (3) the Secretary of State was not such a tribunal and (4) there was insufficient judicial control of the decisions to satisfy art 6(1) ECHR, since the statutory appeals available did not provide for a rehearing on the merits. The House of Lords broadly approved points (1)–(3), but (reversing the Divisional Court) rejected point (4): art 6(1) ECHR did not require a court to rehear the merits of the decisions, and the statutory appeals to the High Court provided sufficient review of their legality. Lord Clyde said: 'We are concerned with an administrative process and an administrative decision. Planning is a matter for the formation and application of policy. The policy is not matter for the courts but for the executive' (para 139).

Earlier, in *Bryan v United Kingdom*,[79] the Strasbourg Court had held that no breach of art 6(1) ECHR occurred where an inspector's decision on a planning appeal was subject to an appeal to the High Court that extended to all grounds of judicial review; such control by the national court overcame the fact that the position of the inspector was not an independent court or tribunal for the purposes of art 6(1). Because of *Bryan v United Kingdom*, the challenge in *Alconbury* focused on the fact that the decisions were made by the minister, not by an inspector.

The strain placed upon the inquiry in relation to proposals of national importance has been evident in inquiries such as that conducted (exceptionally) by a High Court judge into the proposal by British Nuclear Fuels Ltd to establish a nuclear fuel reprocessing plant at Windscale,[80] the marathon inquiry conducted into the proposal by the Central Electricity Generating Board to build a PWR nuclear power station in Suffolk[81] and the even longer inquiry into the projected fifth air terminal at Heathrow.[82]

---

[77] [1981] AC at 118.
[78] [2001] 2 All ER 929. See D Elvin and J Maurici [2001] JPL 883.
[79] (1995) 21 EHRR 342, applying *Albert and Le Compte v Belgium* (1983) 5 EHRR 533.
[80] See the Parker Report 1978 and P McAuslan (1979) 2 Urban Law and Policy 25.
[81] See M Purdue et al. [1985] PL 475, [1987] PL 162; O'Riordan et al., *Sizewell B: An Anatomy of the Inquiry*.
[82] Report by R. Vandernieer QC on the Heathrow Terminal Five inquiry; and see HC Deb, 20 November 2001, col 177.

Lengthy and expensive as such inquiries are and difficult as it is for interest groups to take part, they afford a means of scrutinising in public the technical and environmental aspects of a proposal and of ventilating issues of public concern. This scrutiny may not lead to a reversal of government policies, but it would be rash to suppose that better decisions would be made if there were no public inquiries. Could the system be improved? In 1988, the government gave guidance on the procedures that should be followed for major public inquiries.[83]

Important new powers of authorising transport projects (including railway and guided transport systems) and schemes affecting harbours and canals were given to ministers by the Transport and Works Act 1992, which aimed to reduce the need for special powers to be obtained by private Acts.[84] For schemes of national significance, before the Secretary of State may make an order for a scheme, each House of Parliament must first have adopted a resolution approving the proposal. The Secretary of State may (and in some cases must) hold a public local inquiry or grant a hearing into objections to such schemes that are received, but these proceedings are held within the limits of any parliamentary approval that has been given.

In December 2001, shortly after the decision on terminal 5 at Heathrow, the government issued fresh proposals for dealing with major infrastructure projects, by which its policies would be stated in advance before an inquiry was held and approval of such projects would be a matter for Parliament.[85]

C. Tribunals of inquiry

Both tribunals and inquiries form part of the regular structure of administrative justice and many thousands of decisions are made each year by recourse to these procedures. The 'tribunal of inquiry' is a much rarer happening, only 24 having been appointed since the Tribunals of Inquiry (Evidence) Act 1921 was passed. In the 19th century, parliamentary committees were occasionally appointed to inquire into matters of concern, for example allegations of corruption among officials or politicians. The use of such committees was discredited in 1913 when a Commons committee investigated the conduct of members of the Liberal government in the Marconi Company affair and in reaching its conclusions produced three conflicting reports.[86] Under the 1921 Act, when both Houses of Parliament resolve that it is expedient that a tribunal be appointed to inquire into a matter of urgent public importance, a tribunal may be appointed by Her Majesty or by a Secretary of State. The instrument of appointment may confer on the tribunal all the powers of the High Court, or in Scotland the Court of Session, with regard to the examination of witnesses and production of documents. Where a person summoned as a witness before the tribunal fails to attend or refuses to answer any question which the tribunal may legally require to be answered, or commits any other contempt, the chairman of the tribunal may report the matter to the High Court or the Court of Session for inquiry and punishment.[87]

---

[83] See Cm 43, 1988; also Joint Circular 10/88. See now Circular 00/05, annex 4, 'Preparing for Major Planning Inquiries in England, a Code of Practice'.

[84] For the background, see HL 97 (1987–88) and Cm 1110, 1990. Also report of Council on Tribunals for 1989–90, pp 42–5, and for 1991–92, pp 44–7.

[85] See J Popham and M Purdue [2002] JPL 137 and HC Deb, 20 July 2001, col 521W.

[86] See Donaldson, *The Marconi Scandal*.

[87] See *A-G v Mulholland and Foster* [1963] 2 QB 477 (imprisonment of two journalists for refusing to disclose their sources); and ch 18 D.

Tribunals of inquiry have been appointed to investigate serious allegations of corruption or improper conduct in the public service or to investigate a matter of concern which requires thorough and impartial investigation to allay public anxiety. In the former category fall the tribunals appointed in 1936 to inquire into a leakage of Budget secrets, in 1948 to investigate bribery of ministers and civil servants, in 1957 to investigate the premature disclosure of information relating to the raising of the bank rate, in 1971 to investigate circumstances relating to the collapse of the Vehicle and General Insurance Company, and in 1978 to investigate the disastrous financial operations of the Crown Agents in 1968–74.[88] In the latter category fall the tribunal of inquiry into the Aberfan coal-tip disaster in 1966, the inquiry into the 'Bloody Sunday' shootings in Londonderry in 1972, Lord Cullen's inquiry in 1996 into the Dunblane shootings and the inquiry into abuse of children in care in North Wales.[89] In 1998 Lord Saville, together with two judges from Canada and Australia, was appointed to make a second inquiry into the 'Bloody Sunday' events. That inquiry's procedural decisions were successfully challenged by judicial review[90] and the inquiry was still taking evidence at the end of 2001.

The task of a tribunal of inquiry is to investigate certain allegations or events with a view to producing an authoritative account of the facts, attributing responsibility or blame where it is necessary to do so. Tribunals of inquiry do not make decisions as to what action should be taken in the light of their findings of fact, but they may make recommendations for such action. The chairman is normally a senior judge, assisted by one or two additional members or expert assessors. The subject-matter is presented publicly to the tribunal by senior counsel, instructed by the Treasury Solicitor, whose duty it is to call all relevant witnesses, whether or not they are suspected of impropriety. The tribunal allows witnesses to be legally represented and their costs may be met ex gratia out of public funds. There may be cross-examination of witnesses by counsel appearing at the tribunal and witnesses may be questioned by the tribunal. Because of the inquisitorial nature of the proceedings, it is difficult to provide the same facilities to a witness for answering an accusation as he or she would have in answering a criminal charge. If steps are not taken to guard against this, a witness might be inculpated on charges which had not been formulated in advance and which he or she had no chance of contesting.[91] The Attorney-General may, however, inform a witness that no criminal proceedings will be brought against him or her in respect of matters arising out of the evidence.

In 1966, a royal commission on tribunals of inquiry under the chairmanship of Salmon LJ reported that tribunals of inquiry should be appointed only in cases of vital public importance, but that it was necessary to retain the possibility of inquisitorial procedure.[92] The commission did not favour changes such as a preliminary inquiry or a subsequent right of appeal. In what have come to be known as the six Salmon 'cardinal principles', the commission laid emphasis on protecting persons whose reputations might be involved; for example, a witness should be told beforehand of any allegations affecting him or her and should be entitled to legal representation, to cross-examine those giving evidence adverse to him or her and to call relevant witnesses. Independent counsel to the tribunal should be appointed rather than using the Law Officers in this role.

---

[88] See Cmd 5184, 1936; Cmd 7616, 1948; Cmnd 350, 1957; HC 133 (1971–72); HC 364 (1981–82). And see Keeton, *Trial by Tribunal*; and Z Segal [1984] PL 206.

[89] HC 553 (1966–67); HC 220 (1971–72); Cm 3386, 1996; and HC 201 (1999–2000).

[90] See *R v Lord Saville of Newdigate, ex p A* [1999] 4 All ER 860. And B Hadfield [1999] PL 663.

[91] This criticism was made of the tribunal which investigated the collapse of the Vehicle and General Insurance Company: HC 133 (1971–72); and ch 7.

[92] Cmnd 3121, 1966.

In 1966, concern arose about the extent of press comment on the Aberfan disaster, having regard to the uncertain operation of the *sub judice* rule once the tribunal had been appointed. In 1969, a departmental committee, also chaired by Salmon LJ, examined the rules of contempt of court in relation to tribunals of inquiry.[93] When the law of contempt of court was reformed in 1981, the changes then made were in general extended to tribunals of inquiry; in particular, the proceedings of such a tribunal are deemed to be 'active' from the time at which the tribunal is appointed until its report is presented to Parliament.[94]

The public procedures of a tribunal of inquiry were not considered suitable for a review of events leading to the Falklands Islands hostilities that involved access to many secret diplomatic and intelligence documents; instead, a committee of privy councillors was appointed.[95]

Relatively few tribunals of inquiry have been appointed under the 1921 Act, but inquiries are often held under other legislation, for example into rail accidents, the collapse of large companies, or the conduct of the police or of health authorities.[96] These inquiries are often but not always conducted by a serving or retired judge. In 1963, Lord Denning's inquiry into the Profumo affair was conducted informally and with no statutory powers: the Salmon commission recommended that such inquiries should not be repeated to investigate any matter causing nation-wide concern.[97] However, in 1992 Bingham LJ completed a non-statutory inquiry into the role of the Bank of England in the collapse of BCCI; and from 1992 to 1996 Sir Richard Scott carried out his inquiry into the Matrix Churchill affair and the export of arms from Britain to Iraq.[98] Such inquiries are 'judicial' in that they are conducted by a judge. But their procedure is investigative and they have no power to compel witnesses to attend. Since they are not protected by the law of contempt of court, the subject-matter can be discussed freely in the media. In the Matrix Churchill inquiry, Sir Richard Scott was assured that if he needed them, powers under the 1921 Act would be granted; in fact, he was eventually satisfied that he had full access to all official witnesses and papers.[99] Despite abundant efforts made by the inquiry to avoid unfairness, the procedure for taking evidence orally in public received some criticism for its effect on witnesses, who could have legal assistance but not representation.[100] In Sir Richard's view, the Salmon 'principles' mentioned earlier did not apply fully to an investigatory inquiry and a balance was needed between aspects of fairness, efficiency and cost.[101] As a sequel to the Scott inquiry, the Council on Tribunals advised the Lord Chancellor on procedural issues affecting such inquiries, stressing that the Salmon 'principles' were recommendations, not rules of law, and that it was 'wholly impracticable' to devise a single set of rules to govern every inquiry.[102]

---

[93] Cmnd 4078, 1969. And see Cmnd 5313, 1973.

[94] Contempt of Court Act 1981, s 20; and see ch 18 D.

[95] Cf the abortive proposals for a joint parliamentary committee into the Rhodesian oil sanctions affair: HC Deb, 1 February 1979, cols 1709 et seq, and HL Deb, 8 February 1979, cols 849 et seq.

[96] See e.g. the (Macpherson) inquiry into the killing of Stephen Lawrence, Cm 4262, 1998; the (Kennedy) inquiry into the Bristol Royal Infirmary, Cm 5207, 2001; and the (Phillips) inquiry into the government response to BSE, HC 887 (1999–2000).

[97] Cmnd 2152, 1963; and Cmnd 3121, 1966, pp 19–21.

[98] See respectively HC 198 (1992–93) and HC 115 (1995–96) (the Scott report), on which see articles at [1996] PL 357–527; also I Leigh and L Lustgarten (1996) 59 MLR 695.

[99] Scott report, section A, ch 1.

[100] See Lord Howe [1996] PL 445; and Scott report, app A, part D. Also B K Winetrobe [1997] PL 18; L Blom-Cooper [1993] CLP 204 and [1994] PL 1; C Clothier [1996] PL 384; M C Harris [1996] PL 508; Leigh and Lustgarten, pp 694–701; and H Grant [2001] PL 377.

[101] Scott report, sections B and K, ch 1; and R Scott (1995) 111 LQR 596.

[102] Report of Council on Tribunals for 1995–96, app A.

D. The Parliamentary Ombudsman

Before the creation of the Parliamentary Ombudsman, the main safeguards for the citizen against oppressive or faulty government were the following: judicial review of administrative action, through remedies to be described in chapter 31; the right of appeal to a tribunal against an administrative decision; the opportunity of taking part in a public inquiry held before a ministry's decision was made; redress by parliamentary means with the aid of an MP; and a request for administrative review of a decision already taken. Although each of these procedures may be effective in particular situations, each has its limitations.[103] For example, many discretionary decisions affecting the individual are made without the possibility of recourse to a tribunal. Judicial review is expensive and often uncertain and is not an ideal procedure for investigating the course of official decision-making. Parliamentary procedures are not well suited to the impartial finding of facts or to the objective application of principles of good administration.

The office of Parliamentary Commissioner for Administration was created in 1967. The statutory title of the office is very cumbrous and in 1994 the government agreed that 'at the first opportunity' of legislation it would be changed to 'Parliamentary Ombudsman'.[104] Although it derived from the Ombudsman in Scandinavian countries and New Zealand,[105] the British model was designed to fit within existing British institutions, without detracting from existing remedies. While the Parliamentary Ombudsman has close links with the executive, the office is designed as an extension of Parliament; and it has virtually no links with the judicial system. As Sir Cecil Clothier, then the Ombudsman, said in 1984:

> The office . . . stands curiously poised between the legislative and the executive, while discharging an almost judicial function in the citizen's dispute with his government; and yet it forms no part of the judiciary.[106]

On one view, the essence of the Ombudsman idea for the ordinary person is accessibility, flexibility and informality. On another view, the Ombudsman provides an authoritative means of 'judging' the behaviour of officials, thus helping to maintain standards of administration that are publicly acceptable. In the British version of the Ombudsman, the latter view often seems to prevail over the former.

Status and jurisdiction[107]

The Parliamentary Ombudsman is appointed by the Crown and holds office during good behaviour, although he or she may be removed by the Crown following addresses by both Houses (s 1). By a practice dating from 1977, the government consults the chairman of the House of Commons committee on the Ombudsman before making an appointment.[108] The Ombudsman's salary is charged on the Consolidated Fund (s 2).

---

[103] Cf *The Citizen and the Administration* (the Whyatt report), ch 27 above; Cmnd 2767, 1965; and Birkinshaw, *Grievances, Remedies and the State*.

[104] See HC 619 (1993–94).

[105] On comparative aspects, see Rowat (ed.), *The Ombudsman*; Gellhorn, *Ombudsmen and Others*; Hill, *The Model Ombudsman*; Stacey, *Ombudsmen Compared*.

[106] Report for 1983 (HC 322 (1983–84)), p 1.

[107] References in the text are to the Parliamentary Commissioner Act 1967, as amended subsequently. The literature includes Gregory and Hutchesson, *The Parliamentary Ombudsman*; Seneviratne, *Ombudsmen in the Public Sector*; Harlow and Rawlings, *Law and Administration*, chs 12, 13; A W Bradley [1980] CLJ 304; C Clothier [1986] PL 204; G Drewry and C Harlow (1990) 53 MLR 745.

[108] Cmnd 6764, 1977. See HC 619 (1993–94) for the government's agreement to amend the law so that appointment by the Crown would give effect to an address by the Commons moved after consultation with the Opposition.

He or she appoints the staff of the office, subject to Treasury consent as to numbers and conditions of service (s 3). Of the seven Ombudsmen who served between 1967 and 2002, five came to the post after civil service careers and two were practising Queen's Counsel.

The main task of the Ombudsman is to investigate the complaints of private persons that they have suffered injustice in consequence of maladministration by government departments and many non-departmental public bodies in the exercise of their administrative functions (s 5). The area of jurisdiction is defined by the 1967 Act, Sch 2 of which (as amended in 1987) lists the departments and other bodies subject to investigation. This list may be amended by Order in Council (s 4), a power which is exercised when departments are abolished or created. Section 4 in its 1987 version restricts the bodies which may be entered in Sch 2 to (a) government departments; (b) bodies exercising functions on behalf of the Crown; (c) bodies established under an Act of Parliament or Order in Council or by a minister that fulfil certain criteria as to the source of their income and the power of appointment to them.[109]

The Ombudsman has no jurisdiction over authorities which are outside central government, for example, local authorities, the police and universities, although he or she may investigate complaints about the way in which central departments have discharged their functions in these fields. However, many matters are excluded from investigation for which ministers are or may be responsible to Parliament (s 5(3) and Sch 3). Thus the Ombudsman may not investigate:

(a)   action taken in matters certified by a Secretary of State to affect relations between the UK government and other governments, or international organisations;
(b)   action taken outside the UK by any officer representing or acting under the authority of the Crown;[110]
(c)   the administration of dependent territories outside the UK;
(d)   action taken by a Secretary of State under the Extradition Acts;
(e)   action taken by or with the authority of a Secretary of State for investigating crime or protecting the security of the state, including action so taken with respect to passports;
(f)   (1) the commencement or conduct of civil or criminal proceedings before any court in the United Kingdom, court martial or international court; (2) action taken by persons appointed by the Lord Chancellor as administrative staff of courts or tribunals, and being action taken on the direction or by authority of persons acting in a judicial capacity;[111]
(g)   any exercise of the prerogative of mercy;
(h)   action taken on behalf of central government by authorities in the National Health Service;
(i)   matters relating to contractual or other commercial transactions on the part of central government;[112]
(j)   appointments, discipline and other personnel matters in relation to the civil service and the armed forces, and decisions of ministers and departments in respect of other branches of the public service;
(k)   the grant of honours, awards or privileges within the gift of the Crown.

---

[109] Bodies within jurisdiction include the Arts Council, the Charity Commission, the Commission for Racial Equality, OFSTED and the utility regulators such as OFTEL and OFWAT.

[110] The acts of British consuls abroad, other than honorary consuls, are within jurisdiction, if the complainant is resident or has a right of abode in the United Kingdom: 1967 Act, s 6(5).

[111] By the Parliamentary Commissioner Act 1994, acts of the Appeals Service (note 20 above) may be investigated, although the Service is not appointed by the Lord Chancellor.

[112] This is subject to an exception for transactions relating to compulsorily purchased land and other land bought under threat of compulsory powers. But for this exception, a latter-day Crichel Down affair (ch 7) would be outside the Commissioner's jurisdiction.

In respect of each exclusion, different policy considerations arise. It was these restrictions that led to criticism that the legislation sought to carve up areas of possible grievances in an arbitrary way.[113] Those restrictions which have been most criticised are in (i) and (j) in the preceding list. The government has power by Order in Council to revoke any of these restrictions (s 5(4)), but despite frequent recommendations from the House of Commons committee that the restriction on personnel matters in (j) should be revoked, successive governments have refused to do so.[114]

Another limitation is that the Ombudsman may not normally investigate any action in respect of which the complainant has or had a right of recourse to a tribunal or a remedy by proceedings in any court of law, although he or she may do so if in a particular case the citizen could not reasonably be expected to exercise the right (s 5(2)). Thus, if an individual wishes to challenge a decision about tax or social security, he or she should appeal to the relevant tribunal. But the Ombudsman often accepts that a complainant cannot be reasonably expected to embark on the hazardous course of litigation.[115]

There is no rule that the complainant must be a British citizen, but in general he or she must either be resident in the United Kingdom or have been present in the United Kingdom or on a British ship or aircraft when the offending action occurred, or the action concerned must relate to rights or obligations arising in the United Kingdom (s 6(4)).

There is also a time bar: the Ombudsman may investigate a complaint only if it is made to an MP within 12 months from the date when the citizen first had notice of the matter complained of, except where special circumstances justify the Ombudsman in accepting a complaint made after a longer interval (s 6(3)).

It is for the Ombudsman to determine whether a complaint is duly made under the Act; in practice, many complaints identify the injustice that has been suffered more closely than the maladministration that caused it.[116] The Ombudsman has an express discretion to decide whether to investigate a complaint.[117] But the Act does not protect the Ombudsman if he or she takes up a complaint on a matter outside jurisdiction and the Ombudsman's acts are subject to judicial review, although the court is unlikely to intervene concerning his or her discretionary decisions.[118] If the Ombudsman were to act outside jurisdiction, for instance by investigating the actions of a university, no one could be held liable for obstruction or contempt for refusing to supply information (s 9). Questions as to the extent of the Ombudsman's powers may involve difficult legal issues, for example regarding the extent to which the acts of court officials may be investigated.[119]

Procedure

One important feature of the Ombudsman idea is that the Ombudsman should be accessible to the individual. But in Britain the citizen has no right to present a complaint to

---

[113] HC Deb, 18 October 1966, col 67 (Quintin Hogg MP). Cf report by Justice, *Our Fettered Ombudsman*, 1977.

[114] See e.g. HC 615, 1977–78; and Cmnd 7449, 1979.

[115] Cf *R v Commissioner for Local Administration, ex p Croydon BC* [1989] 1 All ER 1033, 1044–5.

[116] Cf *R v Local Commissioner for Administration, ex p Bradford Council* [1979] QB 287, 313.

[117] Section 5(5), 1967 Act. And see *Re Fletcher's Application* [1970] 2 All ER 527.

[118] *R v Parliamentary Commissioner for Administration, ex p Dyer* [1994] 1 All ER 375. In *R v PCA, ex p Balchin* [1998] 1 PLR 1 (Sedley J) and (*the same*) No 2 [2000] 2 LGR 87 (Dyson J), decisions by successive Ombudsmen rejecting a complaint against the Department of Transport were quashed; see P Giddings [2000] PL 201. Cf. *R v Local Commissioner for Administration, ex p Liverpool Council* [2001] 1 All ER 462.

[119] See Courts and Legal Services Act 1990, s 110 (extending jurisdiction to certain staff of courts and tribunals, but not if acting on judicial authority), and the Parliamentary Commissioner Act 1994.

the Parliamentary Ombudsman. In the first instance, a complaint must be addressed by the person who claims to have suffered injustice to an MP (s 5(1)). It is for the MP to decide whether to refer the complaint to the Ombudsman. Usually complainants will send the complaint to their constituency MP but the Act does not require this. When the Ombudsman receives a complaint from a private person that is clearly investigable, it may be sent with the complainant's agreement to his or her MP, with a statement that the Ombudsman will investigate it if the MP wishes this is to be done.[120] Although many critics would wish to see it removed in favour of direct access, the 'MP filter' was upheld by the select committee of the Commons on the Parliamentary Ombudsman in 1993.[121]

When the Ombudsman receives a complaint from an MP, it is first decided whether it falls within jurisdiction. If so, and if the Ombudsman decides to conduct an investigation, the department concerned and any person named in the complaint must be given an opportunity of commenting on any allegations made (s 7(1)). The investigation must be carried out in private (s 7(2)); normally one of the Ombudsman's staff examines the relevant department files. The Commissioner has wide powers of compelling ministers and officials to produce documents and has the same powers as the High Court in England or the Court of Session in Scotland to compel a witness to give evidence (s 8). The Ombudsman's investigation is not restricted by the doctrine of public interest immunity (s 8(3)). The only documents which are privileged are those certified by the Secretary of the Cabinet, with the approval of the Prime Minister, to relate to proceedings of the Cabinet or a committee of the Cabinet (s 8(4)).

If the investigation is carried through to the point of completion (and the present practice of the Ombudsman is to do this only if necessary to obtain an appropriate outcome),[122] the Ombudsman must send to the MP concerned a report on the investigation (s 10(1)). If the Ombudsman considers that injustice was caused through maladministration and has not been remedied, he or she may lay a special report before Parliament (s 10(3)). Such a report and other communications relating to an investigation are absolutely privileged in the law of defamation (s 10(5)). A minister has no power to veto an investigation, but may give notice to the Ombudsman that publication of certain documents or information would be prejudicial to the safety of the state or against the public interest; this notice binds the Ombudsman in making his or her report (s 11(3)).

The Ombudsman has no executive powers. Thus he or she cannot alter a departmental decision or award compensation to a citizen, although an appropriate remedy may be suggested. A minister will usually be under a strong obligation to accept the Ombudsman's findings, but a report might have such political implications that a minister could come under pressure not to accept it.[123] To support the Ombudsman in such a situation, and to watch over the office, a select committee of the Commons (the Committee on Public Administration) examines the Ombudsman's reports and takes evidence from departments that have been criticised. The committee has been more successful in helping to ensure the provision of adequate remedies and the improvement of defective procedures than in efforts to remove limits upon the Ombudsman's jurisdiction.[124] In 1993, the committee made a valuable study of the powers and work of the Parliamentary Ombudsman and the Health Service

---

[120] Report of PCA for 1978 (HC 205 (1978–79)), p 4.
[121] See HC 33–I (1993–94), pp xv–xx.
[122] Report of PCA for 2000–01 (HC 5 (2001–02)), ch 2.
[123] In 1975, the government was supported by the Commons in rejecting the Ombudsman's finding that the government had some responsibility for holidaymakers' losses arising from the collapse of the Court Line group: HC Deb, 6 August 1975, col 532.
[124] R Gregory [1982] PL 49.

Ombudsman,[125] following this in 1995 with a report on the theme of maladministration and redress.[126] In 2000, the committee reported on a wide-ranging review of public sector ombudsmen made by the Cabinet Office.[127]

The Ombudsman's casework

What is meant by the phrase, 'injustice to the person aggrieved in consequence of maladministration' (s 10(3))? No definition and no illustrations of maladministration and injustice are given in the Act. Maladministration includes such defects as 'neglect, inattention, delay, incompetence, ineptitude, perversity, and arbitrariness'.[128] Many examples of maladministration may be found in the Ombudsman's reports. They include failure to give effect to assurances given to a citizen;[129] incorrect advice about social security or tax matters; failure to give proper effect to a department's policy guidance;[130] dilatory enforcement of regulations against asbestosis;[131] failure to make departmental policy known in the press;[132] and even the making of misleading statements by a minister in Parliament.[133] In 1984, Home Office officials were criticised severely for having failed to deal promptly with complaints from a prisoner that his conviction for murder had been based on evidence from a forensic scientist whose evidence in other trials was known to be incompetent and unreliable.[134]

Even if maladministration has occurred, this does not in itself mean that injustice has thereby been caused to the individual. Conversely, injustice or hardship may exist which has been caused not by maladministration but, for example, by an Act of Parliament or a judicial decision. Injustice for this purpose means not merely injury of a kind that a court may remedy, but includes 'the sense of outrage aroused by unfair or incompetent administration, even where the complainant has suffered no actual loss'.[135]

One difficult matter has been the relation between maladministration and discretionary decisions. Unlike the New Zealand Ombudsman, who is empowered to find that a discretionary decision was wrong, the British Ombudsman may not question the merits of a discretionary decision taken without maladministration (s 12(3)). Where errors have been made in the procedures leading to a discretionary decision, the Ombudsman can report accordingly. But what if a discretionary decision has caused manifest hardship to the individual, but no identifiable defect has occurred in the procedures leading up to it? In such a case, the Ombudsman may infer an element of maladministration from the very decision itself. Similarly he has been prepared to inquire into harsh decisions which may have been based on the over-rigorous application of departmental policies.[136] A catalogue of maladministration for the 1990s prepared by Sir William Reid, Ombudsman from 1990 to 1996, includes 'unwillingness to treat the

[125] HC 33–I (1993–94). See also HC 619 (1993–94); R Gregory et al. [1994] PL 207; P Giddings and R Gregory [1995] PL 45.

[126] HC 112 and 316 (1994–95).

[127] See HC 612 (1999–2000) responding to *Review of Public Sector Ombudsmen in England*, Cabinet Office, April 2000.

[128] HC Deb, 18 October 1966, col 51 (R H S Crossman MP).

[129] See A W Bradley [1981] CLP 1, 8–11.

[130] A R Mowbray [1987] PL 570. See also A R Mowbray [1990] PL 68 and P Brown, in Richardson and Genn (note 7), ch 13 (remedies for misinformation).

[131] HC 259 (1975–76), p 189.

[132] HC 680 (1974–75).

[133] HC 498 (1974–75).

[134] HC 191 (1983–84). On the PCA's response to official delay generally, see S N McMurtrie [1997] PL 159.

[135] Both judgments in *R v PCA, ex p Balchin*, above, approved this quotation from Mr Crossman's speech to Parliament in 1966.

[136] HC 9 (1968–69); HC 350 (1967–68), and see G Marshall [1973] PL 32.

complainant as a person with rights' and 'failure to mitigate the effects of rigid adherence to the letter of the law where that produces manifestly inequitable treatment'.[137]

Two leading examples of the Ombudsman's investigations may be given. The Sachsenhausen case was the first occasion on which he found a department to be seriously at fault.[138]

> Under the Anglo-German Agreement of 1964, the German government provided £1 million for compensating UK citizens who suffered from Nazi persecution during the Second World War. Distribution of this money was left to the discretion of the UK government and in 1964 the Foreign Secretary (Mr Butler) approved rules for the distribution. Later the Foreign Office withheld compensation from 12 persons who claimed under these rules because of their detention within the Sachsenhausen concentration camp. Pressure from many MPs failed to get this decision reversed and a complaint was referred to the Ombudsman. By this time the whole of the £1 million had been distributed to other claimants. After extensive investigations, the Ombudsman reported that there were defects in the procedure by which the Foreign Office reached its decisions and subsequently defended them, and that this maladministration had damaged the reputation of the claimants. When this report was debated in the Commons, the Foreign Secretary (Mr George Brown) assumed personal responsibility for the decisions of the Foreign Office, which he maintained were correct. He nonetheless made available an additional £25,000 in order that the claimants might receive the same rate of compensation as successful claimants on the fund.[139]

At the time, the prevailing view was that the 'Butler rules' were not enforceable in law since they conferred no rights on the claimants, but on similar facts today the claimants could seek judicial review of the Foreign Office decisions, based on the legitimate expectations created by the rules.[140] In 1968, parliamentary pressure alone would not have been successful. Indeed, the Ombudsman's report was based on information about the Foreign Office decisions which parliamentary procedures could not have discovered.

The most elaborate investigation ever undertaken by the Ombudsman was into the Barlow Clowes affair, which no fewer than 159 MPs had referred to him:[141]

> In 1988, the Barlow Clowes investment business collapsed, leaving millions of pounds owing to investors, many of whom were elderly persons of modest means. The Department of Trade and Industry had licensed the business under the Prevention of Fraud (Investments) Act 1958 (which later gave way to the more rigorous Financial Services Act 1986), though there were indications that the business was not properly conducted. The Ombudsman found that there had been maladministration in five respects on the part of civil servants. As a result, the eventual losses to investors exceeded what they would have been had the department exercised its regulatory powers with a 'sufficiently rigorous and enquiring approach'.[142]

The government took the unusual course of rejecting the findings of maladministration, but nonetheless undertook ex gratia to provide £150 million to compensate investors for up to 90% of their loss. Had the investors attempted to sue the DTI in negligence, they would almost certainly have been unable to establish in law that the department owed them any duty of care.[143]

---

[137] Report of PCA for 1993, HC 290 (1993–94), p 4.
[138] HC 54 (1967–68); HC 258 (1967–68); G K Fry [1970] PL 336; and Gregory and Hutchesson (note 107), ch 11.
[139] HC Deb, 5 February 1968, cols 105–17.
[140] Ch 30 C.
[141] See PCA, HC 76 (1989–90); also HC 671 (1987–88) (the Le Quesne report); HC 99 (1989–90); and R Gregory and G Drewry [1991] PL 192, 408.
[142] HC 76 (1989–90), para 8.12.
[143] *Yuen-Kun Yeu v A-G of Hong Kong* [1988] AC 175 and *Davis v Radcliffe* [1990] 2 All ER 536; ch 31 A.

At one time, the services of the Ombudsman were not well publicised and seemed under-used. During the 1990s, the number of complaints made each year rose from 801 in 1991 to a record figure of 1,933 in 1996 before falling back slightly. In 2000–01, 1,721 new complaints were received and the Ombudsman disposed of 1,787 cases.[144] The cases proceeding to a full investigation (247) fell compared with earlier years, because the Ombudsman (Sir Michael Buckley) adopted a more flexible policy of discontinuing investigations when it became clear that the complaint was justified or that no worthwhile outcome seemed likely. Ninety-nine cases were disposed of as being clearly outside the Ombudsman's jurisdiction; 777 were disposed of on the papers. Of those in which inquiry was made of the department concerned but no investigation made, in 252 cases the outcome was negative; in 313 cases, it was positive. Of 247 cases that were fully investigated, 157 complaints were found to be justified, 69 complaints partly justified and only 21 unjustified. The department receiving most complaints (720) was Social Security (mainly in respect of the Benefits Agency or the Child Support Agency), while 214 complaints were made against the Inland Revenue.

A finding of maladministration may lead to a payment of ex gratia compensation. Thus the Benefits Agency paid a claimant who had been wrongly advised about sickness and retirement benefits nearly £37,000 for lost entitlement and £11,300 interest for late payment; where a claim for disablement benefit had been mishandled, £24,000 was paid including interest. Where there had been serious delays in the arable area payments scheme, the Ministry of Agriculture paid out £550,000 in interest payments to nearly 3,000 farmers.

The Ombudsman has no power to compel a department to provide a remedy; but where injustice caused by maladministration has not been remedied, he or she may lay a report before Parliament (s 10(3)). The first such report in 1978 led to a government decision to introduce legislation enabling the injustice to be remedied.[145] In 1995, the second such report resulted from the government's refusal to accept that the Department of Transport had acted wrongly over the planned Channel Tunnel rail link and the blight on properties in Kent affected by the plans.[146] In 1997, the department adopted a scheme for compensating certain owners which the Ombudsman considered acceptable.

The 1967 Act does not allow the Ombudsman to give publicity to an individual's complaint, but a quarterly selection of reports is published in an anonymised form. In the mid-1990s, Sir William Reid issued several reports on investigations which he considered to be of general interest: these included reports on the Department of Agriculture's deliberate decision to deprive poultry farmers of their full right to compensation and the innumerable errors made by the Child Support Agency.[147] His successor, Sir Michael Buckley, reported on a remarkable failure by Social Security to advise pensioners of a statutory change that cut the value of earnings-related retirement pensions for a surviving partner, and on the steps taken to provide redress for this.[148]

In 1994 an additional role was assumed by the Ombudsman under the code of practice on access to official information, issued under the government's policy of open government.[149] Where a department fails to make available information which should under the code be produced, the individual's complaint can be referred to the

---

[144] Report of PCA for 2000–01 (HC 5 (2001–02)).

[145] HC 598 (1977–78); Local Government, Planning and Land Act 1980, s 113; [1982] PL at pp 61–3.

[146] HC 193 (1994–95); report of PCA for 1995, HC 296 (1995–96), pp 42–5. Also HC 270 and 819 (1994–95) and HC 453 (1996–97); R James and D Longley [1996] PL 38.

[147] See HC 519 (1992–93) and HC 135 (1994–95). Also A W Bradley [1992] PL 353, [1995] PL 345; and W Reid [1993] PL 221.

[148] See HC 305 (1999–2000) and HC 271 (2000–01).

[149] See *Open Government* (Cm 2290, 1993). A revised version of the code was issued in 1997. See ch 13 F.

Ombudsman, who may deal with it as a complaint under the 1967 Act. Details of investigations made into these complaints are regularly published by the Ombudsman.

Other ombudsmen in the public sector

The Ombudsman model has been applied in other areas of government. Although complaints about the National Health Service were excluded from the jurisdiction of the Parliamentary Ombudsman, a scheme of Health Service Commissioners (Ombudsmen) for England, Wales and Scotland was later introduced.[150] Complaints about the acts of health authorities, NHS trusts and other bodies may be referred directly to the appropriate Ombudsman by a member of the public. In 1996, the jurisdiction was enlarged to include complaints against those providing primary health functions such as general medical, dental and ophthalmic services and by the removal of the statutory bar which had prevented the Ombudsman from investigating complaints about clinical judgment.[151] Many aspects of the Health Service Ombudsmen are modelled directly on the Parliamentary Commissioner Act 1967; in practice the Parliamentary Ombudsman also holds the three posts of Health Service Ombudsman, whose reports in that capacity are considered by the Commons' select committee on public administration.

As far as local government is concerned, there are Commissions for Local Administration in England and in Wales (of which the Parliamentary Ombudsman is an ex officio member) and a Commissioner for Local Administration in Scotland.[152] Again the scheme resembles the Parliamentary Ombudsman model, with certain differences. Individuals may complain to the Local Government Ombudsman for their area regarding alleged maladministration by local authorities, joint boards, police authorities and other local bodies. Since 1988, the individual has been able to complain either directly to the Ombudsman or by referring the matter to a member of the body in question, but before the Ombudsman may investigate, the complaint must have been brought to the notice of the authority in question. The complainant must specify the conduct which he or she considers to be maladministration or at least identify the action giving rise to complaint.[153] Certain matters are excluded from investigation, including complaints about action which affects all or most of the inhabitants in the local area and matters that relate to teaching, discipline and management in local authority schools. Reports on cases investigated are sent to the local authority and to the complainant. The greatest number of complaints relate to housing and town planning.[154] As with the Parliamentary Ombudsman, the local Ombudsman has no means of compelling the provision of a remedy for maladministration, although a council has power to pay compensation where the Ombudsman reports in favour of a complaint.[155] If no satisfactory response is made by the council to the Ombudsman's first report, he or she may issue a second report with a recommendation on the action that should be taken, and may require local publicity to be given to the matter.[156] A strong case may be made

[150] See the consolidating Health Service Commissioners Act 1993; also Seneviratne, *Ombudsmen in the Public Sector*, ch 3.
[151] Health Service Commissioners (Amendment) Act 1996. Even before this enlargement, the number of complaints increased from 990 in 1990–91 to 1,784 in 1995–96: report of Health Service Commissioners for 1995–96, HC 465 (1995–96).
[152] Local Government Act 1973, Part III; Local Government (Scotland) Act 1975, Part II.
[153] *R v Local Commissioner, ex p Bradford Council* [1979] QB 287.
[154] Seneviratne, (note 107), ch 3. See generally Justice, *The Local Ombudsman*; D C M Yardley [1983] PL 522; C Crawford [1988] PL 246; G Marshall [1990] PL 449.
[155] Local Government Act 1974, s 31(3), as amended.
[156] Ibid, s 31(1)–(2H), as amended by the Local Government and Housing Act 1989. In 2000–01 only two 'second reports' were issued in England: report of Commission for Local Administration for 2000–01.

for imposing a legal obligation on a council to provide a remedy in such circumstances.[157] As with the NHS, the work of the Local Government Ombudsmen has emphasised the need for councils to have in place effective complaints procedures.[158]

Although there are statutory provisions which enable the various Commissioners to cooperate with one another,[159] it would take an exceptional citizen to know how and to whom he or she could refer complaints about officialdom. One consequence of devolution to Scotland and Wales is that there is now a Scottish Parliamentary Ombudsman and a Welsh Administration Ombudsman who investigate maladministration by the devolved authorities.[160] In 2001, the Parliamentary Ombudsman held both these posts, as well as the three posts of Health Ombudsman in England, Scotland and Wales. From the individual's viewpoint, a uniform and simple right of access to all Ombudsmen is highly desirable. In April 2000, a Cabinet Office review of public sector ombudsmen in England[161] concluded that the current legislation needed a radical overhaul; integrated arrangements for complaints of maladministration should be made for central and local government, the NHS and other public bodies. Individuals should have a common right of access to the new-style ombudsmen and the 'MP filter' applying to the Parliamentary Ombudsman should disappear. There should be a collegiate body (or commission) to enable the ombudsmen to exercise a common jurisdiction, but individual ombudsmen could in practice exercise specialised roles. The commission would be answerable to Parliament and would be expected to adopt flexible working methods. The review was welcomed by the select committee on public administration,[162] but no government decision on the review had been made by March 2002.

The desire for joined-up ombudsmen is, however, not easy to satisfy in a simple way, given the increasing complexity of levels of government and forms of public administration. During the 1990s, in response to the Citizen's Charter initiative in 1991,[163] some departments appointed so-called 'lay adjudicators' to deal promptly with grievances that had not been dealt with satisfactorily by the officials concerned. Thus the Inland Revenue appointed a Revenue Adjudicator[164] and the Home Office appointed a Prisons 'Ombudsman' for England and Wales.[165] Further, by art 195 (ex art 138e) of the EC Treaty, the European Parliament appoints an Ombudsman to hear complaints from EU citizens of maladministration on the part of Community institutions, except for the Court of Justice and the Court of First Instance acting in their judicial role.

Although the concept of an ombudsman originated as a safeguard against abuses in government, in modified form it has spread to the private sector, with the building societies, banks, insurance companies and others appointing ombudsmen to deal with complaints from dissatisfied consumers.[166] In some areas, the appointment of an

[157] Cf Commissioner for Complaints Act 1969 (Northern Ireland), s 7 (power of county court to award damages). See also HC 448 (1985–86), C M G Himsworth [1986] PL 546 and Justice/All Souls Committee report, *Administrative Justice – Some Necessary Reforms*, ch 5.
[158] See Lewis, Seneviratne and Cracknell, *Complaints Procedures in Local Government*; Commission for Local Administration, *Devising a Complaints System* (1992).
[159] E.g. Local Government Act 1974, s 33; Health Service Commissioners Act 1993, s 18.
[160] See the Scotland Act 1998, s 91 and SI 1999 No 1351 (amended by SI 1999 No 1595); Government of Wales Act 1998, ss 111, 112 and Sch 10.
[161] See note 127 above.
[162] See HC 612 (1999–2000).
[163] See Cm 1599, 1991; HC 158 (1991–92). Also A W Bradley [1992] PL 353; A Barron and C Scott (1992) 55 MLR 526.
[164] See P Morris [1996] PL 309.
[165] The title is inappropriate, because of potential confusion with the Parliamentary Ombudsman: see HC 33–I (1993–94), p x.
[166] See A R Mowbray in Finnie, Himsworth and Walker (eds), *Edinburgh Essays in Public Law*, pp 315–34.

ombudsman is required to ensure that professionals deal properly with complaints from the public – as in the case of the Legal Services Ombudsman, appointed by the Lord Chancellor.[167] Finally, the fact that demarcation between the private and public sectors is becoming increasingly blurred with privatisation and the exposure of public administration to market forces, will necessarily have an impact on the ombudsman model as it has done on parliamentary modes of redress and on judicial review of administration.

[167] Courts and Legal Services Act 1990, ss 21–6; and for Scotland, see Law Reform (Miscellaneous Provisions) Act 1990, s 34.

Chapter 30

JUDICIAL CONTROL OF ADMINISTRATIVE ACTION – I

The judicial review of administrative action is an essential process if the rule of law is to be observed in a modern democracy. Whether powers are exercised directly by officials or ministers with no right of appeal, or whether there is a right of appeal to a court or tribunal against their decisions, it is salutary that all decision-makers exercising public power should know that the superior courts exercise jurisdiction over the *legality* of their decisions, on such matters as the extent of their powers and the proper observance of procedure. Certainly, judicial review is no substitute for administrative or political control of the *merits*, *expediency* or *efficiency* of decisions, and matters such as the level of expenditure that should be permitted to local councils are not inherently suitable for decision by a court.[1] But the courts can ensure that decisions made by public authorities conform to the law and that standards of fair procedure are observed.

In exercising this jurisdiction, the courts take account of the principles of administrative law that have developed from judicial decisions and also the specific legislation that applies to the subject matter. The role of the judiciary has been said to be essentially that of a football referee, the judge's task being to intervene when a breach of the rules has occurred. While the background of common law rules does not change overnight, 'Parliament, understandably and indeed inevitably, tends to lay down different rules for different situations'; the judges 'are continually being faced with the need to study, interpret and apply new versions of the rules'.[2]

The legislation that applies to public authorities is made up of many separate Acts, varying widely in the powers conferred, the agencies in whom they are vested and the extent of protection for private interests. In its operation judicial control always has a tendency to fragment into disparate branches of law, such as education, housing and immigration law. Yet general principles have emerged from numerous judicial decisions affecting public authorities and awareness of those principles is essential when specific statutes are before the court.

Judicial review of administrative action involves the judges in the task of developing legal principles against a complex and often changing legislative background. In this dynamic branch of the law, precedents must be used with care. As Lord Diplock warned in 1981: 'Any judicial statements on matters of public law if made before 1950 are likely to be a misleading guide to what the law is today.'[3] Some areas of government (such as immigration) give rise to many more cases of judicial review than others, and it has been said that judicial review of administrative action 'is inevitably sporadic and peripheral' when set against the entire administrative process.[4] But the general principles which emerge from the judicial process should not be haphazard, incoherent or contradictory.[5]

---

[1] *R v Environment Secretary, ex p Hammersmith Council* [1991] 1 AC 521; p 662.
[2] *R v Environment Secretary, ex p Hammersmith Council* at 561 (Lord Donaldson MR).
[3] *R v IRC, ex p National Federation of Self-Employed* [1982] AC 617, 640.
[4] De Smith, Woolf and Jowell, *Judicial Review of Administrative Action*, p 3.
[5] For a perceptive critique of the underlying theories, see D J Galligan (1982) 2 OJLS 257.

The legal solution to many administrative disputes inevitably involves some form of judicial discretion. Even if the relevant principles are clear, their application to a particular dispute is seldom clear-cut. This fact, taken with the political impact that a judicial decision may have when it concerns the policy of a minister or large local authority, may lead to criticism of the judges for political bias.[6] A prominent instance of this occurred in 1981, when the cheap fares policy for London of the (Labour) Greater London Council (GLC) was challenged in the courts by the (Conservative) Bromley Council. Some extravagant language was used by two judges in the Court of Appeal (Lord Denning MR and Watkins LJ) in condemning the actions of the GLC, but that court's decision was upheld in more restrained terms by a unanimous House of Lords.[7] During the 1990s, many cases of judicial review arose to a greater or lesser extent out of political controversy, but it is fundamental that the judges should decide such cases on legal grounds, not for reasons relating to the judge's own political views. The landmark decision in *M v Home Office*[8] that the Conservative Home Secretary (Kenneth Baker) was in contempt of court concerning the removal from Britain of a Zairean asylum seeker may have affected his political standing: but the decision owed nothing to party political factors and everything to what the judges considered should be the proper relationship between the executive, the courts and the individual and the authority that the courts must have in that evolving relationship.

This chapter outlines the grounds on which the courts exercise the function of judicial review.[9] Some are of long standing in the common law, such as the rule against bias and the right to a fair hearing, others are still being developed, such as proportionality and legitimate expectations. Before we consider these grounds, three preliminary matters must be mentioned.

First, the foundations of judicial review have been the subject of vigorous scholarly debate.[10] It is accepted by both sides in the debate that the grounds of judicial review were developed by the judges within the common law and have never been the subject of comprehensive legislation. Nonetheless, one side of the debate holds that judicial review is founded on the presumption that whenever it legislates, Parliament intends statutory powers to be exercised according to the principles of judicial review. The argument is that a key ground of judicial review, namely the ultra vires rule as broadly understood, implies that all grounds of review have developed through statutory interpretation and depend on the presumed intention of Parliament. The opposing side in the debate denies that the ultra vires rule is the foundation of judicial review, arguing that it is wrong to found judicial review on a fiction, namely the intent of Parliament, since the grounds of judicial review are judge-made: hence, the courts' authority is not derived from Parliament but, under the rule of law, is coordinate with the authority of Parliament. Positions have shifted since the debate began and the common ground has increased, but it is difficult to see why a debate about the foundations of judicial review should become a debate about the supremacy of Parliament. It is not contended by either side that Parliament has no authority to legislate on the scope of judicial review.

---

[6] E.g. Griffith, *The Politics of the Judiciary*, chs 3–7.

[7] *Bromley Council v Greater London Council* [1983] AC 768; and see the sequel *R v London Transport Executive, ex p GLC* [1983] QB 484. Also J Dignan (1983) 99 LQR 605; H Sales [1991] PL 499.

[8] [1994] 1 AC 377.

[9] For the procedure of judicial review, see ch 31.

[10] The articles include D Oliver [1987] PL 543, C Forsyth [1996] CLJ 122, P Craig [1998] CLJ 63 and M Elliott [1999] CLJ 129; all appear, with other articles, in Forsyth (ed.) *Judicial Review and the Constitution*. Also Elliott, *The Constitutional Foundations of Judicial Review*; PA Joseph [2001] PL 354; P Craig and N Bamforth [2001] PL 763.

The second matter relates to the classification of the grounds of judicial review. In the GCHQ case in 1984, Lord Diplock classified the grounds on which administrative action is subject to judicial control under three heads, namely illegality, irrationality and procedural impropriety; he accepted that further grounds (for example, proportionality) might be added as the law developed.[11] In 1986, the President of the New Zealand Court of Appeal commented that 'the substantive principles of judicial review are simply that the decision-maker must act in accordance with law, fairly and reasonably'.[12] This is an admirable summary of the policy behind the law, but a great deal needs to be known about the meaning attached to each of its three strands if it is to serve as a guide to decision-making.

Third, we must note the impact of the Human Rights Act 1998.[13] By s 6(1) of the Act, it is unlawful for public authorities (except where they are required to do so by primary legislation) to act in a way which is incompatible with Convention rights. Thus, the existing grounds of judicial review were joined by a ground of great breadth, namely acting inconsistently with a Convention right. Further, by ss 7–8 of the 1998 Act, judicial review serves as a residual procedure for the protection of Convention rights.

A. Judicial review on substantive grounds

This section is concerned with grounds of review relating to the substance or content of the official decision or action that is under review; grounds relating to the procedure by which a decision was made are considered in the following section. Although the emphasis is on English law, the principles of judicial review in the law of Scotland are very similar.[14]

The ultra vires rule (excess of powers)

When a power vested in a public authority is exceeded, acts done in excess of the power are invalid as being ultra vires. The ultra vires doctrine cannot be used to question the validity of an Act of Parliament; but it serves to control those who exceed the powers which an Act has given. The simplest instance of the rule is where a local council, whose capacity to act and to regulate private activities is derived from statute, acts outside the scope of that authority. Two examples may be given.

In R v *Richmond upon Thames Council, ex p McCarthy and Stone Ltd*, a local planning authority began charging a fee of £25 for informal consultations between its planning officers and developers intending to seek planning permission for new development. The council was required by law to determine all applications for planning permission that were made, whether or not such informal consultations had been held. *Held*, by the House of Lords, while it was conducive or incidental to the council's planning functions that its officers should have informal consultations with intending developers, the fee of £25 was not lawful, since making such a charge was not incidental to those functions. The House applied the principle that no charge on the public can be levied by a public body without clear statutory authority.[15]

In *Hazell* v *Hammersmith and Fulham Council*, the local authority (as other councils had done) in 1983 established a fund for conducting transactions in the capital money market, by which the council could benefit from future movements in interest rates. These transactions

---

[11] *CCSU v Minister for Civil Service* [1985] AC 374, 410; cf p 414 (Lord Roskill).
[12] Sir Robin Cooke, in Taggart (ed.), *Judicial Review of Administrative Action in the 1980s*, p 5.
[13] See also text at notes 112–15 below.
[14] See *Stair Memorial Encyclopedia of the Laws of Scotland*, vol 1, Administrative Law (reissue, 2000) and Clyde and Edwards, *Judicial Review*.
[15] [1992] 2 AC 48.

included interest rate swaps, options to make such swaps, forward rate agreements and so on. If interest rates fell, the council would benefit; in fact, rates went up and large capital losses were made by the council. In a second stage of the policy, the council made further swaps, but solely to limit the extent of its losses while extricating itself from the market. The district auditor applied for a declaration that all the transactions were unlawful. *Held*, by the House of Lords, a local council had no power to enter into interest swap transactions, which by their nature involved speculation in future interest rates, since they were inconsistent with the statutory borrowing powers of the council and were not 'conducive or incidental to' those powers.[16]

As these cases illustrate, the powers of an authority include not only those expressly conferred by statute but also those which are reasonably incidental to those expressly conferred.[17] While it was held to be within the management powers of a housing authority to enable its tenants to insure their household goods with a particular insurance company,[18] a council's implied powers do not protect what on other grounds is objectionable.

In *Crédit Suisse* v *Allerdale Council*, the council set up a company to provide a leisure pool complex (which was plainly within the council's powers) together with time-share accommodation (which eventually was held not to be); since the council was restricted from itself borrowing the necessary capital, it guaranteed repayment of a loan of £6 million made by the plaintiff bank to the company. The company did not earn enough from selling time-shares to repay the loan. *Held*, the guarantee was void and unenforceable, as the Local Government Act 1972 had established a comprehensive code of borrowing powers. The project was 'an ingenious scheme designed to circumvent the no doubt irksome controls imposed by central government'.[19]

Decisions such as these created much uncertainty relating to the private funding of new developments by local councils. In 1997, Parliament widened the power of councils to enter into contracts for the provision of assets, services and goods and associated finance and authorised councils to certify certain contracts as being within their powers.[20] The ultra vires rule itself applies to all public authorities, but its application in any particular case necessarily depends on the powers vested in the public body. Government departments benefit from the rule that the Crown as a legal person is not created by statute and has capacity at common law to own property, enter into contracts, employ staff etc.[21] However, a department that is exercising statutory powers of regulation may not use them so as to conflict with other statutes or exceed its powers in other ways.

In *R* v *Social Security Secretary, ex p Joint Council for the Welfare of Immigrants*[22] the minister had power under the Social Security Contributions and Benefits Act 1992 to make regulations regarding eligibility for income support. To discourage asylum seekers from coming to the United Kingdom, the minister made regulations that barred certain asylum seekers from receiving income support, although they were entitled to remain in the country while their appeals under the Asylum and Immigration Appeals Act 1993 were determined.

---

[16] [1992] 2 AC 1; and see M Loughlin [1990] PL 372, [1991] PL 568.
[17] In the case of local authorities, see Local Government Act 1972, s 111; Local Government (Scotland) Act 1973, s 69.
[18] *A-G* v *Crayford UDC* [1962] Ch 575.
[19] [1997] QB 306 (Neill LJ); and see *Crédit Suisse* v *Waltham Forest Council* [1997] QB 362.
[20] Local Government (Contracts) Act 1997: certification does not protect a contract from judicial review, but the court may for certain reasons determine that a certified contract that would otherwise be ultra vires should have effect in law.
[21] See B V Harris (1992) 108 LQR 626.
[22] [1996] 4 All ER 385. For other unlawful decisions by ministers, see *Laker Airways Ltd* v *Department of Trade* [1977] 1 QB 643 (GR Baldwin [1978] PL 57); *R* v *Transport Secretary, ex p Richmond Council* [1994] 1 All ER 577; and *R* v *Foreign and Commonwealth Secretary, ex p Bancoult* [2001] QB 1067.

The Court of Appeal held, by 2–1, that the regulations would, for some asylum seekers, render nugatory their appeal rights; as they conflicted with the 1993 Act, the regulations were ultra vires.

Nor may a department incur expenditure which does not meet the relevant conditions imposed by Parliament.[23] When a public body's conduct is challenged as ultra vires or contrary to statute, the court's attention focuses on the Act which is claimed to be the source of its authority. Often an answer is found by interpreting that Act. But the process of judicial review is not a narrow exercise in statutory interpretation. One reason for this is that acts taken under the prerogative or from another non-statutory source may themselves be subject to judicial review.[24] A second reason is that many statutes confer broad discretion on public authorities; judicial control of such discretion, to which we now turn, goes well beyond the process of statutory interpretation.[25]

Abuse of discretionary powers[26]

We have already seen that the concept of a discretion involves the possibility of choosing between several decisions or courses of action, each of which may be lawful.[27] However, in exercising a discretion, an official or public body may (intentionally or inadvertently) make a decision or embark on action which the court considers to be unlawful. For centuries, the courts have supervised such decisions.[28] While the court will not substitute its own decision for the decision made by the official or body to whom the law entrusts the discretion, it may intervene where a discretion appears not to have been lawfully exercised. It is settled law that, even if the language of a statute seeks to confer an absolute discretion, the courts will be very reluctant to hold that their power to review the action taken is excluded. The attitude of the courts to claims that a minister has unfettered discretion is shown in *Padfield* v *Minister of Agriculture*.

> Under the Agricultural Marketing Act 1958, the milk marketing scheme included a complaints procedure by which a committee of investigation examined any complaint made about the operation of the scheme 'if the Minister in any case so directs'. Padfield, a farmer in south-east England, complained about the prices paid to farmers in that region by the Milk Marketing Board. The minister refused to direct that the complaint be referred to the committee of investigation, and claimed that he had an unfettered discretion in deciding whether or not to refer such complaints. *Held*, the minister would be directed to deal with the complaint according to law. The reasons given by the minister for his refusal were not good reasons in law and showed that he had not exercised his discretion in a manner which promoted the intention and objects of the Act of 1958. 'The policy and objects of the Act must be determined by construing the Act as a whole, and construction is always a matter of law for court'.[29]

This decision was also significant in that the judges, after examining the reasons given by the Minister of Agriculture to see whether they conformed to the Act, were

---

[23] *R v Foreign Secretary, ex p World Development Movement* [1995] 1 All ER 611.

[24] See *CCSU v Minister for the Civil Service* [1985] AC 374; *R v Panel on Take-overs, ex p Datafin plc* [1987] QB 815.

[25] J Jowell and A Lester [1987] PL 368.

[26] See de Smith, Woolf and Jowell, *Judicial Review of Administrative Action*, ch 6; Wade and Forsyth, *Administrative Law*, chs 11, 12; Craig, *Administrative Law*, chs 16, 17. And see Galligan, *Discretionary Powers*.

[27] See ch 27, text at notes 61–4.

[28] See e.g. *Rooke*'s case (1598) 5 Co Rep 99b: ' "Discretion" means . . . that something is to be done according to the rules of reason and justice, not according to private opinion.'

[29] [1968] AC 997, 1030 (Lord Reid). In *R v Environment Secretary, ex p Spath Holme Ltd* [2001] 2 AC 349, 396, Lord Nicholls said: 'The discretion given by Parliament is never absolute or unfettered.'

prepared to assume that he had no better reasons for his decision. The willingness of the judges to impose limits upon the minister's discretion in *Padfield* matches the way in which they have frequently cut down the width of local authority discretions. Thus a local planning authority may grant planning permission 'subject to such conditions as they think fit', but the courts have severely limited the apparent width of this power.[30]

The distrust of excessive discretion explains why even the Home Secretary's power to refuse naturalisation to an alien without giving reasons is subject to a procedural requirement of fairness;[31] and why a power to grant what would otherwise be a 'conclusive' certificate may be reviewed if the power is inconsistent with Community law.[32] In the past the courts were readier to accept that executive discretion was immune from judicial review than they are today. An extreme instance of the courts' refusal to review executive discretion arose during the Second World War: in *Liversidge* v *Anderson*,[33] the House of Lords, Lord Atkin dissenting, held that the power of the Home Secretary to detain anyone whom he had reasonable cause to consider to be of hostile origin or association was a matter for executive discretion and that the courts must accept a statement by the Home Secretary that he believed he had cause to order the detention. This is an example of extreme judicial deference to executive decision-making, best explained by the context of wartime.

We now consider various grounds on which the exercise of discretion may be reviewed by the courts. In practice, these grounds may overlap and a poorly reasoned decision may be defective on several grounds.[34]

1 *Irrelevant considerations.* Powers are not lawfully exercised if the decision-maker takes into account factors that in law are irrelevant or leaves out of account relevant matters. Thus the Home Secretary acted unlawfully when, in deciding whether it was justified to release from prison two young men who as children had been convicted of murder, he took into account an irrelevant matter (public petitions demanding that the murderers be imprisoned for life) and refused to take account of a relevant matter (their progress and development in detention).[35] A decision to award a council house to a councillor, enabling her to get ahead of others on the housing list, was unlawful, having been influenced by the view of the chairman of the housing committee that it would help her to be re-elected.[36] Where rates of over £50,000 had been overpaid to a council on an unoccupied warehouse, the council did not lawfully exercise its statutory discretion to refund overpaid rates when it refused to do so for reasons which the House of Lords held to be irrelevant and in disregard of the statutory purpose of the discretion.[37]

The court's power to rule that certain considerations are irrelevant may severely limit the scope of general words in a statute,[38] but the courts do not always interpret statutory discretion narrowly.[39] The converse of the proposition that an authority must

---

[30] E.g. *Hall and Co Ltd* v *Shoreham-by-Sea UDC* [1964] 1 All ER 1; *R* v *Hillingdon Council, ex p Royco Homes Ltd* [1974] QB 720.

[31] *R* v *Home Secretary, ex p Fayed* [1997] 1 All ER 228.

[32] E.g. *Case C-222/84 Johnston* v *Chief Constable, RUC* [1987] QB 129.

[33] [1942] AC 206. See R F V Heuston (1970) 86 LQR 33, (1971) 87 LQR 161; Simpson, *In the Highest Degree Odious.*

[34] See e.g. *R* v *Home Secretary, ex p Venables* [1998] AC 407.

[35] Ibid.

[36] *R* v *Port Talbot Council, ex p Jones* [1988] 2 All ER 207.

[37] *R* v *Tower Hamlets Council, ex p Chetnik Developments Ltd* [1988] AC 858.

[38] See e.g. *Mixnam's Properties Ltd* v *Chertsey UDC* [1965] AC 735 (G Ganz (1964) 27 MLR 611).

[39] E.g. *Roberton* v *Environment Secretary* [1976] 1 All ER 689 (risk of assassination of Prime Minister relevant to diversion of footpath on Chequers Estate); *R* v *Westminster Council, ex p Monahan* [1990] 1 QB 87 (relevant to permission for office development near Covent Garden that profits would fund improvements in opera house).

not take into account irrelevant considerations is that it must take into account relevant considerations. However, to invalidate a decision it is not enough that considerations have been ignored which *could* have been taken into account: it is only when the statute 'expressly or impliedly identifies considerations *required to be taken into account* by the authority as a matter of legal obligation' that a decision will be invalid because relevant considerations were ignored.[40] Thus there are factors which the decision-maker *may* take into account, but need not do so.[41] While it is for the court to rule whether particular factors are relevant or irrelevant and whether they were taken into consideration, it is for the decision-maker to decide what weight to give to a relevant consideration that is taken into account.[42]

2 *Improper purposes.* The exercise of a power for an improper purpose is invalid. Improper purposes include malice or personal dishonesty on the part of the officials making the decision, but examples of this kind are rare. Most instances of improper purpose have arisen out of a mistaken interpretation by a public authority of its powers, sometimes contributed to by an excess of zeal in the public interest. Thus a city council which was empowered to buy land compulsorily for the purpose of extending streets or improving the city could not validly buy land for the purpose of taking advantage of an anticipated increase in value of the land.[43] In *Congreve* v *Home Office*, where the Home Office had threatened certain holders of television licences that their licences would be revoked by the Home Secretary if they did not each pay an extra £6, the Court of Appeal held that it was an improper exercise of the Home Secretary's power of revocation 'to use a threat to exercise that power as a means of extracting money which Parliament had given the Executive no mandate to demand'.[44] In *Porter* v *Magill*,[45] it was held unlawful for the Conservative majority on the Westminster council to adopt a policy of selling council houses in certain parts of the city in the belief that home owners were more likely than council tenants to vote Conservative. The House of Lords accepted that councillors are elected and in due course may stand for re-election, but stressed that a council's powers must be used for the purposes for which they were conferred, not to promote the electoral advantage of a political party.

Difficulty arose in an earlier case from Westminster when the council was motivated both by lawful and unlawful purposes.

The Westminster Corporation was empowered to provide public conveniences but not pedestrian subways. Underground conveniences were designed so that the subway leading to them provided a means of crossing a busy street. It was sought to stop the scheme on the ground that the real object was the provision of a crossing and not public conveniences. The court refused to intervene. 'It is not enough to show that the corporation contemplated that the public might use the subway as a means of crossing the street. In order to make out a case of bad faith, it must be shown that the corporation constructed the subway as a means of crossing the street under colour and pretence of providing public conveniences not really wanted.'[46]

---

[40] *CREEDNZ Inc* v *Governor-General* [1981] 1 NZLR 172, 183 (Cooke J) (emphasis supplied), approved in *Re Findlay* [1985] AC 318, 333.

[41] See *R* v *Somerset CC, ex p Fewings* [1995] 3 All ER 20, at 32 (Simon Brown LJ). (By 2–1, ban on hunting deer on council's land held unlawful as council had not based ban on its powers of land management; but belief that deer hunting was cruel was not necessarily an irrelevant consideration.)

[42] *Tesco Stores* v *Environment Secretary* [1995] 2 All ER 636; *R* v *Cambridge Health Authority, ex p B* [1995] 2 All ER 129.

[43] *Municipal Council of Sydney* v *Campbell* [1925] AC 338. In *Crédit Suisse* v *Allerdale Council* (above), the scheme was designed to evade a statutory borrowing restriction.

[44] [1976] QB 629, 662 (Geoffrey Lane LJ).

[45] [2002] 2 WLR 37. See also *R* v *Lewisham Council, ex p Shell UK Ltd* [1988] 1 All ER 938.

[46] *Westminster Corpn* v *London and North Western Railway Co* [1905] AC 426, 432 (Lord Macnaghten); cf *Webb* v *Minister of Housing* [1965] 2 All ER 193.

In such cases a distinction has sometimes been drawn between purpose and motive, so that where an exercise of power fulfils the purposes for which the power was given, it matters not that those exercising it were influenced by an extraneous motive. But the motive–purpose distinction is difficult to maintain and it has sometimes given way to the test of what was the dominant purpose or to the rather stricter rule, already outlined, that the presence of any extraneous or irrelevant considerations invalidates the decision.[47]

3 *Error of law.* An authority which is entrusted with a discretion must direct itself properly on the law or its decision may be declared invalid.

> In *R* v *Home Secretary, ex p Venables*, the Home Secretary increased from 10 to 15 years the 'tariff period' which two young murderers would have to serve before being considered for release. The Home Secretary stated that young offenders sentenced to detention during Her Majesty's pleasure would be dealt with on the same basis as adult offenders on whom mandatory life sentences had been imposed. *Held*, by 3–2, the Home Secretary by this statement misdirected himself in law. 'His legal premise was wrong: the two sentences are different. A sentence of detention during Her Majesty's pleasure requires the Home Secretary to decide from time to time . . . whether detention is still justified. The Home Secretary misunderstood his duty. This misdirection by itself renders his decision unlawful.'[48]

So too, where a county council decided to ban deer hunting over its land, but without considering the extent of its powers, the policy was quashed.[49] Decisions such as these illustrate Lord Diplock's statement that 'the decision-maker must understand correctly the law that regulates his decision-making power and must give effect to it'.[50]

The notion of error of law goes wider than a mere mistake of statutory interpretation. A minister commits an error of law if (inter alia) he or she acts when there is no evidence to support the action or comes to a conclusion to which, on the evidence, he or she could not reasonably have come.[51] These principles were highlighted in 1976 when a Labour Secretary of State and a Conservative council clashed over the re-organisation of secondary education.

> Under the Education Act 1944, s 68 (now s 496 of the Education Act 1996), if the Secretary of State was satisfied that an education authority was proposing to act unreasonably, he or she could issue such directions to the authority as appeared expedient. When in May 1976 the newly elected Tameside council proposed, contrary to an earlier plan, to continue selection for entry to five grammar schools in the coming September, the Secretary of State directed the council to adhere to the earlier plan. The House of Lords refused to enforce this direction, holding that it was valid only if the Secretary of State had been satisfied that no reasonable authority could act as the council was proposing to. 'Unreasonable' in s 68 did not mean conduct which the Secretary of State thought was wrong. On the facts, there was no material on which the Secretary of State could have been satisfied that the council was acting unreasonably. He must therefore have misdirected himself as to the grounds on which he could act.[52]

Reliance on error of law as a ground for controlling discretion places the courts in a position of strength vis-à-vis the administration since it is peculiarly for the courts to identify errors of law. As the *Tameside* case indicated, error of law is a sufficiently

---

[47] De Smith, Woolf and Jowell, op cit, pp 340–6.
[48] *R* v *Home Secretary, ex p Venables* [1998] AC 407, 518–19 (Lord Steyn).
[49] *R* v *Somerset CC, ex p Fewings* [1995] 3 All ER 20.
[50] *Council of Civil Service Unions* v *Minister for the Civil Service* [1985] AC 374, 408.
[51] *Edwards* v *Bairstow* [1956] AC 14; applied to ministers' decisions in *Ashbridge Investments Ltd* v *Minister of Housing* [1965] 3 All ER 371; *Coleen Properties Ltd* v *Minister of Housing* [1971] 1 All ER 1049. On error of law generally, see J Beatson (1984) 4 OJLS 22. See also note 108 below.
[52] *Education Secretary* v *Tameside Council* [1977] AC 1014 (D Bull (1987) 50 MLR 307).

pliable concept to enable the judges, if they feel it is necessary, to make a very close scrutiny of the reasons for a decision and the facts on which it was based. We consider later in this chapter whether it is now a general rule that a tribunal which makes an error of law in reaching a decision must be held to be exceeding its jurisdiction.

4 *Unauthorised delegation.*   A body to which the exercise of discretion has been entrusted by statute may not delegate the exercise of that discretion to another person or body unless the statute can be read as having authorised such delegation. In general, a statute that authorises one level of delegation does not thereby authorise further delegation. In *Barnard* v *National Dock Labour Board*, the national board lawfully delegated disciplinary functions over registered dockers to local boards; a local board acted unlawfully when it sub-delegated the power to suspend dockers to the port manager.[53]

The rule against unauthorised delegation of powers might seem to require all powers vested in a minister to be exercised by him or her personally. However, in the case of central government the courts have accepted that powers and duties conferred on a minister may properly be exercised by officials for whom the minister is responsible to Parliament or by a junior minister.[54] But where a statutory duty is vested in one minister, he or she may not adopt a policy by which the decision is effectively made by another minister.[55] And, where a discretion is vested in a subordinate officer, it may not be taken away by orders from a superior.[56] Similar principles apply to statutory agencies. Thus the Police Complaints Board could not adopt a rule of taking no action on complaints which the Director of Public Prosecutions had decided should not lead to criminal proceedings;[57] but the Commission for Racial Equality might delegate to its staff the task of conducting formal investigations into alleged discrimination.[58] In local government, there is now wide authority for councils to delegate their functions to committees, sub-committees and officers.[59]

5 *Discretion may not be fettered.*   Public bodies often exercise discretion in deciding whether to grant a benefit sought by an individual – be it planning permission, licence, grant of money or admission to a school – or to impose a penalty (such as revoking a licence or excluding a pupil for misconduct). In law, the body must consider the matter on its merits, including the individual circumstances. But it is impossible to assess the merits of a particular case without considering general matters, such as any relevant standards or policies or decisions made in earlier cases. The exercise of discretion must not be prejudged or fettered by a binding rule. The decision-maker may adopt a general policy and indicate that it will be applied in the absence of exceptional circumstances,[60] but may not have a rule that certain applications will always be refused.[61]

---

[53] [1953] 2 QB 18. And e.g. *Young* v *Fife Regional Council* 1986 SLT 331.
[54] *Carltona Ltd* v *Commissioners of Works* [1943] 2 All ER 560; *Re Golden Chemical Products* [1976] Ch 300. See also *R* v *Home Secretary, ex p Oladehinde* [1991] 1 AC 254; D Lanham (1984) 100 LQR 587; *R* v *Home Secretary, ex p Doody* [1994] 1 AC 531, 566 (power of Home Secretary to determine penal element of life sentence for murder); and ch 13 D.
[55] *Lavender & Son Ltd* v *Minister of Housing* [1970] 3 All ER 871.
[56] *Simms Motor Units Ltd* v *Minister of Labour* [1946] 2 All ER 201.
[57] *R* v *Police Complaints Board, ex p Madden* [1983] 2 All ER 353.
[58] *R* v *Commission for Racial Equality, ex p Cottrell & Rothon* [1980] 3 All ER 265.
[59] Local Government Act 1972, s 101; Local Government (Scotland) 1973, s 56.
[60] *R* v *Torquay Licensing Justices, ex p Brockman* [1951] 2 KB 784.
[61] *R* v *Port of London Authority, ex p Kynoch* [1919] 1 KB 176, 184 (dictum of Bankes LJ). See D J Galligan [1976] PL 332 and *R* v *Police Complaints Board, ex p Madden*, note 57. See *R* v *Home Secretary, ex p Venables* [1998] AC 407 (Home Secretary's discretion fettered by rigid policy of ignoring child's development in prison) and *R* v *Home Secretary, ex p Hindley* [2001] 1 AC 410 (Home Secretary prepared to reconsider decision on whole life tariff at any time).

These principles apply to the exercise of discretionary powers vested in government departments. In practice, it is often essential that departments should formulate policies and apply them.

> Under a scheme for discretionary investment grants to industry, the Board of Trade applied a rule that grants could not be paid in respect of items costing less than £25 and refused to pay a grant to a firm which had spent over £4 million on gas cylinders costing £20 each: the House of Lords accepted that the department was entitled to make such a rule or policy, provided that it was prepared to listen to arguments for the exercise of individual discretion.[62]

In such a case, individuals may find it very difficult to persuade officials that they should receive preferential treatment. Their right might be more realistically described as a right to ask that the general policy should be changed.[63] Even so, the courts could be readier than they are to hold that public authorities are entitled to adopt definite policies without this interfering with the proper exercise of discretion.[64] Thus, as regards discretionary awards for further and higher education, local authorities have found it difficult to reconcile budgetary constraints with the need for fair and consistent treatment of individuals.[65]

6 *Breach of a local authority's financial duties.* One controversial ground of review in local government is that councils are expected to observe due standards of financial responsibility to local taxpayers. In *Roberts v Hopwood*, the House of Lords held invalid a decision by the Poplar council in 1923 to pay a minimum wage of £4 per week to all adult employees, regardless of the work which they did, their sex and the falling cost of living; the judges considered that the council had exceeded its power to pay such wages as it saw fit, by making gifts or gratuities to its staff which it had no power to do.[66] Fifty years later, the principle that local authorities owe a fiduciary duty to their ratepayers in financial management was prominent in *Bromley Council v Greater London Council*.[67] The House of Lords held that the Greater London Council must exercise its powers in relation to London transport with due regard to business principles; the decision that fares be cut by 25% had caused a big increase in the subsidy payable by ratepayers and a sharp loss in rate support grant paid from central government. The council was thus in breach of the fiduciary duty which it owned to London ratepayers. However, a modified scheme of subsidy for London fares later survived legal challenge.[68] In *Pickwell v Camden Council* the court accepted as lawful a local pay settlement made by the council during national strikes which was more favourable to workers in Camden than was the national settlement.[69]

7 *Unreasonableness (irrationality).* A judge may not on judicial review set aside an official decision merely because he or she considers that the matter could have been decided differently. Judicial review does not provide a right to appeal on the merits of

---

[62] *British Oxygen Co v Board of Trade* [1971] AC 610. And see *Cumings v Birkenhead Corpn* [1972] Ch 12.

[63] *British Oxygen Co v Board of Trade* at 631 (Lord Dilhorne).

[64] Cf *A-G ex rel Tilley v Wandsworth BC* [1981] 1 WLR 854 and *R v Rochdale BC, ex p Cromer Ring Mill Ltd* [1982] 3 All ER 761.

[65] E.g. *R v Warwick CC, ex p Collymore* [1995] ELR 217; *R v London Borough of Bexley, ex p Jones* [1995] ELR 42.

[66] [1925] AC 578. And see *Prescott v Birmingham Corpn* [1955] Ch 210.

[67] [1983] AC 768.

[68] *R v London Transport Executive, ex p GLC* [1983] QB 484.

[69] [1983] QB 962 (and C Crawford [1983] PL 248). See to opposite effect, *Allsop v North Tyneside Council* (1992) 90 LGR 462.

the decision. However, a decision may be set aside for unreasonableness. The difficulty is to know when a decision may be said to be unreasonable.

Associated Provincial Picture Houses Ltd v *Wednesbury Corporation*[70] concerned the Sunday Entertainments Act 1932, that gave a local authority power to permit cinemas to open on Sundays, 'subject to such conditions as the authority think fit to impose'. A local council allowed cinemas to show films on Sundays, on the condition that no children under 15 should be admitted to the performances, with or without an adult. This prevented parents taking their children to the cinema on a Sunday. *Held*, the condition was neither ultra vires nor unreasonable.

In his much-quoted judgment, Lord Greene MR set out what is now termed the *Wednesbury* test, namely that a court may set aside a decision for unreasonableness only when the authority has come to a conclusion 'so unreasonable that no reasonable authority could ever have come to it'.[71] The judgment emphasises that unreasonableness is closely related to other grounds of review, such as irrelevant considerations, improper purposes and error of law.

The meaning of 'unreasonable' was central to the *Tameside* case, as we have seen. Lord Diplock said there that 'unreasonable' denotes 'conduct which no sensible authority acting with due appreciation of its responsibilities would have decided to adopt'.[72] In the GCHQ case, Lord Diplock called the test one of irrationality: it applied 'to a decision which is so outrageous in its defiance of logic or of accepted moral standards that no sensible person who had applied his mind to the question to be decided could have arrived at it'.[73] In 1998, Lord Cooke of Thorndon regretted that some *Wednesbury* phrases had become 'established incantations' and preferred 'the simple test' of whether the decision under review 'was one which a reasonable authority could reach'.[74]

What none of these formulations brings out is that the test of reasonableness does not apply uniformly to all kinds of decision. There are some decisions (for instance, allocating financial resources to local councils) where the court would intervene for unreasonableness only in exceptional circumstances.[75] By contrast, if fundamental human rights are in issue, as where the life of an asylum seeker may be at risk, 'the basis of the decision must surely call for the most anxious scrutiny'.[76] In 1996 the Court of Appeal held that an unreasonable decision was

one beyond the range of responses open to a reasonable decision-maker. But in judging whether the decision-maker has exceeded this margin of appreciation the human rights context is important. The more substantial the interference with human rights, the more the court will require by way of justification before it is satisfied that the decision is reasonable in the sense outlined above.[77]

Despite this significant development, the *Wednesbury* test was founded on an approach which was deferential to the decisions of public authorities. Some lawyers

---

[70] [1948] 1 KB 223.
[71] On the principles of *Wednesbury* review, see P Walker [1995] PL 556, Lord Irvine of Lairg [1996] PL 59, R Carnwath [1996] PL 245 and J Laws in Forsyth and Hare (eds) *The Golden Metwand and the Crooked Cord*, pp 185–201.
[72] *Education Secretary* v *Tameside Council*, at p 1064.
[73] *Council of Civil Service Unions* v *Minister for the Civil Service* [1985] AC 374, 410.
[74] *R* v *Chief Constable of Sussex, ex p International Trader's Ferry Ltd* [1999] 2 AC 418, 452. See also Lord Cooke's speech in *R (Daly)* v *Home Secretary* [2001] 2 AC 532, 548.
[75] *R* v *Environment Secretary, ex p Nottinghamshire CC* [1986] AC 240.
[76] *R* v *Home Secretary, ex p Bugdaycay* [1987] AC 514, 531.
[77] *R* v *Ministry of Defence, ex p Smith* [1996] QB 517, 554 (Sir Thomas Bingham MR), applied in *R* v *Lord Saville, ex p A* [1999] 4 All ER 860.

believed that the test of unreasonableness was too high a hurdle to surmount and that the European test of proportionality provided a better approach to the control of discretion. A determined attempt to get British courts to adopt the test of proportionality was made in *R v Home Secretary, ex p Brind*.[78] The House of Lords held that, without incorporation of the European Convention on Human Rights, British courts could not (except when rights in Community law were affected)[79] review executive decisions on the basis of proportionality. Applying the *Wednesbury* test, the House upheld a government ban on the broadcasting of direct statements by representatives of proscribed organisations in Northern Ireland: the ban was not one that no reasonable Home Secretary could have imposed.

The position of proportionality altered dramatically when the Human Rights Act 1998 came into effect.

8 *Proportionality.* In varying forms, the concept of proportionality is found in the constitutional law of countries such as Germany and Canada,[80] as well as in Community law and in European human rights law.[81] In outline, if action to achieve a lawful objective is taken in a situation where it will restrict a fundamental right, the effect on the right should not be disproportionate to the public purpose sought to be achieved. The test applies in respect of European Convention rights, many of which (for instance, the right to freedom of expression) are subject to such restrictions 'as are prescribed by law and are necessary in a democratic society' for specified public purposes.[82] A restriction cannot be regarded as 'necessary in a democratic society' unless it is proportionate to the legitimate aim pursued.[83] If in a given situation there is a need for public action to restrict the right, the restriction 'must be necessary and proportionate to the damage which the restriction is designed to prevent'.[84] Any further restriction is unjustifiable.

By the Human Rights Act 1998, British courts must take account of Strasbourg case law where it is relevant to Convention rights. In *R v Home Secretary, ex p Daly*,[85] a prison policy that barred a prisoner in a closed prison from being present while his cell was searched, even when letters between him and his solicitor were examined, was held by the House of Lords to be unlawful on common law grounds. It was also held to infringe Daly's right under art 8(1) ECHR to respect for his correspondence to a greater extent than was necessary. Lord Steyn observed that proportionality was likely to mean a greater intensity of review than the *Wednesbury* test or even the heightened scrutiny test applied in *R v Ministry of Defence, ex p Smith*,[86] but he denied that this meant there had been a shift to merits review. Certainly the test of proportionality is likely to have an extensive effect on judicial review.[87] In 2001, Lord Slynn urged that,

---

[78] [1991] 1 AC 696 (note 74).

[79] As in the *International Trader's Ferry* case.

[80] See *R v Oakes* (1986) 26 DLR (4th) 200. For instances from the Caribbean, see *De Freitas v Permanent Secretary of Ministry of Agriculture* [1999] 1 AC 69 and *Thomas v Baptiste* [2000] 2 AC 1.

[81] See J Jowell and A Lester, in Jowell and Oliver (eds), *New Directions in Judicial Review*, pp 51–72; M Fordham and T de la Mare, in Jowell and Cooper (eds) *Understanding Human Rights Principles*, pp 27–89; Craig, *Administrative Law*, pp 586–603; Ellis (ed), *The Principle of Proportionality in the Laws of Europe*; and Schwarze, *European Administrative Law*, ch 5.

[82] Art 10(2) ECHR. See *Sunday Times v UK* (1979) 2 EHRR 245; and ch 19 C.

[83] As in *Dudgeon v UK* (1981) 4 EHRR 149.

[84] *R v Home Secretary, ex p Brind* [1991] 1 AC 696, 751 (Lord Templeman).

[85] [2001] 2 AC 532.

[86] See text at note 77.

[87] See e.g. *South Bucks DC v Porter* [2002] 1 All ER 425 (whether proportionate for court to restrain gipsies from occupying mobile homes in breach of planning control); and *Lindsay v Customs & Excise Commissioners* [2002] STI 238(CA, *The Times*, 27 February 2002: blanket policy of confiscating vehicles used in smuggling held disproportionate).

quite apart from European law, proportionality should be recognised as part of English law.[88]

Failure to perform a statutory duty

We have so far been considering how a public authority may exceed its powers or misuse its discretion. Such a body may also act unlawfully if it fails to perform a duty imposed upon it by statute. Thus a local authority acted unlawfully when it decided not to fund the provision required by certain children with special educational needs, leaving this to be paid for by the governors of the children's school; the governors successfully applied for judicial review of the decision.[89] In that case a specific statutory duty was enforced, but there are many duties which are more general in character and may not be clearly enforceable in the courts. Thus the Education Act 1996, s 9, obliges both the Secretary of State and local education authorities to pay regard 'to the general principle that pupils are to be educated in accordance with the wishes of their parents, so far as that is compatible with the provision of efficient instruction . . . and the avoidance of unreasonable public expenditure'. How far does this statutory duty create enforceable rights in the parents of children of school age? This duty has been held to require local authorities to take parental wishes into account but does not oblige the authorities to give effect to them.[90] Thus in regard to school admission policies, it was only in 1980 (now, the School Standards and Framework Act 1998, s 86) that local authorities were placed under an enforceable duty to respect parental preferences.

By contrast, under s 8 of the Education Act 1944, education authorities had a duty 'to secure that there shall be available for their areas sufficient schools . . . for providing full time education' suitable to their pupils. In *Meade* v *Haringey BC*, a local authority was faced with strike action by caretakers and ancillary staff and decided that all schools should close until further notice. The Court of Appeal held that parents who suffered as a result of this decision to close the schools had a remedy in court and that the council would be in breach of its duty if it decided to close the schools in sympathy with a trade union's claims at a time when the closure could reasonably have been avoided.[91] However, later decisions have referred to the duty in issue in *Meade* as a 'target duty': 'The metaphor recognises that the statute requires the relevant public authority to aim to make the prescribed provision but does not regard failure to achieve it without more as a breach.'[92] Thus the duty may be enforceable by the Secretary of State under default powers[93] but not by a private individual.

Even if an individual is entitled to seek judicial review (as a public law remedy), it does not follow that he or she also has the right (in private law) to sue for damages caused by the breach of duty. Thus prison authorities must observe the statutory rules made for the conduct and discipline of the prisons, but no right to sue for damages accrues to prisoners who are affected if the rules are broken.[94]

Two other matters may be mentioned. First, all public authorities have a duty under the Human Rights Act 1998, s 6, to act consistently with an individual's Convention

---

[88] In the *Alconbury Developments* case [2001] 2 All ER at [51].
[89] *R v Hillingdon Council, ex p Queensmead School* [1997] ELR 331.
[90] *Watt v Kesteven CC* [1955] 1 QB 408, applied in *Cumings v Birkenhead Corpn* [1972] Ch 12.
[91] [1979] 2 All ER 1016. The duty is now found in the Education Act 1996, s 14.
[92] *R v London Borough of Islington, ex p Rixon* [1997] ELR 66, citing *R v ILEA, ex p Ali* (1990) 2 Admin LR 822.
[93] See e.g. *R v Environment Secretary, ex p Norwich Council* [1982] QB 808.
[94] *R v Deputy Governor of Parkhurst Prison, ex p Hague* [1992] 1 AC 58. See also *X v Bedfordshire CC* [1995] 2 AC 633; and ch 32 A.

rights unless they are prevented from doing so by primary legislation. Breach of this duty could give rise to a claim for judicial review and in some cases a claim for compensation. Second, the statutory language is not always decisive of whether a public authority has a duty or a discretion on a certain matter. In some circumstances, the word 'may' used in legislation is equivalent to 'must'.[95]

The concept of jurisdiction[96]

Our discussion so far of the ultra vires doctrine has been phrased in terms of powers, discretion and duties. In many cases, however, use is made of the language of jurisdiction. For historical reasons, as we saw in chapter 27, the concepts of vires (powers) and jurisdiction are closely linked. Often it makes no difference whether a certain matter is regarded as being ultra vires or in excess of jurisdiction. An inferior tribunal or a body such as a licensing authority may be said to have jurisdiction to hear and determine certain questions, whether it be a claim for a social security benefit or a taxi driver's licence. These decisions are subject to control by the superior courts on jurisdictional grounds. This supervision does not provide a fresh decision on the merits but ensures that the body in question has observed the limits which are a condition of its power to make binding decisions. According to a famous dictum in *R v Nat Bell Liquors*:

> That supervision goes to two points: one is the area of the inferior judgment and the qualifications and conditions of its exercise; the other is the observance of the law in the course of its exercise.[97]

In other words, the supervision of a tribunal by means of judicial review ensures that the tribunal acts within the limits of its powers and observes the law while it is dealing with a matter that is within its powers. On this approach, it was formerly possible for a tribunal to act within its jurisdiction, but at the same time to commit an error of law that was subject to judicial review. For reasons of a procedural kind, it was often advantageous for a challenge to a tribunal's decision to be presented as a challenge to the tribunal's jurisdiction. Many older cases are concerned with the distinction between (*a*) an error made by a tribunal on a point of jurisdiction and (*b*) an error of law made by a tribunal 'within jurisdiction'. A superior court would often review the merits of a decision when it considered that a mistake had been made by a tribunal, while justifying the review on jurisdictional grounds.

Today, by a tortuous chapter of legal history, the law has fortunately developed to a point at which we need no longer struggle with the concept of an 'error of law within jurisdiction', for the reason that all errors of law made by a tribunal now give rise to judicial review. It is necessary to outline only the most recent pages of that history, beginning with a House of Lords decision that illustrates the difficulties of distinguishing between jurisdictional and non-jurisdictional matters, namely *Anisminic Ltd v Foreign Compensation Commission*.[98]

> The Foreign Compensation Commission was a tribunal created by the Foreign Compensation Act 1950. It had rejected a claim made by a British company (Anisminic) under a scheme for compensating British subjects who had lost property in Egypt during the Suez affair in 1956. The reason for rejection was that, on the commission's interpretation of the relevant Order

---

[95] *Padfield v Minister of Agriculture* [1968] AC 997.
[96] See de Smith, Woolf and Jowell, op cit, ch 5; Wade and Forsyth, op cit, ch 9; and (for a rewarding restatement) Craig, op cit, ch 15. Also Rubinstein, *Jurisdiction and Illegality*.
[97] [1922] 2 AC 128, 156.
[98] [1969] 2 AC 147; and see H W R Wade (1969) 85 LQR 198, B C Gould [1970] PL 358, L H Leigh [1980] PL 34.

in Council, it was fatal to the claim that Anisminic's assets in Egypt had after 1956 been acquired by an Egyptian company, since the order required that any 'successor in title' to the British claimant had to be of British nationality. In the absence of any right to appeal, Anisminic had to establish not only that the commission's interpretation of the order was erroneous, but also that the commission's decision rejecting the claim was a nullity, since the 1950 Act excluded the power of the High Court to review errors of law made within the jurisdiction of the commission. *Held*, by a majority in the House of Lords, the commission's interpretation of the Order in Council was wrong (since the Egyptian company was not Anisminic's 'successor in title'); and that this error had caused the commission to take into account a factor (the nationality of the Egyptian company) which was irrelevant to Anisminic's claim. Thus the commission had exceeded the limits of its jurisdiction and the decision rejecting the claim was a nullity.

The main issue for present purposes is whether the *Anisminic* case established the rule that *all* errors of law made by a tribunal cause the tribunal to exceed its jurisdiction. On a reading of the speeches in *Anisminic*, this does not seem to have been intended, but in *Pearlman* v *Keepers and Governors of Harrow School*, Lord Denning MR said that the distinction between an error which entails absence of jurisdiction and an error made within the jurisdiction should be abandoned and that the new rule should be that 'no court or tribunal has any jurisdiction to make an error of law on which the decision of the case depends'.[99] In supporting this view, Lord Diplock said:

> The breakthrough made by *Anisminic* was that, as respects administrative tribunals and authorities, the old distinction between errors of law that went to jurisdiction and errors of law that did not was for practical purposes abolished.[100]

Other judges for a time sought to maintain the traditional rule that tribunals might commit errors of law while remaining within their jurisdiction.[101] One reason for this was found in the ancient remedy of certiorari, which for a long time was available to review matters affecting jurisdiction and also errors of law 'on the face of the record', i.e. those errors of law which were apparent from the text of the tribunal's decision.[102] The consequence of this was that errors of law which neither went to jurisdiction nor were apparent from the decision itself could not be reviewed. This is no longer the case. In *R v Hull University Visitor, ex p Page*, the House of Lords held unanimously that *Anisminic* had rendered obsolete the distinction between error of law on the face of the record and other errors of law 'by extending the doctrine of ultra vires'. Parliament must be taken to have conferred power on a tribunal subject to it being exercised 'on the correct legal basis'; a misdirection in law in making the decision therefore rendered the decision ultra vires.[103]

An important proposition that is not affected by the *Anisminic* and *Hull University* decisions is that no tribunal or other decision maker has power conclusively to determine the limits of its own jurisdiction. Lord Mustill has said that the question of jurisdiction is 'a hard-edged question. There is no room for legitimate disagreement'.[104] What has been called the doctrine of jurisdictional fact arises when a decision maker's jurisdiction depends on a 'precedent fact' which must if necessary be established by

---

[99] [1979] QB 56, 70 (and H F Rawlings [1979] PL 404).

[100] *Re Racal Communications Ltd* [1981] AC 374, 383, and see *O'Reilly v Mackman* [1983] 2 AC 237, 278 (Lord Diplock).

[101] *Re Racal Communications Ltd* at 390 and *South East Asia Fire Bricks v Non-Metallic etc. Union* [1981] AC 363.

[102] *R v Northumberland Compensation Appeal Tribunal, ex p Shaw* [1952] 1 KB 388.

[103] [1993] AC 682, 701. This reasoning is criticised by I Hare, in Forsyth and Hare (eds), *The Golden Metwand and the Crooked Cord*, pp 112–39.

[104] *R v Monopolies and Mergers Commission, ex p South Yorkshire Transport Ltd* [1993] 1 All ER 289, 293. Lord Mustill accepted that a criterion on which a body's jurisdiction depends may be 'broad enough to call for the exercise of judgment'.

the court and not by the decision-maker. To take the example of the Home Secretary's power to deport an alien when he or she considers that this would be conducive to the public good: if X is being detained with a view to deportation under this power and claims that he is a British citizen, and thus not subject to deportation, the issue of his nationality must be decided by the court. Thus the court must examine the evidence relevant to X's nationality and must decide the matter for itself; on this issue the court is not confined to a supervisory role.

This fundamental principle was re-established by the House of Lords in *R v Home Secretary, ex p Khawaja*.[105] The case concerned the power of the Home Secretary to remove from the United Kingdom those who were 'illegal entrants' under the Immigration Act 1971. The House applied the principle that (in Lord Scarman's words) 'where the exercise of an executive power depends upon the precedent establishment of an objective fact, it is for the court, if there be a challenge by way of judicial review, to decide whether the precedent requirement has been satisfied'.[106] On this test, it was not sufficient that the immigration officers believed Khawaja to be an illegal entrant; his status as an illegal entrant had to be established by evidence before the power to remove him could be exercised. This strict test is particularly suitable when someone's liberty is at stake.[107]

Mistake of fact

Apart from the jurisdictional fact doctrine mentioned earlier, an attempt to seek judicial review of a decision based on the claim that the decision-maker made an error of fact will be met by the reply that judicial review does not provide a right of appeal. This is the more likely if there was some evidence for and some against the disputed finding, since the claimant is, in effect, asking the court to substitute itself for the decision maker in deciding an issue of fact. But suppose that there has been an evident mistake in a finding of fact that is directly material to the decision – for example, a decision based on a statement that is incorrect (such as a planning decision to refuse development on land that is said to be in the green belt, when this has never been the case). Here, a claim for review may well succeed on other grounds – such as taking into account an irrelevant consideration (the false description of the land), coming to a conclusion for which there is no evidence (which is an error of law),[108] unfairness (if the claimant had no opportunity to deal with the issue) or *Wednesbury* unreasonableness. However, there is developing authority for the view that a decision may be subject to review where there has been an error as to a material fact.[109] In *R v Criminal Injuries Compensation Board, ex p A*,[110] four members of the House of Lords accepted that a decision could be quashed for a material error of fact. The effect of the Human Rights Act 1998 may well be to confirm this position. Under art 6(1) ECHR, where (as in the *Alconbury Developments* case) a decision affecting civil rights is made by the Secretary of State, a reviewing court must be able to control essential findings of fact, although it is not required to provide a rehearing on every evidentiary issue.[111]

---

[105] [1984] AC 74, reversing *R v Home Secretary, ex p Zamir* [1980] AC 930.

[106] [1984] AC at 108.

[107] *Khawaja* was applied in *Tan Te Lam v Superintendent of Tai A Chau Detention Centre* [1997] AC 97.

[108] On the law/fact distinction, see W A Wilson (1936) 26 MLR 609, (1969) 32 MLR 361; and E Mureinik (1982) 98 LQR 587. And see text at note 51 above; and *Edwards v Bairstow* [1956] AC 14.

[109] In the *Tameside* case (note 52), Lord Wilberforce said that a decision founded 'upon an incorrect basis of fact' could be reviewed ([1977] AC 1014, 1047). And see T H Jones [1990] PL 507.

[110] [1999] 2 AC 330 (on a matter of 'crucial importance' to A's claim for compensation, Board proceeded on basis of inaccurate police evidence about a medical examination).

[111] And see *R (Alconbury Developments Ltd) v Environment Secretary* [2001] 2 All ER 929, esp Lord Slynn at [53] and Lord Nolan at [61].

Acting incompatibly with Convention rights

The Human Rights Act 1998 provides by s 6(1): 'It is unlawful for a public authority to act in a way which is incompatible with a Convention right.' While an act for this purpose includes a failure to act, it does not include a failure to introduce in Parliament a proposal for legislation or a failure to make any primary legislation (s 6(6)). The act of a public authority is not unlawful if as a result of a provision of primary legislation, the authority could not have acted differently or if it is giving effect to or enforcing legislation that cannot be read or given effect in a way which is compatible with Convention rights.[112]

The 1998 Act does not use the term 'ultra vires', but one effect of s 6(1) is to create a new and discrete ground on which an act, decision or failure to act may on judicial review be held unlawful, even if apart from the Human Rights Act the case would not succeed. In practice, most applicants for judicial review are likely to join arguments based on Convention rights to grounds for review that would have been available apart from the Human Rights Act. Sometimes such arguments will not affect the outcome;[113] but they may make all the difference. For example, the Court of Appeal would now have to deal with the right to respect for private life under art 8 ECHR in considering the policy of excluding all homosexuals from the Armed Forces;[114] and cases involving the right to freedom of expression would now be decided on the basis of art 10.[115] If individuals rely on Convention rights in their dealings with a public authority, the authority must in the exercise of its functions decide whether they are relevant and, if so, what their effect may be. If the authority ignores the Convention issues, the authority is at risk of failing to take relevant considerations into account, committing an error of law or of making a disproportionate decision.

B. Review on procedural grounds

Even if an official decision is within the powers of the body taking it, the decision may be challenged on procedural grounds; the issue then is whether the procedural requirements on which the decision's validity depends have been observed. Many such requirements are found in the statutes which confer the power of decision. Others are derived from the common law doctrine of natural justice or, as it is now widely known, the doctrine of fairness.

Statutory requirements

Where statute authorises a certain power to be exercised after a stated procedure has been followed, failure to observe the procedure may result in the purported exercise of the power being declared a nullity.

In *Ridge v Baldwin*, the Brighton police committee summarily dismissed their chief constable following his trial at the Central Criminal Court on charges of conspiracy; his acquittal had been accompanied by serious criticism of his conduct by the trial judge. Disciplinary regulations made under the Police Act 1919 laid down a procedure by which a formal inquiry had to be held into charges brought against a chief constable before he could be dismissed. The committee contended that this procedure did not apply to the power of dismissal under the

---

[112] For the meaning of 'public authority' and for an account of Convention rights, see ch 19 C.
[113] See e.g. *R (B) v Alperton Community School* [2001] ELR 359.
[114] Cf *R v Ministry of Defence, ex p Smith* [1996] QB 517.
[115] Cf *Wheeler v Leicester City Council* [1985] AC 1054; *R v Barnet Council, ex p Johnson* (1991) 89 LGR 581.

Municipal Corporations Act 1882. The House of Lords held inter alia that the disciplinary regulations did apply; 'inasmuch as the decision was arrived at in complete disregard of the regulations it must be regarded as void and of no effect'.[116]

But not every procedural error invalidates administrative action. The courts have often distinguished between procedural requirements which are mandatory (breach invalidates) and those which are directory (breach does not invalidate). But this distinction does not take account of whether there has been a total failure to observe the procedure or substantial compliance with it; or of whether the procedural defect caused any real prejudice to the individual.[117] In 1979 Lord Hailsham, commenting on the distinction, suggested that the courts are faced with 'not so much a stark choice of alternatives but a spectrum of possibilities'. He continued: 'The jurisdiction is inherently discretionary, and the court is frequently in the presence of differences of degree which merge almost imperceptibly into differences of kind.'[118] In that case, a planning authority's failure to notify landowners about their right of appeal to the secretary of state invalidated a decision by the authority which adversely affected the land. In 1999, the Court of Appeal held that where a required procedure has not been observed, to ask if the requirement was mandatory or directory was no more than a first step leading to such questions as whether there was substantial compliance; whether the non-compliance was capable of being waived; and what was the consequence if it had not been or could not be waived.[119] In such a situation, a reviewing court has an important discretion to exercise.

Natural justice

The requirements of natural justice are essentially rules of the common law, which are now buttressed under the Human Rights Act 1998 by art 6(1) ECHR:

> In the determination of his civil rights and obligations or of any criminal charge against him, everyone shall be entitled to a fair and public hearing within a reasonable time by an independent and impartial tribunal established by law.

On many matters, the common law rules have been embodied in enacted law, for example where statutory procedures enable someone who objects to a proposed decision to be heard at a public inquiry. As an unwritten principle, natural justice evolved largely through the control exercised by the central courts over bodies of inferior jurisdiction, such as local justices and the governing bodies of corporations.[120] The rules of natural justice were also applied to arbitrators, and to the disciplinary functions of professional bodies and voluntary associations. With the growth of governmental powers affecting an individual's property or livelihood, natural justice served to supplement the shortcomings of legislation. Public authorities were bound to observe natural justice in many of their functions and it was for the courts to determine the limits of this obligation. Before considering how the courts have performed this task, it is convenient first to illustrate the two main rules of natural justice with examples drawn from the ordinary courts.

---

[116] [1964] AC 40, 117 (Lord Morris of Borth-y-Gest).
[117] Compare *Coney v Choyce* [1975] 1 All ER 979 (no prejudice from failure to notify school closure at school entrance) with *Bradbury v London Borough of Enfield* [1967] 3 All ER 434 (complete failure to notify proposed changes in composition of schools).
[118] *London and Clydesside Estates Ltd v Aberdeen DC* [1979] 3 All ER 876, 883; and see *Wang v Commissioner of Inland Revenue* [1995] 1 All ER 367.
[119] *R v Immigration Appeal Tribunal, ex p Jeyeanthan* [1999] 3 All ER 231, applied in *Attorney-General's Reference (No 3 of 1999)* [2001] 1 All ER 577 (HL).
[120] Ch 27; and see De Smith, Woolf and Jowell, *Judicial Review*, chs 7–12; Wade and Forsyth, *Administrative Law*, chs 13–15; Craig, *Administrative Law*, chs 13, 14; Flick, *Natural Justice*.

1 *The rule against bias.*   The essence of a fair judicial decision is that it has been made by an impartial judge. This has been the subject of many decisions at common law, to which must now be added decisions of the European Court of Human Rights, interpreting the right under art 6(1) ECHR to a fair hearing before an 'independent and impartial tribunal'.[121] The main rule against bias[122] is that a judge may be disqualified from acting in a case on two grounds. First, where he or she has a direct pecuniary interest, however small, in the subject matter of the case; thus a judge who is a shareholder in a company appearing as a litigant must decline to hear the case, except with consent of the parties.[123] The automatic disqualification of a judge also applies where there is no financial interest, but the judge would be deciding a case which would affect the promotion of a cause in which he or she is closely involved with one of the parties.[124] This form of disqualification arose when, as one of five judges in the House of Lords who heard an appeal concerning General Pinochet's extradition, Lord Hoffmann was chair and director of a charitable branch of Amnesty International, which had argued at the appeal in support of the extradition and had thus become a party to the case. The judge's involvement with Amnesty International was not known to the parties during the hearing. Second, apart from a pecuniary interest or identification with one of the parties, a judge is disqualified from sitting when (in Lord Hope's words) *'the fair-minded and informed observer, having considered the facts* [relating to an allegation of bias], *would conclude that there was a real possibility that the tribunal was biased'*.[125] Under this form of the test, approved by the House of Lords in 2001, disqualification is not automatic but depends on whether an informed observer would conclude there was a 'real possibility of bias' once the facts had been ascertained.

Three comments may be made on the italicised test. First, where bias is alleged, the reviewing court does not have to decide whether the judge was in fact biased, since 'bias operates in such an insidious manner that the person alleged to be biased may be quite unconscious of its effect'.[126] Second, the test acknowledges that 'in any case where the impartiality of a judge is in question the appearance of the matter is just as important as the reality'.[127] Lord Hewart's dictum, that it is 'of fundamental importance that justice should not only be done but should manifestly and undoubtedly be seen to be done', comes from *R* v *Sussex Justices, ex p McCarthy*:

> The acting clerk to the justices was a member of a firm of solicitors who were to represent the plaintiff in civil proceedings as a result of a collision in connection with which the applicant was summoned for a road traffic offence. The acting clerk retired with the bench, but was not asked to advise the justices on their decision to convict the applicant. *Held*, that, as the clerk's firm was connected with the case in the civil action, he ought not to advise the justices in the criminal matter and therefore could not, had he been required to do so, have discharged his duties as clerk. The conviction was quashed, despite the fact that he had taken no part in the decision.[128]

Third, the test for judicial bias approved in *Porter* v *Magill* resolves a long-standing uncertainty as to whether in establishing bias it was enough that an observer had a 'reasonable suspicion' that a tribunal might be biased or whether it must beyond this

---

[121] The leading Convention cases on judicial bias are reviewed in *Hoekstra* v *HMA* 2001 SLT 28. Recent articles include D Williams [2000] PL 45 and K Malleson [2002] 22 LS 53.

[122] *R* v *Rand* (1866) LR 1 QB 230; *R* v *Sunderland Justices* [1901] 2 KB 357; and *Wildridge* v *Anderson* (1897) 25 R (J) 27.

[123] *Dimes* v *Grand Junction Canal (Proprietors of)* (1852) 3 HLC 759. And see R Cranston [1979] PL 237. Cf *R* v *Mulvihill* [1990] 1 WLR 438.

[124] *R* v *Bow Street Magistrate, ex p Pinochet Ugarte (No 2)* [2000] 1 AC 119.

[125] *Porter* v *Magill* [2002] 2 WLR 37, at [103] (Lord Hope).

[126] *R* v *Gough* [1993] AC 646, 672 (Lord Woolf).

[127] *Ex p Pinochet Ugarte*, at 139 (Lord Nolan).

[128] [1924] 1 KB 256.

be shown that in fact there was a 'real likelihood' or 'real danger' of bias. On this issue there was divergence between the English and Scottish courts. An earlier formula adopted by the House of Lords, that sought to lay down a single test for all purposes,[129] was not followed in some Commonwealth decisions.[130] Nor was it necessarily consistent with the Strasbourg case-law on Article 6(1) ECHR.

The need for integrity in the judicial process runs through recent decisions on bias. In *Locabail (UK) Ltd* v *Bayfield Properties Ltd*,[131] the Court of Appeal gave authoritative guidance in five cases where judicial bias was alleged in respect of such matters as a judge's opinions, social relationships and former professional activities and the importance of full disclosure. A judge 'would be as wrong to yield to a tenuous or frivolous objection as he would to ignore an objection of substance'; but 'if in any case there is real ground for doubt, that doubt should be resolved in favour of recusal'.[132] There was, however, no room for doubt in a Scottish case, when a senior judge who had newly retired but was still sitting as an appeal judge, published a colourful newspaper article in which he referred to the European Convention as offering 'a field day for crackpots, a pain in the neck for judges and legislators, and a goldmine for lawyers'. The Scottish High Court held that the article would create an apprehension that the judge would be biased in presiding over a criminal appeal in which Dutch appellants were relying on their Convention rights.[133]

2 *The right to a fair hearing.* It is equally fundamental to a just decision that each party should have the opportunity of knowing the case against him or her and of stating his or her case. Both parties must have the chance to present their version of the facts and to make submissions on the relevant rules of law. Each side must be able to comment on all material considered by the judge and neither side must communicate with the judge behind the other's back. Although the rules of court procedure embody these general principles, the unwritten right to a hearing may operate even in the courts. Thus the High Court could not order a solicitor personally to bear costs caused by his misconduct without giving the solicitor an opportunity to meet the complaint,[134] nor could a witness to proceedings for assault be bound over to keep the peace unless the magistrates gave him or her an opportunity of being heard.[135] The requirements of natural justice are not invariable: although a party to civil proceedings is normally entitled to know all the material considered by the judge, the nature of the High Court's inherent jurisdiction over children was such that in exceptional cases the judge might take into account confidential medical reports on the children which were not disclosed to the parents.[136] But the Court of Appeal acted in breach of natural justice when in a case concerning the wardship of children the court read and acted on a letter by a social worker which the parties had not seen.[137]

---

[129] *R* v *Gough* [1993] AC 646.

[130] E.g. *Webb* v *R* (1994) 181 CLR 41.

[131] [2000] QB 451. See also *Metropolitan Properties Ltd* v *Lannon* [1969] 1 QB 577 (bias of chairman of rent assessment committee); *R* v *Inner West London Coroner, ex p Dallaglio* [1994] 4 All ER 139 (refusal to resume inquest into *Marchioness* disaster); and *In re Medicaments and Related Classes of Goods* [2001] 1 WLR 700.

[132] *Locabail*, at [21] and [25]. And see *Taylor* v *Lawrence* [2002] 2 All ER 353.

[133] *Hoekstra* v *HMA* (note 121).

[134] *Abraham* v *Jutsun* [1963] 2 All ER 402.

[135] *Sheldon* v *Bromfield Justices* [1964] 2 QB 573; cf *R* v *Woking Justices, ex p Gossage* [1973] QB 448. And *R* v *Lincoln Crown Court, ex p Jude* [1997] 3 All ER 737.

[136] *Re K (Infants)* [1965] AC 201. Contrast *McMichael* v *UK* (1995) 20 EHRR 205. For the position in adoption proceedings, see *Re D (Minors) (Adoption reports: confidentiality)* [1996] AC 593.

[137] *B* v *W, Wardship: Appeal* [1979] 3 All ER 83.

Natural justice and administrative authorities

The rules of natural justice have been applied to many decisions made outside the courts. From the rules of natural justice has developed what is now in effect a universal rule that public authorities must act fairly in making decisions. Before that rule developed, a court was likely to ask whether in relation to the particular decision before it there was a duty to observe the rules of natural justice. Thus, if the exercise of power affected a person's rights, property or character, it was more likely to be subject to natural justice; so was a decision which followed a procedure involving the confrontation of two opposing views, in a manner resembling litigation.[138] Thus the rules of natural justice (including the right to notice of charges made against the individual and a right to reply) were held to apply to the exercise of disciplinary powers, including such penalties as expulsion, by bodies such as universities[139] and trade unions.[140] The same rules were applied in a classic 19th-century decision to action by a local authority under statutory powers directed against an individual's property.

> In *Cooper v Wandsworth Board of Works*, the plaintiff recovered from the board damages in trespass for demolishing his partly built house. He had failed to notify his intention to build the house to the board, which by statute thereupon had power to demolish the building. *Held*, that the board should have given a hearing to the plaintiff before exercising their statutory power of demolition. 'Although there are no positive words in a statute requiring that the party shall be heard, yet the justice of the common law shall supply the omission of the legislature'.[141]

In a similar manner the rule against bias has been applied to local authorities. Thus a local authority's decision to grant planning permission for the development of an amusement park by a private company was declared to be void because the council had previously made a contract with the company by which it was liable to the company in damages if planning permission was not granted.[142] And when the Barnsley markets' committee revoked a stallholder's licence for a trivial and isolated misdemeanour, that decision was also quashed: not only did the committee hear the evidence of the market manager (who was in the position of a prosecutor) in the absence of the stallholder, but the manager was present throughout the committee's deliberations.[143]

Natural justice and ministers' powers

The older instances of natural justice date from the period before the development of modern government. Today when new powers are granted, they are generally accompanied by statutory procedures intended to provide safeguards against arbitrary use of the powers. To what extent may additional unwritten rules of fair procedure be applied by the courts?[144] Is the rule that no person should be judge in their own cause relevant if the settlement of disputes arising from the execution of policy is entrusted to the minister whose department is responsible for that policy?[145] There are some powers

---

[138] See R B Cooke [1954] CLJ 14. Cf *Durayappah v Fernando* [1967] 2 AC 337, 349.

[139] *Dr Bentley's* case (1723) 1 Stra 557; cf *Ceylon University v Fernando* [1960] 1 All ER 631.

[140] *Annamunthodo v Oilfield Workers' TU* [1961] AC 945; cf *Breen v AEU* [1971] 2 QB 175.

[141] (1863) 14 CB (NS) 180, 194 (Byles J).

[142] *Steeples v Derbyshire CC* [1984] 3 All ER 486, distinguished in *R v Amber Valley DC, ex p Jackson* [1984] 3 All ER 501. See also *R v Environment Secretary, ex p Kirkstall Valley Campaign Ltd* [1996] 3 All ER 304.

[143] *R v Barnsley Council, ex p Hook* [1976] 3 All ER 452.

[144] See *Wiseman v Borneman* [1971] AC 297, 308 (Lord Reid); *Lloyd v McMahon* (note 179 below).

[145] In the context of the Human Rights Act 1998, this question was raised in the *Alconbury Developments* case: n 111 above.

where the courts have allowed little scope for natural justice, notably in relation to the deportation of aliens where aspects of national security are affected.[146] Where ministers' powers have involved public inquiries, the courts have had to decide how far common law principles of natural justice may supplement the procedure adopted by the department in question. In 1915, the House of Lords in *Local Government Board* v *Arlidge* held that natural justice required little more from a department than the carrying out in good faith of its usual procedures.

A public inquiry had been held by the Local Government Board into an appeal brought by Arlidge, the owner of a house that had been declared unfit for human habitation. After receiving a report from the inspector who conducted the inquiry, the board confirmed the order. Arlidge challenged the decision, arguing that he had not seen the inspector's report, that he did not know which official of the board had decided to confirm the order, and that he should have had an oral hearing before that official. The House of Lords rejected these claims, holding that Parliament, having entrusted judicial duties to an executive body, must be taken to have intended it to follow the procedure which was its own and was necessary if it was to be capable of doing its work efficiently. So long as the officials dealt with the question referred to them without bias, and gave the parties an adequate opportunity of presenting the case, the board could follow its own established procedures, even though they were not those of a court of law.[147]

Similarly, in *Board of Education* v *Rice* it was held that in disposing of an appeal the Board of Education was bound to act in good faith and to listen fairly to both sides, since that was a duty which lay on everyone who decided anything. The board was not, however, bound to follow the procedure of a trial. It could obtain information in any way it thought best, always giving a fair opportunity to those who were parties in the controversy to correct or contradict any relevant statement prejudicial to their view.[148]

These decisions, particularly *Arlidge*, rejected the approach that departments should adopt court-like procedures in deciding questions 'which were more or less of a judicial character'.[149] In the 1930s, in cases concerned with procedures for slum clearance and the compulsory purchase of land, the courts found great difficulty in applying common law rules of natural justice to the duties of the minister. An exceptional case was *Errington* v *Minister of Health*, in which the court quashed a slum clearance order made by the Jarrow council: after the public inquiry into the order, councillors discussed the issues with Whitehall and a civil servant visited the houses without notice being given to the owner.[150] In such cases, the courts attempted to distinguish between the judicial and administrative functions of the minister. Thus the judges accepted that the final decision of the minister could be based on matters of policy and was thus administrative, but asserted that the department exercised judicial or quasi-judicial functions at the public inquiry stage.[151] This approach was called into question in *Franklin* v *Minister of Town and Country Planning* where, under the New Towns Act 1946, a public inquiry had been held into objections to a controversial draft order that the minister had made designating Stevenage as a new town. Rejecting the objectors' argument that the minister was biased in confirming his own order, the House of Lords held that there was no evidence that the minister had not genuinely considered the report of the inspector on the inquiry. The House stated that at no stage was a judicial or quasi-judicial duty imposed on the minister: his duty to consider the inspector's report

---

[146] See e.g. *R* v *Home Secretary, ex p Cheblak* [1991] 2 All ER 319. And ch 20 B.
[147] [1915] AC 120.
[148] [1911] AC 179.
[149] See Dicey, *Law and the Constitution*, app 2 (reprinting his influential article in (1915) 31 LQR 148).
[150] [1935] 1 KB 249.
[151] This followed the analysis made in the Ministers' Powers Report, 1932; see ch 27.

was purely administrative.[152] Such conceptual analysis has long been out of fashion, but aspects of the analysis are being revisited as the courts apply the requirements of art 6(1) ECHR to established administrative procedures.[153]

Today, as a consequence of the Franks report in 1957, most public inquiries are governed by detailed procedural rules which set high standards of fairness.[154] But such rules have not been applied to all public inquiries; and common law rules of natural justice may still be relevant.[155] In *Bushell* v *Secretary of State for the Environment*, which concerned a controversial motorway inquiry, the House of Lords adopted an approach which, as in *Franklin*'s case, stressed the administrative character of the minister's decision and protected crucial aspects of the official process from full investigation at the inquiry.[156]

The present scope of natural justice

The importance of natural justice in the judicial review of administrative action has not been in doubt since the landmark decision of the House of Lords in *Ridge* v *Baldwin*, the facts of which we have already considered in relation to statutory procedures.

> The power of the Brighton police committee under an Act of 1882 was to dismiss 'any constable whom they think negligent in the exercise of his duty or otherwise unfit for the same'. Claiming to act under this power, they dismissed the chief constable without giving him a hearing. The Court of Appeal held that in dismissing the chief constable, 'the defendants were acting in an administrative or executive capacity just as they did when they appointed him'.[157] The House of Lords overruled this view: quite apart from the procedure laid down by the discipline regulations, natural justice required that a hearing should have been given before the committee exercised its power. The failure to give a hearing invalidated the dismissal, and the subsequent hearing given to Ridge's solicitor did not cure the earlier defect.[158]

This decision could have been regarded narrowly as an interpretation of a particular statute. In fact, *Ridge* v *Baldwin* was the first of a group of House of Lords decisions during the 1960s which laid the foundations for the operation of judicial review today. Of first importance was the holding in *Ridge* that the duty to observe natural justice was not confined to powers classified as 'judicial' or 'quasi-judicial'. This enabled the courts to apply natural justice in a very wide variety of situations. By 1970, this development led Megarry J to remark that the courts were tending to apply principles of natural justice to all powers of decision unless the circumstances indicated to the contrary.[159] The benefits of *Ridge* v *Baldwin* spread to many other persons, including students,[160] police officers,[161] school teachers,[162] market stallholders,[163] residents of local

---

152 [1948] AC 87 (criticised by H W R Wade (1949) 10 CLJ 216).
153 See the *Alconbury Developments* case, note 88 above.
154 See ch 29 B.
155 *Fairmount Investments Ltd* v *Environment Secretary* [1976] 2 All ER 865.
156 [1981] AC 75; ch 29 B. Cf the approach taken in the *Alconbury Developments* case (n 88).
157 [1963] 1 QB 539, 576 (Harman LJ).
158 [1964] AC 40; and see A W Bradley [1964] CLJ 83.
159 *Gaiman* v *National Association for Mental Health* [1971] Ch 317, 333 (power to expel members of company limited by guarantee); cf *Bates* v *Lord Hailsham* [1972] 3 All ER 1019 (delegated legislation).
160 E.g. *R* v *Aston University Senate, ex p Roffey* [1969] 2 QB 538; and *Glynn* v *Keele University* [1971] 2 All ER 89. And see, on the visitor's jurisdiction, *Thomas* v *University of Bradford* [1987] AC 795; and *R* v *Hull University Visitor, ex p Page* [1993] AC 682.
161 *R* v *Kent Police Authority, ex p Godden* [1971] 2 QB 662; *Chief Constable of North Wales* v *Evans* [1982] 3 All ER 141.
162 *Hannam* v *Bradford Corpn* [1970] 2 All ER 690; *Malloch* v *Aberdeen Corpn* [1971] 2 All ER 1278.
163 *R* v *Barnsley Council, ex p Hook* [1976] 3 All ER 452; *R* v *Wear Valley Council, ex p Binks* [1985] 2 All ER 699.

authority homes at risk of closure,[164] those affected by decisions of self-regulatory bodies[165] and, most notably, convicted prisoners in respect of prison discipline and the parole system.[166] In 1980, on an appeal from the Bahamas concerning refusal of an individual's constitutional right to citizenship, the Judicial Committee held that natural justice must be observed by any person with authority to determine questions affecting the rights of individuals.[167] But natural justice is not limited to situations in which individuals can show that their private rights are in issue, and the courts protect a wide variety of individual interests against unfair action by public bodies.[168]

Fairness and natural justice

The scope of natural justice is best understood against the broad perception that it is the duty of the courts to ensure that *all* administrative powers are exercised fairly, that is, in accordance with principles of fair procedure. It has always been difficult to describe the contents of natural justice except in general terms. As Tucker LJ said in 1949:

> There are . . . no words which are of universal application to every kind of inquiry and every kind of domestic tribunal. The requirements of natural justice must depend on the circumstances of the case, the nature of the inquiry, the rules under which the tribunal is acting, the subject-matter that is being dealt with and so forth.[169]

In *Ridge* v *Baldwin*, in rebutting the view that natural justice was so vague as to be meaningless, Lord Reid referred to the test of what a reasonable person would regard as fair procedure in given circumstances.[170] In 1967, in *Re HK*, which concerned the inquiry that an immigration officer should make when seeking to discover the age of a potential immigrant, Lord Parker CJ said that good administration required that the immigration officer should act fairly: 'only to that limited extent do the so-called rules of natural justice apply, which in a case such as this is merely a duty to act fairly'.[171] Even where an executive body does not need to conduct an adversarial hearing before reaching a decision, it must act fairly.[172]

The courts came to explain natural justice purely in terms of fairness.[173] Lord Diplock stated that whenever statutes give power to make decisions which 'affect to their detriment the rights of other persons or curtail their liberty to do as they please', Parliament is presumed to have intended that the administrative body should act fairly towards them.[174] In 1988, the position was summarised by Lord Bridge in *Lloyd* v *McMahon*:

> [The] so-called rules of natural justice are not engraved on tablets of stone. To use the phrase which better expresses the underlying concept, what the requirements of fairness demand when

---

[164] *R* v *Devon CC, ex p Baker* [1995] 1 All ER 73.

[165] *R* v *LAUTRO, ex p Ross* [1993] QB 17; and A Lidbetter [1992] PL 533.

[166] E.g. *R* v *Hull Prison Visitors, ex p St Germain* [1979] QB 425 and (the same) *(No 2)* [1979] 3 All ER 545; *Leech* v *Deputy Governor of Parkhurst Prison* [1988] AC 533; *R* v *Home Secretary, ex p Doody* [1994] 1 AC 531.

[167] *A-G* v *Ryan* [1980] AC 718.

[168] Cf *O'Reilly* v *Mackman* [1983] 2 AC 237, 275, 283 (Lord Diplock). For the protection of new social interests, see e.g. *R* v *Wandsworth Council, ex p P* (1989) 87 LGR 370; *R* v *Norfolk CC Social Services Dept, ex p M* [1989] QB 619.

[169] *Russell* v *Duke of Norfolk* [1949] 1 All ER 109, 118.

[170] [1964] AC 40 at 65.

[171] [1967] 2 QB 617, 630, applied in *R* v *Home Secretary, ex p Mughal* [1974] QB 313.

[172] *Pearlberg* v *Varty* [1972] 2 All ER 6.

[173] E.g. *Wiseman* v *Borneman* [1971] AC 297; *Maxwell* v *Dept of Trade* [1974] QB 523; and *Selvarajan* v *Race Relations Board* [1976] 1 All ER 12.

[174] *R* v *Commission for Racial Equality, ex p Hillingdon Council* [1982] AC 779, 787.

any body, domestic, administrative or judicial, has to make a decision which will affect the rights of individuals depends on the character of the decision-making body, the kind of decision it has to make and the statutory or other framework in which it operates. In particular, it is well established that when a statute has conferred on any body the power to make decisions affecting individuals, the courts will not only require the procedure prescribed by the statute to be followed, but will readily imply so much and no more to be introduced by way of additional procedural safeguards as will ensure the attainment of fairness.[175]

In *Lloyd v McMahon* itself, councillors who were in breach of duty by preventing their council from setting the level of local rates, claimed the opportunity of making oral representations to the district auditor before statutory sanctions were imposed. It was held that the auditor had acted fairly, as he had given them notice of the case against them and had received and considered their written representations. In 1993, concerning parole for convicted murderers serving mandatory life sentences, Lord Mustill said that it was for the courts 'to decide what the elements of fairness demand' in the regime by which Home Secretaries had chosen to exercise their powers; he stressed that standards of fairness are not immutable and depend on the context of those powers.[176]

The procedural effects of natural justice and fairness

On the basis that a public authority must act fairly in making its decisions and remembering that fairness is concerned with procedural matters, not with the substance of a decision, what in practical terms must the public authority do? A great deal depends on the nature of the decision. In a situation where a public office or other benefit is being withdrawn for reasons of misconduct or incompetence, the 'irreducible minimum' at the core of natural justice is (a) the right to a decision by an unbiased tribunal; (b) the right to have notice of the charges against the individual; and (c) the right to be heard in answer to those charges.[177]

In cases where no misconduct is alleged (for example, in the case of school or residential home closures, where parents or residents must in fairness be consulted by the local authority), then (a) consultation must take place at a time when the proposals are at a formative stage; (b) sufficient reasons must be given for the proposal to permit intelligent consideration and response; (c) adequate time must be allowed; and (d) the product of consultation must be conscientiously taken into account.[178]

Many detailed procedural questions arise to which there are no general answers. We have seen that in some contexts individuals do not have the right of an oral hearing,[179] but if the body in question has to decide questions as to someone's conduct or competence, the individual is entitled to know what evidence is given against him or her and must have a fair opportunity to rebut it.[180] Regulatory bodies that expect officials to do preliminary work for them must nonetheless be in a position to come to their own decisions.[181] Where a soldier claimed that he had been subject to racial harassment, members of the Army Board could not decide on the complaint judicially

---

[175] [1987] AC 625, 702–3.
[176] *R v Home Secretary, ex p Doody* [1994] 1 AC 531, 557.
[177] Lord Hodson in *Ridge v Baldwin* [1964] AC 40, at 132.
[178] *R v Brent Council, ex p Gunning* (1985) 84 LGR 168 (P Meredith [1988] PL 4); and *R v Devon CC, ex p Baker* [1995] 1 All ER 73. Cf *R v North Devon Health Authority, ex p Coughlan* [2001] QB 213 [108]–[117].
[179] *Lloyd v McMahon* [1987] AC 625.
[180] *Kanda v Government of Malaya* [1962] AC 322; *Chief Constable of North Wales v Evans* [1982] 3 All ER 141.
[181] *Selvarajan v Race Relations Board* [1976] 1 All ER 12; and *R v Commission for Racial Equality, ex p Cottrell and Rothon* [1980] 3 All ER 265.

without meeting to consider the matter; and the soldier was entitled to see all the material on which the board reached its decision, other than documents for which public interest immunity was properly claimed.[182] An individual has no universal right to be legally represented regardless of the nature of the proceedings in question,[183] but there may be circumstances in which a body with power to permit legal representation may not reasonably refuse it.[184] No breach of natural justice occurs when the opportunity of being heard is lost through the fault of a party's lawyer.[185]

There is no absolute rule that natural justice does not apply in the case of preliminary investigations, inspections or suspensions pending a final decision,[186] but the right to a hearing is often excluded because of the need for urgent action or because the individual's rights will be observed at a later stage.[187]

Many aspects of procedure raise issues of fairness: thus it may be unfair for a tribunal to refuse adjournment of a hearing.[188] The manner in which evidence is obtained by tribunals is subject to constraints of natural justice[189] but hearsay evidence is usually permitted.[190] Natural justice may entitle a party to cross-examine those giving evidence against him or her[191] or obtain the names of potential witnesses from the other side.[192] But it is sometimes sufficient that only the gist of allegations against an individual is made known.[193] Considerations of national security may seriously reduce the scope for natural justice.[194] It has been held contrary to natural justice for a commission of inquiry with investigative powers to make findings of fact that individuals have been guilty of serious misconduct, when the findings are supported by no evidence of probative value and individuals have had no opportunity to rebut them.[195]

Three matters may be mentioned briefly. First, if fairness or natural justice would otherwise entitle someone to be heard, a court should be slow to brush aside that right on the ground that a hearing would make no difference to the outcome.[196] The second matter is whether the failure by an authority to give a hearing to which the individual is entitled is cured by a full and fair hearing given later by an appellate body. No absolute rule applies: sometimes the appeal proceedings may take the form of a full rehearing and this may cure the earlier defect, but in other situations the individual may be entitled to a fair hearing at both stages. In intermediate cases, the court must decide 'whether, at the end of the day, there has been a fair result, reached by fair methods'.[197]

---

[182] *R v Army Board of Defence Council, ex p Anderson* [1992] QB 169.

[183] *R v Maze Prison Visitors, ex p Hone* [1988] AC 379.

[184] *R v Home Secretary, ex p Tarrant* [1985] QB 251.

[185] *R v Home Secretary, ex p Al-Mehdawi* [1990] 1 AC 876 (and J Herberg [1990] PL 467).

[186] *Rees v Crane* [1994] 2 AC 173 (Trinidad judge entitled to notice of complaints against him at initial stage of dismissal procedure).

[187] *Wiseman v Borneman* [1971] AC 297; *Furnell v Whangarei High Schools Board* [1973] AC 660; *Norwest Holst Ltd v Trade Secretary* [1978] Ch 201.

[188] *R v Cheshire CC, ex p C* [1998] ELR 66.

[189] *R v Deputy Industrial Injuries Commissioner, ex p Moore* [1965] 1 QB 456; *Crompton v General Medical Council* [1982] 1 All ER 35.

[190] *T A Miller Ltd v Minister of Housing* [1968] 2 All ER 633.

[191] *R v Board of Visitors, ex p St Germain (No 2)* [1979] 3 All ER 545. Cf *R v Commission for Racial Equality, ex p Cottrell and Rothon.*

[192] *R v Blundeston Board of Visitors, ex p Fox-Taylor* [1982] 1 All ER 646.

[193] *R v Gaming Board, ex p Benaim and Khaida* [1970] 2 QB 417; *Maxwell v Dept of Trade* [1974] QB 523.

[194] *R v Home Secretary, ex p Hosenball* [1977] 3 All ER 452; *R v Home Secretary, ex p Cheblak* [1991] 2 All ER 319.

[195] *Mahon v Air New Zealand Ltd* [1984] AC 808.

[196] *John v Rees* [1970] Ch 345, 402; and *R v Chief Constable, Thames Valley, ex p Cotton* [1990] IRLR 344, 352. And see Lord Bingham [1991] PL 64.

[197] *Calvin v Carr* [1980] AC 574, discussed by M Elliott (1980) 43 MLR 66.

The third matter concerns the legal effect, if any, of a decision reached in breach of natural justice. When a breach of natural justice is established, then on the authority of *Ridge* v *Baldwin* the decision in question is void and a nullity. In *Durayappah* v *Fernando*, however, the Judicial Committee held that failure to give a hearing when one was due made the decision voidable and not void.[198] This decision was plainly contrary to legal principle. In 1979, the Judicial Committee accepted that a decision reached in breach of natural justice was void rather than voidable, but added that until it was declared to be void by a court it was capable of having some effect in law and could be the basis of an appeal to a higher body.[199]

Does fairness require reasons to be given?

Although the giving of reasons 'is one of the fundamentals of good administration',[200] at common law there is no general duty to give reasons for decisions.[201] In many situations, legislation requires reasons to be given. Thus, by the Tribunals and Inquiries Act 1992, s 10, tribunals must on request supply reasons for their decisions and so must ministers in the case of decisions made following a public inquiry. Many statutes or procedural regulations go further and require reasons to be given whenever certain kinds of decision are made (for example, the refusal of planning permission). Despite the absence of a general duty to give reasons, the courts often require reasons to be given. Thus, reasons must be stated for an exercise of discretion if a right of appeal is valueless without this.[202] Fairness may in some situations require the giving of reasons, because of the impact of the decision on the individual's rights and interests.[203] Thus a prisoner sentenced to a mandatory life sentence was entitled to know the reasons for the Home Secretary's decision as to the minimum period that he must serve. In the leading case, Lord Mustill said:

> The giving of reasons may be inconvenient, but I can see no grounds at all why it should be against the public interest: indeed, rather the reverse. That being so, I would ask simply: Is refusal to give reasons fair? I would answer without hesitation that it is not.[204]

This approach, although taken in a specific context, is capable of applying to many decisions that affect the individual. Moreover, reasons must be given if a decision in the absence of explanation may appear arbitrary, harsh, mistaken or unreasonable:[205]

> if all other known facts and circumstances appear to point overwhelmingly in favour of a different decision, the decision-maker who has given no reasons cannot complain if the court draws the inference that he had no rational reason for his decision.[206]

---

[198] [1967] 2 AC 337, criticised by H W R Wade (1967) 83 LQR 499 and (1968) 84 LQR 95; see M B Akehurst (1968) 31 MLR 2, 128 and D Oliver [1981] CLP 43.

[199] *Calvin* v *Carr*. And see S Sedley [1989] PL 32.

[200] *Breen* v *AEU* [1971] 2 QB 175, 191 (Lord Denning MR). See also G Richardson [1986] PL 437; P Neill, in Forsyth and Hare (eds), *The Golden Metwand and the Crooked Cord*, pp 161–84; P P Craig [1994] CLJ 282.

[201] *R* v *Trade Secretary, ex p Lonrho plc* [1989] 2 All ER 609; *R* v *Higher Education Funding Council, ex p Institute of Dental Surgery* [1994] 1 All ER 651; *Public Service Board of New South Wales* v *Ormond* (1986) 63 ALR 559.

[202] *Minister of National Revenue* v *Wright's Canadian Ropes* [1947] AC 109.

[203] *R* v *Home Secretary, ex p Doody* [1994] 1 AC 531; *R* v *Kensington and Chelsea Council, ex p Grillo* (1996) 28 HLR 94.

[204] *Ex p Doody* at 564–5.

[205] *R* v *Civil Service Board, ex p Cunningham* [1991] 1 All ER 310 (and J Herberg [1991] PL 340).

[206] *R* v *Trade Secretary, ex p Lonrho plc* [1989] 2 All ER 609, 620 (Lord Keith).

Although the courts indirectly require the giving of reasons in such situations, they have not yet held that reasons should be given for all decisions.[207] A general ruling to this effect is overdue, even if it were accompanied by an exception for situations in which public interest considerations had to prevail over the general rule.

As it is, the practice of judicial review supports the giving of reasons. Thus, if an individual receives no reasons for a decision and obtains permission for full judicial review, the decision-maker will be expected to disclose relevant information so that the court can properly decide the application for review.[208] Aspects of fairness merge with principles of good administration: a court is likely to hold that operative reasons must have existed when the decision was made and will place little weight on reasons created subsequently. When a statute excluded the giving of reasons for the refusal of naturalisation, the Home Secretary's duty to act fairly meant that he must give sufficient information on the matters that concerned him to enable the applicants to make such representations as they could on those matters.[209]

European Community law requires that reasons be given when this is necessary to secure effective protection of a Community right.[210] Where art 6(1) ECHR entitles the individual to a fair hearing before an independent and impartial court or tribunal, the court or tribunal is expected to give reasons for its decision, so that the parties and the public may understand the basis for it.[211] This last point is already recognised in national law: where there is a duty to give reasons, 'proper and adequate reasons must be given' which are intelligible and deal with the substantial points in issue.[212] Concise reasons may be sufficient, but a general formula that does not deal with the individual issues in a case is unlikely to be acceptable. In some situations, the court may accept evidence as to the reasoning of the decision-maker even if it was not explained at the time, but breach of a statutory duty to give reasons with the decision may in itself cause the court to quash the decision for error of law.[213]

C. Legitimate expectations

A developing concept of public law linked with fairness is that of legitimate expectations.[214] The concept exists in other systems of law (including those of Australia, Germany and the EU)[215] and is an aspect of legal certainty. In their dealings with public agencies, private persons need to know if they can rely on statements by officials or on decisions that have been notified to them. In business and commercial affairs, an individual may hold others to their word when a *contract* has been concluded between them. But decisions like the issue of a licence or the grant of a permission do not usually take a contractual form. When is an individual (X) entitled to hold a public authority to its word? Is the authority free to change its mind or to disavow an official who has led

---

[207] See *Stefan* v *General Medical Council* [1999] 1 WLR 1293. And see Lord Bingham's summary of the law in *R* v *Ministry of Defence, ex p Murray* [1998] COD 134.

[208] Cf *R* v *Lancashire CC, ex p Huddleston* [1986] 2 All ER 941 (and A W Bradley [1986] PL 508).

[209] *R* v *Home Secretary, ex p Al Fayed* [1997] 1 All ER 228.

[210] See e.g. Case 222/86 *UNECTEF* v *Heylens* [1989] 1 CMLR 901.

[211] *Hadjianastassiou* v *Greece* (1992) 16 EHRR 219.

[212] *Re Poyser and Mills' Arbitration* [1964] 2 QB 467, 478. On the adequacy of reasons for a planning decision, see *Save Britain's Heritage* v *Number 1 Poultry Ltd* [1991] 2 All ER 10.

[213] *R* v *Westminster City Council, ex p Ermakov* [1996] 2 All ER 302.

[214] See R Baldwin and D Horne (1986) 49 MLR 685; C F Forsyth [1988] CLJ 238; P P Craig (1992) 108 LQR 79; Craig, *Administrative Law*, ch 19.

[215] Schwarze, *European Administrative Law*, ch 6; and Schønberg, *Legitimate Expectations in Administrative Law*. See also *Minister of State for Immigration* v *Teoh* (1995) 128 ALR 353 (ratification of treaty creates expectation that executive decisions will conform to the treaty); and ch 15 B.

X to believe that a certain decision would be made? The term 'legitimate expectation' was used in 1969 by Lord Denning MR in distinguishing between aliens who had to leave Britain when their leave to remain expired and those whose leave to remain was terminated by the Home Office prematurely: the latter, but not the former, had a 'legitimate expectation, of which it would not be fair to deprive [them] without hearing what [they have] to say'.[216]

There are four main situations to be discussed:[217]

(1)   the authority has made a decision affecting X that it later seeks to replace with a fresh decision;

(2)   the authority gives an assurance that it will apply certain procedure or policy to a matter affecting X, but in fact acts differently;

(3)   without any assurance being given, the authority has long followed a consistent practice, so that X believes that the practice will continue in the absence of notice that it has been changed;

(4)   the authority states the policy that it will follow on a matter, but changes that policy before deciding X's case, making a different decision from that which X had expected.

We may assume in each case that the outcome is less favourable than the individual had expected it to be. It may not always be clear on the evidence into which, if any, of these categories a situation falls. Thus in case (2), X's perception of a conversation with an official, Y, may be very different from Y's (for instance, X insists that Y assured him that X's application would succeed; Y remembers stating that applications like X's often stood a fair chance of success). If the exchanges were in writing, questions arise as to the fair meaning of the letters. In some cases, Y may have gone outside the limits of his authority and another private individual may have an interest that conflicts with X's.

In case (1), *revocation of a decision*, legal certainty requires that if an agency takes a decision affecting rights of the individual and communicates it to him/her, not qualifying it as 'provisional' or 'subject to review', the agency has exercised its discretion in the matter and may not alter the decision to the individual's disadvantage.[218] This principle is subject to express statutory provision. Thus the social security statutes authorise earlier decisions to be reviewed, for example when fresh information is available.[219] Planning permission that has been given may be revoked, but only on payment of compensation.[220] Apart from legislation, an authority that has conferred a continuing benefit on someone under a mistake of fact may revoke the benefit for the future when it discovers the true position.[221] And where the original benefit was based on a mistake of law, the authority may make a fresh decision based on a correct view of the law.[222]

In case (2), *breach of an assurance*, the authority has departed from an assurance given to the individual. It is well established that the courts may enforce the legitimate expectation created by such an assurance. Thus, an express undertaking by a public body to receive and consider an individual's representations entitles him or her to a hearing on the matters in question: 'When a public authority has promised to follow

---

[216] *Schmidt* v *Home Secretary* [1969] 2 Ch 149.

[217] Cf the analysis in Schønberg, *Legitimate Expectations*, p 5; and in Craig, *Administrative Law*, ch 19.

[218] *Re 56 Denton Road Twickenham* [1953] Ch 51; and see G Ganz [1965] PL 237.

[219] E.g. Social Security Administration Act 1992, ss 25, 30.

[220] Town and Country Planning Act 1992, ss 97, 107.

[221] *Rootkin* v *Kent* CC [1981] 2 All ER 227.

[222] *Cheung* v *Herts* CC, *The Times*, 4 April 1986; C Lewis [1987] PL 21.

a certain procedure, it is in the interest of good administration that it should act fairly and implement its promise, so long as implementation does not interfere with its statutory duty.'[223] If the individuals otherwise have no right to a hearing, it will be vital for them to show that such an undertaking was given.

Fairness may require an assurance to be enforced although the legislation does not provide for this. Where a Nigerian woman (without indefinite leave to remain in the United Kingdom) wished to return home for Christmas and was given a firm assurance by the Home Office (confirmed in her passport) that she would be readmitted if she came back by 31 January, the immigration officer could not refuse to admit her when she returned before that date.[224] Many cases are less clear-cut. As Bingham LJ said, where revenue officials had indicated to taxpayers that an element in proposed dealings would be treated as capital and not as income, but later dealt with it as income:

> If a public authority so conducts itself as to create a legitimate expectation that a certain course will be followed it would often be unfair if the authority were permitted to follow a different course to the detriment of one who entertained the expectation ... But fairness is not a one-way street. It imports the notion of equitableness, of fair and open dealing, to which the authority is as much entitled as the citizen. The Revenue's discretion ... is limited. Fairness requires that its exercise should be on a basis of full disclosure.[225]

In that case, no legitimate expectation arose to prevent the Revenue from collecting the tax that was legally due. In such situations, the fairness claimed by an individual may conflict with a broader notion of fairness in the public interest and with the principle of legality.[226] Where the Revenue give a definite assurance to the taxpayer as to what the tax consequences of a transaction will be, the Revenue are bound by it if the assurance would between private persons create a contractual duty or an estoppel.[227] But the taxpayer must have 'put all his cards face upwards on the table' and the assurance must be 'clear, unambiguous and devoid of relevant qualification'.[228]

In case (3), the expectation arises from the *consistent practice* of the authority. In the GCHQ case, the invariable practice of government had been to consult with civil service unions before changing terms of employment for civil servants; apart from the factor of national security, the unions had a legitimate expectation of being consulted before the government withdrew from staff at GCHQ the right to join a union.[229] Where for 25 years tax refund claims had invariably been accepted without regard to a statutory time limit, the Revenue could not without notice begin to refuse refunds on the basis that the claims were late.[230]

In case (4), *change of policy*, the complaint is that the individual did not receive the expected decision because the policy had changed. Such a complaint may be joined with a complaint of lack of consultation,[231] but it may be a claim that the case should have been decided according to the original policy. It may be difficult to make this claim without claiming that the policy should not have been changed at all. Related to this is the controversial issue of the relief that follows a successful claim: does an

---

[223] *A-G of Hong Kong v Ng Yuen Shiu* [1983] AC 629, 638 (Lord Fraser).

[224] *R v Home Secretary, ex p Oloniluyi* [1989] Imm AR 135. Also *R v Home Secretary, ex p Khan* [1985] 1 All ER 40 (A R Mowbray [1985] PL 558).

[225] *R v IRC, ex p MFK Ltd* [1990] 1 All ER 91, 110. Also *R v Jockey Club, ex p RAM Racecourses Ltd* [1993] 2 All ER 225, 236 (Stuart-Smith LJ).

[226] See the cases on estoppel mentioned at p 726 below.

[227] *R v IRC, ex p Preston* [1985] AC 835. The comparison with private law may not now be apt: see *R v East Sussex CC, ex p Reprotech (Pebsham) Ltd* [2002] UKHL 8.

[228] See *R v IRC, ex p MFK Ltd* above.

[229] *Council of Civil Service Unions v Minister for the Civil Service* [1985] AC 375.

[230] *R v IRC, ex p Unilever plc* [1996] STC 681.

[231] As in *R v Health Secretary, ex p US Tobacco International Inc* [1992] QB 353.

expectation merely go to procedure (so that the court holds that X should have had a hearing before the adverse decision was made) or does it go to matters of substance (so that the court may grant X the benefit that he had expected to receive)?[232]

In *Re Findlay*, the Home Secretary changed the policy on the granting of parole to convicted prisoners, causing certain prisoners to become eligible for parole much later than would have been the case under the former policy. Lord Scarman said: 'But what was their *legitimate* expectation? Given the substance and purpose of the legislative provisions governing parole, the most that a convicted prisoner can legitimately expect is that his case will be examined individually in the light of whatever policy the Secretary of State sees fit to adopt . . .'[233]

Notwithstanding *Re Findlay*, the courts have since decided that a legitimate expectation arising from an existing policy may go much further than this.

In *R v Ministry of Agriculture, ex p Hamble Fisheries Ltd*, under a policy regulating the catching of certain species of fish, a company planned to obtain an 'aggregated' licence for a larger trawler by transferring licences from other vessels. After the company bought two small trawlers for this purpose, but before it applied for the 'aggregated' licence, the ministry ended the aggregation policy, acting under pressure from Europe to preserve fish stocks. The new policy included transitional provision for licence applications that had been submitted to the ministry but not yet decided. The company was refused a licence under the new policy. *Held* by Sedley J, reviewing both European and national law: (1) a legitimate expectation could give rise to a substantive claim for the benefit sought, and could (if fairness required) require the ministry to make an exception to its policy; (2) here, the ministry had made transitional provision for claims already submitted; (3) no one had a legitimate expectation that policy would not change, and fairness did not require a further exception to be made to the new policy.[233a]

This judgment was controversial for two reasons: (*a*) it held that a legitimate expectation enabled the court to confer the substantive benefit that the claimant was seeking (and not merely a procedural remedy); (*b*) it held that the court must conduct a balancing exercise in considering whether the effect of a changed policy on a claimant was 'fair', not merely whether the policy met the *Wednesbury* test of unreasonableness. In respect of (*b*), the judgment was initially described by the Court of Appeal as heresy,[234] but it was approved in *R v North Devon Health Authority, ex p Coughlan*.[235]

In 1993, a health authority moved geriatric patients into a new facility after assuring them that they could live there for as long as they chose. In 1998, the authority decided to close the facility and transfer the patients to local authority care. *Held*, the decision to terminate care in the NHS was based on a mistaken view of the legislation. The promise to the patients had created a legitimate expectation of a substantive benefit, the frustration of which would be so unfair as to amount to an abuse of power. There was no 'overriding public interest' to justify departure from the promise.

The decision in *Coughlan* is welcome, but future courts will face difficult questions in balancing individual expectations against the necessity for public authorities to act in the public interest as they see it.[236] This developing area of law owes much to European law. *Coughlan* increases the likelihood that the test of proportionality will supersede the *Wednesbury* test.

---

[232] See *R v North and East Devon Health Authority, ex p Coughlan* [2001] QB 213.
[233] [1985] AC 318, 338; *R v Home Secretary, ex p Hargreaves* [1997] 1 All ER 397 (minimum eligibility of prisoners for home leave raised from one-third of sentence to a half); T R S Allan [1997] CLJ 246 and S Foster (1997) 60 MLR 727.
[233a] [1995] 2 All ER 714.
[234] *R v Home Secretary, ex p Hargreaves*.
[235] [2001] QB 213, distinguishing *ex p Hargreaves*.
[236] See P Craig and S Schønberg [2000] PL 684, 698–700; cf M Elliott [2000] Judicial Review 27, arguing that *Wednesbury* provides the proper standard of review.

Estoppel and government action

This discussion has focused on the concept of legitimate expectations. At an earlier time, a public authority's promise as to how it would exercise a statutory function was usually ignored since it was thought that it could have no legal effect.[237] The courts then invoked the doctrine of estoppel in easing the plight of someone who had relied on an assurance from an official only to find that it was not binding. In a notable decision, *Robertson v Minister of Pensions*,[238] Denning J applied this principle:

> Whenever government officers, in their dealings with a subject, take on themselves to assume authority in a matter with which the subject is concerned, he is entitled to rely on their having the authority which they assume. He does not know and cannot be expected to know the limits of their authority, and he ought not to suffer if they exceed it.

This valuable principle was rejected by a conservative House of Lords,[239] because it was thought to allow officials to play fast and loose with legal rules, whether relating to criminal law[240] or to the limits of a public authority's powers, duties or jurisdiction.[241] But even though an estoppel (which is a rule of evidence) could not prevail over a rule of law, there were good reasons why public authorities, including the Crown, should be subject to the operation of estoppel in administrative matters. It was said in 1962 that estoppel could not hinder the exercise of a statutory discretion,[242] but some scope was found for estoppel in later cases where informal assurances given by planning officials had been relied on by individuals.[243] In 2002, these planning cases were considered by the House of Lords. It was argued to the House that an informal opinion given in 1991 by a local official that planning permission was not required for a certain use of land should be treated as a binding decision by the local authority acting under statutory powers. The House rejected this argument, since the planning legislation required a formal application to be made for such a decision and imposed other procedural requirements on the process. Even if the local council had been a private party, there was no material for an estoppel. Referring to the concept of legitimate expectation and to the difficulties of applying estoppel to planning decisions, Lord Hoffmann said: 'It seems to me that in this area, public law has already absorbed what is useful from the moral values which underlie the private law concept of estoppel and the time has come for [public law] to stand upon its own two feet.'[244] The implications of this decision for planning law will be considerable. Future cases concerning the effect of informal procedures will have to be decided with reference to legitimate expectations rather than estoppel. In appropriate situations, however, the various rules of estoppel may continue to have some application to public authorities and private individuals alike.

Legitimate expectations, compensation and the Ombudsman

We have seen that the concept of legitimate expectations may be invoked by those who, on judicial review, either claim that an authority's decision should be quashed or seek

---

[237] Cf *ex p Coughlan*, at [55].

[238] [1949] 1 KB 227.

[239] *Howell v Falmouth Boat Construction Co* [1951] AC 837.

[240] Cf *R v Arrowsmith* [1975] QB 678 and authorities there cited.

[241] *Maritime Electric Co v General Dairies Ltd* [1937] AC 610; *Rhyl UDC v Rhyl Amusements Ltd* [1959] 1 All ER 257; *Essex Congregational Union v Essex CC* [1963] AC 808.

[242] *Southend Corporation v Hodgson (Wickford) Ltd* [1962] 1 QB 416.

[243] *Lever Finance Ltd v Westminster Council* [1971] 1 QB 222, criticised in *Western Fish Ltd v Penwith DC* [1981] 2 All ER 204. Cf *Newbury Council v Environment Secretary* [1981] AC 578. Also A W Bradley [1981] CLP 1.

[244] *R v East Sussex CC, ex p Reprotech (Pebsham) Ltd* [2002] UKHL 8, Times Law Report, 5 March 2002.

a substantive benefit that has been denied to them (as in the *Coughlan* case). In the next chapter, we will see that the award of damages is not typically the remedy that judicial review provides. By contrast, decisions of the Parliamentary Ombudsman often lead to compensation when individuals have suffered injustice through maladministration.[245] In many cases in which a claimant has suffered loss arising from a legitimate expectation against a public authority, it is very likely that the same facts would found a complaint of maladministration.

---

[245] See ch 29 D.

Chapter 31

JUDICIAL CONTROL OF ADMINISTRATIVE ACTION – II

In chapter 30 we considered the principles which the courts apply to the exercise of administrative powers by public authorities. We now examine the procedures by which the courts exercise their supervisory jurisdiction.[1] Review may take place indirectly, when an issue as to the validity of administrative action is decided in the course of ordinary civil or criminal proceedings.[2] So too the validity of action by a public authority may be relevant to a private law action in contract or tort (chapter 32). But here we are concerned with the procedures enabling there to be a direct review by the court of acts and decisions of public authorities.

The primary procedure in English law is now that of *application for judicial review*, often referred to in short as 'judicial review'.[3] It was brought into being by a group of reforms between 1977 and 1982 which, like many procedural reforms of the common law, did not go back to first principles and make a fresh start. In particular, the sphere of application of the new procedure was not defined, and certain aspects of the common law appeared to have been left intact. Since then, some limited reforms of the procedure have been made, particularly in 2000. In this chapter we look briefly at the earlier position in English law before we deal with the procedure of application for judicial review itself. Thereafter this chapter will deal with statutory remedies created for the review of certain decisions, the exclusion of judicial review and the different system of remedies in Scots law. The chapter concludes with an account of habeas corpus. This ancient writ is an important remedy against executive action which takes away individual liberty.

Forms of relief

When administrative action is challenged in the courts, the individual will ask the court to provide one or more of the following forms of relief:

(*a*) to quash, or set aside as a nullity, a decision that is ultra vires or otherwise unlawful;
(*b*) to restrain the authority from acting ultra vires or otherwise unlawfully;
(*c*) to order the authority to perform its lawful duties;
(*d*) to declare the rights and duties of the parties;
(*e*) to order the authority to provide financial redress for loss or injury suffered; and
(*f*) to secure temporary relief, pending the outcome of the proceedings.

---

[1] In addition to the books on administrative law already cited, informative works on procedural aspects are Gordon, *Judicial Review and Crown Office Practice*; Supperstone and Goudie (eds), *Judicial Review*; and Lewis, *Judicial Remedies in Public Law*.
[2] See pp 742–3 below.
[3] A similar but not identical procedure was created in Scotland in 1985; p 748 below. For Northern Ireland, see P Maguire, in Hadfield (ed.), *Judicial Review, A Thematic Approach*, app.

The main defect in English law used to be that while procedures existed for all these forms of relief to be obtained, there was no single procedure for doing so. Often the procedures for obtaining one or more of these reliefs were mutually incompatible and the law was fragmented into the law of different remedies. Today, there is a comprehensive procedure for securing whatever relief is appropriate. The main effect of the reforms was that certain remedies which had long been available – notably the prerogative orders (mandamus, prohibition and certiorari), injunctions and declarations – were for purposes of administrative law transformed into *forms of relief*[4] obtainable by a single procedure known as an application for judicial review. These changes in procedure were accompanied by judicial reorganisation so that, according to one expert view, without Parliament having directly authorised it, an administrative court had been established.[5] But it was not until 2000 that the court, which exists within the Queen's Bench Division of the High Court, was named the Administrative Court.[6]

The prerogative orders

The prerogative writs of mandamus, prohibition and certiorari (later restyled orders)[7] were the principal means by which the former Court of King's Bench exercised jurisdiction over local justices and other bodies.[8] Although the writs issued on the application of private persons, the word 'prerogative' was apt because they were associated with the right of the Crown to ensure that justice was done by inferior courts and tribunals. The Crown as such played no part in the proceedings, but orders could be sought by or against a minister or a government department. Since the prerogative orders upheld the public interest in the administration of justice, aspects of the procedure (for example, the need for leave from the court, the summary procedure and the discretionary remedies) were vitally different from litigation designed to protect the plaintiff's private rights.

Mandamus is an order from the High Court commanding a public authority or official to perform a public duty, in the performance of which the applicant has a sufficient legal interest. The order does not lie against the Crown as such. However, mandamus may enforce performance of a duty imposed by statute on a minister or on a department or on named civil servants, provided that the duty is one which is owed to the applicant and not merely to the Crown.[9] In practice, mandamus is used to enforce the performance of many duties which directly affect the individual.[10]

Mandamus will not lie if the authority has complete discretion whether to act or not. But there may be a duty to exercise a discretion, such as the duty of a tribunal to hear and determine a case within its jurisdiction. Thus the Home Secretary was required by mandamus to hear and determine the application made by the wife of a UK citizen for a certificate of patriality.[11] So too the duty of a tribunal to give reasons for its

---

[4] Supreme Court Act 1981, s 31(1).

[5] L Blom-Cooper [1982] PL 250, 260.

[6] Practice Direction (Administrative Court: Establishment) [2000] 4 All ER 1072.

[7] Administration of Justice (Miscellaneous Provisions) Acts 1933, s 5, and 1938, s 7. Part 54 of the Civil Procedure Rules, that took effect in 2000, calls mandamus a 'mandatory order', prohibition a 'prohibiting order' and certiorari a 'quashing order'. But the Supreme Court Act 1981, s 31 speaks of mandamus, prohibition and certiorari, and has not been amended. In 1994, the Law Commission recommended that the names be changed by amending the 1981 Act: *Administrative Law: Judicial Review and Statutory Appeals*, para 8.3.

[8] De Smith, Woolf and Jowell, *Judicial Review of Administrative Action*, ch 14; Henderson, *Foundations of English Administrative Law*.

[9] R v *Special Commissioners for Income Tax* (1888) 21 QBD 313, 317. Cf R v *Lords of the Treasury* (1872) LR 7 QB 387. And see Harding, *Public Duties and Public Law*, pp 87–96.

[10] E.g. *Padfield v Ministry of Agriculture* [1968] AC 997.

[11] R v *Home Secretary, ex p Phansopkar* [1976] QB 606.

decisions under the Tribunals and Inquiries Act 1992, s 10, may be enforced by mandamus. Where a minister has power to give directions to a local authority, for example in the exercise of default powers, such a direction may be enforced by mandamus, provided that the direction is lawful.[12] Failure to comply with an order of mandamus constitutes contempt of court and is punishable accordingly.

Prohibition is an order issued primarily to prevent an inferior court or tribunal from exceeding its jurisdiction, or acting contrary to the rules of natural justice, where something remained to be done which could be prohibited. *Certiorari* served originally to bring a case or decision from an inferior court into the Court of King's Bench for review. Today it is a means of quashing decisions by inferior courts, tribunals and public authorities where one or more grounds for judicial review are established. By setting aside a defective decision, certiorari prepares the way for a fresh decision to be taken.

As means of jurisdictional control, prohibition and certiorari cover broadly the same ground. The main difference is that certiorari quashes an order or decision already given, and prohibition prevents an order or decision being made which if made would be subject to certiorari. It is convenient to seek both remedies in the same proceedings when a decision in excess of jurisdiction has already been made and other similar decisions have yet to be made.[13] Likewise certiorari and mandamus may be sought in the same proceedings, certiorari to quash a decision in excess of jurisdiction and mandamus to compel the tribunal to hear and determine the case according to law.[14]

Although both certiorari and prohibition originated as means of supervising inferior courts and tribunals, they have long been available against ministers, departments, local authorities and other administrative bodies. It is not necessary now to examine the steps by which this broadening in the application of the remedies took place.[15] Without this enlargement, the remedies could not have provided the basis for an effective system of administrative law. But it is salutary to remember that it was only in 1979 that the Court of Appeal held that prison visitors exercising disciplinary powers over prisoners were subject to review by certiorari, after argument which included debate as to the scope of the remedy.[16] In 1988, the House of Lords held that the governor of a prison was also subject to judicial review and Lord Bridge spoke in terms that made clear how much the language of debate had changed, even since 1979:

> The principle is now as well established as any principle can be in the developing field of public law that where any person or body exercises a power conferred by statute which affects the rights or legitimate expectations of citizens and is of a kind which the law requires to be exercised in accordance with natural justice, the court has jurisdiction to review the exercise of that power.[17]

In other words, if the jurisdiction existed, no separate issue arose as to the availability of certiorari. The 1979 and 1988 decisions concerned the exercise of statutory powers, but the court's supervisory jurisdiction through certiorari extended also to prerogative powers and to regulatory powers, even if they did not derive from statute.[18]

---

[12] *Education Secretary v Tameside MB* [1977] AC 1014.

[13] *R v Paddington Rent Tribunal, ex p Bell Properties Ltd* [1949] 1 KB 666.

[14] E.g. *R v Hammersmith Coroner, ex p Peach* [1980] QB 211.

[15] Leading judgments that show the development are in *R v Electricity Commissioners, ex p London Electricity Joint Committee* [1924] 1 KB 171, 205 (Atkin LJ); *Ridge v Baldwin* [1964] AC 40 (Lord Reid); *R v Criminal Injuries Compensation Board, ex p Lain* [1967] 2 QB 864, 882 (Lord Parker CJ); and *O'Reilly v Mackman* [1983] 2 AC 237, 279 (Lord Diplock).

[16] *R v Board of Visitors of Hull Prison, ex p St Germain* [1979] QB 425.

[17] *Leech v Deputy Governor of Parkhurst Prison* [1988] AC 533, 561.

[18] Respectively *R v Criminal Injuries Compensation Board, ex p Lain* (note 15); and *R v Panel on Takeovers, ex p Datafin plc* [1987] QB 815.

Another necessary development concerned the individual's standing (or *locus standi*) to seek review of a decision. English law has never recognised an *actio popularis* (the right of anyone to challenge the conduct of a public authority regardless of whether he or she is affected by it). Formerly, the rules on what right or interest must be shown by an applicant for a prerogative order might vary with the particular remedy being sought.[19] Fortunately, this is no longer the case, even though aspects of the law of standing to sue are not yet settled.[20]

Injunctions[21]

While the prerogative orders enabled the courts to exercise a supervisory jurisdiction over inferior tribunals and public authorities, the injunction is an equitable remedy available in all branches of law, public and private, to protect a person's rights against unlawful infringement. In the public law field an injunction may be claimed against a public authority or official, to restrain unlawful acts which are threatened or are being committed, for example unlawful interference with private rights[22] or ultra vires action such as improper expenditure of local funds.[23] An important exception relates to the position of the Crown. Injunctions are not available against the Crown as a legal entity, and they are not available in private law proceedings brought directly against the Crown.[24] In place of an injunction in private law proceedings against the Crown, the court may make an order declaring the rights of the parties, and if necessary the court may grant an interim declaration, which the Crown would be expected to observe.[25] However, Community law may require injunctive relief to be available against the Crown[26] and such relief may also be given in judicial review proceedings against government departments, ministers and civil servants.[27]

Where the injunction concerns private rights (for example, liability in private nuisance), the ordinary rules of the law of property or tort apply as to who may seek an injunction. But when the injunction concerns a matter of public right (for example, the public nuisance caused by the obstruction of a highway), an injunction can be obtained by the Attorney-General, either at his own instance or at the instance of a relator (i.e. one who informs). A relator need have no personal interest in the subject-matter of the claim save his or her interest as a member of the public. The consent of the Attorney-General to the proceedings prevents any objection being taken to the relator's standing in the matter.

There are two cases where a person can sue without joining the Attorney-General:

(*a*)   if interference with the public right also constitutes an interference with the claimant's private right; for example, where an obstruction on a highway is also an interference with a private right of access to the highway;[28]

---

[19] De Smith, Woolf and Jowell, op cit, pp 626–31, 634–5; Thio, *Locus Standi and Judicial Review*.

[20] See p 739 below.

[21] De Smith, Woolf and Jowell, op cit, pp 637–42; Wade and Forsyth, op cit, pp 553–60.

[22] E.g. *Pride of Derby Angling Association* v *British Celanese Ltd* [1953] Ch 149.

[23] *A-G* v *Aspinall* (1837) 2 My & Cr 406.

[24] Crown Proceedings Act 1947, s 21; ch 32 C.

[25] Civil Procedure Rules, 25.1(1). For the former position, see *R* v *IRC, ex p Rossminster Ltd* [1980] AC 952.

[26] *R* v *Transport Secretary, ex p Factortame Ltd* [1990] 2 AC 85; *(The same) (No 2)* [1991] 1 AC 603. See also the Public Supply Contracts Regulations 1991, SI 1991 No 2679, reg 26, authorising injunctive relief against the Crown for breach of the regulations.

[27] *M* v *Home Office* [1994] 1 AC 377; and note 62 below.

[28] *Boyce* v *Paddington BC* [1903] 1 Ch 109; *Barrs* v *Bethell* [1982] Ch 294.

(*b*) where no private right of the claimant is interfered with, but he or she suffers special damage from the interference with a public right, for example, where as a result of a public nuisance a plaintiff's premises have been rendered unhealthy.[29]

A third exception, under the Local Government Act 1972, is that a local authority may institute proceedings in its own name when it considers it expedient for promoting or protecting the interests of inhabitants of its area, even though the object of the proceedings is to enforce public rights which before the 1972 Act would have required the Attorney-General's consent to relator proceedings.[30]

Relator actions are rare today and are not used to restrain action by a public authority where a claim for judicial review is available. One use of relator proceedings, that goes far outside administrative law, is to provide a means of enforcing the criminal law when existing penalties and procedures are inadequate to deter repeated breach.

In *Attorney-General* v *Sharp*, the owner of a fleet of buses had been prosecuted 48 times for breach of local regulations in operating his buses without a licence. He continued to run his buses without a licence, since despite the fines he found it profitable to do so. *Held* that, since the rights of the public were involved and as the remedies provided by the local Act had proved ineffective, there was jurisdiction to grant an injunction at the instance of the Attorney-General by way of ancillary relief.[31]

In comparable circumstances, relator proceedings have been used to enforce planning control and fire precautions against those who find it profitable to break the law.[32]

In practice, the Attorney-General appears to have absolute discretion in deciding whether to consent to relator proceedings. Although he is accountable to Parliament for his decisions, he cannot be required to justify them to the courts nor may the courts overrule the decisions. These questions were settled in 1977 in *Gouriet*'s case:

The Union of Post Office Workers had asked its members to boycott South African mail for one week as a protest against apartheid. Gouriet, claiming that the boycott would be criminal conduct under the Post Office Act 1953, asked the Attorney-General to consent to proceedings for an injunction against the union. This consent was refused. Gouriet then obtained an interim injunction against the union from the Court of Appeal. On appeal to the House of Lords, *held* that when the Attorney-General has refused consent to relator proceedings, a private citizen who asserts that the public interest is affected by a threatened breach of the criminal law, may not go to the civil courts for a remedy, whether injunction or declaration. Public rights may be asserted in a civil action only by the Attorney-General as representing the public. The Attorney-General's discretion may not be reviewed in the courts.[33]

In the sensitive political circumstances of the *Gouriet* case, a difficult discretion had to be exercised in the public interest and it would have broken new ground for the Attorney-General's decision to be subject to judicial review. Yet in not dissimilar circumstances involving the imminent breach of a local authority's duty to maintain its schools, the court was willing to assume jurisdiction.[34] The proposition of the Lords in *Gouriet* that public rights can be asserted only by the Attorney-General applies both to injunctions and to declarations sought by ordinary action. However, the Lords were not dealing with applications for judicial review by which, as we shall see, individuals

---

[29] *Benjamin* v *Storr* (1874) LR 9 CP 400.
[30] *Stoke-on-Trent Council* v *B & Q (Retail) Ltd* [1984] AC 754; *Kirklees Council* v *Wickes Building Supplies Ltd* [1993] AC 227. And see B Hough [1992] PL 130.
[31] [1931] 1 Ch 121; and see *A-G* v *Harris* [1961] 1 QB 74.
[32] *A-G* v *Bastow* [1957] 1 QB 514; *A-G* v *Chaudry* [1971] 3 All ER 938.
[33] *Gouriet* v *Union of Post Office Workers* [1978] AC 435; and see P P Mercer [1979] PL 214, B Hough (1988) 8 LS 189, and Edwards, *The Attorney-General, Politics and the Public Interest*, pp 120–58.
[34] *Meade* v *Haringey BC* [1979] 2 All ER 1016.

may with leave of the court bring proceedings against public authorities in which the Attorney-General plays no part.

The High Court may grant an injunction to restrain a person from acting in an office to which he or she is not entitled and may also declare the office to be vacant. This procedure takes the place of the ancient procedure of an information in the nature of a writ of *quo warranto*.[35]

Declaratory judgments[36]

A declaratory judgment is one which merely declares the legal relationship of the parties and is not accompanied by any sanction or means of enforcement. The authority of a court's ruling on law is such that a declaratory judgment will normally restrain both the Crown and public authorities from illegal conduct. By the Civil Procedure Rules, 40.20: 'The courts may make binding declarations whether or not any other remedy is claimed.'

It is a convenience in many public law disputes to be able to have the law determined in relation to particular facts without seeking a coercive remedy. An early example arose in *Dyson v Attorney-General*, where a taxpayer obtained a declaration against the Crown that the tax authorities had no power to request certain information from him on pain of a £50 penalty for disobedience.[37] The jurisdiction to grant declarations is as wide as the law itself, except that the judges may as a matter of discretion impose limits on its use. Thus an action for a declaratory judgment must be based on a concrete case which has arisen. The courts will not give answers to questions propounded in the form of hypothetical cases and are reluctant to grant a bare declaration that can have no legal consequences;[38] however, courts have reviewed the legality of advisory guidance which in itself has no legal effect.[39]

The court will not give a declaratory opinion in civil proceedings as to a matter that is in issue in concurrent criminal proceedings[40] and, even at the request of the Attorney-General, will not grant a declaration that conduct would be criminal except in a very clear case.[41] Where a statute both creates a duty and provides the procedure for enforcing it, this may exclude declaratory proceedings.[42] But the existence of a statutory procedure for obtaining a decision on whether planning permission was needed did not prevent a landowner from coming to court for a declaration as to the extent of existing development rights.[43]

Actions for a declaration formerly had some procedural advantages over the prerogative orders and were brought for this reason. Thus, instead of being quashed by certiorari, the decision of a tribunal could be declared invalid as being in excess of jurisdiction or in breach of natural justice,[44] but the court could not by a declaration decide afresh a question entrusted by statute to a minister or tribunal.[45] The use of

---

[35] Supreme Court Act 1981, s 30; cf Local Government Act 1972, s 92.

[36] De Smith, Woolf and Jowell, op cit, ch 18; Zamir and Woolf, *The Declaratory Judgment*.

[37] [1912] 1 Ch 158.

[38] *Maxwell v Dept of Trade* [1974] QB 523.

[39] E.g. *Gillick v West Norfolk Health Authority* [1986] AC 112. In 1994, the Law Commission recommended that the High Court be authorised in its judicial review jurisdiction to make advisory declarations on points of general importance: Law Com No 226, pp 74–6. And see J Laws (1994) 57 MLR 213.

[40] *Imperial Tobacco Ltd v A-G* [1981] AC 718.

[41] *A-G v Able* [1984] QB 795. Special considerations arise in medical cases where a patient cannot consent to treatment; e.g. *F (Mental Patient: Sterilisation)* [1990] 2 AC 1; *Airedale NHS Trust v Bland* [1993] AC 789; cf *R (Pretty) v DPP* [2002] 1 All ER 1.

[42] *Barraclough v Brown* [1897] AC 615.

[43] *Pyx Granite Co Ltd v Ministry of Housing* [1960] AC 260.

[44] *Anisminic Ltd v Foreign Compensation Commission* [1969] 2 AC 147; *Ridge v Baldwin* [1964] AC 40.

[45] *Healey v Minister of Health* [1955] 1 QB 221; *Argosam Finance Ltd v Oxby* [1965] Ch 390.

the declaration in this way was greatly restricted when the procedure of application for judicial review was created in 1977–82.[46]

The creation of the procedure of application for judicial review

In 1976, the main reasons why reform in the remedies available in administrative law was essential were the following:[47]

(*a*)   While two or more of the prerogative orders could be sought in the same proceedings and an injunction and declaration could be sought together, the two classes of remedy could not be combined nor could a litigant who made the wrong choice convert one procedure into the other. Damages could be sought with an injunction or declaration, but not with the prerogative orders.

(*b*)   The rules of standing to sue differed as between the prerogative orders and injunctions/declarations.

(*c*)   The summary procedure used for the prerogative orders did not allow for discovery of documents or the cross-examination of witnesses.

(*d*)   Certiorari had to be sought within six months, but no fixed limit of time applied to the declaration.

(*e*)   Leave from the court was required for prerogative order proceedings but not for injunctions/declarations.

(*f*)   The declaration lay in respect of all forms of official act, including delegated legislation, and against all public authorities, including the Crown. But a declaration could not quash a decision made by a tribunal within jurisdiction.

Accordingly, the Law Commission proposed a draft Bill to create the procedure of application for judicial review. The Commission emphasised that the new procedure was not to be an exclusive remedy and litigants would remain free to seek an injunction or declaration if they so chose. In the event the procedure of applying for judicial review was created first by amending the Rules of the Supreme Court to provide a new Order 53; this was soon amended so that judicial review decisions in civil cases could be made by a single judge instead of by a Divisional Court (two or three judges).[48] It was by the Supreme Court Act 1981, s 31, that the procedure of judicial review was authorised by Parliament. Moreover, the business of the High Court was reorganised by forming a Crown Office list, to include judicial review, statutory appeals to the High Court and similar matters.[49] In 1982, the House of Lords in *O'Reilly* v *Mackman* gave impetus to the reforms by holding that, for most purposes in public law, the procedure of application for judicial review had become an exclusive remedy.[50]

Minor changes were made in 1990 as the first effects of Lord Woolf's review of civil procedure were felt, but a more extensive reform occurred after a review of the Crown Office list by an expert group chaired by Sir Jeffery Bowman. In October 2000, Order 53 gave way to Part 54 of the Civil Procedure Rules; the name Administrative Court was given to the court that would hear cases on the Administrative Court list.[51]

---

[46] See the discussion of *O'Reilly* v *Mackman* [1983] 2 AC 286 (p 741 below).

[47] Report on Remedies in Administrative Law, Cmnd 6407, 1976.

[48] See SI 1977 No 1955, amended by SI 1980 No 2000.

[49] *Practice Direction* [1981] 3 All ER 61.

[50] See pp 741–3 below.

[51] CPR, Part 54 and Part 54 Practice Direction; also *Practice Direction* (*Administrative Court: Establishment*) [2000] 4 All ER 1071. See Bowman, *Review of the Crown Office List*, March 2000. For text of the rules and comment, see the journal Judicial Review: 1999 (pp 72–95, 207–17); 2000 (pp 164–70, 209–39); and 2001 (pp 197–204).

Applications for judicial review: the procedure

By s 31 of the Supreme Court Act 1981, applications to the High Court for an order of mandamus, prohibition or certiorari (and for an injunction restraining a person from acting in a public office to which he or she is not entitled) *must* be made, in accordance with rules of court, by an application for judicial review. In the Civil Procedure Rules, 54.1, the prerogative orders are called mandatory, prohibiting and quashing orders respectively, but their scope is unchanged. The High Court has a discretionary power (by s 31(2) of the 1981 Act) to make a declaration or grant an injunction whenever an application for judicial review has been made seeking that relief, if it would be 'just and convenient' to do so. In exercising this discretion the court must have regard inter alia to the nature of the matters in respect of which the prerogative orders apply, the nature of the persons and bodies against whom the orders lie and all the circumstances. Thus within the scope of the prerogative orders, concerning matters of public law, declarations and injunctions may be granted on an application for judicial review. But the Act leaves it entirely open whether within this field an application for judicial review is to be the sole means of obtaining an injunction or declaration.

Leave of the court is needed for every application for judicial review (s 31(3)). This rule, derived from earlier procedure for the prerogative orders, means that a two-stage process is followed: (*a*) when the court decides whether to give leave (permission) for an application for judicial review to proceed and if so (*b*) the substantive hearing of the application.

Under the Civil Procedure Rules, the claimant files a claim form, stating the action or decision to be reviewed, the relevant facts, the grounds of the claim and the remedy sought. Notice must be given to the defendant (the body or official who took the action or decision) and other interested parties; the defendant and others notified must within 21 days state whether they intend to contest the claim and, if so, must give a summary of the grounds they will rely on. The granting of permission is generally decided on the papers by a single judge,[52] but the judge may request a short hearing in open court. A hearing is held if interim relief is sought. If permission is refused or granted in part or subject to conditions, the claimant may ask for the matter to be reconsidered at a hearing. If permission is still withheld, the claimant may appeal to the Court of Appeal.[53] In the past, the 'filter' stage has operated very unevenly, but it is a safeguard against a flood of 'hopeless' cases and vexatious challenges.[54] Once permission has been granted, further evidence may be filed and the substantive hearing takes place before a single judge or a divisional court.

An important rule is that claims must be made promptly and 'in any event not later than three months after the grounds to make the claim first arose', but the period may be shorter if legislation so provides for a particular claim.[55] If the court considers that the case is one which requires urgent action (for instance, a challenge to school admission decisions), it may refuse permission for a claim that is not made promptly, even within the three-month period. The court may extend time if there is a good reason to do so, but the parties may not agree to extend time.[56] Under the Supreme

---

[52] In 2001, 24 judges were designated to sit in the Administrative Court.
[53] CPR 52.15. If the Court of Appeal refuses leave the House of Lords has jurisdiction to grant leave to appeal: *R v London Borough of Hammersmith, ex p Burkett* [2002] UK HL 23, overruling, *Re Poh* [1983] 1 All ER 287.
[54] See A Le Sueur and M Sunkin [1992] PL 102; Bridges, Meszaros and Sunkin, *Judicial Review in Perspective*, chs 7, 8 and (same authors) [2000] PL 651.
[55] CPR 54.5. For the operation of these rules, see *R (Burkett) v Hammersmith LBC* [2001] JPL 775. Also N Pleming and K Marcus [2000] Judicial Review 6; G Roots and R Walton [2001] JPL 775; M J Beloff in Forsyth and Hare (eds) *The Golden Metwand and the Crooked Cord*, pp 267–95.
[56] CPR 3.1(2)(a); 54.5(2).

Court Act 1981, s 31(6), the court may refuse to grant leave for an application or may refuse relief sought by the claimant if it considers that the granting of the relief 'would be likely to cause substantial hardship to, or substantially prejudice the rights of, any person or would be detrimental to good administration'. The interaction of this provision with the procedure rules has caused much difficulty. It is now established that where permission has been granted for judicial review, the court at the substantive hearing may not set aside that permission on the ground that there had been unjustified delay in the claim being made; however, delay may be a reason for withholding relief that would otherwise be justified.[57]

If permission to proceed with a claim for judicial review is given, the court may order a stay of proceedings to which the claim relates.[58] The court may grant other interim relief, including mandatory orders and interim declarations,[59] applying the test of balance of convenience that is appropriate in civil proceedings generally,[60] but with regard to special considerations applicable to public law litigation.[61]

The 1981 Act did not expressly provide for interim relief against the Crown, as recommended by the Law Commission, but in *M v Home Office*[62] it was held that the language of s 31 enabled coercive orders (including interim injunctions) to be made against ministers of the Crown in judicial review proceedings.

On an application for judicial review, the court may award damages if these have been sought by the applicant and the court is satisfied that damages could have been obtained by an action brought for the purpose (s 31(4)). But the 1981 Act did not alter the substantive rules of liability in damages and the fact that an individual suffered financial loss because of a decision that is quashed as invalid gives rise to no liability.[63] Thus even successful applicants for judicial review seldom obtain damages.

A claim for judicial review must be supported by such written evidence as is available and a witness statement confirming the truth of the facts relied on; the defendant authority may file evidence in reply. The claimant is under a duty to the court to disclose all relevant material of which he or she is aware, even if it weakens the claim. The court may order disclosure of documents, further information and cross-examination of witnesses. In practice, many cases turn on the documents that record the decision-making process. It is sometimes said that a claim for judicial review is unsuitable for resolving disputes of fact. However, the court must decide issues of fact that are essential to a claim (such as a disputed claim that a decision-maker was biased or that proper consultation did not occur). Where an order is granted to quash the decision under review, the court remits the matter to the decision-maker, with an appropriate direction, but if there is no purpose in remitting it the court may take the decision itself.[64] The Civil Procedure Rules permit claims begun by ordinary procedure to be transferred, with permission of the court, into a claim for judicial review and, conversely, a claim for judicial review may be transferred into an ordinary claim.[65]

[57] See *R v Criminal Injuries Compensation Board, ex p A* [1999] 2 AC 330; *R v Dairy Produce Tribunal, ex p Caswell* [1990] 2 AC 738 (and A Lindsay [1995] PL 417).

[58] CPR 54.10. Under the former RSC Order 53, r 10, 'stay of proceedings' was interpreted broadly in *R v Education Secretary, ex p Avon Council* [1991] 1 QB 558, but see *Minister of Foreign Affairs v Vehicles and Supplies Ltd* [1991] 4 All ER 65.

[59] CPR 25.1(1). This power was not formerly available: *R v IRC, ex p Rossminster Ltd* [1980] AC 952.

[60] *American Cyanamid Co v Ethicon Ltd* [1975] AC 396.

[61] See e.g. *R v Kensington and Chelsea BC, ex p Hammell* [1989] QB 518 and *R v Inspectorate of Pollution, ex p Greenpeace Ltd* [1994] 4 All ER 322.

[62] [1994] 1 AC 377 (H W R Wade (1991) 107 LQR 4; M Gould [1993] PL 368). For the Crown Proceedings Act 1947, s 21, see ch 32 C.

[63] Ch 32 A; e.g. *Dunlop v Woollahra Council* [1982] AC 158.

[64] Supreme Court Act 1981, s 31(5); and CPR 54.19.

[65] CPR, Part 30 and 54.20.

Significant issues which have arisen in relation to the public law character of applications for judicial review include (*a*) the scope and extent of review, (*b*) standing to apply for review, (*c*) the effect of alternative remedies, (*d*) whether judicial review is exclusive and (*e*) the discretion of the court in granting review.

Scope and extent of judicial review

Much greater use is made of the procedure for judicial review than was formerly made of the prerogative orders. If an application for review concerns decisions of any public authority or official, the courts readily accept jurisdiction in judicial review, except if a reason to the contrary is shown.[66] Thus decisions taken under prerogative powers are subject to review, unless in their subject matter the court considers them to be non-justiciable.[67] Also reviewable are decisions by local authorities in controlling access to public property, initiating legal proceedings and in matters preliminary to the award of contracts.[68] Such decisions arise from an exercise of public power susceptible to control on principles of public law. Two broad exceptions to the availability of judicial review exist. First, some decisions are subject to statutory appeals and similar procedures which, to a greater or lesser extent, exclude judicial review under CPR Part 54.15.[69] Second, public authorities are in general subject to the ordinary law of contract, tort and property. Since *O'Reilly* v *Mackman*,[70] such branches of law may be said to be within 'private law' to distinguish them from the rules of 'public law' applied on judicial review. A claim for judicial review may not be used in place of an ordinary action in contract or tort, just because the defendant is a public authority.

Thus, when such an authority dismisses an employee, the employee's primary remedy is a claim for unfair dismissal or a claim under the contract of employment.[71] However, depending on the circumstances, decisions by public authorities as employers may stem from or involve issues of public law.[72] Public sector employees such as NHS hospital staff[73] and civil servants[74] must generally use procedures open to them in employment law rather than seek judicial review. This does not apply to holders of public office such as police and prison officers[75] whose position is based on statute. Judicial review may be available if a public employment dispute raises issues as to the powers of the public authority or other matters suitable for redress by judicial review.[76]

A difficult question is what constitutes a 'public law dispute' for judicial review purposes. The prerogative orders were not, and judicial review is not, available against bodies such as trade unions or commercial companies. Membership of a trade union is based on contract. If a trade unionist complains that his or her expulsion from the

[66] See de Smith, Woolf and Jowell, op cit, ch 3; Lewis, *Judicial Remedies in Public Law*, ch 4.
[67] See the CCSU case, note 72 below; and e.g. *R* v *Ministry of Defence, ex p Smith* [1996] QB 517. Cf *Reckley* v *Minister of Public Safety (No 2)* [1996] AC 527.
[68] Respectively *Wheeler* v *Leicester City Council* [1985] AC 1054; *Avon CC* v *Buscott* [1988] QB 656; and *R* v *Enfield Council, ex p TF Unwin (Roydon) Ltd* [1989] 1 Admin LR 51.
[69] See pp 743–8 below.
[70] [1983] 2 AC 237, p 741 below.
[71] *R* v *BBC, ex p Lavelle* [1983] 1 All ER 241.
[72] E.g. *CCSU* v *Minister for Civil Service* [1985] AC 374; cf H W R Wade (1985) 101 LQR 180, 190–6.
[73] *R* v *East Berks Health Authority, ex p Walsh* [1985] QB 152, and p 773 below.
[74] *R* v *Lord Chancellor's Department, ex p Nangle* [1992] 1 All ER 897.
[75] *R* v *Home Secretary, ex p Benwell* [1985] QB 554. By the Criminal Justice and Public Order Act 1994, s 126, prison officers acquired the same employment rights as other civil servants: G S Morris [1994] PL 535.
[76] See *McLaren* v *Home Office* [1990] ICR 824. Also S Fredman and G Morris [1988] PL 58, [1991] PL 484, (1991) 107 LQR 298.

union was in breach of union rules or infringed natural justice, he or she may sue the union for damages and an injunction. Bodies such as the National Greyhound Racing Club and the Jockey Club are not subject to judicial review, even if they regulate major areas of sport, but contractual remedies will often be available.[77] Neither are decisions by religious bodies subject to judicial review.[78] The position of the universities is unduly complex. In older colleges and universities that have a visitor, in general, complaints by a student or staff member about the university must be taken to the visitor, whose decisions are subject to judicial review on limited grounds.[79] But many recently created universities have no visitor and their decisions are subject to judicial review on the usual grounds.[80]

The most difficult case is that of regulatory bodies which derive their powers neither directly from statute[81] nor from contract. Despite having no formal legal status, the City Panel on Take-overs and Mergers is subject to judicial review, since its functions 'de facto' are in the nature of public law powers and are indirectly supported by statutory sanctions.[82] The effect of privatisation and 'market testing' of public services has produced some conflicting decisions.[83] Publicly owned undertakings are subject to judicial review in respect of some of their functions.[84] Inferior courts, such as magistrates' courts and county courts, are subject to judicial review. So is the Crown Court, 'other than its jurisdiction in matters relating to trial on indictment'.[85] This limitation expresses an important principle that makes it necessary to distinguish between those decisions of the Crown Court that are subject to judicial review and others which can be challenged only by appeal after a trial.

This discussion has been based on judicial decisions made before the Human Rights Act 1998 took effect. As we have seen,[86] the Act obliges public authorities (and bodies that exercise functions both of a public nature and of a private nature) to act consistently with Convention rights. Some bodies that were outside the scope of judicial review may now rank as public authorities;[87] they may be subject to judicial review if their decisions are not subject to another remedy. However, where the dismissal of a public sector employee involves breaches of his or her Convention rights, in principle the remedy may continue to lie in the employment tribunal, not the Administrative Court.

---

[77] *Law* v *National Greyhound Racing Club Ltd* [1983] 3 All ER 300; *R* v *Disciplinary Committee of the Jockey Club, ex p Aga Khan* [1993] 2 All ER 853. And see M Beloff [1989] PL 95; N Bamforth [1993] PL 239. Cf *Finnigan* v *New Zealand Rugby Football Union Inc* [1985] 2 NZLR 159 (private association exercising function of major national importance).

[78] *R* v *Chief Rabbi, ex p Wachmann* [1993] 2 All ER 249.

[79] *R* v *Hull University Visitor, ex p Page* [1993] AC 682.

[80] See e.g. *R* v *Metropolitan University of Manchester, ex p Nolan* [1994] ELR 380 and cf *Clark* v *University of Lincolnshire and Humberside* [2000] 3 All ER 752.

[81] Unlike the Law Society; see e.g. *Swain* v *Law Society* [1983] 1 AC 598.

[82] *R* v *Panel on Take-overs and Mergers, ex p Datafin plc* [1987] QB 817 (C F Forsyth [1987] PL 356; D Oliver [1987] PL 543); *R* v *Advertising Standards Agency, ex p Insurance Service plc* (1990) 2 Admin LR 77.

[83] Compare *R* v *Lord Chancellor, ex p Hibbit & Saunders* [1993] COD 326 (D Oliver [1993] PL 214) and *R* v *Legal Aid Board, ex p Donn & Co* [1996] 3 All ER 1.

[84] *R* v *British Coal Corpn, ex p Vardy* [1993] ICR 720. See ch 14.

[85] Supreme Court Act 1981, s 29(3); R Ward [1990] PL 50; *in re Ashton* [1994] 1 AC 9 and *R* v *Manchester Crown Court, ex p DPP* [1993] 4 All ER 928; and see *R* v *DPP, ex p Kebeline* [2000] 2 AC 326 (decision to prosecute subject to criminal process, not to judicial review).

[86] See ch 19 C.

[87] See D Oliver [2000] PL 475, 486–8; and *Aston Cantlow Parochial Church Council* v *Wallbank* [2001] 3 All ER 393.

Standing to apply for judicial review

At the stage when leave is sought for an application for judicial review, the court must not grant leave 'unless it considers that the applicant has a sufficient interest in the matter to which the application relates' (s 31(3)). The test of 'sufficient interest' was proposed by the Law Commission in 1976 as a formula which would allow for further development in the rules of standing. It plainly allows the court discretion to decide what is to constitute 'sufficient interest'. To what extent did it alter existing rules of locus standi?

> In *R v Inland Revenue Commissioners, ex p National Federation of Self-employed and Small Businesses*, a body of taxpayers challenged arrangements made by the Commissioners for levying tax on wages paid to casual employees on Fleet Street newspapers. For many years the employees had given fictitious names to evade tax, but the Commissioners agreed with the employers and unions on a scheme for collecting tax in future and for two previous years, in return for an undertaking by the Commissioners not to investigate any earlier years. The Federation, complaining that their members were never treated so favourably, applied for a declaration that the arrangement was unlawful, and a mandamus ordering the Commissioners to collect tax as required by law. The Court of Appeal held, assuming the agreement to be unlawful, that the Federation had sufficient interest in the matter for their application to be heard. The House of Lords *held* that the question of sufficient interest was not merely a preliminary issue to be decided when leave was being sought on an application for judicial review, but had to be resolved in relation to what was known by the court of the matter under review. On the evidence, the tax agreement was a lawful exercise of the Commissioners' discretion. In general, unlike local ratepayers,[88] a taxpayer did not have an interest in challenging decisions concerning other taxpayers' affairs. In the circumstances, the National Federation did not have sufficient interest to challenge the Commissioners' decisions.[89]

The speeches in this case contain a perplexing diversity of opinions about the test of 'sufficient interest'. The account just presented seeks to summarise the views of three judges (Lords Wilberforce, Fraser and Roskill), although Lord Fraser also stressed that the test of 'sufficient interest' was a logically prior question which had to be answered before any question of the merits arose. Lord Scarman paid lip service to the existence of a test of standing separate from the merits, but his conclusion (that the Federation had no sufficient interest *because* they had not shown that the tax authorities had failed in their duties) virtually eliminated any prior test of standing separate from the merits. Lord Diplock, who advocated a very broad test of standing, was alone in holding that the Federation had sufficient interest in the matter; in his view the case simply failed on its merits. What emerges from the various speeches is that the judges were reluctant to turn away the applicants without hearing something of their case, and unwilling to hold that the tax authorities were immune from judicial review.

In most applications for judicial review, the question of sufficient interest presents no problems, although for the parties not to raise the issue does not confer on the court jurisdiction that is otherwise absent.[90] An ordinary taxpayer had interest to challenge the government's proposal to designate as a 'Community treaty' a treaty providing extra funds to the Community.[91] The Equal Opportunities Commission had standing to challenge statutory provisions which discriminated against women employees in breach of their Community rights.[92] Organisations such as trade unions acting in their

---

[88] *Arsenal FC v Ende* [1979] AC 1.
[89] [1982] AC 617 (P Cane [1981] PL 322). And see de Smith, Woolf and Jowell, ch 2.
[90] *R v Social Services Secretary, ex p CPAG* [1990] 2 QB 540.
[91] *R v HM Treasury, ex p Smedley* [1985] QB 657; *R v Foreign Secretary, ex p Rees-Mogg* [1994] QB 552. See also *R v Felixstowe Justices, ex p Leigh* [1987] QB 582.
[92] *R v Employment Secretary, ex p EOC* [1995] 1 AC 1.

members' interests and environmental groups have standing to challenge decisions on relevant issues,[93] but difficulties may arise when an applicant is not personally affected by a decision and is acting in the public interest.[94] Thus a non-profit-making company formed to protect the site of a Shakespearian theatre had no standing to review a minister's decision refusing to schedule the site as a historic monument.[95] It has been said that at the leave stage, the test of sufficient interest should be applied only to exclude those without a legitimate concern ('in other words a busybody'),[96] but at the substantive hearing other questions of standing may be raised. Relatives of someone who was murdered were held to have no standing to seek review of a decision by the Lord Chief Justice as to the minimum period in detention that the murderers should serve.[97]

A new test of standing is created by the Human Rights Act 1998, s 7: a claim that a public authority has acted incompatibly with a Convention right, in breach of s 6 of the Act, may be brought only by someone who is a 'victim' of the act within the meaning of art 34 ECHR. Strasbourg case-law does not permit cases to be brought by representative bodies and pressure groups unless they themselves are victims of a breach of their Convention rights.[98] Such bodies must thus ensure that one or more 'victims' are claimants for judicial review in order to be able to rely on s 6 of the 1998 Act. Fortunately, there is no victim test for persons who wish to rely on other provisions of the Act, such as the duty under s 3 to interpret legislation consistently with the Convention, wherever this is possible.

Alternative remedies

Another issue considered at the leave stage stems from the principle that the prerogative orders are a residual remedy. In a leading 19th century case, mandamus was refused where a statute created both a duty and a specific remedy for enforcing it (complaint to central government).[99] Today, an individual must use an express right of appeal if this will meet the substance of the complaint.[100] Tribunals exist for deciding claims to social security, disputes over tax, immigration claims and so on.[101] Judicial review is not an optional substitute for an appeal to a tribunal with appropriate jurisdiction.[102] The existence of an alternative remedy does not deprive the Administrative Court of jurisdiction, but requires the court to exercise its discretion: whether leave for judicial review to proceed is granted will depend on whether the statutory remedy is a satisfactory and effective alternative to review.[103] Thus, the default powers of ministers concerning social service complaints may deal with the factual issues raised by a complaint, but do not enable important points of law to be resolved.[104] Sometimes the reason for

---

[93] *R v Inspectorate of Pollution, ex p Greenpeace (No 2)* [1992] 4 All ER 329; *R v Home Secretary, ex p Fire Brigades Union* [1995] 2 AC 513; *R v Foreign Secretary, ex p World Development Movement* [1995] 1 All ER 611. And P Cane [1995] PL 276.

[94] See Law Com No 226, pp 41–44 and report by Justice, *A Matter of Public Interest* (1996).

[95] *R v Environment Secretary, ex p Rose Theatre Trust Co* [1990] 1 QB 504. See also Sir K Schiemann [1990] PL 342 and P Cane [1990] PL 307.

[96] *R v Somerset CC, ex p Dixon* [1998] Env LR 111.

[97] *R (Bulger) v Home Secretary* [2001] 3 All ER 449. The claim was also rejected on its merits.

[98] See Clayton and Tomlinson, *The Law of Human Rights*, ch 22 B.

[99] *Pasmore v Oswaldtwistle Council* [1898] AC 387. And see *Barraclough v Brown* [1897] AC 615 (declarations).

[100] *R v Paddington Valuation Officer, ex p Peachey Property Co* [1996] 1 QB 380.

[101] See ch 29 A.

[102] *R v IRC, ex p Preston* [1985] AC 835.

[103] *Leech v Deputy Governor of Parkhurst Prison* [1988] AC 533.

[104] *R v Devon CC, ex p Baker* [1995] 1 All ER 73.

withholding permission is merely that the application for judicial review is premature, as, for instance, where a right of appeal is open to the individual. In other cases, a judicial remedy may be justified, if the decision at first instance is manifestly ultra vires[105] or there has been abuse of statutory procedure by the authority.[106] But where to protect consumers the sale of an unsafe product was banned by a local authority, the manufacturer was required to appeal to the magistrates' court and could not seek judicial review.[107] In such cases, the court considers such matters as the comparative speed, expense and finality of the alternative processes, the need for fact-finding and the desirability of an authoritative ruling on points of law.[108]

Does judicial review provide an exclusive procedure?[109]

Although the House of Lords failed to sound a clear note in the *National Federation* case, the House in two later cases was unanimous in holding that litigants seeking judicial review must proceed by application under the then Order 53. The question arose because the Supreme Court Act 1981 did not expressly exclude the individual in public law cases from suing for an injunction or declaration, or for damages for breach of statutory duty. The issue had arisen in numerous cases concerning immigrants, prisoners, homeless persons and others.

> In *O'Reilly* v *Mackman*, convicted prisoners who had lost remission of sentence in disciplinary proceedings after riots at Hull prison sued for a declaration that the decisions were null and void because of breaches of natural justice.[110] The defendants applied to have the action struck out on the ground that the decisions of boards of visitors could be challenged only by an application for judicial review. *Held* (House of Lords) while the High Court had jurisdiction to grant the declarations sought, the prisoners' case was based solely on rights and obligations arising under public law. Order 53, by its requirement of leave from the court and by its time limit, protected public authorities against groundless or delayed attacks. It would 'as a general rule be contrary to public policy, and as such an abuse of the process of the court, to permit a person seeking to establish that a decision of a public authority infringed rights to which he was entitled to protection under public law to proceed by way of ordinary action and by this means to evade the provision of Order 53 for the protection of such authorities' (Lord Diplock).[111] And in *Cocks* v *Thanet DC*, the House held that a homeless person who sought to challenge a decision by a local authority that he was not entitled to permanent accommodation must do so under Order 53, and not by suing in the county court for a declaration and damages for breach of statutory duty.[112]

Although neither the Supreme Court Act 1981 nor Order 53 had established the application for judicial review as an exclusive remedy, these two decisions left no doubt that the Lords wished to carry further than Parliament had done the reforms associated with Order 53. The step taken in *O'Reilly* was justified on practical grounds, namely that litigants could be required to use the judicial review procedure as the former

---

[105] *R* v *Hillingdon Council, ex p Royco Homes Ltd* [1974] 1 QB 720.
[106] *R* v *Chief Constable, Merseyside, ex p Calveley* [1986] QB 424.
[107] *R* v *Birmingham Council, ex p Ferrero Ltd* [1993] 1 All ER 530.
[108] *R* v *Falmouth Port Health Authority, ex p South West Water Ltd* [2001] QB 445.
[109] See De Smith, Woolf and Jowell, pp 191–201; Wade and Forsyth, pp 649–666; Craig, ch 23; A Tanney [1994] PL 51.
[110] See *R* v *Board of Visitors of Hull Prison, ex p St Germain* [1979] QB 425.
[111] [1983] 2 AC 237, 285. And see C F Forsyth [1985] CLJ 415; and Justice/All Souls Report, *Administrative Justice*, ch 6.
[112] [1983] 2 AC 286. In *O'Rourke* v *Camden Council* [1998] AC 188, the decision in *Cocks* was applied but other aspects of the case were disapproved.

defects hampering use of the prerogative orders had been cured. But in expressly seeking to protect public authorities from a flood of litigation,[113] *Reilly* relied heavily on the public law/private law distinction, despite the difficulties that this presents in English law.[114]

One consequence of *O'Reilly* has been that much effort in litigation has been spent in testing the procedural choices made by litigants, rather than in deciding the merits of their grievances. Sir William Wade's view in 2000 was dramatic: 'The need for law reform is clearly greater now than it was before 1977.'[115] However, this understates the general benefits resulting from the 1977 reforms, and the Law Commission in 1994 did not share this view of the difficulties created by *O'Reilly*.[116] Decisions by the Lords since *O'Reilly* have shown that the rule of procedural exclusivity is not absolute. An action for negligence against a planning authority relating to an agreement over a disputed enforcement notice was held to raise no question of public law, since the action did not seek to quash the notice and assumed that it was valid.[117] In *O'Reilly*, Lord Diplock stated that an exception to the rule might exist where the invalidity of an official decision arose 'as a collateral issue in a claim for infringement of a right of the plaintiff arising under private law'.[118] The converse of this situation arose when a local council sued one of its tenants for non-payment of rent and the tenants raised the defence that rent increases made by the council were ultra vires. Although the tenant could have sought judicial review of the increases (and had not done so), the defence was held to be no abuse of process but a proper defence of the tenant's private rights.[119] In 1992, Lord Diplock's suggested exception was applied directly in *Roy* v *Kensington Family Practitioner Committee*. An NHS committee, acting under statutory powers, had deducted 20% from money which was due to Dr Roy for providing medical services to the NHS; in suing by ordinary action for the full amount, Dr Roy was entitled to seek a declaration that the deduction had not been properly made.[120] This decision by the House of Lords was a significant step towards reassessing the proper limits of the exclusivity rule. It appeared that Lords Bridge and Lowry would favour restricting the *O'Reilly* rule to situations in which the individual's *sole* aim was to challenge a public law act or decision and would not apply it when an action to vindicate private rights might involve some questions as to the validity of a public law decision.[121] In 1995, the Lords further limited the effect of *O'Reilly*, holding that a decision by the regulator of telecommunications interpreting a statutory licence might be questioned by originating summons in the Commercial Court; Lord Slynn emphasised the need for greater procedural flexibility.[122] Subsequent decisions reinforced the trend away from the rigid exclusivity rule and discouraged reliance on procedural defences.[123] Also significant have been new rules of civil procedure that facilitate transfer into and out

---

[113] See Woolf, *Protection of the Public – A New Challenge*, ch 1; and (the same) [1986] PL 220; [1992] PL 221, 231.
[114] Ch 27.
[115] Wade and Forsyth, op cit, p 653.
[116] See Law Com No 226, part 3.
[117] *Davy* v *Spelthorne Council* [1984] AC 262.
[118] [1983] 2 AC 237, 285.
[119] *Wandsworth Council* v *Winder* [1985] AC 461.
[120] [1992] 1 AC 624 (and P Cane [1992] PL 193).
[121] [1992] 1 AC 624, at 629 and 653 respectively.
[122] *Mercury Communications Ltd* v *Director General of Telecommunications* [1996] 1 All ER 575.
[123] *British Steel plc* v *Customs & Excise Commissioners* [1997] 2 All ER 366 (action of restitution to recover money paid after unlawful demand for tax); *Rye (Dennis) Pension Fund* v *Sheffield Council* [1997] 4 All ER 747 (county court action to secure payment of housing grant); *Steed* v *Home Secretary* [2000] 3 All ER 226 (compensation for surrendered firearm).

of judicial review proceedings, subject to control by the court where, for instance, delay might indicate an abuse of process.[124]

An exaggerated view of the procedural exclusivity required by *O'Reilly* v *Mackman* threatened for a time to erode the rights of individuals who have to defend themselves against enforcement action by public authorities. It is now settled that an individual who is prosecuted for breach of subordinate legislation such as byelaws can as a defence plead that the legislation is invalid and is not barred from doing so by failure to seek judicial review.[125] And tribunals whose task it is to decide whether a statutory disability benefit should be paid to an individual are able to decide on the validity of the relevant regulations.[126]

Judicial discretion in granting relief [127]

It has been said that judicial discretion is at the heart of administrative law.[128] Certainly, a judge has discretion to exercise at the permission stage, for instance in relation to any issue of delay or alternative remedy. At the substantive hearing, the court exercises further discretion in deciding whether to grant relief even if grounds for review have been established. Although a judge may often be reluctant to withhold relief in such a case,[129] relief has been denied for reasons such as the applicant's conduct and motives[130] and the public inconvenience that a remedy might entail.[131] Relief was withheld where planning permission had been granted on the basis of a factual error, but the court was satisfied that it would have been granted apart from this.[132] Similar flexibility was shown when, in reviewing decisions of the City's Take-over Panel, the Court of Appeal stated that in that context the court would see its role as 'historic rather than contemporaneous', i.e. that the court would seek to guide the panel in its future conduct of affairs, not to intervene in ongoing takeover battles.[133]

Statutory machinery for challenge

The technicalities of the prerogative and other remedies in their unreformed state often led in the past to legislation providing a simpler procedure for securing judicial review. Such legislation was always related to specific powers of government and usually included provisions excluding other forms of judicial review. An important example is provided by the standard procedure for the compulsory purchase of land. After a compulsory purchase order has been made by the local authority and, where objections have been raised, an inquiry has been held into the order, the minister must decide whether to

---

[124] *Clark* v *University of Lincolnshire and Humberside* [2000] 3 All ER 753 (where Lord Woolf MR discusses the effect of the Civil Procedure Rules on *O'Reilly* v *Mackman*).

[125] See *Boddington* v *British Transport Police* [1999] 2 AC 143 (C Forsyth [1998] PL 364) and authorities cited at p 663, note 93 above.

[126] *Chief Adjudication Officer* v *Foster* [1993] 1 All ER 705 (D Feldman (1992) 108 LQR 45 and A W Bradley [1992] PL 185).

[127] De Smith, Woolf and Jowell, ch 20.

[128] See Lord Cooke, in Forsyth and Hare (eds) *The Golden Metwand and the Crooked Cord*, pp 203–20. Also *Williams* v *Bedwellty Justices* [1997] AC 225.

[129] See Sir T Bingham [1991] PL 64. Also S Sedley [1989] PL 32 (criticising the use of discretion in *R* v *Chief Constable of North Wales* [1982] 3 All ER 141).

[130] E.g. *R* v *Commissioners of Customs and Excise, ex p Cooke* [1970] 1 All ER 1068. See generally Sir T Bingham [1991] PL 64.

[131] *R* v *Social Services Secretary, ex p Association of Metropolitan Authorities* [1986] 1 All ER 164.

[132] *R* v *North Somerset Council, ex p Cadbury Garden Centre Ltd*, *The Times*, 22 November 2000.

[133] *R* v *Panel on Take-overs and Mergers, ex p Datafin plc* [1987] QB 815. And see C Lewis [1988] PL 78.

confirm the order. If the decision is to confirm, there is a period of six weeks from the confirmation during which any person aggrieved by the purchase order may challenge the validity of the order in the High Court[134] on two grounds: (1) that the order is not within the powers of the enabling Act; or (2) that the requirements of the Act have not been complied with and that the objector's interests have been substantially prejudiced thereby.[135] These grounds have been interpreted as covering all grounds upon which judicial review may be sought, including in (1) matters affecting vires, abuse of discretion and natural justice and in (2) observance of all relevant statutory procedures.[136] When an aggrieved person makes an application to the High Court, the court may make an interim order suspending the purchase order, either generally or so far as it affects the applicant's property. If the order is not challenged in the High Court during the six-week period, the order is statutorily protected from challenge; any other form of judicial review of the order is excluded, before or after the confirmation of the order.[137]

This effective method of challenge was first provided by the Housing Act 1930 at a time when there was strong feeling against legislative attempts to exclude judicial review of ministers' actions altogether. Today it provides a statutory form of judicial review in respect of many decisions relating to the control of land.[138] Resort to this remedy has often enabled the High Court to give its entire attention to the principles of judicial review in issue, uncomplicated by procedural or jurisdictional questions.[139] The time limit on the right of challenge is necessary in order that, if no objection is taken promptly, the authorities concerned can put the decision into effect. Other statutory remedies include the right to appeal to the High Court on matters of law from many tribunals[140] and on points of law in respect of planning decisions.[141] Although these remedies are not applications for judicial review within the meaning of the Supreme Court Act 1981, s 31, they are heard in the Administrative Court.[142] By enabling there to be judicial control of executive decisions, they help to satisfy the requirements of art 6 ECHR.[143]

It is, however, necessary for an applicant to the court to come within the scope of the procedure and the question of locus standi depends on the statutory provisions. The six-week right to challenge compulsory purchase orders and planning decisions is given to 'any person aggrieved'. This clearly includes owners who object to their land being compulsorily purchased but in 1961 it was held not to include neighbouring owners who had objected at a public inquiry to proposed new development; they were considered to have no legal interest that would render them aggrieved persons in law.[144] In 1973 Ackner J gave a more generous interpretation to the phrase 'person aggrieved', including within it the officers of an amenity association who had opposed new development at a public inquiry.[145] Today, there are many reasons why the

---

[134] Or in Scotland in the Court of Session. On when the six weeks begin to run, see *Griffiths* v *Environment Secretary* [1983] 2 AC 51.

[135] Acquisition of Land Act 1981, s 23 (consolidating earlier Acts).

[136] *Ashbridge Investments Ltd* v *Minister of Housing* [1965] 3 All ER 371; *Coleen Properties Ltd* v *Minister of Housing* [1971] 1 All ER 1049.

[137] Acquisition of Land Act 1981, s 23; and see p 745 below.

[138] E.g. Town and Country Planning Act 1990, ss 284–8 and Transport and Works Act 1992, s 22.

[139] See e.g. *Bushell* v *Environment Secretary* [1981] AC 75; p 680 above.

[140] Tribunals and Inquiries Act 1992, s 11.

[141] Town and Country Planning Act 1990, ss 289, 290.

[142] See CPR, Part 52 (esp 52.17, 18 and section III).

[143] See *R (Alconbury Developments Ltd)* v *Environment Secretary* [2001] 2 All ER 929 and *Bryan* v *UK* (1995) 21 EHRR 342.

[144] *Buxton* v *Minister of Housing* [1961] 1 QB 278; cf *Maurice* v *London CC* [1964] 2 QB 362.

[145] *Turner* v *Environment Secretary* (1973) 72 LGR 380.

term 'person aggrieved' should be given a meaning consistent with the broad test of 'sufficient interest' that applies to judicial review in general.

Statutory exclusion of judicial control[146]

There is a strong presumption that the legislature does not intend access to the courts to be denied. Where Parliament has appointed a specific tribunal for the enforcement of new rights and duties, it is necessary to have recourse to that tribunal in the first instance. Unless an equivalent to judicial review is provided by the statute, the tribunal's decisions will be subject to judicial review. But many statutes have contained words designed to oust the jurisdiction of the courts. Such provisions have been interpreted by the judges so as to leave, if at all possible, their supervisory powers intact. At one time the prerogative orders were often excluded by name, but even the express exclusion of certiorari was not effective against a manifest defect of jurisdiction or fraud committed by a party procuring an order of the court.[147] One frequent clause was that a particular decision 'shall be final', but this does not exclude judicial review, whether for jurisdictional defects or for error of law.[148] Such a clause means simply that there is no right of appeal from the decision. Another clause which does not deprive the courts of their supervisory jurisdiction is where it is stated that a statutory order when made shall have effect 'as if enacted in the Act' which authorised it; the court may nonetheless hold the order to be invalid if it conflicts with provisions of the Act.[149]

It is then only by an exceptionally strong formula that Parliament can effectively deprive the High Court or the Court of Session of supervisory jurisdiction over inferior tribunals and public authorities. Exclusion clauses today frequently accompany the granting of an express right to challenge the validity of an order or decision during a limited time. Thus the statute which permits challenge of a compulsory purchase order within six weeks of its confirmation provides that subject to the possibility of challenge in that time, 'a compulsory purchase order . . . shall not, either before or after it has been confirmed, made or given, be questioned in any legal proceedings whatsoever . . .'.[150]

> In *Smith* v *East Elloe Rural District Council* the plaintiff, whose land had been taken compulsorily for the building of council houses nearly six years previously, alleged that the making of the order had been caused by wrongful action and bad faith on the part of the council and its clerk. She submitted that the exclusion clause did not exclude the court's power in cases of fraud and bad faith. The House of Lords held by a bare majority that the effect of the Act was to protect compulsory purchase orders from judicial review except by statutory challenge during the six-week period. Although the validity of the order could no longer be challenged, the action against the clerk of the council for damages could proceed.[151]

A very different attitude towards an exclusion clause was taken by the House of Lords in 1968 in a decision which we have already considered in relation to jurisdictional control.

> In *Anisminic Ltd* v *Foreign Compensation Commission*, the Foreign Compensation Act 1950, s 4(4), provided that the determination by the commission of any application made under the Act 'shall not be called in question in any court of law'. The commission was a judicial body responsible for distributing funds supplied by foreign governments as compensation to British

---

[146] De Smith, Woolf and Jowell, pp 231–49; Wade and Forsyth, pp 697–720; Craig, ch 24.
[147] *Colonial Bank of Australasia* v *Willan* (1874) 5 PC 417.
[148] *R* v *Medical Appeal Tribunal, ex p Gilmore* [1957] 1 QB 574.
[149] *Minister of Health* v *R* [1931] AC 494.
[150] Acquisition of Land Act 1981, s 25.
[151] [1956] AC 736.

subjects. It rejected a claim made by Anisminic for a reason which the company submitted was erroneous in law and exceeded the commission's jurisdiction. *Held*, by a majority in the House of Lords, s 4(4) did not debar a court from inquiring whether the commission had made in law a correct decision on the question of eligibility to claim. 'Determination' meant a real determination, not a purported determination. By taking into account a factor which in the view of the majority was irrelevant to the scheme, the commission's decision was a nullity. Lord Wilberforce said, 'What would be the purpose of defining by statute the limits of a tribunal's powers, if by means of a clause inserted in the instrument of definition, those limits could safely be passed?'[152]

The decision is a striking example of the ability of the courts to interpret privative clauses in such a way as to maintain the possibility of judicial review. Although the authority of *Smith* v *East Elloe RDC* was questioned in the *Anisminic* case, the former decision was not overruled: indeed, the issues involved in considering the finality of a compulsory purchase order are different from those involved in considering how far an award of compensation should be subject to review. A further distinction is between a statute that seeks to exclude the jurisdiction of the courts entirely (as in *Anisminic*) and a statute that confers a right to apply to the courts for review within a stated time (as in the case of a compulsory purchase order) but excludes judicial review thereafter. In 1976, the statutory bar on attempts to challenge the validity of a purchase order after the six-week period was held to be absolute: an aggrieved owner could not bring such a challenge some months later, even though he alleged that the order had been vitiated by a breach of natural justice and good faith which he had only discovered after the six-week period.[153] Even if the purchase order must stand, this should not prevent the owner from seeking compensation from those responsible for the alleged acts of bad faith.

Parliamentary authority to exclude judicial review

We have seen that in the recent debate about the foundations of judicial review, even those who denied that parliamentary intent was the basis of judicial review accepted that Parliament could restrict or exclude judicial review in specific instances.[154] Today an attempt by Parliament to do so might conflict with European law. Thus a certificate issued by the Secretary of State for Northern Ireland that purported to be 'conclusive evidence' that a police decision was taken for reasons of national security was held to be contrary to the principle of effective judicial control in European Community law.[155] When a similar certificate prevented a Roman Catholic company from pursuing a complaint of religious discrimination in the award of contracts, the 'conclusive evidence' rule was held to be a disproportionate restriction on the right of access to a court and thus it breached art 6 ECHR.[156] Where a matter concerns 'civil rights and obligations', as in that case, exclusion of access to a court will violate art 6.[157] According to the Strasbourg case-law, a national legislature may impose reasonable time limits on access to a court, but such restrictions must not impair the essence of

---

[152] [1969] 2 AC 147, 208 (and ch 30 A above). For the legislative sequel, see Foreign Compensation Act 1969, s 3.
[153] *R* v *Environment Secretary, ex p Ostler* [1977] QB 122 (N P Gravells (1978) 41 MLR 383 and J E Alder (1980) 43 MLR 670). Also *Hamilton* v *Scottish Secretary* 1972 SLT 233 and *R* v *Cornwall CC, ex p Huntington* [1994] 1 All ER 694.
[154] Ch 30, at page 696.
[155] Case 222/84 *Johnston* v *Chief Constable RUC* [1987] QB 129.
[156] *Tinnelly & Sons Ltd* v *UK* (1998) 27 EHRR 249.
[157] See e.g. *Zander* v *Sweden* (1993) 18 EHRR 175 and *Fayed* v *UK* (1994) 18 EHRR 393.

the right.[158] The rule that judicial review must be sought promptly and in any event within three months would be likely to comply with art 6; so in most cases would the six-week rule on challenges to planning and compulsory purchase decisions. But an absolute exclusion of review after six weeks might be disproportionate in a case where relevant information is concealed by officials until after the right of access to a court has lapsed. No issues as to art 6 of the ECHR are raised by the exclusion of judicial review on matters that do not involve an individual's 'civil rights and obligations', such as the validity of an Act of the Scottish Parliament[159] or a Speaker's certificate under the Parliament Act 1911.[160]

Parliament has an uneven record in relation to the exclusion of the courts. The Franks committee in 1957 recommended that no statute should seek to oust the prerogative orders. In response, successive Tribunals and Inquiries Acts (in 1958, 1971 and now 1992, s 12) have provided that:

(a) any provision in an Act passed before 1 August 1958 that any order or determination shall not be called into question in any court; or

(b) any provision in such an Act which by similar words excludes any of the powers of the High Court

shall not prevent the remedies of certiorari or mandamus from being available. A similar provision, but not restricted to specific remedies, protects the supervisory jurisdiction of the Court of Session. These provisions do not apply in two cases: (i) to an order or determination of a court of law, or (ii) where an Act makes provision for application to the High Court within a stated time (for example, the power to challenge a town planning decision within six weeks). Because of (ii), the 1992 Act does not apply to the situation in *Smith* v *East Elloe RDC*.[161]

For several reasons, s 12 of the 1992 Act is far from being a full response to the problem of ouster clauses. First, the protection given to certiorari and mandamus in English law should be replaced by broader protection (as in Scotland) for judicial review in general. Second, s 12 has been held not to apply to 'conclusive evidence' clauses.[162] Third, the Act's effect is limited to legislation enacted before August 1958 and does not apply to later statutes.[163] It may be said that since 1958 Parliament must be taken to have been aware of the undesirability of excluding judicial review, but this does not mean that all exclusion clauses enacted since 1958 are necessarily justifiable. Fourth, it was not until long after 1958 that Parliament could have become aware of the protection for judicial review in European law. In summary, Parliament's concern about exclusion clauses should not be limited to pre-1958 Acts and to matters falling within European Community law and human rights law. Arguably, there is a need for a statute to create a strong rule of interpretation to preserve the possibility of judicial review that would apply to all legislation, whenever enacted, on the lines of the Human Rights Act 1998, s 3. Such a rule would not block a determined attempt by the executive to remove judicial review from one or more areas of government. But if such an attempt

---

[158] *Stubbings* v *UK* (1996) 23 EHRR 213.
[159] Scotland Act 1998, s 28(5).
[160] Parliament Act 1911, s 3.
[161] *Hamilton* v *Secretary of State for Scotland* (note 153 above).
[162] *R* v *Registrar of Companies, ex p Central Bank of India* [1986] QB 1114. A different view of 'conclusive evidence' clauses might be taken in other contexts.
[163] E.g. Security Service Act 1989, s 5(4); Intelligence Services Act 1994, s 9(4); Police Act 1997, s 91(10); Regulation of Investigating Powers Act 2000, s 67(8). The last of these provides that decisions by the tribunal set up by the Act '(including decisions as to whether they have jurisdiction) shall not be subject to appeal or be liable to be questioned in any court.'

were made in Parliament, it must be hoped that the political process would rigorously scrutinise the government's proposals and motivation.[164]

Remedies in Scots administrative law[165]

The prerogative orders have never been part of Scots law, except to the extent that they were introduced into Scotland by legislation for the purposes of revenue law, nor did a separate court of equity develop in Scotland. Apart from statutory remedies like the six-week right to challenge a compulsory purchase order, which apply both in Scotland and England, administrative law remedies in Scotland are essentially the same remedies as are available in private law to enforce matters of civil obligation. The most important of these remedies (which are now available subject to procedural changes made in 1985 and subsequently) are (a) the ancient remedy of *reduction*, by which any document (including decisions of tribunals, local byelaws, the dismissal of public servants and disciplinary decisions) may be quashed as being in excess of jurisdiction, in breach of natural justice or in other ways contrary to law;[166] (b) the no less ancient remedy of *declarator*, from which the English declaration of right was derived; (c) the remedies of *suspension* and *interdict*, which together serve broadly the same purposes as injunction and prohibition in English law; (d) the action for damages for breach of civil obligation; and (e) a summary remedy to enforce performance of statutory duties, comparable with but not identical to mandamus.[167] By contrast with the former English law, all relevant forms of relief may be sought in the same proceedings.[168]

Several points of comparison with English law may be noted. First, it was established in *Watt* v *Lord Advocate* that while the remedy of reduction may be used to quash decisions of tribunals which are in excess of their jurisdiction, it is not available to review errors of law made by a tribunal within jurisdiction.[169] However, at a time before the right of appeal on points of law from decisions of the Social Security Commissioners had been created,[170] the Court of Session also held that the error of law in question had led the tribunal to exceed its jurisdiction, since it had caused a statutory entitlement to unemployment benefit to be withheld on an extraneous consideration. This decision applied to Scots law the principle in *Anisminic Ltd* v *Foreign Compensation Commission*.[171]

Second, in Scots law there is no direct equivalent to relator proceedings. The Lord Advocate in this respect never assumed the role played by the Attorney-General. For this reason, and because Scots law does not favour the granting of an interdict by a civil court to restrain further criminal conduct, *Gouriet*'s case[172] has no direct application in Scotland. The lack of relator proceedings is partly made good by broader rules on title and interest to sue, which permit individuals to sue directly to enforce many

---

[164] For consideration of legislation that removed or substantially impaired the role of the High Court in judicial review, see Lord Woolf at [1995] PL 57, 68; cf the comments of Lord Irvine at [1996] PL 59, 75–78.

[165] *Stair Encyclopedia of the Laws of Scotland*, vol I, reissue, part 4; C M G Himsworth, in Supperstone and Goudie (eds), *Judicial Review*, ch 19; and in Hadfield (ed.), *Judicial Review, A Thematic Approach*, ch 10; T Mullen et al [1995] PL 52; Clyde and Edwards, *Judicial Review*, part 5.

[166] See e.g. *Malloch* v *Aberdeen Corpn* [1971] 2 All ER 1278; *Barrs* v *British Wool Marketing Board* 1957 SC 72.

[167] Court of Session Act 1988, s 45(b); *T Docherty Ltd* v *Burgh of Monifieth* 1971 SLT 12.

[168] E.g. *Macbeth* v *Ashley* (1874) LR 2 HL (Sc) 352.

[169] 1979 SC 120.

[170] See now Social Security Administration Act 1992, s 24; ch 29 A.

[171] Note 152 above. And see *Stair Encyclopedia*, paras 45, 47–50; Clyde and Edwards, pp 597–603.

[172] Note 33 above.

public rights.[173] In *Wilson* v *Independent Broadcasting Authority*, members of a group campaigning in the referendum on devolution had title and interest to sue for an interdict to restrain a series of political broadcasts which did not maintain a balance between the two sides. The judge, Lord Ross, could see 'no reason in principle why an individual should not sue in order to prevent a breach by a public body of a duty owed by that public body to the public.'[174] This welcome statement of principle departed from some earlier decisions.[175] In 1987, the organisation Age Concern Scotland was held to have title but no interest to challenge as ultra vires official guidance that limited the making of supplementary payments to old people for severe weather conditions.[176] Although a teachers' association had title and interest to challenge a university's unlawful action where its members could not be expected to do so individually,[177] the test of standing in Scotland is applied more strictly than the test of 'sufficient interest' in English law.[178]

Third, difficult situations brought about by official failures may sometimes be resolved by the power of the Court of Session to exercise an extraordinary equitable jurisdiction in the form of the *nobile officium* of the court.[179]

Finally, since 1985 Scotland has had its own procedure of application for judicial review, which is similar to but not identical with the English model.[180] It was introduced later in Scotland than in English law because the procedural difficulties relating to the prerogative orders did not exist in Scots law. However, the ordinary procedures of civil litigation were not suitable for the prompt resolution of disputes arising in areas such as housing and immigration; and the decision of the House of Lords in *Brown* v *Hamilton DC* that the sheriff court had no power at common law to review decisions of local authorities caused Lord Fraser to recommend the introduction of a new summary procedure in the Court of Session.[181]

In 1985, rules of court[182] established a procedure of petition, known as an application for judicial review, which *must* be used whenever an application is made to the supervisory jurisdiction of the Court of Session for one or more of the remedies mentioned earlier. The rules seek to provide for the rapid handling of every application, with the main procedural steps being under the control of individual judges designated for the purpose. The leave of the court is not required for an application, but an application without merits can be briskly rejected by the judge for that reason. Although the rules impose no time limit on petitions for judicial review, under general principles of Scots law a petition may fail on a plea of *mora* (delay), taciturnity and acquiescence.[183] The major problem that has arisen is that the 'supervisory jurisdiction' of the Court of Session is not defined in legislation, though it has often been described in judgments.[184] It cannot be identified with the scope of the remedies that may be granted

---

[173] *Duke of Atholl* v *Torrie* (1852) I Macq 65; *Ogston* v *Aberdeen Tramways Co* (1896) 24 R 8. Also *Stair Encyclopedia*, paras 122–38; Clyde and Edwards, ch 10.

[174] 1979 SC 351.

[175] *D & J Nicol* v *Dundee Harbour Trustees* 1915 SC (HL) 7; *Simpson* v *Edinburgh Corp* 1960 SC 313.

[176] *Scottish Old People's Welfare Council, Petitioners* 1987 SLT 179. Clyde and Edwards (p 377) suggest that prematurity was the reason why there was no interest.

[177] *Educational Institute of Scotland* v *Robert Gordon University, The Times*, 1 July 1996.

[178] See Lord Hope [2001] PL 294, discussing *Rape Crisis Centre and Brindley, Petitioners* 2000 SCLR 807 (petitioners had no title to review Home Secretary's decision to admit an American boxer and rapist to fight in Glasgow). But cf *Uprichard* v *Fife Council* 2000 SCLR 949.

[179] *Ferguson, Petitioners* 1965 SC 16.

[180] See A W Bradley [1987] PL 313.

[181] 1983 SLT 397 at 418, and see *Stair Encyclopaedia*, p 191.

[182] See now Rules of the Court of Session (made by SI 1994 No 1443), ch 58.

[183] *Stair Encyclopedia*, para 121; and e.g. *Hanlon* v *Traffic Commissioners* 1988 SLT 802; *Uprichard* v *Fife Council* 2000 SCLR 949.

[184] E.g. *Moss Empires Ltd* v *Glasgow Assessor* 1917 SC (HL) 1.

on a successful application for judicial review since those remedies are available throughout the civil law. Some judgments after 1985 drew for this purpose upon the private law/public law distinction made in English law,[185] but in 1992 the Court of Session in *West v Secretary of State for Scotland*[186] robustly rejected that distinction. It held that the court has power under its supervisory jurisdiction 'to regulate the process by which decisions are taken by any person or body to whom a jurisdiction, power of authority has been delegated or entrusted by statute, agreement or any other instrument', in particular where there was a 'tripartite relationship' between the decision-maker, the individual affected and the person or body from whom the power to decide was derived. On the facts in *West*, a prison officer could not obtain judicial review of a decision made by the Scottish Office that he should not receive removal expenses after he had been transferred from one penal institution to another. This dispute was seen as one arising from a contract of employment, with no features bringing the dispute within the 'supervisory jurisdiction'.[187] The court's approach to jurisdiction was based on an analysis of the process of decision-making and its review. Later judgments have doubted whether a 'tripartite relationship' is always essential.[188] There is no divergence between the substantive grounds of judicial review in English and Scots law, but *West* may enable the Scottish courts to apply their supervisory jurisdiction to regulatory and similar powers of private organisations, where in England this would be impeded by the private/public distinction.

Habeas corpus[189]

As has already been seen,[190] the prerogative writ of habeas corpus is in English law an important remedy in respect of public or private action which takes away individual liberty. Today its use as a means of securing judicial control of executive acts arises frequently in extradition law and to a lesser extent in other areas involving powers of detention, such as immigration control,[191] mental health[192] and child care.[193] Unlike the prerogative orders, the writ has not recently been the subject of legislative reform. The writ originally enabled a court of common law to bring before itself persons whose presence was necessary for pending proceedings. In the 15th and 16th centuries, King's Bench and Common Pleas used habeas corpus to assert their authority over rival courts and to release persons imprisoned by such courts in excess of their jurisdiction. In the 17th century, the writ was used to check arbitrary arrest by order of the King or the King's Council.[194]

---

[185] Including *Tehrani v Argyll Health Board (No 2)* 1990 SLT 118 and *Watt v Strathclyde Council* 1992 SLT 324. See Himsworth in Supperstone and Goudie (note 165) and Lord Clyde, in Finnie, Himsworth and Walker (eds), *Edinburgh Essays in Public Law*, pp 281–93.

[186] 1992 SLT 636. See W J Wolffe [1992] PL 625; *Stair Encyclopedia*, para 115; Clyde and Edwards, pp 344–7.

[187] See also *Naik v Stirling University* 1994 SLT 449 and *Blair v Lochaber Council* 1995 SLT 407.

[188] See *Naik v Stirling University* 1994 SLT 449; *McIntosh v Aberdeenshire Council* 1999 SLT 93, 97; and cf *Blair v Lochaber Council* 1995 SLT 407.

[189] See Sharpe, *The Law of Habeas Corpus* and Clark and McCoy, *The Most Fundamental Legal Right*. On the history, see HEL IX 108–25 and Forsyth, *Cases and Opinions in Constitutional Law*, ch 16. See also Sir S Brown [2000] PL 31.

[190] Ch 21 E.

[191] E.g. *R v Durham Prison (Governor), ex p Hardial Singh* [1984] 1 All ER 983; and *Tan Te Lam v Superintendent of Tai A Chau Detention Centre* [1997] AC 97.

[192] E.g. *Re S-C (mental patient)* [1996] QB 599. Cf *Johnson v UK* (1999) 27 EHRR 296.

[193] *LM v Essex CC* (1999) 1 FLR 988.

[194] For *Darnel*'s case and the Petition of Right, see ch 12 D.

It was of the essence of habeas corpus that it was a procedure by which the court could determine the legality of an individual's detention, effectively and without delay. Habeas Corpus Acts were enacted in 1679, 1816 and 1862,[195] not to widen the jurisdiction of the courts but to enhance the effectiveness of the writ and to ensure that applications were dealt with promptly. Thus the 1679 Act prohibited evasion of habeas corpus by transfer of prisoners detained for 'any criminal or supposed criminal matter' to places outside the jurisdiction of the English courts on pain of heavy penalties. The 1816 Act inter alia gave the judge power in civil cases to inquire summarily into the truth of the facts stated in the gaoler's return to the writ, even though the return was 'good and sufficient in law'.[196] The 1862 Act provided that the writ was not to issue from a court in England into any colony or foreign dominion of the Crown where there were courts having authority to grant habeas corpus. Detention within Northern Ireland and Scotland is a matter for the courts in those jurisdictions.[197]

Habeas corpus is described as a writ of right which is granted *ex debito justitiae*. This means that a prima facie case must be shown before it is issued but, unlike the prerogative orders, it is not a discretionary remedy and it may not be refused merely because an alternative remedy exists.[198] Habeas corpus is a remedy against *unlawful* detention: thus it enabled the court to decide whether a profoundly retarded and autistic person incapable of giving consent could be detained under the Mental Health Act 1983 without an order being made for compulsory detention.[199] This decision concerned the limits of a hospital trust's statutory powers of detention, but is habeas corpus a remedy for correcting every error made by a body with power to detain?

Certainly, the writ does not provide a right of appeal for those detained by order of a court or tribunal. It might be supposed that habeas corpus lies whenever there are grounds for judicial review of a decision to detain someone, but the position is much less clear-cut than this.[200] Indeed, the reforms in judicial review procedure that we have considered in this chapter did not apply to habeas corpus, and the two procedures remain separate. In *Rutty*'s case,[201] the High Court, acting under the Habeas Corpus Act 1816 to examine the truth of the facts stated in the return, held that there had been no evidence before the magistrate eight years earlier to justify an order that an 18-year-old woman with learning difficulties be detained. But in a line of immigration cases during the 1970s, the courts were most reluctant to make effective use of habeas corpus as a means of reviewing executive decisions, for example in the case of someone about to be removed from the country as an illegal entrant.[202] We have seen that in *Khawaja*'s case the House of Lords reversed this trend.[203] During the 1990s the Court of Appeal distinguished between the scope of habeas corpus and the grounds of judicial review, holding that habeas corpus could mount a challenge to the jurisdiction or vires of a detention decision, but not if the decision was 'within the powers' of the decision-maker but was defective for reasons such as procedural error, mistake of law, or unreasonableness. The reason given for this limitation on habeas corpus was that, in the latter class of cases, the decision was lawful until it had been

---

[195] For the detail, see Taswell-Langmead, *English Constitutional History*, pp 432–6.
[196] See e.g. *R v Board of Control, ex p Rutty* [1956] 2 QB 109.
[197] *Re Keenan* [1972] 1 QB 533; *Re McElduff* [1972] NILR 1; *R v Cowle* (1759) 2 Burr 834, 856.
[198] *R v Governor of Pentonville Prison, ex p Azam* [1974] AC 18, 31 (CA).
[199] *R v Bournewood NHS Trust, ex p L* [1999] 1 AC 458.
[200] De Smith, Woolf and Jowell, p 678; and see Rubinstein, *Jurisdiction and Illegality*, pp 105–16, 176–86.
[201] Note 196 above.
[202] The decisions include *R v Home Secretary, ex p Mughal* [1974] 1 QB 313 and *R v Home Secretary, ex p Zamir* [1980] AC 930. And see C Newdick [1982] PL 89.
[203] *R v Home Secretary, ex p Khawaja* [1984] AC 74 and ch 30 A.

quashed by an order of certiorari.[204] Yet this approach seems deeply flawed: it is based on an out-dated distinction (between 'errors as to jurisdiction' and 'errors within jurisdiction') which has ceased to apply in judicial review generally. It is now settled that breaches of natural justice, errors of law and so on cause a decision to be ultra vires:[205] how then can such a decision be held to be 'within powers' in the law of habeas corpus? When individual liberty is at stake, it would be unjust for the court to refuse habeas corpus to someone who had shown that the decision to detain him or her was ultra vires but required to be quashed by certiorari: to avoid the injustice, the court would need to grant the detainee permission to apply for judicial review and to quash the decision concerned forthwith, without new proceedings being necessary. Although this approach has been authoritatively criticised for eroding habeas corpus,[206] it was applied in 1996 where young persons had been wrongly imprisoned for non-payment of fines, but the court held that their detention could be challenged by judicial review, but not by habeas corpus.[207]

This uncertainty affecting habeas corpus is reflected in case law at Strasbourg: the European Court of Human Rights held in the case of a mental patient that habeas corpus did not enable the English court to determine both the substantive and formal legality of the detention,[208] but reached the opposite conclusion in the case of persons suspected of terrorist offences.[209] By Art 5(4) ECHR, every person who is detained is entitled to take proceedings by which the lawfulness of the detention is decided speedily by a court and release is ordered if the detention is not lawful. The awkward interface that has developed between habeas corpus and judicial review needs to be resolved.[210] One possible reform would be to amend the Supreme Court Act 1981, s 31, to add an order of habeas corpus to the forms of relief that may be granted on an application for judicial review. This would leave intact the law on the writ of habeas corpus, but would provide an alternative form of access to the same relief.

Normally the applicant for habeas corpus will be the person detained, but any relative or other person may apply on his or her behalf if the detainee cannot do so. Application is made to the High Court ex parte (that is, without the other side being heard) supported by an affidavit or statement of fact.[211] If prima facie grounds are shown, the court ordinarily directs that notice of motion be given to the person having control of the person detained (for example, a prison governor) but notice may also be served on a minister (for example, the Home Secretary) who is responsible for the detention and who may file evidence in reply. On the day named, the merits of the application will be argued. If the court decides that the writ should issue, it orders the prisoner's release forthwith. Under this practice the respondent need not produce the prisoner in court at the hearing: exceptionally, an applicant may be allowed to present his or her

---

[204] *R v Home Secretary, ex p Cheblak* [1991] 2 All ER 319; *R v Home Secretary, ex p Muboyayi* [1992] 1 QB 244. In *Muboyayi*, habeas corpus was issued urgently to restrain the removal of an individual pending decision of his application for judicial review; the court could now issue an interim injunction against the removal: *M v Home Office* (note 62 above).

[205] See *Ridge v Baldwin* [1964] AC 40; *Anisminic Ltd v Foreign Compensation Commission* [1969] 2 AC 147; *R v Hull University Visitor, ex p Page* [1993] AC 682.

[206] Law Commission, Law Com No 226, part XI, and H W R Wade (1997) 113 LQR 55. Also A Le Sueur [1992] PL 13; M Shrimpton [1993] PL 24.

[207] *R v Oldham Justices, ex p Cawley* [1997] QB 1. And see Sir S Brown [2000] PL 31. Cf *Re S-C (mental patient)* [1996] QB 599 (habeas corpus granted where social worker's application for S-C's detention was untruthful).

[208] *X v UK* (1981) 4 EHRR 188.

[209] *Brogan v UK* (1988) 11 EHRR 117.

[210] See e.g. *B v Barking, Havering and Brentwood NHS Trust* (1999) 1 FLR 106; *Sheikh v Home Secretary* [2001] ACD 93; and O Davies [1997] Judicial Review 11.

[211] RSC, Ord 54 (kept in being by the Civil Procedure Rules).

case in person.[212] No return to the writ is made as the writ itself has not been issued. In exceptional cases the court may order the issue of the writ on the ex parte application if, for example, the detainee is at risk of being taken outside the jurisdiction. Disobedience to the writ is punishable by fine or imprisonment for contempt of court and there may be penalties under the Act of 1679. Officers of the Crown are subject to the writ.[213] Rights of appeal from the High Court's decision are subject to detailed provision in the Administration of Justice Act 1960 (ss 5, 14, 15) as amended by the Access to Justice Act 1999: in a civil matter, the appeal goes via the Court of Appeal to the House of Lords and in a criminal matter (for example, in extradition proceedings) from the Divisional Court to the Lords, with leave.[214]

The writ of habeas corpus has no exact counterpart in Scots law, but ever since the Scottish Parliament's Act in 1701 for preventing Wrongous Imprisonment there has been strict provisions restricting the length of time within which a person committed for trial may be held in custody.[215] As regards civil detention, the Court of Session have jurisdiction to order the release of any person who is unlawfully detained. If no more convenient remedy is available (for example, by a suspension and interdict), the detained person may petition the Inner House of the Court of Session for release in the exercise of the nobile officium of the court.

---

[212] *Re Wring* [1960] 1 All ER 536.
[213] *Re Thompson* (1889) 5 TLR 565; *Secretary of State v O'Brien* [1923] AC 603.
[214] On the civil/criminal distinction, see e.g. *Amand v Home Secretary* [1943] AC 147, 156.
[215] For the '80 day' and '110 day' rules, see the Criminal Procedure (Scotland) Act 1995, s 65.

Chapter 32

LIABILITY OF PUBLIC AUTHORITIES
AND THE CROWN

In chapters 30 and 31, we examined the law that enables the courts to review the decisions of public authorities on grounds such as ultra vires, error of law and breach of natural justice. We now consider the position of public authorities in relation to civil liability.[1] In principle, public authorities in English law are subject to the same rules of liability in tort and contract as apply to private individuals. There is no separate law of administrative liability for wrongful acts.[2] In practice, however, public authorities require powers to enable them to maintain public services and perform regulatory functions; these powers are generally not available to private individuals. Many new public works, such as motorways and power stations, could not be created unless there was power in the public interest to override private rights that might be adversely affected. Parliament has often legislated to give public authorities special powers or protection from liability. The courts have recognised that the public interest may require a public authority to be treated differently from private individuals.

At several points in this chapter, the special position of the Crown will be emphasised. In the past, important distinctions were drawn between (a) the Crown, including departments of central government and (b) other public bodies, such as local authorities and statutory corporations. While many of these distinctions have been removed, notably by the Crown Proceedings Act 1947, others still survive. This chapter deals, in section A, with the liability of public authorities and the Crown in tort and, in section B, with contractual liability. Section C deals with other aspects of the law relating to the Crown, including such procedural immunities and privileges as survive and the rules of evidence relating to the non-disclosure of evidence in the public interest.

As with many aspects of public law, the liability of public authorities has been much affected by European Community law. The liability of Community organs under art 288 (ex 215) EC Treaty to compensate for serious breaches of Community law that they commit is paralleled by the duty of member states 'to make good loss and damage caused to individuals by breaches of Community law for which they can be held responsible',[3] for example by failure to implement a Community directive. We have already noted the impact of Community law on the supremacy of Parliament that was made manifest in the *Factortame* litigation concerning the Merchant Shipping Act 1988, enacted to protect British fishing interests from other European interests.[4] Later in the same litigation, the House of Lords held, after analysing the decision-making that lay behind the 1988 Act, that the Act was a 'sufficiently serious infringement' of

---

[1] Wade and Forsyth, *Administrative Law*, chs 20–21; Craig, *Administrative Law*, chs 25, 26; de Smith, Woolf and Jowell, *Judicial Review of Administrative Action*, ch 19; Hogg, *Liability of the Crown*; Harlow, *Compensation and Government Torts*; Kneebone, *Tort Liability of Public Authorities*.
[2] As was stressed in Dicey's account of the 'rule of law': ch 6.
[3] *Francovitch v Italy* C-6/90 and C-9/90 [1991] I-ECR 5357, para 37. Also *Brasserie du Pêcheur SA v Germany* and *R v Transport Secretary, ex p Factortame Ltd* C-46/93 and C-48/93 [1996] ECR I-1029; P Craig (1993) 109 LQR 595 and (1997) 113 LQR 67; C Lewis and S Moore [1993] PL 151; and C Lewis in Forsyth and Hare (eds) *The Golden Metwand and the Crooked Cord*, p 319.
[4] See ch 4 C and ch 8.

Community law to justify the award of compensatory damages.[5] The criteria which led to this decision were derived from Community law, which requires, for a finding that a breach is 'sufficiently serious', that a member state has 'manifestly and gravely disregarded the limits on the exercise of its discretion'. But the procedure and other aspects of a claim in damages for such breaches may be governed by national law, provided that this does not discriminate against Community law and does not in practice prevent individuals from enforcing their Community rights.[6]

In respect of human rights, by art 41 ECHR, where a Convention right has been violated and national law does not allow full reparation to be made, the Strasbourg Court 'shall, if necessary, afford just satisfaction to the injured party', by requiring the state to pay compensation. By the Human Rights Act 1998, s 8, a national court with power to award damages in civil proceedings may (if necessary) order a public authority to pay damages for breach of a Convention right; in doing this, the court must take account of the principles of compensation applied at Strasbourg.[7] Such an award is, of course, not needed if compensation payable under national law is adequate to meet Convention requirements.

The impact of the new rules of liability in European Community law and human rights law is being felt at a time when key principles of the liability of public authorities in UK law are in a volatile state. This can be seen in the many recent decisions by the House of Lords in this area, including two by a seven-judge court.[8] It is, in fact, impossible to study this subject without regard both to European law and to the developing body of national law.

Relevant aspects of the law in Scotland will be mentioned briefly in each section. Although the common law in Scotland regarding the position of the Crown differed from the law in England, the same broad approach to the liability of public authorities in general has been followed in both legal systems, especially since the Crown Proceedings Act 1947.

A. Liability of public authorities and the Crown in tort

Individual liability

In the absence of statutory immunity, every individual is liable for wrongful acts that he or she commits and for such omissions as give rise to actions in tort at common law or for breach of statutory duty. This applies even if an officer representing the Crown claims to be acting out of executive necessity.

> In *Entick* v *Carrington*[9] the King's Messengers were held liable in an action of trespass for breaking and entering the plaintiff's house and seizing his papers, even though they were acting in obedience to a warrant issued by the Secretary of State. This was in law no defence as the Secretary had no legal authority to issue such a warrant.

Obedience to orders is not normally a defence whether the orders are those of the Crown, a local authority,[10] a company or an individual employer.[11] The principle that

---

[5] *R* v *Transport Secretary, ex p Factortame Ltd (No 5)* [2000] 1 AC 524.
[6] See e.g. the rejection of the Community law claim in *Three Rivers DC* v *Bank of England (No 3)* [2000] 3 All ER 1.
[7] See ch 19 C; A R Mowbray [1997] PL 647; English and Scottish Law Commissions, *Damages under the Human Rights Act 1998* (2001); D Fairgrieve [2001] PL 695.
[8] *Murphy* v *Brentwood Council* [1999] 1 AC 398 and *Phelps* v *Hillingdon Council* [2001] 2 AC 619.
[9] (1765) 19 St Tr 1030; ch 6 A.
[10] *Mill* v *Hawker* (1875) LR 10 Ex 92.
[11] For the position of the armed forces, see ch 16.

superior orders are no defence to an action in tort would, if unqualified, have placed too heavy a burden on many subordinate officials. At common law an officer of the court, such as a sheriff, who executes an order of the court, is protected from personal liability unless the order is on its face clearly outside the jurisdiction of the court.[12] Moreover, it has been found necessary to provide protection for certain classes of official. Thus certain statutes exempt officials from being sued in respect of acts done bona fide in the course of duty.[13] The Constables Protection Act 1750 protects constables who act in obedience to the warrant of a magistrate, though the magistrate acted without jurisdiction in issuing the warrant. Again, the Mental Health Act 1983, s 139, affords constables and hospital staff protection against civil and criminal liability in respect of acts such as the compulsory detention of a mental patient, unless the act was done in bad faith or without reasonable care.[14] The liability of individual officials will therefore turn both on the powers which they may exercise and also on the privileges and immunities which they may enjoy. But no general immunity is enjoyed by officers or servants of the Crown.[15]

Vicarious liability of public authorities

While the individual liability of public officials was historically important in establishing that public authorities were themselves subject to the law, individual liability is not today a sufficient basis for the liability of large organisations. It is now essential to be able to sue an individual's employing authority, if only because the authority is a more substantial defendant: a successful claimant wants the certainty of knowing that any damages and costs awarded will in fact be paid.

We examine in the following sections the process by which vicarious liability came to be imposed on central government. In cases not involving the Crown, it has long been the law that a public authority is, like any other employer, liable for the wrongful acts of its servants or agents committed in the course of their employment. It was established in 1866 that the liability of a public body whose servants negligently execute their duties is identical with that of a private trading company.

> In *Mersey Docks and Harbour Board Trustees* v *Gibbs*,[16] a ship and its cargo were damaged on entering a dock by reason of a mud bank left negligently at the entrance. The trustees were held liable and appealed to the House of Lords on the ground that they were not a company deriving benefit from the traffic, but a public body of trustees constituted by Parliament for the purpose of maintaining the docks. That purpose involved authority to collect tolls for maintenance and repair of the docks, for paying off capital charges and ultimately for reducing the tolls for the benefit of the public. It was held that these public purposes did not absolve the trustees from the duty to take reasonable care that the docks were in such a state that those who navigated them might do so without danger.

In spite of the argument that a corporation should not be liable for a wrongful act, since a wrongful act must be beyond its lawful powers, a corporation is, like any other employer, liable for the torts of its employees acting in the course of their employment. Thus a hospital authority is liable for negligence in the performance of their

---

[12] *The Case of the Marshalsea* (1613) 10 Co Rep 76a.
[13] E.g. National Health Service Act 1977, s 125; Financial Services Act 1986, s 187.
[14] On the earlier law, see *R* v *Bracknell Justices, ex p Griffiths* [1976] AC 314; and *Ashingdane* v *UK* (1985) 7 EHRR 528.
[15] The suggestion to the contrary in *R* v *Transport Secretary, ex p Factortame Ltd* [1990] 2 AC 85, 145 was rightly disapproved in *M* v *Home Office* [1994] 1 AC 377.
[16] (1866) LR 1 HL 93 (discussed fully in Kneebone (note 1), ch 2).

professional duties by physicians and surgeons employed by the authority.[17] Under general principles of vicarious liability, a public authority is not liable for acts committed by an employee who is acting outside the course of employment 'on a frolic of his own'. But where a prisoner is ill-treated by prison officers, the Home Office may be vicariously liable even if those acts amount to misfeasance in public office, when the ill-treatment is a misguided or unauthorised method of performing their duties;[18] and the owners of a school were liable for sexual abuse of boys by a house warden, the abuse being very closely connected with his employment.[19] An exception to vicarious liability may arise when an official, although appointed and employed by a local authority, carries out functions under the control of a central authority or in the exercise of a distinct public duty imposed by the law.[20] There was formerly no vicarious liability in respect of police officers, but the chief constable is now vicariously liable for their acts committed in the performance of their functions,[21] and the vicarious liability extends to acts of racial discrimination.[22]

Tortious liability of the Crown

There were two main rules which until 1948 governed the liability of the Crown: (*a*) the rule of substantive law that the King could do no wrong; (*b*) the procedural rule derived from feudal principles that the King could not be sued in his own courts. The survival of these rules into the 20th century meant that before 1948 the Crown could be sued neither in respect of wrongs that had been expressly authorised nor in respect of wrongs such as negligence committed by Crown servants in the course of their employment.[23] Nor were government ministers vicariously liable for the tortious acts of staff in their departments, since in law ministers and civil servants are alike servants of the Crown.[24] It was anomalous that this immunity of the Crown applied to the activities of central government. The rigour of the immunity was eased before 1948 by concession. Acting through the Treasury Solicitor, departments were often prepared to defend an action against a subordinate official and pay damages if he or she were found personally liable for a wrongful act. From this there developed the practice by which the Crown might nominate a defendant on whom a writ could be served. This practice was disapproved by the House of Lords in 1946, in a case in which the nominated defendant could not have been personally liable for the alleged tort.[25] It became urgently necessary for the law to be changed to permit the Crown to be sued in tort. As early as 1927 a draft Bill had been recommended by a government committee, but opposition from within government prevented reform of the law.[26] The law was at last placed on a new basis by the Crown Proceedings Act 1947.

---

[17] *Cassidy v Minister of Health* [1951] 2 KB 343. For the vicarious liability of education and social service authorities, see *X v Bedfordshire CC* [1995] 2 AC 633.
[18] *Racz v Home Office* [1994] 2 AC 45; and p 767 below.
[19] *Lister v Hesley Hall Ltd* [2001] 2 All ER 769.
[20] *Stanbury v Exeter Corpn* [1905] 2 KB 838.
[21] Police Act 1964, s 48 (now 1996, s 88); Police (Scotland) Act 1967, s 39; ch 21 E.
[22] Race Relations (Amendment) Act 2000, s 4, reversing *Farah v Metropolitan Police Commissioner* [1997] 1 All ER 289.
[23] See e.g. *Viscount Canterbury v A-G* (1842) 1 Ph 306 (negligence of Crown servants causing Houses of Parliament to burn down).
[24] *Raleigh v Goschen* [1898] 1 Ch 73; *Bainbridge v Postmaster-General* [1906] 1 KB 178. And see *M v Home Office* [1994] 1 AC 377, 408–9.
[25] *Adams v Naylor* [1946] AC 543.
[26] Cmd 2842, 1927. And see J Jacob [1992] PL 452 and Jacob, *The Republican Crown*, ch 2.

With important exceptions, this Act (which applies only to proceedings by and against the Crown in right of Her Majesty's Government in the United Kingdom)[27] established the principle that the Crown is subject to the same liabilities in tort as if it were a private person of full age and capacity (*a*) in respect of torts committed by its servants or agents, (*b*) in respect of the duties which an employer at common law owes to his servants or agents, and (*c*) in respect of any breach of the common law duties of an owner or occupier of property (s 2(1)). The Crown is therefore vicariously liable for the torts of its servants or agents, for example, negligent driving by a Crown servant while in the course of his or her employment.

The Crown is also liable for breach of a statutory duty, provided that the statute is one which binds the Crown as well as private persons (s 2(2)) such as the Occupiers' Liability Act 1957. The Act of 1947 imposes no liability enforceable by action in the case of statutory duties which bind only the Crown or its officers.

Although the principle of Crown liability is established, the Act of 1947 elaborates this in some detail. Thus the vicarious liability of the Crown is restricted to the torts of its officers as defined (s 2(6)). This definition requires that the officer shall (*a*) be appointed directly or indirectly by the Crown and (*b*) be paid in respect of his duties as an officer of the Crown at the material time wholly out of the Consolidated Fund,[28] moneys provided by Parliament or a fund certified by the Treasury. This excludes, for example, the police. There is no vicarious liability for officers acting in a judicial capacity or in execution of judicial process (s 2(5))[29] or for acts or omissions of a Crown servant unless apart from the Act the servant would have been personally liable in tort (s 2(1)). The general law relating to indemnity and contribution applies to the Crown as if it were a private person (s 4). The Act does not authorise proceedings against the Sovereign in her personal capacity (s 40(1)) and does not abolish any prerogative or statutory powers of the Crown, in particular those relating to the defence of the realm and the armed forces (s 11(1)).

Under the 1947 Act, there were formerly two principal exceptions from liability in tort. The first related to the armed forces. By s 10, neither the Crown nor a member of the armed forces was liable in tort in respect of acts causing death or personal injury which were committed by a member of the armed forces while on duty, where (*a*) the victim was a member of the armed forces on duty at the time or, if not on duty as such, was on any land, premises, ship, aircraft or vehicle which was being used for the purposes of the armed forces and (*b*) the injury was certified by the secretary of state as attributable to service for purposes of pension entitlement. This certificate did not guarantee an award of a pension unless the conditions for entitlement were fulfilled.[30] There certainly must be a public scheme for compensating members of the armed forces who suffer injury or death during their service. But should this exclude the right to sue for common law damages? In 1987, Parliament legislated to put into suspense s 10 of the 1947 Act.[31] Section 10 can be revived if it appears to the Secretary of State

---

[27] S 40(2)(b), (c). And see *Franklin* v *A-G* [1974] QB 185; *Tito* v *Waddell (No 2)* [1977] Ch 106; *Mutasa* v *A-G* [1980] QB 114; *R* v *Foreign Secretary, ex p Indian Assn of Alberta* [1982] QB 892.

[28] Ch 17.

[29] On s 2(5), see *Jones* v *Department of Employment* [1989] QB 1 (functions of adjudication officer not judicial) and *Welsh* v *Chief Constable of Merseyside Police* [1993] 1 All ER 692 (prosecutor's administrative functions not judicial). Immunity for judicial acts done in good faith is maintained by the Human Rights Act 1998, s 9(3), except that damages may, where an individual's right to liberty is violated, and to comply with art 5(5) ECHR, be awarded against the Crown. And see I Olowofoyeku [1998] PL 444.

[30] *Adams* v *War Office* [1955] 3 All ER 245. On s 10, see also *Pearce* v *Defence Secretary* [1988] AC 755, overruling in part *Bell* v *Defence Secretary* [1986] 1 QB 322 and *Derry* v *Ministry of Defence* (1999) 49 BMLR 62.

[31] Crown Proceedings (Armed Forces) Act 1987; and see F C Boyd [1989] PL 237. The 1987 Act was not retrospective: *Derry* v *Ministry of Defence*. Also *Matthews* v *Ministry of Defence* [2002] All ER (D) 137 (Jan) (immunity of Crown declared incompatible with art 6(1) ECHR).

necessary or expedient to do so, for example by reason of imminent national danger or for warlike operations outside the United Kingdom. Until it is so revived, members of the armed forces (and in the event of death, their dependants) may sue fellow members (and the Crown vicariously) for damages in respect of injuries or death arising out of their service. When a soldier sued for personal injury caused during the Gulf operations in 1991 (for which s 10 was not revived), the Court of Appeal held that no duty of care was owed to him by his fellow soldiers during battle conditions.[32]

The second exception from liability for tort formerly applied to the Post Office, at that time a government department, for acts or omissions in relation to postal packets or telephonic communications (s 9). Neither was there any liability in contract.[33] When the Post Office became a public corporation, the existing limitations on liability for postal and telephone services were continued.[34]

Subject to these two exceptions, the Crown Proceedings Act 1947 in principle assimilated the tortious liabilities of the Crown to those of a private person. However, in many situations involving the potential liability of the government the analogy of private liability is not directly helpful. Some claims against the Crown are held to be non-justiciable,[35] but in general the courts apply to governmental action rules derived from, for example, the ordinary law of negligence.[36]

In Scotland, the position of the monarch in respect of Crown proceedings was not identical with the position in English law, the Court of Session being less willing than the English courts to grant the King immunity from being sued.[37] However, it was held in 1921 that the Crown was not vicariously liable for the wrongful acts of Crown servants.[38] Section 2 of the 1947 Act established such liability in Scotland, although the terminology is modified. Thus 'tort' in the Act's application to Scotland means 'any wrongful or negligent act or omission giving rise to liability in reparation'.[39]

The Act of 1947 thus enabled the Crown to be sued in England in the law of torts and, in Scotland, in the law of delict or reparation. We will now consider some aspects of the substantive law governing the liability in tort of public authorities generally.

Statutory authority as a defence

Where acts of a public body interfere with an individual's rights (whether these concern property, contract or liberty), those acts will be unlawful unless legal authority for them exists. Such authority may be found in legislation or in common law. Where Parliament expressly authorises something to be done, to do it in accordance with that authority cannot be wrongful. It will depend on the legislation whether compensation is payable for the rights which Parliament has authorised to be taken away. The construction of many public works affecting private rights of property (for example, nuclear installations or motorways) is subject to detailed rules of compensation in the relevant legislation.[40] But express provision for compensation is not always made. It is then for the court in interpreting the legislation to decide what powers are authorised and whether any compensation is payable. In that process of interpretation, it is assumed that, when

---

[32] *Mulcahy v Ministry of Defence* [1996] QB 732; and ch 16.
[33] *Triefus & Co Ltd v Post Office* [1957] 2 QB 352.
[34] Post Office Act 1969, ss 6(5), 29, 30; British Telecommunications Act 1981, s 70.
[35] E.g. *Tito v Waddell (No 2)* and *Mutasa v A-G* (note 27 above).
[36] E.g. *Dorset Yacht Co v Home Office* [1970] AC 1004; note 77 below.
[37] See J D B Mitchell [1957] PL 304.
[38] *MacGregor v Lord Advocate* 1921 SC 847.
[39] Crown Proceedings Act 1947, s 43(b).
[40] See e.g. Nuclear Installations Acts 1965 and 1969 (as amended by Energy Act 1983, Part II); Land Compensation Act 1973.

discretionary power is given to a public body, there is no intention to interfere with private rights, unless the power is expressed in such a way as to make interference inevitable.

> In *Metropolitan Asylum District* v *Hill*, hospital trustees were empowered by statute to build hospitals in London. A smallpox hospital was built at Hampstead in such a way as to constitute a nuisance at common law. *Held*, in the absence of express words or necessary implication in the statute authorising the commission of a nuisance, the building of the hospital was unlawful. 'Where the terms of the statute are not imperative, but permissive, when it is left to the discretion of the persons empowered to determine whether the general powers committed to them shall be put into execution or not, . . . the fair inference is that the Legislature intended that discretion to be exercised in strict conformity with private rights and did not intend to confer licence to commit nuisance in any place which might be selected for the purpose'.[41]

If, however, the exercise of a statutory power or duty inevitably involves injury to private rights, there is no remedy unless the statute makes provision for compensation.[42]

> In *Allen* v *Gulf Oil Refining Ltd*, the House of Lords held that a local Act which envisaged the building of an oil refinery at Milford Haven, though it gave the company no express power to construct the refinery and did not define the site, did give authority for the construction and use of the refinery. Such authority protected the company against liability for nuisance to neighbouring owners which was the inevitable result of the construction of the refinery, though the Act gave the owners no compensation for the loss of their rights.[43]

The courts adopt a strict approach in considering whether a nuisance that has occurred is an inevitable consequence of the statute. To establish a defence of statutory authority, the defendant must show that no reasonable or practicable steps could have been taken to prevent the nuisance occurring.[44] While, as in *Allen* v *Gulf Oil Refining Ltd*, the right to sue for nuisance may have been taken away, the courts will rarely hold that a body exercising statutory powers is at liberty to do so carelessly. As a leading dictum of Lord Blackburn put it,

> . . . no action will lie for doing that which the legislature has authorised, if it be done without negligence, although it does occasion damage to anyone; but an action does lie for doing that which the legislature has authorised, if it be done negligently.[45]

This statement must be read in context: it applies only where a statute authorises an act to be done which will necessarily cause some injury to private rights, and where the act is performed carelessly so causing unnecessary injury to those rights.[46] Such additional injury is outside the protection afforded by the statute. However, if a public authority which merely has a power to act, and not a duty, decides to take action but acts inefficiently, it is not liable unless the inefficiency causes extra damage to an individual: this was so held in 1941, in the difficult case of *East Suffolk Catchment Board* v *Kent*, when the use by a river board of an ineffective method of removing flood water from a farmer's land was held to create no liability towards the farmer.[47]

---

[41] (1881) 6 App Cas 193, 212–13 (Lord Watson).
[42] *Hammersmith Rly Co* v *Brand* (1869) LR 4 HL 171.
[43] [1981] AC 1001.
[44] *Marcic* v *Thames Water Utilities Ltd* [2002] 2 All ER 55 (defendant liable for discharge from sewers on to M's property).
[45] *Geddis* v *Proprietors of Bann Reservoir* (1878) 3 App Cas 430, 455–6.
[46] *X* v *Bedfordshire CC* [1995] 2 AC 633, 733.
[47] [1941] AC 74. And see M J Bowman and S H Bailey [1984] PL 277. Cf *Fellowes* v *Rother DC* [1983] 1 All ER 513, 522 and *Stovin* v *Wise* (note 64 below).

Statutory duties[48]

It was at one time the view that anyone harmed by a failure to perform a statutory duty could bring an action for damages against the person or body liable to perform it.[49] If this were the law today, it would have a very broad impact on public bodies required to provide services or to exercise regulatory or protective functions. However, the enormous variety of duties imposed by statute means that there can be no single form of proceedings for enforcing public duties. Some duties, for example the duty of the Secretary of State for Education to promote the education of the people of England and Wales,[50] are effectively unenforceable by legal proceedings of any kind.[51] Some public duties may be enforced by proceedings for an injunction brought by the Attorney-General in the public interest, or by a local authority in exercise of statutory powers.[52] Some are enforceable only by recourse to statutory compensation.[53] Very many duties may, as we have seen, be enforced by an order of mandamus obtained by judicial review.[54] Some statutes provide for a criminal penalty in the event of a breach of duty. Where the statute that creates a duty expressly provides a sanction for breach (for example, prosecution of the person responsible) or a remedy for those affected to use, the courts may hold that no other means of enforcing the duty exists.[55]

In some situations, particularly where the statutory duty closely parallels a common law duty (for example, to use care not to cause personal injury) the breach of statutory duty gives rise to a private right of action for damages; such an action is akin to an action for negligence, except that liability depends on the breach of the duty itself, not on there being a lack of care.[56] Such an action for breach exists if it can be shown by interpretation of the statute that the duty was imposed for the protection of a certain class and that the legislature intended to confer on members of that class the benefit of a right of action.[57] It is notoriously difficult to evaluate all the factors that may be relevant when a court is deciding whether a statutory duty is enforceable by an action for damages, where the statute is silent on the point.[58] In 1969, the English and Scottish Law Commissions recommended that the courts should be able to assume in interpreting statutes that the remedy of damages was available for breach of statutory duty, unless the statute expressly provided to the contrary.[59] This proposal, which was not adopted, did not take account of the fact that many statutory duties relate to public services; as such, they are now considered to be enforceable by judicial review, not by suing for damages. Recent judicial policy has severely limited the availability of damages as a remedy for breach of public duties.

---

[48] R A Buckley (1984) 100 LQR 204; Harding, *Public Duties and Public Law*, ch 7.
[49] Dicta to this effect in *Couch v Steel* (1854) 3 E & B 402 were disapproved in *Atkinson v Newcastle Waterworks Co* (1877) 2 Ex D 441.
[50] Education Act 1996, s 10.
[51] Ch 30 A, p 707 above.
[52] Ch 31.
[53] Note 40 above.
[54] Ch 31.
[55] See *Cutler v Wandsworth Stadium Ltd* [1949] AC 398; *Lonrho Ltd v Shell Petroleum Co Ltd* [1982] AC 173, 185; *Scally v Southern Health Board* [1992] 1 AC 294; *Wentworth v Wiltshire CC* [1993] QB 654.
[56] E.g. *Reffell v Surrey CC* [1964] 1 All ER 743.
[57] See *X v Bedfordshire CC* [1995] 2 AC 633, 731.
[58] See Bennion, *Statutory Interpretation*, Code, s 14. Such difficulties do not arise where an Act specifies the means of enforcement; see e.g. Local Government Act 1988, s 19(7) (excluding criminal penalties but authorising judicial review and claims for damages).
[59] HC 256 (1968–69), para 38.

In *X (minors)* v *Bedfordshire CC*,[60] the House of Lords considered a group of claims for damages arising from the defective performance by local councils of duties relating to the education and welfare of children. The alleged breaches included the failure of a social service authority to take children into care who were badly in need of protection against abuse; a converse error by social workers in taking a child into care believed to be at risk of sexual abuse, when the identity of her abuser was mistaken; and failures by education authorities to identify the special educational needs of children and to provide appropriate special schooling. The councils had applied to have these claims struck out as disclosing no cause of action. *Held*, so far as the actions were based on breach of statutory duty, they were disallowed. The duties in question gave rise to no private rights of action; nor were the councils under a duty of care in performing the statutory duties. The education cases were allowed to proceed so far as they were based on the councils' vicarious liability for the professional negligence of teachers and educational psychologists; there was held to be no such vicarious liability for social workers and psychiatrists reporting to the councils on alleged child abuse.

This decision is notable for Lord Browne-Wilkinson's analysis of the common law rules of liability that apply to statutory functions of local authorities. He emphasised that very different policy considerations applied to (*a*) public law remedies obtainable by judicial review and (*b*) the private right to sue for damages. In a different context, an earlier decision of the House reflects a similar approach to that in *X* v *Bedfordshire CC*: a prisoner adversely affected by a breach of prison rules was held to have no action in damages arising from the breach. Lord Jauncey said:

> The fact that a particular provision was intended to protect certain individuals is not of itself sufficient to confer private law rights upon them, something more is required to show that the legislature intended such conferment.[61]

In *O'Rourke* v *Camden Council*, a homeless person sued the council for breach of its duty under the Housing Act 1985 to provide temporary accommodation. The Lords held that the duty was enforceable by judicial review as a matter of public law, but did not give rise to an action for damages.[62] The House of Lords later confirmed that there was no claim for breach of statutory duty against an education authority in respect of a failure to diagnose and identify a child's special needs, but that the authority was liable vicariously for the failure of its employee (an educational psychologist) to show the professional skill that could reasonably have been expected.[63]

Tort liability and judicial review

As *X* v *Bedfordshire CC* and similar decisions[64] illustrate, in an era when the use of judicial review has expanded dramatically, as has liability for breaches of duties owed in European law, the courts have resisted an equivalent expansion in the liability of public bodies to be sued for damages. We have seen that in France both the judicial review of decisions and the power to award compensation for wrongful acts committed by public authorities are entrusted to the administrative courts.[65] Under the French

---

[60] [1995] 2 AC 633; see P Cane (1996) 112 LQR 13, L Edwards (1996) 1 Edin Law Rev 115; S H Bailey and M J Bowman [2000] CLJ 85.

[61] *R* v *Deputy Governor of Parkhurst Prison, ex p Hague* [1992] 1 AC 58, 171 (Lord Jauncey); see also *Calveley* v *Chief Constable, Merseyside Police* [1989] AC 1228.

[62] [1998] AC 188, reversing *Thornton* v *Kirklees Council* [1979] QB 626; see Sir R Carnwath [1998] PL 407.

[63] *Phelps* v *Hillingdon Council* [2001] 2 AC 619.

[64] See e.g. *Hill* v *Chief Constable of West Yorkshire* [1989] AC 53; *Elguzouli-Daf* v *Commissioner of Metropolitan Police* [1995] QB 335; and *Stovin* v *Wise* [1996] AC 923.

[65] Ch 27. Brown and Bell, *French Administrative Law*, ch 8. Also Bell and Bradley (eds), *Governmental Liability* and Markesinis et al., *Tortious Liability of Statutory Bodies* (comparing English, French and German law).

system, rules of public liability have developed which differ from the rules of liability in civil law. In English law, by contrast, public authorities and officials are in principle subject to the same law of civil liability as private persons. Thus a claim in damages against a public authority must be based on an ordinary tort (including negligence, nuisance, trespass to the person and breach of statutory duty) or on a specific right of action created by statute. Yet the existing categories of tort do not include all instances in which a public body may cause loss to an individual through acts or omissions that as a matter of public law are in some way wrongful.

In particular, English law does not accept that an individual has a right to be indemnified for loss caused by invalid or ultra vires administrative action.[66] Although a claimant for judicial review may seek damages together with quashing, mandatory, declaratory and restraining orders, this has not changed the substantive rules of liability.[67] Thus a prisoner may successfully seek judicial review of a prison governor's decision to put him in solitary confinement for 28 days, but has no right to sue the governor or the Home Office for damages, whether for breach of prison rules or for false imprisonment.[68]

When a trader's licence for a market stall is cancelled in breach of natural justice, he or she may by judicial review recover the licence[69] but has no right to compensation for the intervening loss of income unless, exceptionally, the market authority acted with malice.[70] The Judicial Committee has twice affirmed that a public authority's decision may be invalid, in the sense of being ultra vires, without this giving rise to a right to damages.

In *Dunlop* v *Woollahra Council*, an owner of building land suffered financial loss when the local council imposed restrictions on prospective development which were later quashed as ultra vires. *Held*, the owner had no claim in damages for the loss resulting from the invalid restrictions. Moreover, the council had not acted negligently in imposing the restrictions, having taken legal advice before so doing. The council had acted in good faith and, in the absence of malice, could not be liable for the tort of abuse of public office.[71] In *Rowling* v *Takaro Properties Ltd*, a New Zealand Cabinet minister had acted ultra vires in refusing consent to the proposed development of a luxury hotel; this had caused the Japanese investors to lose interest in the project. When the minister was sued for damages by the developer, the Judicial Committee *held* (reversing the New Zealand Court of Appeal) that even assuming that a duty of care was owed by the minister to the developer, he was not in breach of that duty: his decision had been based on a tenable view of his powers and was neither unreasonable nor negligent.[72]

In 1986, a similar stance on the question of remedy was adopted by the Court of Appeal when French turkey farmers had been adversely affected by a ban on importing turkeys into Britain that had been imposed in breach of the EEC Treaty (art 28, ex 30) by the Ministry of Agriculture; the majority held that it was a sufficient remedy for the French farmers that they could have sought judicial review of the ban.[73] It has since become clear that, as Oliver LJ held in dissent, the protection of rights under

---

[66] *Hoffmann-La Roche* v *Secretary of State for Trade* [1975] AC 295, 358 (Lord Wilberforce).
[67] See ch 31; and see e.g. *Page Motors Ltd* v *Epsom and Ewell BC* (1982) 80 LGR 337, and P Cane [1983] PL 202; *Davy* v *Spelthorne BC* [1984] AC 262.
[68] *R* v *Deputy Governor of Parkhurst Prison, ex p Hague* [1992] 1 AC 58.
[69] *R* v *Barnsley Council, ex p Hook* [1976] 3 All ER 452.
[70] See p 767 below.
[71] [1982] AC 158.
[72] [1988] AC 473.
[73] [1986] QB 716. The claim of misfeasance in public office against the Minister of Agriculture was allowed to proceed.

Community law requires the payment of compensation to cover the period between imposition of the ban and its revocation.[74]

In some circumstances, maladministration by a government department or local authority may cause an individual to suffer injustice. In this event, by complaining to the appropriate Ombudsman the individual may obtain compensation, but the authority is not liable to be sued in damages for such maladministration.[75] It was against this background that in 1988 the Justice/All Souls committee on administrative law recommended that the law should permit compensation to be recoverable by any person who sustains loss as a result of acts or decisions that are for any reason wrongful or contrary to law or are a result of any excessive delay.[76] This proposal was not acceptable to the government and in practice the liability of public authorities continues to depend on tort law, in particular the tort of negligence, as it develops under the influence of European law.

Public authorities and liability for negligence

Although the Crown Proceedings Act 1947 assimilated the tort liability of government to that of a private person, the duties of government give rise to issues of liability which are not easily resolved by applying legal principles that relate primarily to the acts of private persons. Indeed, the analogy with private persons is of limited value. Most actions by public authorities stem from legislation. And many disputes as to liability turn directly on the relationship between (*a*) common law rules on the duty of care; (*b*) the legislation, which broadly will confer either a duty or a power to act; and (*c*) the rules of administrative law that apply when judicial review is sought.

> In *Dorset Yacht Co v Home Office*,[77] the Home Office was sued for the value of a yacht which had been damaged when seven borstal boys absconded at night from a borstal summer camp on an island in Poole harbour. The plaintiffs alleged that the boys were able to abscond because of the negligence of their officers. The Home Office argued that the system of open borstals would be jeopardised if any liability was imposed on the government for the wrongful acts of those who absconded. The House of Lords *held*, Lord Dilhorne dissenting, that the Home Office was liable for the negligence of the officers; in the circumstances the officers owed a duty of care to the yacht owners, the damage to the yacht being reasonably foreseeable as the direct consequence of a failure by the officers to take reasonable care.

This decision had broad consequences for the developing law of negligence, but it did not hold that the Home Office was liable regardless of negligence; nor did it govern the situation in which it was alleged that an executive discretion (for example, to transfer someone to an open prison) had been improperly exercised. Lord Diplock in *Dorset Yacht* suggested that questions of liability for the exercise of discretion were to be settled by applying the public law concept of ultra vires rather than the civil law concept of negligence.[78] The relationship between the two concepts arose again in *Anns v Merton Council*,[79] in which the Lords held that both a failure by local inspectors to inspect, and a failure to inspect properly, the foundations of a new building (which later suffered structural damage because the foundations were inadequate) could make the council liable for the cost of repairing the building. In the leading speech, Lord

---

[74] See e.g. the *Francovitch* and *Factortame (No 5)* cases, at notes 3 and 5 above.
[75] Ch 29 D; and *R v Knowsley BC, ex p Maguire* (1992) 90 LGR 653. And see M Amos [2000] PL 21.
[76] *Administrative Justice, Some Necessary Reforms*, ch 11.
[77] [1970] AC 1004; and see C J Hamson [1969] CLJ 273, G Semar [1969] PL 269 and M A Millner [1973] CLP 260.
[78] [1970] AC 1004, at 1067; cf Harlow, *Compensation and Government Torts*, pp 54–7.
[79] [1978] AC 728.

Wilberforce distinguished between the discretion of the council in adopting its policy as to inspection, and the operational tasks involved in carrying out that policy: the more 'operational' a power or duty might be, the easier it might be to impose a duty of care.[80]

An immense amount of litigation arose directly from *Anns v Merton Council*, caused in part by Lord Wilberforce's analysis of the approach which the courts should adopt in applying the law of negligence to new fact situations, and in part by the broad way in which *Anns* caused public authorities to be liable for not having prevented the commission of wrongs by others.[81] In *Murphy v Brentwood Council*, on similar facts to those in *Anns*, a seven-judge House of Lords declared that *Anns* had been wrongly decided and held (inter alia) that the defendant council owed no duty of care to the plaintiff when it approved the plans for defective foundations for the plaintiff's house.[82] Moreover, in *Caparo Industries plc v Dickman*,[83] the House adopted a three-part test applying to new situations in which it was sought to establish liability for negligence: (1) whether the harm to the claimant was foreseeable; (2) whether the parties were in a relationship of proximity; and (3) whether it was 'fair, just and reasonable' that the defendant should owe a duty of care to the claimant. This decision confirmed[83a] that 'novel categories of negligence' would develop 'incrementally and by analogy with established categories, rather than by a massive extension of a prima facie duty of care', restrained only by indefinable policy considerations seeking to limit the scope of the duty of care. In applying criterion (3) to new claims brought against a public body, judges exercise discretion in assessing what may be the consequences for public policy of holding the body liable.

The courts have indeed sought to restrict the imposition of liability in several contexts, particularly in respect of claims for economic loss arising out of regulatory functions[84] and of claims seeking to impose a private law duty of care on the public functions of the police[85] and on the civil servants who decide claims for social security benefits.[86] Inevitably, the outcome of judicial policy-making will often be uncertain.

> In *Stovin v Wise*, a county council as highway authority had statutory power to remove an earth bank that it knew restricted visibility at a dangerous road junction, but it failed to do so. When an accident occurred at the junction, was the council liable for failure to exercise its power? The House of Lords held (by 3–2) that a duty of care to users of the highway to remove the bank arose only if (*a*) it was 'irrational' (in the public law sense) for the power *not* to be used and (*b*) there were exceptional factors indicating that the policy of the legislation was to confer a right to sue on a person injured when the power was not exercised. The majority held that neither condition was satisfied, adding that it was 'important, before extending the duty of care owed by public authorities, to consider the cost to the community of the defensive measures which they are likely to take to avoid liability'.[87] The dissenting judges

---

80   See D Oliver [1980] CLP 269, S H Bailey and M J Bowman [1986] CLJ 430; P P Craig (1978) 94 LQR 428. Also *X v Bedfordshire CC* [1995] 2 AC 633, 736–8 and *Stovin v Wise* (below).

81   E.g. *Peabody Donation Fund v Sir Lindsay Parkinson & Co* [1985] AC 210 and *Curran v Northern Ireland Co-ownership Association* [1987] AC 718. See M J Bowman and S H Bailey [1984] PL 277; T Weir [1989] PL 40; A W Bradley (1989) 23 The Law Teacher 109.

82   [1991] 1 AC 398. And see I N D Wallace (1991) 107 LQR 177.

83   [1990] 2 AC 605.

83a   Quoting from *Sutherland Shire Council v Heyman* (1985) 60 ALR 1, 43–4 (Brennan J).

84   *Yuen Kun-yeu v A-G of Hong Kong* [1988] AC 175; *Davis v Radcliffe* [1990] 2 All ER 536. And see H McLean (1988) 8 OJLS 442.

85   *Rigby v Chief Constable of Northampton* [1985] 2 All ER 985; *Hill v Chief Constable of West Yorkshire* [1989] AC 53; *Calveley v Chief Constable, Merseyside* [1989] AC 1228. But cf *Swinney v Chief Constable of Northumbria* [1997] QB 464 and *Waters v Commissioner of Metropolitan Police* [2000] 4 All ER 934.

86   *Jones v Department of Employment* [1989] QB 1; W J Swadling [1988] PL 328.

87   [1996] AC 923, 958 (Lord Hoffmann). And see S H Bailey and M J Bowman [2000] CLJ 85, 101–19.

held that, being aware of the danger, the council was under a common law duty of care towards road users to use its powers to remove the cause of the danger.

Judicial reluctance to impose duties of care on public authorities has caused some claimants to have recourse to Strasbourg. In *Osman* v *Ferguson*, despite strong facts, the Court of Appeal struck out a claim against the police for negligently failing to prevent a fatal attack, holding that the claim was 'doomed to failure';[88] the court applied the ruling in *Hill* v *Chief Constable of West Yorkshire*[89] that it would be against public policy for the police to be under any liability to the victims of crimes committed by those whom the police failed to apprehend. The Strasbourg court held in 1998 that this decision to strike out *Osman* v *Ferguson* was in breach of art 6(1) ECHR, since the effect was to afford the police a blanket immunity from being sued in respect of their acts and omissions relating to criminal offences.[90]

This decision was much criticised for having transformed the right to a fair hearing under art 6(1) into an evaluation of the substantive rights that should exist in national law.[91] Remarkably, three years later, in *Z* v *UK*,[92] a sequel to the House of Lords' decision in *X* v *Bedfordshire Council*, the Strasbourg court changed its position, holding by 12–5 that for an English court to strike out an action did not breach art 6(1) since there would have been a full and fair hearing, argued in law on the basis that all facts were as claimed by the claimants. Further, the court held on the evidence in *Z* v *UK* that the fact that young children had been left by the local authority to live with cruel and abusive parents for over four years breached their right under art 3 ECHR to be protected against inhuman or degrading treatment; their right under art 13 ECHR to an effective remedy had also been breached by the English legal system. In this serious case, the court ordered the UK government to pay substantial sums to the claimants by way of compensation.

Even though the Strasbourg court erred in its reasoning in *Osman* v *UK*, the knowledge that national decisions on public liability must take account of Convention rights seems to have had a salutary effect on recent case-law about the liability of local authorities responsible for social services and education.[93] Whether or not such authorities are under a common law duty of care in making their decisions, the Human Rights Act 1998 now requires the courts to decide whether the defective provision of public services affects the Convention rights of those concerned.

By contrast with difficulties that arise when a claimant seeks to impose a duty of care on a public body in a new situation, some aspects of negligence are readily applied in the public sector. Thus, under *Hedley Byrne & Co* v *Heller*,[94] someone who relies to his or her detriment on inaccurate statements made by an official in the course of

---

[88] [1993] 4 All ER 344, 354. A 15-year-old boy and his family had suffered extreme harassment from the boy's former teacher over several months, culminating when he fired at them, severely injuring the boy and killing his father. The police knew of the harassment and of threats by the assailant before the fatal attack occurred.

[89] [1989] AC 53 (a case brought by the family of the last victim of the 'Yorkshire ripper').

[90] *Osman* v *UK* (1998) 29 EHRR 245.

[91] See e.g. C A Gearty (2001) 64 MLR 159.

[92] (2001) 34 EHRR 3; see C A Gearty (2002) 65 MLR 87 and R English (2001) 151 NLJ 973. The applicant children complained that the council had delayed for four years before taking them into care, despite the extreme circumstances, and that this had caused them serious physical and emotional harm.

[93] See *Barrett* v *Enfield Council* [2001] 2 AC 550 (arrangements for child taken into care of council may be subject to a duty of care, as acts pursuant to the lawful exercise of discretion: see P Craig and R Fairgrieve [1999] PL 626); *W* v *Essex CC* [2001] 2 AC 592 (arguable that council owed duty of care to foster parents in placing with them a 15-year-old boy who sexually assaulted the foster parents' children); and *Phelps* v *Hillingdon Council* (see note 63 above).

[94] [1964] AC 465.

the latter's duties may have a remedy in negligence for loss suffered: a local authority was liable when an environmental health officer, acting in an advisory role, negligently required expensive and unnecessary alterations to be made to a farm guest-house.[95]

Misfeasance in public office

It is a fundamental assumption of the law that those who exercise public functions should do so in good faith and without malicious or spiteful motives. Bad faith may not, of course, be assumed merely because a public body has made a decision that is corrected by judicial review. But where it is shown that a body or official was not acting in good faith, liability in tort may exist.[96] Instances of the tort are infrequent, but in *Bourgoin SA* v *Ministry of Agriculture*, where it was conceded that the minister knew that he did not have the powers that he purported to exercise, the Court of Appeal held that liability for misfeasance would arise.[97] The tort of misfeasance arises only from the conduct of a public officer in the exercise of his or her power. Liability depends on the state of mind of the officer in question and takes two forms:

> First there is the case of targeted malice by a public officer, i.e. conduct specifically intended to injure a person or persons. This type of case involves bad faith in the sense of the exercise of public power for an improper or ulterior motive. The second form is where a public officer acts knowing that there is no power to do the act complained of (or reckless as to whether there is) and that the act will probably injure the plaintiff. It involves bad faith inasmuch as the public officer does not have the honest belief that his act is lawful.[98]

The tort is founded upon the dishonest conduct of the official and is distinct from other torts such as negligence or breach of statutory duty; an omission to act is not sufficient, unless there has been a dishonest decision not to act. As regards the first form of the tort, it makes no difference whether the official exceeds his or her powers or acts according to the letter of the power.[99] It appears that local councillors could be liable for misfeasance if, intending to damage the interests of a particular lessee, they voted for a resolution requiring the council's rights as owner of property to be exercised against the lessee.[100] Misfeasance in public office was committed when the corporate officer of the House of Commons breached the rules that governed the placing of a contract to provide the windows of a costly new building for the House.[101] Vicarious liability may arise for misfeasance in office where this is an improper way of performing an officer's duties or is very closely connected with the performance of those duties.[102] Exemplary damages may be payable for misfeasance in public office.[103]

---

[95] *Welton* v *North Cornwall DC* [1997] 1 WLR 570. See also *Harris* v *Wyre Forest DC* [1990] 1 AC 831 and *T (minor)* v *Surrey CC* [1994] 4 All ER 577.

[96] See e.g. *Roncarelli* v *Duplessis* (1959) 16 DLR (2d) 689; *David* v *Abdul Cader* [1963] 3 All ER 579 (malicious refusal of licence) (A W Bradley [1964] CLJ 4); *Micosta SA* v *Shetland Islands Council* 1986 SLT 193; and J McBride [1979] CLJ 323.

[97] [1986] QB 716.

[98] *Three Rivers Council* v *Bank of England (No 3)* [2000] 3 All ER 1, 8 (Lord Steyn). For a full review of the case-law, see Clarke J in this case [1996] 3 All ER 558 (and C Hadjiemmanuil [1997] PL 32). See also refusal of the Lords to strike out the case [2001] 2 All ER 513.

[99] [2000] 3 All ER 1, 49 (Lord Millett, citing *Jones* v *Swansea Council* [1989] 3 All ER 162).

[100] *Jones* v *Swansea Council* [1990] 3 All ER 737.

[101] *Harmon CFEM Facades (UK) Ltd* v *Corporate Officer of the House of Commons* (2000) 67 Con LR 1.

[102] *Racz* v *Home Office* [1994] 2 AC 45. See also *Lister* v *Hesley Hall Ltd* (at note 19 above).

[103] *Kuddus* v *Chief Constable of Leicestershire* [2001] 3 All ER 193; and see note 106 below.

Other aspects of governmental liability

Two other aspects of the liability of public authorities may be briefly mentioned.

First, ever since the general warrant cases in the 1760s in which exemplary damages were awarded for unlawful search and seizure, the courts have had power to award exemplary damages for oppressive, arbitrary or unconstitutional acts in the exercise of public power.[104] It was formerly considered that the power was limited to certain torts for which exemplary damages had been awarded before 1964,[105] but in 2001, in a case of alleged misfeasance in public office by a police officer, the House of Lords held that this limitation was not justified and that such a rigid rule would limit the future development of the law.[106] Juries considering the award of exemplary damages against the police must be directed by the trial judge as to the permissible range of such awards.[107]

Second, the developing law of restitution was applied by the House of Lords in resolving a fundamental question as to the obligations of public authorities in *Woolwich Building Society v Inland Revenue Commissioners (No 2)*.[108] Nearly £57 million in tax had been paid under protest by the society under regulations which were later held to be ultra vires.[109] The House held by a majority of 3–2 that there was a general restitutionary principle by which money paid pursuant to an ultra vires demand by a public authority was recoverable as of right, not at the discretion of the authority. This, said the majority, was required both by common justice and by the principle in the Bill of Rights that taxes should not be levied without the authority of Parliament.[110] Amongst the questions left open by Lord Goff's speech was whether the same principle applies if taxes are levied wrongly because the tax inspector misconstrued a statute or regulation. On this point Lord Goff commented that 'it would be strange if the right of the citizen to recover overpaid charges were to be more restricted under domestic law than it is under Community law'.[111]

B. Contractual liability[112]

As a legal institution, the making of contracts (binding agreements) between two or more persons is the means whereby an infinite number of transactions occur in a modern economy. Legislation is the primary means of creating duties and rights in public law, such as the duty to pay taxes or the right to receive free education. Often government must decide how far to rely on legislative commands to achieve a certain goal: thus, for the armed forces, the policy may be to employ a wholly professional army based on recruiting volunteers or to compel all persons of a certain age to serve alongside a nucleus of regular soldiers. Legislation is needed both to authorise conscription

---

[104] *Wilkes v Wood* (1763) Lofft 1; *Rookes v Bernard* [1964] AC 1129, 1226. And see *Lancashire CC v Municipal Mutual Insurance Ltd* [1997] QB 897.

[105] *AB v South West Water Services Ltd* [1993] QB 507, applying *Cassell and Co Ltd v Broome* [1972] AC 1027.

[106] *Kuddus v Chief Constable of Leicestershire* [2001] 3 All ER 193, overruling *AB v South West Water Services Ltd*. And see Law Commission, *Aggravated, Exemplary and Restitutionary Damages* (Law Com No 247), 1997. In *Kuddus*, Lord Scott was opposed to exemplary damages generally, and in cases of vicarious liability in particular ([2001] 3 All ER at 225–8).

[107] *Thompson v Metropolitan Police Commissioner* [1998] QB 498.

[108] [1993] AC 70; see P B H Birks [1980] CLP 191, [1992] PL 580; J Beatson (1993) 109 LQR 401.

[109] *R v IRC, ex p Woolwich Building Society* [1991] 4 All ER 92.

[110] See chs 2 A and 17.

[111] [1993] AC 70, at 177. For the duties of public bodies to make restitution, see also *Westdeutsche Landesbank Girozentrale v Islington Council* [1994] 4 All ER 890 (CA).

[112] Street, *Governmental Liability*, ch 3; Mitchell, *The Contracts of Public Authorities*; Turpin, *Government Procurement and Contracts*; Hogg, *Liability of the Crown*, ch 9.

and to levy taxation to pay for the armed forces, but a significant distinction may be drawn in achieving certain ends between (*a*) reliance on legislative commands (*imperium*) and (*b*) use of government's economic resources (*dominium*).[113] The government, formerly the monarch, has long met many of its needs by making contracts in the market.[114] Political trends since 1979 have expanded the purposes for which contracts are used: instances include the contracts placed by the Home Office for companies to manage prisons and detention centres;[115] the authority given by Parliament for 'contracting out' statutory functions;[116] and the privatisation of public utilities.[117] Sometimes the shell of a contract is used, without legal content, as with the creation of the 'internal market' in the NHS in 1990[118] and the use of 'framework agreements' to govern executive agencies.[119] The 'private finance initiative' and public–private partnerships enable new projects to be financed and managed, to a greater or lesser extent, jointly by the public and private sectors. One commentator has written: 'The techniques of public administration have been refashioned in the mould of the private commercial sector. . . . Contract has replaced command and control as the paradigm of regulation.'[120] These trends increase the significance of the contract, as the means by which public bodies obtain the supplies, services or public works that they need.

In English law, the contracts of public authorities are in general subject to the same law that governs contracts between private persons. There is no separate body of law governing administrative contracts, as there is in France.[121] There are however certain qualifications which must be made to these general statements. First, while contracts are made against the background of common law, the terms of a contract may disapply the general rules (for example, by providing for arbitration in the event of disputes). Moreover, contracts made on behalf of the Crown are subject to exceptional rules, which will be examined together with relevant provisions of the Crown Proceedings Act 1947. Contracts made by statutory bodies such as local authorities are subject to the rules of ultra vires, both as regards substance and procedure. Thus a contract which it is beyond the power of a local authority to make is void and unenforceable;[122] but effect has been given to certain contracts that would otherwise fail under this rule.[123] A contract made by a public authority is void if it seeks to fetter the future exercise of the authority's discretionary powers.[124] Thus where a planning authority in Cheshire agreed with Manchester University to discourage new development within the vicinity of the Jodrell Bank radio telescope, the purported agreement was without legal effect.[125] Moreover, a local authority remains free to exercise its power to make byelaws even though the effect of doing so may be to render the future performance of contracts it

---

[113] This distinction is developed by T C Daintith [1979] CLP 41 and (same author) in Jowell and Oliver (eds), *The Changing Constitution* (3rd edn, 1994, ch 8).

[114] Government contracts typically involve the exercise of *dominium*. See e.g. *The Bankers' case* (1695) Skin 601. And George IV rented jewels to display in his crown that he could not afford to buy.

[115] Criminal Justice Act 1991, ss 84–91, Sch 10; Criminal Justice and Public Order Act 1994, ss 7–15.

[116] Deregulation and Contracting Out Act 1994, Part II.

[117] See ch 14. Also Craig, *Administrative Law*, ch 4; Harlow and Rawlings, *Law and Administration*, ch 5.

[118] See D Longley [1990] PL 527 and J Jacob [1991] PL 255.

[119] On the role of contracts in government generally, see Harden, *The Contracting State*; Craig, *Administrative Law*, ch 5; Harlow and Rawlings, *Law and Administration*, chs 8, 9. Also M Freedland [1994] PL 86, [1998] PL 288.

[120] M Hunt, in Taggart (ed.) *The Province of Administrative Law*, p 21.

[121] Mitchell (note 112), ch 4; Brown and Bell, *French Administrative Law*, pp 202–11.

[122] *Rhyl UDC v Rhyl Amusements Ltd* [1959] 1 All ER 257; *Hazell v Hammersmith Council* [1992] 2 AC 1; *Crédit Suisse v Allerdale Council* [1997] QB 306; and ch 30 A.

[123] Local Government (Contracts) Act 1997; ch 30 A.

[124] *Ayr Harbour Trustees v Oswald* (1883) 8 App Cas 623; *Triggs v Staines UDC* [1969] 1 Ch 10; *Dowty Boulton Paul Ltd v Wolverhampton Corpn (No 2)* [1973] Ch 94.

[125] *Stringer v Minister of Housing* [1971] 1 All ER 65.

has made impossible or unprofitable for the contractor.[126] In the case of a local authority, its standing orders normally regulate the procedure by which contracts are placed and these may not be ignored by a council.[127] Criminal sanctions apply if a councillor takes part in considering a contract or proposed contract in which he or she has a pecuniary interest.[128] Where the officers of a local council purport to execute a contract in terms which have never been approved by the council, the contract is wholly void and not binding on the council.[129] An important control in the public interest is that contracts entered into by local authorities are subject to retrospective scrutiny by the system of local government audit.[130] The contractual freedom of local authorities is subject to legislative intervention, as between 1988 and 1999 when councils were required to apply compulsory competitive tendering to specified activities, a policy that was superseded by various measures to secure 'best value'.[131] Councils were also barred from taking into account 'non-commercial' considerations in the placing of contracts for works and supplies, a restriction that was eased by the Local Government Act 1999.

The economic importance of public procurement contracts has long been recognised in Community law and the Community directives on this matter are the subject of delegated legislation within the United Kingdom, creating rights and duties enforceable in the ordinary courts.[132] The public procurement rules require public authorities who enter into contracts within the scope of the rules to follow open procedures for the tendering process for contracts with a value above a stated amount, to observe certain criteria in awarding the contract, to specify lawful policy objectives, and to state reasons for choosing a particular contractor. If these duties are breached, a company whose tender has not succeeded may sue the authority for damages.[133]

Contractual liability of the Crown

In English law before 1948, the Crown's immunity from being sued directly in the courts was not confined to liability in tort and extended to all other aspects of civil liability. But it had long been regarded as essential that an individual should be able to obtain judicial redress under a contract made with the Crown or government department. The petition of right was originally a remedy for recovering property from the Crown, but it became available to enforce contractual obligations. The practice was simplified by the Petitions of Right Act 1860. A petition of right lay in respect of any claim arising out of contracts by which the Crown could be bound, but not in respect of claims in tort. It lay also for the recovery of real property, for damages for breach of contract[134]

---

126 *William Cory & Son Ltd* v *City of London* [1951] 2 KB 476.
127 *R* v *Hereford Corpn, ex p Harrower* [1970] 3 All ER 460. Also *R* v *Enfield Council, ex p Unwin (Roydon) Ltd* (1989) 1 Admin LR 51.
128 Local Government Act 1972, s 94.
129 *North West Leicestershire DC* v *East Midlands Housing Assn* [1981] 3 All ER 364.
130 Audit Commission Act 1998.
131 Local Government Acts 1988 and 1999.
132 The EC directives deal with public works (93/97), public supplies (93/36), public services (92/50), public sector remedies (89/665) and utilities contracts (93/38). The UK regulations are SIs 1991 No 2680 (public works contracts), 1993 No 3228 (public services contracts), 1995 No 201 (public supply contracts) and 1996 No 2911 (utilities contracts). See Arrowsmith, *The Law of Public and Utilities Procurement*.
133 In *Harmon CFEM Facades (UK) Ltd* v *Corporate Officer, House of Commons* (2000) 67 Con LR 1, 72 Con LR 21, the claimant submitted the lowest tender but was not awarded the contract; it won substantial damages for breaches of duty (including failure to state relevant criteria and unlawful post-tender negotiations) and breach of implied contract. See also *R* v *Portsmouth Council, ex p Coles* (1997) 1 CMLR 1135.
134 *Thomas* v *R* (1874) LR 10 QB 31.

and to recover compensation under a statute.[135] Before a petition could be heard by the court, it had to be endorsed with the words *fiat justitia* (let right be done) by the Crown on the advice of the Home Secretary, who acted on the opinion of the Attorney-General. A judgment in favour of a suppliant on a petition of right took the form of a declaration of the suppliant's rights and, being observed by the Crown, was as effective as a judgment in an ordinary action.

By s 1 of the Crown Proceedings Act 1947, in all cases where a petition of right was formerly required, it is possible to sue the appropriate government department or, where no department is named for the purpose, the Attorney-General, by ordinary process either in the High Court or in a county court. No prior fiat from the Crown is required.

While the Petitions of Right Act 1860 was repealed by the Crown Proceedings Act 1947, it appears to have been kept in being for proceedings in matters of contract or property against the Sovereign personally.[136] The 1947 Act applies only to proceedings against the Crown in right of the government of the United Kingdom, not in claims against the Crown that arise in respect of the surviving colonies.[137]

In Scotland the petition of right procedure had never existed, since it was always possible to sue the Crown as of right in the Court of Session on contractual claims or for the recovery of property.[138] Accordingly, s 1 of the Crown Proceedings Act 1947 does not apply to Scotland.

In general the ordinary rules of contract apply to the Crown: thus an agent need have only ostensible authority to bind the Crown and there is no rule requiring the actual authority of the Crown.[139] Those who make contracts on behalf of the Crown, as its agents, are in accordance with the general rule not liable personally.[140] Statutory authority is not needed before the Crown can make a contract, but payments due under the Crown's contracts come from money provided by Parliament; if Parliament exceptionally provides that no money is payable to a certain contractor, payments that would otherwise be due may not be enforced.[141] If a contract expressly provides that payments are to be conditional on Parliament appropriating the money, the Crown is not liable if Parliament does not do so. But, in general, 'the prior provision of funds by Parliament is not a condition preliminary to the obligation of the contract'.[142] Payments due under contract are made out of the general appropriation for the class of service to which the contract relates and not from funds specifically appropriated to a particular contract. It is usually accepted that the Crown has full contractual capacity as a matter of common law,[143] but this cannot entitle the Crown to make contracts which are contrary to statute. There is moreover a rule of law, the exact extent of which it is not easy to determine, that the Crown cannot bind itself so as to fetter its future executive action.

In *Rederiaktiebolaget Amphitrite v R*, a Swedish shipping company, Sweden being a neutral in the First World War, was aware that neutral ships were liable to be detained in British

---

[135] *A-G v De Keyser's Royal Hotel* [1920] AC 508.

[136] Crown Proceedings Act 1947, s 40(1); *Franklin v A-G* [1974] QB 185, 194.

[137] Before Rhodesia achieved lawful independence as Zimbabwe, difficulties as to Crown proceedings arose over the non-payment of interest to holders of Rhodesian government stock; see *Franklin v A-G* [1974] QB 185; *Franklin v R* [1974] QB 202.

[138] Mitchell, *Constitutional Law*, p 304.

[139] See *A-G for Ceylon v Silva* [1953] AC 461 on the difficulties of establishing ostensible authority in relation to the Crown. Cf *Re Selectmove Ltd* [1995] 2 All ER 531.

[140] *Macbeath v Haldimand* (1786) 1 TR 172; and see *Town Investments Ltd v Department of the Environment*, note 175 below.

[141] *Churchward v R* (1865) LR 1 QB 173.

[142] *New South Wales v Bardolph* (1934) 52 CLR 455, 510 (Dixon J); Street, *Governmental Liability*, pp 84–92.

[143] See e.g. BV Harris (1992) 108 LQR 626; cf M Freedland [1994] PL 86, 91–5.

ports. They obtained an undertaking from the British government that a particular ship, if sent to this country with certain cargo, would not be detained. Accordingly the ship was sent with such a cargo, but the government withdrew the undertaking and refused clearance for the ship. On trial of a petition of right, *held*, the undertaking of the government was not enforceable as the Crown was not competent to make a contract which would have the effect of limiting its power of executive action in the future.[144]

It has been suggested that the defence of executive necessity only 'avails the Crown where there is an implied term to that effect or that is the true meaning of the contract';[145] or again that the defence has no application to ordinary commercial contracts. A preferable view is that the *Amphitrite* case illustrates a general principle that the Crown, or any public authority, cannot be prevented by an existing contract from exercising powers which are vested in it either by statute or common law for the protection of the public interest.[146]

> In *Commissioners of Crown Lands* v *Page*, the Crown sued for arrears of rent due under a lease of Crown land that had been assigned to the defendant. The defence was that the land had been requisitioned by a government department and that this constituted eviction by the Crown as landlord. The Court of Appeal held that the arrears were payable. Devlin LJ said: 'When the Crown, in dealing with one of its subjects, is dealing as if it too were a private person, and is granting leases or buying and selling as ordinary persons do, it is absurd to suppose that it is making any promise about the way in which it will conduct the affairs of the nation.'[147]

Other problems arise from the contracts of public authorities to which English law provides no answer: for example, the power of a public body to decide with whom to contract and to remove a firm from its list of approved contractors.[148] This power was used by the Labour government in 1975–78 to require companies who were granted contracts to observe a non-statutory pay policy.[149] This is an outstanding example of a government's ability to achieve public goals without recourse to formal legislation,[150] a power that was denied to local councils by the Local Government Act 1988.[151]

We have seen that where contracts are subject to European rules on public procurement, the pre-contractual procedures observed by public authorities are controlled, with recourse to the courts if the rules are breached. Where these rules do not apply, the position is uncertain. In one case the Lord Chancellor's Department was held to have acted unfairly in awarding a contract, but the process was held not to be subject to judicial review.[152] The courts should, however, uphold fairness and legitimate expectations in this situation. Thus, the National Lottery Commission acted unlawfully in deciding not to award the next licence for the Lottery to the existing licensee (Camelot) but to enter into negotiations with the rival bidder (the People's Lottery).[153] In Northern Ireland, the right not to be discriminated against on religious grounds was held by the Strasbourg

---

[144] [1921] 3 KB 500.
[145] *Robertson* v *Minister of Pensions* [1949] 1 KB 227, 237 (Denning J).
[146] Street (note 112), pp 98–9; Mitchell (note 112), pp 27–32, 52–65.
[147] [1960] 2 QB 274, 292; see also *William Cory & Son Ltd* v *City of London* [1951] 2 KB 476.
[148] Turpin, *Government Procurement and Contracts*, ch 4.
[149] G Ganz [1978] PL 333.
[150] T C Daintith [1979] CLP 41. Until it was rescinded by the House of Commons on 16 December 1982, the Fair Wages Resolution had for many years required uniform conditions on fair wages to be included in all government contracts.
[151] See text at note 131 above.
[152] *R* v *Lord Chancellor, ex p Hibbit & Saunders* [1993] COD 326. Reliance on the public/private law distinction here is unconvincing (D Oliver [1993] PL 214). Cf *R* v *Legal Aid Board, ex p Donn & Co* [1996] 3 All ER 1, and see S Arrowsmith, *Government Procurement and Judicial Review* and (1990) 106 LQR 277.
[153] *R* v *National Lottery Commission, ex p Camelot Group plc* (2001) EMLR 43.

Court to apply to public procurement decisions.[154] Control over government contracts is exercised by the Comptroller and Auditor-General. Much government practice in placing and administering contracts derives from rulings of the Public Accounts Committee.[155] In view of the number of government contracts awarded each year, remarkably few disputes arising from such contracts reach the courts. Disputes in practice are resolved by various forms of consultation, negotiation or arbitration. The Review Board for Government Contracts, established in 1969 under an agreement between the government and the Confederation of British Industry, regularly reviews the profit formula for non-competitive government contracts and it may also examine in relation to a particular contract a complaint that the price paid is not 'fair and reasonable.' Government contracts are excluded from the jurisdiction of the Parliamentary Ombudsman.[156]

Service under the Crown

Service under the Crown is another instance of the special contractual position of the Crown; for it is generally held to be part of the prerogative that the Crown employs its servants at its pleasure, whether in the civil service or the armed forces.[157] The Crown has always claimed that its freedom to dismiss its servants at will is necessary in the public interest. Certainly the case law suggests that at common law Crown servants have few rights if any against the Crown. Thus, in the absence of statutory provision,[158] no Crown servant has a remedy for wrongful dismissal. Where a colonial servant failed in a claim that he had been engaged for three years certain, Lord Herschell said: 'Such employment being for the good of the public, it is essential for the public good that it should be capable of being determined at the pleasure of the Crown, except in exceptional cases where it has been deemed to be more for the public good that some restriction should be imposed on the power to dismiss its servants.'[159]

While at common law civil servants lacked any tenure of office, in practice they have enjoyed a high degree of security. This security by tradition depended on convention rather than law and the collective agreements on conditions of service which were applied to civil servants did not give rise to contractual rights.[160] Indeed, it was for long uncertain whether Crown service is a contractual relationship at all. Thus it was formerly doubtful whether civil servants could even sue for arrears of their pay.[161] However, most provisions of the Employment Rights Act 1996 now apply to civil servants, who are protected against unfair dismissal.[162] They are also protected against racial and sexual discrimination in relation to their employment.[163] In 1991, it was held that civil servants are employed by the Crown under contracts of employment, since all the incidents of such a contract were present in that case and the civil service pay and conditions code dealt in detail with many aspects of the relationship; despite the statement

---

[154] *Tinnelly & Sons Ltd v UK* (1998) 27 EHRR 249.
[155] Ch 17.
[156] Ch 29 D.
[157] See *CCSU v Minister for the Civil Service* [1985] AC 374 and cf Sir William Wade (1985) 101 LQR 180.
[158] E.g. the rule that judges hold office during good behaviour (ch 18 C), *Gould v Stuart* [1896] AC 575 and *Reilly v R* [1934] AC 176.
[159] *Dunn v R* [1896] 1 QB 116; G Nettheim [1975] CLJ 253. See also *Dunn v MacDonald* [1897] 1 QB 401.
[160] *Rodwell v Thomas* [1944] KB 596; cf *Riordan v War Office* [1959] 3 All ER 552. And see *CCSU v Minister for the Civil Service* [1985] AC 374.
[161] *Kodeeswaran v A-G of Ceylon* [1970] AC 1111; cf *Cameron v Lord Advocate* 1952 SC 165.
[162] Employment Rights Act 1996, s 191.
[163] Sex Discrimination Act 1975, s 85 and Race Relations Act 1976, s 75 (as amended). Ch 19 A.

in the code that the relationship was governed by the prerogative and civil servants could be dismissed at pleasure, neither the Crown nor civil servants intended the contents of the code to be merely voluntary.[164] However, the same court held that an aggrieved civil servant could not seek judicial review of a dismissal or other action.[165]

The law on Crown employment of civil servants is both clearer and more contractual in nature than was once the case, but some particular limitations continue to exist. Thus the Crown may in the interests of state security exempt classes of civil servants from enjoying employment rights. This power was used in 1984 to exempt the civilian staff of the Government Communications Headquarters at Cheltenham from the Act. At the same time, the government used the prerogative powers of the Crown to impose a new condition of service barring GCHQ staff from union membership.[166] Members of the armed forces have distinctly less protection in law than civil servants, but the system of command and discipline stands in the way of assimilating service in the Armed Forces to that of civilian employment. Some provisions of the Employment Rights Act 1996 now apply to the armed forces.[167] In respect of racial and sex discrimination, a member of the forces has a right of recourse to an employment tribunal but only after having pursued a complaint by means of the internal redress of complaints procedure.[168] Members of the armed forces may well benefit in various respects from the Human Rights Act 1998.[169]

C. The Crown in litigation: privileges and immunities

As we have already seen,[170] 'the Crown' is a convenient term in law for the collectivity that now comprises the Sovereign in her governmental capacity, ministers, civil servants and the armed forces. Lord Templeman said in 1993: 'The expression "the Crown" has two meanings, namely the monarch and the executive.'[171] When the Sovereign governed in person, royal officials properly benefited from the Sovereign's immunities and privileges. But despite the ending of personal government by the Sovereign, the personnel of central government continued to benefit from Crown status. The shield of the Crown extended to what was described not very satisfactorily as the general government of the country or 'the province of government',[172] but not to local authorities or to other public corporations. Notwithstanding the Crown Proceedings Act 1947, for several reasons it may be necessary to know whether a public authority has Crown status.[173] It is good legislative practice for an Act which creates a new public body to state whether and to what extent it should enjoy Crown status,[174] but this does not

---

[164] *R v Lord Chancellor's Department, ex p Nangle* [1992] 1 All ER 897 (and see S Fredman and G Morris [1991] PL 485 and (1991) 107 LQR 298). For proposals to provide senior civil servants with full written contracts, see Cm 2627, 1994 and M Freedland [1995] PL 224.

[165] For the reasons for this, see p 373 above.

[166] *CCSU v Minister for the Civil Service* [1985] AC 374; and Employment Rights Act 1996, s 193.

[167] Employment Rights Act, s 192, as amended by Armed Forces Act 1996, s 26.

[168] Armed Forces Act 1996, ss 20–23. For the former position, see *R v Army Board, ex p Anderson* [1992] QB 169. For a detailed account, see R Watt in Sunkin and Payne (eds) *The Nature of the Crown*, ch 11.

[169] Cf *R v Ministry of Defence, ex p Smith* [1996] QB 517.

[170] Ch 12, text at notes 1–7. And see in Sunkin and Payne (eds), *The Nature of the Crown*, ch 2 (Sir W Wade) and ch 3 (M Loughlin).

[171] *M v Home Office* [1994] 1 AC 377, 395.

[172] *Mersey Docks Trustees v Cameron* (1861) 11 HLC 443, 508; *BBC v Johns* [1965] Ch 32.

[173] E.g. liability to taxation and the criminal law; whether staff are Crown servants (*R v Barrett* [1976] 3 All ER 895). And see ch 14.

[174] See e.g. National Health Service and Community Care Act 1990, Sch 6, para 21 (NHS trusts not to be servants or agents of Crown).

always happen. Whether because of express legislation or judicial interpretation, a public agency may be regarded as having Crown status for some purposes, but not for others.

In regard to central government, the concept of 'the Crown' has various consequences. Contracts are generally concluded in the name of individual departments and ministers, acting expressly or impliedly for the Crown.

> In *Town Investments Ltd* v *Department of the Environment*, it had to be decided whether a rent-freeze imposed by counter-inflation legislation applied to two office blocks in London, of which the Secretary of State for the Environment was the lessee 'for and on behalf of Her Majesty'; the offices were occupied by a variety of departments, and in part by the US navy. The House of Lords *held* (Lord Morris dissenting) that the Crown was the tenant and that the premises were occupied for the purpose of a business carried on by the Crown; the leases were therefore subject to the rent freeze. Lord Diplock stated that it was public law that governed the relationships between the Queen in her political capacity, government departments, ministers and civil servants: executive acts of government done by any of them 'are acts done by "the Crown" in the fictional sense in which that expression is now used in English public law'.[175]

This decision revealed a striking anomaly in the legislation, namely that the Crown as tenant could take the benefit of the rent-freeze, whereas the Crown as landlord was not barred from increasing the rents which its tenants had to pay. The legal reasons for this inequity will be examined later. Although in 1991 the Court of Appeal considered 'the Crown' not to be a legal person, the House of Lords later held that 'at least for some purposes' the Crown has legal personality.[176] Whether the Crown is to be described as a corporation sole or a corporation aggregate[177] seems immaterial, given that the longstanding practice of Parliament has been to. legislate on the basis that the Crown is a continuing legal entity.

Application of statutes to Crown[178]

As we have seen, under the 1947 Act the Crown may be sued for breach of statutory duty. But nothing in the Act affects 'any presumption relating to the extent to which the Crown is bound by an Act of Parliament' (s 40(2)(f)). The rule that Acts do not bind the Crown, that is, that the Crown's rights and interests are not prejudiced by legislation unless a statute so enacts by express words or by necessary implication, significantly limits governmental liability for breach of statutory duty. It is by this rule, for example, that Crown property is in law exempt from taxation and much environmental legislation. This immunity of central government from regulation that applies to private persons goes much further than is justifiable, and Parliament has begun to remove the immunity piecemeal.[179] In 1947, the Judicial Committee took a strict view of the test of 'necessary implication', holding that in the absence of express words the Crown is bound by a statute only if the purpose of the statute would be 'wholly frustrated' if the Crown were not bound.[180] In 1989, as we saw in chapter 12, in *Lord Advocate* v *Dumbarton Council*, the House of Lords for the first time considered the legal basis of Crown immunity. The Court of Session had held that in some instances

---

[175] [1978] AC 359, 381 (and see C Harlow (1977) 40 MLR 728).
[176] *M v Home Office* [1992] QB 270; [1994] 1 AC 377, 424.
[177] E.g. *Re Mason* [1928] Ch 385.
[178] Street, *Governmental Liability*, ch 6; Hogg, *Liability of the Crown*, ch 11; Bennion, *Statutory Interpretation*, pp 139–45.
[179] E.g. National Health Service and Community Care Act 1990, s 60.
[180] *Province of Bombay* v *Municipal Corpn of Bombay* [1947] AC 58 and *Madras Electric Supply Co Ltd* v *Boarland* [1955] AC 667.

(for example, where its property was not affected) the Crown could be bound by town planning and highways legislation. Reversing this decision, the House held that the Crown is not bound by any statutory provision 'unless there can somehow be gathered from the terms of the relevant Act an intention to that effect'.[181] For an Act to bind the Crown it is sufficient for it to be shown that if the Act did not do so its purpose would be frustrated in a material respect, not that its purpose would be wholly frustrated. It is good legislative practice for new Acts to state expressly whether and to what extent they apply to the Crown.[182] Where an Act does not apply to the Crown or its servants acting in the course of duty, a Crown servant is not liable criminally if he or she disregards the statute.[183] But these rules do not prevent the Crown deriving benefits from legislation. Even though the Crown is not named in an Act, the Crown may take advantage of rights conferred by the Act, as in the *Town Investments* case.[184]

Procedure

Where the Act of 1947 enables proceedings to be brought against the Crown in English courts, whether in tort or contract or for the recovery of property, in principle the normal procedure of litigation applies. The action is brought against the appropriate department, the Minister for the Civil Service being responsible for publishing a list of departments and naming the solicitor for each department to accept process on its behalf; in cases not covered by the list, the Attorney-General may be made defendant. The trial follows that of an ordinary civil action, but differences arise in respect of remedies and enforcement. The most important is that in place of an injunction or a decree of specific performance, the court makes an order declaring the rights of the parties (s 21(1)); and no injunction may be granted against an officer of the Crown if the effect 'would be to give any relief against the Crown which could not have been obtained in proceedings against the Crown' (s 21(2)). Although at common law an injunction lay against an officer of the Crown who was threatening to commit a wrong such as a tort,[185] for many years after 1947 section 21 was interpreted broadly so as to deprive the court of power to grant such relief.[186] The inability of the court to grant injunctions excluded the power to grant interim injunctions, and, at that time, English law did not allow an interim declaration to be made.[187]

It is now clear that the powers of the court in respect of the executive are not so limited as previously seemed to be the case. First, the court may grant injunctive relief where necessary to protect rights under Community law.[188] Second, the House of Lords held in M v *Home Office*, applying ss 23(2) and 38(2) of the 1947 Act, that the restrictions on injunctive relief do not apply to applications for judicial review, which are not 'proceedings against the Crown' for the purposes of the 1947 Act.[189] Third, it was also held in M v *Home Office* that s 21(2) of the 1947 Act does not prevent injunctive

---

[181] [1990] 2 AC 580, 604 (ch 12 D and J Wolffe [1990] PL 14). Contrast *Bropho* v *State of Western Australia* (1990) 171 CLR 1 (and S Kneebone [1991] PL 361).

[182] E.g. Race Relations Act 1976, s 75, considered in *Home Office* v *Commission for Racial Equality* [1982] QB 385.

[183] *Cooper* v *Hawkins* [1904] 2 KB 164. See now Road Traffic Regulation Act 1984, s 130.

[184] Crown Proceedings Act 1947, s 31; and note 175 above.

[185] *Tamaki* v *Baker* [1901] AC 561.

[186] *Merricks* v *Heathcoat-Amory* [1955] Ch 567.

[187] See *R* v *IRC, ex p Rossminster Ltd* [1980] AC 952. On the case for interim declaratory relief, see Law Com No 226 (1994), pp 61–4. For the power, see now Civil Procedure Rules, r 25.1(1)(b).

[188] *Case C-213/89, R* v *Transport Secretary, ex p Factortame Ltd (No 2)* [1991] 1 AC 603; ch 8 D.

[189] [1994] 1 AC 377; S Sedley, in Forsyth and Hare (eds), *The Golden Metwand and the Crooked Cord*, pp 253–66; T Cornford, in Sunkin and Payne (eds), *The Nature of the Crown*, ch 9; M Gould [1993] PL 568.

relief being granted against officers of the Crown (including ministers) who have personally committed or authorised a tort and applies only in respect of duties laid on the Crown itself. As Lord Woolf said, 'it is only in those situations where prior to the Act no injunctive relief could be obtained that s 21 prevents an injunction being granted.'[190] But he added that declaratory relief against officers of the Crown should normally be appropriate.

Other provisions maintaining the special position of the Crown may be briefly mentioned:

(*a*)   judgment against a department cannot be enforced by the ordinary methods of levying execution or attachment; the department is required by the Act to pay the amount certified to be due as damages and costs (s 25);[191]

(*b*)   there can be no order for restitution of property, but the court may declare the plaintiff entitled as against the Crown (s 21(1));

(*c*)   in lieu of an order for the attachment of money owed by the Crown to a debtor, a judgment creditor may obtain an order from the High Court directing payment to himself or herself and not to the debtor (s 27).[192]

An action for a declaration may be brought against the Crown without claiming other relief, for example where a wrong is threatened,[193] but not to determine hypothetical questions which may never arise; for example, as to whether there is a contingent liability to a tax.[194]

In private litigation, when the claimant seeks an interim injunction against the defendant to maintain the status quo pending the final decision, the court grants such a request only if the claimant gives an undertaking as to damages, so that the defendant's loss may be made good if the action ultimately fails. When the Crown is seeking to assert rights of property or contract, the Crown may be expected to give such an undertaking. But when the Crown takes proceedings to enforce the law, an undertaking as to damages is generally not appropriate.[195]

In Scotland, where civil procedure is different from that in England, actions in respect of British or United Kingdom departments (like the Ministry of Defence or the Inland Revenue) may be brought against the Advocate-General for Scotland, an office created by the Scotland Act 1998; in respect of departments of the devolved Scottish Administration, actions are brought against the Lord Advocate.[196] So far as remedies against the Crown are concerned, the Court of Session in *McDonald v Secretary of State for Scotland*[197] held that the reasoning in *M v Home Office* did not apply in Scotland, where the statutory and procedural background differs from that in England; ss 21(1) and 42 of the 1947 Act permit a declarator but not interdict to issue against the Crown and ministers. Actions may be raised by and against the Crown in either the Court of Session or the sheriff court.

---

[190] [1994] 1 AC 377, 413, disapproving *Merricks v Heathcoat-Amory* above; and see H W R Wade (1991) 107 LQR 4.

[191] Cf *Gairy v A-G of Grenada* [2002] 1 AC 167 (rule of no coercive relief against Crown yields to G's constitutional right not to be deprived of property without compensation).

[192] And see *Brooks Associates Inc v Basu* [1983] 1 All ER 508.

[193] *Dyson v A-G* [1912] 1 Ch 158.

[194] *Argosam Finance Co v Oxby* [1965] Ch 390.

[195] *Hoffmann-La Roche & Co v Trade Secretary* [1975] AC 295 (department seeking to compel company to observe price control for drugs.) And see *Kirklees Council v Wickes Building Supplies Ltd* [1993] AC 227.

[196] Crown Suits (Scotland) Act 1857 as amended by the Scotland Act 1998, Sch 8, para 2.

[197] 1994 SLT 692. This decision was confirmed in *Scott Davidson, Petitioner* (Court of Session, 18 December 2001).

Non-disclosure of evidence: public interest immunity

Disclosure of documents (formerly termed discovery) is a procedure in civil litigation by which a party may inspect all documents in the possession or control of an opponent which relate to the matters in dispute. Formerly it could not be used against the Crown. By s 28 of the 1947 Act, the court may order discovery against the Crown and may also require the Crown to answer interrogatories, that is, written questions to obtain information from the other party on material facts. But the Act expressly preserves the existing rule of law (formerly known as Crown privilege) that the Crown may refuse to disclose any document or to answer any question on the ground that this would be injurious to the public interest; the Act even protects the Crown from disclosing the mere existence of a document on the same ground. Public interest immunity (which became known as PII in the wake of the Matrix Churchill trial in 1992 discussed below) is not restricted to proceedings in which the Crown is a party and applies also to civil proceedings between private individuals. Although PII is important also for the police, its main significance is as a means of keeping secret aspects of central government. Vital defence and security interests must be protected against the harmful exposure of information in judicial proceedings (as is recognised in European human rights law). It is more difficult to define what matters must not be disclosed, since ministers and civil servants are likely to exaggerate the harm that would be done by disclosing information they wish to keep secret. A secretive and closed system of government permits less disclosure than an open and participatory system. In fact, this branch of public law has seen a remarkable development over five decades, primarily by an important sequence of judicial decisions that are outlined later.

We can start at the height of the Second World War with the decision in *Duncan* v *Cammell Laird & Co*.[198]

> Early in 1939 a new submarine sank while on trial with the loss of 99 lives, including civilian workmen. Many actions in negligence were brought by the personal representatives against the company, who had built the submarine under contract with the Admiralty. In a test action, the company objected to the production of documents relating to the design of the submarine. The First Lord of the Admiralty directed the company not to produce the documents on the ground of Crown privilege, since disclosure would be injurious to national defence. *Held* (House of Lords) the documents should not be disclosed. Although a validly taken objection to disclosure was conclusive, and should be taken by the minister himself, the decision ruling out such documents was that of the judge. In deciding whether it was his duty to object, a minister should withhold production only where the public interest would otherwise be harmed, for example, where disclosure would be injurious to national defence or to good diplomatic relations, 'or where the practice of keeping a class of documents secret is necessary for the proper functioning of the public service'.[199]

On this basis, documents might be withheld either because the *contents* of those documents must be kept secret (as in *Duncan*'s case itself) or on the much wider ground that they belonged to a *class* of document which must as a class be treated as confidential, for example civil service memoranda and minutes, to guarantee freedom and candour of communication on public matters. Thereafter the practice developed of withholding documents simply on the minister's assertion that they belonged to a class of documents which it was necessary in the public interest for the proper functioning of the public service to withhold.[200] It seemed that the courts could not overrule the minister's objection if taken in correct form.

---

[198] [1942] AC 624. For the subsequent history, see J Jacob [1993] PL 121. And see Cross and Tapper, *Evidence*, ch 11.1.
[199] [1942] AC at 642.
[200] See *Ellis* v *Home Office* [1953] 2 QB 135 and *Broome* v *Broome* [1955] P 190 for the harsh operation of the rule; and J E S Simon [1955] CLJ 62.

Concern at these wide claims of privilege was eased by government concessions. In 1956, the Lord Chancellor stated that privilege would not be claimed in certain types of litigation for various kinds of documents in a department's possession; these included factual reports about accidents involving government employees or government premises and, where the Crown or a Crown employee was being sued for negligence, medical reports by service or prison doctors. In 1962, the government stated that statements made to the police during criminal investigations would not be withheld where the police were sued for malicious prosecution or wrongful arrest and that in other civil proceedings the question of whether statements to the police should be withheld would be left to the trial judge, subject in each case to the names of police informers not being revealed.[201] Despite these concessions, it was still considered that in English law the courts were bound by the minister's objection. By contrast, it was already established in Scotland that a court must take account of the minister's decision but could in exceptional circumstances overrule it if the interests of justice so required.[202] After decisions of the Court of Appeal had cast doubt on the conclusiveness of the minister's objection,[203] in 1968 the House of Lords overruled an objection taken by the Home Secretary to the production of certain police reports.

In *Conway* v *Rimmer*[204] a former probationary constable sued a police superintendent for malicious prosecution after an incident of a missing electric torch had led to the acquittal of the plaintiff on a charge of theft and to his dismissal from the police. The Home Secretary claimed privilege for (*a*) probationary reports on the plaintiff and (*b*) the defendant's report on the investigation into the incident. He certified that these were confidential reports within a class of documents production of which would be injurious to the public interest. *Held*, the court has jurisdiction to order the production of documents for which immunity is claimed. The court will give full weight to a minister's view, but this need not prevail if the relevant considerations are such that judicial experience is competent to weigh them.

The House of Lords thus established that it is for the courts to hold the balance in the contest between secrecy and disclosure, although the correctness of the decision in *Duncan* v *Cammell Laird* was not doubted. *Conway* v *Rimmer* enabled English law on this matter of public policy to be brought broadly into line with Scots law. In later cases, the issues for decision included (*a*) the use as evidence of material which is subject to constraints of confidentiality; (*b*) the disclosure of documents relating to the formulation of government policy; (*c*) the grounds which must be shown before the court will inspect documents; and (*d*) the use of public interest immunity in criminal proceedings.

In *Rogers* v *Home Secretary*,[205] the House of Lords refused to order production of a secret police report to the Gaming Board about an applicant for a gaming licence, holding that the report fell into a class of documents which should not be disclosed. It was emphasised that power to withhold evidence on grounds of public interest was not a privilege of the Crown as such and that 'Crown privilege' was a misnomer. The fact that documents may be regarded as confidential by their authors is no reason why they should as a class be immune from disclosure on grounds of public interest. Where a government department holds material supplied to it in confidence by companies regarding commercial activities, the court's decision on public interest immunity will depend

---

[201] See HL Deb, 6 June 1956, cols 741–8 and 8 March 1962, col 1191.
[202] *Glasgow Corpn* v *Central Land Board* 1956 SC (HL) 1; *Whitehall* v *Whitehall* 1957 SC 30.
[203] *Merricks* v *Nott-Bower* [1965] 1 QB 57 and *Re Grosvenor Hotel London (No 2)* [1965] Ch 1210; D H Clark (1967) 30 MLR 489.
[204] [1968] AC 910; D H Clark (1969) 32 MLR 142.
[205] [1973] AC 388.

on an assessment of factors such as the reasons for disclosure and the harm that disclosure might cause to the public interest.[206]

In *D v National Society for the Prevention of Cruelty to Children*, the House of Lords held that public interest as a ground for non-disclosure of confidential material was not confined to the efficient functioning of government departments.[207] The Court of Appeal had ordered the NSPCC to reveal the identity of someone who had informed the society of a suspected case of child battering. The society, established by royal charter, had a statutory responsibility to take proceedings for the care of children. The Lords held, by analogy with the rule protecting the identity of police informers from disclosure, that the names of informants to the society should be immune from disclosure.

In *Science Research Council v Nassé*,[208] the House of Lords held that on an employee's complaint of unlawful discrimination in employment, no question of public interest immunity could arise in respect of confidential reports on other employees held by the employer. Lord Scarman stated that public interest immunity was restricted 'to what must be kept secret for the protection of government at the highest levels and in the truly sensitive areas of executive responsibility'.[209] However, the language of public interest immunity was used in *Campbell v Tameside Council*, where a teacher had been assaulted by an 11-year-old pupil and wished to see psychologists' reports held by the council; the Court of Appeal ordered discovery after inspecting the reports, since the public interest in the administration of justice outweighed any harm to the public service resulting from production of the reports.[210] When in unfair dismissal proceedings a former diplomat wished to rely on material relating to the security and intelligence services, the Court of Appeal, without inspecting the documents, upheld the Secretary of State's certificate claiming immunity for them in view of the actual or potential risk to national security.[211]

In *Conway v Rimmer*, Lord Reid had expressed the opinion that Cabinet minutes and documents concerned with policy-making within departments were protected against disclosure, so that the inner working of government should not be exposed to ill-informed and biased criticism.[212] In *Burmah Oil Co Ltd v Bank of England*,[213] the House of Lords had to consider the extent to which such high-level documents should be protected from disclosure.

In 1975 Burmah Oil had with government approval agreed to sell its holdings in BP stock to the Bank of England as part of an arrangement protecting the company from liquidation. Later the company sought to have the sale set aside as unconscionable and inequitable. It wished to see documents held by the bank, including (*a*) ministerial communications and minutes of meetings attended by ministers and (*b*) communications between senior civil servants relating to policy matters. The Crown contended that it was 'necessary for the proper functioning of the public service' that the documents be withheld. The House of Lords *held* that the Crown's claim of immunity was not conclusive. If it was likely (or reasonably probable) that the documents contained matter that was material to the issues in the case, the court might inspect them to determine where the balance lay between the competing public interests. Having inspected the documents, the House ordered that they be not produced since they did not contain

---

[206] Compare *Crompton Amusement Machines Ltd v Commissioners of Customs and Excise* [1974] AC 405 and *Norwich Pharmacal Co v Commissioners of Customs and Excise* [1974] AC 133.
[207] [1978] AC 171.
[208] [1980] AC 1028.
[209] [1980] AC at 1088.
[210] [1982] QB 1065.
[211] *Balfour v Foreign and Commonwealth Office* [1994] 2 All ER 588.
[212] [1968] AC 910, 952; see also Lord Upjohn at 993.
[213] [1980] AC 1090; D G T Williams [1980] CLJ 1.

material necessary for disposing fairly of the case. Lord Wilberforce dissented from the decision to inspect; in his view, it was a plain case of 'public interest immunity properly claimed on grounds of high policy'.[214]

In the *Burmah Oil* case, judicial opinion had moved far beyond the position in *Conway v Rimmer*. Even Lord Wilberforce envisaged that there might be circumstances in which a high-level governmental interest must give way before the interests of justice.[215] Even Cabinet papers are not immune from disclosure in an exceptional case where the interests of justice so require.[216] In the Watergate tapes case, it was the public interest in criminal justice that led the US Supreme Court to order President Nixon to deliver his tapes to the special investigator.[217]

Apart from such exceptional circumstances, did *Burmah Oil* mean that the judges should regularly inspect and if necessary order the production of documents relating to policy-making within government departments? In *Air Canada* v *Trade Secretary*[218] the House of Lords upheld the Secretary of State's claim for immunity and refused to inspect the documents. In civil litigation, as the rules then stood, one party might inspect relevant documents held by the other side when discovery was *necessary* either for disposing fairly of the action or for saving costs.[219] In *Air Canada*, the House applied to a case alleging ultra vires acts by a department stricter rules than would apply to litigation between private parties where public interest immunity was not claimed. The majority (Lords Fraser, Wilberforce and Edmund-Davies) held that for a court to exercise the power of inspection, it was not sufficient that the documents *might* contain information relevant to the issues in dispute; the party seeking access to the documents must show that it was reasonably probable that the documents were likely to help his or her case. A speculative belief to this effect was not enough. The minority considered that the applicant must show only that disclosure of the documents was likely to be necessary for fairly disposing of the issues in dispute; on the facts, Air Canada had failed to do this.

The decision in *Air Canada* is a reminder that even where the applicant is seeking judicial review, the litigation has an adversary character and the court does not have an inquisitorial power to inspect documents held within government. The *Air Canada* case makes more severe the obstacle which an applicant for discovery must surmount to persuade the court to exercise its powers.

In *R* v *Chief Constable of West Midlands Police, ex p Wiley*,[220] the House of Lords held, overruling decisions by the Court of Appeal,[221] that confidential statements made during investigation of complaints against the police were not as a class immune from disclosure in civil litigation. In Lord Woolf's view: 'The recognition of a new class-based public interest immunity requires clear and compelling evidence that it is necessary'; no sufficient case had been made to justify a general immunity for such statements held by the police. The House accepted that a specific statement need not be disclosed if, for instance, it revealed the identity of a police informer.

---

[214] [1980] AC at 1117.

[215] [1980] AC at 1113.

[216] As in the Australian case of *Sankey* v *Whitlam* (1978) 21 ALR 505. See also *Air Canada* v *Trade Secretary* [1983] 2 AC 394, 432 (Lord Fraser); I G Eagles [1980] PL 263.

[217] *US* v *Nixon* 418 US 683 (1974).

[218] [1983] 2 AC 394; Lord Mackay (1983) 2 CJQ 337 and T R S Allan (1985) 101 LQR 200.

[219] RSC Ord 24. See now Civil Procedure Rules, part 31, esp r 31.19.1.

[220] [1995] 1 AC 274.

[221] *Neilson* v *Laugharne* [1981] QB 736; *Makanjuola* v *Metropolitan Police Commissioner* [1992] 3 All ER 617; and *Halford* v *Sharples* [1992] 3 All ER 624. *Neilson* had been distinguished in *Peach* v *Metropolitan Police Commissioner* [1986] 1 QB 1064 and *Ex p Coventry Newspapers Ltd* [1993] QB 278.

Although public interest immunity has mainly arisen from the civil procedure of discovery, the immunity extends to criminal proceedings, albeit in a different form.[222] Plainly the public interest in keeping material secret can be damaged by disclosure wherever it occurs, but the public interest in the administration of justice is at its strongest when, if evidence were to be withheld from production in a criminal trial, this would prevent the accused from establishing a defence. While all or part of a trial under the Official Secrets Acts may be held in camera,[223] if material is too secret for the judge to decide the issue of immunity under such restrictions, any prosecution must be abandoned.[224] In November 1992, the collapse of the Matrix Churchill trial for unlawful export of arms to Iraq brought these issues into public controversy. Before the trial, four ministers had signed PII certificates for documents that related to whether the defendants' involvement in the export of machinery to Iraq was known to the security services and thus to the government. The claims for PII were made on a variety of 'class' grounds, including the protection of the proper functioning of government as well as the interest in keeping secret security and intelligence operations. Having inspected the documents, the trial judge ordered disclosure.[225] Sir Richard Scott's subsequent inquiry into the export of defence equipment and other goods to Iraq extended to the issue of PII certificates in the Matrix Churchill case.[226] His report contained a penetrating study of the use which departments had made of PII certificates. Of their use in Matrix Churchill, his main criticisms were:

> (i) class claims were made which ought to have had no place in a criminal trial; (ii) the claims extended to some documents 'of which no more could be said than that they were confidential'; (iii) ministers were advised that they could not take into account when considering the class claims whether the documents were so material to the trial that they ought to have been disclosed to the defence; (iv) one minister, Mr Heseltine, had been advised that it was his duty to make the PII claim, despite his view that the overall public interest required disclosure.[227]

On this last point, the Attorney-General's advice to Mr Heseltine had been based on a view of the law[228] which had been widely held but was declared to be wrong during the course of the Scott inquiry. In *R v Chief Constable of West Midlands Police, ex p Wiley*, the House of Lords held that, in principle, documents which are relevant and material to litigation should be produced unless disclosure would cause substantial harm. 'A rubber stamp approach to public interest immunity by the holder of a document is neither necessary nor appropriate.'[229] This was a welcome clarification of the duty of ministers, but other questions relating to the use of PII certificates required to be answered.

In 1996, the Attorney-General announced the results of a review into the operation of PII in relation to government documents in England and Wales. He stated that the

---

[222] *R v Governor of Brixton Prison, ex p Osman (No 1)* [1992] 1 All ER 108; *R v Davis* [1993] 2 All ER 643. See now Criminal Procedure and Investigation Act 1996, Parts I, II and, e.g., Corker, *Disclosure in Criminal Proceedings*, ch 6. The non-disclosure by the prosecution, with the approval of the judge, of relevant evidence by reason of PII, does not cause a criminal trial to be unfair in breach of art 6(1) of the ECHR: *Jasper v UK* (2000) 30 EHRR 441. Cf *McGinley & Egan v UK* (1999) 27 EHRR 1.

[223] Official Secrets Act 1920, s 8; and ch 25 above.

[224] *R v Ward* ([1993] 2 All ER 577) at p 633; and cf *R v Davis* (above).

[225] See A W Bradley [1992] PL 514, A T H Smith [1993] CLJ 1, I Leigh [1993] PL 630. On the Scott report, see [1996] PL 357–507; also I Leigh and L Lustgarten (1996) 59 MLR 695.

[226] In the Scott report (HC 115, 1995–96), see on PII vol III, chs G.10–15 and G.18; vol IV, ch K.6. Also R Scott [1996] PL 427; A Tomkins, *The Constitution after Scott*, ch 5; I Leigh in Thompson and Ridley (eds), *Under the Scott-light*, pp 55–70.

[227] Scott report, para G18.104.

[228] Derived mainly from the *Makanjuola* case (note 221 above).

[229] [1995] 1 AC 274, 281 (Lord Templeman). Cf *Savage v Chief Constable of Hampshire* [1997] 2 All ER 631.

government would no longer rely on the former division into 'class' and 'contents' claims. Ministers would in future claim PII 'only when it is believed that disclosure of a document would cause real harm to the public interest'. Future PII certificates would seek to identify in more detail the contents of a document and the damage which disclosure would do, and this 'will allow even closer scrutiny of claims by the court, which is always the final arbiter'. It was hoped that the effect of *ex p Wiley* and the government's new approach woud be to reduce the number of PII claims.[230]

The law has thus come a very long way since *Duncan* v *Cammell Laird* first distinguished between 'contents' and 'class' as a basis for witholding documents in the public interest. The government's decision in 1996 to cease withholding documents on 'class' grounds appears to have achieved its objectives, judging by the recent absence of controversy affecting public interest immunity.

---

[230] HC Deb, 18 December 1996, cols 949–50. And see M Supperstone [1997] PL 211.

Bibliography

ADLER, M, & BRADLEY, A W (eds), *Justice, Discretion and Poverty*, 1976

AITKEN, J, *Officially Secret*, 1971

AKDENIZ, Y, WALKER, C, & WALL, D (eds), *The Internet, Law and Society*, 2000

ALDERMAN, G, *Pressure Groups and Government in Great Britain*, 1984

ALDERMAN, R K, & CROSS, J A, *The Tactics of Resignation*, 1967

ALEXANDER, L (ed), *Constitutionalism: Philosophical Foundations*, 1998

ALLAN, T R S, *Law, Liberty and Justice: The Legal Foundations of British Constitutionalism*, 1993

ALLEN, C K, *Law and Orders*, 3rd edn, 1965

ALLEN, T R S, *Constitutional Justice: a Liberal Theory of the Rule of Law*, 2001

ALLASON, R, *The Branch: A History of the Metropolitan Police Special Branch 1883–1983*, 1988

ALLISON, J W F, *A Continental Distinction in the Common Law: a Historical and Comparative Perspective on English Public Law*, rev edn, 2000

ALSTON, P (ed), *Promoting Human Rights through Bills of Rights: Comparative Perspectives*, 1999

ALSTON, P (ed), *The EU and Human Rights*, 1999

AMERY, L S, *Thoughts on the Constitution*, 2nd edn, 1953

ANDREW, C, *Secret Service: The Making of the British Intelligence Community*, 1985

ANDREWS, J A (ed), *Welsh Studies in Public Law*, 1970

ANSON, W R, *The Law and Custom of the Constitution*, vol I, *Parliament* (ed. M L Gwyer), 5th edn, 1922; vol II, *The Crown* (ed. A B Keith), 4th edn, 1935

ARLIDGE, A, & EADY, D, *The Law of Contempt*, 1982

ARMSTRONG, W (ed), *Budgetary Reform in the United Kingdom*, 1980

ARNSTEIN, W L, *The Bradlaugh Case*, 1965

ARONSON, M, & WHITMORE, H, *Public Torts and Contracts*, 1982

ARROWSMITH, S, *The Law of Public and Utilities Procurement*, 1996

ARROWSMITH, S, *Civil Liability and Public Authorities*, 1992

ARROWSMITH, S, *Government Procurement and Judicial Review*, 1988

ARTHURS, H W, *Without the Law: Administrative Justice and Legal Pluralism in the 19th Century*, 1985

ASHTON, C, & FINCH, V, *Constitutional Law in Scotland*, 2000

AUBREY, C, *Who's Watching You?*, 1981

AUST, A, *Modern Treaty Law and Practice*, 2000

AUSTIN, J, *The Province of Jurisprudence Determined* (ed. H L A Hart), 1954

BAGEHOT, W, *The English Constitution* (introduction R H S Crossman), 1963

BAILEY, S H (ed), *Cross on Local Government Law*, 8th edn, 1991

BAILEY, S H, HARRIS, D J, & JONES, B L, *Civil Liberties: Cases and Materials*, 5th edn, 2002

BAILEY, S H, JONES, B L, & MOWBRAY, A R, *Cases and Materials on Administrative Law*, 2nd edn, 1992

BAINBRIDGE, D, *Data Protection Law*, 2000

BALDWIN, J R, WIKELEY, N, & YOUNG, R, *Judging Social Security: The Adjudication of Claims for Benefit in Britain*, 1992

BALDWIN, R, *Rules and Government*, 1995

BALDWIN, R, *Regulating the Airlines*, 1985

BALDWIN, R, & KINSEY, R, *Police Powers and Politics*, 1982

BALDWIN, R, & MCCRUDDEN, C, *Regulation and Public Law*, 1987

BARENDT, E, *Broadcasting Law: a Comparative Study*, 1993

BARENDT, E, *Freedom of Speech*, 1987

BARKER, A (ed), *Quangos in Britain*, 1982

BARKER, A, BYRNE, I, & VEALL, A, *Ruling by Task Force*, 2000

BARNARD, C, *EC Employment Law*, 1996

BARNETT, A, *This Time: our Constitutional Revolution*, 1997

BARNETT, J, *Inside the Treasury*, 1982

BASSETT, R G, *1931: Political Crisis*, 1958

BATES, T ST J N, et al, *In Memoriam J D B Mitchell*, 1983

BEATSON, J, & CRIPPS, Y (eds), *Freedom of Expression and Freedom of Information*, 2000

BEATSON, J, & MATTHEWS, M H, *Administrative Law, Cases and Materials*, 2nd edn, 1989

BEDDARD, R, *Human Rights and Europe*, 2nd edn, 1980

BEER, S H, *Modern British Politics*, 1965

BEER, S H, *Treasury Control*, 2nd edn, 1957

BELL, J S, *French Constitutional Law*, 1992

BELL, J S, & BRADLEY, A W (eds), *Governmental Liability: A Comparative Study*, 1991

BENNION, F, *Statutory Interpretation*, 3rd edn, 1997

BENTHAM, J, *Handbook of Political Fallacies* (ed. H A Larrabee), 1962

BERCUSSON, B, *European Labour Law*, 1996

BERGER, R, *Impeachment*, 1973

BERKELEY, H, *The Power of the Prime Minister*, 1968

BETTEN, L, & GRIEF, N, *EU Law and Human Rights*, 1998

BIRCH, A H, *Representative and Responsible Government*, 1964

BIRKINSHAW, P, *Freedom of Information*, 3rd edn, 2001

BIRKINSHAW, P, *Grievances, Remedies and the State*, 2nd edn, 1994

BIRKINSHAW, P, *Reforming the Secret State*, 1991

BIRRELL, D, & MURIE, A, *Policy and Government in Northern Ireland: Lessons of Devolution*, 1980

BISHOP, M, KAY, J, & MAYER, C, *Privatisation and Economic Performance*, 1994

BISHOP, M, KAY, J, & MAYER, C, *The Regulatory Challenge*, 1995

BLACKBURN, R, *The Electoral System in Britain*, 1995

BLACKBURN, R (ed), *Constitutional Studies: Contemporary Issues and Controversies*, 1992

BLACKBURN, R, *The Meeting of Parliament*, 1990

BLACKBURN, R, & PLANT, R (eds), *Constitutional Reform*, 2001

BLACKBURN, R, & POLAKIEWICZ, J (eds), *Fundamental Rights in Europe: the European Convention on Human Rights and its Member States 1950–2000*, 2001

BLACKSTONE, *Commentaries on the Laws of England*, 10th edn, 1787; 14th edn, 1803

BLOM-COOPER, L J, & DREWRY, G, *Final Appeal*, 1972

BOGDANOR, V (ed), *The British Constitution in the Twentieth Century* (forthcoming)

BOGDANOR, V, *Devolution in the United Kingdom*, 1999

BOGDANOR, V, *Politics and the Constitution*, 1996

BOGDANOR, V, *The Monarchy and the Constitution*, 1995

BOGDANOR, V, *Multi-party Politics and the Constitution*, 1983

BOGDANOR, V, *The People and the Party System*, 1981

BOLINGBROKE, H ST J, *Political Writings* (ed. D Armitage), 1997

BONNER, D, *Emergency Powers in Peacetime*, 1985

BOTTOMLEY, A (ed), *Feminist Perspectives on the Foundational Subjects of Law*, 1996

BRAGG, B, *A Genuine Expression of the Will of the People*, 2001

BRAZIER, R, *Constitutional Practice*, 3rd edn, 1999

BRAZIER, R, *Constitutional Reform: Re-shaping the British Political System*, 2nd edn, 1998

BRAZIER, R, *Ministers of the Crown*, 1997

BRAZIER, R, *Constitutional Texts: Materials on Government and the Constitution*, 1990

BREWER-CARIAS, A R, *Judicial Review in Comparative Law*, 1989

BRIDGES, Lord, *The Treasury*, 2nd edn, 1966

BRIDGES, L, MESZAROS, G, & SUNKIN, M, *Judicial Review in Perspective*, 2nd edn, 1995

BROMHEAD, P A, *The House of Lords and Contemporary Politics, 1911–1957*, 1958

BROMHEAD, P A, *Private Members' Bills in the British Parliament*, 1956

BROWN, A N, *Criminal Evidence and Procedure*, 1996

BROWN, R G S, & STEEL, D R, *The Administrative Process in Britain*, 2nd edn, 1979

BROWN, L N, & BELL, J S, *French Administrative Law*, 4th edn, 1993

BROWN, L N, & KENNEDY, T, *The Court of Justice of the European Communities*, 5th edn, 2000

BROWNLIE, I, *Basic Documents on Human Rights*, 3rd edn, 1993

BROWNLIE, I, *Principles of Public International Law*, 5th edn, 1998

BRYCE, J, *Studies in History and Jurisprudence*, 1901

BUCK, T, *The Social Fund – Law and Practice*, 2nd edn, 2000

BUCKLAND, P, *The Factory of Grievances*, 1979

BUNYAN, T, *The Political Police in Britain*, 1976

BURROWS, F, *Free Movement in Community Law*, 1987

BURROWS, N, *Devolution*, 2000

BUTLER, D (ed), *Coalitions in British Politics*, 1978

BUTLER, D, *Governing without a Majority: Dilemmas for Hung Parliaments in Britain*, 1983

BUTLER, D, & HALSEY, A H (ed), *Policy and Politics*, 1978

BUTLER, D E, *The Electoral System in Britain since 1918*, 2nd edn, 1963

BYRNE, T, *Local Government in Britain*, 6th edn, 1994

CALVERT, H, *Constitutional Law in Northern Ireland*, 1968

CALVERT, H (ed), *Devolution*, 1975

CAMPBELL, C, *Emergency Law in Ireland 1918–1925*, 1994

CAMPBELL, C M (ed), *Do We Need a Bill of Rights?*, 1980

CAMPBELL, T D, EWING, K D, & TOMKINS, A (eds), *Sceptical Essays in Human Rights*, 2001

CANE, P, *An Introduction to Administrative Law*, 3rd edn, 1996

CARD, R, *Public Order: The New Law*, 1989

CAREY, P, *Data Protection in the UK*, 2000

CARMICHAEL, P, & DICKSON, B, *The House of Lords*, 1999

CARNALL, G, & NICHOLSON, C (eds), *The Impeachment of Warren Hastings*, 1989

CARR, C, *Concerning English Administrative Law*, 1941

CARTWRIGHT, T J, *Royal Commissions and Departmental Committees in Britain*, 1975

CHAPMAN, L, *Your Disobedient Servant*, rev edn 1979

CHESTER, D N, *The Nationalization of British Industry, 1945–51*, 1975

CHESTER, D N, & BOWRING, N, *Questions in Parliament*, 1962

CHITTY, J, *Prerogatives of the Crown*, 1820

CHRISTIE, M, *Breach of the Peace*, 1990

CHUBB, B, *The Control of Public Expenditure*, 1952

CLARK, D, & MCCOY, G, *The Most Fundamental Legal Right: Habeas Corpus in the Commonwealth*, 2000

CLARKE, R, *New Trends in Government*, 1971

CLAYTON, R, & TOMLINSON, H, *The Law of Human Rights*, 2000

CLAYTON, R, & TOMLINSON, H, *Civil Actions Against the Police*, 2nd edn, 1992

CLAYTON, R J (ed), *Parker's Law and Conduct of Elections*, 1996

CLYDE, Lord, & EDWARDS, D J, *Judicial Review*, 2000

COLLINS, H, EWING, K D, & MCCOLGAN, A, *Labour Law*, 2001

CONVERY, J, *The Governance of Scotland*, 2000

COOMBES, D, *The Member of Parliament and the Administration*, 1966

CORKER, D, *Disclosure in Criminal Proceedings*, 1996

COSGROVE, R A, *The Rule of Law: Albert Venn Dicey, Victorian Jurist*, 1980

COWLEY, P (ed), *Conscience and Parliament*, 1998

CRAIES, W F, *Statute Law* (ed. S G C Edgar), 7th edn, 1971

CRAIG, P P, *Administrative Law*, 4th edn, 1999

CRAIG, P P, *Public Law and Democracy in the UK and the USA*, 1991

CRAIG, P P, & DE BURCA, G, *EU Law: Text, Cases and Materials*, 2nd edn, 1998

CRAUFURD SMITH, R, *Broadcasting Law and Fundamental Rights*, 1997

CRICK, B, *The Reform of Parliament*, 2nd edn, 1968

CRIPPS, Y, *The Legal Implications of Disclosure in the Public Interest*, 2nd edn, 1994

CRITCHLEY, T A, *The Conquest of Violence*, 1970

CRITCHLEY, T A, *A History of the Police in England and Wales*, 2nd edn, 1978

CROMBIE, J, *Her Majesty's Customs and Excise*, 1962

CROSS, R, & TAPPER, C, *Evidence*, 9th edn, 1999

CROSS, R, *Precedent in English Law* (eds R Cross & J W Harris), 4th edn, 1991

CROSS, R, *Statutory Interpretation* (eds J Bell & G Engle), 2nd edn, 1987

CROSSMAN, R H S, *The Diaries of a Cabinet Minister* (vol I), 1975

CURRAN, J, & SEATON, J, *Power without Responsibility*, 4th edn, 1991

CYGAN, A J, *The United Kingdom Parliament and European Union Legislation*, 1998

DAALDER, H, *Cabinet Reform in Britain, 1914–1963*, 1964

DAINTITH, T C, & PAGE, A C, *The Executive in the Constitution: Structure, Autonomy and Internal Control*, 1999

DALE, W, *The Modern Commonwealth*, 1983

DALYELL, T, *Devolution, The End of Britain?*, 1977

DASH, S, *Justice Denied*, 1972

DAVIES P L, & FREEDLAND, M R, *Labour Legislation and Public Policy: A Contemporary History*, 1993

DAVIS, G, WIKELEY, N, & YOUNG, R, *Child Support in Action*, 1998

DAVIS, K C, *Discretionary Justice*, 1969

DAY, A J, *Directory of European Political Parties*, 2000

DENNING, LORD, *What Next in the Law?*, 1982

d'ENTREVES, A P, *The Notion of the State*, 1967

de SMITH, S A, *Constitutional and Administrative Law* (ed. R Brazier), 7th edn, 1994

de SMITH, S A, *The New Commonwealth and its Constitutions*, 1964

de SMITH, S A, WOOLF, Lord, & JOWELL, J, *Judicial Review of Administrative Action*, 5th edn, 1995

DEAKIN, S, & MORRIS, G S, *Labour Law*, 3rd edn, 2001

DEVINE, T M, *The Scottish Nation 1700–2000*, 1999

DEVLIN, Lord, *The Criminal Prosecution in England*, 1960

DICEY, A V, *The Law of the Constitution* (ed. E C S Wade), 10th edn, 1959

DICEY, A V, & RAIT, R S, *Thoughts on the Union between England and Scotland*, 1920

DONALDSON, A G, *Some Comparative Aspects of Irish Law*, 1957

DONALDSON, F, *The Marconi Scandal*, 1962

DONALDSON, G, *Edinburgh History of Scotland*, vol 3, *James V–James VII*, 1965

DOUGLAS-SCOTT, S, *The Constitutional Law of the European Union*, 2002

DOYLE, B, *Disability, Discrimination and Equal Opportunities*, 1995

DREWRY, G (ed), *The New Select Committees*, 2nd edn, 1989

DRUCKER, H (ed), *Scottish Government Yearbook 1980*, 1980

DRZEMCZEWSKI, A, *European Human Rights Convention in Domestic Law*, 1983

DUFF, A (ed), *The Treaty of Amsterdam*, 1997

DUMMETT, A, & NICOL, A, *Subjects, Citizens, Aliens and Others: Nationality and Immigration Law*, 1990

DWORKIN, R, *Taking Rights Seriously*, 1977

EDWARDS, J LI J, *The Attorney-General, Politics and the Public Interest*, 1984

EDWARDS, J LI J, *The Law Officers of the Crown*, 1964

ELLIOTT, M, *The Constitutional Foundations of Judicial Review*, 2001

ELLIS, E, *The Principle of Proportionality in the Laws of Europe*, 1999

ELLIS, E, & TRIDIMAS, T, *Public Law of the European Community: Text, Materials and Commentary*, 1995

ELTON, G R, *Studies in Tudor and Stuart Politics and Government* (2 vols), 1974

EMERY, C T, & SMYTHE, B, *Judicial Review: Legal Limits of Official Power*, 1986

ENGLEFIELD, D (ed), *Commons Select Committees*, 1984

ERNST, J, *Whose Utility?: The Social Impact of Public Utility Privatisation and Regulation in Britain*, 1994

ERSKINE MAY, *Parliamentary Practice (The Law, Privileges, Proceedings and Usage of Parliament)* (ed. D Limon & W R McKay), 22nd edn, 1997

EVANS, G (ed), *Labor and the Constitution, 1972–1975*, 1977

EVANS, J M, *Immigration Law*, 2nd edn, 1983

EVATT, H V, *The King and His Dominion Governors*, 1936

EVELEGH, R, *Peace Keeping in a Democratic Society*, 1978

EWING, K D (ed), *The Funding of Political Parties: Europe and Beyond*, 1999

EWING, K D, *Britain and the ILO*, 2nd edn, 1994

EWING, K D, *The Funding of Political Parties in Britain*, 1987

EWING, K D, *Trade Unions, the Labour Party and the Law*, 1983

EWING, K D, & FINNIE, W, *Civil Liberties in Scotland: Cases and Materials*, 2nd edn, 1988

EWING, K D, & GEARTY, C A, *The Struggle for Civil Liberties: Political Freedom and the Rule of Law in Britain 1914–1945*, 2000

EWING, K D, & GEARTY, C A, *Democracy or a Bill of Rights*, 1991

EWING, K D, & GEARTY, C A, *Freedom under Thatcher: Civil Liberties in Modern Britain*, 1990

EWING, K D, GEARTY, C A, & HEPPLE, B A (eds), *Human Rights and Labour Law*, 1994

FARMER, J A, *Tribunals and Government*, 1974

FARRAR, J H, *Law Reform and the Law Commission*, 1974

FAWCETT, J E S, *The British Commonwealth in International Law*, 1963

FELDMAN, D J, *Civil Liberties and Human Rights in England and Wales*, 2nd edn, 2002

FENWICK, H, *Civil Rights: New Labour, Freedom and the Human Rights Act*, 2000

FERGUSON, W, *Edinburgh History of Scotland*, vol 4, *1689 to the Present*, 1968

FFORDE, J S, *The Bank of England and Public Policy 1941–1958*, 1992

FINDLATER, R, *Banned!*, 1967

FINE, B, & MILLER, R (eds) *Policing the Miners' Strike*, 1985

FINER, S E (ed), *Adversary Politics and Electoral Reform*, 1975

FINNIE, W, HIMSWORTH, C, & WALKER, N (eds), *Edinburgh Essays in Public Law*, 1991

FISHER, J, *British Political Parties*, 1996

FLICK, G A, *Natural Justice*, 1979

FOLEY, M, *The Politics of the British Constitution*, 1999

FOLEY, M, *The Rise of the British Presidency*, 1993

FOLEY, M, *The Silence of Constitutions: Gaps, 'Abeyances' and Political Temperament in the Maintenance of Government*, 1989

FORD, P & G (ed), *Luke Graves Hansard's Diary, 1814–1841*, 1962

FORSEY, E A, *The Royal Power of Dissolution of Parliament in the British Commonwealth*, 1943

FORSYTH, C (ed), *Judicial Review and the Constitution*, 2000

FORSYTH, C, & HARE, I (eds), *The Golden Metwand and the Crooked Cord: Essays in honour of Sir William Wade* (1998)

FORSYTH, W, *Cases and Opinions on Constitutional Law*, 1869

FOULKES, D L, *Administrative Law*, 8th edn, 1995

FRANKLIN, M N, & NORTON, P (eds), *Parliamentary Questions*, 1993

FRANSMAN, L, *British Nationality Law*, 1989

FREDMAN, S, & MORRIS, G S, *The State as Employer: Labour Law in the Public Services*, 1989

FREEMAN, E A, *The Growth of the English Constitution*, 1872

FRIEDMANN, W G, *Law in a Changing Society*, revised 1964

FRIEDMANN, W G (ed), *Public and Private Enterprise in Mixed Economies*, 1974

FRIEDMANN, W G, & GARNER, J F (ed), *Government Enterprise*, 1970

FRYDE, E B, & MILLER, E (ed), *Historical Studies of the English Parliament 1399–1603*, 1970

FULLBROOK, J, *Administrative Justice and the Unemployed*, 1978

FULLER, L L, *The Morality of Law*, 1964

GALLIGAN, D J, *Discretionary Powers: A Legal Study of Official Discretion*, 1987

GANZ, G, *Quasi-Legislation: Recent Developments in Secondary Legislation*, 1987

GEARTY, C A (ed), *European Civil Liberties and the European Convention on Human Rights*, 1997

GEARTY, C A, *Terror*, 1991

GEARTY, C A, & KIMBELL, J A, *Terrorism and the Rule of Law*, 1995

GEARTY, C A, & TOMKINS, A, *Understanding Human Rights*, 1996

GELLHORN, W, *Ombudsmen and Others*, 1966

GENN, H, *The Effectiveness of Representation at Tribunals*, 1989

GERHARDT, M J, *The Federal Impeachment Process: A Constitutional and Historical Analysis*, 2nd edn, 2000

GIBBONS, T, *Regulating the Media*, 2nd edn, 1997

GIDDINGS, P J (ed), *Parliamentary Accountability: A Study of Parliament and Executive Agencies*, 1995

GILBERT, G, *Aspects of Extradition Law*, 1991

GILL, P, *Policing Politics*, 1994

GOLDSWORTHY, J, *The Sovereignty of Parliament: History and Philosophy*, 1999

GOODWIN-GILL, G, *The Refugee in International Law*, 2nd edn, 1996

GORDON, G H, *Criminal Law of Scotland*, 2nd edn, 1978

GORDON, R, *Crown Office Proceedings*, 1990

GORDON, R, *Judicial Review and Crown Office Practice*, 1998

GOUGH, J W, *Fundamental Law in English Constitutional History*, 1955

GRAHAM, C, *Regulating Public Utilities*, 2000

GRAHAM, C, & PROSSER, T (eds), *Waiving the Rules: The Constitution under Thatcherism*, 1988

GRANT, J P (ed), *Independence and Devolution, the Legal Implications for Scotland*, 1976

GRANT, W, & MARSH, D, *The Confederation of British Industry*, 1977

GREGORY, R, & HUTCHESSON, P G, *The Parliamentary Ombudsman*, 1975

GREY, Earl, *Parliamentary Government*, 1864

GRIFFITH, J A G, *Central Departments and Local Authorities*, 1966

GRIFFITH, J A G (ed), *From Policy to Administration*, 1976

GRIFFITH, J A G, *Parliamentary Scrutiny of Government Bills*, 1974

GRIFFITH, J A G, *The Politics of the Judiciary*, 4th edn, 1991

GRIFFITH, J A G, & RYLE, M, *Parliament*, 1989

GUEST, A G (ed), *Oxford Essays in Jurisprudence*, 1961

GURRY, F, *Breach of Confidence*, 1984

HADDEN, T, & BOYLE, K, *The Anglo-Irish Agreement*, 1989

HADFIELD, B (ed), *Judicial Review, A Thematic Approach*, 1995

HADFIELD, B (ed), *Northern Ireland: Politics and the Constitution*, 1992

HADFIELD, B, *The Constitution of Northern Ireland*, 1989

HAGUE, D C, MACKENZIE, W J M, & BARKER, A (ed), *Public Policy and Private Interests*, 1975

HAILSHAM, Lord, *On the Constitution*, 1992

HAILSHAM, Lord, *The Dilemma of Democracy*, 1978

HALL, P, *Royal Fortune: Tax, Money and the Monarchy*, 1992

HANHAM, H J, *The Nineteenth Century Constitution, 1815–1914*, 1969

HANSON, A H, *Parliament and Public Ownership*, 1961

HARDEN, I, *The Contracting State*, 1992

HARDING, A J, *Public Duties and Public Law*, 1989

HARLOW, C, *Compensation and Government Torts*, 1982

HARLOW, C, & RAWLINGS, R, *Law and Administration*, 1984

HARMAN, H, & GRIFFITH, J A G, *Justice Deserted*, 1979

HARRIS, D J, *The European Social Charter*, 1984

HARRIS, D, & DARCY, J, *The European Social Charter*, 2nd edn, 2001

HARRIS, D J, O'BOYLE, M, & WARBRICK, C, *Law of the European Convention on Human Rights*, 1995

HARRIS, M, & PARTINGTON, M (eds), *Administrative Justice in the 21st Century*, 1999

HARRIS, N (ed), *Social Security Law in Context*, 2000

HARRIS, N, *Special Educational Needs and Access to Justice: the Role of the Special Educational Needs Tribunal*, 1997

HARRIS, N, & EDEN, K, *Challenges to School Exclusions: Exclusions, Appeals and the Law*, 2000

HARRISON, A J, *The Control of Public Expenditure, 1979–1989*, 1989

HART, H L A, *The Concept of Law*, 1961

HART, H L A, & HONORE, A M, *Causation in the Law*, 1959

HARTLEY, T C, *The Foundations of European Community Law*, 4th edn, 1998

HARVEY, B W (ed), *The Lawyer and Justice*, 1978

HARVEY, C, *Seeking Asylum in the UK: Problems and Prospects*, 2000

HATHAWAY, J, *The Law of Refugee Status*, 1991

HAWKINS, W, *Pleas of the Crown*, 6th edn (by T Leach), 2 vols, 1787

HAYEK, F A, *The Constitution of Liberty*, 1963

HAYEK, F A, *The Road to Serfdom*, 1944

HAZELL, R (ed), *The State and the Nations: the First Year of Devolution in the United Kingdom*, 2000

HEALEY, D, *The Time of My Life*, 1989

HEARD, A, *Canadian Constitutional Conventions: the Marriage of Law and Politics*, 1991

HEARN, W E, *The Government of England*, 1867

HECLO, H, & WILDAVSKY, A, *The Private Government of Public Money*, 1974

HEDLEY, P, & AYNSLEY, C, *The D-Notice Affair*, 1967

HENDERSON, E G, *Foundations of English Administrative Law*, 1963

HENLEY, D, et al, *Public Sector Accounting and Financial Control*, 1984

HENNESSY, P, *The Prime Minister: the Office and its Holders since 1945*, 2000

HENNESSY, P, *Cabinet*, 1986

HENNESSY, P, *Whitehall*, rev edn, 1990

HEPPLE, B A, *Race, Jobs and the Law in Britain*, 2nd edn, 1970

HEPPLE, B A, et al, *Equality: a New Framework*, 2000

HERBERT, A P, *Uncommon Law*, 1935

HEUSTON, R F V, *Essays in Constitutional Law*, 2nd edn, 1964

HEUSTON, R F V, *Lives of the Lord Chancellors 1885–1940*, 1964

HILL, L B, *The Model Ombudsman*, 1976

HIMSWORTH, C M G, *Local Government Law in Scotland*, 1995

HIMSWORTH, C M G, & MUNRO, C R, *The Scotland Act 1998*, 1999

HOBBY, C, *Whistleblowing and the Public Interest Disclosure Act 1998*, 2001

HOFFMANN, Lord, *A Sense of Proportion* (J M Kelly Memorial Lecture, 1996), 1997

HOGG, P W, *Constitutional Law of Canada*, 4th edn, 1997

HOGG, P W, & MONAHAN, P, *Liability of the Crown*, 3rd edn, 2000

HOGGETT, B, *Mental Health Law*, 4th edn, 1996

HOLDSWORTH, W, *A History of English Law* (14 vols), 1923–64

HOLLAND, P, *The Governance of Quangos*, 1981

HOLT, J C, *Magna Carta*, 2nd edn, 1992

HOOD PHILLIPS, O, *Reform of the Constitution*, 1970

HOOD PHILLIPS, O, & JACKSON P, *Constitutional and Administrative Law*, 8th edn (by P Jackson and P Leonard), 2001

HOPKINS, P, *Parliamentary Procedures and the Law Commission*, 1994

HOWARD, C, *Australian Federal Constitutional Law*, 3rd edn, 1985

HUNNINGS, N M, *Film Censors and the Law*, 1967

HUNT, M, *Using Human Rights Law in English Courts*, 1997

INGMAN, T, *The English Legal Process*, 8th edn, 2000

JACKSON, J, & DORAN, S, *Judge without Jury*, 1995

JACOB, J M, *The Republican Crown: Lawyers and the Making of the State in 20th Century Britain*, 1996

JACOBS, F G, & WHITE, R C A, *The European Convention on Human Rights*, 2nd edn, 1996

JACONELLI, J, *Enacting a Bill of Rights, the Legal Problems*, 1980

JAMES, S, *British Cabinet Government*, 1992

JANIS, M, KAY, R, & BRADLEY, A W, *European Human Rights Law: Text and Materials*, 2nd edn, 2000

JEFFERSON, T, & GRIMSHAW, R, *Controlling the Constable: Police Accountability in England and Wales*, 1984

JEFFERY, K, & HENNESSY, P, *States of Emergency: British Governments and Strikebreaking since 1919*, 1983

JENKINS, R, *A Life at the Centre*, 1991

JENKINS, R, *Mr Balfour's Poodle*, 1954

JENNINGS, A (ed), *Justice under fire: the Abuse of Civil Liberties in Northern Ireland*, 1990

JENNINGS, I, *Cabinet Government*, 3rd edn, 1959

JENNINGS, I, *The Law and the Constitution*, 5th edn, 1959

JENNINGS, I, *Parliament*, 2nd edn, 1957

JENNINGS, I, *The Sedition Bill Explained*, 1934

JENNINGS, R, & WATTS, A, *Oppenheim's International Law: the Law of Peace*, 9th edn, 1992

JOHNSON, N, *In Search of the Constitution*, 1977

JOHNSON, N, *Parliament and Administration; the Estimates Committee 1945–65*, 1966

JOHNSTON, A, *The Inland Revenue*, 1965

JONES, A, *Extradition and Mutual Assistance*, 2001

JONES, J M, *British Nationality Law*, 2nd edn, 1956

JONES, R (ed), *Mental Health Act Manual*, 6th edn, 1999

JONES, T, *Whitehall Diary*, vol 3 (ed. R K Middlemas), 1971

JONES, T, & NEWBURN, T, *Policing after the Act: Police Governance after the Police and Magistrates' Courts Act 1994*, 1997

JOSEPH, K, *Freedom under the Law*, 1975

JOWELL, J, & COOPER, J (eds), *Understanding Human Rights Principles*, 2001

JOWELL, J L, & OLIVER, D H (eds), *New Directions in Judicial Review*, 1988

JOWELL, J L, & OLIVER, D H (eds), *The Changing Constitution*, 3rd edn, 1994 and 4th edn, 2000

JUSTICE, All Souls Committee, *Administrative Justice: Some Necessary Reforms*, 1988

JUSTICE, *The Local Ombudsman*, 1980

KEATING, M J, & MIDWINTER, A, *The Government of Scotland*, 1983

KEETON, G W, *Trial by Tribunal*, 1960

KEIR, D L, & LAWSON, F H, *Cases in Constitutional Law*, 6th edn, 1979

KELLAS, J G, *The Scottish Political System*, 4th edn, 1989

KELLY, J M, *The Irish Constitution*, 3rd edn, 1994

KERMODE, D G, *Devolution at Work: A Case Study of the Isle of Man*, 1979

KERR, J, *Matters for Judgment*, 1979

KERSELL, J E, *Parliamentary Supervision of Delegated Legislation*, 1960

KING, A, *Does the United Kingdom still have a Constitution?*, 2001

KINLEY, O, *The European Convention on Human Rights: Compliance Without Incorporation*, 1993

KITSON, F, *Low Intensity Operations*, 1971

KNEEBONE, S, *Tort Liability of Public Authorities*, 1998

LASKI, H J, *A Grammar of Politics*, 5th edn, 1967

LATHAM, R T E, *The Law and the Commonwealth*, 1949

LAUNDY, P, *The Office of Speaker*, 1964

LAWRENCE, R J, *The Government of Northern Ireland*, 1965

LAWSON, N, *The View from No. 11*, 1993

LEE, H P, HANKS, P, & MORABITO, V, *In the Name of National Security: the Legal Dimensions*, 1995

LEGGATT, A, *Tribunals for Users: One System, One Service*, 2001

LEGOMSKY, S H, *Immigration and the Justiciary: Law and Politics in Britain and America*, 1987

LEIGH, D, *The Frontiers of Secrecy*, 1980

LESTER, A, & BINDMAN, G, *Race and Law*, 1972

LESTER, A, & PANNICK, D (eds), *Human Rights Law and Practice*, 1999

LEVY, H P, *The Press Council*, 1967

LEWIS, A, *Make No Law*, 1991

LEWIS, C B, *Judicial Remedies in Public Law*, 1992

LEWIS, N, SENEVIRATNE, M, & CRACKNELL, S, *Complaints Procedures in Local Government*, 1987

LEWIS, N, & GATESHILL, B, *The Commission for Local Administration*, 1978

LIKIERMAN, J A, *Cash Limits and External Financing Limits*, 1981

LINKLATER, M, & LEIGH, D, *Not Without Honour*, 1986

LODGE, J (ed), *Institutions and Policies of the European Community*, 1983

LOUGHLIN, M, *Legality and Locality: the Role of Law in Central–Local Government Relations*, 1996

LOUGHLIN, M, *Local Government in the Modern State*, 1986

LOUGHLIN, M, *Public Law and Political Theory*, 1992

LOVELAND, I, *Political Libels: a Comparative Study*, 2000

LOVELAND, I, *By Due Process of Law? Racial Discrimination and the Right to Vote in South Africa 1850–1960*, 1999

LOVELAND, I D, *Constitutional Law, A Critical Introduction*, 1996

LOVELAND, I D (ed), *Frontiers of Criminality*, 1995

LOWE, N V, & SUFRIN, B E, *Borrie and Lowe's Law of Contempt*, 3rd edn, 1996

LOWELL, A L, *The Government of England*, 1908

LUSTGARTEN, L, *Legal Control of Racial Discrimination*, 1980

LUSTGARTEN, L, *The Governance of the Police*, 1986

LUSTGARTEN, L, & LEIGH, I, *In From the Cold: National Security and Parliamentary Democracy*, 1994

MACCORMICK, N, *Questioning Sovereignty: Law, State, and Nation in the European Commonwealth*, 1999

MACDONALD, I A, & WEBBER, J, *Immigration Law and Practice in the United Kingdom*, 5th edn, 2001

MACGREGOR, L, PROSSER, T, & VILLIERS, C (eds), *Regulation and Markets beyond 2000*, 2000

MCCABE, S, & WALLINGTON, P, *The Police, Public Order and Civil Liberties: Legacies of the Miners' Strike*, 1988

MCCOLGAN, A, *Discrimination Law: Text, Cases and Materials*, 2000

MCCRUDDEN, C (ed), *Regulation and Deregulation: Policy and Practice in the Utilities and Financial Services Industries*, 1999

MCCRUDDEN, C, & CHAMBERS, G (eds), *Individual Rights and the Law in Britain*, 1993

MCELDOWNEY, J F, *Public Law*, 2nd edn, 1998

MCFADDEN, J, & LAZAROWICZ, M, *The Scottish Parliament: an Introduction*, 1999

MCILWAIN, C H, *Constitutionalism, Ancient and Modern*, 1947

MCILWAIN, C H, *The High Court of Parliament*, 1910

MACKINTOSH, J P, *The British Cabinet*, 3rd edn, 1977

MACKINTOSH, J P, *The Devolution of Power*, 1968

MACKINTOSH, J P, *The Government and Politics of Britain* (ed. P G Richards), 7th edn, 1988

MACKINTOSH, J P, *Specialist Committees in the House of Commons – have they failed?* (rev), 1980

MCNAIR, Lord, *Law of Treaties*, 2nd edn, 1961

MCNAIR, Lord, & WATTS, A D, *The Legal Effects of War*, 4th edn, 1966

MAITLAND, F W, *The Constitutional History of England*, 1908

MAJOR, J, *The Autobiography*, 1999

MALLORY, J R, *The Structure of Canadian Government*, 1971

Manual of Military Law, 13th edn, 1992

MANN, F A, *Foreign Affairs in English Courts*, 1986

MARGACH, J, *The Abuse of Power*, 1978

MARKESINIS, B S, *The Theory and Practice of Dissolution of Parliament*, 1972

MARKESINIS, B S, AUBY, J-B, COESTER-WALTJEN, D, & DEAKIN, S F, *Tortious Liability of Statutory Bodies: a Comparative and Economic Analysis of Five English Cases*, 1999

MARSHALL, G, *Constitutional Conventions*, 1984

MARSHALL, G, *Constitutional Theory*, 1971

MARSHALL, G, *Parliamentary Sovereignty and the Commonwealth*, 1957

MARSHALL, G, *Police and Government*, 1965

MARSHALL, G, & MOODIE, G C, *Some Problems of the Constitution*, 5th edn, 1971

MATHIJSEN, P S R F, *A Guide to European Community Law*, 7th edn, 1999

MEGARRY, R E, & WADE, H W R, *The Law of Real Property*, 5th edn, 1984

MICHAEL, J, *The Politics of Secrecy*, 1982

MIDDLEMAS, K, & BARNES, J, *Baldwin*, 1969

MIERS, D R, & PAGE, A C, *Legislation*, 2nd edn, 1990

MILIBAND, R, *Capitalist Democracy in Britain*, 1982 . . .

MILL, J S, *Representative Government*, 1861

MILLER, C J, *Contempt of Court*, 2nd edn, 1989

MILLER, J D B (ed), *Survey of Commonwealth Affairs: Problems of Expansion and Attrition, 1953–1969*, 1974

MILLETT, J D, *The Unemployment Assistance Board*, 1940

MILNE, D, *The Scottish Office*, 1957

MITCHELL, J D B, *Constitutional Law*, 2nd edn, 1968

MITCHELL, J D B, *The Contracts of Public Authorities*, 1954

MOORE, W H, *Act of State in English Law*, 1906

MORE, J S, *Lectures on the Law of Scotland* (ed. J McLaren), 1864

MORGAN, J, *Conflict and Order: The Police and Labour Disputes in England and Wales 1900–39*, 1987

MORGAN, J P, *The House of Lords and the Labour Government, 1964–1970*, 1975

MORGAN, R, & NEWBURN, T, *The Future of Policing*, 1997

MORISON, J, & LIVINGSTONE, S, *Reshaping Public Power: Northern Ireland and the British Constitutional Crisis*, 1995

MORRIS, A (ed), *The Growth of Parliamentary Scrutiny by Committee*, 1970

MORRIS, G S, *Strikes in Essential Services*, 1986

MORRIS, H F, & READ, J S, *Indirect Rule and the Search for Justice*, 1972

MORRISON, H, *Government and Parliament*, 3rd edn, 1964

MORTON, J, *Criminal Justice and Public Order Act 1994*, 1994

MOSLEY, R K, *The Story of the Cabinet Office*, 1969

MOUNT, F, *The British Constitution Now: Recovery or Decline?*, 1992

MOWBRAY, A R, *Cases and Materials on the European Convention on Human Rights*, 2001

MUNRO, C R, *Television, Censorship and the Law*, 1979

MUNRO, C R, *Studies in Constitutional Law*, 2nd edn, 1999

NICOLSON, I F, *The Mystery of Crichel Down*, 1986

NICOLSON, H, *King George V*, 1952

NOBLES, R, & SCHIFF, D, *Understanding Miscarriages of Justice*, 2000

NOEL, E, *Working Together – The Institutions of the European Community*, 1994

NOLAN, Lord, & SEDLEY, S, *The Making and Remaking of the British Constitution*, 1997

NORMANTON, E L, *The Accountability and Audit of Governments*, 1966

NORTON, P, *The Commons in Perspective*, 1981

NORTON, P, *The Constitution in Flux*, 1982

NORTON, P, *Dissension in the House of Commons 1945–1974*, 1975; *1974–1979*, 1980

O'CONNELL, D P, & RIORDAN, A, *Opinions on Imperial Constitutional Law*, 1971

O'HIGGINS, P, *Censorship in Britain*, 1972

OLIVER, D, *Common Values and the Public-Private Divide*, 1999

OLIVER, D, & DREWRY, G, *The Law and Parliament*, 1998

OLOWOFOYEKO, A, *Suing Judges: a Study of Judicial Immunity*, 1993

O'RIORDAN, T, KEMP, R, & PURDUE, M, *Sizewell B: An Anatomy of an Inquiry*, 1988

PAGE, A, REID, C, & ROSS, A, *A Guide to the Scotland Act 1998*, 1999

PAINE, T, *Rights of Man* (ed. H Collins), 1969

PANNICK, D, *Judicial Review of the Death Penalty*, 1982

PARRIS, H, *Constitutional Bureaucracy*, 1969

PARRY, C, *Nationality and Citizenship Laws of the Commonwealth*, 2 vols, 1957–60

PARTINGTON, M, *Introduction to the English Legal System*, 2000

PARTINGTON, M, *Secretary of State's Powers of Adjudication in Social Security Law*, 1991

PATERSON, A, *The Law Lords*, 1982

PATERSON, A, & BATES, T ST J, *The Legal System of Scotland: Cases and Materials*, 3rd edn, 1993

PATTEN, J, *Political Culture, Conservatism and Rolling Constitutional Change*, 1991

PEERS, S, *EU Justice and Home Affairs Law*, 2000

PELLING, H, *The British Communist Party: A Historical Profile*, 1975

PIMLOTT, B, *The Queen: A Biography of Elizabeth II*, 1996

PINTO-DUSCHINSKY, M, *British Political Finance 1830–1980*, 1981

PLIATZKY, L, *The Treasury under Mrs Thatcher*, 1989

POLLOCK, F, & MAITLAND, F W, *History of English Law*, vol 1, 1898

POLYVIOU, P G, *The Equal Protection of the Laws*, 1980

POLYVIOU, P G, *Entry, Search and Seizure: Constitutional and Common Law*, 1982

PONTING, C, *The Right to Know: The Inside Story of the Belgrano Affair*, 1985

PORT, F J, *Administrative Law*, 1929

PROSSER, T, *Laws and the Regulators*, 1997

PROSSER, T, *Nationalised Industries and Public Control: Legal, Constitutional and Political Issues*, 1986

RAWLINGS, H F, *The Law and the Electoral Process*, 1988

RAZ, J, *Ethics in the Public Domain: Essays in the Morality of Law and Politics*, 1994

REID, G, *The Politics of Financial Control*, 1966

REINER, R, *The Politics of the Police*, 1992

RENTON, R W, & BROWN, H H, *Criminal Procedure in Scotland*, 6th edn, 1996 (by G H Gordon & C H W Gane)

RICHARD, I, & WELFARE, D, *Unfinished Business: Reforming the House of Lords*, 1999

RICHARDS, P G, *Parliament and Conscience*, 1970

RICHARDS, P G, *Patronage in British Government*, 1963

RICHARDSON, G, & GENN, H (eds), *Administrative Law and Government Action: The Courts and Alternative Mechanisms of Review*, 1994

RIDER, B, ABRAMS, C, & FERRAN, E, *Guide to the Financial Services Act 1986*, 1989

RILEY, P W J, *The Union of England and Scotland*, 1978

RIMINGTON, S, *Open Secret: the Autobiography of the former Director-General of MI5*, 2001

ROBERTS, C, *The Growth of Responsible Government in Stuart England*, 1966

ROBERTS-WRAY, K, *Commonwealth and Colonial Law*, 1966

ROBERTSON, A H, & MERRILLS, J G, *Human Rights in Europe: A Study of the European Convention on Human Rights*, 3rd edn, 1993

ROBERTSON, G, *Freedom, the Individual and the Law*, 7th edn, 1993

ROBERTSON, G, *Obscenity*, 1979

ROBERTSON, G, *The People against the Press*, 1983

ROBINSON, A, *Parliament and Public Spending – The Expenditure Committee 1970–76*, 1978

ROBSON, W A, *Justice and Administrative Law*, 3rd edn, 1951

ROBSON, W A, *Nationalised Industries and Public Ownership*, 2nd edn, 1962

RODGER, B J, & MCCULLOUGH, A (eds), *The UK Competition Act*, 2000

ROLPH, C H, *The Trial of Lady Chatterley*, 1961

ROSEVEARE, H, *The Treasury*, 1969

ROWAT, D C, *The Ombudsman*, 2nd edn, 1968

ROWE, P, *Defence: The Legal Implications*, 1987

ROWE, P (ed), *The Gulf War 1990–91 in International and English Law*, 1993

RUBIN, G R, *Private Property, Government Requisition and the Constitution 1914–1927*, 1994

RUBINSTEIN, A, *Jurisdiction and Illegality*, 1965

RUSSELL, M, *Reforming the House of Lords: Lessons from Overseas*, 2000

RYLE, M, & RICHARDS, P G (eds), *The Commons under Scrutiny*, 3rd edn, 1988

SAWER, G, *Federation under Strain*, 1977

SCARMAN, Lord, *English Law – The New Dimension*, 1974

SCHØNBERG, S, *Legitimate Expectations in Administrative Law*, 2000

SCHWARZE, J, *European Administrative Law*, 1992

SENEVIRATNE, M, *Ombudsmen in the Public Sector*, 1994

SHARPE, R J, *The Law of Habeas Corpus*, 2nd edn, 1989

SHELL, D, *The House of Lords*, 2nd edn, 1992

SIMPSON, A W B, *Human Rights and the End of Empire: Britain and the Genesis of the European Convention*, 2001

SIMPSON, A W B, *In the Highest Degree Odious*, 1992

SIMPSON, A W B, *Pornography and Politics – the Williams Report in Retrospect*, 1983

SINGER, P, *Democracy and Disobedience*, 1973

SMITH, A T H, *Offences Against Public Order*, 1987

SMITH, I T, & THOMAS, G H, *Industrial Law*, 7th edn, 2000

SMITH, J C, & HOGAN, B, *Criminal Law*, 9th edn, 1999

SMITH, T B (ed), *The Laws of Scotland: Stair Memorial Encyclopedia*, vols 1 & 5, 1987

SORENSEN, M (ed), *Manual of Public International Law*, 1968

SPENCER, J R, *Jackson's Machinery of Justice*, 8th edn, 1989

SPENCER, S, *Called to Account*, 1985

STACEY, F, *Ombudsmen Compared*, 1978

STALKER, J, *Stalker*, 1988

STANBROOK, I, & C, *Extradition Law and Practice*, 2nd edn, 2000

STEEL, D, *A House Divided; the Lib-Lab Pact and the Future of British Politics*, 1980

STEEL, D, *No Entry*, 1969

STEPHEN, J F, *Digest of Criminal Law*, 1877

STEPHEN, J F, *History of the Criminal Law of England* (3 vols), 1883

STEVENS, R, *Law and Politics: the House of Lords as a Judicial Body, 1800–1976*, 1979

STEVENS, R B, *The Independence of the Judiciary, The View from the Lord Chancellor's Office*, 1993

STEWART, J D, *British Pressure Groups*, 1956

STEWART, J, & STOKER, G (eds), *Local Government in the 1990s*, 1995

STONE, R T H, *Entry, Search and Seizure: A Guide to Civil and Criminal Powers of Entry*, 3rd edn, 1997

STREET, H, *Freedom, the Individual and the Law*, 5th edn, 1982

STREET, H, *Governmental Liability*, 1953

STREET, H, *Justice in the Welfare State*, 2nd edn, 1975

SUNKIN, M, & PAYNE, S (eds), *The Nature of the Crown: a Legal and Political Analysis*, 1999

SUPPERSTONE, M, *Brownlie's Law of Public Order and National Security*, 2nd edn, 1981

SUPPERSTONE, M, & GOUDIE, J (eds), *Judicial Review*, 1991

SWINFEN, D B, *Imperial Appeal: The debate on the appeal to the Privy Council, 1833–1986*, 1987

TAGGART, M (ed), *The Province of Administrative Law*, 1997

TAGGART, M (ed), *Judicial Review of Administrative Action in the 1980s*, 1987

TARNOPOLSKY, W S, *The Canadian Bill of Rights*, 2nd edn, 1975

TASWELL-LANGMEAD, T P, *English Constitutional History* (ed. T F T Plucknett), 11th edn, 1960

TERRY, C S, *The Scottish Parliament 1603–1707*, 1905

THAIN, C, & WRIGHT, M, *The Treasury and Whitehall*, 1995

THIO, S M, *Locus Standi and Judicial Review*, 1971

THOMPSON, B, & RIDLEY, F F (eds), *Under the Scott-light: British Government seen through the Scott Report*, 1997

THOMPSON, E P, *Whigs and Hunters: the Origin of the Black Act*, 1975

THOMPSON, E P, *Writing by Candlelight*, 1980

TILEY, J, *Revenue Law*, 4th edn, 2000

TOMKINS, A, *The Constitution after Scott: Government Unwrapped*, 1998

TOWNSHEND, C, *Making the Peace: Public Order and Public Security in Modern Britain*, 1993

TRENCH, A (ed), *The State of the Nations 2001: the Second Year of Devolution in the United Kingdom*, 2001

TRIBE, L, *Constitutional Choices*, 1985

TRIDIMUS, T, *The General Principles of EC Law*, 2000

TURNBULL, M, *The Spycatcher Trial*, 1989

TURPIN, C C, *British Government and the Constitution: Text, Cases and Materials*, 3rd edn, 1995

TURPIN, C C, *Government Procurement and Contracts*, 1989

UGLOW, S, *Policing a Liberal Society*, 1988

UNSWORTH, C, *The Politics of Mental Health Legislation*, 1987

VAN DIJK, P, & VAN HOOF, G, *Theory and Practice of the European Convention on Human Rights*, 2nd edn, 1990

VERCHER, A, *Terrorism in Europe: An International Comparative Legal Analysis*, 1992

VILE, M J C, *Constitutionalism and the Separation of Powers*, 1967

VOGLER, R, *Reading the Riot Act: the Magistracy, the Police and the Army in Civil Disorder*, 1991

WACKS, R, *Personal Information*, 1989

WACKS, R, *The Protection of Privacy*, 1980

WADE, H W R, *Constitutional Fundamentals*, 1980

WADE, H W R, & FORSYTH, C F, *Administrative Law*, 8th edn, 2000

WADHAM, J, & MOUNTFIELD, H, *Guide to the Human Rights Act 1998*, 2nd edn, 2000

WALKER, C, *The Prevention of Terrorism in British Law*, 2nd edn, 1992

WALKER, D M, *The Scottish Legal System*, 6th edn, 1992

WALKER, J, *The Queen has been Pleased*, 1986

WALKER, N, *Policing in a Changing Constitutional Order*, 1998

WALKER, P GORDON, *The Cabinet*, rev 1972

WALKER, S, *In Defense of American Liberties*, 1990

WALKER, C P, & STARMER, K, *Justice in Error*, 1993

WALKLAND, S A (ed), *The House of Commons in the Twentieth Century*, 1979

WALLINGTON, P T, & MCBRIDE, G, *Civil Liberties and a Bill of Rights*, 1976

WARD, I, *A Critical Introduction to European Law*, 1996

WEATHERILL, S, & BEAUMONT, P R, *EC Law*, 3rd edn, 1999

WEATHERILL, S, *Law and Integration in the European Union*, 1995

WEBB, P, *The Modern British Party System*, 2000

WEILER, J H H, *The Constitution of Europe: 'Do the new clothes have an emperor?' and Other Essays on Eurpean Integration*, 1999

WEILER, P, *In the Last Resort*, 1974

WEIR, S, & BEETHAM, D, *Political Power and Democratic Control in Britain*, 1999

WEST, N, *A Matter of Trust: MI5, 1945–72*, 1982

WEST, N, *MI5: British Security Service Operations 1909–45*, 1983

WHEARE, K C, *Modern Constitutions*, 2nd edn, 1966

WHEARE, K C, *The Constitutional Structure of the Commonwealth*, 1960

WHEARE, K C, *The Statute of Westminster and Dominion Status*, 5th edn, 1953

WHEELER-BENNETT, J, *King George VI*, 1958

WHITE, F, & HOLLINGSWORTH, K, *Audit, Accountability and Government*, 1999

WHITE, R M, & WILLOCK, I D, *The Scottish Legal System*, 1999

WHITLAM, G, *The Truth of the Matter*, 1979

WHITTINGTON, K E, *Constitutional Construction: Divided Powers and Constitutional Meaning*, 1999

WHITTY, N, MURPHY, T, & LIVINGSTONE, S, *Civil Liberties Law: the Human Rights Act Era*, 2001

WILLIAMS, G, *Media Ownership and Democracy*, 2nd edn, 1996

WILLIAMS, D G T, *Not in the Public Interest*, 1965

WILLIAMS, D G T, *Keeping the Peace*, 1967

WILLIAMS, E N, *The 18th Century Constitution, 1688–1815*, 1960

WILLIAMS, O C, *History of Private Bill Procedure*, 2 vols, 1949

WILLSON, F M G, *The Organization of British Central Government, 1914–1964*, 2nd edn, 1968

WILSON, H, *The Governance of Britain*, 1976

WILSON, H, *The Labour Government, 1964–70*, 1974

WILSON, S S, *The Cabinet Office to 1945*, 1975

WINDLESHAM, Lord & RAMPTON, R, *Report on 'Death on the Rock'*, 1989

WINETROBE, B K, *Realising the Vision: a Parliament with a Purpose*, 2001

WINTERTON, G, *Monarchy to Republic: Australian Republican Government*, 1994

WOLFE, J N (ed), *Government and Nationalism in Scotland*, 1969

WOODHOUSE, D, *The Office of Lord Chancellor*, 2001

WOODHOUSE, D, *Ministers and Parliament: Accountability in Theory and Practice*, 1994

WOOLF, Sir H, *Protection of the Public – A New Challenge*, 1990

WRAITH, R E, & HUTCHESSON, P G, *Administrative Tribunals*, 1973

WRAITH, R E, & LAMB, G B, *Public Inquiries as an Instrument of Government*, 1971

WYATT, D, & DASHWOOD, A, *European Union Law*, 4th edn, 2000 (ed. Amull, Dashwood, Ross and Wyatt)

WYATT, D, & DASHWOOD, A, *European Community Law*, 3rd edn, 1993

YOUNG, H, *The Crossman Affair*, 1976

YOUNG, T, *Incitement to Disaffection*, 1976

ZAMIR, I, WOOLF, Lord, & WOOLF, J, *The Declaratory Judgement*, 2nd edn, 1993

ZANDER, M, *Cases and Materials on the English Legal System*, 7th edn, 1996

ZANDER, M, *A Bill of Rights?*, 4th edn, 1997

ZANDER, M, *The Police and Criminal Evidence Act 1984*, 3rd edn, 1995

Index